Come with us to the French-speaking world!

Allez, viens!

—a fully integrated French program—makes it possible for you to accomplish all your teaching objectives as never before! *Allez, viens!* ensures development of language proficiency in French and builds students' language skills, so they can communicate effectively and express themselves with confidence.

- The FOUR LANGUAGE SKILLS—listening, speaking, reading, and writing—plus CULTURE are all interwoven throughout the program.

- Strong GRAMMAR support lays an invaluable foundation for proficiency.

- Authentic READING material and process-WRITING projects offer in-depth opportunities for enhanced skill development.

- All three levels of *Allez, viens!* are PACED so that you can finish each text within the year. And because the first two chapters of the Level 2 and Level 3 *Pupil's Editions* are review, the program provides an easy transition from level to level.

- Designed for LEARNERS OF ALL TYPES, *Allez, viens!* is the program of choice for every one of your students.

- VIDEO CORRELATIONS let you easily integrate video segments into your instruction.

- A COMPLETE AUDIO PROGRAM—available on audiocassettes or compact discs—reinforces the text material and gives students another learning option.

- Constant SPIRALING and RE-ENTRY of material from earlier chapters provide consistent reinforcement and review.

See and hear native speakers in authentic locations around the francophone world!

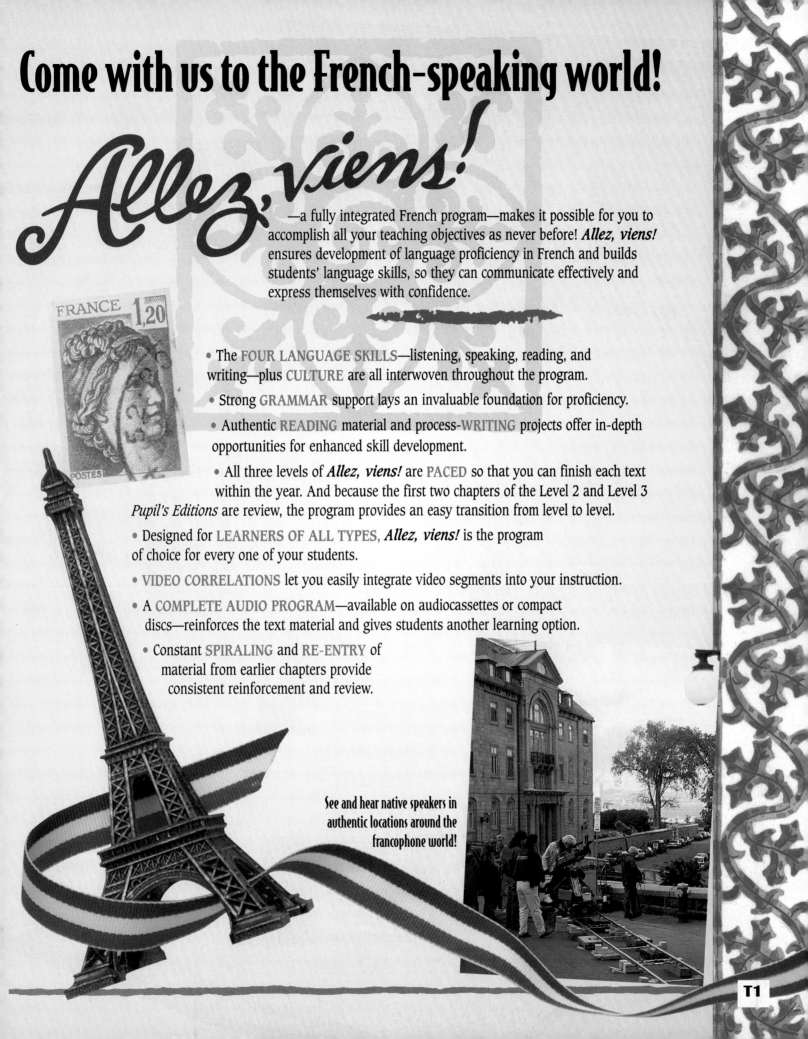

Allez, viens en Afrique francophone!

L'Afrique francophone

	Le Maroc	La Tunisie	Le Sénégal	La République centrafricaine
Population	26.181.000	8.400.000	7.952.000	2.875.000
Superficie (km²)	710.000	164.000	197.000	640.000
Capitale	Rabat	Tunis	Dakar	Bangui
Spécialités	pastilla, thé à la menthe	couscous, tajine	couscous, maffé, chawarma	dengbé

Autres états et régions francophones : l'Algérie, le Bénin, le Burkina-Faso, le Burundi, le Cameroun, les Comores, le Congo, la Côte-d'Ivoire, le Djibouti, le Gabon, la Guinée, l'île Maurice, le Mali, la Mauritanie, Madagascar, la Mayotte, le Niger, le Rwanda, la Réunion, le Sahara Occidental, les Seychelles, le Tchad, le Togo, le Zaïre.

Une mosquée en Afrique

106 cent six

cent sept 107

Where Will We Go?

Each Location Opener introduces your students to the diversity of French-speaking countries with four pages of colorful photos and cultural information.

CHAPITRE **3**

Soyons responsables!

① En Suisse, on protège l'environnement!

54 cinquante-quatre

How Will We Get There?

Chapter Openers serve as advance organizers, identifying learner outcomes and stimulating interest.

Viens avec nous en Suisse où les montagnes sont reines et la propreté est une tradition. Dans ce petit pays d'Europe, la nature et la civilisation essaient de coexister harmonieusement. En plus, les Suisses, disons «Vive l'écologie!»

In this chapter you will learn
- to ask for, grant, and refuse permission; to express obligation
- to forbid; to reproach; to justify your actions and reject others' excuses

And you will
- listen to teenagers asking for permission
- read fables about personal responsibility
- write a brochure for an environmental cause
- find out about Swiss efforts to protect the environment

② Eh! Tu ne sais pas que c'est interdit de jeter les papiers par terre?

③ Il faut que je tonde la pelouse d'abord.

cinquante-cinq 55

Mise en train

Mon look, c'est mon affaire

Axcelle entre dans le salon avec le courrier qu'elle vient d'aller chercher...

① JEROME Ah, tu es allée chercher le courrier? Il y a quelque chose pour moi?
AXCELLE Non, rien pour toi, comme d'habitude.
JEROME Et ça, c'est quoi? Un magazine?
AXCELLE Non, c'est le catalogue printemps-été de Quelle. J'espère qu'il y a des trucs bien.
JEROME Tu es vraiment obsédée par la mode, toi! De toute façon, il n'y a que ça qui vous intéresse, vous, les filles!

Axcelle regarde le catalogue...

AXCELLE Ouah! Génial, cet ensemble! Tu n'aimes pas?
JEROME Lequel?
AXCELLE Celui-là, le noir avec le pantalon à pattes d'eph.

② JEROME Ah! Ne me dis pas que tu aimes vraiment ça! C'est affreux!
AXCELLE Tu comprends vraiment rien à la mode, toi! C'est super branché comme style et puis, si tu sortais un peu, tu verrais que tout le monde s'habille comme ça.
JEROME Ouais, ben, c'est peut-être à la mode, mais je trouve quand même ça ridicule! ... Ça, par contre, je trouve que c'est très classe.
AXCELLE Le tailleur rose, là?
JEROME Oui, comment tu le trouves?

③ AXCELLE Pas mal, mais bon, je ne me vois pas aller à l'école comme ça. Ça fait un peu trop sérieux.
JEROME Peut-être, mais au moins, c'est élégant.
AXCELLE Tiens, regarde ce qu'elle porte, la fille, là.
JEROME Laquelle?

④ AXCELLE Celle avec le caleçon imprimé et le grand tee-shirt. J'aime bien ça. C'est sympa, ça peut se porter partout et c'est moins sérieux que ton tailleur. Qu'est-ce que tu en dis?
JEROME Ouais... J'aime bien ce genre de vêtements. C'est cool et puis... c'est moins bizarre que ton pattes d'eph. Bon, à mon tour de regarder un peu!
AXCELLE Ben, je croyais qu'il n'y avait que les filles qui s'intéressaient à la mode!
JEROME ... ça va, hein! Elle est où, la section «hommes»?
AXCELLE ... enfant.

⑤ JEROME Ah, voilà... Oh là là, c'est nul! Il n'y a rien qui me plaît!
AXCELLE Du calme. Tu n'as pas tout vu. Tiens, il est chouette, ce gilet, non?
JEROME Ouah! Un gilet en cuir pour 299 F! C'est hyper-cool! Je crois que je vais le commander. En plus, j'ai vraiment plus rien à me mettre.
AXCELLE Tiens, au fait, tu as quelque chose pour le mariage de Joël et Virginie?
JEROME Tu fais bien d'en parler. Non, j'ai rien et je me demande ce que je pourrais bien mettre. A ton avis, un pantalon à pinces et une chemise, ça irait?
AXCELLE Euh... si j'étais toi, je mettrais plutôt un costume et une cravate.
JEROME Tu crois?
AXCELLE Ben, oui, c'est quand même un mariage! Et puis, je suis sûre que c'est ce que la plupart des hommes vont mettre.
JEROME Ce n'est pas trop habillé?
AXCELLE Ecoute! Au pire, tu seras le mieux habillé de tous, pour une fois!
JEROME Ah, très drôle. Va un peu à la page des costumes au lieu de dire n'importe quoi... Tiens, il te plaît, celui-là?

⑥ AXCELLE Ouais, je trouve qu'il est très chic. En tout cas, si tu l'achètes, prends aussi la cravate, elle va très bien avec.
JEROME Ouais, peut-être... Enfin, j'ai encore le temps d'y penser. Il reste deux mois avant le mariage.
AXCELLE Bon, retourne à la section «femmes» que je trouve quelque chose pour ce mariage, moi aussi... Tiens, voilà. Elle est parfaite, cette robe, non?

⑦ JEROME Tu rigoles ou quoi?
AXCELLE Non, pourquoi? Tu as quelque chose contre les robes à pois?
JEROME Ben, euh... T'étonne pas si je fais semblant de ne pas te connaître si tu mets ça au mariage!

CHAPITRE 4 Des goûts et des couleurs

MISE EN TRAIN

quatre-vingt-trois 83

Authentic Locations & Language

Mise en train and *Remise en train* features introduce the functions, vocabulary, and grammar targeted in the chapter and are reproduced in the audio program.

Your Building Blocks to Proficiency

The function, grammar, and vocabulary features in each chapter of *Allez, viens!* are linked to give your students the building blocks they need to develop complete language proficiency.

The *Grammaire* presentation provides strong grammar support for the function-driven base of *Allez, viens!*, the perfect combination to help your students develop their French proficiency.

The *Vocabulaire* found in each chapter relates to the theme and language function, and is presented visually whenever possible.

In this function-driven program, each *Comment dit-on?* presentation equips your students for specific language tasks appropriate to the chapter theme.

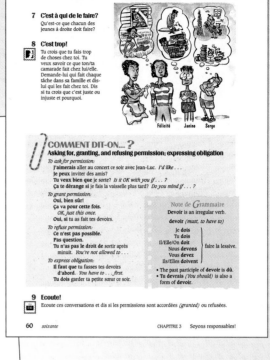

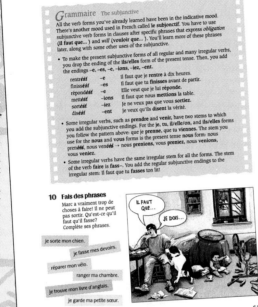

An Abundance of Activities

Throughout *Allez, viens!*, activities flow from controlled and structured through transitional to open-ended, communicative activities. Plenty of activities are contained within the program to build competency in each of the four language skills. Types of activities included in each chapter are:

- Contextualized listening activities
- Pair and group work
- Journal writing activities (can be used as portfolio assessment activities)
- Reading, writing, and role-playing activities
- Discovery questions and discussions of culture topics

Critical Thinking Through Multicultural Awareness

The *Panorama Culturel* is designed to give your students a chance to meet people from around the French-speaking world who share their views, opinions, and thoughts on a variety of topics that are thematically related to the chapters in ***Allez, viens!***. Filmed on location, authentic interviews with native speakers can be found in the text, on the *Video Program,* and in the *Audio Program.* The result: total video, audio, and text integration for complete language development. The *Panorama Culturel* also contains critical-thinking activities that expand upon what students learn from the interviews.

An Encounter of Cultures

Have you ever wished for a fresh new way to introduce French-speaking peoples and cultures to your students? ***Allez, viens!***'s *Rencontre Culturelle* offers just that! Mini photo-essays present francophone cultures, both exotic and familiar, from around the world. Students learn about the history of Belgium, the peoples of the Central African Republic, the cultural diversity of Montreal, traditional markets in Morocco, and much more. Each presentation includes critical-thinking questions that encourage students to compare the culture they are studying to their own. They'll see the similarities among worldwide cultures, as well as the differences that make each culture unique.

Allez, viens!

Holt French
Level 3

ANNOTATED
TEACHER'S EDITION

HOLT, RINEHART AND WINSTON
Harcourt Brace & Company

Austin • New York • Orlando • Atlanta • San Francisco • Boston • Dallas • Toronto • London

Printed in the United States of America

ISBN 0-03-094022-2

2 3 4 5 6 7   071   99 98 97 96

In the *Annotated Teachers's Edition:*
Photography Credits
Abbreviations used: (t) top, (c) center, (b) bottom, (l) left, (r) right.
Front Matter: Page T23(b), Pierre Berger/Photo Researchers; T25(t), Victor Englebert; T32(br), HRW Photo by Marty Granger/Edge Productions; T37(b), HRW Photo by Marty Granger/Edge Productions; T45(bl), HRW Photo/Michelle Bridwell; T47(bl), HRW Photo/Lance Shriner; T47(br), HRW Photo/Helen Kolda. **Chapter 1:** Page 3E, P. J. Sharpe, SuperStock; 3F(br), Robert Fried. **Chapter 5:** Page 109F(bl), HRW Photo by Patrice Maurin-Berthier; 109F(br), HRW Photo by Patrice Maurin-Berthier. **Chapter 6:** Page 135E(bl), Noboru Komine/Photo Researchers Inc.; 135E(br), HRW Photo by Mark Antman. **Chapter 7:** Page 161E, HRW Photo by Patrice Maurin-Berthier; 161F(tl), E. R. Degginger/Bruce Coleman, Inc.; 161F(bl), Anne Kaiser/SuperStock. **Chapter 8:** Page 187E(br), Steve Vidler/SuperStock; 187F(bl), SuperStock; 187F(br), Guido Cozzi/Bruce Coleman, Inc. **Chapter 9:** Page 217E(b), HRW Photo by May Polycarpe.

Illustration Credits
Front Matter: Page T38, Jocelyne Bouchard; T49, Jocelyne Bouchard. **Chapter 2:** Page 27D, Anne Stanley; 27F, Pascal Garnier. **Chapter 3:** Page 53E, Julian Willis; 53F, Julian Willis. **Chapter 4:** Page 79E, Pierre Fouillet; 79F, Gwenneth Barth. **Chapter 5:** Page 109E, Jocelyne Bouchard. **Chapter 6:** Page 135F, Jocelyne Bouchard. **Chapter 9:** Page 217F, Jocelyne Bouchard. **Chapter 10:** Page 243C, David Gothard; 243F, David Gothard. **Chapter 12:** Page 295E, Alain Massicotti; 295F, Lisa Nigro.

In the *Pupil's Edition:*
For permission to reprint copyrighted material, grateful acknowledgment is made to the following sources:

ASBL Association de Gestion des Domaines Touristiques du Vallon de la Lambrée: Advertisement, "Château Fort de Logne," from *Guide des attractions touristiques & musées, Belgique.*

asbl: Attractions et Tourisme: Advertisement, "Château Fort de Logne," "Musée de la Dentelle," and "Parc de Récréation Mont Mosan" from *Guide des attractions touristiques musées, Belgique.*

Bayard Presse: From *Albert nez en l'air* by Paul Martin, illustrations by Mario Ramos. Photograph captions from pages 40, 41, 43, 50, and 51 from *Images Doc,* no. 25, January 1991. Copyright © 1991 by Bayard Presse. From "Basket-ball," from "Escrime," from "Gymnastiqué," and from "Tir à l'arc" from "Sportez-vous bien!" from *Okapi,* October 1-15, 1986. Copyright © 1986 by Bayard Presse. "Béatrice," "Raul," and "Stéphanie" from "Le sport, c'est quoi pour vous?" from *Okapi,* November 15–30, 1986. Copyright © 1986 by Bayard Presse. From "Quel rôle joue la mode dans votre vie?" from *Okapi,* July 15–31, 1989. Copyright © 1989 by Bayard Presse. From "Aimez–vous la BD?" from *Okapi,* no. 534, February 15–28, 1994. Copyright © 1994 by Bayard Presse. "Tous aiment me voir danser," "La musique est un langage universel," "La musique, c'est beau!," and "La musique m'accompagne dans la vie," from "Quelle musique écoutez-vous?" from *Okapi,* no. 548, October 15–22, 1994. Copyright © 1994 by Bayard Presse.

Jérôme Bonnefroy: Photographs of clothing from "Vanessa, Hélène, Charlotte, Shannen... Exploitent leurs combines" from *Bravo Girl,* no. 56, April 25–May 8, 1994.

ACKNOWLEDGMENTS continued on page 398, which is an extension of the copyright page.

Annotated Teacher's Edition

CONTRIBUTING WRITERS

Jennie Bowser Chao
Consultant
East Lansing, MI
Ms. Chao was the principal writer of the Level 3 *Annotated Teacher's Edition*.

Judith Ryser
San Marcos High School
San Marcos, TX
Ms. Ryser contributed teaching suggestions and notes for the reading and writing sections of the Level 3 *Annotated Teacher's Edition*.

Jayne Abrate
The University of Missouri
Rolla Campus
Rolla, MO
Ms. Abrate contributed teaching suggestion, notes, and background information for the Location Openers of the Level 3 *Annotated Teacher's Edition*.

Margaret Sellstrom
Consultant
Austin, TX
Ms. Sellstrom contributed answers to activities of the Level 3 *Annotated Teacher's Edition*.

FIELD TEST PARTICIPANTS

Marie Allison
New Hanover High School
Wilmington, NC

Gabrielle Applequist
Capital High School
Boise, ID

Jana Brinton
Bingham High School
Riverton, UT

Nancy J. Cook
Sam Houston High School
Lake Charles, LA

Rachael Gray
Williams High School
Plano, TX

Priscilla Koch
Troxell Junior High School
Allentown, PA

Katherine Kohler
Nathan Hale Middle School
Norwalk, CT

Nancy Mirsky
Museum Junior High School
Yonkers, NY

Myrna S. Nie
Whetstone High School
Columbus, OH

Jacqueline Reid
Union High School
Tulsa, OK

Judith Ryser
San Marcos High School
San Marcos, TX

Erin Hahn Sass
Lincoln Southeast High School
Lincoln, NE

Linda Sherwin
Sandy Creek High School
Tyrone, GA

Norma Joplin Sivers
Arlington Heights High School
Fort Worth, TX

Lorabeth Stroup
Lovejoy High School
Lovejoy, GA

Robert Vizena
W.W. Lewis Middle School
Sulphur, LA

Gladys Wade
New Hanover High School
Wilmington, NC

Kathy White
Grimsley High School
Greensboro, NC

REVIEWERS

Khaled Bendakhlia
Consultant
Austin, TX

Jeannette Caviness
Mount Tabor High School
Winston-Salem, NC

Joseph F. Herney
Briarcliff High School
Briarcliff Manor, NY

Patricia Rebac
Clarksville High School
Clarksville, TN

Jo Anne Wilson
Consultant
Glen Arbor, MI

Tony Zaunbrecher
Calcasieu Parish School Board
Lake Charles, LA

PROFESSIONAL ESSAYS

Standards for Foreign Language Learning
Robert LaBouve
Board of National Standards in Foreign Language Education
Austin, TX

Multi-Level Classrooms
Dr. Joan H. Manley
The University of Texas
El Paso, TX

Teaching Culture
Nancy A. Humbach
The Miami University
Oxford, OH

Dorothea Brushke
Parkway School District
Chesterfied, MO

Learning Styles and Multi-Modality Teaching
Mary B. McGehee
Louisiana State University
Baton Rouge, LA

Higher-Order Thinking Skills
Dr. Audrey L. Heining-Boynton
The University of North Carolina
Chapel Hill, NC

Using Portfolios in the Foreign Language Classroom
Jo Anne S. Wilson
J. Wilson Associates
Glen Arbor, MI

Pupil's Edition

Authors

Emmanuel Rongiéras d'Usseau
Le Kremlin-Bicêtre, France

Mr. Rongiéras d'Usseau contributed to the development of the scope and sequence for the chapters, created the basic material and listening scripts, selected realia, and wrote activities.

Contributing Writers

Jayne Abrate
The University of Missouri
Rolla Campus
Rolla, MO

Judith Ryser
San Marcos High School
San Marcos, TX

Consultant

John DeMado
Washington, CT

Reviewers

Deana Allert
U.S. Peace Corps volunteer
Senegal, 1991-1992
Berkeley, CA

Donna Clementi
Appleton West High School
Appleton, WI

Donald Doehla
Vallejo Senior High School
Vallejo, CA

Amina Elaisammi
Embassy of the Kingdom of Morocco
Washington, DC

Zohra Ben Hamida
Tunisian Information Office
Washington, DC

Joseph F. Herney
Briarcliff High School
Briarcliff Manor, NY

Sam Leone
Freehold Township High School
Freehold, NJ

Patricia Norwood
The University of Texas at Austin
Austin, TX

Joann K. Pompa
Mountain Pointe High School
Phoenix, AZ

Marc Prévost
Austin Community College
Austin, TX

Field Test Participants

Marie Allison
New Hanover High School
Wilmington, NC

Gabrielle Applequist
Capital High School
Boise, ID

Jana Brinton
Bingham High School
Riverton, UT

Nancy J. Cook
Sam Houston High School
Lake Charles, LA

Rachael Gray
Williams High School
Plano, TX

Priscilla Koch
Troxell Junior High School
Allentown, PA

Katherine Kohler
Nathan Hale Middle School
Norwalk, CT

Nancy Mirsky
Museum Junior High School
Yonkers, NY

Myrna S. Nie
Whetstone High School
Columbus, OH

Jacqueline Reid
Union High School
Tulsa, OK

Judith Ryser
San Marcos High School
San Marcos, TX

Erin Hahn Sass
Lincoln Southeast High School
Lincoln, NE

Linda Sherwin
Sandy Creek High School
Tyrone, GA

Norma Joplin Sivers
Arlington Heights High School
Fort Worth, TX

Lorabeth Stroup
Lovejoy High School
Lovejoy, GA

Robert Vizena
W.W. Lewis Middle School
Sulphur, LA

Gladys Wade
New Hanover High School
Wilmington, NC

Kathy White
Grimsley High School
Greensboro, NC

To the Student

*Some people have the opportunity to learn a new language by living in another country.
Most of us, however, begin learning another language and getting acquainted with a foreign
culture in a classroom with the help of a teacher, classmates, and a book.
To use your book effectively, you need to know how it works.*

Allez, viens! *(Come along!)* takes you to French-speaking locations on three different continents. Each location is introduced with photos and information in a four-page photo essay.

There are twelve chapters in the book, and each one follows the same pattern.

First, the two Chapter Opener pages announce the chapter theme and list the objectives. These objectives set goals that you can achieve by the end of the chapter.

Mise en train *(Getting started)* The next part of the chapter may be a conversation among French-speaking people, a letter, or even a magazine article, involving language you'll be learning in the chapter. You'll also be able to listen to this on audiocassette or CD.

Première Etape *(First Part)* This is the first of two sections, or **étapes**, in the chapter. At the beginning of each **étape** there's a reminder of the objective(s) you'll be aiming for in this part. In order to communicate, you'll need the French expressions listed in one or more boxes labeled **Comment dit-on... ?** *(How do you say . . . ?)*. You'll also need vocabulary; look for new words under the heading **Vocabulaire**. You won't have trouble finding grammar, for you're sure to recognize the headings **Grammaire** and **Note de grammaire**. Now, all you need is plenty of practice. In each **étape** there are listening, speaking, reading, and writing activities for you to do individually, with a partner, or in groups. By the end of an **étape**, you'll have achieved your objective(s).

Remise en train *(Getting started again)* After practicing the language that was presented in the **Mise en train**, you're ready to continue. In this part of the chapter, additional conversations, letters, or articles introduce a new situation involving the language you'll be learning and using in the next **étape**. You'll hear this material, too, on audiocassette or CD.

Deuxième Etape *(Second Part)* As in the first **étape**, there's a reminder of your new objective(s). Look for the same features you became familiar with in the first **étape**: French expressions in **Comment dit-on... ?** boxes, new words under the heading **Vocabulaire**, and any grammar you'll need in boxes labeled **Grammaire** or **Note de grammaire**. Of course, there will be plenty of listening, speaking, reading, and writing practice.

Allez, viens! will also help you get to know the cultures of the people who speak French.

Panorama Culturel *(Cultural Panorama)* On this page of the chapter you'll read interviews with French-speaking people around the world. They'll talk about themselves and their lives, and you can compare their culture to yours. You'll watch these interviews on video or listen to them on audiocassette or CD.

Note Culturelle *(Culture Note)* These notes provide a lot of interesting cultural information.

Rencontre Culturelle *(Cultural Encounter)* In nine of the chapters, this page offers you, through photos and interesting information, a firsthand encounter with the French-speaking country where the chapter is set.

Lisons! *(Let's read!)* After the second **étape**, one or more reading selections related to the chapter theme will help you to continue developing your reading skills.

Ecrivons! *(Let's write!)* Writing is an important means of communication. It takes many forms and has many purposes. It's also a skill that takes practice to develop. In this section, you'll have a chance to develop this skill as you learn to be expressive, creative, informative, and persuasive in your new language.

Mise en pratique *(Putting into practice)* A variety of activities gives you opportunities to put into practice what you've learned in the chapter in new situations. You'll improve your listening skills and practice communicating with others orally and in writing.

Que sais-je? *(What do I know?)* On this page at the end of the chapter, a series of questions and short activities will help you decide how well you can do on your own.

Vocabulaire *(Vocabulary)* On the last page of the chapter, you'll find a list of new words and phrases from the chapter. The words are grouped by **étape** and listed under the objectives they support. Make sure you also know the words and expressions you've already learned that appear in each of the boxes labeled **Comment dit-on... ?** and **Vocabulaire**—You'll need to know all of them for the Chapter Test!

Throughout the book, you'll get a lot of help.

De bons conseils *(Good advice)* Check out the helpful hints in these boxes to improve your study habits and your reading and writing.

Tu te rappelles? *(Do you remember?)* Along the way, these notes will remind you of things you might have forgotten.

A la française *(The French way)* Be on the lookout for these boxes, too. They'll give you additional language tips to help you communicate more like a native speaker.

Vocabulaire à la carte *(Your choice of vocabulary)* From these lists, you'll be able to choose extra words and expressions you might want to use when you talk about yourself and your interests.

At the end of your book, you'll find more helpful material, including a list of the communicative expressions you'll need, a summary of the grammar you've studied, supplementary vocabulary, and French-English, English-French vocabulary lists with the words you'll need to know in bold type.

Allez, viens! Come along on the next lap of your exciting trip to new cultures.

Bon voyage!

ANNOTATED TEACHER'S EDITION

Contents

Contents

ALLEZ, VIENS

en Europe!

LOCATION • CHAPITRES 1, 2, 3, 4 XXIV

VISIT FRANCOPHONE EUROPE AND—

Learn about the traditional clothing and foods of France • CHAPITRE 1
Read about comics in the francophone world • CHAPITRE 2
Learn about environmentalism in French-speaking countries • CHAPITRE 3
Find out about French fashion • CHAPITRE 4

CHAPITRE 1

France, les régions 4

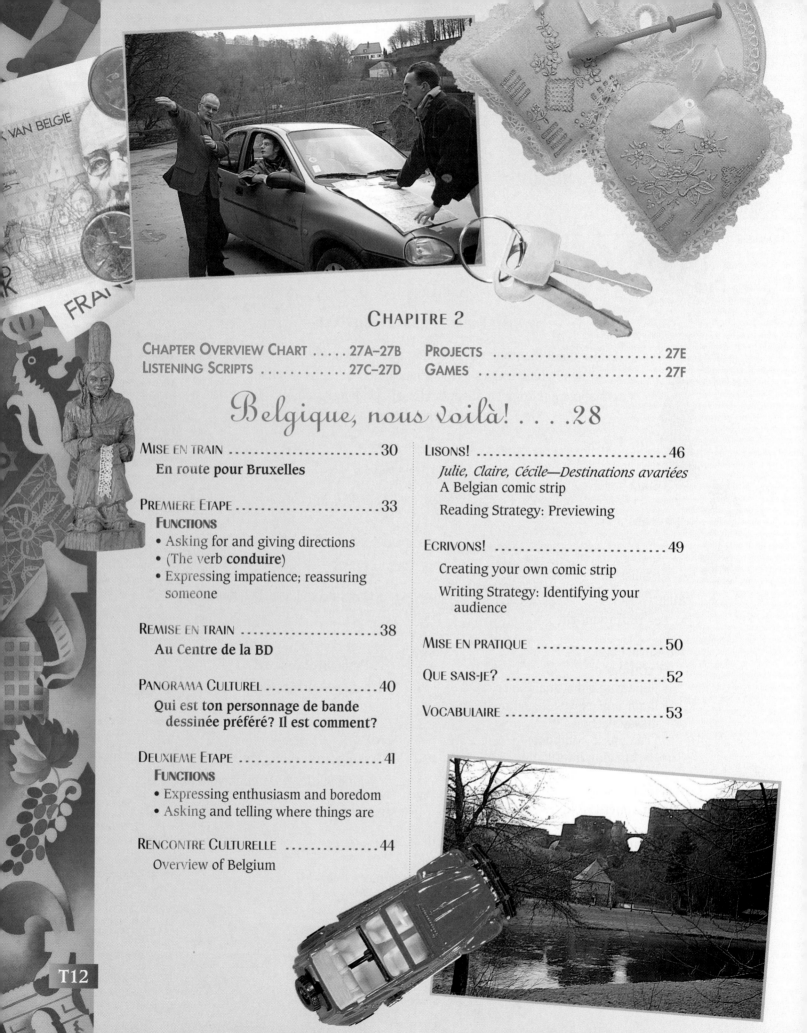

CHAPITRE 2

Belgique, nous voilà! 28

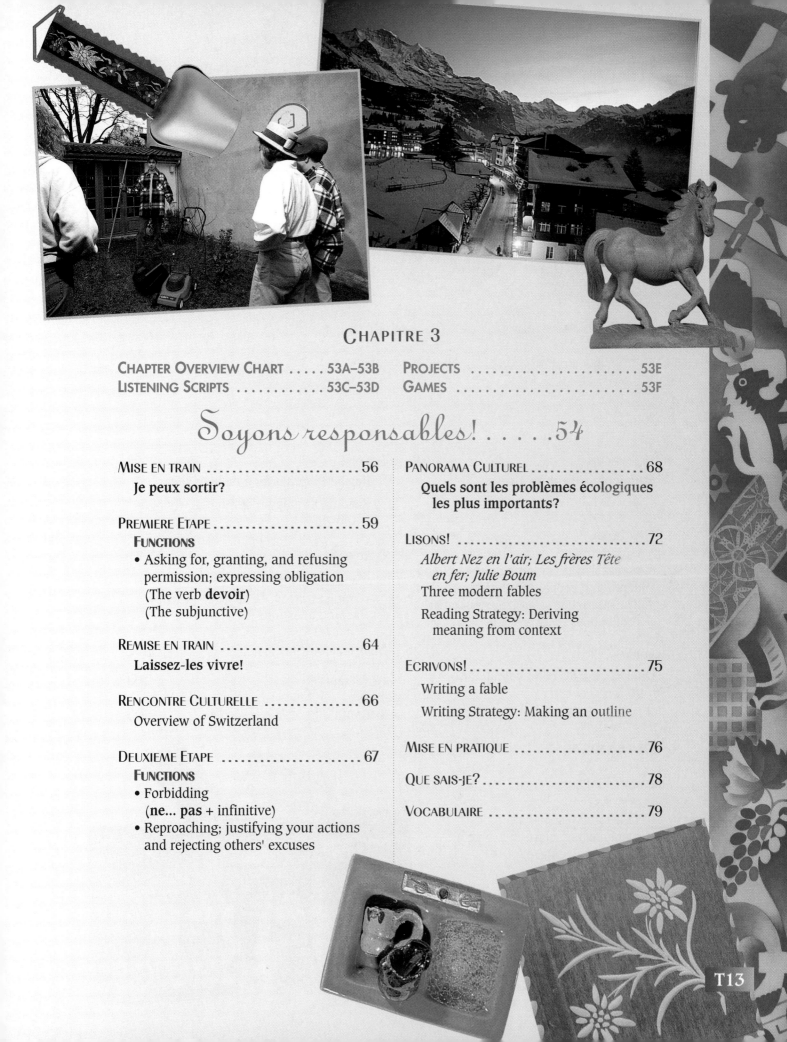

Chapitre 3

Soyons responsables! 54

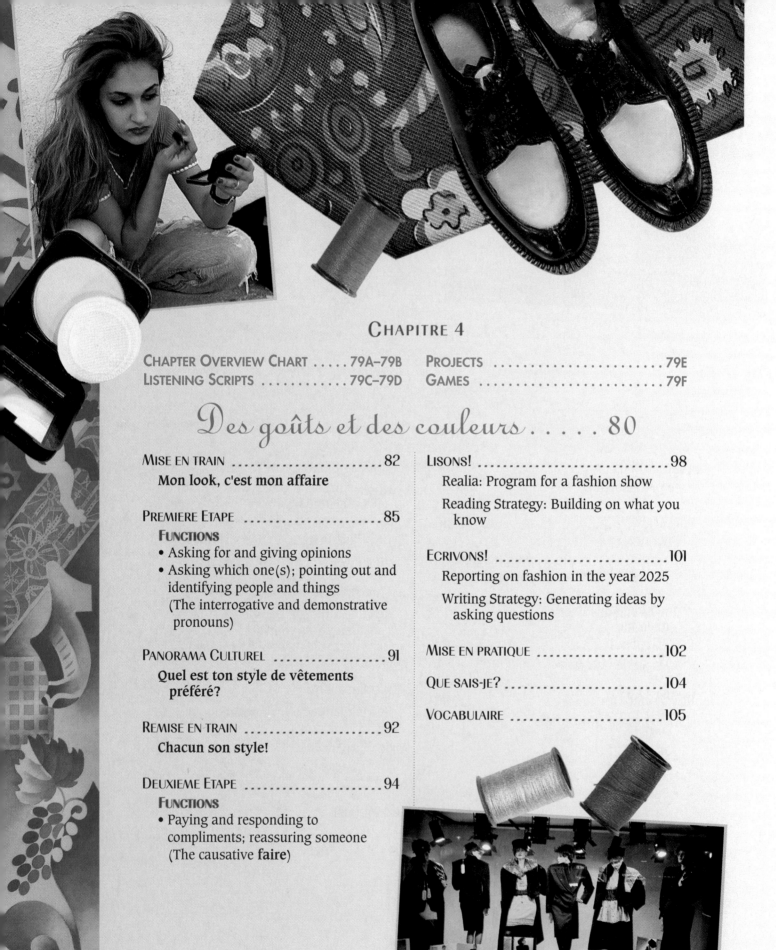

CHAPITRE 4

Des goûts et des couleurs 80

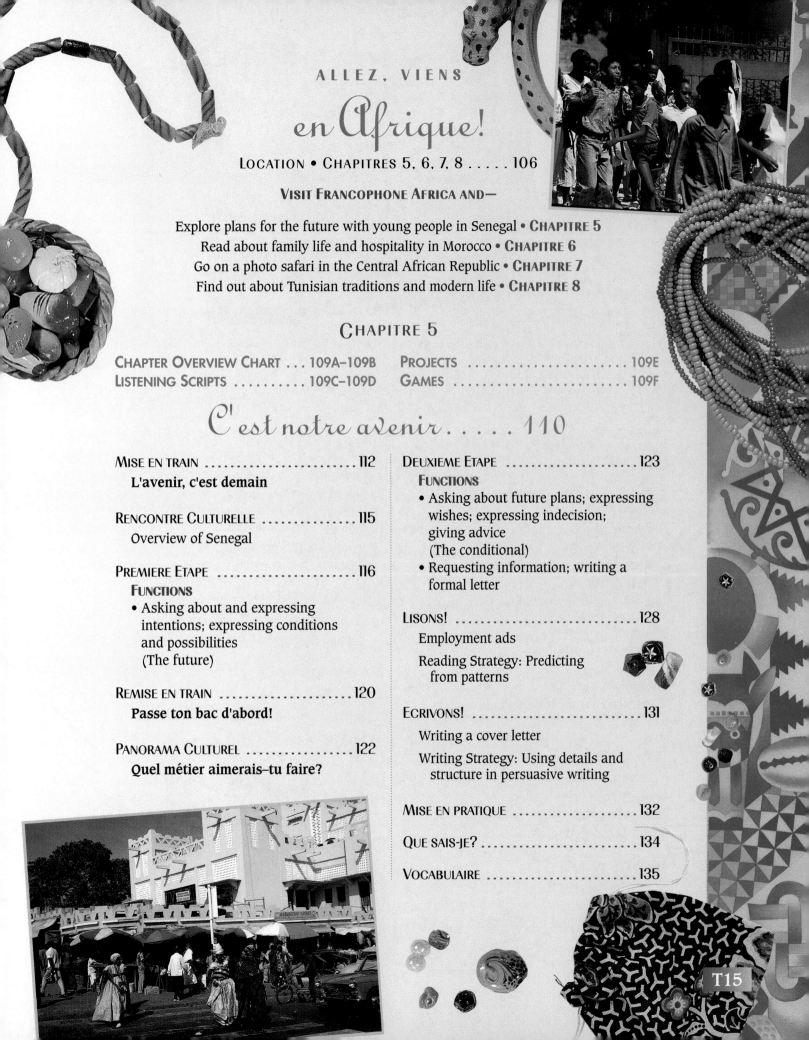

ALLEZ, VIENS

en Afrique!

LOCATION • CHAPITRES 5, 6, 7, 8 106

VISIT FRANCOPHONE AFRICA AND—

Explore plans for the future with young people in Senegal • CHAPITRE 5
Read about family life and hospitality in Morocco • CHAPITRE 6
Go on a photo safari in the Central African Republic • CHAPITRE 7
Find out about Tunisian traditions and modern life • CHAPITRE 8

CHAPITRE 5

C'est notre avenir 110

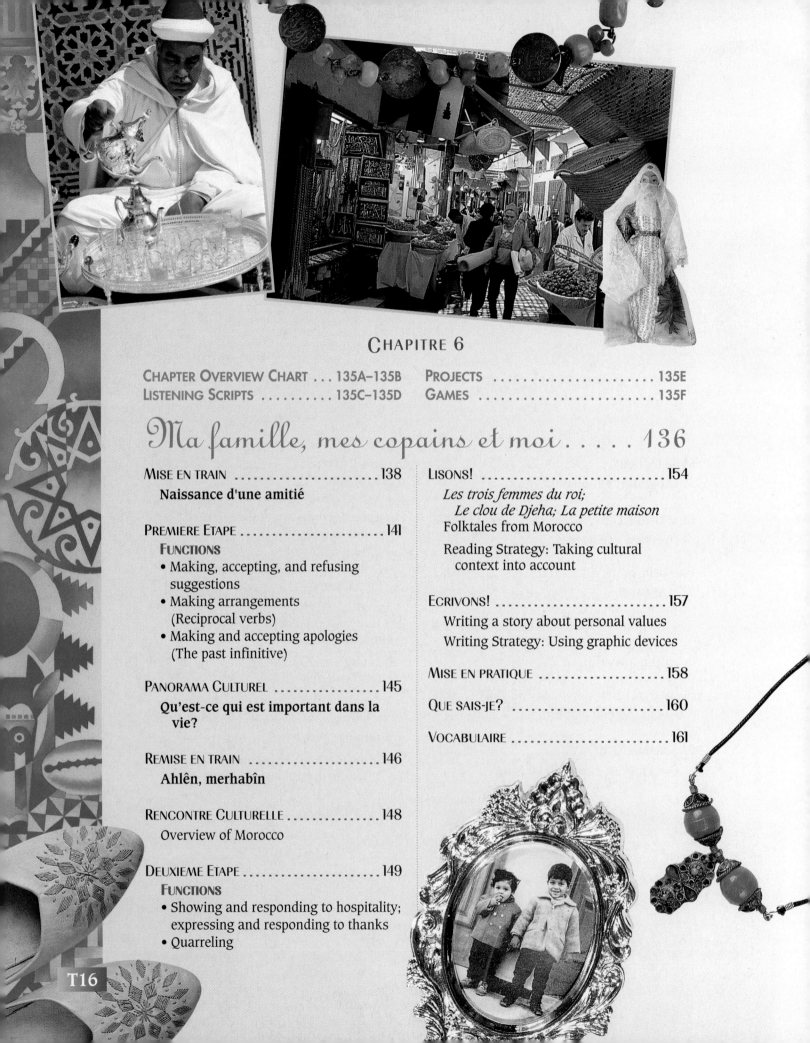

CHAPITRE 6

Ma famille, mes copains et moi 136

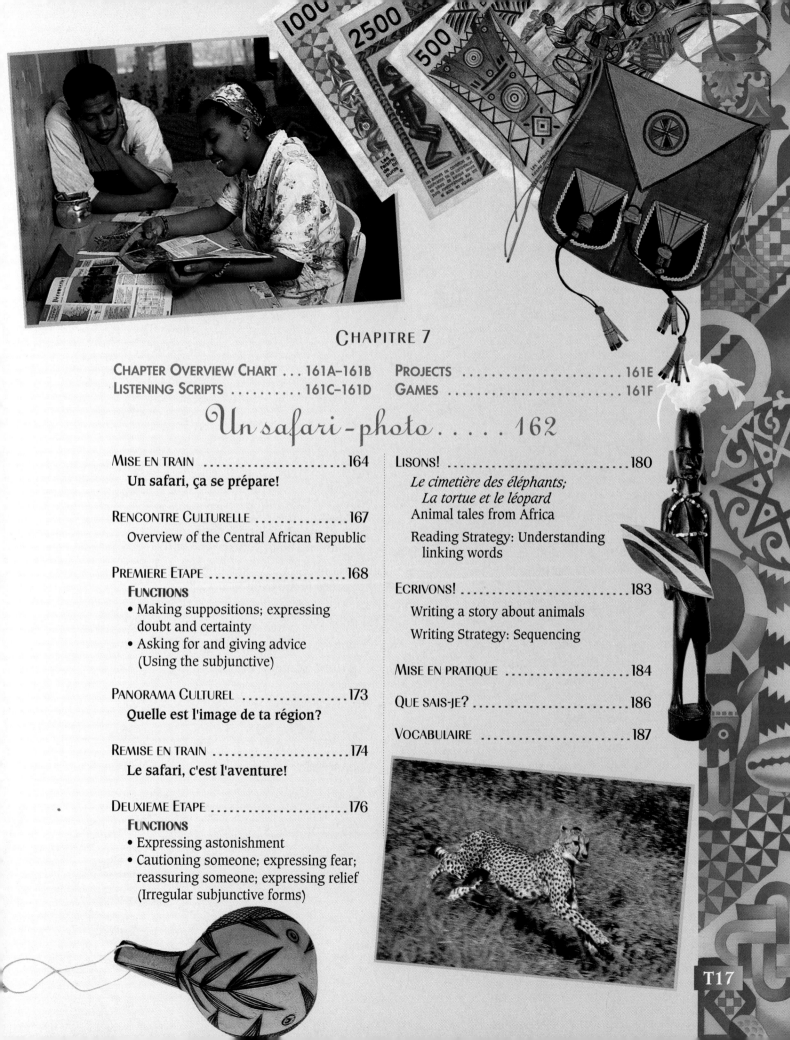

CHAPITRE 7

Un safari-photo 162

CHAPITRE 8

La Tunisie, pays de contrastes 188

**VISIT FRANCOPHONE NORTH AMERICA
AND THE CARIBBEAN AND—**

Talk about movies and television shows • CHAPITRE 9
Learn about everyday life in Guadeloupe • CHAPITRE 10
Read about Cajun food and festivals • CHAPITRE 11

CHAPITRE 9

C'est l'fun! 218

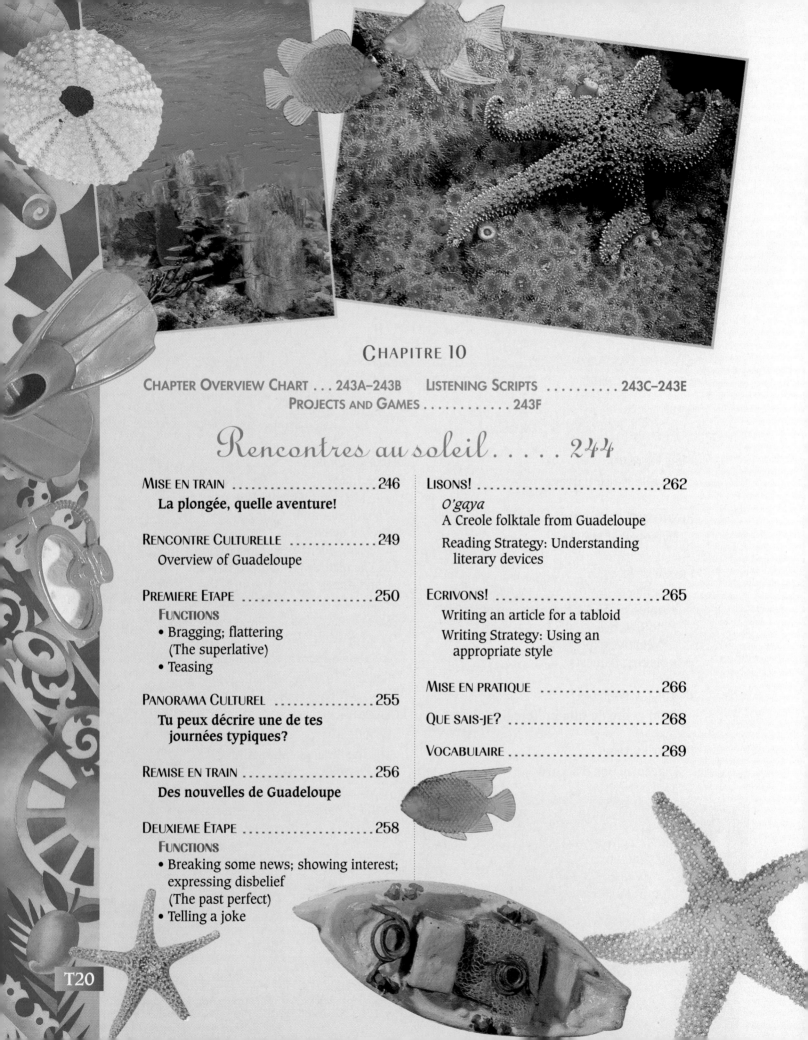

CHAPITRE 10

Rencontres au soleil 244

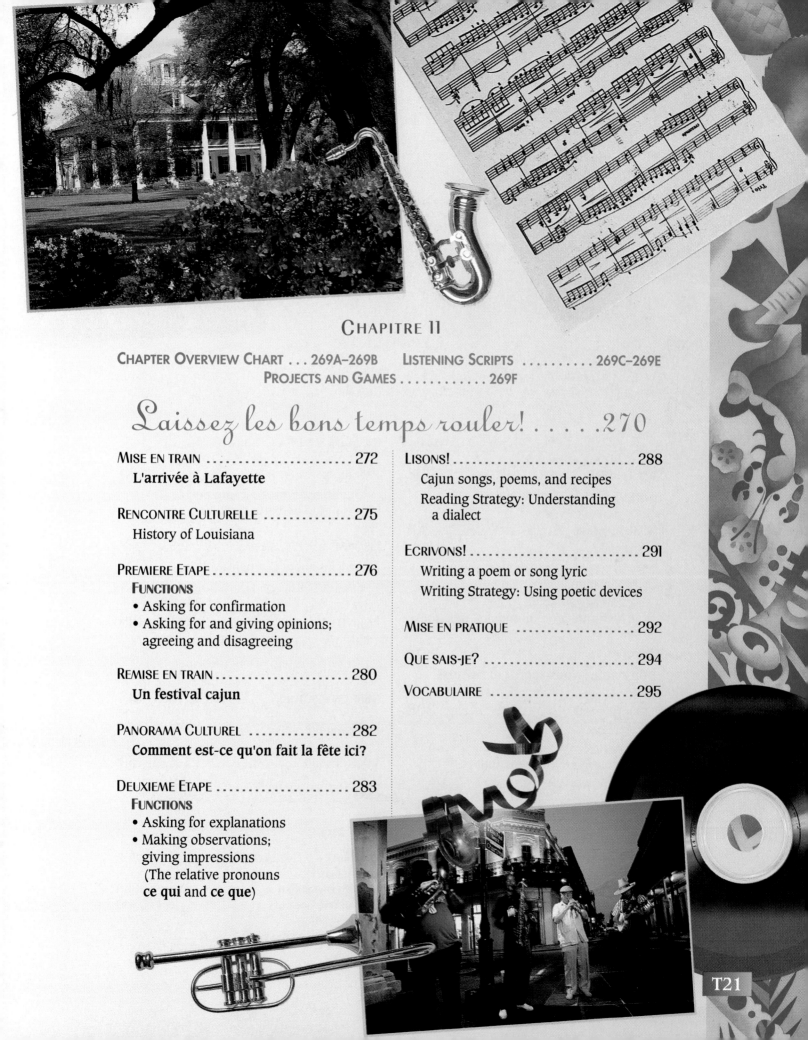

CHAPITRE 11

VISIT A GATHERING OF NATIONS
AT THE OLYMPICS AND—

Meet athletes
from around the
world • CHAPITRE 12

CHAPITRE 12

Echanges sportifs et culturels ... 296

REFERENCE SECTION

Cultural References

Page numbers referring to material in the Pupil's Edition *appear in regular type. When the material referenced is located in the* Annotated Teacher's Edition, *page numbers appear in **boldface type**.* ◆

Maps

L'Europe francophone

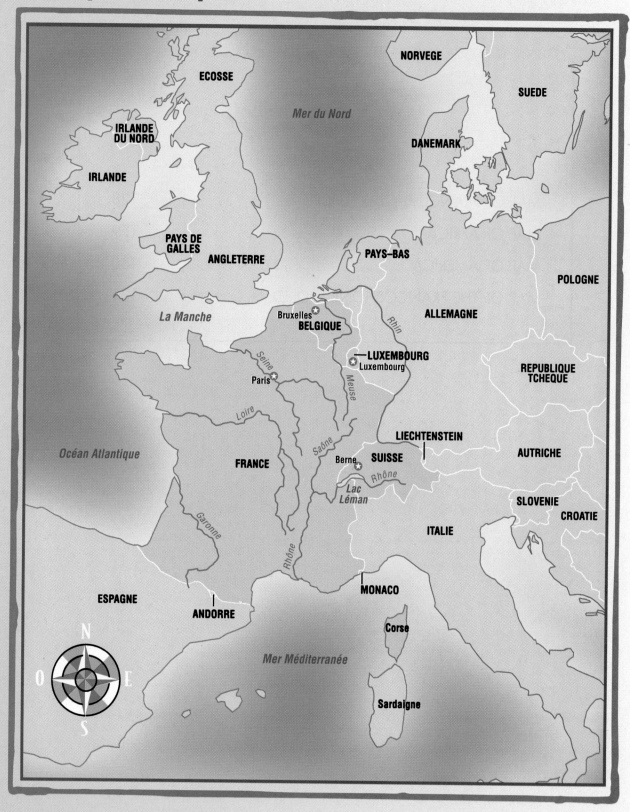

NORVEGE

ECOSSE

SUEDE

Mer du Nord

IRLANDE DU NORD

DANEMARK

IRLANDE

PAYS DE GALLES

PAYS-BAS

POLOGNE

ANGLETERRE

ALLEMAGNE

La Manche

Bruxelles

BELGIQUE

Rhin

Seine

LUXEMBOURG

Luxembourg

REPUBLIQUE TCHEQUE

Paris

Meuse

Loire

Saône

LIECHTENSTEIN

Océan Atlantique

AUTRICHE

Berne

SUISSE

FRANCE

Rhône

Lac Léman

SLOVENIE

Garonne

ITALIE

CROATIE

Rhône

ESPAGNE

MONACO

ANDORRE

Corse

Mer Méditerranée

Sardaigne

N
O   E
S

L'Afrique francophone

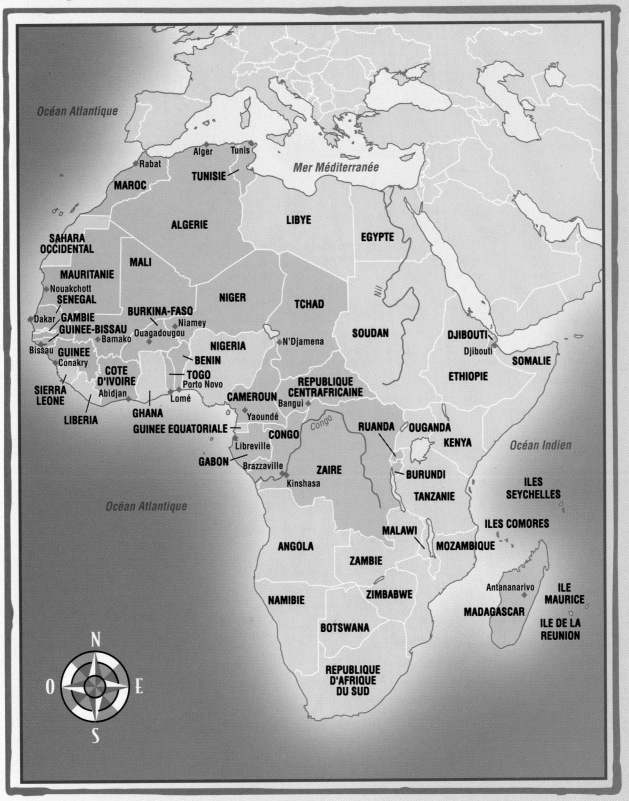

Océan Atlantique

Mer Méditerranée

MAROC
Rabat
Alger
Tunis
TUNISIE

ALGERIE
LIBYE
EGYPTE

SAHARA
OCCIDENTAL

MALI

MAURITANIE
Nouakchott
SENEGAL
NIGER
TCHAD
SOUDAN
DJIBOUTI
Djibouti

Dakar
GAMBIE
BURKINA-FASO
Niamey
Ouagadougou
N'Djamena
SOMALIE

Bamako
GUINEE-BISSAU
NIGERIA
ETHIOPIE

Bissau
GUINEE
BENIN

Conakry
COTE
D'IVOIRE
TOGO
Porto Novo
REPUBLIQUE
CENTRAFRICAINE

SIERRA
LEONE
Abidjan
Lomé
CAMEROUN
Bangui

LIBERIA
GHANA
Yaoundé
RUANDA
OUGANDA

GUINEE EQUATORIALE
CONGO
KENYA
Océan Indien

Libreville
Congo
BURUNDI

GABON
Brazzaville
ZAIRE
ILES
SEYCHELLES

Kinshasa
TANZANIE

ILES COMORES

ANGOLA
MALAWI
MOZAMBIQUE

ZAMBIE

Océan Atlantique

NAMIBIE
ZIMBABWE
Antananarivo
ILE
MAURICE

MADAGASCAR
ILE DE LA
REUNION

BOTSWANA

REPUBLIQUE
D'AFRIQUE
DU SUD

N
O   E
S

xxi

L'Amérique francophone

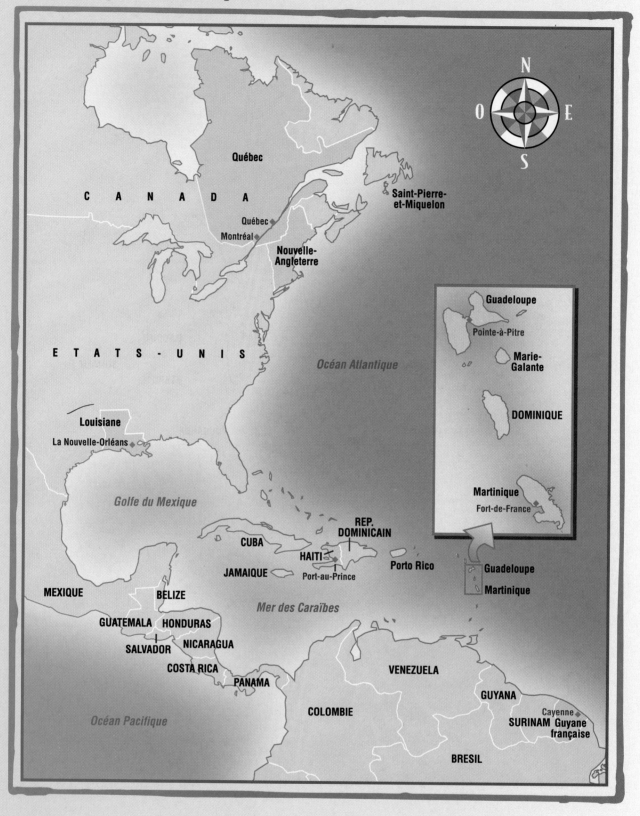

T30

Le Monde francophone

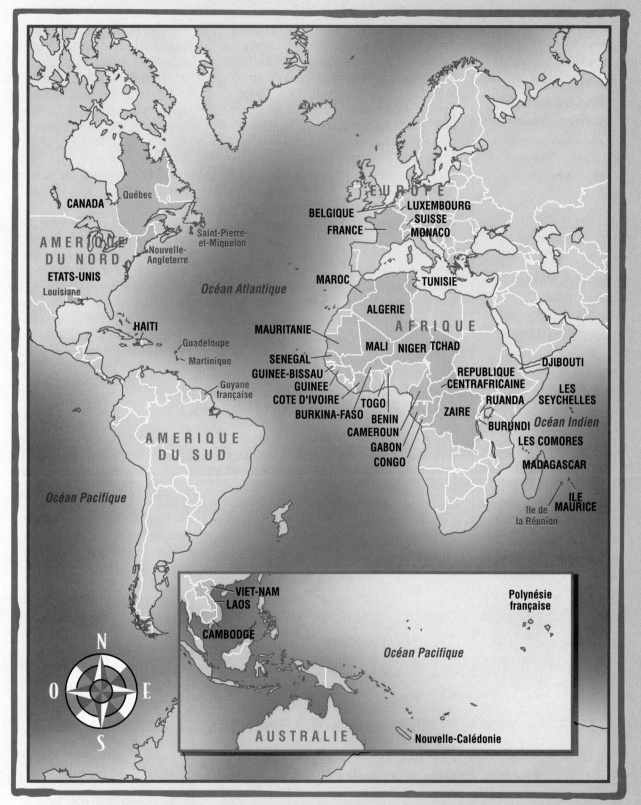

CANADA
Québec
AMÉRIQUE DU NORD
Saint-Pierre-et-Miquelon
Nouvelle-Angleterre
ÉTATS-UNIS
Louisiane
Océan Atlantique
HAÏTI
Guadeloupe
Martinique
Guyane française
AMÉRIQUE DU SUD
Océan Pacifique

EUROPE
BELGIQUE
LUXEMBOURG
SUISSE
FRANCE
MONACO
MAROC
TUNISIE
ALGERIE
AFRIQUE
MAURITANIE
MALI
NIGER
TCHAD
SENEGAL
DJIBOUTI
GUINEE-BISSAU
REPUBLIQUE
CENTRAFRICAINE
GUINEE
COTE D'IVOIRE
TOGO
RUANDA
LES SEYCHELLES
BURKINA-FASO
BENIN
ZAIRE
CAMEROUN
BURUNDI
Océan Indien
GABON
LES COMORES
CONGO
MADAGASCAR
ILE MAURICE
Ile de la Réunion

VIET-NAM
LAOS
Polynésie française
CAMBODGE
Océan Pacifique
AUSTRALIE
Nouvelle-Calédonie

N O E S

xxiii

Since the early eighties, we have seen significant advances in modern foreign language curriculum practices:

(1) a redefinition of the objectives of foreign language study involving a commitment to the development of proficiency in the four skills and in cultural awareness;

(2) a recognition of the need for longer sequences of study;

(3) a new student-centered approach that redefines the role of the teacher as facilitator and encourages students to take a more active role in their learning;

(4) the inclusion of students of all learning abilities.

The new Holt, Rinehart and Winston foreign language programs take into account not only these advances in the field of foreign language education, but also the input of teachers and students around the country. ◆

PRINCIPLES AND PRACTICES

As nations become increasingly interdependent, the need for effective communication and sensitivity to other cultures becomes more important. Today's youth must be culturally and linguistically prepared to participate in a global society. At Holt, Rinehart and Winston, we believe that proficiency in more than one language is essential to meeting this need.

The primary goal of the Holt, Rinehart and Winston foreign language programs is to help students develop linguistic proficiency and cultural sensitivity. By interweaving language and culture, our programs seek to broaden students' communication skills while at the same time deepening their appreciation of other cultures.

◆◆

We believe that all students can benefit from foreign language instruction. We recognize that not everyone learns at the same rate or in the same way; nevertheless, we believe that all students should have the opportunity to acquire language proficiency to a degree commensurate with their individual abilities.

Holt, Rinehart and Winston's foreign language programs are designed to accommodate all students by appealing to a variety of learning styles.

◆◆

We believe that effective language programs should motivate students. Students deserve an answer to the question they often ask: "Why are we doing this?" They need to have goals that are interesting, practical, clearly stated, and attainable.

Holt, Rinehart and Winston's foreign language programs promote success. They present relevant content in manageable increments that encourage students to attain achievable functional objectives.

We believe that proficiency in a foreign language is best nurtured by programs that encourage students to think critically and to take risks when expressing themselves in the language. We also recognize that students should strive for accuracy in communication. While it is imperative that students have a knowledge of the basic structures of the language, it is also important that they go beyond the simple manipulation of forms.

Holt, Rinehart and Winston's foreign language program reflects a careful progression of activities that guides students from comprehensible input of authentic language through structured practice to creative, personalized expression. This progression, accompanied by consistent re-entry and spiraling of functions, vocabulary, and structures, provides students with the tools and the confidence to express themselves in their new language.

◆◆

Finally, we believe that a complete program of language instruction should take into account the needs of teachers in today's increasingly demanding classrooms.

At Holt, Rinehart and Winston, we have designed programs that offer practical teacher support and provide resources to meet individual learning and teaching styles.

Using the Pupil's Edition of Allez, viens!

Allez, viens! offers an integrated approach to language learning. Presentation and practice of functional expressions, vocabulary, and grammar structures are interwoven with cultural information, language learning tips, and realia to facilitate both learning and teaching. The technology, audiovisual materials, and additional print resources integrated throughout each chapter allow instruction to be adapted to a variety of teaching and learning styles. ◆

ALLEZ, VIENS! LEVEL 3

Allez, viens! Level 3 consists of twelve instructional chapters. To ensure successful completion of the book and to facilitate articulation from one level to the next, Chapters 1 and 12 are review chapters and Chapters 2 and 11 introduce minimal new material.

Following is a description of the various features in *Allez, viens!* and suggestions on how to use them in the classroom. While it is not crucial for students to cover all material and do all activities to achieve the goals listed at the beginning of each chapter, the material within each chapter has been carefully sequenced to enable students to progress steadily at a realistic pace to the ultimate goal of linguistic and cultural proficiency. You, the teacher, as presenter, facilitator, and guide, will determine the precise depth of coverage, taking into account the individual needs of each class and the amount and type of alternative instructional material to be used from the *Allez, viens!* program.

STARTING OUT...

In *Allez, viens!,* chapters are arranged by location. Each new location is introduced by a **Location Opener,** four pages of colorful photos and background information that can be used to introduce the region and help motivate students.

The two-page **Chapter Opener** is intended to pique students' interest and focus their attention on the task at hand. It is a visual introduction to the theme of the chapter and includes a brief description of the topic and situations students will encounter, as well as a list of objectives they will be expected to achieve.

SETTING THE SCENE...

Language instruction begins with the **Mise en train** and the **Remise en train,** the comprehensible input that models language in a culturally authentic setting. Accompanied by the audiocassette or compact disc recording, the highly visual presentation ensures success as students practice their receptive skills and begin to recognize some of the new functions and vocabulary they will encounter in the chapter. Following the **Mise en train** and the **Remise en Train** is a series of activities that can be used to help guide students through the story and check comprehension.

BUILDING PROFICIENCY STEP BY STEP...

Première and **Deuxième étape** are the two core instructional sections where the greater part of language acquisition will take place. The communicative goals in each chapter center on the functional expressions presented in **Comment dit-on... ?** boxes. These expressions are supported and expanded by material in the **Vocabulaire, Grammaire,** and **Note de grammaire** sections. Activities immediately following the above features are designed to practice recognition or to provide closed-ended practice with the new material. Activities then progress from controlled to open-ended practice where students are able to express themselves in meaningful communication. Depending on class size, general ability level, and class dynamics, you may wish to proceed sequentially through all activities in a chapter, supplementing presentation or practice at various points with additional materials from *Allez, viens!,* or to proceed more quickly to open-ended pair and group work.

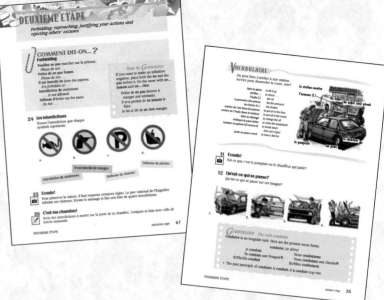

DISCOVERING THE PEOPLE AND THE CULTURE...

Cultural information has been incorporated into activities wherever possible. There are also two major cultural features to help students develop an appreciation and understanding of the cultures of French-speaking countries.

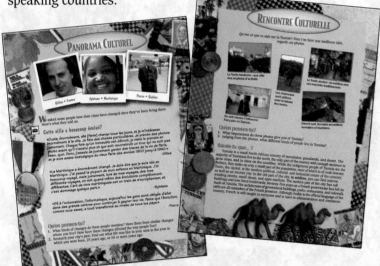

Panorama Culturel presents spontaneous interviews conducted in various countries in the French-speaking world on a topic related to the chapter theme. The interviews may be presented on video or done as a reading supplemented by the audiocassette or compact disc recording. Culminating activities on this page may be used to verify comprehension and encourage students to think critically about the target culture as well as their own.

Rencontre Culturelle presents an overview of francophone cultures from around the world in photo-essay format and invites students to compare and contrast the foreign culture with their own.

Note Culturelle provides tidbits of both "big C" and "little c" culture that can be used to enrich and enliven activities and presentations at various places throughout each chapter.

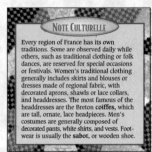

UNDERSTANDING AUTHENTIC DOCUMENTS...

Lisons! presents reading strategies that help students understand authentic French documents. The reading selections vary from advertisements to letters to short stories in order to accommodate different interests and familiarize students with different styles and formats. The accompanying activities progress from prereading to reading to postreading tasks and are designed to develop students' overall reading skills and challenge their critical thinking abilities.

Ecrivons! presents writing strategies that help students develop their writing skills. The strategies are integrated with prewriting, writing, and postwriting tasks designed to develop students' expressive and creative writing abilities in French.

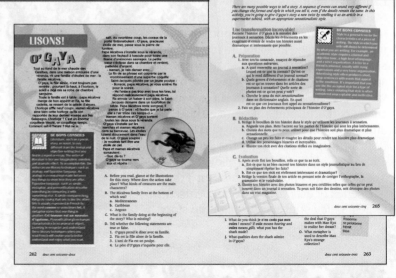

TARGETING STUDENTS' NEEDS...

In each **étape** several special features may be used to enhance language learning and cultural appreciation.

De bons conseils suggests effective ways for students to learn a foreign language.

A la française provides students with tips for speaking more natural-sounding French.

Vocabulaire à la carte presents optional vocabulary related to the chapter theme. These words are provided to help students personalize activities; students will not be required to produce this vocabulary on the Chapter Quizzes and Test.

Tu te rappelles? is a re-entry feature that lists and briefly explains previously learned vocabulary, functions, and grammar that students might need to review at the moment.

Si tu as oublié... is a handy page reference to either an earlier chapter where material was presented or to a reference section in the back of the book that includes such aids as the Summary of Functions and the Grammar Summary.

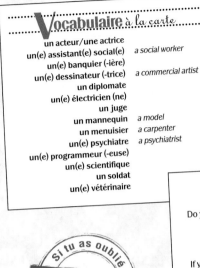

De bons conseils

You've probably noticed that the names of some careers in French have only a masculine form. You can use the masculine form to refer to both women and men, for example; **C'est un médecin** (He or she is a doctor). If you want to make it clear that you're talking about a woman, you can add the word **femme** to the masculine form; **C'est une femme médecin.**

Vocabulaire à la carte

un acteur/une actrice
un(e) assistant(e) social(e)   *a social worker*
un(e) banquier (-ière)
un(e) dessinateur (-trice)   *a commercial artist*
un diplomate
un(e) électricien (ne)
un juge
un mannequin   *a model*
un menuisier   *a carpenter*
un(e) psychiatre   *a psychiatrist*
un(e) programmeur (-euse)
un(e) scientifique
un soldat
un(e) vétérinaire

A la française

Sometimes you're not exactly sure what you're going to say next and you need a second to think. You can fill in gaps in your speech with these words that French-speaking people commonly use:
Bon,... Eh bien,... Euh,... Voyons,...
Attends,... Tu sais,... Alors,... and **Ben,...**

Si tu as oublié
the imperfect
va à la page 349.

Tu te rappelles?

Do you remember how to make the forms of the conditional?
Add the endings of the imperfect tense,
to the infinitive or to the irregular future stem.
Est-ce que tu **pourrais** le faire?
If you're unsure which stems are irregular, turn to page 125.
Remember to drop the **e** from **-re** infinitives.
Je viv**rais** à la campagne si je pouvais.

WRAPPING IT ALL UP...

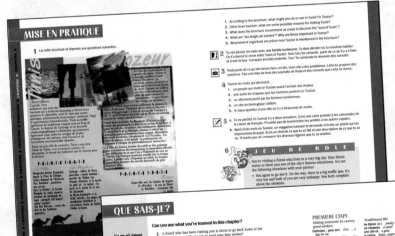

Mise en pratique, at the end of each chapter, gives students the opportunity to review what they have learned and to apply their skills in new communicative contexts. Focusing on all four language skills as well as cultural awareness, the **Mise en pratique** can help you determine whether students are ready for the Chapter Test.

Que sais-je? follows the **Mise en pratique** and is a checklist that students can use on their own to see if they have achieved the goals stated on the Chapter Opener. Each communicative function is paired with one or more activities for students to use as a self-check. Page references are given for students who need to return to the chapter for review.

Vocabulaire presents the chapter vocabulary grouped by **étape** and arranged according to communicative function or theme. This list represents the active words and expressions that students will be expected to know for the Chapter Quizzes and Test.

The Annotated Teacher's Edition

The *Allez, viens!* Annotated Teacher's Edition *is designed to help you meet the increasingly varied needs of today's students by providing an abundance of suggestions and strategies. The* Annotated Teacher's Edition *includes the reduced pages of the* Pupil's Edition *with teacher annotations, wrap-around teacher text with video references and bar codes, notes, suggestions, answers, and additional activities, as well as interleafed pages of scripts, projects, and games before each chapter.* ◆

USING THE LOCATION OPENER

Each reduced student page is wrapped with background information for you about the photographs and settings. In addition, teaching suggestions help you motivate students to learn more about the history, geography, and culture of French-speaking countries.

USING THE CHAPTER INTERLEAF

The chapter interleaf includes a chapter overview correlation chart for teaching resources, *Pupil's Edition* listening scripts, and suggestions for projects and games.

The **Chapter Overview** chart outlines at a glance the functions, grammar, culture, and re-entry items featured in each **étape**. A list of corresponding print and audiovisual resource materials for each section of the chapter is provided to help integrate video and ancillaries into your lessons. The reading and review features for each chapter are also referenced, as well as a variety of assessment and portfolio options.

Textbook Listening Activities Scripts provide the scripts of the chapter listening activities for reference or for use in class. The answers to each activity are provided below each script for easy reference.

Projects propose extended four-skills activities based on the chapter theme and content. **Projects** suggestions are provided to give students the opportunity to personalize the information they've learned in the chapter. Individual projects offer students the chance to explore topics related to the chapter theme that are of personal interest to them. Group and cooperative learning projects encourage students to work together to apply what they've learned in the chapter by creating a poster, brochure, or report, often accompanied by an oral presentation.

Games provide students with informal, entertaining activities in which they can apply and reinforce the functions, structures, vocabulary, and culture of the chapter. **Games** appeal to a variety of learners and encourage teamwork and cooperation among students of different levels and learning styles.

USING THE WRAP-AROUND TEACHER TEXT

Wrap-around teacher text gives point-of-use suggestions and information to help you make the most of class time. The wrap-around style of the *Annotated Teacher's Edition* conveniently presents bar codes, video references, teacher notes, suggestions, and activity answers together on the same page with the reduced *Pupil's Edition* page.

TEACHING CYCLE

For each **étape**, a logical instructional sequence includes the following steps to enable you to:
- **Jump Start!** your students with an individual writing activity that focuses their attention on previously-learned material while they wait for class to begin.
- **Motivate** students by introducing the topic in a personalized and contextualized way.
- **Teach** the functions, vocabulary, structures, and culture with a variety of approaches.
- **Close** each **étape** with activities that review and confirm the communicative goals.
- **Assess** students' progress with a quiz and/or performance assessment activity. **Performance Assessment** suggestions provide an alternative to pen and paper tests and give you the option of evaluating students' progress by

having them perform communicative, competency-based tasks. These may include teacher-student interviews, conversations, dialogues, or skits that students perform for the entire class. These tasks can also be recorded or videotaped for evaluation at a later time.

Portfolio icons signal activities that are appropriate for students' oral or written portfolios. They may include lists, posters, letters, journal entries, or taped conversations or skits. A variety of suggestions are provided within each chapter so that you can work with your students to select the activities that would best document their strengths and progress in the language. Portfolio information, including checklists and suggestions for evaluation, is provided in the *Assessment Guide,* pages 2–13. On pages 14–25 of the *Assessment Guide,* there are suggestions for the expansion of the two designated portfolio activities from the *Pupil's Edition.* In each chapter overview, these two activities (one written and one oral) are listed under "Portfolio Assessment." The portfolio suggestions will help students to further develop their oral and written language skills, often in the context of real-life situations. For a discussion of portfolio creation and use, see *Using Portfolios in the Foreign Language Classroom,* page T52.

FOR INDIVIDUAL NEEDS

Suggestions under the following categories provide alternate approaches to help you address students' diverse learning styles.
- **Visual, Auditory, Tactile, and Kinesthetic Learners** benefit from activities that accommodate their unique learning styles.
- **Slower Pace** provides ideas for presenting material in smaller steps to facilitate comprehension.

- **Challenge** extends activities into more challenging tasks that encourage students to expand their communicative skills. For more information on diverse learning styles, see the essay *Learning Styles and Multi-Modality Teaching* by Mary B. McGehee on pages T48–T49.

Making Connections

To help students appreciate their membership in a global society, suggestions for linking French with other disciplines, their community, and other cultures appear under the following categories:

- **Math...Geography...Health...Science ...History...Language Arts Links** relate the chapter topic to other subject areas, making French relevant to the students' overall academic experience.
- **Multicultural Links** provide students the opportunity to compare and contrast their language and culture with those of French-speaking countries and other parts of the world.
- **Community...Family Links** encourage students to seek opportunities for learning outside of the classroom by interacting with neighbors and family members. These suggestions also call on students to share their learning with their family and community.

Developing Thinking Skills

Thinking Critically helps students develop their higher-order thinking skills.

Drawing Inferences, Comparing and Contrasting, Analyzing, Observing, and Synthesizing offer suggestions to extend activities beyond an informational level. They increase comprehension of language and culture, and they help students exercise and develop higher-order thinking skills. For more information on different learning levels, see the essay *Higher-Order Thinking Skills* by Dr. Audrey L. Heining-Boynton on pages T50–T51.

Establishing Collaborative Learning

Cooperative Learning allows students to work together in small groups to attain common goals by sharing responsibilities. Students are accountable for setting the group objectives, completing the assignment, and ensuring that all group members master the material. Working together in cooperative groups allows students to take an active role in the classroom, to develop more self-esteem as they contribute to the success of the group, and to experience less anxiety by working in small groups. Cooperative learning enables students to improve interpersonal communication skills by encouraging them to listen to and respect other opinions, and to share their own.

Total Physical Response (TPR) techniques visually and kinesthetically reinforce structures and vocabulary. They are active learning exercises that encourage students to focus on class interaction while learning French.

Teaching Lisons!

Teacher's notes and suggestions in **Lisons!** offer prereading, reading, and postreading activities to help students develop reading skills. Background information and useful terms related to the reading are provided as well.

Ecrivons! suggestions provide teachers with innovative ideas on how to best use process writing in the classroom. The suggestions include teacher notes, prewriting, writing, and postwriting instructional and communicative tips. These types of activities help students gain the most advantage from the brainstorming, draft, editing, and revision processes of writing.

Allez, viens! *Video*

Allez, viens! *Video Program and* Allez, viens! *Expanded Video Program bring the textbook to life and introduce your students to people they will encounter in every chapter of the* Pupil's Edition. *Filmed entirely on location in French-speaking countries around the world, these video programs feature native speakers of French in realistic, interesting situations.*

Video is an ideal medium for providing authentic input needed to increase proficiency in French. Both informative and entertaining, the episodes of the **Video Program** *and* **Expanded Video Program** *provide rich visual clues to aid comprehension and motivate students to learn more.* ◆

*A*LLEZ, VIENS! VIDEO PROGRAM

The video program is fully integrated and correlates directly with the *Allez, viens! Pupil's Edition:*

PANORAMA CULTUREL Authentic interviews with native speakers of French bring the French-speaking world to life as real people talk about themselves, their country, and their way of life. The unscripted language spoken at a normal rate of speed will give students a taste of "real" French. Students will be exposed to a wide range of French speakers and will be introduced to several regional accents. The opinions and reactions expressed by the interviewees give students increased insight into French-speaking cultures. Each interview topic is thematically related to the chapter and is introduced by two hosts in a talk show format.

VIDÉOCLIPS Students will enjoy the authentic footage from French television: music videos, commercials, human interest stories, and more. While carefully selected to meet pedagogical objectives, in order to preserve authenticity this material was not edited for the classroom. You may want to preview the **Vidéoclips** and adapt them to your classroom needs. These short segments of video give students confidence as they realize that they can understand and enjoy material that was produced for native speakers of French!

*A*LLEZ, VIENS! VIDEO GUIDE

Allez, viens! **Video Guide** provides background information together with suggestions for presentation and pre- and post-viewing activities for all portions of the **Video Program** and the **Expanded Video Program.** In addition, the **Video Guide** contains a transcript and synopsis of each episode, supplementary vocabulary lists, and reproducible student activity sheets that help students focus on the pertinent information and make the language accessible to them.

Allez, viens! *Ancillaries*

The **Allez, viens!** *French program offers a state-of-the-art ancillary package that addresses the concerns of today's teachers. Because foreign language teachers are working with all types of students, the activities in our ancillaries accommodate all learning styles. The activities provided in the* **Allez, viens!** *ancillary materials are both innovative and relevant to students' experiences.* ◆

TEACHING RESOURCES WITH PROFESSIONAL ORGANIZER

The *Allez, viens!* ancillaries are packaged in three **Chapter Teaching Resources** booklets along with a tri-fold **Professional Organizer**. Each **Chapter Teaching Resources** booklet puts a wealth of resources at your fingertips!

CHAPTER TEACHING RESOURCES, BOOKS 1-3

Oral communication is the language skill that is most challenging to develop and test. The *Allez, viens!* **Situation Cards** and **Communicative Activities** help students develop their speaking skills and give them opportunities to communicate in a variety of situations.

Additional Listening Activities, in combination with the **Audiocassette** and **Audio CD Program,** provide students with a unique opportunity to actively develop their listening skills in a variety of authentic contexts.

The *Allez, viens!* **Realia** reproduce real documents to provide your students with additional reading and language practice using culturally authentic material. Included with the **Realia** are teacher suggestions and student activities.

The **Student Response Forms** are provided for your convenience. These copying masters can be reproduced and used as answer forms for all the textbook listening activities.

The **Assessment Program** provides a method of evaluation that is fair to all students and that encourages students to work towards realistic, communicative goals. The **Assessment Program** includes the following components:

- Three **Quizzes** per chapter (one per **étape**)

- One **Chapter Test** per chapter; each **Chapter Test** includes listening, reading, writing, and culture sections and a score sheet for easy grading. Part of each test can be corrected on ScanTron®.

- **Speaking tests,** provided in the **Assessment Guide.**

Also included in the **Chapter Teaching Resources:**

- **Answer Key** for the **Practice and Activity Book**

- **Teaching Transparency Masters** and suggestions for use

- **Listening Scripts** and **Answers** for the **Additional Listening Activities, Quizzes,** and **Chapter Tests.**

GRAMMAR AND VOCABULARY WORKSHEETS

The *Grammar and Vocabulary Reteaching and Practice Worksheets,* found in the **Teaching Resources with Organizer,** re-present all major grammar points and offer additional focused practice with the structures, words, and phrases targeted in each **étape.**

ASSESSMENT GUIDE

The **Assessment Guide** describes various testing and scoring methods. This guide also includes:

- **Portfolio Assessment** suggestions and rubrics

- **Speaking Tests** to be used separately or as part of the **Chapter Test**

- A **Midterm** and a **Final Exam** with scripts and answers

TEACHING TRANSPARENCIES

The **Teaching Transparencies** benefit all students, and the visual learner in particular. These colorful transparencies add variety and focus to your daily lesson plans. Suggestions for using the transparencies can be found in the **Chapter Teaching Resources** books.

AUDIO PROGRAM

All recorded material is available in either the **Audiocassette Program** or the **Audio CD Program.** The listening activities, pronunciation activities, interviews, and dialogues help students further develop their listening and pronunciation skills by providing opportunities to hear native speakers of French in a variety of authentic situations.

PRACTICE AND ACTIVITY BOOK

The **Practice and Activity Book** provides further practice with the functions, grammar, and vocabulary presented in each **étape.** Additional reading, culture, and journal activities for each chapter give students the opportunity to apply the reading and writing strategies they've learned in relevant, personalized contexts.

TEST GENERATOR

The **Test Generator** software program enables you to create customized worksheets, quizzes, and tests for each chapter in *Allez, viens!* The **Test Generator** is available for IBM® PC and Compatibles and Macintosh® computers.

Chapter 6 Sample Lesson Plan

The following lesson plan suggests how the material in Chapter 6 may be distributed over twelve days. You may choose to prepare similar plans to guide you through the other chapters of **Allez, viens!**, adjusting the daily schedule and selecting appropriate activities and ancillary material that best suit your individual needs and those of your students. (Page numbers set in **boldface** type refer to activities in the Annotated Teacher's Edition.) ◆

CHAPITRE 6 : MA FAMILLE, MES COPAINS ET MOI

DAILY PLANS	RESOURCES
DAY 1 **OBJECTIVE:** To find out about Moroccan hospitality	

Chapter Opener, pp. 136–137
    Motivating Activity, **p. 136**
    Focusing on Outcomes, **p. 137**
Mise en train, pp. 138–140
    Motivating Activity, **p. 138**
    Presentation: **Naissance d'une amitié, p. 138**
    Activities 1–5, p. 140
Close: Activity 6, p. 140
Assignment: Activity 1, *Practice and Activity Book*, p. 61
	Textbook Audiocassette 3B/Audio CD 6
	Practice and Activity Book, p. 61
	Video Program, Videocassette 1

DAY 2 **OBJECTIVE:** To make, accept, and refuse suggestions	

Review Assignment from Day 1
Première étape, p. 141
    Jump Start!, **p. 141**
    Motivate, **p. 141**
    Presentation: **Comment dit-on... ?, p. 141**
    Activities 7–8, p. 141
Close: Activity 9, p. 141
Assignment: Activity 3, *Practice and Activity Book*, p. 62
	Textbook Audiocassette 3B/Audio CD 6
	Practice and Activity Book, pp. 62–65
	Chapter Teaching Resources, Book 1
	    Teaching Transparency 6-1, pp. 62, 64

DAY 3 **OBJECTIVE:** To make arrangements	

Review Assignment from Day 2
    Presentation: **Comment dit-on... ?, p. 141**
    Activity 10, p. 142
    Presentation: **Grammaire, p. 142**
    Activity 11, p. 142
    Activities 12–13, p. 143
Close: Activity 2, *Practice and Activity Book*, p. 62
Assignment: Activities 4–6, *Practice and Activity Book*, pp. 63–64
	Textbook Audiocassette 3B/Audio CD 6
	Practice and Activity Book, pp. 62–65
	Grammar and Vocabulary Worksheets,
	    pp. 54–57
	Chapter Teaching Resources, Book 1
	    Teaching Transparency 6-1, pp. 62, 64

DAY 4 **OBJECTIVE:** To make and accept apologies; to find out about the personal values of francophone people	

Review Assignment from Day 3
    Presentation: **Comment dit-on... ?, p. 143**
    Activity 14, p. 143
    Presentation: **Grammaire, p. 143**
    Activities 15–16, p. 144
Panorama Culturel, p. 145
    Motivating Activity, **p. 145**
    Presentation: **p. 145**
Close: Close, **p. 144**
Assignment: Activity 17, p. 144; Activity 18a, p. 144; Activity 8, *Practice and Activity Book*, p. 65
	Textbook Audiocassette 3B/Audio CD 6
	Practice and Activity Book, pp. 62–65
	Grammar and Vocabulary Worksheets,
	    pp. 58–59
	Chapter Teaching Resources, Book 1
	    Teaching Transparency 6-1, pp. 62, 64
	Video Program, Videocassette 1

DAY 5 **OBJECTIVE:** To find out about family life in Morocco	

Review assignment from Day 4
    Option: Activity 18b, c, p. 144
    Teaching Transparency 6-1
Quiz 6-1
    Assessment: Performance Assessment, **p. 144**
Remise en train, pp. 146–147
    Motivating Activity, **p. 146**
    Presentation: **Ahlên, merhabîn, p. 146**
    Activities 19–21, p. 146
    Activities 22–23, p. 147
Close: Activity 24, p. 147
Assignment: Activities 9–10, *Practice and Activity Book*, p. 66
	Textbook Audiocassette 3B/Audio CD 6
	Practice and Activity Book, pp. 62–66
	Chapter Teaching Resources, Book 1
	    Teaching Transparency 6-1, pp. 62, 64
	    Quiz 6-1, pp. 77–78
	Assessment Items
	    Audiocassette 7B/Audio CD 6

DAILY PLANS	RESOURCES

DAY 6   **OBJECTIVE:** To find out about Morocco; To show and respond to hospitality; to express and respond to thanks

Review Assignment from Day 5
Rencontre Culturelle, p. 148
  Motivating Activity, **p. 148**
  Presentation: **p. 148**
Deuxième étape, p. 149
  Jump Start!, **p. 149**
  Motivate, **p. 149**
  Presentation: **Comment dit-on... ?, p. 149**
  Activity 25, p. 149
Close: Activity 26, p. 150
Assignment: Activity 11, *Practice and Activity Book,* p. 67
	Textbook Audiocassette 3B/Audio CD 6
	Practice and Activity Book, pp. 67–71
	Chapter Teaching Resources, Book 1
	  Teaching Transparency 6-2, pp. 63, 64

DAY 7   **OBJECTIVE:** To describe family relationships

Review Assignment from Day 6
  Activity 27, p. 150
  Presentation: **Vocabulaire, p. 151**
  Activity 29, p. 151
  Option: Building on Previous Skills, **p. 151**
  Activities 30–31, p. 152
Close: Students present scenes from Activity 31
Assignment: Activities 12–13, *Practice and Activity Book,* pp. 68–69
	Textbook Audiocassette 3B/Audio CD 6
	Practice and Activity Book, pp. 68–71
	Grammar and Vocabulary Worksheets,
	  pp. 60–62
	Chapter Teaching Resources, Book 1
	  Teaching Transparency 6-2, pp. 63, 64

DAY 8   **OBJECTIVE:** To quarrel

Review Assignment from Day 7
  Motivating Activity, **p. 152**
  Presentation: **Comment dit-on... ?, p. 152**
  Activity 32, p. 152
  Activities 33–35, p. 153
  Option: Cooperative Learning, **p. 153**
Close: Close, **p. 153**
Assignment: Activities 14–16, *Practice and Activity Book,* p. 70
	Textbook Audiocassette 3B/Audio CD 6
	Practice and Activity Book, pp. 68–71
	Chapter Teaching Resources, Book 1
	  Teaching Transparency 6-2, pp. 63, 64

DAY 9   **OBJECTIVE:** To read folktales from Morocco

Review Assignment from Day 8
  Option: Activity 36, p. 153
  Teaching Transparency 6-2
Quiz 6-2
Assessment: Performance Assessment, **p. 153**
Lisons!, pp. 154–156
  Motivating Activity, **p. 154**
  Activities A–B, p. 154
Close: Have students predict the end of the story
Assignment: Activity G, p. 155
	Textbook Audiocassette 3B/Audio CD 6
	Practice and Activity Book, pp. 68–72
	Chapter Teaching Resources, Book 1
	  Teaching Transparency 6-2, pp. 63, 64
	  Quiz 6-2, pp. 79–80
	Assessment Items
	  Audiocassette 7B/Audio CD 6

DAY 10   **OBJECTIVE:** To read folktales from Morocco; to write a story about personal values

Review Assignment from Day 9
  Activities C–I, p. 155
  Activities J–O, p. 156
Ecrivons!, p. 157
  Part A, p. 157
  Teaching Suggestions, **p. 157**
Close: Activity P, p. 155
Assignment: Part B, p. 157; Activities 1–11, **Que sais-je?,** p. 160
	Textbook Audiocassette 3B/Audio CD 6
	Practice and Activity Book, p. 72
	Chapter Teaching Resources, Book 1

DAY 11   **OBJECTIVE:** To use what you have learned; to prepare for Chapter Test

Review Assignments from Days 9 and 10
  Part C, p. 157
Mise en pratique, pp. 158–159
  Activity 1, p. 158
  Activities 2–4, 6 p. 159
  Option: Games, **p. 135F**
Assignment: Activity 5, p. 159; **Mon journal,** *Practice and Activity Book,* p. 150
	Textbook Audiocassette 3B/Audio CD 6
	Chapter Teaching Resources, Book 1
	Video Program, Videocassette 1

DAY 12   **OBJECTIVE:** To assess progress

Chapitre 6 Chapter Test	*Chapter Teaching Resources, Book 1,*
	  pp. 81–86
	Assessment Guide
	  Speaking Test, p. 30
	  Portfolio Assessment, pp. 2–13, 19
	Assessment Items
	  Audiocassette 7B/Audio CD 6

Standards for Foreign Language Learning

BY ROBERT LaBOUVE

STANDARDS AND SCHOOL REFORM

In 1989 educational reform in the United States took on an entirely different look when state and national leaders reached consensus on six national educational goals for public schools. In 1994 a new law, *Goals 2000: Educate America Act,* endorsed these six goals and added two more. The most important national goal in the law for foreign language educators is Goal Three, which establishes a core curriculum and places foreign languages in that core. As a result of this consensus on national goals, the Federal government encouraged the development of high standards in the core disciplines.

We must first define "standards" in order to fully understand the rationale for their development. Content standards ask: What should students know and be able to do? Content standards have recently been developed by the foreign language profession as a collaborative project of the American Council on the Teaching of Foreign Languages, the American Association of Teachers of French, the American Association of Teachers of German, and the American Association of Teachers of Spanish and Portuguese. Performance standards ask: How good is good enough? Opportunity-to-learn standards ask: Did the school prepare all students to perform well? There is a growing consensus that states and local districts should address the last two types of standards.

DEVELOPMENT OF FOREIGN LANGUAGE STANDARDS

A task force of foreign language educators began work on the standards in 1993 by establishing specific foreign language goals. They then set content standards for each goal. The task force sought feedback from the foreign language profession through an extensive dissemination program and produced a draft of the standards document for introduction at a number of sites around the United States during the 1994–1995 school year. The final version, published in 1996, incorporated suggestions from the sites where the standards were introduced and reaction from volunteer reviewers and the field in general.

While the standards are world class, they are realistic and attainable by most students. The task force also realized that the general set of goals and standards would have to be made language specific in a curriculum development process and that continuing staff development would be essential.

FOREIGN LANGUAGE GOALS AND STANDARDS

Communication Communicate in Languages Other Than English	**Standard 1.1**	Students engage in conversations, provide and obtain information, express feelings and emotions, and exchange opinions.
	Standard 1.2	Students understand and interpret written and spoken language on a variety of topics.
	Standard 1.3	Students present information, concepts, and ideas to an audience of listeners or readers on a variety of topics.
Cultures Gain Knowledge and Understanding of Other Cultures	**Standard 2.1**	Students demonstrate an understanding of the relationship between the practices and perspectives of the culture studied.
	Standard 2.2	Students demonstrate an understanding of the relationship between the products and perspectives of the culture studied.
Connections Connect with Other Disciplines and Acquire Information	**Standard 3.1**	Students reinforce and further their knowledge of other disciplines through the foreign language.
	Standard 3.2	Students acquire information and recognize the distinctive viewpoints that are only available through the foreign language and its cultures.
Comparisons Develop Insight into the Nature of Language and Culture	**Standard 4.1**	Students demonstrate understanding of the nature of language through comparisons of the language studied and their own.
	Standard 4.2	Students demonstrate understanding of the concept of culture through comparisons of the cultures studied and their own.
Communities Participate in Multilingual Communities at Home and Around the World	**Standard 5.1**	Students use the language both within and beyond the school setting.
	Standard 5.2	Students show evidence of becoming life-long learners by using the language for personal enjoyment and enrichment.

FOREIGN LANGUAGE GOALS AND STANDARDS

The goals and standards describe a K–12 foreign language program for *all* students, presenting languages, both modern and classical, as part of the core curriculum for every student, including those whose native language is not English. Broad goals establish the basic framework of the language program. The proposed content standards set for these goals describe what students should know and be able to do in a language. The chart on page T42 shows how the standards are arrayed alongside the goals.

The first two goals in this expanded language program describe today's typical school language program. The last three are often identified by teachers as important, but are not always implemented. The standards-based program moves beyond an emphasis on skills to a redefinition of the content of a language program itself.

Sample progress indicators are provided for Grades 4, 8, and 12 as examples of what students can do to meet the standards and accomplish the goals of the language program. A higher level of performance will be expected as students progress from one benchmark grade to another. For example, Standard 1.1 at Grade 4 suggests that students can "ask and answer questions about such things as family, school events, and celebrations in person or via letters, e-mail, or audio and video tapes," but Standard 1.1 at Grade 12 suggests that students can "exchange, support, and discuss their opinions and individual perspectives with peers and/or speakers of the target language on a variety of topics dealing with contemporary and historical issues."

IMPACT OF THE STANDARDS

While there is an assumption that foreign language goals and standards will have a great impact upon the states and local districts, the national standards themselves are voluntary. Clearly, standards will influence instruction and curriculum development in districts that choose to align their language programs with the national standards. Assessment programs will most likely begin to reflect the influence of the standards. The

standards will also have an impact on the preparation of future teachers and on staff development for teachers now in the classroom.

A curriculum based on the standards will encourage students to take responsibility for their learning by making the language curriculum coherent and transparent to them. Students will know from the beginning what they should be able to do when they exit the program and they will be able to judge for themselves how they are progressing, especially at Grades 4, 8, and 12.

The standards will direct instruction in the classroom by providing curriculum developers and teachers with a broad framework upon which to construct the expanded language program. Standards for each goal will ensure that no goal is treated informally or left to chance. Teachers who use the content standards should play a critical role in their district by deciding how good is good enough for students who exit the program.

The standards will also have a significant impact on the demand for sequential, cross-disciplinary instructional materials for a K–12 language program. Another challenge will be the development of new technologies that increase learning in order to meet high standards.

Probably the greatest benefit that national standards may bring will be in the area of making possible articulation that is horizontal (linking languages to other disciplines) and vertical (grade to grade, school to school, and school to college). Language teachers will join their English and social studies colleagues in helping students become language-competent, literate citizens of the world. A language program that is at once coherent and transparent to students and others will provide all language educators a basis for reaching consensus about their expectations on what students should know and do. To those of us who feel that foreign language education is basic education for all students, the national standards document should become a strong advocate for languages in the curriculum of every school and for the extended sequences of study presented by the goals and standards. The standards document will make it easier for language educators to present a solid rationale for foreign languages in the curriculum.

To receive information on ordering the standards document, *Standards for Foreign Language Learning: Preparing for the 21st Century,* please contact the project office:

National Standards in Foreign
Language Education
c/o ACTFL
6 Executive Plaza
Yonkers, NY 10701-6801
(914) 963–8830
FAX: (914) 963-1275

Allez, viens!

supports the Foreign Language Goals and Standards in the following ways:

THE PUPIL'S EDITION

- Encourages students to take responsibility for their learning by providing clearly defined objectives at the beginning of each chapter.

- Provides a variety of pair- and group-work activities to give students an opportunity to use the target language in a wide range of settings and contexts.

- Offers culture-related activities and poses questions that develop students' insight and encourage them to develop observational and analytical skills.

THE ANNOTATED TEACHER'S EDITION

- Provides a broad framework for developing a foreign language program and offers specific classroom suggestions for reaching students with various learning styles.

- Offers ideas for multicultural and multidisciplinary projects as well as community and family links that encourage students to gain access to information both at school and in the community.

THE ANCILLARY PROGRAM

- Provides students with on-location video footage of native speakers interacting in their own cultural and geographic context.

- Includes multiple options for practicing new skills and assessing performance, including situation cards, portfolio suggestions, speaking tests, and other alternatives.

- Familiarizes students with the types of tasks they will be expected to perform on exit exams.

Multi-Level Classrooms

BY JOAN H. MANLEY

So you have just heard that your third-period class is going to include both Levels 2 and 3! While this is never the best news for a foreign language teacher, there are positive ways, both psychological and pedagogical, to make this situation work for you and your students. ◆

There are positive ways, both psychological and pedagogical, to make this situation work for you and your students.

RELIEVING STUDENT ANXIETIES

Initially, in a multi-level class environment, it is important to relieve students' anxiety by orienting them to their new situation. From the outset, let all students know that just because they "did" things the previous year, such as learn how to conjugate certain verbs, they may not yet be able to use them in a meaningful way. Students should not feel that it is demeaning or a waste of time to recycle activities or to share knowledge and skills with fellow students. Second-year students need to know they are not second-class citizens and that they can benefit from their classmates' greater experience with the language. Third-year students may achieve a great deal of satisfaction and become more confident in their own language skills when they have opportunities to help or teach their second-year classmates. It is important to reassure third-year students that you will devote time to them and challenge them with different assignments.

EASING YOUR OWN APPREHENSION

When you are faced with both Levels 2 and 3 in your classroom, remind yourself that you teach students of different levels in the same classroom every year, although not officially. After one year of classroom instruction, your Level 2 class will never be a truly homogeneous group. Despite being made up of students with the same amount of "seat time," the class comprises multiple layers of language skills, knowledge, motivation, and ability. Therefore, you are constantly called upon to make a positive experience out of a potentially negative one.

Your apprehension will gradually diminish to the extent that you are able to . . .

- make students less dependent on you for the successful completion of their activities.
- place more responsibility for learning on the students.
- implement creative group, pair, and individual activities.

How can you do this? Good organization will help. Lessons will need to be especially well-planned for the multi-level class. The following lesson plan is an example of how to treat the same topic with students of two different levels.

TEACHING A LESSON IN A MULTI-LEVEL CLASSROOM

▶ **LESSON OBJECTIVES**

Relate an incident in the past that you regret.
Level 2: Express surprise and sympathy.
Level 3: Offer encouragement and make suggestions.

▶ **LESSON PLAN**

1. **Review and/or teach the past tense.** Present the formation of the past tense. Model its use for the entire class or call upon Level 3 students to give examples.
2. **Practice the past tense.** Have Level 3 students who have mastered the past tense teach it to Level 2 students in pairs or small groups. Provide the Level 3 student instructors with several drill and practice activities they may use for this purpose.
3. **Relate your own regrettable past experience.** Recount a personal regrettable incident—real or imaginary—to the entire class as a model. For example, you may have left your automobile lights on, and when you came out of school, the battery was dead and you couldn't start your car. Or you

may have scolded a student for not doing the homework and later discovered the student had a legitimate reason for not completing the assignment.

4. **Prepare and practice written and oral narratives.** Have Level 2 students pair off with Level 3 students. Each individual writes about his or her experience, the Level 3 partner serving as a resource for the Level 2 student. Partners then edit each other's work and listen to each other's oral delivery. You might choose to have students record their oral narratives.

5. **Present communicative functions.**
   A. Ask for a volunteer to recount his or her own regrettable incident for the entire class.
   B. Model reactions to the volunteer's narrative.
      (1) Express surprise and sympathy (for Level 2): "Really! That's too bad!"
      (2) Offer encouragement and make suggestions (for Level 3): "Don't worry. You can still..."

6. **Read narratives and practice communicative functions.** Have Level 2 students work together in one group or in small groups, listening to classmates' stories and reacting with the prescribed communicative function. Have Level 3 students do the same among themselves. Circulate among the groups, listening, helping, and assessing.

7. **Assess progress.** Repeat your personal account for the entire class and elicit reactions from students according to their level. Challenge students to respond with communicative functions expected of the other level if they can.

Every part of the above lesson plan is important. Both levels have been accommodated. The teacher has not dominated the lesson. Students have worked together in pairs and small groups, while Level 3 students have helped their Level 2 classmates. Individual groups still feel accountable, both within their level and across levels.

Any lesson can be adapted in this way. It takes time and effort, but the result is a student-centered classroom where students share and grow, and the teacher is the facilitator.

Allez, viens!

facilitates work in a multi-level classroom in the following ways:

THE PUPIL'S EDITION

- Provides creative activities for pair and group work that allow students at different levels to work together and learn from one another.

THE ANNOTATED TEACHER'S EDITION

- Offers practical suggestions for Projects and Cooperative Learning that engage students of different levels.

- Provides For Individual Needs teaching suggestions throughout the program. Second-year students will benefit from the Slower Pace activities, while third-year students will take advantage of the Challenge exercises.

- Provides a clear, comprehensive outline of the functions, vocabulary, and grammar that are recycled in each chapter. The Chapter Overview of each chapter is especially helpful to the teacher who is planning integrated or varied lessons in the multi-level classroom.

THE ANCILLARY PROGRAM

- Provides a variety of materials and activities to accommodate different levels in a multi-level classroom.

- Facilitates collective learning so that groups of students at different learning levels may work together, pacing an activity according to their specific abilities.

Teaching Culture

BY NANCY HUMBACH AND DOROTHEA BRUSCHKE

Ask students what they like best about studying a foreign language. Chances are that learning about culture, the way people live, is one of their favorite aspects. Years after language study has ended, adults remember with fondness the customs of the target culture, even pictures in their language texts. It is this interest in the people and their way of life that is the great motivator and helps us sustain students' interest in language study.

We must integrate culture and language in a way that encourages curiosity, stimulates analysis, and teaches students to hypothesize and seek answers to questions about the people whose language they are studying. Teaching isolated facts about how people in other cultures live is not enough. This information is soon dated and quickly forgotten. We must go a step beyond and teach students that all behavior, values, and traditions exist because of certain aspects of history, geography, and socio-economic conditions.

There are many ways to help students become culturally knowledgeable and to assist them in developing an awareness of differences and similarities between the target culture and their own. Two of these approaches involve critical thinking, that is, trying to find reasons for a certain behavior through observation and analysis, and putting individual observations into larger cultural patterns. ◆

We must integrate culture and language in a way that encourages curiosity, stimulates analysis, and teaches students to hypothesize.

FIRST APPROACH: QUESTIONING

The first approach involves questioning as the key strategy. At the earliest stages of language learning, students begin to learn ways to greet peers, elders, and strangers, as well as the use of **tu** and **vous.** Students need to consider questions such as: "How do French-speaking people greet each other? Are there different levels of formality? Who initiates a handshake? When is a handshake or kisses on the cheeks **(la bise)** appropriate?" Each of these questions leads students to think about the values that are expressed through word and gesture. They start to "feel" the other culture, and at the same time, understand how much of their own behavior is rooted in their cultural background.

Magazines, newspapers, advertisements, and television commercials are all excellent sources of cultural material. For example, browsing through a French magazine, one finds a number of advertisements for food items and bottled water. Could this indicate a great interest in eating and preparing healthy food? Reading advertisements can be followed up with viewing videos and films, or with interviewing native speakers or people who have lived in French-speaking countries to learn about customs involving food selection and preparation.

Students might want to find answers to questions such as: "How much time do French people spend shopping for and preparing a meal? How long does a typical meal **en famille** last? What types of food and beverages does it involve?" This type of questioning might lead students to discover different attitudes toward food and mealtimes.

An advertisement for a refrigerator or a picture of a French kitchen can provide an insight into practices of shopping for food. Students first need to think about the refrigerator at home, take an inventory of what is kept in it, and consider when and where their family shops. Next, students should look closely at a French refrigerator. What is its size? What could that mean? (Shopping takes place more often, stores are within walking distance, and people eat more fresh foods.)

Food wrappers and containers also provide good clues to cultural insight. For example, since bread is often purchased fresh from a **boulangerie,** it is usually carried in one's hand or tote bag, with no packaging at all. Since most people shop daily and carry their own groceries home, heavier items like sodas often come in bottles no larger than one and one-half litres.

SECOND APPROACH: ASSOCIATING WORDS WITH IMAGES

The second approach for developing cultural understanding involves forming associations of words with the cultural images they suggest. Language and culture are so closely related that one might actually say that language *is* culture. Most words, especially nouns, carry a cultural connotation. Knowing the literal equivalent of a word in another language is of little use to students in understanding this connotation. For example, **ami** cannot be translated simply as *friend*, **pain** as *bread,* or **rue** as *street.* The French word **pain,** for instance, carries with it the image of a small local bakery stocked with twenty or thirty different varieties of freshly-baked bread, all warm from a brick oven. At breakfast, bread is sliced, covered with butter and jam, and eaten as a **tartine;** it is eaten throughout the afternoon and evening meals, in particular as an accompaniment to the cheese course. In French-speaking countries, "bread" is more than a grocery item; it is an essential part of every meal.

When students have acquired some sense of the cultural connotation of words—not only through teachers' explanations but, more importantly, through observation of visual images—they start to discover the larger underlying cultural themes, or what is often called deep culture.

These larger cultural themes serve as organizing categories into which individual cultural phenomena fit to form a pattern. Students might discover, for example, that French speakers, because they live in much more crowded conditions, have a great need for privacy (cultural theme), as reflected in such phenomena as closed doors, fences or walls around property, and sheers on windows. Students might also discover that love of nature and the outdoors is an important cultural theme, as indicated by such phenomena as flower boxes and planters in public places—even on small traffic islands—well-kept public parks in every town, and people going for a walk or going hiking.

As we teach culture, students learn not only to recognize elements of the target culture but also of their American cultural heritage. They see how elements of culture reflect larger themes or patterns. Learning what constitutes American culture and how that information relates to other people throughout the world can be an exciting journey for a young person.

As language teachers, we are able to facilitate that journey into another culture and into our own, to find our similarities as well as our differences from others. We do not encourage value judgments about others and their culture, nor do we recommend adopting other ways. We simply say to students, "Other ways exist. They exist for many reasons, just as our ways exist due to what our ancestors have bequeathed us through history, traditions, values, and geography."

Learning Styles and Multi-Modality Teaching

BY MARY B. McGEHEE

The larger and broader population of students who are enrolling in foreign language classes brings a new challenge to foreign language educators, calling forth an evolution in teaching methods to enhance learning for all our students. Educational experts now recognize that every student has a preferred sense for learning and retrieving information: visual, auditory, or kinesthetic. Incorporating a greater variety of activities to accommodate the learning styles of all students can make the difference between struggle and pleasure in the foreign language classroom. ◆

Incorporating a greater variety of activities to accommodate the learning styles of all students can make the difference between struggle and pleasure in the foreign language classroom.

ACCOMMODATING DIFFERENT LEARNING STYLES

A modified arrangement of the classroom is one way to provide more effective and enjoyable learning for all students. Rows of chairs and desks must give way at times to circles, semicircles, or small clusters. Students may be grouped in fours or in pairs for cooperative work or peer teaching. It is important to find a balance of arrangements, thereby providing the most comfort in varied situations.

Since visual, auditory, and kinesthetic learners will be in the class, and because every student's learning will be enhanced by a multi-sensory approach, lessons must be directed toward all three learning styles. Any language lesson content may be presented visually, aurally, and kinesthetically.

Visual presentations and practice may include the chalkboard, charts, posters, television, overhead projectors, books, magazines, picture diagrams, flashcards, bulletin boards, films, slides, or videos. Visual learners need to see what they are to learn. Lest the teacher think he or she will never have the time to prepare all those visuals, Dickel and Slak (1983) found that visual aids generated by students are more effective than ready-made ones.

Auditory presentations and practice may include stating aloud the requirements of the lesson, oral questions and answers, paired or group work on a progression of oral exercises from repetition to communication, tapes, CDs, dialogues, and role-playing. Jingles, catchy stories, and memory devices using songs and rhymes are good learning aids. Having students record themselves and then listen as they play back the cassette allows them to practice in the auditory mode.

Kinesthetic presentations entail the students' use of manipulatives, chart materials, gestures, signals, typing, songs, games, and role-playing. These lead the students to associate sentence constructions with meaningful movements.

A SAMPLE LESSON USING MULTI-MODALITY TEACHING

A multi-sensory presentation on greetings might proceed as follows.

▶ FOR VISUAL LEARNERS

As the teacher begins oral presentation of greetings and introductions, he or she simultaneously shows the written forms on transparencies, with the formal expressions marked with an adult's hat, and the informal expressions marked with a baseball cap.

The teacher then distributes cards with the hat and cap symbols representing the formal or informal expressions. As the students hear taped mini-dialogues, they hold up the appropriate card to indicate whether the dialogues are formal or informal. On the next listening, the students repeat the sentences they hear.

▶ FOR AUDITORY LEARNERS

A longer taped dialogue follows, allowing the students to hear the new expressions a number of times. They write from dictation several sentences containing the new expressions. They may work in pairs, correcting each other's work as they "test" their own understanding of the lesson at hand. Finally, students respond to simple questions using the appropriate formal and informal responses cued by the cards they hold.

▶ FOR KINESTHETIC LEARNERS

For additional kinesthetic input, members of the class come to the front of the room, each holding a hat or cap symbol. As the teacher calls out situations, the students play the roles, using gestures and props appropriate to the age group they are portraying. Non-cued, communicative role-playing with props further enables the students to "feel" the differences between formal and informal expressions.

Helping students learn how to use their preferred mode

Since we require all students to perform in all language skills, part of the assistance we must render is to help them develop strategies within their preferred learning modes to carry out an assignment in another mode. For example, visual students hear the teacher assign an oral exercise and visualize what they must do. They must see themselves carrying out the assignment, in effect watching themselves as if there were a movie going on in their heads. Only then can they also hear themselves saying the right things. Thus, this assignment will be much easier for the visual learners who have been taught this process, if they have not already figured it out for themselves. Likewise, true auditory

students, confronted with a reading/writing assignment, must talk themselves through it, converting the entire process into sound as they plan and prepare their work. Kinesthetic students presented with a visual or auditory task must first break the assignment into tasks and then work their way through them.

Students who experience difficulty because of a strong preference for one mode of learning are often unaware of the degree of preference. In working with these students, I prefer the simple and direct assessment of learning styles offered by Richard Bandler and John Grinder in their book *Frogs into Princes*, which allows the teacher and student to quickly determine how the student learns. In an interview with the student, I follow the assessment with certain specific recommendations of techniques to make the student's study time more effective.

It is important to note here that teaching students to maximize their study does not require that the teacher give each student an individualized assignment. It does require that each student who needs it be taught how to prepare the assignment using his or her own talents and strengths. This communication between teacher and student, combined with teaching techniques that reinforce learning in all modes, can only maximize pleasure and success in learning a foreign language.

▶ REFERENCES

Dickel, M.J. and S. Slak. "Imaging Vividness and Memory for Verbal Material." *Journal of Mental Imagery* 7, i (1983):121–6.

Bandler, Richard, and John Grinder. *Frogs into Princes*. Real People Press, Moab, UT. 1978.

Allez, viens!

accommodates different learning styles in the following ways:

THE PUPIL'S EDITION

- Presents basic material in audio, video, and print formats.
- Includes role-playing activities and a variety of multi-modal activities, including an extensive listening strand and many art-based activities.

THE ANNOTATED TEACHER'S EDITION

- Provides suggested activities for visual, auditory, and kinesthetic learners, as well as suggestions for slower-paced learning and challenge activities.
- Includes Total Physical Response activities.

THE ANCILLARY PROGRAM

- Provides additional reinforcement activites for a variety of learning styles.
- Presents a rich blend of audiovisual input through the video program, audio program, transparencies, and blackline masters.

The following is an example of an art-based activity from *Allez, viens!*

Regarde les bureaux de José et de Jocelyne. A ton avis, qu'est-ce qu'ils aiment faire?

Le bureau de José   Le bureau de Jocelyne

Higher-Order Thinking Skills

BY AUDREY L. HEINING-BOYNTON

Our profession loves acronyms! TPR, ALM, OBI, and now the HOTS! HOTS stands for higher-order thinking skills. These thinking skills help our students listen, speak, write, and learn about culture in a creative, meaningful way, while providing them with necessary life skills. ◆

Introduce students to the life skills they need to become successful, productive citizens in our society.

WHAT ARE HIGHER-ORDER THINKING SKILLS?

Higher-order thinking skills are not a new phenomenon on the educational scene. In 1956, Benjamin Bloom published a book that listed a taxonomy of educational objectives in the form of a pyramid similar to the one in the following illustration:

Bloom's Taxonomy of Educational Objectives

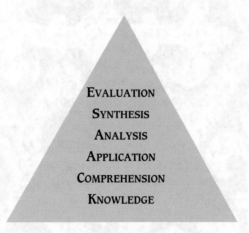

EVALUATION
SYNTHESIS
ANALYSIS
APPLICATION
COMPREHENSION
KNOWLEDGE

Knowledge is the simplest level of educational objectives, and is not considered a higher-order thinking skill. It requires the learner to remember information without having to fully understand it. Tasks that students perform to demonstrate knowledge are recalling, identifying, recognizing, citing, labeling, listing, reciting, and stating.

Comprehension is not considered a higher-order thinking skill either. Learners demonstrate comprehension when they paraphrase, describe, summarize, illustrate, restate, or translate.

Foreign language teachers tend to focus the most on knowledge and comprehension. The tasks performed at these levels are important because they provide a solid foundation for the more complex tasks at the higher levels of Bloom's pyramid. However, offering our students the opportunity to perform at still higher cognitive levels provides them with more meaningful contexts in which to use the target language.

When teachers incorporate **application, analysis, synthesis,** and **evaluation** as objectives, they allow students to utilize **higher-order thinking skills.**

- **Application** involves solving, transforming, determining, demonstrating, and preparing.

- **Analysis** includes classifying, comparing, making associations, verifying, seeing cause-and-effect relationships, and determining sequences, patterns, and consequences.

- **Synthesis** requires generalizing, predicting, imagining, creating, making inferences, hypothesizing, making decisions, and drawing conclusions.

- Finally, **evaluation** involves assessing, persuading, determining value, judging, validating, and solving problems.

Most foreign language classes focus little on higher-order thinking skills. Some foreign language educators mistakenly think that all higher-order thinking skills require an advanced level of language ability. Not so! Students can demonstrate these skills by using very simple language available even to beginning students. Also, higher-order thinking tasks about the target culture or language can be conducted in English. The use of some English in the foreign language class in order to utilize higher cognitive skills does not jeopardize progress in the target language.

Higher-order thinking skills prepare our students for more than using a foreign language. They introduce students to the life skills they need to become successful, productive citizens in our society. When we think about it, that *is* the underlying purpose of education.

Why Teach Higher-Order Thinking Skills?

There is already so much to cover and so little time that some teachers may question the worth of adding these types of activities to an already full schedule. Yet we know from experience that simply "covering" the material does not help our students acquire another language. Incorporating higher-order thinking skills in the foreign language classroom can help guide students toward language acquisition by providing meaningful experiences in a setting that can otherwise often feel artificial.

Also, we now know that employing higher-order thinking skills assists all students, including those who are at risk of failing. In the past, we felt that at-risk students were incapable of higher-order thinking, but we have since discovered that we have been denying them the opportunity to experience what they are capable of doing and what they need to do in order to be successful adults.

Sample Activities Employing Higher-Order Thinking Skills

There are no limitations to incorporating higher-order thinking skills in the foreign language classroom. What follows are a few sample activities, some of which you might already be familiar with. Use *your* higher-order thinking skills to develop other possibilities!

► LISTENING

HOTS:	Analysis
TASKS:	Patterning and sequencing
VOCABULARY NEEDED:	Three colors
MATERIALS REQUIRED:	Three colored-paper squares for each student

After reviewing the colors, call out a pattern of colors and have the students show their comprehension by arranging their colored pieces of paper from left to right in the order you give. Then have them finish the pattern for you. For example, you say: **rouge, vert, bleu, rouge, vert, bleu...** now what color follows? And then what color?

This is not only a HOTS activity; it also crosses disciplines. It reviews the mathematical concept of patterning and sequencing. You can have the students form patterns and sequences using any type of vocabulary.

► READING

HOTS:	Synthesis
TASKS:	Hypothesizing and imagining
VOCABULARY NEEDED:	Determined by level of students
MATERIALS REQUIRED:	Legend or short story

After the students have read the first part of the story, have them imagine how the story would end, based on the values of the target culture.

► SPEAKING

HOTS:	Evaluation
TASKS:	Assessing and determining value
VOCABULARY NEEDED:	Numbers 0-25, five objects students would need for school
MATERIALS REQUIRED:	Visuals of five school-related objects with prices beneath them

Tell students that they each have twenty-five dollars to spend on back-to-school supplies. They each need to tell you what they would buy with their money.

► WRITING

HOTS:	Analysis
TASKS:	Classifying
VOCABULARY NEEDED:	Leisure activities
MATERIALS REQUIRED:	Drawings of leisure activities on a handout

From the list of activities they have before them, students should write the ones that they like to do on the weekend. Then they should write those that a family member likes to do. Finally, students should write a comparison of the two lists.

Commitment to Higher-Order Thinking Skills

Teaching higher-order thinking skills takes no extra time from classroom instruction since language skills are reinforced during thinking skills activities. What teaching higher-order thinking skills does require of teachers is a commitment to classroom activities that go beyond the objectives of Bloom's knowledge and comprehension levels. Having students name objects and recite verb forms is not enough. Employing HOTS gives students the opportunity to experience a second language as a useful device for meaningful communication.

► REFERENCES

Bloom, Benjamin. *Taxonomy of Educational Objectives. Handbook 1: Cognitive Domain.* New York: David McKay Company, 1956.

Allez, viens!

encourages higher-order thinking skills in the following ways:

THE PUPIL'S EDITION

- Develops critical thinking skills through a variety of activities, including interpretation of the visually-presented **Mise en train**, journal writing, interviews, **Rencontre Culturelle** presentations, application of reading strategies, and situational role-plays.

THE ANNOTATED TEACHER'S EDITION

- Includes Thinking Critically and Multicultural Links features that provide the teacher with suggestions for activities requiring students to draw inferences, compare and contrast, evaluate, and synthesize.

THE ANCILLARY PROGRAM

- Incorporates higher-order thinking skills in Communicative Activities, Additional Listening Activities, and the chapter-related realia. In the *Practice and Activity Book,* students are guided carefully from structured practice to open-ended tasks that require higher-order thinking.

Using Portfolios in the Foreign Language Classroom

BY JO ANNE S. WILSON

The communicative, whole-language approach of today's foreign language instruction requires assessment methods that parallel the teaching and learning strategies in the proficiency-oriented classroom. We know that language acquisition is a process. Portfolios are designed to assess the steps in that process. ◆

Portfolios offer a more realistic and accurate way to assess the process of language teaching and learning.

WHAT IS A PORTFOLIO?

A portfolio is a purposeful, systematic collection of a student's work. A useful tool in developing a student profile, the portfolio shows the student's efforts, progress, and achievements for a given period of time. It may be used for periodic evaluation, as the basis for overall evaluation, or for placement. It may also be used to enhance or provide alternatives to traditional assessment measures, such as formal tests, quizzes, class participation, and homework.

WHY USE PORTFOLIOS?

Portfolios benefit both students and teachers because they

- **Are ongoing and systematic.** A portfolio reflects the real-world process of production, assessment, revision, and reassessment. It parallels the natural rhythm of learning.

- **Offer an incentive to learn.** Students have a vested interest in creating the portfolios through which they can showcase their ongoing efforts and tangible achievements. Students select the works to be included and have a chance to revise, improve, evaluate, and explain the contents.

- **Are sensitive to individual needs.** Language learners bring varied abilities to the classroom and do not acquire skills in a uniformly neat and orderly fashion. The personalized, individualized assessment offered by portfolios responds to this diversity.

- **Provide documentation of language development.** The material in a portfolio is evidence of student progress in the language learning process. The contents of the portfolio make it easier to discuss student progress with the students as well as with parents and others interested in the student's progress.

- **Offer multiple sources of information.** A portfolio presents a way to collect and analyze information from multiple sources that reflect a student's efforts, progress, and achievements in the language.

PORTFOLIO COMPONENTS

The foreign language portfolio should include both oral and written work, student self-evaluation, and teacher observation, usually in the form of brief, non-evaluative comments about various aspects of the student's performance.

THE ORAL COMPONENT

The oral component of a portfolio might be an audio- or videocassette. It may contain both rehearsed and extemporaneous monologues and conversations. For a rehearsed speaking activity, give a specific communicative task that students can personalize according to their individual interests (for example, ordering a favorite meal in a restaurant). If the speaking activity is extemporaneous, first acquaint students with possible topics for discussion or even the specific task they will be expected to perform. (For example, tell them they will be asked to discuss a picture showing a sports activity or a restaurant scene.)

THE WRITTEN COMPONENT

Portfolios are excellent tools for incorporating process writing strategies into the foreign language classroom. Documentation of various stages of the writing process—brainstorming, multiple drafts, and peer comments—may be included with the finished product.

Involve students in selecting writing tasks for the portfolio. At the beginning levels, the tasks might include some structured writing, such as labeling or listing. As students become more proficient, journals, letters, and other more complicated writing tasks are valuable ways for them to monitor their progress in using the written language.

STUDENT SELF-EVALUATION

Students should be actively involved in critiquing and evaluating their portfolios and monitoring their own progress. The process and procedure for student self-evaluation should be considered in planning the contents of the portfolio. Students should work with you and their peers to design the exact format. Self-evaluation encourages them to think about what they are learning (content), how they learn (process), why they are learning (purpose), and where they are going in their learning (goals).

TEACHER OBSERVATION

Systematic, regular, and ongoing observations should be placed in the portfolio after they have been discussed with the student. These observations provide feedback on the student's progress in the language learning process.

Teacher observations should be based on an established set of criteria that has been developed earlier with input from the student. Observation techniques may include the following:

- Jotting notes in a journal to be discussed with the student and then placed in the portfolio
- Using a checklist of observable behaviors, such as the willingness to take risks when using the target language or staying on task during the lesson
- Making observations on adhesive notes that can be placed in folders
- Recording anecdotal comments, during or after class, using a cassette recorder.

Knowledge of the criteria you use in your observations gives students a framework for their performance.

HOW ARE PORTFOLIOS EVALUATED?

The portfolio should reflect the process of student learning over a specific period of time. At the beginning of that time period, determine the criteria by which you will assess the final product and convey them to the students. Make this evaluation a collaborative effort by seeking students' input as you formulate these criteria and your instructional goals.

Students need to understand that evaluation based on a predetermined standard is but one phase of the assessment process; demonstrated effort and growth are just as important. As you consider correctness and accuracy in both oral and written work, also consider the organization, creativity, and improvement revealed by the student's portfolio over the time period. The portfolio provides a way to monitor the growth of a student's knowledge, skills, and attitudes, and shows the student's efforts, progress, and achievements.

HOW TO IMPLEMENT PORTFOLIOS

Teacher-teacher collaboration is as important to the implementation of portfolios as teacher-student collaboration. Confer with your colleagues to determine, for example, what kinds of information you want to see in the student portfolio, how the information will be presented, the purpose of the portfolio, the intended purposes (grading, placement, or a combination of the two), and criteria for evaluating the portfolio. Conferring among colleagues helps foster a departmental cohesiveness and consistency that will ultimately benefit the students.

THE PROMISE OF PORTFOLIOS

The high degree of student involvement in developing portfolios and deciding how they will be used generally results in renewed student enthusiasm for learning and improved achievement. As students compare portfolio pieces done early in the year with work produced later, they can take pride in the progress as well as reassess their motivation and work habits.

Portfolios also provide a framework for periodic assessment of teaching strategies, programs, and instruction. They offer schools a tool to help solve the problem of vertical articulation and accurate student placement. The more realistic and accurate assessment of the language learning process that is provided by portfolios is congruent with the strategies that should be used in the proficiency-oriented classroom.

Professional References

This section provides information about several resources that can enrich your French class. Included are addresses of government offices of francophone countries, pen pal organizations, subscription agencies, and many others. Since addresses change frequently, you may want to verify them before you send your requests. ◆

CULTURAL AGENCIES

For historic and tourist information about France and francophone countries, contact:

French Cultural Services
972 Fifth Ave.
New York, NY 10021
(212) 439-1400

French Cultural Services
540 Buth St.
San Francisco, CA 94108
(415) 397-4330

TOURIST OFFICES

Maison de la France
1007 Slocum St.
Dallas, TX 75027
(214) 742-1222

Délégation du Québec
53 State Street
Exchange Place Bldg., 19th floor
Boston, MA 02109
(617) 723-3366

Caribbean Tourism Association
20 E. 46th St., 4th floor
New York, NY 10017
(212) 682-0435

INTERCULTURAL EXCHANGE

American Field Service
220 East 42nd St.
New York, NY 10017
(212) 949-4242

CIEE Student Travel Services
205 East 42nd St.
New York, NY 10017
(212) 661-1414

PEN PAL ORGANIZATIONS

For the names of pen pal groups other than those listed below, contact your local chapter of AATF. There are fees involved, so be sure to write for information.

Student Letter Exchange (League of Friendship)
630 Third Avenue
New York, NY 10017
(212) 557-3312

World Pen Pals
1694 Como Avenue
St. Paul, MN 55108
(612) 647-0191

PERIODICALS

Subscriptions to the following cultural materials are available directly from the publishers. See also the section on Subscription Services.

- *Phosphore* is a monthly magazine for high school students.
- *Okapi* is a bimonthly environmentally-oriented magazine for younger teenagers in France.
- *Vidéo-Presse* is a monthly magazine, aimed at 9- to 16-year-olds in Quebec schools.
- *Le Monde* is the major daily newspaper in France.
- *Le Figaro* is an important newspaper in France. Daily or Saturday editions are available by subscription.
- *Elle* is a weekly fashion magazine for women.
- *Paris Match* is a general interest weekly magazine.
- *Le Point* is a current events weekly magazine.
- *L'Express* is a current events weekly magazine.

SUBSCRIPTION SERVICES

French-language magazines can be obtained through subscription agencies in the United States. The following companies are among the many that can provide your school with subscriptions.

EBSCO Subscription Services
P. O. Box 1943
Birmingham, AL 35201-1943
(205) 991-6600

Continental Book Company
8000 Cooper Ave., Bldg. 29
Glendale, NY 11385
(718) 326-0572

PROFESSIONAL ORGANIZATIONS

The two major organizations for French teachers at the secondary-school level are:

The American Council on the Teaching of Foreign Languages (ACTFL)
6 Executive Blvd.
Upper Level
Yonkers, NY 10701
(914) 963-8830

The American Association of Teachers of French (AATF)
57 East Armory Ave.
Champaign, IL 61820
(217) 333-2842

A Bibliography for the French Teacher

This bibliography is a compilation of several resources available for professional enrichment. ◆

SELECTED AND ANNOTATED LIST OF READINGS

▶ I. METHODS AND APPROACHES

Cohen, Andrew D. *Assessing Language Ability in the Classroom,* 2/e. Boston, MA: Heinle, 1994.
- Assessment processes, oral interviews, role-playing situations, dictation, and portfolio assessment.

Hadley, Alice Omaggio. *Teaching Language in Context,* 2/e. Boston, MA: Heinle, 1993.
- Language acquisition theories and models and adult second language proficiency.

Krashen, Stephen, and Tracy D. Terrell. *The Natural Approach: Language Acquisition in the Classroom.* New York: Pergamon, 1983.
- Optimal Input Theory: listening, oral communication development, and testing.

Oller, John W., Jr. *Methods That Work: Ideas for Language Teachers,* 2/e. Boston, MA: Heinle, 1993.
- Literacy in multicultural settings, cooperative learning, peer teaching, and CAI.

Shrum, Judith L., and Eileen W. Glisan. *Teacher's Handbook: Contextualized Language Instruction.* Boston, MA: Heinle, 1993.
- Grammar, testing, using video texts, microteaching, case studies, and daily plans.

▶ II. SECOND LANGUAGE THEORY

Krashen, Stephen. *The Power of Reading.* New York: McGraw, 1994.
- Updates Optimal Input Theory by incorporating the reading of authentic texts.

Liskin-Gasparro, Judith. *A Guide to Testing and Teaching for Oral Proficiency.* Boston, MA: Heinle, 1990.
- Oral proficiency through interview techniques and speech samples.

Rubin, Joan, and Irene Thompson. *How To Be a More Successful Language Learner,* 2/e. Boston, MA: Heinle, 1993.
- Psychological, linguistic, and practical matters of second language learning.

▶ III. VIDEO AND CAI

Altmann, Rick. *The Video Connection: Integrating Video into Language Teaching.* Boston, MA: Houghton, 1989.
- Diverse strategies for using video texts to support second language learning.

Dunkel, Patricia A. *Computer-Assisted Language Learning and Testing.* Boston, MA: Heinle, 1992.
- CAI and computer-assisted language learning (CALL) in the foreign language classroom.

Kenning, M. J., and M.M. Kenning. *Computers and Language Learning: Current Theory and Practice.* New York, NY: E. Horwood, 1990.
- Theoretical discussions and practical suggestions for CAI in second language development.

▶ IV. PROFESSIONAL JOURNALS

Calico
(Published by Duke University, Charlotte, N.C.)
- Dedicated to the intersection of modern language learning and high technology. Research articles on videodiscs, using computer-assisted language learning, how-to articles, and courseware reviews.

The Foreign Language Annals
(Published by the American Council on the Teaching of Foreign Languages)
- Consists of research and how-to-teach articles.

The French Review
(Published by the American Association of Teachers of French)
- Articles on French-language literature.

The IALL Journal of Language Learning Technologies
(Published by the International Association for Learning Laboratories)
- Research articles as well as practical discussions pertaining to technology and language instruction.

The Modern Language Journal
- Primarily features research articles.

Scope and Sequence: French Level 1

CHAPITRE PRELIMINAIRE : ALLEZ, VIENS!

Functions
- Introducing yourself
- Spelling
- Counting
- Understanding classroom instructions

Grammar
- French alphabet
- French accent marks

Culture
- The French-speaking world
- Famous French-speaking people
- The importance of learning French
- French gestures for counting

CHAPITRE 1 : FAISONS CONNAISSANCE!

Location: Poitiers

Functions
- Greeting people and saying goodbye
- Asking how people are and telling how you are
- Asking someone's name and age and giving yours
- Expressing likes, dislikes, and preferences about things
- Expressing likes, dislikes, and preferences about activities

Grammar
- ne... pas
- The definite articles le, la, l', and les and the gender of nouns
- The connectors et and mais
- Subject pronouns
- -er verbs

Culture
- Greetings and goodbyes
- Hand gestures
- Leisure-time activities

Re-entry
- Introductions
- Numbers 0–20
- Expressing likes, dislikes, and preferences about things

CHAPITRE 2 : VIVE L'ECOLE!

Location: Poitiers

Functions
- Agreeing and disagreeing
- Asking for and giving information
- Telling when you have class
- Asking for and expressing opinions

Grammar
- Using si instead of oui to contradict a negative statement
- The verb avoir

Culture
- The French educational system/le bac
- L'heure officielle
- Curriculum in French schools
- The French grading system

Re-entry
- Greetings
- The verb aimer
- Numbers for telling time

CHAPITRE 3 : TOUT POUR LA RENTREE

Location: Poitiers

Functions
- Making and responding to requests
- Asking others what they need and telling what you need
- Telling what you'd like and what you'd like to do
- Getting someone's attention
- Asking for information
- Expressing thanks

Grammar
- The indefinite articles un, une, and des
- The demonstrative adjectives ce, cet, cette, and ces
- Adjective agreement and placement

Culture
- Bagging your own purchases
- Buying school supplies in French-speaking countries
- French currency

Re-entry
- The verb avoir
- Expressing likes and dislikes
- Numbers

CHAPITRE 4 : SPORTS ET PASSE-TEMPS

Location: Quebec

Functions
- Telling how much you like or dislike something
- Exchanging information
- Making, accepting, and turning down suggestions

Grammar
- Contractions with à and de
- Question formation
- de after a negative verb

- The verb faire
- Adverbs of frequency

Culture
- Old and new in Quebec City
- Celsius and Fahrenheit
- Sports in francophone countries
- Maison des jeunes et de la culture

Re-entry
- Expressing likes and dislikes
- The verb aimer; regular -er verbs
- Agreeing and disagreeing

CHAPITRE 5 : ON VA AU CAFE?

Location: Paris

Functions
- Making suggestions and excuses
- Making a recommendation
- Getting somone's attention
- Ordering food and beverages
- Inquiring about and expressing likes and dislikes
- Paying the check

Grammar
- The verb prendre
- The imperative

Culture
- Food served in a café
- Waitpersons as professionals
- La litote
- Tipping

Re-entry
- Accepting and turning down a suggestion
- Expressing likes and dislikes
- Numbers 20–100

CHAPITRE 6 : AMUSONS-NOUS!

Location: Paris

Functions
- Making plans
- Extending and responding to invitations
- Arranging to meet someone

Grammar
- Using le with days of the week
- The verb aller and aller + infinitive
- The verb vouloir
- Information questions

Culture
- Going out
- Dating in France
- Conversational time

Re-entry
- Expressing likes and dislikes
- Contractions with **à**
- Making, accepting, and turning down suggestions
- **L'heure officielle**

CHAPITRE 7 : LA FAMILLE
Location: Paris
Functions
- Identifying people
- Introducing people
- Describing and characterizing people
- Asking for, giving, and refusing permission

Grammar
- Possession with **de**
- Possessive adjectives
- Adjective agreement
- The verb **être**

Culture
- Family life
- Pets in France

Re-entry
- Asking for and giving people's names and ages
- Adjective agreement

CHAPITRE 8 : AU MARCHE
Location: Abidjan
Functions
- Expressing need
- Making, accepting, and declining requests
- Telling someone what to do
- Offering, accepting, or refusing food

Grammar
- The partitive articles **du, de la, de l'**, and **des**
- **avoir besoin de**
- The verb **pouvoir**
- **de** with expressions of quantity
- The pronoun **en**

Culture
- The Ivorian market
- Shopping for groceries in francophone countries
- The metric system
- Foods of Côte d'Ivoire
- Mealtimes in francophone countries

Re-entry
- Food vocabulary
- Activities
- Making purchases

CHAPITRE 9 : AU TELEPHONE
Location: Arles
Functions
- Asking for and expressing opinions
- Inquiring about and relating past events
- Making and answering a phone call
- Sharing confidences and consoling others
- Asking for and giving advice

Grammar
- The **passé composé** with **avoir**
- Placement of adverbs with the **passé composé**
- The -**re** verbs: **répondre**
- The object pronouns **le, la, les, lui,** and **leur**

Culture
- History of Arles
- The French telephone system
- Telephone habits of French-speaking teenagers

Re-entry
- Chores
- Asking for, giving, and refusing permission
- **aller** + infinitive

CHAPITRE 10 : DANS UN MAGASIN DE VETEMENTS
Location: Arles
Functions
- Asking for and giving advice
- Expressing need; inquiring
- Asking for an opinion; paying a compliment; criticizing
- Hesitating; making a decision

Grammar
- The verbs **mettre** and **porter**
- Adjectives used as nouns
- The -**ir** verbs: **choisir**
- The direct object pronouns **le, la,** and **les**
- **c'est** versus **il/elle est**

Culture
- Clothing sizes
- Fashion in francophone countries
- Responding to compliments

Re-entry
- The future with **aller**
- Colors
- Likes and dislikes

CHAPITRE 11 : VIVE LES VACANCES!
Location: Arles
Functions
- Inquiring about and sharing future plans
- Expressing indecision; expressing wishes
- Asking for advice; making, accepting, and refusing suggestions
- Reminding; reassuring
- Seeing someone off
- Asking for and expressing opinions
- Inquiring about and relating past events

Grammar
- The prepositions **à** and **en**
- The -**ir** verbs: **partir**

Culture
- **Colonies de vacances**
- Vacations

Re-entry
- **aller** + infinitive
- Asking for advice
- Clothing vocabulary
- The imperative
- Weather expressions
- The **passé composé**
- The verb **vouloir**

CHAPITRE 12 : EN VILLE
Location: Fort-de-France (Review)
Functions
- Pointing out places and things
- Making and responding to requests
- Asking for advice and making suggestions
- Asking for and giving directions

Grammar
- The pronoun **y**

Culture
- Store hours in France and Martinique
- Making "small talk" in francophone countries
- Getting a driver's license in francophone countries
- **DOMs** and **TOMs**
- Public areas downtown

Re-entry
- Contractions with **à**
- The partitive
- Contractions with **de**
- Family vocabulary
- Possessive adjectives
- The **passé composé**
- Expressing need
- Making excuses
- Inviting

Scope and Sequence: French Level 2

CHAPITRE 1 : BON SEJOUR!

Location: Paris region (Review)

Functions

- Describing and characterizing yourself and others
- Expressing likes, dislikes, and preferences
- Asking for information
- Asking for and giving advice
- Asking for, making, and responding to suggestions
- Relating a series of events

Grammar

- Adjective agreement
- The imperative
- The future with **aller**

Culture

- Travel documents for foreign countries
- Ethnic restaurants
- Studying abroad

Re-entry

- Adjectives to characterize people
- Pronunciation: **liaison**
- Family vocabulary
- Clothing and colors
- Weather expressions and seasons
- Telling time

CHAPITRE 2 : BIENVENUE A CHARTRES!

Location: Paris region (Review)

Functions

- Welcoming someone and responding to someone's welcome
- Asking how someone is feeling and telling how you're feeling
- Pointing out where things are
- Paying and responding to compliments
- Asking for and giving directions

Grammar

- Irregular adjectives
- Contractions with **à**

Culture

- Paying and receiving compliments
- Teenagers' bedrooms in France
- **Notre-Dame-de-Chartres**
- Houses in francophone countries

Re-entry

- Use of **tu** versus **vous**

- Pronunciation: intonation
- Prepositions of location
- Contractions with **de**
- Making suggestions

CHAPITRE 3 : UN REPAS A LA FRANÇAISE

Location: Paris region

Functions

- Making purchases
- Asking for, offering, accepting, and refusing food
- Paying and responding to compliments
- Asking for and giving advice
- Extending good wishes

Grammar

- The object pronoun **en**
- The partitive articles
- The indirect object pronouns **lui** and **leur**

Culture

- Neighborhood stores
- Typical meals in the francophone world
- Courses of a meal
- Polite behavior for a guest
- Special occasions

Re-entry

- Giving prices
- Expressions of quantity
- Food vocabulary

CHAPITRE 4 : SOUS LES TROPIQUES

Location: Martinique

Functions

- Asking for information and describing a place
- Asking for and making suggestions
- Emphasizing likes and dislikes
- Relating a series of events

Grammar

- The use of **de** before a plural adjective and noun
- Recognizing reflexive verbs
- The reflexive verbs **se coucher** and **se lever**
- The present tense of reflexive verbs

Culture

- **La ville de Saint-Pierre**
- Places to visit in different regions
- **Yoles rondes**
- The **créole** language
- **Carnaval**
- Music and dance in Martinique

Re-entry

- Connectors for sequencing events
- Adverbs of frequency
- Pronunciation: **e muet**
- Sports vocabulary

CHAPITRE 5 : QUELLE JOURNEE!

Location: Touraine

Functions

- Expressing concern for someone
- Inquiring; expressing satisfaction and frustration
- Sympathizing with and consoling someone
- Giving reasons and making excuses
- Congratulating and reprimanding someone

Grammar

- The **passé composé** with **avoir**
- Introduction to verbs that use **être** in the **passé composé**

Culture

- **Carnet de correspondance**
- Meals at school
- French grades and report cards
- School life in francophone countries

Re-entry

- Connector words
- Sports and leisure activities
- Pronunciation: the nasal sound [ɛ̃]
- Question words
- Reflexive verbs

CHAPITRE 6 : A NOUS LES CHATEAUX!

Location: Touraine

Functions

- Asking for opinions; expressing enthusiasm, indifference, and dissatisfaction
- Expressing disbelief and doubt
- Asking for and giving information

Grammar

- The phrase **c'était**
- The **passé composé** with **être**
- Formal and informal phrasing of questions
- The verb **ouvrir**

Culture

- Types of châteaux in France
- Buses and trains in France
- Historical figures of Chenonceau
- Studying historical figures in school

Re-entry

- Pronunciation: [y] versus [u]

Scope and Sequence: French Level 3

CHAPITRE 1 : FRANCE, LES REGIONS
Location: France (Review)

Functions
- Renewing old acquaintances
- Inquiring; expressing enthusiasm and dissatisfaction
- Exchanging information
- Expressing indecision
- Making recommendations
- Ordering and asking for details

Grammar
- The passé composé

Culture
- Traditional regional clothing
- Regional specialties
- Eating out in France
- Regional foods

Re-entry
- Food vocabulary
- Question formation

CHAPITRE 2 : BELGIQUE, NOUS VOILA!
Location: Belgium (Review)

Functions
- Asking for and giving directions
- Expressing impatience
- Reassuring someone
- Expressing enthusiasm and boredom
- Asking and telling where things are

Grammar
- The verb conduire

Culture
- Languages in Belgium
- Favorite comic book characters
- Overview of Belgium

Re-entry
- Extending invitations
- The imperative
- Direct and indirect object pronouns
- The forms of the imperfect
- Making, accepting, and refusing suggestions

CHAPITRE 3 : SOYONS RESPONSABLES!
Location: Switzerland

Functions
- Asking for, granting, and refusing permission
- Expressing obligation
- Forbidding
- Reproaching
- Justifying your actions and rejecting others' excuses

Grammar
- The verb devoir
- The subjunctive
- ne... pas + infinitive

Culture
- Swiss work ethic
- Switzerland's neutrality
- Overview of Switzerland
- Environmental issues
- La minuterie

Re-entry
- Complaining
- Chores
- Negative expressions

CHAPITRE 4 : DES GOUTS ET DES COULEURS
Location: France

Functions
- Asking for and giving opinions
- Asking which one(s)
- Pointing out and identifying people and things
- Paying and responding to compliments
- Reassuring someone

Grammar
- The interrogative and demonstrative pronouns
- The causative faire

Culture
- French clothing stores
- Fashion and personal style
- French sense of fashion

Re-entry
- Clothing vocabulary
- Adjectives referring to clothing
- Family vocabulary
- Chores

CHAPITRE 5 : C'EST NOTRE AVENIR
Location: Senegal

Functions
- Asking about and expressing intentions
- Expressing conditions and possibilities
- Asking about future plans
- Expressing wishes
- Expressing indecision
- Giving advice
- Requesting information
- Writing a formal letter

Grammar
- The future
- The conditional

Culture
- Careers and education in Senegal
- Overview of Senegal
- Planning for a career
- Types of job training

Re-entry
- The subjunctive
- Giving advice
- The passé composé
- The imperfect
- Making a telephone call
- Expressing likes and preferences

CHAPITRE 6 : MA FAMILLE, MES COPAINS ET MOI
Location: Morocco

Functions
- Making, accepting, and refusing suggestions
- Making arrangements
- Making and accepting apologies
- Showing and responding to hospitality
- Expressing and responding to thanks
- Quarreling

Grammar
- Reciprocal verbs
- The past infinitive

Culture
- Bargaining in North Africa
- Values of francophone teenagers
- Overview of Morocco
- Hospitality in Morocco

Re-entry
- Reflexive verbs
- Accepting and refusing suggestions
- Making plans
- Describing and characterizing yourself and others
- Family vocabulary
- Expressing thanks

CHAPITRE 7 : UN SAFARI-PHOTO
Location: Central African Republic

Functions
- Making suppositions
- Expressing doubt and certainty
- Asking for and giving advice
- Expressing astonishment
- Cautioning someone

- Expressing fear
- Reassuring someone
- Expressing relief

Grammar
- Structures and their complements
- Using the subjunctive
- Irregular subjunctive forms

Culture
- Overview of the Central African Republic
- Animal conservation in the Central African Republic
- Stereotypical impressions of francophone regions

Re-entry
- The subjunctive
- The rain forest
- Travel items
- Adjectives to describe animals
- The conditional

CHAPITRE 8 : LA TUNISIE, PAYS DE CONTRASTES

Location: Tunisia

Functions
- Asking someone to convey good wishes
- Closing a letter
- Expressing hopes or wishes
- Giving advice
- Complaining
- Expressing annoyance
- Making comparisons

Grammar
- **Si** clauses
- The comparative

Culture
- Overview of Tunisia
- Traditional and modern life in Tunisia
- Carthage
- Modernization in francophone countries
- Traditional and modern styles of dress in Tunisia

Re-entry
- The imperfect
- Formation of the conditional
- Intonation
- Adjective agreement
- Describing a place

CHAPITRE 9 : C'EST L'FUN!

Location: Canada

Functions
- Agreeing and disagreeing
- Expressing indifference

- Making requests
- Asking for and making judgments
- Asking for and making recommendations
- Asking about and summarizing a story

Grammar
- Negative expressions
- The relative pronouns **qui, que,** and **dont**

Culture
- Multilingual broadcasting in Canada
- Overview of Montreal
- Favorite types of movies
- The Canadian film industry

Re-entry
- Expressing opinions
- Quarreling
- Agreeing and disagreeing
- Types of films
- Summarizing a story
- Continuing and ending a story
- Relating a series of events
- Relative pronouns

CHAPITRE 10 : RENCONTRES AU SOLEIL

Location: Guadeloupe

Functions
- Bragging; flattering; teasing
- Breaking some news
- Showing interest
- Expressing disbelief; telling a joke

Grammar
- The superlative
- The past perfect

Culture
- Climate and natural assets of Guadeloupe.
- Overview of Guadeloupe
- **La Fête des Cuisinières**
- Daily routines of francophone teenagers
- Greetings in Guadeloupe

Re-entry
- Forms of the comparative
- Adjective agreement
- The **passé composé**
- Breaking some news

CHAPITRE 11 : LAISSEZ LES BONS TEMPS ROULER!

Location: Louisiana

Functions
- Asking for confirmation
- Asking for and giving opinions

- Agreeing and disagreeing
- Asking for explanations
- Making observations
- Giving impressions

Grammar
- The relative pronouns **ce qui** and **ce que**

Culture
- **Mardi Gras** and festivals in Louisiana
- Cajun French
- Cajun music
- History of Louisiana
- Parties and celebrations in francophone countries

Re-entry
- Renewing old acquaintances
- Food vocabulary
- Types of music
- Agreeing and disagreeing
- Asking for and giving opinions
- Emphasizing likes
- Making suggestions
- Expressing opinions

CHAPITRE 12 : ECHANGES SPORTIFS ET CULTURELS

Location: Worldwide (Review)

Functions
- Expressing anticipation
- Making suppositions
- Expressing certainty and doubt
- Inquiring
- Expressing excitement and disappointment

Grammar
- The future after **quand** and **dès que**

Culture
- International sporting events in francophone countries
- Stereotypes of people in francophone countries

Re-entry
- Sports vocabulary
- Making suppositions
- Expressing certainty and doubt
- The future
- Prepositions with countries
- Greeting people
- Introducing people
- Asking someone's name and age and giving yours
- Offering encouragement

Allez, viens en Europe francophone!

pp. T62–105

Motivating Activity

Ask students to name the countries and other political entities in Europe where French is spoken (France, Switzerland, Belgium, Luxembourg, Monaco). Have them tell what they know about these places, including well-known monuments, topography, food specialties, and famous people.

Background Information

France, Belgium, and Switzerland are francophone countries because the land these countries now occupy was at one time under the control of the Franks. Charlemagne, a Frankish king and emperor, formed a huge empire that included not only these areas, but parts of northern Spain, Italy, Germany, Austria, and even Denmark.

History Link

The area ruled by Charlemagne was divided among his three grandsons in 842, according to the Treaty of Verdun **(le Traité de Verdun)**. Charles II, known as **le Chauve** *(the Bald)*, received most of what is now France and western Belgium; Louis II **(le Germanique)** received most of present-day Germany and Austria; Lothaire was awarded the region in between, from Holland to Rome, Italy. French language, culture, and politics predominated in the western area and German in the east, but the central area, encompassing Belgium, Luxembourg, and Switzerland, became a heterogeneous mix of cultures.

CHAPITRES 1, 2, 3, 4

Allez, viens en Europe francophone!

La ville de Genève au bord du lac Léman

History Link

The current borders of France were fixed in 1860, when Nice and Savoie were annexed. The provinces of Alsace and Lorraine, however, have changed hands several times between France and Germany. Germany controlled the areas from 1870–1918 and from 1940–1945. After the second world war, Alsace and Lorraine were returned to France and have remained French ever since. However, the influences of German culture are still evident throughout these regions.

L'Europe francophone

	La Belgique	La France	La Suisse
Population	9.900.000	58.000.000	6.400.000
Superficie (km²)	30.540	549.000	41.293
Capitale	Bruxelles	Paris	Berne
Autres villes importantes	Liège	Lyon	Zurich
	Anvers	Marseille	Genève
	Charleroi	Bordeaux	Lausanne
	Mons	Nice	Bâle
	Gand	Strasbourg	

Autres états francophones :
Le Luxembourg, La principauté de Monaco

un **1**

Using the Almanac and Map

Terms in the Almanac

- **Paris** was named after the Celtic tribe that first inhabited the area, the **Parisii.** It has been the capital of France since the reign of Philippe-Auguste (1180–1223).
- **Marseille,** founded by the Greeks as **Massilia** in 600 B.C., is one of France's largest cities and a major port.
- **Bordeaux** was the birthplace of Michel de Montaigne, a sixteenth-century essayist and philosopher. Le Baron de Montesquieu, famous for his *L'Esprit des lois* in which he discusses the separation of powers in government, was also a native of Bordeaux.
- **Bruxelles,** the capital of Belgium, is also the site of the headquarters of NATO and the EU. It is famous for its beautiful tapestries into which golden threads have been woven (**tapis d'or**).
- **Anvers,** which means **les jetées** *(the throwaways),* is a Flemish city on the Escaut River. Its name comes from a legend telling how the town was terrorized by a giant whose hand was cut off and thrown into the river by the local hero.
- **Berne** was founded in 1191 by the Duke of Zähringen, who pledged to name the town after the first animal captured during the hunt, which was a bear.
- **Genève** was once known as the "Rome of Protestantism" because Jean Calvin came here in the sixteenth century to try to apply his principles during the Protestant Reformation.
- **Bâle** is a major port on the Rhine River. In 1521, it became the home of the Dutch humanist Erasmus, who preached tolerance.

Art Link

The Flemish artist Peter Paul Rubens painted for many of the monarchs of Europe. Some of his paintings are on display in the Louvre in Paris. When Rubens died in 1604, he was buried in the cathedral of Anvers.

Using the Map

Have students look at the map and describe France's borders with its neighbors (the ocean, rivers, mountains).

Language Note

You might have students look up the origins of the various place names. Sources include the Greek names **Massilia** (Marseille) and **Nicaea** (Nice); Celtic tribal names such as the **Parisii** (Paris); Roman names such as **Lugdunum** (Lyons) and **Belgica Prima** (Belgium); Germanic names such as **Francs** (France) and **Burgondes** (Bourgogne); and places named after people like **Carcassonne** for Dame Carcas or **Charleroi** for Charles II of Spain.

Using the Photo Essay

① **Mont Cervin**, located near the border with the Italian province of Aosta, is 4,505 meters high. A British climber was the first to scale it in 1865.

② Known for its thirteenth-century Gothic abbey, **Mont-Saint-Michel,** an island in the Gulf of Saint-Malo between Normandy and Brittany, has been the destination of pilgrims since the Middle Ages. In the past, the island was accessible only at low tide, when the receding waters revealed a passage to the island. Since the tides in the bay would come in dangerously fast, many pilgrims lost their lives trying to outrun a swift, incoming tide. Today, the island is connected to the mainland by a mile-long causeway.

Geography Link

② The Couesnon River empties into the bay near **Mont-Saint-Michel.** Once known for its severe flooding, it is now controlled by dams and dikes. The flood control projects, however, have yielded an unexpected consequence for the island. The dams prevent the flooding that flushed out sand and sediment from the bay. Without this flooding, sediment remains in the bay and Mont-Saint-Michel is truly an island only during high tides.

Ecology Link

② Construction will begin soon to replace half of the causeway that connects **Mont-Saint-Michel** to the mainland with a bridge to allow the tide to flow freely, thereby restoring the natural ecology.

③ Brussels' historic **Grand-Place** is the site of a flower market where vendors carpet the square with their colorful blooms to form the **tapis de fleurs.**

L'Europe de l'Ouest n'est pas très grande, mais elle présente beaucoup de régions différentes qui ne correspondent pas exactement aux frontières politiques. La langue contribue à accentuer ces différences parce qu'elle correspond à une culture. Par exemple, en Belgique, on parle français dans le sud et flamand dans le nord. En Suisse, on parle français, italien et allemand et au Luxembourg on parle français, luxembourgeois et allemand. Il y a six millions de francophones en Europe qui vivent dans des pays autres que la France.

① «Matterhorn» est le nom allemand du **Mont Cervin** dans les Alpes suisses. Il domine la célèbre station de sports d'hiver de Zermatt, un village où les automobiles ne sont pas autorisées.

③ Bruxelles est la capitale de la Belgique et sa population est bilingue français-flamand.

2 *deux*

② En Normandie, dans le nord-ouest de la France, l'abbaye gothique du **Mont-Saint-Michel** est un grand lieu touristique.

🌐 Culture Note

In Luxembourg, French is the official language, **Letzeburgesch (Luxembourgeois)** is the Germanic national language, and German is also spoken. Operating under a constitutional monarchy similar to Belgium's, Luxembourg is a highly industrialized country with a high standard of living and an extremely low illiteracy rate.

Multicultural Link

Have students compare the regional differences in francophone Europe with those in the United States. Have them list the different nationalities and languages in francophone Europe and the United States.

④ **Les Ardennes,** a rugged forest where Charlemagne once hunted, covers northern France, eastern Belgium, and Luxembourg. It was the site of the final German offensive in World War II, the Battle of the Bulge, which took place in December of 1944 and January of 1945.

⑤ Les fortifications de **la ville de Carcassonne** sont un bel exemple d'architecture médiévale.

④ La région **des Ardennes** est partagée entre la France, le Luxembourg et la Belgique.

⑤ **Carcassonne** is the largest fortified city in Europe. It is surrounded by an inner wall and an outer wall that connects fourteen towers. The current structure dates from the thirteenth century, when Carcassonne came into French hands. The Romans established an encampment here as a trading center between the Mediterranean Sea and the city of Toulouse. About 300 people presently live in the old fortified city, and thousands more live in the more modern city **(la ville basse)** outside the ramparts.

⑥ En Europe, le chemin de fer est très développé et permet de passer partout et de visiter un maximum de régions.

⑥ The construction of roads and railroads into the mountainous areas of France and Switzerland has eased the previous isolation of the inhabitants. Although the mountains did not prevent major invasions over the centuries, they did isolate the people from much of the outside world.

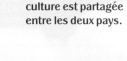

⑦ **La ville de Strasbourg** est la capitale de l'Alsace, à la frontière franco-allemande. Sa culture est partagée entre les deux pays.

⑦ **Strasbourg** is located near the Rhine River, which forms the border with Germany. An important commercial, manufacturing, and transportation center, Strasbourg has a long and eventful history. It was destroyed by the Huns in the fifth century, and after the Franks helped rebuild the city, it became part of the Holy Roman Empire. In 1681, Louis XIV took possession of Strasbourg and it became part of France.

trois **3**

Culture Note

⑤ Legend has it that in the Middle Ages, Carcassonne was running low on food as it was besieged by Charlemagne. The leader of the city, Dame Carcas, thought of a clever ruse to fool the surrounding troops. She ordered that the last bit of wheat be fed to the only remaining pig, and the pig be tossed over the town wall. The pig landed at Charlemagne's feet and burst open. Believing that the inhabitants had plenty of food since the pig was so well fed, Charlemagne decided to withdraw. As he and his troops were leaving, Dame Carcas stood on the wall, blew a horn, and said «**C'est Dame Carcas qui te sonne!**»

Science Link

⑦ Johannes Gens-Fleisch, known as Gutenberg, developed his revolutionary printing press in Strasbourg in 1434.

Chapitre 1 : France, les régions
Chapter Overview

| Mise en train
pp. 6–8 | **Les retrouvailles** | | | Note Culturelle, Traditional regional clothing, p. 8 | |

	FUNCTIONS	GRAMMAR	CULTURE	RE-ENTRY
Première étape pp. 9–13	• Renewing old acquaintances, p. 9 *Review* • Inquiring, p. 10 • Expressing enthusiasm and dissatisfaction, p. 10 • Exchanging information, p.12	*Review* The **passé composé**, p. 11		Chapters 1 and 2 are a global review of Holt French, Levels 1 and 2.

| Remise en train
pp. 14–15 | **Bon appétit!** | | | |

	FUNCTIONS	GRAMMAR	CULTURE	RE-ENTRY
Deuxième étape pp. 16–19	• Expressing indecision; making recommendations, p. 17 • Ordering and asking for details, p. 18		• **Panorama Culturel,** Regional specialties, p. 16 • **Note Culturelle,** Eating out in France, p. 17 • **Note Culturelle,** Regional foods, p. 18	

| **Lisons!**
pp. 20–22 | **Il faut être raisonnable**
Reading Strategy: Identifying the point of view of the narrator |

| **Ecrivons!**
p. 23 | **Une brochure touristique**
Writing Strategy: Defining your purpose |

| **Review**
pp. 24–27 | • **Mise en pratique,** pp. 24–25
• **Que sais-je?** p. 26
• **Vocabulaire,** p. 27 |

Assessment Options

Etape Quizzes
• *Chapter Teaching Resources, Book 1*
  Première étape, Quiz 1-1, pp. 23–24
  Deuxième étape, Quiz 1-2, pp. 25–26
• *Assessment Items, Audiocassette 7A/Audio CD 1*

Chapter Test
• *Chapter Teaching Resources, Book 1*, pp. 27–32
• *Assessment Guide, Speaking Test, p. 28*
• *Assessment Items, Audiocassette 7A/Audio CD 1*

Test Generator, Chapter 1

RESOURCES: Print	RESOURCES: Audiovisual
Practice and Activity Book, p. 1	Textbook Audiocassette 1A/Audio CD 1
Practice and Activity Book, pp. 2–5 Grammar and Vocabulary Worksheets, pp. 1–4 Chapter Teaching Resources, Book 1 • Communicative Activity 1-1, pp. 4–5 • Teaching Transparency Master 1-1, pp. 8, 10 . . . . • Additional Listening Activities 1-1, 1-2, 1-3, pp. 11–12 . . . . . • Realia 1-1, pp. 15, 17 • Situation Cards 1-1, pp. 18–19 • Student Response Forms, pp. 20–22 • Quiz 1-1, pp. 23–24	Textbook Audiocassette 1A/Audio CD 1 Teaching Transparency 1-1 Additional Listening Activities, Audiocassette 9A/Audio CD 1 Assessment Items, Audiocassette 7A/Audio CD 1
Practice and Activity Book, p. 6	Textbook Audiocassette 1A/Audio CD 1
Practice and Activity Book, pp. 7–10 Grammar and Vocabulary Worksheets, pp. 5–8 Chapter Teaching Resources, Book 1 • Communicative Activity 1-2, pp. 6–7 • Teaching Transparency Master 1-2, pp. 9, 10 . . . . • Additional Listening Activities 1-4, 1-5, 1-6, pp. 12–13 . . . . . • Realia 1-2, pp. 16, 17 • Situation Cards 1-2, 1-3, pp. 19–20 • Student Response Forms, pp. 20–22 • Quiz 1-2, pp. 25–26 . . . . Video Guide	Textbook Audiocassette 1A/Audio CD 1 Teaching Transparency 1-2 Additional Listening Activities, Audiocassette 9A/Audio CD 1 Assessment Items, Audiocassette 7A/Audio CD 1 Video Program, Videocassette 1
Practice and Activity Book, p. 11	
Video Guide	Video Program, Videocassette 1

Alternative Assessment

• Performance Assessment
  Première étape, p. 13
  Deuxième étape, p. 19

• Portfolio Assessment
  Written: **Mise en pratique,** Activity 4, *Pupil's Edition*, p. 25
    Assessment Guide, p. 14
  Oral: **Mise en pratique,** Activity 6, *Pupil's Edition*, p. 25
    Assessment Guide, p. 14

Chapitre 1 : France, les régions
Textbook Listening Activities Scripts

For Student Response Forms, see *Chapter Teaching Resources, Book 1,* pp. 20–22.

Première étape

8 Ecoute! p. 9

1. — Salut! Comment vas-tu? Ça fait longtemps qu'on s'est pas vus!
   — Oui, ça fait bien deux ans! Qu'est-ce que tu deviens?
   — Oh, rien de neuf.
2. — Tiens, Jean-Paul! Je suis contente de te revoir!
   — Oui, moi aussi. Ça fait combien de temps qu'on s'est pas vus?
   — Ça fait trois mois au moins. Ça va?
   — Oui, super.
3. — Quoi de neuf?
   — Oh, tu sais, toujours la même chose. Et toi?
   — Rien de neuf. Dis donc, ça fait combien de temps qu'on s'est pas vus?
   — Depuis le mois de juin, je crois.

Answers to Activity 8
1. b   2. a   3. d

10 Ecoute! p. 10

1. — Alors, c'était comment, tes vacances à la mer?
   — Génial. Je me suis bien amusée.
2. — C'était comment, ce voyage?
   — Pas trop bien. Ça s'est mal passé.
3. — Tu t'es bien amusée chez tes cousins?
   — Pas du tout. C'était vraiment pas terrible comme vacances.
4. — Tiens, Véronique. Ça s'est bien passé, ce week-end?
   — Non, je me suis ennuyée.
5. — Raconte-moi un peu ce séjour. C'était comment la Martinique?
   — Super. On a passé des vacances formidables.
6. — Comment ça s'est passé, cette journée à la campagne?
   — Ça s'est très bien passé. On a fait un pique-nique.

Answers to Activity 10
1. contente   2. non   3. non   4. non   5. contente   6. contente

12 Ecoute! p. 11

1. — Mon père a un bateau. Alors, en ce moment, je fais du ski nautique tous les jours.
   — Tu en as de la chance. Moi, je travaille.
2. — Tu sais, elle a parlé à ses parents de la situation avec sa sœur.
   — Et alors? Qu'est-ce qu'ils ont dit?
3. — Mademoiselle, l'addition, s'il vous plaît.
   — Déjà?

— Oui, le film commence dans un quart d'heure.
4. — Qu'est-ce qui t'est arrivé?
   — Je suis restée une semaine au lit avec une mauvaise grippe!
   — Alors, il y avait de bons programmes à la télé?
5. — Tu ne pars pas en Afrique?
   — Si, au mois d'août.
6. — Qu'est-ce que tu as fait pendant tes vacances à Montpellier?
   — Tu sais, j'adore la mer, alors j'y suis allé tout le temps.
7. — Dis donc, tu crois que tu es prête pour le permis de conduire?
   — Ben, oui, je pense. En ce moment, je prends des leçons trois fois par semaine.
8. — Dis, au fait, tu as payé l'addition?
   — Oui. Ne t'inquiète pas, j'ai fait un chèque pour nous deux.

Answers to Activity 12

1. présent	3. présent	5. présent	7. présent
2. passé	4. passé	6. passé	8. passé

15 Ecoute! p. 13

— Salut, Marie-Claire! Ça fait longtemps qu'on ne s'est pas vues!
— Oui, ça fait deux mois.
— Alors, ça s'est bien passé, tes vacances?
— Oh, pas mal. Je suis allée à la plage.
— Quand?
— Fin août.
— Avec qui?
— Avec ma famille.
— Comment ça s'est passé?
— La première semaine, c'était pas terrible. Il a plu tous les jours.
— Qu'est-ce que tu as fait alors?
— Tu sais, je me suis beaucoup ennuyée. Je suis restée avec mes parents.
— Et après ça?
— Enfin, ce vendredi-là, je suis allée au cinéma. Et tu sais qui était là? Nicole! Je l'ai vue devant le cinéma. Elle était en vacances avec sa famille aussi.
— Donc, vous vous êtes bien amusées?
— Oui, et samedi, il a fait beau temps, enfin! On est donc allés faire du ski nautique. Tu sais ce qui est arrivé? J'ai rencontré un garçon mignon.
— C'est vrai?
— Oui, nous avons fait de la plongée dimanche. C'était super. Nous avons passé beaucoup de temps ensemble après ça. Il m'a dit qu'il allait me téléphoner à Paris.

Answers to Activity 15
c,   b,   a,   d

*R*emise en train

24 Ecoute! p. 15

PATRICIA   Toi, Julien, tu as pris la quiche à vingt-huit francs... tu as bu de l'eau. Avec ton plat et ton dessert, ça fait cent quarante-huit francs.

Pauline... le plat du jour à quarante-quatre francs, les crudités à trente-cinq francs et ton coca. Voyons... Ça fait quatre-vingt-onze francs.

Toi, Hector, ça te fait seulement soixante-dix-neuf francs.

Yasmine, ton presskopf et ta choucroute, ça te fait cent trente francs.

Et moi, j'ai pris le potage à vingt-cinq francs, la truite, l'assiette de crudités et la crème brûlée. Ça fait cent soixante francs.

HECTOR   Quel festin! Heureusement qu'on n'a pas partagé en cinq.

Answers to Activity 24

1. Julien: cent quarante-huit francs (148 F)
2. Pauline: quatre-vingt-onze francs (91 F)
3. Hector: soixante-dix-neuf francs (79 F)
4. Yasmine: cent trente francs (130 F)
5. Patricia: cent soixante francs (160 F)

*D*euxième étape

26 Ecoute! p. 17

1. — Hum. Fromage ou dessert? Je n'arrive pas à me décider.
2. — Je ne sais pas quoi prendre. Tout a l'air si bon!
3. — Pourquoi tu ne prends pas la tarte aux pommes? Elle est très bonne ici.
4. — J'ai tellement faim. Tout me tente. Qu'est-ce que je pourrais bien prendre?
5. — A mon avis, tu devrais boire plus de jus de fruits. C'est excellent pour la santé.
6. — Voyons... J'hésite entre le poisson et le poulet.

Answers to Activity 26

1. hésite	4. hésite
2. hésite	5. recommande quelque chose
3. recommande quelque chose	6. hésite

28 Ecoute! p. 18

— Excusez-moi, monsieur, qu'est-ce que vous avez pris comme entrée?
— Comme entrée, attendez... Ah oui, j'ai pris une salade de tomates.
— Et comme plat?
— Du poulet.
— Avec des frites?
— Non, avec des haricots verts. Voyons... mon fromage... et comme dessert, j'ai pris une tarte aux pommes.
— C'est noté. Merci monsieur.

Answer to Activity 28

b

30 Ecoute! p. 19

1. — Vous avez choisi?
2. — Que voulez-vous comme entrée?
3. — Et comme boisson?
4. — Comment désirez-vous votre viande?
5. — Que voulez-vous comme dessert?

Answers to Activity 30

1. Oui, je vais prendre le steak-frites.	4. A point.
2. Les crudités.	5. La crème caramel, s'il vous plaît.
3. De l'eau minérale.	

*M*ise en pratique

5 p. 25

1. — Qu'est-ce qu'on mange aujourd'hui?
   — Des raviolis au gratin et une glace.
2. — Tu as choisi?
   — Non, j'hésite entre les spaghettis et le veau aux petits pois.
3. — Quel dilemme! Je n'arrive pas à me décider. La raie ou le coq au riesling?
   — Tu devrais prendre le poisson. C'est bon pour la mémoire.
4. — Je voudrais manger du caviar et du filet mignon.
   — Pas de chance. Aujourd'hui, c'est spaghettis ou raviolis.
5. — Qu'est-ce que c'est, le filet de lingue avec des blettes?
   — Je ne sais pas, mais c'est le plat du jour.

Answers to Mise en pratique Activity 5

1. Collège Molière	4. Lycée Camille Sée
2. Institution Saint-Jean	5. Collège Berlioz
3. Cité Technique	

Chapitre 1 : France, les régions
Projects

Les régions de la France
(Cooperative Learning Project)

ASSIGNMENT

Groups of students will research the history, specialties, products, and traditional dress of a region of France, display their information on a poster, and give a short oral presentation.

MATERIALS

✂ **Students may need**

- Posterboard
- Colored pencils or markers
- Scissors
- Glue
- Travel brochures and encyclopedias
- Travel guide books

SUGGESTED SEQUENCE

1. In groups of four, students choose a region of France to research. They might choose Provence, Bretagne, Savoie, Alsace, Lorraine, Normandie, Bourgogne, Ile-de-France, or any other region. Then, group members decide who will be the writer, illustrator, proofreader, and presenter.

2. All group members do research. Each member may choose a specific topic (traditional clothing, food specialties, products, geographic features, language/dialect). Group members then share their information with one another and decide what to include in the final project.

3. The writer organizes and writes a rough draft of the oral presentation. The proofreader edits the information and proposes the final draft. In collaboration with the other group members, the illustrator determines the visuals that will be used for the poster, assembles the necessary materials, and makes the visuals. The presenter assists the other group members and begins to plan out the presentation.

4. The group organizes and assembles their poster. They should all help the presenter prepare. They might serve as the audience for a rehearsal. Finally, the presenter conveys the group's findings to the class, using the poster as a visual aid.

5. You might display students' posters around the classroom or school.

GRADING THE PROJECT

Since this is a cooperative learning project, you might want to give each member a grade for the work of the entire group, based on content, language use, and appearance of visuals. Each member should also receive an individual grade for his or her effort and participation in the project.

Suggested Point Distribution (total = 100 points)

Content . . . . 25 points

Language use . . . . 25 points

Appearance of visuals . . . . 25 points

Effort/participation . . . . 25 points

 *Games*

L'ADDITION, S'IL VOUS PLAIT

In this game, students will practice recognizing French menu items.

Procedure To begin, copy the items and prices from one of the menus in the chapter onto a transparency. Then, divide the class into two or more teams. Have one player from each team come to the board. Read aloud an order from the menu. The players find each item on the menu, note the prices, and race to add up the cost of the meal and give the total. The first player to give the correct total in French wins a point for his or her team. You might also want to create your own menu for this game.

J'AI TROUVE!

In this game, students will practice locating the various regions of France.

Procedure Before students play the game, make an answer key by listing cities and regions in France and marking them on a copy of a map of France. Then, hang up a large map of France. Divide the class into two teams and have one player from each team stand by the map. For larger classes, you might form four teams and hang two maps. Name a city or region of France. The first player to point to it and say **J'ai trouvé!** wins a point for his or her team. Give each team member a chance to play. Make sure you or the players point out each city for the rest of the class.

Le Routier Sympa
Menu à 59 francs

LES ENTREES

les carottes râpées
grated carrots with vinaigrette

la salade de tomates

le céleri rémoulade
grated celery root with mayonnaise
and vinaigrette

l'assiette de crudités
plate of raw vegetables with
vinaigrette

l'assiette de charcuterie
plate of pâté, ham, and cold sausage

le pâté

LES PLATS

le steak-frites
le poulet haricots verts
l'escalope de dinde purée
sliced turkey breast with
mashed potatoes

le filet de sole riz
champignons
filet of sole with rice and mushrooms

la côtelette de porc pâtes
porkchop with pasta

LA SALADE VERTE

L'ASSIETTE DE FROMAGES

camembert
brie
roquefort

fromage de chèvre
goat cheese

LES DESSERTS

les glaces: vanille, fraise, chocolat

les tartes aux fruits
fruit pies/tarts

la crème caramel
caramel custard

Chapitre 1
France, les régions
pp. 4–27

𝒰sing the Chapter Opener

 **Video Program**

Videocassette 1

Teacher Notes

• Chapter 1 is a review chapter that reintroduces functions, grammar, and vocabulary from *Allez, viens!* Levels 1 and 2.

• Before you begin the chapter, you might want to preview the *Video Program* and consult the *Video Guide.* Suggestions for integrating the video into each chapter and activity masters for video selections can be found in the *Video Guide.*

Motivating Activity

Have students name different regions of the United States and tell what they know about them. Then, show *Map Transparency 1* (**L'Europe francophone**) and ask students what they already know about the different regions of France.

Photo Flash!

① This photo shows Colmar's **Quai de la Poissonnerie,** with its sixteenth- and seventeenth-century half-timbered houses decorated with multicolored flowers. Such houses are typical of Alsace, Normandy, Champagne, and the Basque country. In this construction, the areas in between the timbers are filled with *wattle and daub,* or interwoven poles and twigs that are covered with plaster or clay.

CHAPITRE **1**
France, les régions

① La belle ville alsacienne de Colmar

4　*quatre*

Geography Link

Have students locate Alsace and Colmar on a map of France. You might also have students draw or trace a map of France on a piece of posterboard and label the different regions. Have them recall what they know about the different regions of France and draw illustrations of the various regional specialties and traditional costumes in the appropriate areas on their maps. This activity could be used as an additional chapter project.

Culture Note

Point out the banknotes on this page. The 50-franc note bears the image of Antoine de Saint-Exupéry, a famous aviator and writer. The 20-franc bill shows Eugène Delacroix, a nineteenth-century Romantic painter. His famous painting, *Liberté guidant le peuple,* is reproduced on the reverse side of the bill. Ask students to identify the people on American bills and to name their major accomplishments.

Viens avec nous en France, pays connu pour la diversité de ses régions. Chaque région se différencie des autres par son histoire, sa culture et ses traditions. Mais ce n'est pas tout : chaque région est aussi fière de ses spécialités gastronomiques dont la renommée est mondiale.

In this chapter you will review and practice

- renewing old acquaintances; inquiring; expressing enthusiasm and dissatisfaction; exchanging information
- expressing indecision; making recommendations; ordering and asking for details

And you will

- listen to French teenagers talk about their vacations and order in a restaurant
- read a short story
- write a travel brochure
- find out about the varied regions of France

② Je suis contente de te revoir!

③ Je n'arrive pas à me décider.

Focusing on Outcomes

Have students match the functional objectives to the photos. You might have them brainstorm useful words or expressions they already know in French to accomplish these objectives. NOTE: The self-check activities in **Que sais-je?** on page 26 help students assess their achievement of the objectives.

Photo Flash!

② In this photo, two schoolmates are greeting each other after a summer apart. You might want to ask students what or whom they missed over the summer. Remind students that **la bise** is appropriate for girls greeting boys or other girls and that boys shake hands when they greet each other.

Teaching Suggestion

In Levels 1 and 2, students learned about people and places in Poitiers, Paris, Arles, areas around Paris, and Touraine, including Chenonceaux and Amboise. Have students recall their favorite location in France, point it out on a map, and tell why they like it.

Culture Note

Call students' attention to the round of Camembert shown at the top of this page. Normandy is famous for its cheeses, particularly the soft, mild Camembert. The more pungent Livarot and the creamy Pont l'Evêque cheeses are also from Normandy.

Teacher Note

Some activities suggested in the *Annotated Teacher's Edition* ask students to contact various people, businesses, and organizations in the community. Before assigning these activities, it is advisable to request parental permission. In some cases, you may also want to obtain permission from the parties the students will be asked to contact.

Language Note

② Have students deduce the meaning of **revoir** from the root verb **voir** and the prefix **re-**. Ask them if the students in this photo have seen each other before. Ask them what **au revoir** means literally *(until we see each other again)*. You might compare this phrase to the Spanish **hasta la vista** or the German **auf Wiedersehen.**

Summary

In **Les retrouvailles**, Pauline, Julien, Patricia, Hector, and Yasmine are meeting in a restaurant at the end of the summer. They get reacquainted and discuss where they went on vacation, what they did, and how they liked it.

Motivating Activity

Ask students what they might talk about with their friends at the beginning of the school year. Ask what they did or would like to have done during the summer.

Reteaching

Sports and leisure activities
Before students read **Les retrouvailles,** you might use flashcards or magazine pictures to review the months of the year and sports and leisure activities.

Presentation

Have students look at the photos and the introduction and guess what the conversation is about. Then, play the recording and have them follow along in their books. After each person's account of his or her vacation, ask a few comprehension questions, such as **Où est-ce qu'il/elle a passé les vacances? Qu'est-ce qu'il/elle a fait?** Next, have pairs or small groups read the conversation aloud and do Activity 1 on page 8.

Language Note

Have students look at the title of the **Mise en train** and find a root word that looks familiar **(trouv-)**. Ask them what they think **Les retrouvailles** means, based on the prefix **re-** and the root **trouv-** *(reunion)*.

Mise en train

Les retrouvailles

A Colmar, de jeunes Alsaciens se réunissent au restaurant pour parler de leurs vacances avant la rentrée.

❶

HECTOR Salut, les copains. Ça fait plaisir de vous revoir.

PAULINE Bonjour. J'ai l'impression que ça fait une éternité qu'on ne s'est pas vus.

JULIEN Dis donc, Patricia, tu as l'air en forme. Ça te réussit, les vacances.

PATRICIA Toi aussi, tu es bien bronzé. C'était bien, Biarritz?

JULIEN Oui, super! Il a fait un temps magnifique.

PAULINE Eh, on pourrait aussi bien parler assis.

YASMINE Alors, on se met où?

HECTOR Là, non? Il y a une table pour cinq.

❷ HECTOR Alors, Yasmine, c'était bien, tes vacances?

YASMINE Oui, pas mal. J'ai passé une semaine à Paris avec mes parents. J'ai visité la tour Eiffel, Notre-Dame, le Louvre, bref, tous les monuments parisiens! Il a fait tellement chaud et lourd qu'à la fin, j'en avais marre des visites. Mais je ne connaissais pas Paris et je suis ravie d'y être allée.

Nord-Pas-de-Calais

Haute-Normandie

Basse-Normandie

Paris

Bretagne

PARIS — MUSÉE DU LOUVRE

Pays de la Loire

Chenonceaux

Centre

Poitou-Charentes

Limousin

Aquitaine

Biarritz

Midi-Pyrénées

Languedoc-Roussillon

6 *six*

CHAPITRE 1 France, les régions

RESOURCES FOR MISE EN TRAIN

Textbook Audiocassette 1A/Audio CD 1
Practice and Activity Book, p. 1

Culture Notes

• The beach town of Biarritz in south-western France is a fashionable resort. Known as "the queen of resorts and the resort of kings," Biarritz has boasted visits by Queen Victoria, Edward VII, and Alfonse XIII of Spain.

• The controversial modern glass pyramid in the Louvre courtyard was built in the late 1980s by the Chinese-American architect I. M. Pei, who is noted for his use of large geometrical designs in public buildings. The pyramid is controversial because some feel that its modern style clashes with the Louvre's classic construction.

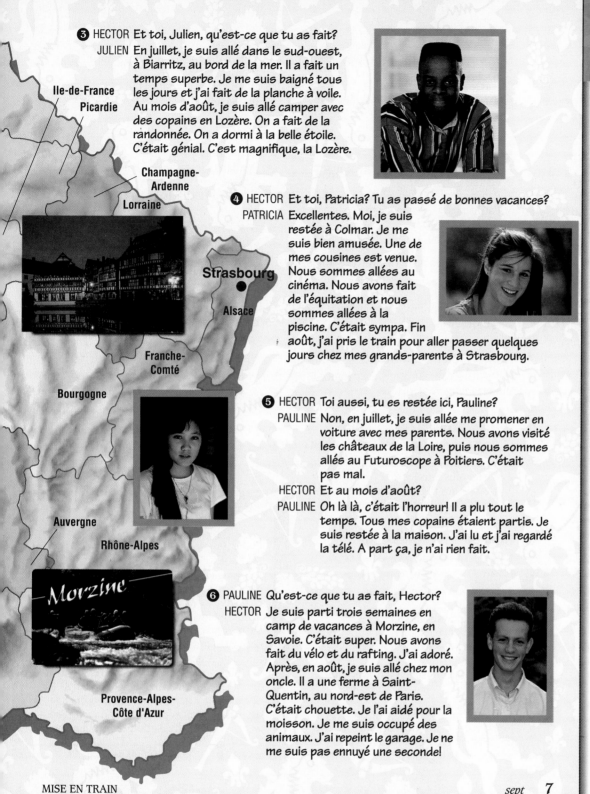

3 HECTOR Et toi, Julien, qu'est-ce que tu as fait?

JULIEN En juillet, je suis allé dans le sud-ouest, à Biarritz, au bord de la mer. Il a fait un temps superbe. Je me suis baigné tous les jours et j'ai fait de la planche à voile. Au mois d'août, je suis allé camper avec des copains en Lozère. On a fait de la randonnée. On a dormi à la belle étoile. C'était génial. C'est magnifique, la Lozère.

Ile-de-France
Picardie
Champagne-
Ardenne
Lorraine

Strasbourg
Alsace

4 HECTOR Et toi, Patricia? Tu as passé de bonnes vacances?

PATRICIA Excellentes. Moi, je suis restée à Colmar. Je me suis bien amusée. Une de mes cousines est venue. Nous sommes allées au cinéma. Nous avons fait de l'équitation et nous sommes allées à la piscine. C'était sympa. Fin août, j'ai pris le train pour aller passer quelques jours chez mes grands-parents à Strasbourg.

Franche-
Comté

Bourgogne

5 HECTOR Toi aussi, tu es restée ici, Pauline?

PAULINE Non, en juillet, je suis allée me promener en voiture avec mes parents. Nous avons visité les châteaux de la Loire, puis nous sommes allés au Futuroscope à Poitiers. C'était pas mal.

HECTOR Et au mois d'août?

PAULINE Oh là là, c'était l'horreur! Il a plu tout le temps. Tous mes copains étaient partis. Je suis restée à la maison. J'ai lu et j'ai regardé la télé. A part ça, je n'ai rien fait.

Auvergne
Rhône-Alpes

Morzine

Provence-Alpes-
Côte d'Azur

6 PAULINE Qu'est-ce que tu as fait, Hector?

HECTOR Je suis parti trois semaines en camp de vacances à Morzine, en Savoie. C'était super. Nous avons fait du vélo et du rafting. J'ai adoré. Après, en août, je suis allé chez mon oncle. Il a une ferme à Saint-Quentin, au nord-est de Paris. C'était chouette. Je l'ai aidé pour la moisson. Je me suis occupé des animaux. J'ai repeint le garage. Je ne me suis pas ennuyé une seconde!

MISE EN TRAIN

sept **7**

Teaching Suggestions
• Ask students which of the friends in **Les retrouvailles** enjoyed their vacation. (**Qui a passé de bonnes vacances?**) Have them find the words or phrases that support their answers. (**Julien;** "**Oui, super! Il a fait un temps magnifique.**") Then, ask them which ones they would use to describe their own summer vacation.
• Have students write down any important words they don't know. Then, have groups use the context to guess the meanings of the words.
• Once students are familiar with **Les retrouvailles,** write the names of the characters on the board, quote them at random, and have students identify the speakers. Then, have students choose quotes to read aloud to a partner, who identifies the speaker.

Geography Link
Using a large map of France, have students locate each of the places mentioned in **Les retrouvailles.** You might also play the game **J'ai trouvé!** described on page 3F.

Teaching Suggestions

2 If the statements are true, have students cite proof from the text; if they are false, have students correct them.

4 Have students tell whether they would feel the same or differently if they had taken the same vacations as the French teenagers.

5 Ask students these same questions about their area. They might want to say **Nulle part** *(Nowhere).*

Building on Previous Skills

6 List the expressions students find on the board or on a transparency. Then, have them give previously-learned expressions that accomplish the same purposes.

Language Note

Sabot is the root of the French word **sabotage,** which is also used in English. The word was used in the nineteenth century when factory workers protested poor working conditions by throwing their wooden shoes **(sabots)** into the machinery. It came to mean deliberately poor workmanship or damage to equipment.

Multicultural Link

Have students investigate traditional clothing, music, food, and dances of different ethnic groups from around the world. As an added challenge, you might have them find out why particular clothing is worn or on what occasions special food is served.

---

1 **Tu as compris?** See answers below.
1. Where are these young people meeting?
2. What time of year is it? How do you know?
3. How long has it been since they've seen one another?
4. Where did the teenagers go during their vacations?
5. What sort of activities did they participate in?

2 **Vrai ou faux?**
1. C'était la première fois que Yasmine visitait Paris. *vrai*
2. Pendant l'été, Julien a fait du camping. *vrai*
3. Patricia est partie en camp de vacances. *faux*
4. Pendant ses vacances, Pauline a voyagé avec ses parents. *vrai*
5. L'oncle d'Hector habite à Morzine. *faux*

3 **C'est qui?**
Parmi les jeunes dans **Les retrouvailles,** qui...
1. ne s'est pas amusé(e) pendant le mois d'août? *Pauline*
2. a visité des monuments pendant ses vacances? *Yasmine*
3. est allé(e) dans une ferme pendant ses vacances? *Hector*
4. aime faire du camping? *Julien*
5. aime faire de l'équitation? *Patricia*

4 **Content ou pas content?**
Qui est très content(e) de ses vacances?
Qui est moins content(e)?
Très content(e): Julien, Patricia, Hector
Moins content(e): Yasmine, Pauline

5 **Qu'est-ce qu'on peut y faire?**
D'après **Les retrouvailles,** où est-ce qu'on peut...
1. se baigner dans l'océan? *à Biarritz*
2. visiter des musées? *à Paris* 3. *à Morzine*
3. trouver des rivières avec des torrents?
4. voir de magnifiques châteaux? *dans la vallée de la Loire*

6 **Cherche les expressions**
What do the young people in **Les retrouvailles** say to . . . See answers below.
1. greet one another after a long absence?
2. compliment someone?
3. make a suggestion?
4. express dissatisfaction with a vacation?
5. express enthusiasm for a vacation?

7 **Et maintenant, à toi**
Regarde les cartes postales aux pages 6 et 7. Où est-ce que tu aimerais aller en vacances? Pourquoi?

Bretagne

NOTE CULTURELLE

Every region of France has its own traditions. Some are observed daily while others, such as traditional clothing or folk dances, are reserved for special occasions or festivals. Women's traditional clothing generally includes skirts and blouses or dresses made of regional fabric, with decorated aprons, shawls or lace collars, and headdresses. The most famous of the headdresses are the Breton **coiffes,** which are tall, ornate, lace headpieces. Men's costumes are generally composed of decorated pants, white shirts, and vests. Footwear is usually the **sabot,** or wooden shoe.

8 *huit*

CHAPITRE 1   France, les régions

Answers

1 1. in a restaurant
2. fall; They are just back from summer vacation.
3. all summer
4. Yasmine: Paris; Julien: Biarritz et Lozère; Patricia: Colmar et Strasbourg; Pauline: les châteaux de la Loire et le Futuroscope à Poitiers; Hector: Morzine et Saint-Quentin
5. *Possible answers:* sightseeing, swimming, windsurfing, camping, hiking, going to the movies, horseback riding, visiting relatives, reading, watching TV, biking, rafting, helping with the harvest, repainting the garage

6 1. Ça fait plaisir de vous revoir. Ça fait une éternité qu'on ne s'est pas vus.
2. ... tu as l'air en forme. Ça te réussit, les vacances. ... tu es bien bronzé.
3. Eh, on pourrait aussi bien parler assis.
4. ... j'en avais marre des visites. C'était l'horreur.
5. Je suis ravie d'y être allée. Je me suis bien amusée. Je ne me suis pas ennuyé une seconde! C'était génial/sympa/pas mal/super.

Renewing old acquaintances; inquiring; expressing enthusiasm and dissatisfaction; exchanging information

COMMENT DIT-ON... ?
Renewing old acquaintances

Les cigognes font partie du paysage alsacien. Dès les premiers froids, elles partent vers l'Afrique et reviennent en Alsace au printemps.

To greet someone you haven't seen recently:

Ça fait longtemps qu'on ne s'est pas vu(e)s. *It's been a long time since we've seen each other.*

Je suis content(e) de te revoir. *I'm glad to see you again.*

Qu'est-ce que tu deviens? *What's going on with you?*

Quoi de neuf? *What's new?*

To respond:

Ça fait deux mois. *It's been . . .*

Depuis l'hiver. *Since . . .*

Moi aussi.

Toujours la même chose! *Same old thing!*

Rien (de spécial). *Nothing (special).*

---

8 Ecoute!   1. b   2. a   3. d

Ecoute les dialogues et choisis la phrase qui correspond à chaque dialogue.

a. Ils ne se sont pas vus depuis trois mois.
b. Ils ne se sont pas vus depuis deux ans.
c. Ils ne se sont pas vus depuis janvier.
d. Ils ne se sont pas vus depuis le mois de juin.

9 Il y a belle lurette... ! *It's been ages!*

Ça fait longtemps que tu n'as pas vu un(e) de tes ami(e)s. Qu'est-ce que vous vous dites?

RESOURCES FOR **PREMIERE ETAPE**

Chapter Teaching Resources, Book 1
- Teaching Transparency Master 1-1, pp. 8, 10
  Teaching Transparency 1-1
- Additional Listening Activities 1-1, 1-2, 1-3, pp. 11–12
  Audiocassette 9A/Audio CD 1
- Realia 1-1, pp. 15, 17
- Situation Cards 1-1, pp. 18–19
- Student Response Forms, pp. 20–22
- Quiz 1-1, pp. 23–24
  Audiocassette 7A/Audio CD 1

ADDITIONAL RESOURCES

Textbook Audiocassette 1A
OR *Audio CD 1*

Practice and Activity Book, pp. 2–5

🅙ump Start!

Have students choose a location from **Les retrouvailles**, list two activities available there, and tell whether they've done or would like to do each activity.

MOTIVATE

Have students recall greetings they've already learned. Ask what they would say in English to greet someone they haven't seen for a long time.

TEACH

Presentation

Comment dit-on? Rehearse the greetings with several students before class. In class, act as if you are just recognizing a student and say **Sarah? Ça fait longtemps qu'on ne s'est pas vu(e)s! Qu'est-ce que tu deviens?** Then, prompt one of the prepared students to recognize you, and respond appropriately. Have pairs read the expressions together.

✜ For Individual Needs

Visual Learners Write the expressions from **Comment dit-on... ?** on strips of transparency and scatter them on the projector. Then, have students rearrange them to make a conversation and have partners read it aloud.

8 Slower Pace Before you play the recording, have students read the choices. You might also review numbers and months.

9 Challenge Students might include the expression **Il y a belle lurette... !** in their conversations and expand them to talk about what they've done during their time apart.

Presentation

Comment dit-on... ? Tell students about your imaginary summer vacation, miming or showing pictures of activities as you discuss them. Express enthusiasm about some activities and boredom about others, using appropriate facial expressions. Then, ask students **Qu'est-ce que tu as fait ce week-end/pendant les vacances? Ça s'est bien passé?** After you've questioned several students, ask the class about other students' vacations (**C'était comment, les vacances de Steve?**)

Additional Practice

Write **C'était chouette!** and **C'était pas terrible** on the board. Have students suggest activities in French that evoke each remark.

For Individual Needs

10 Kinesthetic Learners
Students might respond by writing + or – signs, or by making the thumbs-up or thumbs-down gesture.

11 Auditory Learners
Read aloud possible conversations and have students match them to the illustrations.

11 Visual Learners/ Challenge Have students draw their own illustrations depicting a good or bad situation, exchange drawings, and write conversations based on them.

Group Work

11 Have students work in groups to create a conversation for one of the illustrations. Groups might volunteer to present their conversations to the class.

COMMENT DIT-ON... ?
Inquiring; expressing enthusiasm and dissatisfaction

To inquire about someone's trip or vacation:

C'était comment, tes vacances?
How was your vacation?
Ça s'est bien passé?
Comment ça s'est passé?
Tu t'es bien amusé(e)? *Did you have fun?*

To express enthusiasm:

C'était chouette!
Ça s'est très bien passé.
Super!
Je me suis beaucoup amusé(e).
I had a lot of fun.

To express dissatisfaction:

C'était pas terrible. *It wasn't so great.*
Ça ne s'est pas très bien passé.
Pas trop bien.
Je me suis ennuyé(e). *I was bored.*

10 Ecoute!

Ecoute ces dialogues. Est-ce que ces personnes sont contentes ou non? Answers on p. 3C.

11 Qu'est-ce qu'ils disent?

Christophe téléphone à ses amis dimanche soir pour savoir comment leur week-end s'est passé. Utilise les expressions dans le **Comment dit-on... ?** pour recréer leurs conversations.
See answers below.

a.

b.

c.

d.

10   *dix*   CHAPITRE 1   France, les régions

Possible answers

11 1. — Comment ça s'est passé à l'Auto Ecole?
       — Ça ne s'est pas très bien passé. J'ai eu un accident.
    2. — C'était comment, ton week-end?
       — Super! J'ai gagné la compétition.
    3. — C'était comment, tes vacances?
       — C'était pas terrible. Je me suis ennuyé.
    4. — Comment ça s'est passé, le week-end de ski?
       — Pas trop bien. Je me suis cassé le bras.

Grammaire   The passé composé (Review)

Do you remember how to form the **passé composé**? It has two parts: a present-tense form of **avoir** or **être**, and the past participle of the main verb.

Elle **a fini** tout le gâteau.   Elles **sont parties** en vacances.
Nous **avons attendu** le train.   Nous **sommes resté(e)s** une semaine.
Elle **s'est ennuyée.**
Nous **nous sommes amusés.**

You use **être** as the helping verb with these verbs: **aller, sortir, partir, retourner, mourir, naître, venir, devenir, arriver, rester, entrer, monter, descendre, tomber, rentrer, revenir.**

• Don't forget to make the past participles of these verbs agree with the subject of the sentence.

• Remember that you use **être** as the helping verb with all reflexive verbs.

• Make the past participle of reflexive verbs agree with the reflexive pronoun, if there is no direct object following the verb.

Some verbs have irregular past participles. You use **avoir** as the helping verb with those listed here.

dire	**dit**	prendre	**pris**	voir	**vu**	boire	**bu**
écrire	**écrit**	être	**été**	lire	**lu**	pouvoir	**pu**
mettre	**mis**	faire	**fait**	avoir	**eu**	vouloir	**voulu**

12   Ecoute!

Au restaurant, tu entends les conversations des gens autour de toi. Est-ce qu'ils parlent au présent ou au passé? Answers on p. 3C.

A good way to get ready for this year of French study is to review and practice what you learned before.
1. Use the flashcards you've made to review vocabulary and expressions. Pay close attention to those you use the most.
2. Look at the charts in the back of this book to refresh your memory of important grammar points.
3. With a classmate, practice short conversations on the topics you learned about last year, such as food, clothing, activities, and so on.

Presentation

Grammaire   Hold up pictures illustrating different verbs as you use the verbs in sentences. For example, as you show a picture of a train, say **Je suis parti(e) en train.** Write your sentences on a transparency and ask how the **passé composé** was formed. Review the verbs that take **être** in the **passé composé** by drawing a house on the board or on a transparency. Have students call out what they did to enter and leave the house and to go upstairs and downstairs (**Je suis entré(e)**, **Nous sommes descendu(e)s**). Use stick figures and arrows to illustrate the verbs they call out. Next, hold up pictures to suggest various activities (bowl of hot chocolate) and ask questions, such as **Qu'est-ce que j'ai pris au petit déjeuner?** Finally, have pairs of students tell two or three things they did yesterday.

Reteaching

Reflexive verbs   Ask students how reflexive verbs are different from other verbs and what they need to remember when they form the past tense of these verbs (use a reflexive pronoun, use **être**, make the past participle agree). Then, tell students what you did this morning (**Je me suis levé(e) à six heures, puis je me suis brossé les dents**) as you demonstrate the activities, using props (an alarm clock, a toothbrush). Repeat the demonstration and have students tell what you did. (**Vous vous êtes levé(e) à six heures.**) Then, have a volunteer mime the activities and have the class tell what he or she did. (**Il/Elle s'est brossé les dents.**)

For Individual Needs

12   Slower Pace   Ask students to recount in French something that happened in the past. Then, have them tell you something that is going on now and explain the difference between the verb forms.

Additional Practice

12   Have students write sentences in the **passé composé** or in the present tense and read them to a partner, who tells whether they describe a past event or a present situation.

Teaching Suggestion

De bons conseils   You might suggest that students find and organize old vocabulary cards, go over last year's portfolio, and view posters or projects from last year's class. You might display posters from last year's projects around the room.

For Individual Needs

13 Slower Pace Have students write where each place is (**à la montagne, à la plage, en ville**). Then, have them suggest expressions associated with each place. Have them turn in these notes along with the final postcard and include them in their written portfolios.

Presentation

Comment dit-on... ? Act out one side of a phone conversation in which you ask for details about a friend's vacation. Next, act out the other side of the phone conversation, giving details about an imaginary vacation. For each detail you give, call on students to guess what the question was. Then, write the questions on the board and point to them to prompt students to ask you about your imaginary vacation.

Game

MÉMOIRE Draw a 12-square grid on a transparency. Write questions from **Comment dit-on... ?** in some of the squares and their answers in others. Cover the squares with adhesive notes. Form two or more teams. The first player from the first team removes two of the notes. If the player matches a question and its answer, he or she keeps the notes and earns a point for the team. If not, he or she replaces them, and the next team takes a turn.

Reteaching

Forms of transportation

Review the forms of transportation by holding up magazine pictures to prompt answers to the question **Tu es parti(e) comment?**

---

13 Un petit mot

Choisis une de ces cartes postales. Imagine que c'est là que tu es allé(e) pour tes vacances. Maintenant, écris un petit mot à un(e) ami(e) pour lui dire ce que tu as fait là-bas.

COMMENT DIT-ON... ?

Exchanging information

To ask about someone's vacation:

Est-ce que tu es resté(e) ici?
Did you stay here?

Quand est-ce que tu y es allé(e)?

Avec qui est-ce que tu y es allé(e)?

Tu es parti(e) comment?
How did you get there?

Où est-ce que tu as dormi?
Where did you stay?

Quel temps est-ce qu'il a fait?
What was the weather like?

To answer:

Oui, je suis resté(e) ici tout le temps. *Yes, I stayed here the whole time.*

Non, je suis parti(e) dix jours en août. *No, I went away for . . .*

J'y suis allé(e) début/fin juillet. *I went there at the beginning/ end of . . .*

J'y suis allé(e) seul(e)/avec mes parents. *I went alone/with . . .*

Je suis parti(e) en train. *I went by . . .*

A l'hôtel. *In a hotel.*

Chez des amis. *With . . .*

Il a fait un temps magnifique. *The weather was . . .*

Il a plu tout le temps. *It rained the whole time.*

14 Cherche la réponse

Les copains de Norbert lui posent des questions sur ses vacances. Choisis les bonnes réponses.

1. Où est-ce que tu es allé?
2. Quand est-ce que tu y es allé?
3. Avec qui est-ce que tu y es allé?
4. Vous êtes partis comment?
5. Quel temps est-ce qu'il a fait?

Du canoë.

Dans les Alpes. 1

Fin août. 2

En train. 4

3

Avec un groupe de jeunes.

Super beau! 5

12 *douze* CHAPITRE 1 France, les régions

Language Notes

• Remind students to use **à** with most cities, **en** with feminine countries, and **au** with masculine countries. **En** Arles is one exception.

• Remind students that, to form a question, they can put a question word at the beginning or end of a statement and use intonation. (**Tu es parti(e) quand?**) To ask a yes-no question, students should put **est-ce que** before a statement. (**Est-ce que tu es parti(e) à midi?**)

Teacher Note

Additional answers to the question **Où est-ce que tu as dormi?** are **Dans une auberge de jeunesse, Chez mes grands-parents,** and **A la belle étoile.** You might review months of the year and weather expressions and use them as possible answers for the other questions in **Comment dit-on... ?**

15 Ecoute!

Ecoute le dialogue entre Amina et son amie Marie-Claire. Mets les dessins dans le bon ordre d'après la conversation. c, b, a, d

a.

b.

c.

d.

16 Quoi d'autre?

A ton avis, qu'est-ce que Marie-Claire a fait d'autre pendant ses vacances à la plage? Ecris un récit pour raconter tout ce qui lui est arrivé.

17 Qu'est-ce que tu as fait?

Demande à ton/ta camarade ce qu'il/elle a fait pendant ses vacances. Puis, changez de rôles.

18 Mon journal

Les vacances sont finies. Qu'est-ce que tu as fait? Ecris tes souvenirs d'été—vrais ou imaginaires—dans ton journal.

19 Interview

a. Avec un(e) camarade, pense à une personne célèbre. Il/Elle rentre de vacances. Tu es journaliste et tu l'interviewes sur ses vacances. Tu es payé(e) à la ligne, donc pose un maximum de questions pour écrire ton article. Jouez cette scène et puis, changez de rôles.

b. Ecris ton article. Avant publication, tu le soumets à l'éditeur (ton/ta camarade), qui en fait la critique et fait quelques petites corrections, si nécessaire.

For Individual Needs

15 Slower Pace Before playing the recording, have students describe what is happening in each illustration.

Teaching Suggestion

16 Before students get started, have them recall as many activities as they can in French. Write their suggestions on the board and have students use the ones that would apply to Marie-Claire's situation in their narrative.

Mon journal

18 For an additional journal entry suggestion for Chapter 1, see *Practice and Activity Book*, page 143.

Portfolio

19 Oral/Written Part **a** is an appropriate oral portfolio entry, and Part **b** is an appropriate written entry. For portfolio information, see *Assessment Guide*, pages 2–13.

CLOSE

Have students write a few sentences on a card, telling where they went for a real or imaginary vacation, how they got there, where they stayed, and what it was like. Collect and redistribute the cards. Have students circulate, asking questions to try to find the student who has the card describing their vacation. (Où est-ce que tu es allé(e)? Tu es parti(e) comment?)

ASSESS

Quiz 1–1, *Chapter Teaching Resources, Book 1,* pp. 23–24

Assessment Items, Audiocassette 7A
Audio CD 1

Performance Assessment

In groups of three or four, have students act out a scene similar to **Les retrouvailles.** Have them greet one another and ask about one another's vacation. You might have groups turn in their written scripts. Base students' grades on content, language use, creativity, and oral presentation.

Teacher Note

When giving assignments that entail the disclosure of personal information, keep in mind that some students and their families may consider these matters private. In some cases, you may want to give an alternate assignment in which students may substitute fictitious information.

Summary

In **Bon appétit!**, the five friends order meals in an Alsatian restaurant, including the Alsatian specialty **press-kopf.** The restaurant menu is included in the scene.

Motivating Activity

Have students name French foods they are familiar with. Ask if they ever have problems deciding what to order.

Presentation

Before playing the recording, have students read the questions in Activity 20 and scan the menu and dialogue for words related to food. Then, play the recording, pausing after each person orders to ask **Qu'est-ce qu'il/elle va prendre?** You might want to have groups of five read the dialogue aloud together.

Teaching Suggestion

Have students make a timeline of the duration of the meal, from the group's arrival to their paying the check. Then, ask students **Le repas a duré combien de temps? Tes repas durent plus ou moins longtemps?**

Thinking Critically

Comparing and Contrasting

Have students compare what the teenagers in **Bon appétit!** ordered with what they might order in an American restaurant. Have them compare how the food is ordered as well.

For Individual Needs

21 Challenge Have students write two or three additional true-false statements and quiz a partner.

Remise en train

Bon appétit!

Regarde la carte. Est-ce que tu reconnais certains de ces plats? Lesquels?

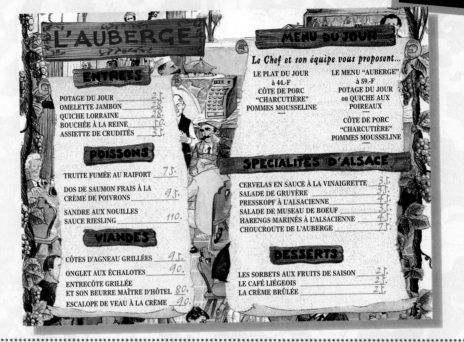

L'AUBERGE

ENTRÉES

POTAGE DU JOUR	2.5
OMELETTE JAMBON	28.
QUICHE LORRAINE	28.
BOUCHÉE À LA REINE	40.
ASSIETTE DE CRUDITÉS	35.

POISSONS

TRUITE FUMÉE AU RAIFORT	75.
DOS DE SAUMON FRAIS À LA CRÈME DE POIVRONS	95.
SANDRE AUX NOUILLES SAUCE RIESLING	110.

VIANDES

CÔTES D'AGNEAU GRILLÉES	95.
ONGLET AUX ÉCHALOTES	90.
ENTRECÔTE GRILLÉE ET SON BEURRE MAÎTRE D'HÔTEL	80.
ESCALOPE DE VEAU À LA CRÈME	90.

MENU DU JOUR

Le Chef et son équipe vous proposent...

LE PLAT DU JOUR à 44.-F	LE MENU "AUBERGE" à 59.-F
CÔTE DE PORC "CHARCUTIÈRE" POMMES MOUSSELINE	POTAGE DU JOUR ou QUICHE AUX POIREAUX
	CÔTE DE PORC "CHARCUTIÈRE" POMMES MOUSSELINE

SPÉCIALITÉS D'ALSACE

CERVELAS EN SAUCE À LA VINAIGRETTE	35.
SALADE DE GRUYÈRE	35.
PRESSKOPF À L'ALSACIENNE	45.
SALADE DE MUSEAU DE BOEUF	35.
HARENGS MARINÉS À L'ALSACIENNE	45.
CHOUCROUTE DE L'AUBERGE	75.

DESSERTS

LES SORBETS AUX FRUITS DE SAISON	25.
LE CAFÉ LIÉGEOIS	25.
LA CRÈME BRÛLÉE	25.

---

20 Tu as compris?

1. What are the teenagers in **Bon appétit!** talking about? what to order
2. Who has difficulty making a decision? Patricia
3. What do the teenagers ask the waitress to bring to the table? bread and water
4. Why can't they divide the check evenly? Pauline and Yasmine didn't have dessert.

21 Vrai ou faux?

1. D'habitude, Yasmine prend du poulet et des frites. vrai
2. Pauline n'a jamais mangé de presskopf. faux
3. Hector a pris le plat du jour. vrai
4. Tout le monde a pris un dessert. faux

22 Entrée ou fromage?

Regarde encore la carte de L'Auberge et dis si ces plats sont des entrées, des poissons, des viandes ou des desserts.

entrée — la quiche lorraine

poisson — la truite fumée

poisson — le sandre

viande

dessert — le café liégeois

les côtes d'agneau

dessert — la crème brûlée

le potage — entrée

viande — l'escalope de veau

viande — l'entrecôte grillée

l'omelette jambon — entrée

14 *quatorze*   CHAPITRE 1   France, les régions

Building on Previous Skills

22 Have students name other dishes for each category, either from memory or from the menu.

Culture Note

The term **à la carte** refers to items chosen from anywhere on the menu. **Le menu** usually refers to a fixed-price menu (**un prix fixe**), where the diner may choose from among several specified dishes for each course. Eating **à la carte** is usually more expensive.

Midi et quart...

PATRICIA   Qu'est-ce que vous allez prendre? Je n'arrive pas à me décider.

JULIEN   Moi non plus, tout me tente. Comme entrée, j'hésite entre une bouchée à la reine et de la quiche. Et toi, Yasmine?

YASMINE   Aucune idée. Je ne sais pas quoi prendre.

JULIEN   Toi, évidemment, si tu n'as pas ton poulet rôti et tes frites, tu préfères mourir de faim.

YASMINE   Oh, ça suffit, les sarcasmes.

PAULINE   Essaie le presskopf. C'est un plat alsacien délicieux.

LA SERVEUSE   Vous avez décidé?

HECTOR   Non, pas encore. Un instant, s'il vous plaît.

Midi vingt-cinq...

LA SERVEUSE   Vous avez choisi, maintenant?

PAULINE   Oui, je crois. Comme entrée, je vais prendre l'assiette de crudités. Et ensuite, le plat du jour.

23 Cherche les expressions

Look back at **Bon appétit!** to find ways to . . . See answers below.

1. ask someone what he or she is going to have.
2. express indecision.
3. tell what you're going to have.
4. ask someone to pass you something.
5. ask a server to bring you something.
6. ask how much the check is.

HECTOR   Moi aussi, la même chose.

PATRICIA   Je voudrais la choucroute... ou, non, donnez-moi plutôt l'entrecôte grillée. Ou bien...

JULIEN   Bon, tu te décides!

PATRICIA   OK, OK! Je vais prendre... Ah, non! Voilà, j'ai trouvé! La truite!

Une heure...

PAULINE   Alors, il est comment, ton presskopf?

YASMINE   Pas mal... Euh, passe-moi le sel, s'il te plaît. Et la moutarde.

PATRICIA   Madame, est-ce qu'on pourrait avoir du pain, s'il vous plaît? Ah! Et une carafe d'eau!

LA SERVEUSE   Oui, tout de suite.

Deux heures et quart...

PATRICIA   Bon, on y va?

HECTOR   D'accord... Madame? L'addition, s'il vous plaît?

LA SERVEUSE   Oui, tout de suite... Voilà.

JULIEN   Ça fait combien?

HECTOR   595 F. Divisé par cinq, ça fait... 120 F par personne.

PAULINE   Eh, moi, j'ai pas pris de dessert! Et Yasmine non plus!

HECTOR   C'est vrai, tu as raison. Bon, eh bien, chacun paie sa part.

24 Ecoute! Answers on p. 3D.

Ecoute le dialogue. Combien est-ce que chaque personne doit payer?

| Julien | Pauline | Hector |
| Yasmine | Patricia |

25 Et maintenant, à toi

Pense à des plats américains. Qu'est-ce que tu préfères manger comme entrée, poisson, viande et dessert?

quinze 15

Answers

23 1. Qu'est-ce que vous allez prendre?
  2. Je n'arrive pas à me décider; J'hésite entre... et... ; Je ne sais pas quoi prendre.
  3. Je vais prendre... ; Je voudrais...; Donnez-moi...
  4. Passe-moi...
  5. Est-ce qu'on pourrait avoir... ?
  6. Ça fait combien?

Culture Notes

• **Presskopf** is a type of sausage made from pig's or calf's head cooked in bacon rind. It may be served cold as an appetizer or warm as a main dish.

• To request tap water in a French restaurant, ask for **une carafe d'eau,** which is usually free of charge.

Group Work

Assign each character in **Bon appétit!** to a group of five students. They should read their character's role in the conversation carefully, as if studying for a part in a play. Groups should give a report on their person's character and role in the scene.

Language Note

Students may want to know the following food-related vocabulary: **l'escalope** (*thin slice of veal or turkey*); **le potage** (*soup*); **le sandre** (*pikeperch*); **le café liégeois** (*resembles an ice cream sundae; coffee ice cream with crème Chantilly or whipped cream, sometimes also served with coffee syrup*).

Teaching Suggestion

24 Before playing the recording, review higher numbers using flashcards or simple arithmetic problems.

Teacher Note

24 Remind students that the tip is usually included in the price (**service compris**), so they don't need to figure the tip in their calculations.

Teaching Suggestion

25 You might ask vegetarian students **Qu'est-ce que tu préfères manger comme plat?** instead of **Qu'est-ce que tu préfères manger comme viande?**

Additional Practice

Have students tell what they would order at **l'Auberge.** Have students take a class poll of the most and least popular dishes and present the results.

Math Link

Have students order from the menu and then figure out how much their meal would cost in francs and in dollars.

PANORAMA CULTUREL

Marie • France

Christian • France

Célestine • Côte d'Ivoire

We asked some people about the specialties of their regions. Here's what they had to say.

Quelles sont les spécialités de ta région?

«La bouillabaisse. C'est un plat provençal surtout marseillais... C'est une soupe de poissons... On fait ça avec divers poissons et du pain, des petits croûtons de pain... Voilà.»

-Marie

«Euh... les spécialités [de Cherbourg], elles sont des petits homards que nous appelons «les demoiselles de Cherbourg» et qui sont des grosses crevettes... En Normandie, nous avons du cidre que nous faisons avec des pommes, [de] la crème fraîche, du boudin et du thon.»

-Christian

«En Côte d'Ivoire il y a d'abord l'attiéké, qu'on peut exporter [et] importer du moins d'ailleurs. Et aussi, il y a le foutou. Le foutou, c'est de la banane mélangée [avec] du manioc. On fait cuire et on pile. Ensuite, [il est] accompagné de la sauce graine généralement et ensuite, il y a la sauce arachide accompagnée du riz.»

-Célestine

Qu'en penses-tu?

1. What are the specialties these people mention?
2. What are the specialties of your area? What are the specialties of other states?
3. Choose a region of France or another francophone country and find out what its specialties are.

1. la bouillabaisse, "les demoiselles de Cherbourg," le cidre, la crème fraîche, le boudin, le thon, l'attiéké, le foutou, la sauce graine, la sauce arachide

---

Teacher Notes

- See *Video Guide* and *Practice and Activity Book* for activities related to the **Panorama Culturel.**
- Remind students that cultural material may be included in the Chapter Quizzes and Test.
- The interviewees' language represents informal, unrehearsed speech. Occasionally, edits have been made for clarification.

Motivating Activity

Ask students question 2 under **Qu'en penses-tu?** Ask if there are local stores or restaurants that offer ethnic specialties.

Presentation

Have students recall food specialties they've learned about (**pissaladière, ratatouille, attiéké, foutou**). Then, play the video. Write the specialties mentioned on a transparency and have volunteers write the name of the interviewee that mentions each one next to it. Then, ask the **Questions** below.

Multicultural Link

Have students plan a multicultural and ethnic food-tasting for the class.

Teacher Note

For specific information on Ivorian and French food specialties, check the Cultural References section of *Allez, viens!* Levels 1 and 2.

Questions

1. La bouillabaisse est une spécialité de quelle région? (la Provence, Marseille)
2. Quelles sont les spécialités de Cherbourg? (des petits homards) de Normandie? (du cidre, de la crème fraîche, du boudin, du thon)
3. Quelles sont les spécialités de la Côte d'Ivoire? (l'attiéké, le foutou, la sauce graine, la sauce arachide)
4. Comment est-ce qu'on prépare le foutou? (On mélange la banane avec du manioc. On le fait cuire et on pile.)

Culture Note

Tell students about regional dialects as well as specialties. France used to have a number of dialects. **Breton, alsacien,** and **provençal** are still spoken in some areas of France.

DEUXIÈME ETAPE

Expressing indecision; making recommendations; ordering and asking for details

COMMENT DIT-ON... ?

Expressing indecision; making recommendations

A server might ask:
Qu'est-ce que vous allez prendre?

To express indecision:
Je ne sais pas.
Tout me tente.
   Everything looks tempting.
Je n'arrive pas à me décider.
   I can't make up my mind.
J'hésite entre le saumon **et** la truite fumée.
   I can't decide between . . . and . . .

To make recommendations:
Tu devrais prendre les côtelettes d'agneau.
Pourquoi tu ne prends pas l'escalope de veau à la crème?
Essaie les tomates farcies.
   Try . . .
Prends le saumon.

26 Ecoute!

Ecoute les phrases suivantes. Est-ce que les personnes hésitent ou recommandent quelque chose? Answers on p. 3D.

VOCABULAIRE

Voici un menu typiquement français :

NOTE CULTURELLE

Quand les Français sortent dîner, ils passent souvent deux ou trois heures à table pour pouvoir apprécier leur repas aussi bien que leur sortie. En principe, les serveurs n'apportent pas l'addition tant que le client ne l'a pas demandée; s'ils le faisaient, les clients auraient l'impression qu'on essaie de les mettre dehors.

Le Routier Sympa
Menu à 59 francs

LES ENTREES
les carottes râpées
grated carrots with vinaigrette
la salade de tomates
le céleri rémoulade
grated celery root with mayonnaise and vinaigrette

l'assiette de crudités
plate of raw vegetables with vinaigrette
l'assiette de charcuterie
plate of pâté, ham, and cold sausage
le pâté

LES PLATS
le steak-frites
le poulet haricots verts
l'escalope de dinde purée
sliced turkey breast with mashed potatoes

le filet de sole riz champignons
filet of sole with rice and mushrooms
la côtelette de porc pâtes
porkchop with pasta

LA SALADE VERTE

L'ASSIETTE DE FROMAGES
camembert
brie
roquefort
fromage de chèvre
goat cheese

LES DESSERTS
les glaces: vanille, fraise, chocolat
les tartes aux fruits
fruit pies/tarts
la crème caramel
caramel custard

DEUXIEME ETAPE

dix-sept **17**

RESOURCES FOR DEUXIEME ETAPE

Chapter Teaching Resources, Book 1
• Communicative Activity 1-2, pp. 6–7
• Teaching Transparency Master 1-2, pp. 9, 10
   Teaching Transparency 1-2
• Additional Listening Activities 1-4, 1-5, 1-6, pp.12–13
   Audiocassette 9A/Audio CD 1
• Realia 1-2, pp. 16, 17
• Situation Cards 1-2, 1-3, pp. 18–19
• Student Response Forms, pp. 20–22
• Quiz 1-2, pp 25–26
   Audiocassette 7A/Audio CD 1

ADDITIONAL RESOURCES
Textbook Audiocassette 1A
OR *Audio CD 1*
Practice and Activity Book, pp. 7–10
Video Program, Videocassette 1
Video Guide

Jump Start!

Have students write out an "order" of five things they'd like to have for dinner, using food and drink items they already know.

MOTIVATE

Have students recall expressions they already know in French that would be useful in a restaurant.

TEACH

Presentation

Comment dit-on... ? Have students look at the menu on page 14 as you express indecision and make recommendations, using appropriate facial expressions. Then, ask students **Qu'est-ce que vous allez prendre?** as you stand ready to take their orders. As students express indecision, prompt others to make recommendations by handing them cards on which you have written food items.

Vocabulaire Tape pictures of the food items to the board. Point to each one and ask either-or questions. (**C'est un steak-frites ou du camembert?**) Then, call for volunteers to come forward. Ask them **Qu'est-ce que vous prenez comme entrée/fromage/dessert?** and have them point to a picture and say **Je voudrais l'assiette de crudités.** Encourage them to hesitate and ask the class to make recommendations.

Building on Previous Skills

Ask students which of the foods pictured in the Vocabulaire they have tasted and if they like them. (**C'était bon/délicieux/pas bon/dégoûtant.**)

27 Pas américain, ça!

Regarde la carte à la page 17. A ton avis, quels plats est-ce qu'on ne trouve pas aux Etats-Unis?

Possible answers: les carottes râpées, la salade de tomates, le céleri rémoulade, l'assiette de crudités, l'assiette de fromages, la crème caramel

28 Ecoute!

 Ecoute ce dialogue. Le serveur a mélangé les commandes et demande à son client ce qu'il a mangé. Laquelle des commandes suivantes est la bonne? b

salade de tomates
poulet frites
salade verte
tarte aux pommes

salade de tomates
poulet haricots verts
assiette de fromages
tarte aux pommes

salade de tomates
poulet haricots verts
salade verte
tarte aux prunes

a. b. c.

29 Vous désirez?

 Et toi, qu'est-ce que tu prends? Regarde la carte du **Routier Sympa** et choisis une entrée, un plat et un dessert. Ensuite, demande à un(e) camarade de classe ce qu'il/elle prend.

COMMENT DIT-ON... ?
Ordering and asking for details

A server might ask:
Vous avez choisi?
Have you made your selection?
Vous avez décidé?

Que voulez-vous comme entrée?
What would you like for an appetizer?
Et comme boisson? *And to drink?*
Comment désirez-vous votre viande? *How do you like your meat cooked?*

To ask for details:
Qu'est-ce que vous avez comme spécialités? *What kind of . . . do you have?*
Qu'est-ce que vous me conseillez? *What do you recommend?*
Qu'est-ce que c'est, le presskopf? *What is . . .?*

To respond to the server:
Non, pas encore.
Un instant, s'il vous plaît.
Oui, je vais prendre la soupe à l'oignon.
Comme entrée, j'aimerais le pâté de campagne.

De l'eau, s'il vous plaît.
Saignante. *Rare.*
A point. *Medium rare.*
Bien cuite. *Well-done.*

NOTE CULTURELLE

Dans chaque région de France, on peut manger des plats traditionnels variés; par exemple, **la bouillabaisse** en Provence, **le foie gras** dans le Périgord, **les crêpes** en Bretagne, **le cassoulet** dans le Languedoc et **la choucroute** en Alsace.

18 *dix-huit* CHAPITRE 1   France, les régions

Culture Notes

• Most French people prefer their meat less cooked than Americans. They might even ask for it to be served **bleue** (with only the outside layer browned). If you prefer that your meat be more thoroughly cooked, ask specifically for your meat to be **à point** or **bien cuite**.

• **Bouillabaisse** is a type of seafood soup from Marseilles. **Foie gras** is duck or goose liver pâté often served as an **entrée** with small pieces of toast. **Crêpes** resemble thin pancakes and are usually rolled up and stuffed with sugar, jam, or chocolate spread. **Cassoulet** is a casserole of white beans, various meats, vegetables, and herbs that is slowly simmered. **Choucroute** is *sauerkraut,* chopped cabbage that is salted and fermented in its own juice.

30 Ecoute!

Tu es au restaurant. Le serveur te pose des questions. Choisis la meilleure réponse.

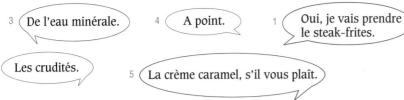

3 De l'eau minérale.

4 A point.

1 Oui, je vais prendre le steak-frites.

2 Les crudités.

5 La crème caramel, s'il vous plaît.

31 Méli-mélo!

Mets dans l'ordre ce dialogue entre un serveur et un client. Ensuite, joue la scène avec ton/ta camarade.

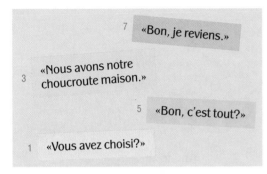

7 «Bon, je reviens.»

2 «Non, pas encore… euh… qu'est-ce que vous avez comme spécialités?»

3 «Nous avons notre choucroute maison.»

4 «OK, une choucroute.»

5 «Bon, c'est tout?»

1 «Vous avez choisi?»

6 «Ah non, finalement, je vais prendre le poulet haricots verts et une carafe d'eau.»

32 De notre cuisine à votre table

Tu travailles dans un restaurant qui livre à domicile *(delivers to customers' homes)*. Crée une carte avec trois entrées, trois plats principaux, trois desserts et trois boissons. Ensuite, au téléphone, un(e) client(e) te demande ce que tu as comme entrée, plat principal, etc. et il/elle passe sa commande. Joue cette scène avec ton/ta camarade. Changez de rôles.

33 Mon journal

Où es-tu allé(e) la dernière fois que tu as mangé au restaurant? Tu étais avec qui? Qu'est-ce que tu as mangé? C'était comment?

34 Jeu de rôle

You're a server at **L'Auberge.** Your classmates will look at the menu on page 14. They'll ask you questions about the menu and then order. Answer their questions and take down their orders. Change roles.

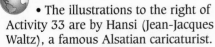

For Individual Needs

30 Visual/Kinesthetic Learners Give pictures of the food items to five students, who stand in front of the class. As you play the recording, the class writes down the name of the student that is holding the food item being discussed. Then, as you play the recording again, have the students at the front step forward as they hear the question that corresponds to their picture. The class confirms or corrects.

31 Kinesthetic Learners In groups of seven, each student writes one of the sentences on a sheet of paper and holds it up. Group members arrange themselves in the proper order and read the dialogue aloud.

Portfolio

32 Written/Oral The menu is appropriate for students' written portfolios. The conversation is appropriate for their oral portfolios. For portfolio information, see *Assessment Guide,* pages 2–13.

CLOSE

List the courses of a meal on the board (**entrée, plat principal, fromage, dessert,** and **boisson**). Ask students **Qu'est-ce que vous voulez comme… ?** Have them hesitate and then order a dish for that course.

ASSESS

Quiz 1–2, *Chapter Teaching Resources, Book 1,* pp. 25–26

Assessment Items, Audiocassette 7A/Audio CD 1

Performance Assessment

Have students act out the **Jeu de rôle** from Activity 33. They might want to use the menus they created in Activity 32.

Culture Notes

• The illustrations to the right of Activity 33 are by Hansi (Jean-Jacques Waltz), a famous Alsatian caricaturist.
• The girl in the middle of the lower illustration is holding **Kugelhopf,** a special Alsatian bread that is usually sprinkled with powdered sugar and eaten with coffee, or in the afternoon as a **goûter.**

• The other girls in the lower illustration are wearing a **coquarde,** the tricolor symbol of revolutionary France, on their hats. Alsatians began wearing these after World War I to show their pride in once again being a part of France.
• The girl in the upper illustration is wearing **sabots,** wooden shoes that are part of traditional costumes in several regions of France.

chouette!

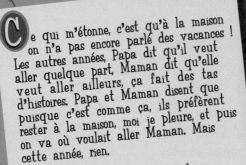

READING STRATEGY

Identifying the point of view of the narrator

Teacher Note

For an additional reading, see *Practice and Activity Book*, page 11.

PREREADING
Activities A and B

Motivating Activity

Ask students to list famous little boys or girls from movies, television, or comics (Calvin of *Calvin and Hobbes*®, Dennis the Menace, Lucy of *Peanuts*®, Kevin of *Home Alone*®). Have them think of words or expressions to describe them. Why are these children funny?

Teaching Suggestions

A. You might remind students that scanning involves looking over a text quickly to find specific information. Have them find clues in the story to determine the speaker's approximate age.

B. Have students also look at the illustrations and anticipate what the story might be about.

READING
Activities C–P

Teaching Suggestion

C.–E. Have pairs or small groups of students read the story and answer the questions in these activities. You might have students give quotations from the story to support their answers.

Terms in Lisons!

Students might want to know the following words: **maîtresse** (*elementary school teacher*); **mouchoir** (*handkerchief*); **tousser** (*to cough*); **épaules** (*shoulders*).

Ce qui m'étonne, c'est qu'à la maison on n'a pas encore parlé des vacances ! Les autres années, Papa dit qu'il veut aller quelque part, Maman dit qu'elle veut aller ailleurs, ça fait des tas d'histoires. Papa et Maman disent que puisque c'est comme ça, ils préfèrent rester à la maison, moi je pleure, et puis on va où voulait aller Maman. Mais cette année, rien.

Pourtant, les copains de l'école se préparent tous à partir. Geoffroy, qui a un papa très riche, va passer ses vacances dans la grande maison que son papa a au bord de la mer.

DE BONS CONSEILS

Identifying the point of view of the narrator of a story is a key to understanding the story itself. A foreign tourist, a small child, and an eighty-year-old woman would probably relate the same incident very differently. When you read, think about the person who is telling the story. Who is he? Where does he live? What is his age? What kind of person does he seem to be? Answering these kinds of questions will help you to understand the narrator's point of view, and so get more out of the story.

A. Scan the first paragraph. From whose point of view is the story told? How old would you say this person is? a child; around seven or eight

B. Knowing who the narrator is, what do you think you'll read about in the story? See answer below.

Agnan, qui est le premier de la classe et le chouchou de la maîtresse, s'en va en Angleterre passer ses vacances dans une école où on va lui apprendre à parler l'anglais. Il est fou, Agnan.

Alceste va manger des truffes en Périgord, où son papa a un ami qui a une charcuterie. Et c'est comme ça pour tous : ils vont à la mer, à la montagne ou chez leurs mémés à la campagne. Il n'y a que moi qui ne sais pas encore où je vais aller, et c'est très embêtant, parce qu'une des choses que j'aime le mieux dans les vacances, c'est d'en parler avant et après aux copains.

Alors, je suis allé dans le jardin et j'ai attendu Papa, et quand il est arrivé de son bureau, j'ai couru vers lui ; il m'a pris dans ses bras, m'a fait « Oupla ! » et je lui ai

C. What is Nicolas' relationship to . . .
   1. Geoffroy, Agnan, and Alceste? classmate
   2. Maman and Papa? son

D. What is Nicolas concerned about at the beginning of the story? uncertain vacation plans

E. Match Nicolas' schoolfriends with their vacation destinations and planned activities.
See answers below.

Alceste
Geoffroy
Agnan

apprendre à parler anglais
Périgord
Angleterre
manger des truffes
au bord de la mer

Literature Link

Ask students for examples of other stories told in the first person that they've read either in English class or for pleasure. How does a first person narrator affect the tone of the story?

Teacher Note

In 1960, the humorist René Goscinny began his collaboration with the illustrator Jean-Jacques Sempé. The result was the publication of *Le Petit Nicolas*. Nicolas shares his world with a child's typical innocence and simplicity.

Answers

B *Possible answer:* The story will probably be a cute, humorous account of a childhood event, told in simple language.

E Alceste - Périgord - manger des truffes
Geoffroy - au bord de la mer
Agnan - Angleterre - apprendre à parler anglais

demandé où nous allions partir en vacances. Alors, Papa a cessé de rigoler, il m'a posé par terre et il m'a dit qu'on allait en parler dans la maison, où nous avons trouvé Maman assise dans le salon.

— Je crois que le moment est venu, a dit Papa.

— Oui, a dit Maman, il m'en a parlé tout à l'heure.

— Alors, il faut le lui dire, a dit Papa.

— Eh bien, dis-lui, a dit Maman.

Alors, Papa s'est assis dans le fauteuil, il m'a pris par les mains et il m'a tiré contre ses genoux.

— Mon Nicolas est un grand garçon raisonnable, n'est-ce pas ? a demandé Papa.

Moi, j'aime pas trop quand on me dit que je suis un grand garçon, parce que d'habitude, quand on me dit ça, c'est qu'on va me faire des choses qui ne me plaisent pas.

— Et je suis sûr, a dit Papa, que mon grand garçon aimerait bien aller à la mer !

— Oh ! oui, j'ai dit.

— Aller à la mer, nager, pêcher, jouer sur la plage, se promener dans les bois, a dit Papa.

— Il y a des bois, là où on va ? j'ai demandé. Alors c'est pas là où on a été l'année dernière ?

— Écoute, a dit Maman à Papa. Je ne peux pas. Je me demande si c'est une si bonne idée que ça. Je préfère y renoncer. Peut-être, l'année prochaine...

— Non ! a dit Papa. Ce qui est décidé est décidé. Un peu de courage, que diable ! Et Nicolas va être très raisonnable ; n'est-ce pas, Nicolas ?

Moi j'ai dit que oui, que j'allais être drôlement raisonnable.

— Et on va aller à l'hôtel ? j'ai demandé.

— Pas exactement, a dit Papa. Je... je crois que tu coucheras sous la tente. C'est très bien, tu sais...

Alors là, j'étais content comme tout.

— Sous la tente, comme les Indiens dans le livre que m'a donné tante Dorothée ? j'ai demandé.

— C'est ça, a dit Papa.

— Chic ! j'ai crié. Tu me laisseras t'aider à monter la tente ? Et à faire du feu pour cuire le manger ? Oh ! ça va être chic, chic, chic !

F. How do you know that Nicolas' parents don't want to tell him something? Find five things they say that show you this. Then find three actions or gestures that illustrate their nervousness. *See answers below.*

G. Which of the following sentences do they say to make him accept the idea? *See answers below.*

> Ce qui est décidé est décidé.

> Ce soir, pour le dessert, il y aura de la tarte.

> Tu iras seul, comme un grand.

> Mon Nicolas est un grand garçon raisonnable, n'est-ce pas?

> C'est la première fois que tu seras séparé de nous...

H. Why does Nicolas dislike it when his parents call him **grand garçon**? *See answers below.*

I. Where do Nicolas' parents plan for him to go on vacation? What will he do there? Where will he sleep? *See answers below.*

J. Match the words from the story on the left with their synonyms on the right.

a. cesser de 2	1. leurs grands-mères
b. des tas de 6	2. s'arrêter de
c. ce qui m'étonne, c'est que 5	3. autre part
d. leurs mémés 1	4. rire
e. puisque 7	5. je suis surpris que
f. ailleurs 3	6. beaucoup de
g. rigoler 4	7. parce que

vingt et un **21**

LISONS!
CHAPITRE 1

Teaching Suggestion

You might want to do Activities F through H with the entire class. Then, have students break into small groups or pairs to do Activities J through M.

For Individual Needs

G. Slower Pace Ask for examples of words or expressions in English that a parent might say to placate a child. Have a volunteer read the choices for this activity one at a time and have the class decide which ones apply.

Teaching Suggestions

H. Ask students if they would have the same reaction as Nicolas. Is there an expression that they've heard adults use in English to preface something unpleasant?

J. Remind students that they don't need a dictionary for this activity. If they're uncertain, encourage them to go back to the story and use the context to try to guess the meaning of the word.

For Individual Needs

J. Slower Pace Have students find the expression in the story and write the sentence in which it appears. Then, have them replace the synonyms in the second column until they find one that logically completes the sentence.

Answers

F *Possible answers*

They hesitate to tell Nicolas the news. They try to break the news to him gently. They act nervous.

1. — Je crois que le moment est venu.
2. — Alors, il faut le lui dire, a dit Papa.
3. — Écoute, a dit Maman à Papa. Je ne peux pas.
4. — Non! a dit Papa... Un peu de courage, que diable!
5. — Il faut que tu sois très raisonnable.

Papa a cessé de rigoler. Papa s'est essuyé la figure avec son mouchoir. Papa a toussé un peu dans sa gorge.

G — Tu iras seul, comme un grand.
— Mon Nicolas est un grand garçon raisonnable, n'est-ce pas?
— Ce soir, pour le dessert, il y aura de la tarte.

H This usually means they are going to do something he won't like.

I summer camp; swim, fish, play on the beach, walk in the woods; in a tent

Literature Link

N. You might explain to your students that the word *ironic* describes an event or situation that is contrary to what was expected or intended. Ask them for examples of irony from books they've read or movies or TV programs they've seen.

Thinking Critically

O. Comparing and Contrasting Have students list adjectives or phrases to describe Nicolas. Then, have them compare this list to the one they created to describe famous boys and girls from American cartoons (see Motivating Activity on page 20). How is Nicolas similar to them? How is he different? If *Le Petit Nicolas* were translated into English, do students think it would be popular?

POSTREADING
Activity Q

Teaching Suggestion

Q. Have students write a brief, humorous, first-person account of a childhood event told from the child's point of view. They might choose a comic like *Dennis the Menace* that they've read recently or a scene from a child-centered movie to recount.

For Individual Needs

Challenge/Tactile Learners
Bring in several comic strips from the Sunday paper. Have students choose a strip, cut blank speech bubbles out of construction paper, and paste the blank bubbles over the originals. Then, have them create new French dialogues and write them in the blank speech bubbles.

Papa s'est essuyé la figure avec son mouchoir, comme s'il avait très chaud, et puis il m'a dit :

– Nicolas, nous devons parler d'homme à homme. Il faut que tu sois très raisonnable.

– Et si tu es bien sage et tu te conduis comme un grand garçon, a dit Maman, ce soir, pour le dessert, il y aura de la tarte.

Alors Papa a toussé un peu dans sa gorge, il m'a mis ses mains sur mes épaules et puis il m'a dit :

– Nicolas, mon petit, nous ne partirons pas avec toi en vacances. Tu iras seul, comme un grand.

– Comment, seul ? j'ai demandé. Vous ne partez pas, vous ?

– Nicolas, a dit Papa, je t'en prie, sois raisonnable. Maman et moi, nous irons faire un petit voyage, et comme nous avons pensé que ça ne t'amuserait pas, nous avons décidé que toi tu irais en colonie de vacances. Ça te fera le plus grand bien, tu seras avec des petits camarades de ton âge

et tu t'amuseras beaucoup...

– Bien sûr, c'est la première fois que tu seras séparé de nous, Nicolas, mais c'est pour ton bien, a dit Maman.

– Alors, Nicolas, mon grand... qu'est-ce que tu en dis ? m'a demandé Papa.

– Chouette ! j'ai crié, et je me suis mis à danser dans le salon. Parce que c'est vrai, il paraît que c'est terrible, les colonies de vacances : on se fait des tas de copains, on fait des promenades, des jeux, on chante autour d'un gros feu, et j'étais tellement content que j'ai embrassé Papa et Maman. Ce qui est drôle, c'est que Papa et Maman me regardaient avec des gros yeux ronds. Ils avaient même l'air un peu fâché.

> *Pourtant, je ne sais pas, moi, mais je crois que j'ai été raisonnable, non ?*

K. Look for these words and expressions in the story. Use context to figure out what they mean. the teacher's pet

le chouchou de la maîtresse

He pulled me against his knees

Il m'a tiré contre ses genoux.

Papa s'est essuyé la figure.
Papa wiped his face.

Je préfère y renoncer.

Je me suis mis à danser... I'd rather give up the idea.

I started to dance . . .

L. What is Nicolas' reaction to his parents' news? Why? He dances around; He's excited.

M. How do Nicolas' parents feel about his reaction? Are they really relieved that he took it so well? How do you know? See answers below.

N. What is the significance of the title **Il faut être raisonnable**? Why is the title ironic, in light of the story? See answers below.

O. Based on what you've read, how would you describe Nicolas? How would you describe his parents? See answers below.

P. This story is told from a child's point of view. Find five examples in the text of language typical of the way a child would express himself. See answers below.

Q. How would you feel if you were in Nicolas' situation?

22 *vingt-deux*

Answers

M They feel surprised, a bit angry, and a little hurt; No; "... Papa et Maman me regardaient avec de gros yeux ronds. Ils avaient même l'air un peu fâché."

N Nicolas' parents tell him he must be reasonable, and then they are surprised when he is.

O *Possible answers:* Nicolas has a sense of adventure and doesn't understand his parents' annoyance at his eagerness to attend camp alone. Nicolas' parents worry about his feelings, thinking he is more dependent than he is.

P *Possible answers:* Il est fou, Agnan; ... chez leurs mémés... ; ... j'allais être drôlement raisonnable; ... j'étais content comme tout; Sous la tente, comme les Indiens... ? Chic! j'ai crié; Chouette! j'ai crié... ; Il paraît que c'est terrible, les colonies de vacances...

ECRIVONS!

In the story you've just read, Nicolas talks about places all over France where his friends are going for their vacation. America also has many unique regions. In this activity, you'll select a region of America where you would like to take a vacation. Then, you'll write a travel brochure for that region, including anything a vacationer might need to know.

Une brochure touristique

Choisis une région des Etats-Unis que tu trouves intéressante. Ecris une brochure pour convaincre des touristes de visiter cette région.

A. Préparation

1. Connais-tu bien la région que tu as choisie? Commence par écrire ce que tu sais déjà.
2. Si tu as besoin de plus d'informations, renseigne-toi à la bibliothèque. Essaie de trouver des renseignements sur les activités, les points d'intérêt, les spécialités régionales et la géographie de la région que tu vas décrire.
3. Réfléchis un peu. Dans quel but *(purpose)* est-ce que tu écris?
4. Pense à des mots que tu vas utiliser dans ta brochure pour atteindre ton but.
   a. Fais une liste d'adjectifs emphatiques comme «formidable» ou «extraordinaire» pour décrire la région.
   b. Maintenant, fais une liste de mots ou d'expressions qui décrivent les caractéristiques de ta région; par exemple, «montagneux» ou «Il y a beaucoup de soleil».

DE BONS CONSEILS
You always have a purpose for writing. You may want to explain something to someone, to relate a funny incident, to create, or just to put your thoughts down on paper. Whatever your reason is, it will influence the way you write. You will determine the tone, the language, and even the organization of your writing according to your purpose.

B. Rédaction

1. Fais un brouillon *(rough draft)* de ta brochure. N'oublie pas de diviser ta présentation en trois parties :
   a. Une brève introduction où l'on apprend de quelle région tu parles.
   b. Toutes les informations sur les aspects les plus intéressants de la région.
   c. Une partie finale qui puisse convaincre les gens de venir découvrir la région.
2. Pour illustrer ta brochure, trouve des photos dans des magazines ou fais tes propres dessins.

C. Evaluation

1. Est-ce que ta brochure peut vraiment convaincre quelqu'un de choisir cet endroit pour y passer ses vacances? Montre-la à un(e) camarade de classe et demande-lui son opinion.
2. Vérifie l'orthographe *(spelling)* et la grammaire de ton brouillon. Fais les révisions nécessaires. Mets ta brochure au propre.

vingt-trois **23**

WRITING

For Individual Needs

B. 1. Visual/Tactile Learners Have students organize their brochures by rewriting the words they listed in Activity A.4. on different-colored paper, using one color for each part of the presentation (introduction, body of information, conclusion).

POSTWRITING

Teaching Suggestion

Remind students that peer evaluation should focus on content and organization as well as on spelling and grammar. Partners should point out both strengths and weaknesses and make specific suggestions to help the writer improve his or her brochure.

ECRIVONS!
CHAPITRE 1

WRITING STRATEGY
Defining your purpose

Teacher Notes

- To encourage the writing process in **Ecrivons!,** make sure students do each step of the writing assignment.
- You may want to use the portfolio evaluation forms (Evaluating Written Activities, Forms A and B) found in the *Assessment Guide* to help you evaluate students' final products.

 Portfolio

Written Have students include all their preliminary work for Parts A-C in their written portfolios to show the entire writing process. For portfolio information, see *Assessment Guide,* pages 2–13.

PREWRITING

Motivating Activity

Pass several travel brochures around the class. Have students suggest techniques the designers use to attract people to a particular area (content of photos, layout, language, special offers).

For Individual Needs

A. 1. Visual Learners Have students begin by drawing sketches or gathering photos and pamphlets of their region.

Teaching Suggestion

A. 3. Have students brainstorm reasons for writing (personal expression, to inform, to persuade). Then, have them decide which purposes apply to a travel brochure. Have them also consider the audience they're targeting.

The **Mise en pratique** reviews and integrates all four skills and culture in preparation for the Chapter Test.

 Video Wrap-Up

VIDEO PROGRAM
Videocassette 1

Teacher Note

You might want to use the *Video Program* as part of the chapter review.

Teaching Suggestion

1 Ask students what the headings of the survey mean. Have them use cognates and context to figure out what the categories mean.

Game

JEU-CONCOURS Form two teams. Have each team write 5–10 questions about the survey. (**Quel pourcentage de Français est déjà allé à la mer en été?**) Then, collect the questions. Have one player from each team come to the front of the room. Ask them a question. The first player to find and call out the correct answer in French wins a point for his or her team. Continue until all the questions have been asked.

For Individual Needs

2 Slower Pace You might have students write out their questions before they interview their partner.

MISE EN PRATIQUE

 1 a. Regarde les résultats de ce sondage sur les vacances des jeunes Français. Ensuite, utilise le sondage comme modèle pour préparer un questionnaire sur les vacances des jeunes Américains.

 b. Pose tes questions aux autres élèves pour savoir où ils sont allés, comment, avec qui, etc. Compare leurs réponses avec le sondage sur les Français.

 2 C'est le premier jour d'école. Tu rencontres un(e) ami(e) qui te demande comment tes vacances se sont passées, ce que tu as fait, mangé, etc. Joue cette scène avec ton/ta camarade.

 3 Regarde les menus et fais une liste de deux entrées, trois plats principaux et trois desserts.

LES VACANCES DES 14/19 ANS	Vacances d'été 1990	Vacances d'hiver 89/90
Taux de départ (en %)	61,9	28,2
Nombre moyen de journées	25,7	11,9
Nombre de séjours (milliers)	4 091	1 925
En France (en %)	76,3	80,5
A l'étranger (en %)	23,7	19,5
Genre de séjour (en %)		
Circuit	6,2	3,1
Mer	47,1	14,3
Montagne (hors sports d'hiver)	12,9	5,4
Sports d'hiver	-	31,5
Campagne	21,0	24,4
Ville et autres	12,8	21,3
Mode d'hébergement (en %)		
Hôtel	5,1	10,6
Location	16,8	14,1
Résidence secondaire	8,6	13,3
Parents et amis	39,5	45,9
Village de vacances	5,7	4,9
Tente, caravane	18,5	1,5
Autres	5,8	9,7

Un petit mot de ta correspondante à Colmar. Je t'envoie les menus scolaires qui sont publiés dans l'Alsace, notre journal régional. Les spécialités comme les spaetzlé (ce sont des pâtes alsaciennes) et la salade au gruyère, c'est typique de chez nous. En général, on a deux heures pour manger. On peut manger à la cantine ou rentrer à la maison. Moi, je préfère manger au lycée. Ecris-moi pour me dire comment ça se passe, les repas du midi chez vous.

Salut,
Martine

▬ A LA SOUPE LES POTACHES ▬

Les menus suivants seront servis mardi à midi dans les cantines scolaires:

CITÉ TECHNIQUE: aile de raie, sauce aux câpres, pommes vapeur ou coq au riesling et spaetzlé, entrée au choix, dessert au choix.

LYCÉE BARTHOLDI: assiette de charcuterie, filet de poisson sauce nantua, riz, orange.

LYCÉE CAMILLE SÉE: spaghetti à la bolognaise ou gratin de ravioli au poulet, entrée et dessert au choix.

COLLÈGE BERLIOZ: choux-fleurs ou brocolis en salade, filet de lingue, blettes et pommes de terre à la crème, Danette.

COLLÈGE MOLIÈRE: potage, ravioli au gratin, salade verte, cône glacé.

COLLÈGE SAINT-ANDRÉ: côte de porc, gratin de choux-fleurs ou émincé de dinde, pâtes, entrée, fromage et dessert au choix.

INSTITUT DE L'ASSOMPTION: omelette-frites, entrée, fromage et dessert au choix.

INSTITUTION SAINT-JEAN: spaghetti bolognaise ou émincé de veau, petits pois à la française, entrée, fromage et dessert au choix.

ÉCOLES MATERNELLES: salade au gruyère, rôti de boeuf, choux-fleurs au gratin, salade de fruits.

3. *Possible answers:*
Entrées: assiette de charcuterie, potage
Plats: aile de raie, filet de poisson, spaghetti à la bolognaise
Desserts: cône glacé, orange, salade de fruits

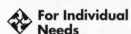 **Culture Note**

Une salade au gruyère is an appetizer consisting only of shredded **gruyère** cheese (similar to Swiss cheese) served with a light dressing. **Spaetzlé** is a dish of handmade egg noodles, usually served with a sauce as a side dish at the noon meal.

Math Link

1 Students might show the comparison between the French survey and their own in the form of a bar graph.

Teacher Note

Remind students that when saying numbers in French, a comma (**virgule**) is used instead of a decimal. Therefore, *1.5* would be written **1,5** and read as **un virgule cinq**.

4 Réponds à ta correspondante Martine et explique-lui comment le repas de midi se passe dans ton école. N'oublie pas de donner des exemples de menus typiques.

 5 Ecoute les lycéens suivants. Décide dans quelle école ils vont en t'aidant des menus à la page 24. Answers on p. 3D.

Le Cygne

☞ Les Entrées

Potage du jour	20,-
Salade de crudités	35,-
Escargots maison Dz . . 72, -1/2 Dz . . 36,-	
Champignons frais sautés à l'ail	40,-
Salade frisée au chèvre chaud	45,-
Salade de foie de veau	45,-

☞ Les Viandes

Faux-filet au poivre	85,-
Filet mignon	75,-
Steak Tartare	78,-
Emincé de veau au curry	85,-
Steak de saumon grillé, sauce à l'oseille	85,-

Les Plats Régionaux et les Petits Plats

Tarte flambée gratinée	40,-	Cervelle d'agneau	72,-
Tripes au vin blanc	64,-	Brochette garnie	72,-
Tête de veau vinaigrette	64,-	Steak foie de veau lyonnaise	76,-
Rognons de porc aux champignons	64,-	Pâté en croûte garni	58,-
Foies de lapins sautés	68,-	Salade de bœuf garnie	64,-

☞ Les fromages

Assortiment de fromages	32,-
Munster	24,-
Camembert	20,-
Gruyère	20,-
Chèvre	24,-
Bleu	24,-

☞ Les desserts

Assiette de sorbets	36,-
Gâteau au chocolat, aux deux sauces	32,-
Soupe de kiwis à la sauce menthe	35,-
Pommes Grand-Mère au miel	32,-
Brochette de fruits	35,-
Tarte flambée aux pommes ou bananes	35,-

6 J E U   D E   R O L E

You're at a restaurant with friends. One of you plays the server. The others, playing the customers, look at the menu but are unsure about what to order. Ask each other questions, make recommendations, and order.

MISE EN PRATIQUE

vingt-cinq **25**

Thinking Critically

6 Analyzing Have students consider the advantages of a long, relaxing meal spent with friends and family (more time to develop social relationships, better digestion). What are the disadvantages? (can be more expensive, takes time from work and school)

Language Note

Students might want to know the following words from the menu: **lapin** *(rabbit)*; **brochette** *(shishkabob)*; **miel** *(honey)*; **cervelle** *(brains)*.

Teaching Suggestion

4 Remind students to mention whether they usually go home for lunch. They might also discuss the pros and cons of an open campus for lunch.

📁 Portfolio

4 Written This activity is appropriate for students' written portfolios. For portfolio suggestions, see *Assessment Guide,* page 14.

◈ For Individual Needs

5 Slower Pace Before you play the recording, have students note the similarities and differences among the school menus. You might also pause the recording after each conversation and have students decide which school the speakers attend.

6 Slower Pace Have students look through the menu and note the foods they like and those they don't like.

6 Kinesthetic Learners Have students stage the scene, using a table, chairs, menus they create, props, and costumes. They might act out an extended scene, entering the restaurant one at a time, greeting one another as if they haven't seen one another for a long time, being seated at a table, asking for their menus, ordering their food, eating, and paying the check.

📁 Portfolio

6 Oral This activity is appropriate for students' oral portfolios. For portfolio suggestions, see *Assessment Guide,* page 14.

This page is intended to help students prepare for the test. It is a brief checklist of the major points covered in the chapter. The students should be reminded that this is only a checklist and does not necessarily include everything that will appear on the test.

Teaching Suggestions

4–6 Have students write a short description of their last vacation, real or imaginary, using the **passé composé** and the **imparfait**.

5 Students might interview one another, using the questions they've written.

8 Ask students to recommend their favorite Alsatian specialty from the chapter.

Additional Practice

8 Have students list 3–4 of their favorite French or Alsatian dishes and recommend them to a partner.

For Individual Needs

9 Kinesthetic Learners
You might have partners act out the roles of server and customer, using the questions as a guide.

Additional Practice

10 You might also have students tell what the server would ask to elicit these orders.

QUE SAIS-JE?

Can you renew old acquaintances?
p. 9

Can you inquire and express enthusiasm and dissatisfaction? p. 10

Can you exchange information? p. 12

Can you express indecision? p. 17

Can you make recommendations?
p. 17

Can you order and ask for details?
p. 18

Can you use what you've learned in this chapter?

1 How would you . . .
1. Ça fait longtemps qu'on ne s'est pas vu(e)s. Je suis content(e) de te revoir.
1. greet a friend you haven't seen in a while?
2. inquire about your friend's activities?
Qu'est-ce que tu deviens? Quoi de neuf?

2 How would you respond if . . .
1. a friend you haven't seen in a while greeted you? Ça fait... ; Depuis...
2. your friend wanted to know what you've been doing?
Toujours la même chose! Rien (de spécial).

3 How would you ask a friend how his or her vacation was?
C'était comment, tes vacances?

4 How would these people describe their vacations? *Possible answers:*

1. C'était pas terrible.

2. Ça ne s'est pas très bien passé.

3. Super! Ça s'est très bien passé.

4. C'était chouette! Je me suis beaucoup amusée.

5 What questions would you ask to find out . . .
1. where your friend went on vacation? Où est-ce que tu es allé(e)?
2. who he or she went with? Avec qui est-ce que tu es allé(e)?
3. how he or she got there? Tu es parti(e) comment?
4. where he or she stayed? Où est-ce que tu as dormi?
5. what the weather was like? Quel temps est-ce qu'il a fait?

6 How would you answer the questions in number 5? See answers below.

7 What would you say if you were in a restaurant and couldn't decide what to order? *Possible answers:* Je ne sais pas. Tout me tente. Je n'arrive pas à me décider. J'hésite entre... et...

8 How would you recommend that someone order a certain dish?
Tu devrais prendre... ; Pourquoi tu ne prends pas... ; Essaie... ; Prends...

9 How do you ask the server . . .
1. what the restaurant's specialties are? Qu'est-ce que vous avez comme spécialités?
2. what kinds of appetizers there are? Qu'est-ce que vous avez comme entrées?
3. for a recommendation? Qu'est-ce que vous me conseillez?

10 How would you order each of the following items? See answers below.
1. un café   2. du poulet   3. de la glace aux fraises

Possible answers
6 1. Je suis allé(e)...
2. J'y suis allé(e) seul(e)/avec...
3. Je suis parti(e) en...
4. A l'hôtel. Chez...
5. Il a fait un temps magnifique. Il a plu tout le temps.
10 1. Un café, s'il vous plaît.
2. Je vais prendre du poulet.
3. Comme dessert, j'aimerais de la glace aux fraises.

PREMIERE ETAPE

Renewing old acquaintances

Ça fait longtemps qu'on ne s'est pas vu(e)s. *It's been a long time since we've seen each other.*
Je suis content(e) de te revoir. *I'm glad to see you again.*
Ça fait... *It's been . . .*
Depuis... *Since . . .*
Qu'est-ce que tu deviens? *What's going on with you?*
Quoi de neuf? *What's new?*
Toujours la même chose! *Same old thing!*
Rien (de spécial). *Nothing (special).*

Inquiring; expressing enthusiasm and dissatisfaction

C'était comment, tes vacances? *How was your vacation?*
Tu t'es bien amusé(e)? *Did you have fun?*
Je me suis beaucoup amusé(e). *I had a lot of fun.*
C'était pas terrible. *It wasn't so great.*
Je me suis ennuyé(e). *I was bored.*

Exchanging information

Est-ce que tu es resté(e) ici? *Did you stay here?*
Oui, je suis resté(e) ici tout le temps. *Yes, I stayed here the whole time.*
Non, je suis parti(e)... *No, I went away for . . .*
J'y suis allé(e) début/fin... *I went at the beginning/end of . . .*
J'y suis allé(e) seul(e)/avec... *I went alone/with . . .*
Tu es parti(e) comment? *How did you get there?*
Je suis parti(e) en... *I went by . . .*
Où est-ce que tu as dormi? *Where did you stay?*
A l'hôtel. *In a hotel.*
Chez... *With . . .*
Quel temps est-ce qu'il a fait? *What was the weather like?*
Il a fait un temps... *The weather was . . .*
Il a plu tout le temps. *It rained the whole time.*

DEUXIEME ETAPE

Expressing indecision

Tout me tente. *Everything looks tempting.*
Je n'arrive pas à me décider. *I can't make up my mind.*
J'hésite entre... et... *I can't decide between . . . and . . .*

Making recommendations

Tu devrais prendre... *You should have . . .*
Essaie... *Try . . .*

French menu

les entrées (f.) *appetizers*
l'assiette (f.) de charcuterie *plate of pâté, ham, and cold sausage*
l'assiette de crudités (f.) *plate of raw vegetables with vinaigrette*
les carottes râpées *grated carrots with vinaigrette dressing*
le céleri rémoulade *grated celery root with mayonnaise and vinaigrette*
les plats principaux *main dishes*
la côtelette de porc pâtes *porkchop with pasta*
l'escalope (f.) de dinde purée *sliced turkey breast with mashed potatoes*
le filet de sole riz champignons *filet of sole with rice and mushrooms*
le poulet haricots verts *roasted chicken with green beans*
le steak-frites *steak with French fries*
la salade verte *salad*
l'assiette de fromages *a selection of cheeses*
le fromage de chèvre *goat cheese*
les desserts (m.) *desserts*
la crème caramel *caramel custard*
les tartes (f.) aux fruits *fruit pies/tarts*

Ordering and asking for details

Vous avez choisi? *Have you made your selection?*
Que voulez-vous comme entrée? *What would you like for an appetizer?*
Comme entrée, j'aimerais... *For an appetizer, I would like . . .*
Et comme boisson? *And to drink?*
Comment désirez-vous votre viande? *How do you like your meat cooked?*
Saignante. *Rare.*
A point. *Medium rare.*
Bien cuite. *Well-done.*
Qu'est-ce que vous avez comme...? *What kind of . . . do you have?*
Qu'est-ce que vous me conseillez? *What do you recommend?*
Qu'est-ce que c'est,...? *What is . . .?*

Chapitre 2 : Belgique, nous voilà!

Chapter Overview

Mise en train pp. 30–32	**En route pour Bruxelles**			

	FUNCTIONS	GRAMMAR	CULTURE	RE-ENTRY
Première étape pp. 33–37	• Asking for and giving directions, p. 33 • Expressing impatience; reassuring someone, p. 36	The verb **conduire**, p. 35	• **Note Culturelle,** Languages in Belgium, p. 33 • Realia: Map of Belgium, p. 34	• Extending invitations • The imperative

Remise en train pp. 38–39	**Au Centre de la BD**			

	FUNCTIONS	GRAMMAR	CULTURE	RE-ENTRY
Deuxième étape pp. pp. 40–45	• Expressing enthusiasm and boredom, p. 41 • Asking and telling where things are, p. 43		• **Panorama Culturel,** Favorite comic book characters, p. 40 • **Rencontre Culturelle,** Overview of Belgium, p. 44 • Realia: Tourist map of central Brussels, p. 45	• Direct and indirect object pronouns • The forms of the imperfect • Making, accepting, and refusing suggestions

Lisons! pp. 46–48	**Julie, Claire, Cécile—Destinations avariées** Reading Strategy: Previewing

Ecrivons! p. 49	**Ma propre bande dessinée** Writing Strategy: Identifying your audience

Review pp. 50–53	• **Mise en pratique,** pp. 50–51 • **Que sais-je?** p. 52 • **Vocabulaire,** p. 53

Assessment Options	**Etape Quizzes**
	• *Chapter Teaching Resources, Book 1*
	  Première étape, Quiz 2-1, pp. 77–78
	  Deuxième étape, Quiz 2-2, pp. 79–80
	• *Assessment Items, Audiocassette 7A/Audio CD 2*
		Chapter Test
		• *Chapter Teaching Resources, Book 1,* pp. 81–86
		• *Assessment Guide,* Speaking Test, p. 28
		• *Assessment Items, Audiocassette 7A/Audio CD 2*
		
		Test Generator, Chapter 2

RESOURCES: Print	RESOURCES: Audiovisual
Practice and Activity Book, p. 13	*Textbook Audiocassette 1B/Audio CD 2*
Practice and Activity Book, pp. 14–17 *Grammar and Vocabulary Worksheets*, pp. 9–12 *Chapter Teaching Resources, Book 1* • Communicative Activity 2-1, pp. 58–59 • Teaching Transparency Master 2-1, pp. 62, 64 . . . . • Additional Listening Activities 2-1, 2-2, 2-3, pp. 65–66 . . . . . • Realia 2-1, pp. 69, 71 • Situation Cards 2-1, pp. 72–73 • Student Response Forms, pp. 74–76 • Quiz 2-1, pp. 77–78.	*Textbook Audiocassette 1B/Audio CD 2* *Teaching Transparency 2-1* *Additional Listening Activities, Audiocassette 9A/Audio CD 2* *Assessment Items, Audiocassette 7A/Audio CD 2*
Practice and Activity Book, p. 18	*Textbook Audiocassette 1B/Audio CD 2*
Practice and Activity Book, pp. 19–22 *Grammar and Vocabulary Worksheets*, pp. 13–17 *Chapter Teaching Resources, Book 1* • Communicative Activity 2-2, pp. 60–61 • Teaching Transparency Master 2-2, pp. 63, 64 . . . . • Additional Listening Activities 2-4, 2-5, 2-6, pp. 66–67 . . . . . • Realia 2-2, pp. 70, 71 • Situation Cards 2-2, 2-3, pp. 72–73 • Student Response Forms, pp. 74–76 • Quiz 2-2, pp. 79–80. . . . . • Video Guide.	*Textbook Audiocassette 1B/Audio CD 2* *Teaching Transparency 2-2* *Additional Listening Activities, Audiocassette 9A/Audio CD 2* *Assessment Items, Audiocassette 7A/Audio CD 2* *Video Program, Videocassette 1*
Practice and Activity Book, p. 23	
Video Guide	*Video Program, Videocassette 1*

Alternative Assessment
• Performance Assessment
  Première étape, p. 37
  Deuxième étape, p. 45
• Portfolio Assessment
  Written: **Mise en pratique,** Activity 2, *Pupil's Edition*, p. 50
    Assessment Guide, p. 15
  Oral: **Mise en pratique,** Activity 5, *Pupil's Edition*, p. 51
    Assessment Guide, p. 15

For Student Response Forms, see *Chapter Teaching Resources, Book 1,* pp. 74–76.

Première étape

7 Ecoute! p. 33

— Bon, bien. Vous continuez tout droit. Vous allez voir le panneau qui indique l'entrée de l'autoroute. C'est la N. soixante-trois. Suivez l'autoroute pendant à peu près cinq kilomètres et sortez à Court St.-Etienne. C'est un petit village. Après le village, vous traversez un grand pont. Prenez la première route à gauche. Vous allez arriver à un carrefour. Là, vous tournez à droite, et cette route vous conduira au centre du village. Vous ne pouvez pas le manquer.

— D'accord. Je crois que je comprends. Merci, monsieur.

— Je vous en prie.

Answer to Activity 7
Malmédy

11 Ecoute! p. 35

1. — Le plein de super, s'il vous plaît.

2. — Vous avez besoin d'huile, madame.

3. — Vous pourriez vérifier les pneus?

4. — Oh, là là! Je suis tombé en panne d'essence! Il y a une station-service près d'ici?

5. — Vous pourriez me nettoyer le pare-brise, s'il vous plaît?

6. — Voilà. J'ai mis de l'air dans les pneus et j'ai vérifié l'huile. Ça va.

7. — Eh bien, le plein de super, ça vous fait cent soixante-cinq francs.

8. — Et les freins ne marchent pas très bien. Vous pouvez les vérifier?

Answers to Activity 11
1. chauffeur
2. pompiste
3. chauffeur
4. chauffeur
5. chauffeur
6. pompiste
7. pompiste
8. chauffeur

17 Ecoute! p. 37

1. — Mais qu'est-ce que tu fais? Le film va commencer dans dix minutes!

2. — Et moi aussi, j'ai faim, mais on n'a pas le temps d'aller manger. On va rater le train!

3. — Attends! Je dois trouver mes lunettes de soleil. Ça ne va pas prendre longtemps.

4. — Mais on va arriver, il n'y a pas le feu!

5. — Eh bien, tu m'embêtes, là. Grouille-toi! On a encore un tas de choses à faire.

6. — Le musée n'ouvre pas avant dix heures de toute façon. On a largement le temps!

7. — Eh, du calme, du calme. On peut changer le pneu.

8. — Tu peux te dépêcher un peu? Moi aussi, j'ai besoin du téléphone.

Answers to Activity 17
1. impatient
2. impatiente
3. calme
4. calme
5. impatient
6. calme
7. calme
8. impatient

Deuxième étape

28 **Ecoute! p. 41**

1. — Tu as lu ça? Lucky Luke®, c'est ma BD préférée. C'est marrant comme tout.

2. — Eh regarde! Tintin®! Ce que c'est bien, Tintin. Tu sais, lire Tintin, ça me branche!

3. — Tu vois? C'est Spirou®. Tu aimes, toi? Moi, non. C'est mortel!

4. — Et voilà un album de Boule & Bill®. Tu vas le lire? Moi, je trouve que c'est ennuyeux à mourir. Je vais chercher autre chose.

5. — Tu n'as jamais lu Tif et Tondu®? Tu devrais en lire. C'est rigolo comme tout!

6. — Tu l'as trouvé, ton Gaston®? Oh, c'est rasant, Gaston. Je ne sais pas pourquoi tu aimes tant ça.

7. — Tiens! Les Mousquetaires®! Tu vois? Qu'est-ce qu'ils sont dingues!

8. — Dis donc, tu n'as pas dit que tu préférais Jojo®? Moi, ça m'embête. Et c'est tellement bébé!

Answers to Activity 28

| 1. s'amuse | 3. s'ennuie | 5. s'amuse | 7. s'amuse |
| 2. s'amuse | 4. s'ennuie | 6. s'ennuie | 8. s'ennuie |

33 **Ecoute! p. 43**

1. — Vous pourriez me dire où est le café?

   — Oui. Prenez l'escalier, montez au premier étage et c'est tout suite à gauche.

2. — Excusez-moi, où sont les toilettes?

   — Elles sont tout au fond, à droite, à côté de l'entrée.

3. — Excusez-moi, vous savez où est la fusée de Tintin?

   — Bien sûr. Prenez l'escalier, et elle sera juste en face de vous, au premier étage.

4. — Excusez-moi, je cherche l'ascenseur.

   — Il est sur votre gauche, après l'escalier, à côté des téléphones.

5. — Pardon madame, où se trouve la bédéthèque, s'il vous plaît? En haut ou en bas?

   — Au rez-de-chaussée. Elle est au fond, à gauche, après l'ascenseur.

6. — Pour aller à la boutique de souvenirs, s'il vous plaît?

   — C'est en haut, sur votre droite, juste après la fusée de Tintin.

Answers to Activity 33

1. d 2. b 3. e 4. c 5. a 6. f

Mise en pratique

3 **p. 50**

1. — Ecoute! Tu viens ou pas? On n'a pas le temps de s'arrêter!

   — Oh! Tu as raison! Le spectacle va bientôt commencer!

2. — Tu peux te dépêcher? J'ai faim!

   — Du calme, du calme. On y arrive.

3. — Mais qu'est-ce que tu fais?! Allons-y!

   — Je dois vérifier le plan du parc. Ça ne va pas prendre longtemps.

4. — Je suis vraiment impatient de voir les feux d'artifice!

   — Moi aussi! Ça va être super!

5. — Plus vite! Je dois téléphoner à ma mère à une heure!

   — Du calme, du calme. On a largement le temps!

Answers to Mise en pratique Activity 3

1. impatiente	4. impatiente
2. essaie de rassurer	5. essaie de rassurer
3. essaie de rassurer	

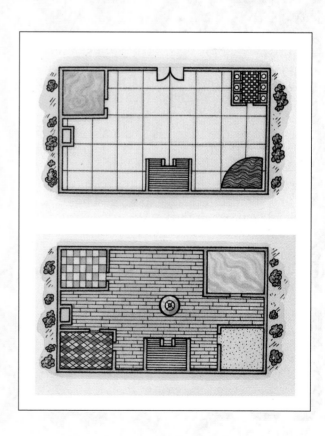

Un manuel
(Individual or Group Project)

ASSIGNMENT

Students will create a driver's manual, including a labeled diagram or picture of the car and specific instructions for the vehicle's care and maintenance.

MATERIALS

✂ **Students may need**

- Construction paper
- Old magazines with car ads
- Colored markers
- Car manuals
- French-English dictionary
- Stapler

SUGGESTED SEQUENCE

1. Students should choose the type of car for which they plan to design the manual, and either find a picture of it in a magazine or draw it by hand on construction paper. Then, have them label all its parts. If students are mechanically oriented, they might even sketch a cut-out diagram of the engine and look up and label important interior parts.

2. Next, have students brainstorm the information they'd like to include in their manuals (how often to change the oil, air pressure for the tires, what type of gas to use, the proper use of seat belts and headlights, and so on). They might borrow a parent or friend's car manual for ideas or call local mechanics for maintenance suggestions.

3. Have students write a clear, concise manual for the car's use and maintenance. They might need to look up additional words or expressions in the dictionary.

4. Have them exchange rough drafts with a partner or give them to you for corrections and suggestions. Then, students should write their final drafts on construction paper.

5. Have students design and draw a cover for their manual. Then, they should staple the cover, illustration, and instructions together.

Le code de la route
(Individual or Group Project)

ASSIGNMENT

Students will create a poster promoting safe driving habits.

MATERIALS

✂ **Students may need**

- Posterboard
- Glue
- Scissors
- Pens
- Colored markers
- French-English dictionary

SUGGESTED SEQUENCE

1. Have students decide which safety rules they will feature. Students might contact local defensive driving schools or the Department of Transportation for brochures and information on safe driving tips.

2. Have students look up any unfamiliar words. They might also research French and Belgian traffic signs. Have them come up with a slogan or a promotional character to feature in their poster.

3. Have students write out the slogans, captions, and safety tips they intend to use in their posters. They should exchange and edit papers with a partner or another group.

4. Have students organize and sketch the layout of their posters. You might have them exchange papers at this point to get advice from their peers on how to make the layout and message more attractive and attention-getting.

5. Students should incorporate their peers' suggestions and corrections into the final text and arrangement of the illustrations for the poster.

6. You might want to display students' posters around the classroom or the school.

GRADING THE PROJECTS

To evaluate both projects, you might base students' grades on appropriate content, language use, creativity, and appearance of the manual or poster.

Suggested Point Distribution (total = 100 points)

Content	25 points
Language use	25 points
Creativity	25 points
Appearance	25 points

SENTENCE SCRAMBLER

In this game, students will practice arranging vocabulary words into sentences.

Procedure   To prepare for this game, write the individual words of various sentences on strips of transparency. Several sentences are suggested below. Put the transparency strips for each sentence in a separate bag. To play the game, divide the class into two teams. Scatter the transparency strips for the first sentence on the overhead projector. Have two students from the first team come to the overhead and try to rearrange the words in the correct order within ten or twenty seconds. If they form the sentence within the allotted time, they win a point for their team. Then, the opposing team takes a turn. Award a point for each correct sentence. You might play until one team has earned five or ten points.

Suggested sentences:

1. Ça ne va pas prendre longtemps!
2. Comment on va à Bruxelles?
3. Vous allez voir un panneau qui indique l'entrée de l'autoroute.
4. Après Bruxelles, vous allez tomber sur un petit village.
5. Cette route vous conduira au centre-ville.

LE JEU DU PENDU *("HANGMAN")*

In this game, students will review and practice the chapter vocabulary.

Procedure   Divide the class into two teams. Draw two scaffolds on the board or on a transparency. Then, choose a word or phrase from the chapter vocabulary list and draw a blank to represent each letter of the word or expression. Each team should have a different word or expression. Have the first player from the first team suggest a letter. If the letter appears in the word(s), write it in the appropriate blanks as many times as it appears. The next player on the team will then suggest another letter. If the suggested letter does not appear in the word, draw the noose on that team's scaffold, and the turn passes to the opposing team. The rope and body are drawn in the following order: noose, head, torso, each arm, each leg, each hand, each foot, and hair. The game continues until a complete body has been drawn on one team's scaffold or until one team guesses the word or expression.

CHARADES

In this game, students will practice service-station vocabulary and expressions for giving directions.

Procedure   To prepare for this game, write vocabulary words and expressions from the chapter on index cards and place them in a bag. Divide the class into two teams. Then, write categories on the board, such as **à la station-service** and **les indications.** You might include additional categories related to the vocabulary. To play the game, have one player from the first team choose a category. He or she then draws a card from the bag and mimes the word or expression. The player's team has 30 seconds to try to guess the word or expression. If the player's team does not guess correctly, the other team has a chance to guess. The turn then passes to the second team. You might play until one team wins a given number of points.

2
Belgique, nous voilà!

① La Grand-Place, cœur de la ville de Bruxelles

28   vingt-huit

Chapitre 2
Belgique, nous voilà!
pp. 28–53

Using the Chapter Opener

 Video Program

Videocassette 1

Before you begin this chapter, you might want to preview the *Video Program* and consult the *Video Guide.* Suggestions for integrating the video into each chapter and activity masters for video selections can be found in the *Video Guide.*

Motivating Activity

Ask students if they have ever gotten lost, run out of gas, or had a flat tire. Ask them what they did in these situations.

Teaching Suggestions

• Have students look at the title, text, and illustrations on pages 28–29 and predict what the chapter will be about.
• Show *Map Transparency 1* (**L'Europe francophone**) and have students locate Belgium. Ask them to share what they already know about Belgium.

Teacher Note

The comic strip frame shown at the top right of this page is from *Astérix chez les Belges.* If possible, bring some Astérix® comic books to class.

Thinking Critically

① **Comparing and Contrasting**   Have students look at this photo of the center of Brussels and compare what they see with the center of their own city or town.

Photo Flash!

① The historical **Grand-Place,** at the congruence of six major streets in the center of Brussels, is famous for its richly decorated Gothic and Baroque façades. Dating back to the Middle Ages, the square was reconstructed after being bombarded by Louis XIV's army in 1695. Many beautiful houses (**hôtels particuliers**) and former medieval guild halls, which are now restaurants and cafés, define the square's perimeter. The magnificent **Hôtel de Ville,** constructed in the fifteenth century in the elaborate High Gothic style, is the square's hallmark.

Viens visiter la Belgique, pays de la bande dessinée! C'est là que sont nés quelques-uns des personnages de bande dessinée les plus célèbres. A Bruxelles, on peut découvrir une petite merveille, le Centre Belge de la Bande Dessinée.

In this chapter you will review and practice

- asking for and giving directions; expressing impatience; reassuring someone
- expressing enthusiasm and boredom; asking and telling where things are

And you will

- listen to two teenagers as they tour a comic book museum
- read a French comic strip
- write your own comic strip
- find out about specialty items produced in Belgium

② Vous allez voir un panneau qui indique l'entrée de l'autoroute.

③ Vous pourriez me dire où se trouve le Palais Royal?

vingt-neuf 29

Focusing on Outcomes

Have students read the introductory paragraph. Ask them what they would expect to find at the **Centre Belge de la Bande Dessinée.** Then, have students look at the outcomes and tell which ones are represented in the photos. Have students list French words or expressions they already know that accomplish these functions. (*Asking for and giving directions:* **Je cherche... , s'il vous plaît. Tournez à gauche.** *Reassuring someone:* **Ça va aller mieux.** *Expressing enthusiasm and boredom:* **C'est sensas/mortel/sinistre.** *Asking and telling where things are:* **Où se trouve... ? ... se trouve dans le nord. C'est à gauche de...**) NOTE: The self-check activities in **Que sais-je?** on page 52 help students assess their achievement of the objectives.

Photo Flash!

③ The student in this photo is asking for information at an information desk. Tourist offices and information desks are often identified by the international symbol for information, a lowercase **i.** Ask students what types of questions they might ask at an information desk.

Teaching Suggestion

Have students tell of recent occasions when they used these functions in English.

Building on Previous Skills

Have students recall vocabulary for buildings and places in town and suggest other places that might complete the caption of Photo 3. (**Vous pourriez me dire où se trouve _____?**) You might also have them suggest possible answers to the question.

🌐 Culture Note

Call students' attention to the lace shown on pages 28–29. In the early seventeenth century, lace became a popular fabric and luxury item in Europe. Handmade lace was worn and coveted by both men and women. In the seventeenth and eighteenth centuries, Flanders, now part of Belgium, was one of the major centers of lace production, along with France and Italy. In later centuries, cotton clothing became more popular, and electric bobbins made handmade lace expensive and less practical than more durable fabrics. However, traditional handmade lace is still proudly produced in the town of Bruges and is quite popular with tourists.

Summary

In **En route pour Bruxelles**, Stéphane and Hervé leave France and stop at a gas station on their way to the comic-book museum in Brussels. They fill up and have the oil and tires checked. As they drive through Bouillon, they ask for directions to the highway. Later, the impatient Hervé is annoyed when they have a flat tire, but Stéphane knows just what to do.

Motivating Activity

Ask students if they prefer using a map or asking for directions. Ask them if they know the significance of the colors used on road signs in the United States. (yellow—caution; green—highway information; brown—parks; blue—services such as water, phone, camping, and restrooms; orange—construction; red—stop or danger)

Teaching Suggestion

Poll students to find out how many know how to check the oil and air and change a flat tire. Ask what they need to do to prepare for a car trip.

Presentation

Play the recording, stopping after each scene. Have students tell what they understood. Remind them to use the illustrations to figure out what is happening. Ask questions 1–3 of Activity 1 on page 32 after the first scene and 4–5 after the fourth scene.

Culture Note

In France, some cars still take **super** (*regular gasoline*), although many recent models take **sans plomb** (*unleaded*) or **gazole** (*diesel*), which is less expensive than regular or unleaded gas.

Mise en train

En route pour Bruxelles

Dans une station-service à Sedan, juste avant de partir pour la Belgique...

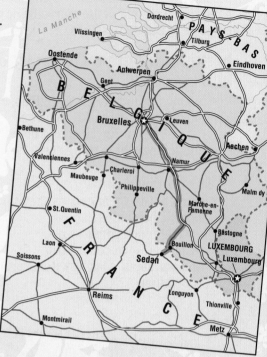

❶ LE POMPISTE Bonjour!

STEPHANE Le plein de super, s'il vous plaît.

HERVE A quelle heure tu crois qu'on va arriver à Bruxelles?

STEPHANE Bruxelles, c'est à environ 170 kilomètres d'ici. Donc, ça va nous prendre une heure et demie au plus et le Centre ouvre à dix heures. On a largement le temps.

HERVE Chouette! Je suis vachement content d'aller au Centre de la BD.

LE POMPISTE Voilà. Ce sera tout?

HERVE Euh... Vous pourriez vérifier l'huile, s'il vous plaît? Ah! Et les pneus aussi!

Essences

LE POMPISTE Oui, bien sûr.

STEPHANE Qu'est-ce qu'on va faire après la visite du Centre?

HERVE On pourrait aller à la Grand-Place, au palais, au musée de l'Armée...

STEPHANE Hé! N'oublie pas qu'on doit rentrer ce soir.

LE POMPISTE L'huile, ça va. J'ai mis de l'air dans les pneus. Ça fait 125 francs.

STEPHANE Hervé, tu me passes 63 francs?

HERVE Euh... Moi, j'ai juste assez pour Bruxelles...

STEPHANE Oh, tu pousses, quand même! C'est toujours la même chose!

30 *trente*

CHAPITRE 2   Belgique, nous voilà!

RESOURCES FOR MISE EN TRAIN

Textbook Audiocassette 1B/Audio CD 2
Practice and Activity Book, p. 13

Math Link

Have students figure out the distance between Sedan and Brussels (about 170 km) in miles. To convert kilometers to miles, multiply by .62 (105 miles).

Geography Link

Have students find the answers to the following questions: **Quelle est la population de la Belgique?** (environ 9.900.000) **Avec quels pays est-ce que la Belgique partage ses frontières?** (les Pays-Bas, l'Allemagne, le Luxembourg et la France) **Quelle est la superficie** (*area*) **de la Belgique?** (30.540 **kilomètres carrés et 11.784 miles carrés**) Have students compare the size and population of Belgium to that of their own state.

Ils traversent la ville de Bouillon...

② STEPHANE   *Tiens, tu as vu le château? Super! On s'arrête?*

HERVE   *Oh, non, écoute! On n'a pas le temps!*

STEPHANE   *En tout cas, on doit s'arrêter pour demander comment on arrive à l'autoroute.*

③ STEPHANE   *Pardon, monsieur. La route pour Bruxelles, s'il vous plaît?*

LE MONSIEUR   *Alors, pour Bruxelles... Vous suivez la N. 89 pendant à peu près 12 kilomètres. Là, vous allez voir un panneau qui indique l'entrée de l'autoroute. Prenez la direction de Bruxelles. C'est la E. 411. Elle vous conduira tout droit au centre-ville. Vous ne pouvez pas le manquer.*

STEPHANE   *Ah ben, ça n'a pas l'air compliqué. Merci, monsieur.*

Sur la E. 411, près de Namur...

④ HERVE   *Je suis vraiment impatient d'arriver! Va plus vite, bon sang! Tu n'avances pas!*

STEPHANE   *Du calme, du calme! Il n'y a pas le feu! Il est seulement neuf heures. Tu es toujours... Oh là là! Qu'est-ce qui se passe?*

HERVE   *On a un pneu crevé! Arrête-toi! Arrête-toi!*

STEPHANE   *Zut, alors!*

HERVE   *Euh, tu sais changer les pneus, toi?*

STEPHANE   *Ouais, mais tu vas m'aider quand même!*

HERVE   *Euh, ouais. Mais je ne sais pas comment on fait, moi.*

STEPHANE   *Tu es vraiment nul comme type! Bon, je vais chercher la roue de secours. Prends la boîte à outils et le cric.*

HERVE   *Grouille-toi! On va être en retard! Je voulais arriver à l'heure d'ouverture pour éviter la foule.*

STEPHANE   *Oh, écoute. Ça ne va pas prendre longtemps.*

MISE EN TRAIN   *trente et un*   **31**

Language Notes

• **Le type** is slang for *boy* or *guy*.
• Tell students that **Oh là là!** is an expression of dismay or annoyance, not admiration.

History Link

Bouillon, situated in the lush Ardennes forest, is the setting of an imposing medieval castle that served as a stronghold during the first crusade, led by Godefroi de Bouillon.

Culture Note

Roads in France and Belgium are identified by both a letter and number. The letters indicate the type of road: **N** designates a **route nationale** while **D** signifies a **route départementale.** **E** indicates international highways that traverse several European countries. These roads have no tolls. An **A** road is an **autoroute,** which often requires a toll. **B** and **C** indicate smaller, local roads.

Teaching Suggestions

• Have students look at the map on page 30 and describe alternate routes from Sedan to Brussels. Did the boys take the most efficient route?
• Have students scan **En route pour Bruxelles** to find the following: two services a gas station attendant might perform, three things to see in Brussels, two highways, and a tool one might carry in a car (**faire le plein, vérifier l'huile et les pneus; la Grand-Place, le palais, le musée de l'Armée; la N. 89, la E. 411; le cric**).

For Individual Needs

Visual/Auditory Learners
On the board or on a transparency, draw a gas pump, the Bouillon château fort, and a flat tire and number them from 1–3. Then, play excerpts of the recording and have students call out the number of the appropriate illustration.

Kinesthetic Learners   Have partners mime the action in one of the scenes for the class. The first person to call out the number of the scene in which the action takes place chooses a partner and mimes a different action.

Culture Note

The French often complain about the high price of gasoline, which usually costs about as much per liter in France as it does per gallon (about 4 liters) in the United States. For this reason, **gazole,** or diesel fuel, has become popular.

For Individual Needs

2 Tactile Learners Have students write these and additional sentences on strips of paper and arrange them in the correct order.

2 Kinesthetic Learners Have six students act out the sentences and have the class put them in order.

3 Auditory Learners Have students close their books. Write **Stéphane, Hervé, le pompiste,** and **le monsieur** on the board. Then, read the quotes aloud and have students match each one to the speaker.

Teaching Suggestions

3 Ask individuals to suggest additional quotes and have the class try to guess who the speakers were.

4 Have students support their answers with quotations from **En route pour Bruxelles.** Have them suggest other adjectives to describe Stéphane and Hervé.

For Individual Needs

5 Slower Pace Write the expressions from the **Mise en train** that serve these functions on a transparency and have students match them with the appropriate questions from this activity.

Teaching Suggestion

6 Have partners ask and answer these questions together. Students might then volunteer information about their partner. (**Suzanne est allée en Californie en voiture.**)

---

1 Tu as compris?

1. Where are Stéphane and Hervé going? Brussels
2. What do they plan to do there? visit the Comic Book Center
3. Where do they stop along the way? Why? service station, for gas, oil, and air for their tires; Bouillon, to ask directions
4. Who seems to be more impatient? Why? Hervé; He keeps telling Stéphane to hurry.
5. What happens at the end? flat tire

2 Mets en ordre

Mets ces phrases en ordre d'après **En route pour Bruxelles.** 6, 3, 2, 5, 1, 4

1. Ils ont un pneu crevé.
2. Stéphane veut visiter le château.
3. Le pompiste vérifie l'huile.
4. Stéphane va chercher la roue de secours.
5. Ils s'arrêtent pour demander la route.
6. Le pompiste fait le plein de super.

3 Qui dit quoi?

Hervé **Stéphane**   **Hervé**   Hervé **le pompiste**   Stéphane **le monsieur**

Grouille-toi! On va être en retard!

Le Centre ouvre à dix heures. On a largement le temps.

Moi, j'ai juste assez pour Bruxelles.

Ah ben, ça n'a pas l'air compliqué.

Vous allez voir un panneau qui indique l'entrée de l'autoroute.

Voilà. Ce sera tout?
Le pompiste

Stéphane

Tu es vraiment nul comme type!
Stéphane

L'huile, ça va. Ça fait 125 francs.
Le pompiste

Le monsieur

4 Comment sont-ils?

Comment est Stéphane? Et Hervé? Choisis les adjectifs qui les décrivent le mieux.

Stéphane   Stéphane   Hervé

impatient   sûr de lui   patient   embêtant
Hervé   calme   grippe-sou (stingy)   énervé   égoïste
Stéphane   Hervé   Hervé   Hervé

5 Cherche les expressions

What do the young people in **En route pour Bruxelles** say to . . . See answers below.

1. have the gas tank filled?
2. have the oil checked?
3. suggest places they should visit?
4. point out something?
5. express impatience?
6. ask for directions?
7. express annoyance?
8. reassure someone?

6 Et maintenant, à toi

Est-ce que tu as déjà fait un long voyage en voiture? Où est-ce que tu es allé(e)? Avec qui? Est-ce que vous vous êtes arrêté(e)s en route? Pourquoi?

32   *trente-deux*   CHAPITRE 2   Belgique, nous voilà!

Answers

5 1. Le plein de super, s'il vous plaît.
2. Vous pourriez vérifier l'huile, s'il vous plaît?
3. On pourrait aller à...
4. Tiens, tu as vu... ?
5. Oh, non, écoute! On n'a pas le temps! Je suis vraiment impatient d'arriver! Va plus vite, bon sang! Tu n'avances pas! Grouille-toi! On va être en retard!

6. La route pour... , s'il vous plaît?
7. Oh, tu pousses, quand même! C'est toujours la même chose. Tu es vraiment nul comme type.
8. On a largement le temps. Du calme, du calme! Il n'y a pas le feu. Oh, écoute. Ça ne va pas prendre longtemps.

PREMIERE ETAPE

Asking for and giving directions; expressing impatience; reassuring someone

COMMENT DIT-ON...?
Asking for and giving directions

To ask for directions:

La route pour Bruxelles, **s'il vous plaît?**

Comment on va à Namur?

To give directions:

Pour (aller à) Bruxelles, **vous suivez la** N. (Nationale) 89 **pendant à peu près** 35 **kilomètres.** *To get to . . . , follow . . . for about . . . kilometers.*

Vous allez voir un panneau qui indique l'entrée de l'autoroute. *You'll see a sign that points out the freeway entrance.*

Vous traversez un grand pont. *You cross . . .*

Après le pont, **vous allez tomber sur** un petit village. *After . . . , you'll come across . . .*

Cette route vous conduira au centre-ville. *This road will lead you into the center of town.*

Vous continuez tout droit, jusqu'au carrefour. *You keep going straight ahead, up to the intersection.*

7 Ecoute!

Ecoute cette conversation. Est-ce que cette jeune fille va à Spa, Malmédy ou Verviers? Malmédy

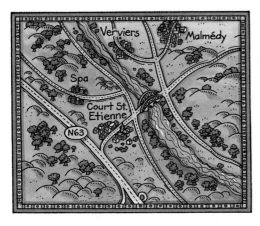

> ## NOTE CULTURELLE
>
> Belgium has two official languages, French and Dutch. Flemish, a dialect of Dutch, is spoken in **la Flandre,** the northern half of the country, and French is spoken in **la Wallonie,** the southern half. This division has always been a source of friction between the two language groups. It led to constitutional revisions in 1971 that created the present linguistic regions and made Brussels, the capital, officially bilingual. Travelers to Belgium will notice that maps include both Dutch and French names for many cities, for example **Antwerpen/Anvers** and **Brugge/Bruges.**

RESOURCES FOR PREMIERE ETAPE

Chapter Teaching Resources, Book 1
- Communicative Activity 2-1, pp. 58–59
- Teaching Transparency Master 2-1, pp. 62, 64
  Teaching Transparency 2-1
- Additional Listening Activities 2-1, 2-2, 2-3, pp. 65–66
  Audiocassette 9A/Audio CD 2
- Realia 2-1, pp. 69, 71
- Situation Cards 2-1, pp. 72–73
- Student Response Forms, pp. 74–76
- Quiz 2-1, pp. 77–78
  Audiocassette 1B/Audio CD 2

ADDITIONAL RESOURCES
Textbook Audiocassette 1B
  OR *Audio CD 2*
Practice and Activity Book, pp. 14–17

Jump Start!

Have students use the following direction words they've already learned to tell where a classmate is seated in relation to their own seat: **à droite, à gauche, près de, loin de, devant, derrière. (Il est derrière moi, à gauche.)** You might have volunteers read their descriptions aloud and have the class guess whose location is being described.

MOTIVATE

Ask students to give detailed directions in English from the school to their house or to a grocery store or movie theater. Then, have them list French expressions they've already learned for giving directions.

TEACH

Presentation

Comment dit-on... ? Draw a city map on a transparency. Bring in a toy car and move it along the map as you say the various directions. Then, have a volunteer come to the overhead and move the car as you give directions. Next, move the car yourself as students give the appropriate directions.

For Individual Needs

7 Challenge Have students give directions to Spa, Verviers, and Court St.-Etienne.

Multicultural Link

Note Culturelle Have students name bilingual countries, regions, or states (Morocco, Florida), and then find out what each culture has contributed to the community.

 TPR

To review prepositions of location, direct students to stand or sit in various places in the classroom (**Phil, mets-toi derrière Simone. Lisa, assieds-toi à côté de moi**) and have them respond appropriately.

For Individual Needs

8 Slower Pace/Tactile Learners Have students identify the sentences spoken by the girl asking for directions and those spoken by the woman giving them. Then, have them copy the girl's lines onto strips of paper of one color and the woman's lines onto strips of a different color and put the dialogue in order.

8 Visual Learners After doing the activity, have students sketch a map according to the directions in the dialogue. Have a volunteer draw his or her map on a transparency. Then, have the class compare their maps to the one projected and suggest any corrections.

Teaching Suggestion

10 Have students write directions to another city shown on the map. Then, collect the papers and redistribute them. Students should follow the directions on the paper they receive, and then write where they lead at the bottom. Return the papers to the original writers, who verify the answer.

Portfolio

10 Oral This activity is appropriate for students' oral portfolios. For portfolio information, see *Assessment Guide*, pages 2–13.

---

8 Méli-mélo!

Mets dans l'ordre ce dialogue entre Adrienne et Mme Zidan. Ensuite, joue la scène avec ton/ta camarade.

11 «Merci, madame.»

5 «Oui, jusqu'au feu rouge, et...»

3 «Est-ce que vous pourriez me dire où se trouve la N. 44?»

7 «Et puis?»

1 «Pardon, madame.»

9 «Et c'est là, à environ 10 kilomètres?»

12 «Je vous en prie.»

8 «Et puis, vous continuez pendant à peu près 10 kilomètres.»

4 «Bien sûr. Vous suivez cette route jusqu'au feu rouge.»

2 «Oui?»

6 «Au feu rouge, vous tournez à droite.»

10 «Oui, vous allez tomber sur une vieille église. Juste après l'église, vous allez voir le panneau.»

9 La route pour Liège, s'il vous plaît?

Tu voyages en Belgique près de Salmchâteau. Tu t'arrêtes à une station-service pour demander la route pour Liège. Joue cette scène avec ton/ta camarade.

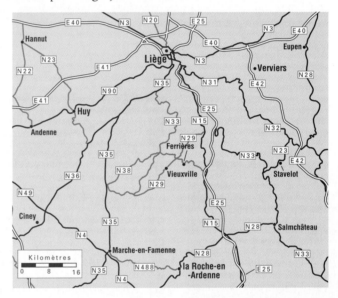

10 Devine!

Regarde la carte et choisis une ville. Explique à ton/ta camarade comment y arriver de Liège. Il/Elle doit deviner de quelle ville tu parles. Ensuite, changez de rôles.

34 *trente-quatre*   CHAPITRE 2   Belgique, nous voilà!

Culture Notes

• The highest legal speed limit in Belgium is 120 kilometers per hour. You might have students convert this into miles per hour (1 km = .62 miles, so 120 km equals about 75 miles).

• Liège is the cultural capital of Wallonia. Its diverse cultural events and numerous museums, including museums of Walloon life and art, have earned the city the nickname **l'Athènes du Nord**. Liège is famous for its crystal and special puppets (**marionnettes liégeoises**).

Vocabulaire

On peut bien s'arrêter à une station-service pour demander la route, non?

faire le plein	to fill it up
vérifier ...	to check ...
l'huile (f.)	the oil
la pression des pneus	the tire pressure
les freins (m.)	the brakes
mettre de l'air dans les pneus	to put air in the tires
mettre de l'huile dans le moteur	to put oil in the motor
faire la vidange	to change the oil
nettoyer le pare-brise	to clean the windshield
tomber en panne (d'essence)	to break down (run out of gas)
avoir un pneu crevé	to have a flat tire

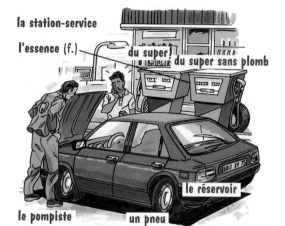

la station-service

l'essence (f.)

du super?

du super sans plomb

le réservoir

le pompiste

un pneu

11 Ecoute!

Est-ce que c'est le pompiste ou le chauffeur qui parle? Answers on p. 27C.

12 Qu'est-ce qui se passe?

Qu'est-ce qui se passe sur ces images?

1. Il vérifie l'huile.

2. Elle a un pneu crevé.

3. La pompiste nettoie le pare-brise.

4. Il est tombé en panne.

Grammaire The verb conduire

Conduire is an irregular verb. Here are the present tense forms.

conduire *(to drive)*

Je **conduis**	Nous **conduisons**
Tu **conduis** une Peugeot®.	Vous **conduisez** une Citroën®.
Il/Elle/On **conduit**	Ils/Elles **conduisent**

• The past participle of **conduire** is **conduit**: Il **a conduit** trop vite.

PREMIERE ETAPE

trente-cinq 35

Culture Note

Peugeot® and Citroën® are makes of French cars. Most French cars are smaller and more economical than American cars because of narrow streets, limited parking in cities, and the high price of gasoline.

Language Notes

• **Une** is used with brand names to refer to all car brand names (**une Peugeot**) because **voiture** is feminine.
• When discussing driving at a certain speed, the verb **rouler** is used. (**On roule à 60 kilomètres à l'heure.**)

Presentation

Vocabulaire Mime the new activities as you say them. Then, give students commands (**Vérifiez l'huile! Nettoyez le pare-brise!**) and have them respond by miming the actions. You might also call on individuals to mime an action and have the others try to identify the action.

For Individual Needs

11 Slower Pace Before they listen to the recording, have students give examples of what a gas station attendant and a customer might say.

Presentation

Grammaire Bring in photos of different makes of cars from magazines and hold them up as you introduce the verb forms. (**Je conduis une (Peugeot). Elle conduit une...**) Then, give the pictures to various students and ask the class **Qu'est-ce qu'il/ elle conduit?** Ask questions to pairs or groups of students to practice the plural forms. Next, point to two boys or two girls together and ask **Qu'est-ce qu'ils/elles conduisent?** Then, ask them **Qu'est-ce que vous conduisez?** to elicit **Nous conduisons...** Finally, ask students if they know how to drive (**Tu sais conduire?**) and if they drive well or badly (**Tu conduis bien ou mal?**)

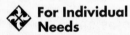
13 En voiture

Est-ce que ces chauffeurs conduisent bien ou mal?

1. Il conduit mal. 2. Elles conduisent bien. 3. On conduit mal. 4. Ils conduisent mal.

14 Le code de la route

Pendant ton voyage en Belgique, tu tombes sur les panneaux suivants. Quelle est la phrase qui correspond à chacun de ces panneaux?

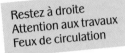

Restez à droite
Attention aux travaux
Feux de circulation

Vitesse limitée
Défense de tourner
à gauche

1. Défense de tourner à gauche 2. Attention aux travaux 3. Restez à droite 4. Vitesse limitée 5. Feux de circulation

15 Viens chez moi!

 Ton ami(e) habite chez une famille belge à Stavelot. Ecris une lettre et invite-les à passer un week-end chez toi à Hannut. N'oublie pas de leur donner les indications nécessaires pour y venir en voiture. Consulte la carte à la page 34.

Si tu as oublié extending invitations va à la page 320.

16 Pour arriver chez nous...

 Un(e) ami(e) de ta famille vous téléphone pour annoncer sa visite. Il/Elle ne connaît pas très bien la route. Donne-lui les indications nécessaires pour arriver chez vous. Joue cette scène avec ton/ta camarade.

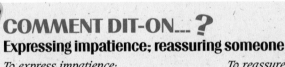

COMMENT DIT-ON... ?
Expressing impatience; reassuring someone

To express impatience:
Mais qu'est-ce que tu fais?
Tu peux te dépêcher? *Can you hurry up?*
Grouille-toi! *Get a move on!*
On n'a pas le temps!
Je suis vraiment impatient(e) d'arriver!

To reassure someone:
Ça ne va pas prendre longtemps!
Sois patient(e)! *Be patient!*
On a largement le temps! *We've got plenty of time!*
Il n'y a pas le feu. *Where's the fire?*
Du calme, du calme.

36   *trente-six*   CHAPITRE 2   Belgique, nous voilà!

17 Ecoute!

Est-ce que ces personnes sont impatientes ou plutôt calmes? *Answers on p. 27C.*

18 Qu'est-ce qu'ils sont énervés!

Rassure ces gens. *Possible answers:*

1. Sois patiente!

ZUT, ALORS!... LE MUSÉE VA ÊTRE FERMÉ!

2. Du calme, du calme.

AH, NON!... QU'EST-CE QUE JE VAIS FAIRE MAINTENANT?

3. Il n'y a pas le feu.

JE SUIS VRAIMENT IMPATIENT D'ARRIVER!

4. On a largement le temps!

MAIS ON N'A PAS LE TEMPS!... ILS ARRIVENT À HUIT HEURES!

BOUTIQUE

Tu te rappelles ?

Do you remember how to give commands and make suggestions? You use the **tu** and **vous** forms of the verb for commands and the **nous** form for suggestions. When you write the **tu** form of an **-er** verb as a command, you drop the **s**.

> **Regarde!**
> **Faites** le plein!
> **Allons** à Bruxelles!

Remember to place reflexive or object pronouns after a positive command or suggestion. You place a hyphen between the verb and pronoun when writing.

> **Grouille-toi!**
> **Dépêchons-nous!**

Don't forget to place the pronouns before the verb in negative commands and suggestions, though.

> Ne **vous** inquiétez pas!

Almost all verbs follow this pattern. The verb **être** has irregular command forms.

> **Sois** gentil!
> **Soyez** patients!
> **Soyons** à l'heure!

À la française

Sometimes French speakers communicate their ideas with gestures instead of words. Look at the pictures to the left. Can you find a gesture you might use to tell someone to hurry up?

19 Pas encore prêt(e)?!

Tu es venu(e) chercher ton ami(e) pour aller à un concert. Il/Elle n'est pas encore prêt(e) et veut faire les choses suivantes. Qu'est-ce que tu lui dis? Joue cette scène avec ton/ta camarade.

changer de chaussures

mettre un pull

trouver son appareil-photo

aller aux W.-C.

téléphoner à un(e) ami(e)

chercher les billets

boire quelque chose

20 On est en retard!

Vous êtes enfin parti(e)s pour le concert. Tu ne sais pas comment y arriver, donc tu demandes des indications à ton ami(e). En route, vous tombez en panne d'essence. Comme vous êtes déjà en retard, tu es très impatient(e)! Ton ami(e) va te rassurer et proposer une solution.

PREMIERE ETAPE
trente-sept 37

For Individual Needs

17 Challenge Play the recording a second time and have students describe the situations.

Game

JACQUES A DIT Divide the class into small groups. On slips of paper, write various activities, using infinitives, and put them into several bags. Give a bag to one member of each group, who will be the leader. The leader draws a slip (**regarder à droite**) and tells his or her group to do the activity. (**Regardez à droite!**) If the leader says **Jacques a dit** before the command, the members of the group should perform that activity. If not, the players should remain still. If a player moves when the leader did not say **Jacques a dit,** he or she is out, but remains involved by acting as judge.

For Individual Needs

18 Challenge After students complete the activity, act out one of the scenes shown (**Zut alors! Le musée va être fermé!**), and then point to a student. That student stands and reads aloud the response he or she wrote to reassure that person. (**Sois patient!**) Then, that student chooses a different scene, plays the role of the impatient person, and calls on another student to respond.

Portfolio

20 Oral Students might perform this activity for the class. They might vary the kind of car trouble they have or add other problems. This item is appropriate for students' oral portfolios. For portfolio information, see *Assessment Guide,* pages 2–13.

CLOSE

To close this **étape,** play the game "Sentence Scrambler" described on page 27F.

ASSESS

Quiz 2-1, *Chapter Teaching Resources, Book 1,* pp. 77–78

*Assessment Items, Audiocassette 7A
Audio CD 2*

Performance Assessment

On a transparency, draw a map that includes several different highways, a bridge, several cities or towns, and some intersections. Label the towns and highways, using Belgian designations (see Culture Note on page 31). Then, play the role of a lost motorist and ask students how to get to various cities from a specified point.

Summary

In **Au Centre de la BD**, Stéphane and Hervé ask for information on where to begin their tour, and then take the center's Art Nouveau staircase to a gallery where they see Tintin's rocket. Later, at the **bédéthèque**, Hervé reads *Le Sceptre d'Ottokar*, while Stéphane reads his first **Schtroumpfs®** *(Smurfs)* comic book.

Motivating Activity

Ask students if they read comic books or the comics in the newspaper, and if they have a favorite.

Presentation

Have students look at the illustrations and tell all they can about the comic-book center. Have them look at the book covers and tell which one(s) they might like to read. Then, play the recording. After the first scene, ask **Comment est le Centre de la BD? Qu'est-ce que les garçons voient là-bas?** Next, play the second scene. Read aloud the titles of the comic books mentioned and have students tell whether Stéphane or Hervé liked them.

Culture Note

Victor Horta was an outstanding architect of the Art Nouveau style in Belgium. His organic, curvilinear forms adorn several of Brussels' public buildings. The building in which the **Centre de la Bande Dessinée** is housed, the former Wauquez department store (1905), was designed by Horta in his later, simplified style.

Remise en train

Au Centre de la BD

CENTRE BELGE DE
LA BANDE DESSINEE

ouvert tous les jours (sauf lundi) de 10 à 18 heures
20 rue des Sables - B- 1000 Bruxelles
Tél.: 02/219.19.80
Fax : 02/219.23.76

BELGISCH CENTRUM
VAN HET BEELDVERHAAL

open alle dagen behalve op maandag
van 10 tot 18 uur.
Zandstraat 20 - B.1000 Brussel
Tel.: 02/219.19.80
Fax : 02/219.23.76

A l'accueil...

STEPHANE Tu as vu ça? C'est grandiose ici. Je n'imaginais pas ça comme ça. Regarde un peu cet escalier.

HERVE «1905. Art nouveau. Architecte Horta. C'est un ancien magasin qui... »

STEPHANE Arrête, ça suffit. Une vraie encyclopédie, ce garçon. Tu as les billets? Tu viens?

HERVE Attends, je voudrais demander quelque chose. Pardon, mademoiselle, on n'est jamais venus ici. On commence par où?

HOTESSE Vous pouvez commencer où vous voulez, mais surtout ne manquez pas la bédéthèque. C'est là, juste en face.

HERVE Merci, mademoiselle.

STEPHANE Alors, on monte?

21 Tu as compris?   See answers below.

1. Where are Hervé and Stéphane? What kind of place is it?
2. What is Hervé's favorite comic book series?
3. What does Stéphane decide to read? Does he like it?
4. What is the **bédéthèque**? Can you guess how the word was formed?*

22 Trouve....   Possible answers:

1. le nom d'un album de BD. *On a marché sur la lune, Le Sceptre d'Ottokar*
2. le nom d'un personnage de BD. *Tintin*
3. le nom d'un architecte. *Horta*

23 Vrai ou faux?

1. Stéphane a déjà visité le Centre de la BD.   faux
2. La bédéthèque est au premier étage.   faux
3. Hervé a lu tous les Tintin.   faux
4. D'habitude, Stéphane lit de la science-fiction.   vrai
5. *Le Sceptre d'Ottokar* est un album de Tintin.   vrai
6. Le Centre est fermé le lundi.   vrai
7. Le Centre est ouvert jusqu'à huit heures du soir.   faux

* **Bandes dessinées** are often referred to as **BD** (pronounced **bédé**). The word **bédéthèque** is formed from the abbreviation **bédé** and the ending -**thèque**, as in **bibliothèque**.

RESOURCES FOR REMISE EN TRAIN

Textbook Audiocassette 1B/Audio CD 2
Practice and Activity Book, p. 18

Answers

21 1. Comic Book Center; a renovated store in the Art Nouveau style, built in 1905 and later transformed into a museum for comic books
2. Tintin
3. **les Schtroumpfs** *(the Smurfs);* Yes
4. a comic book library; **Bédéthèque** is formed from **bédé** *(BD, bandes dessinées)* and -**thèque** (as in **bibliothèque**).

STEPHANE Eh, regarde. C'est la fusée de Tintin dans *On a marché sur la lune.* Tu l'as lu?

HERVE Bien sûr. J'ai lu tous les Tintin, sauf *Le Sceptre d'Ottokar.*

A la bédéthèque...

STEPHANE Regarde toutes ces bandes dessinées! Je pourrais passer toute la journée ici.

HERVE Moi, je vais chercher le Tintin que je n'ai pas encore lu. Et toi, qu'est-ce que tu vas lire?

STEPHANE Je ne sais pas. Tu as une idée?

HERVE Tiens, regarde! On est juste devant toute la série des Schtroumpfs, les petits hommes bleus. Tu en as déjà lu?

STEPHANE Non, jamais.

HERVE Tu devrais. C'est rigolo comme tout.

STEPHANE Bon, donne. Ça me changera de la science-fiction.

Plus tard...

STEPHANE Alors, ça t'a plu, ton *Sceptre d'Ottokar*?

HERVE Oui, c'était drôle et plein d'action. Et toi, les Schtroumpfs, qu'est-ce que tu en penses?

STEPHANE J'ai «schtroumpfé» que c'était bien!

---

24 Mets en ordre

Mets les activités de Stéphane et d'Hervé en ordre d'après **Au Centre de la BD.** 5, 6, 3, 2, 1, 4

1. Hervé cherche le Tintin qu'il n'a pas encore lu.
2. Ils voient la fusée de Tintin.
3. Ils montent au premier étage.
4. Hervé conseille à Stéphane de lire les Schtroumpfs.
5. Ils se trouvent à l'accueil.
6. Hervé demande à l'hôtesse par où commencer la visite.

25 Cherche les expressions

What do the people in **Au Centre de la BD** say to . . . See answers below.

1. point out something?
2. tell where something is?
3. give advice?
4. ask an opinion?
5. express enthusiasm?

26 Et maintenant, à toi

Quel est ton personnage de bande dessinée préféré? Pourquoi?

Answers

25 1. Tu as vu ça? Regarde un peu... Tiens, regarde!
2. C'est là, juste en face.
3. Tu devrais...
4. ... ça t'a plu,... ? Qu'est-ce que tu en penses?
5. Je pourrais passer toute la journée ici. C'est rigolo comme tout. ... c'était drôle et plein d'action. ... que c'était bien!

Culture Note

The first **Tintin** comic book, *Tintin au pays de Soviets,* appeared in 1930. **Tintin** is currently published in over forty languages. Several of the books have even been made into full-length cartoon films, such as *Le mystère de la toison d'or* and *Le temple du soleil.*

Thinking Critically

Drawing Inferences Have students look at the covers of the comic books shown on pages 38 and 39 and try to guess what the main characters are like. Have them make a list of adjectives in French and/or English to describe them.

For Individual Needs

Tactile Learners Bring in comics from the Sunday paper and cut out the speech bubbles. Have students write new speech bubbles for the comics and glue or tape them on.

24 Challenge After students complete this activity, have them summarize **Au Centre de la BD**, using the sequencing expressions **d'abord, ensuite, après ça,** and **enfin.**

Teacher Note

Stéphane says **J'ai "schtroumpfé" que c'était bien!**, imitating the language of the Smurfs, who often substitute a form of the word **schtroumpf** for various parts of speech. You might have your students guess what Stéphane meant (**J'ai trouvé**). Students might enjoy **"schtroumpfing"** their own sentences. You might have them read their sentences aloud and have their classmates try to guess the original word.

Teaching Suggestion

26 Poll the class to find the most popular comic-strip characters. You might also ask what students would put in a comic-book museum.

VIDEO PROGRAM
Videocassette 1

Teacher Notes

- See *Video Guide* and *Practice and Activity Book* for activities related to the **Panorama Culturel**.
- Remind students that cultural material may be included in the Chapter Quizzes and Test.
- The interviewees' language represents informal, unrehearsed speech. Occasionally, edits have been made for clarification.

Motivating Activity

Ask students to describe their favorite comic book or cartoon characters and tell why they like them.

Presentation

On the board, write the names of the comic-book characters and adjectives describing them from the interviews in two columns. Play the video and have students match the characters with their descriptions. Then, ask students the **Questions** below. Have pairs or groups of students read the interviews together.

Culture Notes

- The *Astérix* series is about one small Gallic village's struggle to resist conquest by the Romans.
- **Tintin** is an adventurous young reporter who travels around the world with **Capitaine Haddock** and **Professeur Tournesol** (*Professor Sunflower*).
- **Iznogoude** is a scheming advisor (**vizir**) to the **calife**, the Arab ruler.

PANORAMA CULTUREL

Olivier • Martinique

Onélia • France

Bosco • Côte d'Ivoire

We asked some French-speaking people about their favorite comic book characters. Here's what they had to say.

Qui est ton personnage de bande dessinée préféré? Il est comment?

«En général, *Les Aventures de Tintin* sont les bandes dessinées que je lis et que je préfère. Tintin, pour moi, c'est un bon moyen de se distraire, qui trouve des énigmes de façon très loufoque, très drôle. Tintin, [il est] un peu maigrichon, vraiment, par rapport à moi, intelligent et très futé.»

-Olivier

«Mon personnage de bande dessinée préféré, c'est Iznogoud. Le titre de la bande dessinée, c'est *Le Calife qui voulait devenir*. Il est assez méchant, mais très drôle. Il y a beaucoup d'humour dans cette bande dessinée. Et je trouve ça très drôle, même si c'est un peu cynique comme histoire. J'aime beaucoup.»

-Onélia

«Moi, j'adore énormément les bandes dessinées. Mon personnage préféré de bande dessinée est Donald. C'est un canard. Il est toujours dans les bandes dessinées de Walt Disney. Ce qui me plaît beaucoup dans ce personnage-là, c'est que... c'est toujours à lui qu'arrivent les malheurs par rapport à Gontran, et oncle Picsou qui est très avare. J'adore beaucoup celui-là parce que vraiment il est très strict et puis il se met beaucoup en colère et puis, enfin, il est très rigolo, quoi.»

-Bosco

Qu'en penses-tu?

1. Which of the comic book characters mentioned have you heard of?
2. Which French comic books would you most like to read? Why?

Language Notes

- Students may want to know the following words from the interviews: **loufoque** (*wild, crazy*); **maigrichon** (*scrawny*); **futé** (*cunning*); **avare** (*miserly*); **en colère** (*angry*).
- You might have students say **"Iznogoude"** aloud and suggest an English phrase that it sounds like (*Is no good*). From this pun, have students imagine what Iznogoude's character is like.

Questions

1. **Quelle bande dessinée est-ce qu'Olivier préfère?** (Tintin)
2. **Comment est Tintin, d'après Olivier?** (un peu maigrichon, intelligent et très futé)
3. **Comment est *Le Calife qui voulait devenir*, d'après Onélia?** (très drôle, un peu cynique)
4. **Comment est oncle Picsou?** (très avare, très rigolo)

DEUXIEME ETAPE

Expressing enthusiasm and boredom; asking and telling where things are

VOCABULAIRE

rigolo(te)	*funny, hysterical*	rasant(e)	*boring*	
fou (folle)	*crazy, funny*	mortel(le)	*deadly boring*	
dingue	*wild, crazy, funny*	de mauvais goût	*in poor taste*	
marrant(e)	*funny*	bébé	*childish, stupid*	

VOUS ÊTES TOUS DES DINGUES!!!

27 Elles sont comment? *Possible answers:*

Quels mots du **Vocabulaire** décrivent ces bandes dessinées? Quels autres mots est-ce que tu peux utiliser pour décrire ces personnages?

À la française

Look at these gestures that French speakers commonly use to express enthusiasm or boredom. Can you tell which is which?

1. marrante; Calvin est amusant. Hobbes est mignon.

2. rigolote; Snoopy est génial.

3. rasante; Garfield est gros.

COMMENT DIT-ON... ?

Expressing enthusiasm and boredom

To express enthusiasm:

Qu'est-ce que c'est rigolo! *That is so . . . !*

Ce que c'est bien! *Isn't it great!*

C'est marrant **comme tout!** *It's as . . . as anything!*

Ça me branche! *I'm crazy about that!*

To express boredom:

C'est mortel!

Ça me casse les pieds! *That's so boring!*

Ça m'embête! *That bores me!*

Ça m'ennuie à mourir! *That bores me to death!*

28 Ecoute!

Stéphane et Hervé visitent la bédéthèque. Est-ce qu'ils s'amusent ou s'ennuient? *Answers on p. 27D.*

Jump Start!

Have students give directions to a nearby city.

MOTIVATE

Have students list expressions they already know for giving opinions of books or movies (**C'est drôle/bête/un navet/du n'importe quoi.**)

TEACH

Presentation

Vocabulaire Say each expression, using appropriate facial expressions and intonation. Then, list movies and ask either-or questions about them. (**C'est rigolo ou rasant?**) Have students complete sentences such as **C'est marrant,...** with book or movie titles.

Comment dit-on... ? Hold up two comic books and express enthusiasm for one and boredom for the other. Then, write each expression on a large card and give the cards to eight students. Write *Expressing enthusiasm* and *Expressing boredom* at opposite ends of the board. As each of the eight students says the expression on his or her card, have the class tell under which category he or she should stand. Then, have students list books and movies they find boring or really interesting. Read from their lists and ask questions about them. (**... , ça te branche ou ça t'embête?**)

Language Notes

• **Ça me casse les pieds!** and **Ça m'embête** can be used to express annoyance as well as boredom.

• Students might want to use the verb **rigoler** *(to joke, to have fun)* or the expression **être plié(e)** *(to "crack up")*.

RESOURCES FOR DEUXIEME ETAPE

Chapter Teaching Resources, Book 1

- Communicative Activity 2-2, pp. 60–61
- Teaching Transparency Master 2-2, pp. 63, 64
  Teaching Transparency 2-2
- Additional Listening Activities 2-4, 2-5, 2-6, pp. 66–67
  Audiocassette 9A/Audio CD 2
- Realia 2-2, pp. 70, 71
- Situation Cards 2-2, 2-3, pp. 72–73
- Student Response Forms, pp. 74–76
- Quiz 2-2, pp. 79–80
  Audiocassette 7A/Audio CD 2

ADDITIONAL RESOURCES

Textbook Audiocassette 1B
  OR *Audio CD 2*

Practice and Activity Book, pp. 19–22

Video Program, Videocassette 1
Video Guide

 **For Individual Needs**

29 Challenge Have students give reasons for their opinions. (**Les maths? C'est mortel! C'est trop difficile. Je n'aime pas ça parce qu'il faut toujours étudier.**)

Reteaching

Object pronouns Write sentences such as **Je regarde la télévision** and **Elle parle à Jean** on a transparency, using a red pen for **la télévision** and **à Jean**. Then, cut the subjects, verbs, and objects into strips. Ask students which words can be replaced with a pronoun (**la télévision, à Jean**). Remove those strips and replace them with new strips on which the appropriate object pronouns (**la, lui**) are written in red and rearrange the strips to form the new sentences **Je la regarde** and **Elle lui parle**. Have groups create their own sentences and exchange them with another group, who will rewrite the sentences, using object pronouns.

Additional Practice

Tu te rappelles? You might use vocabulary flashcards to review verbs that take different objects, such as **expliquer (à quelqu'un)**, **écouter, chercher**, and **téléphoner (à quelqu'un)**.

Building on Previous Skills

30 You might have students describe the comic if their partner isn't familiar with it. (**De quoi ça parle? Ça parle de...**)

---

29 Qu'est-ce que tu en penses?

Qu'est-ce que ton/ta camarade pense de ces choses?

—Euh, les maths? Qu'est-ce que tu en penses?
—Oh, c'est rasant, les maths.

les devoirs   les livres
les profs   les films
les examens   la télé
les BD   les musées

Tu te rappelles ?

Do you remember the direct and indirect object pronouns?

me	*me, to me*	**la**	*her, it*	**vous**	*you, to you*
te	*you, to you*	**les**	*them*	**lui**	*to him, to her*
le	*him, it*	**nous**	*us, to us*	**leur**	*to them*

Remember to place these pronouns before the conjugated verb.

Je **la** regarde.   Elle **lui** parle.   Ils **m'**attendaient.   Je **leur** ai donné de l'argent.

In positive commands and suggestions, put the pronoun after the verb.

Téléphone-**leur**!   Cherchons-**la**!

If an infinitive follows the verb, place the pronoun before the infinitive.

Il ne veut pas **le** lire.

Remember, not all French verbs take the same object as English verbs. If you're unsure about which verbs take a direct and an indirect object, study the list on page 351.

30 Tu les connais?

Est-ce que tu connais ces personnages de bande dessinée?

—Tu le connais?
—Oui, je le connais.   *ou*   —Non, je ne le connais pas.
C'est Tintin. Je le trouve...

1.

2.

3.

4.

31 Qu'est-ce que c'est?

Pense à une phrase. Remplace le nom par un pronom. Ton/ta camarade va deviner de quoi tu parles suivant le contexte.

—Je vais **la** lire.
—C'est une bande dessinée?
—Oui.

regarder	laver	écouter
conduire	apporter	faire
mettre	oublier	étudier

32 Mon journal

Quelles sont les bandes dessinées américaines que tu as lues? Lesquelles préfères-tu? Lesquelles est-ce que tu n'aimes pas? Décris tes personnages préférés.

 **For Individual Needs**

31 Slower Pace Before students do the activity, have them make sentences, using the verbs given here. (**Je regarde la télé.**) Write the sentences on the board or on a transparency. Then, call on individual students to replace a direct or indirect object in each sentence with a pronoun. (**Je la regarde.**)

Mon journal

32 For an additional journal entry suggestion for Chapter 2, see *Practice and Activity Book*, page 146.

COMMENT DIT-ON... ?

Asking and telling where things are

To ask where something is:

Vous pourriez me dire où il y a un téléphone?

Pardon, vous savez où se trouve l'ascenseur?

Tu sais où sont les toilettes?

To tell where something is:

Par là, au bout du couloir. *Over there, at the end of the hallway.*

Juste là, à côté de l'escalier. *Right there, next to . . .*

En bas. *Downstairs.*

En haut. *Upstairs.*

Au fond. *Towards the back.*

Au rez-de-chaussée. *On the ground floor.*

Au premier étage. *On the second floor.*

En face du guichet. *Across from . . .*

A l'entrée de la bédéthèque. *At the entrance to . . .*

33 Ecoute!

Ecoute ces personnes qui demandent des renseignements à l'accueil du Centre de la BD. Regarde le plan du Centre et choisis la lettre qui correspond à leur destination.

1. d   2. b   3. e   4. c   5. a   6. f

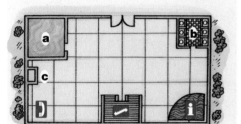
Rez-de-chaussée

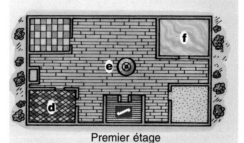
Premier étage

34 Pardon, vous savez où....

En visitant le Centre Belge de la Bande Dessinée, tu rencontres des gens qui cherchent les téléphones, la boutique de souvenirs et les escaliers. Dis-leur où ils se trouvent. Joue cette scène avec ton/ta camarade.

35 Dis-moi où se trouve....

Ton ami(e) belge passe sa première journée dans ton école. Il/Elle te demande où se trouvent les endroits suivants. Tu lui réponds. Joue cette scène avec ton/ta camarade.

la cantine   la salle d'informatique

le gymnase   les toilettes

l'auditorium   la bibliothèque

le laboratoire de chimie

Presentation

Comment dit-on... ? Draw the floor plan of your school on butcher paper and tape it to the board. Ask questions such as **Vous pourriez me dire où est la cantine?** and answer them yourself, pointing to the floor plan. Then, ask students where things are, such as **Où est la cantine, en haut ou en bas?** Point to the floor plan as you give the choices. You might also ask yes-no questions, such as **Les toilettes sont au fond du couloir?**

Teaching Suggestion

Stack two boxes with the open end facing students. Position a stuffed animal in a box and ask questions, such as **M. Flouflou est en haut ou en bas? Il est au fond ou à l'entrée?** Then, have a student position the animal and ask the class to describe its location. (**Où est M. Flouflou?**)

(TPR) Using the boxes and stuffed animal described above, give individual students commands (**Mets M. Flouflou en haut!**) and have them move the animal in response.

Group Work

Have groups draw a plan of their ideal school on butcher paper. Have them place a stuffed animal or other object on the plan and then give directions to the other group members, who move the animal accordingly.

For Individual Needs

33 Slower Pace Before playing the recording, describe the floor plans in detail in French.

Additional Practice

34 Students might also ask their partner about the **fusée de Tintin**, the staircase, and the information desk.

35 You might have students list other places, such as their locker (**mon casier**), the water fountain (**la fontaine d'eau potable**), or the parking lot (**le parking**).

35 Have students write out their directions. Then, have them read them aloud as the class tries to guess the destinations.

35 Have students draw a floor plan of an imaginary school, and then describe it to a partner. The partner should try to draw the plan, according to the description.

Motivating Activity

Form small groups. Give groups two minutes to brainstorm and write down words or expressions for the following categories: *Information an encyclopedia might list about Belgium* and *What I'd like to find out about Belgium* (population, size, history; famous actors/actresses, typical foods). When two minutes have elapsed, collect the papers, award one point for each appropriate item, and announce the winning group. You might have a group member read their list for the class.

Presentation

Have students look at the photos and answer the questions in **Qu'en penses-tu?** You might also have students draw other inferences about Belgium from the photos. Then, ask them the following questions: **Quelles langues est-ce qu'on parle en Belgique? Qu'est-ce qu'on peut faire en Belgique? Quelles sont les villes principales de la Belgique?**

For Individual Needs

Visual Learners Hold up some items that are produced in Belgium and others that are not (lace, chocolate, potato, endives, cheese) and have students tell which items are distinctly Belgian.

Challenge Have students find out more information about Belgium. Ask them to choose either a time period, a town, or a cultural or political topic. This could be used as a chapter project.

RENCONTRE CULTURELLE

Qu'est-ce que tu sais sur la Belgique? Pour t'en faire une meilleure idée, regarde ces photos.

Quelques produits de Belgique : le chocolat, la dentelle et l'endive

La ville de Bruges

Les deux langues officielles de la Belgique

Le quartier financier à Bruxelles

Les pêcheurs de la mer du Nord

La ville de Liège

Qu'en penses-tu?

1. What impression do these photos give you of Belgium?
2. How do you think the location of Belgium influences its people and their lifestyles?

Possible answers: Due to its central location, Belgium is influenced by the political and economic fluctuations of its neighboring countries. Its proximity to France and the Netherlands has resulted in two language groups (French and Dutch).

Savais-tu que... ?

Belgium is one of the smallest and most densely populated European countries. Its name comes from the Belgae tribes who settled the area in the second century B.C. Bordered by France, Luxembourg, Germany, and the Netherlands, the country's central location has been a source of both prosperity and hardship, for throughout its history it has served as a battleground for other countries. Today, Belgium has one of the most highly developed economies in the world, and Belgians enjoy a high standard of living. Popular sports include bicycle racing and soccer, and many Belgians enjoy fishing, pigeon racing, and camping in the Ardennes forest in the southeastern part of the country. The country is famous for its chocolates, **gaufres** (thick waffles eaten with whipped cream or other toppings), and **frites,** which are sold at sidewalk stands and eaten with a variety of sauces such as mustard, mayonnaise, and vinegar. Belgian lace, or **dentelle,** has been renowned for its quality since the Middle Ages and is still made by hand in Bruges and Brussels.

History Link

Belgium, which was originally part of the Netherlands, gained independence after revolting against Dutch rule in 1830. Prince Leopold of Saxe-Coburg was elected king of the new country and was known thereafter as Leopold I. After a period of much social unrest and tensions over linguistic differences, in 1930 the Belgian parliament finally divided the country into two separate administrative areas, the French-speaking south and the Dutch- and Flemish-speaking north.

Geography Link

Have students locate Liège, Brussels, Bruges, and the North Sea on a map of Belgium. You might also have them identify the French-speaking and the Flemish-speaking regions.

36 Qu'elle est belle, la ville de Bruxelles!

Tu fais la visite de Bruxelles avec ton ami(e). Regarde les activités sur les photos suivantes et sur le plan en bas de la page. Dis ce que tu veux faire. Ton ami(e) va accepter ou refuser et dire s'il/si elle trouve ces activités amusantes ou ennuyeuses.

Si on allait... ?

Si tu as oublié the forms of the imperfect *va à la page 348.*

Tu te rappelles?

Do you remember how to make, accept, and refuse suggestions?

To make a suggestion:
Si on allait à la Grand-Place?
On pourrait voir la cathédrale.
Ça te dit d'aller à Bruges?

To accept:
Bonne idée.
Pourquoi pas?
Je veux bien.

To refuse:
Je n'ai pas envie.
Ça ne me dit rien.
Non, je préfère...

au théâtre de marionnettes de Toone

acheter de la dentelle

au Palais Royal

goûter du chocolat belge

37 Ça se trouve où?

Vous avez trouvé des endroits où vous voulez aller, mais vous ne connaissez pas la ville. Ton ami(e) regarde le plan de Bruxelles et t'explique comment arriver aux endroits que vous avez choisis. Note ses indications.

38 Absolument incroyable!

Ecris une lettre à ton/ta camarade de classe. Explique-lui tout ce que tu as vu et fait à Bruxelles. N'oublie pas d'exprimer ton enthousiasme ou ton ennui.

❶ **La Bourse,** rue Henri Maus,2
❷ **Cathédrale St-Michel,** Parvis Sainte-Gudule
❸ **Les Galeries St-Hubert,** rue du Marché-aux-Herbes
❹ **La Grand-Place**
❺ **Musée d'Art Ancien,** rue de la Régence,3
❻ **Musée de Cire,** boulevard Anspach,36
❼ **Musée du Costume et de la Dentelle,** rue de la Violette,6
❽ **Palais des Beaux-Arts,** rue Ravenstein,23
❾ **Palais Royal,** place des Palais
❿ **Musée du Théâtre de Toone VII,** Petite rue des Bouchers,21

DEUXIEME ETAPE

quarante-cinq **45**

DEUXIEME ETAPE
CHAPITRE 2

Additional Practice

Tu te rappelles? Have partners make and respond to suggestions by replacing the places and activities mentioned with local alternatives. You might also have students list two or three things they'd like to do in their favorite francophone city or region and suggest them to a partner. (**Si on allait à la plage des Salines?**)

Teaching Suggestion

37 Have students choose a point of departure before they give their directions.

📁 Portfolio

38 Written This activity is appropriate for students' written portfolios. For portfolio information, see *Assessment Guide,* pages 2–13.

CLOSE

On a transparency, write a list of popular book and movie titles. Have students write how they feel about each one.

ASSESS

Quiz 2-2, *Chapter Teaching Resources, Book 1,* pp. 79–80
Assessment Items, Audiocassette 7A/Audio CD 2

Performance Assessment

Have groups of three or four students role-play a scene in which they go to the mall by car (perhaps with a minor mishap on the way!), ask for directions to a bookstore or music store, and discuss books or music that they like or don't like.

🌍 Culture Notes

• Belgium is a constitutional monarchy much like Great Britain. The **Palais Royal,** an imposing building in an eclectic architectural style, is the official residence of the king and the site of official ceremonies and the Changing of the Guard.
• **La Bourse,** the Belgian stock exchange, dates from the time of the French Revolution.
• **La Cathédrale St-Michel** dates from 1266, and its façade, from the fifteenth century. Originally built in the Romanesque style, its elaborate Gothic accents were added later.
• **Les Galeries St-Hubert,** constructed in 1846, was the first enclosed shopping arcade in Europe. It now houses many boutiques and tempting chocolate and coffee shops.
• **Le Musée de Cire** is a wax museum that depicts 2,000 years of Belgian history.

READING STRATEGY
Previewing

Teacher Note
For an additional reading, see *Practice and Activity Book,* page 23.

PREREADING
Activities A–B

Motivating Activity
Ask students if they ever go on vacation with their friends. If they could plan a summer vacation with their friends, where would they go and why? Do they think it would be difficult to get their friends to agree on a destination? Why or why not?

Thinking Critically
Analyzing Ask students if they think it would be easy or difficult to translate a comic book and why (slang, puns, cultural context).

Teaching Suggestions
A. Ask students what types of language they would expect to find in a comic book (sound effects, exclamations, slang words, narration).

A. Have students identify the cognate in the title of the comic strip (**destinations**) and predict what the story will be about (deciding on a vacation destination).

A. You might have students work in small groups or pairs to answer the questions in Activity A. Remind them not to read the text, but to infer the answers to the questions from the illustrations.

B. Ask students what other predictions they can make about the tone and plot of the story.

LISONS!

DE BONS CONSEILS
Previewing is a great way to get an idea of what's going to happen before you actually begin to read. When you preview, you take note of such things as the title, subheadings, pictures, captions, charts, and graphs in order to see how the text is organized and what its function is. Once you've done that, you're able to make predictions about what kind of information and vocabulary you will probably encounter. Taking time to preview a text and make predictions will make a new reading easier and more fun.

For Activity A, see answers below.

A. Preview the comic strip before you begin to read and make predictions about what's going to happen.

46 *quarante-six*

1. A girl is talking on the phone. Who might she be talking to?
2. Two other girls arrive. What are they carrying? What might the girls be planning?
3. What emotions do the girls display during their discussion? Do the emotions change as the story progresses?
4. What can you predict about the outcome of the story based on the girls' expressions in the last frame?
   Possible answers: informal,
B. What predictions can you make about   slang the language you'll find in the comic strip?
C. Now, read the dialogue in the first frame.

Answers
A 1. *Possible answers:* a friend, a boyfriend
   2. *Possible answers:* books, brochures, papers; a vacation, leisure activities
   3. excitement, anger, amusement, happiness, satisfaction; Yes.
   4. One girl will be happy, and the other two won't be quite as happy with the outcome.

READING
Activities C–K

For Individual Needs

D. Challenge Have students suggest additional reasons for going to each country. Collect their suggestions and read them aloud. Have the class guess which country is being described.

Geography Links

D. Have students locate the three suggested countries on a map of Europe or on *Map Transparency 1* (**L'Europe francophone**). Which of the three countries is the closest to Belgium? Which one is the farthest away?

D. Have students name countries or states that have the same characteristics as those mentioned in the comic strip. (**les plages:** la Côte d'Azur, Florida, California; **les montagnes:** Colorado, les Alpes)

Building on Previous Skills

E. Have students first list expressions they already know for expressing disagreement. (**Pas question!**) Ask them what types of facial expressions and gestures they associate with these expressions. Then, have them look for those gestures and expressions in the comic strip to find the frames in which the characters are disagreeing.

Teaching Suggestion

G. You might have students give English equivalents of some of these slang expressions.

Is the comic strip about friends getting together to . . .
a. leave for vacation?
b. talk about a vacation they took?
c. talk about where to go on vacation?

D. Match each destination with the reasons each person gives for wanting to go there.
See answers below.

l'Irlande

l'Espagne

la Suisse

les plages   vert
les montagnes
sauvage   le soleil
moins de monde

E. What words and phrases in the text express

For Activities E and F, see answers below.

the girls' disagreement about where to go?

F. Why do Claire and Cécile change their minds about where they want to go? What causes them to get angry once again?

G. The characters in this story use many slang expressions. Match the slang expression on the left with its standard French equivalent on the right.

a. une tonne de 3
b. se marrer 4
c. faire la noubat 1
d. terrible 5
e. c'est dingue 2

1. faire la fête
2. c'est incroyable
3. beaucoup de
4. s'amuser
5. merveilleux

quarante-sept **47**

Answers

D *l'Irlande:* vert, sauvage
l'Espagne: les plages, le soleil
la Suisse: les montagnes, moins de monde

E ... faudra discuter! Y a pas à discuter: pour moi, c'est l'Espagne. Y a des plages terribles. Ah, non! Flûte! La Suisse, c'est mieux! Il y a des montagnes et aussi moins de monde! Moins de monde! Et moi, je ne veux pas aller chez... C'est fini, oui? Tu rêves? Tandis que l'Irlande, c'est vert, peu peuplé, sauvage!

F They change their minds because Julie insists that they compromise; They get angry again because they still disagree.

Teaching Suggestion

H. You might have students work in pairs to figure out the phrases. Remind them not to look them up in a dictionary, but to use the context to determine their meaning.

Thinking Critically

I. Synthesizing Have students think of words or expressions in English or their native language where sounds are dropped or words are run together *(gonna, hafta, gotta, I dunno)*. You might want to have groups make lists and then compile a list as a class.

For Individual Needs

J. Visual Learners Have students look at the emotional changes pictured on this page. As they look at the last frame of the comic strip, have them suggest who or what might be the reason for the girls' change in attitude.

Teaching Suggestion

Have students review the predictions they made on page 46. Were they confirmed? How accurate were their predictions?

Language Arts Link

K. Ask students what a play on words is called in English (a pun) and if they can think of any examples.

POSTREADING
Activity L

Group Work

L. Have small groups create and act out a skit involving a disagreement. They might choose one of the following topics: deciding on a movie to see, choosing a restaurant, choosing a vacation destination, or dividing up household chores.

H. Find these expressions in the text. Use contextual clues to tell what they mean. *See answers below.*

> Et tout et tout.   C'est bien parce que c'est toi.

> Mener quelqu'un par le bout du nez.   Assez ri.

I. Some dialogues are written to represent the way people speak in everyday language. Such is the case in this story, where the writers have omitted many words and sounds that are often dropped in normal speech. Look through the dialogues to find . . . *See answers below.*

1. four instances where **ne** is dropped.
2. one instance where **tu** becomes **t'**.
3. three instances where **il y a** becomes **y a**.
4. one instance where **je** becomes **j'**.

J. Why is Julie so happy at the end of the story? Why are the other two girls suspicious? *See answers below.*

K. If **avarié** means *ruined,* what does the title mean? How is this a play on words? *See answers below.*

L. Have you and your friends ever disagreed strongly about something? How did you resolve the disagreement?

48 *quarante-huit*

Answers

H Et tout et tout. *(And so on and so forth.)* C'est bien parce que c'est toi. *(Just because it's you.)* Mener quelqu'un par le bout du nez. *(To lead someone by the nose.)* Assez ri. *(Enough joking around.)*

I 1. ... t'as pas oublié... ; Ça va pas être facile... ; Y a pas à discuter... ; ... j'veux pas aller...
2. ... t'as pas oublié...
3. ... y a des questions plus désagréables... ; Y a pas à discuter... ; Y a des plages terribles; ... en Suisse, y a des gens aussi!
4. ... j'veux pas aller...

J Julie is happy because they are going where she wanted to go; The other girls realize that Julie "won" without having to fight for her choice of destination by encouraging the others to compromise.

K "Ruined Destinations;" The girls' vacation plans were almost ruined **(avariées)** because their destinations were varied **(variées)**.

Have you ever tried to create your own comic strip? Telling an entire story in just a few frames can be very challenging; there isn't much room for dialogue, so it's important to choose your words carefully. In this exercise, you'll create a comic strip in French with your own characters, story, and illustrations.

Ma propre bande dessinée

Maintenant, tu vas créer ta propre bande dessinée. Imagine des personnages et crée une situation amusante ou intéressante. Ensuite, raconte ton histoire sans la rendre trop longue!

A. Préparation

Avant d'écrire ta BD, n'oublie pas de suivre les étapes suivantes.
1. Réfléchis bien à ces questions.
   a. A quel public est-ce que tu t'adresses? A des enfants? A tes camarades de classe?
   b. Quel ton est approprié à ton sujet? Sérieux? Amusant?
   c. Quels types de personnages et quel genre d'histoire est-ce que tu veux créer?
2. Ecris une description de tes personnages et de ce qui leur arrivera.
3. Pense au nombre d'images nécessaires pour raconter ton histoire.

B. Rédaction

1. Pour créer tes illustrations, dessine des images ou découpe-les dans un magazine ou une autre BD.
2. Ecris les dialogues dans les bulles de ta BD.

C. Evaluation

1. Fais une évaluation de ta BD. Pose-toi ces questions.
   a. Est-ce que ta BD est amusante ou intéressante?
   b. Est-ce que chaque image montre la progression de l'histoire?
   c. Est-ce que tu as utilisé un vocabulaire approprié à tes lecteurs?
   d. Est-ce que tu as raconté toute l'histoire sur le même ton?
2. Fais les révisions nécessaires. N'oublie pas de vérifier l'orthographe et la grammaire.

DE BONS CONSEILS

Just as the way you talk depends on who you're talking to, the way you write should also be directed by the people who will be reading your writing, your *audience*. Before you begin to write, ask yourself the following questions: For what audience is this intended? How much does my audience know about this topic? What strong feelings might the audience have about the topic? Should I use formal or informal language in addressing the audience? How can I make my message interesting to this particular audience? Your writing will be much more effective and meaningful if you tailor it to fit the interests, knowledge, and experience of the people for whom it is intended.

WRITING STRATEGY
Identifying your audience

Teacher Notes
- Encourage the process aspect of the **Ecrivons!** activities by making sure students always do each step of the writing assignment.
- You may want to use the portfolio evaluation forms (Evaluating Written Activities, Forms A and B) found in the *Assessment Guide* to help you evaluate students' final products.

Portfolio

Written You might have students include all their work for Parts A–C in their written portfolios. For portfolio information, see *Assessment Guide,* pages 2–13.

PREWRITING

Motivating Activity

Ask students if they have ever clipped a comic strip from the paper or recounted a cartoon episode to a friend. Have them give examples.

Reading/Writing Link

A. 1. Have students also consider the level of language that they plan to use in their comic strips. They might look back at Activity G on page 47 and decide if they would like to use any of these slang expressions.

For Individual Needs

A. 3. Visual/Tactile Learners Have students write each event on a small piece of paper. Then, have them tape the pieces in order on full sheets of paper, which represent frames of the comic strip.

WRITING

Teaching Suggestion

To help students make the beginning, middle, and end of their stories clear, write phrases such as **Lundi matin à 8 heures,... ; Plus tard,... ; Chez Hélène,... ; Le lendemain, au cours d'histoire,...** on the board.

POSTWRITING

Teaching Suggestion

C. 1. Once students have evaluated their comic strips according to these criteria, have them exchange papers with a partner and evaluate each other's work. Remind them to make specific suggestions for improving the comic strip.

MISE EN PRATIQUE

The **Mise en pratique** reviews and integrates all four skills and culture in preparation for the Chapter Test.

 Video Wrap-Up

VIDEO PROGRAM
Videocassette 1

You might want to use the *Video Program* as part of the chapter review. See the *Video Guide* for teaching suggestions and activity masters.

 For Individual Needs

1 Auditory Learners
Before students open their books, write the questions submitted by Marie-Céline on the board. Make sure students understand them. Then, tell students to listen carefully for the gist of the responses as you read the letters aloud. Then, discuss each one with students.

1 Challenge Have students summarize each person's letter in French, as if they were telling a friend about it. (**Bénédicte pense que le rôle des BD est d'enseigner l'histoire et la politique.**)

Additional Practice

1 For additional reading and speaking practice, have students take turns choosing lines from the letters to read aloud to a partner, who tries to name the person who wrote them.

 Portfolio

2 Written This activity is appropriate for students' written portfolios. For portfolio suggestions, see *Assessment Guide,* page 15.

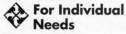 **For Individual Needs**

3 Challenge Have students tell why the first speaker is impatient.

---

1 Lis les lettres suivantes et réponds aux questions.

Aimez-vous la BD?

«Je voudrais vous poser une question : que pensez-vous des bandes dessinées ? Aimez-vous Tintin, Astérix, Gaston et les autres? Lisez-vous plus de BD que de romans? D'avance, merci ! » Marie-Céline, Le Chesnay

«Buenos dias, Marie-Céline ! Ta question est très intéressante. Personnellement, je trouve que si l'histoire est bien tournée et les dessins sont bien faits, les BD feront exploser les librairies.
Mais je pense qu'on devrait s'en servir pour expliquer aux enfants et aux adolescents la vie ou la politique ; parfois on ne comprend plus rien ! Et peut-être que les BD pourront nous apprendre plein de choses faciles ou compliquées, tout en rigolant ! On pourrait apprendre la vie de Napoléon ou celle de César !
Entre nous, ça serait plus drôle que les explications de nos parents, non? Enfin, je t'ai donné mon avis là-dessus. Vive les bandes dessinées et vive le dessin artistique !»
Bénédicte, Pontoise

«Moi, je préfère les romans aux bandes dessinées. D'abord parce que je suis un rêveur et que les romans chassent les idées noires de notre tête et peuplent celle-ci de songes merveilleux.
J'ai peu de BD, mais je lis tout de même quelques BD : Tintin, Astérix, Boule et Bill, Gaston et d'autres.
Je voudrais laisser un message : «Ceux qui n'ont pas encore découvert les romans ne doivent pas avoir peur de ceux-ci, car une BD ne remplacera jamais un roman !» Bonne lecture ! Plongez-vous vite dans Alexandre Dumas, Jules Verne, Victor Hugo !»
Julien, Alès

«Salut Marie-Céline ! Moi, j'adore les bandes dessinées. Je bouquine beaucoup. Mais dans les BD, il n'y a pas ce qu'il y a dans les autres livres. Même si on ne sait pas lire, les images nous aident à comprendre le thème, et si on n'aime pas lire, rien ne vaut de feuilleter les BD. J'ai toute la collection Tintin, Lucky Luke, et Astérix. Quand on n'a pas envie de se plonger dans des romans mieux vaut lire une bande dessinée.»
Aurélie, Toulouse

«Je réponds à la question : "Aimez-vous la BD ?"
Oui, j'aime la BD car il y a les personnages qui s'expriment avec leurs gestes, leurs habits. Alors que les romans ou livres sont barbants, on ne comprend pas tout le temps qui est-ce qui parle et puis c'est bien mieux d'avoir des images.»
Pierre, Toulouse

1. What kind of letters do you think these are? teen forum
2. What question are these teenagers answering? What is your opinion of comic books?
3. How many of these teenagers prefer to read comic books? How many prefer novels? 3; 1
4. Why do some of the teenagers prefer comic books? And novels?
   Comics can be used to explain difficult subjects with humor; Comics are amusing, with illustrations that aid understanding; Novels stimulate the imagination and the intellect.

 2 Ecris ta réponse à la question posée par Marie-Céline. Est-ce que tu lis souvent des bandes dessinées? Plus souvent que des romans? Pourquoi ou pourquoi pas?

 3 Ecoute les conversations de ces jeunes qui se trouvent dans un parc d'attractions. Est-ce que la personne qui répond est impatiente ou est-ce qu'elle essaie de rassurer l'autre?
Answers on p. 27D.

50 *cinquante*   CHAPITRE 2   Belgique, nous voilà!

Language Note

Students might want to know the following words from the letters: **rêveur** *(dreamer)*; **songe** *(dream)*; **bouquiner** *(to read)*; **feuilleter** *(to leaf through)*; **se détendre** *(to relax).*

4 Donne le nom de quelques produits typiques de la Belgique. Qu'est-ce que tu voudrais acheter si tu allais en Belgique? *Possible answers:* le chocolat, la dentelle, les gaufres

 5 Avec ton/ta camarade, choisissez un de ces endroits pour y passer la journée. N'oubliez pas de donner votre opinion sur chaque endroit.

CHATEAU FORT DE LOGNE
Vieuxville-Ferrières — F9

L'un des plus fameux châteaux de la vallée de l'Ourthe (IXᵉ - XVᵉ siècles) et néanmoins injustement méconnu !
Antique forteresse des abbés de Stavelot, le Château de Logne devint au XVᵉ siècle une base importante des de la Marck, les "Sangliers des Ardennes".
Sur place, le guide vous fera revivre le Moyen Age avec ses coutumes et ses guerres; il vous mènera dans de mystérieux souterrains que hante encore la Gatte d'Or, gardienne d'un fabuleux trésor. Du haut de son enceinte, le Château vous offrira un point de vue u

A proximité, le Musée d découverts lors des foui

Ouvert du 1/7 au 31/8, de mai à octobre : de 1 70 FB; grp.: ad. 80 FB, en F, NL (GB sur den Bouverie 1 • Tél.: 086.

MUSEE DE LA DENTELLE
Marche-en-Famenne — Ⓑ G9

Histoire de la dentelle à travers siècles et costumes.
Spécimens de dentelles les plus renommées.
Ancien centre dentellier wallon, la ville et les villages environnants comptaient 850 dentellières au XVIIIe siècle.
Dentelles aux fuseaux d'hier et d'aujourd'hui - Travaux de l'école de dentelles.
Outillage et travaux de dentellières de Belgique, France, Italie, Allemagne, Russie...

En saison (juin, juillet, août, sept.) ouvert du lundi au samedi de 9.00 à 12.00 h. et de 13.30 à 17.30 h. - le dimanche, de 10.00 à 12.00 h. et de 14.00 à 17.00 h. • Hors saison : fermé les dimanche, lundi et jours fériés • Pour groupes sur rendez-vous unts 40 FB • V : 30 min. • P site : le Pot d'Etain, Maison imenne, rue des Brasseurs 7

PARC DE RECREATION MONT MOSAN
Huy — Ⓑ F8

Il y a toujours du nouveau au Mont Mosan!
Enfin un vrai parc de récréation à la portée de toutes les bourses.
Le spectacle des otaries (trois espèces différentes), les phoques, l'exposition sur les mammifères marins, la vaste plaine de jeux, les châteaux gonflables, la cafétéria et sa petite restauration, etc...
Pour une journée de détente, pensez Mont Mosan.
Ouvert du 2/4 au 31/10/94 : de 10h00 à 20h00 • Prix : 100 FB, Grp 70 FB • p, P • B-4500 Huy, Plaine de la Sarte • Tél.: 085/23.29.96 • Fax : 085/21.30.61.

JEU DE ROLE

6 You've chosen where to go, but you don't know how to get there! You have to call the tourist bureau to ask where the town is and how to get there from Stavelot. Your friend will play the role of the tourist bureau employee. He/She can use the map on page 34. Write the directions that he/she gives you. Don't forget to repeat them to make sure you understood. Ask the employee what he/she thinks of the attraction you plan to visit.

MISE EN PRATIQUE

cinquante et un **51**

Teaching Suggestion
4 You might also ask students the following questions: **Qu'est-ce que tu voudrais voir en Belgique? Quelles villes est-ce que tu voudrais visiter? Pourquoi?**

Group Work
5 You might have students do this activity in small groups. Students might also suggest the places on the tourist map of Brussels on page 45 or other places mentioned in the chapter.

Additional Practice
5 Have students take turns imagining they went to one of the places pictured and telling a partner one activity they did there. (**J'ai vu des otaries.**) The partner names the place (**Parc de récréation Mont Mosan**).

📁 Portfolio
5 Oral This activity is appropriate for students' oral portfolios. For portfolio suggestions, see *Assessment Guide,* p. 15.

Teaching Suggestion
6 You might have students do this activity with toy phones, sitting back-to-back to simulate a phone conversation.

Language Note
Students might want to know the following words from the brochures: **guerre** *(war);* **souterrain** *(underground);* **fuseau** *(bobbin);* **otaries** *(sea lions);* **phoques** *(seals);* **gonflable** *(inflatable).*

This page is intended to help students prepare for the test. It is a brief checklist of the major points covered in the chapter. The students should be reminded that this is only a checklist and does not necessarily include everything that will appear on the test.

 **For Individual Needs**

2 Auditory/Visual Learners You might have students record the directions on audiocassette or draw a map to accompany their written directions.

Teaching Suggestions

5 Encourage students to vary their responses and use as many expressions as they can recall.

8 Have volunteers read their directions aloud as their classmates try to guess the destination.

Game

LA VOILÀ! Write the questions from **Que sais-je?** on one set of cards and the answers on another set. Tape the question cards on the board at random and place the answer cards in a bag. Then, form two or more teams. Have the first player from each team come to the front. On your cue, the players each select one card from the bag, find the matching question on the board, and call out **La voilà!** The first player to find the correct question wins a point for his or her team. Repeat the process with the next two players. Play until one team has earned ten or fifteen points.

QUE SAIS-JE?

Can you use what you've learned in this chapter?

Can you ask for and give directions? p. 33

1 How would you ask someone for directions to Brussels?
La route pour Bruxelles, s'il vous plaît? Comment on va à Bruxelles?

2 How would you give someone directions from your home to . . .
1. your school?
2. your best friend's house?
3. the nearest grocery store?

Can you express impatience? p. 36

3 How would you express your impatience if . . . See answers below.
1. you wanted to leave, but your friend wouldn't get ready?
2. your friend wanted to stop and look in a music store on the way to the movies?
3. you were hurrying to a class with a friend who suddenly stopped to talk to someone?

Can you reassure someone? p. 36

4 For each of the situations in number 3, what would the other person say to reassure you? *Possible answers:* 1. Il n'y a pas le feu. Sois patient(e)! 2. Ça ne va pas prendre longtemps. 3. Du calme, du calme! On a largement le temps!

Can you express enthusiasm and boredom? p. 41

5 How would you express your enthusiasm for these TV shows and comic strips to a friend? See answers below.

The Simpsons   Calvin and Hobbes
The Far Side   Saturday Night Live
Seinfeld   The Quigmans

6 How would you express boredom with these activities? See answers below.

playing golf   going to a museum
doing homework   cleaning the house
watching a documentary listening to a lecture

Can you ask and tell where things are? p. 43

7 What questions would you ask to find . . . See answers below.
1. a telephone?
2. a bathroom?
3. the elevator?

8 How would you tell a new student to your school where to find . . .
1. the toilets?
2. the cafeteria?
3. the science lab?
4. the principal's office?

ET LE SOLEIL SE COUCHE. FIN DE L'ÉPISODE. IL VA SE REMETTRE À CHANTER QU'IL EST UN COW-BOY SOLITAIRE...

52   *cinquante-deux*   CHAPITRE 2   Belgique, nous voilà!

Answers
3 *Possible answers*
1. Grouille-toi! Tu peux te dépêcher?
2. On n'a pas le temps. Je suis vraiment impatient(e) d'arriver!
3. Mais, qu'est-ce que tu fais? Tu peux te dépêcher?
5 Qu'est-ce que c'est rigolo! Ce que c'est bien! C'est marrant comme tout! Ça me branche!

6 C'est mortel! Ça me casse les pieds! Ça m'embête! C'est rasant! Ça m'ennuie à mourir!
7 *Possible answers*
1. Vous pourriez me dire où il y a un téléphone?
2. Tu sais où sont les toilettes?
3. Pardon, vous savez où se trouve l'ascenseur?

VOCABULAIRE

PREMIERE ETAPE

Asking for and giving directions

La route pour..., s'il vous plaît? *Could you tell me how to get to . . . ?*

Comment on va à... ? *How can I get to . . . ?*

Pour (aller à)..., vous suivez la... pendant à peu près... kilomètres. *To get to . . . , follow . . . for about . . . kilometers.*

Vous allez voir un panneau qui indique l'entrée de l'autoroute. *You'll see a sign that points out the freeway entrance.*

Vous traversez... *You cross . . .*

Après..., vous allez tomber sur... *After . . . , you'll come across . . .*

Cette route vous conduira au centre-ville. *This road will lead you into the center of town.*

Vous continuez tout droit, jusqu'au carrefour. *You keep going straight ahead, up to the intersection.*

conduire *to drive*

At the gas station

avoir un pneu crevé *to have a flat tire*

l'essence (f.) *gas*

faire le plein *to fill it up*

faire la vidange *to change the oil*

mettre de l'air dans les pneus *to put air in the tires*

de l'huile dans le moteur *oil in the motor*

nettoyer le pare-brise *to clean the windshield*

le/la pompiste *the gas station attendant*

le réservoir *the gas tank*

une station-service *a gas station*

du super *regular leaded*

du super sans plomb *unleaded*

tomber en panne (d'essence) *to break down (run out of gas)*

vérifier... *to check . . .*

les freins (m.) *the brakes*

l'huile *the oil*

la pression des pneus *the tire pressure*

Expressing impatience

Mais qu'est-ce que tu fais? *What are you doing?*

Tu peux te dépêcher? *Can you hurry up?*

Grouille-toi! *Get a move on!*

On n'a pas le temps! *We don't have time!*

Je suis vraiment impatient(e) de... ! *I'm really anxious to . . . !*

Reassuring someone

Ça ne va pas prendre longtemps! *It's not going to take long!*

Sois patient(e)! *Be patient!*

On a largement le temps! *We've got plenty of time!*

Il n'y a pas le feu. *Where's the fire?*

Du calme, du calme. *Calm down.*

DEUXIEME ETAPE

Expressing enthusiasm and boredom

Qu'est-ce que c'est... ! *That is so . . . !*

Ce que c'est bien! *Isn't it great!*

C'est... comme tout! *It's as . . . as anything!*

Ça me branche! *I'm crazy about that!*

Ça me casse les pieds! *That's so boring!*

Ça m'embête! *That bores me!*

Ça m'ennuie à mourir! *That bores me to death!*

Adjectives

rigolo(te) *funny, hysterical*

fou (folle) *crazy, funny*

dingue *wild, crazy, funny*

marrant(e) *funny*

rasant(e) *boring*

mortel(le) *deadly boring*

de mauvais goût *in poor taste*

bébé *childish, stupid*

Asking and telling where things are

Vous pourriez me dire où il y a... ? *Could you tell me where I can find . . . ?*

Pardon, vous savez où se trouve... ? *Excuse me, could you tell me where . . . is?*

Tu sais où sont... ? *Do you know where . . . are?*

Par là, au bout du couloir. *Over there, at the end of the hallway.*

Juste là, à côté de... *Right there, next to . . .*

En bas. *Downstairs.*

En haut. *Upstairs.*

Au fond. *Towards the back.*

Au rez-de-chaussée. *On the ground floor.*

Au premier étage. *On the second floor.*

A l'entrée de... *At the entrance to . . .*

VOCABULAIRE

cinquante-trois **53**

Teaching Suggestions

- Encourage students to make and use vocabulary flashcards to review the vocabulary from the chapter.
- Have students write a sentence or two-line dialogue for each word or expression in the chapter vocabulary to help them remember it. (**Ma meilleure amie est dingue. Vous traversez le pont.**)

CHAPTER 2 ASSESSMENT

CHAPTER TEST

- *Chapter Teaching Resources, Book 1,* pp. 81–86
- *Assessment Guide,* Speaking Test, p. 28
- *Assessment Items, Audiocassette 7A Audio CD 2*

TEST GENERATOR, CHAPTER 2

ALTERNATIVE ASSESSMENT

Performance Assessment

You might want to use the **Jeu de rôle** (p. 51) as a cumulative performance assessment activity.

Portfolio Assessment

- **Written: Mise en pratique,** Activity 2, *Pupil's Edition,* p. 50
  Assessment Guide, p. 15
- **Oral: Mise en pratique,** Activity 5, *Pupil's Edition,* p. 51
  Assessment Guide, p. 15

Game

LÈVE-TOI! Prepare a stack of yellow and blue cards and form two teams. Call out categories from the **Vocabulaire** (*Asking for and giving directions, At the service station*). Tell students to stand if they can give a word or expression from that category. Call on the first person to stand and have him or her respond. If the student gives an appropriate response, his or her team wins a point, and he or she receives a yellow card. If the answer is not correct, the other team may try to answer. The second time a student answers correctly, he or she gets a blue card and may no longer answer questions for the team. Students with blue cards help keep score, determine who stood first, and judge the accuracy of the answers. The team with the most points wins.

Chapitre 3 : Soyons responsables!
Chapter Overview

Mise en train pp. 56–58	**Je peux sortir?**			Note Culturelle, Swiss work ethic, p. 58	

	FUNCTIONS	**GRAMMAR**	**CULTURE**	**RE-ENTRY**	
Première étape pp. 59–63	• Asking for, granting, and refusing permission, p. 60 • Expressing obligation, p. 60	• The verb **devoir**, p. 60 • The subjunctive, p. 61	• Realia: Party invitation, p. 62 • Realia: Anti-smoking ad, p. 63	• Complaining • Chores	

Remise en train pp. 64–65	**Laissez-les vivre!**			Note Culturelle, Switzerland's neutrality, p. 65	

	FUNCTIONS	**GRAMMAR**	**CULTURE**	**RE-ENTRY**	
Deuxième étape pp. 66–71	• Forbidding, p. 67 • Reproaching, p. 69 • Justifying your actions and rejecting others' excuses, p. 69	**ne... pas** + infinitive, p. 67	• **Rencontre Culturelle,** Overview of Switzerland, p. 66 • **Panorama Culturel,** Environmental issues, p. 68 • **Note Culturelle, La minuterie,** p. 69 • Realia: Letters on environmental issues, p. 70	Negative expressions	

Lisons! pp. 72–74	**Albert Nez en l'air; Les frères Tête en fer; Julie Boum** Reading Strategy: Deriving meaning from context

Ecrivons! p. 75	**Ta fable à toi** Writing Strategy: Making an outline

Review pp. 76–79	• Mise en pratique, pp. 76–77 • Que sais-je? p. 78 • Vocabulaire, p. 79

**Assessment
Options**
	Etape Quizzes
	• *Chapter Teaching Resources, Book 1*
	  Première étape, Quiz 3-1, pp. 131–132
	  Deuxième étape, Quiz 3-2, pp. 133–134
	• *Assessment Items, Audiocassette 7A/Audio CD 3*
		Chapter Test
		• *Chapter Teaching Resources, Book 1,* pp. 135–140
		• *Assessment Guide,* Speaking Test, p. 29
		• *Assessment Items, Audiocassette 7A/Audio CD 3*
		
		Test Generator, Chapter 3

RESOURCES: Print	RESOURCES: Audiovisual
Practice and Activity Book, p. 25	Textbook Audiocassette 2A/Audio CD 3
Practice and Activity Book, pp. 26–29 Grammar and Vocabulary Worksheets, pp. 18–26 Chapter Teaching Resources, Book 1 • Communicative Activity 3-1, pp. 112–113 • Teaching Transparency Master 3-1, pp. 116, 118 . . . . • Additional Listening Activities 3-1, 3-2, 3-3, pp. 119–120. . . • Realia 3-1, pp. 123, 125 • Situation Cards 3-1, pp. 126–127 • Student Response Forms, pp. 128–130 • Quiz 3-1, pp. 131–132	Textbook Audiocassette 2A/Audio CD 3 Teaching Transparency 3-1 Additional Listening Activities, Audiocassette 9A/Audio CD 3 Assessment Items, Audiocassette 7A/Audio CD 3
Practice and Activity Book, p. 30	Textbook Audiocassette 2A/Audio CD 3
Practice and Activity Book, pp. 31–34 Grammar and Vocabulary Worksheets, pp. 27–28 Chapter Teaching Resources, Book 1 • Communicative Activity 3-2, pp. 114–115 • Teaching Transparency Master 3-2, pp. 117, 118 . . . . • Additional Listening Activities 3-4, 3-5, 3-6, pp. 120–121. . . • Realia 3-2, pp. 124, 125 • Situation Cards 3-2, 3-3, pp. 126–127 • Student Response Forms, pp. 128–130 • Quiz 3-2, pp. 133–134 . . . . Video Guide	Textbook Audiocassette 2A/Audio CD 3 Teaching Transparency 3-2 Additional Listening Activities, Audiocassette 9A/Audio CD 3 Assessment Items, Audiocassette 7A/Audio CD 3 Video Program, Videocassette 1
Practice and Activity Book, p. 35	
Video Guide	Video Program, Videocassette 1

Alternative Assessment
- Performance Assessment
  Première étape, p. 63
  Deuxième étape, p. 71
- Portfolio Assessment
  Written: **Ecrivons!,** Pupil's Edition, p. 75
    Assessment Guide, p. 16
  Oral: **Mise en pratique,** Activity 2, Pupil's Edition, p. 76
    Assessment Guide, p. 16

For Student Response Forms, see *Chapter Teaching Resources Book 1,* pp. 128–130.

*M*ise en train

3 Ecoute! p. 58

1. — Si je me souviens bien, tu n'as pas eu de très bonnes notes en français.
2. — Ecoute, tu es déjà fatiguée. Tu travailles beaucoup en semaine.
3. — Pas question. Tu ne vas pas faire tes devoirs à onze heures du soir.
4. — Oui, si tu ne rentres pas trop tard. Tes grands-parents viennent dîner et tu dois mettre la table.

Answers to Activity 3
1. Gilles   2. Karine   3. Mélanie   4. Charles

*P*remière étape

6 Ecoute! p. 59

1. — Tu veux aller voir un film?
   — Euh, oui, bien sûr. Mais j'étais en train de faire la vaisselle. Tu peux attendre une demi-heure?
   — Oui. Ça va. Ça ne commence pas avant vingt heures.
2. — C'est chouette, le camping, non?
   — Oui, s'il ne pleut pas. Moi, j'ai peur qu'il... Ah zut alors! J'ai oublié d'arroser le jardin.
   — Ben, ça ne fait rien. Regarde, il commence à pleuvoir!
3. — Tu n'es pas encore prête?
   — Euh, non. Il faut que je donne à manger au chat d'abord.
   — Allez, dépêche-toi! On part!
4. — Ginette m'a dit de la retrouver au café à cinq heures. Tu viens?
   — Je ne sais pas. Je voudrais bien, mais je dois d'abord rentrer pour sortir le chien.
   — Bon, je viens avec toi. On peut la retrouver après, d'accord?
   — D'accord.
5. — Tu viens avec nous à la plage samedi?
   — Ce serait chouette! Mais j'ai un tas de choses à faire à la maison samedi. Je dois faire la lessive, passer l'aspirateur, nettoyer le parquet...
   — Allez, bon week-end!!!
6. — C'est toujours comme ça avec les parents. Il faut, il faut, il faut! Faire les devoirs, ranger la chambre, faire la vaisselle...
   — Oui, moi c'est pareil. Et ce que je déteste plus que tout, c'est laver les vitres. Tu fais ça, toi?
7. — Tu veux venir faire les vitrines avec nous cet après-midi?
   — J'aimerais bien, mais je n'ai vraiment pas le temps, je dois faire le repassage.
   — Bon, tant pis, ce sera pour la prochaine fois peut-être.
8. — Zut alors! C'est demain le pique-nique?
   — Oui.

— C'est mon jour de ménage à la maison. J'ai beaucoup de choses à faire.
— Ta mère te permettra peut-être de faire tout ça plus tard?
— Ben, non. C'est une vraie prison ici. Pendant que vous vous amusez, moi, je serai en train de nettoyer les salles de bains.

Answers to Activity 6
1. Christiane   3. Amina   5. Amina   7. Christiane
2. Christiane   4. Christiane 6. Christiane 8. Amina

9 Ecoute! p. 60

1. — Dis donc, tu veux bien que je sorte avec Roger après le dîner?
   — Il faut d'abord que tu débarrasses la table et que tu fasses la vaisselle.
   — Mais, ça va être trop tard après.
   — Bon. Ça va pour cette fois.
2. — Papa, je peux dîner chez mes copains ce soir?
   — Pas question. Tes grands-parents viennent dîner à la maison.
   — Mais papa...
   — J'ai dit non.
3. — Dites, Michel m'a invité à sa boum ce soir. Je peux y aller?
   — Oui, si tu as fini tes devoirs.
   — Euh, je n'ai pas encore fini. Je pourrais les finir demain.
   — Je regrette, mais si je dis oui, ça va être la même chose la prochaine fois.
   — Mais c'est son anniversaire!
   — Pas question!
4. — J'aimerais partir en vacances aux Etats-Unis.
   — Tu as de l'argent pour y aller?
   — Euh, non.
   — Alors, je suis désolé, mais ce n'est pas possible.
5. — Papa, j'aimerais aller au concert de Vanessa Paradis avec mes copains.
   — Et tu vas rentrer à quelle heure?
   — Euh, ça dure jusqu'à minuit, et puis je dois revenir.
   — Ah, non. Ça veut dire deux heures du matin, ça! Tu sais bien que tu n'as pas le droit de rentrer après minuit.
6. — Tu veux bien que je sorte ce soir?
   — Où veux-tu aller?
   — Au restaurant avec un copain.
   — Oui, si tu rentres à onze heures au plus tard.
   — D'accord.
7. — Maman, tu veux bien que j'invite Ali à dîner?
   — Quand ça?
   — Demain soir.
   — Oui, bien sûr.

Answers to Activity 9
1. accordée   3. refusée   5. refusée   7. accordée
2. refusée   4. refusée   6. accordée

*R*emise en train

19 Ecoute! p. 64

— Tu dois constamment te tenir au courant du temps qu'il fait.
— Tu ne dois jamais aller faire une randonnée tout seul.
— Il faut que tu emportes un équipement approprié.
— Si tu n'es pas sûr du chemin, il vaut mieux revenir sur tes pas.
— Il faut que tu fasses un plan de ta randonnée avant de partir.
— N'oublie pas de dire l'heure de ton départ et de ton arrivée à un adulte.

Answers to Activity 19
1. the fifth rule
2. the third rule
3. the second rule
4. the sixth rule
5. the first rule
6. the fourth rule

*D*euxième étape

25 Ecoute! p. 67

Mesdames, messieurs, afin de préserver le parc, nous attirons votre attention sur certaines règles. Il est interdit de cueillir des fleurs, de chasser ou de pêcher dans le parc. Défense également de fumer dans les cafétérias et les toilettes du parc. De même, il est interdit de jeter des papiers ou des ordures par terre. Pour cela, nous avons des poubelles. Enfin, veuillez ne pas amener d'animaux domestiques dans le parc. Nous vous remercions et vous rappelons que respecter la nature, c'est respecter les autres.

Possible answers to Activity 25
1. Don't pick the flowers.
2. No hunting or fishing.
3. No smoking in the cafeterias or restrooms.
4. No littering.

27 Ecoute! p. 69

1. — Eh bien, ma mère, elle utilise des aérosols presque tous les jours, ou pour nettoyer la maison ou pour faire sa toilette.
2. — Mes cousins habitent loin de leur travail, mais ils prennent des transports en commun tout de même. Mes cousins François et Gilbert prennent le bus tous les jours, et ma cousine, Alice partage sa voiture avec ses copains pour aller au travail.
3. — Mon frère Jean-Marc, il est pénible! Il n'arrête pas de déranger les autres en faisant du bruit. C'est la même chose tous les jours. Après l'école, il met sa musique tellement fort! Et puis, on lui a dit mille fois d'éteindre la télé et les lumières, mais il ne le fait jamais!
4. — Mon père continue à prendre des douches très longues, vingt minutes ou plus quelquefois! Je lui

ai dit à quel point il gaspille l'eau, mais ça lui est égal, évidemment.
5. — Ma sœur Jeannine, c'est elle qui m'a appris à recycler l'aluminium et le papier. Et la semaine prochaine, nous allons planter des arbres avec notre groupe de scouts.

Answers to Activity 27
1. mauvaise   2. bonne   3. mauvaise   4. mauvaise   5. bonne

28 Ecoute! p. 69

1. — Tu sais bien que tu as tort de fumer, Etienne!
2. — Eh oui, je sais que c'est pas bien de gaspiller l'énergie, mais je suis pas le seul à le faire après tout, hein?
3. — Tu ferais mieux de marcher de temps en temps. Ce n'est pas bien de prendre ta voiture pour aller partout.
4. — Oui, bien sûr que tu n'es pas le seul, mais ce n'est pas une raison!
5. — Je n'ai pas le temps de recycler. Et puis, je ne suis pas obligé. Je suis quand même libre...
6. — Ce n'est pas parce que tout le monde gaspille l'eau que tu dois la gaspiller aussi.
7. — Et encore une fois, j'ai trouvé toutes les lumières allumées, et personne dans la pièce! Tu sais bien que tu ne dois pas oublier d'éteindre les lumières, Florence.

Answers to Activity 28
1. reproche   3. reproche   5. excuse   7. reproche
2. excuse   4. reproche   6. reproche

*M*ise en pratique

1 p. 76

— Maman, j'aimerais aller au Festival international du jazz. Mélanie m'a invitée à y aller avec elle. Tu veux bien que j'y aille?
— Tu penses passer la nuit à Montreux?
— Euh, oui.
— Tu as de l'argent pour ça?
— Mais, euh, non.
— Alors, je regrette, mais ce n'est pas possible.
— Bon. Et si je rentrais après le concert?
— Mais tu sais bien que tu n'as pas le droit de sortir après minuit, Sabine.
— Mais, maman!
— N'insiste pas, Sabine, c'est non!
— Et si Mélanie peut me prêter de l'argent? Je peux y passer la nuit?
— Oui, si tu as fait tes devoirs. Et n'oublie pas que tu dois faire la vaisselle et la lessive avant de partir.
— D'accord, d'accord.
— Et je veux absolument que tu ranges ta chambre avant.
— Bon, bon.

Answers to Mise en pratique Activity 1
1. to the International Jazz Festival
2. Sabine doesn't have the money to spend the night in Montreux; She can go if Mélanie lends her the money.
3. She must do her homework, do the dishes, do the laundry, and pick up her room.

L'environnement
(Group Project)

ASSIGNMENT

Groups of students will create posters in French that describe an environmental problem and propose a solution. They will also give an oral presentation to the class, based on their posters.

MATERIALS

✂ **Students may need**
- Posterboard
- Colored markers or pens
- Scissors
- Glue
- Recent current events magazines

SUGGESTED SEQUENCE

1. Have students form small groups and select a topic related to the environment. Possible topics include air/water/noise pollution, industrial waste, endangered species, and garbage disposal. Students might choose to feature a local environmental concern, or one unique to a certain area of the world.

2. Students should research the problem. Have them use current magazines and newspapers to find relevant statistics and popular opinions about the issue. They should also find or draw pictures to illustrate the problem.

3. Have group members share and compile their research and propose a solution. Once they have decided on the content of their posters, have them plan the graphics and layout. They might create a slogan or a symbol, such as Woodsy Owl. If students have access to computers, encourage them to create charts and graphs to present the statistics that they've gathered. They should also find or draw pictures to illustrate their solution.

4. Have students exchange their rough drafts and layouts with another group. Remind students to check not only French spelling and grammar, but also the content and design of the poster. They might make suggestions for additional or alternative graphics and illustrations.

5. Have groups plan the final layout of their posters. They should arrange their illustrations and copy the text onto the poster.

6. Have group members present their poster to the class. Each member should take part in describing and explaining the environmental problem and the proposed solution. You might want to videotape students' presentations.

7. Display students' posters around the classroom or the school.

GRADING THE PROJECT

Each group should receive a collective grade based on the inclusion of all required elements, accuracy of language, and creativity and overall appearance of the poster. Each member of the group should also receive an individual grade for his or her effort and participation in the project and for the oral presentation.

Suggested Point Distribution (total = 100 points)

Inclusion of requirements	20 points
Language use	20 points
Creativity/overall appearance	20 points
Effort/participation	20 points
Oral presentation	20 points

VERB TENSE RACE

In this game, students will practice various verb forms.

Procedure   This game can be played by two or more teams. Begin by giving the infinitive of a verb, a subject pronoun, and a tense or mood **(finir, tu, subjonctif)**. Players should write a sentence, using the elements you called out. **(Il faut que tu finisses tes devoirs.)** Vary the subjects and tenses/mood. If two teams are playing, have one student from each team race to the board to write their sentence. If there are three or more teams, provide each team with sheets of construction paper and a thick marker. Have students work together to figure out and write down an answer. The first team to hold up a correct answer wins. If you need a tiebreaker, give two points for correct irregular verb forms or past participles.

JEU DE SOCIETE

In this game, students will practice expressing obligation and social responsibilities.

Procedure   In small groups, students will make and play their own board game. They will need construction paper, markers, and dice. Students should draw a path or a road divided into 20-30 squares. They should mark a starting point **(Départ)** and an ending point **(Arrivée)**. In the squares, have them write examples of both pro- and anti-environmental behavior and a positive or negative point value for each. For example, they might write **Tu jettes des ordures dans la rue** (–3) or **Tu prends une douche de 3 minutes** (+4). They should also create "free" squares with environmental messages, such as **Sauvons les forêts tropicales!** To start the game, players place playing pieces such as coins or paper clips at the starting point. Then, each player rolls a die and moves his or her playing piece the number of spaces indicated. When a student lands on a square with a negative point value **(Tu jettes des ordures dans la rue)**, the other students must reproach him or her **(Il ne faut pas que tu jettes des ordures dans la rue!)** in order for the points to be deducted from the player's score. When a player lands on a square with a positive point value **(Tu prends une douche de trois minutes)**, he or she must tell the other players to do that activity in order to earn the points. **(Vous devriez prendre une douche de trois minutes!)** You might appoint a scorekeeper in each group to keep track of each player's points. The player with the most points at the end of the game wins.

LE BASE-BALL

In this game, students will practice household chores and expressing obligation.

Procedure   Draw a baseball diamond on the board. Gather or draw large pictures of various household chores. To begin the game, one team member chooses a base hit (single, double, or triple) that he or she would like to try for. To hit a single, a player must name in French the chore that is illustrated by the picture you hold up. To hit a double, the player must say a logical sentence including the chore. To hit a triple, the player must say a sentence that begins **Il faut que...** and includes the chore. If the student responds correctly, write his or her initials on the appropriate base. Then, the next player chooses a hit to try for and responds. Players on base advance ahead of the hitter. When a player crosses home plate, his or her team scores a run. A team makes an out when a player does not give an appropriate response. Then, the turn passes to the other team. There are no home runs. You might play for a specified amount of time or for a certain number of runs.

Chapitre 3
Soyons responsables!

pp. 54–79

**sing the Chapter Opener**

🖵 **Video Program**

Videocassette 1

Before you begin this chapter, you might want to preview the *Video Program* and consult the *Video Guide*. Suggestions for integrating the video into each chapter and activity masters for video selections can be found in the *Video Guide*.

Motivating Activity

Ask students to name environmental groups they are familiar with and tell what these groups do to protect the environment. Ask students what they can do personally to protect the environment.

Teaching Suggestion

Ask students to tell everything they can about the photos in French. If any words in the captions are unfamiliar, have them try to guess the meaning from context.

Photo Flash!

① This photo shows Lake Geneva (**Lac Léman**), overshadowed by the mountains of the Jorat heights in French-speaking Switzerland. In the southern part of the country, the Swiss Alps tower over 12,000 feet. Students may want to know that the highest peak in the Swiss Alps is not the Matterhorn (14,691 feet), but Dufourspitze peak, which measures over 15,000 feet.

CHAPITRE

3
Soyons responsables!

① En Suisse, on protège l'environnement!

54   *cinquante-quatre*

🌐 Culture Note

Ecology is an important part of everyday life in Switzerland. Many laws have been passed to protect the country's forested areas, and strict controls on automobile emissions help to decrease air pollution. Explorations into the widespread use of alternative energy sources have been successful. Over 400 hydroelectric plants supply energy to the country, without the negative effects of fossil fuels.

Teaching Suggestion

Have students find the answers to the following questions: **Combien de langues officielles est-ce qu'il y a en Suisse? (4) Lesquelles? (français, allemand, italien, romanche) Où se trouve la Suisse? (à l'est de la France, au nord de l'Italie) Quels sont les produits typiques qu'on trouve en Suisse? (le chocolat, les montres, le fromage)**

Viens avec nous en Suisse où les montagnes sont reines et la propreté est une tradition. Dans ce petit pays d'Europe, la nature et la civilisation essaient de coexister harmonieusement. Avec les Suisses, disons «Vive l'écologie!»

In this chapter you will learn

- to ask for, grant, and refuse permission; to express obligation
- to forbid; to reproach; to justify your actions and reject others' excuses

And you will

- listen to teenagers asking for permission
- read fables about personal responsibility
- write a brochure for an environmental cause
- find out about Swiss efforts to protect the environment

② Eh! Tu ne sais pas que c'est interdit de jeter des papiers par terre?

③ Il faut que je tonde la pelouse d'abord.

cinquante-cinq **55**

For Individual Needs

Challenge Have students rewrite the introduction so that it describes the United States.

Language Note

Tell students that **propreté** *(cleanliness)* is a false cognate; it is related to **propre** *(clean)*, not **propriété** *(property)*.

Focusing on Outcomes

Have students match each photo with a functional objective. (Photo 2, *expressing obligation;* Photo 3, *reproaching*) You might want to have students recall French words or expressions they already know that they can use to express the functions. (**Tu devrais… ; Tu ferais bien de… ; Désolé(e), j'ai des trucs à faire. J'ai quelque chose à faire.**) NOTE: The self-check activities in **Que sais-je?** on page 78 help students assess their achievement of the objectives.

Photo Flash!

③ This photo shows a teenager who is declining his friends' invitation because he has to mow the lawn. In France and in other French-speaking countries, houses are rarely built on large lots. In large cities, enclosed courtyards, often shared by two or three apartment buildings, are common.

Teaching Suggestions

- Ask students how they think the people in Photos 2 and 3 are feeling and why. Have them replace the interdiction in the caption for Photo 2 with others that might apply to school. (**Il est interdit de parler en classe.**)
- Have students skim the introduction to determine the general message and then scan it to find words associated with Switzerland. (**petit, la nature, la civilisation, harmonieusement**). Then, have them guess what **Vive l'écologie!** means.
- Have students tell what chores are represented by the objects on pages 54 and 55. Ask them to name additional chores that parents might ask teenagers to do.

Summary

In **Je peux sortir?**, several teenagers ask their parents for permission to do various things. Despite Mélanie's protests, her father doesn't let her go to the movies because she hasn't done her homework. Gilles' parents give him permission to go hiking over Easter vacation, provided he improves his French grades. Karine gets permission to go to a birthday party if she comes home by midnight. Charles can watch a video with his friends if he cleans his room first.

Motivating Activity

Ask students if they ever have to ask their parents' permission to do something. Do their parents usually consent? Do they ever give conditional approval? Have students list reasons parents give for refusing permission.

Presentation

Have students look at the photos in the **Mise en train**. Ask what they think will happen in this episode. Then, play the recording as students read along. Stop the recording after each scene and ask **Qu'est-ce qu'il/elle veut faire? Il/Elle a le droit de le faire? Pourquoi ou pourquoi pas?**

Teaching Suggestion

Assign partners one of the following scenes to practice reading aloud together: 1, 3, 5, or 7. Then, ask the rest of the class to close their books. Call on partners at random to read their scene to the class, and have students tell what the teenager is asking permission to do, and whether it is granted.

Mise en train

Je peux sortir?

A Lausanne, en Suisse francophone, comme partout ailleurs, quand on veut sortir, il faut demander la permission aux parents.

❶ Chez Mélanie...

MELANIE Papa, est-ce que je peux aller au cinéma ce soir?

M. BONVIN Ce soir? Est-ce que tu as fait tes devoirs?

MELANIE Euh non, pas encore.

M. BONVIN Alors, c'est non.

MELANIE Mais papa... Je peux les faire après le film!

M. BONVIN Pas question. Tu ne vas pas faire tes devoirs à onze heures du soir.

MELANIE Ecoute, papa...

M. BONVIN N'insiste pas, c'est comme ça.

MELANIE J'en ai marre! C'est toujours la même chose!

❷ Mélanie au téléphone...

MELANIE Claire? Je suis désolée, je n'ai pas le droit de sortir. Il faut que je fasse mes devoirs.

CLAIRE Tant pis.

MELANIE Ce sera pour la prochaine fois.

CLAIRE D'accord. Salut.

❸ Chez Gilles...

GILLES Dites, vous voulez bien que je parte faire une randonnée en montagne avec des copains?

MME FORNEREAU Quand ça?

GILLES Pendant les vacances de Pâques.

M. FORNEREAU Et ton examen d'entrée au lycée?

GILLES C'est-à-dire que...

M. FORNEREAU Si je me souviens bien, tu n'as pas eu de très bonnes notes en français.

GILLES Non, c'est vrai, elles n'étaient pas terribles.

MME FORNEREAU Alors, pour ta randonnée, on est d'accord si tu as de bonnes notes en français. Sinon, tu restes ici pour réviser.

GILLES D'accord.

56 *cinquante-six*   CHAPITRE 3   Soyons responsables!

RESOURCES FOR MISE EN TRAIN
Textbook Audiocassette 2A/Audio CD 3
Practice and Activity Book, p. 25

Culture Note

Lausanne is located on the northern shore of Lake Geneva in French-speaking Switzerland. An important cultural center, Lausanne was the birthplace of several famous writers, including the nineteenth-century novelist Benjamin Constant, author of the Romantic novel *Adolphe*. Lausanne is also home to the International Olympic Committee, which oversees and promotes the Olympic Games.

④ Gilles au téléphone...

GILLES   Cyrille? J'ai parlé avec mes parents de notre projet de vacances.

CYRILLE   Ah oui? Qu'est-ce qu'ils ont dit?

GILLES   Ils ne sont pas très chauds.

CYRILLE   Ah, dommage!

GILLES   Attends, ils veulent bien. Mais il faut que je travaille mon français.

CYRILLE   C'est drôle! Mes parents m'ont dit la même chose!

⑤ Chez Karine...

KARINE   Dites, je suis invitée à une soirée d'anniversaire. Est-ce que je peux y aller?

MME LABORIT   Chez qui?

KARINE   Chez Jean-Michel. Samedi soir.

M. LABORIT   Hmm..., d'accord, mais il faut que tu rentres à minuit au plus tard.

KARINE   Mais papa, la soirée commence à neuf heures. C'est trop tôt, minuit.

M. LABORIT   J'ai dit minuit au plus tard.

KARINE   Mais je n'ai pas école le lendemain.

MME LABORIT   Ecoute, tu es déjà fatiguée. Tu travailles beaucoup en semaine.

KARINE   Mais le week-end, c'est fait pour s'amuser!

⑥ Karine au téléphone...

KARINE   Jean-Michel? C'est d'accord pour samedi. Mais je dois rentrer à minuit.

JEAN-MICHEL   Dommage. Mais c'est pas grave. Tu auras quand même le temps de manger et de danser.

⑦ Chez Charles...

CHARLES   Maman, ça te dérange si je vais chez Gabriel regarder une vidéo cet après-midi?

MME PANETIER   Tu n'as pas de devoirs à faire?

CHARLES   Non, j'ai tout fait.

MME PANETIER   Tu as rangé ta chambre?

CHARLES   Euh, non.

MME PANETIER   Alors, il faut d'abord que tu ranges ta chambre.

CHARLES   Je peux y aller après?

MME PANETIER   Oui, si tu ne rentres pas trop tard. Tes grands-parents viennent dîner et tu dois mettre la table.

CHARLES   D'accord. Je fonce ranger ma chambre.

⑧ Charles au téléphone...

CHARLES   Gabriel, je ne peux pas venir tout de suite. Il faut d'abord que je fasse des trucs à la maison.

GABRIEL   OK. A quelle heure est-ce que tu viens, alors?

CHARLES   Vers trois heures.

GABRIEL   Bien. On t'attend pour regarder le film.

Language Note

The verb **foncer** as used by Charles in Part 7 of **Je peux sortir?** means *to jump (to a task),* "to get to it."

Culture Note

The film that Charles would like to see, *La soif de l'or,* is by Gérard Oury, a popular French director of comic films. The film stars Christian Clavier, a comic actor, who began his career as part of a sketch comedy team called **Le splendide,** and later starred in the comic film *Les visiteurs.*

Teacher Notes

- Gilles wants to go hiking during Easter vacation (**les vacances de Pâques**). French students plan for this vacation just as American students plan for spring break.
- Remind students that a **carnet de correspondance** is a notebook in which students' grades and behavior at school are recorded.

Teaching Suggestions

- Have students react to each situation. Do they think the parents are being reasonable? Would they react in the same way as these teenagers?
- Have students try to guess the meaning of Gilles' statement about his parents, **Ils ne sont pas très chauds.** *(They aren't thrilled with the idea.)*
- Ask students if they agree with Karine that the weekend is for having fun and staying up late.

Thinking Critically

Analyzing   Ask students to list all the reasons the parents gave for granting or refusing permission. Do they think the reasons were valid? Why or why not? If students were parents, would they place the same restrictions on their children? Why or why not?

Additional Practice

Ask students the following questions about the report card at the top of this page: **Comment s'appelle l'élève?** (Foinereau) **En quelle matière il est le plus fort?** (en histoire-géo) **Il a eu quoi en français?** (huit)

Teaching Suggestion

1 You might ask these questions during the presentation to check comprehension.

✦ For Individual Needs

2 Kinesthetic Learners
Write the sentence starters on one set of large cards and their completions on another set. Give each card to one of ten students. Have the students stand at the front of the room and hold up their cards. Call on members of the class to match two people and read aloud the resulting sentence. Continue until all the starters have been paired with appropriate completions. Then, have students indicate which teenager from the **Mise en train** is represented by each pair of students.

3 Slower Pace As students listen, encourage them to take notes on the most important details to help them answer. Stop the recording after each statement to allow students time to write. You might play each statement twice.

3 Challenge For additional listening practice, have students give other quotations from the text and have the class tell whether the adult or the young person is speaking.

4 Challenge Once students have listed the expressions, have them work with a partner to use them to create a logical dialogue.

---

1 Tu as compris?

1. What are the teenagers asking their parents? for permission to go out/away
2. Who gets permission and who doesn't? Gilles, Charles, and Karine do; Mélanie does not.
3. On what conditions do the parents give their permission?
   Gilles must improve his French grades. Karine must return by midnight. Charles must clean his room.

2 Qui suis-je?

Joins ces bouts de phrases et dis quel(le) jeune de **Je peux sortir?** parle.

a.   b.   c. 3 c   d. 5 b

1. «Moi, je n'ai pas...
2. «Moi, je voudrais bien...
3. «Moi, il faut d'abord que...
4. «Moi, je dois...
5. «Moi, il faut que...

je fasse des trucs à la maison.»   je travaille mon français.»

faire une randonnée en montagne.»   le droit de sortir.»

rentrer à minuit.»   2 b   1 d

4 a

3 Ecoute!

C'est le parent de quel(le) jeune qui parle? Answers on p. 53C.

Mélanie		Karine	
	Charles		Gilles

4 Cherche les expressions

What do the people in **Je peux sortir?**
say to . . . See answers below.

1. ask permission?
2. grant permission?
3. refuse permission?
4. protest?
5. put an end to a conversation?
6. express disappointment?
7. express obligation?

5 Et maintenant, à toi

Est-ce que tes parents te permettent toujours de sortir? Sinon, leurs raisons sont-elles similaires à ou différentes de celles que donnent les parents dans **Je peux sortir?**

NOTE CULTURELLE

On dit des Suisses qu'ils sont disciplinés, travailleurs et minutieux. Ils sont contents lorsqu'ils parviennent à faire quelque chose de constructif. Les enfants suisses doivent apprendre à travailler dur très jeunes. Même les plus jeunes doivent participer à quelques tâches ménagères et, plus ils grandissent, plus ils ont de responsabilités. Lorsque les adolescents sortent de l'école, ils savent que des heures de travail—devoirs pour l'école aussi bien que tâches ménagères—les attendent à la maison. Tout ce temps passé à travailler ensemble est peut-être l'une des raisons pour lesquelles les Suisses restent si proches de leur famille.

58   *cinquante-huit*   CHAPITRE 3   Soyons responsables!

Answers
4 1. Est-ce que je peux... ? Vous voulez bien que je... ? Ça te dérange si je... ?
2. On est d'accord si... ; ... d'accord, mais il faut que... ; ... il faut d'abord que tu...
3. ... c'est non. Pas question.
4. Mais... ; Ecoute...
5. N'insiste pas, c'est comme ça.
6. Tant pis; ... dommage.
7. Il faut que je... ; Je dois...

PREMIÈRE ÉTAPE

Asking for, granting, and refusing permission; expressing obligation

VOCABULAIRE

Chez toi, qui...

enlève la neige?

lave les vitres?

fait la lessive?

fait la poussière?

nettoie le parquet?

fait le repassage?

arrose le jardin?

tond la pelouse?

mettre la table	sortir le chien	faire son lit	nettoyer la salle de bains
débarrasser la table	garder les enfants	faire la vaisselle	ramasser les feuilles
passer l'aspirateur	donner à manger au chat	faire la cuisine	*to rake leaves*

6 Ecoute!

Regarde les listes de tâches ménagères *(household chores)* que Christiane et Amina doivent faire. Ecoute les conversations et dis si c'est Christiane ou Amina qui parle.
Answers on p. 53C.

Christiane
débarrasser la table
faire la vaisselle
sortir le chien
faire la poussière
laver les vitres
arroser le jardin
faire le repassage

Amina
faire la lessive
faire la cuisine
mettre la table
passer l'aspirateur
nettoyer le parquet
donner à manger au chat
nettoyer les salles de bains

Jump Start!

Write the following lists on the board or on a transparency and have students match them and then write sentences, telling how often they do each one.

1. **faire**   a. **le chien**
2. **tondre**   b. **la voiture**
3. **promener**   c. **la vaisselle**
4. **laver**   d. **la pelouse**

MOTIVATE

Have students list all the chores they usually do at home and rate them on a scale of 1 to 10, with 1 being the least demanding and 10 the most demanding.

TEACH

Presentation

Vocabulaire Mime the expressions and have students mimic your actions. Then, hold up props (a dog leash), and ask **Qu'est-ce qu'on doit faire aujourd'hui?** Finally, have partners ask each other who does various chores in their homes. (**Chez toi, qui nettoie le parquet?**)

TPR Give commands (**Enlève la neige!**) and have students respond by miming the appropriate action.

Additional Practice

• Name various rooms of a house (**la cuisine**) and have students suggest chores associated with each room (**faire la vaisselle**).

• Play the game "**Le jeu du pendu**" on page 27F, using the new vocabulary.

For Individual Needs

6 Slower Pace Have students copy the two lists and check off each chore they hear mentioned.

RESOURCES FOR PREMIERE ETAPE

Chapter Teaching Resources, Book 1
• Communicative Activity 3-1, pp. 112–113
• Teaching Transparency Master 3-1, pp. 116, 118
   Teaching Transparency 3-1
• Additional Listening Activities 3-1, 3-2, 3-3, pp. 119–120
   Audiocassette 2A/Audio CD 3
• Realia 3-1, pp. 123, 125
• Situation Cards 3-1, pp. 126–127
• Student Response Forms, pp. 128–130
• Quiz 3-1, pp. 131–132
   Audiocassette 7A/Audio CD 3

ADDITIONAL RESOURCES
Textbook Audiocassette 2A
   OR *Audio CD 3*
Practice and Activity Book, pp. 26–29

Teaching Suggestion

7 Give props (a watering can) to various students, who tell what they must do with them. (**Je dois arroser le jardin.**) The class identifies which child in the illustration each student is portraying. (**C'est Serge.**)

Building on Previous Skills

8 Have students tell how often they do each chore, using (**deux**) **fois par semaine, le** (**lundi**), **souvent,** and so on.

Presentation

Comment dit-on... ? Say the expressions of refusal in a strict tone of voice and the expressions for granting permission in a pleasant one. Pass out cards with these expressions written on them. Then, ask students for permission to go out. Have them respond with the expression on their card. Have students list in French chores or other obligations that might be given as the basis for a refusal (**faire ton lit, faire tes devoirs**). Ask for permission to do something. Students should grant you permission on the condition that you do one of the chores listed first.

Additional Practice

• Write each of the four functions in **Comment dit-on... ?** on the board and have students copy them. Write the expressions in random order on a transparency. Have students copy the expressions under the appropriate function on their paper.
• Say the expressions at random and have students check the appropriate function on their paper.

---

7 **C'est à qui de le faire?**
Qu'est-ce que chacun des jeunes à droite doit faire?
See answers below.

8 **C'est trop!**

Tu crois que tu fais trop de choses chez toi. Tu veux savoir ce que ton/ta camarade fait chez lui/elle. Demande-lui qui fait chaque tâche dans sa famille et dis-lui qui les fait chez toi. Dis si tu crois que c'est juste ou injuste et pourquoi.

Félicité   Janine   Serge

COMMENT DIT-ON... ?
Asking for, granting, and refusing permission; expressing obligation

To ask for permission:
J'aimerais aller au concert ce soir avec Jean-Luc. *I'd like . . .*
Je peux inviter des amis?
Tu veux bien que je sorte? *Is it OK with you if . . . ?*
Ça te dérange si je fais la vaisselle plus tard? *Do you mind if . . . ?*

To grant permission:
Oui, bien sûr!
Ça va pour cette fois.
 OK, just this once.
Oui, si tu as fait tes devoirs.

To refuse permission:
Ce n'est pas possible.
Pas question.
Tu n'as pas le droit de sortir après minuit. *You're not allowed to . . .*

To express obligation:
Il faut que tu fasses tes devoirs **d'abord.** *You have to . . . first.*
Tu dois garder ta petite sœur ce soir.

> ### Note de *Grammaire*
> **Devoir** is an irregular verb.
>
> **devoir** *(must, to have to)*
>
> | | |
> |---|---|
> | Je **dois** | |
> | Tu **dois** | |
> | Il/Elle/On **doit** | faire la lessive. |
> | Nous **devons** | |
> | Vous **devez** | |
> | Ils/Elles **doivent** | |
>
> • The past participle of **devoir** is **dû.**
> • **Tu devrais** *(You should)* is also a form of **devoir.**

9 **Ecoute!**
Ecoute ces conversations et dis si les permissions sont accordées *(granted)* ou refusées.
Answers on p. 53C.

Teaching Suggestion

Note de grammaire Have students write down one chore they must do. Then, ask individuals **Qu'est-ce que tu dois faire?** Students respond with the chore they wrote down. After several students respond, ask the rest of the class **Qu'est-ce que Kim doit faire? Maria et David, qu'est-ce qu'ils doivent faire ce soir?** You might also call out a chore and have students recall who has to do it. (**faire la vaisselle; Craig, Alicia et Houng doivent la faire.**)

For Individual Needs

9 **Challenge** To extend this activity, ask students what the people are asking permission to do.

Answers
7 Félicité: laver les vitres, tondre la pelouse
Janine: faire le repassage, faire la lessive
Serge: arroser le jardin, faire la vaisselle

Grammaire The subjunctive

All the verb forms you've already learned have been in the indicative mood. There's another mood used in French called **le subjonctif**. You have to use subjunctive verb forms in clauses after specific phrases that express *obligation* (**Il faut que...**) and *will* (**vouloir que...**). You'll learn more of these phrases later, along with some other uses of the subjunctive.

- To make the present subjunctive forms of all regular and many irregular verbs, you drop the ending of the **ils/elles** form of the present tense. Then, you add the endings –e, –es, –e, –ions, –iez, –ent.

rentr~~ent~~	–e	Il faut que je **rentre** à dix heures.
finiss~~ent~~	–es	Il faut que tu **finisses** avant de partir.
répond~~ent~~	–e	Elle veut que je lui **réponde**.
mett~~ent~~	–ions	Il faut que nous **mettions** la table.
sort~~ent~~	–iez	Je ne veux pas que vous **sortiez**.
dis~~ent~~	–ent	Je veux qu'ils **disent** la vérité.

- Some irregular verbs, such as **prendre** and **venir**, have two stems to which you add the subjunctive endings. For the **je, tu, il/elle/on,** and **ils/elles** forms you follow the pattern above: que je **prenne**, que tu **viennes**. The stem you use for the **nous** and **vous** forms is the present tense **nous** form: nous pren~~ons~~, nous ven~~ons~~ → nous **prenions**, vous **preniez**, nous **venions**, vous **veniez**.

- Some irregular verbs have the same irregular stem for all the forms. The stem of the verb **faire** is **fass**–. You add the regular subjunctive endings to the irregular stem: Il faut que tu **fasses** ton lit!

10 Fais des phrases

Marc a vraiment trop de choses à faire! Il ne peut pas sortir. Qu'est-ce qu'il faut qu'il fasse? Complète ses phrases. *See answers below.*

je sorte mon chien.

je fasse mes devoirs.

réparer mon vélo.

ranger ma chambre.

je trouve mon livre d'anglais.

je garde ma petite sœur.

For Individual Needs

11 Visual Learners Have one student come to the board and sketch one of the chores suggested by the illustration (**débarrasser la table**). He or she then calls on a classmate to tell what Marina and her brother must do. (**Il faut qu'ils débarrassent la table.**)

Portfolio

13 Oral This activity may be recorded or videotaped for students' oral portfolios. For portfolio information, see *Assessment Guide,* pages 2–13.

For Individual Needs

13 Slower Pace Before students begin, the student who will play the teenager writes down all of the necessary information about the party. Those who will play the parents make a list of the tasks they will require the teenager to do.

Presentation

Vocabulaire Using sock puppets, create and act out a dialogue about a parent reprimanding a child for the actions listed in the **Vocabulaire**. Then, have the teenage puppet say or do something that will provoke one of these reprimands from students. (Be impolite, act disrespectful to someone, tell a fib, and so on.) Finally, ask students questions, such as **Tu partages toujours tes affaires?** If they answer no, prompt another student to tell them they should. (**Il faut que tu partages tes affaires.**)

---

11 Quel désordre!

Regarde la maison de Marina après sa soirée! Qu'est-ce qu'il faut que Marina et son frère fassent?
See answers below.

12 Un drame!

Avec ton/ta camarade, écris des dialogues pour illustrer les situations ci-dessous. Jouez les scènes.

1. Michel veut aller au cinéma et demande la permission à son père. Son père veut bien, si Michel a fini ses devoirs.
2. Malika aimerait regarder un film à dix heures du soir. Sa mère refuse parce que c'est trop tard et que Malika a école demain. Malika insiste. Sa mère met un point final à la discussion.

13 Je peux?

a. Tu as reçu cette invitation pour une soirée. Demande à tes parents la permission d'y aller. Ils veulent en savoir plus : chez qui? avec qui? quand? à quelle heure? Ensuite, ils te donnent la permission à condition que tu fasses quelques tâches d'abord. Prépare et joue cette scène avec deux autres camarades.

b. Téléphone à Viviane pour accepter son invitation. Dis-lui que tu as des tâches à faire, mais que tu peux venir après ça.

A la française

You can use words such as **dis donc** (*hey*), **dites** (*say*), **au fait** (*by the way*), and **alors** to start up a conversation or bring up a particular topic.

Tu es invité(e) à une boum!
Où? Avenue de Tivoli 60, Lausanne
Quand? Le samedi 12 mars à partir de 21 h
Pourquoi? Les 17 ans de Viviane Gervais
(Si tu comptes venir, téléphone au 234 68 70 avant le 10 mars).

VOCABULAIRE

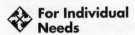

IL FAUT QUE TU...

dises la vérité.	*tell the truth.*
manges mieux.	*eat better.*
respectes tes profs et tes parents.	
aides les personnes âgées.	
partages tes affaires.	*share your things.*
prennes tes propres décisions.	*make up your own mind.*
conduises prudemment.	*drive safely.*
sois attentionné(e).	*be considerate.*
sois prudent(e).	*be careful, aware.*
sois plus responsable.	
sois tolérant(e).	
sois poli(e).	*be polite.*

62   *soixante-deux*   CHAPITRE 3   Soyons responsables!

Culture Note

Point out to students that the phone number on the invitation consists of one group of three digits and two groups of two digits each. Phone numbers in Switzerland vary by **canton** *(district)*. Numbers in Zurich, Geneva, and Lausanne, the most densely populated areas, have seven digits.

Phone numbers for smaller **cantons** might have only five or six digits. Ask students to recall how French phone numbers are given (four sets of two digits: 42.13.76.23) and what Canadian phone numbers look like (like American phone numbers, one set of three digits and one set of four digits: 243–3982).

Possible answers
11 Il faut qu'ils fassent la vaisselle, nettoient le parquet, fassent la lessive, lavent les vitres, sortent le chien.

14 C'est pas bien, ça! *Possible answers:*

Ces gens n'ont pas une attitude très responsable. Dis-leur ce qu'il faut qu'ils fassent.

1. Il faut que tu partages tes affaires.

2. Il faut que vous mangiez mieux.

3. Il faut que vous soyez attentionnés.

4. Il faut que tu respectes ta mère.

15 Il faut que tu....

Quelles sont les choses que tes parents te rappellent constamment? Fais-en une liste et compare-la avec celle de ton/ta camarade.

16 Voilà ce qu'il faut faire

Ton ami(e) te téléphone pour discuter des problèmes suivants. Dis-lui ce qu'il/elle doit faire, à ton avis.

Il/Elle s'est foulé la cheville.

Il/Elle s'est fâché(e) parce que sa sœur a voulu emprunter son nouveau jean.

Il/Elle a raté une interro et l'a caché à ses parents.

Son grand-père ne peut plus conduire.

Il/Elle a grossi.

Il/Elle s'est disputé(e) avec ses parents.

Fumer, c'est pas ma nature!

17 Que c'est compliqué, tout ça!

D'après toi, quelles sont les responsabilités et obligations d'un(e) adolescent(e)? Fais-en une liste et compare ta liste avec celle de ton/ta camarade.

For Individual Needs

14 Auditory Learners

Read aloud possible responses and have students write the number of the appropriate illustrations.

Teaching Suggestion

16 Have students write down their suggestions. Collect them and read them aloud. Have the class guess which problem the advice is for.

CLOSE

To close this **étape,** have students form small groups and assign a location to each one (**à la maison, au lycée, au café**). Two members of each group assume the roles of **"Philippe Falloir"** and **"Véronique Vouloir."** Everything these students say must begin with **Il faut que...** or **Je veux que...** The group members work together to write a skit that takes place in their assigned location.

ASSESS

Quiz 3-1, *Chapter Teaching Resources, Book 1,* pp. 125–126

Assessment Items, Audiocassette 7A/Audio CD 3

Performance Assessment

Write the different rooms of the house on index cards. Have students choose a card and tell a friend three chores that they both need to do in that room before going out. The friend might protest, but the student should be firm.

Language Notes

• Students might recognize **sois, soyez,** and **soyons** as the imperative forms of **être.**

• **Affaires** refers to a person's belongings in general. A parent might tell a child **Range tes affaires!** (*Put away your things!*) It can also mean *business* or *dealings.* Students might want to use the expressions **Ce n'est pas tes/mes affaires** (*It's none of your/my business*) or **Mêle-toi de tes affaires** (*Mind your own business*).

Family Link

Have students ask an adult friend, teacher, or family member what they were often reprimanded for as a child (slumping, having their elbows on the table, talking back). In class, ask students to list activities that were mentioned in their interviews. When assigning Family Link activities, keep in mind that some students and their families may consider family matters private.

Summary

In **Laissez-les vivre!**, Isabelle and Gilles are hiking in a Swiss park. Isabelle reproaches Gilles for picking a bouquet of flowers, which is not allowed in the park. She reluctantly accepts the bouquet, however, when she learns he picked them as a gift for her. Gilles promises he won't do it again. Brochures on hiking safety and protecting the forest are reproduced on these pages.

Motivating Activity

Come to class carrying a backpack stocked with first-aid supplies, a flashlight, a compass, and other camping safety equipment. Ask students to describe what you're wearing and try to guess what is in your pack. Ask for advice on what else to bring for a hike in a national park.

Presentation

Read aloud the advice from the **Equipement adéquat** brochure. After each one, have students remind you what to pack for the trip as suggested by the advice (**Pense à prendre...**). Have students read the second brochure together. Then, play the recording. Have two students act out the scene between Isabelle and Gilles, using a bouquet of flowers as a prop.

Teaching Suggestion

Ask the following questions: **Pourquoi est-ce qu'il faut un équipement approprié?** (Le temps peut changer soudainement.) **Est-ce qu'il est permis d'allumer un feu en forêt?** (non) **Qu'est-ce qu'il faut faire de ses déchets?** (les emporter)

Remise en train

Laissez-les vivre!

Finalement, les parents de Gilles lui ont donné la permission de partir avec ses copains. Ils sont allés faire une randonnée...

Equipement adéquat

En montagne, le temps peut changer soudainement et de manière inattendue (pluie, orage, grêle, neige jusqu'en basse altitude, même en été et en automne). Un équipement approprié est donc d'une importance vitale:

Chaussures de montagne à tige montante, avec semelles de caoutchouc profilées

Vêtements permettant de faire face à un changement de temps inattendu. Aujourd'hui, le principe de «couches superposées» s'est imposé de manière générale; on préfère à une seule veste très chaude plusieurs vêtements légers portés les uns par-dessus les autres.

Protection contre le froid: pull-over, bonnet, gants, pantalons longs

Protection contre le soleil: chapeau, lunettes de soleil, crème solaire

Protection contre le vent et la pluie

Sac à dos avec bretelles larges et bien ajustées, et ceinture sur les hanches

Cartes pédestres et cartes nationales précises, à l'échelle 1:50 000 ou 1:25 000, guides d'excursions, éventuellement altimètre et boussole

Vivres et boissons: en particulier pour les enfants, prendre suffisamment à boire. Pas de boissons alcoolisées pendant les randonnées en montagne!

Pour les cas d'urgence: bande élastique et pansements rapides (sparadrap), éventuellement couverture de sauvetage, sifflet à roulette, lampe de poche

Les bâtons de marche peuvent apporter une aide précieuse à la descente, car ils soulagent les articulations.

Les six règles des randonnées en montagne

Planifiez soigneusement chaque randonnée en montagne.

Ayez un équipement approprié et complet.

Ne vous lancez jamais seul(e) dans une randonnée en montagne.

Informez un parent, ou une connaissance, de votre randonnée.

Surveillez constamment l'évolution du temps.

Respectez le principe: «Dans le doute, faire demi-tour».

---

18 Tu as compris? See answers below.

1. What are the two brochures about?
2. Where are Gilles and Isabelle?
3. What is the disagreement between them?
4. How does Gilles justify his action?
5. What are Isabelle's feelings?

19 Ecoute!

Isabelle fait savoir à Gilles les six règles de la randonnée. De laquelle est-ce qu'elle parle? Answers on p. 53D.

20 Des reproches

Dans la forêt, Isabelle fait des reproches à Gilles. Combine logiquement ses morceaux de phrases.

- N'allume jamais
- Ne coupe pas inutilement
- Ramasse soigneusement tes déchets
- et emporte-les avec toi.
- de feu en forêt.
- des branchages et des fleurs.

64 *soixante-quatre*

CHAPITRE 3   Soyons responsables!

RESOURCES FOR REMISE EN TRAIN

Textbook Audiocassette 2A/Audio CD 1
Practice and Activity Book, p. 30

Language Note

Students might want to know the following words: **caoutchouc** *(rubber)*; **grêle** *(hail)*; **sifflet à roulette** *(whistle)*.

Answers

18 1. proper hiking equipment and safety rules for hiking in the mountains, ways to protect the forest
2. in the mountains
3. whether it is all right to pick flowers
4. Everyone does it.
5. Isabelle thinks he shouldn't pick flowers, but she accepts them since they're already picked.

Isabelle surprend Gilles en train de cueillir des fleurs.

ISABELLE	Dis donc, tu n'as pas lu la brochure?
GILLES	Quoi?
ISABELLE	Il est interdit de cueillir des fleurs!
GILLES	Mais c'est pour faire un tout petit bouquet.
ISABELLE	Tu ne devrais pas. Regarde la brochure!
GILLES	Je ne suis pas le seul... tout le monde fait pareil!
ISABELLE	Eh bien, ce n'est pas une raison.
GILLES	Tant pis. C'était pour toi, ces fleurs.
ISABELLE	Pour moi? Euh... Eh bien, c'est gentil... Mais ce n'est pas une excuse!
GILLES	Tu ne les veux pas?
ISABELLE	Euh... Maintenant qu'elles sont cueillies. C'est pas bien, mais... je te remercie quand même.
GILLES	Je te promets, c'est la dernière fois!

21 Qu'est-ce qu'on emporte?

Nomme au moins dix objets qu'il faut emporter quand on fait une randonnée en montagne. See answers below.

22 Cherche les expressions

What expressions do the teenagers in **Laissez-les vivre!** use to . . . See answers below.

1. say that something is not allowed?
2. make an excuse?
3. reproach someone?
4. reject an excuse?
5. make a promise?

23 Et maintenant, à toi

Est-ce que tu es déjà allé(e) dans un parc national? Quelles règles est-ce qu'il fallait respecter? Est-ce que tu as suivi ces règles? Pourquoi ou pourquoi pas?

REMISE EN TRAIN

soixante-cinq 65

Answers

21 *Possible answers:* chaussures de montagne, pull-over, bonnet, gants, pantalons longs, chapeau, lunettes de soleil, crème solaire, sac à dos, cartes pédestres, boissons, bande élastique

22 1. Il est interdit de...

2. Mais c'est pour... ; Tout le monde fait pareil!

3. Tu ne devrais pas.

4. ... ce n'est pas une raison; ... ce n'est pas une excuse!

5. Je te promets,...

Community Link

After students read the **Note Culturelle,** have them find out if the organizations mentioned have branches in their city. They might also make a list of local organizations that have functions similar to those mentioned. You might even arrange for a representative from one of these groups to speak to the class.

For Individual Needs

22 Slower Pace Write the French expressions that serve the functions listed in questions 1–5 on strips of transparency and scatter them across the overhead. Have students write the functions *(making an excuse)* from numbers one through five and copy each expression under the appropriate function.

Thinking Critically

Comparing and Contrasting Ask students to compare the rules for the Swiss park with rules for local parks. Do they think the Swiss rules are more or less strict than those they're familiar with?

Analyzing Ask students if they think the park rules are fair and reasonable. Why or why not?

Teaching Suggestions

- In English, ask students if they would pick the flowers if they were in Gilles' position. If they were in Isabelle's position, would they accept the flowers? Why or why not?
- Have students rewrite the dialogue as if Gilles had violated one of the other rules in the brochure.

Culture Note

The International Movement of the Red Cross and Red Crescent is familiarly known as the Red Cross, or Red Crescent in Muslim countries. It was founded in 1863 as a humanitarian relief agency. Its founder, Jean Henri Dunant, was a Swiss philanthropist who organized emergency aid services at the Battle of Solferino in 1859 during the war for Italian independence. The organization's famous red cross was inspired by the Swiss flag, which shows a white cross on a red background.

Motivating Activity

Have students draw or bring in pictures of things they associate with Switzerland. Make a collage of all the pictures and ask students to generalize about the class' impressions of the country.

Presentation

Have students test their observational skills by looking at the photos for 30 seconds, closing their books, and then describing the photos that they remember. Then, ask students **Comment sont les maisons en Suisse? Quelles langues est-ce qu'on parle là-bas? Qu'est-ce qu'il y a à faire là-bas? Qu'est-ce qu'on peut acheter comme souvenir?**

♜ Game

LA SUISSE After students have read **Savais-tu que... ?**, have them write two or three either-or questions about Switzerland. **(En Suisse, il y a quatre ou cinq langues officielles?)** You might have them do extra research to write additional questions. Then collect the questions and form two teams. Read aloud one of the questions. The first player to answer the question correctly wins a point.

History Link

Switzerland has had a policy of neutrality since the seventeenth century. Its neutrality was officially guaranteed by the Congress of Vienna in 1815. Although Switzerland mobilized its armies to defend the country during World War II, it remained essentially neutral in the conflict. Swiss voters have even rejected membership in the United Nations to avoid conflicts with their historical policy of neutrality.

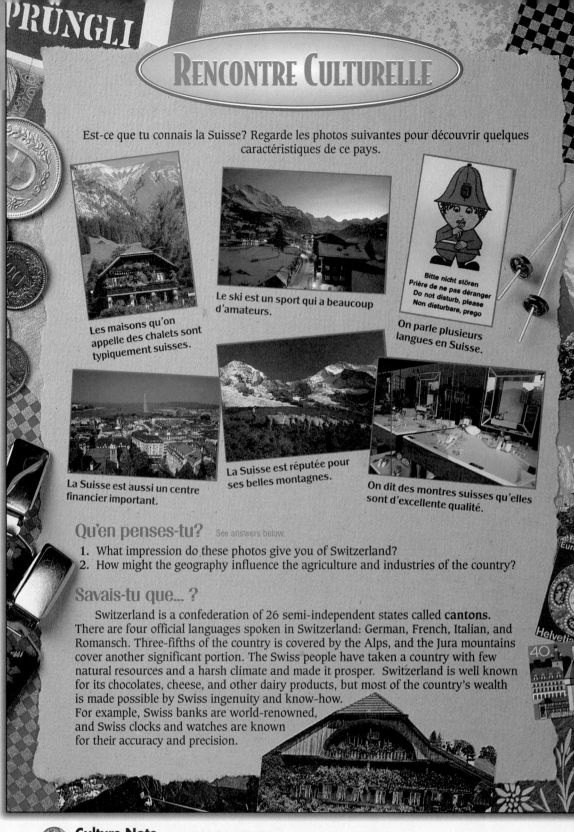

RENCONTRE CULTURELLE

Est-ce que tu connais la Suisse? Regarde les photos suivantes pour découvrir quelques caractéristiques de ce pays.

Les maisons qu'on appelle des chalets sont typiquement suisses.

Le ski est un sport qui a beaucoup d'amateurs.

On parle plusieurs langues en Suisse.

La Suisse est aussi un centre financier important.

La Suisse est réputée pour ses belles montagnes.

On dit des montres suisses qu'elles sont d'excellente qualité.

Qu'en penses-tu? See answers below.

1. What impression do these photos give you of Switzerland?
2. How might the geography influence the agriculture and industries of the country?

Savais-tu que... ?

Switzerland is a confederation of 26 semi-independent states called **cantons**. There are four official languages spoken in Switzerland: German, French, Italian, and Romansch. Three-fifths of the country is covered by the Alps, and the Jura mountains cover another significant portion. The Swiss people have taken a country with few natural resources and a harsh climate and made it prosper. Switzerland is well known for its chocolates, cheese, and other dairy products, but most of the country's wealth is made possible by Swiss ingenuity and know-how. For example, Swiss banks are world-renowned, and Swiss clocks and watches are known for their accuracy and precision.

🌐 Culture Note

Romansch (**romanche**), one of the four official languages of Switzerland, is spoken by fewer than 50,000 people. Although there are attempts to keep the language alive, it is declining under the widespread use of German. German is the most common language in Switzerland (spoken by approximately 65% of the population), followed by French (18%) and Italian (10%).

Possible answers

1. cold, mountainous, known for banks and watches, multilingual, skiing popular
2. Crops and livestock would need to be adapted to cold, mountainous region. Industries would need to capitalize on natural resources (skiing) or on ingenuity (watches, banking).

DEUXIEME ETAPE

Forbidding; reproaching; justifying your actions and rejecting others' excuses

COMMENT DIT-ON... ?

Forbidding

Veuillez ne pas marcher sur la pelouse.
  Please do not . . .
Prière de ne pas fumer.
  Please do not . . .
Il est interdit de jeter des papiers.
  It's forbidden to . . .
Interdiction de stationner.
  . . . is not allowed.
Défense d'écrire sur les murs.
  Do not . . .

Note de *Grammaire*

If you want to make an infinitive negative, place both the **ne** and the **pas** before it. Do the same with **ne... jamais** and **ne... rien.**

> Prière de **ne pas** donner à manger aux animaux.
> Il m'a promis de **ne jamais** le faire.
> Je lui ai dit de **ne rien** manger.

24 Les interdictions

Trouve l'interdiction que chaque symbole représente.

a.   b.   c.   d.

d
Il est interdit de manger.

a
Défense de pêcher.

c
Interdiction de stationner.

b
Défense de chasser.

25 Ecoute!

Pour préserver la nature, il faut respecter certaines règles. Le parc national de l'Engadine informe ses visiteurs. Ecoute le message et fais une liste de quatre interdictions.
Answers on p. 53D.

26 C'est ma chambre!

Ecris des interdictions à mettre sur la porte de ta chambre. Compare ta liste avec celle de ton/ta camarade.

DEUXIEME ETAPE

---

*J*ump Start!

Have students complete these sentences, using a different verb for each:
Chez moi, il faut que je...
Il ne faut pas que tu...
Le prof veut que nous...

MOTIVATE

Ask students to list things they aren't allowed to do at school. Write them on a transparency. Ask what the consequences are for breaking these rules, and if there are any rewards for following them. You might also ask if they think the rules are fair and why or why not.

TEACH

Presentation

Comment dit-on... ? Introduce the new expressions while acting out the forbidden activities. You might also use props (a toy car, a food wrapper, a crayon) to get the meaning across. Then, project the list of rules generated for the activity under Motivate, write their French equivalents, and have students tell you what is forbidden at school.

For Individual Needs

24 Auditory Learners Read aloud the rules given here and have students call out the letter of the corresponding symbol.

24 Challenge Have groups illustrate school rules or humorous rules they would like to see. Display the signs in the classroom.

25 Slower Pace Play the recording four times. Have students listen for and note only one prohibited activity each time.

RESOURCES FOR DEUXIEME ETAPE

Chapter Teaching Resources, Book 1
• Communicative Activity 3-2, pp. 114–115
• Teaching Transparency Master 3-2, pp. 117, 118
  Teaching Transparency 3-2
• Additional Listening Activities 3-4, 3-5, 3-6, pp. 120–121
  Audiocassette 9A/Audio CD 3
• Realia 3-2, pp. 124, 125
• Situation Cards 3-2, 3-3, pp. 126–127
• Student Response Forms, pp. 128–130
• Quiz 3-2, pp. 133–134
  Audiocassette 7A/Audio CD 3

ADDITIONAL RESOURCES
Textbook Audiocassette 2A
  OR *Audio CD 3*
Practice and Activity Book, pp. 31–34
Video Program, Videocassette 1
Video Guide

VIDEO PROGRAM
Videocassette 1

Teacher Notes

- See *Video Guide* and *Practice and Activity Book* for activities related to the **Panorama Culturel.**
- Remind students that cultural material may be included in the Chapter Quizzes and Test.
- The interviewees' language represents informal, unrehearsed speech. Occasionally, edits have been made for clarification.

Motivating Activity

Ask students which environmental issues they think are the most important and why.

Presentation

Play the video, having students listen for and list key words they recognize. Remind them not to be discouraged if they don't understand every word on the first viewing, especially since the issues are complex. Play the video a second time and have students tell what they understood. Then, have them compare the issues they listed for the Motivating Activity with the ones the interviewees mentioned.

Teaching Suggestion

Write the interviewees' names on slips of paper. Have each student select a paper and write speech bubbles containing reprimands or interdictions that the interviewee might say. **(Il faut que tu penses à l'ozone! Défense de jeter des papiers par terre!)**

PANORAMA CULTUREL

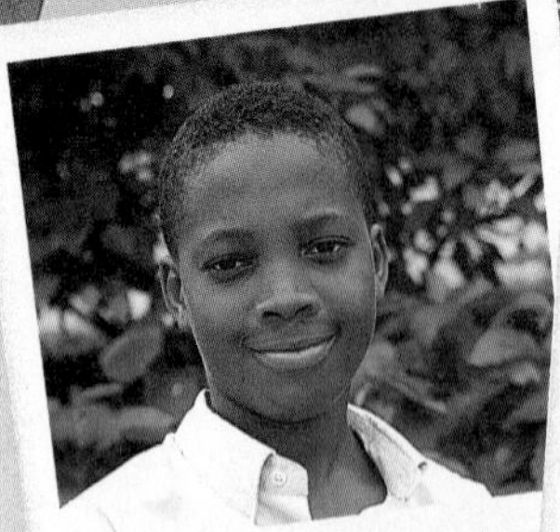

Alexandre • Côte d'Ivoire

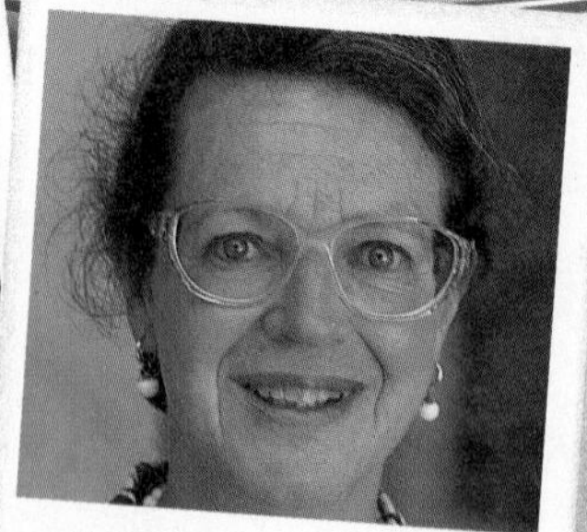

Micheline • Belgique

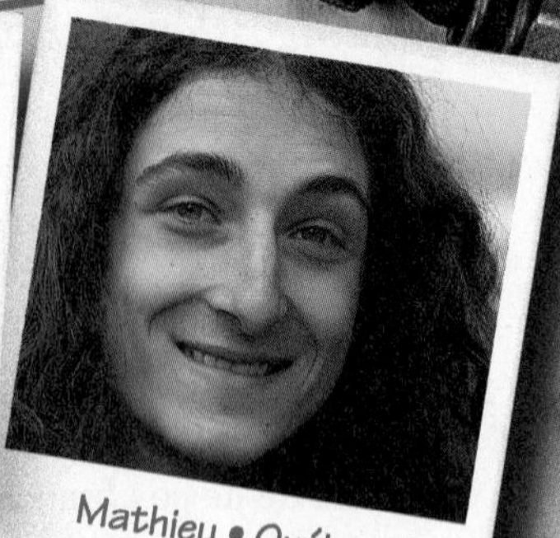

Mathieu • Québec

We asked people what environmental issues they were most concerned about. Here's what they had to say.

Quels sont les problèmes écologiques les plus importants?

«Les problèmes qui me gênent dans ma vie sont les saletés que l'on jette dans les rues... Quand on se promène dans la rue, on voit les saletés. Bon, si on est avec un étranger, il voit les saletés. Bon, ça ne lui fait pas plaisir. J'aimerais que le maire organise la population à nettoyer la ville.»

-Alexandre

«Il y a surtout le problème des trous dans l'ozone qui sont en train de réchauffer l'atmosphère. Si on ne fait pas quelque chose rapidement, il y aura de gros problèmes. On risque même de tous disparaître.»

-Micheline

«Ce qu'on a détruit durant le siècle, on ne peut pas tout refaire... parce qu'on est dans un système où l'on consomme beaucoup. On consomme beaucoup trop. Et puis, c'est la consommation, c'est ça qui nous détruit. Il faut consommer moins, qui veut dire faire attention à ce qu'on prend et recycler. Je veux dire, quand on prend quelque chose, puis on le jette, mais on peut le reprendre et faire quelque chose d'autre.»

-Mathieu

Qu'en penses-tu?

1. Among the environmental issues mentioned by the interviewees, which concern you the most? Why?
2. Do any of these problems occur in your area? What solutions have been proposed?
3. What can you do personally to care for the environment?

Questions

1. **Qu'est-ce qui gêne Alexandre? (les saletés dans la rue)**
2. **Qu'est-ce qu'Alexandre veut que le maire fasse? (organise la population à nettoyer la ville)**
3. **Pour Micheline, quel problème est le plus important? (les trous dans l'ozone)**
4. **D'après Mathieu, qu'est-ce qu'il faut faire? (consommer moins, recycler)**

Multicultural Link

Have students research "green" political parties in different countries and international environmental organizations to find out what their goals are.

Language Note

Students may want to know the following words: **saletés** *(litter);* **trous** *(holes);* **siècle** *(century);* **détruire** *(to destroy).*

VOCABULAIRE

jeter des ordures...   *to throw trash . . .*
    par terre
    dans l'eau
gaspiller...   *to waste . . .*
    l'énergie (f.)
    l'eau
utiliser des aérosols
faire du bruit
fumer

recycler...   *to recycle . . .*
    les boîtes (f.)   *cans*
    le verre   *glass*
    le plastique
    le papier
éteindre...   *to turn off/out . . .*
    la télé
    les lumières (f.)
planter un arbre
partager son véhicule
prendre les transports en commun

27 Ecoute!

Isabelle parle des habitudes de sa famille. Est-ce qu'elles sont bonnes ou mauvaises?

Answers on p. 53D.

COMMENT DIT-ON... ?

Reproaching; justifying your actions; rejecting others' excuses

To reproach someone:
Vous (ne) devriez (pas) gaspiller l'eau. *You should(n't) . . .*
Tu as tort de fumer. *You're wrong to . . .*
Ce n'est pas bien de cueillir des fleurs. *It's not good to . . .*
Tu ferais mieux de ne pas utiliser d'aérosols. *You'd do better not to . . .*

To justify your actions:
Je suis quand même libre, non?
  I'm free, aren't I?
Tout le monde fait pareil.
  Everybody does it.

Je ne suis pas le/la seul(e) à fumer.
  I'm not the only one who . . .

To reject others' excuses:
Pense aux autres.
  Think about other people.
Ce n'est pas une raison.
Ce n'est pas parce que tout le
  monde le fait que tu dois le faire.

> **NOTE CULTURELLE**
>
> **La minuterie** is an invention designed to save electricity. In many apartment buildings and other public structures, there is a system of switches in the hallways and stairways to light the way for residents or visitors. When you press a switch, the lights go on and then go off automatically, giving you time to reach either your own door or the next switch.

28 Ecoute!

Est-ce que ces personnes font des reproches ou trouvent des excuses?

Answers on p. 53D.

DEUXIEME ETAPE   *soixante-neuf* **69**

Presentation

Vocabulaire Write the new expressions on large index cards. Present the expressions to the class one at a time, illustrating their meaning through gestures. Then, show the cards at random and have the class give the thumbs-up or thumbs-down gesture. If the thumbs-down gesture is given, throw the card in a trash can. If the response is thumbs-up, tape the card to the board and have volunteers create sentences, using the expression **Il faut que tu...**

Additional Practice

Have students write down an activity one should or shouldn't do. Then, appoint one student to stand on one side of the room, holding a box on which is drawn the thumbs-up sign, and another student to stand on the other side of the room holding a box on which is drawn the thumbs-down sign. Give students twenty seconds to put their slip in the appropriate box. Then, read each slip aloud and have students indicate if it's in the appropriate box by responding **oui** or **non**.

Presentation

Comment dit-on... ? After having students repeat the new expressions, spray an aerosol can, pretend to light up an imaginary cigarette, or throw some papers on the floor. Have students reproach you. Use every excuse to justify your actions. Have volunteers reject each excuse. Then, have a student mime one of the negative actions and have the class reproach him or her.

Thinking Critically

Analyzing–Note Culturelle–Ask students if they think the **minuterie** is an effective way to save electricity. Ask for other suggestions on how to be energy-efficient.

For Individual Needs

28 Kinesthetic Learners Have students shake their index finger if they hear a reproach and extend their palms up and shrug their shoulders if they hear an excuse.

Portfolio

30 Oral This activity may be recorded for students' oral portfolios. For portfolio information, see *Assessment Guide*, pages 2–13.

Teaching Suggestions

30 Write the situations on slips of paper and put them in a box. Have partners select a slip and create an appropriate dialogue. Have them act out the scene for their classmates, who will write a one-sentence description of the situation with books closed.

31 Have students skim the survey to get a general idea of what it is about. Ask them what topics are discussed. Then, ask students the following questions: **Qu'est-ce que Julie fait pour protéger l'environnement?** (Elle ne détruit rien et elle ramasse ses ordures.) Est-ce que Geneviève pense que c'est bien de jeter des aliments par terre? (non) Pourquoi pas? (Ça prend beaucoup de temps pour se désintégrer.) D'après Jacquie, qu'est-ce qu'il faut faire à cause des personnes irresponsables? (débourser beaucoup d'argent) Pourquoi est-ce qu'Annie critique les gens qui utilisent des pesticides? (Ils éliminent les animaux.)

Thinking Critically

Analyzing Ask students which of the teenagers' complaints and concerns they consider the least and most important and why. Which one is the easiest to rectify? Which problem is the broadest and most difficult to solve?

Language Note

Students might want to know the following words: **débourser** *(to pay out);* **nuisible** *(harmful);* **dépotoir** *(dump).*

---

29 Pense aux autres!

Quels reproches est-ce que tu peux faire à ces personnes?
Possible answers:

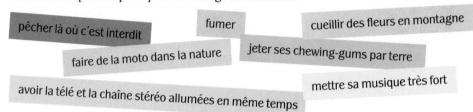

1. Tu ferais mieux de ne pas jeter des ordures par terre.
2. Tu devrais recycler.
3. Tu as tort de faire du bruit.
4. Vous devriez éteindre la télé et les lumières avant de partir.

30 Mais non!

Certaines personnes ne respectent pas l'environnement. Qu'est-ce que tu peux leur dire? Ton/ta camarade fait les choses suivantes. Il/Elle va trouver des excuses pour se justifier. Toi, tu vas lui faire des reproches pour qu'il/elle change ses habitudes.

pêcher là où c'est interdit

fumer

cueillir des fleurs en montagne

faire de la moto dans la nature

jeter ses chewing-gums par terre

avoir la télé et la chaîne stéréo allumées en même temps

mettre sa musique très fort

31 L'environnement, ça regarde les jeunes

Lis ces remarques faites par quelques jeunes francophones et réponds aux questions.
See answers below.

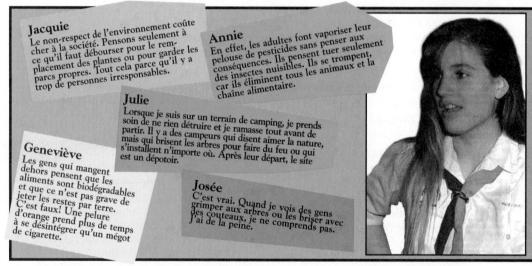

Jacquie
Le non-respect de l'environnement coûte cher à la société. Pensons seulement à ce qu'il faut débourser pour le remplacement des plantes ou pour garder les parcs propres. Tout cela parce qu'il y a trop de personnes irresponsables.

Annie
En effet, les adultes font vaporiser leur pelouse de pesticides sans penser aux conséquences. Ils pensent tuer seulement des insectes nuisibles. Ils se trompent, car ils éliminent tous les animaux et la chaîne alimentaire.

Julie
Lorsque je suis sur un terrain de camping, je prends soin de ne rien détruire et je ramasse tout avant de partir. Il y a des campeurs qui brisent les arbres pour faire du feu ou qui s'installent n'importe où. Après leur départ, le site est un dépotoir.

Geneviève
Les gens qui mangent dehors pensent que les aliments sont biodégradables et que ce n'est pas grave de jeter les restes par terre. C'est faux! Une pelure d'orange prend plus de temps à se désintégrer qu'un mégot de cigarette.

Josée
C'est vrai. Quand je vois des gens grimper aux arbres ou les briser avec des couteaux, je ne comprends pas. J'ai de la peine.

1. What are these quotations about? Who do you think might have made them?
2. Who's particularly worried about pesticides? Who's worried about littering?
3. What does Julie do to help protect the environment? What is her criticism of others?
4. What is a result of people's disrespect of the environment, according to Jacquie?

Family Link

Have students ask teachers, staff members, or a relative what environmental concerns they have and what they think should be done about them. Have students write a brief comparison of their family's concerns with those discussed in the survey in Activity 31. Students might want to use this information as the basis for the project described on page 53E.

Answers

31 1. how people harm the environment; teenagers
2. Annie; Geneviève
3. She is careful not to destroy anything, and she picks up her trash when camping; others break off branches to build fires, camp anywhere, and leave trash.
4. Society pays by having to replace plants and clean parks.

32 Un test

Fais ce test pour savoir si tu respectes l'environnement. Inscris le nombre de tes points sur une feuille de papier. Ensuite, calcule ton score. Compare tes résultats avec ceux de ton/ta camarade.

En général, tu...
- ❑ jettes tes chewing-gums par terre — 1 point
- ❑ les mets dans une poubelle — 5 points
- ❑ ne manges pas de chewing-gums — 6 points

Comme sport, tu pratiques...
- ❑ le vélo — 6 points
- ❑ la moto — 2 points
- ❑ le ski — 3 points

Quand tu écris, tu utilises...
- ❑ du papier recyclé — 6 points
- ❑ du papier normal — 4 points
- ❑ ce que tu as sous la main — 4 points

Tu prends des douches de...
- ❑ deux minutes — 6 points
- ❑ cinq minutes — 3 points
- ❑ dix minutes — 1 point

Chez toi, quand tu ne regardes pas la télé...
- ❑ tu l'éteins automatiquement — 6 points
- ❑ tu la laisses allumée — 1 point
- ❑ tu ne sais pas — 1 point

Tu mets ta chaîne stéréo...
- ❑ uniquement quand tu veux écouter de la musique — 6 points
- ❑ dès que tu es dans ta chambre — 4 points
- ❑ toute la journée — 3 points

Tu circules à pied ou à vélo...
- ❑ le plus souvent possible — 6 points
- ❑ rarement — 3 points
- ❑ uniquement lorsque tu es obligé(e) — 1 point

L'addition...

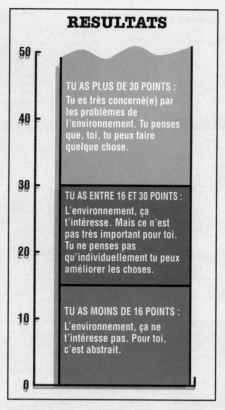

RESULTATS

TU AS PLUS DE 30 POINTS :
Tu es très concerné(e) par les problèmes de l'environnement. Tu penses que, toi, tu peux faire quelque chose.

TU AS ENTRE 16 ET 30 POINTS :
L'environnement, ça t'intéresse. Mais ce n'est pas très important pour toi. Tu ne penses pas qu'individuellement tu peux améliorer les choses.

TU AS MOINS DE 16 POINTS :
L'environnement, ça ne t'intéresse pas. Pour toi, c'est abstrait.

33 Mon journal

Tu as pris des résolutions! Ecris quelques phrases dans ton journal pour décrire tes mauvaises habitudes ou celles de tes amis quant à l'environnement et ce qu'il faut que tu fasses ou qu'ils fassent pour les changer.

34 Une annonce publique

With two friends, write the script for a public service announcement. Create a scene in which someone acts irresponsibly. The other group members reproach this person, who tries to make excuses for his or her behavior. Finally, you'll show why it's necessary to act responsibly. Act out this scene for your classmates.

DEUXIEME ETAPE

soixante et onze **71**

ASSESS

Quiz 3-2, *Chapter Teaching Resources, Book 1,* pp. 133–134

Assessment Items, Audiocassette 7A Audio CD 3

Performance Assessment

Distribute an equal number of squares of green and blue construction paper. Each "green" pairs up with a "blue," and they act out a brief skit in which the "green" reprimands the "blue" for irresponsible behavior and gives advice on how to be more considerate or environmentally conscious. The "blue" may choose to be receptive or to protest and make excuses. The "green" should reject any excuses for inappropriate behavior.

 For Individual Needs

32 Visual Learners

Form eight groups and have each group illustrate one of the test items. Students may choose to show what one shouldn't do (littering) or what one should do (recycling). Have them write captions for their illustrations. You might display their illustrations around the room.

Mon journal

33 For an additional journal entry, see *Practice and Activity Book,* page 147.

Portfolio

34 Oral Students might include this item in their oral portfolios. Encourage them to add background music and a narrator to their commercial. If the resources are available, have students videotape their commercials. For portfolio information, see *Assessment Guide,* pages 2–13.

Group Work

Show *Teaching Transparency 3-2* and have small groups write and act out a dialogue based on the scene. One member acts as the park ranger and reproaches the visitors, who justify their actions.

CLOSE

To close this **étape,** have students act out their dialogues from Activity 30 on page 70. After each dialogue, ask the class what the person did wrong, how he or she tried to justify the behavior, and how the other student countered the excuse.

LISONS!   ALBERT NEZ EN L'AIR

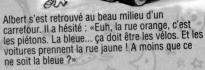

LISONS!

Dans la vie, il y a des malins, à qui il n'arrive jamais rien, et les nigauds, à qui il arrive plein d'accidents idiots. Comme les malins, il ne leur arrive jamais rien, c'est difficile de raconter leurs histoires. Les nigauds, c'est beaucoup plus rigolo. Voici donc quelques histoires de nigauds, pour tous les malins qui veulent rester malins, et les nigauds qui veulent devenir malins...

Albert Nez en l'air vivait sur une petite base de l'espace nommée Val-Fleuri. On y faisait pousser des plantes venues de toute la galaxie. Albert était très étourdi, ce qui est ennuyeux quand on habite dans l'espace.

Albert s'est retrouvé au beau milieu d'un carrefour. Il a hésité : «Euh, la rue orange, c'est les piétons. La bleue... ça doit être les vélos. Et les voitures prennent la rue jaune ! A moins que ce ne soit la bleue ?»

Un jour, les parents d'Albert l'ont envoyé voir son tonton à Villeneuve-sur-Orbite, une grande ville de l'espace. Avant le départ, ils lui ont fait des recommandations :

«Attention à la circulation. A Villeneuve-sur-Orbite, les rues bleues sont réservées aux piétons, les rues orange aux voitures et les rues jaunes aux vélos. Et on ne peut traverser que si le feu est rouge.»

Albert a regardé le feu, qui était vert. Il s'est dit : «Bon, c'est vert, alors je peux passer !» Albert est parti droit vers la rue orange. Manque de chance, un énorme camion à réaction arrivait à pleine vitesse...

Dans la fusée pour Villeneuve-sur-Orbite, Albert rêvassait un peu. A travers le hublot, il voyait la ville de l'espace se rapprocher... Il n'a pas entendu l'hôtesse qui lui demandait d'attacher sa ceinture.

L'arrivée de la fusée sur la ville a été un peu brutale mais il faut dire qu'elle allait à 20 000 kilomètres à l'heure. Tout le monde est resté bien accroché à son siège, sauf Albert qui a été projeté à travers le hublot !

Le camion a culbuté Albert à une telle vitesse que l'étourdi a traversé toute la ville, est passé à travers la bulle de verre et est parti comme une fusée dans l'espace...

C'est pourquoi aujourd'hui, si vous demandez : «Où est Albert ?», tout le monde vous répond : «Dans la Lune !»

DE BONS CONSEILS

You probably encounter unfamiliar words every time you read French, but turning to the dictionary for every new word is time-consuming and can take all the fun out of reading. Instead, try figuring out the meaning of words from their context. What does the rest of the sentence say? How is the unfamiliar word related to the words around it? Is the word a noun? A verb? An adjective? What clues do you get from illustrations or photos that accompany the text? Using contextual clues will make reading French quicker and more enjoyable.

For Activities A–C, see answers below.

A. Does the picture at the top of the reading give you any clue to what it will be about?

B. The introduction mentions people who are **nigauds** and **malins**. Can you figure out the meanings of these words from their context? What part of speech are they? How are they related to each other?

Albert Nez en l'air

C. Where does Albert live? Why is it a problem that he is **étourdi**?

D. Which of the following is *not* a warning that Albert's parents make when he goes on a trip?
1. Attention à la circulation.
2. Traverse seulement quand le feu est rouge.
3. Ne traverse pas sans regarder.
4. Prends les rues bleues.

LISONS!
CHAPITRE 3

READING STRATEGY
Deriving meaning from context

Teacher Note
For an additional reading, see *Practice and Activity Book*, page 35.

PREREADING
Activities A–B

Motivating Activity
Ask students if they remember stories from their childhood and, if so, what messages they conveyed. Have them recall the themes of different fables and give popular morals for children's stories. You might even read a fable by Aesop or La Fontaine in English and have students tell what the moral is.

Teaching Suggestion
A. Have students predict the moral of each story from the illustrations and the titles.

Additional Practice
Have students imagine the plot of *Albert Nez en l'air* from the illustrations on this page. Have them write a caption in French for each illustration and then combine the captions into a brief plot summary.

READING
Activities C–Q

◆ For Individual Needs

C.–E. Slower Pace Remind students to scan the text and use the illustrations to locate the answers to these questions. For example, for Activity D, students should find the illustration of Albert's parents warning him and scan the text next to it for the specific answers.

Teaching Suggestion
Have students list colors mentioned in *Albert Nez en l'air* (bleu, orange, jaune, rouge). In what context are they being used? (traffic lights, streets) Ask students to explain how the colors are related to Albert's problem. (They are signals and warnings that he misinterprets or ignores.)

Answers
A Yes, the story will be about an absent-minded, accident-prone boy

B *Un nigaud* is a simpleton, and *un malin* is a crafty person; nouns; The two nouns are antonyms (opposites).

C in a space station named Val-Fleuri; His absent-mindedness gets him into trouble in space.

Robert, Hubert et Herbert Tête en fer étaient les fils d'un marchand de boudin. A force de manger du boudin, ils étaient devenus très forts.

Les frères Tête en fer pouvaient jouer à plein de jeux dangereux sans jamais se faire mal. Ils s'amusaient bien, jusqu'au jour où leurs parents les ont envoyés à l'école du village d'à côté...

Mais les trois frères n'avaient pas l'habitude de jouer avec des amis si légers. Ils les ont lancés avec tant de force qu'Alain Maigrichon s'est retrouvé sur le clocher de l'église et Fanny... on la cherche encore !

Le troisième jour, évidemment, plus personne ne voulait jouer avec les frères Tête en fer. Il faut dire qu'il n'y avait plus que deux élèves intacts : Michel Porcelaine et Sophie Fêlée.

Les trois frères ont alors eu une mauvaise idée : ils ont organisé entre eux une partie de Boule qui roule. Ils sont montés sur un talus et se sont laissé rouler jusque dans la cour.

LES FRÈRES TÊTE EN FER

Le premier jour, à la récré, ils ont invité Jérôme Minus et Suzie Plume à faire une partie de Tape en fer. Les trois frères ont gagné facilement : ils avaient tapé si fort que leurs copains s'étaient enfoncés sous terre !

Malheureusement, au passage, ils ont bousculé Michel Porcelaine et Sophie Fêlée avec une telle force que leurs deux camarades se sont cassés en mille morceaux !

Les frères Tête en fer ont terminé leur course dans la piscine de l'école et comme il n'y avait plus personne pour les aider, ils sont encore au fond, en train de rouiller !

Le second jour, les frères Tête en fer ont proposé à Alain Maigrichon et Fanny Faiblarde de faire une partie de Lance moi haut, un jeu de leur invention.

For Activities G–L, see answers below.

E. Albert was hurled out of the spaceship because he forgot to . . .
　a. sit down when the spaceship landed.
　b. close the porthole.
　c. fasten his seatbelt.

F. Select the definition on the right that matches the word on the left.
　c **1.** étourdi　　　**a.** une petite fenêtre ronde
　a **2.** hublot　　　**b.** se tenir à
　b **3.** s'accrocher à　**c.** qui oublie tout
　d **4.** culbuter　　**d.** renverser

G. How did Albert end up on the moon?

H. Can you guess what the expression **être dans la lune** means? Why is it used at the end of the story?

Les frères Tête en fer

I. What was so unusual about **Robert, Hubert, and Herbert Tête en fer?**

J. Describe the games the brothers played with their schoolmates. What was the outcome of each game?

K. What is significant about the last names of the other students in the story?

L. Find the following words in the story and tell what they mean, using the illustrations as clues.

| boudin | clocher |
| enfoncé | talus | rouiller |

Drawing Inferences Knowing that *Les frères Tête en fer* is a fable, have students look at the illustrations and try to predict the moral. If students have difficulty, have them first tell as much as they can about each illustration in English.

Teaching Suggestions

• Ask students to find sequencing words and time expressions in *Les frères Tête en fer* (**le premier jour, second, troisième**). Have students list the classmates that the brothers played with on each day.
• You might also ask students why the brothers were so strong (from eating sausage).
• Ask students what the moral or lesson of this story is.

Thinking Critically

Synthesizing You might ask students if they ever played with children like the **frères Tête en fer** when they were younger. Ask them if they enjoyed playing with them and why or why not.

For Individual Needs

Visual Learners Trace the illustrations onto a transparency. Then, read aloud short excerpts from the story and have students match the quotations to the illustrations.

Answers

G He crossed on a green light and was hit by a truck.

H **Etre dans la lune** means *to have one's head in the clouds;* the French expression applies both literally and figuratively to Albert.

I They were very strong, with skin so hard they could not be hurt.

J **Tape en fer:** This game is played by hitting people with an iron mallet; The brothers knocked their playmates into the ground.
　Lance moi haut: This game is played by throwing people in the air; They threw a boy up to the steeple and a girl so far away she has never been found.
　Boule qui roule: This game is played by curling into a ball and rolling. They broke their two remaining classmates to pieces and ended up themselves at the bottom of the pool, rusting.

K **Minus** *(very small kid, or loser)* suggests inferiority or defeat; **Plume** *(feather)* lightness; **Maigrichon** *(skinny little kid)* and **Faiblarde** *(weakling)* weakness; **Porcelaine** *(porcelain)* and **Fêlée** *(cracked)* fragility.

L **boudin:** blood sausage
　enfoncé: buried
　clocher: steeple
　talus: embankment
　rouiller: rust

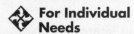

For Individual Needs

M.–Q. Slower Pace Have students look at the illustrations and tell in English everything they think happened in the story. You might have students form small groups and pool their impressions. Then, have them work together to answer the questions in Activities M through Q.

Teaching Suggestion

Q. Have students correct the false statements.

For Individual Needs

Q. Challenge Have partners write additional true-false statements and provide an answer key. Then, collect their papers and read the statements aloud to the class. You might make this activity a game, with players from two teams competing to respond to the statements.

POSTREADING
Activity R

Reading/Writing Link

R. Have groups list other common morals for stories (Don't put all your eggs in one basket. The grass is always greener on the other side of the fence.) You might have groups compete to see who can create the longest list. Have each member of the group keep a copy of the list to use in the **Ecrivons!** activities on page 75.

Teaching Suggestion

Have students write a short summary of one of the stories. Remind them to include only the essential events. Have them first list three or four events from the story, and then compose their summary. You might have students read their summaries aloud and have the class tell which story is being summarized.

JULIE BOUM

Julie Boum était la fille du célèbre savant, le professeur Jim Boum. C'était une fille très curieuse mais vraiment pas très maligne. Elle avait toujours envie de faire des expériences comme son papa… Un après-midi, Julie s'ennuyait un peu. Elle se promenait dans la maison quand elle a trouvé la porte du laboratoire ouverte.

Julie a ouvert le placard à pilules et a hésité un instant. Il y avait des pilules vertes et des bleues. «Le plus simple, c'est d'en prendre une de chaque !» s'est dit Julie.

Elle est entrée, bien décidée à explorer cet endroit mystérieux. Une drôle de machine, avec un bouton rouge, était accrochée au mur. On aurait dit une sorte de jouet… Julie a appuyé sur le bouton mais rien ne s'est passé. Quelle déception ! Julie s'est approchée un peu de la machine. Zouf ! elle a senti que ses cheveux étaient aspirés à l'intérieur. Elle a relevé la tête mais trop tard : sa tresse gauche avait été coupée net.

Julie aimait beaucoup cette tresse. Elle a regardé dans la machine pour voir où étaient passés ses cheveux. Horreur ! la deuxième tresse a disparu à son tour.

Julie était bien embêtée. Elle a décidé de se faire repousser ses tresses grâce à la pilule pousse-minute, une invention de son papa. Il suffisait d'en avaler une pour que les cheveux poussent très vite !

On n'a jamais bien su ce qui s'était passé. Les voisins ont entendu un grand «Bang» : le laboratoire a explosé en 726 morceaux. On a juste retrouvé les tresses de Julie, recrachées par la machine…

Julie Boum For Activities M and N, see answers below.

M. Who is Julie Boum? What is she like?

N. What happens one day when Julie finds the door to her father's laboratory open?

O. Which of the following did *not* happen?
1. Julie est entrée dans le laboratoire de son père.
2. Une machine a coupé les tresses de Julie.
3. <u>Julie a démonté la machine pour retrouver ses tresses.</u>
4. Julie a mélangé des pilules vertes et des pilules bleues.
5. Le laboratoire a explosé en quelques centaines de morceaux.

P. The highlighted words in these sentences are false cognates. Use context clues to figure out their true meanings.

1. Elle avait toujours envie de faire des **expériences** comme son papa. experiments
2. Julie a appuyé sur le bouton mais rien ne s'est passé. Quelle **déception!** disappointment
3. Elle a relevé la tête mais trop tard : sa tresse gauche avait été coupée **net.** clean (off)

Q. Vrai ou faux?
- F 1. Julie Boum était une fille très maligne.
- F 2. Le père de Julie lui a permis de faire des expériences.
- V 3. Julie a joué avec une machine de son père.
- F 4. Jim Boum avait inventé une pilule pour faire exploser sa fille.
- V 5. On n'a retrouvé que les tresses de Julie.

R. What are the lessons to be learned from the three fables you've just read? See answers below.

74 *soixante-quatorze*

Cooperative Learning

Have students form small groups and choose one of the stories on pages 72–74 to act out. One student is the narrator, one is the director, and the others are actors. Have students perform their story for the class. You might also want to videotape their performances and use them to introduce the reading next year.

Answers

M She is the daughter of a famous scientist; She is very curious but not very bright.

N She goes into the laboratory and puts her head in a machine, which cuts her braids off.

R *Possible answers*
Albert Nez en l'air: Pay attention.
Les frères Tête en fer: Treat your friends with care because you never know when you will need them.
Julie Boum: Too much curiosity and too little knowledge can get you in trouble.

ECRIVONS!

As you've seen, a fable is simply a story with the purpose of teaching a moral, a lesson about life. There are many traditional fables, such as those told by the Greek writer Aesop, but fables can also be modern and funny, like the ones you've just read. In this activity, you're going to create your own fable.

Ta fable à toi

Maintenant, tu vas inventer une fable. Raconte une histoire qui a une morale.

A. Préparation

1. Choisis d'abord une morale dont tu veux parler. Pense à quelque chose qu'il ne faut pas faire ou à quelque chose qu'il est bon de faire. Voici quelques sujets possibles pour t'inspirer.

> ne pas être attentionné(e)   ne penser qu'à soi   ne rien vouloir partager
>
> ne pas protéger l'environnement   ne pas être prudent(e)
>
> faire des commérages (gossip)   ne pas bien manger

2. Invente l'histoire d'une personne qui ne fait pas ce qu'elle devrait faire et raconte ce qui lui arrive.
3. Fais un plan.
   a. Ecris les événements principaux de ton histoire dans l'ordre où ils vont arriver.
   b. Pense aux détails de chaque événement et écris-les.

DE BONS CONSEILS

Sometimes writers know exactly how they want a story to end even before they start to write, and sometimes they allow the story to develop and create its own ending. When you know your ending beforehand, it's very important that you structure the story so that it leads steadily and logically to its conclusion. Making a brief outline of the events and details that you want to include in your story, in their proper order, will help you to do this.

B. Rédaction

Fais un brouillon de ta fable en suivant ton plan.

C. Evaluation

1. Relis ton brouillon en essayant de répondre aux questions suivantes.
   a. Est-ce que tu as respecté l'ordre de ton plan?
   b. Est-ce que tu as oublié quelque chose?
   c. Est-ce qu'il y a des passages ou des détails qui ne sont pas importants pour comprendre l'histoire?
   d. Est-ce que les lecteurs vont comprendre la morale de ton histoire?
2. Fais les corrections nécessaires pour améliorer ton histoire. Ajoute plus de détails s'il le faut.
3. Rédige la version finale de ta fable. N'oublie pas de corriger les fautes d'orthographe, de grammaire et de vocabulaire.

soixante-quinze 75

WRITING STRATEGY
Making an outline

Teacher Notes
- Encourage the process aspect of the **Ecrivons!** activities by making sure students always do each step of the writing assignment.
- You may want to use the portfolio evaluation forms (Evaluating Written Activities, Forms A and B) found in the *Assessment Guide* to help you evaluate students' final products.

 Portfolio

Written You might want to have students include all their work for Parts A-C in their written portfolios. For portfolio suggestions, see *Assessment Guide,* page 16.

PREWRITING

Motivating Activity
Ask students for examples of sayings or moralistic stories that parents might tell young children. (If you keep making faces, your face will freeze like that. *The Little Engine that Could*)

Reading/Writing Link
A. 1. Have students refer to the lists they created for **Lisons!** (see Reading/ Writing Link for Activity R on page 74). Compile a class list on a transparency.

Teaching Suggestion
A. 3. Have students do a clustering (mapping) activity. They should write the main events in large circles, and then write relevant details in smaller circles connected to the main ones, so that the drawing resembles a wheel with spokes.

WRITING

Teaching Suggestion
B. Encourage students to use sequencing words such as **d'abord, ensuite, et après,** and **enfin** to clarify the organization of their fable. You might give them the phrase **Il était une fois...** *(Once upon a time . . .).*

POSTWRITING

Teaching Suggestion
C. Have students exchange papers. After the reviewer has read the story, he or she summarizes the story in English, listing the main events in order and giving the moral. If the reviewer's summary and the author's outline and intent differ, they should examine the story together to suggest how the problems could be rectified.

The **Mise en pratique** reviews and integrates all four skills and culture in preparation for the Chapter Test.

 Video Wrap-Up

VIDEO PROGRAM
Videocassette 1

You might want to use the *Video Program* as part of the chapter review. See the *Video Guide* for teaching suggestions and activity masters.

Teaching Suggestion

1 Have students read the questions before you play the recording. Ask them what they think the conversation will be about.

 Portfolio

2 Oral This item is appropriate for students' oral portfolios. For portfolio suggestions, see *Assessment Guide,* page 16.

Motivating Activity

Ask students how much water they think the average person uses each day. Have them list the different ways we consume water (showers, laundry, drinking, and so on). Then, have them try to guess which use consumes the most water. You might also ask them what percentage of the world population they think has running water (10%).

MISE EN PRATIQUE

1 Ecoute cette conversation entre Sabine et sa mère et réponds aux questions. Answers on p. 53D.

1. Où est-ce que Sabine veut aller?
2. Pourquoi est-ce que sa mère ne veut pas qu'elle y aille? A quelle condition est-ce qu'elle pourrait y aller?
3. Quelles sont trois choses que Sabine doit faire avant de partir?

2 Pense à quelque chose que tu voudrais faire et demande la permission à ton père/ta mère. Il/Elle te rappelle ce qu'il faut que tu fasses et refuse. Tu insistes. Enfin, tu obtiens la permission, à certaines conditions. Joue cette scène avec ton/ta camarade.

3 Lis cette brochure et réponds aux questions suivantes. See answers at the bottom of p. 77.

AIDEZ-NOUS A...

Nous sommes parmi les 10% de privilégiés, sur cette planète, qui n'avons qu'à tourner un robinet pour obtenir de l'eau potable.

Si nous souhaitons conserver ce privilège, pensons aussi à tourner le robinet dans l'autre sens, afin que cette eau précieuse ne s'écoule pas inutilement.

Une des tâches du Département des travaux publics est de veiller sur la qualité de l'eau restituée à la nature. Pour y parvenir, il a besoin de votre aide sous deux formes:

EVITER LE GASPILLAGE
LIMITER LA POLLUTION

Votre récompense sera de bénéficier plus longtemps d'une eau de bonne qualité. Vos petits-enfants vous en seront reconnaissants. Les arbres, les fleurs et les oiseaux aussi.

Pour éviter le gaspillage

LE PETIT TRUC:
Remplissez entièrement la machine lorsque vous lavez le linge ou la vaisselle. Et n'ajoutez que le minimum de produit en fonction de la dureté de l'eau.

LE GESTE JUSTE:
Ne videz pas complètement votre chasse d'eau lorsque ce n'est pas nécessaire. Un petit geste économique à faire: rabattre le clapet ou remonter la manette!

LE BONS SENS:
Ne faites pas la vaisselle sous l'eau courante. Préférez la douche au bain!

TOUT CE QUE VOUS MELEZ A L'EAU DOIT ETRE TOT OU TARD RETIRE.

PROTEGER LES EAUX!

250 litres par personne et par jour

Savez-vous que chaque Genevois, pour son usage privé, utilise environ 250 litres d'eau par jour? Mais si on tient compte des besoins de l'industrie, de l'artisanat, du commerce et de l'agriculture, cette moyenne grimpe à 550 litres par personne.

Ces 550 litres disparaissent dans les canalisations et aboutissent aux stations d'épuration, où ils sont traités avant d'être rejetés dans le lac ou des rivières.

Le traitement de ces eaux est complexe et coûteux. Il nécessite une surveillance permanente. Pensez-y chaque fois que vous êtes tenté de laisser un robinet inutilement ouvert.

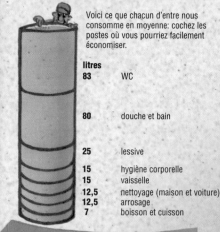
Voici ce que chacun d'entre nous consomme en moyenne: cochez les postes où vous pourriez facilement économiser.

litres	
83	WC
80	douche et bain
25	lessive
15	hygiène corporelle
15	vaisselle
12,5	nettoyage (maison et voiture)
12,5	arrosage
7	boisson et cuisson

76 *soixante-seize*

CHAPITRE 3 Soyons responsables!

Language Note

Students might want to know the following words from the brochure: **robinet** *(faucet);* **s'écouler** *(to flow);* **reconnaissant** *(grateful);* **dureté** *(hardness);* **courante** *(running);* **vider** *(to empty);* **chasse d'eau** *(toilet tank);* **aboutir** *(to end up);* **cuisson** *(cooking).*

1. What sort of brochure is this? Who do you think distributes it?
2. What are the two main things this brochure asks people to do?
3. What are a few things you can do to save water?
4. How much water does an average person in Geneva use? What happens to the water after it is used?
5. Which activity requires the most water? Which activity requires the least water?

4 Tu veux préserver ton environnement. Avec deux autres élèves, pensez à un site naturel que vous voulez préserver. Ensuite, préparez une brochure pour attirer l'attention sur ce site et ce qu'il faut que tout le monde fasse pour le préserver.

5 Avec ton/ta camarade, crée quelques panneaux contenant les messages suivants.

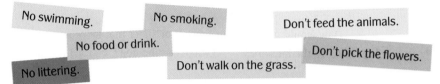

No swimming.

No smoking.

Don't feed the animals.

No food or drink.

Don't pick the flowers.

No littering.

Don't walk on the grass.

6

JEU DE ROLE

You and your friends are going to participate in a demonstration. Choose a good cause, such as forest conservation, animal protection, or water and air pollution. Make signs with slogans and plan what you're going to say to the crowd of onlookers. Act out this scene. The rest of the class will act as the onlookers, who aren't very interested in the environment. Remind them of their obligations.

CE TERRAIN A ETE SAUVE POUR LES PETITS-ENFANTS DE NOS ENFANTS GRACE A L'ASSISTANCE DU **WORLD WILDLIFE FUND** LA FONDATION INTERNATIONALE POUR LA SAUVEGARDE DE LA FAUNE ET DES ENDROITS ET TERRITOIRES SAUVAGES

Thinking Critically

3 Analyzing Ask students for their reactions to the brochure. Were they surprised by the information? Have them evaluate the suggestions that are made for conserving water. Do they consider them reasonable? Do students do these things? Have students suggest additional ways to conserve water.

Teaching Suggestion

4 Have students find pictures, take photos, or draw illustrations of the site they will feature in their brochures. Remind them to make the brochure colorful and attention-getting. You might want to supply colored markers and old magazines and catalogues to students. This project is explained in more detail on page 53E.

 For Individual Needs

5 Challenge As an extension of this activity, have students provide media coverage of the event. A student who has experience with video cameras films the demonstration, and additional volunteers act as reporters and interview the participants.

Answers

3 1. brochure about water conservation; distributed by public utilities company
2. avoid waste and limit pollution
3. *Possible answers:* Run dishwasher and washing machine only when full. Don't wash dishes under running water. Take a shower instead of a bath.
4. 250 liters per day; It is channeled to a purification station, treated, and returned to the lakes or rivers.
5. WC; drinking and cooking

This page is intended to help students prepare for the test. It is a brief checklist of the major points covered in the chapter. The students should be reminded that this is only a checklist and does not necessarily include everything that will appear on the test.

♜ Game

SERPENT! Prepare a game board on a sheet of paper on which squares "snake" across the page. Number each square and label the first one **Départ** and the last one **Arrivée**. In each square, write an answer to one of the questions in **Que sais-je?** On a separate sheet of paper, type the numbers of the questions in **Que sais-je?** that correspond to the squares on the board game. Form groups of three (two players and one judge). Give a copy of the board and a die to the players and an answer sheet to the judge. The players take turns rolling the die and moving game pieces (a coin or paper clip) from square to square. When they land on a square, they must give the question from **Que sais-je?** that is answered on that square. The judge verifies the responses. If the player responds incorrectly, he or she returns to the square from which he or she began the turn. The first person to reach the **Arrivée** square wins the game.

QUE SAIS-JE?

Can you ask for, grant, and refuse permission? p. 60

Can you express obligation? p. 60

Can you forbid someone to do something? p. 67

Can you reproach someone? p. 69

Can you justify your actions and reject others' excuses? p. 69

Can you use what you've learned in this chapter?

1 How would you ask permission to do something with a friend this weekend? J'aimerais... ; Je peux... ? Tu veux bien que je... ? Ça te dérange si je... ?

2 If you were a parent, how would you give your teenager permission to do something? How would you refuse permission? See answers below.

3 What would you say to a friend who wanted to borrow your favorite cassette or CD? Oui, bien sûr! Ça va pour cette fois. Ce n'est pas possible. Pas question.

4 How would you tell your brother or sister that he or she has to . . .
1. do the laundry?   2. take out the dog?   3. mow the lawn?
See answers below.

5 How would you tell what these signs forbid? *Possible answers:*

1.
Défense de fumer.
2.
Interdiction de stationner.
3.
Il est interdit de manger et de boire.

6 What would you say to someone who . . . *Possible answers:*
1. throws trash out of the car window? Tu ne devrais pas jeter d'ordures par la vitre de ta voiture.
2. uses aerosol sprays around the house? Tu as tort d'utiliser des aérosols.
3. smokes? Ce n'est pas bien de fumer. Tu ferais mieux de ne pas fumer.

7 How would you reproach these people? *Possible answers:*

1.
Tu ne devrais pas faire du bruit.
2.
Vous devriez éteindre la télé et les lumières avant de partir.

8 What would you say to justify an action of yours that angered someone? See answers below.

9 What would you say to a child who makes excuses for doing something wrong? *Possible answers:* Pense aux autres. Ce n'est pas une raison. Ce n'est pas parce que tout le monde le fait que tu dois le faire.

Answers
2 *Give:* Oui, bien sûr! Je veux bien. Ça va pour cette fois. Oui, si...
Refuse: Ce n'est pas possible. Pas question. Tu n'as pas le droit de...
4 *Possible answers*
1. Tu dois faire la lessive.
2. Tu dois sortir le chien.
3. Il faut que tu tondes la pelouse.
8 *Possible answers:* Je suis quand même libre, non? Tout le monde fait pareil. Je ne suis pas le/la seul(e) à...

PREMIERE ETAPE

Asking for, granting, and refusing permission

J'aimerais...   *I'd like . . .*
Tu veux bien que... ?   *Is it OK with you if . . . ?*
Ça te dérange si... ?   *Do you mind if . . . ?*
Ça va pour cette fois.   *OK, just this once.*
Tu n'as pas le droit de...   *You're not allowed to . . .*

Expressing obligation

Il faut que... d'abord.   *You have to . . . first.*

Household chores

arroser le jardin   *to water the garden/yard*

donner à manger à   *to feed*
enlever la neige   *to shovel snow*
faire la cuisine   *to cook*
faire la lessive   *to do the laundry*
faire son lit   *to make one's bed*
faire la poussière   *to dust*
faire le repassage   *to do the ironing*
laver les vitres   *to wash the windows*
mettre la table   *to set the table*
nettoyer le parquet   *to clean the floor*
nettoyer la salle de bains   *to clean the bathroom*
ramasser les feuilles   *to rake leaves*
sortir le chien   *to take out the dog*
tondre la pelouse   *to mow the lawn*

Personal responsibilities

aider les personnes âgées   *to help elderly people*
conduire prudemment   *to drive safely*
dire la vérité   *to tell the truth*
Il faut que tu sois . . .   *You must be . . .*
  attentionné(e)   *considerate*
  poli(e)   *polite*
  prudent(e)   *careful, aware*
  responsable   *responsible*
  tolérant(e)   *tolerant*
manger mieux   *to eat better*
partager tes affaires   *to share your things*
prendre tes propres décisions   *to make up your own mind*
respecter tes profs et tes parents   *to respect your teachers and parents*

Teaching Suggestions

- Have students supply a completion for each expression under *Asking for, giving, and refusing permission*, *Forbidding*, and *Reproaching*.
- Have partners or small groups make lists of things they should do and things they shouldn't do.
- Have partners take turns calling out a verb from one of the expressions under *Household chores*, *Personal responsibilities*, or *Social responsibilities* (**enlever**). The other student responds by completing the expression (**enlever la neige**).

DEUXIEME ETAPE

Forbidding

Veuillez ne pas...   *Please do not . . .*
Prière de ne pas...   *Please do not . . .*
Il est interdit de...   *It's forbidden to . . .*
Interdiction de...   *. . . is not allowed.*
Défense de...   *Do not . . .*

Social responsibilities

éteindre les lumières (f.)   *to turn off/out the lights*
partager son véhicule   *to share one's vehicle*
planter un arbre   *to plant a tree*
prendre les transports en commun   *to take public transportation*
recycler   *to recycle*
  les boîtes (f.)   *cans*

le papier   *paper*
le plastique   *plastic*
le verre   *glass*
faire du bruit   *to make noise*
fumer   *to smoke*
gaspiller   *to waste*
  l'énergie (f.)   *energy*
jeter des ordures   *to throw trash*
  par terre   *on the ground*
  dans l'eau   *in the water*
utiliser des aérosols   *to use aerosol sprays*

Reproaching

Vous (ne) devriez (pas)...   *You should(n't) . . .*
Tu as tort de...   *You're wrong to . . .*
Ce n'est pas bien de...   *It's not good to . . .*
Tu ferais mieux de ne pas...   *You'd do better not to . . .*

Justifying your actions; rejecting others' excuses

Je suis quand même libre, non?   *I'm free, aren't I?*
Tout le monde fait pareil.   *Everybody does it.*
Je ne suis pas le/la seul(e) à...   *I'm not the only one who . . .*
Pense aux autres.   *Think about other people.*
Ce n'est pas une raison.   *That's no reason.*
Ce n'est pas parce que tout le monde le fait que tu dois le faire.   *Just because everyone else does it doesn't mean you have to.*

CHAPTER 3 ASSESSMENT

CHAPTER TEST

- *Chapter Teaching Resources, Book 1*, pp. 135–140
- *Assessment Guide,* Speaking Test, p. 29
- *Assessment Items, Audiocassette 7A Audio CD 3*

TEST GENERATOR, CHAPTER 3

ALTERNATIVE ASSESSMENT

Performance Assessment

You might want to use the **Jeu de rôle** (p. 77) as a cumulative performance assessment activity.

 **Portfolio Assessment**

- **Written: Ecrivons!**, *Pupil's Edition*, p. 75
  Assessment Guide, p. 16
- **Oral: Mise en pratique,** Activity 2, *Pupil's Edition*, p. 76
  Assessment Guide, p. 16

VOCABULAIRE

soixante-dix-neuf   **79**

Chapitre 4 : Des goûts et des couleurs
Chapter Overview

| **Mise en train**
pp. 82–84 | **Mon look, c'est mon affaire** | | | Note Culturelle, French clothing stores, p. 84 | |

	FUNCTIONS	GRAMMAR	CULTURE	RE-ENTRY
Première étape pp. 85–91	• Asking for and giving opinions, p. 86 • Asking which one(s), p. 88 • Pointing out and identifying people and things, p. 88	The interrogative and demonstrative pronouns, p. 89	• Realia: Teen quote on fashion from *Okapi* magazine, p. 90 • **Panorama Culturel,** Fashion and personal style, p. 91	• Clothing vocabulary • Adjectives referring to clothing

| **Remise en train**
pp. 92–93 | **Chacun son style!** | | | Note Culturelle, The French sense of fashion, p. 93 | |

	FUNCTIONS	GRAMMAR	CULTURE	RE-ENTRY
Deuxième étape pp. 94–97	• Paying and responding to compliments, p. 96 • Reassuring someone, p. 96	The causative **faire,** p. 95	Realia: *Mannequins d'un jour,* p. 96	• Family vocabulary • Chores

Lisons! pp. 98–100	**Christian Lacroix Collection Automne/Hiver 1994–1995** Reading Strategy: Building on what you know

Ecrivons! p. 101	**La Mode en l'an 2025** Writing Strategy: Generating ideas by asking questions

Review pp. 102–105	• **Mise en pratique,** pp. 102–103 • **Que sais-je?** p. 104 • **Vocabulaire,** p. 105

Assessment Options	**Etape Quizzes**
	• *Chapter Teaching Resources, Book 1*
	  Première étape, Quiz 4-1, pp. 185–186
	  Deuxième étape, Quiz 4-2, pp. 187–188
	• *Assessment Items, Audiocassette 7B/Audio CD 4*
		Chapter Test
		• *Chapter Teaching Resources, Book 1,* pp. 189–194
		• *Assessment Guide,* Speaking Test, p. 29
		• *Assessment Items, Audiocassette 7B/Audio CD 4*
		
		Test Generator, Chapter 4

RESOURCES: Print	RESOURCES: Audiovisual
	Textbook Audiocassette 2B/Audio CD 4
Practice and Activity Book, p. 37	
Practice and Activity Book, pp. 38–41 *Grammar and Vocabulary Worksheets,* pp. 29–37 *Chapter Teaching Resources, Book 1* • Communicative Activity 4-1, pp. 166–167 • Teaching Transparency Master 4-1, pp. 170, 172 .... *Teaching Transparency 4-1* • Additional Listening Activities 4-1, 4-2, 4-3, pp. 173–174... *Additional Listening Activities, Audiocassette /Audio CD* • Realia 4-1, pp. 177, 179 • Situation Cards 4-1, pp. 180–181 • Student Response Forms, pp. 182–184 • Quiz 4-1, pp. 185–186 .... *Assessment Items, Audiocassette 7B/Audio CD 4* *Video Guide* .... *Video Program, Videocassette 1*	Textbook Audiocassette 2B/Audio CD 4
Practice and Activity Book, p. 42	Textbook Audiocassette 2B/Audio CD 4
Practice and Activity Book, pp. 43–46 *Grammar and Vocabulary Worksheets,* pp. 38–40 *Chapter Teaching Resources, Book 1* • Communicative Activity 4-2, pp. 168–169 • Teaching Transparency Master 4-2, pp. 171, 172 .... *Teaching Transparency 4-2* • Additional Listening Activities 4-4, 4-5, 4-6, pp. 174–175... *Additional Listening Activities, Audiocassette 9B/Audio CD 4* • Realia 4-2, pp. 178, 179 • Situation Cards 4-2, 4-3, pp. 180–181 • Student Response Forms, pp. 182–184 • Quiz 4-2, pp. 187–188 .... *Assessment Items, Audiocassette 7B/Audio CD 4*	Textbook Audiocassette 2B/Audio CD 4
Practice and Activity Book, p. 47	
Video Guide .... *Video Program, Videocassette 1*	

Alternative Assessment
- Performance Assessment
  Première étape, p. 90
  Deuxième étape, p. 97
- Portfolio Assessment
  Written: **Mise en pratique,** Activity 2, *Pupil's Edition,* p. 102
    Assessment Guide, p. 17
  Oral: **Mise en pratique,** Activity 3, *Pupil's Edition,* p. 102
    Assessment Guide, p. 17

For Student Response Forms, see *Chapter Teaching Resources, Book 1,* pp. 182–184.

Première étape

7 Ecoute! p. 85

1. — Oui, elle était là.

— Et qu'est-ce qu'elle portait?

— Un pattes d'eph et un col roulé gris foncé. Elle aime bien la mode des années soixante-dix, tu sais.

2. — Oui, je lui ai parlé un peu.

— Il va bien?

— Oui, mais il a raté son examen d'anglais.

— Oh, zut! Alors, il avait l'air de quoi?

— Tu sais, il est toujours rigolo. Il portait un pantalon à pinces, une chemise à rayures, un gilet en laine et une cravate à pois. C'était trop drôle!

3. — Oui, elle est venue avec Ahmed.

— Elle était en jean?

— Non, elle avait sa jupe écossaise, un pull noir et ses bottes en cuir. Elle avait aussi un foulard imprimé. Ça faisait cloche, à mon avis.

4. — Si, je t'assure, elle est venue.

— Alors là vraiment, ça m'étonne. Je lui ai téléphoné mercredi, et elle m'a dit qu'elle s'était disputée avec Antoine, et qu'elle n'irait pas à la boum.

— Ecoute, elle a dû changer d'avis parce que moi, je suis sûre que c'était elle. Elle portait son caleçon imprimé et le tee-shirt forme tunique que Corinne lui a offert pour son anniversaire.

5. — Tu sais, ça faisait longtemps que je ne l'avais pas vue, elle.

— Tu trouves pas qu'elle a changé?

— Si, beaucoup. Et puis, elle ne s'habille plus du tout comme avant.

— Tu trouves? Qu'est-ce qu'elle portait? J'ai pas fait attention.

— Elle avait une robe à col en V et des hauts talons.

Answers to Activity 7
1. Tatiana   3. Brigitte   5. Lian
2. Antoine   4. Nathalie

10 Ecoute! p. 86

1. — Comment tu trouves cette jupe?

— Je la trouve pas mal. Surtout en bleu.

2. — Il te plaît, ce pantalon à pinces?

— Non, pas du tout. Je préfère celui-là.

3. — Tu n'aimes pas cette cravate en soie?

— Si, je l'aime bien. Elle est cool.

4. — Qu'est-ce que tu penses de ces hauts talons?

— Je trouve qu'ils font vieux.

5. — Il est pas mal, ce gilet, non?

— Ah, non. Il ne me plaît pas du tout.

6. — Regarde ces bottes. Qu'en penses-tu?

— Je trouve qu'elles sont chic. J'aime bien ce genre de bottes.

Answers to Activity 10
1. aime   3. aime   5. n'aime pas
2. n'aime pas   4. n'aime pas   6. aime

15 Ecoute! p. 88

1. — Eh, comment tu trouves cette robe?

— Laquelle?

— Celle de la fille là-bas.

— Mais quelle fille?

— Là, la fille avec les lunettes.

— Je la trouve jolie.

2. — Tiens, tu n'aimes pas le pantalon du garçon, là-bas?

— Quel garçon?

— Le garçon qui porte un chapeau.

— Ah! Oui, il est pas mal, son pantalon.

3. — Il ne te plaît pas, le gilet?

— Lequel?

— Celui du garçon là-bas?

— Quel garçon?

— Eh bien, celui qui a un imperméable!

— Oui, je l'aime bien.

4. — Tu n'aimes pas les bottes de cette fille?

— Quelle fille?

— Là, celle qui a une jupe à carreaux.

— Bof, elles sont pas mal.

Answers to Activity 15
1. Michèle   3. Valentin
2. Sylvain   4. Annette

16 Ecoute! p. 89

1. — Comment tu le trouves?

— Lequel?

— Celui-là, à deux cents francs.

— Il est pas mal. Mais je préfère celui-là.

— Lequel?

— Celui à deux cent soixante francs.

2. — Elle est chouette, non?

   — Laquelle?

   — Celle-ci, là, dans la vitrine.

   — Oui, tu as raison, elle est jolie.

   — Celle-là aussi est pas mal.

   — Bof, je ne l'aime pas tellement.

3. — Ceux-ci, ils ne te plaisent pas?

   — Non, pas vraiment. Ils font trop vieux, je trouve.

   — Et ceux-là?

   — Ah oui, je préfère ceux-là. Ils sont cool.

4. — Elles sont géniales, celles-ci, tu ne trouves pas?

   — Lesquelles?

   — Là, les noires.

   — Oh non, je ne les aime pas du tout. Tu ne préfères pas celles-là?

   — Celles-là? Elles sont horribles!

Answers to Activity 16

1. un caleçon   3. des hauts talons

2. une jupe écossaise   4. des bottes

Deuxième étape

26 Ecoute! p. 94

1. — Qu'est-ce que ce sera aujourd'hui?

   — Vous pourriez me couper les cheveux en brosse?

2. — Qu'est-ce que je vous fais?

   — J'aimerais avoir les cheveux frisés, s'il vous plaît.

3. — Vous voulez une permanente?

   — Euh, non, vous pouvez plutôt me défriser les cheveux? Je voudrais un nouveau look, des cheveux raides peut-être.

4. — J'aimerais avoir les cheveux teints en bleu, s'il vous plaît.

   — D'accord.

5. — Pouvez-vous me couper les cheveux très courts?

   — Bien sûr!

6. — Comment les voulez-vous?

   — Je voudrais une coupe au carré, s'il vous plaît.

Answers to Activity 26

1. Sylvain   3. Fatima   5. Germain

2. Fabienne   4. Romain   6. Nathalie

31 Ecoute! p. 96

1. — Elle est délirante, ta coupe à la Mohawk! Je te trouve très bien comme ça!

   — Tu crois?

2. — Il ne fait pas trop vieux, ce gilet?

   — Fais-moi confiance, il est très classe.

3. — Oh, je ne sais pas. Tu ne trouves pas que c'est un peu tape-à-l'œil?

   — Crois-moi, c'est tout à fait toi!

4. — Elle est jolie, ta jupe. Elle va très bien avec tes yeux.

   — Oh, c'est un vieux truc.

5. — Tu es sûr? C'est pas trop bizarre, cette couleur?

   — Mais non! Et je ne dis pas ça pour te faire plaisir.

6. — Que tu es belle avec cette robe! Ça te va comme un gant!

   — Oh, tu sais, je ne l'ai pas payée cher.

7. — Je ne sais pas si ça me va, cette coupe. Qu'en penses-tu?

   — Je t'assure, elle est très réussie.

8. — Dis, qu'est-ce que tu penses de ce pull?

   — Il est super.

   — Vraiment?

   — Oui, fais-moi confiance.

Answers to Activity 31

1. répond   3. rassure   5. rassure   7. rassure

2. rassure   4. répond   6. répond   8. rassure

Mise en pratique

1 p. 102

1. — Ce que je préfère, moi, c'est être la plus naturelle possible.

2. — Mon look, c'est dans le style des années soixante-dix!

3. — Je passe la plupart de mon temps à la campagne, donc je préfère porter des vêtements confortables.

4. — J'aime mettre mes yeux en valeur. J'utilise une ombre à paupières violette.

5. — Quand je ne travaille pas, je ne me maquille pas. Si je sors avec mes copains, je n'utilise pas beaucoup de maquillage.

6. — Mes vêtements préférés, c'est les chaussures à plate-forme, les pattes d'eph et les mini-jupes. C'est hyper-cool!

Answers to Mise en pratique Activity 1

1. Hélène   3. Hélène   5. Hélène

2. Vanessa   4. Vanessa   6. Vanessa

Un magazine de mode
(Group Project)

ASSIGNMENT

Students will create advertisements for a fashion magazine.

MATERIALS

✄ **Students may need**
- Construction paper or posterboard
- Colored markers or pens
- Fashion magazines
- French-English dictionaries

SUGGESTED SEQUENCE

1. Have students imagine a product or a line of products to advertise. They might choose articles of clothing, accessories, hair products, skin products, cologne, or other fashion-related items. You might have them look through several fashion magazines for ideas. Tell students they have the option of satirizing existing products instead of creating their own.

2. Have students name their products, design the packaging, and organize the scope of their advertising campaign. They should decide what claims they will make about their products (it makes your hair softer; it makes you look more chic); what audience they are appealing to (teenagers, working mothers, executives); and what the major selling point will be (the price, the "mystique," the effectiveness). Have them create a slogan for their products.

3. Have students write the text for their ads. They should look up any unfamiliar words in the dictionary. Have them hand in the text or exchange it with another group for editing.

4. Students should plan the layout of their ads. Have them sketch the products and decide on the placement of the text and the illustrations.

5. Have students finalize their ads on sheets of construction paper or posterboard.

GRADING THE PROJECT

Students should receive a collective grade for appropriate and complete content, language, variety of vocabulary, and creativity and overall appearance. Each member of the group should receive an individual grade for his or her effort and participation in the project.

Suggested Point Distribution (total = 100 points)

Content . . . . 20 points
Language use . . . . 20 points
Variety of vocabulary . . . . 20 points
Creativity/appearance . . . . 20 points
Effort/participation . . . . 20 points

loubard   grunge   baba   BCBG   punk

QUI A QUOI?

In this game, students will practice recognizing vocabulary for clothing and clothing styles.

Procedure   For this game, you will need to prepare a stack of index cards with an article of clothing and a color (and style, if desired) written on them, such as **des gants à pois rouges**. In class, have students fold a piece of notebook paper to make nine squares or draw a large tic-tac-toe board on a sheet of paper. Give each student several crayons or markers in the following colors: blue, green, red, black, and yellow. Then, have a volunteer call out an article of clothing (and a style, if desired), such as **un polo (à rayures)**. Students draw the item described in one of their squares. Repeat with eight additional volunteers. Be sure students change colors after each item. Then, draw a card from your stack and ask who has that item of clothing in that color: **Qui a un foulard bleu?** If a student has drawn that article of clothing in the same color, he or she marks that square on the paper. After you call out ten or fifteen items, have students total the number of squares they've marked. The student with the most marked squares wins.

CHASSE AU TRESOR

In this game, students will practice vocabulary for clothing and clothing styles, as well as for hair and hairstyles.

Procedure   To prepare for this game, make a list of twenty "scavenger hunt" items, such as **Trouve quelqu'un qui... (1) a un foulard à rayures; (2) s'est fait couper les cheveux la semaine dernière; (3) a une permanente.** Distribute copies to students. Then, have students circulate around the room and try to find someone who can affirmatively answer each of their questions. If a student answers **oui**, he or she signs next to the item on the list. Students may not use their own names, and they may use each student's name only once. Give students five minutes to try to complete the list. The student who has completed the most items on the list when you call time is the winner. Have the winner read each item, along with the name of the person who answered "yes" to the question (**Gloria a un foulard à rayures. Bill s'est fait couper les cheveux la semaine dernière.**) Then, you might ask the class which other students answered each question affirmatively. (**Qui a un foulard à rayures?**)

Chapitre 4
Des goûts et des couleurs

pp. 80–105

*U*sing the Chapter Opener

 **Video Program**

Videocassette 1

Before you begin this chapter, you might want to preview the *Video Program* and consult the *Video Guide*. Suggestions for integrating the video into each chapter and activity masters for video selections can be found in the *Video Guide*.

Motivating Activity

Have students list and describe the "looks" that are currently popular. Ask them what items of clothing are essential for each look and what type of person wears them. You might even ask volunteers who are wearing a particular style to model it for the class and tell why they like it.

Teaching Suggestion

Have students name famous French clothing, cosmetics, and jewelry designers. You might also have several students research a designer and report their findings to the class. Ask them if they think having designer clothing and accessories is important, and why or why not.

Photo Flash!

① In this photo, mannequins sport the latest Parisian fashions. Such window displays are often elaborate and artistically designed creations, especially in the fashionable **Faubourg Saint-Honoré** district of Paris, where many **couturiers** have boutiques.

CHAPITRE

4
Des goûts et des couleurs

① Paris, centre de la mode

80 *quatre vingts*

Culture Notes

• Yves St-Laurent is known as one of the masters of **haute couture.** His designs have garnered numerous awards, such as the Neiman-Marcus Oscar and the Harper's Bazaar Oscar.

• Christian Dior's concept of fashion is carried on today by the House of Dior. Although his hallmark was the chemise, his fashions, unlike those of other designers, were known for their constant change.

• Pierre Cardin, an Italian-born Paris intellectual, is known for his avant-garde fashions that tend toward the extreme. For an idea of his style, see the costumes for Jean Cocteau's 1947 film *Beauty and the Beast*.

• Coco Chanel, born in 1883, is often considered this century's foremost **couturière.** Her new concept of fashion was casual and simple. She is famous for perfecting the simple suit, the design of which would be translated to simple, understated evening wear.

La France est bien connue pour son influence sur la mode. Le look est une notion importante dans la vie des Français. Quel que soit leur âge, style ou niveau social, ils font attention à ce qu'ils portent. Et toi, quels styles de vêtements et de coiffure est-ce que tu aimes?

In this chapter you will learn

- to ask for and give opinions; to ask which one(s); to point out and identify people and things
- to pay and respond to compliments; to reassure someone

And you will

- listen to French teenagers talk about fashion
- read about a Paris fashion designer's line of clothing
- write a fashion report for the year 2025
- find out about the French sense of style

② Ça fait vraiment cloche!

③ Crois-moi, c'est tout à fait toi!

quatre-vingt-un **81**

Focusing on Outcomes

Have students look at the photos on pages 80–81 and match them to the chapter outcomes. Then, have them list English expressions that they might use to express the outcomes. You might also have students suggest French expressions they already know that accomplish the functions listed. Have a student compile a list of these expressions on a transparency. NOTE: You may want to use the video to support the objectives. The self-check activities in **Que sais-je?** on page 104 help students assess their achievement of the objectives.

Teaching Suggestions

② Have students guess whether the teenagers in this photo are complimenting or criticizing the fashion. Have them suggest what **cloche** might mean *(stupid)*.

③ Ask students what they think of the hairstyle in this photo. You might also have them describe hairstyles that they think are conservative, and others that they find bizarre.

② ③ Have students look at these photos and suggest additional captions. You might project the transparency of French expressions from the Focusing on Outcomes activity to get them started.

History Link

Students might be interested to know that in eighteenth-century France, women wore huge **paniers** under their long skirts, which created a boxlike frame on either side of the hips. **Mouches,** or artificial moles, were often applied to the face. In the nineteenth century, both men and women tossed aside the powdered wigs and makeup associated with court life in favor of simpler, more austere styles.

Men's clothing was usually black and complimented by a silk top hat. In women's clothing, the tight waist was fashionable throughout the nineteenth century and was combined with a full skirt or even a bustle to create an hourglass effect. You might have students research other aspects of the history of fashion. They might choose a particular country or time period to research, and then report back to the class with their findings.

Summary

In this scene, Jérôme and Axcelle discuss the fashions in the *Quelle* catalogue, which has just arrived in the mail. Axcelle comments on a pair of bell-bottoms that she likes, but thinks that the suit Jérôme points out is too serious. They both agree that leggings and oversized T-shirts are cool. Then, Jérôme looks at the men's section and finds a black leather vest that he likes. Next, they discuss what to wear to an upcoming wedding. Jérôme would like to wear pants and a shirt, but Axcelle recommends that he wear a suit. Axcelle finds a pink polka-dot dress that she'd like to wear, but Jérôme jokes that he'll pretend not to know her if she wears it.

Motivating Activity

Bring in fashion magazines and hold up pictures of various trendy styles. Have students give their opinions of each style.

Presentation

Have students look at the photos on pages 82–83. Ask them to describe the styles illustrated. Point to the various outfits and ask **Comment tu trouves ça?** Then, have students make a chart with the outfits (**le pantalon à pattes d'eph, le tailleur rose, le caleçon imprimé et le grand tee-shirt, le gilet en cuir, le costume, la robe à pois**) in a vertical column on the left, and **Axcelle** and **Jérôme** across the top. Play the recording and have students fill in the chart with a check mark if the person likes the item and an "X" if not. Then, name each item and have volunteers tell whether Axcelle and Jérôme liked it.

Mise en train

Mon look, c'est mon affaire

Axcelle entre dans le salon avec le courrier qu'elle vient d'aller chercher...

❶ JEROME Ah, tu es allée chercher le courrier? Il y a quelque chose pour moi?

AXCELLE Non, rien pour toi, comme d'habitude.

JEROME Et ça, c'est quoi? Un magazine?

AXCELLE Non, c'est le catalogue printemps-été de Quelle. J'espère qu'il y a des trucs bien.

JEROME Tu es vraiment obsédée par la mode, toi! De toute façon, il n'y a que ça qui vous intéresse, vous, les filles!

Axcelle regarde le catalogue...

AXCELLE Ouah! Génial, cet ensemble! Tu n'aimes pas?

JEROME Lequel?

AXCELLE Celui-là, le noir avec le pantalon à pattes d'eph.

❷ JEROME Ah! Ne me dis pas que tu aimes vraiment ça! C'est affreux!

AXCELLE Tu comprends vraiment rien à la mode, toi! C'est super branché comme style et puis, si tu sortais un peu, tu verrais que tout le monde s'habille comme ça.

JEROME Ouais, ben, c'est peut-être à la mode, mais je trouve quand même ça ridicule! ... Ça, par contre, je trouve que c'est très classe.

AXCELLE Le tailleur rose, là?

JEROME Oui, comment tu le trouves?

❸ AXCELLE Pas mal, mais bon, je ne me vois pas aller à l'école comme ça. Ça fait un peu trop sérieux.

JEROME Peut-être, mais au moins, c'est élégant.

AXCELLE Tiens, regarde ce qu'elle porte, la fille, là.

JEROME Laquelle?

❹ AXCELLE Celle avec le caleçon imprimé et le grand tee-shirt. J'aime bien ça. C'est sympa, ça peut se porter partout et c'est moins sérieux que ton tailleur. Qu'est-ce que tu en dis?

JEROME Ouais... J'aime bien ce genre de vêtements. C'est cool et puis... c'est moins bizarre que ton pattes d'eph. Bon, à mon tour de regarder un peu!

AXCELLE Ben, je croyais qu'il n'y avait que les filles qui s'intéressaient à la mode!

JEROME Oh, ça va, hein! Elle est où, la section «hommes»?

AXCELLE Après les enfants.

82 *quatre-vingt-deux* · · · · · · CHAPITRE 4 Des goûts et des couleurs

RESOURCES FOR MISE EN TRAIN

Textbook Audiocassette 2B/Audio CD 4
Practice and Activity Book, p. 37

Language Note

Have students look at the photo of the bell-bottoms next to the second scene and try to guess the literal meaning of **les pattes d'eph** *(elephant feet)*. Tell them that **eph** (pronounced "eff") is an abbreviated form of the word **éléphant**.

⑤ JEROME   Ah, voilà... Oh là là, c'est nul! Il n'y a rien qui me plaît!

AXCELLE   Du calme. Tu n'as pas tout vu. Tiens, il est chouette, ce gilet, non?

JEROME   Ouah! Un gilet en cuir pour 299 F! C'est hyper-cool! Je crois que je vais le commander. En plus, j'ai vraiment plus rien à me mettre.

AXCELLE   Tiens, au fait, tu as quelque chose pour le mariage de Joël et Virginie?

JEROME   Tu fais bien d'en parler. Non, j'ai rien et je me demande ce que je pourrais bien mettre. A ton avis, un pantalon à pinces et une chemise, ça irait?

AXCELLE   Euh... si j'étais toi, je mettrais plutôt un costume et une cravate.

JEROME   Tu crois?

AXCELLE   Ben, oui, c'est quand même un mariage! Et puis, je suis sûre que c'est ce que la plupart des hommes vont mettre.

JEROME   Ce n'est pas trop habillé?

AXCELLE   Ecoute! Au pire, tu seras le mieux habillé de tous, pour une fois!

JEROME   Ah, très drôle. Va un peu à la page des costumes au lieu de dire n'importe quoi... Tiens, il te plaît, celui-là?

⑥ AXCELLE   Ouais, je trouve qu'il est très chic. En tout cas, si tu l'achètes, prends aussi la cravate, elle va très bien avec.

JEROME   Ouais, peut-être... Enfin, j'ai encore le temps d'y penser. Il reste deux mois avant le mariage.

AXCELLE   Bon, retourne à la section «femmes» que je trouve quelque chose pour ce mariage, moi aussi... Tiens, voilà. Elle est parfaite, cette robe, non?

⑦ JEROME   Tu rigoles ou quoi?

AXCELLE   Non, pourquoi? Tu as quelque chose contre les robes à pois?

JEROME   Ben, euh... T'étonne pas si je fais semblant de ne pas te connaître si tu mets ça au mariage!

MISE EN TRAIN   *quatre-vingt-trois*   **83**

For Individual Needs

Visual/Tactile Learners

Write the descriptions of the clothing shown on pages 82–83 on strips of transparency. Write the corresponding prices on another set of transparency strips. Scatter the strips across the projector. Then, read a description aloud (**une robe à pois**) and have a student match that item with its price (**179F**). Continue until all the items and prices are matched.

Building on Previous Skills

Have students tell how much Jérôme would pay for the suit and the vest (1298F — **mille deux cent quatre-vingt-dix-huit francs**). How much would Axcelle pay for the dress and the bell-bottoms? (378F — **trois cent soixante-dix-huit francs**).

Teaching Suggestions

- You might ask students if they mind being overdressed for an event and if they would rather be overdressed or underdressed.
- Ask students **Qu'est-ce que tu aimes mettre pour aller à un mariage?**
- Assign scenes to pairs of students. Have them read their scene together. You might ask for volunteers to read their scene aloud for the class.
- Read aloud lines from the dialogue and have students raise their right hand if it's Axcelle's line and their left hand if it's Jérôme's.

Math Link

Have students convert the clothing prices from francs to dollars. Current exchange rates should be available in local newspapers.

Culture Note

Quelle, La Redoute, and *3 Suisses* are French fashion catalogues. Most French catalogues come out twice a year, with a spring/summer issue and a fall/winter issue. Orders can be placed by phone, by mail, or by Minitel. Minitel is often the preferred mode, since most French people have access to it, and it is in service 24 hours a day, seven days a week. For more information on the Minitel, see page 283 of *Allez, viens!* Level 2.

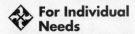

1 Tu as compris?   2. trendy, latest styles; He prefers a more classic style.

1. What does Axcelle receive in the mail? a clothing catalogue
2. What sort of clothes does Axcelle like? What does Jérôme think about them?
3. For what upcoming event do they try to select outfits? a wedding
4. What is Jérôme thinking of wearing? What about Axcelle? a suit and tie; a polka-dot dress

2 Qui parle de quoi?   See answers below.

C'est l'opinion d'Axcelle ou de Jérôme? De quels vêtements est-ce qu'ils parlent?

1. Ça peut se porter partout.

3. Ne me dis pas que tu aimes vraiment ça! C'est affreux!

5. Je ne me vois pas aller à l'école comme ça. Ça fait un peu trop sérieux.

2. Si tu l'achètes, prends aussi la cravate, elle va très bien avec.

4. T'étonne pas si je fais semblant de ne pas te connaître si tu mets ça au mariage!

3 Les styles

Quels vêtements de **Mon look, c'est mon affaire** sont...
See answers below.

décontractés?   chic?   élégants?
très à la mode?   excentriques?
branchés?   sérieux?

4 Quels vêtements?

Quel est le vêtement de **Mon look, c'est mon affaire** qui correspond à chacune des descriptions suivantes?

le costume   la robe à pois   le gilet en cuir   le pantalon à pattes d'eph

Une élégance raffinée pour ce costume réalisé dans un mélange de coton et polyester. Veste coupe classique avec fente dos, 1 poche poitrine et 2 poches intérieures. Pantalon à pinces, montage ville : fermeture par glissière.

Imprimé pastilles pour cette robe fluide. Entièrement boutonnée devant, taille appuyée par découpes devant et dos. Encolure en V, pinces sous poitrine. Manches courtes. Épaulettes. Base ample et dansante. Long. 90cm.

Une qualité de cuir superbe pour ce gilet sans manches. Empiècement avec double surpiqûre. 2 poches passepoilées. Fermeture par pressions. Dos 100% polyester rehaussé d'un lien et d'une boucle. 100% cuir (agneau).

Bien mode, le pantalon «patte d'eph» avec base en dentelle. Taille élastique. Entrejambes 72 cm env. 55% coton, 43% polyamide, 2% élasthanne.

5 Cherche les expressions

In **Mon look, c'est mon affaire**, what expressions do Axcelle and Jérôme use to . . .   See answers below.

1. ask an opinion?
2. ask which one(s)?
3. point out an item?
4. give a favorable opinion?
5. give an unfavorable opinion?

6 Et maintenant, à toi

Est-ce que tu t'es déjà habillé(e) pour une occasion spéciale? Laquelle? Quels vêtements est-ce que tu as choisis? Quel est ton look préféré?

NOTE CULTURELLE

La France est réputée pour sa **haute couture**. Mais bien sûr, tout le monde n'a pas les moyens de se payer des vêtements créés par des grands couturiers tels que Christian Dior ou Nina Ricci. Dans les grands magasins comme les **Galeries Lafayette** ou le **Printemps**, on peut trouver des vêtements de bonne qualité à tous les prix. Les jeunes peuvent également acheter des vêtements relativement bon marché dans des boutiques de mode telles que **Kookaï**, **Naf-Naf** et **Ton sur ton**.

PREMIERE ETAPE

Asking for and giving opinions; asking which one(s); pointing out and identifying people and things

Si tu as oublié clothing vocabulary va à la page 335.

VOCABULAIRE

La boîte à mode

un costume
une robe à col en V
une cravate en soie
un gilet en laine
une chemise à rayures
un pendentif
une mini-jupe écossaise
des gants (m.)
un tee-shirt forme tunique
un col roulé
un pantalon à pinces
un caleçon à pois
un sac
un collant
des hauts talons (m.)
des bottes (f.) en cuir

7 Ecoute!

Gabrielle et son amie Suzette parlent de ce que tout le monde portait à la boum hier soir. De qui est-ce qu'elles parlent? Answers on p. 79C.

Nathalie
Liah
Antoine
Brigitte
Tatiana
Ahmed
Etienne

PREMIERE ETAPE

quatre-vingt-cinq **85**

RESOURCES FOR **PREMIERE ETAPE**

Chapter Teaching Resources, Book 1
- Communicative Activity 4-1, pp. 166–167
- Teaching Transparency Master 4-1, pp. 170, 172
  Teaching Transparency 4-1
- Additional Listening Activities 4-1, 4-2, 4-3, pp. 173–174
  Audiocassette 9B/Audio CD 4
- Realia 4-1, pp. 177, 179
- Situation Cards 4-1, pp. 180–181
- Student Response Forms, pp. 182–184
- Quiz 4-1, pp. 185–186
  Audiocassette 7B/Audio CD 4

ADDITIONAL RESOURCES
Textbook Audiocassette 2B
  OR Audio CD 4
Practice and Activity Book, pp. 38–41
Video Program, Videocassette 1
Video Guide

PREMIERE ETAPE
CHAPITRE 4

Jump Start!

Have students describe their favorite outfit and tell why they like it. Have them write a second sentence describing a clothing style they dislike, and telling why.

MOTIVATE

Make two columns on the board and label them **cool** and **nul**. Bring in magazine pictures of different outfits. Show the pictures to the class and have them tell under which column you should tape each one.

TEACH

Presentation

Vocabulaire Bring in the real clothing items pictured here or magazine pictures of them. Hold up an item or picture and ask students questions about it. For example, you might hold up a polka-dot shirt and a striped shirt and say **C'est une chemise à pois. Et voici une chemise à rayures. Et toi, tu préfères les chemises à pois ou à rayures?** You might even ask what students are wearing. (**Qui porte quelque chose à pois aujourd'hui?**)

Group Work

Form four or five groups. Give each group a card with the name of a celebrity and a location or event written on it (**Michael Jordan à un mariage** or **le président à Paris**). Then, have groups go to the board and draw and clothe their person, labeling at least four items of clothing. When the groups have finished, each member describes an article of clothing their person is wearing. As an alternative, have groups draw on transparencies with colored markers.

For Individual Needs

8 Tactile Learners Have partners draw an illustration of each item in the word box on the left on separate pieces of paper and place them face-down in a pile on their desks. Have them do the same with the items in the word box on the right. Then, one student selects a paper from the first pile and asks what to wear with that item. The partner draws a paper from the second pile and suggests that item. Have students take turns drawing from the two piles.

Presentation

Comment dit-on... ? Come to class wearing an outrageous outfit or bring items for a student volunteer to wear. You might include an old hat, an old pair of pants on which you have drawn designs, and brightly-colored shoes that are too large. Write the expressions for giving opinions on a transparency, dividing them into two columns, labeled *Favorable* and *Unfavorable*. Then, give your opinion of each article of clothing you're wearing and ask students what they think of it. (**J'aime bien ce genre de chaussures. Qu'en penses-tu?**)

For Individual Needs

Visual Learners Distribute magazine pictures of various fashions to partners. Have them ask for and give their opinions of the outfit. Then, have pairs pass their picture to the pair on their right. Partners then ask for and give their opinions of the new outfit. Continue until all partners have seen each picture.

---

8 Je mets quoi, alors?

Ton ami(e) ne sait pas quoi mettre. Donne-lui des conseils.

> —Je ne sais pas quoi mettre avec...
> —Tu devrais mettre...

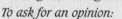

ma mini-jupe écossaise
mon pattes d'eph
mon pantalon à pinces
ma robe à col en V
mon costume
mon caleçon imprimé

ta chemise à rayures
ta cravate en soie
ton tee-shirt forme tunique
ton col roulé
ton foulard bleu foncé
ton débardeur à pois

9 Qu'est-ce qu'on met?

Un(e) ami(e) français(e) te demande ce que les Américains mettent pour aller à ces endroits. Donne-lui des conseils. Joue cette scène avec ton/ta camarade.

au concert
au restaurant
à une boum
à un mariage
à l'école
à une interview pour un job

COMMENT DIT-ON... ?
Asking for and giving opinions

To ask for an opinion:
Comment tu trouves ce pattes d'eph?
Tu n'aimes pas ce pendentif?
Elle te plaît, cette mini-jupe?
Qu'est-ce que tu penses de ces bottes?
Qu'en penses-tu?
  What do you think of it?

To give a favorable opinion:
Je le trouve super.
Si, je l'aime bien.
Elle me plaît beaucoup.
J'aime bien ce genre de bottes.
  I really like this type of . . .
C'est très bien, ça.

To give an unfavorable opinion:
Je le trouve moche.
Non, je ne l'aime pas tellement.
Elle ne me plaît pas du tout.
Je trouve qu'elles font vieux.
  I think they look . . .
Ça fait vraiment cloche!
  That looks really stupid!

10 Ecoute!

Ecoute ces jeunes qui parlent de vêtements. Ils les aiment ou pas?   Answers on p. 79C.

Vocabulaire à la carte

un pattes d'eph	bell bottoms
un débardeur	a tank top
à manches courtes/longues	short/long-sleeved
un coupe-vent	a windbreaker
des bretelles (f.)	suspenders
un foulard	a scarf
des bottines (f.)	ankle boots
des mocassins (m.)	loafers
en toile	linen
en daim	suede
à carreaux	checked
imprimé(e)	printed
bleu clair	light blue
bleu foncé	dark blue

Teaching Suggestion

10 Before playing the recording, say at random the various expressions for giving opinions from **Comment dit-on... ?** Have students make the thumbs-up gesture if the opinion is favorable and the thumbs-down gesture if it is unfavorable.

Reteaching

Object pronouns Ask students how they choose whether to use the object pronoun **le**, **la**, or **les** when giving their opinion. Have them give examples of clothing items that they would replace with **le**, **la**, and **les**. Then, show magazine pictures of various clothing items and ask individual students to give their opinions of them, using object pronouns. (**Comment tu trouves cette cravate? Je la trouve moche.**)

11 Qu'est-ce qu'ils se disent?

Ces jeunes sont en train de faire les magasins. Utilise les expressions dans le **Comment dit-on...?** pour recréer leurs conversations. *Possible answers:*

1. —Qu'en penses-tu?
—Je le trouve cool!

2. —Elle te plaît, cette robe?
—Elle me plaît beaucoup.

3. —Qu'est-ce que tu penses de ces chaussures?
—Je les trouve moches.

4. —Comment tu trouves ce sac?
—Je trouve qu'il fait vieux.

VOCABULAIRE

chic	élégant(e)	super	affreux (-euse)	*hideous*	sobre	*plain*
classe	génial(e)		ringard(e)	*corny*	tape-à-l'œil	*gaudy*
délirant(e) *wild*	hyper-cool		sérieux (-euse)	*conservative*	vulgaire	*tasteless*

12 Qu'en penses-tu?

a. Regarde ces vêtements. Tu penses acheter quelque chose, mais tu veux savoir ce qu'en pense ton/ta camarade. Demande-lui comment il/elle trouve ces vêtements.

Si tu as oublié adjectives referring to clothes va à la page 335.

1. **D. Le gilet écossais sans manches.** Très mode, il ajoute une petite note colorée à toute tenue. Réalisé en 50% acrylique, 45% laine et 5% autres fibres.
Rouge : 231.6946.
3 tailles : 34/36, 38/40, 42/44
279 F

E. Le pull Lambswool double fil. Assorti au gilet. Col roulé côtelé. Emmanchures diminuées. Finitions bord-côtes. En maille jersey 100% laine. Long. 64 cm env.
Bordeaux chiné : 221.0902.
Bleu : 221.0905.
Gris chiné : 221.0906.
Vert chiné : 221.0909.
36/38/40, 42/44/46
229 F

G. La chemise à rayures. Col boutonné, poche poitrine à rabat boutonné, poignets à patte capucin, empiècement dos double avec pli creux et lichette. Entretien facile : elle est en 80% coton, 20% polyester.
Prune : 261.0111.   Bleu : 271.0112.
Vert : 271.0115.   Mousse : 271.0118.
4 encolures :   37/38 169 F
39/40, 41/42 179 F   43/44 189 F
H. La cravate.
Des fleurs imprimées sur de la pure soie.
Larg. 9 cm.   Feuilles : 271.9090 169 F

I. Les bottes drapées. A porter avec ou sans revers. Dessus cuir pleine fleur (bovin). Tige 25 cm doublée en synthétique. Demi-semelle intérieure synthétique. Semelle extérieure en élastomère. Talon enrobé peau 8 cm.
6 pointures : 36, 37, 38, 39, 40, 41
Noir : 521.2376.   479 F
Verni noir : 521.2379.   529 F

b. Choisis ce que tu vas acheter. Téléphone au service clientèle du magasin pour commander *(to order)* ce que tu veux. N'oublie pas de donner le numéro de référence, le prix et la couleur de l'article. Joue cette scène avec ton/ta camarade.

Additional Practice

Have students make a poster depicting their own personal sense of style by gathering magazine pictures or drawing illustrations. Have them include their favorite colors, patterns, and types of fabric on their posters. They might even glue bits of fabric or jewelry to their posters to add texture. Have them label each item and use the opinion expressions from **Comment dit-on...?** to describe their sense of style. (**Je les trouve super, ces cravates imprimées! J'aime bien ce genre de robe. J'aime bien les hauts talons.**) This activity might be done as a chapter project.

[spiral binding]

Presentation

Vocabulaire The day before you plan to present the vocabulary, assign each student one of the vocabulary words to illustrate. Have them find a magazine picture to illustrate their adjective, attach it to a piece of construction paper, and write the adjective on the reverse side. On the day of the presentation, collect the illustrations. Hold up each one, read aloud the adjective written on the back, and ask students if they agree with the opinion. (**C'est ringard, n'est-ce pas? Comment tu trouves ça?**). Then, hold up magazine pictures of various outfits, asking **Comment tu trouves ça? C'est ringard ou hyper-cool?**

For Individual Needs

12 a. Slower Pace Before students pair off, have them write down their impressions of each article of clothing.

12 b. Challenge To make their phone conversations more interesting, have the student who is taking the order play the role comically by misunderstanding everything the customer says.

Building on Previous Skills

12 b. Students might also give and spell their name, address, and phone number for the customer service representative.

Portfolio

12 b. Oral This activity is appropriate for students' oral portfolios. For portfolio information, see *Assessment Guide*, pages 2–13.

Additional Practice

13 Have students close their books. Write the different styles (**punk, grunge, baba, BCBG, loubard**) on the board or on a transparency. Then, call out an article of clothing (**un blouson en cuir noir**) and have students tell which style(s) it represents (**loubard, punk**). For visual learners, you might hold up the real clothing items or pictures of them.

Teaching Suggestion

14 a. Have students consider the following questions: How will the look "feel" (romantic, sporty, professional)? Is the new style for adults or teenagers? Which colors and fabrics would suit their style?

📁 Portfolio

14 b. Written This activity is appropriate for students' written portfolios. For portfolio information, see *Assessment Guide,* pages 2–13.

Presentation

Comment dit-on... ? Begin by holding up two items that are the same except for the color. Ask students **Quelle jupe est-ce que tu préfères, la rouge ou la verte?** Then, have a student ask you the same question. Answer, using **celle. (Je préfère celle-là.)** Ask several students the same question. Repeat the process with two masculine clothing items and **celui.** Finally, ask students who various people in the class are. (**Comment il s'appelle, celui au pull bleu? C'est qui, celle qui me regarde d'un air bizarre?**) Then, have volunteers act as new students in class and describe the people whose names they would like to know. Have other students identify them.

13 **Quel style!**

Demande à ton/ta camarade ce qu'il/elle pense de ces différents styles. Est-ce que tu es d'accord?

loubard   grunge   baba   BCBG   punk

14 **Un style tout nouveau**

a. Tu es styliste de mode. Avec tes camarades, crée une nouvelle ligne de vêtements. Dessine trois ensembles.

b. Maintenant, faites votre publicité. Ecrivez une description de votre nouvelle ligne de vêtements. Créez un slogan pour attirer l'attention de vos clients potentiels. Présentez vos modèles à la classe. Vos camarades vont donner leurs opinions.

COMMENT DIT-ON...?
Asking which one(s); pointing out and identifying people and things

To ask which one(s):
Quelle jupe est-ce que tu préfères?
Laquelle est-ce que tu vas acheter?
Tu essaies un jean? **Lequel?**

To point out and identify things:
Ça, c'est la jupe que je préfère.
Moi, j'aime bien **ces** chaussures-**là**.
Je préfère **celles**-là. . . . *those.*
Celui du garçon là-bas. *The one . . .*
Tu n'aimes pas **le vert?**

To point out and identify people:
Regarde **celui avec** les lunettes!
. . . *the man/boy/one with . . .*
Tu vois **la fille au** pull bleu?
Là-bas, le garçon qui porte un pantalon rouge.
Celle qui parle à la vendeuse.
The woman/girl/one who . . .

15 **Ecoute!**

Pendant que Julien et Marc attendent devant le cinéma, ils parlent des vêtements que portent les jeunes qui passent. De qui est-ce qu'ils parlent? *Answers on p. 79C.*

Sylvain   Michèle   Valentin   Annette

88   *quatre-vingt-huit*   CHAPITRE 4   Des goûts et des couleurs

Teaching Suggestion

You might point out the difference between the suffixes -ci and -là. Demonstrate the difference by first pointing to a student near you and then to one at the back of the class, saying **Ce garçon-ci porte un tee-shirt, mais celui-là porte un pull.** You might also bring in two clothing items, such as scarves, and give them to two students, one who is sitting close by and another who is sitting farther away. Ask a third student **Tu aimes mieux ce foulard-ci ou celui-là?**

*G*rammaire The interrogative and demonstrative pronouns

• When you want to ask *which one(s)*, use the appropriate interrogative
pronoun to refer to the noun.

	masculine	feminine
singular	**lequel?**	**laquelle?**
plural	**lesquels?**	**lesquelles?**

—Je vais acheter ce pantalon.
—**Lequel?**
—Je trouve qu'ils sont moches, ces gants.
—**Lesquels?**

• When you want to say *this one, that one, these,* or *those,* use the appropriate
demonstrative pronoun to refer to the noun.

	masculine	feminine
singular	**celui-là**	**celle-là**
plural	**ceux-là**	**celles-là**

Moi, je vais acheter **celui-là**. (ce sac-là)
Celle-là? Oui, je l'aime bien, mais elle coûte trop cher! (cette jupe-là)
Oh, je déteste **ceux-là**! Qu'est-ce qu'ils sont moches! (ces gilets-là)
Tu n'aimes pas **celles-là**? Moi je les adore! (ces bottes-là)

16 Ecoute!

Ecoute ces conversations qui ont lieu dans des
boutiques de mode. De quoi est-ce qu'on parle?
Answers on p. 79D.

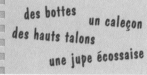
des bottes   un caleçon
des hauts talons
une jupe écossaise

17 C'est bien ça, non?

Fabrice cherche un cadeau d'anniversaire pour sa sœur.
Il ne sait pas quoi acheter. Djamila lui donne des conseils. Complète leur conversation avec
un pronom interrogatif ou démonstratif.

DJAMILA Pourquoi tu ne lui achètes pas
des bottes?

FABRICE Bon. Qu'est-ce que tu penses
de ces bottes-là?

FABRICE __1__ ? Lesquelles

DJAMILA Les blanches. Elles sont chic, non?

FABRICE Moi, je préfère __2__ -là. celles

DJAMILA Bon, d'accord. Et ces gants-là?
C'est une bonne idée, des gants,
non? Lesquels

FABRICE __3__ ?

DJAMILA __4__ -là, les noirs. Ceux

FABRICE Oui, ils sont classe; mais, euh,
je ne sais pas...

DJAMILA Oh, regarde! J'adore ce col roulé.
Qu'en penses-tu? lequel

FABRICE Je ne le vois pas. C'est __5__ ?

DJAMILA __6__ -là, à côté du pull bleu foncé.
Tu vois, là-bas? Celui

FABRICE Oui, il est vachement bien!
Je le prends!

DJAMILA Je me demande ce que tu ferais
sans moi!

Presentation

Grammaire Write **lequel,
laquelle, lesquels, lesquelles,
celui-là, celle-là, ceux-là,**
and **celles-là** on eight large
cards and give them to eight
students. Explain briefly the
use of these forms. Then, give
positive opinions about various clothing items students are
wearing (**Je trouve qu'elles
font très baba, ces chaussettes.**) and have the student
holding the appropriate interrogative pronoun stand up
and read the card in response.
(**Lesquelles?**) Have students
repeat the question. Then,
have the student holding the
card with the appropriate
demonstrative pronoun stand
up, read the card, and point to
the item of clothing in question. (**Celles-là!**) Repeat the
process several times.

Additional Practice

Compliment an item of clothing that a student is wearing
without pointing at it. (**J'aime
bien ce pantalon.**) Call on
another student to ask for
clarification. (**Lequel?**) Respond by using the correct
demonstrative pronoun and
pointing to the item of clothing this time. (**Celui-là!**) Have
partners repeat this process.

**For Individual
Needs**

16 Slower Pace Before
students listen to the recording,
have them write down the
interrogative and demonstrative
pronouns for each item in the
box to the right of the activity.

17 Challenge Have students rewrite the dialogue,
substituting different clothing
items for the ones suggested.
Remind them to change all references to the item, including
colors. (**Les blanches** might
change to **le vert**, for example.)

**Cooperative
Learning**

As a class project, set up a flea market. You
will need to bring in some old ties, plastic
sunglasses, and other small items. The object
is for students to use the interrogative and
demonstrative pronouns as often as possible,
while acting as vendors or customers. The
vendors offer suggestions and compliments,
while the customers try to choose what to

buy. You might model a sample conversation
with a student acting as the vendor.

— J'aime bien ces lunettes.
— Lesquelles? Celles-ci?
— Non, celles-là.
— Elles vous vont très bien, madame/
monsieur!
— Euh, j'hésite. Je peux voir celles-là?
— Lesquelles?
— ...

Teaching Suggestions

18 a. Tell students that they must include the following in their dialogues: at least five clothing items, at least three favorable opinions, at least three unfavorable opinions, at least two interrogative pronouns, at least two demonstrative pronouns, at least one type of fabric, and at least one style of clothing.

18 b. Have students begin their collaboration by circling three of the best lines of their own dialogue. Have them underline one or two additional lines that they like as well. When partners get together, they should combine the best parts of both dialogues and compromise on the rest.

 **Mon journal**

20 For an additional journal entry suggestion for Chapter 4, see *Practice and Activity Book,* page 148.

CLOSE

🏰 Game

🎲 **J'EN DOUTE** Form two teams. On the board, a player from one team writes a vocabulary expression **(en laine)**, which a player from the other team must use correctly in a sentence **(En hiver, j'aime mettre des jupes en laine.)** If a player doesn't know the meaning of a word, he or she might try to bluff the other team by making up a sentence. The other team has the option of calling the player's bluff by saying **J'en doute.** If the challenging team is right, and the player can't give the English definition of the word or expression, that team receives two points. If they are wrong, however, they lose a point.

---

18 **Regarde les gens qui passent!**

a. Rémi et Céline sont à la terrasse d'un café. Ils regardent les passants et ils font des commentaires sur leurs vêtements. Imagine ce qu'ils disent et écris leur conversation.

 b. Echange ton dialogue avec celui d'un(e) camarade. Travaillez ensemble pour faire un seul dialogue, puis jouez ce dialogue.

19 Le rôle de la mode

Lis la question de Sélima et les réponses de quelques jeunes. Ensuite, réponds aux questions.

«Cela peut paraître stupide, mais... quel rôle joue la mode vestimentaire dans votre vie, et comment vous habillez-vous pour aller au lycée? Pour moi, c'est très important, car j'aime bien m'habiller à la mode, et je dépense la plupart de mon argent en bracelets ou en habits. Merci pour vos réponses!»
Sélima, Tunis (Tunisie)

«Bonjour, Sélima. Vois-tu, pour moi aussi, la mode est importante. Elle permet quelquefois de dévoiler une partie de toi, inconnue de tes amis. Dans la mode, il existe des vêtements plus adaptés pour ta personnalité que d'autres, et c'est souvent en regardant la façon de s'habiller de quelqu'un, que l'on découvre son caractère. Mais je ne mettrai jamais un jean à la dernière tendance s'il ne me plaît pas, même pour être «cool»! Gros bisous de France.»
Stéphanie, Megève

«Sélima, je pense que la mode, ce n'est pas très important. La mode ne doit pas être une tenue qu'on vous impose. C'est plutôt une création qui reflète votre personnalité, votre tempérament. Je pense qu'il ne faut pas utiliser tout son argent de poche pour cela. Sers-toi de tes vieux vêtements et rénove-les.
Quant à tes bijoux, mélange-les. Tu obtiendras sûrement quelque chose qui te plaira. Tu seras à l'aise et tu auras fait la mode, celle qui te convient.»
Florence, Verrières-le-Buisson

«Personnellement, je trouve que les gens attachent trop d'importance à la mode. En effet, certaines personnes vont même jusqu'à juger les autres par les habits. Je pense que ça nous empêche de voir d'autres vérités beaucoup plus importantes. Il ne faut pas ignorer totalement la mode, mais ne pas penser qu'à ses habits. Voilà, Sélima, en résumé, ce que je pense de la mode, et j'espère avoir répondu à ta question.»
Caroline, Chêne-Bougeries (Suisse)

1. Why did Sélima write her letter? to find out how important fashion is to others
2. Who thinks that fashion is important? Who doesn't? Stéphanie; Caroline, Florence
3. According to Stéphanie and Florence, what is a purpose of fashion? to express oneself
4. What advice does Florence have for Sélima? Don't spend all your money on clothes.

20 Mon journal

 Qu'est-ce que tu penses de la mode? Est-ce qu'elle a beaucoup d'importance pour toi?

ASSESS

Quiz 4–1, *Chapter Teaching Resources, Book 1,* pp. 185–186

Assessment Items, Audiocassette 7B Audio CD 4

Performance Assessment

Have partners act out a skit about two friends in a clothing store. One tries on bizarre combinations of clothing (striped pants with a plaid shirt) and asks for opinions of them. The other compliments the outfits and makes suggestions for other choices (a white shirt with striped pants).

Language Note

Students might want to know the following words from the letters: **dévoiler** (*to uncover*); **empêche** (*prevent*); **bijoux** (*jewelry*); **convient** (*suits*).

PANORAMA CULTUREL

Mélanie • Québec

Sylviane • Martinique

Céline • Viêt-nam

VIDEO PROGRAM
Videocassette 1

We asked people for their ideas on fashion and personal style. Here's what they had to say.

Quel est ton style de vêtements préféré?

«Moi, c'est un bon gilet, puis un jean, c'est toujours ça que je porte. Des fois, je peux porter d'autres sortes de pantalons, pas de jeans, mais... un bon chandail et puis je suis bien là-dedans. Il faut que je sois confortable. Si je ne suis pas confortable, je ne le porterai pas.»

-Mélanie

«J'aime surtout les vêtements... j'aime surtout les matières. J'aime beaucoup le coton, le lin, les matières naturelles, parce que, bon, on vit dans un pays où il fait très chaud et il faut pouvoir supporter la chaleur. Et j'aime beaucoup aussi les couleurs, parce que bon, je vis dans un pays ensoleillé, donc les couleurs sont des choses très importantes.»

Est-ce que c'est important d'être à la mode?

«Oui, c'est important d'être à la mode, parce que, bon, nous en Martinique, on a quand même ce côté un petit peu français et européen où on aime beaucoup les vêtements et on aime beaucoup se montrer.»

-Sylviane

Quel est ton style de vêtements préféré?

«J'aime tout ce qui est hors du commun. Enfin... qui est pas tellement banal mais qui... qu'on peut pas voir tous les jours, quoi.»

Est-ce que c'est important d'être à la mode?

«Ça dépend. Je veux dire... Il y a certaines filles qui s'habillent mais qui n'ont rien à l'intérieur, qui n'ont pas un esprit très beau à l'intérieur. C'est pas très beau à l'intérieur. Donc, elles ont besoin de bien s'habiller. Mais enfin, ça dépend.»

-Céline

Qu'en penses-tu?

1. Which person do you most agree with? Why?
2. What reasons do these people give to support their opinions about fashion and style?
3. Do you think it's important to follow the latest trends or to be in style? Why or why not?

2. See answers below.

Teacher Notes
• See *Video Guide* and *Practice and Activity Book* for activities related to the **Panorama Culturel**.
• Remind students that cultural material may be included in the Chapter Quizzes and Test.
• The interviewees' language represents informal, unrehearsed speech. Occasionally, edits have been made for clarification.

Motivating Activity

Ask students how they would respond to the question **Est-ce que c'est important d'être à la mode?**

Presentation

Before playing the video, have students suggest words and phrases they expect to hear. Then, play the video. After each interview, ask **Quel est son style de vêtements préféré?** Ask the **Questions** below to check comprehension.

Teaching Suggestion

Ask students which interviewee they agree with most closely. Then, have them form small groups and discuss their answers to the questions in **Qu'en penses-tu?**

Language Note

Students might want to know the following words from the interviews: **chandail** *(thick sweater);* **ensoleillé** *(sunny);* **se montrer** *(to show oneself).*

Answers

2. Mélanie likes to be comfortable. Sylviane lives in a warm climate, so natural materials and fabric color are important. Also, in Martinique, they share somewhat the same sense of fashion as other Europeans. Céline likes to wear clothing that is out of the ordinary. She feels that some people must dress well to make up for what they're lacking inside.

Questions

1. **Qu'est-ce que Mélanie aime mettre? (un bon gilet et un jean, un bon chandail)**
2. **Quelles matières est-ce que Sylviane aime? (le coton, le lin, les matières naturelles)**
3. **Pourquoi est-ce que Céline croit que certaines filles ont besoin de bien s'habiller? (Elles n'ont pas un esprit très beau à l'intérieur.)**

Summary

In **Chacun son style**, Perrine and Larissa are trying to decide what to wear to a concert. Perrine asks for advice on makeup. She then tells about going to the hair stylist to get her usual haircut. At the salon, she saw customers with all types of bizarre hairstyles, so she decided to have her hair curled and dyed orange. Larissa assures her that the haircut looks fine.

Motivating Activity

Ask students if they have ever had a haircut they hated and what they disliked about it. You might also have them find photos of different hairstyles in magazines and glue them to pieces of posterboard to display in the classroom.

Presentation

Have students look at the photos on pages 92 and 93 and guess what the girls are talking about. Play the recording, pausing after each section to ask the related comprehension questions in Activity 21. Then, point to various photos in the **Remise en train** and ask for students' opinions of each style. (**Comment tu trouves ça?**)

For Individual Needs

23 Challenge Have students create their own fill-in-the-blank activity for the **Remise en train**, using Activity 23 as a model. Have pairs or small groups write four or five sentences with a word missing in each one. They should list the missing words below the sentences. Then, have them exchange papers with another pair or group and complete the sentences.

Remise en train

Chacun son style!

PERRINE Oh, ça va être super ce soir!

LARISSA Je parie que Loïc va venir...

PERRINE Je crois pas! Il déteste le heavy metal.

LARISSA Ah oui, c'est vrai. Il est tellement BCBG, tu trouves pas?

PERRINE Eh! Tu penses que je devrais mettre du mascara?

LARISSA Mmm... non. C'est trop tape-à-l'œil.

PERRINE Ah! Et mon rouge à lèvres orange, tu le trouves trop tape-à-l'œil aussi?

LARISSA Je ne sais pas, moi. Qu'est-ce que tu mets?

PERRINE Ben, soit ma mini-jupe noire avec un débardeur vert, soit ma robe violette.

21 Tu as compris? See answers below.

1. What are Perrine and Larissa talking about?
2. Where are they getting ready to go?
3. What are they doing to get ready?
4. Why did Perrine decide to change her hairstyle?
5. Does Larissa approve of her new style?

22 Vrai ou faux?

1. Perrine et Larissa se préparent à sortir. *vrai*
2. Larissa a déjà décidé quoi mettre pour aller au concert. *faux*
3. Les stylistes de Biguine ne font pas de coupes bizarres. *faux*
4. Perrine s'est fait couper les cheveux comme d'habitude. *faux*
5. Perrine va mettre sa mini-jupe noire avec son débardeur vert. *faux*

23 Choisis le bon mot

Complète chaque phrase avec l'expression qui convient. See answers below.

1. Larissa trouve le mascara de Perrine trop ▨ .
2. Perrine veut mettre du ▨ orange pour aller avec sa robe violette.
3. Larissa va emprunter ▨ de Perrine.
4. Les cheveux de Perrine sont ▨ et ▨ .
5. Chez Biguine, il y avait un garçon aux cheveux ▨ .

> tape-à-l'œil   frisés
>
> verts   l'ombre à paupières
>
> rouge à lèvres   orange

92 *quatre-vingt-douze*   CHAPITRE 4   Des goûts et des couleurs

---

RESOURCES FOR REMISE EN TRAIN

Textbook Audiocassette 2B/Audio CD 4
Practice and Activity Book, p. 42

Teacher Note

23 You might keep the fill-in-the-blank activities students create for the For Individual Needs (Challenge) activity to use as introductory material next year.

Answers

21 1. the evening to come, who is going to be there
   2. heavy metal concert
   3. putting on makeup, picking out clothes
   4. She saw other clients getting wild haircuts.
   5. Yes.

23 1. tape-à-l'œil
   2. rouge à lèvres
   3. l'ombre à paupières
   4. frisés, orange
   5. verts

LARISSA Alors, je dirais le rouge à lèvres orange si tu mets ta robe violette. Et moi? Je me demande ce que je vais mettre... Oh, dis donc! Elle est géniale, ton ombre à paupières!

PERRINE Tu peux l'emprunter, si tu veux.

LARISSA Merci. Décidément, j'aime vraiment tes cheveux comme ça!

PERRINE Tu crois? Je suis allée chez Biguine hier. Je voulais juste me faire couper les cheveux comme d'habitude. Mais quand j'ai vu les autres clients! Ils avaient des coupes dingues!

LARISSA Ah oui?

PERRINE Ouais. Il y en avait une qui avait les cheveux tondus d'un côté, et longs et raides de l'autre. Un autre avait une coupe à la Mohawk.

LARISSA C'est pas vrai!

PERRINE Je te jure! Et ils étaient teints en vert.

LARISSA Et c'est pour ça que tu as décidé de te faire friser et teindre en orange?

PERRINE Ben oui. Tu es sûre que c'est pas trop bizarre?

LARISSA Mais non! L'orange te va très bien!

PERRINE Ouais! Justement, j'ai pensé que ça irait bien avec mon rouge à lèvres et avec ma robe violette.

NOTE CULTURELLE

The French sense of fashion tends to be natural and includes a personal touch. Women and teenage girls usually wear very little makeup and tend to prefer simple haircuts. Jewelry is also understated. If a woman is wearing large earrings, she probably wouldn't also wear a large bracelet or necklace. Men typically prefer a simpler style as well, seldom wearing large rings or belts with big buckles. A small scarf tied around the neck is a common fashion accessory for both men and women.

24 Cherche les expressions

In **Chacun son style!** what expressions do Perrine and Larissa use to . . . See answers below.

1. tell who they think will be at the concert?
2. ask for advice?
3. ask for an opinion?
4. give an opinion?
5. pay a compliment?
6. respond to a compliment?
7. express disbelief?
8. reassure a friend?

25 Et maintenant, à toi

Quelle coupe de cheveux est-ce que tu préfères? Est-ce que tu as l'air plus ou moins sérieux que les jeunes dans **Chacun son style!**?

REMISE EN TRAIN

quatre-vingt-treize **93**

Answers

24 1. Je parie que... va venir.
   2. Tu penses que je devrais... ?
   3. Mon rouge à lèvres orange, tu le trouves trop tape-à-l'œil... ? Tu es sûre que c'est pas trop bizarre?
   4. Ça va être super ce soir! C'est trop tape-à-l'œil.
   5. Elle est géniale, ton ombre à paupières! Décidément, j'aime vraiment tes cheveux comme ça!
   6. Tu crois?
   7. C'est pas vrai!
   8. Mais non! L'orange te va très bien!

For Individual Needs

Challenge Give transparencies to small groups and have them write several multiple-choice questions about the **Remise en train,** such as **Perrine est allée...** (a) au restaurant; (b) à un concert de heavy metal; (c) se faire couper les cheveux; (d) dans un grand magasin. Collect the transparencies, project them, and have the class choose the appropriate answers.

Teaching Suggestions

- Ask students for their reactions to Perrine's hairstyle.
- Ask students what they would say if a friend got an unattractive or unusual haircut and asked for their opinion of it.

Thinking Critically

25 Comparing and Contrasting Have students compare the hairstyles shown with those they admire. Ask them to characterize the hairstyles in the **Remise en train** as well as other styles they like.

Teaching Suggestion

Note Culturelle Ask students if the following styles are more American or French: heavy makeup, a small scarf for a man, large earrings and bracelets, big belt buckles, understated jewelry.

Language Note

You might point out that the adjective **tondu** *(shaved)* comes from the verb **tondre** *(to shave, to mow)*.

DEUXIEME ETAPE

Paying and responding to compliments; reassuring someone

Jump Start!

Display a picture of a person with an unusual haircut. Have students use vocabulary they just learned to give their opinion of the hairstyle. (**Ça fait sobre/ringard/délirant.**)

MOTIVATE

Ask students to describe their own hair in French. (**J'ai les cheveux blonds. Je suis brune.**) Then, have them list in English all the hairstyles they can think of, including types of hairstyles that were popular in the fifties, sixties, seventies, and eighties.

Family Link

Have students ask older relatives what hairstyles were popular when they were younger and then report their findings.

TEACH

Presentation

Vocabulaire Bring in or draw pictures of different types of haircuts. Hold up each picture, name the style, and have students repeat. Then, hold up the pictures again, asking **Comment sont ses cheveux?** Next, have a volunteer come to the board and draw a representation of a hairstyle. The first student to correctly name the hairstyle takes the next turn. Continue until all the vocabulary items have been drawn.

For Individual Needs

27 Slower Pace Before students begin, write **C'est qui, cette femme/cet homme?** on the board and have them give the interrogative and demonstrative pronouns they would use to respond.

94 **DEUXIEME ETAPE**

VOCABULAIRE

une coupe	a haircut
un shampooing	
une permanente	
une natte	a braid
une queue de cheval	a pony tail
un chignon	a bun
la frange	bangs
une moustache	
une barbe	a beard
des pattes (f.)	sideburns

 26 Ecoute!

Regarde le **Vocabulaire** et écoute ce que chaque personne a dit au coiffeur. C'était qui? Answers on p. 79D.

 27 Voilà ma famille

Dominique te montre une photo de sa famille. Demande-lui qui sont les gens sur la photo. Joue cette scène avec ton/ta camarade.

—C'est qui, cette femme?
—Laquelle?
—Celle aux cheveux...
—C'est ma...

94 *quatre-vingt-quatorze* CHAPITRE 4 Des goûts et des couleurs

RESOURCES FOR DEUXIEME ETAPE

Chapter Teaching Resources, Book 1
- Communicative Activity 4-2, pp. 168–169
- Teaching Transparency Master 4-2, pp. 171, 172
  Teaching Transparency 4-2
- Additional Listening Activities 4-4, 4-5, 4-6, pp. 174–175
  Audiocassette 9B/Audio CD 4
- Realia 4-2, pp. 178, 179
- Situation Cards 4-2, 4-3, pp. 180–181
- Student Response Forms, pp. 182–184
- Quiz 4-2, pp. 187–188
  Audiocassette 7B/Audio CD 4

ADDITIONAL RESOURCES
Textbook Audiocassette 2B
  OR *Audio CD 4*
***Practice and Activity Book**, pp. 43–46*

*G*rammaire   The causative **faire**

- If you want to say that you're going to *have something done*, use the verb **faire** with the infinitive of the verb that tells what you want done.

  Je **fais nettoyer** mon costume. Elle **a fait réparer** ses bottes.
  I'm having my suit cleaned. *She had her boots repaired.*

- If the verb that tells what you want done is reflexive, place the reflexive pronoun before the conjugation of **faire**.

  Je **me fais couper** les cheveux. (**se couper**) *I'm having my hair cut.*
  Il **s'est fait raser** la moustache. (**se raser**) *He had his mustache shaved.*
  Tu vas **te faire friser**? (**se friser**) *Are you going to get your hair curled?*

28   Une journée bien remplie

Qu'est-ce que M. Mouchet fait faire aujourd'hui?

tondre sa pelouse   se couper les cheveux
nettoyer ses vêtements   vérifier l'huile

1. Il se fait couper les cheveux.   2. Il fait nettoyer ses vêtements.   3. Il fait vérifier l'huile de sa voiture.   4. Il fait tondre sa pelouse.

29   Qu'est-ce que je leur dis?

Ton ami(e) va chez le coiffeur mais ne sait pas comment il/elle veut se faire coiffer. Donne-lui des conseils. Ensuite, changez de rôles.

—Qu'est-ce que tu en penses, toi?
—Tu devrais te faire couper les cheveux en brosse.

se couper les cheveux
se friser
se raser la barbe
se teindre
se faire une permanente

A la **française**

You've already learned that French speakers drop certain words and letters when they speak informally.

C'est pas vrai!   J'le trouve hyper-cool!
Je crois pas!   T'as pas l'temps?

They also tend to run certain syllables and words together. Look at the pronunciation of these common phrases:

/shai pa/	(Je ne sais pas.)
/y'en a/	(Il y en a.)
/kes tu/	(Qu'est-ce que tu…)
/wes que tu/	(Où est-ce que tu…)
/ifait/	(Il fait…)
/ifont/	(Ils font…)

Remember, though, that it is not correct to write this way.

Presentation

Grammaire Have students suggest in French services that they or their parents might have done by a professional. Write their suggestions (**nettoyer ses vêtements**) on strips of transparency with a red pen. Then, call on various students to write each form of the verb **faire** with a blue pen on a strip of transparency until all the forms are written. Write the subject pronouns in green on a final set of strips. Then, call on a student to use one strip of each color to form a sentence. (**Il fait nettoyer ses vêtements.**) Have the class repeat the sentence. Repeat the process until all the verbs have been used. Note: If the verb is reflexive, students will have to place the reflexive pronoun before the form of **faire**.

Additional Practice

28 Have students rewrite the sentences as if they were having each service done. (**Je me fais couper les cheveux.**)

Portfolio

29 Oral This activity is appropriate for students' oral portfolios. For portfolio information, see *Assessment Guide*, pages 2–13.

Teaching Suggestion

A la française Have partners write and act out dialogues, using at least three of these expressions. You might even award a prize to the pair that includes the most expressions in their dialogue and one to the pair with the best pronunciation.

Language Notes

- Tell students that when you say you've had something done, the past participle will not show agreement. (**Elle s'est fait couper les cheveux.**)
- You might also explain that the person performing the service can be specified by using **par** followed by the person: **Je me suis fait couper les cheveux par ma sœur.**

- Students might be interested in the following colloquial and idiomatic uses of the vocabulary words: **barbe à papa** *(cotton candy)*; **à la barbe de quelqu'un** *(under someone's nose)*; **raser** *(to bore)*; **se faire des cheveux blancs** *(to worry oneself gray)*; **tiré par les cheveux** *(far-fetched)*.

Building on Previous Skills

30 After students have answered **avant** or **après** for each item, have them write sentences, using the **imparfait** or the present tense. (**Elle avait les cheveux longs et raides. Maintenant, elle a une coupe dégradée.**)

Motivating Activity

Have students recall expressions for paying and responding to compliments in French. (**C'est tout à fait ton style. Il/Elle va très bien avec... ; Tu trouves?**)

Presentation

Comment dit-on... ? Write the new expressions on a transparency and use them to compliment students' clothing. After students respond to the compliment (**Tu crois?**), reassure them, using one of the new expressions, and have the class repeat. Then, have a student compliment something you're wearing. Act uncertain, prompting the student to reassure you. Write the categories *Paying a compliment, Responding to a compliment,* and *Reassuring someone* at the head of three columns on the board. Then, call on a student to choose an expression from the transparency and write it under the appropriate heading on the board. Continue until all the expressions have been copied.

Additional Practice

31 After students have completed the activity, you might type copies of the script, eliminating some words. Have students work in pairs to fill in the blanks and then take turns reading the scripts aloud.

---

30 **Mannequin d'un jour** See answers below.

Lis cet article et fais les activités suivantes.

a. Associe les mots AVANT et APRES à ces phrases.

> Elle porte un chemisier à rayures.
>
> Elle a une coupe dégradée.
>
> Elle porte un pull noir.
>
> Elle a les cheveux longs et raides.

b. Quel maquillage a été utilisé? De quelles couleurs?

> rouge à lèvres   blush   crayon
> poudre
> fond de teint   ombre à paupières

AVANT

Les cheveux raides avec peu de volume, une peau fine et fragile.

DEUXIEME ETAPE

LE MAQUILLAGE

Application d'une poudre libre abricot pour faire ressortir son teint. Ses sourcils sont redessinés au crayon. Ensuite, pour agrandir son regard, pose d'un crayon noir sur les paupières supérieures et inférieures, avec une touche de mascara noir sur les cils supérieurs. Avec, pour la touche finale, un blush framboise coordonné au rouge à lèvres.

PREMIERE ETAPE

LA COUPE DE CHEVEUX

Les cheveux de Liliane sont coupés sur une base de carré. Ils sont ensuite effilés tout autour de son visage. La frange est dégradée pour donner un effet déstructuré à l'ensemble de la coiffure (Coiffure réalisée par Arnaud pour Franck Provost).

APRES

Un caleçon noir avec un petit pull chaussette très mode, et des bottines coordonnées (Vêtements et chaussures offerts par La Blanche Porte).

COMMENT DIT-ON... ?

Paying and responding to compliments; reassuring someone

To pay a compliment:

Je te trouve très bien comme ça.
Ça fait très bien.
C'est tout à fait toi.
Ça va avec tes yeux.
Ça te va comme un gant.
Que tu es jolie avec ça!
  You really look . . . in that!
C'est assorti à ton pull.
  That matches . . .

To reassure someone:

Crois-moi, c'est tout à fait toi.
Je t'assure, c'est réussi.
  Really, . . .
Fais-moi confiance, c'est très classe.
  Trust me, . . .
Je ne dis pas ça pour te faire plaisir.
  I'm not just saying that.

To respond to a compliment:

Ça te plaît vraiment?
Tu crois?
C'est gentil.
Oh, c'est un vieux truc.
  This old thing?
Oh, tu sais, je ne l'ai pas payé(e) cher.

Fais-moi confiance! c'est tout à fait toi!

---

31 **Ecoute!**

Ecoute ces conversations. Est-ce que ces gens répondent à un compliment ou est-ce qu'ils rassurent quelqu'un? Answers on p. 79D.

Language Note

Students might be interested in the following expressions involving clothing items: **Il ne s'agit pas de mettre des gants.** *(There's no point in trying to be gentle);* **tourner les talons** *(to turn on one's heels and walk away).*

Answers

30 a. Avant, elle a les cheveux longs et raides. Après, elle a une coupe dégradée. Avant, elle porte un chemisier à rayures. Après, elle porte un pull gris.

b. une poudre abricot, un crayon à sourcils, un crayon noir, un blush framboise, du rouge à lèvre framboise

32 On bavarde!

Mets en ordre les éléments de chacune des conversations que tu entends à cette boum.

a. Oui, elle te plaît? 2
Ah, tu t'es acheté une nouvelle jupe? 1
Je la trouve jolie. Elle va bien avec tes yeux. 3
C'est gentil. Tu sais, je ne l'ai pas payée cher. 4

b. Euh, non. 2
Crois-moi, c'est tout à fait toi! 3
En tout cas, je te trouve très bien comme ça. 5
Dis donc, il est nouveau, ton coupe-vent? 1
Oh, c'est un vieux truc. 4

c. Tu crois? 4
Oui, ça me va comment? 2
Dis-moi, tu t'es maquillée! 1
Je t'assure, ça va bien avec tes yeux. 5
Ça te va très bien. 3

d. Je t'assure, c'est tout à fait toi. 5
Tiens, tu es allée chez le coiffeur! 1
Ça te va très bien. 3
Comment tu trouves? 2
Ah oui? 4

e. Ça va avec ton style. 3
Oui. Qu'en penses-tu? 2
Vraiment? 4
Tu t'es fait couper les cheveux? 1
Fais-moi confiance, c'est très réussi. 5

33 Un nouveau look

a. Ton/ta camarade te téléphone pour te dire qu'il/elle s'est fait couper les cheveux. Il/Elle te raconte son rendez-vous chez le coiffeur.

b. Tu rencontres ton/ta camarade. Tu lui fais des compliments sur sa coupe de cheveux. Tu dois le/la rassurer parce qu'il/elle n'est pas certain(e) qu'il/elle aime ce nouveau style.

34 Jeu de rôle

a. You're going to the school prom. Discuss with your friend what you're going to wear. What "look" do you prefer? What are you going to do to get ready? Are you going to the barber/hair stylist?

b. You're at the prom. You meet a friend who pays you a compliment. You respond and pay him/her a compliment. Your friend isn't very confident about how he/she looks, so you reassure him/her.

For Individual Needs

32 Visual Learners/ Challenge Once partners have arranged and practiced the conversations, hold up a picture of a windbreaker, some makeup, a skirt, or a hairstyle, and point to a pair of students. They should then perform for the class the dialogue that corresponds to that item.

Teaching Suggestions

32 Type copies of the scrambled dialogues and distribute them to students. Have students number the dialogues in the correct order, recopy them, and read them aloud with a partner. For additional listening practice, call on partners to read a dialogue and have the class give the letter of the corresponding illustration.

33 Have students write out these dialogues. They might exchange papers with a partner for editing and then turn in the final copy.

Portfolio

34 Oral Parts **a** and **b** of this activity are appropriate for students' oral portfolios. For portfolio information, see *Assessment Guide*, pages 2–13.

Teaching Suggestion

You might play the game "Chasse au trésor," described on page 79F.

CLOSE

Make complimentary statements or ask personalized questions, such as **John, je te trouve très bien comme ça. Tu t'es fait couper les cheveux, Marie? Qu'est-ce que tu penses de mon foulard, Lucien? Sam, que tu es branché avec ça!** Have students respond appropriately.

ASSESS

Quiz 4–2, *Chapter Teaching Resources, Book 1,* pp. 187–188

Assessment Items, Audiocassette 7B Audio CD 4

Performance Assessment

Have partners create and act out a skit in which two friends choose new outfits and hairstyles for a special event (a concert, a family reunion, a school dance). They should ask for and give opinions about various clothing and hair styles, as well as compliment and reassure each other on their final choices.

Teacher Note

For an additional reading, see *Practice and Activity Book,* page 47.

PREREADING
Activities A–D

Motivating Activity

Ask students for their opinion of high fashion (**haute couture**) and if they have ever been to a fashion show or seen one on TV. Ask them if they would like to wear fashions by famous designers. Have them list words and expressions that they associate with high fashion.

Teaching Suggestion

A.–D. You might do these activities as a class and then have pairs or groups do the remaining activities.

 Culture Note

French fashion shows vary from informal parades to grandiose, choreographed runway events. A formal show might include original music scores, creative lighting, and specialized stage sets. Sponsors from the textile or garment industry might fund a formal event, either to promote a new fabric or line, or as a charity function. On a smaller level, many department stores have more intimate "in-house" fashion shows, in which the fashions are modeled in the store.

LISONS!

HAUTE-COUTURE
AUTOMNE-HIVER 1994/1995

DIX
Trois-quart silhouetté en satin jade. Sweater en plumes rouges et roses. Jupe en velours incarnat.

ONZE
Veste cintrée en tweed artisanal bleu, bordeaux et argent à poignets de renard roux. T-shirt en crêpe cyclamen brodé d'un collier trompe-l'œil. Jupe en velours pourpre.

DOUZE
Veste-corset en tissage artisanal pourpre et mordoré à poignets brodés. Pantalon masculin en lainage marine fileté de rouge.

DE BONS CONSEILS
If a reading seems difficult at first, you can use your deductive reasoning skills to develop meaning. Start with a word you know and use it to figure out the words and phrases around it. How are they related to the familiar word? Do they modify it, like an adjective or adverb? Do they show its action, like a verb? Once you understand whole phrases, link them together into longer passages. By building on what you know, you can turn a difficult reading into something coherent and understandable.

CHRISTIAN LACROIX
COLLECTION HAUTE-COUTURE
AUTOMNE-HIVER 1994/95

«Il y a incontestablement chez moi l'envie d'un vêtement net, épuré, structuré. Après les formes souples de ces dernières saisons, la mode se reconstruit. Les hanches sont dessinées, la taille étranglée avec des corselets. La jupe-cloche s'évase pour donner à la silhouette une forme sablier que souligne encore le retour de l'épaule. Bref, un structuré léger, qui ne verse jamais dans la roideur, et dont les matières très élaborées, les ornements, les détails de broderies servent encore à gommer tout ce qu'il pourrait avoir d'autoritaire. Tout en ayant le sentiment de demeurer fidèle à moi-même, cette collection me paraît à des années-lumière de l'an passé.»

PRET-A-PORTER
AUTOMNE-HIVER
1994/1995

QUARANTE-TROIS
Bustier en patches de maille et dentelle naturelle. Jupe longue en dentelle noire et or.

QUARANTE-QUATRE
Parka en cuir noir argenté à parements de Mongolie et brodé d'ex-votos. Mini-jupe de dentelle argent sur fuseau de velours noir à bandes dorées.

QUARANTE-CINQ
Parka en cuir «platine».

QUARANTE-SIX
Veste trapèze gansée à motifs de chenille «cœurs» noir et blanc. Liquette et pantalon large en crêpe imprimé «d'étoile» coordonné.

For Activities A–D, see answers below.

A. What is this reading selection about? Who is Christian Lacroix?

B. What kind of vocabulary do you expect to find in this type of reading?

C. What are the names of the three collections of clothing? What do the names suggest about the type of clothing you would find in each collection?

D. On the first two pages, what information do you find in the paragraphs? In the short, numbered items?

 Culture Note

Surprisingly, Christian Lacroix has never studied fashion. He is an art historian who loved sketching the traditional costumes of his hometown, Arles, as a child. His most famous feature is the "pouf" or "bubble," a playful innovation launched in 1986 that has been his trademark ever since. Throughout his career, Lacroix has believed that fashion should be colorful and fun, even foolish, and should never be taken too seriously.

Answers
A fashion; a French designer
B kinds of clothing, fabrics, colors, sizes, textures
C Haute Couture (high fashion, very expensive, high quality); Prêt-à-Porter (ready-to-wear, high quality, off the rack, less expensive than Haute Couture); Bazar (a mixture of styles and influences)
D general description of collection; specific designs

PRET-A-PORTER
AUTOMNE-HIVER 1994/1995

QUATRE-VINGT-TROIS
Caraco de taffetas «chaîne» fleuri bleu pastel brodé d'or et bordé de dentelle noire.

QUATRE-VINGT-QUATRE
Sweater de maille artisanale orné d'arabesques de gomme cuivrée et empierrée. Jupe de taffetas orange à fleurs chinoises sur jupon de taffetas à carreaux.

QUATRE-VINGT-CINQ
Bustier de maille artisanale orné d'arabesques de gomme cuivrée et empierrée à manches et basques de mousseline rousse. Jupe à trois étages en patches de taffetas bordé de dentelle.

BAZAR
AUTOMNE-HIVER 1994/1995

SEPT
Blouson en satin imper à col de peau lainée. Gilet XVIIIe en peau lainée. Pull ras-du-cou en shetland. Jeans surteint.

HUIT
Coupe-vent en satin imper. Veste de gardian en velours gansé. Gilet de gardian en velours gansé. Chemise cintrée en jean. Jupon en madras de laine.

NEUF
Mini-blouson en satin imper et gilet de peau lainée. Gilet en shetland rayé. Col roulé en shetland rayé. Jupon en madras de laine contrasté.

BAZAR DE CHRISTIAN LACROIX
AUTOMNE-HIVER 1994-1995

«Cette collection «Bazar» n'a pas été pensée comme une ligne secondaire, «bis» ou «ter» mais comme une ligne complémentaire à la fois «autonome» et faite pour coexister avec le Prêt-à-Porter et même la Couture (une cliente de Haute-Couture vient souvent faire ses essayages en jeans et en T-shirt : autant qu'ils viennent de chez nous !) et pourquoi pas imaginer, ce n'est pas pour moi une utopie, une femme dont la tenue serait composée d'éléments des trois lignes confondues (Haute-Couture, Prêt-à-Porter et Bazar). Enfin, en tant que styliste, je ressentais le besoin de préparer le prochain millénaire en prouvant que la Maison Christian Lacroix, symbolique des années 80 qui l'ont vue naître, pouvait avoir sa propre version des années 90 et 2000, parler à la rue sans rien perdre de ses racines (le Sud, le métissage des cultures, l'histoire revisitée, toujours d'actualité).»

E. Which of these words does Lacroix NOT use to describe his **Haute Couture** line?

> net
> structuré
> souple
> léger
> élaboré
> autoritaire

F. How does Lacroix feel about clothing from his three lines being worn together? They can be worn separately or combined.

G. Can you tell which descriptions match the outfits in the four sketches? See answers below.

H. Can you describe what these clothes look like? See answers below.

> jupe en velours pourpre
> sweater de plumes
> parka en cuir noir
> mini-jupe de dentelle argent
> veste trapèze
> jupe à trois étages

quatre-vingt-dix-neuf **99**

READING
Activities E–M

Teaching Suggestion

F. Have small groups read Christian Lacroix's comments on the **Bazar** line. Then, ask them the following questions: How does Lacroix think of this line? (It is complementary to his other lines.) What does he consider to be at the root of all his designs? (the South, multiculturalism, history revisited).

For Individual Needs

H. Challenge Divide students into small groups. Type the French descriptions of the articles of clothing listed in this activity and distribute copies to students. Next to each item, have them list one additional article of clothing that is part of the same outfit. For example, next to **jupe en velours pourpre**, they might write **tee-shirt en crêpe cyclamen brodé.**

Teaching Suggestion

H. For each item listed in this activity, have students suggest an article of clothing that one might wear with it. (**Avec la jupe en velours pourpre, on pourrait mettre un chemisier en soie blanc.**)

Terms in Lisons!

Students might want to know the following words from the reading: **taille** *(waist);* **épaule** *(shoulder);* **léger** *(light);* **mordoré** *(bronze);* **dentelle** *(lace);* **racines** *(roots);* **revendiquez** *(demand).*

Answers

G Sketch 1: onze
Sketch 2: quarante-quatre
Sketch 3: quatre-vingt-quatre
Sketch 4: neuf

H purple velvet skirt, feathered sweater, black leather parka, silver lace mini-skirt, trapezoid jacket, three-tiered skirt

Language Notes

- **Haute couture,** or *high fashion,* refers to exclusive designs, usually extremely expensive, that are custom-tailored for individual patrons. **Prêt-à-porter,** or *ready-to-wear* clothing, is relatively affordable mass-produced clothing that can be bought in stores.

- The term **bis,** used in the opening quotation for the **Bazar** line, means *twice.* It is also used with apartment buildings to indicate two parts: 12 is *12A,* 12 bis is *12B,* and 12 ter is *12C.*

Building on Previous Skills

L. Have students use their background knowledge to try to guess the meanings of the following words: **tissage** *(weave);* **automnaux** *(fall);* **tressés** *(braided);* **fleuri** *(flowered);* **chinoises** *(Chinese);* **rayé** *(striped);* **vieilli** *(aged).*

 For Individual Needs

Tactile Learners Bring in or have students bring in samples of the different types of fabric mentioned in the program (leather, tweed, plaid, velour, satin, silk, taffeta, fake fur, feathers, lace, nylon, and denim). Have them feel the fabrics and ask them which ones they prefer.

Challenge Have students draw one of the fashions described on pages 98–100 and exchange papers with a partner, who will try to identify which outfit was drawn.

POSTREADING
Activity N

Thinking Critically

N. Analyzing Ask students whether they agree with Christian Lacroix's definition of elegance. Ask them how they would define elegance. Have them name celebrities or other people they consider elegant.

COLLECTION HAUTE-COUTURE

FORMES
Vestes cintrées, épaulées et parfois corsetées, longues, silhouettées ou même étriquées. Jupes «trapèze», «cloche» ou ondulées. Quelques pantalons. Tuniques fluides, robes souples et corolles architecturées pour le cocktail, grandes jupes libres ou crinolines craquantes à minces hauts très-précieux le soir, quelques fourreaux.

ORNEMENTS
Plumes, fourrures et dorures. Patches, pochoirs et peintures. Tubes, paillettes et sequins de music-hall, night-club et fête foraine dégradés, nacrés et irisés. Broderies orientalisantes.

ACCESSOIRES
Variations sur les chapeaux d'homme. Bijoux composites autour du cou. Sacs minuscules en bandoulière. Bottes, richelieux et sandales.

MATIERES
Cachemire, tweeds artisanaux et plumes, maille enrichie, jerseys enluminés et velours travaillés. Faille froissée, satin duchesse et brocarts métallisés. Dentelles toujours. Soies peintes, ombrées ou changeantes.

PRET-A-PORTER

TISSUS
Mohair, tweeds artisanaux, rayures masculines, écossais, velours vieilli ou frappé d'or, crêpes, tulles de laine et georgette imprimés, satin damassé oriental, soies reliéfées, mousseline ombrée, taffetas «chaîne», cuirs platines ou pyrogravés, fausse fourrure et dentelles métalliques.

ACCESSOIRES
Chapeaux composites, bijoux ethniques, collants-dentelles, étoles patchworks, «guillies», boots et escarpins à talons aiguilles, ornements de cheveux, clous, ex-votos, passementeries, arabesques d'or et de sequins, motifs de gomme cuivrée empierrée.

FORMES
Manteaux folkloriques trenches, parkas ethniques, vestes étriquées, cardigans «historiques», smokings en patchworks de noirs, panoplies militaires, mini-kilts ou maxi-jupes «châlet», les robes sont des tuniques et parfois des maillots du soir.

MOTIFS
Carreaux et rayures, tartans, cachemires et fleurs géantes, peaux de bête et camouflage, bouquets chinois, tapis et tapisseries, pochoirs de dentelle.

BAZAR

ACCESSOIRES
Chapeaux de cuir et bérets jacquard, gants tricotés ou imprimés, gourmettes, bracelets, sautoirs, boucles d'oreilles, pendentifs et boutons de manchettes «Lettres, croix et clochettes», jambières et collants-dentelles, ceintures, «colliers-de-chien» et «poignets-de-force» en peau lainée, mouchoirs à breloques.

MATIERES
Du nylon matelassé ou non, du drap caban, des lainages à carreaux, des rayures masculines, du satin, du crêpe, de la peau, du jean, des tweeds, de la maille, du jersey et du tissu-cravate.

CHAUSSURES
Bottes hautes lacées à bouts ronds en cuir frappé chocolat ou noir. Richelieux à semelle crantée et talon bobine en cuir frappé ou en satin et vernis noir. Mocassins effilés à bouts carrés en satin et vernis noir ou en cuir frappé.

Christian Lacroix

Q : Quelles sont les qualités que vous revendiquez chez les femmes qui sont fidèles au style Lacroix ?

C.L. : La liberté qu'elles prennent d'être différentes. Ma cliente n'est pas de celles qui cherchent à passer inaperçues. Elle étonne, elle détone, elle choque, au meilleur sens du terme. Parce qu'avant tout, elle est libre. Sans doute nous inscrivons-nous dans une évolution générale de la mode. Il me semble cependant qu'aujourd'hui les notions de passé, de présent, de futur sont dépourvues de signification. Le mot contemporain a bien vieilli en ce qui concerne le goût. Désormais, l'élégance la plus pointue mélange toutes les époques, tous les styles, toutes les catégories de vêtements, et même les catégories de prix.

I. What kind of information is given on the third page of the reading? *See answers below.*

J. Give examples of what elements make up the look of each of Lacroix's lines. *See answers below.*

K. Match each item with its proper category:

chapeaux de cuir *Accessoires*
lainages à carreaux *Matières*
bottes hautes lacées *Chaussures*
robes souples *Formes*
plumes, fourrures et dorures *Ornements*
collants-dentelles *Accessoires*
fleurs géantes *Motifs*

L. Use the root word to figure out the meaning of these adjectives.

1. métallisé *metallic*   4. lainé *woolen*
2. argenté *silvery*   5. épaulé *with shoulder pads*
3. doré *golden*   6. bordé *edged*

M. How does Christian Lacroix characterize his average client? *free to be different*

N. According to Lacroix, elegance is a mixture of what things? *all periods, styles, categories, price ranges*

100 *cent*

Answers

I examples of the styles, fabrics, decorations, motifs, materials, and accessories that were used in the three lines of clothing and Lacroix's characterization of his average client

J *Possible answers*

Haute Couture: *Formes* - vestes cintrées, épaulées et parfois corsetées; *Accessoires* - variations sur les chapeaux d'homme; *Ornements* - plumes, fourrures et dorures; *Matières* - cachemire, tweeds artisanaux et plumes

Prêt-à-Porter: *Tissus* - mohair, rayures masculines; *Formes* - manteaux folkloriques trenches, parkas ethniques; *Accessoires* - chapeaux composites, bijoux ethniques; *Motifs* - Carreaux et rayures, tartans

Bazar: *Accessoires* - chapeaux de cuir et bérets jacquard, gants tricotés ou imprimés; *Matières* - du nylon matelassé ou non, du drap caban; *Chaussures* - bottes hautes lacées à bouts ronds en cuir frappé chocolat ou noir, Richelieux à semelle crantée et talon bobine en cuir frappé

You've just seen some fashions created by a famous French designer in 1994. In this activity, you'll have the chance to use your imagination to decide what kinds of fashions people will be wearing in the future. You'll take on the role of a TV fashion correspondent in the year 2025 and report on what people are wearing.

La mode en l'an 2025

On est en 2025. Tu es journaliste de mode pour l'émission **Paris branché** et tu dois faire un reportage sur la mode actuelle.

A. Préparation

1. Qu'est-ce qu'on porte en l'an 2025? Quel est le look à la mode? Pour t'en faire une idée, pose-toi les questions suivantes.
   a. Comment est-ce que le monde a changé? Comment sont les gens en 2025? Comment est-ce que cela influence leurs goûts?
   b. Est-ce qu'il y a de nouveaux tissus ou de nouvelles matières dont on peut faire des vêtements?
   c. Est-ce qu'il y a des styles du passé qui reviennent à la mode?
2. Choisis un genre de vêtements particulier pour ton reportage, par exemple, les vêtements de soirée, les vêtements de sport ou les vêtements préférés des adolescents.

DE BONS CONSEILS

Sometimes it's hard to come up with ideas for writing about an imaginary situation. One good way to jump-start your imagination is to ask yourself questions about the topic. For example, if you're asked to write about an imaginary place, you might ask yourself: How are the people there different from us? What's important to them? What do they do? Where do they live? How do they dress? Asking yourself these kinds of questions is a great way to generate ideas and help you get started. Don't be afraid to turn your imagination loose!

B. Rédaction

Fais un brouillon de ton reportage.

1. Décris le type de vêtements que tu as choisi. N'oublie pas d'ajouter quelques informations sur...
   a. le style général des vêtements : décontracté, classique, habillé, sportif, etc.
   b. les couleurs et les motifs
   c. les tissus et les matières
   d. les endroits où on porte ce genre de vêtements
   e. le prix de ces vêtements
   f. le genre de boutiques ou de magasins où on peut les acheter
2. A la fin du reportage, parle des catégories suivantes pour compléter le look.
   a. accessoires
   b. chaussures
   c. maquillage
3. Fais quelques dessins des vêtements que tu as décrits pour illustrer ton reportage.

C. Evaluation

1. Relis ton brouillon. Est-ce que tu peux ajouter quelques détails pour rendre ton reportage plus intéressant?
2. Corrige la grammaire, l'orthographe et le vocabulaire de ton reportage et rédige la version finale.
3. Devant la classe, joue le rôle du/de la journaliste et présente ton reportage à la télé.

cent un **101**

WRITING STRATEGY
Generating ideas by asking questions

 Portfolio

Written You might want to have students include all their work for Parts A–C in their written portfolios. For portfolio information, see *Assessment Guide,* pages 2–13.

PREWRITING

Motivating Activity

Bring in fashion magazines from five, seven, and ten years ago. (They should be available at the local library.) As an alternative, have students describe the clothing styles of the sixties, seventies, and eighties. Ask students to describe the styles and tell how they've changed over the years. You might also have them suggest societal factors that make specific fabrics and "looks" popular at certain times.

Teaching Suggestion

A. 1. b. Have students suggest trendy fabrics of the past (crushed velvet, mohair, polyester, lamé, crochet). You might also have them describe futuristic fabrics they imagine or have seen on television science-fiction shows.

WRITING

For Individual Needs

B. 1. Visual Learners
Have students visualize the outfits that they will be describing. You might also have them sketch the outfits, including accessories and colors, before attempting to produce a written description of the fashions. If the resources are available, have students create their designs using computer-generated graphics.

POSTWRITING

Teaching Suggestions

C. 1. Have students write down the following questions and use them as a checklist, making sure that each one is clearly answered in their report: **Quel est le style des vêtements? Quels tissus sont populaires? Pourquoi? Où est-ce qu'on porte ces vêtements? Combien coûtent ces vêtements? Quels accessoires est-ce qu'on peut mettre avec ces vêtements?** Have them give their report and checklist to a partner to assure that his or her answers match theirs.

C. 3. For the oral report, have students write their notes on a series of five to ten cards with one sentence or phrase on each one. Encourage them to practice their presentations at home or with a friend and not to read directly from the cards. Remind them to use their summarizing skills when planning their oral reports.

The **Mise en pratique** reviews and integrates all four skills and culture in preparation for the Chapter Test.

 Video Wrap-Up

VIDEO PROGRAM
Videocassette 1

You might want to use the *Video Program* as part of the chapter review. See the *Video Guide* for teaching suggestions and activity masters.

 For Individual Needs

1 Challenge You might ask students the following comprehension questions about the article: **Vanessa Paradis aime utiliser quelle sorte de maquillage? Elle aime quel style de vêtements? Qu'est-ce qu'Hélène prend au petit déjeuner? Elle aime se maquiller? Pourquoi pas? Qu'est-ce qu'elle aime mettre comme vêtements?**

Teaching Suggestions

2 You might collect pictures of celebrities and distribute them to partners. Have them base their interview on the celebrity whose picture they receive.

2 Have partners act out their interviews for their classmates, who try to guess the identity of the celebrity being interviewed.

Portfolio

2 Written/3 Oral These activities are appropriate for students' portfolios. For portfolio suggestions, see *Assessment Guide,* page 17.

 For Individual Needs

3 Visual Learners Have students use the photos on pages 82–83 as the basis for their dialogue.

MISE EN PRATIQUE

 1 Lis ce que ces stars françaises disent à propos de leur look. Ensuite, écoute bien. Est-ce que c'est Vanessa ou Hélène qui parle? Answers on p. 79D.

Vanessa Paradis
Beauté

«J'aime faire ressortir mes yeux. Je les mets en valeur en appliquant une ombre à paupières dans les tons violets. Pour qu'on les remarque encore plus, je dessine un trait de crayon noir à l'intérieur de l'œil et surtout un trait d'eye-liner noir au ras des cils supérieurs. Deux couches de mascara sur les cils, un trait de crayon à lèvres pour dessiner le contour de ma bouche, que je coordonne à un rouge à lèvres mat. Cela fait plus soigné ! Mon teint, je l'unifie avec un fond de teint clair et de la poudre transparente.»

Beauté

«Moi, mon truc, c'est d'être la plus naturelle possible. Je démarre ma journée par un petit déjeuner équilibré : thé au lait, tartines au miel, croissants, jus de fruits frais bourrés de vitamines. Ça me donne la pêche ! Quand je ne travaille pas, je ne me maquille pas. En revanche, pour sortir avec mes copains ou pour les concerts, j'utilise une crème teintée hydratante que je matifie avec un nuage de poudre très claire. Une légère touche de mascara sur mes cils, un soupçon de brillant à lèvres sur ma bouche et du vernis transparent sur mes ongles. C'est suffisant ! Pour avoir des cheveux impeccables, je les lave tous les matins avec un shampooing doux.»

Hélène Rolles
look

«Comme je passe la plupart de mon temps à la campagne, je me sens très bien dans les vêtements confortables. C'est l'idéal pour faire des balades avec mon chien, pêcher à la ligne ou faire de la poterie. Mes coups de cœur : une parka en toile, un jean et un denim bleu ou d'autre couleur, le bon gros pull col camionneur, la chemise trappeur et la paire de chaussures de marche.»

look

«Il est dans le style des années 70 ! J'adore aller aux puces pour fouiner. Mes coups de cœur : une paire de chaussures à plate-forme, un pantalon pattes d'eph, une chemise unie ou imprimée à fleurs, une brassière en crochet, une mini-jupe ou un short.»

250-F 315 F 495 F 240 F 306 F 479 F

2
a. Tu travailles pour un magazine de mode français. Tu vas interviewer une célébrité sur son look. Joue cette scène avec ton/ta camarade. Puis, changez de rôles.

b. Ecris ton article pour le magazine. N'oublie pas de dire quels sont les vêtements préférés de la célébrité, comment il/elle préfère se coiffer (se maquiller) et pourquoi.

3
a. Ton ami(e) a un entretien d'embauche *(job interview)*. Il/Elle ne sait pas quoi mettre. Discute avec lui/elle d'un ensemble possible. Dis-lui ce que tu penses de ses idées et il/elle va aussi te donner son opinion.

b. Ton ami(e) a choisi quelque chose à mettre. Il/Elle l'essaie pour voir si ça lui va bien. Fais-lui des compliments et rassure-le/-la.

102 *cent deux* CHAPITRE 4 Des goûts et des couleurs

Culture Notes

1 Vanessa Paradis is a French pop singer whose music recalls the vintage sounds of the sixties. Her music has been compared to the Monkeys, Motown, and the Velvet Underground. In 1993, she teamed up with Lenny Kravitz to produce an album for her English language debut.

1 Hélène Rolles is the star of a popular French TV sitcom, *Hélène et les garçons.* The program is set on a college campus in the Parisian suburb of Saint-Denis, where a group of students spend most of their time discussing relationships. The series is popular in several European countries, a rare event for French television, which usually features American sitcoms and soap operas.

4 Qu'est-ce que tu penses du look de ces mannequins français? Avec ton/ta camarade, parle de leurs vêtements et de leur look.

Brian porte un pantalon en coton blanc cassé extra large et une chemise rouge et blanche à carreaux. Comme chaussures, il porte des bottines en daim marron. Sur la tête, il a noué un bandana blanc et bleu qui apporte une note d'originalité à son style cool et confortable.

Patrice porte une veste et un gilet en lin gris clair, un pantalon en lin gris foncé, une chemise en coton, une cravate en soie rayée et un chapeau en paille. Le tout, création Hermès

5

J E U   D E   R O L E

With group members, create outfits to present in a fashion show. Make sketches of outfits and ask other group members their opinions. Then, decide together which outfits you're going to present and write descriptions of them. During the fashion show, take turns being models and the commentator who describes the clothing. As the audience, your classmates will point out the outfits that they find interesting and tell what they think of them. They'll also write down their opinions of each outfit. Which outfits are the most popular?

MISE EN PRATIQUE

cent trois **103**

Language Note

Students might want to know the following terms from the clothing advertisement: **en daim** *(suede)*; **noué** *(knotted)*; **en paille** *(straw)*.

Teaching Suggestion

4 Encourage students to bring in pictures of additional looks to discuss.

Portfolio

4, 5 Oral These activities are appropriate for students' oral portfolios. For portfolio information, see *Assessment Guide,* pages 2–13.

Teaching Suggestion

5 Have students design a program for their fashion show. First, have them describe their style. They should list fabrics, patterns, and articles of clothing that they would like to feature. Have them draw several fashions and write a description of each article underneath the outfit. They should also write a paragraph telling about the philosophy behind their line of clothing. This activity could serve as an additional chapter project.

Cooperative Learning

5 Have students do this activity in small groups. You might also have them put together outfits with articles of clothing they own and model them instead of drawing them. Have some students act as models. Others should take turns being the commentator. If possible, record the fashion show on videotape. You might also collect students' written opinions of the outfits and give them a grade for their participation in the activity.

QUE SAIS-JE?

This page is intended to help students prepare for the test. It is a brief checklist of the major points covered in the chapter. The students should be reminded that this is only a checklist and does not necessarily include everything that will appear on the test.

Group Work

Have students answer all the questions in **Que sais-je?** Then, have small groups write and act out skits in which they use as many of their answers as possible. You might even have a competition to see which group can use the most expressions in their skit. As students perform their skits, assign a scorekeeper and give him or her a list of the answers. The scorekeeper checks off each answer that is used. After all the groups have performed their skits, the scorekeeper announces which group used the most expressions.

Additional Practice

3 For more practice, have students ask "which one(s)?" for the photos on pages 82–83 of the **Mise en train.**

Can you use what you've learned in this chapter?

Can you ask for and give opinions? p.86

1 How would you ask your friend's opinion of these items? See answers below.

 1.   2.   3.

2 How would you give your opinion of the items in number 1 if you liked them? If you disliked them? See answers below.

Can you ask which one(s)? p.88

3 Your friend is pointing out some things she likes, but you can't tell which one(s) she's talking about. How do you ask? *Possible answers:*

 1.
Lequel?

 2.
Laquelle?

 3.
Lesquels?

Can you point out and identify people and things? p.88

4 How would your friend answer your questions in number 3? *Possible answers:* **1.** Celui-là. **2.** Celle-là. **3.** Ceux-là, les noirs.

5 How would you identify the following people if you didn't know their names? *Possible answers:* **1.** Là-bas, le garçon qui porte un chapeau. Celui avec un chapeau. **2.** Celle avec les lunettes. La fille aux lunettes.

 1.  2.

Can you pay and respond to compliments? p.96

6 How would you compliment a friend on an article of clothing? See answers below.

7 How would you respond if someone complimented you on your clothing? *Possible answers:* Ça te plaît vraiment? Tu crois? C'est gentil. Oh, c'est un vieux truc. Oh, tu sais, je ne l'ai pas payé(e) cher.

Can you reassure someone? p.96

8 What would you say to reassure a friend who is uncertain about a new haircut or article of clothing? *Possible answers:* Crois-moi, c'est tout à fait toi. Je t'assure, c'est réussi. Fais-moi confiance, c'est très classe. Je ne dis pas ça pour te faire plaisir.

Possible answers

1 1. Elle te plaît, cette chemise? Qu'en penses-tu?
2. Tu n'aimes pas ce pantalon? Qu'est-ce que tu penses de ce pantalon?
3. Comment tu trouves ce pendentif?

2 1. *Like:* Elle me plaît beaucoup. Je la trouve super.
Dislike: Elle ne me plaît pas du tout. Je la trouve moche.

2. *Like:* J'aime bien. J'aime bien ce genre de pantalon.
Dislike: Je n'aime pas tellement. Je trouve qu'il fait vieux.
3. *Like:* Il est super.
Dislike: Il fait vraiment ringard!

6 Je te trouve très bien comme ça. Ça fait très bien. C'est tout à fait toi. Ça va avec tes yeux. Ça te va comme un gant. Que tu es... avec ça! C'est assorti à...

PREMIERE ETAPE

Asking for and giving opinions

Qu'est-ce que tu penses de... ? *What do you think of . . .?*
Qu'en penses-tu? *What do you think of it?*
J'aime bien ce genre de... *I like this type of . . .*
Je trouve qu'ils/elles font... *I think they look . . .*
Ça fait vraiment cloche! *That looks really stupid!*

Clothing and styles

un caleçon *leggings*
un collant *panty hose, tights*
un col roulé *a turtleneck sweater*
un costume *a man's suit*
des gants (m.) *gloves*
un gilet *a vest*
des hauts talons (m.) *high heels*
une mini-jupe *a miniskirt*
un pendentif *a pendant*

un sac *a purse*
à col en V *V-necked*
à pinces *pleated*
à pois *polka-dot*
à rayures *striped*
écossais(e) *plaid*
en laine *wool*
en soie *silk*
forme tunique *tunic style*

Describing clothing or hairstyles

affreux(-euse) *hideous*
classe *classy*
délirant(e) *wild*
élégant(e) *elegant, sophisticated*
hyper-cool *super cool*
ringard(e) *corny*
sérieux(-euse) *conservative*
sobre *plain*
tape-à-l'œil *gaudy*
vulgaire *tasteless*

Asking which one(s)

Quel(s)/Quelle(s)... ? *Which . . . ?*
Lequel/Laquelle? *Which one?*
Lesquels/Lesquelles? *Which ones?*

Pointing out and identifying people and things

Celui-là/Celle-là. *That one.*
Ceux-là/Celles-là. *Those.*
Celui du... *The one . . .*
Celui avec... *The man/boy/one with . . .*
Celle qui... *The woman/girl/one who . . .*
La fille au... *The girl in the/with the . . .*
Là-bas, le garçon qui... *Over there, the boy who . . .*

DEUXIEME ETAPE

Paying and responding to compliments

Je te trouve très bien comme ça. *I think you look very good like that.*
Ça fait très bien. *That looks good.*
C'est tout à fait toi. *That's really you.*
Que tu es... avec ça! *You really look . . . in that!*
Ça te va comme un gant. *That fits you like a glove.*
C'est assorti à... *That matches . . .*
Oh, c'est un vieux truc. *This old thing?*
Oh, tu sais, je ne l'ai pas payé(e) cher. *Oh, it wasn't expensive.*

Reassuring someone

Crois-moi, ... *Believe me, . . .*
Je t'assure, ... *Really, . . .*
Fais-moi confiance, ... *Trust me, . . .*
Je ne dis pas ça pour te faire plaisir. *I'm not just saying that.*

Hair and hairstyles

une barbe *a beard*
les cheveux courts *short hair*
   en brosse *a crew cut*
   frisés *curly hair*
   longs *long hair*
   teints *dyed hair*
   raides *straight hair*

un chignon *a bun*
un coiffeur/une coiffeuse *a hair stylist/barber*
une coupe *a haircut*
une coupe au carré *a square cut*
la frange *bangs*
une moustache *a mustache*
une natte *a braid*
des pattes (f.) *sideburns*
une permanente *a perm*
une queue de cheval *a pony tail*
un shampooing *a shampoo*
faire + inf. *to have (something) done*
se friser *to curl one's hair*
se raser *to shave*

CHAPTER 4 ASSESSMENT

CHAPTER TEST

- *Chapter Teaching Resources, Book 1*, pp. 189–194
- *Assessment Guide*, Speaking Test, p. 29
- *Assessment Items, Audiocassette 7B Audio CD 4*

TEST GENERATOR, CHAPTER 4

ALTERNATIVE ASSESSMENT

Performance Assessment

You might want to use the **Jeu de rôle** (p. 103) as a cumulative performance assessment activity.

📁 Portfolio Assessment

- **Written: Mise en pratique,** Activity 2, *Pupil's Edition,* p. 102
  Assessment Guide, p. 17
- **Oral: Mise en pratique,** Activity 3, *Pupil's Edition,* p. 102
  Assessment Guide, p. 17

🏰 Game

TROUVEZ LES CINQ! Begin by writing on a transparency five words or expressions from one of the vocabulary categories. Then, form rows of five or six students. The first student in each row has a sheet of paper and a pen, and the others have pens. Call out the category. Beginning with the first student in each row, each student writes a word or expression from that category on the paper and then passes it to the student behind him or her. Call time after one minute has elapsed and show the transparency with the expressions you've written. One student from each row counts the number of correctly-written matching expressions and gives the results. The team that matches the most expressions wins.

Allez, viens en Afrique francophone!

pp. 106–213

Motivating Activity

Ask students to identify the countries that make up francophone Africa as well as any information that is unique to this region. Ask students if they can name any sub-Saharan African countries outside of the francophone region that were influenced by countries other than France (Liberia—the United States; Ghana—England; Angola—Portugal). Have students recall what they already know about Africa concerning history, food, animals, climate, famous people, and other aspects.

Background Information

There is no single francophone culture in Africa. The territory is too vast and the diversity of ethnic groups too great. **L'Afrique francophone** can be divided into North, West, and Central Africa. This region can be further defined by religion (Islam, Christianity, animism, and others) and by ethnic composition (countries with somewhat heterogeneous populations as opposed to those with a multitude of ethnic groups within their borders). Since independence, nearly all these nations have been plagued by serious social problems, such as governmental instability, disease, and illiteracy. Nevertheless, through it all, the peoples of Africa have maintained their cultural traditions and close family ties within village and tribal groups, have continued developing art, music, and crafts, and have created impressive works of African literature and cinema.

CHAPITRES 5, 6, 7, 8

Une mosquée en Afrique

106 *cent six*

Culture Notes

• The photo on pages 106–107 shows a mosque, a Muslim place of worship. Mosques are generally large, elaborate buildings that not only serve as places of prayer, but also as tombs and as places of religious instruction. The word *mosque* comes from the Arabic **masjid**, which means *a place of kneeling*. Mosques generally have a **mihrab** *(prayer niche)* that faces the holy city of Mecca and between one and six **minarets** *(towers)*, from which the faithful are called to prayer by the **muezzins** *(criers)*.

• A Muslim's chief responsibilities are summarized in the Five Pillars of Faith: The profession of faith (**shahadah**), prayer (**salat**) five times a day, almsgiving, fasting during the holy month of Ramadan, and a pilgrimage, or **hajj,** to Mecca once during his or her lifetime.

Using the Almanac and Map

L'Afrique francophone

	Le Maroc	La Tunisie	Le Sénégal	La République centrafricaine
Population	26.181.000	8.400.000	7.952.000	2.875.000
Superficie (km²)	450.000	164.000	197.000	640.000
Capitale	Rabat	Tunis	Dakar	Bangui
Spécialités	pastilla, thé à la menthe	couscous, tajine	maffé, chawarma	dengbé

Autres états et régions francophones : l'Algérie, le Bénin, le Burkina-Faso, le Burundi, le Cameroun, les Comores, le Congo, la Côte d'Ivoire, Djibouti, le Gabon, la Guinée, l'île Maurice, le Mali, la Mauritanie, Madagascar, Mayotte, le Niger, le Ruanda, la Réunion, le Sahara Occidental, les Seychelles, le Tchad, le Togo, le Zaïre

cent sept 107

Terms in the Almanac

- **Le Maroc** is located in North Africa on the southern side of the Strait of Gibraltar. The country primarily has an agricultural economy although it is one of the top world producers of phosphates and barite. Oranges and sheep are also important exports. Morocco was the first Arab country to discover oil.
- **Rabat,** the capital of Morocco, is the center of an important textile industry and is known for its carpets, blankets, and leather goods.
- **thé à la menthe:** tea made with a special variety of mint.
- **La Tunisie** is located on the Mediterranean coast halfway between Gibraltar and the Suez Canal. Tourism is an important industry, and Tunisia's main exports are oil, natural gas, phosphates, and olive oil.
- **couscous:** kernels of cracked wheat or semolina boiled or steamed and eaten with chicken or other meat and vegetables.
- **tajine:** a stew made with various meats and vegetables.
- **Le Sénégal,** which forms a flat plain barely above sea level on the westernmost point of Africa, is one of the world's largest producers of peanuts.
- **mafé:** beef, chicken, or lamb cooked in peanut sauce and served with rice.
- **chawarma:** grilled meat in pita bread.
- **La République centrafricaine,** one of the world's leading diamond producers, is a tropical, landlocked country located nearly in the center of Africa.
- **dengbé:** wild game eaten with a sauce made with peanut butter or okra.

Using the Map

Using a map of Africa, have students determine which countries in the almanac are in the desert, which are islands, which are located in North Africa, which in Central Africa, and which in West Africa. Have them identify which countries are bordered by the Mediterranean Sea, and which by the Atlantic and Indian Oceans. Ask students to locate the French-speaking countries that are landlocked and to consider how this might affect their economy. Ask them if they know anything about the countries listed in the almanac above.

Language Note

The Arabic word **maghreb** refers to the region formed by Morocco, Algeria, and Tunisia and means *time or place of sunset* or *island of the west.* The term is used to distinguish the region from the **mashriq** *(the eastern Islamic world).*

Using the Photo Essay

① **Le baobab,** a short tropical tree with a large trunk up to nine meters (30 feet) in diameter, is known for its pulpy, yellow fruit called monkey bread. This tree has a number of practical uses. Its immense trunk has the ability to store water, and its leaves can be eaten either fresh or dried. The monkey bread fruit can be made into a sherbet-like refreshing drink, and the shell, which resembles a gourd, can be used as a container. The bark serves as material for musical instruments, packing paper, rope, and even cloth.

② **Casablanca,** the largest city and main port of Morocco, is also a commercial and industrial center. The city, familiarly called **Casa,** was modeled after the French city of Marseilles and is the site of the **Grande Mosquée Hassan II,** named after the present king of Morocco.

③ **Le désert du Sahara,** the largest desert in the world, stretches west to east 5,000 kilometers from the Atlantic Ocean to the Red Sea and north to south for 2,000 kilometers. The Sahara, which means *desert* in Arabic, covers parts of Morocco, Algeria, Tunisia, Libya, Egypt, the Sudan, Chad, Niger, Mali, Mauritania, and the Western Sahara. Inhabited by nomads and camel herders, the area receives very little rainfall. Over the years, the Sahara has been expanding, sometimes naturally, and sometimes because of man's assault on the fragile ecology of the region.

*E*n *Afrique, la francophonie ne représente pas tout à fait la culture traditionnelle française telle qu'on la trouve en Europe. La langue française a été introduite par les colons français. Dans certains de ces pays, le mélange des cultures a été très bien accepté par les populations. Beaucoup de jeunes parlent français et continuent leurs études en France avec l'aide de bourses du gouvernement français; ils rentrent alors dans leur pays avec un diplôme qui leur donne accès à des postes importants. Par contre, dans d'autres pays comme l'Algérie, l'union des cultures ne se fait pas aussi parfaitement parce qu'il y a un mouvement très puissant qui cherche à préserver les traditions religieuses et culturelles.*

① **Le baobab** est un arbre typiquement africain. Souvent, les villages sont construits près d'un baobab.

② Au Maroc, Casablanca, ou «Casa la Blanche», est un des plus grands ports artificiels du monde.

③ **Le désert du Sahara** recouvre une grande partie de l'Afrique du Nord.

Culture Notes

③ Camels are truly animals of the desert. Their stomachs are especially adapted to conserve water, and they can live off water, fat, and nutrients stored in their hump for several days, if necessary. Their wide feet and long eyelashes protect them from the heat and sand of the desert.

• Three francophone African countries that have changed their names in the last 20 years are **Zaïre** (formerly the Belgian Congo), **Bénin** (formerly Dahomey), and the most recent, **Burkina Faso** (formerly Upper Volta). **Burkina** means *honor, dignity, respect, and honesty.* **Faso** means *country of worthy men.*

• **Griots** are praise singers, entertainers, and oral historians found primarily in West Africa. Often wanderers, they form a social caste of their own in many places. Many play a five-stringed, leather-covered, wooden instrument.

④ **Abidjan** est la ville principale de la Côte d'Ivoire, avec ses gratte-ciel et ses larges avenues.

⑤ Au marché marocain qu'on appelle **un souk,** on trouve des fruits et des légumes. En plus, tout l'artisanat africain est souvent représenté.

⑥ Malgré l'influence culturelle de la langue française, les peuples africains sont restés très proches de leurs traditions. Partout en Afrique, les gens portent toujours des costumes traditionnels.

⑦ La République centrafricaine est un pays de savanes. On peut y voir de nombreux animaux sauvages.

④ **Abidjan** is the economic capital and largest city of Côte d'Ivoire.

⑤ **Souks** *(outdoor markets)* are commonplace throughout Morocco. Smaller villages and towns generally have a particular market day (**Souk el Tnine** - *Monday market,* **Souk el Arba** - *Wednesday market*). They also have their own special **souk** quarter, whereas larger cities have several individual **souks,** each of which is devoted to a particular craft. Village markets are not open on Fridays, when the main prayers are held in the mosques.

⑥ While the **costumes traditionnels** vary throughout the continent of Africa, there is some similarity in the way the people in sub-Saharan francophone African countries dress. For important occasions, it is common for both men and women to wear long, embroidered robes (**boubous**). For daily wear, women often wear a colorful **pagne** *(a length of cloth)* wrapped around their waist as a skirt, a matching scarf, and a loose top. The same cloth is used to make men's casual clothes, which consist of loose-fitting shirts and pants.

Geography Link

⑦ The savanna regions of West Africa are tropical grasslands. There are two types of savanna: one caused by fire and the other by climate. In parts of Africa where there are marked wet and dry seasons, the savanna is generally formed as a result of the climate. During the dry season, there is not enough water to support the growth of trees. This fragile ecological balance is altered by overgrazing, which removes the protective grasses and causes desertification.

Teaching Suggestion

Have each student choose a francophone African country to research.

Thinking Critically

Observing Have students examine the photos for examples of arid, desert climates as opposed to more moderate climates. They might notice sand as opposed to grass, the scarcity of trees, and the whitewashed buildings.

Language Link

A **lingua franca** is a third language used between two speakers of different languages. For example, in the Central African Republic, Sango, originally a trading language spoken along the Ubangi River (**Oubangui** in French), is the national language and is spoken by nearly everyone.

Chapitre 5 : C'est notre avenir
Chapter Overview

Mise en train pp. 112–114	**L'avenir, c'est demain**		**Note Culturelle,** Careers and education in Senegal, p. 114	

	FUNCTIONS	**GRAMMAR**	**CULTURE**	**RE-ENTRY**
Première étape pp. 115–119	• Asking about and expressing intentions, p. 117 • Expressing conditions and possibilities, p. 117	The future, p. 118	**Rencontre Culturelle,** Overview of Senegal, p. 115	• The subjunctive • The **passé composé**

Remise en train pp. 120–121	**Passe ton bac d'abord!**

	FUNCTIONS	**GRAMMAR**	**CULTURE**	**RE-ENTRY**
Deuxième étape pp. 122–127	• Asking about future plans, p. 124 • Expressing wishes, p. 124 • Expressing indecision, p. 124 • Giving advice, p. 124 • Requesting information, p. 127 • Writing a formal letter, p. 127	The conditional, p. 125	• **Panorama Culturel,** Planning for a career, p. 122 • **Note Culturelle,** Types of job training, p. 123 • Realia: Employment office forms, p. 126	• Giving advice • The imperfect • Making a telephone call • Expressing likes and preferences

Lisons! pp. 128–130	**Employment ads** **Reading Strategy:** Predicting from patterns

Ecrivons! p. 131	**Une lettre de candidature** **Writing Strategy:** Using details and structure in persuasive writing

Review pp. 132–135	• Mise en pratique, pp. 132–133 • Que sais-je? p. 134 • Vocabulaire, p. 135

Assessment Options	**Etape Quizzes**
	• *Chapter Teaching Resources, Book 2*
	  Première étape, Quiz 5-1, pp. 23–24
	  Deuxième étape, Quiz 5-2, pp. 25–26
	• *Assessment Items, Audiocassette 7B/Audio CD 5*
		Chapter Test
		• *Chapter Teaching Resources, Book 2,* pp. 27–32
		• *Assessment Guide,* Speaking Test, p. 30
		• *Assessment Items, Audiocassette 7B/Audio CD 5*
		
		Test Generator, Chapter 5

RESOURCES: Print	**RESOURCES: Audiovisual**
Practice and Activity Book, p. 49	*Textbook Audiocassette 3A/Audio CD 5*
Practice and Activity Book, pp. 50–53 *Grammar and Vocabulary Worksheets*, pp. 41–48 *Chapter Teaching Resources, Book 2* • Communicative Activity 5-1, pp. 4–5 • Teaching Transparency Master 5-1, pp. 8, 10 . . . . • Additional Listening Activities 5-1, 5-2, 5-3, pp. 11–12 . . . . . • Realia 5-1, pp. 15, 17 • Situation Cards 5-1, pp. 18–19 • Student Response Forms, pp. 20–22 • Quiz 5-1, pp. 23–24	*Textbook Audiocassette 3A/Audio CD 5* *Teaching Transparency 5-1* *Additional Listening Activities, Audiocassette 9B/Audio CD 5* *Assessment Items, Audiocassette 7B/Audio CD 5*
Practice and Activity Book, p. 54	*Textbook Audiocassette 3A/Audio CD 5*
Practice and Activity Book, pp. 55–58 *Grammar and Vocabulary Worksheets*, pp. 49–53 *Chapter Teaching Resources, Book 2* • Communicative Activity 5-2, pp. 6–7 • Teaching Transparency Master 5-2, pp. 9, 10 . . . . • Additional Listening Activities 5-4, 5-5, 5-6, pp. 12–13 . . . . . • Realia 5-2, pp. 16, 17 • Situation Cards 5-2, 5-3, pp. 18–19 • Student Response Forms, pp. 20–22 • Quiz 5-2, pp. 25–26 . . . . *Video Guide*	*Textbook Audiocassette 3A/Audio CD 5* *Teaching Transparency 5-2* *Additional Listening Activities, Audiocassette 9B/Audio CD 5* *Assessment Items, Audiocassette 7B/Audio CD 5* *Video Programs, Videocassette 1*
Practice and Activity Book, p. 59	
Video Guide	*Video Program, Videocassette 1*

Alternative Assessment

• Performance Assessment
  Première étape, p. 119
  Deuxième étape, p. 127

• Portfolio Assessment
  Written: **Ecrivons!,** *Pupil's Edition,* p. 131
    Assessment Guide, p. 18
  Oral: Activity 27, *Pupil's Edition,* p. 126
    Assessment Guide, p. 18

Chapitre 5 : C'est notre avenir
Textbook Listening Activities Scripts

For Student Response Forms, see *Chapter Teaching Resources, Book 2,* pp. 19–21.

Première étape

6 Ecoute! p. 116

1. — Tu te souviens de nos années au lycée? C'était pas facile quand même à notre époque, hein?
  — Ah, c'est sûr! Moi, j'ai passé mon bac deux fois avant de l'avoir. J'avais vingt ans quand je l'ai eu.
2. — Ah bon? Je ne m'en rappelle pas. Remarque, j'étais sûrement déjà au service militaire, je l'ai fait juste après le bac.
3. — C'était quand même moins difficile de trouver du travail dans notre jeunesse. J'ai arrêté mes études après le lycée et j'ai trouvé un emploi tout de suite.
4. — Moi, j'ai fait le bon choix quand j'ai décidé de faire une école technique. Je n'ai jamais eu de problèmes pour trouver un emploi.
5. — Moi, si. Après l'université, je suis resté au chômage pendant six mois.
6. — Ne te plains pas. Moi, ça a duré un an et demi. Tiens, c'est aussi à cette époque-là que je me suis marié.
7. — Et toi, à quel âge est-ce que tu t'es marié déjà? Vingt-trois ans?
  — Mais, non. Moi, je me suis marié à vingt-sept ans. Dis-moi, c'était quoi déjà ton premier travail?
8. — Souviens-toi, chauffeur. J'ai passé mon permis à vingt-deux ans et juste après, j'ai commencé à travailler pour l'entreprise de Khalid. Ça, c'est vraiment un bon souvenir pour moi.
9. — En tout cas, moi, mon meilleur souvenir, c'est la naissance de ma fille, j'avais vingt-neuf ans.

Answers to Activity 6
1. non 2. oui 3. non 4. non 5. oui 6. non 7. oui 8. non 9. oui

7 Ecoute! p. 117

1. — Dis donc, Prosper, qu'est-ce que tu comptes faire après le lycée?
  — Eh bien, travailler. Si je ne trouve pas de travail, je commencerai un apprentissage en août, à l'hôtel de mon oncle. Mais ce que je veux vraiment faire, c'est travailler comme chauffeur. J'adore conduire. J'ai passé mon permis en mai, tu sais.
2. — Félicitations pour ton bac, Prisca!
  — Merci.
  — Et qu'est-ce que tu penses faire maintenant?
  — Je compte entrer à l'université en septembre.
  — C'est bien, ça.
  — Ouais, mais je dois quitter ma famille si je vais à Dakar. Je pense habiter avec mon oncle et ma tante, mais ils ont beaucoup d'enfants. S'ils sont bruyants, je ne pourrai pas étudier.
  — Ben, qu'est-ce que tu peux faire, alors?
  — Il est possible que je prenne un appartement avec une copine.
  — Bonne idée!
3. — Tiens, Séka. On m'a dit que tu as réussi ton bac.
  — Oui.
  — Félicitations! Alors, qu'est-ce que tu comptes faire?

— J'ai l'intention de ne faire absolument rien cet été. C'était tellement dur, le bac, tu sais. Je vais me reposer cet été. Je pense partir en vacances en juillet et, en août, je compte rendre visite à mon frère à Thiès. Il se peut que je travaille un peu avec lui. Il a une épicerie.
4. — Alors, Angèle, ça s'est bien passé, ton bac?
  — Oui, j'ai réussi.
  — Formidable! Qu'est-ce que tu comptes faire maintenant?
  — Ben, je vais me marier cet été.
  — Vraiment?
  — Oui, et peut-être que je travaillerai après.
  — Qu'est-ce que tu veux faire?
  — Oh, je ne sais pas. Il se peut que j'aie un enfant avant de travailler.
  — Alors, bonne chance!

Answers to Activity 7

PROSPER	trouver un travail, faire un apprentissage, travailler comme chauffeur
PRISCA	entrer à l'université, quitter sa famille, prendre un appartement
SÉKA	se reposer, partir en vacances, rendre visite à son frère
ANGÈLE	se marier, trouver un travail, avoir un enfant

Deuxième étape

19 Ecoute! p. 123

1. — La voiture de Mme Bonfils? Je l'ai réparée. Quelle voiture est-ce que je répare maintenant?
  — La voiture de M. Koré. C'est la bleue, là-bas, à côté de la Mercédes.
  — Bon, d'accord.
2. — J'ai mal à la gorge, à la tête et au ventre. J'ai aussi de la fièvre.
  — C'est la grippe, sans doute. Je vais prendre votre température. Ouvrez la bouche, s'il vous plaît.
3. — Que je suis heureuse que vous soyez arrivé! Vous voyez, il y a de l'eau partout!
  — Ça vient d'où, madame?
  — Du lavabo. C'est par ici, la salle de bains.
4. — Salut, Fabrice. Ça avance, le roman?
  — Oh, pas trop bien. J'ai commencé à écrire, mais je me suis aperçu que j'avais encore des recherches à faire.
  — Donc, tu ne finiras pas à la date prévue?
  — Euh, probablement pas.
5. — Vous pourriez taper cette lettre, Bernard?
  — Bien sûr, madame.
  — Et après ça, n'oubliez pas de téléphoner à M. Raynaud pour arranger un rendez-vous.
  — Oui, madame.
6. — Bonjour.
  — Bonjour, Mlle Kanon.
  — Vous avez des questions avant de commencer l'interro?
7. — On fait construire un nouveau bâtiment ici, alors?
  — Oui, c'est moi qui fais les plans.
  — Ah bon?
  — Oui, il y aura quarante étages. Ce sera très moderne.

Answers to Activity 19

1. mécanicien	3. plombier	5. secrétaire	7. architecte
2. médecin	4. écrivain	6. professeur ou institutrice	

24 Ecoute! p. 125

1. — Alors, Yasmine, tu sais ce que tu vas faire?
   — Bien sûr! J'ai l'intention d'entrer à l'université et d'étudier l'histoire.
2. — Eh, Mamadou, Tu as des projets pour l'année prochaine?
   — Pas vraiment. Je ne sais pas encore ce que je vais faire.
3. — Dis, Fatou, qu'est-ce que tu veux faire plus tard?
   — Je n'en ai aucune idée. Je me demande si je vais continuer mes études.
4. — Omar, tu as des projets pour plus tard?
   — Oui, oui. J'ai plein de projets. Mais mon rêve, c'est de faire du théâtre.
5. — Dis donc, Fatima, tu sais ce que tu vas faire plus tard?
   — Euh, j'ai du mal à me décider. Il y a la boutique de ma famille, mais il y a aussi l'université. Je n'arrive pas à prendre une décision.
6. — Eh Habib, tu sais ce que tu vas faire après le lycée?
   — Ce qui me plairait, c'est de voyager un peu avant de commencer l'université. J'aimerais bien passer du temps en France chez mon oncle.
7. — Alors, Thérèse, qu'est-ce que tu vas faire plus tard?
   — Oh, je ne sais pas trop. Je voudrais trouver un travail, mais je ne sais pas quelle sorte de travail. Je n'en ai vraiment aucune idée.

Answers to Activity 24
1. sait 2. hésite 3. hésite 4. sait 5. hésite 6. sait 7. hésite

28 Ecoute! p. 127

— Institut de promotion industrielle.
— Oui, bonjour monsieur.
— Bonjour, mademoiselle.
— J'aimerais avoir des renseignements sur votre école.
— Oui, mademoiselle.
— Je voudrais savoir ce qu'il y a comme cours.
— Nous offrons des cours de gestion, informatique et techniques de commercialisation.
— Est-ce que les cours sont le jour ou le soir?
— Les deux.
— Et, euh, quand est-ce que les cours commencent?
— Vous pouvez commencer tous les trois mois.
— Il y a des conditions d'inscription?
— Oui, mademoiselle. Il faut que vous ayez au moins vingt et un ans, et que vous ayez votre bac.
— Bien. Pourriez-vous me dire quels sont les frais d'inscription?
— Ça dépend des cours que vous prenez. Ça pourrait faire de trois mille francs à quatre mille francs.
— Mmm... Est-ce que vous pourriez m'envoyer une brochure?
— Bien sûr. Quelle est votre adresse?

Answers to Activity 28
e, b, g, c, a, f, d

Mise en pratique

1 p. 132

— Tiens, Karim! Ça va?
— Oui, ça va bien maintenant que c'est fini, le bac.
— Moi aussi. Quel cauchemar, hein?
— Ouais. Mais, je ne sais pas ce que je veux faire maintenant. J'ai du mal à me décider. Et toi, qu'est-ce que tu penses faire?
— Moi, je compte entrer à l'université en automne. J'habiterai avec la famille de mon oncle. Il se peut que je passe l'été chez eux aussi, pour travailler dans leur boutique. Mais ce que je veux faire, c'est voyager et me reposer un peu avant de commencer l'université.
— C'est bien, ça. Alors, tout est décidé pour toi.
— Et toi, tu n'as pas de projets, alors?
— Mon rêve, c'est de voyager, tu sais. Mais sans argent, ce n'est pas possible.
— Alors, il faudrait que tu travailles.
— Eh oui, mais qu'est-ce que je peux faire? Je n'en ai aucune idée. Je ne sais plus ce que je veux.
— Tu ne veux pas continuer tes études, alors?
— Jamais de la vie! C'est fini les études!
— Mais si tu ne te prépares pas, tu ne trouveras jamais de travail.
— Ouais.
— Tu ferais bien de t'inscrire dans une école technique.
— Mais je me demande laquelle. Ce qui me plairait, c'est de rencontrer beaucoup de gens.
— Bon, tu veux rencontrer des gens et tu aimes voyager, n'est-ce pas?
— Oui.
— J'ai une idée, moi. Pourquoi pas travailler dans un hôtel? Tu n'as pas vu l'article dans le journal d'hier à propos de l'Ecole de Formation Hôtelière et Touristique?
— Ben, non.
— Tu devrais le lire. Ça semble très intéressant. Si j'étais toi, je demanderais des renseignements sur cette école.
— Tu me passes l'article?
— Bien sûr!

Answers to Mise en pratique Activity 1
1. vrai 2. vrai 3. faux 4. faux 5. faux 6. vrai 7. vrai 8. vrai

3 p. 132

Bonjour, j'aimerais avoir des renseignements sur votre village hôtel. Pourriez-vous me dire ce qu'on peut y faire comme sports? Je voudrais également savoir si on peut pêcher. Pourriez-vous me dire si les bungalows sont climatisés? Est-ce que vous pourriez m'envoyer une brochure? Mon nom est Ousmane Loukour. Mon adresse est 6, avenue Georges Pompidou, à Dakar. Je vous remercie.

Answers to Mise en pratique Activity 3
M. Loukour wants to know what sports activities are available at the hotel, if there is fishing, if the bungalows are air-conditioned, and if the hotel could send him a brochure; Karim will send the second, more formal letter.

Chapitre 5 : C'est notre avenir
Projects

Career Day
(Individual Project)

ASSIGNMENT

Students will create a poster to advertise a particular career of their choice. They will also give an oral presentation in which they act as a representative of that field, encouraging other students to consider it as a profession.

MATERIALS

✂ **Students may need**
- French-English dictionaries
- Posterboard
- Colored markers or pens
- Encyclopedias
- Current magazines
- College catalogues

SUGGESTED SEQUENCE

COMMUNITY LINK

Before students begin their projects, invite bilingual members of the community to the class (travel agents, bank representatives, business consultants). Have them talk about their training, what they do, and how they use a second language in their work. Encourage students to ask them questions, either spontaneous or prepared in advance.

1. Have students choose a career from the **Vocabulaire** on page 123. They might refer to the **Vocabulaire à la carte** on page 124, the Supplementary Vocabulary at the back of the book, or French-English dictionaries to find additional careers.

2. Once students have chosen a career, have them do a mapping or clustering activity. They should write their chosen profession (**médecin**) in the center of a sheet of paper and circle it. Then, they should write several major characteristics they associate with that profession in separate circles around the central circle (helps people,

medical school, money). Then, they should continue by surrounding each of these circles with additional circles containing related ideas.

3. Have students research their profession. They might interview a friend, relative, or community member in that field, check the encyclopedia for a definition and history of the profession, and find information in magazines or college catalogues about the necessary training, employment opportunities, average salary, and so on.

4. Have students organize their oral presentation and plan the layout of their posters. Remind them that they are acting as a representative of their profession for a "career day" at school. If they choose to be a doctor, they should be prepared to tell the class why they chose to be a doctor, what training is necessary, what it is like to be a doctor, and what their everyday duties and responsibilities are.

5. Have students give their oral presentations to the class, using their posters to encourage their classmates to choose their profession. Class members should ask questions, just as they would if a guest were visiting the class. The class members will receive grades for their participation in other students' presentations.

GRADING THE PROJECT

You might want to grade students' projects on thoroughness and accuracy of content, creativity of visuals, oral presentation, accuracy of language use, and participation in other students' presentations.

Suggested Point Distribution (total = 100 points)

Content	20 points
Creativity of visuals	20 points
Oral presentation	20 points
Language use	20 points
Participation	20 points

QU'EST-CE QUE TU FERAIS?

In this game, students will practice the conditional by telling what they would do in certain situations.

Procedure To prepare for this game, describe different situations on index cards. (**La voiture tombe en panne.**) Suggestions for situations are given below. Put the cards in a box or a bag. Then, form three to five teams. A player from the first team selects a card and shows it to the other team members. The team members each write one sentence telling what they would do in that situation. For example, if the situation were **La voiture tombe en panne,** an appropriate sentence might be **Je trouverais une station-service.** Players from the first team take turns reading their sentences aloud to the other teams until a member of another team correctly names the situation. The team gets one point for each sentence that its members read before the situation is guessed. The team with the most points at the end of three rounds wins. You might want to appoint a scorekeeper/judge for each group to tabulate the points for each round and to verify the correct answers.

Possible situations:

1. **Tu as oublié tes clés.**
2. **Tu es au chômage.**
3. **Tu dois passer ton bac.**
4. **Tu n'as pas d'argent pour le déjeuner.**

COURSE DE RELAI

In this game, which is geared toward kinesthetic learners, students will practice the vocabulary for different careers.

Procedure This game is played as a relay race. To prepare to play, you will need a card with a profession written on it for each member of the class, and a stopwatch. Form two teams. Then, divide the cards into two sets and put each set in a bag. On your command, the first player from the first team selects a card from the team's bag and mimes that profession. The second player on the team tries to guess the profession. If the second player calls out the correct French word, he or she then selects a card from the box and mimes the word for the third player. Teammates are not allowed to help the player who is guessing. When the last player guesses the last situation, stop the stopwatch and write the team's time on the board. Then, the second team draws cards and mimes the professions in the same manner, racing to beat the first team's time.

Chapitre 5
C'est notre avenir
pp. 110–135

sing the
Chapter Opener

Video Program

Videocassette 1

Before you begin this chapter, you might want to preview the *Video Program* and consult the *Video Guide.* Suggestions for integrating the video into each chapter and activity masters for video selections can be found in the *Video Guide.*

Motivating Activity

Ask students for their definitions of "success." Ask them to name people they think are successful or those they admire, and give reasons for their choices. Have students visualize their own lives in five years. What will they be doing? Where will they be living?

Photo Flash!

① This photo shows the Sandaga Market in Dakar. This oriental-style bazaar is crowded with people buying and selling fruits, fish, cloth, shoes, leather goods, and crafts.

Teaching Suggestion

Have students name the objects on pages 110–111. Make a list on a transparency. Call out objects from the list (a stethoscope) and have students suggest words and expressions in English and French they associate with it (the doctor's office; **j'ai mal au ventre**).

C H A P I T R E
5
C'est notre avenir

① Dakar, centre économique du Sénégal

110 *cent dix*

Culture Note

The Sandaga Market is the largest of the three major markets in Dakar. The main feature of the Kermel Market, the most westernized of the markets in Dakar, is the bright array of multicolored flowers. Flower vendors wear cloth headdresses to match the fabric of their **boubous** *(long, flowing African dresses),* arrange a circle of flowers on their heads, and hold additional bouquets in their hands. At the Tilène Market, the least Europeanized of the three large markets, charms, jewelry, and natural medicines are available. This is the place to buy **gris-gris**, necklaces that are often worn in West Africa as good luck charms.

As-tu déjà pensé à ton avenir? Les jeunes Sénégalais que nous rencontrons ici se demandent ce qu'ils vont faire plus tard. Pour certains, le baccalauréat est une étape importante. D'autres finissent leurs études avant la terminale et commencent à travailler très jeunes. Et pour toi, qu'est-ce que ce sera? L'université? Le travail?

In this chapter you will learn

- to ask about and express intentions; to express conditions and possibilities
- to ask about future plans; to express wishes; to express indecision; to give advice; to request information; to write a formal letter

And you will

- listen to teenagers talk about their plans for the future
- read employment ads
- write a letter to apply for a job
- find out how teenagers in francophone countries choose and prepare for a career

② **Tu ferais mieux de continuer tes études.**

③ **Peut-être que je ferai un apprentissage.**

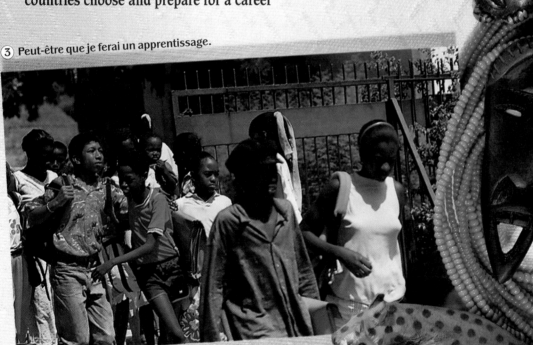

cent onze **111**

Focusing on Outcomes

Have students list expressions in English they associate with the outcomes. Then, have them match the outcomes to the photos. NOTE: You may want to use the video to support the objectives. The self-check activities in **Que sais-je?** on page 134 help students assess their achievement of the objectives.

Teaching Suggestions

- Have students read the introductory paragraph. Then, ask what they think they will learn about in this chapter. Have them suggest words or phrases from the introduction that summarize the chapter theme.
- Have students look at the photos and say as much as they can about them in French.

Language Note

Have students look at the chapter title, **C'est notre avenir.** Ask what words they recognize in **avenir** (à and **venir**). Then, have them try to guess what the title means.

Photo Flash!

③ In this photo, the students are considering their plans for the future. Have students try to guess the meaning of **apprentissage.** They might recognize the English word *apprentice* or the French word **apprendre.**

Group Work

Collect reference materials about Senegal from your local library or travel agencies. Bring them to class and distribute them to small groups. Give students ten minutes to write down as many facts about Senegal as they can find. You might have groups elect one member to report their findings to the class.

Culture Note

Draw students' attention to the craft items displayed on this page. Although the Wolof, the major ethnic group in Senegal, are primarily farmers, they also make a variety of beautiful craft items, including gold and silver ornaments. They are known for their weavings and baskets as well. Another traditional art form is one in which artists draw or paint traditional comic themes (a foolish husband, a hunter being pursued by a lion) onto a sheet of glass.

Teacher Note

For information and brochures on Senegal, you might contact the Senegal Tourist Office at 310 Madison Ave., Suite 724, New York, New York, 10017.

Summary

In **L'avenir, c'est demain**, six Senegalese students tell about their plans for the future. Lamine plans to take his **bac** and go to medical school. Marriage and children are a possibility, he says, but later. Fatima is considering working for her parents in their clothing boutique after taking the **bac**. Omar dreams of becoming a musician. However, he hasn't told his parents yet! Safiétou is considering going to France to work for her brother. Ousmane is awaiting his twenty-first birthday so he can take his driver's test and become a taxi driver. Penda's immediate plans are to relax at the beach. Later, he plans to go to business school.

Motivating Activity

Hold out an imaginary microphone to students and ask them what they'd like to do after high school. You might also have them draw how they picture themselves in five years.

Presentation

Play the recording, pausing after each interview to ask students what they understood. Then, play the recording again, asking about each person's plans after high school.

Teaching Suggestions

- You might ask students these questions about each person: **Qu'est-ce qu'il/elle fera après le bac? Qu'est-ce qu'il/elle veut faire comme métier? Est-ce que le mariage est une possibilité?**
- Have students make a chart containing the names of the students in the **Mise en train**, the activities they are sure of, and the ones they're uncertain about.

Mise en train

L'avenir, c'est demain

L'avenir, c'est dans un ou deux ans. C'est le bac, l'université, le travail, le mariage... Comment est-ce que ces jeunes Sénégalais voient leur avenir après le lycée?

L'année prochaine, j'aurai dix-huit ans et je passerai mon bac. Ensuite, si je le réussis, j'entrerai à l'université. Je voudrais faire des études de médecine. Dans sept ou huit ans, si tout va bien, il se peut que je sois médecin. Bien sûr, si je rencontre une fille que j'aime, il est possible que je me marie et que j'aie des enfants. Mais ça, c'est pour plus tard. Pour l'instant, le principal, c'est de réussir mon bac.

❶ Lamine, 17 ans, Dakar

J'ai du mal à imaginer mon avenir. Je ne sais pas ce que je ferai après le bac. Peut-être que j'arrêterai mes études et que je travaillerai avec mes parents. Ils ont une boutique de vêtements et ils voudraient que je travaille avec eux. Ça ne m'intéresse pas tellement, mais il faut bien que je gagne de l'argent. Et ici, à Dakar, il y a beaucoup de chômage. Enfin, j'ai encore un an pour réfléchir.

❷ Fatima, 17 ans, Dakar

Plus tard, j'ai l'intention d'être musicien. J'espère que je serai célèbre, mais bon, je ne rêve pas trop. En tout cas, après mon bac, j'arrêterai mes études et je me consacrerai entièrement à la musique. Je joue déjà du saxophone dans un petit groupe de World Music. C'est mon rêve et je pense que je réussirai. Le seul problème, c'est convaincre mes parents. Je ne sais pas s'ils seront d'accord. Il faut que j'en parle avec eux. Mais j'attendrai le bon moment!

❸ Omar, 16 ans, Thiès

112 *cent douze*

CHAPITRE 5   C'est notre avenir

RESOURCES FOR MISE EN TRAIN

Textbook Audiocassette 3A/Audio CD 5
Practice and Activity Book, p. 49

Language Note

Students might want to know that **chômage** means *unemployment*. **Au chômage** means *unemployed*.

Culture Note

Thiès, 60 miles east of Dakar, is one of Senegal's largest cities. It is best known for the original tapestries made at the **Manufactures Sénégalaises des Arts Décoratifs.** The scenes on the tapestries, which usually depict everyday life, are based on works by Senegalese artists. Hundreds of artists from all over the country submit their work to be considered for reproduction on the tapestries, but only a few illustrations are selected.

Après le bac, je pense voyager. Mon frère habite en France et j'irai peut-être le rejoindre. Il m'écrit qu'il aime beaucoup la vie là-bas. Au début, c'était difficile, mais il s'est bien intégré. Il travaille dans une entreprise d'import-export. Il fait venir des vêtements sénégalais. Moi, ça me plairait bien comme travail. J'aime beaucoup la mode. Ici, c'est difficile pour une fille de trouver du travail. Mais ce ne sera pas facile d'obtenir un permis de travail pour la France. Et puis, mes parents ne sont pas d'accord. Ils pensent qu'il vaut mieux rester dans son pays que d'aller vivre dans un autre pays. Alors, il faudra que j'attende d'être majeure. Quand j'aurai dix-huit ans, je prendrai une décision.

④ Safiétou, 16 ans, Dakar

⑤ Ousmane, 18 ans, Saint-Louis

Moi, quand j'aurai vingt et un ans, je passerai immédiatement mon permis de conduire pour être chauffeur de taxi, comme mon père. J'aime beaucoup conduire. Et puis, dans un taxi, on rencontre des tas de gens, des touristes, surtout. Je discute beaucoup avec mon père, il aime son métier. Je crois que ça me plaira aussi. Je ne sais pas si je ferai ça toute ma vie, mais, pour l'instant, ça m'intéresse.

Après le bac, moi, j'ai décidé de partir en vacances un mois pour me reposer du lycée! J'ai l'intention d'aller à la plage et de jouer au volley avec les copains. Après, je ferai une école de commerce à Dakar. Là-bas, j'habiterai chez mon oncle. Quand je serai à Dakar, je tiens à aller au cinéma et au concert parce qu'ici, quand on veut sortir, il n'y a pas grand-chose. C'est une petite ville, avec un seul lycée et assez peu de distractions. Une fois en ville, je compte travailler, bien sûr, mais aussi m'amuser! Après, quand j'aurai mon diplôme de l'école de commerce, je chercherai du travail dans une banque. C'est ça qui m'intéresse.

⑥ Penda, 17 ans, Joal-Fadiout

✦ For Individual Needs

Auditory Learners Type the text of the letters from the **Mise en train,** omitting some of the key words. Distribute copies to students. Have them close their books, listen to the recording, and fill in the blanks with the words they hear. Then, have them open their books and check their work.

Group Work

Form small groups and secretly assign one of the letters to each one. Give them one minute to take notes on the writer's plans. Then, have a reporter from each group give a summary of those plans. Have the class guess who is being described.

♜ Game

♜ **C'est moi!** Have students count off from one to six. They should then study the letter that corresponds to the number they have. Then, read aloud a statement from one of the letters. **(J'aime beaucoup la mode.)** The students who have studied that letter should stand up and say **C'est moi!** The first student to recognize the statement and stand up is the winner. Ask the student to give his or her identity **(Safiétou)** and then have him or her open the book and read aloud a statement from another letter to continue the game.

🌐 Culture Notes

• **Saint-Louis,** named after Louis XIII of France, is Senegal's third largest city. It was built on an island at the mouth of the Senegal River in 1859 as the administrative capital of the French West African territories. Famous for its beautiful colonial architecture in pastel shades accented by wooden or wrought iron balconies, Saint-Louis is sometimes called "the New Orleans of West Africa."

• **Joal-Fadiout** is comprised of two separate villages: Joal on the mainland and Fadiout, a small island linked to Joal by a footbridge. Joal is the home of Senegal's former president and world-renowned writer and poet, Léopold Senghor. The island of Fadiout was formed from seashells that piled up over the years, and is held together by the roots of baobab and mangrove trees. Inhabitants of this island pound shells to make cement, which they use to build their houses.

For Individual Needs

3 Challenge Have students react to each of the statements according to their own plans. For example, to react to the statement **Lamine n'a pas l'intention de se marier**, students might say **Moi non plus! Je préfère rester célibataire** or **Moi, si. Je voudrais bien me marier.**

Additional Practice

3 Have students rewrite the false statements to make them true.

♜ Game

4 Play this activity as a game. Before class, make a list of functional expressions from the **Mise en train**, such as **Il est possible que je me marie.** In class, divide students into two or more teams. Place a bell on a desk at the front of the room. Have one player from each team come to the front. Call out the first expression. The first student to ring the bell has the chance to answer by telling which function the expression serves *(expressing a possibility)*. If a player responds correctly, his or her team wins a point. Then, the next players come to the front. Continue until all the expressions have been used.

Teaching Suggestions

5 You might have students write their responses in their journal.

5 Have students interview a classmate about his or her future plans. Then, compile a list of students' plans on the board.

---

1 Tu as compris?

1. At what stage in their life are the writers of the letters you've just read?
2. What question would these letters answer? What are your plans for the future?
3. What are some of the things these teenagers are planning for their future?

1. near the end of secondary school
3. go to a university, work in parents' store, become a musician, travel, become a taxi driver, go on vacation

2 C'est qui?

Associe les jeunes de **L'avenir, c'est demain** aux projets qu'ils ont pour l'avenir.

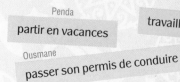

Penda — partir en vacances

Penda — travailler dans une banque

Ousmane — passer son permis de conduire

Safiétou — aller en France

Penda — faire une école de commerce

Ousmane — être chauffeur de taxi

Lamine — faire des études de médecine

travailler avec son frère

Safiétou

3 Vrai ou faux?

1. Lamine n'a pas l'intention de se marier. *faux*
2. Fatima est contente à l'idée de travailler dans la boutique de ses parents. *faux*
3. Il y a beaucoup de chômage à Dakar. *vrai*
4. Omar veut arrêter ses études et se consacrer à sa musique. *vrai*
5. Le frère de Safiétou vend des vêtements sénégalais en France. *vrai*
6. Les parents de Safiétou veulent bien qu'elle habite chez son frère. *faux*
7. Ousmane serait content de pouvoir rencontrer des touristes. *vrai*
8. Penda pense chercher du travail dans une entreprise d'import-export. *faux*
9. La ville de Joal-Fadiout est une grande ville où il y a beaucoup de distractions. *faux*

4 Cherche les expressions

What expressions do the teenagers in **L'avenir, c'est demain** use to . . . See answers below.

1. express a condition?
2. express a possibility?
3. express indecision?
4. express an intention?
5. express an obligation?
6. express interest in something?

5 Et maintenant, à toi

Qu'est-ce que tu penses faire après le lycée? Est-ce que tu vas faire comme un des jeunes de **L'avenir, c'est demain**?

NOTE CULTURELLE

Career opportunities are extremely limited for young people in Senegal, especially those who do not live in big cities. Most of the people in the country work in agriculture, and young people are generally expected to work in the fields as their parents do. Although the law requires that all children complete six years of schooling, in reality only 55% of Senegalese children go to elementary school, and only 10% attend high school. Very few go on to attend Senegal's only university, **l'université de Dakar**.

🌐 Culture Note

All children in Senegal are required to attend school between the ages of 6 and 12. In high school, students are often encouraged to pursue careers in fields that will benefit the country's development, such as business and medicine.

Answers

4 1. . . . si je le réussis . . . ; . . . si tout va bien . . . ; si je rencontre une fille que j'aime . . .
2. . . . il se peut que . . . ; . . . il est possible que . . . ; . . . peut-être que . . .
3. Je ne sais pas ce que je ferai . . .
4. . . . j'ai l'intention de . . . ; je pense . . . ; . . . j'ai décidé de . . . ; . . . je tiens à . . . ; . . . je compte . . .
5. . . . il faut bien que . . . ; . . . il faudra que . . .
6. C'est mon rêve . . . ; . . . ça me plairait bien . . . ; . . . ça m'intéresse.

RENCONTRE CULTURELLE

Qu'est-ce que tu sais sur le Sénégal? Pour t'en faire une meilleure idée, regarde ces photos.

Un marché en plein air

Dakar, la capitale du Sénégal

L'arachide est le produit agricole principal.

La musique traditionnelle est toujours populaire.

La pêche est une activité très importante.

On peut acheter des masques dans les marchés d'artisans.

Qu'en penses-tu?

1. What impression of Senegal do these photos give you?
2. Judging from the photos, what are some of the activities of the people of Senegal? Do people do similar things in cities and towns you know of in other parts of the French-speaking world? In your community? *Possible answers:* **1.** mix of urban and rural, modern and traditional **2.** shopping at outdoor markets, listening to music, fishing, shopping at artisans' markets

Savais-tu que... ?

Senegal, a small country in western Africa, is composed of numerous ethnic groups, including the Wolof, Serer, Diola, and Toucouleur. Many people live in modern urban centers such as Senegal's immense capital, Dakar, which is a business and trade center for all of western Africa. However, most Senegalese live in rural areas and practice customs that date back several hundred years. A chief and group of elders govern each village, deciding on matters such as building a well or a mosque. Agriculture is the mainstay of the economy, and people of all ages participate in cultivating peanuts and other crops, as well as in raising cattle and fishing. People in both cities and villages have strong traditions expressed by their involvement in arts, crafts, music, and dance. Even sports, which are very popular, are sometimes rooted in village traditions, such as **la lutte sans frappe,** a type of wrestling dating back to the seventeenth century.

Culture Notes

• In Senegal, traditional festivals and dances abound. Each ethnic group and region has its own traditional festivals. In Casamance, **Zulane** is a feast for the king of the Oussouye region, and the colorful two-day **Beweng** festival, involving elaborately feathered and beaded costumes, celebrates the harvest. Muslim holidays include **Korité,** on the last day of the fast of Ramadan; **Maouloud,** which celebrates Mohammed's birthday; and **Tamharit,** the Muslim New Year.

• Senegalese families revere their **griots,** or singer-storytellers, whose songs recount everyday life as well as family history.

• Traditional music is accompanied by the **kora,** a harp-like instrument with 21 strings; the **balafon,** a wooden gourd; and the **xalam,** similar to a banjo or guitar. Modern music groups that are becoming popular outside Africa also use many of these instruments.

Motivating Activity

Ask students to locate Senegal on *Map Transparency 2* (**L'Afrique francophone**). Have them imagine what the climate is like. Then, tell them to imagine they are taking a trip to Senegal and ask what they will need to pack.

Presentation

Have small groups study the photos and make notes of their first impressions of Senegal. Have them propose new captions for each photo, based on their impressions. Then, number the photos 1 through 6. Call out a number corresponding to one of the photos and point to a group. The group gives their new caption(s) for the photo. You might write their suggestions on a transparency and have the class select the best caption for each photo.

Thinking Critically

Synthesizing Have students consider what photos might be taken to give an overview of their state. Have them list the subjects of the photos on this page (shopping, the capital city, traditional music, and so on). Then, have them tell what they would photograph to represent their state. You might expand this activity into a project by having students actually take photos and write French captions for them, as if they were making a brochure for an African tourist.

Language Note

The main agricultural product of Senegal is peanuts (**arachides**).

Asking about and expressing intentions; expressing conditions and possibilities

VOCABULAIRE

Regarde les étapes de la vie du père d'Adja.

A dix-huit ans, il **a réussi son bac.**

Ensuite, il **a fait son service militaire.**

Puis, à vingt et un ans, il **a passé son permis de conduire.**

Après, il **est entré à l'université.**

Il **a fini ses études.**

Il **a été** six mois **au chômage.**

Ensuite, il **a trouvé un travail.**

A vingt-sept ans, il **s'est marié.**

Et, à vingt-neuf ans, il **a eu une fille,** Adja.

obtenir son diplôme	choisir un métier *to choose a career*	faire une école technique
arrêter ses études	faire un apprentissage *to do an apprenticeship*	quitter sa famille *to leave home*

6 **Ecoute!** Answers on p. 109C.

Ecoute le père d'Adja et ses amis se rappeler des souvenirs de leur jeunesse et décide si la personne qui parle est le père d'Adja ou non.

🎵 Jump Start!

Have students write three sentences in response to the question **Qu'est-ce que tu vas faire cet été?**

MOTIVATE

Ask students what they want to do next summer or next year and what those plans depend on.

TEACH

Presentation

Vocabulaire Write the new sentences on a transparency and cover it with a sheet of paper. Show props (a diploma, a driver's license, a college T-shirt, the want ads, a plastic wedding ring, a baby doll) as you tell the story, pretending to be Adja's father. Uncover each expression on the transparency as you say it. Then, hold up props (a wedding ring) and ask **Qu'est-ce que j'ai fait? (Vous vous êtes marié(e).)** Next, have students copy the expressions onto separate slips of paper and organize them according to their future plans.

◆ For Individual Needs

6 Tactile/Auditory Learners Have students spread out on their desks the vocabulary slips they created (see Presentation above), or have them write the vocabulary expressions at random on a sheet of paper. As they listen to the recording, have them arrange the slips or number the vocabulary expressions on their paper according to what they hear.

RESOURCES FOR **PREMIERE ETAPE**

Chapter Teaching Resources, Book 2
- Communicative Activity 5-1, pp. 4–5
- Teaching Transparency Master 5-1, pp. 8, 10
  Teaching Transparency 5-1
- Additional Listening Activities 5-1, 5-2, 5-3, pp. 11–12
  Audiocassette 9B/Audio CD 5
- Realia 5-1, pp. 15, 17
- Situation Cards 5-1, pp. 18–19
- Student Response Forms, pp. 20–22
- Quiz 5-1, pp. 23–24
  Audiocassette 7B/Audio CD 5

ADDITIONAL RESOURCES
Textbook Audiocassette 3A
  OR *Audio CD 5*
Practice and Activity Book, pp. 50–53

COMMENT DIT-ON... ?

Asking about and expressing intentions; expressing conditions and possibilities

To ask about intentions:

Qu'est-ce que tu penses faire après le bac?

Qu'est-ce que tu vas faire l'année prochaine?

Qu'est-ce que tu as l'intention de faire en juillet?

Qu'est-ce que tu comptes faire cet été?

To express conditions:

Si je réussis mon bac, j'entrerai à l'université.

Si j'habite à Dakar, je chercherai un travail.

Si je me marie, j'aurai des enfants.

To express intentions:

Après le bac, **je pense** travailler.

En juillet, **j'ai l'intention de** partir en vacances.

Je compte passer mon permis cet été. *I'm planning on . . .*

Je tiens à continuer mes études. *I really want to . . .*

To express possibilities:

Peut-être que je travaillerai.

Il se peut que je fasse un apprentissage.

Il est possible que je fasse des études de médecine.

---

7 Ecoute! Answers on p. 109C.

Ecoute ces jeunes qui parlent de leurs projets après le lycée. Qui a l'intention de... ?

Séka Prisca
Prosper Angèle

se marier trouver un travail entrer à l'université
rendre visite à son frère avoir un enfant
prendre un appartement
se reposer faire un apprentissage quitter sa famille
partir en vacances travailler comme chauffeur

Tu te rappelles ?

Do you remember the forms of the subjunctive that you learned in Chapter 3? Take the **-ent** off of the present tense **ils/elles** form of the verb and add the endings **-e, -es, -e, -ions, -iez, -ent.** Remember that some verbs have irregular stems, but regular endings. Have you noticed some new uses of the subjunctive? There are four expressions you'll learn in this chapter that you'll have to use the subjunctive with: **Il se peut que..., Il est possible que..., Il faudrait que...,** and **Il vaudrait mieux que...**

---

8 Il se peut que je... See answers below.

Qu'est-ce que Bertille pense faire après le lycée? Complète ses phrases.

Il se peut que je...

Presentation

Comment dit-on... ? Make two sets of transparency strips. On the first set, write the phrases for expressing intentions and possibilities. (**Après le bac, je pense...** ; **Avant d'aller à l'université, peut être que...**) On the second set, write logical completions for each sentence in random order (**chercher un travail, je voyagerai**). Have students match each starter with an appropriate completion. Then, write the expressions for asking about intentions on the board. Ask individuals about their plans (**Qu'est-ce que tu comptes faire après le bac?**) and have students answer, using one of the sentences. Next, prompt several students to ask you about your plans for the summer/next year/next month. In some of your answers, express possibility and have students repeat after you.

Language Note

Point out that the expressions **Il se peut que...** and **Il est possible que...** are followed by a verb in the subjunctive. Write them on the board and call on individuals to suggest possible completions.

Reteaching

The subjunctive Write **Il se peut que je ___ mes devoirs** on the board and have a volunteer fill in the blank (**fasse**). Have a second volunteer explain how to form the subjunctive. Then, have students tell about their plans (**Je tiens à finir mes études**) as you write their sentences on the board. Have the class change each sentence to express possibility. (**Il se peut que je finisse mes études.**)

Motivating Activity

Tell students what you plan to do on your trip to Senegal. (**Quand j'irai au Sénégal, j'irai au marché Sandaga.**) Write your sentences on a transparency, and then ask students what they can deduce about the second verb.

Presentation

Grammaire Write **parler**, **choisir**, and **vendre** on the board. Make one set of index cards with the future endings on them and another set with the subject pronouns. Tape a subject pronoun card in front of one of the verbs and the appropriate ending card at the end. Repeat the process with other verbs. For **-re** verbs, erase the final **-e** of the infinitive when you add the endings. Have students repeat the forms after you. Then, make two columns on a transparency. In one column, write sentence starters with **si**. (**Si je réussis mon bac,...**) In the other, write activities in the infinitive form (**... entrer à l'université**). Have students form sentences by matching two phrases and putting the second verb in the future tense.

Teaching Suggestion

9 After students complete the activity, ask them either-or questions. (**Christine dit qu'elle finira ses études ou qu'elle cherchera un travail?**)

 For Individual Needs

Visual Learners Have partners write down three things they plan to do in the future. Then, one student draws an illustration of one of his or her activities. The other student tries to guess the activity. (**Tu te marieras!**) Have partners take turns.

---

*G*rammaire   The future

You've already learned to use **aller** with an infinitive to say that you're *going to do* something. There is also a future tense in French you can use to say that you *will do* something.

> **Je prendrai** une décision.   **Il retrouvera** des amis.
> *I will make . . .*   *He'll meet . . .*

- To form the future tense of most verbs, add the endings **-ai**, **-as**, **-a**, **-ons**, **-ez**, **-ont** to the infinitive. If the infinitive ends in **-re**, drop the final **e** before you add the endings.

> Je **parlerai** français.   Nous **voyagerons** au Sénégal.
> Tu **choisiras** un métier.   Vous **sortirez** après minuit.
> Il/Elle/On **vendra** des fruits.   Ils/Elles **prendront** une décision.

- There are a few irregular verbs that have a special stem to which you add the same endings. You just have to memorize these stems. Here are some of the most common ones:

ser- (être)	devr- (devoir)	pourr- (pouvoir)
aur- (avoir)	voudr- (vouloir)	verr- (voir)
fer- (faire)	viendr- (venir)	enverr- (envoyer)
ir- (aller)	deviendr- (devenir)	saur- (savoir)

> Je **ferai** mes devoirs.   On **viendra** à neuf heures.
> Il **aura** dix-huit ans.   Tu **seras** content.

9   L'avenir de Gérard

Christine imagine l'avenir de Gérard. Complète leur conversation.

GERARD Dis, Christine, à ton avis, qu'est-ce que je __1__ (devenir)? *deviendrai*

CHRISTINE D'abord, tu __2__ (réussir) ton bac. *réussiras*

GERARD Et après?

CHRISTINE Après ça, tu __3__ (entrer) à l'université. *entreras*

GERARD Ah non! J'en ai marre des études! Je __4__ (chercher) un travail. *chercherai*

CHRISTINE Non, tu __5__ (finir) tes études à l'université. *finiras*

GERARD Et pourquoi? Qu'est-ce que je __6__ (faire) après? *ferai*

CHRISTINE Si tu finis, tu __7__ (être) peut-être diplomate. *seras*

GERARD Mais je ne veux pas être diplomate.

CHRISTINE Et pourquoi pas? Comme ça, tu __8__ (pouvoir) voyager partout. *pourras*

GERARD Euh...

CHRISTINE Tu __9__ (aller) dans beaucoup de pays étrangers. Tu __10__ (voir) le monde entier, quoi. Tu __11__ (apprendre) beaucoup de langues... *iras, verras, apprendras*

GERARD Oui, ça pourrait être intéressant, mais j'ai l'intention de me marier. Est-ce que j' __12__ (avoir) des enfants? *aurai*

CHRISTINE Oui. Et ta famille __13__ (vivre) avec toi. *vivra*

GERARD Et on __14__ (avoir) une grande maison? *aura*

CHRISTINE Oui! Ça __15__ (être) nécessaire à cause de tes sept enfants! *sera*

Language Note

Point out that when forming the future of verbs ending in **-oir**, you drop at least the **-oi-** but retain the **-r** (**recevoir—je recevrai**), or you drop and add additional letters. Students should also notice that all regular and irregular future stems end in **-r**, which can serve as a visual and auditory clue.

Family Link

Have students ask friends or family members about their plans for the future. You might have them write a brief report in their journals or have them share their findings. (**Qui a parlé à quelqu'un qui veut être médecin? ... qui veut acheter une maison? ... qui veut se marier?**)

10 Qu'est-ce qu'elle fera?

Qu'est-ce qu'Adjoua fera si elle rend visite à son frère à Paris? *Possible answers:* Elle...

1. visitera le Louvre.

3. ira voir l'Arc de Triomphe.

2. mangera des pâtisseries.

4. fera les magasins.

11 Le temps passe

Safiétou et Penda se marieront cet été. Imagine leur vie pendant les vingt années qui suivront. *See answers below.*

Elle...

être toujours aussi jolie
avoir un travail intéressant
écrire un livre
aller en France

Il...

finir ses études
chercher un travail
devenir banquier
avoir une barbe
être un peu plus gros

Ils...

avoir des enfants
acheter une maison
prendre des vacances chaque année
faire un voyage en Afrique

12 Fais des phrases

Fais des phrases pour décrire des activités que tes amis et toi ferez peut-être après le lycée.

Moi, je	choisir un métier	chercher du travail
Mes amis	se marier	dormir jusqu'à midi
Un(e) de mes ami(e)s	prendre un appartement	aller dans une école technique
Mes amis et moi, nous	entrer à l'université	gagner de l'argent
	sortir tous les soirs	voyager beaucoup

13 Leurs projets d'avenir

Avant le bac, ces jeunes disent à leurs parents ce qu'ils veulent faire plus tard. Avec ton/ta camarade, écris les dialogues entre ces jeunes et un de leurs parents. Puis, jouez ces scènes.

Chakib rêve de devenir footballeur professionnel.

Marina veut trouver un travail et habiter à Dakar.

Aïcha hésite entre aller à l'université et travailler comme vendeuse.

Farouk ne sait pas ce qu'il veut faire.

14 Qu'est-ce que je deviendrai?

Dis à ton/ta camarade ce qui t'intéresse et ce que tu aimes faire. Il/Elle te dira ce que tu deviendras, à son avis. Pose-lui des questions. Changez de rôles.

Possible answers

11 (Elle) sera toujours aussi jolie/aura un travail intéressant/écrira un livre/ira en France.

(Il) finira ses études/cherchera un travail/deviendra banquier/aura une barbe/sera un peu plus gros.

(Ils) auront des enfants/achèteront une maison/prendront des vacances chaque année/feront un voyage en Afrique.

ASSESS

Quiz 5-1, *Chapter Teaching Resources, Book 2,* pp. 23–24

Assessment Items, Audiocassette 7B Audio CD 5

Performance Assessment

Have students find their partners from Activity 13 and act out one of the dialogues from that activity.

Additional Practice

12 Have students write five activities on a sheet of paper (**prendre un appartement, voyager beaucoup**). Collect and redistribute the papers at random. Students write a paragraph about their plans, using the phrases they've received and adding sequencing expressions, such as **ensuite** and **après six mois.**

Portfolio

13 Written/Oral These dialogues are appropriate for students' portfolios. For portfolio information, see *Assessment Guide,* pages 2–13.

For Individual Needs

13 Slower Pace If students have problems getting started, have them read over one of the letters from the **Mise en train** on pages 112–113 that relates to the topic they have selected.

Thinking Critically

Comparing and Contrasting Have students turn to the **Vocabulaire** on page 116 and compare their future plans to what Adja's father did. Then, have them discuss how and why their plans might be different from those of an African student. (They don't have mandatory military service.)

CLOSE

Game

APRÈS LE LYCÉE... Tell students what you plan to do after high school. (**Après le lycée, je compte continuer mes études.**) Then, point to a student at random, who repeats your plan and adds another. (**Après le lycée, je compte continuer mes études, et je tiens à me marier.**) That student then points to another student, who continues in the same manner.

Summary

In **Passe ton bac d'abord!**, Omar tells his parents that he wants to be a musician. His parents argue that there aren't many opportunities for musicians and that he should become a doctor or an engineer instead. He suggests becoming a professor, but his parents still want him to reconsider. Later, he recounts the conversation to his friend Dana, who advises him to write to a music school for information. His letter to the music school is included.

Motivating Activity

Have students reread Omar's letter on page 112 and suggest problems he may have pursuing a career in music and convincing his parents that it's possible. Ask students to describe situations in which they have tried to convince their parents of something.

Presentation

Play the recording and have students listen with their books closed. Stop the recording after the first scene. Ask who is having the discussion, what it is about, what the boy wants to do, and how his parents react to it. Then, play the recording again and have students note the parents' objections and how Omar counters them. Ask students whether they agree with Omar or his parents. Then, play the second scene and have students listen for the advice Dana gives Omar.

Remise en train

Passe ton bac d'abord!

Omar Zidane habite à Dakar, au Sénégal. Pour lui, c'est bientôt la fin du lycée. Qu'est-ce qu'il va faire après? Il a une discussion à ce sujet avec ses parents.

MME ZIDANE Alors, Omar? Tu as réfléchi? Tu sais ce que tu veux faire après ton bac?

OMAR Euh, oui. J'aimerais faire de la musique.

MME ZIDANE De la musique!

OMAR Oui, du saxophone. Je voudrais faire une école de musique.

M. ZIDANE Tu ferais mieux d'entrer à l'université pour faire des études sérieuses.

OMAR Pourquoi? C'est pas sérieux, la musique?

MME ZIDANE Tu sais bien, il n'y a pas beaucoup de débouchés. Il y a tellement de groupes. Tu ferais mieux de devenir médecin ou ingénieur, ou...

OMAR Mais, maman, si je ne réussis pas à percer, je pourrai toujours devenir professeur de musique.

M. ZIDANE Tu sais, ce n'est pas très bien payé, professeur.

OMAR Et alors? Ce n'est pas l'argent qui m'intéresse, c'est la musique!

MME ZIDANE Ecoute, il faut d'abord que tu penses à ton bac. Après, on verra. Mais il faut que tu réfléchisses sérieusement. Musicien, c'est une profession difficile.

OMAR Un jour, je serai célèbre. Et quand on me demandera comment je suis devenu musicien, je dirai : «Ça a été très dur. Mes parents ne voulaient pas que je fasse de la musique!»

15 Tu as compris? See answers below.

1. What are Omar and his parents talking about?
2. What would Omar like to do?
3. What are his parents' concerns?
4. What advice does Dana give to Omar?
5. What information does he provide about himself?
6. What information does Omar request in his letter?

16 Mais moi, je veux! See answers below.

Décide si c'est Omar ou ses parents qui ont dit les phrases suivantes, puis récris leur conversation.

120　*cent vingt*　　　　CHAPITRE 5　C'est notre avenir

RESOURCES FOR REMISE EN TRAIN

Textbook Audiocassette 3A/Audio CD 5
Practice and Activity Book, p. 54

Answers

15 1. his future
2. become a musician
3. limited prospects, poor pay, difficult profession
4. Omar should get information from the music school to convince his parents.
5. He is a prospective student, he has played saxophone for five years, he is in a band that plays World Music.
6. what courses are offered, the price, how long the training lasts, when classes begin

16 a. Omar　　f. ses parents
b. ses parents　g. ses parents
c. ses parents　h. ses parents
d. Omar　　i. Omar
e. Omar

g, d, h, c, e, f, i, b, a

Quelques jours plus tard, Omar parle à son amie Dana de sa conversation avec ses parents.

OMAR Tu sais, j'ai parlé avec mes parents.

DANA Ah oui? Et qu'est-ce qu'ils ont dit?

OMAR Eh bien, ils ne veulent pas que je fasse de la musique.

DANA Pourquoi?

OMAR Ils disent qu'il n'y a pas de débouchés.

DANA Tu leur as expliqué que tu pouvais devenir professeur de musique?

OMAR Oui. Mais ils veulent que je réfléchisse. Bref, ils ne sont pas d'accord.

DANA Tu sais, tu devrais te renseigner auprès d'une école de musique. Peut-être qu'avec plus d'informations, tu pourrais convaincre tes parents.

OMAR Tu as raison, je vais me renseigner un peu mieux.

Omar a finalement écrit une lettre à une école de musique pour avoir plus de renseignements.

Omar Zidane
28, rue Vincent
Dakar

Dakar, le 12 mai 1996

Monsieur le Directeur,
Je me permets de vous écrire parce que j'ai entendu parler de votre école. J'aimerais beaucoup faire des études de musique après mon baccalauréat. Je joue du saxophone depuis cinq ans. Actuellement, je fais partie d'un groupe de World Music, mais j'aimerais me perfectionner. Auriez-vous l'amabilité de m'envoyer des renseignements sur votre école? Je voudrais savoir quels cours sont offerts, le prix, la durée de la formation et quand les cours commencent. Vous serait-il possible de m'envoyer une brochure?

Avec mes remerciements anticipés, veuillez accepter, Monsieur le directeur, l'expression de mes salutations respectueuses.

Omar Zidane

For Individual Needs

17 Kinesthetic Learners
Write all possible answers to these questions on index cards and scatter them around the room face up. Then, call on one student to come to the front. Call out a function (giving advice) and have the student try to find a card with a related expression written on it. (**Tu devrais...**) The other students may help by saying **C'est par ici!**, but they are not allowed to point to a specific card. Once the student has found an appropriate card, have him or her show it to the class. The class verifies that the card applies to the function. Continue until most of the cards have been picked up.

Teaching Suggestions

18 You might have students write a brief entry in their journal about discussions they've had with their parents concerning their future.

• Have students read the letter on the right side of this page. Ask them how the language is different from what they're used to hearing and have them guess why. (It is a business letter and therefore, more formal.) Ask them what formulaic expressions we use in English for formal business letters (*Dear Madam or Sir:, I would greatly appreciate it if . . . , Thank you for your time and attention to this matter, Sincerely,* and so on).

Thinking Critically

Synthesizing Have students suggest informal expressions they use every day and then restate them in more formal English. (*Hey, man. S'up?; Good afternoon, sir. How are you?*)

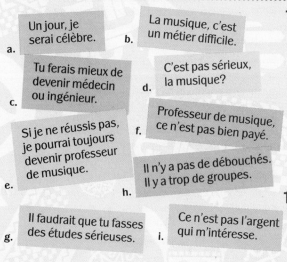

a. Un jour, je serai célèbre.

b. La musique, c'est un métier difficile.

c. Tu ferais mieux de devenir médecin ou ingénieur.

d. C'est pas sérieux, la musique?

e. Si je ne réussis pas, je pourrai toujours devenir professeur de musique.

f. Professeur de musique, ce n'est pas bien payé.

h. Il n'y a pas de débouchés. Il y a trop de groupes.

g. Il faudrait que tu fasses des études sérieuses.

i. Ce n'est pas l'argent qui m'intéresse.

17 Cherche les expressions

According to **Passe ton bac d'abord!**, what expressions would you use to . . .

1. ask about someone's plans?
2. express a wish?
3. give advice?
4. express an obligation?
5. begin a letter?
6. request information?
7. end a letter?

See answers below.

18 Et maintenant, à toi

Et toi? Est-ce que tu as déjà parlé de ton avenir avec tes parents? Est-ce que vous êtes d'accord?

REMISE EN TRAIN

cent vingt et un **121**

Answers

17 1. Tu sais ce que tu veux faire... ?
2. J'aimerais... ; Je voudrais...
3. Tu ferais mieux de... ; ...tu devrais...
4. Il faut d'abord que tu...
5. Monsieur (le Directeur),
6. Auriez-vous l'amabilité de m'envoyer des renseignements sur... ?
   Vous serait-il possible de m'envoyer une brochure?
7. Avec mes remerciements anticipés, veuillez accepter, Monsieur... l'expression de mes salutations respectueuses.

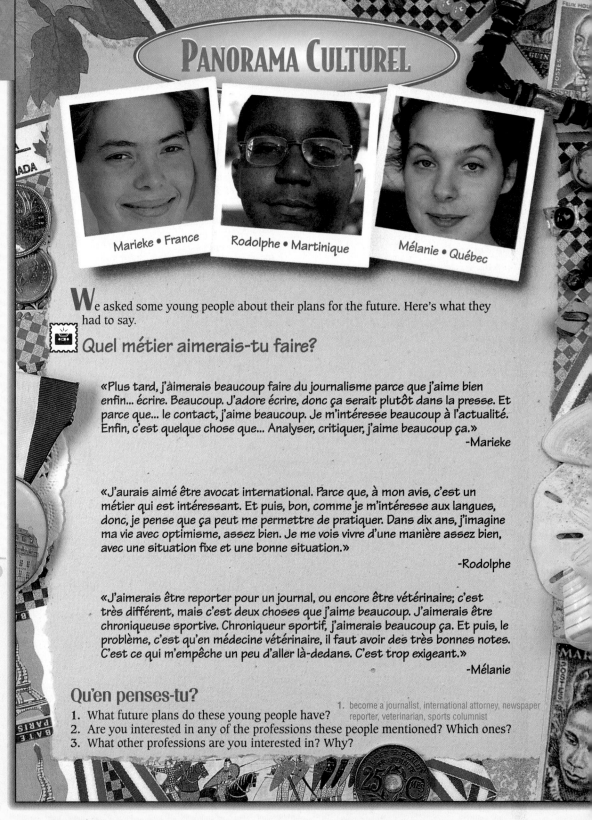

PANORAMA CULTUREL

Marieke • France

Rodolphe • Martinique

Mélanie • Québec

We asked some young people about their plans for the future. Here's what they had to say.

Quel métier aimerais-tu faire?

«Plus tard, j'aimerais beaucoup faire du journalisme parce que j'aime bien enfin... écrire. Beaucoup. J'adore écrire, donc ça serait plutôt dans la presse. Et parce que... le contact, j'aime beaucoup. Je m'intéresse beaucoup à l'actualité. Enfin, c'est quelque chose que... Analyser, critiquer, j'aime beaucoup ça.»

-Marieke

«J'aurais aimé être avocat international. Parce que, à mon avis, c'est un métier qui est intéressant. Et puis, bon, comme je m'intéresse aux langues, donc, je pense que ça peut me permettre de pratiquer. Dans dix ans, j'imagine ma vie avec optimisme, assez bien. Je me vois vivre d'une manière assez bien, avec une situation fixe et une bonne situation.»

-Rodolphe

«J'aimerais être reporter pour un journal, ou encore être vétérinaire; c'est très différent, mais c'est deux choses que j'aime beaucoup. J'aimerais être chroniqueuse sportive. Chroniqueur sportif, j'aimerais beaucoup ça. Et puis, le problème, c'est qu'en médecine vétérinaire, il faut avoir des très bonnes notes. C'est ce qui m'empêche un peu d'aller là-dedans. C'est trop exigeant.»

-Mélanie

Qu'en penses-tu?

1. What future plans do these young people have?
2. Are you interested in any of the professions these people mentioned? Which ones?
3. What other professions are you interested in? Why?

1. become a journalist, international attorney, newspaper reporter, veterinarian, sports columnist

DEUXIEME ETAPE

Asking about future plans; expressing wishes; expressing indecision; giving advice; requesting information; writing a formal letter

VOCABULAIRE

Quel métier est-ce que tu choisiras?

une avocate

un médecin

une institutrice

un ingénieur

un plombier

un tailleur

un(e) architecte	
un(e) avocat(e)	
un chauffeur	
un(e) comptable	*an accountant*
un(e) dentiste	
un écrivain	*a writer*
un homme/une femme d'affaires	*a businessman/woman*
un(e) infirmier (-ière)	*a nurse*
un instituteur/une institutrice	
un(e) journaliste	
un(e) mécanicien(ne)	
un(e) ouvrier (-ière)	*a worker*
un(e) pharmacien(ne)	
un pilote	
un professeur	*a high school/college teacher*
un(e) secrétaire	
un(e) serveur (-euse)	
un(e) technicien(ne)	

NOTE CULTURELLE

In French-speaking countries, as in other places in the world, there is both formal and informal training available for young people who don't want to pursue a university education. In Senegal, an adult who owns a small business or who is skilled at a trade or a craft will teach younger family members, who often work for many years without pay while they're learning. This passing of knowledge and jobs from one generation to the next is especially important in a country such as Senegal where the unemployment rate is 70–80 percent.

19 Ecoute!

Ecoute ces conversations et identifie les métiers des personnes qui parlent.

Answers on p. 109C.

C'est un(e)...

20 Comment on se prépare?

Où est-ce qu'on apprend les métiers donnés dans le **Vocabulaire**? Avec ton/ta camarade, fais une liste de professions sous chaque catégorie de formation.

Université   Ecole technique   Apprentissage

DEUXIEME ETAPE   *cent vingt-trois*   **123**

RESOURCES FOR DEUXIEME ETAPE

Chapter Teaching Resources, Book 2
• Communicative Activity 5-2, pp. 6–7
• Teaching Transparency Master 5-2, pp. 9, 10
  Teaching Transparency 5-2
• Additional Listening Activities 5-4, 5-5, 5-6, pp. 12–13
  Audiocassette 9B/Audio CD 5
• Realia 5-2, pp. 16, 17
• Situation Cards 5-2, 5-3, pp. 18–19
• Student Response Forms, pp. 20–22
• Quiz 5-2, pp. 25–26
  Audiocassette 7B/Audio CD 5

ADDITIONAL RESOURCES
Textbook Audiocassette 3A
  OR *Audio CD 5*
Practice and Activity Book, pp. 55–58
Video Program, Videocassette 1
Video Guide

DEUXIEME ETAPE   123

*J*ump Start!

Have students write a story about an imaginary friend's plans for the future. Tell them to use at least five different verbs.

MOTIVATE

Take a poll of how many students definitely know what profession they want to pursue and how many haven't decided. Ask what they wanted to be when they were five years old. Do students have the same goals now?

TEACH

Presentation

Vocabulaire Find or draw pictures of the professions. Hold up each picture, identify the profession (**Il est journaliste**), and ask **Qu'est-ce qu'il/elle fait?** (**Il écrit pour un journal.**) Then, show the pictures again and ask **Quel est son métier? Et toi, tu veux être (tailleur)?** Have partners ask each other **Et toi, quel métier est-ce que tu veux faire?**

Additional Practice

Have small groups list career fields (medical field, services). Then, have them list in French and English as many professions as possible in each field (**médecin, chauffeur**).

Thinking Critically

Analyzing Have partners read the **Note Culturelle** and consider the advantages and disadvantages of the apprenticeship system. Find out if any students work for their parents, or if they think they might like to work for their parents.

For Individual Needs

21 Kinesthetic Learners

As a variation of this activity, have students work in small groups and take turns miming a profession. The first member to correctly guess the profession (**Tu es médecin!**) takes the next turn. Continue until each student has had at least two turns.

 **Mon journal**

23 For an additional journal entry suggestion for Chapter 5, see *Practice and Activity Book,* page 149.

Presentation

Comment dit-on... ? Write the new expressions on a transparency. Use a different color for each function (blue for asking about future plans, red for expressing wishes, and so on). Then, act out both roles of a conversation between a parent and a student who are discussing the student's future plans. Use as many of the new expressions as possible. As you use each expression, point to it on the transparency. Ask students which function each color represents. Then, tell students about your wishes, and ask about theirs. (**Mon rêve, c'est de voyager partout. Et toi?**)

Additional Practice

Have students refer to the lists on the transparency from the Presentation (see above) as you ask various individuals about their future plans. If a student expresses indecision, call on a classmate to give advice. (**Jessica, tu peux lui donner des conseils?**)

---

 21 Qui suis-je?

Choisis une profession et décris-la. Ton/ta camarade devinera quel métier tu décris.

—Je m'occupe des malades.
—Tu es médecin?
—Non.
—Tu es infirmière?
—Oui.

 22 Sondage

Demande à tes camarades ce qu'ils pensent faire comme métier après le lycée. Quels métiers sont les plus populaires? Pourquoi? Compare tes réponses avec celles de ton/ta camarade.

 23 Mon journal

Quels sont les métiers qui t'intéressent? Pourquoi? Est-ce que tu as déjà décidé ce que tu feras plus tard?

Vocabulaire à la carte

un acteur/une actrice
un(e) assistant(e) social(e)   *a social worker*
un(e) banquier (-ière)
un(e) dessinateur (-trice)   *a commercial artist*
un diplomate
un(e) électricien(ne)
un juge
un mannequin   *a model*
un menuisier   *a carpenter*
un(e) psychiatre   *a psychiatrist*
un(e) programmeur (-euse)
un(e) scientifique
un soldat
un(e) vétérinaire

> **De bons conseils**
>
> You've probably noticed that the names of some careers in French have only a masculine form. You can use the masculine form to refer to both women and men, for example: **C'est un médecin** (*He or she is a doctor*). If you want to make it clear that you're talking about a woman, you can add the word **femme** to the masculine form: **C'est une femme médecin.**

COMMENT DIT-ON... ?

Asking about future plans; expressing wishes; expressing indecision; giving advice

To ask about future plans:
Tu sais ce que tu veux faire?
Tu as des projets?
Qu'est-ce que tu veux faire plus tard?

To express indecision:
Pas vraiment.
Je ne sais pas trop.
Non, je me demande.
  No, I wonder.
Je n'en ai aucune idée.
  I have no idea.
J'ai du mal à me décider.
Je ne sais plus ce que je veux.

To express wishes:
Je voudrais aller à l'université.
J'aimerais bien commencer à travailler.
Ce qui me plairait, c'est de voyager.
Mon rêve, c'est d'être femme d'affaires.

To give advice:
Tu n'as qu'à trouver un travail.
  All you have to do is . . .
Tu devrais te renseigner.
Tu ferais mieux/bien de penser à ton bac.
Il faudrait que tu écrives à l'école de musique.
  You ought to . . .
Il vaudrait mieux que tu travailles.
  It would be better if . . .

 For Individual Needs

Tactile Learners On a sheet of paper, write statements (**Je voudrais aller à l'université**) and corresponding advice in random order. (**Il faudrait que tu étudies.**) Distribute copies to partners. Have them cut apart the statements and advice, match them, and take turns making the statements and responding with the advice.

Language Note

Point out that **Il faudrait que...** and **Il vaudrait mieux que...** require a subjunctive form of the verb that follows.

24 Ecoute!

Est-ce que ces gens savent ce qu'ils vont faire ou est-ce qu'ils hésitent? Answers on p. 109D.

25 Tu ferais bien de....

Ton/ta camarade te parle de ce qu'il/elle voudrait faire. Donne-lui des conseils. Changez de rôles.

> **DESIR**
> acheter une voiture
> être acteur/actrice
> arrêter le lycée
> passer son permis de conduire
> quitter sa famille
> se marier
> devenir musicien(-ne)
> ???

> **CONSEILS**
> chercher un emploi
> choisir un métier pratique
> obtenir son diplôme
> prendre des leçons de conduite
> y réfléchir
> attendre un peu
> aller à l'université
> ???

*G*rammaire The conditional

Generally, you use the conditional in French when you want to tell what you *would* do under certain conditions. You might also use the conditional to be polite. Look at these examples:

> Il **gagnerait** beaucoup d'argent comme médecin. *He would earn . . .*
> Je **voudrais** des renseignements, s'il vous plaît. *I would like . . .*

- To make the forms of the conditional, start with the same stem you use to make the future tense, but add the endings of the imperfect, **-ais, -ais, -ait, -ions, -iez, -aient.** Remember to drop the **e** from infinitives ending in **-re.**

Je **choisirais**		Nous **dirions**	
Tu **choisirais**	le bleu.	Vous **diriez**	la vérité.
Il/Elle/On **choisirait**		Ils/Elles **diraient**	

- The future and the conditional have the same irregular stems. (See page 118.)

> Je **serais** content de continuer mes études.
> Tu **ferais** bien d'étudier.

26 Tes métiers préférés

Discute avec ton/ta camarade du métier que tu voudrais faire. Il/Elle te donnera son opinion.

—Moi, j'aimerais être (METIER)
  parce que je...
—Si j'étais toi, je serais plutôt
  (METIER) parce que tu...

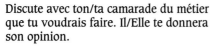

> faire plaisir à ses parents
> devenir riche
> faire un travail qu'on aime
> exploiter ses talents
> rencontrer beaucoup de gens   voyager
> être utile aux autres   être célèbre

DEUXIEME ETAPE

cent vingt-cinq **125**

Presentation

Grammaire Begin by asking students what they would do in certain situations (if they went to college or inherited a million dollars). Have them give their answers as infinitives (**acheter une voiture**), which you write on a transparency. Write the future stem next to each infinitive. Then, write the conditional endings next to the stems. Describe various plans (**J'achèterais une voiture**), and then ask students what they would do. (**Et toi, tu achèterais une voiture?**)

♜ Game

VERB TOSS Write an infinitive on the board. Then, toss a soft ball to a student as you call out a subject pronoun. The student calls out the appropriate conditional form and tosses the ball to another student, while saying a different subject pronoun. After several turns, select a different infinitive and begin a new game.

Teaching Suggestion

26 Have students practice giving advice by responding to your illogical statements, such as **Moi, j'aimerais être pharmacien parce que j'adore les animaux. Je voudrais bien être chauffeur parce que j'adore l'école, et j'aime bien étudier. J'adore dessiner, donc j'aimerais bien être dentiste.** Students might respond with **Si vous adorez les animaux, vous feriez mieux d'être vétérinaire** or **Mais, non! Il faudrait que vous soyez artiste si vous aimez dessiner!**

Teacher Note

The use of the conditional with **si** clauses will be presented in Chapter 8.

Additional Practice

For more practice with the conditional, you might have students play the game "**Qu'est-ce que tu ferais?**" described on page 109F.

Language Note

Point out to students that they should use the conditional in French when they want to say *would* + verb in English. However, tell them that this applies when the action might or could happen *in the future.* To say *When I was young, I <u>would</u> often go to the park,* the **imparfait** should be used.

Portfolio

27 b. Oral This activity is appropriate for students' oral portfolios. For portfolio suggestions, see *Assessment Guide,* page 18.

Teaching Suggestion

27 Type copies of the questionnaire and distribute them to students. Have them mark their responses. Students might also write their choices in complete sentences on a separate sheet of paper. (**J'aime écrire et prendre des initiatives**).

For Individual Needs

27 Slower Pace Before partners act out the interview, have the "guidance counselor" look over the student's questionnaire. The "counselor" should take notes on what the student likes and likes to do, how the student has described his or her personality, and what the student's skills are. Then, have the "counselor" refer to the **Vocabulaire** on page 123 and choose two or three professions that might suit the student. The student should note his or her career choice and the reasons for pursuing it, as well as any questions to ask the "counselor." Have students reverse roles.

Additional Practice

27 As an alternative to the role-playing activity, have students write a letter to the guidance counselor in which they summarize their likes, dislikes, and skills, tell what careers they are interested in, and ask for advice on careers and schooling or training. This letter is appropriate for students' written portfolios.

---

27 **Jeu de rôle**

Tu as du mal à décider ce que tu veux faire après le lycée, donc tu as pris rendez-vous avec le/la conseiller(-ère) d'orientation.

a. En entrant dans son bureau, on te donne cette fiche à remplir. Donne les réponses appropriées.

PARMI CES QUALITES, COCHEZ CELLES DANS LESQUELLES VOUS VOUS RECONNAISSEZ LE MIEUX.

VOUS AIMEZ :

- ❏ prendre des responsabilités
- ❏ manier des chiffres
- ❏ écrire
- ❏ créer des objets décoratifs
- ❏ parler des langues étrangères
- ❏ prendre des initiatives
- ❏ étudier

VOUS ETES :

- ❏ réfléchi(e)
- ❏ prévoyant(e)
- ❏ patient(e)
- ❏ dévoué(e)
- ❏ rêveur(euse)
- ❏ fantaisiste
- ❏ habile de vos mains
- ❏ sensible
- ❏ logique
- ❏ spontané(e)
- ❏ persuasif(ve)
- ❏ original(e)
- ❏ persévérant(e)

Pour chacun des traits suivants, indiquez comment vous vous situez par rapport aux jeunes de votre âge en mettant :
(+ pour très supérieur, = pour moyen, - pour en dessous de la moyenne)

+	=	-	
❏	❏	❏	aptitudes artistiques
❏	❏	❏	tendances à la coopération
❏	❏	❏	tendance à aider autrui
❏	❏	❏	aptitude au commandement
❏	❏	❏	aptitude aux mathématiques
❏	❏	❏	aptitude à la mécanique
❏	❏	❏	originalité
❏	❏	❏	popularité auprès des autres
❏	❏	❏	aptitudes scientifiques
❏	❏	❏	confiance en soi
❏	❏	❏	ordre et soin dans son travail
❏	❏	❏	compréhension des autres

Notez l'importance que vous attribuez aux différents objectifs ou réalisations en mettant :
(+ pour très supérieur, = pour moyen, - pour en dessous de la moyenne)

+	=	-	
❏	❏	❏	être heureux
❏	❏	❏	inventer un produit utile
❏	❏	❏	aider les personnes en difficulté
❏	❏	❏	devenir athlète
❏	❏	❏	assumer un rôle de dirigeant
❏	❏	❏	écrire des romans
❏	❏	❏	travailler de ses mains
❏	❏	❏	contribuer au bien-être de l'humanité
❏	❏	❏	réaliser une œuvre d'art
❏	❏	❏	devenir expert financier ou commercial
❏	❏	❏	avoir beaucoup d'amis
❏	❏	❏	apporter une contribution à la science

Parmi ces différents secteurs professionnels, quels sont ceux qui vous attirent le plus?

- ❏ commerce-vente
- ❏ tourisme-loisirs
- ❏ hôtellerie-restauration
- ❏ coiffure
- ❏ santé
- ❏ carrières sociales
- ❏ banque
- ❏ gestion-comptabilité
- ❏ droit
- ❏ enseignement
- ❏ carrières artistiques
- ❏ informatique
- ❏ armée
- ❏ chimie-biologie
- ❏ agriculture
- ❏ sports
- ❏ mécanique
- ❏ sciences et techniques
- ❏ transport

---

b. Le/La conseiller(-ère) d'orientation examinera tes réponses. Après, tu auras un entretien avec lui/elle. Vous discuterez du métier que tu veux faire et de ce que tes parents veulent que tu fasses. Joue cette scène avec ton/ta camarade. Changez de rôles. N'oublie pas de demander :

- comment tu peux te préparer (université, école technique, etc.);
- combien de temps il te faudra;
- quels débouchés il y a;
- s'il y a d'autres métiers qu'il/elle pourrait suggérer.

126 *cent vingt-six*   CHAPITRE 5   C'est notre avenir

Language Note

Students might want to know the following words from the questionnaire: **chiffres** (*numbers*); **prévoyant(e)** (*having foresight*); **dévoué** (*devoted*); **dirigeant** (*managing*); **comptabilité** (*accounting*); **droit** (*law*); **enseignement** (*teaching*).

COMMENT DIT-ON... ?
Requesting information; writing a formal letter

To request information:

Pourriez-vous m'envoyer des renseignements sur votre école?
Je voudrais savoir quels cours sont offerts.
Vous serait-il possible de m'envoyer une brochure sur votre école?

To begin a formal letter:

Monsieur/Madame,
En réponse à votre lettre du...
Suite à notre conversation
téléphonique,...

To end a formal letter:

Je vous prie d'agréer,
Monsieur/Madame, l'expression
de mes sentiments distingués.

---

28 Ecoute!

Ecoute Armenan qui téléphone à une école technique. Mets les phrases suivantes dans l'ordre d'après la conversation. g, b, d, f, a, e, c

a. Elle demande quels sont les frais d'inscription.

b. Armenan veut savoir quels cours elle pourrait suivre.

c. L'employé demande l'adresse d'Armenan.

d. Elle demande à quelle heure les cours sont offerts.

e. Elle demande à l'employé de lui envoyer une brochure.

f. Elle demande quand les cours commencent.

g. L'employé répond à l'appel d'Armenan.

A la française

You might have noticed that sometimes the subject and verb are reversed in a question. This is called **inversion.** French speakers *invert* subjects and verbs when they want to sound more formal. You'll find inversion in literature, very polite conversations, formal letters or speeches, but not very often in conversational speech.

---

29 Pourriez-vous me renseigner?

Tu voudrais passer ton permis de conduire. Téléphone à une auto-école pour demander combien ça coûte, à quelles heures et quels jours les cours sont offerts et comment s'inscrire. Joue cette scène avec ton/ta camarade.

30 Une lettre de requête

Ecris une lettre à une université ou à une école. Présente-toi, parle de ce que tu voudrais faire et demande des renseignements. N'oublie pas d'utiliser des formules de politesse dans ta lettre.

Motivating Activity

Ask students when they might have to write a formal business letter. Have them look at Omar's letter on page 121 and find polite expressions used in it (**Je me permets de vous écrire,** and so on). Have them tell when to use each expression (to open the letter).

Presentation

Comment dit-on... ? Write a formal business letter on a transparency, using the new expressions. Read it aloud, underlining the new expressions as you read and having students repeat. Write the new expressions on large cards. Draw an outline of a letter on the board, with a place for the address, the salutation, the body of the letter, and the close. Call on students to tape the cards in the appropriate places on the outline.

Teacher Note

A la française You might also tell students that -t- is inserted after third person singular verbs that end in a vowel. (**Demande-t-il l'adresse d'Armenan?**).

Portfolio

30 Written This item is appropriate for students' written portfolios. For portfolio information, see *Assessment Guide,* pages 2–13.

CLOSE

Game

CATÉGORIES Form two teams. Name a topic or function from the chapter, such as *careers* or *expressing indecision.* Have the teams take turns giving related words or expressions until they can't continue. The last team to suggest an appropriate word or expression wins a point.

ASSESS

Quiz 5-2, *Chapter Teaching Resources, Book 2,* pp. 25–26

Assessment Items, Audiocassette 7B
Audio CD 5

Performance Assessment

Have students create and act out a conversation between two indecisive friends who are trying to decide what to do in the future. Challenge students to use as many of the chapter functions as possible in their conversations. You might even award a point for each function or vocabulary item used and offer a small prize to the pair with the most points.

Teacher Note

For an additional reading, see *Practice and Activity Book,* page 59.

PREREADING
Activities A–D

Motivating Activity

Ask students if they have ever looked through the classified ads in the newspaper for a job. Bring in classified ads and distribute them to students. Have groups look over the ads and list the types of jobs available. Ask them what information is given and what abbreviations are used.

Teaching Suggestion

Have students scan the text for cognates and make a list of those they find.

Teacher Note

Graphology, or the analysis of personality through handwriting, is often used in France as a means of screening job applicants. Thus, a **lettre manuscrite** is often requested of applicants. Handwriting samples can reveal general aspects of the applicant's personality that can help the employer decide how well the potential employee would be suited to the workplace.

READING
Activities E–L

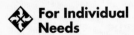

For Individual Needs

E. Visual Learners Type copies of the **Parc Astérix** ad and the **HMC (EUROPE)** ad and distribute them. Have students circle the name of the company and underline the words that describe the type of applicant the company is looking for.

LISONS!

ANNONCES
OFFRE D'EMPLOI

➤ COMMERCE

Agce spécialisée rech. NEGOTIATEUR H/F av. expér. bonne présent. statut agent. % motivant. 44.78.95.26

HMC (EUROPE)
Société Internationale de marketing hôtelier recrute pour un programme de marketing représentant l'hôtel LE MANOIR. Porte Maillot. Vous êtes professionnel, enthousiaste et motivé. Rémunération de base, primes et surtout possibilités de carrières dans le sales management. Pour entretien personnel présentez-vous lundi 28 ou mardi 29 mars entre 9h et 12h ou entre 14h et 17h30 à l'hôtel et demandez Mme Coulanges. Aucun renseignement ne sera donné par téléphone.

Société de distribution concept humanitaire recherche
Directeur de magasin.
Envoyer CV à Monsieur Dantec, 15, rue de la Loge 92220 Bagneux.

Vous êtes jeunes
18-30 ans, libre de tout examen. Rejoignez-nous ! Nous vous offrons une
technique de vente,
une formation, des RDV et un salaire motivant. Si vous disposez d'un véhicule. Si vous êtes libre de 14h à 22h vous êtes sûrement
la (les) personne(s)
qu'il nous faut!
Tel. 42•57•37•24

➤ COMMUNICATION

Jeune Société rech. PERSONNE EN COMMUNICATION anglais courant, min 30 ans. Env. CV + Photo à CODI S.A.,12 rue Henri René 75002 PARIS

recherche pour MENHIR FM... la radio diffusée sur le Parc un(e)
ANIMATEUR RADIO
Doué pour les animations en public, vous possédez une expérience significative de la radio FM d'au moins deux ans. Humour et sens de l'improvisation vous caractérisent. Merci d'adresser votre dossier de candidature, lettre, CV et photo sous réf. V2 au Parc Astérix, BP 8, 60128 PLAILLY

➤ EDITION

Correcteur Editeur rech. profess. ht. niveau pour 1 et 2 lect. de 3200p à 2500s/page. Indispens. avoir connaiss. pers. en gastronomie. Ecr. avec référ. et prétent., lettre manus. à La Page, 6 rue Henry IV 75006 Paris.

STUDIO DE CREATION GRAPHIQUE
recherche
JEUNE ASSISTANT(E)
• compétences graphiques/MAC
• créativité, dynamisme, autonomie et rigueur. Env. CV + lettre sous réf 34810 au journal, qui transmettra

➤ GRAPHISME

CENTRE DE FORMATION RECH. pour des entreprises dans le secteur des Arts Graphiques
46 CANDIDATS
moins de 26 ans. Niveau Bac +2/+3 Pour suivre une spécialisation PAODAO (macintosh) en contrat de qualification. 3/4 temps entreprises. 1/4 temps formation. Formation gratuite et rémunérée.
42.75.24.30/42.49.10.99.

➤ JOURNALISME

Quotidien ch. JOURNALISTE SECRETAIRE DE REDACTION Poste à pourvoir rapidement. Contacter Agence Presse, av. de la Madeleine, 12021 RODEZ Cedex 9

➤ PHOTOGRAPHIE

Labo photo pour pros. urgent. rech. H/F
• standard./réception. bilingue très bonne connaissance photo
• Tireur-filmeur pour contacts couleur (1).47.71.94.10.

➤ RESTAURATION

SERVEURS
à temps complet. Envoyer CV + photo à J.P. 4 rue Maréchal 75006 PARIS.

Restaurant **"La Criée"**
75002 Paris,
recherche serveuses bonne

➤ SECRETARIAT

EDITEUR rech. pour Ouvrage Juridique DACTYLO à domicile

Petite société d'édition et de diffusion de livres sportifs recherche
Secrétaire
à plein temps, 7.000F brut x 13. Envoyer candidature avec CV à Média 8, 29 avenue V. Hugo, 75013 Paris.

➤ TELEMARKETING

GENERATION MARKETING
recrute 100 TELEACTEURS. Dispo. en journée et/ou soirée. Rémunération motivante.
T.42.01.22.22
Sophie.

SALONS PLUS
recherche

30 TELEACTEURS
dispo. en journée ou en après-midi et soirée.
40 TELEACTEURS
Bilingues ou Trilingues Français, Allemand, Néerlandais. Rémunération horaire, primes, av. sociaux. Tél.14.67.45.16

Agence de Télémarketing (92)
recherche
Téléacteurs H/F

DE BONS CONSEILS

There are certain kinds of writing that always follow a predictable pattern. For example, business letters all have a similar formal structure, fairy tales begin with "Once upon a time," and you can usually tell what's going to happen in a "boy-meets-girl" story. If you recognize that the text you're reading has one of these "formulas," you can use that knowledge to help you make some predictions about the kind of information you'll find in the text, how it will be organized, and so on.

For Activities A–D, see answers below.

A. Preview the reading.
  1. What are these reading selections?

2. What "formulas" do you see in this reading? Name four kinds of information you expect to find.

B. Into what categories are the ads on this page organized?

C. Scan the ads on this page.
  1. Find three names of companies.
  2. Give five examples of different types of companies.

D. For each ad on this page, identify the job that is being advertised.

E. Locate the ads for **Parc Astérix** and **HMC (EUROPE).** Answer the following questions for each one: For Activity E, see answers on bottom of p. 129.
  1. What type of company placed the ad?
  2. What are the requirements for getting the job?

Answers

A 1. employment ads
  2. abbreviations, titles of jobs, where to apply for jobs, requirements for jobs, salary

B commerce, communication, publishing, graphic arts, journalism, photography, food service, secretarial, telemarketing

C *Possible answers*
  1. HMC (Europe), Parc Astérix, La Criée, Generation Marketing, Salons Plus
  2. hotel marketing, theme park, newspaper, photo lab, restaurant

D negotiator, hotel marketer, store director, salesperson, communications specialist, radio announcer, proofreader, graphic arts assistant, graphic arts student, newspaper editor, photo lab receptionist, photo lab developer, waiter, waitress, typist, secretary, telemarketers

RAPIDE!

Votre annonce pour le lendemain, téléphonez avant 15h et payez par Carte Bleue

TELEVISION LOCALE

TV10 ANGERS

RECHERCHE POUR SES EMISSIONS EN DIRECT ANIMATEURS(TRICES) A TEMPS PARTIEL EXPERIENCE ANIMATION INDISPENSABLE

Envoyer impérativement : vidéo de présentation (V8, VHS...) + CV + lettre manuscrite à TV10 - rue de la Rame - 49100 ANGERS

ASSISTANT ROUGHMAN

disponible rapidement

Vous avez une formation Arts Graphiques et un minimum d'expérience en réalisation de maquettes, roughs, présentations...

Vous maîtrisez lettrage et dessin et connaissez un minimum la P.A.O.

Vous êtes soigneux, endurant, disponible et apte à travailler en équipe.

Adresser lettre + CV + photo au journal sous réf. Par 2668 qui transmettra.

BOUTIQUE RENOMMEE DE DECORATION INTERIEURE

recherche

son(sa) vendeur(euse) principal(e)

Expérience obligatoire, de préférence dans une activité similaire.

Poste nécessitant : sérieux, sens des responsabilités, goût pour le design, capacité à gérer et à administrer un magasin.

Envoyer CV + photo + motivations sous réf. 3/619 à Paris Annonces 25, rue Pétrarque 75139 Paris cedex 09.

IMPACT MEDECIN

recherche pour son hebdomadaire trois collaborateurs confirmés :

Maquettiste réf 001, Secrétaire de rédaction réf 002, Correcteur réf 003.

Envoyez-nous une lettre accompagnée d'un CV et d'une photo à :

IMPACT MEDECIN
Service ressources humaines
20 Boulevard du Parc 92521
Neuilly sur Seine cedex

✈ Grand-Théâtre ✈
de Bordeaux
DIRECTION ARTISTIQUE ALAIN LOMBARD

CONCOURS DE RECRUTEMENT
CHŒUR DU GRAND-THEATRE
DIRECTION GUNTER WAGNER

LUNDI 28 MARS 1994
1 ALTO II
1 TENOR II
1 BARYTON
ou
1 BASSE

PRISES DE FONCTIONS : SEPTEMBRE 1994
LES EPREUVES AURONT LIEU AU
GRAND-THEATRE DE BORDEAUX

Renseignements : Grand-Théâtre de Bordeaux Régie du chœur
B.P. 95 33025 BORDEAUX

LES RESTAURANTS DU CŒUR

recrutent

BENEVOLES (H/F)
pour La Péniche du Cœur
Centre d'hébergement
des sans-abris

Ecrivez : 221, rue La Fayette

---

3. Where can you apply for the job or receive more information?

F. Can you figure out the meanings of these abbreviations in the ads? *See answers below.*
   1. H/F av. expér. bonne présent.
   2. Editeur rech. profess. ht. niveau
   3. Indispens. avoir connaiss. pers. en gastronomie
   4. Env. CV + lettre sous réf. 34810
   5. dispo. en journée et/ou en soirée

G. Look at the large advertisements on this page and answer the following questions. *See answers below.*
   ### Télévision locale
   1. What job is being advertised?
   2. What must you send that none of the other ads require? Why?

Assistant Roughman
1. What does a "roughman" do?
2. What qualities should an applicant for this job possess?

Grand-Théâtre de Bordeaux
1. What is unusual about the positions being advertised?
2. What must a person do who is interested in one of these positions?

Les restaurants du cœur
1. How does this ad differ from the others?
2. Using the context of the ad, can you tell what **bénévoles** means?

cent vingt-neuf **129**

Game

QUEL EST MON MÉTIER?

Have four panelists imagine they have one of the positions advertised on pages 128–129. Divide the rest of the class into two teams. The teams take turns asking the panelists yes-no questions to try to determine what each person's job is. The first team to correctly identify the positions of all four panelists wins.

Teaching Suggestion

L. To help students generalize the results, first have them write a one-sentence summary of each item. For example, for the first item, students might write *Girls are more concerned than boys with finding a job, and boys are more concerned than girls with being financially secure.* Then, have groups discuss what they consider to be the general trends.

POSTREADING
Activities M–N

Cooperative Learning

M. Have small groups create and administer the poll. In groups, each student writes down one question for the poll. The manager compiles their suggestions. Then, the group members decide together which questions to keep, which ones to reword, and which ones to delete. Each group member asks the class one or two of the questions. Then, the accountant tabulates the group's findings. The designer creates charts to organize the data and plans the layout. All group members comment on and assemble the layout. Groups then present their results, with each group member participating in the oral presentation.

Sondages : les jeunes pour un travail à tout prix

Parmi les choses suivantes, qu'est-ce qui vous paraît le plus important lorsqu'on a un emploi?

Avoir un travail intéressant	70 %	1
Avoir la sécurité de l'emploi	66 %	2
Avoir un bon salaire	49 %	3
Avoir des perspectives de carrière intéressantes	33 %	4
Bien s'entendre avec ses collègues	27 %	5
Avoir des responsabilités	19 %	6
Bien s'entendre avec ses supérieurs	14 %	7
Ne pas être trop accaparé par son travail	9 %	8
Sans opinion	0 %	

Le total est supérieur à 100 %, les personnes interrogées ayant pu donner trois réponses

Pour un jeune comme vous, diriez-vous que pour trouver un emploi aujourd'hui, il vaut mieux :

Faire des études supérieures le plus longtemps possible	23 %	3
Faire des stages en entreprise	40 %	1
Obtenir un diplôme professionnel spécialisé	36 %	2
Sans opinion	1 %	4
Total	100 %	

Quand vous pensez au premier emploi pour un jeune comme vous, diriez-vous:

Qu'il faut prendre le premier emploi qui se présente, même s'il ne correspond pas exactement à ce qu'on cherche	73 %	1
Qu'il faut prendre l'emploi que l'on souhaite, même si cela doit prendre du temps	26 %	2
Sans opinion	1 %	3
Total	100 %	

Pensez-vous que dans les prochaines années il y a de grands risques que vous soyez chômeur?

Oui, pendant longtemps	20 %	2
Oui, mais pendant peu de temps	56 %	1
Non	20 %	2
Sans réponse	4 %	3
Total	100 %	

Les divergences garçons-filles

Ce qui compte le plus pour vous actuellement ?

Trouver un emploi		Etre à l'aise financièrement	
Garçon	50 %	Garçon	53 %
Fille	60 %	Fille	49 %

Ce qui est le plus important quand on a un emploi ?

La sécurité de l'emploi		Un bon salaire	
Garçon	63 %	Garçon	52 %
Fille	69 %	Fille	46 %

Pensez-vous qu'il y ait pour vous des risques d'être chômeur ?

Pendant longtemps		Pendant peu de temps	
Garçon	14 %	Garçon	59 %
Fille	26 %	Fille	53 %

Pour trouver un emploi aujourd'hui, il vaut mieux:

	Faire un stage en entreprise		
Garçon	35 %	Fille	44 %

	Prendre le premier emploi qui se présente		
Garçon	67 %	Fille	79 %

Source : Sofres

For Activities H, I, J, K, and L, see answers below.

H. What is the theme of the poll presented on this page?

I. According to the poll above, what are the best ways to prepare to find a job? Find a job on pages 128 and 129 that might appeal to someone who . . .
1. is looking for an interesting career.
2. would like to have professional training.
3. would like to have responsibility.

J. According to the poll, what are the most important considerations for young French people when it comes to a job?

K. Based on the poll, would you say that young people in France are more optimistic or more pessimistic about employment? Why?

L. Look at the results under the heading **Les divergences garçons-filles**.
1. How do the responses of the boys and girls differ?
2. What general trends can be observed in the results?

M. Take a similar poll in your classroom. Find out what your classmates think is important in a job and how they feel about their job opportunities.

N. Now, choose a job you might like and write an ad for it, modeled on those you've read. Don't forget to use the appropriate abbreviations.

130 *cent trente*

ECRIVONS!

Now that you have read the employment ads, think about what you would do to apply for one of the jobs advertised. You would send the company whatever information was required—résumé, photo, samples of your work—and enclose a cover letter. In this activity, you'll choose one of the ads from **Lisons!** *and write a letter to apply for that position.*

Une lettre de candidature

Maintenant, tu vas écrire une lettre de candidature pour un emploi. Dans cette lettre, il faut convaincre l'employeur que tu es le meilleur candidat/la meilleure candidate pour le poste.

A. Préparation

1. Parmi ces annonces, choisis celle qui t'intéresse le plus :
   a. Parc Astérix
   b. Studio de création graphique
   c. HMC (Europe)
   d. Télévision locale
   e. Assistant roughman
   f. Boutique renommée
2. Fais une liste de tes qualifications et qualités (tu peux les imaginer) pour persuader l'employeur de ton expérience et de ton intérêt.
3. Pense à ce dont l'employeur a besoin. Est-ce qu'il y a d'autres détails que tu pourrais ajouter pour donner une image positive de toi à l'employeur?
4. Mets en ordre les détails que tu as écrits, avec les points les plus forts de ton argumentation à la fin pour avoir le maximum d'effet.

DE BONS CONSEILS

Details and structure are two of the most important elements in persuasive writing. To be as convincing as possible, you must choose facts and examples that will have the greatest impact on your audience. Try to predict your readers' concerns and address them. The structure of your argument also influences the effectiveness of your writing. Begin with your second-best points, followed by the weakest ones, and then put your strongest arguments last. Your most convincing argument will have a bigger impact if it is the last thing your audience reads.

B. Rédaction

Fais le brouillon de ta lettre. N'oublie pas les formules de politesse nécessaires.

C. Evaluation

1. Compare ta lettre à celles que tu as vues dans le chapitre :
   a. Est-ce que tu montres que tu possèdes toutes les qualifications nécessaires pour l'emploi?
   b. Est-ce que ses détails et sa structure rendent ta lettre convaincante?
   c. Est-ce que ton style est adéquat et assez formel?
2. Rédige la version finale de ta lettre. N'oublie pas de corriger les fautes d'orthographe, de grammaire et de vocabulaire.
3. Donne ta lettre à un petit groupe de camarades qui jouent le rôle des employeurs. Ils vont la lire et dire si tu les as persuadés de t'accorder un entretien.

Caroline Lasalle
130, avenue des Amandiers
75006 Paris

Société Marchand
Service du personnel
34, rue Thiers
75012 Paris

Paris, le 25 août 1996

Objet : demande d'emploi de secrétaire trilingue

Madame, Monsieur,

Suite à la parution de votre annonce dans Paris Annonces, je me permets de vous écrire afin de poser ma candidature pour le poste de secrétaire trilingue offert par votre compagnie.
Je vous prie de bien vouloir trouver ci-joint mon *curriculum vitae*.
Sachez également que je me tiens à votre entière disposition pour toutes demandes de renseignements supplémentaires.

Dans l'attente de votre réponse, veuillez accepter, Madame, Monsieur, l'expression de mes sentiments distingués.

cent trente et un **131**

WRITING STRATEGY

Using details and structure in persuasive writing

Portfolio

Written You might have students include all their work for sections A-C in their written portfolios. For portfolio suggestions, see *Assessment Guide,* page 18.

PREWRITING

Motivating Activity

Ask students if they've ever had a job interview or been in a situation in which they had to promote their own abilities and convince someone of their qualifications. If any students have run for student council positions or have completed college entrance applications, you might have them share their experiences.

Teaching Suggestion

A. 3. Have students answer the following questions that an employer might ask: How does your background prepare you for this position? Why are you applying for *this* job in particular? Why should I hire *you* instead of someone else? What makes *you* the best candidate for the job?

For Individual Needs

A. Challenge As students list their qualifications, have them consider the arguments that could be made *against* hiring them as well (too young, not enough experience, won't stay long enough to complete the job). Have them jot down arguments that would pre-empt these objections (I'm consistent, reliable, enthusiastic about the field) and include them in their letters.

WRITING

For Individual Needs

B. Slower Pace Encourage students to borrow appropriate phrases from Omar's letter on page 121. Suggest they use phrases such as **J'ai l'intention de...** or **Je compte...** from **Comment dit-on... ?** on page 117 to relate their future plans to the position.

POSTWRITING

Teaching Suggestion

C. Once students have written their rough draft, have them underline each of their points. Then, have them evaluate the structure of their argument. Are their second-best points first? Is their strongest point last? Have them reread the ad to which they are responding to be sure they mentioned the characteristics the employer requested.

The **Mise en pratique** reviews and integrates all four skills and culture in preparation for the Chapter Test.

 Video Wrap-Up

VIDEO PROGRAM
Videocassette 1

You might want to use the *Video Program* as part of the chapter review. See the *Video Guide* for teaching suggestions and activity masters.

For Individual Needs

1 Slower Pace Before playing the recording, form groups of three and assign either Karim or Sandrine to each one. As they listen to the recording, group members concentrate specifically on their assigned person. Then, have them respond to the true-false statements about their person. Finally, have the groups share their information about Karim and Sandrine.

Building on Previous Skills

2 Have students use their reading strategies to answer these questions. They should use the title to answer the first question. Have them scan the text for the specific answers to the other questions. You might even have a contest to see who can write correct answers to questions 2-5 in the shortest amount of time.

MISE EN PRATIQUE

 1 Ecoute la conversation de Karim et Sandrine et dis si les phrases suivantes sont vraies ou fausses.

1. Karim a réussi son bac.
2. Sandrine compte entrer à l'université.
3. Sandrine ne va pas quitter sa famille.
4. Karim sait ce qu'il veut faire plus tard.
5. Karim a l'intention de continuer ses études.
6. Sandrine conseille à Karim de chercher un travail.
7. Karim voudrait un travail où il puisse rencontrer des gens.
8. Sandrine conseille à Karim de lire un article dans le journal.

2 Lis l'article que Sandrine a donné à Karim. Puis, réponds aux questions.
See answers below.

1. What is this article about?
2. What sort of preparation did these young people receive?
3. According to the school's director, what is the purpose of this program?
4. What does the director expect of the graduates?
5. Who attends this school?

 3 C'est le premier jour d'apprentissage de Karim à l'hôtel. Son supérieur lui a dit de prendre les messages et de répondre aux questions par écrit. Ecoute le message de M. Loukour et fais une liste de ses demandes. Puis, décide laquelle de ces lettres Karim lui enverra.
Answers on p. 109D.

HOTELLERIE -P.B. SAMB
De nouveaux professionnels sur le marché

Une trentaine d'élèves de diverses nationalités de l'Ecole de Formation Hôtelière et Touristique ont reçu vendredi soir leur diplôme.

Tous les candidats ayant réussi cette année, le ministre du Tourisme a félicité la direction et les professeurs de l'école, ainsi que les responsables d'entreprises qui ont contribué à leur formation en les encadrant au niveau des stages pratiques.

Les candidats de cuisine et pâtisserie, restaurant et gestion hôtelière reçoivent une formation de deux ou trois ans axée sur des disciplines relatives à un enseignement pratique doublée de techniques professionnelles, d'expression française ou de langues étrangères.

Il s'agit de «mettre à la disposition des industries hôtelières et touristiques des agents compétents et efficaces», selon le directeur de l'école. En leur souhaitant bonne chance dans leur vie professionnelle, le directeur les a invités à exercer «le plus beau métier du monde avec passion et un plaisir quotidien».

L'EFHT reçoit, en effet, chaque année, outre les élèves sénégalais, des ressortissants d'autres pays africains.

Monsieur,

Comment ça va? Je vous écris cette lettre pour répondre à vos questions. D'abord, je voulais vous dire que nos bungalows, ils sont tous climatisés. Et puis, comme sports, on a du tennis, de la pirogue et de la planche à voile. Ah ! On fait de la pêche aussi. D'ailleurs, voilà une brochure, comme ça, vous pourrez voir par vous-même. Allez, je vous laisse. A bientôt.

Monsieur,

Suite à votre appel téléphonique du 20 juin, nous vous envoyons les renseignements que vous nous avez demandés. Notre établissement offre les sports suivants : tennis, planche à voile, pirogue et pêche. Sachez également que tous nos bungalows sont climatisés, comme vous pourrez le constater dans la brochure que vous trouverez ci-jointe. En vous remerciant d'avance pour votre attention, nous vous prions d'agréer, Monsieur, l'expression de nos sentiments respectueux.

132 *cent trente-deux*

CHAPITRE 5   C'est notre avenir

Answers

2 1. graduation from school of hotels and tourism
   2. training in cooking, restaurant and hotel management
   3. to make available to the hotel and tourist industries competent and efficient staff
   4. to practice the best profession in the world with enthusiasm and daily pleasure
   5. students from various African countries

4 Lis ces lettres que quelques jeunes Sénégalais ont envoyées à un magazine de jeunes francophones. Ecris des réponses que tu enverras au magazine. Compare tes réponses à celles de ton/ta camarade.

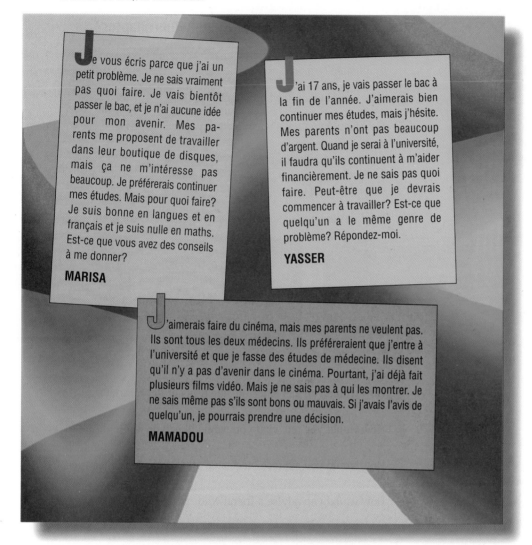

Je vous écris parce que j'ai un petit problème. Je ne sais vraiment pas quoi faire. Je vais bientôt passer le bac, et je n'ai aucune idée pour mon avenir. Mes parents me proposent de travailler dans leur boutique de disques, mais ça ne m'intéresse pas beaucoup. Je préférerais continuer mes études. Mais pour quoi faire? Je suis bonne en langues et en français et je suis nulle en maths. Est-ce que vous avez des conseils à me donner?

MARISA

J'ai 17 ans, je vais passer le bac à la fin de l'année. J'aimerais bien continuer mes études, mais j'hésite. Mes parents n'ont pas beaucoup d'argent. Quand je serai à l'université, il faudra qu'ils continuent à m'aider financièrement. Je ne sais pas quoi faire. Peut-être que je devrais commencer à travailler? Est-ce que quelqu'un a le même genre de problème? Répondez-moi.

YASSER

J'aimerais faire du cinéma, mais mes parents ne veulent pas. Ils sont tous les deux médecins. Ils préféreraient que j'entre à l'université et que je fasse des études de médecine. Ils disent qu'il n'y a pas d'avenir dans le cinéma. Pourtant, j'ai déjà fait plusieurs films vidéo. Mais je ne sais pas à qui les montrer. Je ne sais même pas s'ils sont bons ou mauvais. Si j'avais l'avis de quelqu'un, je pourrais prendre une décision.

MAMADOU

 **5** **J E U   D E   R O L E**

Talk to a parent about what you're thinking of doing after high school. Explain what you want to do with your future and why. Your parent is not very happy with your choice and tries to discourage you from it. Try to convince him or her. Change roles.

MISE EN PRATIQUE   *cent trente-trois* **133**

♜ Game

JE REGRETTE! This game is like "Go Fish." Have partners create a set of 20–25 cards with either **Marisa, Yasser,** or **Mamadou** written on them. Then, have them shuffle the deck, deal three cards to each player, and place the rest of the deck face down. The goal of the game is to have the greatest number of matched cards. The first player then asks a question about one of the people on his or her cards. If the player has a **Marisa** card, he or she might ask **Tu es nulle en maths?** If the other player has a card for the person who would answer yes, he or she gives the card to the first player, who sets the two matching cards aside. If the other player does not have the card, he or she says **Je regrette,** and the first player draws a card from the deck. The game ends when one player empties his or her hand. Players win a point for each pair of matching cards.

Teaching Suggestion

4 Have students write a letter to the magazine in which they describe their own options and ask the readers for advice.

📁 Portfolio

5 Oral This activity is appropriate for students' oral portfolios. You might have students videotape their skits. For portfolio information, see *Assessment Guide,* pages 2–13.

This page is intended to help students prepare for the test. It is a brief checklist of the major points covered in the chapter. The students should be reminded that this is only a checklist and does not necessarily include everything that will appear on the test.

♜ Game

QUE SAIS-JE? Form two teams. Have a player from each team come to the board. Call out a question at random from the **Que sais-je?** The first player to write a correct response on the board wins a point for his or her team. You might offer the winning player the chance to win a bonus point by giving a second possible answer to the question. For question 4, you might hold up magazine pictures of people of various professions. The team with the most points at the end of the game wins.

Additional Practice

4 Have students also write about one or two things that they plan to do.

8 You might have students work with a partner to create a two-line dialogue for each situation.

QUE SAIS-JE?

Can you use what you've learned in this chapter?

Can you ask about and express intentions? p. 117

1 How would you ask a friend what he or she plans to do after graduation? Qu'est-ce que tu penses/vas/comptes faire? Qu'est-ce que tu as l'intention de faire?

2 How would you tell what you plan to do? Je pense/compte/tiens à... ; J'ai l'intention de...

Can you express conditions and possibilities? p. 117

3 How would you tell someone what you will do, given these conditions?
Possible answers:
1. Si je me marie,... j'aurai des enfants.
2. Si j'entre à l'université,... je ferai des études de médecine.
3. Si je gagne de l'argent,... je pourrai prendre un appartement.
4. Si je trouve un travail,... je quitterai ma famille.

4 How would you tell someone that you might do these things?
See answers below.

1.   2.   3.

Can you ask about future plans? p. 124

5 How would you ask someone about his or her future plans? Tu sais ce que tu veux faire? Tu as des projets? Qu'est-ce que tu veux faire plus tard?

Can you express wishes? p. 124

6 How would you tell what you would like to do in the future? Je voudrais... ; J'aimerais bien... ; Ce qui me plairait, c'est de... ; Mon rêve, c'est de...

Can you express indecision? p. 124

7 How would you express indecision about your future plans? Pas vraiment. Je ne sais pas trop. Non, je me demande. Je n'en ai aucune idée. J'ai du mal à me décider. Je ne sais plus ce que je veux.

Can you give advice? p. 124

8 How would you advise a friend who . . . See answers below.

> failed an exam?
> doesn't have any pocket money?
> had a fight with his or her sister?
> forgot to call his girlfriend/her boyfriend?
> is uncertain about his or her choice of profession?

Can you request information and write a formal letter? p. 127

9 How would you request information about courses, costs, and so forth from a school or university? Pourriez-vous m'envoyer des renseignements sur votre école? Je voudrais savoir... ; Vous serait-il possible de m'envoyer une brochure sur votre école?

10 How would you write the closing of the letter in number 9? Je vous prie d'agréer, Monsieur/Madame, l'expression de mes sentiments distingués.

134   *cent trente-quatre*   CHAPITRE 5   C'est notre avenir

Possible answers
4 1. Peut-être que je ferai un apprentissage.
    2. Il est possible que je voyage.
    3. Il se peut que je cherche un travail.

8 *Failed an exam:* Tu n'as qu'à étudier plus.
Doesn't have any pocket money: Tu devrais travailler.
Had a fight with his or her sister: Tu ferais bien de lui parler.
Forgot to call his girlfriend/her boyfriend: Tu devrais t'excuser.
Is uncertain about his or her choice of profession: Il faudrait que tu te renseignes.

PREMIERE ETAPE

Asking about and expressing intentions

Qu'est-ce que tu penses faire?
What do you think you'll do?
Qu'est-ce que tu as l'intention de faire? *What do you intend to do?*
Qu'est-ce que tu comptes faire?
What do you plan to do?
Je pense... *I think I'll . . .*
Je compte... *I'm planning on . . .*
Je tiens à... *I really want to . . .*

Expressing conditions and possibilities

Si... , *If . . . ,*

Peut-être que... *Maybe . . .*
Il se peut que... *It might be that . . .*
Il est possible que... *It's possible that . . .*

Future choices and plans

arrêter/finir ses études *to stop/finish one's studies*
avoir un enfant *to have a child*
choisir un métier *to choose a career*
entrer à l'université *to enter the university*
être au chômage *to be unemployed*

faire un apprentissage *to do an apprenticeship*
faire une école technique *to go to a technical school*
faire son service militaire *to do one's military service*
obtenir son diplôme *to get one's diploma*
se marier *to get married*
passer son permis de conduire *to get one's driver's license*
quitter sa famille *to leave home*
réussir son bac *to pass one's baccalaureat exam*
trouver un travail *to find a job*

DEUXIEME ETAPE

Asking about future plans

Tu sais ce que tu veux faire? *Do you know what you want to do?*
Tu as des projets? *Do you have plans?*

Expressing wishes

J'aimerais bien... *I'd really like . . .*
Ce qui me plairait, c'est de... *What I would like is to . . .*
Mon rêve, c'est de... *My dream is to . . .*

Expressing indecision

Je ne sais pas trop. *I really don't know.*
Non, je me demande. *No, I wonder.*
Je n'en ai aucune idée. *I have no idea.*
J'ai du mal à me décider. *I'm having trouble deciding.*
Je ne sais plus ce que je veux. *I don't know what I want anymore.*

Giving advice

Tu n'as qu'à... *All you have to do is . . .*
Tu ferais mieux/bien de... *You would do better/well to . . .*
Il faudrait que tu... *You ought to . . .*
Il vaudrait mieux que... *It would be better if . . .*

Careers

un(e) architecte *an architect*
un(e) avocat(e) *a lawyer*
un chauffeur *a driver*
un(e) comptable *an accountant*
un(e) dentiste *a dentist*
un écrivain *a writer*
un homme/une femme d'affaires *a businessman/woman*
un(e) infirmier(-ière) *a nurse*
un ingénieur *an engineer*
un(e) instituteur(-trice) *an elementary school teacher*
un(e) journaliste *a journalist*
un(e) mécanicien(ne) *a mechanic*
un médecin *a doctor*
un(e) ouvrier(-ière) *a worker*
un(e) pharmacien(ne) *a pharmacist*

un pilote *a pilot*
un plombier *a plumber*
un(e) secrétaire *a secretary*
un(e) serveur(-euse) *a server*
un tailleur *a tailor*
un(e) technicien(ne) *a technician*

Requesting information

Pourriez-vous m'envoyer des renseignements sur... ? *Could you send me information on . . .?*
Je voudrais savoir... *I would like to know . . .*
Vous serait-il possible de... ? *Would it be possible for you to . . .?*

Writing a formal letter

Monsieur/Madame, *Sir/Madam,*
En réponse à votre lettre du... *In response to your letter of . . .*
Suite à notre conversation téléphonique,... *Following our telephone conversation, . . .*
Je vous prie d'agréer, Monsieur/Madame, l'expression de mes sentiments distingués. *Very truly yours, . . .*

♖ Game

DIS-MOI! Write 20 vocabulary words or expressions on a grid of 20 squares. Make two copies for every three students. Distribute two copies to groups of three. Have two students cut the squares apart and take ten squares each. The third student, who is the judge and timekeeper for the partners, receives a copy of all the words. Then, the partners take turns giving clues to try to get their partner to say each of the words or expressions on the squares within 20 seconds. Students may use French words or gestures to try to get the meaning across. For example, for **un plombier,** the partner might say **Il travaille dans la salle de bains. Il répare les W.C.** The squares containing the words that were not correctly guessed should be put into a pile. At the end of the game, all three students should write a sentence containing each of the words or expressions from this pile.

CHAPTER 5 ASSESSMENT

CHAPTER TEST

• *Chapter Teaching Resources, Book 2,* pp. 27–32
• *Assessment Guide,* Speaking Test, p. 30
• *Assessment Items,* Audiocassette 7B *Audio CD 5*

TEST GENERATOR, CHAPTER 5

ALTERNATIVE ASSESSMENT

Performance Assessment

You might want to use the **Jeu de rôle** (p. 133) as a cumulative performance assessment activity.

📁 Portfolio Assessment

• **Written:** Ecrivons!, *Pupil's Edition,* p. 131
Assessment Guide, p. 18
• **Oral:** Activity 27, *Pupil's Edition,* p. 126
Assessment Guide, p. 18

Chapitre 6 : Ma famille, mes copains et moi
Chapter Overview

Mise en train pp. 138-140	**Naissance d'une amitié**		**Note Culturelle**, Bargaining in North Africa, p. 140	

	FUNCTIONS	GRAMMAR	CULTURE	RE-ENTRY
Première étape pp. 141-145	• Making, accepting, and refusing suggestions, p. 141 • Making arrangements, p. 141 • Making and accepting apologies, p. 143	• Reciprocal verbs, p. 142 • The past infinitive, p. 143	Panorama Culturel, Values of francophone teenagers, p. 145	• Reflexive verbs • Accepting and refusing suggestions • Making plans • Describing and characterizing yourself and others

Remise en train pp. 146-147	**Ahlên, merhabîn**			

	FUNCTIONS	GRAMMAR	CULTURE	RE-ENTRY
Deuxième étape pp. 148-153	• Showing and responding to hospitality, p. 149 • Expressing and responding to thanks, p. 149 • Quarreling, p. 152		• **Rencontre Culturelle,** Overview of Morocco, p. 148 • **Note Culturelle,** Hospitality in Morocco, p. 150	• Family vocabulary • Expressing thanks

Lisons! pp. 154-156	**Les trois femmes du roi; Le clou de Djeha; La petite maison** **Reading Strategy:** Taking cultural context into account

Ecrivons! p. 157	**Une histoire d'attitude** **Writing Strategy:** Using graphic devices

Review pp. 158-161	• **Mise en pratique,** pp. 158-159 • **Que sais-je?** p. 160 • **Vocabulaire,** p. 161

Assessment Options	**Etape Quizzes**
	• *Chapter Teaching Resources, Book 2*
	  Première étape, Quiz 6-1, pp. 77-78
	  Deuxième étape, Quiz 6-2, pp. 79-80
	• *Assessment Items, Audiocassette 7B/Audio CD 6*
		Chapter Test
		• *Chapter Teaching Resources, Book 2,* pp. 81-86
		• *Assessment Guide, Speaking Test,* p. 30
		• *Assessment Items, Audiocassette 7B/Audio CD 6*
		
		Test Generator, Chapter 6

RESOURCES: Print	RESOURCES: Audiovisual
Practice and Activity Book, p. 61	Textbook Audiocassette 3B/Audio CD 6
Practice and Activity Book, pp. 62–65 Grammar and Vocabulary Worksheets, pp. 54–59 Chapter Teaching Resources, Book 2 • Communicative Activity 6-1, pp. 58–59 • Teaching Transparency Master 6-1, pp. 62, 64 . . . . • Additional Listening Activities 6-1, 6-2, 6-3, pp. 65–66 . . . . . • Realia 6-1, pp. 69, 71 • Situation Cards 6-1, pp. 72–73 • Student Response Forms, pp. 74–76 • Quiz 6-1, pp. 77–78.	Textbook Audiocassette 3B/Audio CD 6 Teaching Transparency 6-1 Additional Listening Activities, Audiocassette 9B/Audio CD 6 Assessment Items, Audiocassette 7B/Audio CD 6
Practice and Activity Book, p. 66	Textbook Audiocassette 3B/Audio CD 6
Practice and Activity Book, pp. 67–70 Grammar and Vocabulary Worksheets, pp. 60–62 Chapter Teaching Resources, Book 2 • Communicative Activity 6-2, pp. 60–61 • Teaching Transparency Master 6-2, pp. 63, 64 . . . . • Additional Listening Activities 6-4, 6-5, 6-6, pp. 66–67 . . . . . • Realia 6-2, pp. 70, 71 • Situation Cards 6-2, 6-3, pp. 72–73 • Student Response Forms, pp. 74–76 • Quiz 6-2, pp. 79–80. . . . . Video Guide	Textbook Audiocassette 3B/Audio CD 6 Teaching Transparency 6-2 Additional Listening Activities, Audiocassette 9B/Audio CD 6 Assessment Items, Audiocassette 7B/Audio CD 6 Video Program, Videocassette 1
Practice and Activity Book, p. 71	
Video Guide	Video Program, Videocassette 1

Alternative Assessment
- Performance Assessment
  Première étape, p. 144
  Deuxième étape, p. 153

- Portfolio Assessment
  Written: Mise en pratique, Activity 5, Pupil's Edition, p. 159
  Assessment Guide, p. 19
  Oral: Activity 35, Pupil's Edition, p. 153
  Assessment Guide, p. 19

Midterm Exam
Assessment Guide, pp. 35–42
Assessment Items,
  Audiocassette 7B
Audio CD 6

For Student Response Forms, see *Chapter Teaching Resources Book 2,* pp. 74–76.

Première étape

7 Ecoute! p. 141

1. — Ça t'intéresse d'aller à la piscine avec nous?
   — Impossible, je suis pris. J'ai un cours de piano.
2. — Dis, ça te plairait de faire du camping avec nous pendant les vacances?
   — J'aimerais bien, mais je vais chez mes grands-parents.
3. — Ça t'intéresse d'aller au cinéma ce soir?
   — Bonne idée, ce serait sympa.
4. — Tu ne voudrais pas aller te promener dans le parc cet après-midi?
   — C'est gentil, mais il faut que je rentre. Mes parents m'attendent.
5. — J'ai une idée. Ça te plairait de faire un pique-nique ce week-end?
   — J'aimerais bien, mais je n'ai pas le temps. Il faut que j'étudie mes maths.
6. — Ça vous intéresse d'aller voir Cheb Khaled en concert demain?
   — Moi, j'aimerais bien.
   — Moi aussi, ça me plairait beaucoup.

Answers to Activity 7
1. refuse 2. refuse 3. accepte 4. refuse 5. refuse 6. accepte

10 Ecoute! p. 142

MALIKA Dis, Rachida, ça t'intéresse d'aller faire du shopping dans la médina cet après-midi ?

RACHIDA Impossible, je suis prise. Je dois aller voir ma tante. Tu as des projets pour samedi?

MALIKA Non, je n'ai rien de prévu.

RACHIDA Alors, ça te plairait d'y aller samedi?

MALIKA Oui, ça me plairait bien. Comment on fait?

RACHIDA Si tu veux, on se téléphone demain.

MALIKA Oui... Ou alors, on pourrait se donner rendez-vous à la porte Boujeloud.

RACHIDA D'accord. A quelle heure est-ce qu'on se retrouve?

MALIKA On peut se retrouver après le déjeuner. Vers deux heures.

RACHIDA Ça marche.

MALIKA Alors, à samedi. Deux heures. Porte Boujeloud.

Answers to Activity 10
samedi vers deux heures; à la porte Boujeloud; du shopping

14 Ecoute! p. 143

1. — Oh, ça ne fait rien. C'était une vieille cassette. Je ne l'écoutais plus.
2. — Ne t'inquiète pas. Il n'y a pas de mal. Tu n'oublieras pas la prochaine fois, j'en suis sûr.
3. —Pardonnez-moi. Je ne savais pas qu'il fallait faire ça.
4. — Ne t'en fais pas. Il n'y a pas de mal. J'avais l'intention de la faire nettoyer de toute façon.
5. — Désolé d'avoir oublié notre rendez-vous. J'étais tellement occupé, ça m'est complètement sorti de la tête.
6. — Je m'excuse d'être en retard. C'est la dernière fois. Je te le promets.
7. — Oh, c'est pas grave! Mais n'oublie pas de me téléphoner la prochaine fois que tu rentres tard. Je m'inquiète, tu sais.
8. — Je m'en veux de ne pas lui avoir écrit. Je vais lui envoyer une lettre tout de suite.

Answers to Activity 14
1. répond à une excuse 4. répond à une excuse 7. répond à une excuse
2. répond à une excuse 5. s'excuse 8. s'excuse
3. s'excuse 6. s'excuse

Deuxième étape

25 Ecoute! p. 149

1. — Ça me fait plaisir de vous voir.
   — Moi aussi.
2. — Asseyez-vous, je vous en prie.
   — Merci bien.
3. — Qu'est-ce que je vous sers?
   — Je prendrais bien un verre de thé, s'il vous plaît.
4. — Donnez-moi votre manteau.
   — Merci. Vous êtes bien aimable.

Answers to Activity 25
1. c 2. b 3. d 4. a

29 Ecoute! p. 151

ERIC Salut, Ahmed! Ça va?

AHMED Oui, ça va bien, allez, entre! Eric, je te présente mon père.

M. HABEK Bonjour, Eric.

ERIC Bonjour, monsieur.

AHMED Et ma mère.

MME HABEK Bonjour.

ERIC Bonjour, madame. Je suis content de faire votre connaissance.

MME HABEK Donnez-moi votre veste.

ERIC Merci.

MME HABEK Asseyez-vous, mettez-vous à l'aise.

ERIC Merci, c'est gentil.

AHMED   Eric, viens. Je te présente mon arrière-grand-père. Grand-Papa, c'est Eric.

GRAND-PAPA   Bonjour.

ERIC   Bonjour, monsieur.

AHMED   Allons dans la cuisine. Je vais te présenter ma sœur. C'est l'aînée. Elle s'est mariée l'année dernière. Tu vas rencontrer son mari plus tard.

ERIC   Dis, ton arrière-grand-père, il va bien?

AHMED   Oui. Mais tu sais, il est souvent triste depuis que sa femme est morte. Voilà ma sœur Soumia.

SOUMIA   Bonjour, Eric.

ERIC   Bonjour.

SOUMIA   Qu'est-ce que je peux t'offrir?

ERIC   Je voudrais bien du thé, s'il te plaît.

SOUMIA   Bien sûr.

AHMED   Allal, mon cousin, va arriver dans une minute.

ERIC   Il est jeune?

AHMED   Pas tellement. Il a trente-cinq ans.

ERIC   Il est marié?

AHMED   Non, il est encore célibataire.

M. HABEK   Salut, Allal. Voilà le copain d'Ahmed, Eric. Eric, c'est mon neveu, Allal.

ERIC   Bonjour.

ALLAL   Bonjour.

AHMED   Ah, voilà mon petit frère, Aziz. C'est le benjamin. Viens ici, Aziz. Je te présente Eric.

Answer to Activity 29

a

32 Ecoute! p. 152

1. — Pleurnicheuse!
   — Mais tu n'as pas le droit d'entrer dans ma chambre!
   — Tant pis pour toi!
   — Je vais le dire à Maman!
   — Rapporteuse!

2. — Tu pourrais baisser la musique? C'est tellement fort. J'essaie de faire mes devoirs, tu sais.
   — Tu es casse-pieds!
   — Si tu ne baisses pas, je vais te prendre ton CD.
   — Oh, tu me fais peur.
   — Et voilà.
   — Arrête! Ça suffit! Je baisse. D'accord?

3. — Et voilà, encore une fois j'ai gagné.
   — Tricheur!
   — Mauvaise joueuse! C'est pas de ma faute si tu es nulle.
   — Oh, ça va, hein?
   — Mais c'est toi qui as commencé.
   — Mais t'as triché.
   — Arrête! Y en a marre!

4. — Eh! Arrête de faire ce bruit! Tu le fais exprès?
   — Euh, non.
   — Ben, tu m'énerves, à la fin.
   — Bon, désolé. J'arrête.
   — Eh, tu peux arrêter d'agiter le pied comme ça?
   — Oh, fiche-moi la paix!

5. — Bas les pattes! C'est mon bureau!
   — Mais je cherchais juste un stylo.
   — Va trouver ton stylo ailleurs. T'as pas le droit de fouiller dans mes affaires.
   — Tu me prends la tête! Tu as peur que je lise ton journal? Tiens, justement! Voyons...
   — Eh! Donne-moi ça! Mêle-toi de tes oignons!

Answers to Activity 32

1. Moktar   2. Moktar   3. Amina   4. Amina   5. Moktar

*M*ise en pratique

1 p. 158

MARTIN   Alors, qu'est-ce qu'il y a à voir à Marrakech?

ALI   Oh, il y a plein de choses à voir et à faire. Il y a des musées, des palais, des souks. Et aussi les gens. Il faut rencontrer des Marocains, si tu veux connaître le Maroc.

MARTIN   Et la place Jemaa-el-Fna? On m'a dit que c'est intéressant. Qu'est-ce que tu en penses?

ALI   Oh, c'est dingue! Il y a des conteurs, des musiciens, des vendeurs d'eau...

MARTIN   Il y a des charmeurs de serpents?

ALI   Bien sûr. Ça t'intéresse d'en voir?

MARTIN   Oui.

ALI   Alors, on peut y aller demain matin, si tu veux.

MARTIN   D'accord. A quelle heure est-ce qu'on se donne rendez-vous?

ALI   Vers huit heures, ça va?

MARTIN   Oui. Et où est-ce qu'on se retrouve?

ALI   Place de Bâb Fteuh.

MARTIN   D'accord.

ALI   Tu ne voudrais pas déjeuner chez moi après ça?

MARTIN   Si, ce serait sympa.

ALI   Bon. Après, je t'emmène à la maison pour rencontrer ma famille. Comme ça, tu pourras goûter des plats marocains.

MARTIN   Oh, ce serait chouette!

ALI   Dis donc, ça te plairait de voir le palais de la Bahia?

MARTIN   J'aimerais bien, mais je n'aurai pas le temps. J'ai rendez-vous avec mes parents.

ALI   Bon. D'accord.

Answers to Mise en pratique Activity 1

1. b, d, e   2. b, e   3. vers huit heures   4. c

Une publicité pour le Maroc
(Group Project)

ASSIGNMENT

Students will create and perform a television commercial for the **Office de tourisme du Maroc** to encourage visitors to come to Morocco.

MATERIALS

✂ **Students may need**
- Posterboard
- Construction paper
- Markers
- Scissors
- Glue
- Camcorder
- Videocassette

SUGGESTED SEQUENCE

1. Have students suggest elements of a successful commercial. You might find travel videos from various states or countries (from Morocco, if possible) at the local library and have students analyze them and tell why they are effective.

2. Have groups choose their approach and decide what they will feature in their ad. They should refer to the **Mise en train** on pages 138–139, the **Remise en train** on pages 146–147, and the **Rencontre Culturelle** on page 148 for information on Moroccan culture. If possible, have students visit a travel agency and collect brochures about Morocco.

3. Students should write a script for their commercial. They should suggest at least three interesting things to do and see in Morocco.

4. After the script is written, each group member should proofread it to check for variety of vocabulary and accuracy of language.

5. Have students write the final script and make copies for each member of the group. They should then plan the staging of the commercial, incorporating props or posters made on construction paper. Have them rehearse their commercial in front of another group, who serves as a practice audience.

6. Students perform their commercials for the class. You might videotape their commercials and use them to introduce this chapter next year.

GRADING THE PROJECT

Each group member should receive a collective grade based on completion of the requirements, language use, and creativity and overall presentation. Each group member also receives an individual grade for pronunciation and effort and participation.

Suggested Point Distribution (total = 100 points)

Completion of requirements . . . . 20 points

Language use . . . . 20 points

Creativity/presentation . . . . 20 points

Pronunciation . . . . 20 points

Effort/participation . . . . 20 points

Games

C'EST QUI, ALORS?

In this game, students will practice family vocabulary.

Procedure Write French words for family members on cards and place them face-down on a table at the front of the room. Divide the class into two or more teams. The first player from the first team comes forward and takes a card from the top of the pile. The player then defines the word written on the card by describing how that family member and another member are related. For example, if the card reads **le grand-père**, the player might say **C'est le père de ma mère.** The player's team has ten seconds to try to guess the word on the card. **(C'est le grand-père!)** If the player's team fails to guess the word, the next team has one chance to guess. Whether or not the guess is correct, the turn then passes to the next team. Teams earn one point for each word that they guess correctly. The team with the most points wins.

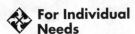

For Individual Needs

Challenge On each card, write an additional word that the players *cannot* use in their definition. On the card that reads **le grand-père**, for example, you might write **à ne pas utiliser : le père.** The player might then define the word by saying **C'est le mari de la mère de ma mère.**

LE FOOTBALL AMERICAIN

In this game, students will practice the functions and vocabulary presented in the chapter.

Procedure To prepare for the game, make one set of cards with the functions written on them (*making suggestions, accepting suggestions,* and so on). Make another set of thirteen cards: eight with *rush,* three with *pass,* one with *interception,* and one with *penalty* written on them. Draw a football field on the board. Write an "X" on one twenty-yard line and an "O" on the other twenty-yard line to represent the teams. Divide the class into two teams. To play the game, a player from the first team draws a card from the pile and follows the appropriate instruction:

- *Pass:* The teacher draws a function card, and the player uses an appropriate word or expression that serves that function in a logical sentence. If the player responds correctly, he or she rolls a die, multiplies that number by ten, and moves his or her team the corresponding number of yards on the field.

- *Rush:* Instructions are the same as those for pass, but the number on the die is doubled.

- *Penalty:* The teacher draws a function card and has a player from the opposing team use a related word or expression in a logical sentence. If the player responds correctly, he or she rolls the die and moves the first team back and his or her team forward the corresponding number of yards.

- *Interception:* The teacher draws a function card and has a player from the opposing team use an appropriate word or expression in a logical sentence. If the player answers correctly, his or her team may take the next turn.

Teams should alternate turns. Teams receive six points for crossing the goal line. When a team crosses the goal line, they may take another turn to try for an extra point. The team with the most points at the end of play wins.

Teacher Note

To review for the Midterm Exam, you might also use functions from preceding chapters to review previously-learned expressions.

*U*sing the Chapter Opener

 Video Program

Videocassette 1

Before you begin this chapter, you might want to preview the *Video Program* and consult the *Video Guide*. Suggestions for integrating the video into each chapter and activity masters for video selections can be found in the *Video Guide*.

Motivating Activity

Ask students if they ever quarrel with their siblings, other family members, or friends. What are the disagreements usually about? How do they solve them? Do they usually apologize? How? You might also have students list any pet peeves they have.

Photo Flash!

① This photo shows two sisters having a minor quarrel. Have students look at the photo and try to guess what the relationship between the two girls is (sisters, friends). Ask students if they recognize a word in **énerves** that would give them a clue to the meaning of the expression. (*nerve*, used in the expression *You're getting on my nerves!*) Then, have them suggest additional French captions for this photo. **(Ma sœur est pénible.)**

CHAPITRE

6
Ma famille, mes copains et moi

① Tu m'énerves, à la fin !

136   *cent trente-six*

Teaching Suggestion

Have students think of a quarrel they recently had with a friend, sibling, or other family member. Have students explain that person's point of view and give reasons for his or her behavior. (she was tired; my music was playing too loud; he tripped over my shoes in the doorway; they worry about me when I come home late)

Culture Note

The Moroccan concept of family extends beyond the nuclear family. In a traditional Moroccan household, the parents, all unmarried children, and any married sons and their families live together under the same roof. When daughters marry, they leave home to live with their husband's family.

P our la plupart d'entre nous, il est important d'avoir de bons rapports avec sa famille et ses amis. Est-ce qu'il t'arrive de te disputer avec tes parents, tes frères et sœurs ou tes copains, et de vouloir te réconcilier ou t'excuser? Chaque culture a sa manière de le faire. Allons au Maroc et observons quelques exemples de savoir-vivre marocain.

In this chapter you will learn

- to make, accept, and refuse suggestions; to make arrangements; to make and accept apologies
- to show and respond to hospitality; to express and respond to thanks; to quarrel

And you will

- listen to teenagers arranging to meet each other
- read about brother/sister relationships in francophone countries
- write about your best friend
- find out about Moroccan hospitality

③ L'hospitalité chez les Marocains

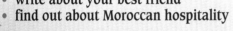

② On se donne rendez-vous à quelle heure?

cent trente-sept 137

Focusing on Outcomes

Have students recall French expressions they've learned that serve these functions. (*Making suggestions:* **Si on allait... ? Ça te dit d'aller... ?** *Accepting and refusing suggestions:* **D'accord. Ça ne me dit rien.** *Making apologies:* **C'est de ma faute. Excuse-moi.** *Accepting apologies:* **Ça ne fait rien. Il n'y a pas de mal.** *Showing hospitality:* **Tu n'as pas soif/faim? Fais comme chez toi.** *Responding to hospitality:* **Merci.**) Have students relate the photos to the outcomes. NOTE: You may want to use the video to support the objectives. The self-check activities in **Que sais-je?** on page 160 help students assess their achievement of the objectives.

Photo Flash!

② The teenager in this photo is arranging to meet a friend. Ask students to give additional reasons for calling their friends (just to talk, to ask for help with a personal problem, to discuss homework).

③ The man in this photo is preparing to serve mint tea (**thé à la menthe**), the national drink of Morocco. Students will learn more about this beverage on pages 138–139 of the **Mise en train**.

Teaching Suggestion

Write the following expressions on butcher paper and have students try to guess which outcome they fulfill. **Ça te plairait d'aller au souk?** *(making suggestions);* **Tu es bête comme tes pieds!** *(quarreling);* **Donnez-moi votre manteau.** *(showing hospitality);* **A quelle heure est-ce qu'on se donne rendez-vous?** *(making arrangements);* **Je vous remercie.** *(expressing thanks);* **Pardonne-moi d'avoir manqué notre rendez-vous.** *(making apologies).*

Language Note

Have students guess what the expression **savoir-vivre** in the introduction means *(good manners)*. They might also be familiar with the expression **savoir-faire** *(know-how)*.

Culture Note

② The scarf that the girl in this photo is wearing is typical of Islamic cultures, in which women usually keep their heads covered in public.

Art Link

Point out the design on the wall in Photo 3. Since the Koran (**le Coran**) forbids the representation of all animals and people, abstract floral and geometric patterns are common motifs in the decorative arts in Islamic countries. These motifs, known as **arabesques,** are often used as decorative architectural features, repeated over and over to produce a sense of stability and symmetry. See also the photo at the top of page 147.

Summary

Naissance d'une amitié takes place in Fez, where the Simenots are on vacation. Since Raphaël doesn't want to shop in the market, he agrees to meet his parents later. While strolling about, he meets a young Moroccan rug vendor named Moktar, who befriends him and offers him the traditional Moroccan mint tea, served scalding hot. Moktar suggests several sites to see in Fez, and they arrange to meet to go to a concert of Moroccan music. The scene ends with Moktar teaching Raphaël how to say *goodbye* in Arabic.

Motivating Activity

Have students describe their impressions of Morocco, based on the photos. Ask them what they think there is to see and do there. Ask them what they would want to know about Morocco before visiting there.

Presentation

On a transparency, write brief summaries of the scenes in random order. To summarize the first scene, you might write **Raphaël et ses parents se séparent.** Then, play the recording. Pause after each scene and have students choose the appropriate summary. As a challenge, you might play the recording first and then have students suggest a brief summary.

Teaching Suggestion

Find a map of Fez in a travel guide or encyclopedia. Distribute copies and have students locate the places mentioned in the **Mise en train** on their maps. Have them locate one or two other attractions and find out about them.

Mise en train

Naissance d'une amitié

La famille Simenot est en vacances à Fès. Ils commencent leur visite par une promenade dans la médina, le vieux quartier du centre-ville.

❶ M. SIMENOT Qu'est-ce que vous voulez voir?

MME SIMENOT Moi, j'aimerais bien voir les magasins de poteries et de tapis.

M. SIMENOT Bonne idée.

RAPHAEL Moi, je préférerais me promener. Ça vous embête si on se sépare?

MME SIMENOT Pas du tout. Mais comment on fait pour se retrouver?

M. SIMENOT On peut se donner rendez-vous devant la Porte Boujeloud.

RAPHAEL D'accord. A quatre heures, ça va?

M. SIMENOT Bon, ça va.

❷ MOKTAR Bonjour. Tu es français?

RAPHAEL Oui.

MOKTAR Je m'appelle Moktar. Et toi?

RAPHAEL Raphaël.

MOKTAR Tu as vu mes beaux tapis? Ils sont pas chers.

RAPHAEL Je te remercie, mais je n'ai pas d'argent. Je viens juste ici pour visiter.

MOKTAR Tu es en vacances?

RAPHAEL Oui.

MOKTAR Ça te dit de prendre un thé?

RAPHAEL Je te remercie, mais...

MOKTAR Tu sais, au Maroc, il ne faut jamais refuser un thé.

RAPHAEL Alors, j'accepte.

❸ MOKTAR Tiens.

RAPHAEL Merci... Aïe! C'est brûlant!

MOKTAR Excuse-moi, j'aurais dû te prévenir. C'est comme ça qu'on boit le thé au Maroc. Très chaud.

RAPHAEL C'est délicieux. Qu'est-ce que tu mets dedans?

MOKTAR De la menthe.

RAPHAEL Tu travailles ici?

MOKTAR Oui, je tiens la boutique quand mes parents sont absents. Ils sont allés acheter des tapis dans le sud.

138 *cent trente-huit*　　　　CHAPITRE 6　Ma famille, mes copains et moi

RESOURCES FOR MISE EN TRAIN

Textbook Audiocassette 3A/Audio CD 6
Practice and Activity Book, p. 61

Teacher Note

You might write to the Moroccan tourist board (**ONMT**) at the following address for maps and additional information: 20 E. 46th St., New York, NY, 10017.

Culture Note

The **Porte Boujeloud,** known as the **Bab Boujeloud** in Arabic, is the brightly-colored polychrome western gate of the district of **Fès El Bali** *(Old Fez).* This older district of the city is an intricate web of intersecting small lanes and alleys. **Fès El Djedid** *(New Fez)* dates from the thirteenth century and consists of royal palaces and gardens.

RAPHAEL	Tu ne vas plus au lycée?
MOKTAR	Non, j'ai arrêté à seize ans. J'ai l'intention de continuer l'affaire de mes parents... Alors, comment tu trouves le Maroc?
RAPHAEL	Tu sais, nous sommes arrivés hier seulement. Mais pour l'instant, je trouve les gens très accueillants.
MOKTAR	Vous allez rester à Fès?
RAPHAEL	Quelques jours seulement. Après, on compte aller à Marrakech.
MOKTAR	C'est chouette, Marrakech. C'est un peu bruyant, mais c'est très animé. Tu aimeras beaucoup.
RAPHAEL	Qu'est-ce qu'il y a à voir à Fès?
MOKTAR	Oh, des tas de choses. C'est d'une richesse! Vous devriez aller voir le Dar el Makhzen. C'est un immense palais où le roi réside quand il vient à Fès. Les portes sont magnifiques.
RAPHAEL	Ah oui?
MOKTAR	Oui. Et surtout, je vous conseille d'aller vous promener sur la place du Vieux Méchouar. C'est très sympa. Il y a des danseurs, des conteurs, des musiciens...

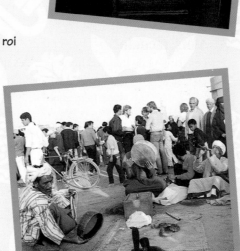

4
RAPHAEL	Je ne sais pas si on aura le temps.
MOKTAR	Encore du thé?
RAPHAEL	Volontiers... Dis-moi, quelle heure il est?
MOKTAR	Quatre heures.
RAPHAEL	Oh là là! Excuse-moi, j'ai rendez-vous avec mes parents. Je suis déjà en retard...

5
MOKTAR	Qu'est-ce que tu fais demain? Tu as des projets?
RAPHAEL	Non, je suis libre. Je n'ai rien de prévu.
MOKTAR	Si tu veux, on peut se revoir.
RAPHAEL	Je veux bien.
MOKTAR	Ça t'intéresse d'aller écouter de la musique marocaine?
RAPHAEL	Oui, ça me plairait bien.
MOKTAR	Si ça te dit, on peut aller à un concert demain soir.
RAPHAEL	Moi, j'aimerais bien. Mais il faut que je demande la permission à mes parents. Comment on fait?

MOKTAR	On peut se téléphoner. Vous êtes à l'hôtel?
RAPHAEL	Oui, on est à l'hôtel Moussafir.
MOKTAR	Bon. Je te téléphone demain matin. Et si tes parents sont d'accord, on peut se retrouver à l'hôtel en fin d'après-midi.
RAPHAEL	Génial. Allez, il faut que j'y aille. Comment on dit «au revoir» en arabe?
MOKTAR	Bes-slama.
RAPHAEL	Bes-slama.

MISE EN TRAIN

cent trente-neuf **139**

Culture Notes

• In Morocco, music and dance are linked to tradition. Music, tied to the oral storytelling tradition, is often a spontaneous account of everyday events. **Ahuash** or **Ahidu** is a musical tradition in which the events of everyday life are recounted to the rhythm of wooden flutes and tambourines. The music, like the arabesque motifs in the visual arts, is often repetitive.

• Arabic is the official language of Morocco, although French is widely spoken. Students might want to learn a few Arabic phrases and use them in the chapter activities: **Salam Walaykoom** (sah LAM wuh LAY kum—*hello*); **Minfadlik** (min FAHD lik—*Please*); **Shokran** (SHOK run—*Thank you*).

For Individual Needs

Challenge After asking students the questions in Activity 1 on page 140, ask about some of the details of the story. (**Pourquoi est-ce que Moktar travaille au magasin? Qu'est-ce qu'il vend? Quelles suggestions est-ce qu'il fait? Comment dit-on «au revoir» en arabe?**)

Teaching Suggestion

Have each student choose a line from the **Mise en train**. (**Encore du thé?**) Give students a few seconds to practice saying their line. Help them with pronunciation. Then, quote from the **Mise en train**. The first student to identify the speaker of your quotation stands up and calls on another student to say his or her line. Continue until all students have spoken.

Culture Note

It is not unusual for Moroccan teenagers to discontinue their schooling in order to work for their parents. Children between the ages of seven and thirteen are required to attend school. At thirteen, they might choose to learn their parents' business.

Photo Flash!

• The photo at the top of this page shows the **Dar el Makhzen**, the vast royal palace that occupies most of **Fès El Djedid**. It is surrounded by extensive gardens and pavilions. Although it is officially a royal residence, the king is rarely seen here.

• Public squares such as the one shown in the second photo are a common sight in large Moroccan cities. In the daytime, they are popular public gathering places, where water sellers and other vendors market their wares, and various performers entertain.

⬧ **For Individual Needs**

2 Tactile Learners Have students copy each of these sentences onto a separate slip of paper, and then arrange them in order on their desks.

2 Challenge Once students have arranged the sentences in the correct order, have them rewrite the sentences as a brief narrative, adding connecting words and, if they desire, personal commentaries on the events.

Additional Practice

3 Have students imagine they are Raphaël's parents and write down one or two additional questions they might ask him. Then, have them ask their questions of a partner, who responds as Raphaël.

Thinking Critically

4 Comparing and Contrasting After students have done the activity, have them do it again, this time imagining that the clues refer to the United States rather than Morocco. For example, in response to the second clue, they would list a typical American drink, perhaps iced tea or cola. Then, have partners compare the Moroccan list to the American one.

Synthesizing–Note Culturelle Ask students to name other places or situations in which bargaining is expected (car dealerships, flea markets, garage sales, real estate purchases).

Language Note

Médina refers to the original Arab part of a Moroccan city. The **kasbah,** or *fortress-palace,* is usually located in this area.

---

1 Tu as compris?

1. What is the Simenot family doing in Fès? vacationing
2. Why does Raphaël leave his parents? to go for a walk
3. Where does he meet Moktar? Why does Moktar speak to him?
4. What plans do they make? 3. carpet store; He hopes to sell a carpet.
   4. to go listen to Moroccan music the next evening.

2 Mets en ordre

Mets ces phrases en ordre d'après **Naissance d'une amitié.** 5, 2, 1, 4, 6, 3

1. Moktar propose un thé à Raphaël.
2. Moktar adresse la parole à Raphaël.
3. Moktar apprend à Raphaël un mot en arabe.
4. Moktar dit à Raphaël ce qu'il devrait voir à Fès.
5. Raphaël et ses parents se donnent rendez-vous.
6. Moktar propose un autre verre de thé à Raphaël.

3 Alors, raconte!

Les parents de Raphaël lui posent des questions sur Moktar. Complète leur conversation.

MME SIMENOT *Qu'est-ce qu'il fait dans la médina?*
RAPHAEL Il... travaille dans la boutique de tapis de ses parents.
M. SIMENOT *Il ne va pas au lycée?*
RAPHAEL Non, il... a arrêté à seize ans.

MME SIMENOT *Qu'est-ce qu'il veut faire plus tard?*
RAPHAEL Il... veut continuer l'affaire de ses parents.
M. SIMENOT *Qu'est-ce qu'il t'a conseillé de voir à Fès?*
RAPHAEL Il... m'a conseillé de voir le Dar el Makhzen et la place du Vieux Méchouar.

4 Ça, c'est le Maroc!

Trouve les choses suivantes dans **Naissance d'une amitié.** See answers below.

1. quelque chose à voir à Fès
2. une boisson typiquement marocaine
3. un objet artisanal marocain typique
4. un endroit où on trouve des danseurs
5. une expression en arabe

NOTE CULTURELLE

Bargaining is an accepted part of doing business in Morocco and other North African countries. While the idea of haggling may embarrass Westerners who are accustomed to paying a set price, merchants in these countries fix their prices knowing that the customer will negotiate. They usually expect a customer to offer half, or even less, of the marked price!

5 Cherche les expressions

What does Moktar or Raphaël say to . . . See answers below.

1. offer tea?
2. accept an offer?
3. apologize?
4. give advice?

5. ask about someone's plans?
6. make a suggestion?
7. accept a suggestion?
8. arrange to meet someone?

6 Et maintenant, à toi

Raconte comment tu as rencontré un(e) de tes ami(e)s. Tu étais où? Dans quelle situation?

140 *cent quarante*   CHAPITRE 6   Ma famille, mes copains et moi

---

Answers

4 1. le Dar el Makhzen
2. le thé à la menthe
3. un tapis
4. la place du Vieux Méchouar à Fès
5. **Bes-slama** (au revoir)

5 1. Ça te dit de prendre un thé? Encore du thé?
2. ... j'accepte. Volontiers...
3. Excuse-moi...
4. Vous devriez... ; Je vous conseille de...
5. Qu'est-ce que tu fais demain? Tu as des projets?
6. Si tu veux, on peut... ; Si ça te dit, on peut... ; Ça t'intéresse de...?
7. Je veux bien. Oui, ça me plairait bien. Moi, j'aimerais bien.
8. On peut se donner rendez-vous... On peut se téléphoner. ... on peut se retrouver à...

Making, accepting, and refusing suggestions; making arrangements; making and accepting apologies

COMMENT DIT-ON... ?

Making, accepting, and refusing suggestions

To make a suggestion:

Ça t'intéresse d'aller écouter de la musique?

Ça te plairait de visiter le musée?

Tu ne voudrais pas aller te promener dans la médina?

To accept a suggestion:

Ce serait sympa.

Oui, ça me plairait beaucoup.

Si, j'aimerais bien.

To refuse a suggestion:

Impossible, je suis pris(e).

J'aimerais bien mais je n'ai pas le temps.

C'est gentil, mais j'ai un rendez-vous.
That's nice of you, but I've got an appointment.

7 Ecoute!

Ecoute ces conversations. Est-ce que ces personnes refusent ou acceptent les suggestions qu'on leur fait? Answers on p. 135C.

8 Qu'est-ce qu'il propose?

Possible answers: Ça te plairait de (d')... **a.** aller à la piscine; **b.** aller au café; **c.** aller au musée; **d.** faire de l'équitation; **e.** jouer au football; **f.** aller au cinéma

Fahmi voudrait sortir ce week-end. Qu'est-ce qu'il propose à son ami Youssef?

a.   b.   c.   d.   e.   f.

9 Tu es libre ce week-end?

Tu es en classe. Tu veux proposer à ton/ta camarade de faire quelque chose ce week-end. Ecris-lui un petit mot et passe-lui le bout de papier. Il/Elle te répond sur la même feuille.

COMMENT DIT-ON... ?

Making arrangements

To make arrangements:

Comment est-ce qu'on fait?
How should we work this out?

Quand est-ce qu'on se revoit?
When are we getting together?

Où est-ce qu'on se retrouve?
Where are we meeting?

A quelle heure est-ce qu'on se donne rendez-vous?
What time are we meeting?

PREMIERE ETAPE

cent quarante et un **141**

Jump Start!

Have students write a note to a friend to suggest two of these activities: **aller au marché, voir un film, se baigner, faire une promenade dans la médina.** Then, have them exchange papers and write a response, accepting or rejecting each suggestion.

MOTIVATE

Have students imagine that they have a friend who is going to visit Morocco. Ask them what they would suggest that their friend see and do in Fez. Write their suggestions on a transparency.

TEACH

Presentation

Comment dit-on... ?
Suggest activities to students, having them respond with expressions they already know. Then, show the transparency from the activity under Motivate and have students suggest the activities to you. Accept or reject their suggestions, using the new expressions. Next, write the responses on separate cards and distribute them to students. Give partners twenty or thirty seconds to suggest and respond to the first activity on the transparency. Students then pass their cards to the next pair and repeat the process, using the second activity.

Comment dit-on... ? Write the new expressions and **Je ne sais pas, lundi après-midi, devant le cinéma,** and **à cinq heures** on transparency strips. Call on individuals to match each question with an answer until all are matched. Then, have students repeat the expressions after you.

Reteaching

Reflexive verbs Have students recall activities they do in the morning. Write their suggestions on a transparency, underlining the reflexive verbs. Then, ask students **Tu t'es levé(e) à quelle heure? Tu t'es brossé les dents à quelle heure?** Have a student explain how to conjugate reflexive verbs in the present and the **passé composé.**

Presentation

Grammaire Show pictures of Romeo and Juliet. Ask **Roméo aime Juliette?** and **Juliette aime Roméo?** Then, say **Ils s'aiment** and write it on the board. Have students try to guess what it means. Then, engage a student in a brief English conversation and say **Nous nous parlons.** Have partners act out other actions, such as **téléphoner** and **écrire,** as you ask the class what they're doing. **(Qu'est-ce qu'ils font? Ils se téléphonent.)** Then, have students write a sentence with a reciprocal verb in the past tense on a slip of paper, cut the words apart, and have a partner reassemble it.

For Individual Needs

11 Challenge Before students open their books, write the verbs from this activity on a transparency and have students tell you in what order they think the actions occurred. Number the verbs according to their directions. Then, have partners create their own version of Laure and Vincent's romance, using connecting words and adding places, times, and even additional characters and events.

---

10 Ecoute!

Malika et Rachida se donnent rendez-vous. Quand est-ce qu'elles vont se retrouver? Où? Qu'est-ce qu'elles vont faire? Answers on p. 135C.

---

*G*rammaire   Reciprocal verbs

Si tu as oublié reflexive verbs *va à la page 348.*

In addition to their reflexive meaning *(himself/herself, ourselves . . .),* the pronouns **se, nous,** and **vous** also have a reciprocal meaning. That is, they mean *(to/for/at) each other* when you add them to any verb. Look at these examples:

On **se** revoit l'année prochaine?
Will we see each other next year?
Ils **s'**aiment.
They love each other.

Nous **nous** sommes parlé hier.
We spoke to each other yesterday.
Vous **vous** êtes rencontrés sur la place?
Did you meet each other on the square?

- You've learned to make past participles agree with a reflexive pronoun when it is a direct object of the verb. The same rule applies to the reciprocal pronouns.

  Nous **nous** sommes rencontrés hier. *(each other)*

- Be careful, though, because you don't change the past participle if the reciprocal pronoun is the indirect object of the verb.

  Ils **se** sont parlé. *(to each other)*

---

11 On s'aime

Raconte l'histoire d'amour de Laure et Vincent d'après les images suivantes.

1. **se voir**
Laure et Vincent se sont vus.

2. **se téléphoner**
Ils se sont téléphoné.

3. **se donner rendez-vous**
Ils se sont donné rendez-vous.

4. **se disputer**
Ils se sont disputés.

5. **se quitter**
Ils se sont quittés.

6. **se réconcilier**
Ils se sont réconciliés.

142 *cent quarante-deux* CHAPITRE 6   Ma famille, mes copains et moi

---

Language Note

Point out that **parler, donner, écrire,** and **téléphoner** take indirect objects and therefore their past participles do <u>not</u> agree with the reciprocal pronouns in the **passé composé. (Ils se sont téléphoné.)** Chercher and **regarder,** however, take direct objects, so their past participles may show agreement. **(Ils se sont regardés.)** You might have students list in two columns the verbs that take a direct object and those that take an indirect object. You might refer them to the appropriate section of the Grammar Summary at the back of the book.

Additional Practice

11 Have students retell the story as if they were Laure or Vincent, using **on.**

12 C'est comme ça

Ecris quelques phrases pour décrire tes rapports avec trois ou quatre des personnes suivantes.

1. ton/ta meilleur(e) ami(e)
2. tes parents
3. ton/ta petit(e) ami(e)
4. tes grands-parents
5. tes profs

se dire tout · se voir souvent · s'entendre bien · se comprendre · s'aimer · se disputer · se téléphoner tous les jours

A la française

French speakers use the subject pronoun **on** more often than **nous**, especially in informal speech. Try using **on** when you mean to say *we*: **On s'aime** (*We love each other*). If you need to emphasize *we*, you can say **Nous, on…**

13 On se téléphone?

Tu as rencontré un garçon/une fille intéressant(e) et tu voudrais le/la revoir. Pose-lui des questions pour fixer un rendez-vous. Joue cette scène avec un(e) camarade.

COMMENT DIT-ON… ?
Making and accepting apologies

To make an apology:

Je m'excuse d'être en retard.
Je suis vraiment désolé(e) d'avoir oublié de te téléphoner.
Pardonne-moi de ne pas avoir répondu.
Je m'en veux d'avoir dit ça.
I feel bad that . . .

To accept an apology:

Ce n'est pas grave.
Ça ne fait rien.
Il n'y a pas de mal.
Ne t'inquiète pas.
Ça arrive à tout le monde.
It happens to everybody.

14 Ecoute!

Ecoute ces dialogues. Est-ce qu'on s'excuse ou est-ce qu'on répond à une excuse?
Answers on p. 135C.

*G*rammaire   The past infinitive

You've already learned that a verb following a conjugated verb must be an infinitive: Je m'excuse d'**être** en retard. The infinitives you've used so far are present infinitives. Infinitives may also express past time: Je suis désolé **d'avoir oublié** *(to have forgotten)*.

- To make the past infinitive, use **avoir** or **être** and the past participle of the verb. Use **être** with the verbs that use **être** in the **passé composé**. Look at these past infinitives:

  Je suis désolé d'**avoir dit** ça. *I'm sorry I said that.*
  Je m'excuse d'**être arrivée** trop tard. *I'm sorry I arrived too late.*
  Pardonne-moi d'**avoir téléphoné** si tard.

♜ Game

DÉSOLÉ(E)! Form two teams. Within each team, have students find a partner, choose an activity for which they might apologize, and create a short skit in which one student apologizes and the other accepts the apology. In their skits, students should not specifically state what they are apologizing for, but give clues about it. For example, if students were acting out an apology for being late, they might say **Je m'excuse. Je n'ai pas entendu mon réveil, et j'ai raté le bus pour aller à l'école.** The other team then must identify the situation (**Tu t'excuses d'être arrivé(e) en retard**) in order to win a point. Have teams take turns performing their skits.

Building on Previous Skills

12 Have students compare their relationships with these people in the past with their relationships now. (**Avant, mes parents et moi, on se disputait souvent, mais maintenant, on s'entend bien.**)

📁 Portfolio

13 **Oral** This activity is appropriate for students' oral portfolios. For portfolio information, see *Assessment Guide*, pages 2–13.

Motivating Activity

Ask students to describe situations in which they might have to apologize. To whom might they apologize? (teacher, parent, sibling, friend, boy/girlfriend) What might they say?

Presentation

Comment dit-on… ? Rush into the classroom and make apologies to several students for being late, using the new expressions. As you apologize to a student, give him or her a card with one of the expressions for accepting an apology written on it. Each student responds, using the expression on the card to accept your apology. Have the class repeat the expressions.

Grammaire Have students suggest in French actions they might apologize for (**arriver en retard**). As they suggest each activity, write the past infinitive form on the board (**être arrivé(e) en retard**). Next, name one of the activities and shake your finger at a student, who apologizes for it. (**Je suis désolé(e) d'être arrivé(e) en retard.**) Then, have students play the game **Désolé(e)!**, described on this page.

Building on Previous Skills

15 Have students write the story of their day as if they were Aïcha, using the given verbs in the **passé composé** and adding background details using the **imparfait**. (**Je jouais au tennis quand j'ai abîmé le jean de ma sœur.**)

Portfolio

18 Written/Oral Part **a** is appropriate for students' written portfolios and Parts **b** and **c** are appropriate for students' oral portfolios. For portfolio information, see *Assessment Guide,* pages 2–13.

Additional Practice

Vocabulaire à la carte

Have students create celebrity personality awards for a magazine. Each student creates a list of celebrities or cartoon characters, identifying **le/la plus ouvert(e), le/la plus bavard(e), le/la plus snob,** and so on. Have a volunteer who is good in math tally the results. You might also have small groups design and draw the layout for the magazine feature.

CLOSE

To close this **étape,** write actions for which one might apologize (**ne pas finir ses devoirs, oublier de téléphoner à sa mère**) on slips of paper and put them in a bag (**le sac des chagrins**). Call on a student to draw a paper from the bag. He or she then turns to a neighbor and apologizes for the action on the paper. The neighbor accepts the apology and names another student in the class, who should then select a paper from the bag and apologize to his or her neighbor.

15 Je m'excuse

Aïcha ne s'est pas très bien comportée *(didn't behave well)* la semaine dernière. Comment est-ce qu'elle s'excusera auprès de tout le monde? See answers below.

Elle...

- a perdu le livre de français de son amie.
- a oublié son rendez-vous avec Jean-Marc.
- s'est disputée avec sa mère.
- n'a pas rendu son CD à sa copine.
- a répété le secret de sa meilleure amie.
- a abîmé *(ruined)* le jean de sa sœur.
- n'a pas téléphoné à son amie.
- est sortie avec le petit ami de son amie.
- est arrivée en classe en retard.
- n'a pas fini ses devoirs.

«Je suis désolée de(d')...»
«Je m'en veux de(d')...»

«Je m'excuse de(d')...»
«Pardonne-moi de(d')...»

16 Un feuilleton

Imagine que tes amis et toi, vous vous trouvez dans les mêmes situations qu'Aïcha. Ecris des dialogues pour raconter ce qui se passe entre vous. N'oublie pas de donner des excuses. Joue ces scènes avec tes camarades.

17 Mon journal

Décris tes rapports avec ton/ta meilleur(e) ami(e). Comment est-il/-elle? Comment es-tu? Pourquoi est-ce que vous vous entendez bien? Est-ce qu'il y a quelque chose que tu n'aimes pas chez lui/elle et qu'il/elle n'aime pas chez toi?

18 A la recherche d'amis

a. Le club de français de ton école va publier des lettres qui parlent de l'amitié. Ecris une lettre dans laquelle tu décris les qualités que tu recherches chez un(e) ami(e).

b. Lis quelques lettres de tes camarades de classe. Choisis la lettre d'une personne que tu aimerais mieux connaître. Présente-toi à cette personne. Propose-lui de faire quelque chose d'intéressant. Continue à faire des suggestions jusqu'à ce qu'il/elle accepte. Prenez rendez-vous.

c. C'est le jour de votre rendez-vous et ton ami(e) n'est pas venu(e)! Il/Elle te téléphone plus tard pour s'excuser. Tu acceptes ses excuses.

Vocabulaire à la carte

ouvert(e)	sensible
bavard(e)	*sensitive*
talkative	réservé(e)
compréhensif (-ive)	timide
understanding	pénible
honnête	bizarre
spontané(e)	froid(e)
généreux (-euse)	égoïste
sociable	snob
discret (-ète)	mal élevé(e)
sincère	*rude*
enthousiaste	versatile
cheerful	*moody*
vif (-ive)	pas futé(e)
quick	*not with it*

ASSESS

Quiz 6-1, *Chapter Teaching Resources, Book 2,* pp. 79–80

Assessment Items, Audiocassette 7B
Audio CD 6

Performance Assessment

Have partners act out a scene like the one in the **Mise en train** in which they do the following: 1. introduce themselves; 2. make suggestions about things to do; and 3. arrange to meet later.

Answers

15 Je suis désolée d(e)/Je m'en veux d(e)/Je m'excuse d(e)/Pardonne-moi d(e)... avoir oublié notre rendez-vous/m'être disputée avec toi/ne pas avoir fini mes devoirs/avoir abîmé ton jean/avoir perdu ton livre de français/ne pas t'avoir rendu ton CD/avoir répété ton secret/ne pas t'avoir téléphoné/être sortie avec ton petit ami/être arrivée en classe en retard.

PANORAMA CULTUREL

Viviane • Côte d'Ivoire

Stanislas • France

Micheline • Belgique

**VIDEO PROGRAM
Videocassette 1**

We asked some people what's important to them. Here's what they told us.

Qu'est-ce qui est important dans la vie?

«Dans la vie, pour moi, ce qui compte, ce sont les parents. D'abord, il faut leur obéir, être à leur service, faire ce qui est mieux, ce qu'ils aiment.»

-Viviane

«Ce qui est important, c'est des... A mon avis, ce qui est important, c'est des relations avec des gens, l'argent, parce qu'il en faut et bien vivre, la qualité de vie.»

-Stanislas

«Trouver justement un métier qu'on aime. Il faut réussir. Pour réussir, il faut être heureux. Et pour être heureux, il faut trouver un métier qu'on aime. Il faut être heureux dans sa famille, d'une façon ou d'une autre. Ça peut être être marié, ne pas être marié. Ça n'a pas d'importance... Et vivre aussi dans un pays qu'on aime.»

Qu'est-ce qui est important dans le choix d'une profession?

«Il faut l'aimer. Il faut aimer le métier que l'on choisit, et si on l'aime pas, il faut avoir le courage de changer rapidement.»

-Micheline

Qu'en penses-tu?

1. What do each of these people think is important?
2. Which person do you most agree with? Why?
3. Do you disagree with any of these people? Why?
4. What other things do you think are important in life?

1. *Viviane:* parents
   Stanislas: interpersonal relationships, money, quality of life
   Micheline: finding a career one likes, having a happy family life, living in a country one likes, having the courage to find the right career

---

Questions

1. Qui pense qu'il est très important de trouver un métier qu'on aime? (Micheline)
2. Qu'est-ce qui est le plus important pour Viviane? (les parents) Et pour Stanislas? (les relations avec des gens et l'argent)
3. Est-ce que Micheline croit qu'il faut se marier pour être heureux? (non)

Community Link

Have students ask the interview question, "What is most important in life?" of people in the community and compare the answers with their own. You might have students share their findings with the class, being sure to respect the privacy of the people they interviewed.

Teacher Notes

- See *Video Guide* and *Practice and Activity Book* for activities related to the **Panorama Culturel**.
- Remind students that cultural material may be included in the Chapter Quizzes and Test.
- The interviewees' language represents informal, unrehearsed speech. Occasionally, edits have been made for clarification.

Motivating Activity

Ask students **Qu'est-ce qui est important dans la vie?** Write their answers on a transparency.

Presentation

Distribute copies of the list from the Motivating Activity. Then, play the video. Have students check each item they hear mentioned. Play the video again. This time, ask students to note additional things the interviewees mention. Compile this list on a transparency and have students rate each item on a scale of 1–10, with 10 being the most important and 1 the least important. Have students use these lists as they discuss the questions in **Qu'en penses-tu?** with a partner.

Thinking Critically

Comparing and Contrasting
Have students compare their lists for the Motivating Activity with the list they compiled from the interviews.

Summary

In this scene, Moktar's parents welcome Raphaël's family into their home. Raphaël reminds his father to take off his shoes when he enters the house. Moktar's sister Amina serves the mint tea, with a little teasing from her brother. M. Moussa invites Raphaël and his parents to his cousin's wedding the next day. At the wedding, Raphaël tries **pastilla,** a pigeon dish, and learns about Moroccan weddings, including the traditional headdress.

Motivating Activity

Ask students what they might say and do to make a guest feel welcome in their home.

Presentation

Have students look at the photos on pages 146–147 and anticipate what will happen in the story. Then, play the recording, pausing after each scene. After the first scene, ask **Qu'est-ce que M. Simenot a oublié de faire? (retirer les chaussures)** After they drink the tea, ask **Combien d'enfants ont les Moussa? (huit) Qu'est-ce que les Moussa proposent de faire le lendemain** (the next day)? **(aller au mariage d'une cousine)** After the wedding scene, ask **Qu'est-ce qu'on mange au mariage? (de la pastilla) Qu'est-ce que la mariée porte? (une coiffe)** Then, ask students for their reactions to Moroccan food and weddings.

Additional Practice

20 Have students create additional true-false statements about the **Remise en train.** Have volunteers read their statements to the class and have students respond **vrai** or **faux.**

Remise en train

Ahlên, merhabîn

Moktar et Raphaël sont allés au concert. Le lendemain, la famille Moussa accueille la famille Simenot chez elle.

MOKTAR	Ça me fait plaisir de te voir.
RAPHAEL	Moi aussi.
MOKTAR	Je vous présente mes parents.
M. SIMENOT	Madame.
MME MOUSSA	Ahlên, merhabîn.
MOKTAR	Ma mère vous souhaite la bienvenue.
M. MOUSSA	Bonjour. Entrez, s'il vous plaît.
M. SIMENOT	Vous êtes bien aimable.
MOKTAR	Mettez-vous à l'aise.
RAPHAEL	Papa, il faut retirer tes chaussures.
M. SIMENOT	Ah, excusez-moi. Je suis navré.
M. MOUSSA	Ça ne fait rien. Vous savez, c'est la coutume ici, mais si ça vous gêne, ce n'est pas important.
M. SIMENOT	Non, non, pas du tout.

M. MOUSSA	Qu'est-ce que je vous sers? Vous savez, ici, nous ne servons pas d'alcool. Mais nous avons des jus de fruits et, bien sûr, du thé à la menthe.
MME SIMENOT	Je prendrais bien du thé.
M. SIMENOT	Oui, ça ira très bien.
RAPHAEL	Pour moi aussi, s'il vous plaît.
M. MOUSSA	Asseyez-vous, je vous en prie.
M. SIMENOT	Merci.

Amina apporte le thé.

AMINA	Bonjour.
M. MOUSSA	Ma fille, Amina...
MOKTAR	Fais gaffe. Amina a le chic pour renverser le thé.
AMINA	Oh, ça va, hein! C'est pas moi qui ai renversé la cafetière hier.

19 Tu as compris? *See answers below.*

1. Where is the Simenot family?
2. What happens when they arrive?
3. What do the two families talk about?
4. Where does the Moussa family invite the Simenot family to go?
5. Why do the Simenots hesitate to accept the invitation?
6. What are the main steps in a Moroccan wedding?

20 Vrai ou faux?

1. On sert du thé à la menthe. vrai
2. Amina renverse souvent le thé. vrai
3. C'est Amina qui a commencé la dispute. faux
4. Les Simenot ont deux enfants. vrai
5. Amina va se marier demain. faux
6. La mariée porte une coiffe très élaborée. vrai

21 Qu'est-ce qu'ils font?

Trouve dans le dialogue des phrases pour décrire les situations suivantes.

1. Il faut retirer tes chaussures.

2. Asseyez-vous, je vous en prie.

3. C'est lui qui a commencé.

4. Qu'est-ce que c'est?

CHAPITRE 6 Ma famille, mes copains et moi

RESOURCES FOR REMISE EN TRAIN

Textbook Audiocassette 3B/Audio CD 6
Practice and Activity Book, p. 66

Culture Note

Because Islam forbids the consumption of alcohol, it is rarely served. Apart from mint tea, popular beverages include orange, almond, banana, and apple juices.

Answers

19 1. at Moktar's home
2. Mme Moussa greets them in Arabic. They have to take off their shoes.
3. Moroccan customs, their families
4. to a cousin's wedding
5. It's a family occasion.
6. The groom's family asks for the woman's hand, the couple signs a contract, the groom gives the bride presents, and everyone celebrates.

MOKTAR	Rapporteuse!
M. MOUSSA	Ça suffit, les enfants!
AMINA	C'est lui qui a commencé.
M. SIMENOT	Euh... et vous avez d'autres enfants?
M. MOUSSA	Nous avons huit enfants. Tous sont mariés sauf Moktar et Amina. Et vous?
M. SIMENOT	Nous avons un autre fils, Jean. Il va se marier en août.
M. MOUSSA	Félicitations. Au fait, nous allons au mariage de ma cousine demain. Vous voulez venir avec nous?
MME SIMENOT	Oh, non. C'est pour la famille.
M. MOUSSA	Mais non! Pas du tout. Ils seront ravis de vous avoir!
MME SIMENOT	Bon, si vous pensez vraiment qu'on ne dérange pas.

A la fête de mariage...

RAPHAEL	Oh, c'est bon, ça! Qu'est-ce que c'est?
MOKTAR	Ça, c'est de la pastilla.
RAPHAEL	C'est fait avec du poulet?
MOKTAR	Non, c'est du pigeon. Il y a aussi des amandes.
RAPHAEL	Mmm... J'adore! Dis donc, c'est quand, la cérémonie?

MOKTAR	Il n'y a pas vraiment de cérémonie comme chez toi. D'abord, la famille de l'homme demande la main de la femme..., puis, les fiancés signent un contrat. Ensuite, le fiancé donne des cadeaux à sa future femme.
RAPHAEL	Et après?
MOKTAR	Et puis, on fait la fête.
RAPHAEL	Oh, dis donc, ta cousine, qu'est-ce qu'elle a sur la tête?
MOKTAR	Les mariées marocaines ont toujours des coiffes très élaborées.
RAPHAEL	Cool. Je parie que le mariage de mon frère ne sera pas aussi chouette.

22 C'est le Maroc?

Après avoir lu **Ahlên, merhabîn,** est-ce que ces traditions te semblent marocaines ou non?

1. En général, les gens sont très accueillants. *oui*
2. On préfère boire du thé glacé. *non*
3. On offre des boissons alcoolisées aux invités. *non*
4. On retire ses chaussures en entrant dans une maison. *oui*
5. Les mariées s'habillent de façon très simple. *non*
6. La cérémonie de mariage a lieu dans une église. *non*
7. On mange du pigeon. *oui*

23 Cherche les expressions

What do the Moussa and Simenot families say to . . . See answers below.

1. welcome someone?
2. introduce someone?
3. offer something to drink?
4. ask someone to sit down?
5. tell someone to be careful?
6. accuse someone of being a tattletale?
7. express congratulations?
8. ask what something is?

24 Et maintenant, à toi

Comment est-ce qu'on accueille des invités dans ton pays? Est-ce que ça se fait comme au Maroc, ou est-ce que c'est différent?

REMISE EN TRAIN

cent quarante-sept **147**

Answers

23 1. **Ahlên, merhabîn.** (Bonjour. Entrez, s'il vous plaît.)
   2. Je vous présente...
   3. Qu'est-ce que je vous sers?
   4. Asseyez-vous, je vous en prie.
   5. Fais gaffe.
   6. Rapporteuse!
   7. Félicitations.
   8. Qu'est-ce que c'est?

Culture Note

Pastilla (**b'stilla** in Arabic), a specialty of Fez, is a pigeon pie made with sugar and cinnamon-coated pastry. Other traditional dishes include **couscous, harira** (a thick, spicy bean soup), and **tajine** (stew). Moroccan pastries, often made with almonds and honey, can be quite rich. **Cornes de gazelles,** sugar-coated pastry horns filled with marzipan, are popular.

Additional Practice

22 Ask students to write additional descriptions of American or Moroccan life. Collect them, read them aloud, and have students identify the culture being described.

For Individual Needs

23 Kinesthetic Learners Write the French expressions that serve the functions described in 1–8 on large cards and distribute them to students. Then, write the functions in questions 1–8 on the board. Say them aloud (express congratulations). A student who has a card bearing an expression that serves that function (**Félicitations!**) tapes the card to the board under the function. Continue until all the cards have been placed.

Thinking Critically

24 Comparing and Contrasting Ask students the following questions: What might a host do instead of asking a guest to remove his or her shoes? (take his or her coat) What might a host offer a guest? (soft drink, iced tea) Would a host invite a guest to a wedding? (no) What invitation might a host make? (to come by for coffee later)

Analyzing Have students compare Moroccan wedding customs with those of the United States. Ask them what could account for the differences.

Culture Note

For traditional Moroccan weddings, the bride's hands, feet, and face are decorated with henna.

Motivating Activity

Have students complete the following sentences, based on their impressions of Morocco from the Location Opener, the **Mise en train,** and the **Remise en train. Le Maroc, c'est... ; Les Marocains sont... ; Au Maroc, on...** Have volunteers share what they wrote. Then, ask the class to generalize about their impressions of Morocco. Remind them that these impressions are based on limited information.

Presentation

Have students look at the photos and answer the questions in **Qu'en penses-tu?** with a partner. Have small groups read the **Savais-tu que... ?** paragraph together. Then, have students close their books. Pretend you're going to visit Morocco, but you don't know anything about it. Have students tell you what they've learned about Morocco.

♜ Game

VRAI OU FAUX? Compose about twenty true–false statements about Morocco, based on the **Savais-tu que... ?,** the **Mise,** and the **Remise en train. (Un souk est un plat marocain. Fès est un centre artistique du Maroc.)** Form two teams. Each team selects a spokesperson. Read aloud a statement to the members of one team, who discuss it and have their spokesperson give their response. If the response is correct, the team wins a point. If not, the next team has a chance to steal the point by either correcting the statement if it is false or by providing an additional fact about the subject if the statement is true.

RENCONTRE CULTURELLE

Est-ce que tu connais le Maroc? Regarde les photos suivantes pour découvrir quelques caractéristiques de ce pays.

Casablanca, la plus grande ville du Maroc

Fès, centre spirituel, intellectuel et artistique du Maroc

Les artisans marocains sont renommés.

Les belles plages des côtes méditerranéenne et atlantique

Le quartier des tanneurs de cuir

Qu'en penses-tu?

1. What impression do these photos give you of Morocco?
2. What differences and similarities do you see between Morocco and the United States?

Possible answers
1. mix of modern and traditional, many crafts, natural beauty
2. *Similarities:* modern cities, natural attractions
   Differences: marketplace instead of mall

Savais-tu que... ?

Morocco is a mountainous country on the northwestern coast of Africa, graced with beautiful beaches on both its Atlantic and Mediterranean coasts. Arabic is the official language of Morocco, but a large percentage of the population speaks French as well. The people of Morocco are mainly of Arab and Berber origins: the Berbers have occupied the area since very ancient times, and the Arab conquest at the end of the seventh century A.D. brought Islam to the country. Morocco is almost 100 percent Islamic, and a mosque can be found in every village. The Moroccan people have a reputation for being master artisans and craftsmen; the high quality of their products is recognized throughout North Africa and Europe. Rugs, pottery, fine leather, copperware, and other goods are sold in Arab markets called **souks.** In a small village there may be only one market, but in large cities such as Fez or Marrakesh, you will find specialized markets such as a **souk de tapis** or **souk de poterie.**

✦ For Individual Needs

Challenge Play the game **Vrai ou faux?** using information questions rather than true-false statements. (**Qu'est-ce que c'est qu'un souk? Quelle ville est le centre artistique et intellectuel du Maroc?**)

🌐 Culture Note

The leather tanneries in Fez, located in the **Souk Dabbaghin,** are a striking sight. Huge vats of brightly-colored dyes are arranged in honeycomb patterns. Vegetable-based dyes, including saffron, indigo, and mint, have replaced the more dangerous chemical dyes used in the past. Once the leather is dyed, it is spread out on the rooftops in colorful sheets to dry in the sun.

DEUXIEME ETAPE

Showing and responding to hospitality; expressing and responding to thanks; quarreling

COMMENT DIT-ON...?

Showing and responding to hospitality; expressing and responding to thanks

To welcome someone:
Entrez, je vous en prie.
Ça me fait plaisir de vous voir.
Donnez-moi votre manteau.
Mettez-vous à l'aise.
Asseyez-vous.

To respond:
Merci.
Moi aussi.
Vous êtes bien aimable.
C'est gentil.

To offer food or drink:
Je vous sers quelque chose?
Qu'est-ce que je peux vous offrir?

To respond:
Je prendrais bien un verre de thé.
Vous auriez des biscuits?

To express thanks:
Merci bien/infiniment/mille fois.
Je vous remercie.
C'est vraiment très gentil
de votre part.

To respond to thanks:
De rien.
Je vous en prie.
(Il n'y a) pas de quoi.
C'est tout à fait normal.

25 Ecoute!

Ecoute M. Ben Assouan qui accueille ses invités. Choisis l'image qui correspond à ce qu'il dit.

1. c 2. b 3. d 4. a

A la française

When someone offers you something in English, and you reply with *Thank you*, people assume that you are accepting the offer. However, when French-speaking people respond to an offer with **merci**, it might mean that they're refusing. So, if you want some of what is offered, say **Oui**, in addition to **merci**.

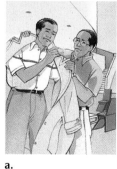
a.

b.

c.

d.

RESOURCES FOR DEUXIEME ETAPE

Chapter Teaching Resources, Book 2
• Communicative Activity 6-2, pp. 60–61
• Teaching Transparency Master 6-2, pp. 63, 64
   Teaching Transparency 6-2
• Additional Listening Activities 6-4, 6-5, 6-6, pp. 66–67
   Audiocassette 9B/Audio CD 6
• Realia 6-2, pp. 70–71
• Situation Cards 6-2, 6-3, pp. 72–73
• Student Response Forms, pp. 74–76
• Quiz 6-2, pp. 79–80
   Audiocassette 7B/Audio CD 6

ADDITIONAL RESOURCES
Textbook Audiocassette 3B
  OR *Audio CD 6*
Practice and Activity Book, pp. 67–70
Video Program, Videocassette 1
Video Guide

Jump Start!

Write the following questions and statements on the board and have students write responses to them: **Ça t'intéresse d'aller au souk? Tu ne voudrais pas goûter de la pastilla? Où est-ce qu'on se retrouve? A quelle heure est-ce qu'on se donne rendez-vous? Pardonne-moi d'avoir oublié notre rendez-vous hier.**

MOTIVATE

Have volunteers act out a skit in English about an American family welcoming the Moussa family to their home.

TEACH

Presentation

Comment dit-on...? Before class, have a student rehearse the responses with you. Bring in a coat, a glass, and some cookies. If possible, make some mint tea. Then, have the student knock on the classroom door. Greet the student, invite him or her inside, and offer a seat and food or drink. Act out the skit again, having students repeat the new expressions. Then, hold up the props (a coat) to elicit the appropriate expression from students. **(Donnez-moi votre manteau.)**

For Individual Needs

25 Slower Pace Have students tell in English what is happening in each illustration and guess what the people might be saying. Then, play the recording, pausing after each dialogue to have students respond.

Thinking Critically

Comparing and Contrasting–Note Culturelle

Have students compare Moroccan and American gestures of hospitality. Have them consider the following questions: In America, is it common to invite acquaintances you've just met to dinner? Is it acceptable to refuse a beverage that is offered?

 For Individual Needs

26 Kinesthetic Learners

Write M. Fikri's lines on separate large cards of one color and distribute them to six students. Do the same with his colleague's lines, using cards of a different color. Have these twelve students stand at the front of the room, holding their cards. Then, have their classmates rearrange them in the logical order of the conversation. Finally, ask for two volunteers to play the roles of M. Fikri and his friend and read aloud the conversation from the cards.

26 Challenge Once students have completed the activity, have them write their own dialogues in which they welcome a friend to their home.

Teaching Suggestion

27 Once students have completed the activity, read the numbered statements aloud and ask for volunteers to offer their responses. Ask students to explain why the other responses are inappropriate.

Additional Practice

27 Once students have completed this activity, have partners create and act out a two- or three-line conversation in which one person is expressing thanks to another.

NOTE CULTURELLE

The concept of hospitality is central to the Arab society of North Africa. It is considered an honor for a host to receive guests in his home, and even a very poor family will prepare a special meal to welcome visitors, providing whatever food it can afford. Mint tea, the national beverage in Morocco, is customarily served to guests. It is considered rude to refuse tea when it is offered, and it is polite to accept several glasses.

26 Méli-mélo!

M. Fikri rend visite à son collègue. Récris leur conversation. *Possible answers:*

«Donnez-moi votre manteau.» 5
«Mettez-vous à l'aise.» 7
«Ça me fait plaisir de vous voir.» 3
«Qu'est-ce que je peux vous offrir?» 9
«Entrez, je vous en prie.» 1
«Bien sûr.» 11

«Vous auriez du thé?» 10
«Moi aussi.» 4
«Vous êtes bien aimable.» 6
«Merci.» 2
«C'est gentil.» 8

27 Merci infiniment!

On te remercie. Choisis la réponse appropriée.

1. Merci bien de m'avoir prêté ton cardigan. J'avais tellement froid!
   a. Vous êtes bien aimable!
   b. De rien.
   c. Tu as toujours froid!

2. Je vous remercie de m'avoir répondu si vite.
   a. Ne vous inquiétez pas.
   b. Mettez-vous à l'aise.
   c. Je vous en prie.

3. Si tu ne m'avais pas aidé, j'aurais raté l'examen. Je ne sais pas comment te remercier!
   a. Fais tes devoirs tous les jours!
   b. C'est tout à fait normal!
   c. Ils sont difficiles, ces examens.

4. Dis donc, on m'a donné le job. Merci mille fois. C'était vraiment gentil de ta part!
   a. Ne sois pas en retard!
   b. Tu aimeras ce travail.
   c. Il n'y a pas de quoi.

150 *cent cinquante*   CHAPITRE 6   Ma famille, mes copains et moi

Culture Note

If you are invited to a Moroccan family's home, it is considered polite to bring a small gift for the hosts, just as in other francophone countries. Sweet pastries or tea and sugar are acceptable gifts. If the family is poor, you might even offer to bring a gift of meat for the hosts.

28 Merci mille fois!

 Ecris un petit mot de remerciement à ton/ta camarade qui...

t'a invité(e) à sa boum.

t'a conseillé(e).

t'a envoyé une carte postale.

t'a donné un CD.

VOCABULAIRE

Voilà la photo de ma famille que tu m'as demandée. Je t'explique qui est tout le monde. La vieille dame, ce n'est pas ma grand-mère, c'est mon **arrière-grand-mère**, Beta. Elle est **veuve**. A côté d'elle, il y a mon père et ma mère. Leurs parents sont morts. Mon père est **le petit-fils** de Beta. Tu te rends compte comme elle est vieille? Bon, il y a aussi ma sœur, Souad. Elle est **mariée**. Là, à côté de moi, c'est son **mari** Karim. De l'autre côté, c'est mon frère, Hassan. C'est **l'aîné**. Il a 25 ans. Il est **célibataire**. Il ne veut pas se marier! Et moi, tu vois, je suis le **benjamin**. Alors, tout le monde attend ton arrivée avec impatience. Tu seras reçu comme un roi.

l'arrière-grand-père	le/la cadet(te)
l'arrière-grand-mère	*the younger child*
le petit-fils	le/la benjamin(e)
la petite-fille	*the youngest child*
le mari	les jumeaux/jumelles
la femme	*twins*
le neveu *nephew*	veuf/veuve *widowed*
la nièce *niece*	mort(e)
l'aîné(e)	marié(e)
the oldest child	célibataire *single*
	divorcé(e)

29 Ecoute!

 Ahmed a invité Eric chez lui. Ecoute leur conversation et décide quelle photo représente la famille d'Ahmed. a

a.

b.

DEUXIEME ETAPE   *cent cinquante et un*   **151**

Language Notes

- Students might want to use the phrase **fils/fille unique** for *only child*.
- The word **benjamin** originates from the Biblical story of Joseph. Benjamin was the youngest son of Jacob and the brother of Joseph. Benjamin was Joseph's favorite brother and the object of much affection and generosity.
- **Les jumelles** also refers to *binoculars,* referring to the "twin" lenses.

📁 Portfolio

28 Written This item is appropriate for students' written portfolios. For portfolio information, see *Assessment Guide,* pages 2–13.

Presentation

Vocabulaire On a transparency, sketch a family tree that illustrates the relationships described in the letter. Label the relationships. You might mark the ages of three children to explain **l'aîné(e)**, **le/la cadet(te)**, and **le/la benjamin(e)**. Read the letter aloud and point to each family member on the tree as you mention the person. Then, ask students to explain the vocabulary. (**Qu'est-ce que c'est qu'un arrière-grand-père? C'est le père d'un de vos grandparents.**) You might also ask the class about their own family relationships (**Qui est l'aîné(e)?**), being sure to respect students' privacy.

Building on Previous Skills

Have students identify the family members from the illustration in the **Vocabulaire,** using **Voici, A sa droite...** , and so on. Have them add details about each person. (**Il est pénible. Elle aime jouer au tennis.**)

Additional Practice

Ask students either–or questions about the marital status of various celebrities. (**Elizabeth Taylor est mariée ou divorcée?**)

🔷 For Individual Needs

29 Slower Pace Before you play the recording, have students point out the differences between the photos.

Motivating Activity

Ask students if they used to argue with their siblings. Ask them to suggest subjects that siblings might argue about.

Presentation

Comment dit-on... ? Create a quarrel between two siblings, using the new expressions. Before class, record one sibling's lines, leaving pauses for the other's responses. In class, play the recording, responding during the pauses with the second sibling's lines. Then, act out the quarrel again, pausing to have students repeat. Next, have partners compose remarks that might provoke someone to say any five of the new expressions. Have them act out their two-line arguments.

Teacher Note

When having students practice the new expressions, remind them to respect others' feelings. Advise them to use these expressions only in the specific, imaginary contexts described here.

Additional Practice

Put on a paper crown and tell students that you are **l'aîné(e)**. Then, make an accusation to a student, who is **le cadet/la cadette** (**Tu me prends la tête!**), and have him or her respond. (**Tant pis!**) Then, that student takes the crown, becomes **l'aîné(e)**, and accuses another student. Continue until all students have played both roles.

152 DEUXIEME ETAPE CHAPITRE 6

---

30 Un arbre généalogique

Décris les membres de ta famille, ou d'une famille imaginaire, et leurs relations. En t'écoutant, ton/ta camarade va dessiner l'arbre généalogique. Il/Elle va te le montrer pour voir s'il/si elle a bien compris. Changez de rôles.

Si tu as oublié
family members
va à la page 335.

31 Mettez-vous à l'aise!

Ta famille a organisé une soirée. Tu accueilles les invités. Ils te remercient. N'oublie pas de présenter tes amis à chaque membre de ta famille. Joue cette scène avec tes camarades. Changez de rôles.

📎 **COMMENT DIT-ON... ?**

Quarreling

To accuse someone:

Rapporteur(-euse)!
Tattletale!
Pleurnicheur(-euse)!
Crybaby!
Tricheur(-euse)!
Cheater!
Tu es bête comme tes pieds!
You're so stupid!
Tu m'énerves, à la fin!
You're bugging me to death!
Tu es vraiment casse-pieds!
You're such a pain!
Tu me prends la tête!
You're driving me crazy!

To justify a quarrel:

C'est toujours la même chose!
C'est lui/elle qui a commencé!
Il/Elle m'a traité(e) d'imbécile!
He/She called me a . . . !
C'est toujours moi qui prends!
I'm always the one who gets blamed!

To respond to an accusation:

Oh, ça va, hein?
Oh, cut it out!
Arrête!
Ça suffit!
Tu le fais exprès?
Are you doing that on purpose?
Mêle-toi de tes oignons!
Mind your own business!
Fiche-moi la paix!
Leave me alone!
Casse-toi!
Get out of here!
Tant pis pour toi!
Tough!
Ferme-la!
Shut up!

32 Ecoute!

Ecoute ces disputes. Comment est-ce qu'elles ont commencé? A ton avis, est-ce que c'est la faute de Moktar ou d'Amina? Answers on p. 135D.

* Ferme-la

À la **française**

Can you guess which of the phrases in the **Comment dit-on...?** this gesture expresses? *

152 *cent cinquante-deux*

CHAPITRE 6 Ma famille, mes copains et moi

🔹 **For Individual Needs**

32 Slower Pace Have students listen to the recording twice, once to determine what caused the disagreement, and again to find out who is at fault.

♜ **Game**

A FINIR Form two teams. Write down the expressions from **Comment dit-on... ?** in random order. Then, have the first player from each team come forward. Call out the first few words of one of the expressions. (**Tu m'énerves,...**) The first player to complete the expression (**... à la fin!**) wins a point. Then, the next two players come forward. Continue until all the expressions have been completed.

33 Les relations frères-sœurs

Lis ces remarques de quelques jeunes francophones et complète les phrases ci-dessous.

Christophe
Il faut toujours que je rende service à ma sœur aînée. Je le fais pour qu'elle me fiche la paix, mais elle, elle ne me rend jamais de service. Si on se dispute pour la télé, ma mère prend toujours sa défense et c'est moi qui dois regarder la télé en noir et blanc dans ma chambre.

Gilles
Mon grand frère m'interdit d'aller dans sa chambre mais lui, il vient toujours fouiller dans la mienne. Il s'imagine qu'il peut me donner des ordres parce qu'il est l'aîné!

Djamila
Pour énerver ma sœur quand on regarde la télé ensemble, je change de chaîne sans lui demander son avis.

Saïd
Je peux parler de mes ennuis à ma grande sœur et je peux aussi lui emprunter de l'argent. On se fait confiance. Après la mort de mon père, je ne pouvais pas m'arrêter de pleurer et ma sœur venait toujours essayer de me réconforter dans ma chambre.

Hélène
Mes frères et sœurs doivent aller au lit plus tôt que moi parce qu'ils sont plus jeunes. Mais si je rentre plus tard que prévu quand je sors, mes parents ne sont pas contents parce qu'ils disent que je donne le mauvais exemple aux petits.

Sylvie
Mes deux frères me font tout le temps des blagues et m'embêtent quand je parle au téléphone avec mes copains. Et quand je fais mes devoirs, ils font beaucoup de bruit juste pour m'embêter.

Martine
Quand ma sœur et moi, nous nous disputons, j'essaie toujours de me réconcilier avec elle. Un jour, je l'ennuyais pendant qu'elle jouait du piano. On a été fâchées un moment. Puis, je lui ai demandé si elle voulait jouer avec moi, elle au piano et moi à la flûte. La dispute s'est arrêtée là.

1. _____ ne peut pas faire ses devoirs parce que ses frères font du bruit. *Sylvie*
2. La sœur de _____ est compréhensive et elle l'aide à résoudre ses problèmes. *Saïd*
3. Quand _____ veut embêter sa sœur, elle change de chaîne sans lui demander. *Djamila*
4. Le frère de _____ entre souvent dans sa chambre pour fouiller dans ses affaires. *Gilles*
5. _____ n'aime pas avoir à donner l'exemple à ses petits frères et sœurs. *Hélène*

34 Arrête!

Ton frère/ta sœur t'énerve quand il/elle fait les choses ci-dessous. Tu le lui dis, et ça provoque une dispute. Joue ces scènes avec ton/ta camarade.

emprunter tes CD sans te le demander

changer de chaîne alors que tu regardes quelque chose à la télé

monopoliser le téléphone

rester trop longtemps dans la salle de bains

se moquer de toi devant tes amis

entrer dans ta chambre et fouiller dans tes affaires

abîmer tes affaires

te tirer les cheveux

35 Les enfants terribles

Tu fais du baby-sitting et tu trouves que les enfants que tu gardes sont insupportables! Tes camarades, qui joueront les enfants, vont imaginer trois disputes qu'ils auront. Tu dois les empêcher de se disputer. Ils se justifient chaque fois.

36 Jeu de rôle

You've decided to throw a party. Unfortunately, you invite people who don't get along with one another. Act out this scene with your friends.
- Invite your guests and make arrangements for the party.
- Welcome your guests and offer refreshments.
- Your guests argue with one another and later apologize.

Cooperative Learning

33 Have students stage a talk show to discuss the letters in this activity. Ask for seven volunteers to act as the guests. Assign one letter to each guest. The guests carefully read the letter assigned to them and assume the identity of the writer. One person is the host of the show. The host prepares a series of questions to ask the guests, based on their letters. The remaining students comprise the studio audience. They should prepare one or two questions to ask each guest during the show. The teacher is the director and stops the show every few minutes for a commercial break to give the host time to redirect the discussion so that everyone has a chance to talk. You might want to videotape the show.

Teaching Suggestion

34 Encourage students to resolve the dispute peacefully after they act out their quarrel. Ask students how these issues might be resolved. You might invite the school guidance counselor to class to discuss how problems can be resolved peacefully.

Portfolio

35 Oral This activity is appropriate for students' oral portfolios. For portfolio suggestions, see *Assessment Guide,* page 19.

CLOSE

To close this **étape,** call on students to give appropriate responses to various expressions from the chapter. (**Tu ne voudrais pas aller au ciné? Qu'est-ce que je peux vous offrir? Je vous remercie. Tu me prends la tête!**)

Language Note

34 Students might want to know the following words: **abîmer** *(to ruin);* **tirer** *(to pull);* **fouiller** *(to look/rummage through).*

ASSESS

Quiz 6-2, *Chapter Teaching Resources, Book 2,* pp. 79–80

Assessment Items, Audiocassette 7B
Audio CD 6

Performance Assessment

Have students act out their skits from Activity 36. You might suggest that the guests take on the roles of celebrities who are known for not getting along well together. You might also videotape or record students' skits. Base students' grades on vocabulary use, creativity, pronunciation, and presentation.

READING STRATEGY

Taking cultural context into account

Teacher Note

For an additional reading, see *Practice and Activity Book,* page 71.

PREREADING
Activity A

Motivating Activity

Begin a discussion about fairy tales. Ask students what the characters in their favorite fairy tales are like, and how the stories end. Have students suggest possible lessons and values that might be taught through a story.

Teaching Suggestion

Call students' attention to the title of the first story, *Les trois femmes du roi.* Ask them to find one element common to fairy tales students are familiar with and one culturally different element in the title (it's about a king; polygamy).

Culture Note

In Islam, polygamy is permitted by the Koran. Men may take up to four wives simultaneously, but they are encouraged to take only as many as their financial means will allow. In *Les trois femmes du roi,* the king is quite wealthy, so three wives is not an unreasonable number.

READING
Activities B–O

For Individual Needs

B. Challenge Have students scan the first paragraph and tell what three claims the three daughters make.

LISONS!

Les trois femmes du roi

Une nuit, le roi dit à son vizir :
– Allons faire le tour de la ville pour voir si tout est tranquille.

Ils se promènent. Les gens dorment ; il n'y a personne dans les rues. Tout à coup, ils voient de la lumière qui passe sous la porte d'une maison.
– Qui a encore sa lampe allumée à cette heure-ci ? dit le roi.

Ils s'arrêtent, mettent l'oreille contre la porte et écoutent ce que l'on dit derrière. Une jeune fille parle et dit à ses sœurs :
– Si le roi m'épousait, je pourrais faire manger tous les gens du pays avec un seul plat de couscous.

Une autre dit :
– S'il m'épousait, je pourrais habiller tous les gens du pays avec un seul morceau de tissu.
– Moi, dit la voix la plus jeune, je lui donnerais un garçon et une fille et ils auraient des cheveux d'argent.

Le lendemain, le roi envoie des gens à la maison où il a entendu du bruit.

Le père des jeunes filles est un homme vieux et pauvre. En entendant frapper à la porte, il demande :
– Qui frappe ?
– Viens ! Le roi veut te parler. Le père a très peur. Il se demande pourquoi le roi veut le voir. Il demande à ses filles :
– Est-ce que vous avez parlé à des gens ? Est-ce que vous vous êtes disputées avec quelqu'un ?
– Non, père, n'aie pas peur ! disent-elles. Nous ne connaissons personne. Nous ne nous sommes disputées avec personne. Jamais nous ne sommes sorties de la maison.

Le vieillard sort et, tremblant de peur, suit les gens qui l'emmènent chez le roi.
– Bon vieillard, lui dit le roi. As-tu des filles ?
– Oui, Seigneur.
– Combien ?
– Trois.
– Veux-tu me les donner en mariage ? Je veux me marier avec toutes les trois, comme cela est permis par Dieu et son Prophète.
– Avec plaisir, ô Roi ! répond le père. Je n'ai pas trouvé de bergers pour devenir leurs maris et toi, Roi, tu les veux toutes les trois !

Le roi fait faire les fêtes du mariage et fait amener ses trois femmes à son palais.

Un jour, le roi dit à l'une de ses trois femmes :
– Tu as dit un jour que, si le roi t'épousait, tu pourrais faire manger tous les gens du pays avec un seul plat de couscous. Fais ce plat de couscous, je veux voir si tu as dit vrai.
– Je ferai ce couscous, ô Roi. Donne-moi seulement un demi-sac de farine.

Le lendemain, quand la femme a reçu du roi un demi-sac de farine, elle envoie quelqu'un acheter un sac de sel. Puis elle fait le couscous en mettant pour chaque part de farine deux parts de sel. Après elle le fait cuire. Alors le roi dit à tous les gens de venir et toute la grande maison est pleine. Il apporte le plat, le pose au milieu de la grande salle et invite tout le monde à manger. Mais chaque fois que quelqu'un prend une boulette de couscous, il la crache aussitôt parce qu'elle est trop salée. Les serviteurs disent :
– Mangez, messieurs !

Mais ils ont peur que le roi se mette en colère et ils répondent :
– Non, merci, nous en avons mangé beaucoup, c'est très bon, mais nous n'avons plus faim.

DE BONS CONSEILS

Stories set in your own culture are easy to understand because you can relate to them. A story about baseball is no problem because baseball is a part of American culture. Even if you haven't played or watched a game, chances are you still know what it is. When you read a story set in another country, however, you may be misled if you assume that the society and customs there are exactly the same as where you live. In order to best understand a story, think about the culture that it represents. What do you know that can help you? If you're not familiar with the country in the story, you may want to find out more about it. Taking the cultural context of a story into account will enable you to understand it better and will make it more enjoyable too.

Les trois femmes du roi

A. Where are the king and his vizier? What do they overhear? See answers below.

B. Which of these statements were not made by one of the three daughters? b, d

«Si le roi m'épousait...

a. je pourrais habiller tous les gens du pays avec un seul morceau de tissu.»

b. je pourrais construire des logements pour tous les gens du pays avec un seul bout de plancher.»

c. je lui donnerais des enfants avec des cheveux d'argent.»

d. je pourrais changer de la paille en or.»

e. je pourrais faire manger tous les gens avec un seul plat de couscous.»

Language Notes

• A **vizir** *(vizier)* is a high official in a Muslim government. An English equivalent might be a prime minister.

• When the king mentions **son Prophète**, he is referring to Mohammed.

• You might tell students that **épouser** means *to marry.*

Teacher Note

B. Before doing this activity, you might tell students that **couscous** is the national dish of Morocco. For more information, see the Location Opener on pages 106–109.

Answers

A outside a house; three sisters telling what they would do if the king married them

Et ils repartent tous chez eux sans dire que le couscous est trop salé. Quand ils sont partis, le roi voit que le plat est encore plein. Il est très heureux et dit :
– Dieu est avec moi ! Ma femme a dit vrai.
Il veut manger un peu de couscous et le crache lui aussi. Il se met en colère et va trouver sa femme :
– Tu as menti ! Personne n'a mangé de ce couscous. Il était trop salé.
– Oui, mais tous les invités ont dit qu'ils en avaient mangé et qu'ils n'avaient plus faim !
– C'est vrai, tu n'as pas menti, répond le roi.
Un autre soir, il dit à son autre femme :
– Tu as dit un jour que, si le roi t'épousait, tu pourrais habiller tous les gens du pays avec un seul morceau de tissu. Fais cela, je le veux !
– Donne-moi un morceau de tissu, ô Roi, et tu verras que j'ai dit vrai.
Le lendemain matin, pendant que le roi appelle tous les gens, la femme coupe le tissu en petits bouts très fins. Puis elle se met au-dessus de la porte de la ville et dit au roi de faire passer tous les gens l'un derrière l'autre. Alors, elle laisse tomber sur chacun d'eux un petit bout de tissu que chacun attrape à la main. Quand ils sont passés, les gens disent au revoir au roi et rentrent chez eux sans rien dire. Ils n'osent pas dire qu'on s'est moqué d'eux parce qu'ils ont peur d'avoir la tête coupée. Le roi dit à sa femme :
– Tu n'as pas habillé tous les gens du pays !
– Si ! Chacun a eu sa part et ils sont tous partis contents.
– C'est vrai ; tu n'as pas menti !
La troisième femme, la plus jeune, avait dit :
– Si le roi m'épousait, je lui donnerais un garçon et une fille et ils auraient des cheveux d'argent.
Elle a peur que le roi se rappelle ce qu'elle a dit. Elle prie Dieu chaque jour et enfin, un enfant grandit dans son ventre. Ses sœurs pensent :
– Le roi va préférer notre sœur à cause de cet enfant. Que faire ?

Elles demandent conseil à une vieille qui leur dit :
– Attendez ! Je vous aiderai.
Quand l'enfant va naître, les deux sœurs appellent la vieille. Elle arrive avec une grande boîte dans laquelle elle a caché deux petits chiens. Elle dit qu'elle va soigner la maman et entre dans la chambre. Deux enfants naissent, un garçon et une fille, et ils ont tous les deux des cheveux d'argent. Alors la vieille prend les deux enfants ; elle les met dans la boîte et, à leur place, elle met les deux petits chiens. Puis elle va dire au roi :
– Votre femme a eu deux enfants, mais ils ressemblent à des chiens !
Alors le roi se met en colère et donne l'ordre d'enfermer sa femme dans la cage où vivent tous les chiens de la maison. Les sœurs et la vieille la conduisent à la cage et là, elle mange et vit avec les bêtes. La vieille va jeter à la mer la grosse boîte où sont les deux enfants. La mer emporte la boîte très loin, vers un pays où vivent un pêcheur et sa femme. Un jour le pêcheur, qui est dans son bateau, voit la boîte. Il s'approche, ouvre la boîte et voit deux petits enfants, avec des cheveux qui brillent comme le soleil. Il rentre chez lui très heureux, montre les enfants à sa femme et tous deux décident de les garder et de les élever. Les enfants grandissent heureux. Ils étudient le Coran et aident le pêcheur et sa femme dans leur travail.
Mes amis, vous voulez connaître la fin de l'histoire. Eh bien, écoutez !
Un jour, les deux enfants se disputent avec d'autres enfants. Ceux-ci leur disent :
– Vous êtes des étrangers ! Le pêcheur et sa femme ne sont pas vos parents. Ils vous ont trouvés dans une boîte sur la mer.
Alors les deux enfants, très tristes, disent au revoir en pleurant au pêcheur et à sa femme et s'en vont en bateau, très loin, sur la mer. Ils arrivent dans

For Activities C, D, E, and F, see answers below.

C. Look over the first page of the story and find some examples of cultural differences. How does this information affect your understanding of the story?

D. When questioned by their father, why do the daughters insist that they have not even left the house? Why would that be important? Is that something important in your culture?

E. What did the first and second wives do when asked to fulfill their vows? Why didn't the people of the kingdom complain? What was the king's reaction?

F. Why are the first and second wives jealous of the third wife? What do they do about it?

G. Vrai ou faux?
1. Les enfants ont des cheveux d'argent. vrai
2. Le roi fait enfermer sa femme dans un donjon. faux
3. Les deux enfants vont en bateau au pays du pêcheur et de sa femme. faux
4. Le pêcheur est très heureux de trouver les enfants. vrai
5. Les enfants savent depuis leur naissance qu'ils sont les enfants du roi. faux
6. A l'âge de quinze ans, les enfants quittent le pays du pêcheur. vrai

H. Why do you think the third wife was treated so harshly? How do you think her punishment was chosen? What punishments would be the most humiliating to people in your culture? See answers below.

I. How are the children finally reunited with their real father? See answers below.

cent cinquante-cinq 155

Thinking Critically

C. Analyzing For each of the cultural differences students found in Activity C, have students explain how the mores of the society affect the characters' behavior or the plot of the story.

Additional Practice

G. For listening practice, read aloud additional true–false statements about the story and have students raise their right hand if the statement you read is true and their left hand if it is false.

Thinking Critically

H. Analyzing Have students compare the means of punishment described in the story with those they are familiar with. Have them give examples of punishments in the past that were intended to humiliate (the public stocks, the dunce cap). Ask students to suggest possible purposes of punishment (to separate from society, to reform, to humiliate).

Reading/Writing Link

Assign partners one paragraph of the story to summarize. Have them write a one- or two-sentence summary on a slip of paper. Then, gather all the papers and put them in a box. Have a student draw the papers from the box one at a time, read them aloud, and tape them on the board in the order of the story, according to the class' instructions.

Answers

C form of government (monarchy vs. democracy), expectations for young women (restrictions against leaving the house or speaking to outsiders vs. relative freedom), and marriage norms (arranged marriages and polygamy vs. choice of mate and monogamy); It explains the sisters' and the king's actions.

D In their culture, young women are not supposed to leave the house or speak to outsiders; They fear punishment if suspected of breaking this restriction; Answers will vary.

E The first wife cooked a dish of couscous so heavily salted no one would eat it, and the second distributed scraps of cloth too tiny to wear; The people did not complain in either case, for fear of angering the king; The king agreed that his wives didn't lie.

F They think the king will prefer the third wife if she fulfills her vow to produce two silver-haired children; They ask an old woman for advice and replace the babies with two dogs.

H She was put in a dog cage and treated like an animal because she supposedly gave birth to dogs, making her a failure as a woman in the eyes of society; Answers will vary.

I When they travel to his country, the king hears about them and sends for them.

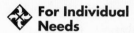

For Individual Needs

Slower Pace Create fill-in-the-blank sentences about *Le clou de Djeha,* such as Djeha veut accrocher un ____ à son ____. Djeha doit vendre sa ____. Djeha ne vend pas le ____ qui est planté dans le mur de sa maison. Après le mariage, l'acheteur va rendre la ____ à Djeha. Djeha et l'acheteur vont chez le ____. Il y a un ____ chez l'acheteur. Type them and distribute copies to students. Have partners work together to fill in the blanks and then number the events in the correct order.

Teaching Suggestions

N. Take a poll of how many students agree with the **cadi's** decision. Ask if they would have made the same decision in his place, knowing they had to justify their decision legally.

O. After students have read *La petite maison,* have them pair off. One partner is a friend who doesn't understand Moroccan culture very well and asks questions about the story. The other partner retells the story and explains the message according to Moroccan culture. Have students role-play this situation. You might ask for volunteers to present their skits to the class.

POSTREADING
Activity P

Thinking Critically

Synthesizing Have students rewrite either the first or the second story as they think it would happen today in the United States, adapting the story to fit American mores. For example, the three wives might become three job applicants for a political position. Students might illustrate their stories and include them in their portfolios.

---

le pays du roi ; et là, ils ont beaucoup d'aventures et beaucoup de malheurs.

Un jour, le roi entend dire qu'il y a dans son pays deux jeunes gens qui ont des cheveux d'argent. Il se rappelle ce que lui a dit sa troisième femme autrefois et il les fait chercher. Quand les deux jeunes gens arrivent devant lui, il leur demande :

– Qui sont vos parents ?

– Nous ne les connaissons pas. Nous avons été trouvés un jour, il y a quinze ans, dans une grande boîte très loin d'ici sur la mer.

– Alors le roi leur tend les bras et s'écrie :

– C'est vous ! Vous êtes mes enfants ! Il y a quinze ans, quand vous êtes nés, on m'a dit que vous ressembliez à des chiens, et j'ai fait jeter votre mère dans une cage !

Et aussitôt il donne l'ordre qu'on aille chercher leur mère et qu'on jette les deux sœurs à sa place dans la cage aux chiens.

Les deux jeunes gens vivent alors heureux auprès du roi et de leur mère. Mais ils n'oublient pas le pêcheur et sa femme et leur envoient souvent de riches cadeaux.

Le clou de Djeha

Un jour, Djeha n'a plus d'argent. Il décide de vendre sa maison. Quelqu'un veut l'acheter, alors Djeha lui dit :

– Je vends ma maison, mais dans cette maison, il y a un clou, planté dans un mur. Ce clou, je ne le vends pas, il est à moi. Et tu n'as pas le droit de l'enlever ni de l'enfoncer.

– D'accord, dit l'acheteur. J'achète la maison.

Et tous les deux vont chez le notaire pour signer la vente. Sur le papier, le notaire écrit que le clou qui est dans le mur ne peut être ni enlevé ni enfoncé.

Quelques jours plus tard, Djeha trouve un vieux cheval mort jeté dans la rue. Il donne de l'argent à des gens et leur dit :

– Allez porter ce cheval mort devant la porte de la maison de Djeha.

Quand ils l'ont porté, Djeha frappe à la porte et dit aux gens de la maison :

– Je veux accrocher ce cheval à mon clou !

– Quoi, mais tu es fou ! Cette maison est à nous !

– Cette maison est à vous mais le clou est à moi, répond Djeha.

– Mais il est mort, ton cheval, et déjà il sent mauvais.

– Le clou est à moi, répète Djeha. Allons chez le cadi.

– Montrez-moi le papier écrit au moment de la vente, dit le cadi. Djeha montre le papier ; le cadi le lit.

– C'est vrai, dit le cadi, le clou est à Djeha. Il peut faire ce qu'il veut avec.

– Mais, monsieur le cadi, dit l'acheteur, aujourd'hui nous avons un mariage chez nous. Cet homme apporte un cheval mort et qui sent mauvais et il veut l'accrocher au clou.

– Tu as signé le papier, répond le cadi. Il est trop tard.

– Monsieur le cadi, dit l'acheteur, c'est d'accord. Je laisse toute la maison à cet homme. Je lui demande seulement qu'il nous laisse finir la fête chez nous et après je lui donnerai la clef.

C'est ainsi que Djeha a retrouvé sa maison.

La petite maison

Un homme construit une petite maison dans un endroit très étroit. Des gens passent et lui disent :

– Ta maison est trop petite !

Il leur répond :

– Vous dites que ma maison est trop petite, mais je serais content si je pouvais un jour la remplir de vrais amis.

J. What happens to the children and their mother at the end of the story? Is the ending fair to everyone? See answers below.

Le clou de Djeha

K. Why does Djeha have to sell his house? What part of it does he not sell? See answers below.

L. What does Djeha want to hang in the house? What problem does this cause? See answers below.

M. Use context to figure out the meanings of these words:

N. What decision does the **cadi** make? Does the decision seem fair to you? How do you think that a different cultural perspective on bargaining and deal-making affect the decision? See answers below.

La petite maison See answers below

O. What is the message of this little story? How does your knowledge of Moroccan culture help you better understand its point?

P. Which of the three stories do you like best? Why? Are any of the stories similar to ones you know?

Answers

J They are reunited and live happily with the king; Yes, within the historical and cultural context of the story. However, according to modern standards, the youngest sister was not treated fairly because she was subjected to a punishment that she didn't deserve.

K He needs money; a nail

L a dead horse; It smells bad and will ruin the buyer's wedding party.

N The *cadi* decides that since the nail belongs to Djeha, he can hang what he wants on it; Some students will find this fair and others unfair; In a culture that values bargaining skills, Djeha's cunning would be admired.

O It emphasizes how difficult it is to find true friends. Moroccan culture places a high value on friendship.

The stories you just read deal with how people relate to each other. In this activity, you'll write your own story of how people relate to each other, in either a positive or a negative way.

Une histoire d'attitude

Maintenant, c'est à toi d'écrire une histoire où tu expliques comment, à ton avis, les gens devraient se comporter les uns envers les autres.

A. Préparation

D'abord, pense à la façon dont les gens agissent les uns envers les autres.
1. Fais un tableau pour organiser tes idées clairement.
   a. Divise ton tableau en deux colonnes : *Positive* et *Negative*.
   b. Remplis chaque colonne avec des choses que les gens font souvent, comme, par exemple, *Lying* ou *Being honest*.
   c. Examine ton tableau. Choisis quelque chose que tu voudrais mettre en valeur dans ton histoire.
2. Imagine le scénario de ton histoire.
   a. Qui est ton personnage principal? Quelle est son attitude?
   b. Quelles vont être les conséquences des actions du personnage principal sur les autres personnages?
   c. Est-ce que le personnage principal va être récompensé pour ses bonnes actions ou bien est-ce qu'il sera puni pour ses mauvaises actions?
3. Esquisse *(Outline)* les événements principaux de ton histoire.

B. Rédaction

Maintenant, fais un brouillon de ton histoire. N'oublie pas...
1. de décrire en détails le comportement de ton personnage principal.
2. d'expliquer les conséquences que ses actions ont sur les autres.
3. de bien montrer le rapport entre l'attitude du personnage principal et la fin de ton histoire.

C. Evaluation

1. Lis ton histoire à ton/ta camarade. Réfléchissez aux questions suivantes.
   a. Est-ce que l'histoire est claire? Est-ce qu'elle suit un ordre logique?
   b. Est-ce que c'est une histoire intéressante? Est-ce que tu pourrais ajouter des détails pour la rendre plus vivante?
2. Corrige les fautes d'orthographe, de grammaire et de vocabulaire.
3. Ecris la version finale de ton histoire.

DE BONS CONSEILS
No matter what the topic or purpose for writing, a writer must organize his or her ideas in a logical way. Many writers find graphic devices to be useful tools for organizing ideas. Time lines, charts, and diagrams are all examples of graphic devices that can help writers to visualize their ideas and clarify their thinking. The type of graphic device you choose will depend on what you're writing about. For example, a time line depicts a chronological progression of events, a comparison-and-contrast chart shows how two things are similar and different, and a flow chart shows the different steps involved in a process. When starting out on a writing task, try using a graphic device appropriate to your topic to help you organize your thoughts.

cent cinquante-sept **157**

WRITING STRATEGY
Using graphic devices

 Portfolio

Written   You might want to have students include all their work for Parts A–C in their written portfolios. For portfolio information, see *Assessment Guide,* pages 2–13.

PREWRITING

Teaching Suggestions

A. 1. Do this activity as a class so students will have a broad range of behaviors from which to choose their topics. Have students include "pet peeve" behaviors and "I like it when . . . " behaviors.

A. 2. You might refer students to some fables or fairy tales *(The Fox and the Crow, Cinderella)* to help them decide how they want their own story to end. Have them discuss how the characters in each story behaved, and why.

 For Individual Needs

A. 3. Visual Learners Have students draw their outline as a timeline. Have them write a description of the main character at one end and how he or she is going to end up at the opposite end. Then, have them write in the main events that will effect this change.

WRITING

Teaching Suggestion

B. To help students focus, suggest they keep these three questions in mind as they write: **Comment est le personnage principal? Quelles sont les conséquences de ses actions? Quelle est la morale de l'histoire?**

POSTWRITING

Teaching Suggestion

C. After students read their stories to a partner, have them ask the partner the questions listed under the Teaching Suggestion for Activity B. If the partner has difficulty describing the main character or finding the moral of the story, the pair should look at the timeline or outline from Part A together and discuss ways to make the message clearer.

 For Individual Needs

C. Visual Learners   Have the writer's partner draw a timeline or chart of the events as he or she listens to the story. Then, they should compare this timeline to the one the writer made in Part A.

The **Mise en pratique** reviews and integrates all four skills and culture in preparation for the Chapter Test.

Video Wrap-up

VIDEO PROGRAM
Videocassette 1

You might want to use the *Video Program* as part of the chapter review. See the *Video Guide* for teaching suggestions and activity masters.

For Individual Needs

1 Slower Pace Have students copy the choices onto a separate sheet of paper. Then, play the recording and have students check off each suggestion they hear. Play the recording a second time and have students mark a + next to the suggestions that Martin accepts. Play the recording a third time and have students answer questions 3 and 4.

1 Challenge Have students close their books. Tell them to listen for and write down the activities Ali suggests and the one he and Martin decide on. Then, play the recording. You might offer a point for each correct activity that students wrote down and two points for correctly identifying the activity the boys decide to do.

Language Note

Students might want to know the following terms from the brochure: **fripes** *(used clothing)*; **couronné** *(crowned, topped)*; **lanternon** *(lantern, decorative ornament)*; **nef** *(nave)*; **cèdre doré** *(gilded cedar)*.

MISE EN PRATIQUE

1 Martin vient de trouver un nouvel ami, Ali, à Marrakech. Ecoute leur conversation et réponds aux questions suivantes.

1. Lesquelles des activités suivantes est-ce qu'Ali propose à Martin? b, d, e

   a. d'aller au souk el-Kebir

   b. de déjeuner chez lui

   c. de prendre un jus d'orange

   d. d'aller voir le palais de la Bahia

   e. d'aller à la place Jemaa-el-Fna

2. Lesquelles des suggestions d'Ali est-ce que Martin accepte? b, e

3. A quelle heure est-ce qu'ils se donnent rendez-vous? vers huit heures

4. Où est-ce qu'ils se retrouvent? c

   a. sur la place Jemaa-el-Fna   **b.** au palais de la Bahia   **c.** sur la place de Bâb Fteuh

Le guide du ROUTARD MAROC

La place Jemaa-el-Fna : Le matin, Jemaa-el-Fna est un immense marché. Cela va des délicieux jus d'orange pressés, aux épices et aux herbes médicinales, en passant par les écrivains publics à l'ombre de leur parapluie noir, et les diseuses de bonne aventure. Puis, peu à peu les vendeurs d'eau font leur apparition. Quand la chaleur se fait moins forte, les principaux acteurs entrent en scène : charmeurs de serpents au son de leur flûte, danseurs gnaouas tournant comme des derviches au son des tambourins, vendeurs de fripes étalant leur frusques sur le sol, restaurants ambulants avec roulante et brasero. Les pickpockets sont à la fête, principalement autour des conteurs qui attirent grand nombre de badauds.

Les souks : Pénétrer seul dans les souks relève de l'exploit, car rares sont ceux qui parviennent à échapper aux guides insistants. Voici quelques conseils :
- Suivre un groupe de touristes et faire semblant d'être avec eux, du moins pour les premiers mètres du parcours, les plus difficiles.
- Ne pas porter de T-shirts ou de sacs évoquant des marques connues de voyagistes. Sinon, vous êtes sûr d'être repéré immédiatement.

Le minaret de la Koutoubia : la Tour Eiffel locale. Tout le monde le connaît et il sert de point de repère. Son décor est différent sur chaque face. Sa tour, aussi haute que celles de Notre-Dame de Paris, est couronnée d'un lanternon surmonté de quatre boules dorées. La légende voudrait nous faire croire qu'elles sont d'or pur et que l'influence des planètes leur permet de tenir en équilibre !

La mosquée de la kasbah : se repère aisément à son minaret aux entrelacs de couleur turquoise qui se détachent du ciel. Vous ne pourrez rien voir d'autre puisque la mosquée, dont la salle de prière ne comprend pas moins de onze nefs, est réservée aux musulmans.

Les tombeaux saadiens : La visite est libre mais payante. Ouvert de 8h30 à 12h et de 14h30 à 17h30 ou 18h. Fermé le mardi. Joli mausolée de Moulay Ahmed el-Mansour, mort de la peste à Fès en 1603, et qui repose, entouré de ses fils, sous une coupole de cèdre doré que supportent douze colonnes de marbre de Carrare. Le jardin est un havre de paix.

Le palais de la Bahia : Visite, obligatoirement accompagnée d'un guide, de 8h30 à 12h et de 14h30 à 18h. Ces horaires peuvent toutefois varier selon la saison. Construite vers 1880, cette riche demeure princière est un chef-d'œuvre de l'art marocain. Sur plus de 8 ha, des appartements superbement décorés débouchent sur des patios fleuris.

A voir aussi : *Le souk des Teinturiers, le souk Chouari (bois), le souk du Cuivre, le souk Smata (cuir), le souk des Bijoutiers, le souk el-Kebir (cuir), le souk Zrabia (caftans, tapis), les kissarias (vêtements, étoffes).*

158 *cent cinquante-huit*   CHAPITRE 6   Ma famille, mes copains et moi

---

Culture Note

The **place Jemaa-el-Fna** is a centrally located square in Marrakesh. In the evening, snake charmers, acrobats, trained monkeys, boy dancers, musicians, and storytellers fill the square. The acrobats, who are primarily from Tazeroulat, often perform in European circuses. Among the music groups are the **Aissaoua,** who play instruments **(ghaitahs)** that resemble oboes, and the Andalusian-sounding string groups, who play fiddles and lute-like instruments called **ouds.**

2 Lis ces extraits d'un guide français sur ce qu'on peut voir à Marrakech et réponds aux questions suivantes. See answers below.

1. What are some things you might see if you visit the **place Jemaa-el-Fna?** What should you be aware of?

2. What kind of souks could you visit? What problem might you run into when going into this area? What does the guidebook suggest you do?

3. With what monument could you compare the **minaret de la Koutoubia?** Why?

4. What can you see at the **tombeaux saadiens?** Is it free?

5. Which of the sites is a masterpiece of Moroccan art? Do you need a guide?

 3 A Marrakech, tu as rencontré quelqu'un avec qui tu voudrais faire un tour de la ville. Propose-lui de visiter des endroits qui sont mentionnés dans le guide. Il/Elle va aussi faire des suggestions. Décidez ensemble de ce que vous allez faire pendant votre séjour. N'oubliez pas de fixer les jours, les heures et les endroits où vous allez vous rencontrer.

 4 Imagine une situation où ton/ta meilleur(e) ami(e) a fait quelque chose qui t'a rendu(e) furieux (-euse). Vous vous disputez. Enfin, il/elle s'excuse. Comme il/elle est vraiment désolé(e), tu acceptes ses excuses.

 **5** Ton correspondant marocain vient bientôt passer une année aux Etats-Unis. Il voudrait savoir si les Américains sont aussi accueillants que les Marocains. Ecris-lui une lettre où tu lui expliques comment on accueille les gens dans la région où tu habites.

6

J E U   D E   R O L E

You're going to a cousin's wedding. Act out the following scenes with classmates.

- When you arrive at your cousin's house, his family greets you and tries to make you feel at home.

- The night before the wedding, your cousin's fiancée shows up looking angry. They have a quarrel. They make up, however, and apologize to each other and to you.

- On the day of the wedding, there are some family members attending whom you don't know. Your cousin tells you who they are and introduces you.

Félicitations pour votre mariage

Answers

2 1. *Possible answers:* public scribes, water vendors, snake charmers, dancers, storytellers; pickpockets

2. *Souks:* dyed goods, wood, copper, leather, jewelry, caftans, carpets, clothes, fabric; self-appointed guides; attach yourself to a group of tourists, avoid dressing like a tourist.

3. the Eiffel Tower, The minaret is a landmark recognized by all.

4. the tomb of Moulay Ahmed el-Mansour and his sons; No.

5. le palais de la Bahia; Yes.

Teaching Suggestion

2 You might also ask students the following questions: **Qu'est-ce qu'on peut acheter à la place Jemaa-el-Fna le matin?** (du jus d'orange, des épices et des herbes médicinales) **Comment est le minaret de la Koutoubia?** (son décor est différent sur chaque face) **Est-ce que les touristes peuvent entrer dans la mosquée de la kasbah?** (non) **Quand est-ce que les tombeaux saadiens sont ouverts?** (du 8h30 à 12h et de 14h30 à 17h30 ou 18h) **Le palais de la Bahia a été construit en quelle année?** (vers 1880)

Additional Practice

2 Type a list of descriptions of the various sites and have students work in pairs to identify each one. For example, you might write

(1) **Son minaret est de couleur turquoise.**
(2) **On peut y acheter des tapis.**
(3) **Son lanternon est surmonté de quatre boules dorées.**
(4) **On joue du tambourin là-bas.**

As an alternative, you might read the descriptions aloud and have the first student to raise his or her hand give the answer.

Teaching Suggestions

3 Have students present their dialogues to the class.

4 Remind students that this situation should be imaginary.

 Portfolio

5 Written This activity is appropriate for students' written portfolios. For portfolio suggestions, see *Assessment Guide,* page 19.

This page is intended to help students prepare for the test. It is a brief checklist of the major points covered in the chapter. The students should be reminded that this is only a checklist and does not necessarily include everything that will appear on the test.

♜ Game

RÉPONSE-QUESTION This game is played like Jeopardy®. Create a 5 X 5 grid on a transparency. Across the top, label the columns A through E. Label the horizontal rows 100 through 500. In each square, write the answer to one of the questions in **Que sais-je?** Cover each of the squares with a small adhesive note. Then, form two teams. The first player from the first team calls out a letter and a point value (A, 100). Uncover that square. The player has ten seconds to supply an appropriate stimulus to evoke the response written in the square. For example, if **C'est gentil, mais j'ai un rendez-vous** were written in the square, a correct question would be *How would you refuse a suggestion?* If the player's question is correct, his team earns the appropriate point value, and the next player from the same team takes a turn. If the player responds incorrectly, the opposing team has a chance to suggest a correct question, win the points, and continue playing by calling out a letter and point value.

QUE SAIS-JE?

Can you use what you've learned in this chapter?

Can you make, accept, and refuse suggestions? p.141

1 How would you suggest the following activities to a friend? See answers below.

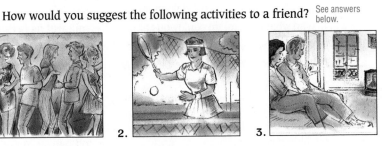

1.   2.   3.

2 How would you accept the suggestions in number 1?
Possible answers: Ce serait sympa. Oui, ça me plairait beaucoup. Si, j'aimerais bien.

3 How would you refuse the suggestions in number 1? *Possible answers:* Impossible, je suis pris(e). J'aimerais bien mais je n'ai pas le temps. C'est gentil, mais j'ai un rendez-vous.

Can you make arrangements? p.141

4 You and your friend have decided to do one of the activities pictured above. What would you say to make the necessary arrangements? See answers below.

Can you make and accept apologies? p.143

5 You've just broken your best friend's CD player. How do you apologize? *Possible answers:* Je m'excuse. Je suis vraiment désolé(e). Pardonne-moi. Je m'en veux d'avoir fait cela.

6 How would you accept the apology in number 5? See answers below.

Can you show and respond to hospitality? p.149

7 What would you say to your guests when . . . See answers below.
 a. they've just arrived at your home?
 b. you've taken their coats and they're standing inside the doorway?
 c. you'd like to offer them something to eat or drink?

8 How would you respond as a guest in each of the situations in number 7? See answers below.

Can you express and respond to thanks? p.149

9 How would you thank these people? Possible answers:
 a. A good friend lends you a new CD. Je te remercie. C'est vraiment très gentil de ta part.
 b. A stranger stops to help pick up some things you've dropped.
 Merci bien/infiniment/mille fois.

10 How would you respond if you were the people in number 9?
Possible answers: **a.** De rien. Je t'en prie.   **b.** (Il n'y a) pas de quoi. C'est tout à fait normal.

Can you quarrel? p.152

11 What would you say in the following situations? See answers below.
 a. Your sister is annoying you while you try to do your homework.
 b. You get in trouble for something your classmate did.
 c. Your little brother enters your room and starts looking through your things.

160 *cent soixante*   CHAPITRE 6   Ma famille, mes copains et moi

Possible answers
1 1. Ça t'intéresse d'aller danser?
 2. Ça te plairait de jouer au tennis?
 3. Tu ne voudrais pas regarder la télé?
4 Comment est-ce qu'on fait? Quand/Où est-ce qu'on se retrouve? A quelle heure est-ce qu'on se donne rendez-vous?
6 Ce n'est pas grave. Ça ne fait rien. Il n'y a pas de mal. Ne t'inquiète pas. Ça arrive à tout le monde.
7 1. Entrez, je vous en prie. Ça me fait plaisir de vous voir. Donnez-moi votre manteau.
 2. Mettez-vous à l'aise. Asseyez-vous.
 3. Je vous sers quelque chose? Qu'est-ce que je peux vous offrir?
8 1. Merci. Moi aussi. Vous êtes bien aimable.
 2. C'est gentil.
 3. Je prendrais bien... ; Vous auriez...?
11 1. Tu m'énerves, à la fin! Tu es vraiment casse-pieds! Tu me prends la tête!
 2. C'est toujours moi qui prends!
 3. Casse-toi!

PREMIERE ETAPE

Making, accepting, and refusing suggestions

Ça t'intéresse de... ?   *Would you be interested in . . .?*
Ça te plairait de... ?   *Would you like to . . .?*
Tu ne voudrais pas... ?   *Wouldn't you like to . . .?*
Ce serait sympa.   *That would be nice.*
Ça me plairait beaucoup.   *I'd like that a lot.*

C'est gentil, mais j'ai un rendez-vous.   *That's nice of you, but I've got an appointment.*

Making arrangements

Comment est-ce qu'on fait?   *How should we work this out?*
Quand est-ce qu'on se revoit?   *When are we getting together?*
Où est-ce qu'on se retrouve?   *Where are we meeting?*
A quelle heure est-ce qu'on se donne rendez-vous?   *What time are we meeting?*

Making and accepting apologies

Je m'excuse de...   *I'm sorry for . . .*
Pardonne-moi de...   *Pardon me for . . .*
Je m'en veux de...   *I feel bad that . . .*
Ça arrive à tout le monde.   *It happens to everybody.*

DEUXIEME ETAPE

Showing and responding to hospitality

Entrez, je vous en prie.   *Come in, please.*
Ça me fait plaisir de vous voir.   *I'm happy to see you.*
Donnez-moi votre manteau.   *Give me your coat.*
Mettez-vous à l'aise.   *Make yourself comfortable.*
Asseyez-vous.   *Sit down.*
Vous êtes bien aimable.   *That's kind of you.*
Je vous sers quelque chose?   *Can I offer you something?*
Qu'est-ce que je peux vous offrir?   *What can I offer you?*
Je prendrais bien...   *I'd like some . . .*
Vous auriez... ?   *Would you have . . . ?*

Expressing and responding to thanks

Merci bien/infiniment/mille fois.   *Thank you very much.*
Je vous remercie.   *Thank you.*
C'est vraiment très gentil de votre part.   *That's very nice of you.*
De rien.   *You're welcome.*

Je vous en prie.   *You're very welcome.*
(Il n'y a) pas de quoi.   *It's nothing.*
C'est tout à fait normal.   *You don't have to thank me.*

Family relationships

l'aîné(e)   *the oldest child*
l'arrière-grand-mère   *great-grandmother*
l'arrière-grand-père   *great-grandfather*
le/la benjamin(e)   *the youngest child*
le/la cadet(te)   *the younger child*
la femme   *wife*
les jumeaux(-elles)   *twins*
le mari   *husband*
le neveu   *nephew*
la nièce   *niece*
la petite-fille   *granddaughter*
le petit-fils   *grandson*
célibataire   *single*
divorcé(e)   *divorced*
marié(e)   *married*
mort(e)   *dead*
veuf(-ve)   *widowed*

Quarreling

Rapporteur (-euse)!   *Tattletale!*
Pleurnicheur (-euse)!   *Crybaby!*
Tricheur (-euse)!   *Cheater!*
Tu es bête comme tes pieds!   *You're so stupid!*
Tu m'énerves, à la fin!   *You're bugging me to death!*
Tu es vraiment casse-pieds!   *You're such a pain!*
Tu me prends la tête!   *You're driving me crazy!*
Oh, ça va, hein?   *Oh, cut it out!*
Arrête!   *Stop!*
Ça suffit!   *That's enough!*
Tu le fais exprès?   *Are you doing that on purpose?*
Mêle-toi de tes oignons!   *Mind your own business!*
Fiche-moi la paix!   *Leave me alone!*
Casse-toi!   *Get out of here!*
Tant pis pour toi!   *Tough!*
Ferme-la!   *Shut up!*
C'est toujours la même chose!   *It's always the same!*
C'est lui/elle qui a commencé!   *He/She started it!*
Il/Elle m'a traité(e) de... !   *He/She called me a . . . !*
C'est toujours moi qui prends!   *I'm always the one who gets blamed!*

Teaching Suggestions

• Have students make flash-cards for the vocabulary expressions. Encourage them to review with a partner by showing the French or English side of the flash-card to a partner, who gives the equivalent word or expression and uses it in a logical sentence.
• Have students write the words for family relationships in two columns, those that refer to males in one and those that refer to females in the other. They might also add other family vocabulary they've already learned to these lists.

CHAPTER 6 ASSESSMENT

CHAPTER TEST

• *Chapter Teaching Resources, Book 2,* pp. 81–86
• *Assessment Guide,* Speaking Test, p. 30
• *Assessment Items, Audiocassette 7B Audio CD 6*

TEST GENERATOR, CHAPTER 6

ALTERNATIVE ASSESSMENT

Performance Assessment

You might want to use the **Jeu de rôle** (p. 159) as a cumulative performance assessment activity.

📁 **Portfolio Assessment**

• **Written:** Mise en pratique, Activity 5, *Pupil's Edition,* p. 159
  Assessment Guide, p. 19
• **Oral:** Activity 35, *Pupil's Edition,* p. 153
  Assessment Guide, p. 19

MIDTERM EXAM

• *Assessment Guide,* pp. 35–42
• *Assessment Items, Audiocassette 7B Audio CD 6*

Chapitre 7 : Un safari-photo
Chapter Overview

Mise en train pp. 164–166	**Un safari, ça se prépare!**		**Note Culturelle,** Wildlife in the Central African Republic, p. 166	

	FUNCTIONS	**GRAMMAR**	**CULTURE**	**RE-ENTRY**
Première étape pp. 167–173	• Making suppositions, p. 169 • Expressing doubt and certainty, p. 169 • Asking for and giving advice, p. 171	• Structures and their complements, p. 169 • Using the subjunctive, p. 172	• **Rencontre Culturelle,** Overview of the Central African Republic, p. 167 • **Note Culturelle,** Animal conservation in the Central African Republic, p. 171 • **Panorama Culturel,** Stereotypical impressions of francophone regions, p. 173	• The subjunctive • The rain forest • Travel items

Remise en train pp. 174–175	**Le safari, c'est l'aventure!**			

	FUNCTIONS	**GRAMMAR**	**CULTURE**	**RE-ENTRY**
Deuxième étape pp. 176–179	• Expressing astonishment, p. 177 • Cautioning someone, p. 178 • Expressing fear, p. 178 • Reassuring someone, p. 178 • Expressing relief, p. 178	Irregular subjunctive forms, p. 179		• Adjectives to describe animals • The conditional

Lisons! pp. 180–182	**Le cimetière des éléphants; La tortue et le léopard** **Reading Strategy:** Understanding linking words

Ecrivons! p. 183	**Une histoire d'animaux** **Writing Strategy:** Sequencing

Review pp. 184–187	• **Mise en pratique,** pp. 184–185 • **Que sais-je?** p. 186 • **Vocabulaire,** p. 187

Assessment Options	**Etape Quizzes**
	• *Chapter Teaching Resources, Book 2*
	  Première étape, Quiz 7-1, pp. 131–132
	  Deuxième étape, Quiz 7-2, pp. 133–134
	• *Assessment Items, Audiocassette 8A/Audio CD 7*
		Chapter Test
		• *Chapter Teaching Resources, Book 2,* pp. 135–140
		• *Assessment Guide,* Speaking Test, p. 31
		• *Assessment Items, Audiocassette 8A/Audio CD 7*
		
		Test Generator, Chapter 7

RESOURCES: Print	RESOURCES: Audiovisual
Practice and Activity Book, p. 73	Textbook Audiocassette 4A/Audio CD 7
Practice and Activity Book, pp. 74–77 *Grammar and Vocabulary Worksheets*, pp. 63–68 *Chapter Teaching Resources, Book 2* • Communicative Activity 7-1, pp. 112–113 • Teaching Transparency Master 7-1, pp. 116, 118 . . . . • Additional Listening Activities 7-1, 7-2, 7-3, pp. 119–120 . . . • Realia 7-1, pp. 123, 125 • Situation Cards 7-1, pp. 126–127 • Student Response Forms, pp. 128–130 • Quiz 7-1, pp. 131–132 . . . . *Video Guide*	Textbook Audiocassette 4A/Audio CD 7 *Teaching Transparency 7-1* *Additional Listening Activities, Audiocassette 10A/Audio CD 7* *Assessment Items, Audiocassette 8A/Audio CD 7* *Video Program, Videocassette 2*
Practice and Activity Book, p. 78	Textbook Audiocassette 4A/Audio CD 7
Practice and Activity Book, pp. 79–82 *Grammar and Vocabulary Worksheets*, pp. 69–72 *Chapter Teaching Resources, Book 2* • Communicative Activity 7-2, pp. 114–115 • Teaching Transparency Master 7-2, pp. 117, 118 . . . . • Additional Listening Activities 7-4, 7-5, 7-6, pp. 120–121 . . . • Realia 7-2, pp. 124, 125 • Situation Cards 7-2, 7-3, pp. 126–127 • Student Response Forms, pp. 128–130 • Quiz 7-2, pp. 133–134	Textbook Audiocassette 4A/Audio CD 7 *Teaching Transparency 7-2* *Additional Listening Activities, Audiocassette 10A/Audio CD 7* *Assessment Items, Audiocassette 8A/Audio CD 7*
Practice and Activity Book, p. 83	
Video Guide	*Video Program, Videocassette 2*

Alternative Assessment
- Performance Assessment
  Première étape, p. 172
  Deuxième étape, p. 179

- Portfolio Assessment
  Written: **Ecrivons!,** *Pupil's Edition,* p. 183
   Assessment Guide, p. 20
  Oral: **Mise en pratique, Jeu de rôle,** *Pupil's Edition,* p. 185
   Assessment Guide, p. 20

Chapitre 7 : Un safari-photo
Textbook Listening Activities Scripts

For Student Response Forms, see Chapter *Teaching Resources Book 2,* pp. 128–130.

Première étape

7 Ecoute! p. 168

1. — Oh, regarde les papillons! Il y en a tellement, et de toutes les couleurs!

2. — Je crois qu'il y a des animaux là-bas, derrière les herbes. Tu les vois?

3. — Chut! Les gazelles viennent boire au point d'eau. Ne fais pas de bruit. Tu vas leur faire peur.

4. — Elles sont immenses, ces chutes d'eau. Et qu'est-ce qu'elles sont bruyantes aussi!

5. — Attention! Tu vas tomber dans l'eau. On ne peut pas se baigner dans la rivière.

6. — Il faut rester dans la voiture. Même si tu ne vois pas d'animaux, il se peut qu'il en arrive un très vite. Et il y a aussi des serpents qu'on ne voit pas dans la brousse.

7. — Regarde les oiseaux! Et ces fleurs tropicales, elles sont vraiment belles, non? Comment elle s'appelle, celle-là?

Answers to Activity 7

1. forêt	5. forêt
2. savane	6. savane
3. savane	7. forêt
4. forêt	

9 Ecoute! p. 169

1. — Je suis sûr qu'il y a de beaux animaux là-bas.

2. — Mais je ne suis pas certain qu'on puisse voir les forêts.

3. — Je ne suis pas certain que la cuisine soit bonne.

4. — Je ne pense pas qu'on puisse se promener dans la savane.

5. — Mais je suis sûr qu'on verra des Pygmées.

6. — Ça m'étonnerait qu'il y ait de bonnes routes.

7. — Je ne suis pas sûr qu'on puisse boire l'eau.

Answers to Activity 9

1. certitude	5. certitude
2. doute	6. doute
3. doute	7. doute
4. doute	

12 Ecoute! p. 170

Salut, c'est Mathieu. Bientôt le grand départ! J'espère que tu n'as rien oublié. Pense à prendre ton caméscope. Emporte aussi trois cassettes. A mon avis, on n'en trouvera pas facilement là-bas. Moi, je prends mon appareil-photo et des pellicules. Au fait, est-ce que tu as pensé à prendre un chapeau? Emporte aussi de la crème solaire. Il va faire très chaud là-bas. Et n'oublie surtout pas ta gourde et ta trousse de premiers soins avec des pansements et un désinfectant. Au fait, est-ce que tu as acheté des jumelles? Bon! A jeudi à l'aéroport. Salut!

Answers to Activity 12

Possible answers: un caméscope, des cassettes, un chapeau, de la crème solaire, une gourde, une trousse de premiers soins, des pansements, un désinfectant, des jumelles

14 Ecoute! p. 171

— Ça me plairait de faire un safari en République centrafricaine. Mais je voulais savoir... est-ce qu'il y a des préparatifs à faire avant de partir?

— Oui, un peu, mais ce n'est pas bien difficile. D'abord, il est très important que vous vous fassiez vacciner contre la fièvre jaune et le choléra. Ensuite, il faut que vous consultiez un médecin car il est essentiel que vous suiviez un traitement contre le paludisme.

— Est-ce qu'il est nécessaire que j'obtienne un visa?

— Euh, non, mais il faut que vous ayez un passeport, bien sûr.

— Bon, ben, qu'est-ce qu'il faut que j'emporte?

— Eh bien, des vêtements légers, en coton de préférence.

— Est-ce qu'il est nécessaire d'emporter un manteau?

— Euh non. Mais prenez un pull pour la nuit.

— Et quoi d'autre?

— Euh... , voyons, il faut que vous emportiez de la lotion anti-moustique et que vous preniez une trousse de premiers soins avec pansements, désinfectant et comprimés pour purifier l'eau.

— Eh bien! Je vais plutôt aller faire du camping dans le sud de la France!

Answers to Activity 14

se faire vacciner, consulter un médecin, prendre son passeport, emporter de la lotion anti-moustique, emporter une trousse de premiers soins

*D*euxième étape

26 Ecoute! p. 177

1. — Oh dis donc! Regarde un peu! Qu'est-ce qu'elle est rapide, cette gazelle!

2. — Oh là là! Il fait chaud et j'ai soif. Quand est-ce qu'on retourne à l'hôtel?

3. — Est-ce qu'il y a des serpents? J'ai peur des serpents, tu sais.

4. — Qu'est-ce qu'elle est drôle, cette autruche.

5. — Ah non! Je n'en peux plus, moi! Ça fait trois heures qu'on les attend, les éléphants!

6. — Ouah! C'est fou comme elle est grande, cette girafe!

7. — Oh, tu as vu? Le lion est en train de tuer le gnou. Je ne peux pas regarder ça.

8. — Tu as vu comme il court vite, ce guépard?

9. — Oh là là! Je n'ai jamais vu un aussi gros éléphant.

10. — Tu vois les vautours, là-bas? C'est dégeu comme ils mangent les restes des animaux morts, non?

11. — Oh, c'est pas vrai! Qu'il est gros, ce rhinocéros. Je parie qu'il est vraiment méchant. Tu as vu sa corne?

Answers to Activity 26

1. exprime étonnement	7. n'exprime pas étonnement
2. n'exprime pas étonnement	8. exprime étonnement
3. n'exprime pas étonnement	9. exprime étonnement
4. exprime étonnement	10. n'exprime pas étonnement
5. n'exprime pas étonnement	11. exprime étonnement
6. exprime étonnement	

29 Ecoute! p. 178

a.

1. — Je vous signale qu'il ne faut pas sortir de la voiture.

2. — Faites gaffe! Il y a des scorpions. N'oubliez pas de regarder où vous marchez.

3. — Calmez-vous! Les éléphants sont gros, mais ils ont peur de vous.

4. — N'ayez pas peur. Les singes vont crier s'il y a un danger.

5. — Attention aux rhinocéros! Ils sont méchants!

6. — Méfiez-vous! Les hyènes ne sont pas grandes, mais elles sont vraiment méchantes!

7. — Pas de panique! Tu vois bien, il y a des antilopes. S'il y avait des lions, les antilopes les sentiraient.

8. — Ne bougez pas! Il y a un serpent derrière vous!

9. — Il serait plus prudent de faire attention aux mouvements des animaux.

10. — Ne vous en faites pas! Il n'y a pas de danger dans la jeep. On peut toujours accélérer.

b.

1. — J'ai très peur des animaux sauvages. Ils sont imprévisibles!

2. — Ouf! On a eu chaud! Tu as vu comme il était furieux, le rhinocéros?

3. — Oh! Il fait tellement noir! J'ai la frousse! Tu entends ces bruits? C'est un animal, tu crois?

4. — On a eu de la chance! Ça arrive souvent que les jeeps tombent en panne?

5. — J'ai peur que ce soit un scorpion. On peut mourir d'une piqûre de scorpion, non?

6. — Ouf! On l'a échappé belle! N'arrête pas la voiture la prochaine fois, d'accord?

Answers to Activity 29

a.

1. avertit	5. avertit	9. avertit
2. avertit	6. avertit	10. rassure
3. rassure	7. rassure	
4. rassure	8. avertit	

b.

1. peur	3. peur	5. peur
2. soulagement	4. soulagement	6. soulagement

*M*ise en pratique

3 p. 185

1. — Et voilà les chutes de Boali. Qu'est-ce qu'elles sont belles! On y a fait un pique-nique. Je n'avais jamais vu d'aussi grandes chutes d'eau. C'était merveilleux!

2. — Et là, c'est notre premier jour dans la brousse. Vous voyez les lions qui dorment? On y est restés deux heures. Ils n'ont pas bougé d'un pouce. C'était mortel.

3. — Là, c'est le jour où on est allés dans la forêt tropicale. On se promenait et tout d'un coup, juste devant nous, on a vu des Pygmées! Ouah! Imaginez un peu! On a même parlé avec eux. Qu'est-ce qu'ils étaient gentils!

4. — Oh ça, c'était le deuxième jour dans la savane. Vous voyez, il n'y avait pas d'animaux! On a attendu pendant des heures. Il faisait chaud. C'était pas amusant!

5. — Ça, c'est ma photo préférée de la forêt. Qu'est-ce qu'elle est belle, cette forêt! Il y avait des papillons partout! Ils étaient super grands! Je n'avais jamais vu de papillons aussi grands!

6. — Et là, c'est l'endroit où nous avons dormi. C'était vraiment horrible! Il y avait des fourmis, des araignées et beaucoup de moustiques. J'avais oublié ma lotion anti-moustique! Et en plus, il y avait des babouins qui arrêtaient pas de s'approcher de notre tente!

Answers to Mise en pratique Activity 3

a, c, e

Mon safari-photo en République centrafricaine
(Group Project)

ASSIGNMENT

Students will prepare a slide show of their photo safari in the Central African Republic, with a commentary on each slide. The "slides" will actually be transparencies that students draw and project.

MATERIALS

✂ **Students may need**
- Travel guides
- Encyclopedias
- Transparencies
- Colored pens for transparencies

SUGGESTED SEQUENCE

1. Have students use travel guides and encyclopedias to find out more about what they might see on a photo safari in the Central African Republic. They might also find out more about the animals they are "photographing." Encourage them to use the information in the Chapter Opener on pages 162–163, the **Mise en train** on pages 164–165, the **Rencontre Culturelle** on page 167, and the **Remise en train** on pages 174–175. They should also invent interesting incidents that will happen during the imaginary trip (a narrow escape from a lion, losing one's camera to the jaws of a crocodile, and so on).

2. Have groups decide what they will "photograph." They should give an account of the entire trip, including the preliminary packing and vaccinations, the plane or train ride there, the animals they see, and any exciting incidents or narrow escapes that occur during the trip.

3. Next, groups should draw their "slides" on transparencies.

4. Once students create the slides, they should write a brief commentary about each one, using the functions from the chapter. If students have difficulty drawing, you might have them trace illustrations from their book onto a transparency. You might have students assign two or three slides to each group member. The entire group edits the commentaries.

5. Students present their slide shows and tell the story of their trip to the class. Each group member should read part of the commentary. One member should be responsible for changing the slides during the presentation.

GRADING THE PROJECT

You might want to base students' grades on thoroughness of content, creativity of visuals, oral presentation, and accuracy of language use. You might also assign individual students a grade based on their individual effort and participation in the project.

Suggested Point Distribution (total = 100 points)

Content	30 points
Creativity of visuals	20 points
Oral presentation	15 points
Language use	15 points
Effort/participation	20 points

MOTS ENCHAINES

In this game, students will practice chapter vocabulary.

Procedure This game may be played by the whole class or in small groups. Assign one vocabulary word to each student. Tell students to write down their word and practice saying it. Then, have each student say his or her word aloud. Next, have students form a circle. If they are playing the game in small groups, have each group form a circle. Appoint a timekeeper within each group. Begin the game by having a student say a sentence that includes both his or her vocabulary word and a second vocabulary word. For example, if a student's word were **un serpent,** he or she might say **Tu as vu le serpent et le rhinocéros là-bas?** The student whose word is **le rhinocéros** continues the game by saying a sentence that includes his or her word and the word of another student. Students must say a logical sentence within five or ten seconds. The goal is to keep the game going as long as possible.

MOTS CROISES

In this game, students will practice chapter vocabulary.

Procedure Draw a 12 × 12 grid on a transparency. Form two or more teams. Have the first player from one team come to the front and write a vocabulary word anywhere on the grid, writing one letter in each square. That player's team wins one point for each letter in the word. For example, if the player wrote **papillon,** his or her team would win eight points. Then, a player from the next team writes a word on the grid. The new word must use one of the letters of a word already on the grid. The game continues until no more words can be added to the grid. The team with the most points wins.

Chapitre 7
Un safari-photo
pp. 162–187

*U*sing the Chapter Opener

 Video Program

Videocassette 2

Before you begin this chapter, you might want to preview the *Video Program* and consult the *Video Guide.* Suggestions for integrating the video into each chapter and activity masters for video selections can be found in the *Video Guide.*

Motivating Activity

Ask students what comes to mind when they think of an African safari, and if they've ever seen any movies set in Africa. Ask them what they would expect to see on a photo safari in Central Africa.

Teaching Suggestion

Have students recall what they already know about Africa. You might ask them to recall what they learned about Côte d'Ivoire in Levels 1 and 2, and what they learned about Senegal and Morocco in Level 3. Ask them what there is to see and do there. (**Qu'est-ce qu'il y a à voir et à faire là-bas?**)

Photo Flash!

① In this photo, a bridge made of tree branches provides passage over the Ubangi River. This river, surrounded by lush green vegetation, forms the border between the Central African Republic and Zaïre.

CHAPITRE

7
Un safari-photo

① La République centrafricaine, pays aux forêts tropicales et aux animaux sauvages

162 *cent soixante-deux*

Culture Notes

• The Ubangi River is a popular thoroughfare, on which nearly 80% of the Central African Republic's visitors are transported by boat. Two river boats from the Congo, **La Ville de Brazza** and **La Ville d'Impfondo**, regularly provide transportation along the river.
• Point out the butterflies at the bottom of this page. The wings of the Central African Republic's numerous species of butterflies are frequently made into colorful collages.

Geography Link

Have students locate **la République centrafricaine** on the map of Africa on page xxi in their book, or you might project *Map Transparency 2* (**L'Afrique francophone**). Re-enter *asking for and giving directions* by asking questions, such as **Où se trouve la République centrafricaine? C'est au nord ou au sud du Zaïre? L'Ethiopie est à l'est ou à l'ouest de la République centrafricaine?**

As-tu déjà vécu une aventure extraordinaire dans un pays étranger ou une région inconnue? Lucie et Joseph Zokoue, eux, sont allés en Afrique faire un safari-photo dans le pays de leurs ancêtres, la République centrafricaine. On peut y admirer de nombreux animaux sauvages au milieu de paysages spectaculaires. Viens avec nous voir la brousse africaine!

In this chapter you will learn

- to make suppositions; to express doubt and certainty; to ask for and give advice
- to express astonishment; to caution someone; to express fear; to reassure someone; to express relief

And you will

- listen to teenagers plan a safari
- read an African animal tale
- write a scene from a movie about an African safari
- find out about endangered African animals

② Est-ce qu'il est nécessaire qu'on se fasse vacciner?

③ Ouah! C'est fou comme il va vite, ce guépard!

cent soixante-trois 163

Focusing on Outcomes

Have students list expressions they've already learned that serve the functions listed on this page. (*making suppositions:* Je crois que... ; Je parie que... ; *expressing doubt and certainty:* C'est possible. Je ne crois pas; *asking for and giving advice:* Qu'est-ce que tu me conseilles? Tu devrais... ; *expressing astonishment:* C'est pas vrai; *cautioning:* Tu ne devrais pas... ; *expressing fear:* J'ai peur de... ; *reassuring someone:* Tu vas t'y faire. Ne t'en fais pas.) Then, have students match the photos to the outcomes. NOTE: You may want to use the video to support the objectives. The self-check activities in **Que sais-je?** on page 186 help students assess their achievement of the objectives.

Teaching Suggestion

Read aloud the introductory paragraph, or ask for a volunteer to read it. Then, reread aloud the second sentence of the paragraph (**Lucie et Joseph Zokoue, eux, sont allés en Afrique...**) and ask students which photo they would associate with this sentence (Photo 2). Repeat the process with the third and fourth sentences of the paragraph (Photos 3 and 1, respectively).

Thinking Critically

Drawing Inferences Have students tell what they would expect to see in the Central African Republic, based on the photos and objects on pages 162–163.

Culture Note

③ The cheetah, capable of attaining speeds of over 60 miles an hour, is the fastest land animal in the world. Characterized by a slim form and long legs, the cheetah's body is built for running at high speeds. Although they can still be seen in the open plains of southern, central, and eastern Africa, cheetahs are currently in danger of extinction.

Math Link

③ Have students calculate the cheetah's average speed in kilometers per hour by multiplying 60 by 1.6 (95 kilometers per hour). The cheetah usually weighs between 110 and 130 pounds. Have students calculate this weight range in kilograms by multiplying the weight in pounds by .45 (50–60 kilograms).

Summary

In **Un safari, ça se prépare!**, Lucie and Joseph try to convince their father to go on a photo safari in the Central African Republic. Once he is convinced, they make preparations for the trip. M. Zokoue calls the embassy to inquire about vaccinations. The employee informs him that a shot for yellow fever is required before entering the country. In the next scene, the family is packing for the trip. They pack sweaters, mosquito repellent, and a first-aid kit, among other items.

Motivating Activity

From their knowledge of the climate and conditions in Africa and from the photos on this page, have students tell what they would need to take on a photo safari to the Central African Republic.

Presentation

Play the recording and tell students to listen for the following: the names of three animals, a disease, and three items to pack for a trip. Then, play the recording again. Pause after the second scene to ask **Pourquoi est-ce que Lucie et Joseph veulent aller faire un safari-photo?** (leur grand-père est né là-bas, pour voir les animaux) Play the third scene and ask **Pourquoi est-ce que M. Zokoue hésite à y aller?** (C'est cher et dangereux.) After the last scene, ask **Qu'est-ce qu'il faut faire avant de partir en République centrafricaine?** (se faire vacciner) Then, have groups of three read the dialogue together.

Mise en train

Un safari, ça se prépare!

1 LUCIE   Oh dis donc! Regarde les éléphants!

JOSEPH   Oh, oui! Ils sont super! Ça serait chouette d'aller en Afrique. On verrait des tas d'animaux sauvages.

LUCIE   Je parie qu'il y a des lions et des tigres partout!

JOSEPH   Tu sais, je ne crois pas qu'il y ait de tigres en Afrique.

LUCIE   Ah, bon... Alors, papa, on va en Afrique pour les vacances? On pourrait faire un safari.

2 M. ZOKOUE   Ah! Bravo! Ma fille veut tuer des éléphants maintenant!

LUCIE   Mais non, papa! Un safari-photo, bien sûr! Les safaris, c'est illégal! Et puis, tu sais bien que je déteste qu'on tue les animaux!

L'éléphant va boire. Avec sa trompe, il pompe 100 litres d'eau par jour.

Pour se cacher dans la savane, les zèbres ont des rayures noires et la girafe, des taches brunes.

3 JOSEPH   Du calme, du calme. On a compris.

M. ZOKOUE   De toute façon, ça coûte très cher, les safaris.

LUCIE   Oh, allez, quoi!

M. ZOKOUE   Et puis, ça doit être très dangereux...

JOSEPH   Mais non, tout le monde va en Afrique maintenant. Et puis, ça serait chouette d'aller en République centrafricaine puisque c'est là où Pépé est né.

LUCIE   Tu imagines si on pouvait aller dans son village pour voir comment c'est...

JOSEPH   Je me demande si on a encore de la famille là-bas... Tu crois qu'ils mangent des araignées?

LUCIE   Ça doit être cool!

M. ZOKOUE   Bon, bon... on verra.

164   *cent soixante-quatre*   CHAPITRE 7   Un safari-photo

RESOURCES FOR MISE EN TRAIN

Textbook Audiocassette 4A/Audio CD 7
Practice and Activity Book, p. 73

Language Notes

• Tell students that **Pépé**, used in the third scene, is a familiar term for *grandfather*.

• **Le paludisme**, which is mentioned on page 165, is *malaria*, a common disease in tropical African countries that is characterized by severe chills and high fever. Female mosquitos carry the disease and transmit it through their bites.

4 Lucie et Joseph ont persuadé leur père d'aller en République centrafricaine. Il est maintenant nécessaire qu'ils organisent leur voyage.

M. ZOKOUE Bon. Si on veut faire un safari cette année, il faut que je prenne les billets maintenant. Ça vous dit toujours?

LUCIE Bien sûr que ça me dit!

M. ZOKOUE Et toi, Joseph?

JOSEPH Moi aussi... mais...

M. ZOKOUE Qu'est-ce qu'il y a?

JOSEPH Euh, je me demande s'il y aura des moustiques.

LUCIE Oh, ils ne vont pas te manger, hein?

M. ZOKOUE Joseph a raison. Les moustiques sont féroces en Afrique. Ils peuvent transmettre des maladies. Il faudra bien se protéger.

JOSEPH Tu vois!

M. ZOKOUE Ah! Au fait, je dois appeler l'ambassade pour savoir ce qu'on doit faire avant de partir.

5 M. ZOKOUE Bonjour madame, je pars en République centrafricaine pour les vacances.

L'EMPLOYEE Oui?

M. ZOKOUE Quelles sont les vaccinations obligatoires?

L'EMPLOYEE Eh bien, il faut que vous vous fassiez vacciner contre la fièvre jaune.

M. ZOKOUE Est-ce qu'il faut un traitement particulier pour le paludisme?

L'EMPLOYEE Oui, pour ça vous devriez consulter un médecin.

M. ZOKOUE Merci beaucoup. Au revoir.

LUCIE Alors, qu'est-ce qu'elle a dit? On doit se faire vacciner?

M. ZOKOUE Oui, c'est obligatoire.

JOSEPH Quoi! Une piqûre!

M. ZOKOUE J'ai bien peur que ce soit nécessaire.

6 JOSEPH Ah non, alors!

LUCIE Quel trouillard, je t'assure!

M. ZOKOUE Ecoutez, c'est simple, les enfants. Pas de piqûre, pas de safari!

7 Enfin, avant de partir, il faut que M. Zokoue et ses enfants fassent leurs valises.

JOSEPH Tu crois que je devrais prendre des cassettes?

M. ZOKOUE Je ne crois pas que ce soit la peine. Tu n'auras pas le temps de les écouter. Mais n'oublie pas ton appareil-photo.

LUCIE Tu seras trop occupé à tuer les moustiques pour écouter de la musique.

JOSEPH Oh, arrête! On ne te demande rien! Papa, tu penses que je prends un pull?

M. ZOKOUE Oui, il vaut mieux. Tu en auras peut-être besoin. Il peut faire froid la nuit.

LUCIE Est-ce qu'on emporte de la crème solaire?

M. ZOKOUE Bien sûr. Il va faire très chaud. Il faut aussi qu'on achète de la lotion anti-moustique. Surtout, c'est très important qu'on emporte une trousse de premiers soins avec des pansements, un désinfectant et des comprimés pour purifier l'eau.

LUCIE Eh ben! C'est vraiment l'aventure!

cent soixante-cinq **165**

Culture Notes

• Although yellow fever is easily prevented by vaccination, it is still common in many African countries. Most countries in Central Africa require vaccination against the disease as a condition for entry. Visitors are also advised to take pre-travel preventive measures against cholera, typhoid, and hepatitis.

• Vistors to Central Africa need water purification tablets (**des comprimés pour purifier l'eau**) when traveling in Central Africa. These tablets are often made with chlorine, iodine, or tincture of iodine.

Science Link

Have volunteers research and explain to the class the chemical processes that occur when purifying water with chlorine or iodine.

CHAPITRE 7

Teaching Suggestion

Have students describe the attitudes of Lucie, Joseph, and M. Zokoue (enthusiastic, squeamish, cautious), using examples from the **Mise en train** to support their ideas. Ask students how they would feel if they were going on a photo safari in Africa.

For Individual Needs

Kinesthetic Learners
Choose several sentences from the **Mise en train** that could easily be acted out. (**Il peut faire froid la nuit. Quoi! Une piqûre! Regarde les éléphants!**) Write the sentences on a transparency and project them. Then, write each sentence on an index card and distribute the cards to students. Have students act out their sentence and have the class call out the sentence they think is being acted out. The first student to say the appropriate sentence takes the next turn. As each sentence is guessed, check it off on the transparency. Continue until all the sentences have been mimed.

Game

Form six small groups. Assign each group a section of the conversation. Groups write several comprehension questions about their section. After the questions are written, each member of the group should edit them. Then, collect all the questions and divide the class into two teams. Players take turns trying to answer the questions. For each correct answer, the team wins a point. The team with the most points wins.

CHAPITRE 7   MISE EN TRAIN   165

Teaching Suggestion

2 As an alternative, rewrite these sentences on a transparency, omitting key words, such as **tigres, dangereux, moustiques, trouillard, piqûre.** List the omitted words below the sentences and have students complete the sentences with the appropriate words.

◈ For Individual Needs

2 Auditory Learners Have partners take turns reading the quotes aloud and identifying the speaker.

3 Slower Pace On a transparency, list the reasons why the Zokoue are taking the various items with them, and have students match the reasons with the items listed in the word box to the right of this activity.

4 Challenge Once students have arranged the events in the proper order, have them write an account of the story as if they were telling it to a friend, using the **passé composé** and the **imparfait.** For #4, give students the word **aurait.**

5 Auditory Learners Play the recording, pausing it each time one of the functional expressions is used to ask students which function is represented by that expression. For example, if you paused the recording after Lucie said **Oh, dis donc! Regarde les éléphants!**, students would answer *to point out something.*

1 Tu as compris?

1. Where is the Zokoue family going for vacation? Central African Republic
2. What are they going to do there? go on a photo safari
3. Why does M. Zokoue hesitate to go? It's expensive and dangerous.
4. What reasons do Lucie and Joseph give to persuade their father to go?
5. What do they have to do before leaving? 4. A lot of people go to Africa. Their grandfather was born there.
   buy the tickets, get vaccinations, pack

2 Qui dit quoi?

Est-ce que c'est Lucie, Joseph ou M. Zokoue qui parle?

1. «Je parie qu'il y a des lions et des tigres partout!» Lucie
2. «De toute façon, ça coûte très cher, les safaris. Et puis, ça doit être très dangereux.» M. Zokoue
3. «Euh, je me demande s'il y aura des moustiques.» Joseph
4. «Quel trouillard, je t'assure!» Lucie
5. «Ecoutez, c'est simple. Pas de piqûre, pas de safari!» M. Zokoue

3 Qu'est-ce qu'on emporte?

D'après **Un safari, ça se prépare!**, lesquels de ces objets est-ce que les Zokoue vont emporter en Afrique? Pourquoi? See answers below.

> une robe   un pull   des cassettes
> de la lotion anti-moustique
> de la crème solaire   des bottes
> des comprimés   des pansements
> de l'aspirine   un appareil-photo

4 Mets en ordre

Mets ces phrases dans l'ordre d'après **Un safari, ça se prépare!** 3, 1, 4, 5, 6, 2

1. Lucie et Joseph proposent de passer les vacances en République centrafricaine.
2. Les Zokoue font leurs valises.
3. Lucie et Joseph lisent un article sur l'Afrique.
4. Joseph se demande s'il y aura des moustiques.
5. M. Zokoue téléphone à l'ambassade.
6. Joseph proteste à l'idée de se faire vacciner.

5 Cherche les expressions

What does Lucie, Joseph, or M. Zokoue say to . . . See answers below.

1. point out something?
2. make a supposition?
3. express doubt?
4. make a strong objection?
5. reassure someone?
6. express necessity?
7. ask for advice?
8. give advice?

6 Et maintenant, à toi

Est-ce que tu aimerais faire un safari-photo? Pourquoi ou pourquoi pas? Quels animaux est-ce que tu aimerais voir?

NOTE CULTURELLE

The Central African Republic has a great variety of wildlife. In the northern savannah regions you will see lions, leopards, buffalo, elephants, hyenas and antelope. The rain forests in the south are one of the few gorilla habitats left in Africa. Here you will also find large populations of chimpanzees, monkeys, and giant squirrels. Along the rivers there are hippopotamuses, crocodiles and rhinoceroses. Many species of birds, snakes, bats, and butterflies can be found throughout the country. The Central African Republic is a true zoologist's paradise!

166 *cent soixante-six*   CHAPITRE 7   Un safari-photo

Answers

3 *Un pull:* Il peut faire froid la nuit. *De la lotion anti-moustique:* Les moustiques sont féroces et ils peuvent transmettre des maladies. *De la crème solaire:* Il va faire très chaud. *Des pansements, des comprimés:* pour purifier l'eau. *Un appareil-photo:* C'est un safari-photo.

5 1. Regarde...
2. Je parie que... ; Ça doit être...
3. ... je ne crois pas que...
4. Mais non... ; Ah non, alors! Je déteste que...

5. Du calme, du calme.
6. ... il faut que... ; Il faudra bien... ; ... je dois... ; ... vous devriez... ; J'ai bien peur que ça soit nécessaire. C'est très important que...
7. Est-ce qu'il faut... ? Tu crois que je devrais... ? ... tu penses que je prends... ? Est-ce qu'on emporte... ?
8. ... il faut que vous... ; Je ne crois pas que ce soit la peine. ... il vaut mieux. Il faut qu'on... ; ... c'est important qu'on...

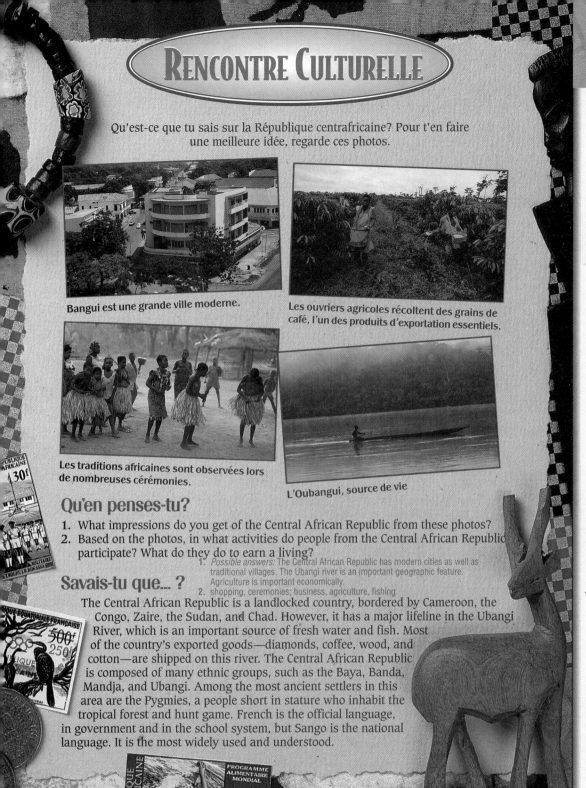

RENCONTRE CULTURELLE

Qu'est-ce que tu sais sur la République centrafricaine? Pour t'en faire une meilleure idée, regarde ces photos.

Bangui est une grande ville moderne.

Les ouvriers agricoles récoltent des grains de café, l'un des produits d'exportation essentiels.

Les traditions africaines sont observées lors de nombreuses cérémonies.

L'Oubangui, source de vie

Qu'en penses-tu?

1. What impressions do you get of the Central African Republic from these photos?
2. Based on the photos, in what activities do people from the Central African Republic participate? What do they do to earn a living?

Possible answers: 1. The Central African Republic has modern cities as well as traditional villages. The Ubangi river is an important geographic feature. Agriculture is important economically.
2. shopping, ceremonies; business, agriculture, fishing

Savais-tu que... ?

The Central African Republic is a landlocked country, bordered by Cameroon, the Congo, Zaire, the Sudan, and Chad. However, it has a major lifeline in the Ubangi River, which is an important source of fresh water and fish. Most of the country's exported goods—diamonds, coffee, wood, and cotton—are shipped on this river. The Central African Republic is composed of many ethnic groups, such as the Baya, Banda, Mandja, and Ubangi. Among the most ancient settlers in this area are the Pygmies, a people short in stature who inhabit the tropical forest and hunt game. French is the official language, in government and in the school system, but Sango is the national language. It is the most widely used and understood.

History Link

The Central African Republic was granted its independence in 1960, after being a French colony for fifty years. Until that time, it was part of French Equatorial Africa and was known as **Oubangui-Chari.** The variety of ethnic groups in the country, as in other countries in Africa, is due to the migration of people from the coasts of Africa who fled the slave trade.

Language Note

Although French is the official language of the Central African Republic, **Sango** is the national language. The country is one of the few African countries whose diverse ethnic groups get along well, primarily because of the existence of this common language.

RENCONTRE CULTURELLE
CHAPITRE 7

Motivating Activity

The day before the presentation, ask students to find out one fact about the Central African Republic. The day of the presentation, have students share their findings. You might ask students for their reactions to the information.

Presentation

Have students read the photo captions and write down the cognates they find. Explain any words students don't understand. Then, have groups write an additional sentence for each caption. Have volunteers read their captions aloud. Finally, have partners read the paragraph under **Savais-tu que... ?**

Teaching Suggestion

Create a categorizing activity based on the **Savais-tu que... ?** Write the categories *The national language, The official language, Exports,* and *Ethnic groups* on the board and have students list the appropriate items under each one. *(French; Sango; diamonds, coffee, wood, cotton; Baya, Banda, Mandja, Ubangi)*

Culture Notes

• Bangui, the capital of the Central African Republic, is a major commercial and industrial center. It also houses the **Musée de Boganda,** which displays African musical instruments and Pygmy utensils.
• The Banda society is primarily agrarian. They raise corn, cassava, peanuts, and sweet potatoes.
• The Baya people identify themselves by clans. Although traditionally they have no official leaders, occasionally chiefs are elected to serve during specific conflicts.

Jump Start!

Have students write a five-sentence letter to a friend who is planning a trip to Africa. They should tell their friend what clothing to bring and what sites to see in various African countries (Côte d'Ivoire, Morocco, Senegal).

MOTIVATE

Ask students what they know about rain forests and what animals they would expect to see in one.

TEACH

Presentation

Vocabulaire Draw or find pictures of the vocabulary items. As you show them, ask questions, such as **Un papillon, c'est beau ou dangereux?** Then, hold up each picture and ask **C'est dans la forêt tropicale ou dans la savane?** Tape the pictures that belong in the forest on one side of the board and those that belong in the savanna on the other. Next, give examples of the vocabulary items, such as Woody Woodpecker, the Seine, or maple, and have students categorize each one. (**C'est un oiseau/une rivière/ un arbre.**)

For Individual Needs

7 Visual Learners As students listen to the recording, have them refer to the vocabulary pictures taped to the board from the Presentation.

Teacher Note

8 The tse-tse fly, mentioned in Joseph's last line of the dialogue, is a carrier of the sleeping sickness virus.

PREMIERE ETAPE

Making suppositions; expressing doubt and certainty; asking for and giving advice

VOCABULAIRE

la forêt tropicale

la savane

7 Ecoute!

Ecoute ces touristes qui visitent la République centrafricaine. Est-ce qu'ils se trouvent dans la forêt tropicale ou dans la savane? Answers on p. 161C.

8 Mais il y a plein de bêtes!

Complète la conversation entre Joseph et Lucie en employant les images données.

JOSEPH Un safari, c'est une bonne idée, mais il y a tellement d'insectes!

LUCIE Non, mais vraiment! Qu'est-ce que tu es trouillard!

JOSEPH Mais pas du tout! Ecoute! Il y a des centaines de moustiques . On peut attraper le paludisme, tu sais.

LUCIE Bon. On peut se faire vacciner, alors.

JOSEPH Et puis, il y a des fourmis et des araignées . Je parie qu'il y a même des scorpions!

LUCIE Il faut que tu fasses attention, c'est tout.

JOSEPH Tu sais bien que j'ai peur des serpents . Et n'oublie pas les mouches tsé-tsé. On pourrait mourir, quoi.

LUCIE Ecoute! Si tu veux, tu peux toujours rester à la maison!

RESOURCES FOR PREMIERE ETAPE

Chapter Teaching Resources, Book 2
• Communicative Activity 7-1, pp. 112–113
• Teaching Transparency Master 7-1, pp. 116, 118
  Teaching Transparency 7-1
• Additional Listening Activities 7-1, 7-2, 7-3, pp. 119–120
  Audiocassette 10A/Audio CD 7
• Realia 7-1, pp. 123, 125
• Situation Cards 7-1, pp. 126–127
• Student Response Forms, pp. 128–130
• Quiz 7-1, pp. 131–132
  Audiocassette 8A/Audio CD 7

ADDITIONAL RESOURCES
Textbook Audiocassette 4A
  OR *Audio CD 7*
Practice and Activity Book, pp. 74–77
Video Program, Videocassette 2
Video Guide

COMMENT DIT-ON... ?
Making suppositions; expressing doubt and certainty

To make a supposition:

On pourrait sûrement voir des chutes d'eau.

Je parie qu'il y a des serpents.

Ça doit être magnifique.
It must be . . .

Il doit y avoir des lions.
There must be . . .

To express doubt:

Ça m'étonnerait qu'il y ait des ours.
I'd be surprised if . . .

Je ne suis pas sûr(e) que ce soit une bonne idée.

Je ne suis pas certain(e) qu'il y fasse chaud la nuit.

Je ne pense pas qu'on puisse sortir de la jeep.

To express certainty:

Je suis certain(e) qu'il y aura des lions.

Je suis sûr(e) qu'il y pleut beaucoup.

Je sais qu'il y a des moustiques.

Je suis convaincu(e) que c'est dangereux.
I'm convinced that . . .

Note de Grammaire

You've probably already noticed that some expressions you learn in the **Comment dit-on... ?** boxes require you to use a certain structure following them. For example: **Il se peut que je** *fasse* **un safari; Peut-être que je** *ferai* **un safari.** Just as you automatically memorize gender with new nouns, always try to memorize what structures follow the expressions you learn.

9 Ecoute!

Ecoute les remarques de ces gens. Est-ce qu'ils expriment une certitude ou un doute? Answers on p. 161C.

10 Ça doit être fou!

Ton ami(e) te propose de faire un safari, mais ça ne te dit pas trop. Vous discutez de votre voyage éventuel en imaginant comment ça serait. See answers below.

—Je parie que(qu')...
—On pourrait sûrement...

—Ça doit être...
—Il doit y avoir...

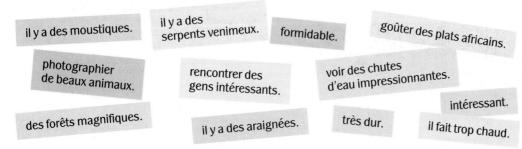

il y a des moustiques.

il y a des serpents venimeux.

formidable.

goûter des plats africains.

photographier de beaux animaux.

rencontrer des gens intéressants.

voir des chutes d'eau impressionnantes.

des forêts magnifiques.

il y a des araignées.

très dur.

intéressant.

il fait trop chaud.

11 Je parie que...

Choisis un pays que tu ne connais pas bien et que tu voudrais visiter. Dis à ton/ta camarade comment tu penses que ça serait. Il/Elle te répondra en exprimant ses doutes ou ses certitudes.

PREMIERE ETAPE · *cent soixante-neuf* **169**

Answers

10 Je parie qu'il y a des moustiques/serpents venimeux/araignées. Je parie qu'il fait trop chaud. On pourrait sûrement goûter des plats africains, photographier de beaux animaux, rencontrer des gens intéressants, voir des chutes d'eau impressionnantes. Il doit y avoir des forêts magnifiques. Ça doit être formidable, intéressant, très dur.

Reteaching

The subjunctive Form small groups and give a transparency to each one. Group members collaborate to write an explanation of the formation of the subjunctive. Have one member from each group present their explanation. You might offer a prize to the group that provides the clearest or the most creative explanation.

Presentation

Comment dit-on... ? Say the expressions for certainty and doubt, using appropriate intonation and gestures, and have students tell whether you are expressing certainty or doubt. Then, ask a student where he or she would like to go on vacation. Make suppositions about the place, such as **Au Mexique? On pourrait sûrement voir des pyramides.** Then, make logical and illogical suppositions about additional locations and have students respond. Finally, use the new expressions to make likely (**Ça m'étonnerait qu'on ait l'école samedi**) and unlikely statements (**Je suis sûr(e) qu'Elvis est vivant**) and have students agree or disagree.

Group Work

Make a poster featuring one of two cartoon characters, **Dominique Doute** or **Cécile Sûre. Dominique Doute** should look doubtful, and **Cécile Sûre** should have an air of certainty. In class, have students write the expressions of doubt or certainty on the appropriate poster. Then, they should find or draw pictures of items that suggest doubt or certainty and write appropriate expressions in speech bubbles next to them. For example, on the poster of **Dominique Doute**, students might glue pictures of UFOs or Santa Claus and write **Je ne suis pas sûr(e) que le père Noël existe.**

Teaching Suggestion

Call students' attention to the verbs in the sentences for expressing doubt and certainty. Ask them what is different about the verbs in the two groups of sentences (one requires the subjunctive, the other the indicative).

Presentation

Vocabulaire Bring in the vocabulary items and a suitcase. After holding up and naming each item, display everything on a table and have students remind you what to pack. **(Vous avez pensé à prendre des jumelles?)** Place each item in the suitcase as they remind you of it. Then, tell students that you've decided to visit Switzerland instead. Have them tell you which items to take out of the suitcase **(Vous n'avez pas besoin de...)** and which one you will still need **(Vous avez toujours besoin de...)**.

 Spread the vocabulary items and a suitcase out on a table. Then, call on students to put various items in the suitcase. **(Jack, mets les jumelles dans la valise!)** You might also ask them to take certain items out of the suitcase. **(Julie, sors mon passeport de la valise.)**

Additional Practice

Suggest situations and have students tell what you need for each one. **(Je me suis fait mal./Il fait nuit, et je ne vois rien.)**

❖ For Individual Needs

12 Visual Learners
Have students make vocabulary cards, spread them out on their desks, and set aside the card for each item they hear mentioned.

Additional Practice

13 Display several items from the **Vocabulaire** on a table. Have students compare the items on display with those on Sabine's list and tell which ones are missing.

VOCABULAIRE

En partant pour un safari, il ne faut pas oublier d'emporter...

- un appareil-photo et des pellicules (f.)
- de la lotion anti-moustique
- une trousse de premiers soins
- un imperméable
- un désinfectant
- des pansements (m.)
- une gourde
- un caméscope et des cassettes (f.)
- un passeport
- des jumelles (f.)
- des lunettes (f.) de soleil
- de la crème solaire
- une torche
- une carte de crédit
- des chèques (m.) de voyage

12 Ecoute!

Mathieu laisse un message sur le répondeur de Frédéric pour lui rappeler ce qu'il doit emporter pour le safari. Fais une liste de six choses qu'il ne doit pas oublier. Answers on p. 161C.

13 N'oublie pas!

Sabine se prépare pour partir faire un safari. Elle te demande de regarder sa liste et de dire ce qu'elle a oublié.

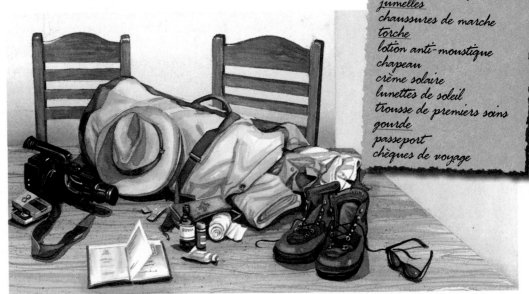

> caméscope, cassettes
> appareil-photo, pellicules
> jumelles
> chaussures de marche
> torche
> lotion anti-moustique
> chapeau
> crème solaire
> lunettes de soleil
> trousse de premiers soins
> gourde
> passeport
> chèques de voyage

♜ Game

LAISSEZ TOMBER! Give each student a vocabulary item or a picture of one. You might also include additional articles of clothing that students can name in French. Then, form two teams. Have two students hold up a sheet of butcher paper between the two teams so that the members of each team can't see each other. Have the first player from each team approach the sheet and hold up their picture or item. When you say **Laissez tomber!**, the students holding the sheet of butcher paper drop it. The two players look at the picture the opposing player is holding and try to name the item in French. The first player to give the French word for the vocabulary item wins a point for his or her team. Team members are not allowed to give help. Then, the students hold up the sheet again, and the next two players approach it. Continue until all players have had a turn.

COMMENT DIT-ON... ?

Asking for and giving advice

To ask for advice:

Tu crois que je devrais emporter des jumelles?
Tu penses qu'il vaudrait mieux se faire vacciner? *Do you think it'd be better to . . . ?*

To respond:

Je crois que ça vaut mieux. *I think that's better.*
A mon avis, c'est plus sûr. *In my opinion, it's safer.*
Ce n'est pas la peine. *It's not worth it.*
Je ne crois pas que ce soit utile. *I don't think it's worthwhile.*

To give advice:

Il faudrait que tu prennes de la lotion anti-moustique. *You ought to . . .*
Il est très important que tu emportes une trousse de premiers soins.
Il est essentiel que tu te fasses vacciner.
Il est nécessaire que tu prennes un imperméable et des bottes.

---

14 Ecoute!

Dans une agence de voyages, tu entends cette conversation entre un client et l'employée. D'après l'employée, lesquels de ces préparatifs sont nécessaires pour aller en République centrafricaine?

Answers on p. 161C.

15 Qu'est-ce que j'emporte?

Tu te demandes quels vêtements prendre pour faire un safari-photo. Ton/ta camarade va te conseiller.

—Tu penses qu'il vaudrait mieux prendre une jupe?
—Je ne crois pas que ce soit utile.

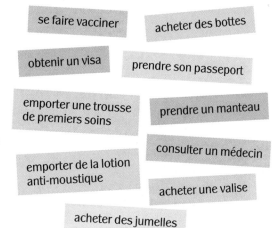

se faire vacciner

acheter des bottes

obtenir un visa

prendre son passeport

emporter une trousse de premiers soins

prendre un manteau

consulter un médecin

emporter de la lotion anti-moustique

acheter une valise

acheter des jumelles

NOTE CULTURELLE

The government of the Central African Republic and the World Wildlife Fund have recently established the Dzanga-Sangha Dense Forest Special Reserve in the extreme southeast of the country. The goal of this pilot project is to protect and preserve an important area of tropical forest, while at the same time allowing for limited use of the land for traditional hunting, tourism, and selective logging. The project also provides for anti-poaching teams, training of forest guards, and computer assistance to reduce illegal hunting in the preserve area.

Presentation

Comment dit-on... ? Introduce a stuffed animal as **Monsieur/Madame Je-sais-tout.** Ask him or her for advice about what to take on your trip to the Central African Republic, and have the animal respond, using the new expressions. Then, have volunteers ask the stuffed animal for advice on what to bring. Have **Monsieur/Madame Je-sais-tout** respond, using the new expressions. Next, project the new expressions on a transparency. Repeat the packing of the suitcase procedure suggested in the Presentation on page 170. This time, ask students for their advice about each item. Prompt them by pointing to an appropriate expression on the transparency.

Teacher Note

You might point out that students must use the subjunctive in all the new expressions for giving advice. The use of the subjunctive with expressions of necessity is presented on page 172.

For Individual Needs

14 Challenge After students have completed the activity, have them use the preparations they've indicated to write a brief note to a friend, advising him or her what to do to prepare for a trip to the Central African Republic.

Additional Practice

15 Write vacation destinations (**à la montagne, à la Martinique, au Canada, en Belgique**) on index cards and distribute them to students. Have partners ask for and give advice about what to take on their vacations.

Culture Note

The Dzanga-Sangha Reserve is one of the best-kept reserves in the Central African Republic. It is a rare example of an undisturbed rainforest. The reserve houses only two parks. The rest of the area is dedicated to hunting zones, Pygmy villages, and research camp sites. The reserve's wildlife has long attracted hunters, but strict regulations have recently been established in order to protect over 40 rare species that live there, including large populations of gorillas and elephants. Bongos (a rare striped antelope), eagles, duiker, and the white-bearded De Brazza's monkey are among the less common species that make their homes in the reserve.

Science Link

Have volunteers research the ecology of the rainforest and report back to the class with their findings.

Presentation

Grammaire Hang four pieces of posterboard around the room. Label them **Norbert Nécessité, Emile Emotion, Dominique Doute,** and **Paul Possibilité.** Write the new expressions on large cards and read them aloud one at a time. Call on students to tape cards to the appropriate poster. When the expressions are placed, form four groups and assign a poster to each one. Groups should write several completions for each expression, according to their "characters." For **Emile Emotion,** students might complete **J'ai peur que (qu')...** with ... **un lion nous mange!**

CLOSE

Game

IL FAUDRAIT QUE VOUS...

Begin the game by saying **Je vais en République centrafricaine. Qu'est-ce que je dois faire?** The first student gives advice, such as **Il faudrait que vous vous fassiez vacciner.** The second student repeats the first piece of advice and adds another. (**Il faudrait que vous vous fassiez vacciner, et il est essentiel que vous emportiez un appareil-photo.**) A player is out when he or she makes a mistake.

ASSESS

Quiz 7-1, *Chapter Teaching Resources, Book 2,* pp. 131–132

Assessment Items, Audiocassette 8A/Audio CD 7

Performance Assessment

Have students act out their skits from Part **b** of Activity 17. Encourage them to use props and to offer explanations for the advice that they give.

Grammaire
Using the subjunctive

You've already learned to use the subjunctive after an expression of *wishing,* such as **vouloir que.** You also use the subjunctive after many expressions of . . .

necessity:

Il est nécessaire qu'on se fasse vacciner.
Il est essentiel que...
Il est important que...
Il faudrait que...
Il vaudrait mieux que...

doubt:

Je ne crois pas qu'il y ait de tigres.
Je ne pense pas que...
Ça m'étonnerait que...
Je ne suis pas sûr(e) que...
Je ne suis pas certain(e) que...

emotion:

Je suis désolé(e) que tu ne puisses pas venir.
Je suis heureux(-euse) que...
J'ai peur que...

possibility:

Il est possible que ce soit dangereux.
Il est fort possible que...
Il se peut que...

Si tu as oublié the subjunctive va à la page 61.

16 A toi de jouer!

Lucie et Joseph parlent de leur voyage en Afrique. Choisis une proposition qui pourrait terminer leurs phrases. See answers below.

il y a de beaux animaux.»
tu restes dans la jeep.»
il y ait des tigres.»
tu ne puisses pas venir.»
on se fasse vacciner.»
il y ait des éléphants.»
ce soit dangereux.»
ce soit une bonne idée.»
on partira en safari.»
il fasse trop chaud.»
on va goûter des plats africains.»

«Il faudrait que(qu')...
«Je suis sûr(e) que(qu')...
«Il est essentiel que(qu')...
«Je parie que(qu')...
«Je ne pense pas que(qu')...
«Je suis désolé(e) que(qu')...
«J'ai peur que(qu')...
«Il se peut que(qu')...
«Il est fort possible que(qu')...
«Je crois bien que(qu')...
«Je ne crois pas que(qu')...

17 On part en Afrique!

a. Tu veux faire un safari, mais tu dois convaincre ton ami(e) qui n'a pas très envie de t'accompagner. Dis-lui ce que tu crois que vous pourrez y faire et y voir.

b. Vous avez décidé de faire le safari! Maintenant, discutez de ce qu'il faut que vous fassiez avant de partir. Demande à ton ami(e) ce que tu devrais emporter.

172 *cent soixante-douze* CHAPITRE 7 Un safari-photo

Possible answers
16 *Il faudrait qu(e)/Il est essentiel qu(e):* tu restes dans la jeep/on se fasse vacciner.
Je suis sûr(e) qu(e)/Je parie qu(e)/Je crois bien qu(e): il y a de beaux animaux/on partira en safari/on va goûter des plats africains.

Je ne pense pas qu(e)/Je ne crois pas qu(e)/Il se peut qu(e)/Il est fort possible qu(e): il y ait des tigres/ce soit dangereux/il y ait des éléphants/ce soit une bonne idée/il fasse trop chaud.
Je suis désolé(e) qu(e): tu ne puisses pas venir.
J'ai peur qu(e): tu ne puisses pas venir/il y ait des tigres/ce soit dangereux/il fasse trop chaud.

PANORAMA CULTUREL

Emmanuel • France

Betty • Martinique

Christian • France

Cities, regions, and even countries can have a reputation. We wanted to know what people thought of specific places. Here's what they told us.

Quelle est l'image de ta région?

«La réputation de la Provence, c'est d'être un peu, surtout à Marseille, d'être un peu bagarreur, d'être un peu «m'as-tu-vu». C'est-à-dire, de se montrer un peu. C'est vrai que c'est souvent le cas à Marseille, hein? Parce que c'est souvent des jeunes qui font ça... Mais les vrais Marseillais sont pas comme ça, quoi.»

-Emmanuel

«Bon alors, les étrangers pensent que la Martinique est une île merveilleuse où il fait toujours très beau, où on peut pratiquer des sports nautiques comme le surf, le ski nautique, où le sable est fin et chaud et où on peut vivre des expériences nouvelles avec un compagnon quelquefois. Ils pensent que la Martinique est une île très accueillante ou très chaleureuse aussi, où il est bon de vivre.»

-Betty

«Ben, en fait, nous [les Français] sommes un peuple assez libre et nous avons inventé la démocratie. Et je crois que beaucoup de pays nous envient notre système politique, d'autre part, bien que ce soit pas un système parfait.»

-Christian

Qu'en penses-tu?

1. What reputation does the area where you live have? Is it justified? Why or why not?
2. What foreign country would you most like to visit? What image do you have of this place?
3. Pick one francophone area and find out what it's known for.

Questions

1. **D'après Emmanuel, quelle est la réputation des Provençaux?** (d'être bagarreurs, m'as-tu-vu)
2. **Est-ce qu'Emmanuel croit que les vrais Marseillais sont comme ça?** (non)
3. **D'après Betty, que pensent les étrangers de la Martinique?** (C'est une île merveilleuse, il fait toujours beau.)
4. **Qu'est-ce que les Français ont inventé, d'après Christian?** (la démocratie)

Language Note

Students might want to know the following words: **bagarreur** *(aggressive)*; **m'as-tu-vu** *(show-off)*; **se montrer** *(to show off)*. Ask students to analyze the term **m'as-tu-vu**. Do they recognize parts of it? (**Tu m'as vu?**) Have them explain how it came to mean *show-off*.

Summary

In *Le safari, c'est l'aventure!*, the Zokoue family is taking a guided tour of the Bamingui-Bangoran national park. They see a gazelle, some monkeys, a family of lions eating a gnu, and some elephants. The guide warns that elephants in general are unpredictable, which makes Joseph a little nervous. When they see a rhinoceros, Lucie gets out of the jeep to take a picture. The family is alarmed when the rhinoceros begins to charge, but Lucie quickly gets back in the jeep and they drive to safety.

Motivating Activity

Ask students to imagine what dangers they might encounter on a safari in Africa.

Presentation

Draw or find pictures of a gazelle, monkeys, lions, elephants, and a rhinoceros and tape them to the board. Then, play the recording. Pause after each scene and have students identify the animal being discussed and the context of the discussion. Then, have volunteers arrange the pictures in the order in which they are mentioned in the recording.

For Individual Needs

Kinesthetic Learners On a transparency, write sentences from the **Remise en train** in which the Zokoues point out the different animals. **(Regardez là-bas! Une famille de lions!)** Then, copy the sentences onto index cards and put them in a bag. Have volunteers select a card and mimic the animal. The class indicates the sentence that refers to the animal.

Remise en train

Le safari, c'est l'aventure!

Les Zokoue sont maintenant en République centrafricaine dans le parc national Bamingui-Bangoran, accompagnés par un guide.

❶ M. ZOKOUE Oh! Regardez comme c'est beau, les enfants!

LUCIE Est-ce que les animaux sont protégés ici?

LE GUIDE Oui, la chasse est illégale. Malheureusement, il y a des braconniers. C'est pour ça qu'on doit surveiller la réserve en permanence.

JOSEPH Des braconniers? Qu'est-ce qu'ils tuent comme animaux?

LE GUIDE Eh bien, les éléphants pour leur ivoire, les singes et les guépards pour leur fourrure et les rhinocéros pour leur corne.

LUCIE C'est dégoûtant! Ça me rend malade!

❷ LUCIE Eh, tu as vu?

JOSEPH Non, qu'est-ce que c'était?

LUCIE Une gazelle... Vous pourriez arrêter la voiture, s'il vous plaît? J'aimerais prendre une photo.

JOSEPH Tu es folle! Reste ici, c'est dangereux!

M. ZOKOUE Méfie-toi, Lucie, j'ai peur qu'il y ait des lions.

LE GUIDE N'ayez pas peur. S'il y avait un lion, la gazelle le sentirait et elle s'enfuirait.

❸ LUCIE Vous avez entendu?

JOSEPH Quoi?

LUCIE Ces bruits horribles! Ces cris! Je me demande ce que c'est.

LE GUIDE Ne vous en faites pas, ce sont des singes. On ne les voit pas facilement. Ils se cachent dans les arbres... Tenez, vous les voyez, là?

LUCIE Ah oui! Oh, super!

18 Tu as compris? *See answers below.*

1. Where is the Zokoue family? What are they doing?
2. What is Lucie's concern?
3. What does Lucie want to take a picture of?
4. Does the guide think it's safe to get out of the car?
5. What does Joseph worry about?
6. What happens when Lucie tries to photograph the rhinoceros?

19 Vrai ou faux?

1. La chasse est illégale dans les réserves. vrai
2. Les singes chantent de belles chansons. faux
3. Le lion laisse les meilleurs morceaux à ses petits. faux
4. On chasse les rhinocéros pour leur corne. vrai
5. Les gnous sont les animaux les plus forts de la brousse. faux
6. Les rhinocéros vont plus vite que les voitures. faux

174 *cent soixante-quatorze* CHAPITRE 7 Un safari-photo

RESOURCES FOR REMISE EN TRAIN

Textbook Audiocassette 4A/Audio CD 7
Practice and Activity Book, p. 78

Answers

18 1. in the Bamingui-Bangoran National Park; taking a guided tour 2. poachers killing animals 3. a gazelle 4. Yes 5. He worries about the vehicle breaking down in the middle of the elephant herd. 6. It charges.

Culture Note

The Bamingui-Bangoran national park, a typical woodland savanna, is home to the animals known as the "big four" (elephants, lions, leopards, and rhinos), among others. New measures have been taken to prevent poaching, which has been a serious problem. Between 1970 and 1990, the rhinoceros population dropped from about 60,000 to 4,000, and the elephant population dropped from 80,000 to about 3,000.

4 M. ZOKOUE Regardez là-bas! Une famille de lions!

LUCIE Qu'est-ce qu'ils mangent?

LE GUIDE Un gnou, sûrement.

LUCIE Mais, c'est horrible!

JOSEPH Mais non, c'est la loi de la nature. Les plus forts mangent les plus faibles.

M. ZOKOUE Vous avez vu comme le lion se garde les meilleurs morceaux? C'est vraiment le roi des animaux!

5 JOSEPH Oh, dis donc! C'est dingue! Qu'est-ce qu'ils sont gros, ces éléphants! Euh, qu'est-ce qu'on ferait si on tombait en panne au milieu du troupeau?

LE GUIDE On ne ferait rien. J'appellerais la base et on attendrait. Mais j'espère que ça ne nous arrivera pas parce que les éléphants sont imprévisibles. Ils pourraient nous attaquer s'ils avaient peur.

JOSEPH Euh... Vous êtes sûr que vous avez fait le plein d'essence avant de partir?

6 M. ZOKOUE Regardez, il y a un rhinocéros là-bas.

LUCIE Vous pourriez vous arrêter, s'il vous plaît?

LE GUIDE Faites attention, les rhinocéros peuvent charger.

M. ZOKOUE Tu ferais peut-être mieux de rester dans la jeep pour prendre ta photo.

LE GUIDE Ne vous inquiétez pas, je le surveille... Mais restez près de nous.

LUCIE D'accord.

Lucie se prépare à prendre une photo du rhinocéros.

LUCIE Souris, petit rhino... Souris.

LE GUIDE Attention, remontez vite!

LUCIE Mais quoi?

M. ZOKOUE Remonte, Lucie, dépêche-toi! Le rhinocéros charge!

LUCIE Aïe! Aïe! Aïe!

LE GUIDE Ne paniquez pas, mais remontez vite.

Elle remonte dans la voiture.

LE GUIDE Accrochez-vous! On va aller très vite!

JOSEPH Ben, dis donc! On l'a échappé belle!

LUCIE Chouette alors! Comme dans les films!

---

20 Ils sont comment, les animaux?

Associe chaque animal à sa description.

Le singe...
L'éléphant...
La gazelle...
Le rhinocéros...
Le lion...
Le guépard...

est le roi des animaux.
est imprévisible.
peut charger.
vit dans les arbres.
sent le lion quand il arrive.
a une belle fourrure.

Le lion
L'éléphant
Le rhinocéros
Le singe
La gazelle
Le guépard

21 Cherche les expressions

What do the people in **Le safari, c'est l'aventure!** say to . . . *See answers below.*

1. express disgust?
2. give a warning?
3. reassure someone?
4. express astonishment?
5. express relief?

22 Et maintenant, à toi

Qu'est-ce que tu penses du massacre des animaux sauvages?

REMISE EN TRAIN

cent soixante-quinze **175**

Answers

21 1. C'est dégoûtant! Ça me rend malade!
  2. Méfie-toi! Faites attention... ; Attention...
  3. N'ayez pas peur. Ne vous en faites pas... ; Ne vous inquiétez pas... ; Ne paniquez pas...
  4. Oh! Regardez comme c'est beau... ! Oh, super! Oh, dis donc! C'est dingue! Qu'est-ce qu'ils sont gros, ces éléphants!
  5. Ben, dis donc! On l'a échappé belle!

Biology Link

There are five different species of rhinoceros, all of which live in Africa and tropical Asia. Students might be interested to know that the rhinoceros' horn is actually made of keratin, which is a protein found in hair. You might have students guess how much the average rhinoceros weighs (three to five tons).

Jump Start!

Write a supposition on the board, such as **Il doit y avoir des lions.** Have students write two sentences, one in which they doubt the statement, and another in which they express their certainty of it.

MOTIVATE

Ask students what animal they would be if they could be any type of animal, and why.

TEACH

Presentation

Vocabulaire Hold up drawings or pictures of the animals and ask students either-or questions about them, such as **Quel animal est gris, la girafe ou l'éléphant?** Then, ask the class **Quel animal a une corne? Quels animaux sont féroces?**, using appropriate gestures to get the meaning across.

For Individual Needs

23 Challenge Have students create additional sentences about the animals in the **Vocabulaire** and the **Vocabulaire à la carte.** They might use the following words: **une queue** *(tail)*; **des crocs** *(fangs, teeth)*; **un carnassier** *(carnivore)*; **un herbivore** *(herbivore)*.

Multicultural Link

Have students choose a country and find out what animals are native to the area. They might also find out about any unique or endangered species that live there and what efforts have been made to protect them. Have students report their findings to the class.

DEUXIEME ETAPE

Expressing astonishment; cautioning someone; expressing fear; reassuring someone; expressing relief

VOCABULAIRE

Chez les lions, c'est la lionne qui chasse. **Le lion**, qui dort à peu près vingt heures par jour, mange les plus gros morceaux. Les lionceaux sont adorables, mais ils deviendront de **féroces** carnassiers.

L'hippopotame (m.) peut respirer dans l'air et dans l'eau. Il se baigne dans les points d'eau pendant la journée. La nuit, il broute l'herbe et les fruits tombés sur le sol.

L'éléphant (m.) est l'animal le plus **lourd** du monde. Il peut peser jusqu'à sept tonnes et boire 100 litres d'eau par jour avec **sa trompe.**

Avec son long cou, **la girafe** peut manger les plus hautes feuilles des arbres. Mais quand elle a soif, elle doit faire le grand écart pour atteindre la surface de l'eau.

Pour saluer, les éléphants se serrent la trompe.

Le singe vit dans les arbres. Quand il est conscient d'un danger, il crie pour prévenir les autres animaux.

Les braconniers chassent **le rhinocéros** pour **sa corne.** C'est un animal très facile à chasser car il ne voit presque rien. Quand deux rhinocéros se battent, ils se donnent des coups de corne. Quand ils s'aiment, ils se frottent l'un contre l'autre à l'aide de leurs cornes.

Le guépard, qui détient le record de vitesse de tous les animaux, peut atteindre 90 km/h. Quand il a attrapé **sa proie,** il la hisse dans un arbre.

Grâce à ses rayures, **le zèbre** peut se cacher dans les hautes herbes pendant qu'il mange. Il ressemble au cheval, mais il pousse des cris comme le hi-han de l'âne.

23 Quel animal?

Complète ces phrases avec le nom de l'animal approprié. 3. Le rhinocéros
4. L'hippopotame

1. Pour se saluer, _____ se serrent la trompe. les éléphants
2. _____ hisse sa proie dans un arbre. Le guépard
3. _____ est très facile à chasser car il ne voit presque rien.
4. _____ se baigne dans les points d'eau pendant la journée.
5. Quand _____ est conscient d'un danger, il crie pour prévenir les autres animaux. le singe
6. _____ ressemble au cheval mais pousse des cris comme le hi-han de l'âne. Le zèbre
7. _____ peut manger les plus hautes feuilles des arbres avec son long cou. La girafe
8. _____ dort à peu près vingt heures par jour. Le lion

Vocabulaire à la carte

une antilope	
une autruche	*an ostrich*
un babouin	*a baboon*
un flamant	*a flamingo*
une gazelle	
un gorille	
une hyène	*a hyena*
un vautour	*a vulture*

RESOURCES FOR DEUXIEME ETAPE

Chapter Teaching Resources, Book 2
• Communicative Activity 7-2, pp. 114–115
• Teaching Transparency Master 7-2, pp. 117, 118
    Teaching Transparency 7-2
• Additional Listening Activities 7-4, 7-5, 7-6, pp. 120–121
    Audiocassette 10A/Audio CD 7
• Realia 7-2, pp. 124, 125
• Situation Cards 7-2, 7-3, pp. 126–127
• Student Response Forms, pp. 128–130
• Quiz 7-2, pp. 133–134
    Audiocassette 8A/Audio CD 7

ADDITIONAL RESOURCES
Textbook Audiocassette 4A
    OR *Audio CD 7*
Practice and Activity Book, pp. 79–82

24 Qu'il est féroce, le lion!

D'après toi, quel est l'animal le plus...?

féroce   méchant   laid   courageux   fort
agile   mignon   lourd   rapide
dangereux   timide   intelligent

25 Devine!

Choisis un animal et fais une phrase pour le décrire. Ton/ta camarade va deviner de quel animal tu parles.

COMMENT DIT-ON...?
Expressing astonishment

Oh, dis donc! *Wow!*
Ça alors! *How about that!*
C'est pas vrai!
Oh là là!
Ouah! *Wow!*
C'est le pied! *Cool! Neat!*
Tiens! Regarde un peu! *Hey! Check it out!*
Qu'est-ce qu'elle est grande, cette girafe!

C'est fou comme elle va vite, cette gazelle! *I can't believe how . . .!*
Quel paysage incroyable!
Tu as vu comme il est gros, l'hippopotame? *Did you see how . . . ?*
Je n'ai jamais vu un aussi gros éléphant.

26 Ecoute!

Ecoute les remarques de ces gens qui visitent la savane. Est-ce qu'ils expriment leur étonnement ou non?

Answers on p. 161D

A la française

French speakers very often begin a sentence with a subject pronoun like **il**, **elle**, or **ça** and then repeat the noun subject at the end of the sentence. Look at these examples: *C'est fou comme* **il est grand, cet éléphant!** or *Ça doit être magnifique,* **la savane.**

27 Ouah!

Voici des photos de ton safari que tu vas envoyer à ta famille et à tes amis. Ecris des phrases qui expriment ton étonnement pour mettre au verso de chaque photo. *Possible answers:*

1. C'est fou comme il va vite, ce guépard!

2. Je n'ai jamais vu une aussi grande bouche!

3. Quels beaux papillons!

4. Qu'est-ce qu'ils sont gros, ces éléphants!

28 Mon journal

Imagine un voyage plein d'aventures. Où est-ce que tu irais? Qu'est-ce que tu y ferais? Comment est-ce que ça serait?

Si tu as oublié the conditional va à la page 125.

Teaching Suggestion

27 Have students create a photo album of their trip to the Central African Republic. They should find or draw pictures of unusual animals and sights that they saw there and tape or glue them to sheets of construction paper. Then, have them write captions underneath each photo, using the new expressions. Have them design and draw an attractive cover for their albums and then fasten all the pages together. This activity could be used as a chapter project.

Mon journal

28 Students might want to write about an adventure story they've read or a movie they've seen. For an additional journal entry suggestion, see *Practice and Activity Book,* page 151.

For Individual Needs

25 Visual Learners As an alternative to this activity, you might have students form small groups and play **Pictionnaire** with the vocabulary. One group member draws a representation of an animal and the others try to guess its name in French.

Presentation

Comment dit-on...? As homework, have students find large pictures of people or things they find impressive. Before class, have several students prepare incredible statements. (**J'ai pêché un poisson de trois mètres!**) In class, have them read their statements. Respond with astonishment to each one, using the new expressions. (**C'est pas vrai!**) Then, have students show their pictures. Express your astonishment as you look at each one (**Je n'ai jamais vu un homme si fort!**) and have students repeat. Next, collect the pictures students brought in, redistribute them, and have partners take turns showing them to each other and responding with astonishment.

Additional Practice

Read statements or show pictures from the *Guinness Book of World Records* and prompt students to react to each one with astonishment.

For Individual Needs

26 Kinesthetic Learners If students hear an expression of astonishment, have them respond by dropping their jaws and loosely cupping both hands over their cheeks. If the person they hear is not expressing astonishment, they should shrug their shoulders.

Presentation

Comment dit-on... ? Create a humorous dialogue about a cowardly lion and his reassuring friend, the mouse. For example:

MOUSE Je te signale que les gens peuvent charger.

LION Mais j'ai peur qu'ils me prennent en photo!

MOUSE Pas de panique! Ne bouge pas...

Using sock puppets or stuffed animals, act out the dialogue for the class. Then, write the new expressions on a transparency. Read them aloud and have students repeat after you. Then, ask students to give expressions that the cowardly lion from *The Wizard of Oz* might say (**J'ai la frousse!**), and expressions that Dorothy might say to reassure him. (**Pas de panique!**)

✦ For Individual Needs

30 Challenge Once students have completed the activity, have them write additional statements that would elicit the remaining responses. For example, for the two remaining responses for #1, **Les araignées sont méchantes** and **Regarde un peu!**, students might write **Comment sont les araignées?** and **Tiens, il y a un guépard!** You might have students exchange papers with a partner, who writes the appropriate response next to each statement.

Teaching Suggestion

31 For writing practice, have students imagine they are on a photo safari and write a diary entry describing what happened to them in each of the instances pictured here.

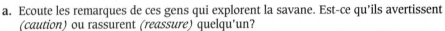

COMMENT DIT-ON...?

Cautioning someone; expressing fear; reassuring someone; expressing relief

To caution someone:

Je vous signale que les animaux peuvent charger. *I'm warning you that* . . .

Il serait plus prudent de rester dans la voiture. *It would be wiser to* . . .

Faites gaffe! *Look out!*

Attention aux araignées! *Watch out for . . . !*

Méfiez-vous! *Be careful!*

Ne bougez pas. *Don't move.*

To express fear:

J'ai très peur des lions.

J'ai peur que ce soit un serpent.

J'ai la frousse! *I'm scared to death!*

To reassure someone:

Ne vous en faites pas.

N'ayez pas peur.

Calmez-vous!

Pas de panique!

To express relief:

On a eu de la chance! *We were lucky!*

Ouf! On a eu chaud! *Whew! That was a real scare!*

On l'a échappé belle! *That was close!*

---

29 Ecoute! Answers on p. 161D.

a. Ecoute les remarques de ces gens qui explorent la savane. Est-ce qu'ils avertissent *(caution)* ou rassurent *(reassure)* quelqu'un?

b. Maintenant, écoute ces gens et dis s'ils expriment leur peur ou leur soulagement *(relief)*.

30 Du calme!

Choisis la réponse appropriée pour rassurer la personne qui a fait les remarques suivantes.

1. «Oh! Il y a des araignées! J'ai très peur des araignées.»
   a. Les araignées sont méchantes.   b. Regarde un peu!   c. N'aie pas peur.
2. «Voilà, on s'est perdus et il fait déjà nuit. J'ai la frousse!»
   a. Tu es trouillard!   b. Ne t'en fais pas!   c. On a eu chaud!
3. «Tu as entendu? J'ai peur que ce soit un lion.»
   a. Quel lion énorme!   b. On l'a échappé belle.   c. Pas de panique!

31 Attention!

Qu'est-ce que tu dirais pour avertir ces gens? See answers below.

1.   2.   3.   4.

Community Link

If possible, organize a field trip to a local zoo and have students observe some of the animals mentioned in the chapter. You might have students take notes on what they learn during the visit, and then write a brief report of their impressions and observations.

Possible Answers

31 1. Ne bougez pas!
2. Méfiez-vous! Je vous singnale que les animaux peuvent charger.
3. Attention aux fourmis!
4 Faites gaffe! Il serait plus prudent de rester dans la voiture.

Grammaire Irregular subjunctive forms

You've already learned some verbs that have irregular stems in the subjunctive. Here are some others.

- To form the subjunctive of the verb **pouvoir**, add the regular subjunctive endings to the stem **puiss-**.

  Je ne pense pas qu'on **puisse** toucher les animaux.

- To form the subjunctive of the verb **aller**, add the regular endings to the stems **all-** (for the **nous** and **vous** forms) and **aill-** (for all other forms).

que j'**aille**	que nous **allions**
que tu **ailles**	que vous **alliez**
qu'il/elle/on **aille**	qu'ils/elles **aillent**

  Je ne veux pas que tu **ailles** en Afrique.
  J'ai peur que vous **alliez** trop vite.

- All the subjunctive forms of the verbs **être** and **avoir** are irregular.

que je **sois**	que nous **soyons**	que j'**aie**	que nous **ayons**
que tu **sois**	que vous **soyez**	que tu **aies**	que vous **ayez**
qu'il/elle/on **soit**	qu'ils **soient**	qu'il/elle/on **ait**	qu'ils **aient**

  Il a peur que ce **soit** trop dangereux.
  Je ne pense pas qu'il y **ait** des panthères.

32 Je ne sais pas, moi!

Fabien et Suzanne parlent d'un voyage qu'ils pourraient faire avec leurs amis. Complète leur conversation en mettant les verbes au subjonctif.

FABIEN Ben moi, j'ai peur que ce __1__ (être) dangereux! *soit*

SUZANNE Moi aussi. Il se peut qu'il y __2__ (avoir) des serpents! *ait*

FABIEN Oui. Et il est fort possible que les animaux __3__ (être) féroces. *soient*

SUZANNE Bien sûr. Je ne crois pas qu'on __4__ (pouvoir) sortir de la voiture. *puisse*

FABIEN Sans doute pas. Il faudra que tu __5__ (prendre) tes photos de l'intérieur de la voiture. *prennes*

SUZANNE En plus, mes parents ne voudront pas que j'y __6__ (aller). Ils auraient trop peur.

FABIEN Et n'oublie pas qu'il est nécessaire qu'on se __7__ (faire) vacciner. *fasse*

SUZANNE Bon, ben, finalement, je ne crois pas que ce __8__ (être) une bonne idée! *soit*

6. *aille*

33 La savane, c'est l'aventure!

With your friends, write a scene for a movie in which the following things happen. Then, act out the scene together.

A group of friends is in the savanna. They express their astonishment at the sight of the wild animals. One person expresses a fear of something, and another reassures him/her. A third person warns the group of some imminent danger. The group finds itself in a dangerous situation, but everyone comes out of it safely and each person expresses relief.

Presentation

Grammaire Write the subject pronouns and the subjunctive stems of each irregular verb on the board and have volunteers add the endings. Then, write sentence starters that require the subjunctive on a transparency. Write subject pronouns and infinitives (**tu/être**) on cards and put them in a bag. Have students select a card and use the subject pronoun and verb to complete one of the sentence starters.

Teaching Suggestion

32 Have students explain why the subjunctive is used in each sentence. Hang the posters illustrating the use of the subjunctive (see Presentation on page 172) and have students point to the appropriate one. For example, for the first sentence (... j'ai peur que ce soit dangereux!), students would point to the poster of **Emile Emotion**, because fear is an emotion.

Portfolio

33 **Oral/Written** This activity is appropriate for students' oral and written portfolios. For portfolio information, see *Assessment Guide*, pages 2–13.

CLOSE

Game

CATÉGORIES Write the five functions from this **étape** on the board. Form two or more teams. Name a function (*expressing astonishment*) and have the teams take turns giving sentences that demonstrate it. (**C'est fou comme le guépard va vite!**) Teams win a point for each sentence. You might use *African animals* as an additional category.

ASSESS

Quiz 7-2, *Chapter Teaching Resources, Book 2,* pp. 133–134

Assessment Items, Audiocassette 8A
Audio CD 7

Performance Assessment

Assign five words or expressions from the vocabulary list on page 187 to each of several small groups. Give groups two or three minutes to create a brief dialogue, using the assigned vocabulary. Call on groups to present their skits to the class. After a group has performed, have the class identify and write down the vocabulary words and expressions from this chapter the group used in the skit.

READING STRATEGY

Understanding linking words

Teacher Note

For an additional reading, see *Practice and Activity Book*, page 83.

PREREADING
Activity A

Motivating Activity

Have students recall stories that have animals as the main characters *(The Tortoise and the Hare, Goldilocks and the Three Bears, Little Red Riding Hood, The Three Little Pigs)*. Have them name the animals in each story. Then, ask them how they would characterize these stories. What do they expect an animal story to be like?

Teaching Suggestion

You might bring in an English text that students are familiar with, read parts of it aloud, and have students raise their hands when they hear a linking word. You might also type the text, give copies to partners, and have them underline the linking words they find.

READING
Activities B–Q

Teaching Suggestion

Have students make two columns, one labeled **Les éléphants** and the other, **Les hommes**. Have them list the advantages of each. For example, under **Les éléphants**, students might write **gros, forts, peau épaisse**.

LISONS!

LE CIMETIERE DES ELEPHANTS

Autrefois, le peuple des éléphants vivait au bord de la rivière Sankourou. Il avait pour roi le puissant et sage Khoro. Un jour, le petit tisserin s'est posé sur la défense de Khoro et lui a raconté, tout effrayé :

«Hélas, puissant Khoro ! C'est terrible ! Une foule d'êtres noirs à deux pattes est arrivée dans notre pays. Ils possèdent de drôles d'objets qui tuent. Ils s'étendent partout et dévastent tout sur leur passage.»

Khoro a souri : « Je connais ces êtres. Ce sont les hommes. Ils sont petits et ne sont pas très forts. Leurs armes ne peuvent pas transpercer l'épaisse peau des éléphants.»

Cependant, peu de temps après, Khoro a cessé de sourire. Les hommes noirs n'étaient ni très grands, ni très forts, mais ils étaient nombreux. Certes, leurs armes ne pouvaient transpercer l'épaisse peau des éléphants.

DE BONS CONSEILS

Understanding linking words can help you see the connection between ideas. Some common French linking words are **pourtant** (yet), **cependant** (however), **néanmoins** (nevertheless), **alors** (so, therefore) and **ainsi** (thus, in this way). Linking words can connect ideas in several different ways. They can continue or expand on an idea, show a cause-and-effect relationship, or express a contradiction. Notice how the linking word functions in this example: **Ce travail est dangereux, il faut cependant le faire.** As you begin to read more sophisticated texts in French, paying attention to the linking words will help you to understand not only the events of the story, but also the more subtle relationship of ideas.

Toutefois, une flèche bien lancée pouvait tuer un éléphant, si elle le frappait à l'œil. Les hommes brûlaient les forêts pour en faire des champs. En outre, une terrible sécheresse éprouvait le pays. Les éléphants étaient aux abois. Ils mouraient de faim et par les armes des hommes noirs. C'est alors que le puissant Roi des Eléphants a rassemblé ses sujets et leur a dit :

«Cette terre n'est plus bénie des dieux. La famine et les hommes noirs nous font souffrir. Nous devons partir d'ici. Nous irons vers le soleil couchant. Notre route sera droite, comme l'était jusqu'à présent notre vie. Nous passerons sur tout ce qui se trouvera sur notre chemin, que ce soient les marécages ou les hommes noirs. Nous sommes peut-être un petit peuple, mais chacun de nous est plus fort que dix fois dix singes. Nous atteindrons notre but. Il n'en reste pas moins que ce pays a toujours été notre terre. Aussi, nous y reviendrons quelques jours chaque année, le premier mois qui suit la saison des pluies. Ainsi, nos enfants le connaîtront, les vieux et les malades pourront y vivre leurs derniers instants.»

Le cimetière des éléphants

A. Who are the **«peuple»** that this story is about? Who is Khoro? elephants; their king

B. Who are **«les êtres noirs à deux pattes»**? What problem do they present? Why isn't Khoro worried about them at first? See answers below.

C. Which is NOT a problem that the elephants experienced after the humans arrive?

Les hommes brûlaient les forêts.

Il y avait une terrible sécheresse.

Une tornade a détruit leur terre.

Les hommes noirs tuaient les éléphants.

Culture Note

The African elephant is the largest living land animal. It weighs over eight tons (7,500 kilograms) and stands ten to thirteen feet tall. These elephants may live in either the jungle or in the savanna. They migrate with the seasons, depending on the availability of food and water. Because they are becoming increasingly rare, regulations against poaching have been established, and conservation parks have been created to protect them.

Answers

B humans; They're taking over and destroying everything in their way; They are small and weak, and their weapons can't pierce an elephant's thick hide.

Ainsi a parlé le puissant Khoro, et il en a été comme il a dit. Le passage des éléphants ressemblait à celui d'une tornade : les arbres ont été arrachés, les champs piétinés, les villages détruits. Beaucoup d'hommes ont péri. La force des éléphants était effrayante.

Cela s'est passé il y a longtemps, très longtemps, mais chaque année, les éléphants continuent à emprunter le même chemin pour montrer leur ancienne patrie à leurs petits et pour que les vieux puissent y mourir. Depuis ce temps, on ne trouve plus de cadavres d'éléphants dans la forêt car ceux-ci vont mourir sur les bords de la rivière Sankourou. Là se trouve leur cimetière bien que personne ne sache l'endroit exact.

LA TORTUE ET LE LEOPARD

Les enfants étaient agités à cause du formidable chasseur qui était passé par leur village ce matin-là. Ce qui les avait impressionnés le plus, c'était la quantité de gris-gris qu'il portait sur lui.

«Quand je serai grand, moi aussi je serai chasseur !» a dit l'un des enfants.

Son oncle, qui l'avait entendu, lui a dit : «Si tu veux vraiment devenir un grand chasseur, il te faudra apprendre beaucoup de choses. Tu devras savoir construire des pièges efficaces pour duper les animaux que tu voudras attraper ; ils sont intelligents, tu sais, et ce n'est pas aussi facile que tu crois de les capturer.»

«Oh, raconte-nous une histoire de pièges !» dit le petit garçon. Les autres enfants voulaient aussi que l'oncle leur raconte une histoire.

«Oui, raconte-nous une histoire! Raconte-nous une histoire !»

Voici ce que l'oncle leur a raconté :

Un jour, Dame Tortue, perdue dans ses pensées, rentrait joyeusement chez elle. En d'autres mots, elle traînait sa carapace un peu plus vite que d'habitude. Mais, elle n'avançait pas très vite car elle s'arrêtait constamment pour sentir une fleur sauvage par ici, ou pour manger un bouton de fleur par là. Elle aurait dû faire attention à des choses plus importantes. Ainsi, sur son chemin, il y avait comme un grand tapis de feuilles de palmier qu'un serpent svelte traversait. Sans réfléchir, la tortue le suivait quand, tout à coup, les feuilles ont cédé sous elle. Boum ! Elle est tombée dans le piège que les chasseurs d'un village alentour avaient creusé au milieu du chemin.

Grâce à sa carapace très dure, elle ne s'est pas blessée. Mais comment allait-elle sortir de ce piège ? Elle savait bien qu'elle devait s'échapper avant le lendemain matin si elle ne voulait pas finir dans la soupe du village.

Alors, Dame Tortue a commencé à réfléchir sérieusement. Elle réfléchissait toujours quand elle a entendu un grand boum... C'était un magnifique léopard, grand, languissant, souple et féroce qui venait de tomber dans le piège, lui aussi. Son grognement montrait bien qu'il n'appréciait pas le stratagème que les chasseurs avaient utilisé pour le capturer.

D. Find three examples of linking words in the third paragraph. What purpose does each of these words serve? How does it connect one idea with another? *See answers below.*

E. What decision does Khoro make to save his subjects? *to leave their territory*

F. Find the sentence that begins **«Aussi, nous y reviendrons...»** near the end of the last paragraph on page 180. In this sentence, **aussi** doesn't mean *also*. Figure out what it means from the way it connects that sentence to the ones before. *therefore*

G. What reasons does Khoro give for returning to the elephants' territory once each year?

H. What are four results of the elephants' passage to their new land? *For Activities G and H, see answers below.*

I. Put these events in the order in which they occur in the story:

4 Les éléphants partent du bord de la rivière.

5 Les éléphants reviennent à la rivière pour mourir.

2 Les hommes font souffrir les éléphants.

Les hommes arrivent à la rivière.

1

3 Le roi Khoro parle à ses sujets.

J. What phenomenon is explained in the last paragraph? *See answers below.*

Answers
D **Cependant** and **mais** express a contradiction.
Certes confirms an idea.
G They return to the elephants' territory so the young elephants can see it, and the old can die there.
H trees uprooted, fields trampled, villages destroyed, many men killed
J why the remains of dead elephants are never found in the forest

LISONS!
CHAPITRE 7

Additional Practice

D. For more practice with linking words, have students look for linking words in the readings *Les trois femmes du roi, Le clou de Djeha,* and *La petite maison* on pages 154–156.

For Individual Needs

G., H. Slower Pace You might make a list of the answers to each of these activities, along with some incorrect answers. Have students choose the correct answers from the lists.

I. Challenge Once students have completed this activity, have them draw or find pictures to illustrate each event listed. You might also have them illustrate additional events from the story. Then, students should write a caption for each picture. Slower-paced students might simply copy the sentences suggested here. More advanced students should paraphrase the story and write new captions. You might have volunteers present their stories to the class, holding up their illustrations as they retell the story in their own words.

Terms in Lisons!

Students might want to know the following words from the readings. From *Le cimetière des éléphants:* **défense** *(tusk);* **pattes** *(paws);* **épais(se)** *(thick);* **champs** *(fields);* **marécage** *(swamp);* **but** *(goal).* From *La tortue et le léopard:* **creuser** *(to dig);* **tacheté** *(spotted).*

Motivating Activity

Have students look at the title of the second story, *La tortue et le léopard.* Ask them what qualities they associate with turtles (slow, shy) and with leopards (fast, sleek, hunters).

Teaching Suggestions

• Ask students who is speaking at the beginning of the story (some children, an uncle of one of the children). What has happened? (A great hunter has entered the village.) What is the effect of the visitor's presence? (The children all want to become hunters.) Who tells the story and why? (the uncle; He is advising the children that a great hunter needs to be able to set good traps.) From this introduction, have students predict the content of the story that the uncle tells.

N. Have students give the contextual clues they used to figure out the meaning of the words.

POSTREADING
Activities R–S

Teaching Suggestion

R. Have students work in groups to discuss what they think the moral of the story might be and report their results to the class.

Thinking Critically
Comparing and Contrasting

Have students compare and contrast the two stories. Have groups draw two columns on a sheet of paper, one titled *Similarities* and the other *Differences.* They should list as much as they can in each column. They might consider the characters involved in each story and their personality traits, the setting, the basic problem, and how the problem was resolved.

Dame Tortue pensait plus vite qu'elle ne marchait. Avant que le léopard ne la remarque, elle s'est mise à crier d'une voix hautaine : «Mais qu'est-ce que tu fais ici, et qui t'a enseigné de pareilles manières ? Tu n'as donc jamais appris qu'on ne s'invite pas chez une dame, comme ça ?»

Le léopard s'est retourné et a regardé Dame Tortue d'un air stupéfait.

«Tu ne sais donc pas que je ne reçois jamais après la tombée de la nuit ?» a continué la tortue. «Sors d'ici, espèce de voyou tacheté !»

C'était plus que le léopard ne pouvait supporter d'une vieille dame aussi laide. Avec un grognement féroce, il a saisi la tortue et l'a lancée en l'air d'un grand coup de patte. «Sors de ce trou toi-même, espèce de vieille gourde osseuse au cou ridé !» il lui a crié. «Je fais ce que je veux !»

«Merci beaucoup, grand léopard» a doucement répondu la tortue de là où elle avait atterri. «Je te conseille d'économiser tes forces pour demain, quand les chasseurs viendront te chercher. Bonne nuit !»

Dame Tortue est alors partie, soulagée et reconnaissante d'avoir eu autant de chance. Elle était aussi très fière d'avoir si bien su échapper à la fois aux chasseurs et au léopard.

La tortue et le léopard

K. Name three things Dame Tortue is doing at the beginning of the story. How do her actions lead her to fall into the trap? See answers below.

L. Who falls into the trap next? a leopard

M. How does the linking word **alors** function at the beginning of the fifth paragraph? It shows cause and effect.

N. Use context to figure out the meanings of these words.

haughty

a trap   bony

hautaine   osseuse

carapace   un piège   languissant   voyou

shell   languid   scoundrel

O. What strategy does Dame Tortue use to get out of the trap? See answers below.

P. What advice does Dame Tortue give the leopard? Why does she feel clever at the end of the story? See answers below.

Q. Are the following statements true or false?

1. Dame Tortue faisait attention à son chemin en rentrant chez elle. false

2. Le léopard est tombé dans le piège avant la tombée de nuit. false

3. Dame Tortue a imaginé un stratagème pour sortir du piège. true

4. Le léopard a gentiment aidé Dame Tortue à sortir du piège. false

5. Le léopard était obligé d'attendre les chasseurs pour sortir du piège. true

6. Dame Tortue n'est pas très maligne. false

R. What lessons does the story suggest? See answers below.

S. Name three elements that are common to both tales. How is the subject of hunting treated differently in the two stories? Why? How do you feel about hunting? See answers below.

182   *cent quatre-vingt-deux*

Teaching Suggestion

Have students suggest adjectives to describe the turtle and the leopard in this story. (*turtle:* resourceful; *leopard:* impatient)

Answers

K She is daydreaming, stopping to smell wildflowers, and eating buds. Not paying attention, she doesn't notice a trap in her path.

O She treats the leopard like an unwanted guest in "her" hole. Angered, he throws her out.

P to save his strength for the hunters; She escaped both the hunters and the leopard.

R *Possible answer:* Cleverness can triumph over adversity and can be more important than physical strength.

S Common elements include animals with human characteristics, physical danger, and escape. The hunters in the first story are killing masses of elephants out of greed for their tusks. The hunters in the second story are trapping individual animals for food.

ECRIVONS!

You've just read two very different stories about animals. Each animal in the stories has a distinct personality, with qualities and flaws that make it seem human. In this activity you'll develop your own animal characters, using them to tell a story that you create.

Une histoire d'animaux
Maintenant tu vas écrire ta propre histoire d'animaux.

A. Préparation
1. Quel type d'histoire est-ce que tu préfères raconter?
   a. Tu peux écrire un mythe. Comme *Le cimetière des éléphants,* ton mythe devra expliquer le comportement particulier d'un groupe d'animaux.
   b. Tu peux choisir d'écrire une fable comme *La tortue et le léopard.* Il doit y avoir, dans ta fable, une morale que tu veux enseigner aux autres.
   c. Si tu préfères, tu peux créer l'histoire de ton choix, à condition qu'elle ait des animaux pour personnages.
2. Imagine l'intrigue de ton histoire. Qu'est-ce qui se passera?
3. Qui vont être les personnages de ton histoire? Fais une courte description de chacun des personnages principaux et explique son rôle dans l'histoire.
4. Fais une liste où tu notes les événements dans l'ordre où ils arriveront. Assure-toi que tu n'as pas oublié d'événements importants.

B. Rédaction
1. Fais un brouillon de ton histoire en suivant ton plan. Vérifie que tu as suivi un ordre logique dans l'action de l'histoire.
2. Utilise quelques-uns des mots suivants pour montrer l'ordre des événements.

ensuite	à la fin
d'abord	au début
puis	pendant que
après	quand

cependant
bien que
néanmoins
ainsi
de plus
en fait
par conséquent
parce que

3. Pour lier les différentes idées et rendre ton histoire plus agréable à lire, utilise certains des mots à droite.

DE BONS CONSEILS
Sequencing, the way you put the events of a story in order, is an important part of storytelling. The action in a story should proceed logically, with no gaps or jumps to break the reader's attention. Sequencing words such as **d'abord, ensuite, puis,** and **enfin** are useful in relating the order of events in a story. Linking words such as those you learned on page 180 can help you relate one sentence to another. Proper sequencing of your sentences and ideas will create a smooth narrative flow in a story.

C. Evaluation
1. Relis ton brouillon.
   a. Est-ce que tu as raconté les événements principaux de l'histoire dans un ordre logique?
   b. Est-ce que tu as utilisé des mots de liaison entre les différents événements?
2. Vérifie la grammaire et l'orthographe de ton histoire et fais les corrections nécessaires.
3. Donne ton histoire à un(e) camarade de classe. Est-ce que le but de l'histoire est clair?

cent quatre-vingt-trois **183**

WRITING STRATEGY
Sequencing

 Portfolio

Written You might want to have students include all their work for sections A–C in their written portfolios. For portfolio suggestions, see *Assessment Guide,* page 20.

PREWRITING

Motivating Activity

Have students list characteristics they associate with various animals (fox—cunning; owl—wise; dog—loyal).

Literature Link

A. Ask students to explain the difference between a myth and a fable. (A myth serves to explain a practice, belief, or natural phenomenon. A fable usually has animals as its main characters and teaches a moral lesson.)

Teaching Suggestion

A. 1. Hold a brief storytelling session in English. Assign several students stories to read and retell (*Paul Bunyan, The Fox and the Crow, The Tortoise and the Hare,* and so on). In class, have students form a circle, and have the storytellers recount their tales.

WRITING

 For Individual Needs

B. 2. Slower Pace Before students try to use these words in their stories, have them write a sentence using each one.

POSTWRITING

Teaching Suggestions

C. 1. Have students number the events on their papers in red, and mark the linking words they used with a highlighter.

• Have students set their stories aside for a day or two after they have finished the rough draft. When they pick them up again, they can evaluate them with a new perspective.

For Individual Needs

Visual Learners Students might also illustrate their story. They should choose several key events, draw pictures for them, and copy the corresponding text underneath.

Family Link

Have students share their stories with their families.

The **Mise en pratique** reviews and integrates all four skills and culture in preparation for the Chapter Test.

Video Wrap-Up

VIDEO PROGRAM
Videocassette 1

You might want to use the *Video Program* as part of the chapter review. See the *Video Guide* for teaching suggestions and activity masters.

Teaching Suggestions

1 Before students attempt to answer the questions, have them look at the pictures and the titles of each section. Have them suggest an English title for this brochure, based on their first observations.

1 Have students try to guess the meaning of the following items mentioned under *Les solutions:* **corail, écailles de tortue, objets en plume** *(coral, tortoiseshell, feather objects)*.

Additional Practice

1 Ask students the following questions about the brochure: **Combien d'espèces d'animaux sont en voie de disparition?** (3.200) **Comment s'appelle le bureau créé pour lutter contre le négoce illégal de la vie sauvage?** (TRAFFIC) **Quels animaux sont touchés par ce problème?** (les singes, les éléphants, les rhinocéros, les félins, les crocodiles, les perroquets, les tortues)

Building on Previous Skills

2 Encourage students to use expressions they've already learned for persuading and reproaching: **Tu (ne) devrais (pas)... ; Tu ferais bien de... ; Tu as tort de... ; Ce n'est pas bien de...**

MISE EN PRATIQUE

1 En Afrique, un gardien d'une réserve que tu visites te donne ce dépliant. Lis-le et réponds aux questions suivantes. See answers below.

PLUS JAMAIS ÇA!

Savez-vous que 3 200 espèces animales et 40 000 espèces végétales sont menacées d'extinction? Le commerce international de la vie sauvage est la deuxième cause de disparition de celles-ci. Malgré la réglementation existante, un négoce illégal important persiste. Pour lutter contre celui-ci, un bureau TRAFFIC vient d'être créé en France. Agissez avec lui, aidez-le...

LES FAITS
Dans le monde entier, singes, éléphants, rhinocéros, félins, crocodiles, perroquets, tortues... sont tués pour leur peau, leurs plumes, leur ivoire, ou capturés vivants : Pour 1 animal vendu jusqu'à 20 meurent durant la capture et les transports. Le bénéfice tiré du trafic illicite de la vie sauvage représente 1/3 du commerce total et profite à une «mafia» internationale. Les collectionneurs, les touristes contribuent à la sur-exploitation de la faune et de la flore sauvages qui participe à l'appauvrissement des pays en développement.

LES RISQUES
Pour la vie sauvage : Dans le monde 3 200 espèces animales sont menacées d'extinction et 40 000 espèces végétales sont en voie de disparition.
Pour l'homme : Le trafic d'animaux véhicule des maladies transmissibles à l'homme ou aux animaux domestiques et d'élevage. Certains animaux sont porteurs de la rage, de la fièvre jaune...

LES SOLUTIONS
Prise de conscience : Vous êtes concernés! Vous êtes la meilleure arme contre la surexploitation de la vie sauvage et de son trafic. Evitez d'acheter : ivoire, corail, écailles de tortue, peaux et fourrures, insectes, objets en plume, animaux sauvages, vivants ou empaillés. Réfléchissez, renseignez-vous!

WWF France   FFSPN

AIDEZ-NOUS A PROTEGER LA VIE

1. What is this brochure about?
2. According to the brochure, why are these animals hunted?
3. Who contributes to the problem besides poachers? How?
4. What risks to people and to animals are mentioned?
5. What does the brochure recommend that each person do to help solve the problem?

2 Après avoir lu le dépliant, tu veux faire quelque chose pour la protection des animaux. Ecris une lettre à tes camarades où tu leur expliques ce qu'il faut faire pour sauver les animaux. A la fin de ta lettre, tu leur demandes de faire un don *(donation)* et de devenir membre du WWF.

☐ Je désire participer à la lutte contre le commerce illégal de la vie sauvage et verse un don de :
  ☐ 100 F   ☐ 200 F   ☐ 500 F et +
☐ Je désire devenir membre du WWF
En étant membre, je reçois la Revue PANDA (au moins 4 fois l'an) et le PANDA Nouvelles (4 à 6 fois l'an)
☐ Mlle ☐ Mme ☐ M. ☐ Famille ☐ Firme

Nom

Prénom

Rue, No

No postal   Localité
Année de
naissance   Signature
          (au-dessous de 16 ans, celle du répondant)

☐ Je m'intéresse aux activités de la section WWF de ma région et désire une information à ce sujet.

☐ J'aimerais également devenir membre de la section WWF de ma région qui agit (par des travaux pratiques) pour la protection de la nature locale. Cotisation annuelle supplémentaire à celle du WWF Suisse: max. Fr.5.- (pour les jeunes membres de moins de 20 ans pas de supplément).

Ecology Link

Before an international ban on ivory was instituted in 1990, the elephant population of some African countries had dropped by as much as 89%. Once the ban was in effect, almost one hundred countries honored it, and the price of ivory fell dramatically. Craft items and jewelry that were once made of ivory are now available in a plastic imitation, which is virtually indistinguishable from authentic ivory.

Answers

1 1. preventing the poaching of endangered species
2. to sell their skins, horns, feathers, fur, or ivory for profit
3. Collectors and tourists contribute by buying animals and products made from them.
4. Wild animals risk extinction. People and domestic animals risk contracting diseases.
5. Refuse to buy products such as ivory and furs that are taken from wild animals.

3 Ecoute Roger qui montre à sa classe les diapositives *(slides)* de son voyage en Afrique. Quels endroits l'ont vraiment impressionné? a, c, e

a.

b.

c.

d.

e.

f.

 4 Tu vas faire un safari avec ton ami(e). Tu lui décris comment sera le paysage et quels animaux vous pourrez y voir, d'après toi. Il/Elle s'est renseigné(e) et te dit s'il/si elle croit que tu as raison. Faites aussi une liste de ce qu'il faut faire avant de partir et de ce qu'il faut emporter. Si ton ami(e) oublie quelque chose, fais-lui des suggestions.

 5 Imagine que tu es dans la brousse africaine. Ecris tes aventures des trois premiers jours. Ensuite, raconte-les à ton/ta camarade.

6

J E U   D E   R O L E

You and your friends are camping in a reserve. Suddenly you hear noises that sound like gunshots. Wondering what the noises could be, you decide to go see what's happening. As you come over a hill, you see poachers. Knowing that you could be in danger, you leave immediately. When you reach a village, you look for a phone to call the reserve patrol. Act out this scene with your classmates. Remember to do these things at the appropriate times:

- express fear
- make suppositions
- reassure one another
- warn your friends
- express your relief

MISE EN PRATIQUE

cent quatre-vingt-cinq **185**

For Individual Needs

3 Visual Learners Type brief descriptions of each slide pictured in this activity. For example, for the first slide, you might write **Les chutes de Boali sont magnifiques!** Make copies of the descriptions, distribute them, and have students match the slides with the descriptions.

3 Auditory Learners As an alternative listening activity, read the items from the listening script aloud in random order and have students indicate which slide is being described.

3 Challenge Have students write captions for each of the slides. They might write captions that Roger would have written, or captions based on their own impressions of Africa. If students write about their own impressions, you might have volunteers read a caption aloud and have the class try to guess which photo it describes.

Portfolio

4 Oral This activity might be included in students' oral portfolios. For portfolio information, see *Assessment Guide,* pages 2–13.

6 Oral This activity is appropriate for students' oral portfolios. You might have students videotape their skits. For portfolio suggestions, see *Assessment Guide,* page 20.

Culture Notes

• The **chutes de Boali,** shown in Photo **a** in Activity 3, are located about one hundred miles northwest of Bangui in the southern part of the Central African Republic. The falls are controlled by a dam, which was built by the Chinese.

• Point out the Pygmies in Photo **c** in Activity 3. The people of this ethnic group are famous for their height, which averages about four feet. Their lifestyle includes hunting and gathering nuts and roots available in the rainforest. A nomadic people, they are constantly moving to areas where food is more plentiful.

This page is intended to help students prepare for the test. It is a brief checklist of the major points covered in the chapter. The students should be reminded that this is only a checklist and does not necessarily include everything that will appear on the test.

Additional Practice

2 Bring in or have students bring in additional pictures of animals that would or would not be seen on a photo safari in the Central African Republic and have students express doubt or certainty about seeing them.

4 Have students suggest additional items that one might need to bring on trips to these places.

Teaching Suggestion

7, 8 Have students combine their answers for Activities 7 and 8 to create a two-line dialogue about one person reassuring a frightened friend.

QUE SAIS-JE?

Can you make suppositions? p.169

Can you express doubt and certainty? p.169

Can you ask for and give advice? p.171

Can you express astonishment? p.177

Can you caution someone? p.178

Can you express fear? p.178

Can you reassure someone? p.178

Can you express relief? p.178

Can you use what you've learned in this chapter?

1 How would you make suppositions about what you would see on a safari? On pourrait sûrement voir... ; Je parie qu'il y a... ; Ça doit être... ; Il doit y avoir...

2 How would you express your doubt or certainty about seeing the following animals on safari in Africa? See answers below.

1. 2. 3. 4.

3 How would you ask whether these items are necessary for a trip?
See answers below.

1. 2. 3.

4 How would you tell a friend whether the items in number 3 are necessary for . . . See answers below.
1. a trip to Africa?   2. a trip to the North Pole?

5 How would you express your feelings about something really impressive? See answers below.

6 How would you warn people in these situations? 1. Méfie-toi!
1. A friend is about to step out into a busy street without looking.
2. A relative is traveling to a country where the mosquitoes carry malaria. Attention aux moustiques!
3. A friend is approached by a mean dog. Fais gaffe!

7 How would you express fear of . . . See answers below.
1. snakes and spiders?   2. a horror movie you're watching?

8 How would you reassure someone who is afraid of the things in number 7? Ne vous en faites pas. Ne t'en fais pas. N'ayez pas peur. N'aie pas peur. Calmez-vous! Calme-toi! Pas de panique!

9 How would you express your relief at . . . Possible answers:
1. not getting bitten by a mean dog? Je l'ai échappé belle! J'ai eu chaud!
2. not getting a bad grade at school? Ouf! J'ai eu de la chance!

Possible answers

2 1. Ça m'étonnerait qu'il y ait des chiens.
2. Je suis sûr(e) qu'il y aura des zèbres.
3. Je ne suis pas certain(e) qu'il y ait des ours.
4. Je suis convaincu(e) qu'il y aura des girafes.

3 Tu crois que je devrais prendre... ; Tu penses qu'il vaudrait mieux emporter...
1. de la lotion anti-moustique?
2. des jumelles?
3. des chèques de voyage?

4 1. Il faudrait que.../ Il est important que.../ Il est essentiel que tu prennes de la lotion anti-moustique/des jumelles/des chèques de voyage.
2. Ce n'est pas la peine de... ; Je ne crois pas que ce soit utile d'emporter de la lotion anti-moustique. Il est nécessaire que tu prennes des jumelles et des chèques de voyage.

5 Oh, dis donc! Ça alors! C'est pas vrai! Oh là là! Ouah! C'est le pied! Tiens! Regarde un peu! Qu'est-ce qu'(e)... ! C'est fou comme... ; Quel(le)... ! Tu as vu comme... ? Je n'ai jamais vu un(e) aussi...

7 1. J'ai très peur des serpents et des araignées.
2. J'ai la frousse!

PREMIERE ETAPE

Making suppositions

On pourrait sûrement... *We'd be able to . . .for sure.*
Ça doit être... *It must be . . .*
Il doit y avoir... *There must be . . .*

Expressing doubt and certainty

Ça m'étonnerait que... *I'd be surprised if . . .*
Je (ne) suis (pas) sûr(e) que... *I'm (not) sure that . . .*
Je (ne) suis (pas) certain(e) que... *I'm (not) certain that . . .*
Je ne pense pas que... *I don't think that . . .*
Je sais que... *I know that . . .*
Je suis convaincu(e) que... *I'm convinced that . . .*

Rain forest and savannah

une araignée *a spider*
un arbre *a tree*

la brousse *the brush*
une fourmi *an ant*
l'herbe (f.) *grass*
une mouche *a fly*
un oiseau *a bird*
un papillon *a butterfly*
un point d'eau *a watering hole*
une rivière *a river*
la savane *the savannah*
un serpent *a snake*
la végétation tropicale *tropical vegetation*

Asking for and giving advice

Tu crois que je devrais...? *Do you think I should . . .?*
Tu penses qu'il vaudrait mieux... ? *Do you think it'd be better to . . .?*
Je crois que ça vaut mieux. *I think that's better.*
A mon avis, c'est plus sûr. *In my opinion, it's safer.*

Ce n'est pas la peine. *It's not worth it.*
Je ne crois pas que ce soit utile. *I don't think it's worthwhile.*
Il faudrait que... *You ought to . . .*
Il est très important que... *It's very important to . . .*
Il est essentiel que... *It's essential to . . .*
Il est nécessaire que... *It's necessary to . . .*

Packing for a safari

un caméscope *a camcorder*
une carte de crédit *a credit card*
de la crème solaire *sunscreen*
un désinfectant *disinfectant*
une gourde *a canteen*
des jumelles (f.) *binoculars*
des pansements (m.) *bandages*
une pellicule *a roll of film*
une torche *a flashlight*

DEUXIEME ETAPE

Expressing astonishment

Oh, dis donc! *Wow!*
Ça alors! *How about that!*
Ouah! *Wow!*
C'est le pied! *Cool! Neat!*
Tiens! Regarde un peu! *Hey! Check it out!*
C'est fou comme... ! *I can't believe how . . . !*
Tu as vu comme... ? *Did you see how . . . ?*
Je n'ai jamais vu un(e) aussi... *I've never seen such a . . .*

African animals

une corne *a horn*
un éléphant *an elephant*
féroce *ferocious*

une girafe *a giraffe*
un guépard *a cheetah*
un hippopotame *a hippopotamus*
un lion *a lion*
lourd(e) *heavy*
la proie *the prey*
un rhinocéros *a rhinoceros*
un singe *a monkey*
une trompe *a trunk*
un zèbre *a zebra*

Cautioning and reassuring someone

Je vous signale que... *I'm warning you that . . .*
Il serait plus prudent de... *It would be wiser to . . .*
Faites gaffe! *Look out!*

Attention à... ! *Watch out for . . . !*
Méfiez-vous! *Be careful!*
Ne bougez pas. *Don't move.*
N'ayez pas peur. *Don't be afraid.*
Calmez-vous! *Calm down!*
Pas de panique! *Don't panic!*

Expressing fear and relief

J'ai très peur de (que)... *I'm very afraid of (that) . . .*
J'ai la frousse! *I'm scared to death!*
On a eu de la chance! *We were lucky!*
Ouf! On a eu chaud! *Whew! That was a real scare!*
On l'a échappé belle! *That was close!*

Game

Loto! Have students make a 5 X 5 grid on a sheet of paper and write in each square one of the expressions from the **Vocabulaire**. While students are making their grids, write the vocabulary expressions on slips of paper and place them in a box. When students have completed their grid, begin the Bingo game by drawing slips and calling out the expressions. Students who have written that expression on their grid should mark it with a scrap of paper or a coin. When a student has marked five squares in a row, he or she calls out **Loto!**, shows you the grid, and reads aloud the French expressions he or she has marked. Then, the entire class writes sentences, using the expressions marked.

CHAPTER 7 ASSESSMENT

CHAPTER TEST
• *Chapter Teaching Resources, Book 2,* pp. 135–140
• *Assessment Guide,* Speaking Test, p. 31
• *Assessment Items, Audiocassette 8A Audio CD 7*

TEST GENERATOR, CHAPTER 7

ALTERNATIVE ASSESSMENT

Performance Assessment
You might want to use the **Jeu de rôle** (p.185) as a cumulative performance assessment activity.

Portfolio Assessment
• **Written: Ecrivons!** *Pupil's Edition,* p. 183
  Assessment Guide, p. 31
• **Oral: Mise en pratique, Jeu de rôle,** *Pupil's Edition,* p. 185
  Assessment Guide, p. 31

Chapitre 8 : La Tunisie, pays de contrastes
Chapter Overview

Mise en train
pp. 190–192

Bisous de Nefta

	FUNCTIONS	GRAMMAR	CULTURE	RE-ENTRY	
Première étape pp. 193–199	• Asking someone to convey good wishes, p. 194 • Closing a letter, p. 194 • Expressing hopes or wishes, p. 196 • Giving advice, p. 196	*si* clauses, p. 197	• **Rencontre Culturelle,** Overview of Tunisia, p. 193 • **Note Culturelle,** Traditional and modern life in Tunisia, p. 194 • **Note Culturelle,** Carthage, p. 198 • **Panorama Culturel,** Modernization in francophone countries, p. 199	• The imperfect • The conditional	

Remise en train
pp. 200–201

Salut de Tunis

	FUNCTIONS	GRAMMAR	CULTURE	RE-ENTRY	
Deuxième étape pp. 202–205	• Complaining, p. 203 • Expressing annoyance, p. 203 • Making comparisons, p. 204	The comparative, p. 204	**Note Culturelle,** Traditional and modern styles of dress in Tunisia, p. 205	• Intonation • Adjective agreement • Describing a place	

Lisons!
pp. 206–208

Enfance d'une fille
Reading Strategy: Relating parts of the story to the main idea

Ecrivons!
p. 209

Un récit familial
Writing Strategy: Brainstorming

Review
pp. 210–213

• **Mise en pratique,** pp. 210–211
• **Que sais-je?** p. 212
• **Vocabulaire,** p. 213

Assessment Options

Etape Quizzes
• *Chapter Teaching Resources, Book 2*
  Première étape, Quiz 8-1, pp. 185–186
  Deuxième étape, Quiz 8-2, pp. 187–188
• *Assessment Items, Audiocassette 8A/Audio CD 8*

Chapter Test
• *Chapter Teaching Resources, Book 2,* pp. 189–194
• *Assessment Guide,* Speaking Test, p. 31
• *Assessment Items, Audiocassette 8A/Audio CD 8*

Test Generator, Chapter 8

RESOURCES: Print	RESOURCES: Audiovisual
Practice and Activity Book, p. 85	*Textbook Audiocassette 4B/Audio CD 8*
Practice and Activity Book, pp. 86–89 *Grammar and Vocabulary Worksheets*, pp. 73–77 *Chapter Teaching Resources, Book 2* • Communicative Activity 8-1, pp. 166–167 • Teaching Transparency Master 8-1, pp. 170, 172 . . . . • Additional Listening Activities 8-1, 8-2, 8-3, pp. 173–174. . . • Realia 8-1, pp. 177, 179 • Situation Cards 8-1, pp. 180–181 • Student Response Forms, pp. 182–184 • Quiz 8-1, pp. 185–186 . . . . *Video Guide*	*Textbook Audiocassette 4B/Audio CD 8* *Teaching Transparency 8-1* *Additional Listening Activities, Audiocassette 10A/Audio CD 8* *Assessment Items, Audiocassette 8A/Audio CD 8* *Video Program, Videocassette 2*
Practice and Activity Book, p. 90	*Textbook Audiocassette 4B/Audio CD 8*
Practice and Activity Book, pp. 91–94 *Grammar and Vocabulary Worksheets*, pp. 78–81 *Chapter Teaching Resources, Book 2* • Communicative Activity 8-2, pp. 168–169 • Teaching Transparency Master 8-2, pp. 171, 172 . . . . • Additional Listening Activities 8-4, 8-5, 8-6, pp. 174–175. . . • Realia 8-2, pp. 178, 179 • Situation Cards 8-2, 8-3, pp. 180–181 • Student Response Forms, pp. 182–184 • Quiz 8-2, pp. 187–188	*Textbook Audiocassette 4B/Audio CD 8* *Teaching Transparency 8-2* *Additional Listening Activities, Audiocassette 10A/Audio CD 8* *Assessment Items, Audiocassette 8A/Audio CD 8*
Practice and Activity Book, p. 95	
Video Guide	*Video Program, Videocassette 2*

Alternative Assessment
- Performance Assessment
  Première étape, p. 198
  Deuxième étape, p. 205
- Portfolio Assessment
  Written: Activity 18, *Pupil's Edition*, p. 198
    Assessment Guide, p. 21
  Oral: **Mise en pratique**, Activity 2, *Pupil's Edition*, p. 211
    Assessment Guide, p. 21

Textbook Listening Activities Scripts

For Student Response Forms, see *Chapter Teaching Resources, Book 2,* pp. 182–184.

Première étape

7 Ecoute! p. 194

1. — Tu sais ce que je vais faire pendant les vacances? De la plongée avec Ahmed.
   — Ah oui? Ça fait longtemps que je ne l'ai pas vu, Ahmed. Salue-le pour moi.
   — D'accord!

2. — Je vais au cinéma avec des copains. Tu veux venir avec nous?
   — Je voudrais bien, mais je ne peux pas. Je dois faire mes devoirs.
   — Dommage. Peut-être la prochaine fois.
   — Oui, j'espère.

3. — Tu as entendu? Malika s'est cassé la jambe.
   — Comment c'est arrivé?
   — Elle est tombée de vélo. Je vais la voir à l'hôpital. Tu veux venir avec moi?
   — Je ne peux pas aujourd'hui. Mais embrasse-la pour moi et dis-lui que je pense à elle.
   — D'accord. Compte sur moi.

4. — Alors, tu reviens en août?
   — Oui, fin août.
   — Bon. Je te téléphonerai. Allez, je parie que ça va être chouette, la Tunisie.
   — Oui, sans doute.
   — Tu nous manqueras. Allez, dépêche-toi. Tu vas rater l'avion.
   — Bon, d'accord. Au revoir.
   — Au revoir.

5. — Alors, bon voyage! Surtout, sois sage. Fais mes amitiés à ton oncle et à ta tante. Et dis-leur que je vais leur écrire.
   — Tu peux compter sur moi.
   — Allez, dépêche-toi, le train va partir!

Answers to Activity 7
1, 3, 5

12 Ecoute! p. 195

1. AMIRA Tu vois comment il trait la vache?
   KARIM C'est cool. Je peux le faire, moi aussi? Tu m'apprends?
   AMIRA Oui, si tu veux, mais je t'assure, c'est pas si cool que ça.

2. KARIM Qu'est-ce qu'elle fait, la femme là-bas?
   AMIRA Oh, elle va donner à manger aux poules. Regarde comme elles sont agitées.

3. AMIRA Attention à la chèvre! Elle mange tout, tu sais. Tu ferais bien de mettre tes mains dans tes poches.

4. KARIM Il est où, ton frère?
   AMIRA Il garde les moutons. Ils sont en train de brouter.
   KARIM Est-ce que vous les tondez?

AMIRA Oui, c'est mon frère et mon père qui les tondent. On utilise leur laine pour faire des tapis.

5. AMIRA Tu vois? Ce sont nos champs de blé.
   KARIM Alors, quand est-ce qu'on récolte le blé?
   AMIRA Bientôt. Nos cousins vont nous aider.

6. KARIM C'est cool, l'artisanat tunisien.
   AMIRA Oui. Regarde cet homme là-bas. Tu vois ce qu'il fait?
   KARIM Oui, il fait de la poterie.
   AMIRA Oui, ici, on est très connus pour notre poterie.

7. KARIM Il est très beau, ce paysage, avec tous ces palmiers et ces dattiers.
   AMIRA Il y en a chez toi?
   KARIM Oh, pas vraiment.
   AMIRA Les dattiers, c'est très important chez nous. Si tu veux, tu peux faire la cueillette des dattes avec nous.
   KARIM Chouette!

Answers to Activity 12
1. f 2. a 3. d 4. e 5. g 6. b 7. c

14 Ecoute! p. 196

1. — Mes parents veulent que j'habite à la ferme avec mon oncle cet été. Bah! Quel cauchemar! Je n'aime pas la campagne, moi.
   — A ta place, je leur en parlerais. Il faut qu'ils sachent ce que tu veux.

2. — Moi, je n'ai aucune idée de ce que je voudrais faire. Et toi?
   — Moi, si j'avais le choix, je partirais en Afrique. Il y a tellement de choses à faire et à voir là-bas!

3. — Je ne pourrai pas y aller si je ne trouve pas de travail, mais il n'y a rien en ce moment.
   — Si j'étais toi, je demanderais au supermarché. J'ai un cousin qui y travaille. Il dit que c'est pas mal.

4. — Si c'était possible, j'habiterais chez mes cousins à la campagne.
   — Mais pourquoi?
   — Parce que c'est tellement tranquille. J'aimerais tellement vivre dans le calme!

5. — Dis Saïd, où est-ce que tu habiterais si tu avais le choix?
   — Oh, ça serait chouette si je pouvais habiter au bord de la mer.

6. — Cet été, j'ai le choix entre aller à la campagne chez mes grands-parents ou aller en ville, chez mon frère. Qu'est-ce que tu en penses?
   — Si j'étais toi, j'irais à la campagne. Tu pourrais découvrir quelque chose de nouveau. Ça te changerait un peu.

7. — Si seulement je pouvais faire un voyage en Tunisie.
   — Ah, oui? Pourquoi?
   — Ben, tu sais que j'adore l'archéologie. J'aimerais visiter les ruines de Carthage. Ce serait super, non?
   — Oui... peut-être.

Answers to Activity 14
1. donne des conseils   4. aimerait faire   7. aimerait faire
2. aimerait faire   5. aimerait faire
3. donne des conseils   6. donne des conseils

Deuxième étape

25 Ecoute! p. 202

1. — Comment? Je ne t'entends pas. La rue est si bruyante à cette heure-ci. Il va falloir qu'on aille à l'intérieur pour parler.

2. — N'oublie pas de donner à manger aux poules, Fatima.

3. — Pardon, madame. Il y a un arrêt de bus près d'ici?

4. — C'est vraiment agréable ici, n'est-ce pas? Les palmiers, les dattiers, les couchers de soleil, qu'est-ce que c'est tranquille!

5. — Zut alors! On va être en retard! C'est toujours la même chose, ces embouteillages!

6. — Eh! Dites donc!! Vous ne pouvez pas regarder où vous allez? Qu'est-ce qu'ils sont mal élevés, ces gens!

7. — Oh, je suis crevé! Ce n'est pas facile de s'occuper des chameaux. Ils sont méchants, tu sais!

8. — Voilà l'immeuble où j'habite. Qu'est-ce tu en penses? Il est vraiment moderne, non?

9. — Désolé, je ne pourrai pas partir tout de suite. On récolte le blé en ce moment. Je viendrai dans un mois, d'accord?

10. — Je trais les vaches tous les jours. J'en ai marre, moi! C'est ton tour, cette fois-ci.

11. — Ben, qu'est-ce qu'on va faire? Il n'y a pas de places de stationnement. On va manquer le début du concert.

12. — Ils sont beaux, ces gratte-ciel, mais ils sont dangereux, non? Qu'est-ce qui se passe s'il y a un feu?

Answers to Activity 25

1. ville	4. campagne	7. campagne	10. campagne
2. campagne	5. ville	8. ville	11. ville
3. ville	6. ville	9. campagne	12. ville

27 Ecoute! p. 203

1. — Ah non! On va manquer le film! J'en ai ras le bol de ces embouteillages!

2. — Tu as entendu, il y a un nouveau cinéma tout près d'ici. Cinq minutes à pied. Cool, non?

3. — Oh, c'est l'horreur, cette pollution, tu sais. Je n'arrive plus à respirer.

4. — Oh, dis donc, il est géant, ce magasin de vidéos. Je parie qu'ils ont absolument tout ce qu'on veut.

5. — Tu sais ce qui m'est arrivé? Quelqu'un m'est rentré dedans et mes lunettes sont tombées. Je commence à en avoir marre de ces gens mal élevés!

6. — C'est tellement animé, la ville. Comme c'est bien d'avoir beaucoup de choses à faire et à voir!

7. — On va essayer le restaurant marocain, ce soir. On m'a dit que c'était très bon. Tu viens avec nous?

8. — On construit un immeuble derrière chez nous. C'est insupportable, à la fin, tout ce bruit.

9. — On dit qu'il va faire encore plus chaud demain. C'est vraiment l'horreur, cette chaleur, et toute cette foule.

10. — Oh! Je commence à en avoir marre! Ils se sont arrêtés en plein milieu du carrefour. On ne pourra pas passer au vert.

Answers to Activity 27

1. non	3. non	5. non	7. oui	9. non
2. oui	4. oui	6. oui	8. non	10. non

28 Ecoute! p. 203

1. — C'est l'horreur!

2. — C'est insupportable, à la fin!

3. — J'en ai ras le bol!

4. — Je commence à en avoir marre!

5. — Vous vous prenez pour qui?

6. — Non mais, surtout, ne vous gênez pas!

7. — Ça va pas, non?!

8. — Ça commence à bien faire, hein?

9. — Dites donc, ça vous gênerait de baisser votre musique?

Mise en pratique

3 p. 211

LEILA Dis Hoda, qu'est-ce que tu penses faire cet été?

HODA Ben, ça serait chouette si je pouvais aller à la mer, mais je ne pense pas que ce soit possible.

LEILA Pourquoi pas?

HODA Ma famille n'y va pas cette année.

LEILA Si j'étais toi, je demanderais à mes parents la permission d'y aller avec des copines.

HODA Mais ils ne seront pas d'accord. Ça, je le sais déjà.

LEILA Dommage. Qu'est-ce que tu pourrais faire d'autre?

HODA Ben, il y a mon oncle et ma tante qui m'ont invitée à passer l'été chez eux en Tunisie.

LEILA Cool!

HODA Si seulement je pouvais y aller, je me baladerais un peu dans le pays.

LEILA Ça serait vachement bien!

HODA Oui, mais, je n'ai pas l'argent pour le billet.

LEILA A ta place, je chercherais du travail. Avec un mois de salaire, tu pourrais te payer le voyage.

HODA Si c'était possible, je m'occuperais des enfants des Marzouk. Ils partent en vacances pendant le mois de juin.

LEILA Pourquoi tu ne le fais pas?

HODA Ils m'ont déjà demandé, mais j'ai refusé parce que je ne savais pas que j'aurais besoin de travailler.

LEILA Si j'étais toi, je leur téléphonerais tout de suite. Il se peut qu'ils n'aient pas encore trouvé quelqu'un.

HODA Oui, c'est peut-être une bonne idée.

Answers to Mise en pratique Activity 3

Souhaits: aller à la mer; passer l'été chez son oncle et sa tante en Tunisie; s'occuper des enfants des Marzouk

Conseils: demander à tes parents la permission d'y aller avec des copines; chercher un travail; téléphoner aux Marzouk.

Projects

Ma ville, hier et aujourd'hui
(Individual Project)

ASSIGNMENT

Students will prepare and videotape a documentary program for French television in which they describe how their city or town has changed in the last fifty years. Students will conduct research in the library or media center and interview some of their city's older residents. Their program should also include visual aids, such as old newspapers and maps, posters they create, or computer-generated graphics.

MATERIALS

✄ Students may need

- Reference materials, such as old newspapers, magazines, and maps
- Cassette recorder
- Audiocassette
- Camcorder

- Videocassette
- Posterboard
- Colored markers
- Computer (for graphics, if available)

SUGGESTED SEQUENCE

1. Have students begin by researching their city's history in the library or media center. You may choose to allow class time for students to do their preliminary research. They should find out how and when the town was founded and what people or businesses were important at that time.

2. Have students prepare a list of interview questions they would like to ask their interviewees. They should also translate the questions into French, since their documentary will be for a French TV station.

3. Then, students should interview at least five people who have lived in the city for the last twenty to fifty years. They might choose to record the interviews on audio- or videocassette so they can play clips of the interviews during their program.

4. Have students organize the information they intend to present for their documentary and write their scripts. Remind them that they need to pique their audience's interest in the first thirty seconds of the program, so they should lead in with their most interesting facts. Then, they should summarize their research and interviews.

5. If students recorded their interviews, they might choose to play short, five- or ten-second clips during their presentation. In this case, they should prepare a voice-over French translation, which they may record at this time or simply read aloud over the recording during the presentation. You might offer help with the translations.

6. Students should create and/or organize any charts, graphs, or photos for their presentation.

7. Have students record their documentaries on videocassette, using all the audiovisual materials they have organized.

GRADING THE PROJECT

You might want to base students' grades on thoroughness of content, organization, use and creativity of audiovisual aids, oral presentation, and language use.

Suggested Point Distribution (total = 100 points)

Content . . . . 25 points
Organization . . . . 25 points
Audiovisual aids . . . . 15 points
Oral presentation . . . . 20 points
Language use . . . . 15 points

Chapitre 8 : La Tunisie, pays de contrastes

 *Games*

SI J'ETAIS...

In this game, students will practice the forms of the imperfect and the conditional.

Procedure Form two teams. A player from one team assumes the identity of a celebrity, a historical figure, or even a cartoon character. Members of the opposing team may then ask up to 20 questions about the player's identity. Questions should include a **si** clause, such as: **Si tu étais des chaussures, quelle sorte de chaussures est-ce que tu serais?** The player answers according to the identity he or she has chosen. For example, if the player chose to be Shaquille O'Neal (NBA basketball player), the response to the question above might be **Je serais des baskets.** You might suggest the following sample questions: **Si tu étais une chanson, laquelle est-ce que tu serais? Si tu suivais un cours au lycée, lequel est-ce que tu suivrais? Si tu étais un plat, quel plat est-ce que tu serais?**

ARRETEZ!

In this game, students will practice chapter vocabulary.

Procedure Choose several words from the **Vocabulaire** page. Write the words on a transparency, and cover it with a sheet of paper. To begin the game, uncover the first word on the list. Students must write new words that begin with the letters of that word. For example, if the word you uncover is **poterie**, students might write **poule** for **p**, **olive** for **o**, **tapis** for **t**, and so on. The student who finishes first calls out **Arrêtez!**, and the other students put down their pens. The student who called out **Arrêtez!** reads his or her words aloud. If the words are all appropriate, that student wins ten points. Then, uncover another word and continue the game.

Variation Give students thirty seconds to write as many words as possible that begin with each letter. Call time and award points for each word that is correctly spelled.

For Individual Needs

Challenge After each round of the game, you might have students write sentences, using the words they wrote during the game.

Chapitre 8
La Tunisie, pays de contrastes

pp. 188–213

*U*sing the Chapter Opener

 Video Program

Videocassette 2

Before you begin this chapter, you might want to preview the *Video Program* and consult the *Video Guide.* Suggestions for integrating the video into each chapter and activity masters for video selections can be found in the *Video Guide.*

Motivating Activity

Have students list things they associate with life a hundred years ago, and things they associate with modern life. Ask them to compare the advantages and disadvantages of living in the past with living today. Ask students if they would prefer to have lived in the past rather than the present, and why.

Teaching Suggestion

Ask students to identify traditional and modern aspects of Tunisian life, based on the photos and objects on pages 188–189.

Photo Flash!

① The Romanesque and Byzantine styles of the cathedral (built in 1882) and the modern office building in this photo coexist harmoniously on the palm-lined **Avenue du 7 novembre** in Tunis. The avenue commemorates the date when the aging Habib Bourguiba, who led Tunisia's independence movement and became the country's first president, was deposed.

CHAPITRE

8
La Tunisie, pays de contrastes

① La Tunisie, un pays au carrefour de la tradition et de la modernité

188   *cent quatre-vingt-huit*

Culture Notes

① In the modern part of the city surrounding Avenue du 7 novembre, the streets are laid out in a grid pattern, resembling nineteenth-century French boulevards. In contrast, the ancient **médina** is a maze of winding, narrow alleys.

① Skyscrapers are a controversial part of Tunis' skyline. After the towering **Hôtel Africa** broke the city's low, unassuming skyline, a policy limiting the height of buildings was established.

Tu connais la Tunisie? C'est un pays à deux visages. D'un côté, c'est de plus en plus moderne. De l'autre côté, les Tunisiens restent très attachés à leurs traditions. Allez, viens! On va faire un tour en Tunisie.

In this chapter you will learn

- to ask someone to convey good wishes; to close a letter; to express hopes or wishes; to give advice
- to complain; to express annoyance; to make comparisons

And you will

- listen to teenagers talk about city life
- read about ancient and modern Tunisia
- write a travel log
- find out about traditional and modern styles of dress in Tunisia

② Salue ton oncle et ta tante.

③ Les embouteillages, c'est l'horreur!

cent quatre-vingt-neuf **189**

Focusing on Outcomes

Have students list French expressions they've already learned that accomplish these functions. Then, have them match the photos to the outcomes listed. NOTE: You may want to use the video to support the objectives. The self-check activities in **Que sais-je?** on page 212 help students assess their achievement of the objectives.

Teaching Suggestions

② Ask students these questions: **Où se trouvent ces gens?** (à l'aéroport) **Qu'est-ce qu'ils font?** (Ils se disent «au revoir»; La fille part en avion.) Then, have students compare the styles of dress of the people shown in this photo. Ask them **Qui est habillé en costume plus traditionnel?** (les femmes à gauche) **Qui porte des vêtements plus modernes?** (les hommes à droite)

③ Have students try to guess the meaning of **embouteillages** *(traffic jams)* from the context and the photo. Ask them how they think the driver in the photo feels.

Language Note

③ Ask students if they can see a familiar word in **embouteillages (bouteille).** Ask them if they know of an expression for traffic jams that uses the corresponding English word *bottle (bottlenecks).*

Thinking Critically

Observing Have students tell what they would expect to see in a typical Tunisian city, based on the photos on pages 188–189 (modern office buildings, older traditional buildings, traffic jams, women in traditional dress, mosques, palm trees, people in modern dress).

Culture Notes

③ Since traffic jams are common and buses aren't air-conditioned, people often choose to walk around Tunis. Bus travel is relatively inexpensive, however, as is the light train metro system.

- Call students' attention to the sandals pictured on this page. In Tunis, average summer temperatures range from 29 to 33 degrees Celsius (84 to 95 degrees Fahrenheit). You might ask students what else they would bring to a country with such a warm climate (a hat or scarf, sunscreen, a water bottle).

Mise en train

Bisous de Nefta

A Nefta, dans un endroit en bordure du désert de Tunisie, vit Zohra, avec son père, sa mère et ses deux frères. Ils habitent dans une petite ferme où on élève des moutons et on cultive l'olivier et le dattier. En plus du lycée, Zohra aide ses parents à la ferme. Quand elle a un moment de libre, elle écrit à sa cousine Aïcha qui habite à Tunis.

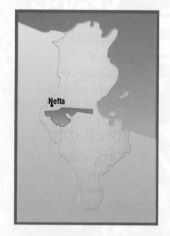

Nefta

Summary

In **Bisous de Nefta**, Zohra, who lives in the small village of Nefta with her family, writes a letter to her cousin Aïcha in Tunis. She describes the beautiful sunsets in her village, and invites Aïcha to come help with the date harvest. She confides that she wants to study archaeology after the **bac**, but her mother, who is more traditional, expects her to marry and work around the house. Zohra asks Aïcha to convey her good wishes to her family and thanks her for her postcard from Tunis.

Motivating Activity

Have students look at the photos on pages 190–191 and tell whether they reflect a traditional or a modern lifestyle. Ask them if the lifestyle depicted in the photos appeals to them, and why or why not.

Teaching Suggestion

Have students read the introduction and the photo captions and try to guess the meaning of the following words: **désert, ferme, moutons, olivier.**

Presentation

Tell students they are going to hear a letter that Zohra wrote to her cousin Aïcha in Tunis. Have them listen for Zohra's complaint and a description of her mother's life. Play the recording. Then, create true-false statements about the letter. (**Zohra va rendre visite à Aïcha.**) Play the recording again, pause it at the appropriate moments, read the statements, and have students respond. For visual learners, you might write your statements on a transparency and uncover them as you say them aloud.

Ils récoltent des dattes.

Chère Aïcha,

Ce soir, il y a un coucher de soleil génial. La lumière se reflète dans les branches des palmiers. Tout est super calme. Je pense à toi, dans ta grande ville. Est-ce qu'il y a des couchers de soleil comme ça à Tunis? J'aimerais tellement que tu sois là. Tu es ma confidente et c'est avec toi que je m'amuse le mieux. Ça serait sympa si tu pouvais venir pendant les vacances. Moi, c'est sûr, je ne pourrai pas aller te voir à Tunis. Quelle barbe! C'est la saison des dattes. Si tu venais, on pourrait les cueillir ensemble. Et puis, le soir, on se baladerait sur l'avenue Bourguiba ou dans la palmeraie. On irait discuter sous les arbres de la Corbeille. On se lèverait tôt le matin pour aller voir le soleil se lever! Et puis, toutes les deux, on s'occuperait des moutons et on aiderait maman aussi. Tu sais, elle est super fatiguée en ce moment. Ça serait vraiment chouette.

Regarde ce beau coucher de soleil!

Qu'est-ce qu'elle est fatiguée, maman!

Voilà nos moutons!

190 *cent quatre-vingt-dix*

CHAPITRE 8 La Tunisie, pays de contrastes

RESOURCES FOR MISE EN TRAIN

Textbook Audiocassette 4B/Audio CD 8
Practice and Activity Book, p. 85

Culture Note

The small town of Nefta in Tunisia is known for its refreshing oasis and for its tradition of **Sufism,** a branch of Islam. The **Corbeille,** a crater-like area surrounded by lush green palm trees, houses a public bath. South of this area, the ten-square-kilometer oasis, fed by over 100 natural springs, offers cool refreshment for swimmers and bathers.

Mais, bon, peut-être que tu as d'autres projets. Je vais te dire un secret : dans deux ans, après mon bac, j'aimerais bien étudier l'archéologie à l'université de Tunis. Enfin, il faut d'abord que j'en parle à papa et maman. J'ai peur qu'ils disent non. Il faudrait que j'arrive à les convaincre. Tu les connais, ils sont archi-traditionnels. Pour eux, une fille n'a pas besoin de faire d'études. A la place, ils voudraient que je me marie et que je m'occupe de ma maison et de mes enfants. Maman m'a même trouvé un mari! Elle voudrait que j'épouse Mustafa, le fils des voisins. Il est gentil, mais il est loin d'être mon prince charmant! Et puis je n'ai que dix-sept ans et j'aimerais quand même bien avoir le droit de choisir mon mari moi-même! Ça, tu vois, c'est un truc que maman ne comprend pas. Elle, elle s'est mariée à quatorze ans. Ce sont ses parents qui lui ont choisi son mari. Et, toute sa vie, elle s'est occupée de nous et de la maison. Encore maintenant, c'est elle qui fait tout à la maison. Elle va chercher l'eau au puits, elle porte le bois sur sa tête, elle fait la cuisine. Elle veut que je fasse comme elle. Tu as de la chance d'avoir des parents modernes, toi! Bon, il faut que je te laisse. Bisous à oncle Khaled et tante Brigitte, et à Rachid aussi. Dis-leur que je pense à eux et que je vais leur écrire. Maman et Papa vous embrassent tous très fort. A bientôt.

Zohra

P.S. Au fait, merci pour ta carte. La vue de Tunis était super. C'est quand même beau, la Tunisie! Ecris-moi vite! Grosses bises.

C'est très tranquille, Nefta.

Les femmes travaillent tout le temps chez nous.

Me voilà avec Ahmed et Hassan.

Teaching Suggestions

• For additional listening practice, read aloud the sentences of the **Mise en train** one at a time, deleting one word or expression from each sentence and blowing a whistle or ringing a bell in its place. (**Il est gentil, mais il est loin d'être mon prince** -ring-.) Students supply the missing words. When deciding which words to omit, you should choose those that can be easily guessed from context or those that students are familiar with.

• Write several sentences from Zohra's letter in random order on a transparency. Have partners copy them in the order in which they appear in the letter.

Thinking Critically

Synthesizing Ask students what they would do if they were in Zohra's position. Remind them that she respects her parents and does not want to offend them.

Teaching Suggestion

Have students think of similar photos they might take of their own city or state, or bring in postcards of local attractions. Have them suggest possible captions for their imaginary photos, such as **C'est très bruyant, New York.**

Language Note

Many Arabic first names have lexical meanings: **Aïcha** means *alive;* **Zohra,** *glowing* or *flower;* **Aziz,** *darling* or *beloved;* **Hassan,** *doer of good;* **Ali,** *of high morals;* **Imed,** *pillar;* **Rachid,** *wise man;* **Samir,** *faithful companion;* **Monia,** *hope.* **Aïcha** is a popular Arab name because it was the name of one of the prophet Mohammed's wives.

Culture Notes

• The family unit is central to the traditional Tunisian social structure. This includes not just parents and children, but the entire extended family, sometimes even married sons. It used to be common to marry within the extended family. In recent years, however, more Tunisians are moving from tight-knit villages to the big cities, and social networks are widening beyond the family unit.

• Tunisian and Moroccan weddings are very similar (see page 147). Visitors are welcome. The festivities, which include the ritual application of henna to the bride's hands and feet, a reception, a ceremony, and a feast with music and dancing usually occur over several days. Today, however, many couples opt for civil ceremonies since the cost of a traditional wedding can be prohibitive.

Additional Practice

3 Have students suggest additional things that Zohra or her parents might say, based on **Bisous de Nefta**, and read them aloud to their classmates, who will try to identify the speakers.

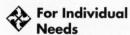
For Individual Needs

4 Slower Pace Provide the missing words on a transparency for students to refer to as they complete the dialogue with a partner.

Game

5 Have students form small groups. Give them one minute to supply as many expressions as possible for numbers 1–6. Students may list previously learned expressions, as well as new expressions from Zohra's letter. After one minute, call time. Groups win one point for each previously learned expression and two points for each new expression on their lists. Tally the points and declare a winner. Have a representative of the winning group read their list aloud.

Thinking Critically

6 Comparing and Contrasting You might have students compare and contrast life in a traditional family versus a more modern one. In this discussion, be careful to respect students' privacy and personal views.

---

1 Tu as compris?

1. To whom is Zohra writing? her cousin Aïcha
2. What time of day is it? sunset
3. What does Zohra like about the place where she lives? quiet, natural beauty
4. What doesn't she like about her family life? traditional gender roles
5. What secret does Zohra share with Aïcha?
6. What does she ask Aïcha to do?

5. She wants to study archeology at the University of Tunis.
6. greet her family, write back

2 Vrai ou faux?

1. Aïcha est la sœur de Zohra. faux
2. Nefta est au nord de la Tunisie. faux
3. Il y de beaux couchers de soleil à Nefta. vrai
4. Aïcha habite un petit village calme. faux
5. Tunis est plus grand que Nefta. vrai
6. A Tunis, il y a une université. vrai
7. Zohra veut faire des études de médecine. faux

3 C'est qui?

A ton avis, qui pourrait dire les phrases suivantes? Zohra ou ses parents?

1. «Ce qui est important, c'est de faire des études.» Zohra
2. «Les femmes doivent s'occuper de la maison.» parents
3. «Une fille devrait se marier très jeune.» parents
4. «Pour une femme, c'est inutile de faire des études.» parents
5. «Il faut pouvoir choisir son mari.» Zohra
6. «Mustafa serait un bon mari.» parents

4 Qu'est-ce qu'elle a dit?

Aïcha dit à sa mère qu'elle a reçu une lettre de Zohra. Complète leur dialogue avec des mots de la lettre.

AICHA   J'ai reçu une lettre de Zohra. Elle vous _____ bien fort. embrasse
SA MERE C'est gentil. Comment va sa mère?
AICHA   Elle est _____. super fatiguée
SA MERE Est-ce que Zohra va venir nous voir?
AICHA   Elle ne pourra pas. C'est la saison des _____. dattes
SA MERE Est-ce qu'elle sait ce qu'elle veut faire après son bac? étudier l'archéologie
AICHA   Elle veut _____. Mais elle a peur que ses parents disent non. Tu sais, ils sont _____.
SA MERE Je vais leur en parler. Si elle venait à Tunis, elle pourrait habiter avec nous. archi-traditionnels
AICHA   Super, je le lui dirai. A propos, elle m'invite chez elle pour les vacances. Elle dit qu'on pourrait _____. Je peux y aller? cueillir des dattes ensemble
SA MERE Si tu as de bonnes notes.

5 Cherche les expressions

What expressions does Zohra use in her letter to . . . See answers below.

1. express a wish?
2. express an obligation?
3. express a concern?
4. convey good wishes to someone?
5. thank someone?
6. end her letter?

6 Et maintenant, à toi

Est-ce que tu préfères que tes parents soient plutôt traditionnels, comme ceux de Zohra, ou plutôt modernes, comme ceux d'Aïcha?

192   *cent quatre-vingt-douze*   CHAPITRE 8   La Tunisie, pays de contrastes

RENCONTRE CULTURELLE

Qu'est-ce que tu sais sur la Tunisie? Pour t'en faire une meilleure idée, regarde ces photos.

Le Tunis moderne : une ville vive et pleine d'activité

Les chameaux sont utilisés pour le labour des terres.

Le Tunis ancien : la médina avec ses marchés traditionnels

On voit encore l'influence française en Tunisie.

Dans le sud, les oasis accueillent nomades et touristes.

Qu'en penses-tu?

1. What impressions do these photos give you of Tunisia?
2. Judging from the photos, what different kinds of people live in Tunisia?

Possible answers: 1. desert climate, mix of modern and traditional, Arab and French.
2. city dwellers, farmers, nomads (herding)

Savais-tu que... ?

Tunisia is a small North African country of mountains, grasslands, and desert. The majority of Tunisians live in the north, the only part of the country with enough moisture to grow crops, and in cities on the coastline. While the indigenous people of Tunisia are the Berbers, they make up only a small part of the population, most of which is of Arab descent. Tunis, the capital, is the modern political, cultural, and industrial center of the country, as well as an ancient city. In the old part of the city, **la médina**, you can find narrow, winding streets, small shops, and open markets. The modern part of the city has tall buildings and tree-lined boulevards. Seventy-five years as a French protectorate has left its mark on Tunisia. The architecture of government buildings, parks, restaurants, and sidewalk cafés are all reminders of the French presence. Although Arabic is the official language of the country, French is still taught to everyone and is used in administration and commerce.

Culture Note

The **médina** was the center of Tunis long before modern office buildings found their way into the city's skyline. It is only in the last century that the city has expanded past the ancient center of town. In the thirteenth century, the decorated doorways to some of the médina's private homes were already famous. Usually blue or beige, these doors are framed by intricate stonework and usually bear a "hand of Fatima" knocker, which is a symbol of good luck.

Language Note

Students might want to know the following Tunisian Arabic phrases: **Assalama** (ahss LEH muh—*Hello*); **Ashnooa ahwalik** ('shnah WEH lik—*How are you?*); **Labes, elhamdulil-lah** (lah BEHS 'hem DOO luh—*Fine, thanks*); **Bisalama** (biss LEH muh—*Goodbye*).

PREMIERE ETAPE

Asking someone to convey good wishes; closing a letter; expressing hopes or wishes; giving advice

COMMENT DIT-ON... ?
Asking someone to convey good wishes; closing a letter

To ask someone to convey good wishes:
Embrasse ta tante **pour moi.**
Give . . . a kiss for me.
Fais-lui/-leur **mes amitiés.**
Give . . . my regards.
Salue-le/-la/-les **de ma part.**
Tell . . . hi for me.
Dis-lui **que je vais** lui écrire.
Dis-lui **que je pense à** elle/lui.

To close a letter:
Bien des choses à tes parents.
All the best to . . .
Je t'embrasse bien fort.
Grosses bises.
Bisous à tes cousins.

7 Ecoute!
Indique les dialogues où quelqu'un transmet ses amitiés. 1, 3, 5

8 Fais nos amitiés à la famille!
Djamil va passer ses vacances chez ses cousins. Imagine la conversation qu'il a avec sa famille avant de partir. Joue cette scène avec ton/ta camarade.

9 Pauvre prof!
Ton professeur de français est à l'hôpital. Tu vas lui rendre visite. Tes camarades te donnent des messages d'amitié à lui transmettre.

10 On pense à toi
a. Tu vas écrire à un(e) camarade qui passe six mois chez ses grands-parents en Tunisie. Quatre de tes camarades de classe te disent de lui transmettre leurs amitiés.
b. Ecris ta lettre. Raconte-lui les dernières nouvelles et n'oublie pas de transmettre les amitiés de chaque camarade.

NOTE CULTURELLE

Tunisia is an extraordinary blend of modern and traditional life. In its cities a visitor can see high-rise buildings, airports, and public transportation. People use computers, drive sports cars, and wear the latest fashions from Paris. In other parts of Tunisia, life has changed very little in hundreds of years. Tunisians in these areas live much as their ancestors did, often in tents or in homes made of sun-hardened mud. They may raise sheep or goats, or migrate with herds of camels, stopping to drink at the same oasis as their ancestors a thousand years before.

194 *cent quatre-vingt-quatorze* CHAPITRE 8   La Tunisie, pays de contrastes

VOCABULAIRE

En Tunisie, on pratique encore des activités traditionnelles.

On fait la cueillette
des dattes (f.),
des olives (f.) et
des figues (f.).

On fait de l'artisanat (m.) :
de la poterie, des objets (m.)
en cuivre, des tapis (m.)
et des bijoux (m.).

On élève des chameaux
(m.), des moutons (m.)
et des chèvres (f.).

On cultive le blé.

On trait les
vaches (f.).

On donne à manger
aux poules (f.).

11 Comme chez nous

Lesquelles des activités du **Vocabulaire** sont aussi bien américaines que tunisiennes?
Answers will vary.

12 Ecoute!

Karim rend visite à ses cousins en Tunisie. Amira lui montre où ils habitent. Quelles images est-ce que tu associes à leurs conversations? 1. f 2. a 3. d 4. e 5. g 6. b 7. c

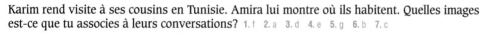

a.　　　b.　　　c.　　　d.

e.　　　f.　　　g.

PREMIERE ETAPE　　　*cent quatre-vingt-quinze* 195

---

13 Qu'est-ce qu'on y fait?

Regarde cette carte. Dis ce qu'on voit et ce qu'on fait en Tunisie selon les régions.

See answers below.

 COMMENT DIT-ON... ?

Expressing hopes or wishes; giving advice

To express a hope or wish:

Si seulement je pouvais, j'habiterais à la campagne.
Si j'avais le choix, j'irais à l'université.
Si c'était possible, j'habiterais à Tunis.
Ça serait chouette si je pouvais étudier l'archéologie.
Qu'est-ce que j'aimerais partir en vacances!

Ça serait chouette si je pouvais aller en Tunisie!

To give advice:

Si c'était moi, je chercherais du travail.
Si j'étais toi, j'en parlerais avec mes parents.
A ta place, j'irais à la campagne.

14 Ecoute!

Ecoute ces dialogues. Est-ce que les gens parlent de ce qu'ils aimeraient faire ou est-ce qu'ils donnent des conseils? *Answers on p. 187C.*

*G*rammaire Si clauses

Here is an English example of a hypothetical situation: *If I lived in the country, I would be happier.* French has a similar structure. To say that *if* something were so, something else *would* happen, begin one part, or clause, of your sentence with si *(if)* and put the verb in the imperfect; in the other part, put the verb in the conditional. Look at these examples:

> **Si** elle **habitait** dans une grande ville, elle **serait** plus stressée.
> *If she lived in a big city, she would be more stressed.*
> **Si** tu **parlais** français, tu **pourrais** parler avec des Tunisiens.
> *If you spoke French, you would be able to speak to Tunisians.*

- You don't always have to begin your sentence with **si.**
  > Ça **serait** chouette **si** j'**habitais** à la campagne.
  > *It would be great if I lived in the country.*
  > J'**irais** à Tunis **si** j'**avais** de l'argent.
  > *I would go to Tunis if I had money.*

Si tu as oublié the imperfect va à la page 348.

Tu te rappelles **?**

Do you remember how to make the forms of the conditional?
Add the endings of the imperfect tense,
to the infinitive or to the irregular future stem.
Est-ce que tu pourr**ais** le faire?
If you're unsure which stems are irregular, turn to page 118.
Remember to drop the **e** from **-re** infinitives.
Je vivr**ais** à la campagne si je pouvais.

15 A toi de jouer

Fais des phrases avec les éléments suivants.
Si j'allais... , je... See answers below.

> en France   en Suisse   en Tunisie
> en République centrafricaine
> au Maroc   au Sénégal   en Belgique

photographier des animaux sauvages

acheter de la dentelle

manger du chocolat

visiter des ruines romaines

boire du thé

emporter des vêtements légers

faire du ski

écouter de la musique exotique

manger du couscous

aller à la plage

acheter une montre

visiter le Louvre

acheter un tapis

Possible answers

15 Si j'allais en France, je visiterais le Louvre; ... en Suisse, je ferais du ski/j'achèterais une montre; ... en Tunisie, je visiterais des ruines romaines; ... en République centrafricaine, je photographierais des animaux sauvages/j'emporterais des vêtements légers; ... au Maroc, je boirais du thé/je mangerais du couscous/j'achèterais un tapis; ... au Sénégal, j'écouterais de la musique exotique; ... en Belgique, je mangerais du chocolat/j'achèterais de la dentelle.

Additional Practice

15 Have students suggest additional activities they might do in these or other countries. You might expand this activity into a game by having students read the last half of their sentences (**... je verrais des rhinocéros).** Their classmates try to guess the first half of the sentence and then read the completed sentence. **(Si j'allais en République centrafricaine, je verrais des rhinocéros.)**

Presentation

Grammaire Have students call out the first person imperfect forms of several verbs (**je faisais, j'habitais**). Write them in one column on a transparency. Then, have students give the first person conditional forms of several verbs (**je deviendrais, j'irais**). Write these in a second column on the transparency. Choose a verb from each column, make a sentence with a **si** clause, and read it aloud. (**Si je faisais de la natation tous les jours, je deviendrais un(e) bon(ne) nageur(euse).**) Then, call on students to do the same. You might have a contest to see who can create the most interesting, yet logical, combinations.

Reteaching

The conditional Have students suggest infinitives of regular verbs at random. Write their suggestions on the board. Then, have a volunteer come to the board and erase the appropriate letters to form the conditional stem. Finally, have a second volunteer act as a student-teacher and conjugate one of the verbs in the conditional, having the class repeat the forms. Have students write sentences, using the verbs on the board.

Additional Practice

Have students write completions for the following sentences: **Si j'étais riche,... ; Si j'habitais en Tunisie,... ; Si j'étais au chômage,...**

For Individual Needs

15 Slower Pace Before beginning the activity, have students write the first person conditional form of the verbs for the activities listed.

Teaching Suggestion

17 Once students have completed the activity as directed, have volunteers repeat aloud some of the advice they gave. (Si j'étais toi, je lui téléphonerais.) Have their classmates try to guess which problem the advice applies to. (Mon/ma meilleur(e) ami(e) ne me parle plus.)

📁 **Portfolio**

18 Written This activity is appropriate for students' written portfolios. For portfolio suggestions, see *Assessment Guide,* page 21.

19 Oral Students might want to include this activity in their oral portfolios. For portfolio information, see *Assessment Guide,* pages 2–13.

CLOSE

To close this **étape,** have students write several sentence starters and their completions on individual strips of paper. (Si j'étais le/la président(e)… / … j'inviterais le professeur à dîner à la Maison Blanche.) Have them exchange all of their strips with a partner, who will match the sentence starters with their completions.

ASSESS

Quiz 8–1, *Chapter Teaching Resources, Book 2,* pp. 185–186

Assessment Items, Audiocassette 8A/Audio CD 8

Performance Assessment

On separate index cards, write the expressions for asking someone to convey good wishes, expressing hope or wishes, and giving advice. Have partners draw two cards each and then create and act out a brief skit, logically incorporating all four expressions.

16 Qu'est-ce qu'ils disent?

Qu'est-ce qu'ils rêvent de faire?

Si je pouvais, je… *Possible answers:*

1. (j')étudierais l'archéologie. 2. (j')aurais une belle voiture. 3. vivrais à la montagne. 4. (j')irais à la plage.

17 Si j'étais toi,…

 Parle d'un problème avec ton/ta camarade. Il/Elle te conseillera.

— J'ai besoin d'argent.
— Si j'étais toi, je chercherais du travail.

Je suis déprimé(e).   J'ai mal à la tête.   Mon/ma meilleur(e) ami(e) ne me parle plus.

Je ne m'entends pas bien avec mes parents.   Je n'ai rien à mettre pour la boum.   J'ai raté mes examens.   Je suis toujours fatigué(e).

18 Je pense à toi

 Ecris une lettre à ton/ta correspondant(e) tunisien(ne) pour lui dire ce que vous feriez s'il/si elle venait chez toi.

19 Te voilà de retour!

Ton ami(e) et sa famille reviennent d'un voyage en Tunisie. Il/Elle te parle de ce qu'ils y ont fait. Pose-lui des questions sur le pays et dis-lui ce que tu voudrais faire si tu y allais. Avant de le/la quitter, transmets tes amitiés à sa famille.

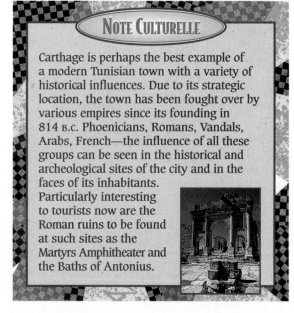

NOTE CULTURELLE

Carthage is perhaps the best example of a modern Tunisian town with a variety of historical influences. Due to its strategic location, the town has been fought over by various empires since its founding in 814 B.C. Phoenicians, Romans, Vandals, Arabs, French—the influence of all these groups can be seen in the historical and archeological sites of the city and in the faces of its inhabitants. Particularly interesting to tourists now are the Roman ruins to be found at such sites as the Martyrs Amphitheater and the Baths of Antonius.

Literature Link

Ask students if they have read about Carthage, and if so, where. Some may have read Virgil's *Aeneid,* in which the mythical hero Aeneas arrives in Carthage while the queen of Phoenicia, Dido, is having the city built. The subsequent romance between the queen and Aeneas, in which the goddess Venus manipulates Dido, and the god Jupiter manipulates Aeneas, comes to a tragic end when Aeneas leaves Dido to pursue his destiny.

History Link

After the Romans destroyed Carthage in 146 B.C., Julius Caesar reestablished it in 46 B.C. The city grew and its population flourished, but it was later ransacked by Vandal and Arab invaders. You might have students find out more about the history of Carthage and other Tunisian cities.

PANORAMA CULTUREL

Gilles • France

Sylviane • Martinique

Pierre • Québec

VIDEO PROGRAM
Videocassette 2

We asked some people how their cities have changed since they've been living there. Here's what they told us.

Cette ville a beaucoup évolué?

«Ouais, énormément, elle [Paris] change tous les jours, et je m'intéresse énormément à la ville. Je fais des choses particulières. Je prends des photos, justement. Chaque fois qu'un immeuble est détruit, je viens le prendre en photo avant qu'il n'existe plus et que soit reconstruit un truc qui ne soit pas beau, quoi. Donc, j'essaie de, justement, garder des traces de la vie de Paris, et je suis assez nostalgique du vieux Paris des années 1900 jusqu'à 1940.»

-Gilles

«La Martinique a énormément changé. Je dois dire que je suis née en Martinique. J'ai passé la plupart de mon enfance en Martinique. J'ai beaucoup voyagé, mais justement, lors de mes voyages, de mes différents voyages, on voit quand même des évolutions complètement différentes. L'art de vivre martiniquais est en train de s'européaniser et c'est dommage quelque part.»

-Sylviane

«Dû à l'automation, l'informatique, aujourd'hui, les gens sont obligés d'aller dans des grands centres pour continuer à gagner leur vie. Parce que l'évolution, comme vous savez, a tout transformé au niveau de tous les pays.»

-Pierre

Qu'en penses-tu?

1. What kinds of changes do these people mention? Have there been similar changes where you live? How have these changes affected the way people live? See answers below.
2. Research your city's past. Find out what life was like in your area in the year in which you were born, 25 years ago, or 50 or more years ago.

Questions

1. Pourquoi est-ce que Gilles prend des photos? (pour garder les traces de la vie de Paris)
2. Est-ce que Sylviane croit que la Martinique a beaucoup changé? (oui)
3. En quoi est-ce que la Martinique a changé, d'après Sylviane? (L'art de vivre est en train de s'européaniser.)

4. Pourquoi est-ce que les gens sont obligés d'aller dans les grands centres, d'après Pierre? (à cause de l'automation, de l'informatique)

Answers

1. *Paris:* old buildings replaced by new ones
   Martinique: lifestyle becoming more European
   Québec: people having to move to large urban centers to earn a living

Summary

In **Salut de Tunis,** Aïcha responds to Zohra's letter. She writes that she is envious of the calm life and beautiful sunsets in Nefta because Tunis is polluted and noisy. She would like Zohra to visit and suggests several things they could do in Tunis. She expresses sympathy for Zohra's situation with her parents, and offers to have her own less traditional parents talk to Zohra's. She tells about her new boyfriend, Chakib, who writes poetry. She mentions that she won't be able to visit during vacation because she got a job working for the Tunis festival.

Motivating Activity

Ask students how they would have responded to Zohra's letter in the **Mise en train.** Then, have them look at the photos on pages 200–201 and predict what Aïcha wrote about.

Presentation

Read aloud the photo captions. Have students make the thumbs-up gesture if Aïcha is describing a positive aspect of the city, and a thumbs-down gesture if she is complaining about Tunis. Then, play the recording. Tell students to listen carefully for differences between Aïcha's lifestyle and Zohra's. Finally, ask the comprehension questions in Activity 20.

Teaching Suggestion

Assign a number to the photos on pages 200–201. Write sentences from the letter that relate to them. For example, **Il y a encore plus de pollution que d'habitude** goes with the upper-left photo on page 200. Then, read the sentences aloud and have students match them with the appropriate photos.

Remise en train

 Salut de Tunis
Aïcha répond vite à la lettre de Zohra.

*Quelle chaleur!
Et quelle pollution!*

Que c'est bruyant, les grandes villes!

Chère Zohra,

Merci pour ta lettre. Elle m'a fait super plaisir. Qu'est-ce que tu as de la chance! Moi aussi, j'aimerais voir de beaux couchers de soleil. Ici, à Tunis, il fait chaud et lourd en ce moment. Résultat, il y a encore plus de pollution que d'habitude. C'est vraiment l'horreur! J'aimerais bien être à ta place au milieu des palmiers. Ça a l'air génial, Nefta! Ici, c'est beaucoup plus bruyant, plus stressant. Il y a trop de voitures et de vélomoteurs. Dès qu'on ouvre les fenêtres, c'est insupportable. Les klaxons, les cris, le bruit des moteurs! D'un autre côté, j'adore vivre ici. C'est super, tous ces cinémas, ces cafés, ces théâtres, cette animation! J'aimerais tellement que tu viennes faire tes études ici. Si tu venais, je te montrerais la ville. On irait se promener dans la médina. On irait voir les derniers films.

---

20 Tu as compris? See answers below.

1. What does Aïcha complain about?
2. How is life different where Aïcha and Zohra live?
3. How does Aïcha offer to help her cousin?
4. What news does Aïcha have for Zohra?

21 Comment est-elle?

Choisis parmis les phrases à droite celles qui décrivent le mieux Aïcha.

✓ Elle aime le cinéma. Elle n'aime pas Tunis.

✓ Elle est dynamique. ✓ Elle est musulmane.

Elle aimerait avoir des parents plus traditionnels. ✓ Elle veut travailler.

Elle ne sort jamais. ✓ La pollution la dégoûte.

✓ Elle aime la nature. Elle cherche un mari.

200 *deux cents* CHAPITRE 8   La Tunisie, pays de contrastes

RESOURCES FOR REMISE EN TRAIN
Textbook Audiocassette 4B/Audio CD 8
Practice and Activity Book, p. 90

Teaching Suggestions

21 Have students respond to each sentence by saying **Moi aussi!, Moi, si!, Moi, non!,** or **Moi non plus.**

• Have students guess the meaning of the word **klaxons** *(car horns)* from context.

Answers

20 1. the heat, pollution, noise, stress, traffic
2. Tunis is a big, noisy, crowded, lively city. Nefta is a small, quiet, slow-paced village.
3. She'll ask her parents to convince Zohra's parents to let Zohra continue her studies.
4. She has a boyfriend.

On s'amuserait bien, tu sais. Essaie de convaincre tes parents. Remarque, je les comprends. Pour eux, c'est pas normal qu'une fille veuille travailler. C'est contre la tradition. Tu sais ce que je vais faire? Je vais demander à Papa et Maman s'ils peuvent parler à tes parents. Je suis sûre qu'ils pourront les convaincre. Heureusement que je n'ai pas ces problèmes avec eux. S'ils voulaient choisir mon mari à ma place, ils m'entendraient! Tout ce qu'ils demandent, c'est que je me marie avec un musulman. Ben, ça, on verra! Pour l'instant, ce qui m'intéresse, moi, c'est de gagner ma vie! Au fait, je ne t'ai pas dit? Figure-toi que j'ai un petit ami. Il s'appelle Chakib. Je crois que tu l'aimerais beaucoup. C'est un poète. Il écrit des poésies géniales. Je pourrais te parler de lui pendant des heures. Bon, je te laisse. Tu sais, je voudrais bien venir te voir pendant les vacances, mais c'est impossible. J'ai trouvé un job pour l'été. Je vais travailler au festival de Tunis. Ça me plaît bien et ça me fera un peu d'argent. C'est vraiment bête, mais j'espère qu'on se verra quand même bientôt. Bien des choses à tes parents et à tes frères. Grosses bises.

Aïcha

Tunis, c'est super animé!

Voilà Chakib,
c'est un vrai poète!

C'est génial de se promener
dans la médina.

Teaching Suggestions
- Have students write down several quotations from Aïcha's letter and from Zohra's letter on pages 190–191, read them aloud at random, and have their classmates try to guess if Aïcha or Zohra wrote the quotation.
- Have students write their answers to Activity 22 on separate, small pieces of paper. Collect them and put them in a box. Select one at a time, read it aloud (**Je suis sûre que...**), and have students tell which function the expression serves (expressing certainty).
- Have students imagine what will happen to Aïcha and Zohra in the future. Do they think that Zohra will be able to convince her parents to let her study at the university, or will she change her mind and stay in Nefta? Will Aïcha stay with Chakib or find someone else?

For Individual Needs

24 Challenge You might have students expand their answers to tell why they prefer the city or the country and write them in their journals.

Culture Note
Students might be interested in the different types of traditional clothing worn in Tunisia. A **burnous** is a heavy wool cloak with a hood, usually draped around the shoulder and worn during the winter. A **djellaba** is a robe of fine cotton or wool with sleeves and a hood, which is worn in Tunisia only by men. A **caftan** is a dressy lounging robe with sleeves but no hood, worn by either men or women.

22 Cherche les expressions

What does Aïcha say in her letter to . . . See answers below.

1. express envy?
2. express a wish?
3. complain?
4. compare Tunis and Nefta?
5. express certainty?
6. break some news?
7. express an impossibility?
8. excuse herself?
9. end her letter?

23 La vie à Tunis

D'après Aïcha, quels sont les avantages de Tunis? Quels en sont les inconvénients? See answers below.

24 Et maintenant, à toi

Où est-ce que tu habites? En ville comme Aïcha ou à la campagne comme Zohra? D'après toi, quels sont les avantages et les inconvénients des deux?

REMISE EN TRAIN

deux cent un **201**

Answers

22 1. Qu'est-ce que tu as de la chance! J'aimerais bien être à ta place.
2. J'aimerais bien/tellement... ; Je voudrais bien... ; J'espère que...
3. C'est vraiment l'horreur! Il y a trop de... ; ... c'est insupportable.
4. Ici, c'est beaucoup plus... ; D'un autre côté,...
5. Je suis sûre que...
6. Au fait, je ne t'ai pas dit?
7. ... c'est impossible.
8. C'est vraiment bête, mais...
9. Grosses bises.

23 *Avantages:* cinémas, cafés, théâtres, animation
Inconvénients: pollution, bruit, stress

Jump Start!

Have students use the following familiar words to write three or more sentences contrasting life in the city and life in the country: **génial, calme, mortel, nul, vivant, bruyant, sale, stressant.**

MOTIVATE

Ask students if they prefer to live in the city or the country, and why. Have them suggest advantages and disadvantages of each place in English.

TEACH

Presentation

Vocabulaire Bring in magazine pictures of the vocabulary items. For **le bruit,** you might cover your ears and exclaim **Quel bruit!** as you show a picture of a busy city thoroughfare. Show the pictures and ask questions about them, such as **C'est un passage pour piétons. Est-ce que les chauffeurs s'arrêtent toujours aux passages pour piétons? Où est-ce qu'on trouve des passages pour piétons?**

Game

MOTS ASSOCIÉS On index cards, make lists of several words grouped by category. For example, **un trottoir, une rue,** and **un tapis** would be categorized as *Things you walk on;* **à un arrêt de bus, chez le médecin,** and **à l'aéroport** would be categorized as *Places where you wait.* Form two or more teams and have the first player from each team stand up. Read a list aloud. The first player to identify the category wins a point for his or her team.

DEUXIEME ETAPE

Complaining; expressing annoyance; making comparisons

VOCABULAIRE

25 Ecoute!

 Ecoute ces conversations. Est-ce que les gens sont à la campagne ou en ville? Answers on p. 187C.

26 C'est pas vrai!

Zohra rend visite à Aïcha qui lui montre son quartier.
Complète leur conversation en employant les images données.

ZOHRA Oh dis donc, Aïcha! Qu'est-ce qu'ils sont grands, les 🏢! gratte-ciel

AICHA Oui. Je suis sûre que tu vas bien t'amuser ici.

ZOHRA Mais, le calme de la campagne me manque. Les gens sont tellement pressés et apparemment, il y a beaucoup de gens 🧍. mal élevés

AICHA Oui, c'est vrai. Et il y a aussi beaucoup de 🖼 et de 🖼. bruit
Tu vois comme ils sont sales, les 🖼? pollution
trottoirs

ZOHRA Oui. Et la circulation, c'est l'horreur, non? Tu as vu cet 🖼? embouteillage
Regarde! Qu'est-ce qui se passe là-bas? Tu vois cette 🖼? foule

AICHA C'est peut-être un accident. On traverse pour voir? Prenons le 🖼.
passage pour piétons

RESOURCES FOR DEUXIEME ETAPE

Chapter Teaching Resources, Book 2
- Communicative Activity 8-2, pp. 168–169
- Teaching Transparency Master 8-2, pp. 171, 172
  Teaching Transparency 8-2
- Additional Listening Activities 8-4, 8-5, 8-6, pp. 174–175
  Audiocassette 10A/Audio CD 8
- Realia 8-2, pp. 178, 179
- Situation Cards 8-2, 8-3, pp. 180–181
- Student Response Forms, pp. 182–184
- Quiz 8-2, pp. 187–188
  Audiocassette 8A/Audio CD 8

Additional Resources
Textbook Audiocassette 4B
  OR *Audio CD 8*
Practice and Activity Book, pp. 91–94

COMMENT DIT-ON... ?

Complaining; expressing annoyance

To complain:

C'est l'horreur!

C'est insupportable, à la fin!

J'en ai ras le bol!
I've really had it!

Je commence à en avoir marre!

To express annoyance at someone:

Non mais, vous vous prenez
pour qui? *Who do you think
you are?*

Non mais, surtout ne vous
gênez pas! *Well just go
right ahead!*

Ça va pas, non?!
Are you out of your mind?!

Ça commence à bien faire, hein?
Enough is enough!

Dites donc, ça vous gênerait de bouger?
Hey, do you think you can . . .?

27 Ecoute!

Ecoute ces conversations. Est-ce que ces gens sont contents d'habiter en ville?
Answers on p. 187C.

28 Ecoute!

Ecoute l'intonation des phrases suivantes et répète-les.

À la française

You've learned that changing the pitch of your voice when you speak is called *intonation*. French speakers use different intonations to express emotions such as excitement or annoyance. The same words can mean something completely different when spoken with different intonations! Remember to pay attention to intonation too when you learn new phrases.

29 Ras le bol!

Nabil et Farid achètent leurs billets de train pour aller chez leurs cousins à la campagne. Imagine et écris leur dialogue d'après les images. *Possible answers:*

1. Je commence à en avoir marre!
2. Non, mais! Vous vous prenez pour qui!
3. Ça commence à bien faire, hein!

30 Ça va pas, non?!

Il y a des gens qui t'embêtent en faisant les choses suivantes. Tu leur demandes poliment d'arrêter, mais ils refusent. Qu'est-ce que tu leur dis? Joue cette scène avec tes camarades.

Quelqu'un...

resquille (*cuts in line*).

te pousse dans le métro.

écoute de la musique très fort.

te marche sur les pieds.

monopolise un téléphone public.

fume là où c'est interdit.

parle très fort au cinéma.

n'arrête pas de te regarder.

Motivating Activity

Ask students to describe situations that make them impatient or annoyed. Have them describe their "pet peeves" (des bêtes noires). Then, have them recall from Chapter 2 French expressions for reassuring someone. (Du calme, du calme.)

Presentation

Comment dit-on... ? Storm into the classroom, complaining about a meeting or a phone call that you just had and using the new expressions. Use gestures and intonation to convey your exasperation. Then, act out one of the situations students suggested for the Motivating Activity above. Express your annoyance at the situation, using appropriate intonation. Have students repeat the expressions, imitating your intonation.

Additional Practice

Project on the overhead a list of annoying situations. Tell a student that he or she is in one of these situations (John, you're in the lunch line, and it's not moving) and have the student react with one of the new expressions. (J'en ai ras le bol!) Then, call on a second student to reassure the first one, using an expression he or she has already learned. (Il n'y a pas le feu!)

For Individual Needs

29 Slower Pace Before students write their dialogues, have them describe each situation in English.

Teaching Suggestion

29, 30 Encourage students to resolve each situation by having one of the parties involved reassure the other.

Architecture Link

Call students' attention to the architecture in the background of the illustrations for Activity 29. Tunisian architecture reflects both Byzantine and Roman influences. The Romanesque arch in illustration 1 and the painted tiles in all the illustrations are common decorative features. The handpainted tiles in particular have been popular since the seventeenth century, adorning the interiors of both private homes and public buildings. These tiles, painted by hand with elaborate geometrical motifs, were originally made in the Tunisian towns of Qellaline and Nabeul. Today, less expensive, factory-made versions from Italy have replaced the hand-painted tiles.

Presentation

Comment dit-on... ? Have students find sentences in Zohra's letter on pages 190–191 and in Aïcha's letter on pages 200–201 that describe their respective cities. **(Ici, c'est beaucoup plus bruyant, plus stressant.)** Compile a list on a tranparency. Then, talk about Nefta or Tunis as if it were your hometown, comparing it to where you live now. **(A Nefta, il y a moins d'embouteillages qu'à Los Angeles.)** As you mention words such as **embouteillage,** hold up pictures to illustrate them. Next, read the sentences about Nefta and Tunis from the transparency and ask students **C'est comme ça chez toi?**

Additional Practice

Have students think of a place where they used to live or an imaginary one. Ask them questions about it. **(C'est plus ou moins tranquille ici? Il y a plus d'embouteillages là-bas?)**

Presentation

Grammaire On a transparency, list in one column adjectives that describe the city and the country. In a second column, write nouns associated with each place, such as **bruit** or **arbres.** Then, compare city and country life, using the adjectives. Have students illustrate comparative sentences on construction paper. For example, to illustrate **Clarksville est moins pollué que New York City,** they might write *Clarksville* and draw a small puff of smoke next to it, a minus sign, and *New York City* with a huge smokestack drawn next to it.

COMMENT DIT-ON...?
Making comparisons

Dans mon village, **ce n'était pas comme ça.**
Ici, c'est stressant, **tandis que** chez moi, c'est tranquille. *Here . . . , whereas . . .*
A la campagne, il y a **moins d'**embouteillages. *less/fewer*
A Tunis, il y a **plus de** bruit. *more*
Tunis est **plus** grand **que** Nefta.
Nefta est une ville **moins** bruyante **que** Tunis.

31 On se dispute

Latifa et Mona vont passer leurs vacances ensemble. Latifa veut aller dans une grande ville mais Mona préfère aller à la campagne. Elles se disputent. Qui fait les remarques suivantes, Latifa ou Mona?

Latifa
«Il y a plus de choses à voir.»

Mona
«Et puis, c'est plus tranquille!»

Latifa
«En tout cas, c'est plus animé.»

Mona
«Peut-être, mais c'est moins stressant.»

Mona   Mona
«Mais il y a moins de pollution.»

Mona
«Oui, mais, il y a moins de monde.»

«D'accord mais, c'est moins ennuyeux!»
Latifa

𝒢rammaire The comparative

- To compare nouns, use **plus de, moins de,** and **autant de** *(as many/much)* before the noun. Use **que** *(than)* to continue the comparison.
  Il fait **plus de** bruit **que** l'autre voisin.
  Elle a **moins d'**argent **que** son frère.
  Tu as **autant de** livres **que** moi.

- To compare adjectives and adverbs, use **plus, moins,** or **aussi** *(as)*.
  Remember to make the adjectives agree with the nouns they refer to.
  Les gens sont **plus** pressé**s** qu'à la campagne.
  Mon village est **moins** pollué **que** la ville.
  La campagne est **aussi** intéressante **que** la ville.

- English uses only one word, *better,* as the comparative of both the adjective *good* and the adverb *well.* There are two words for this in French.

- You use **meilleur(e)(s)** to say that something is *better* than something else.
  Les fruits sont **meilleurs** à la campagne qu'en ville.

- You use **mieux** to say that something is *done better.*
  On mange **mieux** à la campagne qu'en ville.

Teaching Suggestion

Have students suggest two cities or schools for you to compare. Write incomplete comparisons, such as **A Westwood High, il y a plus de (d') ____ qu'à Springdale High,** and have students suggest nouns to complete them **(élèves).** Then, repeat the process with comparisons that require adjectives. **(Westwood High est moins ____ que Springdale High.)** Have students complete similar sentences, comparing Nefta and Tunis.

For Individual Needs

Challenge You might have students write several sentences comparing Nefta and Tunis, and then tell in which city they'd prefer to live and why.

32 Plus ou moins?

Compare la ville et la campagne. See answers below.

> —Il y a moins de chèvres en ville qu'à
> la campagne.

vaches gratte-ciel embouteillages
magasins poules arbres crime
emplois
voitures légumes frais chèvres

33 Autrefois...

M. Fouad habite Tunis, mais il a passé sa jeunesse à la campagne et celle-ci lui manque.
Continue son monologue.

> —Oh, les gens étaient plus polis. Il y avait moins de stress. Et en plus...

vie   nourriture
problèmes   voisins
pollution   bruit
voitures   emploi
gens   stress
campagne   temps libre

pressé   travailleur
simple   bon
difficile   amusant
cher   compliqué
grand   pollué
sympa   énervant
tranquille bruyant

34 Tu as une préférence?

Demande à tes camarades pourquoi ils préféreraient habiter en ville ou à la campagne. Fais une liste des trois raisons les plus souvent données pour chaque endroit. Compare ta liste avec celle de ton/ta camarade.

35 Mon journal

Est-ce que tu habites en ville ou à la campagne? Compare l'endroit où tu vis avec un autre endroit, plus grand ou plus petit.

36 Jeu de rôle

You live in the city and you're unhappy about it. You complain and talk about what you'd do if you lived in the country. Your partner, who lives in the country, is also unhappy about where he/she lives. He/She complains and talks about all the things you can't do in the country. Act out this scene with your partner.

NOTE CULTURELLE

In many francophone countries, traditional dress is still found alongside modern forms of dress. Modern clothing is common in large Tunisian cities, but many people still choose to wear traditional clothing, or to combine the two styles. Tunisian businessmen often wear a suit topped by a **chéchia**, a type of fez, and a Tunisian woman who wears modern clothing will sometimes also wear a **sifsari**. This is a loose, robe-like garment with large folds convenient for carrying packages and even babies!

 Mon journal

35 For an additional journal entry suggestion, see *Practice and Activity Book,* page 152.

Portfolio

36 Oral This activity is appropriate for students' oral portfolios. For portfolio information, see *Assessment Guide,* pages 2–13.

Group Work

Have students organize a formal debate on the topic "City life is better than country life." Divide the class into pros and cons. Have each side prepare their arguments. For larger classes, you might have each side break into small groups. Each side should then choose two debaters. Another French teacher, a French exchange student, or a French-speaking visitor might serve as mediator. The teacher begins the discussion by posing the question. You might videotape this debate and keep the recording to use as introductory material for the chapter next year.

CLOSE

To close this **étape,** walk up to various students and complain about either city or country life. (**Regarde cette foule. C'est insupportable, à la fin!**) After you comment, make either a thumbs-up or a thumbs-down gesture. If you make the thumbs-up gesture, the student should agree with you and commiserate. If you make the thumbs-down gesture, the student should disagree and point out the benefits of living in the city or the country.

Answers

32 Il y a moins de vaches/poules/arbres/légumes frais/ chèvres à la ville qu'à la campagne. Il y a plus de gratte-ciel/embouteillages/magasins/crime/ emplois/voitures à la ville qu'à la campagne.

ASSESS

Quiz 8–2, *Chapter Teaching Resources, Book 2,* pp. 187–188

Assessment Items, Audiocassette 8A
Audio CD 8

Performance Assessment

Write **en ville** or **à la campagne** on cards and put them in a bag. Have partners draw a card. They should create a conversation about living in the area written on their card. They might agree or disagree with each other. Have them present their conversation to the class.

READING STRATEGY

Relating parts of the story to the main idea

Teacher Note

For an additional reading, see *Practice and Activity Book,* page 95.

PREREADING
Activity A

Motivating Activity

Ask students to list stories that recount growing up in a family *(The Diary of Anne Frank, Little House on the Prairie).* Have students imagine what it would be like to grow up in a Tunisian family, according to what they've read in the **Mise en train** and the **Remise en train.**

READING
Activities B–N

Teaching Suggestion

C. Once students have listed the family's expectations for Gisèle, have them give their reactions. You might have them list what they think today's parents expect from their children.

Culture Note

After a restrictive childhood in a traditional Tunisian home, Gisèle Halimi became a persistent advocate of women's rights. In 1971, she co-founded a women's rights group in France, along with the writer Simone de Beauvoir and several others. In 1981, she was elected to the Assemblée nationale, where she served as an active proponent of women's rights until 1984.

LISONS!

Enfance d'une fille

Edouard décroche le téléphone :
- Une petite fille, crie le correspondant... Tu as une petite fille!
- Merci, dit Edouard.
- Une très mignonne petite fille ! précise le correspondant. *Mabrouk* !
- Merci, répète Edouard.

Il raccroche. Pendant une quinzaine de jours, chaque fois qu'on lui demandera si sa femme a accouché, Edouard, mon père, répondra sans sourciller :

«Pas encore... C'est pour bientôt... Mais pas encore... »

Quinze jours pour se faire à l'idée qu'il a cette malchance : une fille...

Puis il finira par se persuader qu'après tout, il a sauvé l'honneur, puisqu' il a déjà un fils aîné. Alors, il avouera enfin :

«Eh bien oui! Elle a accouché : c'est une fille... »

La fille, c'est moi.

Ainsi commence l'aventure...

J'étais toute gosse quand on m'a raconté l'histoire de ma naissance. Ce déclic du téléphone raccroché, ce «mabrouk» crispé, je me souviens les avoir entendus résonner comme un glas. Ils m'ont poursuivie longtemps et continuent de me poursuivre. Ils me disaient la malédiction d'être née femme. Comme un glas, et en même temps, comme un appel, un départ. Je crois que la révolte s'est levée très tôt en moi. Très dure, très violente. Sans aucun doute indispensable pour faire face à ce clivage que j'ai retrouvé dans toute ma vie : j'étais une femme dans un monde pour hommes.

Aussi loin que remontent mes souvenirs, tout, dans mon enfance, dans mon éducation, dans mes études, dans ce qui était permis ou défendu, devait me rappeler que je n'étais née que femme. Ma sœur et moi, nous n'avons absolument pas été élevées comme nos frères.

Notre éducation procédait de ce découpage saignant : «Toi, tu es une fille. Il faut que tu apprennes la cuisine, le ménage. Et tu te marieras, le plus vite possible. Lui, c'est un garçon. Il faut, - on en trouvera les moyens, à tout prix - qu'il fasse des études, qu'il gagne bien sa vie.» Le mariage d'un garçon, c'est affaire personnelle. Le mariage d'une fille, c'est l'affaire des parents : cela ne la regarde pas. D'ailleurs, nos parents nous l'expliquaient : la naissance d'une fille représente une responsabilité épouvantable. Il faut bien sûr l'assumer. Il faut surtout s'en décharger sur un mari, le plus rapidement possible.

Je crois que ma mère a mis un certain acharnement, peut-être inconscient, à maintenir ce clivage. Comme si, au fond, elle voulait reproduire ce qu'elle avait subi. Mon père aussi. Mais d'une certaine manière, il était plus neutre, il avait plus de recul, il était *l'homme*.

Victime de son éducation, ma mère a été mariée à moins de quinze ans. A seize ans, elle avait son premier enfant. Blessée, donc, mais fière, fière de sa maternité et fière de ses blessures, comme certains martyrs. Opprimée dans son plus jeune âge, niée dès son existence, passant sans transition, de la terrible autorité de mon grand-père, authentique *paterfamilias* de tribu, à celle de mon père, son mari, tout naturellement, elle

---

DE BONS CONSEILS

When you read in French, do you sometimes concentrate so much on understanding vocabulary and grammar that you lose track of what the reading itself is about? To solve this problem, first find the main idea, usually located near the beginning of the reading. Then think about how the different parts of the reading relate to the main idea. Do the subtopics act as definitions, summaries, paraphrasings, or illustrations of the main topic? Are they results or consequences of the main idea, or even causes of it?

A. ... j'étais une femme dans un monde pour hommes.

A. In the paragraph that begins **J'étais toute gosse...,** find the sentence that gives the main idea of the reading.

B. How does the first passage relate to the main idea? Why does the author relate the story of her birth? See answers below.

C. What are three things Gisèle was told that a girl is supposed to do? cook, clean house, marry

D. What kind of life had Gisèle's mother known? How are her experiences reflected in the way she raised her daughter? See answers below.

E. Which expression do you associate with:
Perpétuer les choses provoque toujours moins de heurts que vouloir les changer.

Answers

B The anecdote reveals the secondary status of women in traditional Tunisian culture and shows the root of the author's rebellion.

D Married quite young, she was dominated first by her father, then by her husband. She oppressed her own daughters in order to justify her own life.

opprimait à son tour.

Quand je refusais de me marier, à seize ans, elle me disait : « A ton âge, moi j'avais des enfants.» A travers moi, elle voulait revivre sa vie. Comme pour la justifier. Je comprends très bien cette démarche. Perpétuer les choses provoque toujours moins de heurts que vouloir les changer. Un peu comme ces femmes d'aujourd'hui qui ne veulent pas reconnaître l'existence de notre problème. Le reconnaître, les obligerait à se déterminer. Et aussi à admettre que certaines peuvent échapper à ce qui leur est tracé comme un destin. C'est toute l'histoire de cette fameuse quiétude par absence de connaissance.

Pour mes parents, donc, la famille idéale n'était faite que de garçons. Si on leur avait demandé, au moment de ma naissance, ayant déjà un fils, ce qu'ils voulaient, à coup sûr, ils auraient répondu : « Un autre garçon.» Et après ce deuxième garçon? « Encore un garçon... »

Aussi loin que peuvent remonter dans le temps mes souvenirs, je revois d'une manière très précise, les différences ressenties, le clivage fille-garçon. Je sais que très très jeune, vers l'âge de sept, huit ans, ma mère nous obligeait à laver le sol de la maison. (En Tunisie, il n'y avait pas de parquet, il y avait des carreaux par terre.) Il n'était pas question de le demander à mon frère qui était pourtant plus âgé, et beaucoup plus solide, que nous les filles. Je devais ranger, faire la vaisselle. Dans la maison, l'homme n'avait jamais rien à faire. Nous, les filles et ma mère, étions là pour le servir.

C'est quand nos études ont pris une certaine importance, que j'ai ressenti la discrimination. Après le certificat d'études, il a été question que mon frère continue. Dans la famille, on était décidé à se priver de tout pour qu'il ait un diplôme. Pendant ce temps, j'avais progressé toute seule. Mais ça n'avait jamais intéressé personne. Mon frère n'était pas très bon élève, en cinquième. Il avait des colles. Il truquait. Il imitait, sur les bulletins scolaires, la signature paternelle. Et moi, je continuais mon chemin. Je réussissais. Mais personne ne me demandait quoi que ce soit. Au fond, personne ne s'en apercevait.

A dix ans, je savais déjà qu'il ne fallait pas compter sur un effort financier de mes parents pour m'aider à aller au lycée qui était payant. Et même assez cher. Je m'étais renseignée. J'avais appris qu'il existait un concours des bourses, uniquement ouvert à une certaine catégorie sociale d'élèves. Celle à laquelle j'appartenais : les élèves pauvres. Pour réussir, il fallait faire un très bon score. J'ai donc passé cet examen. J'ai même été reçue en tête, autant que je me souvienne. J'obtenais de très bonnes notes, mais elles passaient toujours inaperçues. J'arrivais pour dire : « Je suis première en français.» C'était le moment même où se déclenchait un drame parce que mon frère était dernier en mathématiques. Il était homme et son avenir d'homme occupait toute la place. A en être asphyxiée. Toute l'attention était tournée vers lui. Je ne suis même pas sûre qu'on m'entendait quand je parlais de mes professeurs et de mes cours. Il m'a fallu accumuler beaucoup de succès, réussir mes examens de licence à la faculté pour que mes parents commencent à dire : « C'est pas mal, ce qu'elle fait. Après tout, peut-être est-elle un cas un peu particulier? » Mais à l'époque, ça ne les intéressait pas, c'était secondaire.

Vint le moment où il fallut me décider au mariage. En clair, me marier, c'était arrêter mes études. A l'époque, ma mère aurait beaucoup souhaité me faire épouser un marchand d'huiles,

For Activities G, H, I, and J, see answers below.

a. It's better to give than to receive.
b. Don't make waves; maintain the status quo.
c. Time heals all wounds.

F. Would the following have been said by Gisèle or by her brother?

«Je devais ranger, faire la vaisselle.»
Gisèle

«Mon mariage, c'est mon affaire personnelle.»
brother

«Mon mariage, c'est l'affaire de mes parents.»
Gisèle

«Personne ne s'intéresse à mon éducation.»
Gisèle

«Tout le monde se prive pour que j'aie une éducation.»
brother

«Je ne dois rien faire à la maison.»
brother

G. Why does the author talk about the kind of student her brother was? How does this relate to the main idea?

H. Describe the differences between Gisèle and her brother in regard to . . .
a. their attitudes towards school.
b. their grades.
c. the emphasis placed on education by their parents.

I. How did Gisèle feel about a traditional marriage arrangement? How did her mother react?

J. How did Gisèle save money for her education? Why is this significant, in relation to the main idea?

deux cent sept 207

For Individual Needs

F. Slower Pace Before students do this activity, have them give a general description in English of both Gisèle and her brother. You might even have them compare these characters to characters in a TV program that they are familiar with.

F. Challenge Have students suggest additional things that Gisèle or her brother might say, read them to the class, and have their classmates indicate who might say each statement.

Teaching Suggestion

I. Ask students for their reactions to the traditional marriage arrangement in Tunisia. Do they think they would react as Gisèle did, or would they have a different reaction?

Culture Note

It was a great accomplishment that Gisèle Halimi saved money for her own education because, in traditional Tunisian society, women were rarely allowed to own property. Instead, their dowry or inheritance would be paid to their guardian, either their father or their husband. Since in the past most women did not have jobs and worked in the home, they generally had no way to earn independent incomes.

Answers

G As a student, he was far inferior to his sister, but the parents spent money on his education, not hers, because he was a boy. This is more evidence that the author was "a woman in a man's world."

H a. Gisèle saw the importance of education. Her brother didn't take it seriously.
b. Gisèle made good grades. Her brother did not.
c. Gisèle's parents sacrificed for her brother's education and ignored her academic accomplishments.

I Gisèle rejected a traditional marriage in favor of further education; Her mother didn't understand her.

J She tutored a male student in mathematics. She knew that her parents would not help her pay for her education because she was a girl. It is ironic that she financed her education by tutoring a male student and that her parents had to pay extra for her less gifted brother to be educated, while Gisèle, a bright student, had to earn her own money to finance her education.

Teaching Suggestion

L. As an extension of this activity, you might ask students if they think male and female children are treated differently, based on their experience. If they do, ask them to give examples.

Group Work

N. Have students work in groups to find the answers to the following questions about the news article: How does this article relate to the story? (It begins by mentioning the story and how difficult it was for Gisèle's father to accept her.) What proof is given that, in 1994, female babies are no longer considered a curse? (examples of birth announcements of female babies are given) Who modernized the laws? (the president, Habib Bourguiba)

POSTREADING
Activity O

History Link

O. Significant events for women in American history include the Seneca Falls Convention of 1848, which launched the women's suffrage movement, and the passing of the Nineteenth Amendment in 1920, promoted by Susan B. Anthony, which granted women the right to vote.

Culture Note

Habib Bourguiba once said "When still a young child, I told myself that if one day I had the power to do so, I would make haste to redress the wrong done to women." In 1956, he had the power. He abolished the **sharia,** a civil code based on the Koran, and established reform. Polygamy was outlawed, women obtained the right to vote, and legislation on equal pay was instituted, along with job opportunities for women.

fort riche et sympathique au demeurant. Il avait trente-cinq ans. Moi, j'en avais seize. C'était tout à fait dans les normes du mariage, en Tunisie.

Je ne voulais pas me marier. Je voulais étudier. Je revois toujours ma mère mettre son doigt sur sa tempe et dire : « Gisèle, elle ne veut pas se marier, elle veut étudier... », comme pour expliquer par ce geste : « Elle ne tourne pas rond cette fille! Elle est vraiment bizarre! » On a pensé que cela me passerait.

Mon frère avait redoublé deux fois. Je l'ai donc très vite rattrapé. On s'est finalement retrouvés dans la même classe. C'est à ce moment-là qu'il a quitté le lycée. Renvoyé je crois.

Mes parents ont enregistré cet échec toujours sans commentaire à mon égard. Je me demande cependant si mes succès n'ont pas été considérés, à ce moment-là, comme quelque chose de néfaste. Je bouleversais une règle établie, un ordre. Alors que personne ne s'occupait de moi, que je continue de progresser mais discrètement, comme dans une routine quotidienne, passe encore. Mais que je me fasse remarquer en coiffant au poteau l'homme, l'aîné de la famille, celui à qui on devait passer le flambeau de l'honneur, c'était trop!

L'offensive pour me marier s'est alors faite plus dure, car il fallait rétablir le processus : je me mariais, j'arrêtais mes études et mes parents continuaient à faire des sacrifices pour mon frère. Je me souviens même d'un fait important, compte tenu de notre niveau de vie : on est allé jusqu'à payer au garçon des leçons particulières de mathématiques. Cela représentait pour nous un luxe inouï.

Quelques années plus tard, c'est moi qui donnais des leçons particulières, au fils d'un avocat chez lequel mon père faisait des remplacements de secrétaire. J'étais en seconde, au lycée. Avec ces leçons de mathématiques et de latin, je voulais mettre de l'argent de côté : j'avais décidé que j'irais à l'université en France et je savais que personne ne m'aiderait. C'était assez symbolique : mon frère avait besoin de leçons particulières ; moi, j'en donnais et je gagnais déjà le pouvoir d'apprendre.

Ce que je dis ici peut paraître dur à l'égard d'êtres auxquels je reste *affectivement* très liée, mais j'essaie d'être objective, de dire comment les choses se sont passées. Cela ne change rien à ce que j'éprouve pour ma mère, ma sœur, mon père, ces *victimes*. Je ne veux pas les accabler. Je voudrais les éclairer, de l'*intérieur*. J'explique pour eux et pour moi, l'aliénation qui fut la *nôtre*, qui reste, en grande partie, la leur. Je dénonce. D'une certaine manière, je les réhabilite aussi. De toutes manières, je viens d'eux, de ce milieu, et je ne l'oublie pas. Moi, j'étais déterminée à aller mon chemin, que ça plaise ou non. Et mon chemin passait d'abord par cette envie démesurée que j'avais de lire, d'apprendre, de connaître.

For Activity M, see answers below.

K. How does the author feel about her family today? Does she blame them for the way she was raised? *See answers below.*

L. In your opinion, should male and female children be treated differently?

M. The excerpt on the right is from a magazine article. How much time has passed since the events related by Gisèle Halimi in *Enfance d'une fille* occurred? What changed in her life?

N. What great change took place in Tunisian society in 1956? Name three effects this change had on Tunisian women. *See answers below.*

O. What was the status of women in America in 1927? How has that status changed? *See answers below.*

LES TUNISIENNES EN MARCHE

L'avocate et militante Gisèle Halimi a déjà relaté une anecdote significative entourant sa naissance. Son père, dont elle deviendra l'enfant préféré, mit quinze jours à accepter que son deuxième enfant fut une fille. C'était en 1927. En Tunisie. Aujourd'hui, il est fréquent de lire dans le carnet mondain des trois quotidiens de Tunis des faire-part de naissance ainsi rédigés: La famille est comblée par la nouvelle-née... Inès a donné plus de joie à sa famille... Une jolie poupée prénommée Khaoula est venue égayer le foyer de... En 1994, en Tunisie, les petites filles ne sont plus une malédiction.

C'est le Président Habib Bourguiba qui, dans la foulée de l'indépendance, a entrepris de moderniser les lois. Le 13 août 1956, il promulgue le Code du statut personnel, véritable révolution qui fait de la femme une adulte en lui donnant un statut et des droits juridiques... A partir de là, les femmes, conscientes de leur existence, commencent à se regrouper en associations avec lesquelles il faudra désormais compter.

La Tunisienne, comparée à ses sœurs marocaines et algériennes, avance d'un pas allégé et rapide. «La Tunisie s'est toujours distinguée par une ouverture et un appel — aussi bien des hommes que des femmes — vers une législation plus favorable à ces dernières.»

Answers

K She still cares about them; She doesn't blame them. She considers them all victims.

M about 60 years; She went to France and became a lawyer and a militant. She became her father's favorite child.

N Tunisia gained its independence from France, and President Bourguiba modernized the laws; Tunisian women were given legal rights, women's consciousness seemed to be raised, and they began to form some powerful groups.

O By 1927, women had the right to vote, but they did not yet have equal opportunities in many areas; Now they have additional legal protection, more political power, and better access to education and the professions.

In the exerpt you read from **La cause des femmes,** *author Gisèle Halimi tells about the difficulties she faced growing up in a very traditional Tunisian family. In this activity, you'll write about your family or an imaginary or television family.*

Un récit familial

Maintenant, tu vas écrire un récit familial. Parle de ta propre famille, ou d'une famille imaginaire ou de la télé.

A. Préparation

1. Avant de commencer à écrire, définis une famille traditionnelle et une famille moderne. Réfléchis un peu aux questions suivantes pour préciser tes pensées.
   a. Est-ce que les deux parents travaillent?
   b. Est-ce qu'ils s'occupent tous les deux des enfants?
   c. Est-ce que les enfants bénéficient d'une certaine indépendance?
   d. Comment est-ce que les parents partagent les tâches ménagères?
   e. S'il y a des frères et sœurs, est-ce que les corvées domestiques sont partagées de façon équitable entre les filles et les garçons?
   f. Est-ce que les garçons et les filles ont les mêmes droits et les mêmes responsabilités?
   g. Qu'est-ce que les parents attendent des enfants dans l'avenir? L'université? Une carrière professionnelle? Le mariage? Est-ce qu'ils attendent les mêmes choses des garçons et des filles?
2. Est-ce que cette famille est traditionnelle, moderne ou un mélange des deux? Ecris librement sur ce sujet pendant à peu près dix minutes. Trouve des exemples qui montrent si cette famille est plutôt traditionnelle ou plutôt moderne.
3. Relis ce que tu as écrit pour en garder l'essentiel. Organise tes idées principales dans un plan. Si possible, ajoute des détails et d'autres informations appropriées.

B. Rédaction

Fais un brouillon de ton récit familial en suivant ton plan.

C. Evaluation

1. Fais une évaluation de ton récit. Est-ce que tu as bien suivi ton plan?
2. Est-ce que ton argumentation est logique? Est-ce que tu as clairement expliqué pourquoi tu trouves que cette famille est moderne ou traditionnelle? As-tu choisi de bons exemples?
3. Relis ton récit. Fais attention...
   a. à l'accord du sujet avec le verbe.
   b. aux accents.
   c. à l'orthographe.
   d. à la position et à l'accord des adjectifs.
4. Fais les changements nécessaires.

DE BONS CONSEILS
Brainstorming is a useful technique for generating ideas for your writing. In brainstorming, you quickly write down all the ideas that pop into your head when you think about your topic. Write single words or short phrases instead of complete sentences, and don't worry whether the ideas are good or bad, relevant or too far-fetched. It may even help to give yourself a time limit of thirty seconds or a minute to jot down all your thoughts. Once you've finished, evaluate your ideas: keep the best ones and add information, examples, and details where needed.

deux cent neuf **209**

WRITING STRATEGY
Brainstorming

 Portfolio

Written You might want to have students include all their work for Parts A–C in their written portfolios. For portfolio information, see *Assessment Guide,* pages 2–13.

Motivating Activity

Ask students to describe celebrity families or families from TV or the comics. You might ask **Comment sont les Simpson? Et les Brady du Brady Bunch? C'est une famille moderne ou traditionnelle? Pourquoi? Qu'est-ce que la mère fait? Et le père? Comment sont les enfants?**

Teaching Suggestions

A. Have students take out several sheets of paper. Read over the questions in A. 1. with students. Then, pull out a stopwatch. Tell students they have exactly five minutes to brainstorm. Tell them to label one column **Une famille traditionnelle** and another one **Une famille moderne** and to write down underline everything they can think of to go under each column. At this stage, tell them not to worry about sentence structure, spelling, or punctuation.

A. 3. Once students have brainstormed about their families, have them evaluate their ideas. With a different-colored pen, they should circle the ideas they might want to use, cross out those that they don't, and put a star by the ones they want to feature in their stories.

WRITING

Teaching Suggestion

B. Remind students that they might add to or delete from their original plan.

POSTWRITING

For Individual Needs

C. 2. Auditory Learners Have students summarize the main points of their story for a partner, as if they were giving a speech. If the listener is confused, or if the writer is unable to describe the points clearly, the writer might reevaluate the structure of the essay.

Teaching Suggestion

C. 3. Have students exchange papers with a partner. The partner should check for the four items listed and underline or circle anything that is questionable, writing the letter of the criterion next to it. For example, if the partner thinks that a word may be spelled incorrectly, he or she should circle it and write **c** next to it.

The **Mise en pratique** reviews and integrates all four skills and culture in preparation for the Chapter Test.

Video Wrap-Up

VIDEO PROGRAM
Videocassette 2

You might want to use the *Video Program* as part of the chapter review. See the *Video Guide* for teaching suggestions and activity masters.

Culture Notes

• The **deglet nour** or *finger of light* dates earned their name because of their unique translucence. The origin of these dates, which are unique to Tozeur and Nefta, is explained in a popular myth. The story is about a poor woman who died before she could fulfill the Muslim obligation of a pilgrimage to Mecca. She was buried with a string of beads she'd made from date pits. When the Prophet wept over her unfortunate fate, his tears fell on the pits, from which grew the trees that would bear the new variety of dates.

• Tozeur, along with Nefta, is known for its unique building material, the **brique jaune** mentioned in the last paragraph of the brochure. Traditional houses are constructed with these yellow handmade bricks, which are made from a local clay, dried in a frame in the sun, and then baked for three days. Ornate geometrical designs unique to these towns are etched by hand in bas-relief on the bricks.

MISE EN PRATIQUE

1 Lis cette brochure et réponds aux questions à la page suivante.

Tunis s'affirme Capitale. Non seulement aux yeux des touristes qui y trouvent shopping et distractions sportives et culturelles, mais en tant que centre politique, administratif, économique moderne. Siège d'organisations internationales, Tunis accueille également de nombreux congrès tout au long de l'année. Le festival de Carthage et les Journées cinématographiques et théâtrales, qui prennent également pour cadre les vestiges de la plus prestigieuse cité antique, sont l'occasion de rencontres internationales réputées.

Tunis est une ville de caractère. Tunis a une âme. L'âme de Tunis, c'est à travers le contact, la discussion, le travail des habitants que le visiteur peut la deviner.

P·O·I·N·T·S F·O·R·T·S

En Ville

Perspective Avenue Bourguiba, depuis la Place de l'Afrique.
Centre National de l'Artisanat.
Parc Belvédère : panorama, zoo, piscine
Dans la Médina : la Grande Mosquée, les souks couverts, terrasses de marchands de tapis ; mosquée Sidi Youssef ; musée lapidaire.
Sidi Bou Khrissan ; musée des Arts et des Traditions populaires

En Banlieue

Carthage : colline de Byrsa : panorama ; musée national ; quartier de l'Odéon. Les thermes d'Antonin et le musée de plein air ; le tophet ; les ports et le musée de la mer de Salammbô.
La Marsa-Gammarth et le «Café Saf-Saf» ; les plages, les installations hôtelières et touristiques. Musée du Bardo. Chelles antiques.

Tozeur

Chef-lieu du Gouvernorat et «capitale» du Jerid, Tozeur et les bourgs satellites vivent d'abord des dattes. La palmeraie, masse continue et dense sur la rive Nord-Ouest du chott, compte un million six cent mille palmiers dont plus du quart donne les succulentes «Deglet Nour», les «doigts de lumière».

Deux cents sources jaillissent de dessous le désert d'alentour. Plusieurs de ces sources ont une valeur thérapeutique : à Ras el-Ayoun où l'eau sort à 30° C ; à El-Hamma du Jerid, où affluent les curistes depuis des temps immémoriaux.

Parmi leurs activités, les Syndicats d'Initiative organisent des promenades à travers cet océan de verdure, à pied, en calèche, en voiture, des randonnées chamelières. L'excursion la plus classique consiste à visiter un domaine particulièrement bien soigné, dénommé, en toute modestie, simplement «Le Paradis». Un «zoo du désert» y est accolé : la présentation de serpents d'Afrique est particulièrement instructive.

La ville de Tozeur, écrasée du soleil en été, présente une architecture des monuments et immeubles officiels fort différente de ce que l'on a l'habitude de voir en Tunisie. Ici, l'unique matériau semble être la brique jaune, à peine cuite. Disposées en relief, les briques assemblées forment des motifs décoratifs du plus heureux effet.

P·O·I·N·T·S F·O·R·T·S

Tozeur

Centre-ville avec les maisons de briques
Le «Paradis» - Le zoo du Désert
Le Belvédère - L'ancienne ville
- Le musée

Language Note

Students might want to know the following words from the brochures: **siège** *(seat);* **vestiges** *(remains);* **marché aux puces** *(flea market);* **jaillir** *(to flow);* **désert d'alentour** *(the surrounding desert).*

1. According to the brochure, what might you do or see in Tunis? In Tozeur?

2. Other than tourism, what are some possible reasons for visiting Tunis?

3. What does the brochure recommend as a way to discover the "soul of Tunis"?

4. What are "les doigts de lumière"? Why are these important in Tozeur?

5. What kind of organized excursion near Tozeur is mentioned in the brochure?

2 Tu vas passer six mois avec une famille tunisienne. Tu dois décider où tu voudrais habiter. On t'a donné le choix entre Tunis et Tozeur. Avec ton/ta camarade, parle de ce qu'il y a à faire et à voir là-bas. Compare les deux endroits. Ton/Ta camarade te donnera des conseils.
Answers on p. 187D.

3 Hoda parle de ce qu'elle désire faire cet été, mais elle a des problèmes. Leïla lui propose des solutions. Fais une liste de trois des souhaits de Hoda et des conseils que Leïla lui donne.

4 Trouve les mots qui décrivent...   1. Berbers 2. chéchia

1. un peuple qui vivait en Tunisie avant l'arrivée des Arabes.

2. une sorte de chapeau que les hommes portent en Tunisie.

3. un vêtement porté par les femmes tunisiennes. sifsari

4. un site archéologique célèbre. Martyrs Amphitheater, Baths of Antonius at Carthage

5. le vieux quartier d'une ville où il y a beaucoup de souks. la médina

5 a. Tu es parti(e) en Tunisie il y a deux semaines. Ecris une carte postale à tes camarades de la classe de français. N'oublie pas de transmettre tes amitiés à tes autres copains.

  b. Après trois mois en Tunisie, un magazine tunisien te demande d'écrire un article sur tes impressions du pays. Ecris un récit de ce que tu as fait et une description de ce que tu as vu. N'oublie pas de comparer les diverses régions que tu as visitées.

6

J E U   D E   R O L E

You're visiting a friend who lives in a very big city. Your friend wants to show you one of the city's famous attractions. Act out the following situations with your partner.

- You agree to go see it. On the way, there is a big traffic jam. It's very hot and both of you are very unhappy. You both complain about the situation.

- You finally arrive at your destination, but someone zooms in front of you into the last parking space. You express your annoyance.

- You and your friend stand in line to get tickets and someone cuts in front of you. You're both furious!

- Finally you get to go in, but a few minutes later, someone announces that the attraction is about to close. Now you've really had it!

MISE EN PRATIQUE   *deux cent onze* **211**

Answers
1 1. *Tunis:* shopping, sports and cultural attractions, festivals
   Tozeur: visiting the thermal baths, taking an excursion in the palm grove on foot, in a carriage, by car, or on a camel
 2. business, political activity, the Festival of Carthage, cinema and theater festivals
 3. getting to know its inhabitants
 4. dates; major crop
 5. visiting **Le Paradis,** a desert zoo

📁 **Portfolio**
2 Oral This item is appropriate for students' oral portfolios. For portfolio suggestions, see *Assessment Guide,* page 21.

✦ **For Individual Needs**
3 Challenge Have students tell in French what advice they would give Hoda, including what they would do if they were in Hoda's position.

Teaching Suggestion
4 Refer students to the **Notes Culturelles** in the chapter. You might have several students volunteer to become "experts" on a particular cultural aspect. Assign a **Note Culturelle** or part of the **Rencontre Culturelle** to each volunteer. Have them read over the information carefully, and then prepare a creative presentation of their cultural topic. They might bring in visual aids, such as guide books, or make their own drawings to accompany their presentation.

📁 **Portfolio**
5 Written This activity is appropriate for students' written portfolios. For portfolio information, see *Assessment Guide,* pages 2–13.

Teaching Suggestion
6 Encourage students to have one partner try to reassure and calm the other, using expressions they've already learned from Chapter 2. **(Du calme, du calme. Sois patient(e)! On a largement le temps.)**

This page is intended to help students prepare for the test. It is a brief checklist of the major points covered in the chapter. The students should be reminded that this is only a checklist and does not necessarily include everything that will appear on the test.

Teaching Suggestions

• You might have teams compete to write down the answers to all of the questions in the shortest amount of time.

• Once students have written all of their responses, challenge them to write a letter like the ones in the **Mise** and **Remise en train** in which they use as many of the answers as possible. Have students exchange papers with a partner, who acts as a scorekeeper by counting the number of responses used and declaring a total. You might declare a winner for the class.

QUE SAIS-JE?

Can you ask someone to convey good wishes? p.194

Can you close a letter? p.194

Can you express hopes or wishes? p.196

Can you give advice? p.196

Can you complain? p.203

Can you express annoyance? p.203

Can you make comparisons? p.204

Can you use what you've learned in this chapter?

1 A friend who has been visiting you is about to go back home to her family. What would you say to send your best wishes?
Embrasse... pour moi. Fais-lui/leur mes amitiés. Salue-le/la/les de ma part. Dis-lui que je vais lui écrire. Dis-lui que je pense à elle/lui.

2 How would you end a letter to a friend?
Bien des choses à... ; Je t'embrasse bien fort. Grosses bises. Bisous à...

3 How would you express a wish to . . . See answers below.

1. travel in Africa?   2. buy a new car?   3. go to college?

4 What advice would you give to a friend . . . See answers below.

1. who's having trouble with a school subject?
2. whose parents are very strict?
3. who wants to live in another country?

5 What would you say to complain if you were in these situations? *Possible answers:*

1. J'en ai ras le bol!
2. C'est l'horreur!
3. Je commence à en avoir marre! C'est insupportable à la fin!

6 How would you express your annoyance if . . . See answers below.

1. someone shoved in front of you as you were boarding the bus?
2. someone grabbed an item from you that you wanted to buy?
3. the people behind you at the movies were talking loudly during the film?

7 How would you compare the following? See answers below.

1. your favorite and least favorite school subjects?
2. the last two movies you saw?
3. two places you've lived or visited?

212   *deux cent douze*   CHAPITRE 8   La Tunisie, pays de contrastes

Possible answers

3 1. Ça serait chouette si je pouvais aller en Afrique. Qu'est-ce que j'aimerais aller en Afrique! Si j'avais le choix, j'irais en Afrique.
2. Si c'était possible, j'achèterais une nouvelle voiture.
3. Si seulement je pouvais aller à l'université.

4 1. Si j'étais toi, j'étudierais beaucoup plus.
2. Si c'était moi, j'en parlerais avec eux.
3. A ta place, j'irais en Tunisie.

6 1. Non mais, vous vous prenez pour qui? Non mais, surtout ne vous gênez pas!
2. Ça va pas, non?!
3. Ça commence à bien faire, hein? Dites donc, ça vous gênerait de ne pas parler?

7 1. Le français est plus intéressant que la géométrie.
2. *Aladdin* est moins violent que *Henry V.*
3. New York City, c'est stressant, tandis que Boise, c'est tranquille.

PREMIERE ETAPE

Asking someone to convey good wishes

Embrasse... pour moi.   *Give ... a kiss for me.*
Fais mes amitiés à...   *Give ... my regards.*
Salue... de ma part.   *Tell ... hi for me.*
Dis à... que je vais lui écrire.   *Tell ... that I'm going to write.*
Dis à... que je pense à elle/lui.   *Tell ... that I'm thinking about her/him.*

Closing a letter

Bien des choses à...   *All the best to ...*
Je t'embrasse bien fort.   *Hugs and kisses.*
Grosses bises.   *Hugs and kisses.*
Bisous à...   *Kisses to ...*

Traditional life

le(s) bijou(x) (m.)   *jewelry*
un chameau   *a camel*
une chèvre   *a goat*
le cuivre   *brass, copper*
cultiver le blé   *to grow wheat*
une datte   *a date*
élever   *to raise*
faire de l'artisanat (m.)   *to make crafts*
faire la cueillette   *to harvest*
une figue   *a fig*
un mouton   *a sheep*
une olive   *an olive*
la poterie   *pottery*
une poule   *a chicken*
un tapis   *a rug*
traire les vaches (f.)   *to milk the cows*

Expressing hopes or wishes

Si seulement je pouvais,...   *If only I could, ...*
Si j'avais le choix,...   *If I had a choice, ...*
Si c'était possible,...   *If it were possible, ...*
Ça serait chouette si...   *It would be great if ...*
Qu'est-ce que j'aimerais... !   *I'd really like to ... !*

Giving advice

Si c'était moi, ...   *If it were me, ...*
Si j'étais toi, ...   *If I were you, ...*
A ta place, ...   *If I were in your place, ...*

DEUXIEME ETAPE

City life

un arrêt de bus   *a bus stop*
un embouteillage   *a traffic jam*
une foule   *a crowd*
les gens mal élevés   *impolite people*
les gens pressés   *people in a hurry*
un gratte-ciel   *a skyscraper*
un immeuble   *an apartment building*
un passage pour piétons   *a pedestrian crossing*
une place de stationnement   *a parking place*
la pollution   *pollution*
un trottoir   *a sidewalk*
un vélomoteur   *a moped*

Complaining

C'est l'horreur!   *This is just horrible!*
C'est insupportable, à la fin!   *I won't put up with this!*
J'en ai ras le bol!   *I've really had it!*
Je commence à en avoir marre!   *I've just about had it!*

Expressing annoyance

Non mais, vous vous prenez pour qui?   *Who do you think you are?*
Non mais, surtout, ne vous gênez pas!   *Well just go right ahead!*
Ça va pas, non?!   *Are you out of your mind?!*

Ça commence à bien faire, hein?   *Enough is enough!*
Dites donc, ça vous gênerait de... ?   *Hey, do you think you can ...?*

Making comparisons

Ce n'était pas comme ça.   *It wasn't like this.*
Ici,... tandis que...   *Here ..., whereas ...*
moins de... que   *fewer ... than ...*
plus de... que   *more ... than ...*
autant de... que...   *as many/as much ... as ...*
plus... que...   *more ... than ...*
moins... que...   *less ... than ...*
aussi... que...   *as ... as ...*

♟ Game

DIALOGUES LOGIQUES Have students form small groups. Give a transparency to each one. Then, call out two words or expressions from the **Vocabulaire** (J'en ai ras le bol! A ta place,...). Give groups one minute to write a logical dialogue that includes the two given expressions. Call time and collect the transparencies. Project them, read them aloud to the class, and then award two points to the team that wrote the best dialogue. You might choose to have teams vote on the best dialogue, with the restriction that they cannot vote for their own. Continue the game by calling out two more expressions. You might play for five rounds or to ten points. You might also have two members of the winning group act out their dialogue.

Allez, viens en Amérique francophone!

pp. 214–319

Motivating Activity

Ask students to name places in the Americas where they think French is spoken. Write their suggestions on the board. Then, show *Map Transparency 3* (**L'Amérique francophone**) and have students locate the areas in North and South America where French is spoken. Have them share any related travel experiences or information they already know about these places.

Background Information

France was at one time in possession of much of Canada and what is now the United States west of the Mississippi River. Today, the only vestiges of **La Nouvelle-France**, explored by Jacques Cartier in 1534, are the francophone province of Quebec, scattered francophone areas in other Canadian provinces, and the islands of Saint Pierre and Miquelon, which are French possessions. In the immense territory of the United States, once claimed by La Salle, Joliet, and Marquette, only in Louisiana is the French language spoken. In South America, French Guiana is the sole remaining French enclave. In the Caribbean, French is spoken in Martinique, Guadeloupe, and Haiti.

Culture Note

Montreal's Olympic Stadium is the major feature of the **Parc Olympique**. The stadium, designed by Roger Taillibert, was originally intended to be the site of the 1976 Olympic Games, but it was not completed in time.

CHAPITRES 9, 10, 11, 12

Allez, viens en Amérique francophone!

Le Stade Olympique de Montréal

214   *deux cent quatorze*

Culture Note

Montrealers refer to the Olympic Stadium as "The Big O" because of its circular shape and because the city "owes" a great deal of money for its construction. In order to pay off the debt, the stadium is used year-round for everything from rock concerts to Montreal Expos baseball games.

Architecture Link

The Olympic Stadium also features the highest leaning tower in the world. The tower measures 168 meters tall. The view from the top extends for 80 kilometers. You might have students investigate the location and height of other leaning towers and report their findings to the class.

𝒰sing the Almanac and Map

L'Amérique francophone

	Le Québec	La Louisiane	La Guadeloupe
Population	6.900.000	4.204.000	328.400
Superficie (km²)	1.667.926	125.674	1.709
Villes importantes	Montréal Québec	Nouvelle-Orléans Baton Rouge Lafayette	Pointe-à-Pitre
Spécialités	ragoût de boulettes, tourtière, tarte à la ferlouche	jambalaya, soupe au gombo, écrevisses à l'étouffée	crabes farcis, boudin créole, acras de morue

Autres états et régions francophones :
la Nouvelle-Angleterre (région des Etats-Unis), Haïti, la Martinique, Saint-Pierre-et-Miquelon, la Guyane française

Terms in the Almanac

- **Le Québec** has always played an important role in Canadian politics because of its size, population, and the prominence of its leaders.
- **Montréal,** the largest French-speaking city outside of France, was founded in 1642 on the site of an Indian village called Hochelaga.
- **Québec,** the capital of Quebec province, was founded as a fur-trading post by Samuel de Champlain in 1608.
- **tourtière:** a meat pie eaten especially at Christmas.
- **tarte à la ferlouche:** a pie made with molasses or maple syrup and raisins.
- **La Guadeloupe** has been a French **département d'outre-mer** since 1946. Christopher Columbus landed on the islands in 1493 and named them after a monastery (Santa María de Guadeloupe) in Spain.
- **Pointe-à-Pitre** is Guadeloupe's largest city, main port, and capital.
- **crabes farcis:** stuffed land crab.
- **boudin créole:** a spicy sausage.
- **acras de morue:** cod fritters.
- **La Louisiane** was named by Robert Cavelier de La Salle in honor of King Louis XIV of France. It became a French crown colony in 1731, and was later transferred to the United States as part of the Louisiana Purchase in 1803.
- **La Nouvelle-Orléans** was named for the Duke of Orleans, the brother of Louis XIV.
- **Baton Rouge** is the capital of Louisiana.
- **Lafayette** is located in the heart of Cajun country along the Vermilion River.

Using the Map

Using the map on this page or *Map Transparency 3,* have students locate the areas listed under **Autres états et régions francophones** in the almanac. You might have small groups do research on these areas and report their findings to the class.

History Link

In 1867, the British North American Act created the country of Canada, and Quebec was allowed to keep its French laws, language, and cultural heritage. **La Révolution Tranquille** of the 1960s, during which **les Québécois** sought peacefully to restore the status of the French language and culture in Quebec, led to the declaration in 1977 of French as the official language of Quebec.

Using the Photo Essay

① **L'Acadie** was a francophone region in what is now New Brunswick, Canada. When the area was ceded to the British in 1755, the **Acadiens,** who chose not to swear allegiance to the English, were deported during a period called **le Grand Dérangement.** Families were separated and set adrift in different ships with few provisions and few trained sailors. This period is the setting of Henry Wadsworth Longfellow's poem *Evangeline,* about a woman who is separated from her love during **le Grand Dérangement.** Many Acadians perished during this time, but some were reunited in Louisiana, where they became known as **Cajuns** or **Cadiens.** (See Teacher Note on page 217.)

② The French quarter with its famous wrought-iron balconies has long attracted tourists to New Orleans. The plans for this 180-block district were drawn by the architect Adrien de Pauger in 1722 for the Sieur de Bienville. Many of the district's streets still bear their original names (**rue St. Louis, rue Bourbon, rue Ste Anne**).

③ Only two-thirds of Montreal's population is of French descent. Because of the campaigns of the **Front de Libération du Québec** in the 1960s, nearly 100,000 English speakers left Montreal for Toronto, which benefited greatly from the migration.

History Link

③ The first inhabitants of the island of Montreal were the St. Lawrence **Iroquois.** When the Sieur de Maisonneuve founded the missionary colony of Ville-Marie there in 1642, many conflicts with the Iroquois ensued.

Il y a 11 millions de francophones sur le continent américain. Dans les régions francophones, l'influence de la culture française est très évidente. Mais, en raison de l'éloignement de la France, chaque région a développé sa propre identité culturelle et linguistique. Par exemple, les Québécois ont une interprétation différente de certains mots et ils ont inventé d'autres mots et expressions pour les choses qui n'existaient pas en France. Les langues créoles des Antilles combinent des éléments du français, de l'anglais, de l'espagnol et des langues africaines. Le «cajun» de Louisiane est un mélange de français et d'anglais.

① **Dans la région des bayous, au sud de Baton Rouge et de Lafayette, la musique, la cuisine et la langue sont «cajun».**

② **Le vieux carré** de La Nouvelle-Orléans, avec ses balcons en fer forgé et ses bougainvilliers, attire beaucoup de touristes, en particulier pendant la saison de Mardi Gras.

③ **Montréal est une grande métropole à l'américaine et la deuxième ville francophone du monde.**

216   *deux cent seize*

History Links

① The Cajun city of Lafayette is named after **le Marquis de Lafayette** (1757–1834), a French nobleman and military officer who sympathized with the American cause during the American Revolution. He offered his assistance and became a close associate of George Washington. Later, he returned to France and secured aid for the Americans from the French government.

• The Louisiana Territory was the largest territory added to the United States at any one time. James Monroe was a negotiator who went to Paris in 1803 to try to purchase the city of New Orleans from the French. To his surprise, the French offered him the territory that now comprises all or part of the current states of Arkansas, Missouri, Iowa, Minnesota, North and South Dakota, Oklahoma, Kansas, Montana, Wyoming, Colorado, and Louisiana.

⑤ **La Soufrière** à la Guadeloupe est un volcan actif.

④ **Vermilionville** is a 22-acre historical theme park dedicated to preserving traditional Cajun life. It houses replicas of a Creole plantation home, an overseer's cottage, a cotton gin, a chapel, a blacksmith shop, and a schoolhouse. Cajun storytellers, artisans, and even cooks add to the park's authentic ambiance. The Acadian Village is a similar park that features a model of a nineteenth-century Cajun village.

⑥ The markets of Guadeloupe, like those of Martinique, are filled with a variety of colorful fruits. The following are typical fruits and vegetables of the West Indies: lime, pineapple, guava, sapodilla, star fruit or carambola, sugar cane, cherimoya, mango, papaya, banana, prickly pear, capsicum, bottle gourd, ginger, yam, okra, pumpkin, coconut, maize, chayote or christophene, orange, and chili. Sugar was introduced to the West Indies in the fifteenth century, and Friar Thomas de Berlanga introduced the banana. The cherimoya, lime, melon, and grapefruit were all brought by the Incas.

⑦ The **chutes du Carbet,** a series of three magnificent waterfalls, impressed Columbus when he first arrived on the island. The three falls measure 66 feet, 361 feet, and 375 feet. The river that feeds the falls begins in the Soufrière volcano.

⑦ **Les chutes du Carbet** sont au milieu de la forêt tropicale de la Guadeloupe.

⑥ Comme dans les autres villes des Antilles, **le marché de Pointe-à-Pitre** à la Guadeloupe est très coloré.

④ **Vermilionville** en Louisiane est un village acadien reconstitué pour les touristes.

deux cent dix-sept 217

Teacher Note
You might tell students that **Cadien** is often preferred to **Cajun** by speakers of French in Louisiana.

Culture Note
About one half of the world's supply of sugar comes from sugar cane, which grows in tropical and subtropical climates. The other half comes from sugar beets, which grow in more temperate regions. Many of the tropical islands colonized by Europeans became the sites of huge sugar plantations.

Chapitre 9 : C'est l'fun!
Chapter Overview

Mise en train pp. 220–222	**La télé, ça se partage**		**Note Culturelle,** Multilingual broadcasting in Canada, p. 222	

Première étape pp. 223–229	**FUNCTIONS**	**GRAMMAR**	**CULTURE**	**RE-ENTRY**
	• Agreeing and disagreeing, p. 225 • Expressing indifference, p. 225 • Making requests, p. 227	Negative expressions, p. 226	• **Rencontre Culturelle,** Overview of Montreal, p. 223 • Realia: Television programming guide, p. 228 • **Panorama Culturel,** Favorite types of movies, p. 229	• Expressing opinions • Quarreling • Agreeing and disagreeing

Remise en train pp. 230–231	**D'accord, pas d'accord**			

Deuxième étape pp. 232–235	**FUNCTIONS**	**GRAMMAR**	**CULTURE**	**RE-ENTRY**
	• Asking for and making judgments, p. 233 • Asking for and making recommendations, p. 233 • Asking about and summarizing a story, p. 234	The relative pronouns **qui, que,** and **dont,** p. 234	• **Note Culturelle,** The film industry of Canada, p. 232 • Realia: Movie listing from *L'officiel des spectacles,* p. 232	• Types of films • Summarizing a story • Continuing and ending a story • Relating a series of events • Relative pronouns

Lisons! pp. 236–238	**Fierro... l'été des secrets, a Canadian movie for teenagers** **Reading Strategy:** Visualization

Ecrivons! p. 239	**Un scénario de télévision** **Writing Strategy:** Maintaining consistency

Review pp. 240–243	• **Mise en pratique,** pp. 240–241 • **Que sais-je?** p. 242 • **Vocabulaire,** p. 243

Assessment
Options
	Etape Quizzes
	• *Chapter Teaching Resources, Book 3*
	  Première étape, Quiz 9-1, pp. 23–24
	  Deuxième étape, Quiz 9-2, pp. 25–26
	• *Assessment Items, Audiocassette 8A/Audio CD 9*
		Chapter Test
		• *Chapter Teaching Resources, Book 3,* pp. 27–32
		• *Assessment Guide,* Speaking Test, p. 32
		• *Assessment Items, Audiocassette 8A/Audio CD 9*
		
		Test Generator, Chapter 9

RESOURCES: Print	RESOURCES: Audiovisual
Practice and Activity Book, p. 97	Textbook Audiocassette 5A/Audio CD 9
Practice and Activity Book, pp. 98–101 Grammar and Vocabulary Worksheets, pp. 82–86 Chapter Teaching Resources, Book 3 • Communicative Activity 9-1, pp. 4–5 • Teaching Transparency Master 9-1, pp. 8, 10 . . . . • Additional Listening Activities 9-1, 9-2, 9-3, pp. 11–12 . . . . . • Realia 9-1, pp. 15, 17 • Situation Cards 9-1, pp. 18–19 • Student Response Forms, pp. 20–22 • Quiz 9-1, pp. 23–24 . . . . Video Guide	Textbook Audiocassette 5A/Audio CD 9 Teaching Transparency 9-1 Additional Listening Activities, Audiocassette 10A/Audio CD 9 Assessment Items, Audiocassette 8A/Audio CD 9 Video Program, Videocassette 2
Practice and Activity Book, p. 102	Textbook Audiocassette 5A/Audio CD 9
Practice and Activity Book, pp. 103–106 Grammar and Vocabulary Worksheets, pp. 87–88 Chapter Teaching Resources, Book 3 • Communicative Activity 9-2, pp. 6–7 • Teaching Transparency Master 9-2, pp. 9, 10 . . . . • Additional Listening Activities 9-4, 9-5, 9-6, pp. 12–13 . . . . . • Realia 9-2, pp. 16, 17 • Situation Cards 9-2, 9-3, pp. 18–19 • Student Response Forms, pp. 20–22 • Quiz 9-2, pp. 25–26	Textbook Audiocassette 5A/Audio CD 9 Teaching Transparency 9-2 Additional Listening Activities, Audiocassette 10A/Audio CD 9 Assessment Items, Audiocassette 8A/Audio CD 9
Practice and Activity Book, p. 107	
Video Guide	Video Program, Videocassette 2

Alternative Assessment

- Performance Assessment
  Première étape, p. 228
  Deuxième étape, p. 235
- Portfolio Assessment
  Written: Activity 36, *Pupil's Edition,* p. 235
     Assessment Guide, p. 22
  Oral: **Mise en pratique,** Activity 4, *Pupil's Edition,* p. 241
     Assessment Guide, p. 22

Chapitre 9 : C'est l'fun!
Textbook Listening Activities Scripts

For Student Response Forms, see *Chapter Teaching Resources, Book 3,* pp. 20–22.

Première étape

6 Ecoute! p. 224

Ce soir sur TV Cinq: à dix-huit heures, vous pourrez voir *Le Canada en guerre,* qui comme son titre l'indique, vous fera découvrir le Canada pendant la deuxième guerre mondiale. Filmé de dix-neuf cent quarante et un à dix-neuf cent quarante-cinq par Yves Boisseau, ce programme en noir et blanc présente, entre autres, des interviews de nombreuses personnes qui ont vécu pendant la guerre. Puis à dix-neuf heures trente, vous retrouverez tous nos amis de Zap dans un nouvel épisode intitulé *Vive la rentrée.* Et oui, pour ces jeunes gens aussi, c'est la rentrée des classes. A vingt heures, vous pourrez voir la deuxième partie d'*Emilie, la passion d'une vie.* Pour ceux d'entre vous qui n'ont pas pu voir la première partie, c'est l'histoire d'une jeune institutrice au début du siècle. Puis, à vingt et une heures, *Pour tout dire:* Anne-Marie Dussault présente un reportage sur l'écologie au Canada, le hit-parade des tubes de la semaine et des interviews avec quelques stars qu'on peut voir en ce moment au Festival des Films du Monde. Enfin, à vingt et une heures trente, Annick Maurin présentera la dernière édition du journal télévisé.

Au programme de SRC, tout d'abord, les informations avec *Ce soir* à dix-huit heures. Puis, à dix-neuf heures, Pierre Morel reçoit deux nouveaux candidats qui s'affronteront dans notre émission *Des chiffres et des lettres.* A dix-neuf heures trente, vous pourrez voir un classique d'après l'œuvre d'Hergé. C'est *Tintin et le lac aux requins,* un programme qui ravira les grands comme les petits. Puis, à vingt heures, place à la musique et au cinéma avec *Ad Lib.* Ce soir, l'animatrice Corinne Laroche reçoit notamment Roch Voisine, Céline Dion, le groupe Maracas et de nombreux autres invités. Enfin, à vingt et une heures, Patrice Norton vous fera découvrir le monde d'une des plus grandes stars, Joséphine Baker, dans *J'ai deux amours, la vie de Joséphine Baker.*

Answers to Activity 6
TV5: un documentaire, une série, un feuilleton, un magazine télévisé, les informations
SRC: les informations, un jeu télévisé, un dessin animé, une émission de variétés, un documentaire

10 Ecoute! p. 225

1. — Tu te souviens de la pub pour le parfum où les femmes hurlaient et fermaient les fenêtres?
   — Oui. Elle était bizarre, cette pub.
   — Tu l'as dit!

2. — Les pubs pour les parfums, elles sont toujours trop dramatiques, tu trouves pas?
   — Non, pas du tout. Elles sont quelquefois assez impressionnantes.

3. — Moi, je déteste les pubs pour les lessives. Elles sont d'un stupide. Elles ne sont pas réalistes, et puis, ces lessives, elles sont toutes pareilles, de toute façon.
   — Tu as raison. Moi aussi, ça m'énerve.

4. — Tu regardes les pubs politiques? Elles sont tellement hypocrites, tu trouves pas?
   — A vrai dire, je m'en fiche.

5. — La pub pour la pizza où le grand chien blanc danse le conga, elle est marrante comme tout, non?
   — Tu rigoles? Elle est nulle!

6. — Elle est drôle, la pub où le réparateur attend parce qu'il n'y a pas de machines à laver à réparer, tu ne trouves pas?
   — Tu te fiches de moi? Elle est mortelle.

7. — Elle est sympa, la pub où il y a le petit lapin mécanique. Tu trouves pas?
   — Bof, je ne fais jamais attention aux pubs. Je m'en fiche.

8. — Moi, je trouve que les pubs pour les voitures sont vraiment sexistes!
   — Là, tu as raison! Je ne les aime pas du tout, moi non plus!
   — C'est scandaleux, comme elles exploitent les femmes.

Answers to Activity 10
1. d'accord	3. d'accord	5. pas d'accord	7. indifférent
2. pas d'accord	4. indifférent	6. pas d'accord	8. d'accord

17 Ecoute! p. 227

1. — Il est où, le programme?
   — Chut! Tu ne vois pas que je regarde ce film?

2. — Oh, il est mortel, ce film. Tu as la télécommande? Ça t'embête si je change de chaîne?
   — Ça m'est égal. Je ne regarde pas.

3. — C'est pas vrai! Qu'est-ce qu'il a...
   — Ne parle pas si fort, s'il te plaît.

4. — Eh, Benoît, baisse le son! Ça me casse les oreilles, ton truc.

5. — On peut tout voir comme ça.
   — Ah non! Ça vous gênerait de vous asseoir? On ne voit rien!

6. — Oh! Je commence vraiment à en avoir marre!

7. — Ça vient juste de commencer. On n'en a pas manqué beaucoup. Euh, pardon, je m'excuse...
   — Vous pourriez vous taire, s'il vous plaît? On aimerait bien entendre quelque chose!

8. — Eh, les enfants, vous pourriez faire un peu moins de bruit?

9. — Je suis désolé, Maxime. Je crois que j'ai cassé ton magnétoscope.

— Oh, c'est pas vrai! Tu ne pourrais pas faire attention?

10. — Tais-toi, Emilie. Le prof va t'entendre.

Answers to Activity 17
1, 3, 4, 7, 8, 10

Deuxième étape

28 Ecoute! p. 233

1. — Qu'est-ce que tu as vu comme film?

— J'ai vu *Casablanca.*

— Ah oui? C'était comment?

— Ça m'a beaucoup plu. C'est super, c'est un classique avec Ingrid Bergman et Humphrey Bogart. Si tu veux voir un bon film, je te le recommande.

2. — Comment tu as trouvé *Danse avec les loups?* Il paraît que c'est pas mal.

— C'est très bien fait. Il y a de beaux paysages et l'histoire est intéressante. Kevin Costner joue très bien.

— Tu me le conseilles?

— Sans hésiter. C'est à ne pas manquer!

3. — Qu'est-ce que tu as vu au cinéma dernièrement?

— J'ai vu *Grosse Fatigue,* avec Michel Blanc et Carole Bouquet.

— Ça t'a plu?

— Ça ne m'a pas emballé. Carole Bouquet joue pas mal, mais je n'aime pas le jeu de Michel Blanc. Et puis, l'histoire n'a aucun intérêt.

4. — Au fait, c'était comment, *Maman, j'ai encore raté l'avion?*

— C'est moins bien que le premier, mais c'est pas mal. McCaulay Culkin joue bien et c'est drôle. Je ne me suis pas ennuyé une seconde. Va le voir, c'est génial.

5. — Tu sais ce que j'ai vu ce week-end? *La reine Margot.*

— Alors? Comment tu as trouvé ça?

— Je me suis ennuyée à mourir.

— Ah oui? Pourtant, on m'a dit que c'était pas mal.

— Les acteurs sont mauvais. C'est vraiment nul! N'y va pas!

6. — Si tu veux voir un bon film, je te recommande *La fille de d'Artagnan.*

— C'est vraiment bien?

— Ça m'a beaucoup plu. C'est assez spécial, mais c'est drôle. Et puis, il y a de l'action. Tu verras, si tu vas le voir. Il y a aussi de magnifiques décors.

Answers to Activity 28
1. oui   2. oui   3. non   4. oui   5. non   6. oui

32 Ecoute! p. 234

FABRICE   J'ai vu un bon film hier. Ça se passe à côté de Montréal.

ALINE   De quoi ça parle?

FABRICE   C'est l'histoire de Chomi, un jeune homme qui étudie le cinéma et qui joue au hockey. Il a une amie qui s'appelle Olive. Ils passent tout leur temps ensemble. Et puis, Chomi rencontre une fille qui s'appelle Coyote. Il tombe amoureux d'elle. Olive et Chomi ne se voient plus. C'est très bien fait. Et puis, il y a Mitsou qui joue le rôle de Coyote.

ALINE   Mitsou, la chanteuse?

FABRICE   Oui. Elle joue très bien dans ce film.

ALINE   Et comment est-ce que ça se termine?

FABRICE   Finalement, Olive accepte la relation entre Coyote et Chomi. Je te le recommande. Ça m'a beaucoup plu.

Answers to Activity 32
1. vrai   2. vrai   3. faux   4. faux   5. faux

Mise en pratique

1 p. 240

DIDIER   Oh, c'est vraiment nul, ces feuilletons, tu trouves pas?

SIMONE   Tu l'as dit!

DIDIER   Alors, il y a autre chose?

SIMONE   Attends, je regarde dans le programme. Hmm... , voilà. Il y a un film.

DIDIER   C'est quoi?

SIMONE   Ça s'appelle *Vestiges du jour.*

DIDIER   C'est une histoire d'amour? Bof, les histoires d'amour, ça ne me branche pas trop.

SIMONE   On m'a dit que c'était très bien, en fait, que c'était à ne pas manquer.

DIDIER   Il n'y a pas autre chose?

SIMONE   Evidemment, toi, tu préfères les films d'horreur.

DIDIER   Et alors?

SIMONE   Tu sais bien que je déteste les films d'horreur. Ça a une mauvaise influence sur le public, ça encourage la violence, et puis, c'est révoltant.

DIDIER   Oh, regarde! Il y a *Dracula* à neuf heures moins dix. Passe-moi la télécommande!

SIMONE   Mais, écoute...

DIDIER   Tais-toi. Ça a déjà commencé!

Answers to Mise en pratique Activity 1
e, b, c, d, f, a

Une bande-annonce
(Cooperative Learning Project)

ASSIGNMENT

Students will create a movie plot and write and act out two short clips from their movie to be shown at a class awards ceremony in which the class will act as judges. Students will videotape or perform their clips for the class, preceded by an introduction that includes a brief plot summary and an explanation of how the clips relate to the overall plot of the movie.

MATERIALS

✂ **Students may need**
• Videocassette
• Video camera
• Props appropriate to their scripts

SUGGESTED SEQUENCE

1. Have students form small groups. You might assign a specific type of movie to each group (**une comédie musicale, un film d'espionnage**). Then, have groups create the plot and characters of their film. They should write a one-page summary of the movie, including a brief description of the major characters, the locations, and the basic plot. Group members should edit the summary.

2. Have students choose two scenes they want to feature in their movie clip. Then, have them write short dialogues for these scenes. Remind them that these scenes should not only be representative of the movie, but should get the judges' attention.

3. Groups should assign members to be the actors and actresses in each of the scenes. One or two students should be directors for the scenes. The actors and actresses should memorize their lines and rehearse the scenes according to the director's instructions.

4. Students should write a brief introduction for their clips. They should include the film title and genre, the names of the actors, actresses, and director(s), a brief plot summary, and an explanation of how the clips to be shown relate to the movie's plot.

5. Have students videotape their clips. They might include background music or props to establish the mood.

6. Stage the awards ceremony in class. One student from each group introduces their movie and then shows the clips. If video resources aren't available, have students perform their clips for the class "live" instead. After all the movie clips have been presented, have the class vote on the best movie. Tally their votes and announce the winner.

GRADING THE PROJECT

You might want to give an overall grade to the group, based on appropriate content, creativity, use of visual aids, and language use. You might also assign individual grades for effort and participation in the project.

Suggested Point Distribution (total = 100 points)

Content	20 points
Creativity	20 points
Visual aids	20 points
Language use	20 points
Effort/participation	20 points

Chapitre 9 : C'est l'fun!
Games

MEMOIRE

In this game, students will practice the vocabulary for television programs and types of movies.

Procedure   To prepare for this game, write the French vocabulary words and expressions for television programs and types of movies on index cards. On another set of cards, write the titles of movies or television programs that exemplify the categories in the first set. Number each card on the reverse side. Then, tape the cards to the board so that the numbers are visible. To play the game, form two teams. The first player from the first team calls out two numbers. Turn over the two cards that bear those numbers. If both a category (**une comédie musicale**) and an example of that category *(West Side Story)* are revealed, the player keeps the cards, wins a point for his or her team, and calls out two more numbers. If a player uncovers a match, he or she must express his or her opinion of the program or movie on the cards in order to win the point. If no match is uncovered, the opposing team takes a turn. The team with the most points wins.

LES REPLIQUES *(LINES)*

In this game, students will practice the vocabulary for television programs.

Procedure   To prepare for this game, have students write lines that are typical of different types of movies or TV shows and the appropriate category in parentheses. For example, students might write **Je voudrais acheter une voyelle (un jeu télévisé)**. Collect the papers, shuffle them, and put them in a bag. Then, divide the class into two teams. Have one player from each team come to the front and face each other. Place a bell on a table between the two players. Select a paper from the bag and read aloud the line written on it. Players ring the bell when they are able to identify the type of movie or TV program the line represents. Call on the first player to ring the bell. Teams receive one point for each correct answer. Players then return to their seats, and the next two players come forward. You may want to appoint a moderator to determine who rang the bell first and which answers are acceptable in case of disagreement.

Chapitre 9
C'est l'fun!

pp. 218–243

*U*sing the Chapter Opener

▮ **Video Program**

Videocassette 2

Before you begin this chapter, you might want to preview the *Video Program* and consult the *Video Guide*. Suggestions for integrating the video into each chapter and activity masters for video selections can be found in the *Video Guide*.

Motivating Activity

Have students look at the photos and the objects on pages 218–219 and try to guess what the chapter will be about (television and film). Then, have them close their books and form small groups. Give them one minute to brainstorm words and expressions they associate with television and film. Tell them that they will get one point for each item on their list that other groups didn't list and two points for words or expressions in French. Then, give the signal to start. Call time after a minute or two and have students read their lists. Tally the points and declare a winner.

Teaching Suggestion

Have students name French films and actors or actresses they've heard of and tell what they know about them.

Photo Flash!

① This photo shows the historic district of **Vieux-Montréal**. This area, popular among Montrealers as well as tourists, features historic seventeenth-, eighteenth-, and nineteenth-century buildings.

CHAPITRE 9
C'est l'fun!

① Le vieux quartier de Montréal, avec ses boutiques et ses cafés

218 *deux cent dix-huit*

Culture Notes
• The **Place d'Armes,** located in the center of Vieux-Montréal, features the Neo-Gothic **Basilique Notre-Dame.** Its architect, the Irish-American James O'Donnell, converted to Catholicism after creating the beautiful, imposing basilica.
• The **Place Jacques-Cartier** in Vieux-Montréal, once the city's main marketplace, is now crowded with cafés that serve as popular meeting places for the city's inhabitants.

History Link
At the center of the Place Jacques-Cartier stands the Monument to Lord Nelson. This column, similar to the one in London's Trafalgar Square, was actually constructed a few years before its English counterpart to commemorate Nelson's naval victory at Trafalgar in 1805.

Comme beaucoup de francophones, les Québécois adorent le cinéma et la télévision. Viens avec nous à Montréal, une des capitales médiatiques du monde.

In this chapter you will learn

- to agree and disagree; to express indifference; to make requests
- to ask for and make judgments; to ask for and make recommendations; to ask about and summarize a story

And you will

- listen to teenagers talking about TV and movies
- read a movie script
- create a TV show
- find out about the film industry in Montreal

③ Chut! Ne parle pas si fort!

② N'y va pas! C'est un navet!

deux cent dix-neuf 219

Focusing on Outcomes

Have students read the introductory paragraph and the list of outcomes. Form six small groups and assign a function *(to agree and disagree)* to each one. Have them list French words and expressions they already know to accomplish their function. Then, gather the papers and read each group's list aloud. Have the class try to guess the function the group was assigned, judging from the expressions listed. Have the class tell which functions the photos on page 219 represent. NOTE: You may want to use the video to support the objectives. The self-check activities in **Que sais-je?** on page 242 help students assess their achievement of the objectives.

Photo Flash!

③ In this photo, one teenager is asking another not to speak so loudly. You might point out the wood-burning stove (**un poêle à combustion lente**) in the background. When the tight-fitting door of this fuel-efficient stove is closed, the fire, with minimal access to oxygen, burns slowly. Although the wood-burning stove was once very common, its popularity has decreased in recent years, due to the growing accessibility of hydroelectric power in Quebec.

Teaching Suggestion

Call students' attention to the television program guide in the lower right-hand corner of this page. Ask them to read the cover and tell what they can understand.

Language Notes

② Have students try to guess what **navet** means *(flop, dud)*. You might ask them if they think it's a positive or a negative judgment. Have them suggest additional films that they would consider to be **navets.** Students might be interested to know that, literally, **navet** means *turnip.*

③ Have students guess what the word **Chut!** means *(Shhh!).* Tell them that the final -**t** is pronounced.

Summary

In **La télé, ça se partage,** Danielle and Fabien arrive home after school and try to decide what to watch on TV that evening. Danielle wants to watch *Emilie,* a soap opera set in the early twentieth century, but Fabien wants to watch the comic movie *La chèvre.* They flip a coin, and Danielle wins. That evening, Fabien sets the VCR to record *La chèvre,* and they watch *Emilie.* When a commercial comes on, Fabien is annoyed, but Danielle protests that commercials are interesting.

Motivating Activity

Bring in a TV program guide and distribute copies. Have students tell what they would prefer to watch, at what times, and why. You might have students vote for their favorite program and decide as a class what to watch tonight.

Presentation

Tell students they are going to hear a conversation between a brother and sister who disagree about what to watch on TV. Ask students to listen for what each person wants to watch. Then, play the recording and pause after the second scene. Ask students who they think will win the coin toss. Continue the recording and pause after the third scene to ask who won the toss. Tell students to listen in the next scene for details about *Emilie, la passion d'une vie.* Play the recording, pausing after the scene to have students compare notes. Then, have students listen for Danielle's and Fabien's opinion of commercials as you play the last scene.

Mise en train

La télé, ça se partage
Fabien et Danielle viennent de rentrer de l'école.

19 h 30	20 h 00	20 h 30	21 h 00
Ma Maison	Sous un ciel variable		Enjeux
Zap	Emilie, la passion d'une vie		Pour tout dire...
Le Grand Journal		Détecteurs de mensonges	Visa santé
Piment fort	Cinéma : La Chèvre		
		Columbo : Jeux d'ombre	

❶ FABIEN   Qu'est-ce qu'il y a ce soir à la télé?
DANIELLE   C'est le troisième épisode d'*Emilie, la passion d'une vie.*

❷ FABIEN   Qu'est-ce que c'est, ça?
DANIELLE   C'est un feuilleton super. C'est l'histoire d'une jeune fille, Emilie, qui vit au Québec au début du siècle...
FABIEN   Tu te fiches de moi? Ça a l'air mortel, ton truc! Tu me passes le programme, s'il te plaît... Eh! Il y a *La chèvre,* avec Gérard Depardieu!
DANIELLE   Pas question! Moi, je veux regarder Emilie.
FABIEN   Toi, tu ferais mieux de faire tes devoirs. C'est plus important.
DANIELLE   Tu parles! J'ai une idée, on n'a qu'à tirer à pile ou face.
FABIEN   Euh, tu crois? Je n'ai jamais de chance, moi.
DANIELLE   C'est la seule solution... Alors, pile ou face?

❸ FABIEN   Si je dis pile, ça va être face, et si je dis face, ça va être pile, alors je dis... face!
DANIELLE   Pile! T'as perdu!
FABIEN   C'est pas vrai! C'est toujours la même chose!
DANIELLE   T'inquiète pas, tu pourras le voir, ton film. Tu n'as qu'à l'enregistrer.

220   *deux cent vingt*   CHAPITRE 9   C'est l'fun!

RESOURCES FOR MISE EN TRAIN

Textbook Audiocassette 5A/Audio CD 9
Practice and Activity Book, p. 97

Culture Note

In the 1985 film *La chèvre,* Gérard Depardieu plays a detective who teams up with a clumsy partner to try to find a man's equally clumsy daughter, reported missing in Mexico.

Language Note

Students might want to know that **pile** is also used in several colloquial expressions to mean *just right:* **ça tombe pile** *(that's just what I needed);* **à deux heures pile** *(two o'clock on the dot);* **arriver pile** *(to arrive just at the right moment).*

Ce soir-là, devant la télévision.

4 FABIEN   Ça y est, j'ai mis le magnétoscope en route!

DANIELLE   Chut, le feuilleton commence!

FABIEN   J'espère que je n'ai pas raté le début.

DANIELLE   Mais tais-toi, enfin!

FABIEN   C'est Emilie, celle-là?

DANIELLE   Non, c'est une villageoise. Emilie est plus jeune... Tiens, c'est elle.

FABIEN   Elle est pas terrible.

DANIELLE   Ça te dérangerait de me laisser regarder tranquillement?

FABIEN   Et lui, qui c'est?

DANIELLE   C'est Ovida.

FABIEN   Pourquoi est-ce qu'ils se disputent?

DANIELLE   Parce qu'ils s'aiment.

FABIEN   C'est vraiment nul, ton feuilleton.

DANIELLE   Bon, si tu ne peux pas te taire, va réviser tes maths et fiche-moi la paix!

FABIEN   Oh! Ça va! La télé est à tout le monde.

Un quart d'heure plus tard.

5 FABIEN   Zut, la pub! C'est vraiment barbant, à la fin. Ils coupent toujours les films au meilleur moment.

DANIELLE   Au contraire, c'est pour créer du suspense.

FABIEN   Moi, ces pubs pour des lessives ou des céréales, ça m'énerve!

DANIELLE   Moi, pas du tout. Ça ne me dérange pas. Ça permet de faire une petite pause. Et puis il y a de bonnes pubs. Tiens, regarde celle-là. Elle est chouette, tu trouves pas?

FABIEN   Tu rigoles! Tu es vraiment une esclave de la pub, toi!

DANIELLE   Mais non! Je m'informe, c'est tout. C'est toi qui as tort de tout critiquer comme ça!

6 FABIEN   Bon, ça recommence? J'en ai marre, moi.

DANIELLE   Quoi?

FABIEN   Eh bien, ton feuilleton, là, *Emilie*.

DANIELLE   Ah! Parce que ça t'intéresse maintenant?

FABIEN   Pas du tout, mais je trouve ça tellement bête que ça me fait rire.

DANIELLE   Quel hypocrite!

FABIEN   Pense ce que tu veux, je m'en fiche!

DANIELLE   Ben...

FABIEN   Tais-toi, ça reprend! Monte un peu le son, on n'entend rien.

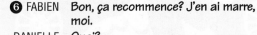

Teacher Note

Students might be interested in the television programs listed in the program guide on page 220. *Emilie* is based on a novel by Arlette Coustine. Emilie is a schoolteacher and the mother of a large family. Another series, *Blanche,* is about the life experiences of one of her daughters. *Zap* is a drama about the school and family issues faced by a group of young friends. *Le grand journal* is a newscast featuring national and international news coverage. *Sous un ciel variable* is a soap opera about the intrigues of the inhabitants of a small town. *Enjeux* is a news magazine hosted by Pierre Maisonneuve.

Teaching Suggestion

Have students name several American soap operas. Ask them if they like soap operas, and why or why not.

Building on Previous Skills

Have students use their reading strategies and their background knowledge to try to guess the meaning of the following words: **feuilleton, enregistrer, magnétoscope, pub, monte** *(soap opera, to record, VCR, commercial, turn up)*.

For Individual Needs

Challenge   Have groups write a summary of each scene of La télé, ça se partage. For example, for the second scene, students might write **Danielle et Fabien ne sont pas d'accord sur ce qu'ils veulent regarder à la télévision ce soir.**

Auditory Learners   Collect students' summaries from the Challenge activity above, read them aloud, and have students call out the number of the scene you're summarizing.

Tactile Learners   On transparency strips, write out the French summaries suggested above and call on students to arrange them in the correct order.

Teaching Suggestion

Ask students if they are annoyed by commercials on TV, like Fabien, or if they enjoy having a break in the program, like Danielle. You might ask if students watch commercials. If not, ask what they do during commercial breaks.

For Individual Needs

2 Auditory Learners
Read these sentences aloud and have students identify the speaker.

3 Auditory Learners/ Slower Pace Have students close their books. Read the sentences and two of the choices aloud as either-or questions. For example, for #1, you might say *Emilie, la passion d'une vie* est une publicité ou un feuilleton?

Teaching Suggestion

Note Culturelle Have students read the **Note Culturelle** in groups. Then, have them write one or two true-false statements about the note. Collect the statements, read them aloud, and have the class respond.

Thinking Critically

5 Analyzing Have students tell how they resolve disputes over minor issues, such as what to watch on television. You might have students share their ideas in small groups and then discuss the merits and disadvantages of each method.

Multicultural Link

Have students compare the programming available in their area with Canadian programming. In the United States, are foreign-language channels or stations available on TV or radio? In what language? On what channel or station?

---

1 Tu as compris? See answers below.

1. What are Fabien and Danielle doing?
2. What does Danielle want to watch on TV? And Fabien?
3. How do they decide which program to watch?
4. What compromise does Danielle suggest?
5. What do Fabien and Danielle think of TV commercials?
6. How does Fabien's opinion of the soap opera change?

2 Qui dit quoi?

Est-ce que c'est Fabien ou Danielle qui parle?

Danielle
«Tu peux enregistrer ton film.»

Danielle
«Ah! Parce que ça t'intéresse maintenant?»

«Ton feuilleton, il a l'air mortel!»
Fabien

«C'est bien, la pub. Ça permet de faire une petite pause.»
Danielle

«Ça m'énerve, la pub!»
Fabien

3 Fais ton choix

1. *Emilie, la passion d'une vie* est...
   a. une publicité.
   b. un feuilleton.
   c. un film avec Gérard Depardieu.
2. Danielle suggère à Fabien...
   a. d'aller voir *La chèvre* au cinéma.
   b. d'aller réviser ses maths.
   c. de regarder *Emilie* avec elle.
3. Quand Danielle et Fabien tirent à pile ou face,...
   a. Danielle gagne.
   b. Fabien gagne.
   c. ils perdent la pièce.
4. Selon Danielle, Emilie et Ovida se disputent parce qu'ils...
   a. ne veulent pas regarder la même émission à la télé.
   b. se détestent.
   c. s'aiment.
5. Pour Fabien, la publicité, c'est...
   a. bon pour permettre une petite pause.
   b. bien pour créer du suspense.
   c. nul.

> ## NOTE CULTURELLE
>
> La radio et la télévision canadiennes reflètent la diversité des cultures que l'on trouve dans le pays. Il y a deux chaînes nationales de télévision, une en français et une en anglais. Il y a également des chaînes de télévision privées comme CTV ou **Réseau de télévision**. Ces chaînes sont locales et leurs programmes sont soit en anglais soit en français. Les stations de radio, elles aussi, offrent des programmes dans les deux langues. Parfois, certains programmes sont même diffusés en dialecte inuit ainsi qu'en de nombreuses autres langues parlées par des Canadiens venus de différentes régions du monde.

4 Cherche les expressions

What expressions do Fabien and Danielle use to . . . See answers below.

1. summarize a plot?
2. disagree?
3. give advice?
4. ask someone to be quiet?
5. express annoyance?
6. express indifference?

5 Et maintenant, à toi

Est-ce que ça t'arrive souvent de te disputer avec quelqu'un pour la télé?

Answers
1 1. discussing what to watch on TV
2. *Emilie; La chèvre*
3. coin toss
4. Fabien can record his film on the VCR.
5. Commercials irritate Fabien, but Danielle likes them.
6. He grows interested in it.
4 1. C'est l'histoire de...
2. Tu te fiches de moi? Pas question! Tu parles! Au contraire. ... pas du tout. Tu rigoles! Mais non! C'est toi qui as tort...

3. Tu ferais mieux de... ; Tu n'as qu'à...
4. Chut! Tais-toi! Ça te dérangerait de me laisser regarder tranquillement? Si tu ne peux pas te taire, va réviser tes maths et fiche-moi la paix!
5. C'est pas vrai! C'est toujours la même chose! Fiche-moi la paix! Zut... ! C'est vraiment barbant... ; ... ça m'énerve! J'en ai marre.
6. Ça ne me dérange pas. ... je m'en fiche!

RENCONTRE CULTURELLE

Qu'est-ce que tu sais sur Montréal? Pour t'en faire une meilleure idée, regarde ces photos.

Les petites rues du Vieux-Montréal sont pleines de charme.

Montréal est aussi un grand port.

Montréal est une ville ultra-moderne et dynamique.

Montréal est un centre artistique et culturel.

Les habitants de Montréal apprécient les activités de plein air.

Qu'en penses-tu?

1. What impression do these photos give you of Montreal?
2. What kinds of things would you be able to do if you visited or lived in Montreal?

Possible answers:
1. busy, modern port city with many fun things to do
2. shop, dine at cafés, sight-see, do business, go to parks, visit the port

Savais-tu que… ?

Montreal is the second largest French-speaking city in the world, but many of its residents also speak English. It is the business center of Quebec province and a major port, even though it is 1,000 miles inland from the Atlantic Ocean! In addition to being an economic center of Canada, Montreal is a very lively city with a rich cultural life. It features popular yearly events, such as the **Festival international du jazz**, growing film and music industries, and an abundance of sports and outdoor activities. Perhaps the most colorful district in the city is **Vieux-Montréal**, where shops and cafes line the cobblestone streets, artists display their wares, and musicians, jugglers, and dancers frequently perform.

History Link

In 1642, the Sieur de Maisonneuve founded the colony of Ville-Marie, which would become Montreal. From 1759 to 1867, the British occupied the area. In 1976, René Lévesque of the separatist **Parti Québécois** came to power and passed the famous **Charte de la langue française**, which established French as the official language of Quebec.

Culture Note

Have students locate the Canadian currency pictured in the border of this page. As in the United States, the monetary unit of Canada is the dollar. Coins are available in denominations of 5, 10, and 25 cents and one dollar. The dollar coin is sometimes referred to as a "loonie" because of the bird depicted on its face.

PREMIERE ETAPE

Agreeing and disagreeing; expressing indifference; making requests

VOCABULAIRE

Qu'est-ce qu'il y a à la télé ce soir?

un feuilleton

une série

un vidéoclip

les informations (f.)

la météo
un documentaire

une publicité
un magazine télévisé

un dessin animé
une émission de variétés

un jeu télévisé
un reportage sportif

6 Ecoute!

Ecoute le programme de la soirée. De quel genre d'émissions est-ce que l'annonceur parle?
Answers on p. 217C.

7 Devine!

Décris une personne célèbre de la télévision et dis dans quel genre d'émissions elle apparaît. Ton/ta camarade va deviner qui c'est. Changez de rôles.

SRC

8 Sondage

Ton/ta correspondant(e) canadien(ne) t'a demandé quelles émissions les jeunes Américains regardent. Demande à tes camarades ce qu'ils regardent le plus souvent. Note les deux émissions les plus populaires pour chaque catégorie du **Vocabulaire**. Compare tes notes avec celles de ton/ta camarade.

TV5	18h00	19h30	20h00	21h00	21h30
	Le Canada en guerre	Zap	Emilie, la passion d'une vie	Pour tout dire	Télé-Journal

SRC	18h00	19h00	19h30	20h00	21h00
	Ce Soir	Des Chiffres et des Lettres	Tintin et le lac aux requins	Ad lib	J'ai deux amours : La vie de Joséphine Baker

CHAPITRE 9   C'est l'fun!

Jump Start!

Have students write a brief description of their favorite TV program for a French pen pal (**C'est l'histoire de...** ; **Il s'agit de...**).

MOTIVATE

Ask students what their favorite TV programs are. Write their nominations on a transparency.

TEACH

Presentation

Vocabulaire Project the transparency suggested for the activity under Motivate or make a similar one now. Then, ask students to regroup the programs by genre. Write the new lists on the board as students make suggestions. Next, identify one of the programs in French by genre as you point to the list (*Animaniacs*® **est un dessin animé**) and ask questions about others. (*Try Your Luck* **est un dessin animé ou un jeu télévisé?**)

Teaching Suggestion

Name characters or celebrities associated with different types of TV programs listed in the **Vocabulaire** (Bugs Bunny, Tweedy). Have students identify the type of program (**un dessin animé**).

Game

VINGT QUESTIONS Have one student think of a TV program. His or her classmates then ask up to twenty yes-no questions to try to determine the show he or she is thinking of. (**C'est un dessin animé? Est-ce que le personnage principal est un chat?**)

RESOURCES FOR PREMIERE ETAPE

Chapter Teaching Resources, Book 3
- Communicative Activity 9-1, pp. 4–5
- Teaching Transparency Master 9-1, pp. 8, 10
  Teaching Transparency 9-1
- Additional Listening Activities 9-1, 9-2, 9-3, pp. 11–12
  Audiocassette 10A/Audio CD 9
- Realia 9-1, pp. 15, 17
- Situation Cards 9-1, pp. 18–19
- Student Response Forms, pp. 20–22
- Quiz 9-1, pp. 23–24
  Audiocassette 8A/Audio CD 9

ADDITIONAL RESOURCES
Textbook Audiocassette 5A
  OR *Audio CD 9*
Practice and Activity Book, pp. 98–101
Video Program, Videocassette 2
Video Guide

9 Mon journal

Quels genres d'émissions est-ce que tu préfères regarder? Pourquoi?

COMMENT DIT-ON... ?

Agreeing and disagreeing; expressing indifference

To express agreement:

Je suis d'accord avec toi.
Moi aussi, j'aime bien les feuilletons.
Moi non plus, je n'aime pas la pub.
Tu as raison.
Tu l'as dit!
Tout à fait! *Absolutely!*

To express disagreement:

Pas du tout.
Tu parles! *No way!*
Tu te fiches de moi? *Are you kidding me?*
Tu rigoles! *You're joking!*
Tu as tort.

To express indifference:

Je m'en fiche. *I don't give a darn.*
Ça m'est vraiment égal. *It's really all the same to me.*
Peu importe. *It doesn't matter much.*

Si tu as oublié expressing opinions va à la page 332.

10 Ecoute!

Ecoute ces gens qui parlent de la publicité. Est-ce que la personne qui répond est d'accord, pas d'accord ou indifférente? Answers on p. 217C.

11 C'est cool, les vidéoclips!

Est-ce que tu as vu le dernier vidéoclip de ces stars? Qu'est-ce que tu en penses? Parles-en avec ton/ta camarade qui te dira s'il/si elle est d'accord avec toi.

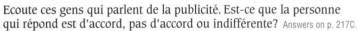

Kenny G   Cranberries   U2
Gloria Estefan   Roch Voisine   Céline Dion
Whitney Houston   MC Solaar
Gipsy Kings   R.E.M.   Boyz II Men

12 Tu rigoles!

Fais une liste de quatre émissions que tu aimes et de quatre autres que tu n'aimes pas. Montre ta liste à ton/ta camarade et donne-lui ton opinion sur chaque émission. Il/Elle va te dire s'il/si elle est d'accord et pourquoi.

13 Les informations

a. Tu es journaliste. Avec ton/ta camarade, prépare un sommaire des événements de la journée.
b. Fais ton reportage devant la classe, comme si tu passais à la télé. Tes camarades, qui jouent le rôle des spectateurs, vont dire ce qu'ils pensent des événements en question et s'ils sont d'accord entre eux ou plutôt indifférents.

Mon journal

9 For an additional journal entry suggestion for Chapter 9, see *Practice and Activity Book,* page 153.

Presentation

Comment dit-on... ? Before class, have one student practice acting as the dummy for your ventriloquist's act. Tell the student to move his or her lips when you place your hand on his or her shoulder and to stop when you remove your hand. In class, have the "dummy" sit at the front. Stand behind him or her. Introduce **Monsieur/Madame Poupée.** Ask him or her about a controversial topic, such as commercials. (**Eh bien, Christophe/ Christine Poupée, tu trouves les pubs marrantes, n'est-ce pas?**) Then, place your hand on the student's shoulder. As he or she moves his or her lips, give a response out of the side of your mouth. (**Mais tu rigoles! Je déteste les pubs!**) Include all of the new expressions in your conversation. Then, make statements about various topics and have students respond with one of the new expressions.

For Individual Needs

11 Visual/Auditory Learners If the resources are available, have students bring in music videos or songs by the artists listed. Show a short segment of a video or play an excerpt of a song, and then call for volunteers to exchange opinions about the video or song and express their agreement or disagreement with each other.

Culture Notes

• Céline Dion was Canada's Entertainer of the Year in 1993, the same year she hosted Canada's Juno music awards and won four Junos. She has already recorded several hit songs in English, including *If You Asked Me To* and *Beauty and the Beast.*

• Originally from Senegal, MC Solaar is a popular French rap musician whose songs promote peace and communication as alternatives to violence.

• Roch Voisine is a popular Canadian singer.

Community Link

Have students call or visit a local radio or TV station to find out about the different types of programs available. They might also find out which programs are the most and least popular.

VOCABULAIRE

14 Voilà comment on fait

Tu veux expliquer à un ami comment enregistrer une émission. Complète le texte en t'inspirant des images.

Alors, d'abord, il faut que tu vérifies l'heure de l'émission dans le [programme télé]. Ensuite, allume ton [téléviseur]. Puis, choisis la [chaîne] qui t'intéresse. Mets une [cassette vidéo] dans ton [magnétoscope]. Quand tu as l' [image] sur l' [écran], prends ta [télécommande] et appuie sur le bouton «enregistrement».

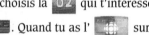

> *Grammaire* Negative expressions
>
> You've already learned **ne... pas, ne... jamais,** and **ne... plus.** Here are some other negative expressions: **ne... rien** *(nothing),* **ne... pas encore** *(not yet),* **ne... aucun(e)** *(no),* **ne... personne** *(no one),* **ne... nulle part** *(nowhere),* and **ne... ni... ni...** *(neither . . . nor . . .).* Study their placement in the following examples.
>
> Je **ne** peux **rien** entendre.   Je **n'**en ai **aucune** idée.
> Ça **n'**a **pas encore** commencé.   **Personne ne** regardait la télé.
> Elle **n'**a rencontré **personne** au cinéma.
> Je **ne** vois la télécommande **nulle part.**
> Il **n'**aime **ni** les feuilletons **ni** les drames.
> **Ni** mon frère **ni** ma sœur **n'**aiment la télé.
>
> - The expression **ne... que** appears to be negative, but has the positive meaning of *only.* Notice the position of **que.**
>
> Il **ne** regarde **que** le sport.   Il **ne** regarde la télé **qu'**avec ses amis.
> *He only watches sports.*   *He watches TV only with his friends.*

15 Questions-réponses

Quelles sont les réponses appropriées aux questions suivantes? See answers below.

Qu'est-ce qu'il y a après le film?

Est-ce que le film est fini?

Tu veux voir un film ou un feuilleton?

Tu as le programme télé?

Il y a quelqu'un devant la télévision?

Où est la télécommande?

Ni l'un ni l'autre. Je préfère voir un reportage.

Je ne sais pas. Je ne la vois nulle part.

Il n'y a plus rien. C'est la fin des programmes.

Non, il n'y a personne.

Non, je n'ai que celui de la semaine dernière.

Non, il n'a pas encore commencé.

16 Tu as vu?

Lisette et Gisèle parlent au téléphone. Choisis une des expressions négatives données pour compléter leur conversation.

LISETTE Hier soir, j'ai regardé *Les meilleures intentions.* Tu l'as vu, toi?

GISELE Non, je __n'__ ai __rien__ regardé hier. Je __ne__ regarde la télé __que__ le samedi soir parce que je __n'__ ai __plus__ le temps.

LISETTE Moi non plus. J'ai trop de devoirs à faire en ce moment.

GISELE Je __n'__ ai __pas encore__ vu le nouveau vidéoclip de Céline Dion. Tu l'as vu, toi?

LISETTE Euh, non. Je __n'__ ai vu __ni__ celui de Céline __ni__ celui de Roch Voisine.

GISELE Dis donc, Lisette, il __n'__ y a __personne__ chez moi. Mes parents sont sortis. Tu veux venir regarder des vidéoclips?

LISETTE Je voudrais bien, mais je __ne__ peux aller __nulle part__ cet après-midi. Je dois travailler. J'ai une interro demain.

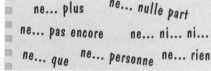

ne... plus   ne... nulle part
ne... pas encore   ne... ni... ni...
ne... que   ne... personne   ne... rien

COMMENT DIT-ON...?
Making requests

To ask someone to be quiet:
Chut! *Shhh!*
Tais-toi! *Be quiet!*
Ne parle pas si fort.
Tu pourrais faire moins de bruit?
Vous pourriez vous taire, s'il vous plaît? *Could you please be quiet?*

To ask someone to adjust the volume:
Baisse le son. *Turn down the volume.*
Monte le son, on n'entend rien. *Turn up . . . the volume.*

17 Ecoute!

Ecoute ces conversations. Dans lesquelles est-ce qu'on demande à quelqu'un de se taire?
1, 3, 4, 7, 8, 10

PREMIERE ETAPE
deux cent vingt-sept **227**

For Individual Needs

15 Auditory Learners
Have students close their books. Read the questions aloud and have students tell which negative expression they would use in the answer. Then, have them open their books and do the activity as directed. When students have matched the questions and answers, have partners read and answer the questions.

16 Challenge Once students have completed the activity as directed, have partners write their own dialogue, using all of the expressions in the word box next to the activity. Have volunteers act out their skits for the class.

Motivating Activity

Ask students to describe situations in which their talking might disturb others (during a test, at the movies, in a library). Then, ask them what they might do or say to others who were talking loudly in these situations.

Presentation

Comment dit-on... ? Draw a TV with a volume control knob on the board and bring in a radio. After turning on the radio (which will represent the sound of the TV), have two volunteers sit in chairs facing the TV and talk quietly. Pull up a chair next to them and ask them to be quiet, using the new expressions. (**Chut!**) Ask them to adjust the volume as well (**Baisse le son!**), having them respond appropriately, using the radio. Then, have volunteers sit in your chair and use one of the new expressions to ask the other viewers watching TV to be quiet.

Portfolio
19 Written/ 20 Oral
Activity 19 is appropriate for students' written portfolios. You might have students videotape or record Activity 20 on audiocassette and have them include it in their oral portfolios. For portfolio information, see *Assessment Guide*, pages 2–13.

Teaching Suggestions
20 Before students begin this activity, you might ask them several comprehension questions about the TV guide. (*Dr. Quinn* **passe à quelle heure?**)

20 Have students scan the TV program guide to find a western, three comedies, a soap opera, a documentary, and a special program. (*Dr. Quinn, Medicine Woman; Poison Ivy; Keeping Up Appearances; The Mommies; Beverly Hills, 90210; National Geographic–Mysteries of Mankind; TVO: One Day in the Life.*)

CLOSE

Game
Write the vocabulary from this **étape** on index cards and put them in a bag. Form two teams and have the first player from the first team come to the front. Select a card from the bag. Depending on the card you draw, you might hold up an item (**la télécommande**), give an example of a TV program (*Bugs Bunny*), mime an expression (**Chut!**), or give an English equivalent. (*You said it!*) If the player correctly identifies the item or program or says the expression, his or her team wins a point, and the turn passes to the next team. Continue until all players have had a turn.

18 Qu'est-ce qu'ils disent? *Possible answers:*
Qu'est-ce que ces personnes peuvent dire pour faire taire ces gens qui font du bruit?

1. Baisse le son! 2. Tu pourrais faire moins de bruit? 3. Vous pourriez vous taire, s'il vous plaît? 4. Chut!

19 Alors, là!
 Qu'est-ce qui se passe sur cette photo? Imagine et écris la conversation de Fabien et Danielle.

Si tu as oublié **quarreling** *va à la page 152.*

20 Jeu de rôle

a. You're going to watch something on TV with a Canadian friend. You try to pick a program from the TV guide that you both want to watch. Unfortunately, you have different preferences and can't agree on anything.

b. You finally make a choice together, but you're not happy with it and you get bored. You annoy your friend by talking several times. Your friend has to ask you to be quiet.

228 *deux cent vingt-huit*

CHAPITRE 9 C'est l'fun!

ASSESS
Quiz 9-1, *Chapter Teaching Resources, Book 3*, pp. 23–24

Assessment Items, Audiocassette 8A Audio CD 9

Performance Assessment
Have students perform their skits from Activity 20. If possible, provide a television, a remote control, and a TV program guide for students to use as props. You might base students' grades on content, language use, and creativity.

PANORAMA CULTUREL

Catherine • Québec

Sébastien • France

Jennifer • France

We asked people about the kinds of movies they like. Here's what they told us.

Quel genre de film préfères-tu?

«J'aime beaucoup les comédies. J'aime aussi les choses historiques, mais je regarde souvent les films pour leurs acteurs. Quand il y a des acteurs qui m'intéressent, je regarde les films. Et puis j'aime, en tout cas... Je suis une des rares qui aiment vraiment les films français. J'aime beaucoup.»

-Catherine

«Les films que je préfère, ce sont les films de science-fiction, Steven Spielberg, parce que j'adore les effets spéciaux, tout ce qui touche au grandiose. Sinon, j'aime bien aussi les comédies, comédies françaises. Je trouve ça assez drôle, et voilà.»

-Sébastien

«J'aime bien tous les films, de préférence les films d'action, les films sur les problèmes de tous les jours, sur les problèmes plus importants.»

-Jennifer

Qu'en penses-tu?

1. Which of these people share your tastes in movies?
2. What French-language films have you seen? Are they different from American films? In what way?
3. Where can you go in your area to see foreign films?

Questions

1. Quel genre de film est-ce que Catherine préfère? (les comédies, les choses historiques)
2. Est-ce que Catherine aime les films français? (oui)
3. Pourquoi est-ce que Sébastien aime les films de science-fiction? (Il aime les effets spéciaux.) Est-ce qu'il aime les comédies? (oui)
4. Quel genre de film est-ce que Jennifer préfère? (les films d'action)

Culture Note

The Canadian film industry is known for its diversity, the high quality of its films, and a lack of commercialization. Several well-known directors are Arthur Lamothe, Pierre Perrault, and Denys Arcand, who has earned numerous film awards.

VIDEO PROGRAM
Videocassette 2

Teacher Notes

- See *Video Guide* and *Practice and Activity Book* for activities related to the **Panorama Culturel.**
- Remind students that cultural material may be included in the Chapter Quizzes and Test.
- The interviewees' language represents informal, unrehearsed speech. Occasionally, edits have been made for clarification.

Motivating Activity

Have students list all the different types of films they can think of (comedy, drama, science-fiction). Write their suggestions on a transparency. You might also have students call out the names of well-known actors and actresses and have the class associate the names with one of the genres. You might also poll the class to find out which type of film is the most popular.

Presentation

Before playing the video, write clues about the interviewees, such as **Cette personne aime les films de science-fiction,** on the board. Then, play the video and have students use the clues to try to guess the identity of the interviewees. Ask the **Questions** to check comprehension. Finally, have partners read the interviews together, and then tell whether they like the same types of films.

Summary

In *D'accord, pas d'accord,* Dina is trying to decide on a film to see with her cousin who is visiting this weekend. Fabien suggests *L'Union sacrée,* a police film starring Patrick Bruel. Marie, unimpressed with Fabien's choice, recommends *Mon père, ce héros* with Gérard Depardieu instead. Another friend, Adrien, suggests *Sidekicks,* a martial arts film with Chuck Norris. Then, Marie suggests *Le grand bleu,* but Adrien thinks it's long and boring. Dina needs more time to decide, but thanks her friends for their ideas.

Motivating Activity

Have students look at the movie advertisements on pages 230–231 and infer the genres of the movies from the ads.

Presentation

Play the recording, pausing after each scene to ask questions about the film being discussed. (*L'Union sacrée* **est un film policier ou un drame?**) Ask who recommends the film and why.

For Individual Needs

22 Auditory Learners
Read these quotations aloud and have students tell which films they refer to.

22 Challenge As an alternative to this activity, have students scan the conversation on pages 230–231 to find one detail about each film: the main actor, the genre, or the director. Ask for volunteers to read their findings aloud and have the class try to identify the movie.

Remise en train

D'accord, pas d'accord

Vendredi, à Montréal, à la sortie du lycée...

1 FABIEN Qu'est-ce que tu vas faire, ce week-end?

DINA Ma cousine vient à Montréal. J'aimerais bien l'emmener au cinéma, mais je ne sais pas trop quoi aller voir. Qu'est-ce que tu as vu comme bons films récemment?

FABIEN De bien, j'ai vu *L'Union sacrée.*

DINA Ah, oui? J'en ai beaucoup entendu parler. C'était comment?

FABIEN C'était super. Tu devrais aller le voir, je suis sûr que ça te plairait. C'est un film policier avec Patrick Bruel et Richard Berry. C'est plein d'action et de suspense; et en plus, c'est drôlement bien fait. Et puis, les acteurs sont super et on ne s'ennuie pas une seconde.

DINA Ça a l'air pas mal. C'est quoi exactement, l'histoire?

FABIEN Alors, tu vois, Berry fait partie des services secrets. Bruel, lui, il est flic. Au début, ils ne s'aiment pas du tout, mais ils sont obligés de travailler ensemble pour arrêter des terroristes. Voilà, je ne t'en dis pas plus. Je t'assure, il faut vraiment que tu ailles voir ce film.

2 MARIE De quel film est-ce que tu parles?

FABIEN De *L'Union sacrée.*

MARIE Bof... c'est pas terrible!

FABIEN Ah non, je ne suis pas d'accord. J'ai trouvé ça très bien, moi.

MARIE Toi, de toute façon, tu aimes tous les films avec Patrick Bruel.

FABIEN Et alors? Il est génial comme acteur!

---

21 Tu as compris?

1. What are the teenagers talking about? movies
2. Do they reach an agreement on which movies are the best? No.
3. Whose recommendation does Dina take? No one's.

22 C'est quel film?

Indique le film dont on parle. See answers below.

«C'est un film policier.»

«C'est avec Patrick Bruel.»

«C'est une comédie.»

«C'est avec Gérard Depardieu.»

«C'est un drame.»

«C'est réalisé par Luc Besson.»

«C'est avec Chuck Norris.»

«C'est un film de karaté.»

230   *deux cent trente*   CHAPITRE 9   C'est l'fun!

Answers
22 C'est un drame: *Le grand bleu*
   C'est avec Patrick Bruel: *L'Union sacrée*
   C'est réalisé par Luc Besson: *Le grand bleu*
   C'est un film policier: *L'Union sacrée*
   C'est avec Chuck Norris: *Sidekicks*
   C'est une comédie: *Mon père, ce héros*
   C'est avec Gérard Depardieu: *Mon père, ce héros*
   C'est un film de karaté: *Sidekicks*

3 MARIE Bof. En tout cas, moi, je te conseille plutôt d'aller voir *Mon père, ce héros* avec Gérard Depardieu.

FABIEN Alors ça, c'est vraiment nul!

MARIE N'importe quoi. C'est très drôle.

DINA De quoi ça parle?

MARIE Ça parle d'une adolescente qui est en vacances avec son père dans une île. Elle rencontre un garçon super mignon et elle lui fait croire que son père est son petit ami.

FABIEN En tout cas, moi, j'ai trouvé ça plutôt lourd et je n'ai pas ri une seule fois.

MARIE Ne l'écoute pas. C'est vraiment marrant.

4 ADRIEN Tu devrais plutôt aller voir *Sidekicks*.

DINA Qu'est-ce que c'est?

ADRIEN C'est l'histoire d'un garçon qui a des problèmes avec les autres enfants du quartier. Dans ses rêves, il vit toutes sortes d'aventures avec son idole, Chuck Norris. A la fin, il décide de prendre des leçons de karaté.

MARIE Ça m'étonnerait que Dina veuille voir un film de karaté!

ADRIEN Et pourquoi pas? Il y a beaucoup d'action et c'est très bien fait.

5 MARIE Moi, je lui conseille plutôt *Le grand bleu*. C'est un film de Luc Besson, un drame.

ADRIEN Il paraît que c'est très mauvais. C'est long, c'est ennuyeux, c'est...

DINA Bon, euh, écoutez, merci pour vos conseils. Finalement, je crois que je ferais mieux de réfléchir et de choisir moi-même!

23 Vrai ou faux?

1. Dans *L'Union sacrée,* Bruel et Berry travaillent ensemble pour arrêter des terroristes. vrai
2. Dans *Mon père, ce héros,* le père croit que sa fille va se marier avec un garçon super mignon. faux
3. Dans *Sidekicks,* Chuck Norris est prof de karaté. faux
4. *Le grand bleu* est un film court mais plein d'action et de suspense. faux

24 Cherche les expressions

See answers below.

What expressions do the teenagers use in *D'accord, pas d'accord* to . . .

1. ask someone to recommend a film?
2. make a recommendation?
3. make a positive judgment?
4. make a negative judgment?
5. ask what a movie is about?
6. summarize a movie?

25 Et maintenant, à toi

Quels genres de films est-ce que tu aimes? Quel est ton film préféré?

For Individual Needs

Challenge Have students scan the conversation and write down all the judgments, positive and negative, that the friends make about the films. Collect their papers, read them aloud, and have students tell whether each remark is positive or negative, who made it, and which film it refers to.

Teaching Suggestions

25 You might have students write their answers to these questions in their journals.

25 Have students ask a partner these questions. You might also take a class poll to determine the three most popular film genres and the three most popular films.

Culture Notes

• Gérard Depardieu, a prolific actor who has played vastly different roles in over 50 films since his début in 1965, has also directed and co-produced several films, notably *Les compères* in 1984. In the 1990s, he made his American film debut, starring in the English-language films *Green Card* and *My Father the Hero.*

• *Le grand bleu* (1988) is a favorite among French film critics. It starred Jean-Marc Barr, Jean Reno, and the American actress Rosanna Arquette. It was filmed in English so it could be more easily dubbed into different languages.

Answers

24 1. Qu'est-ce que tu as vu comme bons films récemment?

2. Tu devrais aller le voir, je suis sûr que ça te plairait. Je t'assure, il faut vraiment que tu ailles voir ce film. Je te conseille plutôt d'aller voir... ; Tu devrais plutôt aller voir... ; Moi, je lui conseille plutôt... ;

3. C'était super. C'est drôlement bien fait/très drôle/vraiment marrant. J'ai trouvé ça très bien, moi. Il est génial comme acteur.

4. ... c'est pas terrible! C'est long/ennuyeux/ vraiment nul. J'ai trouvé ça plutôt lourd et je n'ai pas ri une seule fois. Il paraît que c'est très mauvais.

5. C'est quoi exactement, l'histoire? De quoi ça parle? Qu'est-ce que c'est?

6. C'est un film... ; avec... ; C'est... ; Au début... ; Ça parle de... ; C'est l'histoire de... ; A la fin, ...

*J*ump Start!

List five TV shows and movies, and have students write their opinions of each one, using expressions they already know.

MOTIVATE

Bring in recent movie listings and read aloud several movie titles. Have students tell what type of movie it is. If they haven't heard of the movie, identify the main actors and/or actresses and have them try to guess again.

TEACH

Presentation

Vocabulaire Give examples of each of the genres, using props and gestures to convey meaning. For example, you might say *High Noon* **est un western** while swaggering bow-legged and pretending to draw two guns from your hips. You might also ask which well-known actors might perform in each genre. (**John Wayne jouerait dans un western ou dans un film de science-fiction? Qui jouerait dans un film de science-fiction?**) Then, have partners ask each other which genres they prefer. (**Tu aimes les films d'action?**)

Teaching Suggestions

• Hold up video jackets of different types of movies and have students identify the genre.
• Play the game "**Mémoire**" described on page 217F.

Answers

27 *Le pont de la rivière Kwai:* un film de guerre
Les aventures d'un homme invisible: un film de science-fiction
L'Ami africain: un drame
La Famille Pierreafeu: une comédie
Les Patriotes: un drame
Henry V: un film historique

232 DEUXIEME ETAPE

DEUXIEME ETAPE

Asking for and making judgments; asking for and making recommendations; asking about and summarizing a story

*V*OCABULAIRE

un film d'action
d'espionnage
de guerre
d'horreur
de science-fiction

un film étranger
historique
policier
une histoire d'amour

une comédie
une comédie musicale
un drame
un western

26 Il y en a pour tous les goûts

Devine de quel genre de film il s'agit.

1. C'est drôle. 1. une comédie 2. un film historique
2. Il y a de beaux costumes du XVIᵉ siècle.
3. Ça se passe dans l'espace. un film de science-fiction
4. Un détective cherche l'auteur d'un crime. un film policier
5. Le personnage principal est un monstre. un film d'horreur
6. Ça se passe pendant la guerre du Viêt-nam. un film de guerre
7. C'est une histoire de cow-boys. un western
8. Il y a des sous-titres en anglais. un film étranger

NOTE CULTURELLE

Although its feature-film industry has long been overshadowed by Hollywood, Canada is a major force in the production of non-fiction and noncommercial films. Canada's National Film Board has produced nearly 20,000 documentaries and films, both live-action and animated. Its productions draw praise for their artistic and technical excellence, and some, such as *Mon oncle Antoine* and *Le château de sable,* have won awards at film festivals all over the world. Montreal's own festival, the **Festival des films du monde,** is one of the most important in the world.

27 Qu'est-ce qu'on joue?

Lis ces résumés de films. A quel genre appartient chaque film? See answers below.

PONT DE LA RIVIERE KWAI (LE) — Amér.,coul. (57). De David Lean : Pendant la deuxième guerre mondiale, les Japonais capturent des soldats anglais et les forcent à travailler à la construction d'un pont de chemin de fer. Le Colonel Nicholson, qui au départ refuse de coopérer, finit par voir ce pont comme une source de fierté et un symbole de réussite personnelle. Mais un commando envoyé par l'état-major anglais s'apprête à détruire le pont. Avec Alec Guiness, William Holden.

AVENTURES D'UN HOMME INVISIBLE (LES) — Amér., coul. (92). De John Carpenter : Charmant original, Nick Holloway, par un étrange concours de circonstances, se retrouve invisible, prisonnier dans un bâtiment encerclé par des hommes des services secrets... Avec Chevy Chase, Daryl Hannah, Sam Neill, Michael Mckean.

AMI AFRICAIN (L') — Amér., coul. (94). De Stewart Raffill : Au nord du Kenya, des touristes sont pris en otages par des braconniers, tueurs d'éléphants. La protection inattendue du chef des troupeaux parviendra-t-elle à sauver deux jeunes gens en fuite? Avec Jennifer McComb, Ashley Hamilton, Timothy Ackroyd, Mohamed Nangurai.

FAMILLE PIERREAFEU (LA) — Amér., coul. (94). De Brian Levant : Allez donc voir comment vivaient nos ancêtres de la Préhistoire dans leurs cavernes d'une idyllique banlieue ! Astucieux, rigolards et d'une naïveté qui met l'un d'eux dans un sale pétrin. D'après Hanna et Barbera. Avec John Goodman, Rick Moranis, Elizabeth Perkins, Rosie O'Donnell, Kyle MacLachlan, Halle Berry, Richard Moll, Elizabeth Taylor.

PATRIOTES (LES) — Franç., coul. (93). De Eric Rochant : A 18 ans, Ariel Brenner, d'origine juive, quitte Paris et sa famille pour entrer dans les rangs du Mossad où il va être initié à l'art de la manipulation. Avec Yvan Attal, Richard Masur, Allen Garfield, Yossai Banai, Nancy Allen, Maurice Bénichou, Hippolyte Girardot, Jean-François Stévenin, Christine Pascal, Bernard Le Coq, Roger Mirmont, Myriem Roussel, Sandrine Kiberlain.

HENRY V, de Kenneth Branagh — Brit., coul. (90). De Kenneth Branagh : La conquête de la France, de 1414 à 1420, par Henry V d'Angleterre ; un épisode tumultueux et haut en couleurs de la Guerre de Cent Ans. D'après la tragédie de Shakespeare. Avec Kenneth Branagh, Derek Jacobi, Simon Shepherd, James Larkin, Brian Blessed, James Simmons, Paul Gregory, Charles Kay.

RESOURCES FOR DEUXIEME ETAPE

Chapter Teaching Resources, Book 3
• Communicative Activity 9-2, pp. 6–7
• Teaching Transparency Master 9-2, pp. 9, 10
   Teaching Transparency 9-2
• Additional Listening Activities 9-4, 9-5, 9-6, pp. 12–13
   Audiocassette 10A/Audio CD 9
• Realia 9-2, pp. 16, 17
• Situation Cards 9-2, 9-3, pp. 18–19
• Student Response Forms, pp. 20–22
• Quiz 9-2, pp. 25–26
   Audiocassette 8A/Audio CD 9

ADDITIONAL RESOURCES
Textbook Audiocassette 5A
   OR Audio CD 9
Practice and Activity Book, pp. 103–106

COMMENT DIT-ON... ?

Asking for and making judgments; asking for and making recommendations

To ask for judgments:

C'était comment?

Comment tu as trouvé ça?

To make a positive judgment:

Ça m'a beaucoup plu. *I liked it..*

J'ai trouvé ça amusant/pas mal.

Il y avait de bonnes scènes d'action.

Je ne me suis pas ennuyé(e) une seconde.

Ça m'a bien fait rire. *It really made me laugh.*

To make a negative judgment:

C'est nul/lourd. *It's no good/dull.*

C'est un navet.

Ça n'a aucun intérêt.

Je n'ai pas du tout aimé.

Ça ne m'a pas emballé(e). *It didn't do anything for me.*

Je me suis ennuyé(e) à mourir.

To ask someone to recommend a movie:

Qu'est-ce que tu as vu comme bon film?

Qu'est-ce qu'il y a comme bons films en ce moment?

To recommend a movie:

Tu devrais aller voir *Le château de ma mère.*

Je te recommande *Au revoir les enfants.*

Va voir *Les visiteurs,* **c'est génial comme film.**

C'est à ne pas manquer!

To advise against a movie:

Ne va surtout pas voir *Le jouet!*

Evite d'aller voir *La famille Pierreafeu®.*

N'y va pas!

Ça ne vaut pas le coup! *It's not worth it!*

28 Ecoute!

Ecoute ces conversations. Est-ce que ces gens recommandent les films qu'ils ont vus ou pas? Answers on p. 217D.

29 De bons conseils

Quelques personnes ont fait des recommandations à propos des films qu'elles ont vus. Qu'est-ce qu'elles pourraient ajouter à ce qu'elles ont dit? See answers below.

«Oh, ça m'a beaucoup plu.
«Ça m'a bien fait rire.
«Oh! C'est nul.
«Il y a de beaux costumes.
«Ça n'a aucun intérêt.
«Ça ne m'a pas emballé.

Ça ne vaut pas le coup!»
Je te le recommande.»
C'est à ne pas manquer!»
Evite d'aller le voir.»
N'y va pas!»
Tu devrais aller le voir.»

30 Tu as vu?

Demande à un(e) camarade ce qu'il/elle a vu comme film dernièrement. Ensuite, demande-lui quel genre de film c'était, ce qu'il/elle en a pensé et s'il/si elle te le recommande. Changez de rôles.

Presentation

Comment dit-on... ? Before class, have a student rehearse the questions in the function box and provide him or her with a list of films. In class, have the student ask you for a judgment about one of the films on the list. Use the new expressions to praise some films and give bad reviews of others. Next, have students name some movies they recommend and others they advise against. List them in two columns on a transparency. Recommend some movies and advise against others. Then, make positive judgments and recommendations and ask individuals whether they agree. (**Tu es d'accord ou pas?**) Students should respond with an appropriate expression.

Teaching Suggestion

Have students rewrite the expressions for recommending and advising against a movie, substituting the titles of various movies they've seen. You might have them read their recommendations aloud and have the class express agreement or disagreement by a show of hands.

For Individual Needs

29 Challenge Once students have completed the activity, have partners use two or three of the quotations in a short dialogue. You might have them present their dialogue to the class.

Portfolio

30 Oral This activity is appropriate for students' oral portfolios. For portfolio information, see *Assessment Guide,* pages 2–13.

Game

PAS D'ACCORD Have students form groups of three, one judge and two players. One player makes a judgment about a movie. (**Ça m'a beaucoup plu,** *Henry V.*) The other agrees or disagrees (**Tu rigoles! C'est lourd!**) and makes a judgment about a different movie, using a different expression. (**Mais** *Aladdin,* **j'ai trouvé ça amusant.**) The first player reacts to the judgment, and so on. Players may use previously learned expressions. No repetitions are allowed. The goal is to keep the game going as long as possible.

Possible answers

29 Oh, ça m'a beaucoup plu; Je te le recommande.
Ça m'a bien fait rire; C'est à ne pas manquer!
Oh! C'est nul; Evite d'aller le voir.
Il y a de beaux costumes; Tu devrais aller le voir!
Ça n'a aucun intérêt; N'y va pas!
Ça ne m'a pas emballé; Ça ne vaut pas le coup!

31 Qu'est-ce qu'il y a comme bons films?

Quelqu'un dans ton groupe a envie d'aller voir un film. Chaque élève lui en recommande un. Pour chaque film, les autres disent s'ils sont du même avis ou non. S'ils ne sont pas d'accord, ils lui disent d'éviter ce film et en recommandent un autre.

COMMENT DIT-ON... ?
Asking about and summarizing a story

To ask what a story is about:

De quoi ça parle?
Comment est-ce que ça commence?
Comment ça se termine?

To summarize a story:

Ça parle d'un pays où il y a une guerre civile.
C'est l'histoire d'une femme qui joue du piano.
Il s'agit d'un homme au chômage.
Ça se passe en France.
Au début, ils ne s'aiment pas.
A ce moment-là, il tombe malade.
A la fin, sa femme meurt.

A la française

In French, as in English, you can use the present tense to tell what happened in the past. This makes stories more vivid. For example, if you're telling a story about someone who broke his arm, you might say: "So, he *falls* off the bike and *breaks* his arm!"

32 Ecoute!

Ecoute Fabrice, un jeune Canadien, qui parle d'un film qu'il a vu. Ensuite, dis si les phrases suivantes sont vraies ou fausses. *Answers on p. 217D.*

1. Ça se passe près de Montréal.
2. C'est l'histoire d'un jeune homme qui s'appelle Chomi.
3. Ça parle d'un jeune homme qui est malade.
4. Au début de l'histoire, Chomi passe tout son temps avec Coyote.
5. A la fin de l'histoire, Olive est très fâchée.

Grammaire Relative pronouns

To make longer sentences, you can join two or more clauses by using the words **qui** *(who, that)* and **que** *(whom, that, which)*. Use **qui** as the subject of a clause, and **que** as the object of a clause.

C'est l'histoire d'une femme **qui** est très grande. *(who)*
Ça, c'est la femme **qu'**il a rencontrée au café. *(whom)*

- Since **qui** acts as a subject, it is usually followed by a verb, and since **que** acts as an object, it is normally followed by a subject.
- English speakers often leave out this pronoun but French speakers must use it.
  Il n'a pas aimé le film **qu'**il a vu. *He didn't like the movie (that) he saw.*
- Drop the **e** from **que** before a vowel sound. Never drop the **i** from **qui**.
- Use the word **dont** if you mean *whose* or *about/of/from whom* or *what*.
  Tu connais l'actrice **dont** il parle? *(about whom)*
  Ça, c'est le garçon **dont** la sœur est une actrice célèbre. *(whose sister)*

33 C'est l'histoire de...

Fabien raconte l'intrigue d'un film qu'il recommande à Dina. Complète son récit avec **qui**, **que** ou **dont**.

C'est l'histoire d'un médecin _qui_ fuit. Un soir, il arrive chez lui et découvre _que_ sa femme a été tuée par un homme _dont_ il ne connaît pas l'identité et _qui_ n'a qu'un bras. Personne ne veut croire _que_ l'homme _dont_ le médecin parle existe vraiment et c'est le médecin _qui_ est accusé du meutre. Il est arrêté. Dans le bus _qui_ conduit les prisonniers à la prison, il y a une bagarre _qui_ cause un accident. Le bus est sur le point d'exploser et tout le monde s'échappe. Mais le médecin essaie de sauver quelqu'un _dont_ les mains sont attachées au bus par des menottes. Après, il s'enfuit et il devient «le fugitif» _que_ la police cherche pendant le reste du film. Bon, je ne t'en dis pas plus. Va le voir. C'est génial comme film!

34 C'est à ne pas manquer!

Un de tes camarades écrit à son correspondant pour lui expliquer l'intrigue d'un film qu'il a vu. Récris sa lettre en liant les phrases avec des pronoms relatifs quand c'est possible.
See answers below.

35 Devine!

Ton/ta camarade va te raconter l'intrigue *(plot)* d'un film. Essaie de deviner de quel film il s'agit. Changez de rôles.

36 De quoi ça parle?

Ton correspondant canadien t'a demandé de lui raconter un film américain que tu as vu. Ecris-lui une lettre où tu lui dis le genre du film, qui joue dedans, de quoi ça parle et pourquoi tu as aimé. Recommande-lui d'aller le voir.

37 Une bande-annonce

a. Avec ton/ta camarade, choisissez un film qui vous a plu. Ensuite, créez une bande-annonce *(movie ad)* pour la télé. N'oubliez pas de parler des acteurs, de l'histoire et des qualités du film. Décrivez deux ou trois extraits intéressants du film.

b. Jouez votre bande-annonce devant la classe. Vos camarades vont dire ce qu'ils en pensent et si votre bande-annonce leur donne envie d'aller voir le film.

C'est l'histoire d'un savant. Ce savant s'appelle Frankenstein. Pendant ses études de médecine, Frankenstein rencontre un homme. Cet homme lui parle de ses expériences secrètes pour créer un être humain. Mais, avant de mourir, l'homme dit à Frankenstein de ne pas poursuivre les expériences. L'homme lui avait parlé de ces expériences. Le jeune savant refuse de prendre ces conseils au sérieux. Frankenstein se sert de ces secrets pour créer un être humain. Cet être humain est un monstre. Le monstre est furieux. Le corps et le visage sont horribles. D'abord, il ne comprend pas d'où il vient. Puis, il trouve le journal du savant. Frankenstein avait laissé le journal dans la poche de son manteau. Le monstre est très laid. Il le sait. Et personne ne l'aime. Il demande à Frankenstein de lui créer une compagne. Cette compagne lui ressemble. Je ne te raconte pas la fin... Tu verras. C'est assez terrifiant, mais c'est génial!

····· **V**ocabulaire *à la carte* ·····

les effets spéciaux	
les cascades (f.)	*the stunts*
les scènes (f.) d'action	
les acteurs	
la mise en scène	*the direction*
l'histoire	*the story*
la musique	

Answers

34 C'est l'histoire d'un savant qui s'appelle Frankenstein. Pendant ses études de médecine, Frankenstein rencontre un homme qui lui parle de ses expériences secrètes pour créer un être humain. Mais, avant de mourir, l'homme dit à Frankenstein de ne pas poursuivre les expériences dont il avait parlé. Le jeune savant refuse de prendre ces conseils au sérieux. Frankenstein se sert de ces secrets pour créer un être humain qui est un monstre. Le monstre, qui ne comprend d'abord pas d'où il vient et dont le corps et le visage sont horribles, est furieux. Puis, il trouve le journal que le savant avait laissé dans la poche de son manteau. Le monstre sait qu'il est très laid et que personne ne l'aime. Il demande à Frankenstein de lui créer une compagne qui lui ressemble. Je ne te raconte pas la fin... Tu verras que c'est assez terrifiant, mais c'est génial!

READING STRATEGY
Visualization

Teacher Note
For an additional reading, see *Practice and Activity Book,* page 107.

PREREADING
Activities A–C

Motivating Activity
Choose a dialogue from a story in English that students are familiar with. Tell students to close their eyes and visualize the scene as you read the dialogue aloud. Afterwards, ask students to describe the characters and the setting as they pictured them.

Teaching Suggestions
• Have students look at the photos on pages 236–237 and try to guess what the movie scene will be about.

A. 2. Have students make a list of the main characters and their characteristics to refer to when they read the script.

Additional Practice
B. Ask students these additional questions about the review from *Variety:* Who was responsible for the movie's photography? (Thomas Vamos) For the music? (Osvaldo Montes) Who was the director? (André Melançon) Who wrote the screenplay? (Geneviève Lefèbvre)

LISONS!

Film intelligent qui ne sous-estime pas les jeunes, FIERRO... l'été des secrets confirme une fois de plus la qualité et l'originalité des CONTES POUR TOUS.
— Paul Toutant
RADIO-CANADA

Tous les aspects de ce film sont d'une qualité exceptionnelle: la photographie superbe de Thomas Vamos, la musique admirable de Osvaldo Montes, la réalisation parfaitement maîtrisée de André Melançon, le scénario tout en finesse de Geneviève Lefèbvre, le jeu parfait des comédiens.
— Prat
VARIETY

Des paysages superbes, des images très belles et une histoire qui retient l'attention non seulement des jeunes, mais aussi des grands.
— Claude Bergeron
LE NOUVELLISTE

FIERRO...L'ETE DES SECRETS
SYNOPSIS
Les trois enfants d'une famille de Buenos Aires passent leurs vacances d'été à la ferme de leur grand-père dans la Pampa argentine. Pour le petit Felipe, neuf ans, c'est le bonheur parfait : un nouveau petit chiot et les gâteries de son grand-père. Pour Daniel, 12 ans, c'est l'occasion de prouver qu'il est un homme, en réussissant à dompter un cheval sauvage. Quant à Laura, 13 ans, elle n'est plus une fillette, mais pas encore une femme. Comment va-t-elle aborder l'adolescence dans ce monde traditionnellement macho? Le grand-père Federico, un homme fier et buté, devra exorciser ses vieux principes pour conserver l'amour de ses petits-enfants qui grandissent et surtout celui de Laura. FIERRO... l'été des secrets raconte la fin de l'enfance, ses joies, ses passions, les difficultés de grandir et de vieillir.

DE BONS CONSEILS
Visualization is a technique that helps you to get the most out of what you read. It means that you actively picture in your mind what you are reading; the setting, the way the characters look and are dressed, their actions and speech. Visualization enables you to create a context for what you are reading. Then, if you come across a word you don't know, you can use the context you've created to figure out the meaning of the word.

A. Read the synopsis of the story and answer the following questions. See answers below.
1. Where does the story take place? At what time of year?
2. Who are the main characters in the story and how are they related to one another?
3. What will be significant for Daniel and for Laura this summer?
4. What is the difference between **grandir** and **vieillir**? To what characters do these words apply?

B. What information do you find in the colored boxes over the synopsis? See answers below.
1. What are the five specific aspects of the film praised by the reviewer from *Variety?*
2. What three things does Claude Bergeron mention that are noteworthy about the film?
3. What do you think the **CONTES POUR**

236 *deux cent trente-six*

83. INT. JOUR. SALLE A MANGER

Federico termine son café. Il s'apprête à sortir. Daniel entre.

DANIEL : Ils viennent d'amener Ruano.

Federico se lève en souriant. Il se dirige vers le vestibule.

FEDERICO : J'ai pensé que ça serait plus facile pour toi de le dompter ici.

Daniel s'assoit.

FEDERICO (se méprenant) : Repose-toi un peu aujourd'hui ; tu continueras demain.

Il monte quelques marches d'escalier.

DANIEL : Je ne le monterai pas demain.

FEDERICO : Prends le temps qu'il te faut.

DANIEL : Je ne veux plus le dompter.

Federico s'arrête au milieu de l'escalier.

FEDERICO (surpris) : Qu'est-ce que tu veux dire ?

DANIEL (ferme) : Je ne veux plus le dompter.

Federico le dévisage un moment en silence. Arrivée de Felipe qui vient de la cuisine, suivi d'Anna. Ils se tiennent dans l'encadrement de la porte.

FEDERICO : C'est à cause de l'accident ?

DANIEL : Non, pas du tout.

FEDERICO : Explique-toi.

DANIEL : Ce cheval-là n'est pas pour moi.

FEDERICO : C'est toi qui l'as choisi.

Daniel garde le silence, les yeux dans le vague. Federico poursuit.

FEDERICO : C'est pas possible. Tu ne vas pas te laisser dominer par un cheval... Pas toi...

Laura sort de sa chambre et s'approche de la rembarde de l'escalier. Elle assiste à la conversation.

Daniel ne répond toujours pas.

FEDERICO : Il te fait peur ? C'est ça ?

Daniel lève les yeux et soutient le regard de son grand-père.

DANIEL (ferme) : J'ai pas peur !

FEDERICO : Je ne comprends pas, Daniel... (Un temps.) Je ne comprends pas... Si ce n'est pas de la peur, c'est quoi ? ... de la lâcheté ?

ANNA : Federico !

Daniel s'est durci sous l'accusation.

DANIEL : Tu ne peux pas comprendre. J'ai essayé...

FEDERICO (le coupant): Puis, au premier obstacle, tu démissionnes !

DANIEL (ferme): On n'est pas fait pour aller ensemble, c'est tout.

FEDERICO : C'est trop facile !

DANIEL (il hausse le ton): Non, c'est pas facile !

TOUS could be that Paul Toutant mentions in his review?

C. Where and at what time of day does Scene 83 take place? *dining room; morning*

D. Look over the first dozen lines of the scene and answer these questions. *See answers below.*
  1. Which parts of the scene are the stage directions? What added information do they give?
  2. What information is given by the words in parentheses next to the speaker's name?

E. Why did Federico have the colt Ruano brought to the ranch? *so Daniel could break him*

F. Which of the following is NOT a synonym for **dompter**?

  dominer   imposer sa volonté

  se soumettre

G. What reason does Daniel give for not wanting to continue trying to break Ruano?
  a. He's afraid of the horse because of an accident.
  b. He's found another horse he prefers.
  c. He and the horse just aren't meant for each other.

H. How does Federico react when Daniel refuses to break the horse? *with anger*

I. How does Laura intervene? Why? Does Federico pay any attention to her? *See answers below.*

J. How does Federico treat the people he loves, according to Laura? *He dominates them.*

K. How does Federico react to Laura's outburst? Name two things he does to punish her. *See answers below.*

deux cent trente-sept **237**

READING
Activities D–O

Teaching Suggestions

• Before students begin to read the script, you might ask them to name American movies about childhood experiences.

E.–G. Have students do these activities in groups. They should give the line of the script on which they based their answer to each question.

For Individual Needs

Auditory Learners To help students visualize the scene, you might have five students take the parts of Daniel, Federico, Anna, Laura, and Felipe and read the scene aloud.

E., H., I., J. Slower Pace Write the questions in these activities on a transparency, together with several multiple-choice answers for each one. For example, for E., you might give the following choices: (a) because it was sick; (b) so the family could ride together; (c) so Daniel could break him; (d) as a companion for Laura. Have students choose the correct answer from the choices given. You may want to go over the answers orally, asking students to quote the line from the script that supports their choice.

Terms in Lisons!

Students might want to know the following words from the script: **encadrement de la porte** *(doorway)*; **se durcir** *(to harden)*; **couper** *(to cut)*; **les dents serrées** *(with gritted teeth)*.

Teaching Suggestion

L. If students made lists of the characters' personalities suggested on page 236, have them refer to them now.

For Individual Needs

M. Auditory Learners
Locate the sentence from the scene in which each of these words is used and read it aloud, using appropriate intonation. Then, have students do the activity as directed.

M. Slower Pace Write the definitions of these words on a transparency and have students match the French words with their English equivalents.

Additional Practice

• Have students name the characters for whom the following stage directions were written: **ferme** *(Daniel)*; **indignée** *(Laura)*; **les dents serrées** *(Federico)*; **voix basse** *(Felipe)*; **voix sourde** *(Federico)*; **furieuse** *(Laura)*.

• Write a line on the board from a script, real or imaginary. **(Je m'appelle Inigo Montoya. Tu as tué mon père. Prépare-toi à mourir.)** Give a stage direction **(voix basse)** and ask for volunteers to read the line in the appropriate tone of voice.

POSTREADING
Activity P

Teaching Suggestion

P. Have students describe specific conflicts that they've seen depicted on TV or in a movie and tell how they were resolved. You might have them take notes on the situations described to use for the **Ecrivons!** activities.

FEDERICO : Tu me déçois, Daniel... Tu me déçois beaucoup.

Il ne bouge pas. Laura intervient.

LAURA (indignée mais pas agressive) : T'as pas le droit de lui dire ça.

FEDERICO : Ça, ça ne te regarde pas. Tais-toi !

ANNA : Federico, calme-toi. Tu vas pas faire une scène pour un cheval ?

FEDERICO (voix sourde) : Ne vous mêlez pas de ça. C'est à Daniel que je parle.

Il descend l'escalier.

FEDERICO (à Daniel) : Si tu n'es pas capable d'imposer ta volonté, tu ne seras pas capable de mener ta vie ! Comprends-tu ? Tu n'as pas le choix ; ou tu t'imposes, ou tu te soumets.

Laura descend l'escalier à son tour. Sa voix tremble un peu.

LAURA : Et les gens que tu aimes ? Tu veux les dompter aussi ? C'est ça ?

Federico l'ignore, il continue à s'adresser à Daniel.

FEDERICO : Comprends-tu ?

Laura a atteint le bas de l'escalier. D'un geste impulsif, elle pousse la potiche qui se trouve sur la colonne de l'escalier. La lourde potiche s'effondre avec fracas. Tout le monde sursaute.

LAURA (furieuse) : Ecoute-moi !

Federico se retourne. Felipe et Daniel

regardent Laura, stupéfaits. Elle a l'air d'une furie.

LAURA : Pourquoi ? Pourquoi tu fais ça ? Tu dis que tu veux qu'on soit heureux, mais tu décides toujours pour nous... Tu nous aimes comme tu aimes ton cheval ; va à droite, va à gauche, arrête... Puis quand on fait pas comme tu veux, ça ne fait pas ton affaire ! Pourquoi tu fais ça ? J'en ai assez, moi.

Federico la regarde un moment ; il est blême.

FEDERICO (les dents serrées) : Moi aussi j'en ai assez. Je ne veux plus rien entendre de toi. T'es pas bien ici ? Alors, tu fais tes bagages et tu pars par le prochain train. Et je t'interdis de sortir de ta chambre jusqu'à ton départ. Tu retournes à Buenos Aires !

FELIPE (à voix basse) : Comme grand-maman...

Seul Federico l'a entendu. Il lui jette un regard étrange. Il se tourne alors vers Daniel :

FEDERICO : Toi, on se reparlera ce soir.

Il se dirige vers la porte extérieure et la claque.

L. Whose personality does each of the following statements reflect?

Federico

Federico «Ça ne te regarde pas.»

«Tu me déçois beaucoup.» Daniel

Federico «Je ne veux plus le dompter.»

«Ou tu t'imposes, ou tu te soumets.» Daniel

«On n'est pas fait pour aller ensemble.»

«Tu veux dompter les gens que tu aimes aussi?» Laura

«Tu nous aimes comme tu aimes ton cheval.» Laura

M. Use context to figure out the meaning of these words.

N. According to Federico, why must a person be able to impose his will on others? What does this reveal about his character? *See answers below.*

O. Why do you think Federico finds it more difficult to deal with his grandchildren as they grow up? *See answers below.*

P. What are some typical conflicts that adults and adolescents face as the adolescents grow up and become more independent? *See answers below.*

apprivoiser to tame
aborder to approach
buté stubborn
démissionner to quit, give up
la rembarde railing
blême pale, livid
dévisager to stare at
la lâcheté cowardice

Teaching Suggestion

Have students assume the identity of one of the characters from *Fierro... l'été des secrets* and tell what they would have done in this scene.

Answers
N in order not to be dominated by them; He is domineering.
O They are beginning to become more independent and make their own decisions.
P *Possible answers:* disagreements over adolescents' ability and right to make their own decisions, keeping certain aspects of their lives private

*Now that you have read the scene from **FIERRO... l'été des secrets**, you're going to have a chance to be a screenwriter, too. You and a classmate will write a scene for a television show. Your goal will be to convince a Canadian television producer to buy your idea and produce a Canadian TV series.*

Un scénario de télévision

Avec un(e) camarade, écris une petite scène pour une série télévisée dans laquelle deux personnages essaient de résoudre un désaccord.

A. Préparation

1. Choisissez le genre de série que vous voulez créer : une comédie, un drame, une série policière? Est-ce que vous voulez que votre série soit sérieuse ou drôle?
   a. Qu'est-ce qui se passe dans votre série?
   b. Qui sont les personnages principaux? Voici quelques exemples possibles.

un mari et sa femme
une famille
un enfant et ses parents
deux jeunes qui sont dans la même équipe de sport
deux personnes qui travaillent au même endroit
un garçon et une fille qui sortent ensemble
deux bons/bonnes ami(e)s

DE BONS CONSEILS
A good writer will be careful to maintain consistency in all aspects of writing: mood, point of view, characterization, tone, and so on. For example, a menacing character in a horror story probably wouldn't say something humorous right in the middle of a scary scene. Likewise, a current slang expression would sound out of place in the script of a historical movie. To keep your work consistent, stick to the plan you made before you began to write; when you've finished your writing, read it over and check for things that seem illogical or out of place or character.

   1. Faites une liste d'adjectifs pour décrire leur personnalité.
   2. Rédigez ensuite une brève description de chaque personnage.
   c. Quel genre de relation ont les personnages? Est-ce qu'ils s'entendent bien ou pas? Quel problème ont-ils? Décidez ce qui va se passer dans la scène que vous allez écrire.
2. Jouez votre scène. Improvisez un dialogue adapté à votre scène. Prenez des notes.

B. Rédaction

1. En utilisant vos notes, faites un plan de votre script. Puis, vérifiez que...
   a. le problème des personnages est présenté de façon claire.
   b. les réactions et les commentaires des personnages sont appropriés à la fois au contexte et à leur personnalité.
2. Rédigez votre dialogue en suivant le plan que vous avez fait.
3. Après avoir écrit le dialogue, ajoutez-y des instructions de mise en scène.

C. Evaluation

1. Quand vous avez terminé, relisez votre scène et répondez aux questions suivantes.
   a. Est-ce que le dialogue est réaliste?
   b. Est-ce que les réactions des personnages sont appropriées à leur personnalité et au contexte de l'histoire?
2. Vérifiez la grammaire et l'orthographe de votre histoire et faites les corrections nécessaires.

deux cent trente-neuf **239**

WRITING STRATEGY
Maintaining consistency

 Portfolio

Written You might want to have students include all their work for Parts A–C in their written portfolios. For portfolio information, see *Assessment Guide*, pages 2–13.

PREWRITING

Motivating Activity

Have students name their favorite TV shows and characters and tell why they like them. You might have students use the lists suggested for Activity P on page 238 and describe the situations they listed to the class.

Reading/Writing Link

A. 2. You might have students visualize the setting, action, and mood of their scene before they start writing the dialogue.

For Individual Needs

A. Auditory Learners
Auditory learners may need to "think out loud" in order to hear how their scenes will progress. Encourage them to say the characters' lines aloud, perhaps using sock puppets or stuffed animals.

A. Kinesthetic Learners
These students might need to walk through the actions in their scene with a partner.

WRITING

Teaching Suggestion

B. To avoid inconsistency, encourage students to keep a visual image of their characters in mind as they write their scenes.

POSTWRITING

 Cooperative Learning

Once students have written and edited their "pilot episodes," they might produce and videotape them. Have students form small groups, read each member's script, and decide which one to produce. Then, the writer acts as director and the others are the actors and actresses. Students might even create and record an introductory theme song for the episode. This activity is appropriate for students' oral portfolios.

The **Mise en pratique** reviews and integrates all four skills and culture in preparation for the Chapter Test.

 Video Wrap-Up

VIDEO PROGRAM
Videocassette 2

You might want to use the *Video Program* as part of the chapter review. See the *Video Guide* for teaching suggestions and activity masters.

For Individual Needs

1 Challenge Once students have completed the activity, type the statements in the correct order and distribute copies to partners. Have them reconstruct a conversation, based on the statements. For the first event (**Didier veut la télécommande**), students might write **Tu pourrais me passer la télécommande?**

Teaching Suggestions

2 Once students have completed their lists, have them act out a scene in which they present their ideas to the station's review board. Two or three students should act as board members, asking questions and offering approval or disapproval.

3 Before students read the interview, have them scan the introductory paragraph to find out when the festival is held, what is on the program, and who is being interviewed (from August 22 to September 2; film presentations, appearances by movie stars, and awards; Emma Halvick of *Canada Cinéma* magazine).

Motivating Activity

3 After they read the introductory paragraph, have students suggest questions that they might ask Emma Halvick if they were to interview her about the Montreal film festival.

240 MISE EN PRATIQUE CHAPITRE 9

MISE EN PRATIQUE

 1 Ecoute la conversation entre Didier et Simone. Ensuite, mets le résumé de leur conversation dans le bon ordre. e, b, c, d, f, a

a. Didier demande à Simone de se taire.

b. Didier n'aime pas les histoires d'amour.

c. Simone recommande un film à Didier.

d. Simone n'aime pas les films d'horreur.

e. Simone et Didier sont d'accord.

f. Didier veut la télécommande.

 2 You work for a Canadian TV station and you're responsible for proposing the new fall prime-time programs. Pick programs you think the public will like. Make a timetable of programs that you'll present to your superiors. For each program, be prepared to give the type of show, a title, a summary, and the actors who'll be in it.

3 Lis le texte et réponds aux questions à la page suivante. See answers below.

LE FESTIVAL DES FILMS DU MONDE DE MONTRÉAL

Le festival des films du monde de Montréal a lieu tous les ans du 22 août au 2 septembre. Cette année, c'est la dix-huitième édition. Au programme, présentations des films, rencontres avec les stars et attribution des prix. Nous avons voulu partager cet événement haut en couleurs avec vous. Pour cela, Pierre Arnaud est allé interviewer Emma Halvick du magazine Canada Cinéma.

▶ Quand a lieu le festival des films du monde de Montréal?
- Le festival se déroule du 22 août au 2 septembre.

▶ Quel genre de films est-ce qu'on peut voir au festival et combien y a t-il de présentations?
- C'est un festival où l'on peut voir plus de deux cents films du monde entier, avec chaque année, un hommage rendu à un pays en particulier. Cette année, par exemple, c'est la Turquie.

▶ Combien de catégories différentes de films est-ce qu'il y a?
- Il y a neuf catégories de films. Certains sont en compétition, d'autres sont hors-concours. On peut voir des longs métrages, des courts métrages, des films expérimentaux. Bref, il y en a pour tous les goûts.

▶ C'est la première fois que vous êtes chargée de couvrir ce festival?
- Non, c'est la deuxième année que je viens. Avec autant de plaisir que la première année, d'ailleurs. Vous savez, j'adore le cinéma, alors pour moi, c'est formidable d'avoir l'occasion de faire un reportage sur un festival du cinéma.

▶ Qu'est-ce qui vous plaît tant dans un festival du cinéma?
- Tout me plaît. L'ambiance est vraiment magique, j'ai toujours l'impression d'être dans un conte de fée. C'est merveilleux de pouvoir rencontrer et interviewer toutes ces stars.

▶ Quelle est la star qui vous a le plus marquée au cours d'une interview?
- Il y en a tellement, c'est difficile à dire. Mais je crois que c'est Carole Bouquet. Elle est si belle, si impressionnante et si simple et gentille à la fois. Oui, je crois qu'elle reste mon meilleur souvenir d'interview.

▶ Combien de films voyez-vous en moyenne? Et quel est votre genre de films préféré?
- L'an dernier, j'ai dû voir une trentaine de films à peu près. Cette année, j'espère pouvoir en voir au moins le double. Quant au genre de films que j'aime, ça dépend. Mais en général, j'adore les films de jeunes metteurs en scène. Ici à Montréal, il y a énormément de films qui ont été réalisés par des jeunes, des étudiants qui débutent à peine leur carrière cinématographique.

▶ Comment fonctionne le jury? Qui en sont les membres?
- Le jury est composé de six personnes plus le président. D'ailleurs, cette année, c'est Carole Bouquet qui est présidente. Les membres sont soit des acteurs, soit des producteurs, soit des réalisateurs, soit des critiques de cinéma. Après avoir vu les films en compétition, ils délibèrent jusqu'à ce qu'ils aient attribué les prix.

Language Note

Students might want to know the following words from the interview: **métrage** *(footage);* **conte de fée** *(fairy tale);* **en moyenne** *(on the average).*

Answers

3 1. movies from around the world; long features, short films, experimental films; Each year, homage is paid to a different country.
2. the ambience, meeting and interviewing movie stars
3. films from young directors; at least 60
4. seven; actors, producers, directors, film critics, president

1. What kind of movies are shown at the Montreal film festival? What are some categories of films? What changes each year?
2. What does Emma Halvick particularly like about being at the festival?
3. What kinds of films does she like best? How many would she like to see at the festival?
4. How many people vote on the films? Who are they?

 4 Ton ami(e) et toi, vous vous trouvez à Montréal au moment du Festival des films du monde. Vous regardez passer toutes les stars et vous discutez des films dans lesquels elles jouent. Dites ce que vous en pensez et si vous les recommandez.

 5 Tu es critique de film et tu es au Festival des films du monde avec un/une collègue qui travaille pour la même revue que toi. Choisissez un film à critiquer. Toi, tu en écris une critique positive et ton/ta camarade en écrit une négative. Présentez vos critiques à la classe.

6 **J E U D E R·O L E**

You're a journalist at the **Festival des films du monde** in Montreal. Interview a star. He/She will tell you about a new movie he/she has just made: what kind of movie it is, what it's about, what other actors/actresses are in it, and what he/she thinks about it. Remember to ask his/her opinion about other movies at the festival. Act out this scene with a classmate. Change roles.

Teaching Suggestion

4 Before students begin the activity, have the class name movies that each actor or actress has starred in. You might also name or bring in magazine pictures of additional popular movie stars for students to discuss.

Portfolio

4 Oral This activity is appropriate for students' oral portfolios. You might have them videotape their conversations. For portfolio suggestions, see *Assessment Guide*, page 22.

5 Written This activity is appropriate for students' written portfolios. For portfolio information, see *Assessment Guide*, pages 2–13.

Additional Practice

5 Have students organize and design a program for a film festival in their own town. They should decide where the films could be shown and which films to feature. They should include a map of the locations involved and listings and critiques of all the films featured. This activity could be used as an additional chapter project.

QUE SAIS-JE?

This page is intended to help students prepare for the test. It is a brief checklist of the major points covered in the chapter. The students should be reminded that this is only a checklist and does not necessarily include everything that will appear on the test.

Teaching Suggestions

4 Ask students how these situations differ. (The first involves strangers; the others, family members.)

• You might have students get together with a partner and combine related items, such as questions 11 and 12, into a dialogue.

♜ Game

ALLEZ-Y! Form four teams and give a transparency and a pen to each one. Then, make four sets of index cards, each set bearing the numbers 1–12 (48 cards total), and put each set of cards in a bag. Have one member from each team select four cards from the bag and place them face-down on his or her desk. Then, call out **Allez-y!** Teams turn their cards over and write on their transparency the answers to the questions from **Que sais-je?** that correspond to the numbers they drew. After two minutes, have students put down their pens. Have one member from each team bring their cards and transparency to the front. Show the cards and the transparency and have the class verify that the questions were answered correctly. Award one point for each complete, correct answer. You might play for three such rounds or for a certain number of points.

Can you agree and disagree? p.225

Can you express indifference? p.225

Can you make requests? p.227

Can you ask for and make judgments? p.233

Can you ask for and make recommendations? p.233

Can you ask about and summarize a story? p.234

Can you use what you've learned in this chapter?

1 You and a friend have just seen a movie together. Your friend thought the movie was great. How would you express your agreement with your friend? Je suis d'accord avec toi. Moi aussi, j'ai beaucoup aimé ce film. Tu as raison. Tu l'as dit! Tout à fait!

2 How would you say that you disagree with your friend's opinion of the movie? Pas du tout. Tu parles! Tu te fiches de moi? Tu rigoles! Tu as tort.

3 Your friend wants to know which TV show you want to watch next. What do you say if you really have no opinion? Je m'en fiche. Ça m'est vraiment égal. Peu importe.

4 How would you ask the people in these situations to be quiet?
Chut! Vous pourriez vous taire, s'il vous plaît?

You're at a movie and the people behind you are talking loudly.

Baisse le son!

You're talking on the telephone and your brother has the TV turned up too loud.

You're trying to watch a TV show and your little sister is making noise.
Tu pourrais faire moins de bruit?

5 What would you say to ask a friend her opinion of a TV program you've just seen together? Comment tu as trouvé ça?

6 How would you answer the question in number 5 if you liked the program? See answers below.

7 How would you answer the question in number 5 if you disliked the program? C'était nul/lourd. Ça n'avait aucun intérêt. Je n'ai pas du tout aimé. Ça ne m'a pas emballé(e). Je me suis ennuyé(e) à mourir.

8 How would you ask a friend to recommend a movie? Qu'est-ce que tu as vu comme bon film? Qu'est-ce qu'il y a comme bons films en ce moment?

9 How would you recommend a movie you've just seen to a friend? Tu devrais aller voir... ; Je te recommande... ; Va voir... , c'est génial comme film. C'est à ne pas manquer!

10 What would you say if your friend wanted to go see a movie you thought was terrible? Ne va surtout pas voir... ; Evite d'aller voir... ; N'y va pas! Ça ne vaut pas le coup!

11 How do you ask a friend what a movie was about? De quoi ça parle?

12 How would you tell someone about the last movie you saw? Ça parle de... ; C'est l'histoire de... ; Il s'agit de... ; Ça se passe... ; Au début,... ; A ce moment-là,... ; A la fin,...

Answers

6 Ça m'a beaucoup plu. J'ai trouvé ça amusant/pas mal. Il y avait de bonnes scènes d'action. Je ne me suis pas ennuyé(e) une seconde. Ça m'a bien fait rire.

PREMIERE ETAPE

Agreeing and disagreeing

Tu as raison. *You're right.*
Tu l'as dit! *You said it!*
Tout à fait! *Absolutely!*
Tu parles! *No way!*
Tu te fiches de moi? *Are you kidding me?*
Tu rigoles! *You're joking!*
Tu as tort. *You're wrong.*

Expressing indifference

Je m'en fiche. *I don't give a darn.*
Peu importe. *It doesn't matter.*
ne... aucun(e) *no . . .*
ne... ni... ni... *neither . . . nor . . .*
ne... nulle part *nowhere*
ne... personne *no one*
ne... rien *nothing*

Television programming

un dessin animé *a cartoon*
un documentaire *a documentary*
une émission de variétés *a variety show*
un feuilleton *a soap opera*
les informations (f.) *the news*
un jeu télévisé *a game show*
un magazine télévisé *a magazine show*
la météo *the weather report*
une publicité *a commercial*
un reportage sportif *a sportscast*
une série *a series*
un vidéoclip *a music video*

The television

une cassette vidéo *a videocassette*
une chaîne *a channel*
l'écran (m.) *the screen*
l'image (f.) *the picture*
un magnétoscope *a videocassette recorder*
un programme télé *a TV guide/ listing*
le son *the sound*
la télécommande *the remote*
le téléviseur *the television set*

Making requests

Chut! *Shhh!*
Tais-toi! *Be quiet!*
Ne parle pas si fort. *Don't speak so loudly.*
Tu pourrais faire moins de bruit? *Could you make less noise?*
Vous pourriez vous taire, s'il vous plaît? *Could you please be quiet?*
Baisse/Monte le son. *Turn down/ up the volume.*

DEUXIEME ETAPE

Asking for and making judgments

C'était comment? *How was it?*
Comment tu as trouvé ça? *How did you like it?*
Ça m'a beaucoup plu. *I liked it a lot.*
J'ai trouvé ça amusant/pas mal. *It was funny/not bad.*
Il y avait de... *There were . . .*
Je ne me suis pas ennuyé(e) une seconde. *I wasn't bored a second.*
Ça m'a bien fait rire. *It really made me laugh.*
C'est nul/lourd. *It's no good/dull.*
C'est un navet. *It's trash.*
Ça n'a aucun intérêt. *It's not interesting at all.*
Je n'ai pas du tout aimé. *I didn't like it at all.*
Ça ne m'a pas emballé(e). *It didn't do anything for me.*
Je me suis ennuyé(e) à mourir. *I was bored to death.*

Asking for and making recommendations

Qu'est-ce que tu as vu comme bon film? *What good movies have you seen?*
Qu'est-ce qu'il y a comme bons films en ce moment? *What good movies are out now?*
Tu devrais aller voir... *You should go see . . .*
Je te recommande... *I recommend . . .*
Va voir..., c'est génial comme film. *Go see . . ., it's a great movie.*
C'est à ne pas manquer! *Don't miss it!*
N'y va pas! *Don't go!*
Ne va surtout pas voir... *Really, don't go see . . .*
Evite d'aller voir... *Avoid seeing . . .*
Ça ne vaut pas le coup! *It's not worth it!*

Types of movies

une comédie *a comedy*
une comédie musicale *a musical*
un drame *a drama*
un film d'espionnage *a spy flick*
de guerre *a war movie*
un film étranger *a foreign film*
historique *an historical movie*

Asking about and summarizing a story

De quoi ça parle? *What's it about?*
Comment est-ce que ça commence? *How does it start?*
Comment ça se termine? *How does it end?*
Ça parle de... *It's about . . .*
C'est l'histoire de... *It's the story of . . .*
Il s'agit de... *It's about . . .*
Ça se passe... *It takes place . . .*
Au début,... *At the beginning, . . .*
A ce moment-là,... *At that point, . . .*
A la fin,... *At the end, . . .*

VOCABULAIRE

deux cent quarante-trois **243**

Chapitre 10 : Rencontres au soleil
Chapter Overview

Mise en train pp. 246–248	**La plongée, quelle aventure!**		Note Culturelle, Climate and natural assets of Guadeloupe, p. 248	

Première étape pp. 249–255	**FUNCTIONS**	**GRAMMAR**	**CULTURE**	**RE-ENTRY**
	• Bragging, p. 251 • Flattering, p. 251 • Teasing, p. 254	The superlative, p. 252	• **Rencontre Culturelle,** Overview of Guadeloupe, p. 249 • **Panorama Culturel,** Typical school days, p. 255	• Forms of the comparative • Adjective agreement

Remise en train pp. 256–257	**Des nouvelles de Guadeloupe**		Note Culturelle, Greetings in Guadeloupe, p. 257	

Deuxième étape pp. 258–261	**FUNCTIONS**	**GRAMMAR**	**CULTURE**	**RE-ENTRY**
	• Breaking some news, p. 259 • Showing interest, p. 259 • Expressing disbelief, p. 259 • Telling a joke, p. 261	The past perfect, p. 259		• The **passé composé** • Breaking some news

Lisons! pp. 262–264	**O'gaya, a Creole folktale from Guadeloupe** Reading Strategy: Understanding literary devices

Ecrivons! p. 265	**Une transformation incroyable!** Writing Strategy: Using an appropriate style

Review pp. 266–269	• Mise en pratique, pp. 266–267 • Que sais-je? p. 268 • Vocabulaire, p. 269

Assessment Options

Etape Quizzes
• *Chapter Teaching Resources, Book 3*
  Première étape, Quiz 10-1, pp. 77–78
  Deuxième étape, Quiz 10-2, pp. 79–80
• *Assessment Items, Audiocassette 8B/Audio CD 10*

Chapter Test
• *Chapter Teaching Resources, Book 3,* pp. 81–86
• *Assessment Guide,* Speaking Test, p. 32
• *Assessment Items, Audiocassette 8B/Audio CD 10*

Test Generator, Chapter 10

RESOURCES: Print	RESOURCES: Audiovisual

	Textbook Audiocassette 5B/Audio CD 10
Practice and Activity Book, p. 109	

	Textbook Audiocassette 5B/Audio CD 10
Practice and Activity Book, pp. 110–113 *Grammar and Vocabulary Worksheets*, pp. 89–92 *Chapter Teaching Resources, Book 3* • Communicative Activity 10-1, pp. 58–59 • Teaching Transparency Master 10-1, pp. 62, 64 . . . . *Teaching Transparency 10-1* • Additional Listening Activities 10-1, 10-2, 10-3, pp. 65–66 . . . *Additional Listening Activities, Audiocassette 10B/Audio CD 10* • Realia 10-1, pp. 69, 71 • Situation Cards 10-1, pp. 72–73 • Student Response Forms, pp. 74–76 • Quiz 10-1, pp. 77–78 . . . . *Assessment Items, Audiocassette 8B/Audio CD 10* *Video Guide* . . . . *Video Program, Videocassette 2*	

	Textbook Audiocassette 5B/Audio CD 10
Practice and Activity Book, p. 114	

	Textbook Audiocassette 5B/Audio CD 10
Practice and Activity Book, pp. 115–118 *Grammar and Vocabulary Worksheets*, pp. 93–95 *Chapter Teaching Resources, Book 3* • Communicative Activity 10-2, pp. 60–61 • Teaching Transparency Master 10-2, pp. 63, 64 . . . . *Teaching Transparency 10-2* • Additional Listening Activities 10-4, 10-5, 10-6, pp. 66–67 . . . *Additional Listening Activities, Audiocassette 10B/Audio CD 10* • Realia 10-2, pp. 70, 71 • Situation Cards 10-2, 10-3, pp. 72–73 • Student Response Forms, pp. 74–76 • Quiz 10-2, pp. 79–80 . . . . *Assessment Items, Audiocassette 8B/Audio CD 10*	

Practice and Activity Book, p. 119	

Video Guide . . . . *Video Program, Videocassette 2*	

Alternative Assessment
- Performance Assessment
  Première étape, p. 254
  Deuxième étape, p. 261
- Portfolio Assessment
  Written: Activity 32, *Pupil's Edition*, p. 260
     Assessment Guide, p. 23
  Oral: **Mise en pratique**, Activity 4, *Pupil's Edition*, p. 267
     Assessment Guide, p. 23

For Student Response Forms, see *Chapter Teaching Resources, Book 3,* pp. 74–76.

Première étape

8 Ecoute! p. 250

1. — Eh bien, vous voyez, ça, c'est le requin qu'on a vu. J'avais vraiment peur, moi!
2. — Voilà mon château de sable. Vous voyez, il est entouré de crabes!
3. — Ça, c'est la pieuvre qu'on a vue. Mais elle est partie très vite parce qu'on lui a fait peur.
4. — Ça, c'est un récif de corail. C'est vraiment quelque chose d'extraordinaire!
5. — Ici, ce sont tout simplement des rochers. Vous voyez le nombre d'algues qu'il y a dessus?
6. — Regardez comme elles sont mignonnes, les tortues!
7. — Regardez le nombre de coquillages qu'on peut trouver sur la plage. Mais il faut faire attention, vous voyez, il y a aussi des méduses.
8. — Et là, je cherchais des étoiles de mer et j'ai vu des hippocampes.

Answers to Activity 8
1. h 2. d 3. a 4. c 5. e 6. b 7. f 8. g

11 Ecoute! p. 252

1. BOY C'est pas pour me vanter, mais moi, j'ai escaladé un volcan.
   GIRL Ah ouais? C'était dangereux?
   BOY Oh, j'en ai vu d'autres.
   GIRL Tu en as, du courage.
2. BOY Oh, ça m'énerve, l'algèbre. C'est trop difficile.
   GIRL Mais non, c'est fastoche!
   BOY Vraiment, tu trouves pas ça difficile?
   GIRL Non, pas du tout.
   BOY Ouah! Tu es calée.
3. BOY Alors, tu as gagné?
   GIRL Bien sûr! Oh, tu sais bien que c'est moi qui nage le mieux. Les autres pouvaient aller se rhabiller.
   BOY Oui, c'est vrai. Tu es vraiment la meilleure.
4. GIRL C'est pas vrai! Tu n'as pas piloté l'avion toi-même!
   BOY Mais si. C'était la première fois. Et, c'est pas pour me vanter, mais on m'a dit que je me suis très bien débrouillé.
   GIRL Tu es vraiment le garçon le plus doué que je connaisse.
5. GIRL Pas possible! Tu as gagné le concours?
   BOY Ben oui. C'est moi le meilleur, tu sais bien.
   GIRL Tu es fortiche quand même.
6. BOY Tu es descendue jusqu'à quelle profondeur?
   GIRL Jusqu'à vingt mètres.
   BOY Tu n'as pas eu peur des requins?

GIRL Ben non. J'en ai vu d'autres, tu sais.
BOY Alors là, tu m'épates!

Answers to Activity 11
1. garçon 2. fille 3. fille 4. garçon 5. garçon 6. fille

17 Ecoute! p. 254

1. ANGÈLE Il est super sympa, non?
   BRIGITTE Il essaie de t'impressionner, c'est tout.
   ANGÈLE Moi, je crois qu'il est sincère.
   BRIGITTE Réveille-toi un peu!
   ANGÈLE Oh, ça va, hein?
2. BRIGITTE Il y a un nouveau film que je voudrais voir. Ça te dit d'aller le voir avec moi?
   ANGÈLE Quand ça?
   BRIGITTE Samedi soir.
   ANGÈLE Bon. Où est-ce qu'on se retrouve?
3. BRIGITTE Oh! Attention! Tu vas tomber...
   ANGÈLE Oh!!! Ah zut alors! Je suis toute mouillée maintenant!
   BRIGITTE Ben, t'en rates pas une, toi!
   ANGÈLE Ecoute, ça peut arriver à tout le monde.
4. BRIGITTE Tu as vu? Je suis arrivée la première. C'est moi la meilleure!
   ANGÈLE C'est ça, tu es la meilleure.
   BRIGITTE Ben quoi, c'est vrai!
   ANGÈLE Non mais, tu t'es pas regardée!
5. ANGÈLE Brigitte, dépêche-toi!
   BRIGITTE Mais on a largement le temps.
   ANGÈLE Oui, mais moi, je veux arriver en avance. Comme ça, on pourra trouver de bonnes places.
   BRIGITTE D'accord.
6. BRIGITTE Ça t'a plu, ce film?
   ANGÈLE Bof, ça ne m'a pas emballée. C'était un peu bizarre, à mon avis.
   BRIGITTE Oui, je suis tout à fait de ton avis. Je n'ai pas très bien compris, et puis, c'était ennuyeux à mourir!
7. BRIGITTE Dis, Angèle! On va être en retard! Mais qu'est-ce que tu fabriquais?
   ANGÈLE Euh, je voulais juste lui parler une minute.
   BRIGITTE Et l'interro dans tout ça?
   ANGÈLE Mais il était mignon.
   BRIGITTE Non mais, t'es amoureuse ou quoi?
   ANGÈLE Lâche-moi, tu veux?
8. ANGÈLE Dis donc, Brigitte, qu'est-ce que tu regardes?
   BRIGITTE Rien.
   ANGÈLE Hmm. C'est pas Vincent par hasard?
   BRIGITTE Euh... peut-être. Il est mignon, non?
   ANGÈLE Oui, mais il a vingt-deux ans.
   BRIGITTE Oui, je sais, mais...
   ANGÈLE Oh, arrête de délirer!
   BRIGITTE Et toi, arrête de m'embêter!

Answers to Activity 17
1, 3, 4, 7, 8

Deuxième étape

26 Ecoute! p. 258

1. — Ben, non, ça fait longtemps que je ne l'ai pas vue.
  — Pourtant, vous étiez très copines, non? Vous vous êtes disputées ou quoi?
  — Non, pas du tout. Tu vois, son père a été transféré à Paris et elle a dû déménager en juillet.
  — Tiens, je ne savais pas.

2. — Lui, il a beaucoup changé.
  — Ah bon?
  — Oui, il s'est même trouvé une copine.
  — Ça alors! Pourtant, il était plutôt du genre à ne jamais vouloir sortir.
  — Plus maintenant! Il a complètement changé de style. Et puis, figure-toi qu'il n'a plus de boutons.
  — Pas possible!

3. — Oh là là. Ça a été une vraie catastrophe.
  — Qu'est-ce qui s'est passé?
  — Le jour où il a eu son permis, il a emmené des copains à la plage dans la voiture de son père. Et devine ce qui est arrivé.
  — Je ne sais pas, moi. Raconte!
  — Et ben, il a planté la voiture de son père en revenant.
  — Oh, quelle angoisse!

4. — Et elle? Qu'est-ce qu'elle devient? Toujours aussi sportive?
  — Ben, tu es pas au courant?
  — Non, au courant de quoi?
  — Elle a fait une mauvaise chute de cheval.
  — Ah bon? C'est grave?
  — Ben, elle s'est fait mal au dos et le médecin lui a dit de ne pas faire de sport pendant au moins deux mois.
  — Oh, c'est bête, ça!

5. — Tu sais, elle est beaucoup mieux maintenant.
  — Ah ouais? Qu'est-ce qu'elle a fait?
  — Ben, elle a fait un super régime et elle a perdu beaucoup de poids.
  — Tiens, peut-être que je devrais lui demander comment elle a fait. Moi aussi, j'ai quelques kilos à perdre.

6. — Alors, là, tu vas pas me croire.
  — Raconte.
  — Et ben, l'autre jour, j'ai rencontré sa sœur et tu sais ce qu'elle m'a dit?
  — Non, quoi?
  — Il a rencontré une fille, il est tombé amoureux d'elle et il s'est fiancé avec elle.
  — Pas possible!

7. — C'est arrivé à la boum de Frédéric. Je ne sais pas exactement comment ça a commencé, mais ils se sont bagarrés.

— Oh, ces deux-là, vraiment ils exagèrent! Toujours prêts à se faire remarquer.
  — Ouais. Et puis, c'était pas très sympa pour Frédéric. Le pauvre, ça a complètement cassé l'ambiance à sa fête.

8. — Elle est super contente. Figure-toi qu'à sa dernière visite chez l'orthodontiste, il lui a dit qu'elle n'avait plus besoin de ses bagues et il les lui a enlevées.
  — Génial! Remarque, ça faisait longtemps qu'elle les avait.
  — Oui, au moins deux ans.

Answers to Activity 26

1. Marie-Ange	3. Lucien	5. Sabine	7. Julien et Bruno
2. Germain	4. Mireille	6. Luc	8. Thérèse

28 Ecoute! p. 259

1. — Dis donc, Emilie, tu savais que M. Souchet allait déménager?
  — Ah oui? Qui t'a dit ça?
  — Michel. Il a entendu dire qu'il avait accepté un poste à Paris.
  — Alors, qui va être notre professeur de maths?
  — Aucune idée.

2. — Oh, Sylvie, je suis vraiment désolée de ne pas t'avoir téléphoné.
  — Tu sais, je me demandais où tu étais passée.
  — Ben, j'ai été privée de sortie et de téléphone. Je ne pouvais pas t'appeler.
  — Bon, il n'y a pas de mal.

3. — Dis, Julien, tu connais la dernière?
  — Non, quoi?
  — J'ai entendu dire que Lisette allait rompre avec son petit ami.
  — Oh là là!
  — Ce n'est pas tout. Figure-toi qu'elle a dit à Sophie qu'elle voulait sortir avec toi.
  — Qui t'a dit ça?
  — Leïla.

4. — Oh! J'en ai marre de ce cours!
  — Qu'est-ce qui est arrivé? Pourquoi?
  — J'ai raté un autre examen. Ma moyenne va être nulle.
  — Ne t'en fais pas trop, mais tu sais bien qu'il faut que tu passes plus de temps à étudier.
  — Oui, mais...
  — Tu devrais parler au prof. Peut-être qu'il te permettra de repasser l'examen.

5. — Dis, Than, je vais voir Céline Dion en concert vendredi soir. Ça t'intéresse d'y aller?
  — Peut-être. Je dois demander la permission à mes parents. Je te téléphonerai pour te dire si c'est d'accord ou pas.
  — OK.

6. — Regarde! Voilà Daniel. C'est génial ce qui lui est arrivé!
— Euh, quoi?
— Je ne t'ai pas dit?
— Non. Raconte!
— Ben, l'équipe de l'université l'a accepté.
— Je n'en reviens pas.
— C'est pas tout.
— Quoi?
— Comme il va jouer pour l'université, il va avoir une bourse.

7. — Tu connais la dernière?
— Non.
— Ben, Isabelle est allée au concert de Patrick Bruel.
— Et alors?
— J'ai entendu dire qu'elle l'a rencontré.
— Ça m'étonnerait.
— Si! Et il paraît même qu'il veut sortir avec elle.
— N'importe quoi!

Answers to Activity 28
1, 3, 6, 7

34 Ecoute! p. 261

1. — Est-ce que tu connais l'histoire de l'homme qui a acheté un poisson pour l'anniversaire de sa femme?
— Non, raconte!

2. — Pour arriver de l'autre côté!
— Elle est nulle, ta blague!

3. — ... et alors il dit au policier qu'il n'en sait rien.
— Et puis?

4. — Et le fils dit qu'il ne peut plus mettre sa chaussure.
— Elle est bien bonne! Tu en as une autre?

5. — Quel est le point commun entre un éléphant et une fourmi?
— Je ne sais pas. C'est quoi?

6. — ... et l'autre lui répond «J'en ai marre de tes bêtises!»
— Et alors?

7. — Quelle est la différence entre un prof de français et un prof d'espagnol?
— Euh, je ne sais pas. Dis-moi.

Answers to Activity 34
1. début   3. milieu   5. début   7. début
2. fin   4. fin   6. milieu

Mise en pratique

1 p. 266

1. NATHALIE Non mais, tu t'es pas regardé! T'es même pas capable d'aller le lui dire.
NICOLAS Ben, on va voir!

2. NATHALIE Aïe!
NICOLAS Qu'est-ce qu'il y a?
NATHALIE Je me suis coincé le doigt dans la porte.
NICOLAS T'en rates pas une, toi!
NATHALIE Ben, ça peut arriver à tout le monde!

3. NATHALIE Dis donc, Nicolas! Tu ouvres les portes pour les jeunes filles, toi, maintenant?
NICOLAS Oh, ça va.
NATHALIE T'es amoureux ou quoi?
NICOLAS Lâche-moi, tu veux?
NATHALIE Ben, pourquoi tu n'ouvres pas la porte pour moi?

4. NATHALIE Je parie qu'il va me demander mon numéro de téléphone.
NICOLAS Oh! Arrête de délirer, Nathalie. Tu as vu quel âge il a?
NATHALIE Et alors? Ça veut rien dire, l'âge. Et puis, arrête de m'embêter.

5. NATHALIE Regarde le coquillage que j'ai acheté. Il est beau, non?
NICOLAS Ouais, pas mal. Tu l'as payé combien?
NATHALIE Cent vingt francs.
NICOLAS Quoi? Non mais, réveille-toi un peu! C'est rien qu'un coquillage! C'est incroyable que tu aies payé cent vingt francs pour ça. Il était mignon, le type du magasin ou quoi?
NATHALIE Oh, ça va, hein.

6. NICOLAS Tu vois la fille là-bas?
NATHALIE Oui.
NICOLAS Je crois qu'elle m'aime bien. Elle me regardait pendant que je dansais.
NATHALIE Ben, tu t'es pas regardé? Elle te regardait parce que tu étais ridicule.
NICOLAS Je t'ai pas demandé ton avis.

Answers to Mise en pratique Activity 1
1. Nathalie   3. Nathalie   5. Nicolas
2. Nicolas   4. Nicolas   6. Nathalie

Chapitre 10 : Rencontres au soleil
Projects and Games

Project: Venez à l'aquarium de Pointe-à-Pitre
(Individual Project)

ASSIGNMENT

Students will create a brochure for a new aquarium that will be opening in Pointe-à-Pitre. The brochure should include illustrations of and information about the marine life on display. Since the owners want to attract as many tourists as possible, students should also include several statements emphasizing the size and variety of marine life to be seen there.

MATERIALS

✂ **Students may need**

- Construction paper
- Scissors
- Colored markers
- Old magazines and catalogues
- Tape or glue
- Stapler and staples
- Encyclopedias
- French-English dictionaries

SUGGESTED SEQUENCE

1. Students should list the types of marine life they will feature in their brochure. They might look up additional marine life in the dictionary. Then, have them look up the marine life they've chosen in an encyclopedia and take notes.

2. Have students draw or cut out pictures of some of the marine life in their aquarium.

3. Students should create the slogans they want to use to promote their aquarium. Remind them that they should make sensational claims. They might use the superlative to brag about the size of the aquarium, the variety of marine life on display, the low cost, or the location.

4. Have students plan the layout of their brochure. They should design an attractive cover to catch tourists' attention and make sure that the pages that follow are colorful and interesting.

5. Have students copy the text of their brochure onto construction paper, tape or glue the illustrations in the appropriate places, and staple the pages of the brochure together.

GRADING THE PROJECT

You might base students' grades on content, language use, creativity, and design.

Suggested Point Distribution (total = 100 points)

Content	30 points
Language use	30 points
Creativity	20 points
Design	20 points

 Games

ON A FINI!

In this game, students will practice chapter vocabulary in a fast-paced game.

Procedure   To prepare for the game, write expressions from the chapter vocabulary list on separate index cards, omitting one word from the expression. (**Tu es ___ ou quoi?**) You will need one card for each student in the class. Then, form three teams and have them sit in rows. Put enough cards for each team member in a bag. Give each team's bag to the first team member. Then, call out **Allez-y!** to begin the game. The first player on each team selects a card, writes the missing word on a sheet of paper, keeps the card, and passes the bag to the player behind him or her, who does the same. Players may not pass the bag until they have finished writing their word and have put their pen down. When the last player has finished, he or she calls out **On a fini!** Then, have the players on the winning team read aloud their completed expressions. If all the words are correct, that team wins. You might shuffle and redistribute the cards and play a second round.

JEU DE RYTHME

In this game, students will practice the chapter functions.

Procedure   To play the game, have students sit in a circle. All players should slap both thighs twice, clap their hands twice, and snap their fingers twice. They must keep up this rhythm during the game. Questions and answers must be given on the two beats when players snap their fingers. To begin the game, players start the rhythm. During the finger snaps, ask a question or make a statement that requires a response. (**Je ne t'ai pas dit?**) During the next snaps, call out a student's name (Bob). That student must give an appropriate response during the following snaps. (**Non, raconte!**) Then, during the next snaps, that student names another student (Julie), who must ask a question or make a statement during the following snaps. (**Tu en as, du courage!**) A student who fails to give a correct question, statement, or response during the snaps is out.

Sample questions/statements and responses:

1. **Réveille-toi un peu!/Lâche-moi, tu veux?**
2. **Alors, là, tu m'épates!/Oh, j'en ai vu d'autres.**
3. **Marie a planté sa voiture/Qui t'a dit ça?**
4. **Je me suis fiancé(e)/Je n'en reviens pas!**
5. **Arrête de délirer!/Qu'est-ce que tu en sais?**

Chapitre 10 Rencontres au soleil

pp. 244–269

*U*sing the Chapter Opener

▢ **Video Program**

Videocassette 2

Before you begin this chapter, you might want to preview the *Video Program* and consult the *Video Guide.* Suggestions for integrating the video into each chapter and activity masters for video selections can be found in the *Video Guide.*

Motivating Activity

Ask students what they associate with the beach. Ask them to name marine life they might see underwater and water-related activities that they might do at the beach. Have students recall what they learned about Martinique in Chapter 12 of Level 1 and Chapter 4 of Level 2.

Teaching Suggestion

Have students think of popular activities in Guadeloupe as suggested by the photos shown on pages 244–245 (fishing, scuba diving, beachcombing, swimming). Ask if they have ever done these activities, and if they choose to, have them tell about their experiences. If they haven't done these activities, have them tell whether or not they would like to try them, and why or why not.

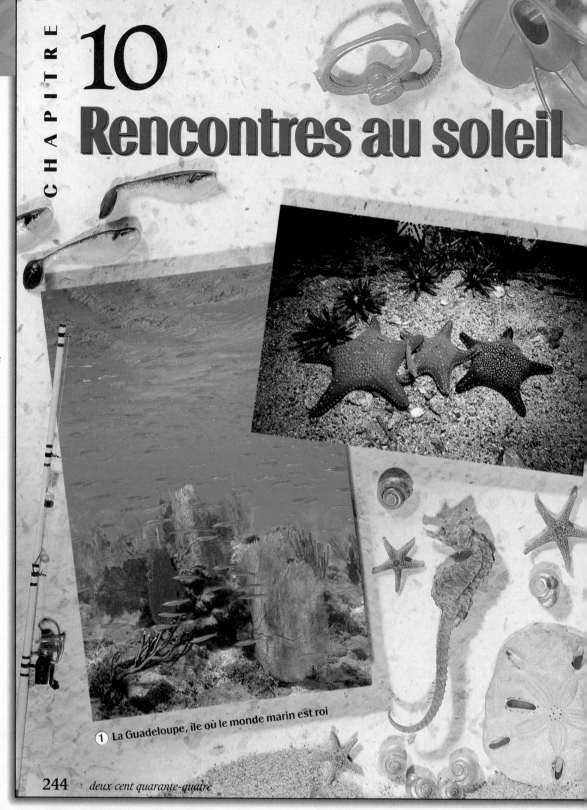

CHAPITRE

10 Rencontres au soleil

① La Guadeloupe, île où le monde marin est roi

244 *deux cent quarante-quatre*

Photo Flash!

① This photo shows an underwater landscape typical of Guadeloupe. Guadeloupe has over 150 miles of coastline, which is home to a variety of marine life. Lobsters, crabs, and shrimp are abundant, as well as murex, conch, triton, abalone, oysters, mussels, and sea urchins. Parrotfish, French angelfish, queen triggerfish, cardinals, and peacockfish are among the more unusual species that inhabit the archipelago's numerous coral reefs.

Marine Biology Link

You might ask students what they know about coral reefs and to find out how they are formed. Coral reefs are living structures formed by the skeletons of various coral polyps (similar to a sea anemone). Their shells, made of calcium carbonate, form a rigid limestone structure. Mud, sediment, and even living algae fall into the holes in the formation and become part of the living structure.

Bienvenue à la Guadeloupe, une île aux paysages paradisiaques où les habitants sont réputés pour leur chaleur. Ici, tout le monde se connaît. Quand on se rencontre, il est normal de s'arrêter pour parler des dernières nouvelles ou pour plaisanter et discuter de choses et d'autres. Allez, viens avec nous à la Guadeloupe!

In this chapter you will learn

- to brag; to flatter; to tease
- to break some news; to show interest; to express disbelief; to tell a joke

And you will

- listen to teenagers talk about diving
- read a folktale from Guadeloupe
- write a newspaper article
- find out about social customs in Guadeloupe

③ C'est fastoche, ça!

② Je n'en reviens pas!

deux cent quarante-cinq 245

Focusing on Outcomes

Have students read the list of outcomes and tell in what situations they might use each one. Then, have them suggest expressions they might use in English to serve each function. Have them associate the two photos on this page with two of the outcomes listed. (Photo 2: *to express disbelief;* Photo 3: *to brag*) NOTE: You may want to use the video to support the objectives. The self-check activities in **Que sais-je?** on page 268 help students assess their achievement of the objectives.

Teaching Suggestions

- Have students read the introductory paragraph and find three words or expressions that indicate that Guadeloupe has a relaxing and hospitable environment (**bienvenue, chaleur, plaisanter**).

② Have students imagine what the girl in this photo told her friend to evoke her surprise.

Building on Previous Skills

Point out the **madras** fabric on this page and ask students what they remember about it. (It is a plaid cotton fabric, usually in bright primary colors, that is used for traditional headdresses as well as everyday clothing in Martinique and Guadeloupe.)

Culture Note

Point out the octopus at the top of this page. Seafood is the basis of many food specialties in Guadeloupe. **Chatroux** is a dish made with a small octopus cooked in a red bean stew. **Blaff,** or creole poached fish, is another specialty. **Calalou** is a thick soup made from crabs, tomatoes, and okra base. **Crabes farcis** are stuffed crabs.

Geography Link

Guadeloupe is actually a group of islands that includes not only the "butterfly" formed by Grande-Terre and Basse-Terre, but also the satellite islands of **Marie-Galante, Les Saintes,** and **La Désirade.** Have students research the origins of the names of these islands. Marie-Galante, known for its beaches and resorts, was named after Columbus' flagship, the **Maria Graciosa.** It was quickly dubbed the "Sombrero" island because of its unusual shape. The archipelago of Les Saintes got its name from All Saint's Day, the day on which it was spotted by Columbus. La Désirade, or *The Sought-After Island,* is a narrow, eight-mile-long island that, ironically, has historically been inhabited by lepers and various political undesirables.

Summary

In **La plongée, quelle aventure!**, Pascal tells his friend Maxime about his first scuba diving experience. Then, Pascal strikes up a conversation with two passing tourists, Brigitte and Angèle. Angèle is impressed with Pascal's account of his scuba diving, and encourages him to tell more. Pascal brags about his courageous encounter with a shark and even offers to teach Angèle how to scuba dive. Brigitte pulls her friend away, and then teases her for flattering Pascal, who was obviously only trying to impress her. Meanwhile, Maxime teases Pascal about his attempt to win Angèle over.

Motivating Activity

Ask students if they have ever had a friend or an acquaintance who exaggerated an experience to impress them. You might have volunteers relate their experiences. Have students give examples of situations in which they might want to brag to impress someone.

Presentation

Have students make suppositions about what happens in **La plongée, quelle aventure!**, based on the photos on pages 246–247. As a challenge, you might have them do this in French, using the expressions for offering possible explanations from Chapter 9 of Level 2 (**Peut-être que… ; Je crois que… ; Je parie que…**). Then, play the recording, pausing after each scene to ask who is involved in the scene and what happened. You might also ask the related questions from Activity 1 on page 248.

Mise en train

La plongée, quelle aventure!

Maxime et Pascal se rencontrent à la plage.

1 PASCAL Salut, Maxime! Ça va?

MAXIME Très bien. Et toi? Tu as passé un bon week-end?

PASCAL Excellent. Devine ce que j'ai fait.

MAXIME Je ne sais pas.

PASCAL De la plongée.

MAXIME Ah oui? De la plongée sous-marine?

PASCAL Oui. C'était la première fois.

MAXIME Alors, comment tu as trouvé ça?

PASCAL Génial. Au début, j'avais un peu peur, mais une fois dans l'eau... Ouah! Regarde un peu les deux filles là-bas. Si on allait leur parler? Je les ai déjà vues hier. Elles ont l'air sympa.

MAXIME Ouais, pourquoi pas?

PASCAL Excusez-moi, mesdemoiselles, on s'est pas déjà rencontrés quelque part?

2 BRIGITTE Euh... non, je crois pas.

PASCAL Ah bon, pourtant... je dois sûrement confondre avec quelqu'un d'autre. Au fait, moi, c'est Pascal. Et lui, c'est Maxime.

BRIGITTE Bonjour. Moi, c'est Brigitte et ma copine, c'est Angèle.

MAXIME Vous êtes d'ici?

BRIGITTE Non, on habite à Paris. On est là pour les vacances.

MAXIME Il fait beau aujourd'hui.

BRIGITTE Oui, un peu chaud, mais bon.

PASCAL Je disais juste à Maxime que ce week-end, j'avais fait de la plongée.

3 ANGELE Ah oui? Mais c'est dangereux ça, non?

PASCAL Oh non. C'est fastoche, ça.

ANGELE Tu es descendu à quelle profondeur?

PASCAL Oh, à une quinzaine de mètres. Au fond de la mer, j'ai vu des poissons magnifiques, de toutes les couleurs, des étoiles de mer, d'énormes crabes. Et puis, vous ne devinerez jamais ce que j'ai vu.

246 *deux cent quarante-six* CHAPITRE 10 Rencontres au soleil

RESOURCES FOR MISE EN TRAIN

Textbook Audiocassette 5B/Audio CD 10
Practice and Activity Book, p. 109

Physics Link

You might ask students if they have ever heard of "the bends" in reference to scuba diving, and if they know why scuba divers must strictly respect time/depth limits. Below 30 feet, the pressure of the water on the diver's body causes various physiological reactions. For example, nitrogen bubbles may be released in the bloodstream. If a diver exceeds the time limits at a given depth, nitrogen builds up in the body, and "the bends," or *decompression sickness* (**un accident de décompression**), can occur, causing severe joint pains, paralysis, or even death.

4
ANGELE Raconte!

PASCAL Un requin!

ANGELE C'est pas vrai!

PASCAL Si, je t'assure. Il est même passé à moins de deux mètres de moi.

ANGELE Pas possible! Dis donc, tu as dû avoir peur, non?

PASCAL Oh, tu sais, j'en ai vu d'autres.

ANGELE Tu en as, du courage!

PASCAL C'est pas pour me vanter, mais moi, j'adore l'aventure.

BRIGITTE Oh, je t'en prie!

PASCAL Enfin, bref, je me suis approché du requin et j'ai essayé de lui faire peur. D'ailleurs, ça a marché. Il m'a regardé et il est parti.

5
ANGELE Alors là, tu m'épates!

PASCAL Si ça vous intéresse, on peut faire de la plongée ensemble.

ANGELE Oh ça serait chouette! Tu pourrais m'apprendre...

BRIGITTE Euh, je ne crois pas qu'on ait le temps.

ANGELE Mais, Brigitte...

BRIGITTE Au fait, tu as vu quelle heure il est? Il faut qu'on rentre à l'hôtel. Bon. Ben à plus tard, hein?

PASCAL Vous savez, on vient souvent par ici. Comme ça, si vous nous cherchez...

Brigitte et Angèle s'en vont.

BRIGITTE Non, mais tu es amoureuse ou quoi?

ANGELE Lâche-moi, tu veux? Il a l'air sympa, c'est tout. Et vachement courageux en plus.

6
BRIGITTE Réveille-toi un peu! Il essayait de nous impressionner, c'est tout. Il n'arrêtait pas de se vanter.

ANGELE Qu'est-ce que tu en sais? Moi, en tout cas, je crois qu'il était sincère.

BRIGITTE Oh! Arrête de délirer!

Pendant ce temps-là...

PASCAL C'est dommage. Je crois que j'avais mes chances avec Angèle.

MAXIME Non mais, tu t'es pas regardé?

7
PASCAL Ben quoi? Elle est folle de moi, cette fille. Je crois que je vais essayer de la revoir.

MAXIME Oh, ça va. Je parie que tu n'en es même pas capable.

PASCAL Tu me crois pas? Eh ben, on va voir!

Marine Biology Link

Have students find out more about the habits of sharks and dolphins and report their findings to the class. Although sharks do live in the Caribbean, the majority of shark attacks reported each year take place off the coasts of Florida and California. Sharks are not often spotted in the coastal waters of Guadeloupe, especially because dolphins, natural enemies of sharks, are often nearby.

Sports Link

Scuba diving is a physically demanding sport that requires specialized training and equipment. Less vigorous sports include snorkeling, which requires no special skills, and "snuba," a combination of snorkeling and scuba diving. Snuba equipment includes an inflatable raft and a compressed-air tank with a 20-foot air supply hose. You might ask students if they might like to try one of these sports, and why or why not.

◆ For Individual Needs

Auditory Learners Describe the photos on pages 246–247 in French. Have students tell which photo you're describing.

Challenge Have students write captions for the photos on pages 246–247. For example, for the photo at the bottom left of page 246, they might write **Pascal fait de la plongée.**

Slower Pace Assign numbers to each of the photos on pages 246–247. Then, write lines from **La plongée, quelle aventure!** on a transparency and have students match them with the photos.

Teaching Suggestions

• Ask students what they would do if they were either Pascal or Angèle. If they were Pascal, would they boast about their scuba experience, or ask Angèle about her vacation? If they were Angèle, would they encourage Pascal or try to steer the conversation away from scuba diving?

• Have students suggest how the story in **La plongée, quelle aventure!** might end.

• Ask students if they have ever gone scuba diving or if they think they might like to try it. Have them suggest the risks (the "bends") and the pleasures (seeing marine life) of the sport.

⊕ Culture Note

SCUBA (Self-Contained Underwater Breathing Apparatus) diving is a popular pastime in Guadeloupe. More than 50,000 divers explore its coastal waters each year, and over twenty diving clubs on the islands offer classes to tourists interested in trying the sport.

Teaching Suggestion

2 Assign four students the roles of Brigitte, Pascal, Angèle, and Maxime. Give them large name tags to identify their characters and have them read aloud the first four scenes of the **Mise en train.** Then, read aloud quotation number 6 and have the class identify the speaker. Have the four students read the next scene. Afterwards, read quotations 2 and 7. Continue in the same manner, reading numbers 3, 4, and 5 after the sixth scene and number 1 after the seventh scene.

 For Individual Needs

2 Visual/Auditory Learners Write the quotations on large strips of posterboard. Write the characters' names across the chalkboard. Then, show each quotation, read it aloud, and have a volunteer tape it to the board under the appropriate name.

3 Challenge Form seven groups and assign a scene from the **Mise en train** to each one. Have them compose a one-sentence summary of their scene and write it on the board or on a transparency. Once all the summaries have been written, have the class arrange them in order according to the **Mise en train.**

5 Auditory Learners You might read aloud the expressions that serve the functions listed in this activity, using appropriate intonation. (**Alors, là, tu m'épates!**) Have students call out the related functions in English (*to flatter someone*).

Answers
1 1. at a beach in Guadeloupe
2. Pascal went scuba diving during the weekend.
3. Angèle and Brigitte

---

1 Tu as compris? See answers below.

1. Where are Maxime and Pascal?
2. What are they talking about?
3. Whom do they meet?
4. What do they talk to the girls about?
5. What is Pascal's attitude?
6. What are the girls' reactions?
7. How does the conversation end?
8. What does Brigitte think of Angèle's behavior? What does Maxime think of Pascal's?

2 Qui dit quoi?

Qui fait les remarques suivantes, Brigitte, Pascal, Angèle ou Maxime?

1. «Elle est folle de moi, cette fille.» Pascal
2. «Non, mais tu es amoureuse ou quoi?»
3. «Je crois qu'il était sincère.» Angèle
4. «Réveille-toi un peu!» 4. Brigitte 2. Brigitte
5. «Non mais, tu t'es pas regardé!» Maxime
6. «C'est pas pour me vanter, mais moi, j'adore l'aventure.» Pascal
7. «Alors là, tu m'épates!» Angèle

3 Mets en ordre

Mets ces phrases en ordre d'après **La plongée, quelle aventure!** 8, 2, 4, 6, 7, 5, 1, 3

1. Brigitte et Angèle s'en vont.
2. Maxime et Pascal engagent la conversation avec les filles.
3. Brigitte se moque *(teases)* d'Angèle.
4. Pascal se vante devant Angèle et Brigitte.
5. Brigitte coupe la conversation.
6. Angèle est très impressionnée.
7. Pascal propose aux filles de faire de la plongée avec eux.
8. Pascal est allé faire de la plongée.

4 Vrai ou faux?

1. C'est la première fois que Pascal voit Angèle et Brigitte. faux
2. Maxime demande à Angèle de sortir avec lui. faux
3. Pascal a vu un requin sous l'eau. vrai
4. Angèle voudrait faire de la plongée. vrai
5. Brigitte est très impressionnée par l'histoire de Pascal. faux

5 Cherche les expressions

What do the teenagers in **La plongée, quelle aventure!** say to . . . See answers below.

1. strike up a conversation?
2. brag?
3. show interest?
4. show disbelief?
5. flatter someone?
6. make an excuse?
7. tease someone?
8. respond to teasing?

6 Et maintenant, à toi

Qu'est-ce que tu penses de la façon dont Pascal et Maxime ont abordé les filles? Comment est-ce que tu abordes quelqu'un que tu aimerais rencontrer?

NOTE CULTURELLE

The islands of Guadeloupe enjoy a warm, tropical climate year-round, with average temperatures of about 80 degrees Fahrenheit on the coast. Only on the summit of the Soufrière volcano can the temperature drop to a chilly 40 degrees! The climate, coupled with a long rainy season, produces a luxuriant plant life, including mangrove swamps and dense forests. The coastline is dotted with bays and fringed with beaches, which are especially beautiful on the island of **Basse-Terre.** The warm water around the islands is home to an abundance of marine life, most notably a wide variety of fish such as tarpon, snapper, and many types of ray fish.

4. Pascal's dive
5. He brags about his courage.
6. Angèle is impressed. Brigitte is not.
7. The girls return to their hotel without committing to seeing the boys again.
8. Brigitte thinks Angèle is naive to be impressed by Pascal. Maxime doesn't think Pascal has a chance with Angèle.

5 1. Excusez-moi,... on s'est pas déjà rencontrés quelque part?
2. C'est fastoche, ça. Oh, tu sais, j'en ai vu d'autres. C'est pas pour me vanter, mais moi...

3. Ah oui? Raconte!
4. Oh, je t'en prie!
5. Tu en as, du courage! Alors là, tu m'épates!
6. Je ne crois pas qu'on ait le temps. Il faut qu'on...
7. Non, mais tu es amoureuse ou quoi? Réveille-toi un peu! Arrête de délirer! Non mais, tu t'es pas regardé? Oh, ça va. Je parie que tu n'en es même pas capable.
8. Lâche-moi, tu veux? Qu'est-ce que tu en sais? Eh ben, on va voir!

RENCONTRE CULTURELLE

Est-ce que tu connais la Guadeloupe? Regarde les photos suivantes pour découvrir quelques caractéristiques de cette île.

On peut voir des fleurs magnifiques dans la forêt tropicale.

Pointe-à-Pitre, chef-lieu de la Guadeloupe

L'agriculture est un secteur important de l'économie de la Guadeloupe.

La Fête des Cuisinières, un événement gastronomique haut en couleurs

La musique fait partie de la vie quotidienne.

Qu'en penses-tu?

1. What impression do these photos give you of Guadeloupe?
2. Judging from the photos, what kinds of activities can people enjoy there?

Possible answers
1. tropical country with urban and natural areas, agriculture and business-based economy, music and cuisine are important
2. visit a tropical forest, attend festivals, play and listen to music

Savais-tu que... ?

La Guadeloupe is the name given to a group of islands located in the West Indies, about 130 kilometers north of Martinique. Discovered by Christopher Columbus in 1493 and first colonized by the French, **la Guadeloupe** became in 1946 a **département d'outre-mer (DOM),** a French overseas department whose residents have the same status and benefits as other French citizens. Agriculture is an important industry in Guadeloupe, with banana plantations and sugarcane cultivation providing the islands' major exports. Music and dance play an important role in Guadeloupe's cultural life, and these combine with its distinctive creole cuisine in the **Fête des Cuisinières.** This annual event displays the talents of the female master chefs of the islands and features a colorful parade of the chefs in flamboyant creole costumes, carrying decorated food baskets.

🌐 Culture Note

The **Fête des Cuisinières** takes place every August in honor of the patron saint of cooks, Saint Laurent. The women chefs of the island dress up in the traditional **madras.** In lieu of the traditional headdress, the women wear elaborate baskets, filled with native fruits such as mangoes, papayas, breadfruit, and christophenes, and decorated with miniature kitchen utensils. This colorful parade winds its way through the streets of Pointe-à-Pitre to the **Cathédrale de Saint-Pierre et de Saint-Paul,** where high mass is held. Then, the festivities continue with a five-hour feast, followed by music and dancing.

Thinking Critically

Comparing and Contrasting Have students compare the **Fête des Cuisinières** with a local event that has similar festivities.

Jump Start!

Have students think of a beach they've been to or have seen pictures of and write answers to the following questions: **Qu'est-ce qu'il y a à voir et à faire là-bas? C'est comment?**

MOTIVATE

Have volunteers read aloud their answers to the Jump Start! activity. Ask them what else they might see at a beach.

TEACH

Presentation

Vocabulaire Using a large sheet of blue or green butcher paper as the "ocean," draw or have students draw a sea scene that portrays the vocabulary items. Then, pretend to swim along the scene. Marvel at the various marine life as you point out each one on your drawing. (**Tiens! Tu as vu cette méduse? Regarde, une tortue! Qu'est-ce qu'il est mignon, cet hippocampe!**) Then, tell what you saw on your snorkeling adventure and have students point to the appropriate items on your drawing.

Possible answers

7 *à manger:* des algues, un crabe, un espadon, une pieuvre, une tortue, un homard, une crevette, un requin
à collectionner: du corail, des hippocampes, des coquillages, des étoiles de mer
animaux dont on peut avoir peur: un requin, un crabe, une pieuvre, une méduse, un espadon

PREMIERE ETAPE
Bragging; flattering; teasing

VOCABULAIRE

L'île de la Guadeloupe est réputée pour la beauté de ses fonds marins.

7 Les fonds marins

Parmi ce que tu vois dans le **Vocabulaire,** qu'est-ce qu'on peut manger? Qu'est-ce qu'on peut collectionner? De quoi est-ce qu'on peut avoir peur? See answers below.

8 Ecoute!

 Dianne montre des diapos *(slides)* de ses vacances à la Guadeloupe à ses camarades de classe. De quelle diapo est-ce qu'elle parle? 1.h 2.d 3.a 4.c 5.e 6.b 7.f 8.g

RESOURCES FOR PREMIERE ETAPE

Chapter Teaching Resources, Book 3
• Communicative Activity 10-1, pp. 58–59
• Teaching Transparency Master 10-1, pp. 62, 64
  Teaching Transparency 10-1
• Additional Listening Activities 10-1, 10-2, 10-3, pp. 65–66
  Audiocassette 10B/Audio CD 10
• Realia 10-1, pp. 69, 71
• Situation Cards 10-1, pp. 72–73
• Student Response Forms, pp. 74–76
• Quiz 10-1, pp. 77–78
  Audiocassette 8B/Audio CD 10

ADDITIONAL RESOURCES
Textbook Audiocassette 5B
  OR *Audio CD 10*
Practice and Activity Book, pp. 110–113
Video Program, Videocassette 2
Video Guide

9 Raconte!

Pascal raconte à Maxime ce qu'il a vu quand il a plongé. Complète leur conversation d'après les images.

MAXIME   Ça s'est bien passé, la plongée?

PASCAL   C'était super.

MAXIME   Qu'est-ce que tu as vu?

PASCAL   Ben, d'abord, j'ai vu des ![tortues] qui mangeaient. Sur les ![rochers], il y avait beaucoup de ![coquillages] et d' ![étoiles de mer].

MAXIME   Et quoi d'autre?

PASCAL   Ensuite, on est passés par un endroit où il y avait beaucoup d' ![algues].

On m'a dit que c'est là qu'il y a des ![crevettes], mais je n'en ai pas vu.

Après quelques mètres, on est arrivés à un récif de ![corail]. C'était beau.

MAXIME   Tu as vu de gros poissons?

PASCAL   Bien sûr. De loin, on a vu un ![espadon], et puis il y a une ![pieuvre] qui est passée tout près de moi.

MAXIME   Cool!

PASCAL   Et juste avant de partir, on a vu un ![requin].

MAXIME   C'est pas vrai!

PASCAL   Si. C'était hyper-cool. On m'a dit qu'il n'était pas dangereux. Par contre, une ![méduse] m'a piqué! Ça m'a fait vraiment mal.

10 C'est cool, la plongée

Tu as fait de la plongée pendant tes vacances à la Guadeloupe. Ecris une carte postale à tes camarades pour leur raconter ce que tu as vu.

Bisous de Guadeloupe!

COMMENT DIT-ON... ?

Bragging; flattering

To brag:

C'est fastoche, ça! *That's so easy!*
C'est pas pour me vanter, mais moi... *I'm not trying to brag, but . . .*
Oh, j'en ai vu d'autres. *I've done bigger and better things.*
C'est moi le/la meilleur(e). *I'm the best.*
C'est moi qui nage le mieux. *I . . . the best.*

To flatter someone:

Tu es fortiche/calé(e). *You're really strong/good at that.*
Alors là, tu m'épates! *I'm really impressed!*
Tu en as, du courage. *You've really got courage.*
Tu es vraiment le/la meilleur(e).
Tu es le garçon le plus cool que je connaisse. *You're the . . . -est . . . I know.*

Game

PICTIONNAIRE Write the vocabulary words from page 250 on separate index cards. Form two teams. Have one player from the first team select a card and draw a picture depicting the word. If his or her team calls out the correct French word within 30 seconds, the team wins a point.

For Individual Needs

9 Auditory/Tactile Learners Have students draw or write the missing vocabulary items on small pieces of paper. Have students listen with their books closed as you read the dialogue aloud, including the omitted vocabulary words. Students arrange the pictures on their desk in the order in which they hear the items mentioned.

Building on Previous Skills

Have partners tell about an activity in which they excel, using expressions they already know (C'est en... que je suis le/la meilleur(e); ... , c'est mon fort).

Motivating Activity

Brag about being the best French teacher (or cook, swimmer, and so on). Then, ask students what they might say in English to flatter someone.

Presentation

Comment dit-on... ? Before class, have five students rehearse the five expressions for flattering. Then, make a five-foot fish out of posterboard. In class, show your fish to students, bragging about your amazing fishing abilities. As you brag, pause to allow one of the prepared students to flatter you.

For Individual Needs

Visual/Auditory Learners Tape numbered pictures of people engaged in various sports to the board. Read aloud boasts each person might make and have students identify the corresponding picture.

Additional Practice

Have students write a sentence bragging about a real or imaginary accomplishment.

(C'est pas pour me vanter, mais j'ai eu cent à l'interro de maths.) Have students exchange papers and write a response.

Language Note

Point out that in the expression **C'est moi qui... le mieux,** the verb that follows **qui** will be in the first person singular form: **C'est moi qui fais le mieux de la plongée.**

Additional Practice

12 Tape pictures of additional activities that Bernard might have done to the board and have students write about them.

Building on Previous Skills

To review the comparative, write various adjectives on the board, such as **grand(e), beau(belle), vieux(vieille), sympa, riche,** and so on. Then, either name or hold up pictures of various celebrities and have students compare them. **(Qui est plus grand, Michael Jordan ou Danny DeVito? Qui est plus riche, Elizabeth Taylor ou moi?)**

Presentation

Grammaire Bring to class three books of various sizes. Ask students to point to the largest and the smallest one. **(Quel livre est le plus grand? Le moins grand?)** Then, demonstrate the superlative by describing one of the books. **(Ça, c'est le meilleur livre des trois. C'est le livre le plus intéressant des trois.)** Then, ask students about their favorites. **(Quel est le meilleur livre/film du monde?)** Have students read the sentences that demonstrate the use of adverbs and infer the rules they exemplify. Then, ask students questions about famous athletes and musicians. **(A ton avis, qui joue le mieux au basket-ball?)**

11 Ecoute!

Ecoute ces conversations. Est-ce que c'est le garçon ou la fille qui se vante? Answers on p. 243C.

12 C'est pas pour me vanter, mais...

Bernard est très fier de lui. Il parle avec son cousin de ce qu'il a fait l'année dernière. Imagine et écris leur dialogue.

*G*rammaire   The superlative

To make the superlative forms in French, you just use the comparative forms along with the appropriate definite articles.

Si tu as oublié forms of the comparative va à la page 204.

Adjectives:

> Ce coquillage est **le plus grand.** Celui-ci est **le moins grand.**
> *the biggest*   *the smallest*
> Ce sont **les meilleures** régions pour la plongée. *the best*

- If the adjective follows the noun, repeat the article.
  > Le requin est l'animal **le plus** dangereux. *the most dangerous*
- Notice that you use **de** to say *in/of* after the superlative.
  > Tu es **la** fille **la plus** courageuse **de** notre classe.
- Don't forget to make the adjectives agree with the nouns.

Adverbs:

> C'est Brigitte qui court **le plus vite.** *the fastest*
> C'est Pascal qui court **le moins vite.** *the slowest*
> C'est moi qui chante **le mieux.** *the best*

252   *deux cent cinquante-deux*   CHAPITRE 10   Rencontres au soleil

♜ Game

C'EST NOUS LES MEILLEURS! To prepare for the game, form two teams. Write words and phrases that would be used in superlative sentences on separate index cards. **(C'est elle qui/danse/le mieux)** Make two identical sets of cards, so that both teams will have the same cards. Distribute one card from each set to each team member, who will be responsible for that word or expression. Then, write several sentences, using the expressions that you wrote on the cards. To play the game, read one of your sentences aloud. **(C'est elle qui danse le mieux.)** The students from each team who hold cards bearing the words and phrases you say race to the board to write the complete sentence together. The first team to write out the correct sentence wins.

13 C'est la mer

Fais des phrases pour dire comment ces animaux sont, à ton avis. *See answers below.*

> Le dauphin est l'animal marin le plus intelligent.

dauphin	laid
requin	mignon
crevette	gros
hippocampe	bizarre
tortue	dangereux
méduse	moche
pieuvre	rapide
étoile de mer	intelligent

14 Pascal est vantard!

Pascal croit qu'il fait tout mieux que les autres. Qu'est-ce qu'il pourrait dire à propos des activités suivantes pour impressionner une fille? *See answers below.*

> De tous les garçons, c'est moi qui cours le plus vite.

courir   parler anglais   conduire   danser
sauter   chanter   nager   s'habiller

bien   haut
prudemment   vite

15 Les vacances à la Guadeloupe

Lis ce texte et dis si les phrases suivantes sont vraies ou fausses.

La Guadeloupe est une destination de rêve. Dès qu'on pose le pied sur son sol, on oublie tout et la vie paraît plus facile. Cette île paradisiaque dont la forme rappelle celle des multiples papillons qu'on peut y trouver est divisée en deux régions : Basse-Terre et Grande-Terre. Sur Grande-Terre, on peut se baigner dans les lagons d'un bleu magnifique et se relaxer sur les plus belles plages du monde ou dans l'un des plus luxueux hôtels du bord de mer. Sur Basse-Terre, on peut admirer une végétation luxuriante que le climat chaud et humide de l'île favorise. La Guadeloupe est réputée pour la gentillesse de ses habitants et pour l'accueil incomparable qu'on y reçoit.

GRANDE-TERRE

BASSE-TERRE

1. La Guadeloupe a la forme d'un papillon. vrai
2. Il est interdit de se baigner dans les lagons. faux
3. Le climat de Basse-Terre est chaud et humide. vrai
4. Les gens sont souvent assez mal élevés. faux
5. La Guadeloupe est une destination de rêve où on voit les plus belles plages du monde. vrai

16 L'endroit le plus beau du monde

Pendant tes vacances à la Guadeloupe, tu téléphones à ton ami(e) pour lui dire ce que tu as fait et vu. Tu es impressionné(e), donc tu exagères. Tu es fier/fière de toi et tu te vantes un peu. Joue cette scène avec ton/ta camarade. Changez de rôles.

PREMIERE ETAPE
deux cent cinquante-trois **253**

Possible answers

13 Le requin est l'animal marin le plus dangereux. La crevette est l'animal marin le plus mignon. L'hippocampe est l'animal marin le plus beau. La tortue est l'animal marin le plus gros. La méduse est l'animal marin le plus embêtant. La pieuvre est l'animal marin le plus laid. L'étoile de mer est l'animal marin le plus bizarre.

14 C'est moi qui parle anglais le mieux de la classe/qui conduis le plus prudemment/qui danse le mieux/qui saute le plus haut/qui chante le mieux/qui nage le plus vite/qui m'habille le mieux.

Additional Practice

13 You might have students expand this activity to describe other animals they've studied in Chapter 12 of Level 2 and Chapter 7 of this book (**orignal, ours, loup, écureuil, renard, raton laveur, mouffette, canard, éléphant, girafe, guépard, hippopotame, lion, rhinocéros, singe, zèbre**).

For Individual Needs

15 Auditory Learners Have students read the statements and keep them in mind as you read the paragraph about Guadeloupe aloud.

15 Challenge/Auditory Learners Have students create additional true-false statements based on the article. Collect them, read them aloud, and have the class respond. Have students correct the false statements.

Teaching Suggestion

16 As an alternative, you might have students write their friend a letter in which they tell about their experiences in Guadeloupe. This activity is appropriate for students' written portfolios.

Geology Link

The islands of Grande-Terre and Basse-Terre have surprisingly different topographies. Grande-Terre is composed mostly of limestone outcroppings called **mornes**. Its coasts are comprised of rocky, jagged cliffs, notably the **Pointe des châteaux**, against which the water crashes dramatically. Basse-Terre, in contrast, is mountainous, with several peaks, deep gorges, cascading waterfalls, mountain streams, and lush tropical rainforests.

Presentation

Comment dit-on... ? Introduce two stuffed animals as
André Amoureux and **Paméla
Parfaite.** Act out a brief scene
between them in which André
falls hopelessly in love with
Paméla. Then, put Paméla
away and tease André for
being foolishly in love, using
the new expressions for teasing. **(Non mais, tu t'es pas
regardé! Arrête de délirer!)**
Have him defend himself,
using the responses. Then,
have a few students tease
André.

For Individual Needs

18 Challenge Once students have completed the activity, have them write a dialogue,
creating a context in which
they use one of the expressions
and the appropriate response.

Portfolio

19 Written This activity is
appropriate for students' written portfolios. For portfolio
information, see *Assessment
Guide,* pages 2–13.

CLOSE

To close this **étape,** call on
students to give appropriate
responses to these remarks:
**C'est moi qui danse le
mieux. Arrête de délirer!
Alors là, tu m'épates! Tu es
vraiment le/la meilleur(e).
Réveille-toi un peu!**

 COMMENT DIT-ON... ?
Teasing

To tease someone:

Tu es amoureux (-euse) ou quoi?
Are you in love or what?
Non mais, tu t'es pas regardé(e)!
If you could see how you look!
Réveille-toi un peu! *Get with it!*
Tu en rates pas une, toi! *You're
batting a thousand!*
Arrête de délirer! *Stop being so silly!*

To respond to teasing:

Lâche-moi, tu veux?
Will you give me a break?
Je t'ai pas demandé ton avis.
Oh, ça va, hein!
Qu'est-ce que tu en sais?
**Ben, ça peut arriver à tout le
monde.**
Et toi, arrête de m'embêter!

17 Ecoute!

Ecoute ces dialogues entre Brigitte et Angèle. Dans quelles conversations est-ce qu'elles se taquinent *(tease)*?
1, 3, 4, 7, 8

18 Qu'est-ce que tu en sais?

Ton/Ta meilleur(e) ami(e) se moque de toi. Choisis la bonne réponse pour te défendre.

1. **Tu en rates pas une, toi!**
   a. Mais le bus n'est pas arrivé à l'heure.
   b. Ben, ça peut arriver à tout le monde!
   c. Oui, c'est vrai. J'ai raté un autre examen.

2. **Tu es amoureux (-euse) ou quoi?**
   a. J'en ai vu d'autres.
   b. Je ne suis jamais tombé(e) amoureux (-euse).
   c. Lâche-moi, tu veux?

3. **Arrête de délirer!**
   a. Mais c'est amusant de délirer!
   b. Et toi, arrête de m'embêter!
   c. Oh, c'est fastoche, ça!

4. **Non, mais tu t'es pas regardé(e)!**
   a. Je t'ai pas demandé ton avis.
   b. Je n'ai pas de miroir.
   c. Si, je suis très beau/belle.

5. **Réveille-toi un peu!**
   a. Je n'ai pas de réveil.
   b. Oh, j'ai sommeil.
   c. Oh, ça va, hein!

19 C'est fastoche, la plongée

Ces jeunes viennent de faire de la plongée. Ils
parlent de ce qu'ils ont vu. Pendant la conversation,
ils se vantent, se flattent et se taquinent. Ecris
leur conversation.

254   *deux cent cinquante-quatre*   CHAPITRE 10   Rencontres au soleil

---

ASSESS

Quiz 9-1, *Chapter Teaching Resources,
Book 3,* pp. 77–78

*Assessment Items, Audiocassette 8B
Audio CD 10*

Performance Assessment

Write the situations students suggested for
the Motivating Activity above on index cards.
Have partners draw a card and act out a brief
skit in which one student teases the other.
You might base students' grades on inclusion
of all the elements, language use, creativity,
and participation.

PANORAMA CULTUREL

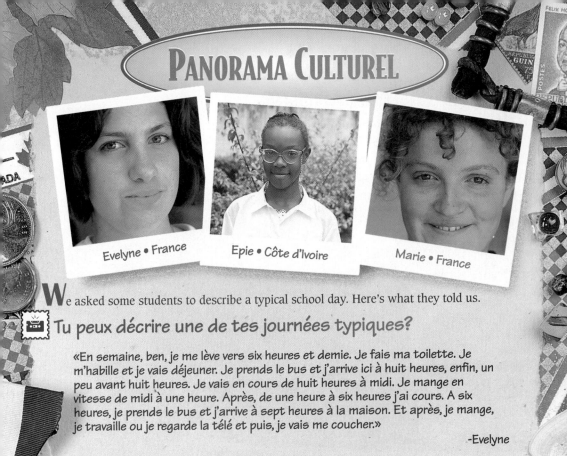

Evelyne • France

Epie • Côte d'Ivoire

Marie • France

We asked some students to describe a typical school day. Here's what they told us.

Tu peux décrire une de tes journées typiques?

«En semaine, ben, je me lève vers six heures et demie. Je fais ma toilette. Je m'habille et je vais déjeuner. Je prends le bus et j'arrive ici à huit heures, enfin, un peu avant huit heures. Je vais en cours de huit heures à midi. Je mange en vitesse de midi à une heure. Après, de une heure à six heures j'ai cours. A six heures, je prends le bus et j'arrive à sept heures à la maison. Et après, je mange, je travaille ou je regarde la télé et puis, je vais me coucher.»

-Evelyne

«Je me réveille à cinq heures. Je me lave. Je fais ma toilette. Je m'habille. Je prends mon petit déjeuner, puis je prends la route de l'école. Arrivée à l'école, je vais en classe. Nous faisons les cours et, à midi, je repars à la maison. Puis, je regarde la télévision et puis, je mange. Dans l'après-midi, je vais me coucher. Si on a cours le soir, je repars à l'école, et puis je reviens. Le soir, j'étudie et puis, je vais dormir.»

-Epie

«Je me lève vers six heures et demie. Je vais dans la salle de bains. Je me lave un petit peu. Je m'habille. Après, je vais donner à manger à mes chevaux. Après, je déjeune, puis ma mère, elle m'emmène avec mes petites sœurs à l'école. Après, la matinée, on travaille. A midi, je mange en ville avec des copines ou des copains, et l'après-midi, je retourne à l'école, et ma mère vient me chercher le soir à six heures. Et après, je me baigne ou je regarde la télé et après, je vais travailler. Et le soir, je mange et après, je donne à manger à mes chevaux et à mon chien, et je vais me coucher.»

-Marie

Qu'en penses-tu?

1. How do the routines of these students differ from a typical school day in the United States? Classes last until 6:00 p.m.
2. Which of these students has a routine most like your own?

VIDEO PROGRAM
Videocassette 2

Questions

1. A quelle heure est-ce qu'Evelyne arrive chez elle le soir? (à sept heures) Qu'est-ce qu'elle fait le soir? (Elle travaille ou elle regarde la télévision.)
2. Qui se lève le plus tôt? (Epie)
3. Qu'est-ce qu'Epie fait l'après-midi? (Elle se couche.)
4. Qu'est-ce que Marie fait que les autres ne font pas? (Elle donne à manger à ses chevaux.)

Thinking Critically

Analyzing Have students read Epie's interview. Ask them what is unusual about her school routine. (She takes a nap in the early afternoon and has classes later in the afternoon.) Have students use their knowledge of Côte d'Ivoire to try to explain her schedule. (It is too hot in the early afternoon to have class or carry on business; most schools and businesses close down during the hottest hours of the day and reopen in the midafternoon.)

Summary

In **Des nouvelles de Guadeloupe**, Joëlle writes her friend Marie-France, relating the latest gossip. She tells about their mutual friends, Paul and Viviane, who broke up but who constantly call Joëlle to talk about the other. She mentions that Prosper broke his leg while hiking up the volcano and that Julie, Raoul's sister, married a boy from Martinique. Another friend, Michel, failed his bac. Joëlle writes that she is also studying for the bac and that she recently won a relay race.

Motivating Activity

Ask students what they would write about in a letter to a pen pal or friend that had moved away. Then, have students look at the photos on page 256 and imagine what the letter on page 257 will be about.

Presentation

Have students read the introduction at the top of this page. Then, assign the names of the people Joëlle mentions in her letter to small groups. Tell them to listen for and note any news pertaining to their assigned person. Then, play the recording and have groups report back to the class.

Answers

20 1. She misses her friend and she wants to share some news.
 2. what has happened since Marie-France left Guadeloupe
 3. Lyon
22 a. Je suis allée écouter un concert de salsa avec Viviane.
 b. Prosper est tombé en faisant une randonnée à la Soufrière.
 c. Julie, la sœur de Raoul, s'est mariée.
 d. Michel travaille dans la boutique de son père en attendant de repasser le bac.

Remise en train

 Des nouvelles de Guadeloupe

Joëlle écrit à une amie, Marie-France, qui a quitté la Guadeloupe il y a quelques mois. Elle lui raconte tout ce qui s'est passé depuis son départ. Et il s'en est passé des choses!

20 Tu as compris? See answers below.
1. Why does Joëlle write the letter?
2. What news does she share with Marie-France?
3. Where will the letter be sent?

21 C'est qui?
Dans la lettre de Joëlle, trouve le nom d'une personne qui...
1. a raté son bac. Michel
2. s'est mariée. Julie
3. s'est disputée avec son petit ami. Viviane
4. a participé à un relais. Joëlle
5. s'est cassé la jambe. Prosper

22 Qu'est-ce qui se passe?
Décris les situations suivantes d'après la lettre de Joëlle. See answers below.

a.

b.

c.

d.

256 *deux cent cinquante-six*   CHAPITRE 10   Rencontres au soleil

---

 RESOURCES FOR REMISE EN TRAIN

Textbook Audiocassette 5B/Audio CD 10
Practice and Activity Book, p. 114

For Individual Needs

21 Visual Learners On a transparency, draw visual cues to represent each event described in the letter (a wedding ring,

a trophy, crutches). If possible, you might bring in these items. Then, point to the pictures or items and call on students to name the person associated with them.

21 Challenge Do the Visual Learners activity described above. Then, have students write a French sentence about the person associated with each item without using their books. For example, the trophy might prompt students to write **Joëlle a participé à un relais.**

Ma chère Marie-France,

Si tu savais comme tu me manques. Quand je sors de l'école, je me dis, «Tiens, si Marie-France était là, on irait se promener dans le vieux centre ou sur la place des Victoires.» Hier, j'ai pensé à toi. Je suis allée écouter un concert de salsa. Tu aurais adoré ça. Tout le monde était debout et dansait. J'y suis allée avec Viviane. Je ne t'ai pas dit? Elle et Paul se sont fâchés. Ils ne se parlent plus depuis trois mois. Paul me téléphone et me parle de Viviane, et Viviane ne me parle que de Paul. Au fait, tu savais que Prosper s'était cassé la jambe? Il est tombé en faisant une randonnée à la Soufrière. Je suis allée le voir à l'hôpital. Il a le moral, mais il a eu peur. Tu connais la dernière? Figure-toi que Julie, la sœur de Raoul, s'est mariée. Non, mais, tu te rends compte! Elle n'a que vingt ans. Je n'ai jamais vu son mari mais j'ai entendu dire qu'il est sympa. Il est martiniquais et je crois qu'elle va aller habiter avec lui à Fort-de-France. Ah, et puis tu connais la meilleure? Tiens-toi bien. Michel a raté son bac. Je me demande vraiment comment il a fait. Il avait toujours des super notes. Il a dû paniquer le jour de l'examen. Il va le repasser cette année. Mais en attendant, il travaille dans la boutique de son père. Le pauvre! Lui qui voulait se lancer dans l'informatique! Comme tu vois, depuis que tu es partie, beaucoup de choses ont changé. Pour ma part, je n'arrête pas. Je suis vachement occupée. Le bac, c'est dans deux mois et je ne me sens pas du tout prête. En plus, j'essaie de continuer mon entraînement. Je cours au moins une heure par jour. Je ne t'ai pas dit? On a gagné à un relais où il y avait les meilleures athlètes des Antilles. C'est génial, non? Écris-moi vite pour me raconter ce que tu fais à Lyon. J'espère qu'il ne fait pas trop froid. Ici, comme tu peux l'imaginer, il fait un temps super. On va à la plage tous les week-ends. Je te laisse. Gros bisous.

Joëlle

NOTE CULTURELLE

In Guadeloupe people tend to take a lot of time talking to one another. For example, acquaintances meeting casually on the street in Guadeloupe wouldn't hesitate to have an extended conversation, discussing their recent activities, current events, and inquiring about other family members. A hurried American greeting of "Hi! How are you doing? Gotta go!" would be considered extremely rude!

24 Cherche les expressions
See answers below.

What expressions does Joëlle use to . . .

1. say she misses someone?
2. describe a hypothetical situation?
3. break some news?
4. make a supposition?
5. express pity?
6. end her letter?

25 Et maintenant, à toi

Est-ce que tu as des amis qui ont déménagé? Est-ce que tu leur écris quelquefois? Qu'est-ce que tu leur dis dans tes lettres?

23 Vrai ou faux?

1. Viviane et Paul se sont réconciliés. faux
2. Joëlle trouve que Julie était trop jeune pour se marier. vrai
3. Michel veut étudier l'informatique. vrai
4. Joëlle va à la plage tous les jours. faux
5. Beaucoup de choses ont changé. vrai

deux cent cinquante-sept 257

Teaching Suggestion

Have students take on the identity of one of the friends that Joëlle writes about in her letter and give clues to their identity. (**Je voudrais me lancer dans l'informatique.**) Their classmates try to guess each friend's name (**Michel**).

Building on Previous Skills

Write bits of gossip from the letter (**Je ne t'ai pas dit? Viviane et Paul se sont fâchés**) on index cards and distribute them to students. Have partners read their news to each other and respond, using expressions they already know. (**Tu plaisantes! Pas possible! C'est pas vrai! N'importe quoi! Mon œil! Oh là là! C'est pas de chance, ça!**) You might list these expressions on a transparency for students to refer to as they exchange gossip.

Teaching Suggestion

25 If a student in your class has moved away recently, you might have the class compose a letter to that person and send it.

Language Note

25 Ask students if they recognize a word within **déménager** (**ménage**). Tell them that **déménager** means *to move* and ask them to explain the literal meaning of the word (*to uproot the household*).

Answers

24 1. Si tu savais comme tu me manques.
2. Si Marie-France était là,...
3. Je ne t'ai pas dit? Au fait, tu savais que... ? Tu connais la dernière? Figure-toi que... ; Ah, et puis tu connais la meilleure?
4. Il a dû paniquer le jour de l'examen.
5. Le pauvre!
6. Je te laisse. Gros bisous.

Culture Note

La Soufrière, which peaks at 4,813 feet, is the highest point in the Lesser Antilles. It erupted in 1590, in 1797–1798, in 1836, and in 1956. Although it is popular among hikers, the 200-foot climb to the top over steep and rocky terrain can be dangerous.

Breaking some news; showing interest; expressing disbelief; telling a joke

VOCABULAIRE

Depuis que Marie-France a quitté la Guadeloupe, il s'en est passé des choses!

Luc **s'est fiancé.**

Sabine **a perdu du poids.**

Etienne **s'est acheté** un vélomoteur.

Marie-Ange **a déménagé.**

Mireille **s'est fait mal au** dos en faisant du cheval.

Lucien **a planté la voiture** de son père.

Thérèse **s'est fait enlever ses bagues.**

Germain **n'a plus de boutons.**

Michel **s'est cassé les jambes.**

Julien et Bruno **se sont bagarrés.**

Ophélia **s'est fait percer les oreilles.**

Agnès **a pris des leçons de conduite.**

26 Ecoute!

Sabine téléphone à son amie qui a déménagé pour lui donner les nouvelles. Regarde les jeunes dans le **Vocabulaire.** De qui est-ce qu'elle parle? Answers on p. 243D.

27 Mon journal

Pense à ce qui t'est arrivé au cours de ces deux dernières années. Choisis les événements les plus importants et parles-en.

258 *deux cent cinquante-huit*   CHAPITRE 10   Rencontres au soleil

---

Jump Start!

Write the following familiar expressions on a transparency: **Tu sais qui... ? Tu connais la nouvelle?** Have students use them to write sentences in which they break two different bits of news to a friend.

MOTIVATE

Have students imagine that they haven't seen you for a year. Ask them what news they would tell you about themselves and their classmates.

TEACH

Presentation

Vocabulaire Act out what happened to each person in the **Vocabulaire** while describing the activities and showing appropriate props. For example, as you say **Luc s'est fiancé,** you might kneel and hold out a ring. Then, read the vocabulary aloud and have students give the thumbs- up or the thumbs-down gesture to indicate whether the event is pleasurable. Finally, say things that the people in the **Vocabulaire** might say (**Youpi! Je me suis fait enlever mes bagues!**) and have students identify the speaker.

Teaching Suggestion

Have students imagine that three of the events from the **Vocabulaire** happened to them. Then, ask them about the activities (**Qui a pris des leçons de conduite?**) and have them answer accordingly.

Mon journal

27 For an additional journal entry suggestion for Chapter 10, see *Practice and Activity Book,* page 154.

RESOURCES FOR DEUXIEME ETAPE

Chapter Teaching Resources, Book 3
- Communicative Activity 10-2, pp. 60–61
- Teaching Transparency Master 10-2, pp. 63, 64
  Teaching Transparency 10-2
- Additional Listening Activities 10-4, 10-5, 10-6, pp. 66–67
  Audiocassette 10B/Audio CD 10
- Realia 10-2, pp. 70, 71
- Situation Cards 10-2, 10-3, pp. 72–73
- Student Response Forms, pp. 74–76
- Quiz 10-2, pp. 79–80
  Audiocassette 8B/Audio CD 10

ADDITIONAL RESOURCES
Textbook Audiocassette 5B
  OR *Audio CD 10*
Practice and Activity Book, pp. 115–118

COMMENT DIT-ON...?
Breaking some news; showing interest; expressing disbelief

To break some news:

Tu savais que... ?

Tu connais la dernière?
  Have you heard the latest?

J'ai entendu dire que...
  I've heard that . . .

Figure-toi que... :

Si tu avais vu ce qu'elle portait!
  If you could have seen . . . !

To show interest:

Raconte!

Oh là là!

Qui t'a dit ça?

Et alors?

To express disbelief:

Mon œil! *No way!*

Je n'en reviens pas. *I don't believe it.*

N'importe quoi! *Yeah, right!*

28 Ecoute!

Tu entends les conversations suivantes à la cantine. Dans quelles conversations est-ce qu'on donne des nouvelles? 1, 3, 6, 7

29 Je n'en reviens pas

Invente trois nouvelles incroyables. Ensuite, annonce ces nouvelles à ton/ta camarade. Il/Elle va exprimer des doutes.

Si tu as oublié the passé composé va à la page 11.

Grammaire The past perfect

Read this English sentence: *She told us that he had already left. Had left* is an example of the past perfect tense in English. You use this tense when you need to say that something happened even farther in the past than something else. This tense is called the **plus-que-parfait** in French and you use it the same way in French as in English.

Elle n'a pas dit ce qu'il **avait fait.**
didn't say   *had done.*

• To form the **plus-que-parfait**, you use the **imparfait** of **avoir** or **être** and add the past participle.

j'**avais dit**	j'**étais allé(e)**
tu **avais dit**	tu **étais allé(e)**
il/elle/on **avait dit**	il/elle/on **était allé(e)(s)**
nous **avions dit**	nous **étions allé(e)s**
vous **aviez dit**	vous **étiez allé(e)s**
ils/elles **avaient dit**	ils/elles **étaient allé(e)s**

• The verbs conjugated with **être** in the **passé composé** are also conjugated with **être** in the **plus-que-parfait**.

• The rules for agreement of past participles are the same for both the **passé composé** and the **plus-que-parfait**.

Additional Practice

Comment dit-on... ? Create a four-line dialogue in which the first speaker breaks some news, the second speaker shows interest, the first speaker tells the news, and the second speaker expresses disbelief. Write the lines in scrambled order on a transparency. Have students number them in the correct order and read the dialogue aloud with a partner.

Grammaire On a sheet of paper, write several sentence starters (**On m'a dit que...** ; **J'ai entendu dire que...**) and several possible endings for each (**... tu étais allé(e) à la boum. ... ils avaient perdu leur chien**). Make one copy for every two students, cut the starters and endings apart, and distribute the pieces to partners. Have them assemble several logical sentences and take turns reading them aloud and responding to the news.

Motivating Activity

Select appropriate articles about celebrities from magazines and read excerpts to students.

Presentation

Comment dit-on... ? The day before the presentation, have students write a statement about an incredible event. In class, call on several students to read their statements aloud. React with interest or disbelief. Then, make up an incredible story (the principal being abducted by space aliens) and break the news to the class. Prompt students to respond, using the new expressions. Then, have partners take turns reading the news they wrote and reacting to it.

Grammaire Before class, write **samedi** on the board and have several students write what they did on Saturday underneath it. (**J'ai planté ma voiture.**) Then, write **lundi** on the board and underneath it, write several different expressions, such as **Pierre m'a dit que...** Write and say a sentence, using one clause from each column. (**Pierre m'a dit qu'il avait planté sa voiture samedi.**) Then, have students use clauses from each column to construct similar sentences.

Teaching Suggestion

Have students write down an activity they did last weekend, real or imaginary. (**J'ai acheté une mobylette.**) Have students exchange papers with a partner, who relates the information to a third student. (**Hélène m'a dit qu'elle avait acheté une mobylette ce week-end**). The third student should respond appropriately. (**Qui t'a dit ça?**)

- Have students look at Joëlle's letter on page 257 and share the news she relates with a partner.

30 Have students write the news in a letter to another friend.

♟ Game

SENTENCE SCRAMBLER To prepare for this game, write the individual words of various sentences on strips of transparency. **(J'ai entendu dire que Monique était tombée amoureuse de Philippe. Julie m'a dit qu'elle s'était cassé la jambe.)** Put the transparency strips for each sentence in a separate envelope. To play the game, divide the class into two teams. Scatter the transparency strips for the first sentence on the overhead. Have two players from the first team come to the overhead and try to re-arrange the words in a logical order within a designated time limit. If they form the sentence within the allotted time, they win a point for their team. Then, the opposing team takes a turn. You might play until one team has earned a specified number of points.

📁 Portfolio

32 Written Activity 32 is appropriate for students' written portfolios. You might have them include real photos or draw pictures to illustrate the events they describe in their letter. For portfolio suggestions, see *Assessment Guide*, page 23.

33 Oral This activity is appropriate for students' oral portfolios. For portfolio information, see *Assessment Guide*, pages 2–13.

---

30 Raconte!

Ta correspondante guadeloupéenne t'a envoyé une lettre. Elle te raconte tout ce qui s'est passé cette année. Tes camarades sont curieux. Raconte-leur ce qu'elle a écrit dans sa lettre. Utilise le plus-que-parfait. See answers below.

Elle m'a dit que...

Je suis tombée malade.

J'ai été opérée.

Je suis allée à l'hôpital.

J'ai obtenu une bourse.

Je suis entrée à l'université.

J'ai perdu du poids.

Je suis partie en vacances.

Je me suis trouvé un petit ami.

Je me suis acheté une voiture.

J'ai travaillé pendant l'été.

31 C'est pas vrai!

Juliette raconte à Lucie ce qui est arrivé à leurs amis. Complète leur conversation en utilisant le passé composé ou le plus-que-parfait.

JULIETTE Tu connais la dernière?

LUCIE Non. Raconte.

JULIETTE Benoît et Delphine ont cassé.

LUCIE C'est pas vrai! Qui t'a dit ça?

JULIETTE Delphine. Elle m'a dit qu'elle (voir) *avait vu* Benoît au café avec une autre fille.

LUCIE Et alors?

JULIETTE Elle lui (téléphoner) *a téléphoné*. Elle lui (demander) *a demandé* s'il (se trouver) *s'était trouvé* une nouvelle petite amie.

LUCIE Et qu'est-ce qu'il a dit?

JULIETTE Ben, il a dit qu'il (inviter) *avait invité* cette fille au café parce qu'elle (venir) *était venue* de Martinique pour rendre visite à son frère qui était occupé.

LUCIE Et Delphine le croit?

JULIETTE Non. Elle lui a dit qu'elle en (finir) *avait fini* avec lui et qu'elle aussi (rencontrer) *avait rencontré* quelqu'un d'autre.

LUCIE Non!

JULIETTE Si, si. Je t'assure. Moi, je lui ai dit que j'(parler) *avais parlé* avec le frère de Benoît et qu'il (ne pas mentir). *n'avait pas menti*

LUCIE Qu'est-ce qui (arriver)? *est arrivé?*

JULIETTE Elle était fâchée. Elle a refusé de m'écouter.

32 Il s'en est passé des choses!

 Ecris à un(e) ami(e) qui a déménagé pour lui dire tout ce qui est arrivé à tes amis depuis l'année dernière.

33 N'importe quoi!

 Parle à ton/ta camarade des dernières aventures des personnages d'un feuilleton ou d'une série télévisée que tu connais. ¡Eɪ ɐl ɥO∗

A la française

Can you guess which of the phrases in the **Comment dit-on... ?** on page 259 this gesture expresses? *

Teacher Note

A la française Remind students of the gesture that accompanies the expression **Mon œil!** They should place their index finger just below one eye and tug gently.

Answers

30 Elle m'a dit qu'elle était tombée malade, avait été opérée, était allée à l'hôpital, avait obtenu une bourse, était entrée à l'université, avait perdu du poids, était partie en vacances, s'était trouvé un petit ami, s'était acheté une voiture, avait travaillé pendant l'été.

COMMENT DIT-ON... ?

Telling a joke

To bring up a joke:
J'en connais une bonne.
I've got a good one.
Est-ce que tu connais l'histoire de... ?
Do you know the one about . . . ?

To continue a story:
... et alors, il dit que...
... et l'autre lui répond...

To relate a joke:
Quelle est la différence entre... et... ?
Quel est le point commun entre... et...?
What do . . . and . . . have in common?
C'est l'histoire d'un mec qui...
It's about a guy who . . .

To respond to a joke:
Elle est bien bonne!
Elle est nulle, ta blague!

34 Ecoute!

Ecoute ces conversations et dis si c'est le début, le milieu ou la fin d'une blague *(joke)*. Answers on p. 243E.

35 Méli-mélo!

Joëlle raconte une blague à Viviane. Mets leur conversation en ordre.

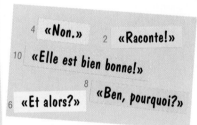

A la française

Sometimes you're not exactly sure what you're going to say next and you need a second to think. You can fill in gaps in your speech with these words that French-speaking people commonly use: **Bon,... Eh bien,... Euh,... Voyons,... Attends,... Tu sais,... Alors,...** and **Ben,...**

7 «Et alors, il dit que les Français sont vraiment nuls.»

5 «Il y a un Texan à Paris avec sa femme. Il regarde la tour Eiffel, d'un air étonné.»

1 «J'en connais une bonne.»

3 «Tu connais l'histoire du Texan à Paris?»

9 «Parce que ça fait cent ans qu'ils ont mis ce derrick, et ils n'ont toujours pas obtenu de pétrole!»

4 «Non.»   2 «Raconte!»

10 «Elle est bien bonne!»

6 «Et alors?»   8 «Ben, pourquoi?»

36 J'en connais une bonne

Pense à une blague que tu pourrais raconter en français. Raconte-la à ton/ta camarade. Changez de rôles.

37 Jeu de rôle

Your French class is on a trip to Guadeloupe. You're camping on the beach. Act out these scenes with your classmates.

a. It's night and you're sitting around the campfire. You're telling jokes and relating the latest news you know.
b. As you go to your sleeping bags, someone sees a snake and everyone is scared. One of you picks up the snake, throws it back into the dunes, and then brags about it. The others flatter this person and tease one another for being scared.

DEUXIEME ETAPE   *deux cent soixante et un*   **261**

Teacher Note

Here are a few jokes you might want to share with your students:

• Un petit Marseillais dit à sa mère : «Maman! Je viens de voir une souris énorme! Une souris grosse comme un hippopotame!» Et sa mère lui répond : «Ecoute, ça fait trente-six millions de fois que je te dis de ne pas exagérer!»

• Un volontaire pour la marine parle au médecin. Le médecin lui demande : «Vous savez nager?» Et le garçon lui répond : «Pourquoi? Vous n'avez pas de bateaux?»

• Un sauveteur voit un baigneur dans la rivière. Et alors, il lui dit qu'il est défendu de nager dans la rivière. Et l'autre lui répond : «Je ne nage pas. Je me noie! *(drown)*» Et le sauveteur dit : «Ah, bon! Alors, faites, faites!»

Motivating Activity

Ask students to list expressions comedians use to begin a joke (Did you hear the one about the... ? Did you ever notice how... ?)

Presentation

Comment dit-on... ? Using a toy telephone, pretend to call a friend and tell the person a joke. (**Est-ce que tu connais l'histoire de la petite fille paresseuse? Une petite fille qui a eu une mauvaise note en histoire dit à son père : «Papa, tu connais la dernière?» Et il lui répond «Euh, non. Raconte.» Et sa fille lui répond «Eh bien, c'est moi!»**) Then, pretend to listen as the other person tells a joke. (**Ben, je ne sais pas. Quelle est la différence?... Elle est nulle, ta blague!**) Finally, write a summary of a joke on the board (see Teacher Note below) and have partners practice telling it.

CLOSE

To close this **étape**, write the vocabulary expressions from page 258 on separate index cards and distribute them to students. Have partners create and act out a skit using 1) the vocabulary item they received; 2) at least one expression for breaking some news; 3) at least one expression for showing interest; and 4) at least one expression of disbelief.

ASSESS

Quiz 10-2, *Chapter Teaching Resources, Book 3,* pp. 79–80

Assessment Items, Audiocassette 8B/Audio CD 10

Performance Assessment

Have students perform their scenes from Activity 37.

LISONS!

Tout au fond de la mer chaude des Caraïbes, dans une maison entourée d'une véranda, vit une famille d'étoiles de mer : la famille Micabwa.

O'gaya, la fille aînée, n'est toujours pas rentrée ; pourtant là-haut, à l'horizon, le soleil a déjà mis sa robe de chambre sanguine.

Toute la famille est à table : papa Micabwa mange de bon appétit et Fia, sa fille cadette, se ressert de la salade d'algues. L'horloge siffle neuf coups. Maman Micabwa aime bien cette horloge qu'ils ont rapportée de leur dernier voyage aux îles Galapagos. L'horloge ? C'est un énorme coquillage bleuté, un coquillage-temps. Comment sait-il l'heure ? Nul ne le

sait. Au neuvième coup, les coraux de la porte tintinnabulent : O'gaya, gracieuse étoile de mer, passe sous la pierre de lumière.

Papa Micabwa s'installe sous la véranda, dans son fauteuil à bascule pour boire une tisane d'anémones sauvages. La petite sœur s'éclipse dans sa chambre et revient, pailletée d'argent.

- Maman, je vais danser avec...

La fin de sa phrase est couverte par le vrombissement d'une superbe coquille Saint-Jacques pilotée par un jeune poulpe :

- Bonsoir, papa Micabwa, je vous enlève Fia pour la soirée.

- Ne l'enlace pas trop avec tous tes bras, lui répond malicieusement papa Micabwa.

Fia envoie un baiser à son père, la Saint-Jacques démarre dans un tourbillon de sable. Papa Micabwa reste songeur, il pense à O'gaya : «Il faudra que je lui parle : elle a l'air triste ces temps-ci.»

Maman Micabwa et O'gaya sortent toutes les deux sous la véranda.

O'gaya s'installe sur les marches et maman Micabwa dans sa berceuse. Les étoiles luisent doucement dans l'eau de la nuit. O'gaya soupire :

- Je voudrais tant être une étoile de ciel.

Papa et maman Micabwa sursautent :

- Que dis-tu ?

O'gaya se tourne vers eux et répète :

A. Before you read, glance at the illustrations for this story. Where does the action take place? What kinds of creatures are the main characters? under the sea; starfish

B. The Micabwa family lives at the bottom of which sea?
   a. Mediterranean
   b. Caribbean
   c. Aegean

C. What is the family doing at the beginning of the story? Who is missing? eating; daughter O'gaya

D. Tell whether the following statements are true or false.
   1. O'gaya prend le dîner avec sa famille. false
   2. Fia est la fille aînée de la famille. false
   3. L'ami de Fia est un poulpe. true
   4. Le père d'O'gaya s'inquiète pour elle. true

262   *deux cent soixante-deux*

Teaching Suggestions

- Have students guess from context the meanings of the following words that appear on this page: **horloge, véranda, sursautent** *(clock; veranda, porch; give a start, jump).*

- Once students have done Activities A–D, ask them for their first impressions of O'gaya (a dreamer, wistful). Have them predict the rest of the story from what they've read so far and what they know of O'gaya's character.

The following is the left teacher-column material

READING STRATEGY
Understanding literary devices

Teacher Note

For an additional reading, see *Practice and Activity Book,* page 119.

PREREADING
Activities A–C

Motivating Activity

Ask students to name stories in which the main characters are animals *(The Three Little Pigs)* and stories that are related to the sea *(The Little Mermaid)*. If students are familiar with *The Little Mermaid,* have them summarize the story and describe the main characters.

Language Arts Link

Before students begin to read, ask them for English examples of the literary devices mentioned in **De bons conseils.** You might have students write down one example of a *simile* (She shone like the sun), one of a *metaphor* (He was a raging bull of a man), and one of *personification* (The tree waved at the family). Then, collect the papers, read the examples aloud, and have students tell which literary device is exemplified by each sentence. As an alternative, you might write the types of devices on a large sheet of butcher paper and have volunteers write examples below each one.

Teaching Suggestion

B., C. Have students read the questions in Activities B and C before reading the first two paragraphs of the story.

Teacher Note

D. The statements in this activity are based on the part of the story that appears on this page only.

- Je voudrais tant être une *étoile de ciel*.
- Hélas ! Nous ne pouvons pas t'aider ma petite fille, répond maman Micabwa.
- Mais, ajoute papa Micabwa, je connais la tortue millénaire Man Dou, elle pourrait te conseiller.
Déjà, O'gaya saute de joie :
- Pourrais-je partir dès demain ?
Papa et maman Micabwa sourient tendrement :
- Mais, bien sûr ma chérie, tu pourras partir demain.
Le lendemain matin, O'gaya est si excitée qu'elle n'arrive pas à boire son lait d'éponge. Elle embrasse ses parents et part. Papa et maman Micabwa ne sont pas trop inquiets ; l'heure est venue pour O'gaya de grandir et de vivre ses rêves.
La voilà partie ! Elle avance vite, quand, tout à coup, une rangée de dents lui barre la route.
- Hé ! Où va-t-on ainsi, sans plus se gêner ? Vous prenez mon domaine pour un jardin public peut-être ? demande Morfyo le requin. O'gaya frissonne, rassemble son courage et répond :
- M. Morfyo, je rêvais, et je suis entrée par

hasard sur vos terres.
- Et à quoi rêves-tu, petite impudente ?
- Je rêve d'être une *étoile de ciel* et je vais voir si la tortue Man Dou peut m'aider !
Morfyo éclate de rire et des milliers de bulles se forment autour de lui.
- Ecoute, petite, des «comme toi», je n'en ai jamais vu. Vouloir vivre dans le ciel ! Je n'en crois pas mes ouïes !
O'gaya n'essaie pas de fuir et fait face au requin :
- Allez-vous me manger M. Morfyo ? demande-t-elle.
- Et en plus, tu as de l'audace ! Décidément, petite, tu m'es bien sympathique. Allez, je t'emmène, grimpe sur mon dos !
Le redoutable requin, son habit noir décoré d'une étrange fleur, O'gaya, se dirige sans hésitation vers la demeure de la tortue Man Dou.
Sur le chemin, ils croisent des poissons-pipelettes en pleine conversation qui, de stupeur, restent bouche-bée.
Morfyo dépose O'gaya à la porte de Man Dou. La petite étoile de mer descend quelques marches et dans un bassin de sable, elle voit une énorme tortue à la carapace brune et jaune comme les gorgones-éventail.
- Man Dou ! Man Dou ! appelle-t-elle timidement.
Une tête apparaît hors de la carapace, deux yeux d'or fondu la fixent.
- Il faut que cela soit bien important pour

E. Find five details that the author uses to draw an analogy between the Micabwa family and a human family. See answers below.

F. What is O'gaya's dream? to become a star in the sky

G. The turtle Man Dou is a thousand years old. Why do O'gaya's parents send her to speak to the turtle? What does this tell you about this culture's attitude toward its elders? See answers below.

H. What is the first creature that O'gaya meets on her journey? a shark

I. What do you think **Je n'en crois pas mes ouïes !** means? If **ouïe** means *hearing* and **ouïes** means *gills,* what pun has the shark made? See answers below.

J. What qualities does the shark admire in O'gaya? her ambition and her audacity

K. What metaphor is found in the sentence that begins **Le redoutable requin...** ? See answers below.

L. What simile do you find in the paragraph that begins **Morfyo dépose O'gaya...** ? See answers below.

M. Find these words in the story and use context to figure out their meaning.

tintinnabulent	tinkle
vrombissement	humming
tourbillon	swirl
luisent	shine
grimpe	climb
frissonne	tremble
se pelotonne	curl up
frémit	shiver
tisse	weave

N. What kind of creature is Man Kya? What is the deal that O'gaya makes with Man Kya to realize her dream?

O. What metaphor is used to describe Man Kya's strange collection? For Activities N and O, see answers below.

deux cent soixante-trois **263**

Answers

E *Possible answers:* house with a porch, dinner table, clock brought back from trip, papa Micabwa having tea on the porch, sister's date

G She can give advice; The culture values the wisdom of its elders.

I *I can't believe my ears.* The shark is making a pun by transforming the usual expression (referring to hearing) to suit his own physiology (gills).

K *habit noir* (shark skin compared to black clothing), *étrange fleur* (O'gaya's star shape compared to a flower)

L *à la carapace brune et jaune comme les gorgones-éventail* (with a brown and yellow shell like fan coral)

N Man Kya is a spider crab; O'gaya must give Man Kya her eyes.

O *fruits étranges et colorés* (strange, colored fruit)

READING
Activities D–S

Teaching Suggestion

You might ask students the following additional questions about the story: How does O'gaya feel about the trip? (excited) How does she show this? (She can't finish her sponge milk.) How do her parents feel about her leaving? (They aren't worried because they know it's time for their daughter to fulfill her own dreams.) How does she feel when she encounters the shark? (frightened) What offer does the shark make to O'gaya? (to carry her on his back) How did the other fish respond to the sight of the shark and O'gaya? (They stood in open-mouthed astonishment.)

Additional Practice

K., L. Have students find a metaphor used to describe Man Dou (**deux yeux d'or fondu**).

For Individual Needs

Challenge Have students write French captions for each of the illustrations on pages 262–263, telling what is happening in the story at that point.

Teaching Suggestion

Have students write a brief description in English of the characters they've encountered in the story so far, as if they were giving actors and actresses descriptions of roles in a play.

For Individual Needs

P. Kinesthetic Learners
Have five volunteers mime the actions described here and have their classmates tell them in what order to stand.

POSTREADING
Activity T

Cooperative Learning

Tell students that they are going to present the story of O'gaya as a play or puppet show for French elementary school students. Have them write a script in French for the play, based on the story they just read. Remind them to include stage directions for the actors and actresses. Group members take on the following roles: director, stage hand, set designer, and actors and actresses. The actors and actresses must memorize their lines. The director plans the staging and directs the production. The stage hand helps with costumes, gathers the props, and keeps them in order. The designer creates the set. Have students perform their play for the class and record it on videotape.

Teaching Suggestion

T. You might have students discuss their answers to these questions in small groups or write their answers in their journals.

For Individual Needs

Visual Learners Have students draw their own illustrations for the story, based on their interpretation of the events and the characters described.

---

que tu oses me réveiller !
- Oh ! Oui, Man Dou, je voudrais être une *étoile de ciel.*
Man Dou cligne des yeux :
- Une étoile de ciel !
Je ne peux rien faire pour toi, mais va voir l'araignée d'eau, Man Kya, elle n'habite pas loin d'ici. Bonne chance !
Man Dou se pelotonne à nouveau dans sa carapace.
O'gaya s'en va. Elle n'est pas longue à trouver la demeure de Man Kya, un antre de fougères marines.
- Man Kya, êtes-vous là ?
- Oui, oui, entrez donc, j'arrive.
O'gaya soulève un rideau de longues et lourdes algues de goëmon : elle se retrouve face à l'araignée d'eau.
- Que désires-tu petite ? demande-t-elle d'une voix aigrelette.
- Etre une étoile de ciel.
- Une étoile de ciel ! Drôle d'idée ; enfin, si tu le désires ! Connais-tu le prix de mes services ?
- Non, répond O'gaya, étonnée.
- Pour ce que tu me demandes, le tarif est de deux yeux.
- Mes yeux ? dit d'une voix angoissée O'gaya.
- Oui, viens voir mon jardin !
Elle sort, O'gaya la suit. Dans l'enclos, poussent des coraux ; pendus aux

branches, des yeux les regardent, fruits étranges et colorés.
- Que penses-tu de ma belle collection ? Alors, que décides-tu ?
O'gaya frémit, mais son rêve est trop profondément gravé en elle pour être effacé par le temps. Elle accepte le marché et donne ses yeux. Alors, l'araignée d'eau Man Kya tisse une échelle avec le fil magique qu'elle sécrète.
L'ouvrage terminé, elle souffle trois notes dans une énorme conque. A la troisième note, un grand oiseau, une frégate noire, plonge. Elle lui met les deux boucles de l'échelle dans le bec et lui ordonne de les accrocher à un croissant de lune. La frégate remonte donc à la surface ; l'échelle se déroule dans toute sa splendeur argentée.
Man Kya guide O'gaya et lui souhaite bon voyage.
La petite étoile de mer se hisse sur l'échelle, fil à fil, jusqu'au ciel.
Alors le soir, doux comme un baiser, se pose sur la mer chaude des Caraïbes ; dans la maison du fond de l'eau, papa et maman Micabwa, assis sous la véranda, pensent tendrement à O'gaya.
Soudain, un reflet inattendu attire leur attention, ils se lèvent et regardent : tout là-haut, une petite étoile luit dans l'eau de la nuit.

P. Put in order the events in the realization of O'gaya's dream.

3 | Man Kya souffle trois notes dans une énorme conque.

O'gaya se hisse sur l'échelle jusqu'au ciel.
5

4 | Un oiseau accroche l'échelle à un croissant de lune.

1 | O'gaya donne ses yeux à l'araignée d'eau.

2 | Man Kya tisse une échelle.

Q. doux comme un baiser (soft as a kiss)

Q. What simile do you find in the paragraph that begins **Alors le soir,... ?**

R. Why is personification an essential part of this story? See answers below.

S. What need do you think O'gaya's dream expresses? What qualities are necessary for her to attain her dream? self-actualization; ambition, courage, self-sacrifice

T. What do you dream of being when you're older? What do you think you'd have to do to attain that dream? Would you make a great sacrifice, if necessary?

264 *deux cent soixante-quatre*

Terms in Lisons!

Students might want to know the following words from the story: **berceuse** *(cradle);* **bulle** *(bubble);* **emmener** *(to take with);* **demeure** *(home);* **cligne** *(blink);* **goëmon** *(wrack).*

Community Link

If students do the cooperative learning activity described above, you might have them perform their play at a local elementary school to promote interest in foreign languages.

Answers
R Because the story is really about human dreams and what it takes to attain them. The characters must seem real in order for the story to have its full impact.

There are many possible ways to tell a story. A sequence of events can sound very different if you change the format and style in which you tell it, even if the details remain the same. In this activity, you're going to give O'gaya's story a new twist by retelling it as an article in a supermarket tabloid, with an appropriate sensationalistic style.

Une transformation incroyable!

Raconte l'histoire d'O'gaya à la manière des journaux à sensation. Décris les événements en les exagérant et essaie de rendre ton histoire aussi dramatique et intéressante que possible.

A. Préparation

1. Avec ton/ta camarade, essayez de répondre aux questions suivantes.
   a. A quoi ressemble un journal à sensation? Lequel est-ce que tu connais? Qu'est-ce qui le rend différent d'un journal normal?
   b. Quels genres d'événements et de citations est-ce qu'on trouve dans les articles des journaux à sensation? Quelle sorte de photos est-ce qu'on peut y voir?
   c. Cherche le sens du mot *sensationalism* dans un dictionnaire anglais. En quoi est-ce que ces journaux font appel au sensationnalisme?
2. Fais un plan des événements principaux de l'histoire d'O'gaya.

DE BONS CONSEILS

Style is a general term for the characteristics of a piece of writing. The style in which you write will always be determined by what you are writing. For example, an academic style requires a formal and objective tone, a high level of language, and a strict organization. A letter to a friend is informal, usually with slang expressions and a very loose organization. Advertising style often produces short, crisp sentences with words that appeal to the emotions. It's important that you use the accepted style for a type of writing, since violating that style is often considered unacceptable and ineffective.

B. Rédaction

1. Rédige le brouillon de ton histoire dans le style qu'utilisent les journaux à sensation.
   a. Regarde ton plan. Mets l'accent sur les parties de l'histoire qui sont les plus intéressantes.
   b. Choisis des mots que tu peux utiliser pour que l'histoire soit plus dramatique et plus sensationnelle.
   c. Change un peu les faits et exagère les détails pour rendre ton histoire plus dramatique.
   d. Utilise des personnages bizarres et incroyables.
   e. Illustre ton récit avec des citations réelles ou imaginaires.

C. Evaluation

1. Après avoir fini ton brouillon, relis ce que tu as écrit.
   a. Est-ce que tu as bien raconté ton histoire dans un style journalistique au lieu de simplement répéter les faits?
   b. Est-ce que ton récit est réellement intéressant et dramatique?
2. Rédige la version finale de ton article en prenant soin de corriger l'orthographe, la grammaire et le vocabulaire.
3. Illustre ton histoire avec des photos bizarres et peu crédibles telles que celles qu'on peut trouver dans un journal à sensation. Tu peux soit faire des dessins, soit découper des photos dans un vrai magazine.

deux cent soixante-cinq **265**

Teaching Suggestion

You might suggest that students ask themselves the following questions to make their stories more sensationalistic: Were the parents devastated by the tragedy? Was O'gaya an exceptional child with extraordinary powers? Did Man Kya have a hidden agenda, perhaps linked to the jealous sister?

POSTWRITING

Teaching Suggestion

Ask the class for sensationalistic words and phrases they used in their papers to exaggerate the story and write them on a transparency. Then, have students reread and edit their stories, perhaps adding some of the words and expressions suggested by their classmates.

WRITING STRATEGY
Using an appropriate style

Portfolio

Written You might want to have students include all their work for Parts A–C in their written portfolios. For portfolio information, see *Assessment Guide*, pages 2–13.

PREWRITING

Motivating Activity

Ask students what subjects are treated in sensationalistic newspapers and how they are presented. Ask them to give examples of sensationalistic language and to bring in examples of sensationalistic headlines from newspapers. You might have groups brainstorm common expressions together.

Teaching Suggestion

Ask students to describe the styles of different types of writing (formal letter, comic book, used car ad, newspaper article, letter to the editor, environmental pamphlet, tabloid article). Have them list words and phrases that they would expect to find in each one.

WRITING

For Individual Needs

Auditory Learners To give students an idea of how to sensationalize the story, read aloud a short factual story you have written or an interesting news article from the paper. Ask students what the facts of the story are. List them on the board. Then, ask students to suggest a sensationalistic headline for the story and to exaggerate the story, adding sensationalistic details.

The **Mise en pratique** reviews and integrates all four skills and culture in preparation for the Chapter Test.

Video Wrap-Up

VIDEO PROGRAM
Videocassette 2

You might want to use the *Video Program* as part of the chapter review. See the *Video Guide* for teaching suggestions and activity masters.

Teaching Suggestion

Ask students the following questions about the articles in *Super!*: Quel est le titre du nouveau téléfilm de Jennie Garth? (*Dites à Laura que je l'aime*) Qui va gagner sept millions de dollars? (Keanu Reeves) A quel âge est-ce que Michael J. Fox a quitté le lycée? (à seize ans) Qui était déguisé en Batman? (Eric Clapton) Mel Gibson va faire un remake de quel film? (*Fahrenheit 451*) Hugh Grant va jouer dans quel film? (un remake de *Neuf mois*) Quel film sort en vidéo en ce moment? (*Blanche Neige*)

Additional Practice

You might ask students to relate additional gossip, real or imaginary, about the stars mentioned in the selection from *Super!*

MISE EN PRATIQUE

 1 Ecoute ces conversations entre Nathalie et son frère, Nicolas. Qui est-ce qui se moque de l'autre, Nathalie ou Nicolas? Answers on p. 243E.

2 Lis cette sélection de *Super*, un magazine pour jeunes francophones. Ensuite, associe les noms des stars donnés aux événements correspondants.

Après son mariage et sa (courte) lune de miel, **Jennie Garth** a joué le rôle de **Laura** dans un téléfilm, **«Tell Laura I Love Her»** («Dites à Laura que je l'aime»). La terrible histoire d'une jeune fille que ses parents font enfermer dans une clinique psychiatrique. On est loin de **Kelly** et de **Beverly Hills!**

Whitney Houston a perdu le deuxième bébé qu'elle attendait de **Bobby**. Leur mariage y survivra-t-il?

Bruce Willis, **Stallone** et **Schwarzie** vont ouvrir un Planet Hollywood à Paris!

JASON ET CHRISTINE ELISE RECONCILIES! A la première du film «The Mask», on a pu constater que Jason et Christine Elise étaient toujours très amoureux l'un de l'autre. Dommage les filles..

Après le triomphe de **«Speed»**, **Keanu Reeves** a la cote. Il a touché 7 millions de dollars pour être à l'affiche de **«Without Remorse»**.

A 33 ans, **Michael J. Fox** a enfin décroché son... bac! «C'est fantastique!», a-t-il déclaré. Il avait quitté le lycée à 16 ans.

Les carnets scolaires de **Michael Douglas** étaient particulièrement nuls! Il a avoué qu'il vibrait plus volontiers pour les bikinis et les sports de plage.

Eric Clapton a participé à un rallye automobile déguisé en **Batman**! Mais il a préféré participer à cette manifestation charitable en **Ferrari** plutôt qu'en **Batmobile**.

C'est officiel! **Tom Cruise** sera le héros du film **«Mission Impossible»**, adapté de la fameuse série T.V.

«Parmi tous mes collègues comédiens, je suis le plus créatif», a déclaré **Michael Keaton**. Monsieur Batman était sérieux?

BRAD PITT: UNE LEGENDE
Première photo du prochain film de Brad Pitt, «Légendes d'automne». Bonne nouvelle, même avec son nouveau look, il est toujours aussi craquant!

Mel Gibson sera le producteur et le héros de **«Fahrenheit 451»**, le remake du film de François Truffaut.

Quant à **Hugh Grant**, la révélation de **«Quatre mariages et un enterrement»**, il sera, lui, la vedette du remake de **«Neuf mois»**, le film de **Patrick Braoudé**.

Peter Gabriel a terminé à Paris le mixage de son futur album **«live»** qui devrait sortir avant la fin de l'année.

James Brown, le papi de la soul music, a lancé une gamme de cookies dont les bénéfices iront à sa fondation pour la prévention de la criminalité dans les quartiers défavorisés.

Keanu Reeves n'arrête pas! Après **«Speed»**, il a tourné **«Johnny Mnemonic»**, un film de science-fiction, et vient de commencer **«A Walk in the Clouds»**, une comédie romantique produite par les frères **Zucker**.

C'est l'événement de l'année! Pour la première fois, **«Blanche Neige»**, le plus beau dessin animé du monde, sort en vidéo! Un film éternel avec une musique et un humour inoubliables!

Sébastien Roch a tourné un téléfilm pour France 2. Dans **«Au nom du fils»**, il sera le fils d'un inspecteur de police. Passionné de rallyes, son personnage, **Cyril**, ne s'entend guère avec son père.

Indiana Jones rempile: **Harrison Ford** a en effet dit **«oui»** pour une suite. Il a ressorti le fouet et feutre mou du placard...mais on ignore encore le nom de sa partenaire.

Robin Wright, Madame Sean Penn et ex-**Kelly** de **«Santa Barbara»**, concocte un bouquin de cuisine **«ultra légère»**.

Language Note

Students might want to know the following terms from the magazine selection: **lune de miel** (*honeymoon*); **gamme** (*line*); **défavorisé** (*disadvantaged*).

Keanu Reeves
Il a tourné un film de science-fiction.

Bruce Willis
Il ouvre un Planet Hollywood à Paris.

James Brown
Il a lancé une gamme de cookies.

Eric Clapton
Il a participé à un rallye automobile.

Jennie Garth
Elle a joué dans un téléfilm.

Michael J. Fox
Il a enfin obtenu son bac.

Tom Cruise
Il sera le héros d'un film adapté d'une série T.V.

Michael J. Fox
Tom Cruise
James Brown
Eric Clapton
Bruce Willis
Keanu Reeves
Jennie Garth

3 Ton/ta correspondant(e) guadeloupéen(ne) voudrait avoir des nouvelles des Etats-Unis. Ecris-lui une lettre dans laquelle tu lui racontes les dernières nouvelles sur quelques célébrités.

 **4** Choisis une des situations suivantes. Tu te vantes. Si ton/ta camarade est impressionné(e), il/elle va te flatter. S'il/si elle ne l'est pas, il/elle va te taquiner. Changez de rôles.

Tu as une nouvelle voiture.

Tu es le/la meilleur(e) dans un sport.

Tu as piloté un avion.

Tu as fait de la plongée.

Tu as fait du deltaplane.

Tu as les meilleures notes de la classe.

5 ## JEU DE ROLE

Your French class is having a party in honor of your pen pal from Guadeloupe, who is visiting. At the party, you'll break some news, tell jokes, brag, flatter and tease each other. With a group of your classmates, write out a scenario of this scene and act it out. Remember to include the following situations.

* Each of you makes up four bits of news to tell the others.
* Two of you tell a joke.
* The pen pal talks about what it's like in Guadeloupe. He/She makes up an event to brag about. The others flatter him/her.
* Each of you teases one of your friends.

For Individual Needs

3 Slower Pace Have volunteers write each bit of news from Activity 2 as if they were relating it to a friend. (**Tu connais la nouvelle? On m'a dit que Jennie Garth avait joué dans un téléfilm.**) If students know additional news about other celebrities, have them write that information as well. Then, have students write their letters as described in the activity.

Portfolio

4 Oral This activity is appropriate for students' oral portfolios. For portfolio suggestions, see *Assessment Guide,* page 23.

Teaching Suggestion

4 You might have partners act out their scenes for their classmates, who try to guess the situation.

Group Work

5 You might want to have students elect a director to help them stage their scene. Since all of the conversations cannot happen simultaneously, the director will need to arrange the blocking and staging so that all the components are included in a natural-sounding conversation. Students may decide to have two or three different scenes, each one focusing on a different character. You might have students videotape their scenes and use them later as a review for the test.

QUE SAIS-JE?

This page is intended to help students prepare for the test. It is a brief checklist of the major points covered in the chapter. The students should be reminded that this is only a checklist and does not necessarily include everything that will appear on the test.

Teaching Suggestion

8–10 You might have students use their answers to these activities to write and act out a brief skit about a friend telling a joke to another friend.

♜ Game

TIC-TAC-TOE Write the questions from **Que sais-je?** on index cards and put them in a bag. If a question has sub-questions, write each one on a separate card. Then, draw a tic-tac-toe grid on the board. In each of the squares, write a number to represent the number of questions that must be answered in order to put a marker in that square. In the top row, write the following numbers: 2 in the first square, 1 in the second, and 2 in the third. In the middle row, write 1, 3, and 1. In the bottom row, write 2, 1, and 2. Then, form two teams and have the first team select a square. Draw the appropriate number of cards from the bag and ask the team the questions. Team members may confer with one another, but only one member may answer. If the team answers all questions correctly, place an X or an O in the square. Then, have the next team take a turn. If the same question is drawn a second time, players must use a different expression to answer it.

Can you use what you've learned in this chapter?

Can you brag? p. 251

1 What would you say to brag in the following situations? *Possible answers:*
  1. You finish an assignment before everyone else. C'était fastoche, ça!
  2. You win a race. C'est moi qui cours le plus vite.
  3. You get the highest grade on a test.
     C'est pas pour me vanter, mais c'est moi le/la meilleur(e).

Can you flatter? p. 251

2 What would you say to flatter a person if he/she were . . . *Possible answers:*
  1. really athletic? Tu es fortiche. Tu es vraiment le/la meilleur(e).
  2. a good student? Tu es calé(e).
  3. very artistic? Alors, là, tu m'épates! Tu es l'artiste le/la plus doué(e) que je connaisse.

3 What would you say to tease the people in these situations?
  1. Your friend seems to have a crush on someone. Tu es amoureux(-euse) ou quoi?

Can you tease? p. 254

  2. Your brother gets dressed to go out on a date and none of his clothes match. Non mais, tu t'es pas regardé(e)!
  3. You're playing tennis with a friend who keeps missing the ball. Réveille-toi un peu!

4 How would you respond to the teasing in number 3? *Possible answers:*
1. Oh, ça va, hein! 2. Lâche-moi, tu veux? 3. Ça peut arriver à tout le monde.

Can you break some news? p. 259

5 What would you say to tell a friend what happened to these people? *Possible answers:*

Ils se sont fiancés.

Elle a déménagé.

Il s'est cassé les (deux) jambes.

Can you show interest? p. 259

6 How would you show interest in something a friend was saying? Ah oui? Qui t'a dit ça? Raconte! Et alors?

Can you express disbelief? p. 259

7 What would you say if you didn't believe what your friend was telling you? Mon œil! Ça m'étonnerait. N'importe quoi!

Can you tell a joke? p. 261

8 How would you introduce a joke? J'en connais une bonne. Est-ce que tu connais l'histoire de... ?

9 What would you say if you heard a joke you liked? Elle est bien bonne!

10 What would you say if the joke were bad? Elle est nulle, ta blague!

PREMIERE ETAPE

Bragging

C'est fastoche, ça!   *That's so easy!*
C'est pas pour me vanter, mais moi...   *I'm not trying to brag, but . . .*
Oh, j'en ai vu d'autres.   *I've done bigger and better things.*
C'est moi le/la meilleur(e).   *I'm the best.*
C'est moi qui... le mieux.   *I . . . the best.*

Flattering

Tu es fortiche/calé(e).   *You're really strong/good at that.*
Alors là, tu m'épates!   *I'm really impressed!*
Tu en as, du courage.   *You've really got courage.*
Tu es vraiment le/la meilleur(e).   *You're really the best.*

Tu es le/la... le/la plus... que je connaisse.   *You're the . . . -est . . . I know.*

Sea life

une algue   *seaweed*
un coquillage   *a shell*
du corail   *coral*
un crabe   *a crab*
une crevette   *a shrimp*
un espadon   *a swordfish*
une étoile de mer   *a starfish*
un hippocampe   *a seahorse*
un homard   *a lobster*
une méduse   *a jellyfish*
une pieuvre   *an octopus*
un requin   *a shark*
un rocher   *rock*
une tortue   *a turtle*

Teasing

Tu es amoureux (-euse) ou quoi?   *Are you in love or what?*
Non mais, tu t'es pas regardé(e)!   *If you could see how you look!*
Réveille-toi un peu!   *Get with it!*
Tu en rates pas une, toi!   *You're batting a thousand!*
Arrête de délirer!   *Stop being so silly!*
Lâche-moi, tu veux?   *Will you give me a break?*
Je t'ai pas demandé ton avis.   *I didn't ask your opinion.*
Oh, ça va, hein!   *Oh, give me a break!*
Qu'est-ce que tu en sais?   *What do you know about it?*
Ben, ça peut arriver à tout le monde.   *It could happen to anyone.*
Et toi, arrête de m'embêter!   *Stop bothering me!*

DEUXIEME ETAPE

Everyday life

s'acheter quelque chose   *to buy oneself something*
avoir des boutons   *to have acne*
se bagarrer   *to fight*
se casser le/la...   *to break one's . . .*
déménager   *to move*
se faire enlever ses bagues   *to get one's braces off*
se faire mal à...   *to hurt one's . . .*
se faire percer les oreilles   *to get one's ears pierced*
se fiancer   *to get engaged*
perdre du poids   *to lose weight*
planter la voiture   *to wreck the car*
prendre des leçons de conduite   *to take driving lessons*

Breaking some news

Tu savais que... ?   *Did you know that . . . ?*
Je ne t'ai pas dit?   *Didn't I tell you?*

Tu connais la dernière?   *Have you heard the latest?*
J'ai entendu dire que...   *I've heard that . . .*
Figure-toi que...   *Can you imagine that . . .*
Si tu avais vu... !   *If you could have seen . . . !*

Showing interest

Oh là là!   *Oh wow!*
Qui t'a dit ça?   *Who told you that?*
Raconte!   *Tell me!*
Et alors?   *And then?*

Expressing disbelief

Mon œil!   *No way!*
Ça m'étonnerait.   *That would surprise me.*
Je n'en reviens pas.   *I don't believe it.*
N'importe quoi!   *Yeah, right!*

Telling jokes

J'en connais une bonne.   *I've got a good one.*
Est-ce que tu connais l'histoire de... ?   *Do you know the one about . . . ?*
Quelle est la différence entre... et... ?   *What's the difference between . . . and . . . ?*
Quel est le point commun entre... ?   *What do . . . and . . . have in common?*
C'est l'histoire d'un mec qui...   *It's about a guy who . . .*
... et alors, il dit que...   *So he says . . .*
... et l'autre lui répond...   *. . . and then the other one answers . . .*
Elle est bien bonne!   *That's a good one!*
Elle est nulle, ta blague!   *What a stupid joke!*

♜ Game

DES BLANCS   To prepare for the game, form five teams and give a transparency to each one. Assign each team five vocabulary expressions. Teams work together to write a logical paragraph or dialogue, using the expressions. Then, they copy it onto a transparency, leaving blank spaces where the vocabulary items should be. Collect the transparencies. To play the game, project the transparencies one at a time for thirty seconds each. Teams will write down the words they would use to fill in the blanks. They should sit out the round involving the transparency they created, so that each team will have four sets of answers. After you have shown the last transparency, have teams read their answers aloud and either verify or correct them. The team that filled in the most blanks correctly wins.

♜ Game

CERCLE DE MOTS   Make two identical sets of flashcards with French words or expressions on one side and their English equivalents on the other. To play the game, form two teams and have each one sit in a circle. Designate one student on each team to be the captain and one to be the judge. Then, distribute one card to each member of both teams. The captain begins by showing the English equivalent on his or her card to the teammate on his or her left. That student responds by giving the French expression. When the judge has verified the response, that student shows the English side of his or her own card to the student on his or her left. When all team members have had a turn, the captain stands up. The first team whose captain stands up wins.

CHAPTER 10 ASSESSMENT

CHAPTER TEST
- *Chapter Teaching Resources, Book 3,* pp. 81–86
- *Assessment Guide,* Speaking Test, p. 32
- *Assessment Items, Audiocassette 8B Audio CD 10*

TEST GENERATOR, CHAPTER 10

ALTERNATIVE ASSESSMENT

Performance Assessment
You might want to use the **Jeu de rôle** (p. 267) as a cumulative performance assessment activity.

📁 Portfolio Assessment

- **Written:** Activity 32, *Pupil's Edition,* p. 260
  Assessment Guide, p. 23
- **Oral: Mise en pratique,** Activity 4, *Pupil's Edition,* p. 267
  Assessment Guide, p. 23

Chapitre 11 : Laissez les bons temps rouler!
Chapter Overview

Mise en train pp. 272–274	L'arrivée à Lafayette		Note Culturelle, Festivals in Louisiana, p. 274	

	FUNCTIONS	GRAMMAR	CULTURE	RE-ENTRY
Première étape pp. 275–279	• Asking for confirmation, p. 276 • Asking for and giving opinions, p. 278 • Agreeing and disagreeing, p. 278		• **Rencontre Culturelle,** Overview of Louisiana, p. 275 • **Note Culturelle,** Music in Louisiana, p. 277 • Realia: Letters from teenagers about music, p. 279	• Renewing old acquaintances • Types of music • Agreeing and disagreeing • Asking for and giving opinions

Remise en train pp. 280–281	Un festival cajun			

	FUNCTIONS	GRAMMAR	CULTURE	RE-ENTRY
Deuxième étape pp. 282–287	• Asking for explanations, p. 283 • Making observations, p. 286 • Giving impressions, p. 286	The relative pronouns **ce qui** and **ce que**, p. 286	**Panorama Culturel,** Parties and celebrations, p. 282	• Food vocabulary • Emphasizing likes • Making suggestions • Expressing opinions

Lisons! pp. 288–290	**Cajun songs, poems, and recipes** **Reading Strategy:** Understanding a dialect

Ecrivons! p. 291	**Un poète en herbe** **Writing Strategy:** Using poetic devices

Review pp. 292–295	• Mise en pratique, pp. 292–293 • Que sais-je? p. 294 • Vocabulaire, p. 295

Assessment Options	**Etape Quizzes**
	• *Chapter Teaching Resources, Book 3*
	  Première étape, Quiz 11-1, pp. 131–132
	  Deuxième étape, Quiz 11-2, pp. 133–134
	• *Assessment Items, Audiocassette 8B/Audio CD 11*
		Chapter Test
		• *Chapter Teaching Resources, Book 3,* pp. 135–140
		• *Assessment Guide, Speaking Test, p. 33*
		• *Assessment Items, Audiocassette 8B/Audio CD 11*
		
		Test Generator, Chapter 11

RESOURCES: Print	RESOURCES: Audiovisual
Practice and Activity Book, p. 121	Textbook Audiocassette 6A/Audio CD 11
Practice and Activity Book, pp. 122–125 Grammar and Vocabulary Worksheets, pp. 96–97 Chapter Teaching Resources, Book 3 • Communicative Activity 11-1, pp. 112–113 • Teaching Transparency Master 11-1, pp. 116, 118 • Additional Listening Activities 11-1, 11-2, 11-3, pp. 119–120 • Realia 11-1, pp. 123, 125 • Situation Cards 11-1, pp. 126–127 • Student Response Forms, pp. 128–130 • Quiz 11-1, pp. 131–132	Textbook Audiocassette 6A/Audio CD 6 Teaching Transparency 11-1 Additional Listening Activities, Audiocassette 10B/Audio CD 11 Assessment Items, Audiocassette 8B/Audio CD 11
Practice and Activity Book, p. 126	Textbook Audiocassette 6A/Audio CD 11
Practice and Activity Book, pp. 127–130 Grammar and Vocabulary Worksheets, pp. 98–101 Chapter Teaching Resources, Book 3 • Communicative Activity 11-2, pp. 114–115 • Teaching Transparency Master 11-2, pp. 117, 118 • Additional Listening Activities 11-4, 11-5, 11-6, pp. 120–121 • Realia 11-2, pp. 124, 125 • Situation Cards 11-2, 11-3, pp. 126–127 • Student Response Forms, pp. 128–130 • Quiz 11-2, pp. 133–134 Video Guide	Textbook Audiocassette 6A/Audio CD 11 Teaching Transparency 11-2 Additional Listening Activities, Audiocassette 10B/Audio CD 11 Assessment Items, Audiocassette 8B/Audio CD 11 Video Program, Videocassette 2
Practice and Activity Book, p. 131	
Video Guide	Video Program, Videocassette 2

Alternative Assessment
- Performance Assessment
  Première étape, p. 279
  Deuxième étape, p. 287
- Portfolio Assessment
  Written: **Mise en pratique,** Activity 5, *Pupil's Edition,* p. 293
   Assessment Guide, p. 24
  Oral: Activity 34, *Pupil's Edition,* p. 287
   Assessment Guide, p. 24

Chapitre 11 : Laissez les bons temps rouler!
Textbook Listening Activities Scripts

For Student Response Forms, see *Chapter Teaching Resources, Book 3*, pp. 128–130.

Première étape

6 Ecoute! p. 276

1. — Tiens, Robert! Dis donc, tu n'as pas changé, toi!
 — Toi non plus! C'est dommage qu'on ne se voit pas plus souvent.
 — Oui, c'est vrai. Pourquoi tu ne me donnes pas ton numéro de téléphone? On pourrait peut-être sortir un de ces soirs.
 — Bonne idée.
2. — Emilie? C'est bien toi? Je ne pensais pas que tu pourrais venir, tu habites si loin. Tu vis toujours à Denver, non?
 — Oui, mais je suis en vacances dans la région en ce moment.
3. — Carole? Non, elle n'est pas venue.
 — Pourquoi?
 — Ben, tu sais, avec son travail, elle est toujours à l'étranger. Je crois qu'elle est en Europe en ce moment d'ailleurs.
 — Ah oui, c'est vrai. Elle est bien journaliste.
4. — Je n'ai jamais revu Simon. Et toi?
 — Moi non plus. Tu sais, on n'était pas très amis tous les deux.
5. — Et qu'est-ce qu'il devient, le frère de Michelle?
 — Si je me souviens bien, il est dans l'armée. Je crois qu'il habite à Austin.
6. — Dis, Laure, tu as vu... zut, comment elle s'appelle, cette fille, déjà?
 — Quelle fille?
 — Tu sais bien, celle qui sortait avec David.
 — Ah! Tu veux dire Jeanne.
7. — Michel, quelle bonne surprise! Je ne m'attendais pas à te voir ici.
 — Je suis venu accompagner ma sœur. Tu sais à quel point elle est timide, elle ne voulait pas venir toute seule.
 — Ta sœur, elle s'appelle Marianne, c'est ça?
 — Oui.
8. — Je me souviens du jour où Monsieur Wilson t'avait envoyée chez le proviseur. Qu'est-ce qu'il était en colère!
 — Tu l'as dit. Remarque, j'étais vraiment insupportable à cette époque.
9. — En tous cas, je te serai toujours reconnaissante de m'avoir aidée avec mes maths, cette année-là. Sans toi, j'aurais jamais réussi.
 — Oh, tu sais, c'était pas grand-chose. Et puis, tu as toujours été tellement sympa avec moi.
10. — Je me demande bien ce que fait Joël aujourd'hui. Après son déménagement, je n'ai jamais su ce qu'il était devenu.
 — Si je ne me trompe pas, il est avocat à Washington. Mais demande à Daniel, ils sont toujours très amis.

Answers to Activity 6
2, 3, 5, 6, 7, 10

9 Ecoute! p. 277

a. 1. [Jazz Music]
 2. [Rock Music]
 3. [Country Music]
 4. [Rap Music]
 5. [Cajun Music]
 6. [Classical Music]
 7. [Blues Music]
 8. [Dance Music]

b. 1. [A Piano]
 2. [A Saxophone]
 3. [A Flute]
 4. [A Bass Guitar]
 5. [Drums]
 6. [A Violin]
 7. [An Accordion]
 8. [A Synthesizer]
 9. [A Trumpet]
 10. [A Drum Machine]

Answers to Activity 9

a. 1. jazz 3. country 5. musique cajun 7. blues
 2. rock 4. rap 6. musique classique 8. dance

b. 1. un piano 5. une batterie 9. une trompette
 2. un saxophone 6. un violon 10. une boîte à rythmes
 3. une flûte 7. un accordéon
 4. une basse 8. un synthétiseur

13 Ecoute! p. 278

ANNE Qu'est-ce que tu penses de ce CD de Miles Davis?
SIMON Je le trouve hyper-cool, moi. Tu sais bien que j'adore le jazz.
ANNE Moi aussi, j'adore. Et le blues, ça te branche?
SIMON Oui, ça m'éclate.
ANNE Quel artiste de blues est-ce que tu préfères?
SIMON Ben moi, j'aime bien Patricia Kaas. Qu'est-ce que tu en penses, toi?
ANNE Ben, moi, je préfère Billie Holiday.
SIMON Tu as entendu parler des Pixies?
ANNE Euh, c'est un groupe de rock, non?
SIMON Oui, c'est ça.
ANNE Ça te branche, le rock?
SIMON Oui, beaucoup. Et toi, ça te plaît?
ANNE Euh, pas tellement. Moi, je préfère la dance.
SIMON Oh. C'est nul, ça.
ANNE Mais non, pas du tout. Moi, j'aime bien ce genre de rythmes.
SIMON Chacun ses goûts.
ANNE Oui, c'est vrai. Il y a des gens qui adorent le rap, par exemple.
SIMON Ben moi, j'aime beaucoup. C'est vachement branché.
ANNE Hmm. Moi, je trouve que c'est pas mal, mais...
SIMON Je suppose que tu préfères le country?
ANNE Ben oui. C'est très bien, le country.
SIMON Tu délires ou quoi? C'est nul comme musique!
ANNE Mais non, tu as tort! C'est très chouette!
SIMON N'importe quoi!

Answers to Activity 13

Simon aime:	Anne est d'accord?
le jazz	oui
le blues	oui
le rock	non
le rap	oui, mais elle préfère le country

*D*euxième étape

23 Ecoute! p. 283

1. — Tu vois le tee-shirt là-bas?
   — Lequel?
   — Celui avec «J'aime la Nouvelle-Orléans» écrit dessus.
   — Oui.
   — Il est chouette, non?

2. — Hmm. C'est très bon. Comment est-ce qu'on appelle ça?
   — Ça, c'est du boudin. Tu aimes ça, vraiment?
   — Oui, c'est délicieux.

3. — Qu'est-ce que ça veut dire, Atchafalaya?
   — Oh, c'est le nom d'un marais très connu ici.

4. — Bon. Ben, à quelle heure est-ce qu'on se donne rendez-vous?
   — A huit heures? Ça te va?
   — Oui, ça me va.

5. — Tu ne sais pas où on vend des pâtisseries?
   — Si. Je connais une excellente pâtisserie qui s'appelle Poupart.

6. — Qu'est-ce que c'est, ça, là-bas?
   — Oh, ça, c'est le musée du jazz. Tu veux le visiter?
   — Oui, bonne idée!

7. — Comment est-ce qu'on fait les bananes Foster?
   — On fait sauter les bananes dans du beurre et puis on les flambe.

8. — D'où vient le nom Nouvelle-Orléans?
   — Ça vient du roi Louis XIV. C'était le roi de France au moment où les Français sont arrivés ici.

9. — Où est-ce que tu as dormi?
   — Dans un Bed & Breakfast installé sur une ancienne plantation.
   — C'était cher?
   — Oui, assez cher.

10. — Comment est-ce qu'on dit *doughnut* en français?
    — Euh... «beignet», je crois.

11. — Qu'est-ce qu'on va faire aujourd'hui?
    — On va faire une promenade dans les bayous.
    — Cool! On va voir des alligators?
    — Peut-être.

12. — Qu'est-ce qu'il y a dans le gombo?
    — Ça dépend. Il y a des okras et du riz, et puis il peut y avoir des crevettes et du crabe ou même du poulet.

Answers to Activity 23
2, 3, 6, 7, 8, 10, 12

26 Ecoute! p. 285

1. SIMON Qu'est-ce que tu vas prendre, toi?
   ANNE Oh, je ne sais pas. J'hésite. Et toi?

SIMON Ben, moi, je vais essayer les crevettes frites. C'est mon plat préféré et on m'a dit qu'elles sont excellentes ici.

2. SIMON Hmm. Ça a l'air bon. Qu'est-ce que c'est?
   ANNE C'est du poisson farci au crabe.
   SIMON Qu'est-ce que tu en penses, toi?
   ANNE C'est délicieux. Je te le recommande.

3. SIMON Dis, c'est bien un sandwich, ça?
   ANNE Oui.
   SIMON Ben, qu'est-ce qu'il y a dedans?
   ANNE Il peut y avoir des écrevisses, des huîtres ou de la viande. Là, tu vois? Celui-là est aux huîtres.
   SIMON Ça a l'air bon.
   ANNE Oui, tu devrais en goûter un.

4. SIMON Qu'est-ce que c'est, les huîtres Rockefeller, déjà?
   ANNE C'est un hors-d'œuvre aux huîtres et aux épinards.
   SIMON Tu as bien dit que c'était assez salé, non?
   ANNE Ah non. Pas du tout. C'est pas très salé.

5. SIMON C'est bien un dessert, ça?
   ANNE Oui.
   SIMON Qu'est-ce qu'il y a dedans?
   ANNE Il y a du pain, du lait, de la crème et des raisins secs.
   SIMON Je vais en prendre.

6. SIMON Comment est-ce qu'on fait le gombo?
   ANNE Tu veux en faire chez toi?
   SIMON Oui, j'adore.
   ANNE Bon. C'est pas trop compliqué. Il faut des okras, du riz, des crevettes, du crabe et quelques épices. Je te donnerai la recette, si tu veux.

7. ANNE Tu devrais goûter ça.
   SIMON C'est bon?
   ANNE Oui. C'est excellent. C'est une de nos spécialités. Tu sais, chez nous, les crustacés sont formidables.
   SIMON D'accord. Bon. Je vais prendre les écrevisses à l'étouffée.

8. SIMON Comment on appelle ça, déjà?
   ANNE Quoi?
   SIMON Ce plat-là, avec du riz.
   ANNE Lequel? Celui avec du poulet, du porc et des saucisses?
   SIMON Oui, celui-là.
   ANNE On appelle ça du «jambalaya».

Answers to Activity 26
1. h 2. d 3. g 4. a 5. c 6. b 7. f 8. e

30 Ecoute! p. 286

1. ELISE Je suis contente d'être venue faire un tour dans ce marché.
   PAUL Tu vois, je t'avais bien dit que ça te plairait.
   ELISE Oui. Ce qui est vraiment intéressant, c'est de voir toutes ces épices qu'on n'a pas en France.

2. PAUL Dis Elise, tu voudrais faire un pique-nique demain?
   ELISE Bien sûr. Où ça?
   PAUL Au parc Audubon. Voyons, qu'est-ce que tu voudrais manger?
   ELISE Pourquoi pas des po-boys?
   PAUL Bonne idée.

3. ELISE   Ce que j'adore ici, c'est l'ambiance. Les gens sont vraiment très accueillants et ils adorent faire la fête.

   PAUL   Tu vois, je t'avais bien dit que la Louisiane était l'endroit idéal pour passer tes vacances.

4. ELISE   Tiens! Regarde un peu. Elle a l'air d'être vraiment vieille, cette maison-là.

   PAUL   Mais bien sûr! C'est une maison ante-bellum. Tu veux en faire la visite?

   ELISE   Oui, pourquoi pas.

5. PAUL   Allez, dépêche-toi! On risque d'être en retard et de rater le début du concert.

   ELISE   Mais on a largement le temps.

   PAUL   Non. Il est déjà huit heures.

   ELISE   Oh, c'est pas vrai! Zut alors!

6. ELISE   Comment est-ce qu'il s'appelle, ce musée, déjà?

   PAUL   Le musée Conti.

   ELISE   C'est la première fois que je visite un musée de cire.

   PAUL   Qu'est-ce que tu en dis?

   ELISE   Ben, les visages sont vraiment bien faits. On dirait que les personnages sont vivants!

7. ELISE   Qu'est-ce que c'est, ces bonbons-là?

   PAUL   Ce sont des pralines. Tu veux goûter? C'est très bon. Tiens.

   ELISE   Mmm, j'adore.

   PAUL   Oui. Moi aussi.

8. ELISE   C'est dingue, les parades que vous avez ici, en Louisiane.

   PAUL   Tu trouves?

   ELISE   Oui. Ce qui saute aux yeux, c'est les couleurs des costumes et des chars.

   PAUL   Oui, c'est délirant.

   ELISE   Et les gens ont l'air de bien s'amuser. C'est fou!

9. PAUL   Je parie que cet alligator viendra si je lui tends mon sandwich.

   ELISE   Attention! Tu ne vois pas que c'est dangereux?

   PAUL   Tu crois que j'ai peur? J'en ai vu d'autres, moi.

   ELISE   Oh, arrête de délirer.

10. ELISE   J'ai l'impression que les bayous sont très sombres.

   PAUL   Euh, oui, on pourrait même dire qu'ils sont mystérieux.

   ELISE   Mais ce que je trouve super, c'est la faune. Comment est-ce qu'on appelle cet oiseau là-bas?

   PAUL   Ah, ça, c'est un oiseau typique de chez nous. C'est un ibis.

Answers to Activity 30
1, 3, 4, 6, 8, 10

*M*ise en pratique

2 p. 293

NADINE   Dis donc, tu ne voudrais pas aller au Village Acadien?

MATHIEU   Ben, je ne sais pas. Qu'est-ce que c'est?

NADINE   C'est un musée en plein air où on peut voir comment vivaient les premiers Cajuns.

MATHIEU   Bof, ça ne me branche pas tellement.

NADINE   Regarde la brochure. Ce qui est intéressant, c'est les costumes. C'est impressionnant.

MATHIEU   Je m'en fiche, moi. Le passé, ça m'ennuie.

NADINE   Je suppose que tu préfères faire le tour des marais, pour voir des alligators?

MATHIEU   Et pourquoi pas?

NADINE   Ça, ça ne me plaît pas du tout. Ça n'a aucun intérêt.

MATHIEU   Tu rigoles? Ce serait dingue!

NADINE   Il y aussi le chêne d'Evangéline.

MATHIEU   C'est bien l'arbre mentionné dans le poème de Longfellow?

NADINE   Ouais.

MATHIEU   Alors, si on y va aujourd'hui, on va dans les marais demain, d'accord?

NADINE   Bon, d'accord.

MATHIEU   Alors, comment tu trouves ça?

NADINE   C'est délicieux.

MATHIEU   Comment est-ce qu'on appelle ça, déjà?

NADINE   Du gombo.

MATHIEU   Qu'est-ce qu'il y a dedans?

NADINE   Il y a des okras, du riz, des crevettes et du crabe.

MATHIEU   C'est épicé?

NADINE   Oui, assez.

MATHIEU   J'ai l'impression que la cuisine cajun est très épicée. Bon, ben, je peux goûter?

NADINE   Bien sûr. Prends-en.

MATHIEU   Mmm, c'est bon.

Answers to Mise en pratique Activity 2
1. Nadine propose d'aller au Village Acadien.
2. Mathieu demande une explication au sujet du Village Acadien.
3. Mathieu en donne une opinion négative.
4. Nadine fait une observation.
5. Mathieu demande à Nadine son opinion sur ce qu'elle mange.
6. Mathieu demande une explication au sujet du gombo.
7. Mathieu donne son impression sur la cuisine cajun.

Project: La cuisine cajun
(Pair Work Project)

ASSIGNMENT

Students will stage a Cajun cooking show.

MATERIALS

✂ **Students may need**
- Cajun cookbooks
- French-English dictionaries
- Food items
- Cooking utensils
- Camcorder
- Videocassette

SUGGESTED SEQUENCE

1. All students should bring cookbooks with Cajun or creole recipes to class to share. Partners will look through the cookbooks and select a recipe to feature on their show.

2. Next, students write a list of the necessary ingredients in French. They should also write out simple, step-by-step instructions on how to prepare the dish they've selected.

3. Have students write the script for their cooking show. This script should include simplified instructions for preparing the recipe, as well as interesting dialogue about Cajun cuisine. For example, when the "chef" is demonstrating the instruction **Ensuite, il faut ajouter du piment,** the helper might comment **Du piment?! Ça va être épicé!** The chef might respond **Dans la cuisine cajun, tu sais, on utilise toujours beaucoup d'épices. On veut qu'on pleure en la mangeant.** You might show excerpts of television cooking shows to give students ideas about what to say in their dialogue.

4. Partners then plan the staging of their show. They should collect the necessary ingredients and utensils. They might also hold several "dress rehearsals" to practice timing and coordination.

5. Although this project does not require it, students might prepare the recipe at home and distribute samples to the class after their demonstration.

6. Have students perform their shows for the class. Have volunteers videotape their classmates' performances.

GRADING THE PROJECT

You might want to base partners' grades on content, inclusion of appropriate vocabulary, creativity, and presentation.

Suggested Point Distribution (total = 100 points)

Content	25 points
Language/vocabulary use	25 points
Creativity	25 points
Presentation	25 points

♜ Games

DIALOGUES SPONTANES

In this game, students will create dialogues, using vocabulary from this and preceding chapters. This game can be used to review vocabulary and expressions in preparation for the final exam.

Procedure Tell partners they are going to write dialogues, each line of which must begin with a different letter of the alphabet in alphabetical order. That is, the first letter of the first speaker's line must be a, the first letter of the second speaker's line must be b, and so on. A sample dialogue is given below. Players take turns writing lines and may refer to the alphabetical glossary at the back of the book. You might give prizes for using the entire alphabet, for the most interesting yet logical dialogue, and for the dialogue that includes the most chapter vocabulary.

Sample dialogue:
— **Alain, c'était comment, tes vacances en Louisiane?**
— **Ben, super!**
— **C'était intéressant, la musique zydeco?**
— **D'habitude, je n'aime pas trop la musique, mais le zydeco, j'adore!**
— **Et tu as vu des alligators?**
— ...

VINGT QUESTIONS

In this guessing game, students will practice vocabulary for Cajun food.

Procedure This game can be played by the entire class or by small groups. Write the names of Cajun dishes on separate index cards and put them in a bag. If several small groups are playing, each group will need a set of cards and a bag. One player draws a card from the bag. Then, the class tries to determine the dish by asking up to twenty yes-no questions. **(C'est un légume? C'est un plat? C'est épicé?)** If you play this game with small groups, you might set a time limit and see which group can guess the most items in that time.

Variation This game could also focus on different kinds of music and musical instruments. Instead of selecting a vocabulary card, the player assumes the identity of a famous musician or singer. (Harry Connick, Jr.) The player's teammates then ask yes-no questions to determine the type of music and instrument the artist plays. **(Tu fais du rap? Tu joues de la flûte?)**

Chapitre 11

Laissez les bons temps rouler!

pp. 270–295

*U*sing the Chapter Opener

 **Video Program**

Videocassette 2

Before you begin this chapter, you might want to preview the *Video Program* and consult the *Video Guide*. Suggestions for integrating the video into each chapter and activity masters for video selections can be found in the *Video Guide*.

Motivating Activity

Name or bring in pictures of crawfish, gumbo, jambalaya, the French Quarter in New Orleans, red beans and rice, Dixieland jazz, po-boys, and Mardi Gras masks or beads. Ask students what region of the United States they associate with these items. Then, ask them if they've ever been to Louisiana. If so, have volunteers share their experiences.

Teaching Suggestions

- Read the photo captions aloud and ask students what is happening in each photo and how it relates to Louisiana.
- Name various foods from Louisiana (gumbo, po-boys, crawfish), as well as others that aren't (crêpes, pastilla, pâté). Have students tell which ones are typical dishes from Louisiana and what country the other dishes are typical of (France, Morocco).

CHAPITRE

11 Laissez les bons temps rouler!

① On fait la fête en Louisiane!

270 *deux cent soixante-dix*

Language Note

Call students' attention to the title **Laissez les bons temps rouler!** and ask them what the equivalent English expression is. (*Let the good times roll.*)

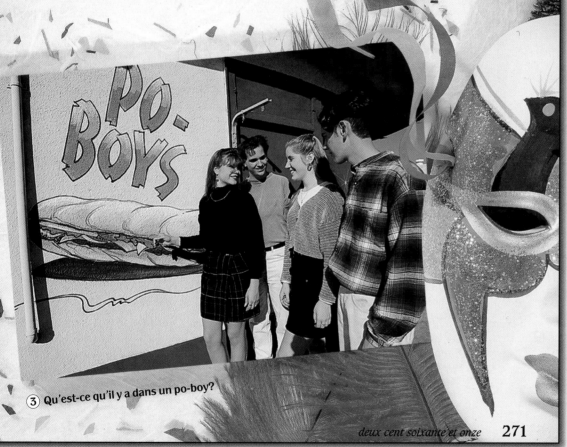

Viens donc en Louisiane, le pays où tous les prétextes sont bons pour faire la fête. Ici, on aime déguster les spécialités gastronomiques locales, danser au rythme de la musique cajun et surtout, on aime s'amuser.

In this chapter you will review and practice

- asking for confirmation; asking for and giving opinions; agreeing and disagreeing
- asking for explanations; making observations; giving impressions

And you will

- listen to teenagers talk about music
- read Cajun poetry, songs, and recipes
- write a poem or a song
- find out about the history of the Cajuns

② Ça te branche, cette musique?

③ Qu'est-ce qu'il y a dans un po-boy?

deux cent soixante et onze 271

Focusing on Outcomes

Have students read the introductory paragraph at the top of this page and the functional outcomes listed below it. Then, call out the numbers of the photos on page 271 and have students tell which function they demonstrate. (Photo 2: *asking for opinions;* Photo 3: *asking for explanations*) Have students list expressions they already know that serve these functions. NOTE: You may want to use the video to support the objectives. The self-check activities in **Que sais-je?** on page 294 help students assess their achievement of the objectives.

Photo Flash!

② In this photo, jazz lovers crowd into the cramped floor space in New Orleans' famous Preservation Hall, where musicians have been playing traditional Dixieland jazz for years.

③ In this photo, a teenager asks her friends about the traditional Louisiana sandwich, the po-boy. This sandwich usually consists of fried seafood stuffed into a length of French-style bread.

Teacher Note

You might tell students that **cadien** is often preferred to **cajun** by speakers of French in Louisiana.

Culture Notes

• You might point out the masks and feathers on this page. For the Mardi Gras celebrations in New Orleans, masked participants often ride colorful floats and toss trinkets, such as beads and plastic doubloons, to onlookers. Costumes for the festivities are often elaborate and always colorful, with beadwork and feathers.

• The Spanish moss at the top of this page is commonly seen dangling from cypress trees in the Atchafalaya (pronounced uh CHA fuh lie uh) swamp. Unlike a parasite, this vegetation is epiphytic: it lives on air and does no damage to the trees to which it clings. The Spanish once called this plant "Frenchman's wig," while the French settlers supposedly called it **barbe espagnole.** In the past, it was used as upholstery stuffing. The plant even filled the cushions of the famous Model T automobile.

Summary

In **L'arrivée à Lafayette,** Simon Laforest arrives in Lafayette from France to visit his American relatives, whom he hasn't seen for a while. M. Laforest asks him about the family in France, and Simon recalls that M. Laforest once gave him a stuffed alligator. M. Laforest recounts some family history about the two Laforest brothers who left Acadia in the eighteenth century, one returning to France and the other going to Louisiana. Anne, Simon's cousin, tells him about the festivals they have in Louisiana, and they discover that they both like jazz. Then, M. Laforest proposes that they go to the Acadian Village, where Simon could learn about the history and traditions of Louisiana.

Motivating Activity

Ask students if they've ever visited relatives they hadn't seen in years. Ask them to imagine what they might talk about in this situation. What do they think an older relative might say to them?

Presentation

Read the introductory paragraph aloud. Then, have students look at the photos on pages 272–273 and tell what they think Simon and his relatives are going to talk about. Write several key words from the **Mise en train** on the board (Paris, Montpellier, grand-mère, alligator, 1982, 1980, Félicie). Tell the students to listen carefully to try to identify each word and its significance. Play the recording, pausing after each scene to have students identify the words. (**Paris, c'est la ville où Simon est né.**)

Mise en train

L'arrivée à Lafayette

Simon Laforest est français. Il vient d'arriver à Lafayette, en Louisiane, pour passer les vacances de Pâques chez ses cousins éloignés qui s'appellent aussi Laforest. Dans la voiture, Simon découvre cette famille et ce pays qu'il ne connaît pas bien.

❶ M. LAFOREST Si je me souviens bien, tu es né à Paris?

SIMON Oui, c'est ça.

M. LAFOREST Et tu habites toujours à Montpellier?

SIMON Oui, oui...

M. LAFOREST Et comment va ta famille?

SIMON Oh, ça va...

M. LAFOREST Et ta grand-mère? Elle est toujours aussi marrante?

SIMON Oh, vous savez, elle, rien ne l'arrête.

M. LAFOREST Je me souviens d'elle, quand elle est venue ici. J'avais onze ans. Je garde un très bon souvenir d'elle. Elle dansait rudement bien sur la musique cajun! Et puis, je l'ai revue quand nous sommes venus chez vous, à Montpellier.

SIMON Vous savez, j'ai toujours le petit alligator en peluche que vous m'aviez offert.

M. LAFOREST Ah, oui?

SIMON C'était en quelle année, déjà?

M. LAFOREST Si je me souviens bien, c'était en 1982. Tu devais avoir deux ou trois ans. Tu es bien né en 1980?

SIMON Oui, c'est ça.

M. LAFOREST Ta sœur, elle, elle n'était pas encore née. Comment elle s'appelle, déjà?

SIMON Félicie.

❷ M. LAFOREST Est-ce que tu connais l'histoire de notre famille?

SIMON Euh, non. Papa me l'a racontée, mais j'ai oublié.

M. LAFOREST Tu vois, au XVIIIème siècle, nos ancêtres ont dû quitter l'Acadie. Un des frères Laforest, Clément, est venu habiter en Louisiane; l'autre, Hubert, est parti en France. Nous, nous sommes les descendants de Clément. Et ta famille descend d'Hubert.

❸ ANNE Oh, papa! On peut parler d'autre chose? Du présent, par exemple? Tu sais, Simon, ici, il y a plein de choses à faire. Il y a des tas de festivals. Tiens, rien que ce mois-ci, il y a le Festival International de Louisiane, ici, à Lafayette, le Festival de l'Ecrevisse à Breaux Bridge et le «Jazz and Heritage Festival» à La Nouvelle-Orléans.

272 *deux cent soixante-douze*   CHAPITRE 11   Laissez les bons temps rouler!

RESOURCES FOR MISE EN TRAIN

Textbook Audiocassette 6A/Audio CD 11
Practice and Activity Book, p. 121

Geography Link

On a world map, have students locate Acadia and trace a path to France and one to Louisiana.

Literature Link

You might read aloud excerpts from Henry Wadsworth Longfellow's poem *Evangeline,* which describes the journey to Louisiana of the Acadians, who were expelled from Canada by the English.

4 ANNE   Tu aimes le jazz, toi?

SIMON   Oui, c'est super!

ANNE   Génial! Moi aussi! Je vis pour le jazz. Mon rêve c'est de devenir musicienne professionnelle de jazz.

SIMON   Tu joues de quoi?

ANNE   De la trompette.

SIMON   Chouette! Moi, je joue de la batterie. Tu aimes le rock aussi?

ANNE   Euh, pas tellement. Je trouve que c'est trop bruyant, trop violent...

SIMON   Tu rigoles! Tu as seize ans et tu n'aimes pas le rock?

ANNE   Ben non. J'aime mieux la dance. Qu'est-ce que tu en penses, toi?

SIMON   Oh, c'est nul!

ANNE   Tu trouves? Bon, on peut toujours écouter du jazz ensemble, puisque tu aimes ça.

SIMON   D'accord.

5 M. LAFOREST   Tu sais, Simon, on a tout un programme pour toi. Pour commencer, on pourrait aller au Village Acadien.

SIMON   Qu'est-ce que c'est?

M. LAFOREST   C'est un musée en plein air qui présente les traditions acadiennes, la manière dont vivaient nos ancêtres, leur histoire...

ANNE   Oui, c'est pas mal. Mais surtout la semaine prochaine, on va aller au Festival International de Louisiane. Tu vas voir, c'est vraiment cool! Il y aura...

M. LAFOREST   Voilà. On est arrivés. Bienvenue chez nous.

MISE EN TRAIN   *deux cent soixante-treize*   **273**

Teaching Suggestion

Assign a number to each photo on this page. Then, have partners choose lines from the conversation to serve as captions for the photos. For example, for the photo at the top right, students might choose **Tu aimes le jazz, toi?** Say the number of a photo and call on a pair of students, who will read their caption aloud.

For Individual Needs

Challenge Have students write new French captions for the photos on pages 272–273.

Kinesthetic Learners Assign partners two lines of the conversation from **L'arrivée à Lafayette (Si je me souviens bien, tu es né à Paris** and **Oui, c'est ça)** and have them rehearse them. Then, have volunteers act out their dialogue and have the class tell which characters they are portraying. Encourage them to use intonation and gestures appropriate to their characters.

Building on Previous Skills

Have students identify the people in the photo on the left side of page 272 and the photos in the center right section of page 273, using expressions they already know for identifying people and family relationships. (**Et voilà, c'est... Ça, c'est... C'est le père de...**)

Community Link

Ask students if their town or state has a museum or organization with programs similar to those at the Acadian Village that promote traditional dances and history. You might have them find out if there is a local heritage society. If so, students might visit it and bring back brochures to share with the class.

Culture Note

The Acadian Village in Lafayette is a replica of a nineteenth-century Cajun town. It is so realistic that it has been used in several movies as an authentic historical set. The home and paraphernalia of the local hero, Dudly LeBlanc, a senator and spokesperson for the Cajun people, are on display there.

History Link

The Acadians were originally French settlers who established agrarian colonies in Nova Scotia in 1604 and 1632. When Britain gained control of this area through the Treaty of Utrecht in 1713, the settlers chose deportation over vowing allegiance to Britain. When the British and the French reconciled in 1763, the Acadians established new colonies in the frontierland of southern Louisiana.

Teaching Suggestion

2 Have students quote from the **Mise en train** to support their choices.

 For Individual Needs

2 Auditory Learners Read these statements aloud and have students tell who might have said them. For further listening practice, create additional statements that Anne, Monsieur Laforest, and Simon might say, read them aloud, and have students identify the speaker.

2 Challenge Have students write additional statements or questions that Anne, Simon, and Monsieur Laforest might say. Have them exchange papers with a partner, identify the speakers, and then return their papers to the writer for correction.

Additional Practice

3 Have students correct the false statements.

 For Individual Needs

4 Kinesthetic Learners Assign each scene from the **Mise en train** to a group of three. Have them read aloud and act out the scene for the class. The other members of the class should listen for the expressions that serve the functions listed in this activity. When they hear one of these expressions used (**Si je me souviens bien...**), have them raise their hands and identify the function (*asking for confirmation*).

Teaching Suggestion

Note Culturelle Have students name what the festivals listed under the **Note Culturelle** celebrate (zydeco, duck, shrimp, Cajun heritage, sugar cane, frogs, folklore, rice).

---

1 Tu as compris?

1. How are Simon, Anne, and M. Laforest related? distant cousins
2. Where does their conversation take place? in the car
3. What does M. Laforest talk about? their families, family history
4. What does Anne talk about? music, festivals
5. What interest do Simon and Anne share? jazz
6. What do M. Laforest and Anne plan to show Simon? Village Acadien, Festival International de Louisiane

2 Qui suis-je?

Qui dirait les phrases suivantes, M. Laforest, Anne ou Simon?

Simon
> Je joue de la batterie parce que j'adore le rock.

Anne
> Je voudrais que Simon s'amuse bien pendant son séjour.

M. Laforest
> Je voudrais raconter à Simon l'histoire de notre famille.

Anne
> Le rock? Ça ne me branche pas tellement. C'est trop bruyant.

Anne
> Je rêve d'aller à La Nouvelle-Orléans et de devenir musicienne de jazz.

Simon
> Qu'est-ce que c'est, le Village Acadien?

3 Vrai ou faux?

1. M. Laforest a visité Montpellier en 1982. vrai
2. La grand-mère de Simon ne sort plus. faux
3. M. Laforest a oublié le nom de la sœur de Simon. vrai
4. La famille de Simon descend de Clément. faux
5. Anne et Simon vont écouter du rock ensemble. faux
6. Le Village Acadien est l'endroit où les musiciens cajuns habitent. faux
7. Il n'y a que deux grands festivals en Louisiane chaque année. faux

4 Cherche les expressions

What expressions do the people in **L'arrivée à Lafayette** use to . . . See answers below.

1. ask for confirmation?
2. give a positive opinion?
3. agree?
4. give a negative opinion?
5. disagree?
6. ask for an explanation?
7. welcome someone?

5 Et maintenant, à toi

Est-ce que tu as déjà voyagé dans un endroit que tu ne connaissais pas? Pourquoi est-ce que tu y es allé(e)? Qu'est-ce que tu y as fait et vu?

NOTE CULTURELLE

Laissez les bons temps rouler! is a popular saying in Louisiana, and with good reason. Louisianans seem to have a talent for having fun, and need no special occasion to indulge their love of food, music, and dance. Any excuse for a party will do, from weekly dances called **fais do-do** (literally, *go night-night*) to festivals that celebrate rice, crawfish, or the sweet potato. Undoubtedly the biggest and most famous celebrations of all are the Mardi Gras events in New Orleans. The Mardi Gras season begins with a series of parties and balls, and culminates in colorful parades and the carnival extravaganza of Mardi Gras night itself, the Tuesday before Lent.

Septembre
Festival du Zydeco du Sud-Ouest de la Louisiane à Plaisance • Festival du Canard à Gueydan, Festival de la Crevette et du Pétrole Louisianais à Morgan City • Festivals Acadiens à Lafayette • Festival et Foire de la canne à sucre à New Iberia • Festival de la "Grenouille" à Rayne

Octobre
Festival du Bétail à Abbeville • Festival de l'Héritage et de la Musique Cajuns à Lafayette • Festival du Coton et "Tournoi de la Ville Platte" • Festival du Folklore Louisianais à Eunice • Festival International du Riz à Crowley • Festival de la "Patate Douce" à Opelousas

---

Culture Note

In Louisiana, festivals abound, occupying almost every weekend of the year. They vary from ethnic celebrations, such as the **Festival International de Louisiane** and the **Festivals Acadiens** in Lafayette, to harvest and food-oriented festivities, such as the Yambilee Yam Festival, the Rice Festival in Crowley, the Breaux Bridge Crawfish Festival, and the World Championship Crawfish Etouffée Cook-off in Eunice.

Answers

4 1. Si je me souviens bien... ; Et tu habites toujours à... ? Elle est toujours... ? Tu es bien né en... ?
2. ... c'est super! Génial! Chouette! ... c'est pas mal.
3. Oui, c'est ça.
4. Je trouve que c'est trop bruyant, trop violent. C'est nul!
5. Tu rigoles! Ben non.
6. Qu'est-ce que c'est?
7. Bienvenue chez nous.

RENCONTRE CULTURELLE

Qu'est-ce que tu sais sur la Louisiane? Pour t'en faire une meilleure idée, regarde les photos.

Les écrevisses sont un plat typique en Louisiane.

Il y a de nombreux bayous en Louisiane.

C'est à La Nouvelle-Orléans que le jazz est né.

Le Café du Monde à La Nouvelle-Orléans

On peut visiter de magnifiques plantations.

Qu'en penses-tu?

1. What impression do these photos give you of Louisiana?
2. Can you identify some different cultural influences illustrated in the photos?

Possible answers: 1. It's a state known for its Cajun cuisine, bayous, jazz music, French influences, and beautiful Southern plantations.
2. Cajun - cuisine, French - cafés

Savais-tu que... ?

Louisiana's French heritage dates from 1682, when millions of acres of land in North America, including what is now Louisiana, were claimed by the explorer Cavelier de La Salle in the name of France. By the early 1700s, Louisiana was a thriving colony and its capital, **La Nouvelle-Orléans,** was an important cultural and political center. Louisiana became part of America when the young United States bought 827,000 square miles of France's North American territory in the Louisiana Purchase of 1803. The French imprint remained strong, however, and it was reinforced by the presence and cultural influence of settlers from the Acadia region of Canada. These people settled in southern Louisiana in large numbers after being driven out of Canada by the British in the 1750s; their descendants are the people we call **Cajuns,** from the word **Acadien.** Cajun French is derived from French forms and idioms from English, Spanish, German, Native-American, and African-American influences.

Culture Notes

• Located in New Orleans' Jackson Square, the Café du Monde is a popular café where residents and tourists come 24 hours a day to relax and enjoy a cup of coffee. It is famous for its coffee and **beignets,** fritters sprinkled with powdered sugar.
• Students might be familiar with the following popular jazz musicians from Louisiana: Louis Armstrong, Harry Connick, Jr., and the Marsalis family.

Language Note

Tell students that Cajun English has its idiomatic expressions, just as Cajun French does. They might hear the expression *to pass a good time* to refer to an enjoyable evening, or *Poo Yi!* to express astonishment.

Motivating Activity

Have students form small groups. Give them two minutes to list words (crawfish), sentences (They celebrate Mardi Gras there), or French expressions (**Laissez les bons temps rouler**) that they associate with Louisiana. After two minutes, have students read their lists aloud.

Presentation

Have students look at the photos and read the captions. Then, ask them what there is to see and do in Louisiana. You might have them rewrite the captions for the photos as if they were making a brochure to encourage tourists to visit Louisiana. For example, instead of **Les écrevisses sont un plat typique en Louisiane,** they might write **Venez en Louisiane! Vous pourrez goûter une spécialité de la région, les écrevisses! C'est délicieux!** Then, have them read the **Savais-tu que... ?**

History Link

Have students research the history of their own state and compare it with Louisiana's history. They might investigate when and by whom their area was first settled, how and when it became part of the United States, and who its key historical figures were.

Language Note

Cajun and *creole* are not interchangeable. *Cajun* refers to descendants of the French settlers (**les Acadiens**) who were driven out of Canada. *Creole,* from the Spanish word **criollo** *(child of the colonies),* has a broad range of meanings. In Louisiana, it often refers to Americans of Caribbean or European descent born in Louisiana.

*J*ump Start!

Have students write answers to the following questions: **Comment tu trouves le jazz? Tu aimes mieux le rock ou le country? Ça te plaît, le rap?**

MOTIVATE

Have volunteers act out a brief skit about running into a relative they haven't seen for years at a family reunion.

TEACH

Presentation

Comment dit-on... ? Create a fictitious family. Write down the names and relationships and what the people are doing now. Before class, have a volunteer acquaint him- or herself with the family. In class, pretend to meet the student after a long separation. Ask about his or her family and have the student answer appropriately. (**Vous habitez toujours à Dallas? Et ta sœur, comment elle s'appelle, déjà?**) Then, confirm students' names and ages, using the new expressions. (**Tu t'appelles Céline, c'est ça? Si je ne me trompe pas, tu as 16 ans.**) Then, have partners confirm each other's name and age, using two of the new expressions.

For Individual Needs

7 Slower Pace Have students number the lines of the conversations in a logical order, rewrite them, read each conversation aloud with their partner, and then tell which one is between two people who haven't seen each other for a long time.

PREMIERE ETAPE

Asking for confirmation; asking for and giving opinions; agreeing and disagreeing

COMMENT DIT-ON... ?
Asking for confirmation

To ask for confirmation:

Vous habitez **toujours** à Bordeaux?
. . . *still* . . .
Vous êtes **bien** trois frères?
Comment elle s'appelle, **déjà?**
. . . *again?*

Ta mère a cinquante ans, **c'est ça?**
Si je me souviens bien, tu es né en 1978. *If I remember correctly, . . .*
Si je ne me trompe pas, tu as 16 ans. *If I'm not mistaken, . . .*

6 Ecoute!

Tu es à la réunion des anciens élèves de ton lycée. Tu entends les conversations suivantes. Dans quelles conversations est-ce que ces gens vérifient des informations? Answers on p. 269C.

7 Méli-mélo!

En employant les phrases ci-dessous, écris les dialogues de deux conversations différentes. Dans quelle conversation est-ce qu'il s'agit de deux personnes qui ne s'étaient pas vues depuis longtemps? la deuxième conversation

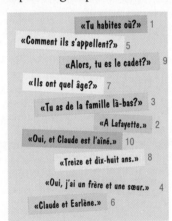
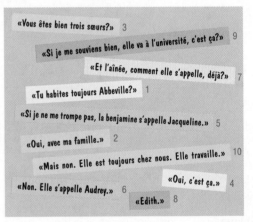

«Tu habites où?» 1
«Comment ils s'appellent?» 5
«Alors, tu es le cadet?» 9
«Ils ont quel âge?» 7
«Tu as de la famille là-bas?» 3
«A Lafayette.» 2
«Oui, et Claude est l'aîné.» 10
«Treize et dix-huit ans.» 8
«Oui, j'ai un frère et une sœur.» 4
«Claude et Earlène.» 6

«Vous êtes bien trois sœurs?» 3
«Si je me souviens bien, elle va à l'université, c'est ça?» 9
«Et l'aînée, comment elle s'appelle, déjà?» 7
«Tu habites toujours Abbeville?» 1
«Si je ne me trompe pas, la benjamine s'appelle Jacqueline.» 5
«Oui, avec ma famille.» 2
«Mais non. Elle est toujours chez nous. Elle travaille.» 10
«Non. Elle s'appelle Audrey.» 6
«Oui, c'est ça.» 4
«Edith.» 8

8 Ça fait longtemps!

A une boum de ton club de français, tu vois un(e) camarade de classe de l'année dernière. Pose-lui des questions pour vérifier ce que tu te rappelles à son sujet. Changez de rôles.

Si tu as oublié renewing old acquaintances va à la page g.

RESOURCES FOR PREMIERE ETAPE

Chapter Teaching Resources, Book 3
- Communicative Activity 11-1, pp. 112–113
- Teaching Transparency Master 11-1, pp. 116, 118
  Teaching Transparency 11-1
- Additional Listening Activities 11-1, 11-2, 11-3, pp. 119–120
  Audiocassette 10B/Audio CD 11
- Realia 11-1, pp. 123, 125
- Situation Cards 11-1, pp. 126–127
- Student Response Forms, pp. 128–130
- Quiz 11-1, pp. 131–132
  Audiocassette 8B/Audio CD 11

ADDITIONAL RESOURCES
Textbook Audiocassette 6A
OR *Audio CD 11*
Practice and Activity Book, pp. 122–125

Vocabulaire

la batterie
la guitare
le rock

l'accordéon (m.)
la musique cajun

le piano
la flûte
le violon
la musique classique

le chant
le blues

le saxophone
la trompette
le jazz

la basse
le country

le micro
la boîte à rythmes
le rap

le synthé
la dance

9 Écoute! Answers on p. 269C.
a. Identifie le genre des extraits de musique suivants.
b. Identifie l'instrument que tu entends.

10 De quoi est-ce qu'on joue?

Regarde ce studio de musique. Qu'est-ce qu'il y a comme instruments? Quels genres de musique est-ce qu'on pourrait produire ici? See answers below.

11 Qu'est-ce qu'on y entend?

A ton avis, quels genres de musique seraient appropriés dans les situations suivantes? See answers below.

> ### Note Culturelle
>
> Music is as much a part of everyday life in Louisiana as eating or sleeping. There are three types of music associated with the state: Cajun, zydeco, and jazz. The French folk music brought to Louisiana by the Acadians has evolved into Cajun music, with its typical sounds of the accordion, the violin, and the metal triangle. African-American musicians created a variation of Cajun music called zydeco by adding the rhythms of the washboard and the spoons. Jazz is often regarded as one of America's great contributions to world culture. Born in New Orleans, it combines elements of traditional African music, spirituals, and brass-band marches.

à une boum
à la mi-temps d'un match
au coin de la rue
dans un restaurant
à un mariage
à un rodéo
dans une discothèque
au bal annuel du lycée

PREMIERE ETAPE

deux cent soixante-dix-sept **277**

Answers

10 *Instruments:* une guitare, une basse, un piano, une batterie, un saxophone, une trompette
Genres de musique: du rock, de la musique classique, du jazz, du country, du blues

11 *Possible answers:* à une boum, au bal annuel du lycée: du rock, du country; à un mariage: de la musique classique; dans un restaurant: du jazz; au coin de la rue: du rap; à la mi-temps d'un match, dans une discothèque: de la dance; à un rodéo: du country

History Link

Note Culturelle Have students research and report on the history of Cajun music, zydeco, or jazz. They might investigate the types of instruments used and find out about famous musicians who are known for each kind of music.

Presentation

Vocabulaire Write each vocabulary item on a large sheet of butcher paper and display the papers around the classroom. Give students a few minutes to write artists and songs under each category. Then, read aloud the names on the lists and have students verify the type of music they play. (**Clint Black, il fait du country?**) You might make mistakes on purpose and have students correct you. (**REM, c'est du blues, c'est ça?**) Next, bring in magazine pictures of musical instruments. Show each one, identify it, and then ask students **Qu'est-ce que je fais comme genre de musique?**

For Individual Needs

Auditory Learners Have students bring in tapes or CDs of their favorite music. Play short excerpts from each one and have students identify the type of music and the instruments they hear. Avoid music selections that might be inappropriate.

Kinesthetic Learners Have small groups play charades. One member tries to convey an instrument or a style of music through mime. The first player to guess correctly takes the next turn.

TPR Bring in or have students bring in CDs or tapes of the various types of music. Hold up each one and have students identify the genre. Then, put the music on a table at the front of the class and have volunteers give instructions to their classmates. (**Stewart, donne un disque de country au prof.**)

Building on Previous Skills

12 In order to review additional previously learned vocabulary, have students play this game, substituting actors for musicians.

Presentation

Comment dit-on... ? Bring in pictures of well-known stars who represent the different types of music. Hold up two of the pictures (the rapper Queen Latifah and the country star George Strait) and create a brief conversation between them.

LATIFAH **Comment tu trouves ça, le rap?**

STRAIT **Je trouve ça nul. Mais le country, c'est cool. Ça te branche, toi?**

LATIFAH **Tu rigoles!**

Repeat the process with the other pictures. Then, hold up a picture (Mozart) and prompt a student to ask the musician for his opinion of any type of music. **(Eh, Mozart, ça te plaît, le rap?)** Then, call on another student to answer as that musician might. **(Tu délires ou quoi?)**

For Individual Needs

13 Slower Pace Have students listen to the recording twice. Have them listen once for the types of music that Simon likes. Then, have them listen again and tell whether Anne agrees.

Portfolio

14 Oral This activity is appropriate for students' oral portfolios. For portfolio information, see *Assessment Guide,* pages 2–13.

---

12   **Devine!**

 Pense à un musicien/une musicienne célèbre. Ensuite, dis aux autres élèves le genre de musique auquel il/elle est associé(e). Les autres élèves te posent des questions pour essayer de deviner qui c'est. Changez de rôles.

COMMENT DIT-ON... ?
Asking for and giving opinions; agreeing and disagreeing

To ask for an opinion:
Comment tu trouves ça, le jazz?
Tu n'aimes pas la dance?
Ça te plaît, le rap?
Qu'est-ce que tu penses du blues?
Ça te branche, le country?

To give a positive opinion:
Je trouve ça hyper-cool.
Si, j'aime beaucoup.
Ça me plaît beaucoup.
Ça m'éclate.
 I'm wild about it.
Je n'écoute que ça.

To agree:
Je suis d'accord avec toi.
Moi aussi, j'aime bien le jazz.
Moi non plus, je n'aime pas la dance.
Ça, c'est sûr.
Tu as raison.

To give a negative opinion:
Je trouve ça nul.
Je n'aime pas du tout.
Ça ne me plaît pas du tout.
Je n'aime pas tellement ça.
Ça ne me branche pas trop.

To disagree:
Pas du tout.
Tu parles!
Tu rigoles!
Tu délires ou quoi?
 Are you crazy or what?
N'importe quoi!

---

13 **Ecoute!**

Ecoute Anne et Simon parler de musique. Quels genres de musique est-ce que Simon aime? Est-ce qu'Anne est d'accord ou pas?
Answers on p. 269C.

14   **Ça te branche?**

Demande à ton/ta camarade ce qu'il/elle aime comme genre de musique. Quels sont ses compositeurs, chanteurs, musiciens ou groupes préférés?

15   **Quel instrument?**

Ton ami(e) voudrait apprendre à jouer d'un instrument mais n'arrive pas à choisir duquel. Demande-lui quel genre de musique il/elle aime. Ensuite, propose-lui quelques instruments. Changez de rôles.

À la française

English speakers must use an object pronoun with verbs such as *like* or *love: Jazz? I love it!* French speakers very often do not, especially if what they're referring to is not a physical object: **Tu aimes le jazz, toi? Moi, j'adore!** or **Le rock? Moi, je n'aime pas trop.**

278 *deux cent soixante-dix-huit*   CHAPITRE 11   Laissez les bons temps rouler!

Teaching Suggestions

14 You might have students stage this activity as an interview, with one student playing the role of the host and the other acting as a guest on a talk show. They might videotape their skits.

15 Before students begin this activity, you might ask those who play instruments to bring them to class and explain how to play them. If students have access to instruments, encourage them to use them in their skits, making sure you are considerate of other classes nearby.

Community Link

You might invite musicians from a community band or orchestra to speak to the class about their personal experiences with music and the musical opportunities that are available in the community.

16 Tu connais?

a. Imagine que tu es français(e). Tu as entendu parler de quelques nouveaux groupes américains. Tu voudrais les connaître. Ecris une lettre à ton/ta correspondant(e) américain(e) pour lui demander qui ils sont et s'il/si elle les aime.

b. Echange ta lettre avec celle de ton/ta camarade. Il/Elle jouera le rôle de ton/ta correspondant(e). Il/Elle va lire ta lettre et y répondre.

17 Quelle musique écoutez-vous?

Lis ces réponses que quelques jeunes francophones ont envoyées à un magazine de jeunes et réponds aux questions suivantes. *See answers below.*

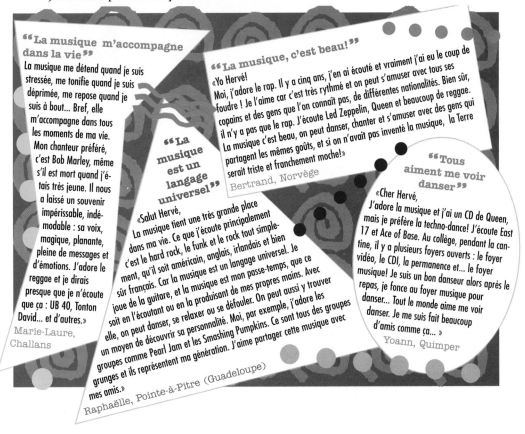

"La musique m'accompagne dans la vie"

La musique me détend quand je suis stressée, me tonifie quand je suis déprimée, me repose quand je suis à bout... Bref, elle m'accompagne dans tous les moments de ma vie. Mon chanteur préféré, c'est Bob Marley, même s'il est mort quand j'étais très jeune. Il nous a laissé un souvenir impérissable, indémodable : sa voix, magique, planante, pleine de messages et d'émotions. J'adore le reggae et je dirais presque que je n'écoute que ça : UB 40, Tonton David... et d'autres.»

Marie-Laure, Challans

"La musique est un langage universel"

«Salut Hervé,
La musique tient une très grande place dans ma vie. Ce que j'écoute principalement c'est le hard rock, le funk et le rock tout simplement, qu'il soit américain, anglais, irlandais et bien sûr français. Car la musique est un langage universel. Je joue de la guitare, et la musique est mon passe-temps, que ce soit en l'écoutant ou en la produisant de mes propres mains. Avec elle, on peut danser, se relaxer ou se défouler. On peut aussi y trouver un moyen de découvrir sa personnalité. Moi, par exemple, j'adore les groupes comme Pearl Jam et les Smashing Pumpkins. Ce sont tous des groupes grunges et ils représentent ma génération. J'aime partager cette musique avec mes amis.»

Raphaëlle, Pointe-à-Pitre (Guadeloupe)

"La musique, c'est beau!"

«Yo Hervé!
Moi, j'adore le rap. Il y a cinq ans, j'en ai écouté et vraiment j'ai eu le coup de foudre ! Je l'aime car c'est très rythmé et on peut s'amuser avec tous ses copains et des gens que l'on connaît pas, de différentes nationalités. Bien sûr, il n'y a pas que le rap. J'écoute Led Zeppelin, Queen et beaucoup de reggae. La musique c'est beau, on peut danser, chanter et s'amuser avec des gens qui partagent les mêmes goûts, et si on n'avait pas inventé la musique, la Terre serait triste et franchement moche!»

Bertrand, Norvège

"Tous aiment me voir danser"

«Cher Hervé,
J'adore la musique et j'ai un CD de Queen, mais je préfère la techno-dance! J'écoute East 17 et Ace of Base. Au collège, pendant la cantine, il y a plusieurs foyers ouverts : le foyer vidéo, le CDI, la permanence et... le foyer musique! Je suis un bon danseur alors après le repas, je fonce au foyer musique pour danser... Tout le monde aime me voir danser. Je me suis fait beaucoup d'amis comme ça... »

Yoann, Quimper

1. What kinds of music do these teenagers like? What are their favorite groups?
2. What are five reasons why music is important to these teenagers?
3. What words do they use to describe the music they like?
4. What are some places where French teenagers can listen to music?
5. Which teenager plays an instrument? Which one likes to dance?

18 Mon journal

Est-ce que la musique est importante pour toi? Quels genres de musique préfères-tu? Quand est-ce que tu en écoutes? Avec qui? Pourquoi?

Answers

17 1. rap, rock, reggae, technopop, hard rock, funk, grunge
Marie-Laure: Bob Marley, UB 40, Tonton David
Raphaëlle: Pearl Jam, Smashing Pumpkins
Bertrand: Led Zeppelin, Queen
Yoann: East 17, Ace of Base

2. *Possible answers:* Music is very rhythmic. It's a way to have fun with friends and strangers. It's relaxing. One can dance to it. One can discover oneself through it.

3. rythmé, beau, magique, planante, pleine de messages et d'émotions, langage universel
4. home, school foyer
5. Raphaëlle; Yoann

Language Note

Students might want to know the following words from the letters: **se détendre** *(to relax);* **se défouler** *(to unwind);* **coup de foudre** *(love at first sight);* **Terre** *(Earth).*

Portfolio

16 Written This activity is appropriate for students' written portfolios. For portfolio information, see *Assessment Guide,* pages 2–13.

Teaching Suggestion

17 Form small groups and assign a letter to each one. Have them write several true-false statements about their letter, exchange papers with another group, write their responses, and return them for correction.

Mon journal

18 For an additional journal entry suggestion, see *Practice and Activity Book,* page 155.

CLOSE

To close this **étape,** have students stand in two lines facing one another. The students in one line should have cards on which a type of music or the name of a musician is written. The students holding the cards ask the students standing opposite them for their opinion of the music or person written on the card. The students facing them respond accordingly. At your signal, one line moves down one student, and the students repeat the process.

ASSESS

Quiz 11-1, *Chapter Teaching Resources, Book 3,* pp. 131–132

Assessment Items, Audiocassette 8B/Audio CD 11

Performance Assessment

Form small groups. Have students take on the identity of various musicians and exchange opinions of various types of music, according to their new identity.

Summary

In **Un festival cajun**, the Laforest family and Simon are at the **Festival International de Louisiane.** Anne and Simon separate from Anne's parents to go hear some Dixieland jazz. Anne proposes that they go to the jazz festival in New Orleans later. Then, they meet her parents at a restaurant. At the restaurant, M. Laforest recommends that Simon try gumbo, and Mme Laforest recommends jambalaya. Later on at the restaurant, a zydeco band begins to play, and Anne's parents get up to dance, much to Anne's embarrassment!

Motivating Activity

Read the following list of activities aloud and have students tell which ones are typical of Louisiana: **écouter du jazz, manger un po-boy, écouter du rap, manger un croissant, manger du jambalaya, danser sur un air de zydeco.**

Presentation

Have students look at the photos on pages 280–281 and try to guess what the Laforest family and Simon did last weekend. Then, tell students to listen for three things that the Laforests do at the festival (**écouter du jazz/du zydéco, manger au restaurant, danser**). Play the recording and ask the questions in Activity 19.

Photo Flash!

The photo in the left corner shows typical houses in the French Quarter of New Orleans. The buildings, usually painted in pastel tones, are accented by black wrought-iron balconies and green bougainvillea plants.

Remise en train

 Un festival cajun

Les Laforest ont emmené Simon au Festival International de Louisiane. Dans la rue, ils s'arrêtent devant un groupe de musique cajun.

ANNE   Dis, Simon, ça te branche vraiment, cette musique?

SIMON   Oh, c'est pas mal. Pourquoi? Qu'est-ce que tu proposes d'autre?

ANNE   Ben, on pourrait aller écouter du jazz.

SIMON   Oui, si tu veux.

ANNE   Papa, maman. Ça vous embête si Simon et moi, on va se balader de notre côté?

M. LAFOREST   Non, pas du tout. On peut se retrouver plus tard au restaurant.

Anne et Simon sont maintenant dans un petit café où un groupe de jazz est en train de jouer.

2 ANNE   Alors, qu'est-ce que tu en penses?

SIMON   C'est vraiment le pied. Ce qui est intéressant, c'est que ce genre de jazz est vraiment différent de ce qu'on entend en France. Comment est-ce qu'on appelle ça, déjà?

ANNE   Dixieland.

SIMON   Ah, oui. C'est ça.

ANNE   Tu sais, si ça te plaît vraiment, on pourrait peut-être aller au festival de jazz à La Nouvelle-Orléans. C'est la semaine prochaine.

SIMON   Ça serait super!

3 ANNE   On pourrait se promener dans le Vieux Carré et aller manger des beignets au Café du Monde. Tu en as entendu parler?

SIMON   Oui, bien sûr.

ANNE   Et je pourrais te montrer un de mes endroits préférés, le musée du jazz... Oh là là! Tu as vu l'heure?

SIMON   Ah, oui. On devait retrouver tes parents à huit heures, non?

ANNE   Oui, au Randol's. On y va?

19   Tu as compris?

1. What event does the Laforest family attend? Festival International de Louisiane
2. Why do Anne and Simon go off on their own? They want to listen to some jazz.
3. What does Anne want to show Simon in New Orleans? the jazz museum
4. Where do they meet M. and Mme Laforest for dinner? What sort of place is it? Randol's; a Cajun restaurant
5. Why is Anne embarrassed? Her parents get up to dance.

20   Mets en ordre

Mets ces phrases en ordre d'après **Un festival cajun.** 2, 4, 5, 3, 1, 6

1. Les Laforest dansent.
2. Simon et Anne écoutent du jazz.
3. Simon hésite entre le gombo et le jambalaya.
4. Anne propose à Simon d'aller visiter La Nouvelle-Orléans.
5. Anne et Simon arrivent au restaurant.
6. Anne a honte.

280   *deux cent quatre vingts*   CHAPITRE 11   Laissez les bons temps rouler!

RESOURCES FOR REMISE EN TRAIN

Textbook Audiocassette 6A/Audio CD 11
Practice and Activity Book, p. 126

Teaching Suggestion

20 Have groups write similar sentences from the **Remise en train** on cards, exchange them with another group, and arrange them in the correct order.

Culture Note

The French Quarter (**le Vieux Carré**) is where francophone residents of the city used to live. The area has been declared a national historic landmark. The former English-speaking area, known as the Garden District, is located a few miles from the center of town. This residential district's stately old homes feature elaborate wrought-iron work.

Au restaurant Randol's. Simon et les Laforest sont en train de regarder la carte.

❹ M. LAFOREST Qu'est-ce que tu veux, Simon?

SIMON Je ne sais vraiment pas quoi prendre. Tout me tente.

M. LAFOREST Pourquoi tu ne prends pas une spécialité d'ici? Du gombo, par exemple?

SIMON Qu'est-ce que c'est?

MME LAFOREST C'est une soupe.

SIMON Qu'est-ce qu'il y a dedans?

MME LAFOREST C'est à base d'okra et de riz avec des crevettes et du crabe. C'est assez épicé.

M. LAFOREST Simon, pourquoi tu n'essaies pas le jambalaya? C'est du riz avec du jambon, des saucisses, des crevettes et du crabe. C'est délicieux.

SIMON Euh, je vous laisse choisir pour moi.

Bienvenue chez Randol's où nous servons les meilleurs fruits de mer du pays cadjin. Restaurant favori des habitants de la région, Randol's, c'est le bon temps à la mode cadjine!

Une abondance de mets cadjins vous attendent chez Randol's, réputé pour ses crabes cuits à la vapeur. La cuisson à la vapeur conserve toute la saveur et nos épices-maison apportent une touche bien cadjine.

Un peu plus tard, toujours au restaurant.

❺ MME LAFOREST Ça y est, le groupe de zydeco commence à jouer! Comment tu trouves ça, Simon?

SIMON J'aime bien, mais je préfère quand même le jazz.

MME LAFOREST Tiens, Boudreaux, si on montrait un peu à Simon comment on danse chez nous?

M. et Mme Laforest se lèvent et vont danser.

❻ ANNE Oh, la honte! C'est pas vrai!

SIMON Ben quoi? Au moins, ils s'amusent! Et puis, ils dansent pas si mal que ça!

ANNE Oh, tu sais, il paraît que c'est de famille.

SIMON Tiens, on dirait que tu as entendu parler de ma grand-mère, toi aussi!

21 Cherche les expressions

What do Simon, Anne, or her parents say to . . . See answers below.

1. ask for an opinion?
2. make a suggestion?
3. ask for permission?
4. make an observation?
5. ask for an explanation?
6. express indecision?
7. give an impression?
8. express embarrassment?

22 Et maintenant, à toi

Est-ce que tu es déjà allé(e) à un festival? C'était comment? Est-ce qu'il y a un festival là où tu habites? C'est un festival de quoi? Qu'est-ce qu'on peut y faire et y manger?

Answers

21 1. ... ça te branche vraiment, cette musique? Alors, qu'est-ce que tu en penses? Comment tu trouves ça?
2. On pourrait... ; ... je pourrais te montrer... ; On y va? Pourquoi tu ne prends pas... ? ... pourquoi tu n'essaies pas... ? ... si on... ?
3. Ça vous embête si... ?
4. ... on dirait que tu as entendu parler de ma grand-mère.
5. Comment est-ce qu'on appelle ça, déjà? Qu'est-ce que c'est? Qu'est-ce qu'il y a dedans?
6. Je ne sais vraiment pas quoi prendre. Tout me tente.
7. Ce qui est intéressant, c'est que...
8. Oh, la honte!

Culture Note

The **Festival International de Louisiane** in April features music, food, crafts, and even films from French-speaking areas, such as Africa, Canada, and the Caribbean.

For Individual Needs

Visual Learners Give transparencies to small groups and assign a scene from **Un festival cajun** to each one. Students should draw an illustration to accompany the scene on the transparency. Then, collect the transparencies and project them. Have the class try to guess which scene of the **Remise en train** each one represents. Then, call on the group that made the transparency to read the corresponding scene aloud.

Teaching Suggestions

• Have volunteers read a quotation from the text (**Oh, la honte! C'est pas vrai!**) and have their classmates try to identify the speaker (**Anne**).
• You might ask students the following questions about the **Remise en train**: Quelle sorte de jazz est-ce qu'on écoute en Louisiane? (Dixieland) Qu'est-ce qu'on peut manger au Café du Monde? (des beignets) Qu'est-ce que c'est, le gombo? (une soupe à base d'okras et de riz avec des crevettes et du crabe) Et le jambalaya? (du riz avec du jambon, des saucisses, des crevettes et du crabe) Quelle sorte de musique est-ce que les Laforest écoutent au restaurant? (zydeco)

For Individual Needs

Slower Pace On a transparency, write the questions listed in the Teaching Suggestion above and number them from 1–5. Write the scrambled answers below, lettered a–e. Have students match the questions with the appropriate responses.

PANORAMA CULTUREL

Sandra • Martinique

Clémentine • France

Jennifer • France

VIDEO PROGRAM
Videocassette 2

Teacher Notes

• See *Video Guide* and *Practice and Activity Book* for activities related to the **Panorama Culturel.**
• Remind students that cultural material may be included in the Chapter Quizzes and Test.
• The interviewees' language represents informal, unre-hearsed speech. Occasionally, edits have been made for clarification.

Motivating Activity

Ask students to name local festivals and celebrations and to explain how they are cele-brated (parades, concerts, dances, parties, fireworks).

Presentation

Read the interview question aloud and have students anti-cipate key words and phrases they might expect to hear in the interviewees' responses. Then, play the video and have students tell what they under-stood. Next, write the **Ques-tions** below on the board or on a transparency, play the video again, and have students try to answer the questions.

Thinking Critically

Comparing and Contrasting
Have small groups discuss how they celebrate national holidays, such as the Fourth of July, Valentine's Day, and so on. Then, have them compare what they do with what the interviewees do.

W e asked people to talk to us about parties and celebrations. Here's what they had to say.

Comment est-ce qu'on fait la fête ici?

«En Martinique, on fait la fête tout le temps, tous les week-ends déjà, c'est la fête. Par contre, on a de très grandes fêtes qui sont d'une part le Carnaval, qui est une très grande fête nationale ici en Martinique et dans la Caraïbe, et c'est au mois de février. On a trois jours de Carnaval pleins, avec des vidés, des gens dans la rue qui dansent, et le soir, avec des soirées extraordinaires, etc. Nous avons aussi la fête de Noël, qui est aussi une fête qui marche bien ici, où il y a pas mal de festivités et d'activités.»

-Sandra

«Alors, la fête... On fait la fête. On trouve toujours quelque chose à fêter, même s'il n'y en a pas vraiment. Donc, on sort le soir ou, des fois les week-ends. On est souvent entre copains, nombreux. Soit on fait des soirées chez d'autres copains, soit on sort dans des discothèques ou bien au restaurant.»

-Clémentine

«Quand je fais la fête, premièrement, j'invite mes amis. Je les appelle par téléphone. On se retrouve chez moi ou chez quelqu'un d'autre. Puis, on achète à manger, des boissons, et on discute toute la soirée. On s'amuse. On danse.»

-Jennifer

Qu'en penses-tu?

1. What occasions do these people celebrate? Carnaval, Christmas, anything at all
2. When you and your friends or family have a party, what do you do? How is this similar to or different from what these people do?

Questions

1. En Martinique, comment s'appelle la grande fête nationale qui a lieu en février? (le Carnaval)
2. Comment est-ce qu'on fête le Carnaval en Martinique? (des gens dansent dans la rue, il y a des soirées extraordinaires)
3. Où est-ce que Clémentine va quand elle sort avec des copains? (dans des dis-cothèques ou au restaurant)
4. Qu'est-ce qu'on fait aux fêtes de Jennifer? (on mange, on discute, on s'amuse, on danse)

DEUXIEME ETAPE

*Asking for explanations; making observations;
giving impressions*

COMMENT DIT-ON... ?

Asking for explanations

To ask for an explanation:

Qu'est-ce que c'est?
Comment est-ce qu'on appelle ça?
Qu'est-ce que ça veut dire, «zydeco»?
Qu'est-ce qu'il y a dans le po-boy?
Comment est-ce qu'on fait le gombo?
D'où vient le mot «cajun»?
Comment on dit «dix» **en anglais?**

23 **Ecoute!**

Ecoute ces personnes parler de leurs séjours en Louisiane. Dans quelles conversations est-ce qu'on demande à quelqu'un d'expliquer quelque chose?
2, 3, 6, 7, 8, 10, 12

A la française

French-speaking people rarely use the passive voice. For expressions such as *French is spoken here, What is that called?* or *How is gumbo made?* use **on** and a verb in the active voice: **On parle français ici, Comment est-ce qu'on appelle ça? Comment est-ce qu'on fait le gombo?**

24 **Qu'est-ce que c'est?**

Trouve les bonnes réponses aux questions de Simon.

1. Qu'est-ce que c'est, le zydeco? b

2. Comment est-ce qu'on appelle ce sandwich? a

3. D'où vient le mot «cajun»? e

4. Qu'est-ce qu'il y a dans le jambalaya? c

5. Qu'est-ce que ça veut dire, «cocodrie»? f

6. Comment on dit «La Nouvelle-Orléans» en anglais?

a. On appelle ça «un po-boy.»

b. C'est un genre de musique.

c. Il y a du riz et du jambon.

d. New Orleans.

e. Ça vient du mot «acadien».

f. Ça veut dire «alligator».

---

*J*ump Start!

Have students write whether they agree or disagree with each of the following statements: **Je trouve le jazz hyper-cool. A mon avis, le rock, c'est nul. Le country, c'est terrible.**

MOTIVATE

Ask students to name food specialties of their state and of other states or regions (New York cheesecake, southern chicken-fried steak, San Francisco sourdough bread). Have them describe each dish as if you were a visiting French person.

TEACH

Presentation

Comment dit-on... ? Point to various objects in the classroom and ask the first two questions. Write the answers to the next five questions in random order on the board (**un genre de musique typique de la Louisiane, des huîtres frites, on y met des okras et du riz et on le fait cuire, du mot «Acadien,»** "ten"). Have students match the questions with their logical responses. Then, ask students the corresponding questions from **Comment dit-on... ?** and have them read aloud the appropriate answer from the board. Then, have partners ask and answer the questions.

Language Note

For more practice with the question **D'où vient le mot... ?**, tell students that the word *zydeco* comes from **les haricots**, in the song entitled *Les haricots sont pas salé. Gumbo* comes from the Kongo or Kimbundu word for peanut, **n-guba.**

RESOURCES FOR DEUXIEME ETAPE

Chapter Teaching Resources, Book 3
• Communicative Activity 11-2, pp. 114–115
• Teaching Transparency Master 11-2, pp. 117, 118
    Teaching Transparency 11-2
• Additional Listening Activities 11-4, 11-5, 11-6, pp. 120–121
    Audiocassette 10B/Audio CD 11
• Realia 11-2, pp. 124, 125
• Situation Cards 11-2, 11-3, pp. 126–127
• Student Response Forms, pp. 128–130
• Quiz 11-2, pp. 133–134
    Audiocassette 8B/Audio CD 11

ADDITIONAL RESOURCES

Textbook Audiocassette 6A
    OR *Audio CD 11*

Practice and Activity Book, pp. 127–130

Video Program, Videocassette 2
Video Guide

For Individual Needs

25 Slower Pace/Visual Learners Before students pair off, have the class explain each sign in French. (Préjean's? C'est un restaurant cajun.) Write their explanations on the board or on a transparency for reference during the activity.

Language Note

25 A bayou is a slow-moving stream which usually runs through marshes and swamps. The word is derived from the Choctaw word **bayuk**.

Teaching Suggestion

25 Once students have completed the activity, write the message from each sign on a transparency. As you show each one, point to a pair of students, who will ask about and explain the meaning of the sign.

Building on Previous Skills

25 Tell partners to imagine that they see these signs during their trip to Louisiana. Have them take turns suggesting the activities advertised on the signs and then finally decide what to do.

Presentation

Vocabulaire Find or draw pictures of the food items. If possible, bring in some of the ingredients as well (spinach, salt, okra, rice, spices, raisins, oysters). Then, put on a chef's hat and apron and stage a Cajun cooking show. Hold up each ingredient or its picture as you mention it. (D'abord, vous mettez des okras et du riz dans une casserole.) Then, tell students you're planning a Cajun meal and have them suggest what to serve.

---

25 Qu'est-ce que ça veut dire?

Tu te promènes dans Lafayette et tu vois des enseignes *(signs)* que tu ne comprends pas. Pose des questions à ton/ta camarade pour qu'il/elle t'explique ce que c'est.

Possible answers:

1. Qu'est-ce que ça veut dire, «two-step»?
2. Qu'est-ce que c'est?
3. Qu'est-ce qu'il y a dans le jambalaya?
4. Qu'est-ce que ça veut dire; «zydeco»?
5. D'où vient le mot «cajun»?
6. Qu'est-ce que c'est, un bayou?

Si tu as oublié foods, va à la page 335.

VOCABULAIRE

La Cuisine Cajun

Le Po-Boy : la spécialité de la Louisiane la plus connue et la moins chère. C'est en fait un sandwich qui peut contenir **du poisson, des écrevisses** (f.) *(crawfish),* **des huîtres** (f.) *(oysters),* **de la viande...** Il constitue un repas à lui tout seul.

Des hors-d'œuvre : des huîtres **cuites** Bienville (**au jambon** et **aux champignons**) ou Rockefeller (**aux épinards**) (m.) *(spinach).* Elles sont plus grosses qu'en France et presque pas **salées** *(salted).*

Des soupes : la grande spécialité régionale, **le gombo,** soupe faite à base **d'okra** (m.) avec **du riz, des crevettes** (f.), **du crabe et des épices** (f.) *(spices).* En hiver, **l'andouille** (f.) *(sausage)* et le **poulet** remplacent souvent les crabes et les crevettes.

Le jambalaya : une autre des grandes spécialités louisianaises, est préparée à partir d'une énorme quantité de riz à laquelle on ajoute du jambon, du poulet, **des saucisses** (f.), **du porc** frais, des crevettes et du crabe.

Les crustacés : la véritable attraction de Louisiane. Les Cajuns connaissent plusieurs recettes pour préparer les crabes, crevettes et écrevisses qui abondent dans les eaux du delta : **en bisque, à la vapeur** *(steamed),* le plus souvent **frits.** La meilleure préparation : **au court-bouillon** *(boiled).* On vous apporte généralement un plateau d'un kilo de ces braves bêtes, **épicées** à souhait.

Des poissons : les eaux des bayous et celles du golfe du Mexique fournissent de nombreuses espèces, dont l'omniprésent catfish que les Louisianais savent préparer de nombreuses façons, **farci au** *(stuffed with)* crabe, par exemple.

Des desserts : les Cajuns sont très amateurs de **pouding au pain,** genre de pain perdu truffé aux **raisins secs.**

Culture Notes

• Cajun and creole cuisine are both popular in Louisiana. Cajun food is typically hearty, country-style fare, prepared with locally available ingredients, such as bay leaves, filé powder (a thickening agent made from ground sassafras leaves), and cayenne pepper. It tends to be spicier than creole cuisine, which originated in New Orleans and features complex recipes that draw on a broad array of spices.

• Additional Cajun dishes are **andouille,** a spicy, smoked sausage stuffed with lean pork or chitterlings; **boudin,** a seasoned rice and pork sausage; **boulette,** a seasoned round meat fritter, similar to a hush puppy; **crawfish étouffée,** peeled crawfish tails smothered in a sauce of pepper, garlic, and onions and thickened with a roux (flour browned in butter or oil) or with butter; and **maque choux,** corn stew.

26 Ecoute!

Ecoute Simon et Anne parler de la cuisine cajun. De quel plat est-ce qu'ils parlent?

1. h **2.** d **3.** g **4.** a **5.** c **6.** b **7.** f **8.** e

a. b. c. d.

e. f. g. h.

27 Ça a l'air bon

Choisis quelques plats du **Vocabulaire** à la page 284. Demande à ton/ta camarade s'il/si elle les a déjà goûtés ou voudrait les goûter. Il/Elle va t'en donner son opinion. Dis-lui si tu es d'accord.

28 Qu'est-ce qu'il y a dedans?

Ton club de français a décidé de faire une fête cajun. Tu vas préparer des plats cajuns avec tes amis. Discutez de ce que vous voudriez cuisiner et de ce que vous devez acheter. Faites une liste des plats et des ingrédients. Joue cette scène avec tes camarades.

29 Moi, je propose...

Tu es en vacances avec un(e) ami(e) en Louisiane et vous voyez ces publicités. Propose à ton ami(e) d'aller dans un de ces endroits. Il/Elle n'est pas d'accord et propose un autre endroit. Vous vous disputez.

POUPART BAKERY, INC.
"La Boulangerie Française de Lafayette"
Petit déjeuner : (Pain Beurre, Croissants, grand choix de patisseries, vrai pain français, baguettes, ficelles...)
Café au lait, expresso, chocolat chaud
Déjeuner : quiches, sandwiches (croissants au jambon ou aux saucisses)
1902 W. Pinhook Rd
Tél : (318) 232-7921

CAJUN BAR-B-QUE
Spécialités de la maison:
Ecrevisses bouillies du Mardi au Samedi
Barbecue le Dimanche
Visa - MC Acceptées
Dwight's
4800 Johnston St.
Tél : (318) 981-1241

LA MAISON DE CAMPAGNE. Lafayette
LIT ET PETIT DÉJEUNER
Maison de style victorien du début du siècle située dans un paisible coin de campagne à 15 minutes de Lafayette.
Petit déjeuner gourmet complet cajun et bonne hospitalité.
Contactez Mr et Mme Mc Lemore pour réservations
825 Kidder Road, Carencro 70520
Tél : (318) 896-6529

Poor Boy's
Riverside Inn
(318) 837-4011
Sert la meilleur cuisine cajun depuis 1932
Crabe Impérial
Homard du Maine
Flétan grillé
Flétan farci
Filet Mignon Riverside
Direction U.S. 90 Est, prenez la route de service, tourner à droite dans Tubing, Lafayette, Louisiana
Les principales cartes de crédit sont acceptées

For Individual Needs

26 Slower Pace Before you play the recording, have students identify each dish in French. Then, play the recording and have students do the activity as directed.

Teaching Suggestions

27 Students might also talk about their own favorite dishes. They should ask their partner if he or she is familiar with the dish, and explain it, if necessary.

28 If the resources are available, have students organize a Cajun and creole food day in class. Some students might investigate the origins of Cajun and creole specialties, while others might find recipes for them in cookbooks and make them for the class to sample. The po-boy sandwich, jambalaya, red beans and rice, and bread pudding are fairly easy to prepare.

Cooperative Learning

28 Have groups plan and hold their Cajun festival. They should decide on the food and the entertainment and choose a date, time, and location. One student is the chef, who makes the grocery list. Another student designs the menu and the program. Finally, all group members prepare a brief skit about what will take place at the festival. At the festival, one student acts as the host and greets the guests, who sit down, taste the food and ask questions about it, compliment the food and the music, and thank the host for the evening.

Teaching Suggestion

29 You might ask students the following questions about the restaurant advertisements: **Quelles sont les spécialités de Dwight's?** (les écrevisses bouillies et le barbecue) **Dans quel établissement est-ce qu'on peut aussi dormir?** (dans la Maison de Campagne) **Où est-ce qu'on peut acheter des pâtisseries françaises?** (à Poupart Bakery, Inc.)

Language Note

Students might want to know that **ficelle** from the Poupart Bakery ad means *a length of French bread,* and that **flétan** in the Riverside Inn ad means *halibut.*

Thinking Critically

Analyzing Ask students if the Poupart Bakery breakfast is typically American or French.

Presentation

Comment dit-on... ? Bring in copies of several works of art by artists with different styles (Matisse, Escher, van Gogh). Make observations about them. (**Ce qui saute aux yeux, c'est les couleurs/les arbres/les oiseaux.**) Then, have students list things they associate with Louisiana (**le zydeco, le Dixieland jazz, les écrevisses**). Write their suggestions on a transparency. Talk about what you like and ask students for their opinions. (**Ce qui me branche vraiment, c'est le zydeco. Et toi, ça te branche?**) Finally, either bring in pictures of people or point to the photos in the **Remise en train** on pages 280–281 and give your impressions of them. (**On dirait qu'on joue souvent de l'accordéon en Louisiane.**) You might also give some obviously erroneous impressions (**Il me semble que les Cajuns n'aiment pas les épices**) and prompt students to respond. (**Vous rigolez ou quoi? Ils adorent les épices!**)

◆ For Individual Needs

30 Challenge Play the recording a second time and have students tell what Elise is commenting on.

Presentation

Grammaire Write several sentence endings on the board or on a transparency. (**... j'aime bien, c'est le gombo; ... m'intéresse, c'est l'histoire des Acadiens.**) Have students complete them, using either **ce qui** or **ce que**.

COMMENT DIT-ON... ?

Making observations; giving impressions

To make an observation:

Ce qui est intéressant/incroyable, c'est les épices.

Ce qui saute aux yeux, c'est les couleurs des costumes.

Ce qui me branche vraiment, c'est le jazz.

Ce que je trouve super, c'est l'architecture coloniale.

Ce que j'adore/j'aime, c'est voir les gens danser.

To give an impression:

On dirait que les Cajuns aiment bien s'amuser.

Il me semble que les bâtiments sont vieux.

J'ai l'impression que le blues est populaire ici.

Ils ont l'air d'aimer danser.

30 Ecoute!

Ecoute Elise parler de son séjour en Louisiane. Dans quelles conversations est-ce qu'elle donne une impression ou fait une observation? 1, 3, 4, 6, 8, 10

*G*rammaire *Relative pronouns*

You've already learned that the pronouns **qui** and **que** join clauses. The words **ce qui** and **ce que** *(what)* can also join clauses.

- **Ce qui** is a subject, and is usually followed directly by a verb.

   Ce qui est incroyable, c'est leurs masques.
   Tu ne comprends pas **ce qui** est important.

- **Ce que** is an object, and it is usually followed directly by a subject.

   Ce que j'adore, c'est le jazz.
   Je ne sais pas **ce qu'**elle fait.

31 Ce qui m'a plu...

Michelle parle du voyage de sa famille en Louisiane. Fais des phrases en employant les mots suivants. See answers below.

| Ce que
Ce qui | était incroyable,
m'a plu,
ma mère a acheté
j'ai trouvé super,
m'a ennuyée,
je ne comprends pas,
mon frère a adoré,
est génial, | c'était les alligators.
c'était la cuisine.
n'était pas très cher.
c'était la musique.
c'était le musée.
c'est pourquoi on porte des masques pendant le Mardi Gras.
c'était de se promener dans le Vieux Carré.
c'est le marché français. |

◆ For Individual Needs

31 Challenge Once students have combined the elements to make complete sentences, have them write a letter that Michelle might have sent to a friend back home.

Possible answers

31 Ce que... ma mère a acheté n'était pas cher/j'ai trouvé super, c'était la musique/je ne comprends pas, c'est pourquoi on porte des masques pendant Mardi Gras/mon frère a adoré, c'était la cuisine. Ce qui... était incroyable, c'était les alligators/m'a plu, c'était de me promener dans le Vieux Carré/m'a ennuyé, c'était le musée/est génial, c'est le marché français.

32 Grosses bises de Louisiane

Marianne est allée en Louisiane pour rendre visite à ses cousins. Elle a écrit cette lettre à sa meilleure amie en France. Complète sa lettre avec **ce qui** ou **ce que**.

Salut Hélène,

Ça va? Moi, ça va très bien. C'est super, la Louisiane! Tu avais raison. Voilà ___ce que___ *j'ai fait pendant les trois premiers jours. Le premier jour, on m'a emmenée à un festival. On a écouté du jazz. C'était super. Tu sais* ___ce que___ *j'ai mangé? Une tarte aux écrevisses.* ___Ce qui___ *m'étonne, c'est que j'ai trouvé ça très bon. Puis, le deuxième jour, on a loué un canoë pour faire un tour du Bassin de l'Atchafalaya. Tu ne devineras jamais* ___ce qui___ *s'est passé. Un alligator s'est approché de nous.* ___Ce que___ *je ne comprends pas, c'est pourquoi le guide l'a encouragé à venir plus près. Il avait l'air d'avoir faim!* ___Ce qui___ *m'a fait peur, c'est qu'il est venu tout près de moi. Mais, évidemment, le guide savait* ___ce qu'___ *il faisait, et l'alligator ne nous a pas attaqués. Puis, le troisième jour, on est allés visiter une plantation.* ___Ce qui___ *était vraiment super, c'était les meubles d'époque, et puis, tu sais* ___ce qu'___ *on a vu dehors? Des champs de cannes à sucre. Demain, on va voir le chêne d'Évangéline. C'est l'arbre du célèbre poème de Longfellow.* ___Ce qui___ *est encore plus intéressant, c'est que c'est un des plus vieux arbres des États-Unis. Bon, je t'écrirai à nouveau la semaine prochaine.*

33 Ce qui saute aux yeux,...

Pendant tes vacances en Louisiane, tu as pris beaucoup de photos. Avant de les envoyer à des amis, écris tes impressions et tes observations au verso *(on the back)*.
See answers below.

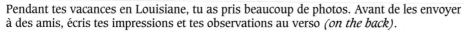

34 Jeu de rôle

You've just returned from your vacation and you show your pictures to a classmate. Act out the scene together.

- Your classmate recognizes what's in the picture.
- You say that he/she is not right.
- He/She asks you to explain what it is.

- He/She makes an observation.
- You give your opinion about it.
- He/She agrees or disagrees.

Possible answers

33 1. Ce qui est incroyable, c'est les alligators.
2. Ce qui est intéressant, c'est les bâtiments.
3. On dirait que les Cajuns aiment bien manger.
4. Ils ont l'air de bien s'amuser pendant Mardi Gras!
5. Ce que je trouve super, c'est l'architecture des plantations.
6. Ce que j'adore, c'est le marché français.

ASSESS

Quiz 11-2, *Chapter Teaching Resources, Book 3,* pp. 133-134

Assessment Items, Audiocassette 8B Audio CD 11

Performance Assessment

Have students perform their skits from Activity 34. You might videotape their performances.

For Individual Needs

32 Challenge Once students have completed the activity, have them write their own letter in which they give their impressions of what they saw in Louisiana.

33 Auditory Learners After students write their captions, have volunteers read one of their captions aloud. Have their classmates try to guess which photo it refers to.

📁 Portfolio

33 Written This activity is appropriate for students' written portfolios. You might also have students bring in real photos they took on a recent vacation, or magazine pictures to represent photos from an imaginary vacation they'd like to take, and give their impressions of those images. For portfolio information, see *Assessment Guide,* pages 2–13.

34 Oral This activity is appropriate for inclusion in students' oral portfolios. You might have them videotape the scene. For portfolio suggestions, see *Assessment Guide,* page 24.

CLOSE

To close this **étape,** have students imagine you have all just returned from a class trip to Louisiana. Start a conversation about the advantages of the visit. Have students make observations about the music, food, and attractions. (**Ce qui me branche vraiment, c'est le zydeco.**) Occasionally, call on students to ask for an explanation of something a student mentions. (**Je ne comprends pas. Charles, demande à Marc d'expliquer ce que c'est que «le zydeco».**)

LISONS!

Freeman's Zydeco

On va aller là-bas
Pour voir Monsieur Zydeco
On va aller là-bas
Chez Freeman Fontenot

Tout le monde dit faudra aller rejoindre
Pour connaître quoi il a fait avec ses mains
Il a bâti eine salle de danse et eine école
Pour tous le voisinage qui est sans nickel

Il avait des richesses de cœur
Il est né pour jouer son vieil accordéon
Il va te donner la chemise de son dos
Eine grande personne, Monsieur Freeman
Fontenot

Chez Denouse McGee

On va aller à Eunice, mais oui, dessous un grand chêne vert
Qu'il a planté lui-même, quand il a trouvé la belle terre
On va aller chez Denouse, eyoù la porte est ouvert
C'est pour voir mon partna, savoir comment il est après faire

On dit «Bonjour» à sa femme, c'est Glad qui va chauffer
Chauffer une gregue de café, goûter et causer en français
Ecouter la belle musique, des chansons qui viennent
d'avant-hier

Ça c'est chez Denouse McGee, 'y a rien que moi je vas faire

Cajun Telephone Stomp

O bébé, j'avais essayé
De causer aujourd'hui.
'Y avait quelque chose qui est
arrivé
Et moi, j'ai commencé d'être
fâché.

Sur le téléphone de l'autre côté,
'Y avait eine 'tite voix mal
enregistrée,
«Après le *beep*,» c'est ça il dit,
«Laisse ton message, 'y a
personne ici.»

Quoi c'est ça, il dit *le beep*?
C'est pas Cadien, ni poli,
S'il n'est pas là, quoi faire sa
voix?
O yé yaille, mon cœur fait mal.

Après dix fois avec cette voix
maudite
C'a commencé de me faire rire,
J'ai oublié à qui je veux parler
Et enfin, j'ai accroché.

Le Chanky-Chank Français

O bébé
Moi, j'amerais ecouter
Ouais, ce soir, s'il vous plait
C'est le chanky-chank français.

Dis à tous tes bons amis
Venez-vous nous rejoindre
Parce qu'on va jamais finir
Ouais, c'est ça moi je veux dire.

L'accordéon et le violon
Font ces tunes toujours ensemble
Pareil comme le vieux temps
'Coute, ça vient eine autre valse
mignonne.

Ca fait la peine d'essayer
De faire danser toute la soirée
C'est rien qui me fait grouiller
Comme le chanky-chank français.

DE BONS CONSEILS

A dialect is a form of a language used in a certain area or by a certain group of people. It may differ from the standard language in grammar, vocabulary, spelling, and pronunciation. Here are a few comprehension strategies that might help you. 1) If you don't recognize the grammatical form of a word, ignore the endings and focus on understanding the root of the word. 2) Look for recurring patterns in unfamiliar grammar and vocabulary and figure them out, using contextual clues. 3) Remember that dialects are often influenced by other languages. Look for words and expressions that are borrowed or translated directly. 4) Be aware that familiar French words may be used with different meanings in a dialect. Remember that your goal is understanding the main message.

Les chansons

A. visiting a friend
B. Eunice; Glad

A. What is **Chez Denouse McGee** about?

B. Where does Denouse McGee live? What is his wife's name?

C. Which of these does the singer NOT say he will do when he visits his friend?

> goûter
> danser
> écouter de la musique
> causer en français
> faire de la cuisine cajun

D. What do you think **le chanky-chank français** is? What instruments are mentioned that are integral to Cajun music? Cajun music; accordion and violin

E. In **Freeman's Zydeco**, why is Freeman Fontenot considered **eine grande personne**?

E. Because of his generosity, he built a dance hall and school for poor people.

READING STRATEGY
Understanding a dialect

Teacher Note

For an additional reading, see *Practice and Activity Book*, page 131.

PREREADING
Activity A

Motivating Activity

Find a pop song in which a lot of slang is used (gonna, whatcha doin', and so on). Write the lyrics on a transparency and have students read them aloud. Ask them which words would be difficult for a French student who had learned standard written English to understand. You might tell students that, although Cajun French may not look familiar, they might often be able to determine meaning by sounding out the words.

Teaching Suggestion

A. Hold a contest to practice skimming. Have students place a bookmark at page 288 and close their books. When you give the signal, students should open their books and skim the song *Chez Denouse McGee* for its general theme. They should raise their hand and close their book when they have an answer. Call on students to give their answers. Repeat the process with the other songs on this page.

READING
Activities B–M, Q–S

Teaching Suggestion

D. Have students scan *Le Chanky-Chank Français* for words related to music (écouter, tunes, valse, danser).

 For Individual Needs

D. Auditory Learners Read aloud the lyrics of *Le Chanky-Chank Français* in a fast-paced, lilting rhythm. Then, bring in selections of different types of music (jazz, pop, country two-step, classical) and have students choose the musical style that most closely matches the rhythm and feel of *Le Chanky-Chank Français* (two-step).

Music Link

D. If students are musically inclined, you might challenge them to adapt the lyrics of one of the songs presented on this page to the tune of an appropriate song with which they are familiar.

Teaching Suggestion

E. You might also ask students what the singer says Monsieur Freeman Fontenot would give you (the shirt off his back).

LEÇON DU BON FRANÇAIS

C'est nécessaire dire:
«Je vais,» plutôt que «Je vas,»
«Près de,» plutôt que «au ras,»
«Beaucoup,» plutôt que «un tas.»
Un tas du monde oublie le «ne»
avec le «pas.»

Écoute, c'est:
«Attendre,» pas «espérer,»
«Pleurer,» pas «brailler,»
«Penser,» pas «jongler.»
Je pense que t'as jamais jonglé
de ça.

Apprends:
«Lentement,» au lieu de
«doucement,»
«Gentil,» au lieu de «vaillant,»
«Beaucoup,» au lieu de «joliment.»
L'essence ce n'est pas du parfum,
tu vois.

Étudie cette liste:
«Une piastre,» c'est «un dollar,»
C'est une «voiture,» pas un «char,»
Une «fête,» c'est un «anniversaire,»
C'est «pourquoi,» pas «quo'faire.»
L'essence va dans ton char, rappelle-
toi!

Tu me demandes quo'faire
Tout ça, c'est nécessaire.
Juste jongle comment vaillant ça
serait,
Si tu rencontrais un vrai Français.

Dégât

HE, AMERICAIN!

Hé, Américain!
Mon droit de grouiller
mon poing
S'arrête à ton nez,
Et ton droit de
grouiller ta langue
S'arrête à la mienne.
Transgression pour
transgression?

Jean Arceneaux
2. février, 1981

PARLEZ EN ANGLAIS?

Combien de temps j'ai entendu,
«You're in America. Speak
English!»
Et chaque fois je me demande,
Pourquoi «Parler en anglais?»
Pourquoi pas en américain?
Selon moi,
L'anglais est une langue aussi
étrange
Que mon français.
Et encore,
C'est la faute à qui
Que vous êtes trop bêtes pour
parler
Deux langues?

Frère Moreau

LE GOMBO DE CADIENS

Quoi c'est ça?
Explique-moi.

D'abord, tu prends un pays:
Le ventre troué du Mississippi,

Ensuite, écoute:
Un peu de Bretons,
De Normands, de Berrichons,
Tu remues longtemps,
Tu écrases les grumeaux,

Et puis:
Un peu d'Allemands,

Remue encore:
Un peu d'Espagnols,

Tourne fort.

Laisse reposer.

Et puis, goûte:
C'est pas encore ça?
Alors, attends un peu,
C'est là que le goût
viendra,
Peu à peu, en douceur,
en douleur,
secrètement.

C'est pas pour rien
Que vous Cadiens,
On vous a fait souffrir
A petit feu...

Isabelle Têche

F. The word **eine** comes from another language that has influenced Cajun French. Can you guess what language it is?

Spanish

German

Italian

G. In the **Cajun Telephone Stomp,** why does the person finally hang up? How do you say **Quoi c'est ça?** in standard French? See answers below.

H. Look through the songs to find three examples of English words or phrases adapted to Cajun French. See answers below.

I. Find an example of the construction **être après + infinitive.** What is its English equivalent? See answers below.

J. Find examples of the following differences between Cajun French and standard French, and tell how they are different. See answers below.
a. one instance where a different grammatical form is used
b. one instance where adjective agreement is different
c. two instances where a syllable is left out
d. two instances where a different word is used to join phrases

Les poèmes

K. What point is Frère Moreau making in his poem **Parlez en anglais?** Is there an American language? What does it or would it consist of? See answers below.

deux cent quatre-vingt-neuf **289**

Multicultural Link

To introduce the poems on this page, bring in telephone directories with the phone numbers blacked out and distribute them to groups. Give students one minute to find and write down last names that represent different ethnic groups (Rodriquez, Liu, Leblanc, Jones, Walkowski). Then, have groups read their lists aloud and have the class identify the country they think is represented by each name (Mexico, China, France, England, Poland). Ask them what this tells them about the ethnic makeup of the United States.

Thinking Critically

K. Analyzing After students have read the poem and answered the questions in Activity K, ask them to consider the pros and cons of making English the official language of the United States (*pros:* all official business would be in the same language, homogeneity; *cons:* loss of ethnic diversity and cultural heritage, discrimination).

Teaching Suggestion

K. After students read the poem, you might have them tell why they are learning a foreign language. Have them list additional advantages to knowing a foreign language.

Answers

G Amused by the answering machine, he forgets whom he was calling; **Qu'est-ce que c'est?**

H *Possible answers:* **le beep** (the beep), **mon partna** (my partner), **sans nickel** (without a nickel)

I ... **savoir comment il est après faire.** (. . . to find out how he's doing.)

J *Possible answers*
a. ... je vas (je vais)
b. ... la porte est ouvert (ouverte)
c. 'tite (petite)
   'coute (écoute)

d. ... quoi il a fait (ce qu'il a fait)
   ... eyoù (là où)

K *Possible answer:* "American" would be a more accurate name for the language spoken in the United States, since its pronunciation, vocabulary, and structure differ from British English. The American language has been shaped by contributions from languages and cultures of various immigrant groups, including the French.

BEIGNETS DE BANANE

2 grosses bananes bien mûres, écrasées
1 tasse (250 ml.) de farine tamisée
2 cuillères à thé (10 ml.) de poudre à pâte
1 gros œuf

1/4 tasse (60 ml.) de lait
1 cuillère à thé (5 ml.) de sucre
1 cuillère à thé (5 ml.) d'essence de vanille
Pincée de sel
Huile

Dans un bol à mélanger, mettre la farine, le sucre, la poudre à pâte et le sel. Battre l'œuf avec le lait et la vanille. Incorporer à la farine et bien mélanger. Ajouter les bananes et bien mélanger à nouveau. Mettre 1 pouce (2.5 cm) d'huile dans une poêle épaisse et chauffer à environ 375°F (190°C). Laisser tomber la pâte par cuillerées dans l'huile chaude et frire jusqu'à ce que les beignets soient bruns et dorés, en les tournant pour les frire également. Retirer et égoutter sur du papier absorbant. Saupoudrer de sucre en poudre.

CREVETTES ET JAMBON JAMBALAYA

2 livres (1 kg.) de crevettes, décortiquées et déveinées
1 tasse (250 ml.) de jambon, haché gros
1 piment vert, haché fin
1/2 tasse (125 ml.) de céleri, haché fin
2 tasses (500 ml.) de tomates, hachées
1 gros oignon, haché fin

1 gousse d'ail, émincée
2 cuillères à table (30 ml.) de persil, émincé
6 cuillères à thé (28 g.) de beurre
1 feuille de laurier (retirer avant de servir)
3 tasses (750 ml.) de riz bouilli chaud
1 cuillère à thé (5 ml.) de sel
6 gouttes de Tabasco

Dans une poêle épaisse, faire fondre 4 cuillères à thé (20 g.) de beurre à feu doux et sauter le piment, le céleri, l'oignon et le persil pour qu'ils soient transparents et légèrement brunis. Ajouter les tomates, l'ail et la feuille de laurier. Brasser constamment. Ajouter le sel et le Tabasco et cuire jusqu'à ce que le mélange commence à bouillir. Baisser le feu et mijoter 20 minutes, pour que le mélange épaississe. Dans une autre poêle, sauter les crevettes et le jambon dans 2 cuillères à thé (10 g.) de beurre. Quand les crevettes sont fermes et rosées, ajouter au mélange de tomates et cuire 5 minutes de plus. Ajouter le riz. Brasser pour bien mélanger jusqu'à ce que le riz soit bien enrobé et qu'il ait absorbé la sauce. Servir immédiatement.

Language Arts Link

L. Ask students what the author of *Leçon du bon français* does at the end of each stanza (uses the French word and its Cajun equivalent in one sentence). Have students write a similar poem in English, comparing American English to local slang. For example, they might write *"Money,"* not *"dough."*

For Individual Needs

Visual Learners Bring in some of the ingredients for the recipes on this page (banana, green pepper, egg, rice, celery). Hold up each ingredient and have students tell which recipe calls for it.

Terms in Lisons!

Students might want to know the following words from the songs and poems: **grouiller** *(to move/mill about);* **poing** *(fist);* **remuer** *(to stir).*

POSTREADING
Activities N–P

Teaching Suggestions

• Ask students for their overall impressions of the Cajun culture in Louisiana, based on the songs, poems, and recipes they've just read.
• You might have volunteers prepare jambalaya and banana fritters at home and distribute samples to the class.

See answers below.

L. What is the significance of the pairs of words in the lines of **Leçon du bon français**? Does the author really believe that the French he speaks is wrong? What is the message of the poem?

M. What ingredients make up **Le Gombo de Cadiens**? How do you have to cook it to make it turn out just right? See answers below.

N. What do you think the author would say the Cajun people have gained through their suffering? See answers below.

O. The words *tongue* and *language* are often synonymous. What right is the author of **Hé, Américain!** eager to protect? See answers below.

P. What is the overall message of these four poems? See answers below.

For Activities Q, R, and S, see answers below.

Les recettes

Q. How would you translate what the cook is saying into English? Into standard French?

R. Which of these recipes seems to be the easier to prepare? Which has the most ingredients?

S. Match each dish with its preparation.

Baisser le feu et mijoter 20 minutes.

Brasser constamment.

Incorporer à la farine et bien mélanger.

Saupoudrer de sucre en poudre.

Ajouter les tomates, l'ail et la feuille de laurier.

Answers

L The first word of each pair is standard French, the second, Cajun French. Cajun French is not "wrong." It is the correct way for Cajuns to communicate with each other. The poet humorously admits that standard French would be nice to know if one ever met a real French person.

M **Le Gombo de Cadiens** is made of many peoples: Bretons, Normands, Berrichons, Germans, and Spaniards. After mixing the ingredients together, wait. The flavor will develop slowly, through pain and suffering.

N The long suffering of the Cajun people has produced a very distinctive, highly flavorful culture.

O He wants to protect the right to speak his own language without interference from others.

P The Cajuns have a right to be proud of their own language, history, and culture.

Q Are you the guy who's been complaining that the crawfish aren't done?; **C'est vous l'homme qui se plaignait que les écrevisses ne sont pas cuites?**

R *Easier:* Beignets de bananes
Most ingredients: Crevettes et jambon jambalaya

S *Beignets de banane:* Incorporer à la farine et bien mélanger. Saupoudrer de sucre en poudre.
Crevettes et jambon jambalaya: Brasser constamment. Ajouter les tomates, l'ail et la feuille de laurier. Baisser le feu et mijouter vingt minutes.

ECRIVONS!

Think again about the poems in the reading selection. What makes them different from a short story or an essay? Poems often tend to focus on a specific experience, emotion, object, or person, and usually contain poetic devices to describe and show hidden meaning in their subjects. In this activity, you'll have the chance to discover and explore some of these poetic devices as you create your own poem or song lyric.

Un poète en herbe

Maintenant, c'est à toi d'écrire un poème ou une chanson.

A. Préparation

1. D'abord, choisis le sujet de ton poème. Tu peux parler d'...
   a. une personne qui joue un rôle important dans ta vie.
   b. un objet que tu aimes beaucoup ou que tu trouves original.
   c. un moment particulier de ta vie, important ou non.
   d. une expérience intéressante que tu as vécue.
2. Pour faire la description de ce que tu as choisi comme sujet, fais une liste d'adjectifs et de verbes pour décrire les caractéristiques particulières de ton sujet.
3. Pour parler de tes sentiments ou de tes émotions, fais une liste de mots ou d'images pour exprimer la joie, la solitude, l'appartenance...

DE BONS CONSEILS
Writers of poetry use a variety of techniques to communicate emotion and meaning, and to create interesting effects with the sounds of language. They use figurative language and **imagery**, words or phrases that appeal to the senses, to create vivid or startling descriptions of a subject. **Rhyme** is often associated with poetry, but **repetition**, repeated sounds, words, or phrases; and **rhythm,** a pattern of stressed and unstressed syllables, are also very effective means of using sounds to convey feeling and mood. Try experimenting with these poetic techniques and see how they add to the depth and intensity of your poetry or song lyrics.

B. Rédaction

1. Fais un brouillon de ton poème/ta chanson. Souviens-toi que ton but principal est de décrire ton sujet de façon vivante et intéressante.
2. Pendant que tu écris ton brouillon, essaie de créer des effets de sons intéressants.
   a. Peux-tu utiliser une série de mots qui commencent par le même son?
   b. Peux-tu terminer tes phrases par des mots qui riment?
   c. Peux-tu combiner tes mots de façon à créer un certain rythme?
3. Essaie de faire ressortir les idées principales en répétant certaines phrases importantes.

C. Evaluation

1. Relis ton brouillon. Est-ce que tu as réussi à décrire ton sujet de façon intéressante ou à bien exprimer une émotion? Essaie de remplacer certains mots par des mots plus forts ou par des mots qui décrivent mieux ton sujet.
2. Maintenant, lis ton poème/ta chanson tout haut. Les sonorités sont-elles agréables? Cherche des endroits où tu peux répéter une phrase importante ou ajouter une nouvelle rime. Fais les changements nécessaires.
3. Corrige les fautes d'orthographe et de grammaire, puis rédige la version finale de ton poème/ta chanson. Fais-le/la lire à ton/ta camarade. Si tu as écrit une chanson et que tu as une idée du genre de musique que tu voudrais, chante ta chanson.

deux cent quatre-vingt-onze **291**

WRITING STRATEGY
Using poetic devices

 Portfolio

Written You might want to have students include all their work for Parts A–C in their written portfolios. For portfolio information, see *Assessment Guide,* pages 2–13.

PREWRITING

Motivating Activity

As a homework assignment, have students find and bring to class a poem that they've read and enjoyed in an English class. Have volunteers read excerpts from their poems aloud. Ask students what they like about the poems (the language, the rhythm, the message, the style).

Language Arts Link

You might copy one of the poems students brought in for the Motivating Activity onto a transparency and have students list poetic devices they find (simile, metaphor, repetition, alliteration, irony). Have students define and give additional examples of these devices.

Building on Previous Skills

A. 2. Before students start writing, have them visualize the subject of their poem. Then, have them list adjectives and verbs to describe what they see and the feelings that the image conveys.

WRITING

 **For Individual Needs**

B. Auditory/Kinesthetic Learners
Auditory learners may need to hear the words and rhythm of their poem in order to write. Encourage them to say the words aloud and to experiment with different combinations of words. Kinesthetic learners might need to hum, clap, or sing to get a feel for the rhythm of their verse.

POSTWRITING

Teaching Suggestion

C. Encourage self-correction. Have students look for words or phrases in their poems that "aren't quite right."

MISE EN PRATIQUE

The **Mise en pratique** reviews and integrates all four skills and culture in preparation for the Chapter Test.

Video Wrap-Up

VIDEO PROGRAM
Videocassette 2

You might want to use the *Video Program* as part of the chapter review. See the *Video Guide* for teaching suggestions and activity masters.

For Individual Needs

1 Challenge Have partners read the brochure together. Then, have them create several fill-in-the-blank sentences. (**Saint Martinville est surnommé «le Petit ____ d'Amérique.»**) They should make an answer key on a separate sheet of paper. Then, have them exchange papers with another pair, complete the activity, and return it for correction.

Teaching Suggestions

1 You might also ask students to describe what one can see and do at each of the attractions listed in the box to the right of this activity. (**Dans le bassin de l'Atchafalaya, on peut voir des castors et des alligators.**)

1 Have students draw illustrations to accompany this brochure.

Language Note

Students might want to know the following words from the brochure: **en plein air** *(outdoor)*; **marais** *(swamp)*; **aigrette** *(egret)*; **chêne** *(oak tree)*.

---

1 Regarde cette brochure touristique sur l'Acadiana et réponds aux questions suivantes.

La paroisse de Lafayette

A Lafayette, au cœur de l'Acadiana, on sent le pouls du pays cajun. Dans la paroisse de Lafayette, le français est toujours utilisé et les étrangers sont reçus comme des amis. Dans plusieurs restaurants de 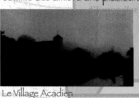 Lafayette vous pourrez, tout en dégustant la délicieuse cuisine cajun et créole, apprécier la musique et la danse traditionnelles.

Le Village Acadien

Le Village Acadien est un musée en plein air qui représente la vie en Acadiana telle qu'elle était au XIXème siècle; Vermilionville est un véritable témoignage vivant du passé cajun et créole. Le Musée de Lafayette a été la maison d'un des premiers habitants de la ville. Le Musée d'Histoire Naturelle et le Planétarium offrent de multiples expositions avec différents thèmes : la nature, les sciences et la technologie. Le Musée d'Art de l'Université du Sud-Ouest de la Louisiane (USL) présente toujours une exposition digne d'intérêt.

En Acadiana, les festivals font partie de la vie de tous les jours comme la bonne nourriture et la bonne musique. Vous entendrez les habitants vous dire—en français— «Laissez les bons temps rouler!» Tout est prétexte à la fête : le Mardi Gras, la culture cajun ou créole et toutes les autres activités liées à la francophonie.

Pour les Cadiens, faire la fête c'est très sérieux, alors amusez-vous à Lafayette, c'est la coutume!

La paroisse de Saint Martin

Vous êtes invités à faire un voyage dans le temps dans la paroisse de Saint Martin. Venez vous balader le long du bayou Teche jusqu'aux premiers refuges des exilés Acadiens. Là, vous rencontrerez des gens qui parlent toujours le français cajun. Sur l'Interstate 10, sortez à Breaux Bridge ou à Henderson pour vous rendre dans les restaurants spécialisés dans les crustacés. Visitez le quartier historique de Breaux Bridge ainsi que son centre ville et profitez-en pour vous rendre dans l'une des salles de danse les plus réputées dans le monde entier.

A partir d'Henderson, explorez le magnifique bassin de l'Atchafalaya à partir de la levée. Pendant la visite des marais, des aigrettes, des hérons, des castors et des alligators viendront saluer votre passage.

A Saint Martinville, surnommé «Le Petit Paris d'Amérique», vous découvrirez ce mélange unique de culture française et d'hospitalité du Sud. Par une visite pédestre vous emprunterez des sentiers dans des paysages somptueux et pourrez contempler le chêne d'Evangéline, le Musée du Mardi Gras, le quartier historique et l'église catholique Saint Martin de Tours, la plus vieille église catholique louisianaise.

Les musiciens cajuns devant le chêne d'Evangéline

1. Est-ce que ces phrases sont vraies ou fausses?

1. En Acadiana un festival est un événement qui se prépare parce que ça n'arrive pas tous les jours. faux

2. Le français est toujours utilisé dans la paroisse de Lafayette. vrai

3. Saint Martinville est surnommé «Le Petit Paris d'Amérique.» vrai

4. L'église Saint Martin de Tours est la plus vieille église catholique des Etats-Unis. faux

2. D'après cette brochure, où est-ce qu'on peut voir... See answers below.

> le bassin de l'Atchafalaya?   des aigrettes
>
> Vermilionville?   le chêne d'Evangéline?
>
> le musée du Mardi Gras?   le Planétarium?

Culture Note

The area that the winding Teche River crosses is known as Teche Country. The name comes from the Indian word **tenche**, meaning *snake*, which describes the river's winding path. Breaux Bridge is known as the Cajun Capital of this area and is also the self-appointed Crawfish Capital of the World.

Answers

1 2. Le bassin de l'Atchafalaya: Saint Martin
Des aigrettes: Saint Martin
Vermilionville: Lafayette
Le chêne d'Evangéline: Saint Martin
Le musée du Mardi Gras: Saint Martin
Le Planétarium: Lafayette

2 Mathieu et Nadine décident ce qu'ils vont faire pendant leur visite en Louisiane. Ecoute leur conversation et mets les événements dans le bon ordre.

5 Mathieu demande à Nadine son opinion sur ce qu'elle mange.

1 Nadine propose d'aller au Village Acadien.

4 Nadine fait une observation.

3 Mathieu en donne une opinion négative.

7 Mathieu donne son impression sur la cuisine cajun.

2 Mathieu demande une explication au sujet du Village Acadien.

6 Mathieu demande une explication au sujet du gombo.

3 Tu vas faire un voyage de cinq jours en Louisiane avec tes camarades. Où est-ce que tu veux aller? Qu'est-ce que tu veux faire? Fais des suggestions. Tes camarades vont te donner leur opinion. S'ils ne sont pas d'accord, ils vont proposer quelque chose d'autre. Quand vous aurez décidé, faites un programme de ce que vous allez faire chaque jour.

4 Tu es en Louisiane et tu as quelques questions à poser à l'employé(e) de l'office de tourisme. Tu lui demandes de t'expliquer les mots suivants. Si tu crois les connaître, vérifie que tu as raison.

«jambalaya»   «cocodrie»
«Atchafalaya»   «zydeco»
«cajun»   «po-boy»   «gombo»
«fais dodo»   «Mardi Gras»

5 Tu es journaliste pour un magazine de tourisme. Tu viens de rentrer d'un voyage en Louisiane. Ecris un article où tu donnes tes impressions et où tu fais des observations sur la Louisiane. N'oublie pas de parler des endroits que tu as visités, de la musique que tu as écoutée et de la cuisine que tu as goûtée.

6

JEU DE ROLE

You're visiting friends in Louisiana. They take you to a Cajun restaurant and dance hall. Act out the following scenes with your partners.

a. You don't know what to order, so your friends make suggestions. Because you're not familiar with the foods they suggest, you ask for some explanation. When you taste what you've ordered, your friends ask your opinion of it. Tell them and add an observation about Cajun food.

b. You and your friends are having a discussion about your music preferences during which you agree or disagree. Suddenly, a live band starts to play. You don't know what kind of music it is, so you ask your friends. They ask you what you think of the music and dancing. Give them your impressions.

MISE EN PRATIQUE · *deux cent quatre-vingt-treize* · **293**

For Individual Needs

2 Tactile Learners Type the sentences on a sheet of paper and distribute copies to students. Have them cut apart each sentence, listen to the recording, and rearrange the slips of paper according to what they hear.

2 Challenge Once students have arranged the sentences in the proper order as described above, have them recreate an approximation of the conversation.

Teacher Note

If students have questions about the words in the box next to Activity 4, have them refer to the **Notes Culturelles** in the chapter.

Portfolio

3, 4 Oral These activities are appropriate for students' oral portfolios. For portfolio information, see *Assessment Guide*, pages 2–13.

5 Written This activity is appropriate for students' written portfolios. If students have access to computers, you might have them design a layout for their article. For portfolio suggestions, see *Assessment Guide*, page 24.

Teaching Suggestion

6 For Part **b**, encourage students to bring in music to use in the skit. They might also have group members act as the band members and dancers mentioned in the discussion.

Culture Note

Saint Martinville was rendered famous by the poet Henry Wadsworth Longfellow in his poem *Evangeline*. The town boasts the bronze Evangeline Statue and the Evangeline Oak, where Gabriel supposedly waited for his lost love.

QUE SAIS-JE?

This page is intended to help students prepare for the test. It is a brief checklist of the major points covered in the chapter. The students should be reminded that this is only a checklist and does not necessarily include everything that will appear on the test.

♜ Game

JEU DE DÉ Form small groups and give a die to each one. The first player in each group rolls the die. He or she then answers the question from **Que sais-je?** with the corresponding number. The other players act as judges. If the question has sub-questions (as in numbers 1, 6, 7, and 8), the player may choose one sub-question to answer. If a player rolls a 6, he or she must roll a second time. If the die lands on 1 or 2, the player must answer question 6. If it lands on 3 or 4, the player answers question 7. If it lands on 5 or 6, the player answers question 8. Then, the next player takes a turn. Players win a point for each correct answer. Tell students that they should listen carefully to other players' answers, since they are allowed to repeat answers if they roll the number of a question that was previously answered.

Can you use what you've learned in this chapter?

Can you ask for confirmation? p.276

1 You run into someone you haven't seen in a long time. How would you ask for confirmation about . . . *Possible answers:*

1. his or her brother's name? Ton frère s'appelle... , c'est ça?
2. where he or she lives? Tu habites toujours à... ?
3. his or her age? Tu as bien... ans, c'est ça?
4. where he or she goes to school? Si je ne me trompe pas, tu vas à... ?

Can you ask for and give an opinion? p.278

2 How would you ask a friend's opinion of your favorite music?
Possible answers: Qu'est-ce que tu penses de... ? Ça te branche,... ?

3 How would you express your opinions about the following types of music?
Possible answers:

> rock   jazz   blues   dance music
> classical   country   rap

Positive opinion: Je trouve ça hyper-cool. J'aime beaucoup. Ça me plaît beaucoup. Ça m'éclate. Je n'écoute que ça.
Negative opinion: Je trouve ça nul. Je n'aime pas du tout. Ça ne me plaît pas du tout. Je n'aime pas tellement ça. Ça ne me branche pas trop.

Can you agree and disagree? p.278

4 A friend gives an opinion about a CD you've just bought. How do you express your agreement? Je suis d'accord avec toi. Moi aussi, j'aime bien... ; Moi non plus, je n'aime pas... ; Ça, c'est sûr. Tu as raison.

5 What do you say if you don't agree with your friend?
Pas du tout. Tu parles! Tu rigoles! Tu délires ou quoi? N'importe quoi!

Can you ask for explanations? p.283

6 What do you say to ask . . . See answers below.

1. what something is?
2. what something is called?
3. what something means?
4. what's in a dish?
5. how to say something in French?

Can you make observations? p.286

7 What observations would you make about . . . See answers below.

1. your town?
2. your school?
3. a place you visited?
4. learning French?

Can you give impressions? p.286

8 How would you give your impressions of these pictures? *Possible answers:*

1. On dirait qu'ils s'amusent bien.

2. Ils ont l'air de s'ennuyer.

3. Il me semble que ce garçon a peur.

Answers

6 1. Qu'est-ce que c'est?
   2. Comment est-ce qu'on appelle ça?
   3. Qu'est-ce que ça veut dire,... ?
   4. Qu'est-ce qu'il y a dans... ?
   5. Comment on dit... en français?

7 *Possible answers*
   1. Ce que j'aime, c'est les musées.
   2. Ce que je trouve super, c'est les professeurs.
   3. Ce qui est incroyable, c'est la cuisine locale.
   4. Ce qui est intéressant, c'est la culture dans les pays francophones.

PREMIERE ETAPE

Asking for confirmation

toujours... ? *still . . . ?*
bien... ? *really . . . ?*
... déjà? *. . . again?*
Si je me souviens bien,... *If I remember correctly, . . .*
Si je ne me trompe pas,... *If I'm not mistaken, . . .*

Musical instruments

l'accordéon (m.) *the accordeon*
la basse *the bass (guitar)*
la batterie *the drums*
la boîte à rythmes *the drum machine*
le chant *singing*
la flûte *the flute*
la guitare *the guitar*

le micro (le microphone) *the mike (the microphone)*
le piano *the piano*
le saxophone *the saxophone*
le synthé (le synthétiseur) *the synthesizer*
la trompette *the trumpet*
le violon *the violin*

Kinds of music

le country *country music*
le blues *blues*
la dance *dance music*
le jazz *jazz*
la musique cajun *Cajun music*
la musique classique *classical music*
le rap *rap*
le rock *rock*

Asking for and giving opinions

Qu'est-ce que tu penses de... ? *What do you think of . . . ?*
Ça te branche,... ? *Are you into . . . ?*
Ça m'éclate. *I'm wild about it.*
Je n'écoute que ça. *That's all I listen to.*
Ça ne me branche pas trop. *I'm not into that.*

Agreeing and disagreeing

Ça, c'est sûr. *That's for sure.*
Tu délires ou quoi? *Are you crazy or what?*

DEUXIEME ETAPE

Asking for explanations

Qu'est-ce que c'est? *What's that?*
Comment est-ce qu'on appelle ça? *What is that called?*
Qu'est-ce que ça veut dire,... ? *What does . . . mean?*
Qu'est-ce qu'il y a dans... ? *What's in . . . ?*
Comment est-ce qu'on fait... ? *How do you make . . . ?*
D'où vient le mot... ? *Where does the word . . . come from?*
Comment on dit... ? *How do you say . . . ?*

Cajun food

à la vapeur *steamed*
l'andouille (f.) *andouille sausage*
au court-bouillon *boiled*
les champignons (m.) *mushrooms*
les crustacés (m.) *shellfish*

les écrevisses (f.) *crawfish*
en bisque *bisque*
épicé(e) *spicy*
les épices (f.) *spices*
les épinards (m.) *spinach*
farci(e) (à) *stuffed (with)*
frit(e) *fried*
le gombo *gumbo*
les hors-d'œuvre (m.) *hors d'oeuvre*
les huîtres (f.) *oysters*
le jambalaya *jambalaya*
des okras (m.) *okra*
le po-boy *po-boy sandwich*
le porc *pork*
le pouding au pain *bread pudding*
les raisins secs *raisins*
salé(e) *salty*
les saucisses (f.) *sausages*
la soupe *soup*
la viande *meat*

Making observations

Ce qui est intéressant/incroyable, c'est... *What's interesting/incredible is . . .*
Ce qui saute aux yeux, c'est... *What catches your eye is . . .*
Ce qui me branche vraiment, c'est... *What I'm really crazy about is . . .*
Ce que je trouve super, c'est... *What I think is super is . . .*
Ce que j'adore/j'aime, c'est... *What I like/love is . . .*

Giving impressions

On dirait que... *It looks like . . .*
Il me semble que... *It seems to me that . . .*
J'ai l'impression que... *I have the impression that . . .*
Ils ont l'air de... *They look like . . .*

Teaching Suggestions

- Have students write a skit, using one word or expression from each category in the **Vocabulaire**.
- Have partners ask each other for explanations of the vocabulary words: **Comment on dit** *drums* **en français? Comment on dit «écrevisses» en anglais?**

CHAPTER 11 ASSESSMENT

CHAPTER TEST

- *Chapter Teaching Resources, Book 3*, pp. 135–140
- *Assessment Guide,* Speaking Test, p. 33
- *Assessment Items, Audiocassette 8B Audio CD 11*

TEST GENERATOR, CHAPTER 11

ALTERNATIVE ASSESSMENT

Performance Assessment

You might want to use the **Jeu de rôle** (p. 293) as a cumulative performance assessment activity.

📁 Portfolio Assessment

- **Written: Mise en pratique,** Activity 5, *Pupil's Edition,* p. 293
  Assessment Guide, p. 24
- **Oral:** Activity 34, *Pupil's Edition,* p. 287
  Assessment Guide, p. 24

VOCABULAIRE
deux cent quatre-vingt-quinze **295**

Chapitre 12 : Echanges sportifs et culturels
Chapter Overview

Mise en train
pp. 298–300

A nous les Jeux olympiques!

Note Culturelle, Sporting events in the francophone world, p. 300

Première étape
pp. 301–305

FUNCTIONS	GRAMMAR	CULTURE	RE-ENTRY
• Expressing anticipation, p. 304 *Review* • Making suppositions, p. 304 • Expressing certainty and doubt, p. 304	The future after **quand** and **dès que**, p. 304		• Sports vocabulary • Making suppositions • Expressing certainty and doubt • The future

Remise en train
pp. 306–307

Un rendez-vous sportif et culturel

Deuxième étape
pp. 308–311

FUNCTIONS	GRAMMAR	CULTURE	RE-ENTRY
Review • Inquiring, p. 309 • Expressing excitement and disappointment, p. 311		**Panorama Culturel,** Regional stereotypes, p. 310	• Prepositions with countries • Francophone cultures • Introducing people • Asking someone's name and age and giving yours • Offering encouragement

Lisons!
pp. 312–314

Articles about Olympic athletes
Reading Strategy: Combining strategies

Ecrivons!
p. 315

Un article de magazine
Writing Strategy: Doing research

Review
pp. 316–319

• Mise en pratique, pp. 316–317
• Que sais-je? p. 318
• Vocabulaire, p. 319

Assessment Options

Etape Quizzes
• *Chapter Teaching Resources, Book 3*
  Première étape, Quiz 12-1, pp. 185–186
  Deuxième étape, Quiz 12-2, pp. 187–188
• *Assessment Items, Audiocassette 8B/Audio CD 12*

Chapter Test
• *Chapter Teaching Resources, Book 3*, pp. 189–194
• *Assessment Guide,* Speaking Test, p. 33
• *Assessment Items, Audiocassette 8B/Audio CD 12*

Test Generator, Chapter 12

RESOURCES: Print	RESOURCES: Audiovisual
Practice and Activity Book, p. 133	Textbook Audiocassette 6B/Audio CD 12
Practice and Activity Book, pp. 134–137 Grammar and Vocabulary Worksheets, pp. 102–104 Chapter Teaching Resources, Book 3 • Communicative Activity 12-1, pp. 166–167 • Teaching Transparency Master 12-1, pp. 170, 172 . . . . • Additional Listening Activities 12-1, 12-2, 12-3, pp. 173–174. . • Realia 12-1, pp. 177, 179 • Situation Cards 12-1, pp. 180–181 • Student Response Forms, pp. 182–184 • Quiz 12-1, pp. 185–186	Textbook Audiocassette 6B/Audio CD 12 Teaching Transparency 12-1 Additional Listening Activities, Audiocassette 10B/Audio CD 12 Assessment Items, Audiocassette 8B/Audio CD 12
Practice and Activity Book, p. 138	Textbook Audiocassette 6B/Audio CD 12
Practice and Activity Book, pp. 139–142 Grammar and Vocabulary Worksheets, pp. 105–107 Chapter Teaching Resources, Book 3 • Communicative Activity 12-2, pp. 168–169 • Teaching Transparency Master 12-2, pp. 171, 172 . . . . • Additional Listening Activities 12-4, 12-5, 12-6, pp. 174–175. . • Realia 12-2, pp. 178, 179 • Situation Cards 12-2, 12-3, pp. 180–181 • Student Response Forms, pp. 182–184 • Quiz 12-2, pp. 187–188 . . . . Video Guide	Textbook Audiocassette 6B/Audio CD 12 Teaching Transparency 12-2 Additional Listening Activities, Audiocassette 10B/Audio CD 12 Assessment Items, Audiocassette 8B/Audio CD 12 Video Program, Videocassette 2
Practice and Activity Book, p. 143	
Video Guide	Video Program, Videocassette 2

Alternative Assessment
- Performance Assessment
  Première étape, p. 305
  Deuxième étape, p. 311

- Portfolio Assessment
  Written: **Mise en pratique,** Activity 4, *Pupil's Edition,* p. 317
    Assessment Guide, p. 25
  Oral: **Mise en pratique,** Activity 3, *Pupil's Edition,* p. 317
    Assessment Guide, p. 25

Final Exam
Assessment Guide, pp. 49–56
Assessment Items,
  Audiocassette 8B
  Audio CD 12

For Student Response Forms, see *Chapter Teaching Resources, Book 3,* pp. 182–184.

Première étape

6 Ecoute! p. 301

1. — Tiens! Regarde un peu! Il est en train de soulever deux cent cinquante-cinq kilos. Il en a les yeux qui lui sortent de la tête!
   — Ah, ouais. Il est vraiment fort, ce Russe. Je crois qu'il va gagner.

2. — Ils sont vraiment étroits, ces bateaux.
   — Oui. Je ne vois pas comment huit personnes peuvent s'asseoir dedans.
   — Et puis, comment est-ce qu'ils font pour ne pas s'emmêler les rames?
   — Je n'en ai aucune idée, moi.

3. — Tu as vu ça, toi?
   — Euh, qu'est-ce qui est arrivé?
   — Le tireur, là, il a manqué son tir.
   — Et alors?
   — Ben, la flèche est arrivée dans le chapeau d'un homme là-bas.
   — Il ferait bien de choisir un autre sport, non?

4. — Dis donc, il y a une faute à chaque fois que le cheval touche un obstacle?
   — Bien sûr.
   — Oh, zut alors!
   — Tu sais, la même chose lui est arrivé l'année passée. Le cheval a eu peur et elle est tombée.
   — Donc, c'est fini, pour elle, la compétition?
   — Ça, c'est sûr.

5. — Ben, dis donc. Regarde le plongeur. Il va partir de cette position, tu crois?
   — Evidemment. Ça a l'air dangereux, tu trouves pas?
   — Oui. J'ai peur qu'il se cogne la tête contre le plongeoir.
   — Moi aussi.

6. — C'est bien pour les filles qu'elles n'aient pas besoin de faire les anneaux.
   — Oui, mais, à la place, il faut qu'elles passent à la poutre.
   — Oui, c'est vraiment dur, ça. Surtout quand on a le trac.
   — Oui, c'est très facile de tomber. Et après ça, bien sûr, c'est fini.

7. — Qu'est-ce qu'elle est grande, cette piscine!
   — Bien sûr, c'est une piscine olympique.
   — Est-ce que c'est le crawl ou le papillon, la prochaine épreuve?
   — C'est le papillon.
   — C'est le Chinois le plus rapide, non?
   — Oui, je crois.

8. — C'est vachement bien de pouvoir regarder d'ici.
   — Oui.
   — Quand je regarde à la télé, ça m'embête parce que tout est mélangé.
   — Moi aussi, ça m'énerve. Ils ne montrent jamais une épreuve en entier. Le lancer du disque, puis le saut à la perche, puis le saut en longueur...
   — Oui. Moi, j'aime bien pouvoir voir tous les concurrents.

9. — Ils sont vraiment bons!

— Tiens! Tu as vu comme il a lancé le ballon à son équipier qui a marqué les deux points?
— Non. Ça s'est passé trop vite.

10. — Tu veux bien m'expliquer ce qui se passe?
   — Bien sûr.
   — Tu sais que je ne comprends rien aux règles. Tout ce que je sais, c'est qu'on porte un kimono blanc avec une ceinture. Je ne verrais pas la différence entre ça et du karaté.
   — Bon. Je t'explique.

Answers to Activity 6

1. haltérophilie	4. équitation	7. natation	10. judo
2. aviron	5. plongeon acrobatique	8. athlétisme	
3. tir à l'arc	6. gymnastique	9. basket-ball	

13 Ecoute! p. 304

1. SÉVERINE Tu crois que je devrais emporter un parapluie? Je parie qu'il pleut beaucoup là-bas.
   FRÈRE C'est pas la peine. Je suis sûr que tu pourras en acheter un sur place, si tu en as besoin.

2. SÉVERINE Oh! J'ai failli oublier mon appareil-photo. Tu veux bien me l'amener?
   FRÈRE Il est où, dans ton placard? Voyons... Je ne pense pas qu'il soit là.

3. SÉVERINE On m'a dit qu'il y fait très chaud en ce moment. Je ne vais pas emporter mon manteau.
   FRÈRE Tu devrais quand même emporter un pull. Je suis sûr qu'il peut faire froid la nuit.

4. SÉVERINE Il doit y avoir des stars, tu crois pas? Quand je verrai Keanu Reeves, je vais lui demander son autographe.
   FRÈRE Tu sais, Séverine, ça m'étonnerait que tu le voies.

5. SÉVERINE Oh là là. J'ai un trac fou. Tu crois que je vais arriver en finale?
   FRÈRE Je n'en ai aucun doute. Tu es la meilleure.

6. SÉVERINE Il me tarde de voir les épreuves de natation. Tu crois que ça va être bien?
   FRÈRE Ça, c'est sûr.

7. SÉVERINE Vivement que j'arrive aux Etats-Unis. Ça doit être vachement intéressant, tu crois pas?
   FRÈRE Oui, mais je ne suis pas certain que tu puisses voir beaucoup de choses. C'est grand, tu sais. Et tu seras tout le temps au village olympique.

8. SÉVERINE Tu crois que je vais trouver des gens qui parlent français?
   FRÈRE Oui, c'est sûr. Il y a une vingtaine de pays francophones qui participent aux Jeux.

9. SÉVERINE Je suis vraiment impatiente de rencontrer des gens intéressants. Je parie que je vais me faire un tas de nouveaux amis.
   FRÈRE J'en suis sûr.

10. SÉVERINE Zut alors! J'en ai marre de cette valise. Tu peux m'aider?
   FRÈRE Oui, mais je ne pense pas qu'on puisse la fermer. Il y a trop de choses dedans.

Answers to Activity 13
Supposition: 1, 4   *Impatience:* 6, 7, 9

Deuxième étape

24 Ecoute! p. 309

1. — Salut. Je m'appelle Odile. Et toi?
   — Saïd.
   — Tu es d'où?
   — De Marrakech, au Maroc.
   — C'est bien comme ville?
   — Oui. C'est super. C'est très animé. Il y a des tas de choses à faire.
2. — Moi, je suis vraiment impatient de voir la natation.
   — Moi aussi.
   — Tu vas voir le deux cents mètres crawl ce soir?
   — Non, malheureusement, je n'ai pas pu avoir de place.
   — Dommage. Je parie que ça va être super!
3. — Tu es africaine?
   — Oui.
   — Cool! C'est comment, la vie là-bas?
   — C'est bien. Il fait toujours beau chez moi, en République centrafricaine.
   — Il ne fait pas trop chaud?
   — Non. Grâce à la forêt tropicale, il fait moins chaud qu'ailleurs.
4. — Et, qu'est-ce qu'on y mange? C'est pareil qu'ici?
   — Euh, je crois qu'on a plus ou moins les mêmes choses, mais on ne mange pas autant de viande que chez toi et puis, il y a quelques plats qu'on ne mange pas chez toi...
   — Par exemple?
   — Et bien, le singe.
   — On mange ça chez toi? Ouah!
5. — Zut alors! On s'est encore perdus. Je crois qu'on est déjà passés devant ce bâtiment il y a dix minutes.
   — Ah non! C'est pas vrai! On va rater le début du match.
   — Bon. Je vais demander à cette jeune fille-là. Pardon, vous savez où se trouve le gymnase?
6. — Dis-moi, est-ce que tout le monde porte ces robes, euh, je ne sais pas comment ça s'appelle, chez toi?
   — Tu veux dire des sifsaris et des djellabas?
   — Oui, c'est ça.
   — C'est un habit assez traditionnel. La plupart des jeunes portent les mêmes vêtements que toi. Mais on peut choisir selon l'occasion.
   — Ah oui?
7. — On va danser dans une discothèque américaine ce soir. Tu viens?
   — Oh, je ne sais pas. J'ai entraînement jusqu'à huit heures. Vous vous retrouvez à quelle heure?
   — A neuf heures.
   — Je serai sûrement fatiguée.
   — Oh, tu es trop sérieuse. Il faut que tu t'amuses aussi.
   — Bon, peut-être.
8. — Alors, qu'est-ce qui est typique de chez vous?
   — Euh, la pastilla. C'est une de nos spécialités les plus connues. C'est une sorte de tarte au pigeon et aux amandes. Vous avez ça, chez vous?
   — Non. C'est bon?
   — Oui, très bon.

Answers to Activity 24

1. pays   3. pays   5. autre chose   7. autre chose
2. autre chose   4. pays   6. pays   8. pays

28 Ecoute! p. 311

1. — La médaille d'argent! Et moi qui pensais que ça serait déjà bien si j'arrivais en finale. J'arrive pas à y croire!
2. — Tout allait bien, jusqu'à ce que le coureur qui était à ma gauche coupe en face de moi. C'est à ce moment-là que je suis tombé. J'ai vraiment pas de chance!
3. — Les Russes nous ont battus. Ils nous ont mis une raclée. Ils ont marqué quatre-vingt-quatre points, et nous seulement trente-huit. Quelle angoisse!
4. — On avait arrêté la compétition parce que le Canadien s'était fait mal. Quand on a recommencé, je voulais m'échauffer à nouveau mais on ne me l'a pas permis. C'est pas juste!
5. — Tu ne devineras jamais ce qui m'est arrivé. C'est trop cool. J'ai eu un dix à l'épreuve de barres asymétriques!
6. — Ecoute! J'ai battu le record de saut à la perche et c'est moi qui détiens le nouveau record! C'est vraiment le pied, non?
7. — Oh, j'en ai vraiment marre! Tu sais, je ne rate jamais mon tir. Je ne comprends vraiment pas ce qui s'est passé.
8. — Si seulement j'avais pu rester sur le cheval. C'est vraiment embarrassant de tomber comme ça! Qu'est-ce que je peux être nul!
9. — Les boules! J'avais le trac et je suis tombée de la poutre. Après ça, j'avais perdu tellement de points que je ne pouvais plus les rattraper.
10. — Tu ne peux pas imaginer à quel point c'est génial quand tu es sur le podium et qu'on joue l'hymne national de ton pays!

Answers to Activity 28

1. gagné   3. perdu   5. gagné   7. perdu   9. perdu
2. perdu   4. perdu   6. gagné   8. perdu   10. gagné

Mise en pratique

2 p. 317

1. — Elle n'a vraiment pas eu de chance, la pauvre. D'abord, elle est tombée des barres asymétriques, et puis le jour suivant, elle est tombée de la poutre.
2. — Les Russes étaient vraiment très bons. On ne pouvait pas les arrêter. Là, vous voyez, c'est le moment où ils ont fait le panier qui les a fait gagner.
3. — Ça, c'est mon athlète préférée, Marie-José Perec. Je l'admire tellement. Là, c'est elle pendant la course de fond. Elle est vraiment bonne!
4. — Vous savez, depuis quelque temps, j'ai envie de faire du judo. C'est vachement intéressant. Cette fille-là, c'est une Française. Elle s'appelle Cathy Fleury. C'est elle qui a gagné.
5. — Et ça, c'est le Chinois qui a gagné la plupart des épreuves de natation. Il est formidable.
6. — Regardez ce pauvre type-là. Je ne sais pas qui c'est, mais je l'ai vu tomber de son cheval. Il ne s'est pas fait mal, heureusement, mais quelle angoisse, hein?
7. — C'est vraiment curieux, cette tenue et ces masques qu'ils portent. Je ne comprends pas très bien les règles de l'escrime, mais c'est fascinant à observer.
8. — Ça, c'était vraiment génial. Vous voyez? Là, c'est le moment où l'Américain a battu le record de saut à la perche. La foule était en délire!

Answers to Mise en pratique Activity 2

1. c   2. g   3. d   4. a   5. h   6. e   7. b   8. f

Cette année-là aux Jeux olympiques
(Individual Project)

ASSIGNMENT

Students will write and produce a booklet that features the host city and champion athletes from the Olympic Games of any given year. The cover of the booklet, illustrated with drawings, cutouts, or computer-generated graphics, will feature information on the Games for that year. The first page of the booklet will give background and tourist information about the host city. Five additional pages will give information on five champion athletes who competed in the Games and information about the events they participated in. Encourage students to incorporate the vocabulary and functions of the chapter in their text.

MATERIALS

✂ **Students may need**
- Encyclopedias
- Construction paper
- Stapler
- Colored pencils or markers
- Magazines or catalogues
- Almanacs
- Typewriter or word processor
- Computer-generated graphics

SUGGESTED SEQUENCE

1. Students research the Olympic Games of a particular year and decide which events to feature.

2. Students research the host city of the Olympic Games they have chosen. They should gather historical information as well as information on local sights that would be of interest to tourists.

3. Students then research the five sporting events they have chosen. They should look up historical information about the sport as well as the basic rules and necessary equipment.

4. Next, students should find out who won the events they've selected in the year they've chosen, where the winning athletes are from, and any pertinent information about them.

5. Students then imagine an interview between one of the athletes and a sports reporter. They might create the interview in three stages: before the athlete leaves his or her home country to attend the Games, at the Games before his or her event takes place, and after the event (or after he or she has received a medal).

6. Students write a rough draft of the information they will include in their booklets, using the notes they have taken during their research, and looking up any French terms they need in the dictionary. Students should edit their papers, and then exchange papers with a partner for additional corrections and comments.

7. Students type or write the text neatly on the pages they will include in the booklet: the cover, the host city information page, and the five pages featuring the champion athletes and their events.

8. Students illustrate the booklet where appropriate.

9. Have students exchange their booklets in class, share them with other French classes, or display them in the school library.

GRADING THE PROJECT

You might base students' grades on content, language use, visual presentation, and creativity.

Suggested Point Distribution (total = 100 points)

Content . . . . 25 points
Language use . . . . 25 points
Visual presentation . . . . 25 points
Creativity . . . . 25 points

D'OU VIENS-TU?

In this game, students will practice using prepositions with the names of countries, departments, or provinces.

To prepare for the game, write the names of different countries in English on separate index cards *(Switzerland)*. On a separate sheet of paper, write their French equivalents including the appropriate form of **de** *(de Suisse)*. Make copies of this score sheet. To play the game, distribute copies of world maps to students. Form groups of six, assign a judge within each group, and give each judge a copy of the score sheet. One player draws a card, points to the appropriate country, department, or province, gives his or her name, and says that he or she comes from that place. **(Je m'appelle Nadine. Je suis du Québec.)** The next player points to the area mentioned by the previous player, repeats the information he or she gave, draws a card, points to the appropriate area on the map, and gives information about him- or herself. **(Elle s'appelle Nadine. Elle est du Québec. Moi, je m'appelle Roger. Je suis d'Haïti.)** The judge verifies that the players maintain the correct order of countries, give the appropriate names, use contractions with **de** correctly, and point to the appropriate area on their map. When a player makes an error, he or she is out, and a new round begins. The player remaining after everyone else is out is the winner.

MOTS ASSOCIES

In this game, students will review all the functional expressions and vocabulary they've learned in Chapters 1–12.

Procedure Distribute several index cards to each student in the class. On one side of the cards, students should write lists of several words and/or expressions grouped by category **(l'escrime, le judo, la gymnastique)**. On the reverse side, they should write the category *(Olympic sports)*. Examples of additional categories are given below. You might assign each student one chapter in the book on which to base his or her categories. Collect the cards and edit them. Then, form two teams and have the first player from each team stand up. Read aloud the list from one of the cards. The first player to identify the category wins a point for his or her team.

Sample categories:
- Places where you wait
- Things to do in Tunisia
- Things your parent might say to you
- Things you might write to an advice columnist
- Things you might write in a business letter

Chapitre 12
Echanges sportifs et culturels

pp. 296–319

*U*sing the Chapter Opener

▦ **Video Program**

Videocassette 2

Before you begin this chapter, you might want to preview the *Video Program* and consult the *Video Guide.* Suggestions for integrating the video into each chapter and activity masters for video selections can be found in the *Video Guide.*

Motivating Activity

Ask students if they have ever been to an Olympic stadium or if they have ever watched the Olympic Games on TV. If so, ask them what events they enjoy watching and why.

Teaching Suggestion

You might ask students to list words and expressions they associate with the Olympics (figure skating, torch, gold medal, international).

Photo Flash!

① This photo shows an Olympic stadium with the Olympic flame in the foreground. The sacred flame is first lit in Olympia in Greece and then carried on foot by various people to the appropriate Olympic location. At the opening ceremonies of the Olympiad, torch-bearing runners circle the stadium track, mount the steps, and ignite the fire, which burns night and day for the duration of the Games.

CHAPITRE

12
Echanges sportifs et culturels

① Les Jeux olympiques, affrontement sportif et union culturelle

296   *deux cent quatre-vingt-seize*

History Link

Have students research the history of the ancient and modern Olympic Games. The Olympic Games date from 8 B.C. when Iphitos, king of Pisa, and Lycurgus, the Spartan law giver, organized sporting competitions in Olympia, Greece. A statue of Zeus was erected there, and the site was declared a sacred space. The winners of the events would attend a banquet and be crowned with an olive wreath. The ancient Games were held for the last time in 393 A.D. Richard Chandler, an Englishman, discovered the site of the sanctuary in 1766, and German archaeologists excavated the site from 1875 to 1881. A French scholar and educator, Baron Pierre de Coubertin, proposed the establishment of the modern Olympic Games and became president of the International Olympic Committee. The first modern Games were held in Athens, Greece in 1896.

② Il me tarde de voir les épreuves de gymnastique.

Viens aux Jeux olympiques! C'est l'endroit idéal pour voir tes athlètes préférés au meilleur de leur forme. Mais ce n'est pas tout. Tu pourras aussi y rencontrer des jeunes du monde entier et découvrir toutes sortes de choses fascinantes sur leur pays, leur culture et leurs habitudes. Et puis, n'oublie pas, il y aura beaucoup de francophones en compétition et ce sera l'occasion pour toi de pratiquer ton français.

In this chapter you will review and practice

- expressing anticipation; making suppositions; expressing certainty and doubt
- inquiring; expressing excitement and disappointment

And you will

- listen to teenagers talking about their countries
- read about an athlete from Quebec
- write an article for a sports magazine
- find out what francophone teenagers think about other cultures

③ C'est comment, la vie là-bas?

deux cent quatre-vingt-dix-sept **297**

Focusing on Outcomes

After students read the introduction and the chapter outcomes, ask them to recall the expressions they learned in Chapter 1 for inquiring. (**C'était comment, tes vacances? Ça s'est bien passé? Tu t'es bien amusé(e)?**) Ask them to recall the expressions they learned in Chapter 7 for making suppositions (**On pourrait sûrement... , Je parie que... , Ça doit être... , Il doit y avoir...**); for expressing doubt (**Ça m'étonnerait que... , Je ne suis pas sûr(e)...**); and for expressing certainty (**Je suis certain(e) que... , Je suis sûr(e) que... , Je sais que... , Je suis convaincu(e)...**). Then, have them tell which photo demonstrates inquiring (Photo 3). NOTE: You may want to use the video to support the objectives. The self-check activities in **Que sais-je?** on page 318 help students assess their achievement of the objectives.

Teaching Suggestions

- Write the following French statements and questions on the board or on a transparency and have students try to match them to the functional outcomes listed on this page: **Je ne crois pas. Qu'est-ce qui est typique de chez toi? J'ai vraiment pas de chance. Ça doit être cool! C'est trop cool! Je suis vraiment impatient(e) de partir.** *(expressing doubt, inquiring, expressing disappointment, making suppositions, expressing excitement, expressing anticipation)*
- Have students list the Olympic events suggested by the objects on pages 296–297 (fencing, soccer, track, gymnastics, basketball).
- Have students suggest additional captions for the photos on pages 296–297.

Geography Links

- Call students' attention to the stamp pictured to the right of Photo 3. Have students locate Niger in central West Africa on the map on page xxi of their book.
- Have students list cities in which Olympic Games have been held (Sarajevo, Barcelona, Atlanta). Write their suggestions on the board. Then, display a large world map and have volunteers mark the cities with pins.

Summary

In **A nous les Jeux olympiques!**, four young athletes are preparing for the Olympic Games. Julie, who will compete in fencing, worries about how she will perform. Lisette reassures and encourages her. Youssef is quite confident that he will do well in the diving competition. Ali reminds Youssef that the American diver is more experienced than he is. Ophélia, a track and field athlete, is feeling the stress of having trained so long. Her trainer, Mr. Duval, encourages her. Mademba, a wrestling champion, tries to calm his mother's fears about his traveling to the United States. Mademba's sister reminds him to get the gymnast Lu Li's autograph, but he warns her that he may not have time.

Motivating Activity

Ask students what they do in order to prepare themselves physically and/or mentally for a competition, a performance, a presentation, or even a test. Ask them what they might say to reassure a friend who is nervous about an upcoming event.

Presentation

Before you play the recording, have students look at the photos and predict what sporting events will be discussed in each dialogue. Then, play the recording. Pause it after each scene to ask what sport the athlete will participate in and how he or she is feeling (nervous, confident, worried, and so on).

Mise en train

À nous les Jeux olympiques!

Lisette téléphone à Julie pour lui souhaiter bonne chance aux Jeux olympiques.

1 LISETTE Allô, Julie? Alors, tu es prête pour le grand départ?

JULIE Ne m'en parle pas! J'ai un trac fou!

LISETTE T'en fais pas. Ça va aller.

JULIE Je suis vraiment impatiente de partir. Tu sais, c'est ma première compétition olympique. Je me demande comment ça sera. En tout cas, je suis sûre que ça va être impressionnant.

LISETTE Moi, je parie que tu vas gagner la médaille d'or!

JULIE Tu parles! Ça m'étonnerait. Il doit y avoir des tas d'escrimeuses beaucoup plus fortes que moi, des championnes qui ont plus d'expérience. Surtout les Allemandes! Je suis certaine que c'est elles qui vont gagner. Si je suis au meilleur de ma forme, je pourrai peut-être arriver en demi-finale. Ça serait déjà très bien.

LISETTE Oh, arrête. Si tu penses comme ça, tu ne gagneras rien du tout. Un conseil : répète trois fois «C'est moi la meilleure!»

JULIE C'est moi la meilleure, c'est moi la meilleure, c'est moi la meilleure!

LISETTE Voilà. Très bien.

JULIE En tout cas, il me tarde d'assister aux épreuves d'athlétisme. Tu imagines un peu! Tous les meilleurs athlètes du monde réunis! Vivement que j'arrive! Au moins, j'aurai cette consolation si je ne gagne pas...

LISETTE Oh non! Tu ne vas pas recommencer! Je parie que tout va très bien se passer. Allez. Je t'embrasse et bonne chance!

Ali entre dans la chambre de son frère Youssef qui est en train de faire ses valises.

2 ALI Salut. Alors, tu as tout ce qu'il te faut?

YOUSSEF Oui, je crois.

ALI Pense à prendre ton maillot.

YOUSSEF Très drôle! Je serai le seul plongeur olympique sans maillot!

ALI Alors, tu as le trac?

YOUSSEF Oh, tu sais, c'est pas pour me vanter, mais je crois que j'ai mes chances.

ALI Oh, arrête de délirer! Tu as vu qui est en compétition? L'Américain, là, il a beaucoup plus d'expérience que toi. C'est la troisième fois qu'il participe aux Jeux olympiques. Ça m'étonnerait que tu le battes.

YOUSSEF Tu es vraiment encourageant, toi. Ça arrive souvent que les plus jeunes concurrents gagnent, tu sais.

ALI Ouais. Bon, ben... bonne chance, hein.

298 *deux cent quatre-vingt-dix-huit*   CHAPITRE 12   Echanges sportifs et culturels

---

RESOURCES FOR MISE EN TRAIN

Textbook Audiocassette 6B/Audio CD 12
Practice and Activity Book, p. 133

Geography Link

Have students look at the flags accompanying the dialogues and find out which countries they represent (France–1 and 3; Morocco–2; Senegal–4).

Teacher Note

You might tell students that fencing competitions involve several different events, related to the three different types of swords used. The foil has a flexible, four-sided blade; the épée has a long, narrow blade; the sabre is a heavier sword with a flexible blade and a cutting edge. All swords used in competition are fixed with blunt ends, and participants wear protective gear to avoid injuries.

A sa dernière séance d'entraînement avant de partir, Ophélia discute avec son entraîneur.

③ M. DUVAL   Eh bien, Ophélia? Tu n'as pas l'air en forme.

OPHELIA   Oh, je ne sais pas. Ça fait tellement longtemps que je m'entraîne. Ça doit être le stress, sûrement.

M. DUVAL   Allez! Encore un effort! C'est pas la mer à boire. Tu y es presque! Tu imagines si Marie-José Perec parlait comme ça? Tu ferais mieux de te concentrer sur ton entraînement. Tu sais ce que je dis toujours...

OPHELIA   Oui, je sais : «On n'arrive à rien sans rien.»

M. DUVAL   C'est ça. Et n'oublie pas que, même si c'est beaucoup de travail maintenant, tu seras vraiment heureuse quand tu seras sur le podium.

OPHELIA   Oui, je sais. Ça va sûrement être génial. Il y aura des champions de tous les pays... Ça sera chouette de parler à des Africains... Je n'ai jamais rencontré d'Africains. Et puis, il me tarde d'aller aux Etats-Unis... Je me demande s'il y a beaucoup d'Américains qui parlent français, parce que mon anglais n'est pas terrible...

M. DUVAL   Oui. Enfin, n'oublie quand même pas l'entraînement.

OPHELIA   Ça, je sais que je peux compter sur vous pour me le rappeler!

Mademba est à l'aéroport avec sa famille qui lui dit au revoir avant son départ pour les Etats-Unis.

④ MME KAUSSI   Tu es sûr que tu as tout ce qu'il te faut?

MADEMBA   Mais oui, maman. T'en fais pas.

MME KAUSSI   Fais attention. Tu sais ce qu'on dit. Ça peut être dangereux de se promener aux Etats-Unis...

MADEMBA   N'aie pas peur. Tu sais, je suis champion de lutte! Je sais me défendre!

MME KAUSSI   Bon. Mais quand même, méfie-toi. Et laisse ton argent dans ta chambre.

MADEMBA   Mais maman, les Etats-Unis, c'est civilisé! Je parie que je vais me faire des tas de copains tout de suite. Il doit y avoir plein de francophones en compétition.

ADJOUBA   Et n'oublie pas que tu m'as promis de demander un autographe à Lu Li.

MADEMBA   Oui, oui. Je sais. Je ferai de mon mieux mais je ne suis pas certain de pouvoir la voir.

ADJOUBA   Pourquoi? Tu ne vas pas aller voir les épreuves de gymnastique?

MADEMBA   Tu sais, ça m'étonnerait que j'aie le temps. J'ai mon entraînement et puis je veux voir autant de matches de basket que possible. Bon. Je dois y aller. Dès que je serai installé, je vous appellerai.

MME KAUSSI   Allez! Au revoir, mon petit et bonne chance! On est fiers de toi.

ADJOUBA   Envoie-nous une carte postale dès que tu pourras... Et n'oublie pas de me rapporter quelque chose.

MADEMBA   Oui, oui! Allez, à bientôt!

Teaching Suggestions

- Play the first two segments of the recording and ask who is more confident, Julie or Youssef (Youssef). Do the same for the third and fourth segments. (Mademba is more confident than Ophélia.)
- In small groups, have students describe each of the four athletes. You might also have them consider how they would feel if they were preparing to participate in the Olympics in a foreign country. Would they be confident or a little nervous? Would they be excited about meeting new people or worried about the competition?

For Individual Needs

Auditory Learners Write several one-sentence descriptions of the various athletes in the **Mise en train**. (**Cette personne fait du plongeon acrobatique. Cette personne aime les matchs de basket.**) Read the sentences aloud and have students identify the athletes they describe.

Challenge Have students assume the identity of one of the athletes from the **Mise en train** and create several one-sentence descriptions of themselves, similar to the ones suggested above. Have them read their descriptions to classmates, who will try to guess their secret identity.

Multicultural Link

Have students research the sports mentioned in the **Mise en train** and gather information about the current Olympic champions, including the country they represent and when and where they won their honors.

Geography Link

Ask students to explain or research the significance of the five rings on the Olympic flag. (They represent the five original continents of the world.) Have them name the continents (Africa, America, Asia, Australia, Europe).

Teaching Suggestions

1 Have students create additional comprehension questions about the **Mise en train** to ask the class.

2 Have students find other quotations from the dialogues to read to a partner, who identifies the speaker.

Note Culturelle After students read the **Note Culturelle**, ask them if they are fans of a particular sport and, if so, have them share what they know about any international competitions in that sport.

Culture Notes

• The **Tour de France** was established in 1903 by Henri Desgrange, a French journalist and cyclist. The annual race covers about 4,000 kilometers over varied terrain throughout France and parts of neighboring countries. The race is divided into 21 day-long segments, or **étapes**. The rider with the lowest overall time wins. From 1903 to 1985, all the winners were from Western Europe, primarily France and Belgium. In 1986, Greg Lemond was the first American to win the **Tour de France**. He won again in 1989 and in 1990.

• The French Open, or the Roland Garros tennis tournament, is one of four major world tennis championships. It is held at the **Stade Roland Garros** in the outskirts of Paris. It has the only hard (clay) court in world competition.

---

1 Tu as compris? See answers below.

1. Where are these teenagers going?
2. When and where does each conversation take place?
3. How does Julie feel about her competition? What about Youssef?
4. What is Ophélia's coach discussing with her?
5. How does Mademba's family feel about his trip to the United States?

2 Qui dit quoi?

Quel(le) jeune fait ces remarques dans **A nous les Jeux olympiques**?

Mademba
> Tu sais, je suis champion de lutte! Je sais me défendre.

Ophélia
> Ça sera chouette de parler à des Africains.

Julie
> Si je suis au meilleur de ma forme, je pourrai peut-être arriver en demi-finale.

> Il doit y avoir des tas d'escrimeuses beaucoup plus fortes que moi.
Julie

> Je me demande s'il y a beaucoup d'Américains qui parlent français, parce que mon anglais n'est pas terrible.
Ophélia

> Oh, tu sais, c'est pas pour me vanter, mais je crois que j'ai mes chances.
Youssef

3 Vrai ou faux?

1. Julie compte gagner la médaille d'or. faux
2. Elle n'a pas envie de voir d'autres sports. faux
3. Youssef a oublié son maillot de bain. faux
4. Il a un trac fou. faux
5. Il se croit le meilleur plongeur du monde. faux
6. M. Duval est satisfait de l'entraînement d'Ophélia. faux
7. Ophélia voudrait rencontrer beaucoup de gens aux Jeux olympiques. vrai
8. Mademba compte assister à beaucoup d'épreuves de gymnastique. faux

4 Cherche les expressions

What do the people in **A nous les Jeux olympiques!** say to . . . See answers below.

1. reassure someone?
2. express anticipation?
3. make a supposition?
4. express doubt?
5. brag?
6. tease?
7. encourage someone?
8. give advice?
9. caution someone?

5 Et maintenant, à toi

Est-ce que tu as déjà participé à une compétition ou à un événement sportif? Comment est-ce que tu t'es préparé(e)? Est-ce que tu étais inquiet/inquiète, impatient(e), sûr(e) de toi?

NOTE CULTURELLE

International sporting events, such as the Olympic Games, are exciting for both spectators and participants. For many people, however, the competition itself is not the most important purpose of such an event. By bringing athletes from all over the world together for friendly competition, these events promote understanding and acceptance among people from many different cultures. Among the most famous international sporting events are the **Tour de France**, regarded as the most grueling bicycle race in the world; the Paris-Dakar Rally, a motorcycle and automobile race between the capitals of France and Senegal; and the Roland Garros tennis tournament, known in the United States as the French Open.

300 *trois cents*   CHAPITRE 12   Echanges sportifs et culturels

---

Answers

1 1. Olympic Games in U.S.
2. as they prepare to leave their home countries
3. Julie is nervous; Youssef is confident of his chances.
4. her training
5. His mother is proud, but concerned for his safety. Adjouba, Mademba's sister, sees a chance to get a gymnast's autograph.

4 1. T'en fais pas. Ça va aller. N'aie pas peur.
2. Je suis vraiment impatiente de... ; Il me tarde de... ; Vivement que... ! Dès que...
3. Je parie que... ; Il doit y avoir... ; Ça doit être...
4. Ça m'étonnerait. ... je ne suis pas certain de... ; Je me demande...
5. C'est moi la meilleure! C'est pas pour me vanter, mais...
6. Oh, arrête de délirer!
7. Allez! Encore un effort! C'est pas la mer à boire. Tu y es presque!
8. Un conseil : ... ; Tu ferais mieux de... ; ... n'oublie pas...
9. Fais attention. ... méfie-toi.

PREMIERE ETAPE

Expressing anticipation; making suppositions; expressing certainty and doubt

VOCABULAIRE

le basket-ball

le ballon

le panier

l'escrime (f.)

l'épée (f.)   le masque

la tenue

le base-ball

le bâton
le casque
le lanceur   la balle   le frappeur

la gymnastique

les barres (f.) asymétriques

les anneaux (m.)

la poutre

l'entraîneur (m.)

l'athlétisme (m.)

le saut à la perche

le lancer du disque   la course de fond

le saut en longueur

le plongeon acrobatique

le plongeoir

plonger

l'aviron (m.)

les rames (f.)

le tir à l'arc

tirer   l'arc (m.)

la flèche

l'haltérophilie (f.)

les haltères (m.)

| la boxe | l'équitation (f.) | la lutte |
| le cyclisme | le judo | la natation |

Si tu as oublié — **sports** — *va à la page 336.*

6 Ecoute!

Ecoute les conversations de ces spectateurs aux Jeux olympiques. A quelles épreuves est-ce qu'ils assistent? Answers on p. 295C.

PREMIERE ETAPE

trois cent un **301**

RESOURCES FOR PREMIERE ETAPE

Chapter Teaching Resources, Book 3
- Communicative Activity 12-1, pp. 166–167
- Teaching Transparency Master 12-1, pp. 170, 172
  Teaching Transparency 12-1
- Additional Listening Activities 12-1, 12-2, 12-3, pp. 173–174
  Audiocassette 10B/Audio CD 12
- Realia 12-1, pp. 177, 179
- Situation Cards 12-1, pp. 180–181
- Student Response Forms, pp. 182–184
- Quiz 12-1, pp. 185–186
  Audiocassette 8B/Audio CD 12

ADDITIONAL RESOURCES
Textbook Audiocassette 6B
OR *Audio CD 12*
Practice and Activity Book, pp. 134–137

Jump Start!

Have students write two or three sentences about sports or activities they participate in, would like to participate in, or enjoy watching.

MOTIVATE

Have students recall as many summer Olympic sporting events as possible.

TEACH

Presentation

Vocabulaire Mime each sport, describing your activities. (**Je fais du basket-ball. Voilà mon ballon et le panier est là-haut.**) If possible, bring in sports equipment as props. Mime each activity again, asking **Qu'est-ce que je fais?** Finally, have volunteers mime the activities and ask the class **Qu'est-ce qu'il/elle fait?** and prompt students to say **Il/Elle fait de la natation.**

Teaching Suggestion

Ask students questions about the sports equipment, such as **Est-ce que j'ai besoin d'un plongeoir pour faire de la gymnastique? (non) De quoi est-ce que j'ai besoin, alors? (Vous avez besoin de barres asymétriques.)**

TPR Bring in and have students bring in pictures of athletes performing the various sports. Tape them to the board. Then, call on a student to be "it." Have volunteers tell the student to identify various pictures. (**Montre-moi la photo de la personne qui fait du judo. Donne-moi la photo de la personne qui fait du tir à l'arc.**)

7 Quel sport?

Associe ces objets à leurs images. Pour quel sport est-ce qu'ils sont nécessaires? See answers below.

8 Sportez-vous bien!

Regarde ce tableau et réponds aux questions suivantes.

1. Trouve un sport...

   a. qui est une bonne préparation pour tous les sports. la gymnastique
   b. qui est bien pour ceux qui sont précis dans leurs gestes. le tir à l'arc
   c. où les plus grands sont favorisés.
   d. pour ceux qui aiment prendre des décisions rapides. c. le basket-ball
   d. l'escrime

2. Qu'est-ce qu'il te faut pour faire... See answers below.

   de la gymnastique?
   de l'escrime?   du basket?
   du tir à l'arc?

3. Vrai ou faux?

   a. Si tu fais de l'escrime, tu pourras te défendre avec politesse. vrai
   b. Le tir à l'arc est le sport le plus populaire en France. faux
   c. La gymnastique peut t'aider à lutter contre le ras-le-bol scolaire. vrai

302 *trois cent deux*   CHAPITRE 12   Echanges sportifs et culturels

9 Sondage

Ton correspondant français voudrait savoir quels sports sont les plus populaires chez toi. Fais un sondage dans ta classe. Demande à tes camarades de nommer par ordre de préférence cinq sports qu'ils aiment faire et cinq sports qu'ils aiment regarder à la télé. Compare tes résultats à ceux de ton/ta camarade.

10 Qu'est-ce que tu en dis?

Ton ami(e) pense essayer un nouveau sport. Il/Elle te demande ton opinion. Tu lui donnes des conseils.

—Je pense faire du plongeon acrobatique. Qu'est-ce que tu en dis?
—Si j'étais toi, je ferais plutôt de la natation. C'est moins dangereux.

> dangereux   cool   fatigant
> ennuyeux   dur   intéressant
> facile   cher   génial
> amusant   bon pour la santé

11 C'est quoi pour vous, le sport?

Lis les remarques faites par quelques jeunes francophones et réponds aux questions.

See answers below.

«RAUL»
Roma (Italie)
J'aime beaucoup le sport, en particulier le foot. Je pense que ça sert à mieux respirer, à faire mieux fonctionner le corps, à organiser ses forces et à s'amuser. Je crois que si tout le monde pratiquait régulièrement un sport, mais bien entendu seulement comme loisir, on ne connaîtrait pas la vieillesse. Personnellement, je préfère les sports d'équipe, parce que je peux connaître des tas d'amis, et aussi parce que la responsabilité de gagner n'est pas concentrée toute sur moi.

«STÉPHANIE»
Limoges
Pour moi, le sport permet de se défoncer, de se marrer, de se mesurer à soi-même et aux autres. Si je fais deux ou trois heures de sport par semaine, j'ai l'impression de ne pas être moi-même, de ne pas m'être assez défoncée. Pendant les vacances, j'ai fait un stage de tennis (trois heures par jour) et de golf (deux heures par jour), et là, j'étais contente et en super forme.

«BÉATRICE»
Annecy-le-Vieux
Tu sais, Stéphanie, moi aussi, je suis une folle de sport. J'adore ça. Je pense que le sport est fait pour se défouler. On bouge, on rigole, et c'est chouette ! Moi, j'ai horreur d'être enfermée toute la journée dans le collège. Alors, quand c'est l'heure du sport, j'en profite beaucoup. Je pratique de la gymnastique aux agrès (barres, poutre et cheval) pendant toute l'année dans un club, et c'est génial. Je fais des compétitions, ce qui m'oblige à bien travailler. J'aime aussi les sports d'équipe que je pratique à l'école, et aussi l'équitation, la natation... Vive les sports !

1. What are six reasons these teenagers give for participating in sports?
2. How does Stéphanie feel if she doesn't devote enough time to sports?
3. Which of the teenagers especially likes team sports? Why?
4. Which of the teenagers goes to competitions? What does she dread?

12 Mon journal

Est-ce que le sport est important pour toi? Pourquoi ou pourquoi pas?

PREMIERE ETAPE   _trois cent trois_   303

Mon journal

12 You might have students expand their journal entries to tell which sports they participate in and how often. They might also compare their attitude towards sports with the attitudes of several of their friends. For an additional journal entry suggestion for Chapter 12, see _Practice and Activity Book,_ page 156.

Answers

11 1. relaxation, fun, personal challenge, competition, health, camaraderie
2. as if she's not herself
3. Raul; friends, shared responsibility for winning
4. Béatrice; she dreads being inside all day at school.

Teaching Suggestion

9 Have several volunteers compile a list on the board of ten sports and activities their classmates suggest. Then, have the entire class decide on a way to take the poll. They might use a yes-no vote, a graded scale (**pas du tout, un peu, beaucoup**), or a numeric scale (1–10). Next, have the volunteers ask students to raise their hands in response to their questions about the various sports. (**Qui aime la natation? Qui aime un peu la natation? Qui croit que la natation mérite un «dix»?**) Have the polltakers count their classmates' raised hands and record the totals on the board.

For Individual Needs

11 Auditory Learners
Call out statements at random from the three articles and have students identify the speaker.

Additional Practice

11 You might ask students the following questions about the teenagers' comments: **Quel sport est-ce que Raul aime en particulier?** (le foot) **Pourquoi est-ce qu'il préfère les sports d'équipe?** (parce qu'il peut connaître des amis et parce que la responsabilité de gagner n'est pas concentrée toute sur lui) **Pourquoi Stéphanie aime-t-elle le sport?** (ça permet de se défoncer, de se marrer, de se mesurer à soi-même et aux autres) **Qu'est-ce que Béatrice déteste?** (être enfermée toute la journée au collège) **Quels autres sports est-ce qu'elle pratique en dehors de la gymnastique?** (l'équitation, la natation)

Presentation

Comment dit-on... ? The day before the presentation, have several pairs of students write brief dialogues, using several of the expressions. In class, write four columns on a transparency: *Expressing anticipation, Expressing certainty, Making a supposition,* and *Expressing doubt.* Have a volunteer come to the overhead projector. Then, have the partners act out their dialogues. After each one, have the class tell the volunteer which functions they heard in the dialogue. The volunteer makes check marks in the appropriate columns. Then, write the expressions on separate transparency strips, scatter them across the projector, and have students tell in which column they belong.

Teaching Suggestion

You might have partners write brief dialogues incorporating one expression from each category.

For Individual Needs

13 Kinesthetic Learners
As students listen to the recording, have them stand up if they hear Séverine making a supposition and raise their hand if they hear her expressing anticipation.

Teaching Suggestion

Note de grammaire Write the following sentence starters on a transparency and have students suggest possible completions: **Je serai heureuse quand...** ; **Dès que je serai à l'université,...** ; **Je vais partir en voyage dès que...** ; **Je regarderai les matchs à la télé quand...**

COMMENT DIT-ON... ?

Expressing anticipation; making suppositions; expressing certainty and doubt

To express anticipation:

Il me tarde de voir les épreuves de judo. *I can't wait to . . .*

Je suis vraiment impatient(e) de partir! *I can hardly wait to . . . !*

Vivement que j'arrive! *I just can't wait to get there!*

Dès que je serai là, je mangerai un hot-dog. *As soon as I get there, . . .*

Quand je verrai mes athlètes préférés, je leur demanderai un autographe.

To express certainty:

Je suis sûr(e)/certain(e) que le basket-ball va être super.

Ça, c'est sûr.

Je n'en ai aucun doute.

To make a supposition:

Ça doit être cool!

Il doit y avoir beaucoup de francophones.

Je parie que les Russes vont gagner.

On pourra sûrement rencontrer des gens intéressants.

To express doubt:

Je ne suis pas sûr(e)/certain(e) que les escrimeurs français puissent gagner.

Je ne pense/crois pas qu'on puisse obtenir des places pour la gymnastique.

Ça m'étonnerait qu'il gagne la médaille d'or.

---

13 Ecoute!

Séverine part aux Etats-Unis. Elle discute avec son frère en faisant ses valises. Indique les conversations où elle fait une supposition et celles où elle exprime son impatience.

Answers on p. 295C.

If you know the word for an activity, you can often guess the word for the person who does that activity. The suffix **-eur/-euse** generally indicates a person who does the action a verb expresses. If **plonger** means *to dive,* who is a **plongeur**? You know the verb **jouer** means *to play.* How would you say *a player*? What are the words for the people who do these activities: **nager, sauter, courir, tirer, recevoir**? Some other less common endings which also indicate a person or a performer are **-ant(e)**, and **-iste**. What do you think the words **gagnant** and **perchiste** mean?

Note de *Grammaire*

You've learned that you generally use the future tense in French in the same way as you do in English. However, when talking about a future event in French, you use the future tense following the conjunctions **quand** and **dès que**, whereas in English, you use the present tense. Look at these examples:

Je serai heureuse **quand** je **serai** sur le podium.
when I am

Je vais lui demander son autographe **dès que** je le **verrai**.
as soon as I see

Game

QUAND JE... Write various infinitives on transparency strips and put them in a bag. On additional transparency strips, have students write sentence starters similar to the ones suggested under the Teaching Suggestion for the Note de grammaire. Collect their sentence starters, edit them, and put them in a separate bag. Then, form two teams. The first player from the first team comes to the front, draws a strip from each bag, and places the strips on the overhead for the teams to see. Then, give the player twenty or thirty seconds to compose a meaningful sentence, using the starter and the verb in the future tense. Players win a point for each correct sentence, and teams alternate turns.

14 Il me tarde de....

Nadine essaie d'imaginer comment ça sera aux Jeux olympiques. Qu'est-ce qu'elle dit?

See answers below.

1.

2.

15 C'est trop cool!

Tu as gagné un voyage pour aller voir un de ces événements sportifs. Tu es impatient(e) d'y aller et tu te demandes comment ça sera. Ton/ta camarade te donnera son avis. Tu lui diras si tu crois qu'il/elle a raison. Changez de rôles.

le Superbowl   le Tour de France
Wimbledon   la Coupe du monde
le rallye Paris-Dakar   Roland-Garros

16 Moi, je suis impatient(e) de voir....

Tu vas inviter ton ami(e) chez toi pour regarder quelques événements des Jeux olympiques à la télé. Regardez le programme. Chacun(e) propose des sports qu'il/elle aime, mais l'autre n'est pas d'accord. Essaie de convaincre ton/ta camarade en disant comment ça sera, d'après toi. Enfin, décidez ce que vous allez regarder et donnez-vous rendez-vous.

Lundi 22 juillet

	17h00	19h00	19h30	22h30
SRC	Athlétisme -Saut à la perche -Saut en hauteur -Saut en longueur	Tir à l'arc Dames Par équipes	Base-ball USA/ Canada	Basket-ball Russie/ Allemagne
	17h00	19h30	20h00	21h30
TVA	Boxe Poids Lourds	Gymnastique -Poutre -Anneaux -Sol	Equitation Concours Complet Individuel	Escrime Dames Fleuret Par équipes
	17h30	18h30	19h00	21h30
CTV	Judo Super Légers	Escrime Epée Messieurs Individuel	Base-ball Japon/ Porto Rico	Haltérophilie Super Lourds

Mardi 23 juillet

	18h00	19h00	22h00	22h30
SRC	Athlétisme - Relais - Saut en hauteur - Course	Basket-ball Espagne/ Suède	Gymnastique Messieurs Exercices au sol	Aviron Dames
	18h00	19h00	19h30	20h30
TVA	Lutte Jusqu'à 68 kg	Plongeon acrobatique Messieurs	Athlétisme -Courses de haies -200m Dames -800m Messieurs	Judo Moyens
	17h00	18h15	19h00	22h15
CTV	Natation 100m Papillon 1500m Nage libre	Athlétisme -Javelot -Lancer du disque	Base-ball Brésil/France	Tir à l'arc Messieurs Individuel

---

For Individual Needs

14 Visual Learners Have students draw their own dream bubble depicting their anticipation of an upcoming event, real or imaginary. Have them write a caption for the illustration.

Culture Note

15 The Paris-Dakar Rally is a car and motorcycle race that takes place every January. On New Year's Day, participants set off from Paris, France to cross the Sahara Desert in the world's most treacherous off-road rally. The course usually takes about twenty days to complete. In 1993, the French swept the awards at the rally, with Bruno Saby taking the grand prize.

Additional Practice

16 Call out, or have students call out, a date, time, and channel (**lundi 22 juillet, 19h30, TVA**), and have the class respond by naming the event that is scheduled for that slot (**la gymnastique**).

CLOSE

Game

On index cards, write the French words for sports and equipment. On the reverse side of each card, write one word students are not allowed to use to define that word. For example, you might write the sport **l'escrime** on one side of a card, and **à ne pas dire : l'épée** on the reverse side. Then, form two teams. The first player from one team selects a card and tries to get his or her teammates to say the word written on the front without saying any form of the word written on the reverse side. For example, if the player drew the card described above, he or she might say **Je porte une tenue blanche et un masque.**

Possible answers

14 1. Quand je verrai mon athlète préféré, je lui demanderai un autographe.

2. Il me tarde de voir les épreuves de natation.

3. Je parie que je vais gagner la médaille d'or!

4. Je pourrai sûrement rencontrer des gens intéressants.

ASSESS

Quiz 12-1, *Chapter Teaching Resources, Book 3,* pp. 185–186

Assessment Items, Audiocassette 8B Audio CD 12

Performance Assessment

Have partners role-play an interview with an athlete's proud parent just after the athlete has left for the Olympic Games.

Summary

In **Un rendez-vous sportif et culturel**, Mademba, Ophélia, and Julie are watching the basketball final. At the game, Mademba meets Yvonne, a volleyball player from Canada, and they discuss life in their home countries. Ophélia is at the game with her new friend, Hélène, and they discuss visiting each other in their respective countries, Guadeloupe and Switzerland. Jean-Paul congratulates Julie on her gold medal and expresses disappointment at his own defeat.

Motivating Activity

Ask students if they have ever had the opportunity to meet people from different cultures. If so, ask them to share their experiences. If not, ask them to imagine what questions they might like to ask them, and what they would like these people to know about their own culture.

Presentation

Ask students questions about the photos on pages 306–307, such as the following: **Mademba et Yvonne assistent à quelle sorte de match?** (un match de basket) Sur la deuxième photo, Yvonne a l'air triste ou plutôt gênée? (gênée) A la page 307, c'est une photo de la France ou de la Guadeloupe? (de la Guadeloupe) Regardez la photo de Julie. Elle a participé à quelle épreuve? (l'escrime) Elle a l'air d'avoir perdu ou d'avoir gagné? (d'avoir gagné) Then, play the recording and ask students the comprehension questions in Activity 17.

Remise en train

Un rendez-vous sportif et culturel

Quelques-uns des athlètes participant aux Jeux olympiques sont allés voir la finale de basket-ball.

1

MADEMBA	You beg my pardon, madame, is it lane euh, vingt-deux?
YVONNE	Yes. Tu peux me parler en français, si tu veux. Je suis du Canada.
MADEMBA	Super! Je m'appelle Mademba. Je suis du Sénégal. Je suis ici pour la lutte. Et toi?
YVONNE	Moi, c'est Yvonne. Je joue au volley.
MADEMBA	Au fait, c'est quoi, le score?
YVONNE	Trente à vingt-sept pour les Etats-Unis.
MADEMBA	Oh, zut alors! Allez, les Russes!
YVONNE	Ah, non! Je suis pour les Américains, moi. Ils sont vraiment bons. Dis, tu as vu leur match contre les Brésiliens?
MADEMBA	Oui, je l'ai vu à la télé avant de venir.
YVONNE	Vous avez la télé au Sénégal?
MADEMBA	Bien sûr. Et on a aussi des téléphones, des ordinateurs, des voitures, des avions... Il n'y a pas que des petits villages au Sénégal, il y a aussi des grandes villes modernes comme Dakar, par exemple.

2

YVONNE	Oh, pardon. Tu dois penser que je suis vraiment stupide.
MADEMBA	Non, pas du tout. Beaucoup de gens pensent comme toi. Je trouve ça dommage que les gens ne s'intéressent pas à la culture des autres.
YVONNE	Oui, c'est vraiment bête. On a vraiment de la chance d'être ici. Tu sais, j'aimerais bien que tu me racontes comment c'est dans ton pays. Dis donc, après le match, on peut aller manger quelque chose et discuter?
MADEMBA	Ça serait super. Et comme ça, tu pourras me parler du Canada.
YVONNE	D'accord.

17 Tu as compris? <small>See answers below.</small>

1. What are these conversations about?
2. What are some things that Hélène wants to do in Guadeloupe?
3. How does Yvonne embarrass herself? 6
4. What did Jean-Paul and Julie enjoy most about their Olympic experience?

18 Mets en ordre

Mets en ordre les événements d'**Un rendez-vous sportif et culturel.**

6 Mademba parle de son pays.

3 Yvonne donne le score à Mademba.

1 Mademba cherche son siège.

2 Mademba rencontre Yvonne.

4 Mademba encourage les Russes.

5 Yvonne fait une gaffe *(blunder).*

306 *trois cent six*   CHAPITRE 12   Echanges sportifs et culturels

RESOURCES FOR REMISE EN TRAIN

Textbook Audiocassette 6B/Audio CD 12
Practice and Activity Book, p. 138

Teaching Suggestion

18 Once students have arranged the events in order, have them compose a brief summary of the **Remise en train.**

Answers

17 1. Mademba/Yvonne: the basketball finals they're watching, Senegal
Ophélia/Hélène: keeping in touch with and visiting each other, Guadeloupe, Switzerland
Jean-Paul/Julie: Julie's gold medal and Jean-Paul's defeat, the experience of attending the Olympics
2. see beaches and tropical forests, walk through markets, meet people, dance the zouk
3. She asks Mademba if they have TV in Senegal.
4. meeting people; learning about their cultures

Ophélia et Hélène passent leur dernière soirée aux Jeux à la finale de basket.

❸ HELENE Dis donc, il est super, ce match. A ton avis, qui va gagner?

OPHELIA Je ne sais pas.

HELENE Qu'est-ce qu'il y a? Tu as l'air triste.

OPHELIA Un peu, oui. Demain tu vas rentrer chez toi et moi aussi. On ne se verra plus.

HELENE C'est vrai. Mais je vais t'écrire et t'envoyer plein de photos.

OPHELIA Moi aussi. Tu sais, je ne t'oublierai pas. Et puis, tu dois absolument venir passer un mois chez moi cet été. D'accord?

❹ HELENE Pas de problème. Il me tarde de voir la Guadeloupe. Ça sera super de voir les belles plages et les forêts tropicales. Et puis, je veux aussi me balader dans les marchés, rencontrer plein de gens et danser le zouk.

OPHELIA Et moi, je suis vraiment impatiente de voir toutes les montagnes couvertes de neige qu'il y a chez toi, en Suisse. N'oublie pas que tu dois m'apprendre à skier.

A la mi-temps, Julie et Jean-Paul échangent leurs impressions des Jeux.

❺ JEAN-PAUL Alors, Julie, ça fait comment d'avoir eu la médaille d'or?

JULIE C'est trop cool! Mais j'arrive toujours pas à y croire.

JEAN-PAUL Félicitations. Tu étais vraiment impressionnante.

JULIE Arrête, tu vas me faire rougir. J'ai eu de la chance, c'est tout.

JEAN-PAUL Moi, par contre, qu'est-ce que j'ai pu être nul! On va se moquer de moi en Belgique. Quelle angoisse!

JULIE Ne t'en fais pas! Ça peut arriver à tout le monde!

JEAN-PAUL C'est vrai. Et puis, tu sais, en venant ici, j'ai rencontré des gens super et j'ai pu apprendre toutes sortes de choses sur leurs pays.

JULIE Oui, moi aussi. Et je pense que ça sera le meilleur souvenir que je garderai de ces Jeux olympiques.

19 Vrai ou faux?

1. Yvonne est pour les Russes. faux
2. Il y a des grandes villes modernes au Sénégal. vrai
3. Mademba voudrait connaître le Canada. vrai
4. Ophélia est impatiente de faire du ski. vrai
5. Hélène ne s'intéresse pas du tout à la culture des autres. faux
6. Julie n'est même pas arrivée en finale. faux
7. Jean-Paul n'a pas aimé venir aux Jeux olympiques. faux

20 Cherche les expressions

What do the people in **Un rendez-vous sportif et culturel** say to . . . See answers below.

1. give their name and nationality?
2. inquire about someone's country?
3. root for a team?
4. express embarrassment?
5. express excitement?
6. congratulate someone?
7. express disappointment?

21 Et maintenant, à toi

Est-ce que tu as déjà rencontré des gens d'un autre pays? Qu'est-ce que tu as appris sur leur pays?

REMISE EN TRAIN

trois cent sept **307**

Answers

20 1. Je m'appelle... ; Moi, c'est... Je suis du...

2. Vous avez... au... ? J'aimerais bien que tu me racontes comment c'est dans ton pays.

3. Allez, les Russes!

4. Oh, pardon. Tu dois penser que je suis vraiment stupide.

5. Ça serait super... ; Super! C'est trop cool!

6. Félicitations. Tu étais vraiment impressionnante.

7. Quelle angoisse!

Teaching Suggestion

Form five groups and assign a section of the dialogue to each one. Have each group write several comprehension questions about their scene. They might write true-false statements, information questions, fill-in-the-blank sentences, or multiple-choice questions. Have the group members edit the questions, copy them onto index cards, and write the answers on the reverse side. After collecting the cards, either ask the questions of the entire class, or divide the class into two teams and have them compete to answer the questions first.

For Individual Needs

20 Visual/Auditory Learners Read aloud each of the French expressions that serve these functions, using appropriate gestures and facial expressions to convey meaning. **(Quelle angoisse!)** Have students tell in English which function you are demonstrating *(expressing disappointment).*

Teaching Suggestions

20 Once students have found these expressions, have them imagine they are participants in the Olympics in a foreign country. Have them write a short dialogue, using the functional expressions from this activity.

• You might also ask students how they think they would feel if they won a medal. Ask what they might say to a reporter in an interview after the event.

DEUXIEME ETAPE

Inquiring; expressing excitement and disappointment

*J*ump Start!

On the board, tape four pictures of athletes engaged in Olympic sports. Have students write a caption for each photo, incorporating one of the following functions for each one: expressing anticipation, expressing certainty, expressing doubt, and making suppositions.

MOTIVATE

Display a large world map with various countries marked with flags or pins. Have students write the names of the marked countries in French, including the appropriate definite articles.

TEACH

Presentation

Vocabulaire Project *Map Transparency 4* (**Le Monde francophone**). As you name the various countries, have a volunteer locate them on the transparency. Then, assume the identity of one of the teenagers in the **Vocabulaire** and give clues about your nationality (**J'habite en Afrique. Chez moi, je fais la cueillette des dattes**) until students guess it correctly. (**Vous venez de la Tunisie!**)

Additional Practice

Call out the names of countries at random (**le Canada**) and have students say that they come from there. (**Je suis du Canada.**)

Geography Link

Display a large world map. Tell volunteers where they are from (**Tu es de Chine**) and have them mark the appropriate country with a pin.

*V*OCABULAIRE

Regarde les gens que Julie a rencontrés aux Jeux olympiques.

 Je suis d'**Algérie**.

 Je suis de **Côte d'Ivoire**.

 Je suis de **Belgique**.

 Je suis de **Guadeloupe**.

 Je suis de **Tunisie**.

 Je suis du **Niger**.

 Je suis du **Maroc**.

 Je suis de **Suisse**.

 Je suis du **Sénégal**.

 Je suis d'**Haïti**.

 Je suis du **Canada**.

 Je suis de **République centrafricaine**

l'Afrique (f.) du Sud
l'Allemagne (f.)
l'Angleterre (f.)

le Brésil
la Chine
l'Espagne (f.)

les Etats-Unis (m.)
l'Italie (f.)
le Japon

le Mexique
la Russie
le Zaïre

22 C'est typique de chez nous

Dans quel pays est-ce qu'on peut voir...?

a. en Belgique

en Côte d'Ivoire

b.

en Tunisie

c.

au Maroc

e.

en République centrafricaine

d.

à la Guadeloupe

f.

g. en Suisse

Tu te rappelles **?**

Do you remember how to say *in* or *to* a country? Use **au** before masculine countries and **en** before feminine countries. Use **en** before any country starting with a vowel, and **aux** before all plural countries.

RESOURCES FOR **DEUXIEME ETAPE**

Chapter Teaching Resources, Book 3
• Communicative Activity 12-2, pp. 168–169
• Teaching Transparency Master 12-2, pp. 171, 172
    Teaching Transparency 12-2
• Additional Listening Activities 12-4, 12-5, 12-6, pp. 174–175
    Audiocassette 10B/Audio CD 12
• Realia 12-2, pp. 178, 179
• Situation Cards 12-2, 12-3, pp. 180–181
• Student Response Forms, pp. 182–184
• Quiz 12-2, pp. 187–188
    Audiocassette 8B/Audio CD 12

ADDITIONAL RESOURCES
Textbook Audiocassette 6B
   OR *Audio CD 12*
Practice and Activity Book, pp. 139–142
Video Program, Videocassette 2
Video Guide

23 Si tu allais...

Après le lycée, ton/ta camarade voudrait voyager. Tu lui proposes des endroits où aller. Il/Elle te dira comment il/elle pense que ça sera là-bas. Dis si tu es d'accord.

> —Si tu allais au Brésil, tu pourrais voir l'Amazone.
> —Je parie que c'est sauvage, là-bas.
> —Oui, c'est sûr.

visiter le Kremlin
voir des mines de diamants
voir des taureaux
visiter la Tour de Londres
aller à Berlin
voir des temples
voir des pyramides mayas
visiter le Vatican
voir la Grande Muraille de Chine

COMMENT DIT-ON... ?
Inquiring

To inquire about someone's country:

Tu es d'où?
C'est comment, la vie là-bas?
Qu'est-ce qu'on y mange?
On porte des chéchias chez toi?
Vous avez/Il y a des téléviseurs **chez vous?**
Qu'est-ce qui est typique de chez toi?

24 Ecoute!

Ecoute ces conversations qui ont lieu au village olympique. Est-ce que ces gens posent des questions sur le pays de quelqu'un ou sur autre chose? Answers on p. 295D.

25 Méli-mélo!

Crée un dialogue entre deux athlètes qui se rencontrent aux Jeux olympiques.

5 «Chouette! C'est comment, la vie là-bas?»

7 «Vous avez des maisons là-bas?»   3 «Tu es d'où?»

9 «Qu'est-ce qu'on y mange?»

11 «C'est fascinant! Qu'est-ce qu'il y a d'autre?»

1 «Salut. Je m'appelle Dianne. Et toi?»

8 «Dans les villes, on a des maisons; dans les villages, il y a des cases (huts).»

10 «Ce qui est typique chez nous, c'est les cassaves.»

6 «C'est super.»   2 «Moi, c'est Koli.»

4 «De République centrafricaine.»

26 C'est comment, la vie là-bas?

Pendant leur séjour au village des Jeux olympiques, ces jeunes francophones se rencontrent à la cantine. Ils voudraient connaître d'autres pays. Ils vont se poser des questions et faire des suppositions. Imagine et écris leurs dialogues.

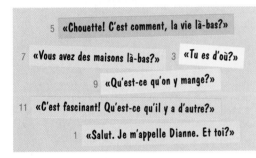

DEUXIEME ETAPE

trois cent neuf **309**

Teaching Suggestion

26 You might have students memorize, rehearse, and act out their dialogues for the class.

📁 Portfolio

26 Written You might have students expand their dialogues by finding out more about their new friends, including what sport they are competing in, how they became interested in the sport, and so on. Students might include their dialogues in their written portfolios. For portfolio information, see *Assessment Guide*, pages 2–13.

Presentation

Comment dit-on... ? Write a dialogue in which a reporter interviews a visiting space alien, using the expressions for inquiring. In class, act out the dialogue, using a sock puppet or a peculiar stuffed animal as your interviewee. Then, ask the class about your interviewee. (**Il/elle est d'où? Qu'est-ce qui est typique de chez lui/elle?**) Then, write the questions in **Comment dit-on... ?** in one column on a transparency. In a second column, write the answers your interviewee gave in random order. Have partners match the questions with the answers and read the dialogue aloud.

Teaching Suggestion

Have students choose to represent one of the countries they've studied this year. You might give them a few minutes to look over the cultural information in the appropriate chapter. Then, have them write answers to the questions in **Comment dit-on... ?** as if they were from that country. Have volunteers read their answers aloud. For each response, have the class give the question that the student is answering. Then, have the class name the country the student comes from.

◆ For Individual Needs

24 Challenge Play the recording again and have students tell what each person is being asked about.

25 Tactile/Visual Learners Have students write each question or statement on a separate strip of paper and arrange the strips to form a logical conversation.

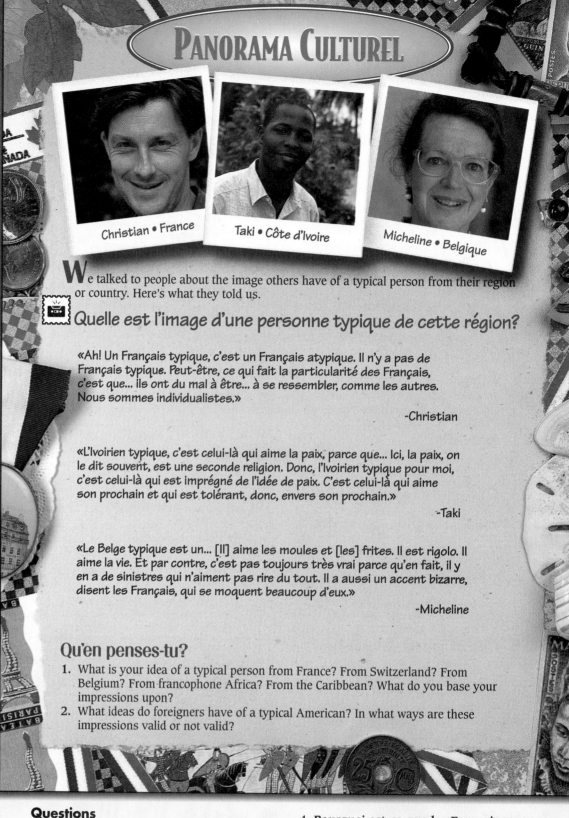

VIDEO PROGRAM
Videocassette 2

Teacher Notes

- See Video Guide and Practice and Activity Book for activities related to the **Panorama Culturel.**
- Remind students that cultural material may be included in the Chapter Quizzes and Test.
- The interviewees' language represents informal, unrehearsed speech. Occasionally, edits have been made for clarification.

Motivating Activity

Ask students to name situations in which they might meet teenagers from other countries (sports competitions, summer camp, exchange programs). Ask what they might want to know about a foreign visitor they just met.

Presentation

Write statements on the board about various stereotypes from the interviews, such as **Il aime les frites. Il a un accent bizarre.** Play the video and have students tell which interviewee mentioned the stereotype. Then, describe the interviewees aloud **(Il ne veut pas ressembler aux autres)** and have students identify the speaker.

Thinking Critically

Analyzing Have students tell why stereotypes are not a fair way of evaluating people. (It does not account for individuality and limits one's cultural perceptions.)

PANORAMA CULTUREL

Christian • France

Taki • Côte d'Ivoire

Micheline • Belgique

We talked to people about the image others have of a typical person from their region or country. Here's what they told us.

Quelle est l'image d'une personne typique de cette région?

«Ah! Un Français typique, c'est un Français atypique. Il n'y a pas de Français typique. Peut-être, ce qui fait la particularité des Français, c'est que... ils ont du mal à être... à se ressembler, comme les autres. Nous sommes individualistes.»

-Christian

«L'Ivoirien typique, c'est celui-là qui aime la paix, parce que... Ici, la paix, on le dit souvent, est une seconde religion. Donc, l'Ivoirien typique pour moi, c'est celui-là qui est imprégné de l'idée de paix. C'est celui-là qui aime son prochain et qui est tolérant, donc, envers son prochain.»

-Taki

«Le Belge typique est un... [Il] aime les moules et [les] frites. Il est rigolo. Il aime la vie. Et par contre, c'est pas toujours très vrai parce qu'en fait, il y en a de sinistres qui n'aiment pas rire du tout. Il a aussi un accent bizarre, disent les Français, qui se moquent beaucoup d'eux.»

-Micheline

Qu'en penses-tu?

1. What is your idea of a typical person from France? From Switzerland? From Belgium? From francophone Africa? From the Caribbean? What do you base your impressions upon?
2. What ideas do foreigners have of a typical American? In what ways are these impressions valid or not valid?

Questions

1. Pourquoi est-ce que Christian dit que les Français sont individualistes? (parce qu'ils ont du mal à se ressembler, à être comme les autres)
2. Qu'est-ce qui est important pour un Ivoirien typique? (l'idée de la paix)
3. D'après Micheline, qu'est-ce que les Belges aiment? (les moules, les frites)
4. Pourquoi est-ce que les Français se moquent des Belges? (parce qu'ils ont un accent bizarre)

Teaching Suggestion

You might want to discuss question 2 under **Qu'en penses-tu?** with the entire class.

27 C'est pareil qu'ici?

Choisis un pays d'un des chapitres du livre. Relis les **Notes Culturelles** et la **Rencontre Culturelle** du chapitre. Imagine que tu es un(e) athlète de ce pays qui participe aux Jeux olympiques. Tu y rencontres un(e) Américain(e) qui va te poser des questions sur ton pays. Tu vas aussi lui poser des questions sur les Etats-Unis. Joue cette scène avec ton/ta camarade. Changez de rôles.

COMMENT DIT-ON... ?

Expressing excitement and disappointment

To express excitement:
Génial!
C'est trop cool!
J'arrive pas à y croire!
C'est pas possible!
C'est vraiment le pied!
Youpi!

To express disappointment:
Les boules! *Darn!*
J'en ai vraiment marre!
J'ai vraiment pas de chance.
C'est pas juste.
Quelle angoisse! *This is the worst!*
Qu'est-ce que je peux être nul(le)!

28 Ecoute!

Ecoute ces jeunes qui téléphonent chez eux pour raconter à leurs parents ce qui leur est arrivé aux Jeux olympiques. Est-ce qu'ils ont gagné ou perdu? Answers on p. 295D.

29 Qu'est-ce qu'ils disent?

Qu'est-ce que ces jeunes athlètes disent à propos de ce qui leur est arrivé aux Jeux olympiques?
Possible answers:

1. C'est trop cool!

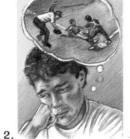

2. Les boules!

3. J'arrive pas à y croire!

4. Quelle angoisse!

30 C'est pas possible!

Imagine que tu as participé aux Jeux olympiques. Ecris une carte postale à un(e) ami(e). Dis-lui comment la compétition s'est passée pour toi et qui tu as rencontré d'intéressant.

31 Jeu de rôle

You're a TV sports reporter covering the Olympics. At the end of the competition, you interview several athletes about their experience. Remember to ask questions about where they're from, how they did in the competition, and what they learned from being at the Games.

Bons baisers des Jeux!

Comment dit-on... ? Tell students about several events and express your excitement over them. You might show pictures to enhance your presentation. For example, show a picture of a sports car and say **Je viens d'acheter cette voiture! Géniale, non? C'est vraiment le pied d'avoir une voiture comme ça!** Then, act out regrettable events, such as dropping and breaking a toy camera, saying **Les boules! Oh là là, quelle angoisse!** Next, project a transparency on which you have written the expressions in **Comment dit-on... ?** Describe situations to students, showing pictures or objects when possible, and prompt them to respond with appropriate expressions. (**Valérie, tu as gagné un voyage en France! Qu'est-ce que tu en dis? Pascal, je suis désolé(e), tu as eu 5 à ton interro de maths.**)

For Individual Needs

29 Slower Pace Before students begin this activity, have them describe what is happening in each illustration and tell whether the participants are excited or disappointed.

Portfolio

30 Written Students might decorate one side of an index card to resemble a postcard, write the text on the reverse side, and include the "postcard" in their written portfolios. For portfolio suggestions, see *Assessment Guide*, pages 2–13.

31 Oral This activity is appropriate for students' oral portfolios. For portfolio information, see *Assessment Guide*, pages 2–13.

CLOSE

To close this **étape**, play the game **"Mots croisés,"** described on page 161F, using the vocabulary and expressions from this chapter. After each round of the game, you might call on volunteers to use each of the words written on the grid in a logical sentence.

ASSESS

Quiz 12-2, *Chapter Teaching Resources, Book 3,* pp. 187–188

Assessment Items, Audiocassette 8B Audio CD 12

Performance Assessment

Have students videotape their TV sports report as described in Activity 31.

Guy Drut, Athlétisme

BARCELONE 92 :
L'or à portée de mains

La 2ᵉ semaine de cette vingt-cinquième olympiade s'ouvre sur l'athlétisme et ses stars : Bubka, Lewis, Powell, Johnson, Ottey. Nos Tricolores seront aussi présents : la championne du monde du 400 m, Marie-José Perec ; le décathlonien Christian Plaziat ; le perchiste Jean Galfione ; Stéphane Diagana sur 400 m haies. Et pourquoi pas l'escrime, l'aviron, le tennis de table, le canoë-kayak ou le tir à l'arc ! Ce sont, en tout cas, les pronostics des consultants de Canal + qui, le temps de ces JO, sont aussi devenus ceux de Télé-Loisirs.

Lionne chasseresse
Championne du monde du 400 m, Marie-José Perec ne devrait pas rencontrer de rivale sur «sa» piste.

« C'est une grande fête. Un sentiment de grande fraternité, d'enthousiasme et de dialogue. Côté stars étrangères, il y a, en premier lieu, Bubka, qui domine le saut à la perche. C'est du 1 contre 1. Au 100 m, l'absence de Carl Lewis m'attriste, c'est un athlète d'une telle qualité. Quant à Leroy Burrell, il sera devant tout le monde s'il retrouve son niveau de l'an dernier. Autre épreuve d'importance, le duel Lewis-Powell à la longueur. Carl est un seigneur, et c'est pour lui un défi fantastique. Il a une telle faculté de concentration qu'il peut très bien atteindre les 30 pieds, soit 9,12 m. Et Merlene Ottey aura une revanche à prendre sur 100 et 200 m. Chez les Français, Jean Galfione peut faire un coup à la perche. Les hommes du 4 x 100 m visent la médaille. Stéphane Diagana sera sans doute la grande satisfaction des Jeux. Pour Plaziat, tout se passe dans la tête. Il a un potentiel extraordinaire. Marie-José Perec va exploser. Je vote sans problème pour une médaille d'or. Et Monique Ewanje-Épée a beaucoup de métier, un punch fantastique. Alors... »

Yannick Noah, Tennis

« Les Jeux olympiques représentent la fête du sport avec toutes ses émotions. Par rapport à la compétition, le tennis est un peu en décalage. Mais d'ici quelques années, il sera complètement accepté. En finale, je vois bien Courier et Sampras, avec une préférence pour ce dernier. Chez les filles, je suis pour Steffi à 100 %. L'Allemande, médaille d'or à Séoul, défend son titre. Mais ce tournoi ressemble à un tournoi du Grand Chelem, puisque les meilleures joueuses seront là, et que Mary Pierce pourrait peut-être faire une perf. Chez les Français, on suivra aussi Leconte et Forget, en simple comme en double. Le tennis, c'est bien, mais je vais suivre avec passion cette équipe de barjos de basketteurs américains avec Magic Johnson et Michael Jordan. »

DE BONS CONSEILS

While each chapter of this book has presented a single reading strategy, in reality you'll usually use a combination of strategies to help you understand and get more out of what you read. For example, if you're reading an autobiographical story written by a person from a different country, it will be important to identify the narrator's point of view and to take the cultural context of the story into account. In addition, you may need to use some of the comprehension strategies you've learned, such as using linking words, contextual clues, and deductive reasoning, in order to understand new words and the relationship of ideas in the reading. The style of the reading may require you to use strategies for understanding literary techniques or dialect, or for relating the subtopics to the main idea. Whatever type of reading you're faced with, remember that you have a variety of strategies available for meeting the challenges it presents.

L'or à portée de mains For Activities B, C, and D, see answers below

A. Preview the article on the first two pages of the reading. What is it about? How is the information organized? *preview of '92 Olympics; by sport*

B. Now, make predictions about the article based on your preview. What kind of information and vocabulary do you expect to find?

C. What French athletes are mentioned in the introduction? In what sports do they participate?

312   *trois cent douze*

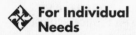

READING STRATEGY
Combining strategies

Teacher Note
For an additional reading, see *Practice and Activity Book*, page 143.

PREREADING
Activities A–B

Motivating Activity
Ask students what their favorite Olympic events are. Ask them if certain countries usually seem to excel in particular sports. Have students name a favorite Olympic athlete and tell whether they prefer the Summer or Winter Olympic Games, and why.

READING
Activities C–O

For Individual Needs

C. Slower Pace On a transparency, write the names of the French athletes in one column and the sports in which they participate in random order in a second column. Have students match the athletes with their sports.

Language Note
Call students' attention to the word **tricolores** in the first paragraph of the article. The French use this term to refer to their national flag, which consists of three colors: blue, white, and red. In this sentence, the term refers to people from France.

History Link
The current French tricolor flag was created during the French Revolution to represent the revolutionary struggle and the new government. The flag of the old monarchy was solid white.

Culture Notes
• Students might be interested to know that the five colors of the Olympic rings (blue, yellow, black, green, and red) represent at least one color from the flag of every country that participates in the Games.
• Marie-José Perec, a French track star, won the gold medal for the 400-meter race at the 1992 Summer Olympic Games in Barcelona, Spain.

Answers
B sports-related (names, events, nationalities, records)
C Marie-José Perec - 400 m
   Christian Plaziat - decathlon
   Jean Galfione - pole vault
   Stéphane Diagana - 400 m hurdles
D Track and field; *Predictions:* Burrell will win if he does as well as last year. Ottey will be out for revenge in the 100 m and 200 m. Galfione may win the pole vault. Diagana will be the big winner. Perec will explode and get the gold medal.

Philippe Riboud, Escrime

«Pour la famille de l'escrime, les jeux sont l'événement le plus attendu dans une carrière. C'est le moment où l'éclairage médiatique met une pression terrible sur les athlètes. Cela revêt une importance énorme pour l'escrime, qui reste un sport confidentiel. On peut compter sur l'équipe de France d'épée pour ramener une médaille, avec notemment Srecki et Lenglet. L'Italien Mazzoni et plusieurs représentants de la CEI ont également leurs chances. Au fleuret masculin, je vois l'Allemand Weiner, ainsi que les Italiens, la CEI et le Français Omnès. Par équipe, la France peut jouer un rôle. Au sabre, je vote tricolore avec Lamour, car il a fait sa meilleure saison. Il devra se méfier des Hongrois, Italiens, et Céistes. Le fleuret féminin est le point faible de la France. En revanche, l'Allemande Fichtel et les Italiennes sont très fortes.»

Le Capitan
Sextuple champion de France, champion du monde 1990 de fleuret, Philippe Omnès possède l'expérience des duels olympiques. Une fine lame qui peut faire mouche !

Dans les sports confidentiels, habituellement traités sur le mode mineur, les chances de médailles sont majeures !

Tennis de table
Née en Chine et naturalisée française, Wang Xiao Ming est avec Gatien, le numéro un mondial, le meilleur atout français.

Canoë-kayak (slalom)
Depuis dix ans, Myriam Jérusalmi collectionne des titres mondiaux en kayak. Le retour du slalom en eau vive aux Jeux olympiques est une aubaine pour la Marseillaise qui, à trente et un ans, pourrait enfin connaître la consécration suprême.

Tir à l'arc
Avoir vingt ans n'empêche pas l'ambition, à l'image du champion d'Europe Sébastien Flute. En individuel comme par équipe, Flute veut enchanter...

D. What sport does Guy Drut write about? What are his predictions for these athletes? See answers on p. 312.

Leroy Burrell
Merlene Ottey
Jean Galfione
Stéphane Diagana
Marie-José Perec

H. Match each athlete to the sport he or she represents. See answers below.

Myriam Jérusalmi
Henri Leconte
Wang Xiao Ming
Sébastien Flute
Jean Galfione

le saut à la perche
le tennis de table
le canoë-kayak
le tennis
le tir à l'arc

E. What sport does Yannick Noah discuss? Who does he predict will win medals? What do you think **simple** and **double** refer to in tennis? tennis; (Pete) Sampras, Steffi (Graf); singles and doubles

F. According to Riboud, which teams are strongest in fencing? What are France's strongest and weakest events in fencing? See answers below.

G. What is a **sport confidentiel**? Which sports are referred to this way in the article? See answers below.

trois cent treize 313

Answers

F France, Italy, Germany, Hungary, representatives from the CEI; France's strong point is **le sabre** (saber). France's weak point is **le fleuret féminin** (women's foil).

G a lesser-known sport; fencing, canoë-kayak, tir à l'arc, tennis de table

H Myriam Jérusalmi - le canoë-kayak
Henri Leconte - le tennis
Wang Xiao Ming - le tennis de table
Sébastien Flute - le tir à l'arc
Jean Galfione - le saut à la perche

Teaching Suggestions

G. Ask students if they participate in or would like to participate in any of these **sports confidentiels**.

• Create several true-false statements about the athletes featured in the article. (Yannick Noah joue au tennis (vrai). Philippe Omnès est champion de tennis de table (faux).) Read the statements aloud and have students respond.

• You might ask students additional questions about the athletes featured on pages 312–313, such as **Qui est née en Chine?** (Wang Xiao Ming) **Qui a trente et un ans?** (Myriam Jérusalmi)

• Ask students which of the athletes featured they would most like to interview, and what they would like to know about them. You might also ask what other athletes they would like to interview about their sport.

Reading/Writing Link

Assign one of the athletes featured on pages 312–313 to students. Have them use their paraphrasing skills to summarize the athlete's interview. Remind them that they don't need to understand every word to summarize, just the general idea. Then, have volunteers read their summaries aloud to the class and have the class guess the name of the athlete being described.

Terms in Lisons!

Students might want to know the following words from the reading: **atteindre** *(to reach)*; **revanche** *(revenge)*; **en décalage** *(behind)*; **Grand Chelem** *(Grand Slam)*; **une perf (une performance)**; **fine lame** *(good swordsman)*; **faire mouche** *(to hit the target)*; **aubaine** *(good fortune)*; **atout** *(asset)*; **s'améliorer** *(to improve)*; **virage** *(turn)*; **malgré** *(in spite of)*; **viser** *(to aim)*.

GUYLAINE CLOUTIER
SPÉCIALISTE DE LA BRASSE

Building on Previous Skills

- Have students use the context of the article on Guylaine Cloutier to guess the meaning of the following words: **se consacrer** *(to dedicate oneself)*; **en vue de** *(with plans of)*; **profiter de** *(to benefit from, to use to one's advantage)*.
- Have students imagine what Guylaine's daily schedule might be like. Have them write out a schedule they imagine, describing when she gets up, eats, trains, studies, and goes to bed.

 **For Individual Needs**

O. Challenge Have students write several true-false statements based on the article. They might pass the statements to a partner to answer, or give the statements to you to read aloud to the entire class.

POSTREADING
Activity P

Teaching Suggestion

At this time, have students recall their predictions from Activity B on page 312 and verify whether they were accurate or not. As students look over the reading, have them tell what helped them most in making these predictions.

Si vous aimez la natation, vous connaissez sûrement la nageuse Guylaine Cloutier, une spécialiste du 100 et 200 m brasse. Très déterminée, son grand objectif est de participer pour une troisième fois aux Jeux olympiques. Ce sera à Atlanta, en 1996.

Dans l'eau, Guylaine est perfectionniste et cherche toujours à s'améliorer. «J'aime la natation et je veux toujours battre mes records personnels, toujours aller plus vite», souligne cette étudiante aux Hautes études commerciales (HEC).

C'est à raison de 20 heures et plus par semaine qu'elle s'entraîne, soit au Cepsum de l'Université de Montréal, soit au Club de natation de Laval, avec son entraîneur Stéphane Bédard. «Nous travaillons sur des points techniques comme la fréquence à laquelle je tourne les bras. Entre les deux murs de la piscine je suis très efficace, mais dans les virages je peux perdre des dixièmes de secondes à cause de ma petite taille. Fait à souligner : malgré un entraînement intense, Guylaine poursuit en même temps, aux HEC, un baccalauréat en administration. Après sa carrière de nageuse, elle aimerait devenir une femme d'affaires.

Parmi ses plus beaux souvenirs, il y a sa participation aux Jeux olympiques de Barcelone, à l'été 1992. «J'étais parmi les favorites. Je m'étais préparée pendant une année et mes performances étaient très bonnes.»

Plus experimentée, plus forte musculairement, Guylaine compte prendre toute l'année 1995 pour se consacrer uniquement à son entraînement en vue de ses troisièmes Jeux olympiques à Atlanta, en 1996. Ces Jeux seront son chant du cygne et l'athlète de 23 ans veut terminer sa carrière en beauté.

La vie d'athlète de niveau international comporte des avantages, comme celui de voyager. «J'ai visité plusieurs pays grâce à la natation. J'en profite notamment pour découvrir la nourriture du pays. J'adore voyager et j'ai bien aimé ma visite à Honolulu. J'aimerais y retourner», dit-elle.

En attendant un tel voyage, Guylaine Cloutier désire continuer à améliorer toujours ses meilleurs temps et vise sûrement monter sur le podium olympique à Atlanta. Pourquoi pas?

SON PALMARÈS

Depuis 1985, membre de l'équipe canadienne.

1988 - 15e sur 200 m brasse aux Jeux olympiques de Séoul.

1990 - Médaillée d'argent sur 100 et 200 m brasse aux Jeux du Commonwealth à Auckland.

1991 - 4e sur 200 m brasse aux Championnats du monde à Perth.

1992 - 4e sur 100 m brasse et 5e sur 200 m brasse aux Jeux olympiques de Barcelone

1994 - 1re sur 100 m brasse et sur 200 m brasse aux essais pour les Jeux du Commonwealth à Victoria; 1re sur 100 m brasse aux Championnats américains à Seattle.

Guylaine Cloutier For Activities I–N, see answers below.

I. What is this article about? What kind of information do you expect to find in such an article?

J. What is Guylaine's specialty?

K. Where does Guylaine attend school? What does she plan to do after her swimming career is over?

L. In the paragraph that begins **Plus expérimentée...**, find the expression **chant du cygne**. Use the context to figure out what this expression means. Do we have a similar expression in English?

M. What is one advantage of being an international athlete?

N. What are Guylaine's goals?

O. **Vrai ou faux?**

1. Depuis 1985, Guylaine est membre de l'équipe française. faux

2. Elle n'a pas participé aux Jeux de Séoul en 1988. faux

3. Elle a reçu le deuxième prix en 1990. vrai

4. Elle a gagné une médaille aux Jeux de Barcelone. faux

5. Elle n'a jamais fini première à une compétition. faux

P. Do you play or follow any of the sports named in the articles? What athletes do you think might win in these sports in the next Olympics?

314 *trois cent quatorze*

Answers

I Canadian swimmer training for '96 Olympics; events, training, medals, personal records

J 100 m and 200 m breaststroke

K Les Hautes études commerciales; become a businesswoman

L Yes, a *swan song* is one's final performance.

M travel

N to improve her times, to win an Olympic medal

Math Link

Have students convert the different swimming distances (100 and 200 meters) to feet. To convert meters to feet, multiply the number of meters by 3.28. To convert meters to yards, multiply the number of meters by 1.09. After students have found the distances in feet or yards, have them measure the length of the classroom. Then, have them figure how many classroom lengths equal 100 and 200 meters. Finally, have a student walk the appropriate number of classroom lengths to demonstrate the length of the swimming competitions.

You've just read about many world-class athletes, some famous and some relatively unknown. Many people admire athletes for their skill and dedication, and for the determination and character required to become one of the very best in a sport. In this activity you're going to write a magazine article about an athlete whom you admire or find interesting.

Un article de magazine

Tu veux envoyer un article sur un de tes athlètes préférés à un magazine sportif français. Ecris un article sur un(e) athlète que tu admires ou que tu trouves particulièrement intéressant(e).

A. Préparation

1. Choisis une personne que tu admires et sur laquelle tu pourras trouver des informations.
2. Fais des recherches sur cette personne.
   a. Sélectionne des sources d'informations. Tu peux peut-être trouver ces informations dans des livres, des magazines ou des articles de journaux à la bibliothèque de ton école ou à la bibliothèque municipale.
   b. Lis toutes les informations que tu as trouvées et prends des notes ou fais des photocopies de ce que tu peux utiliser.
3. Organise les informations que tu as trouvées.
   a. Fais des catégories, comme par exemple, **Education, Entraînement** ou **Succès**.
   b. Fais un plan de ton article. Mets les catégories que tu as choisies dans l'ordre où elles apparaîtront dans ton devoir. Ensuite, organise les informations que tu as trouvées sous forme de paragraphes.

DE BONS CONSEILS
Of course you know that doing research is important for writing a research paper, but it can also be necessary for many other kinds of writing. Whether it's a movie scene, a tourist brochure, an article, or a letter to the editor, all writing requires complete and accurate information. You may have access to more traditional research materials, such as the card catalogue and the periodicals index, or more modern ones, such as on-line information services and reference works stored on CD-ROM. Whatever the sources and types of information available to you, don't hesitate to do the research necessary to make your writing accurate as well as interesting.

B. Rédaction

1. Fais un brouillon de ton article en suivant le plan que tu as fait.
2. Vérifie que tu as bien utilisé toutes les informations que tu voulais. Consulte à nouveau les sources d'informations que tu as utilisées pour trouver des détails que tu pourrais ajouter.
3. S'il le faut, aide-toi d'un dictionnaire français-anglais pour traduire en français certaines des informations que tu as trouvées.
4. Trouve des photos pour illustrer ton article. Ecris une légende *(caption)* pour chaque photo et donne un titre à ton article.

C. Evaluation

1. Relis ton article et pose-toi les questions suivantes.
   a. Est-ce que tu as bien suivi ton plan?
   b. Est-ce que tu as trouvé des informations intéressantes pour ton article?
   c. Est-ce que tu as parlé des faits les plus importants de la vie de cet(te) athlète?
   d. Est-ce qu'il y a d'autres détails sur cet(te) athlète qui pourraient intéresser tes lecteurs?
2. Rédige la version finale de ton article en n'oubliant pas de corriger les fautes d'orthographe, de grammaire et de vocabulaire.

trois cent quinze **315**

WRITING STRATEGY
Doing research

 Portfolio

Written You might want to have students include all their work for Parts A–C in their written portfolios. For portfolio information, see *Assessment Guide,* pages 2–13.

PREWRITING

Motivating Activity

Have students name several famous athletes they might like to interview. Ask them what they think their readers would want to know about the people they mentioned.

Teaching Suggestion

A. 2. Before students begin their research, ask them to list possible sources they are familiar with. You might also invite the school reference librarian to your class to suggest additional sources and helpful research techniques.

WRITING

For Individual Needs

B. 2. Visual Learners
Have students go over their notes and underline each piece of information that pertains to a certain category (**Famille, Education,** and so on), using a different color of ink for each category. Then, have students write their rough draft, using the appropriate color of ink for each category in their article. Next, have them verify that every underlined note is in the appropriate category in the rough draft.

POSTWRITING

Teaching Suggestion

C. 1. Have students exchange papers and notes and ask these questions about their classmate's article. If they answer no to any of the questions, they should make constructive suggestions for revisions.

 Cooperative Learning

C. 2. Have students work in groups to proofread one another's article. Within each group, have students assign each member a specific proofreading task, such as spelling, vocabulary, or certain points of grammar (subject-verb agreement, noun-adjective agreement, contractions with **à** or **de,** and so on).

MISE EN PRATIQUE

 Video Wrap-Up

VIDEO PROGRAM
Videocassette 2

You might want to use the *Video Program* as part of the chapter review. See the *Video Guide* for teaching suggestions and activity masters.

Teaching Suggestion

Have partners take turns reading parts of the article aloud to each other.

Additional Practice

1 Ask students the following questions:

1. Qui est Gaston Jacques? (un professeur d'éducation physique)
2. Qu'est-ce qu'il a fait pour Chantal? (il lui a appris à nager)
3. Qui est André Viger? (son athlète préféré)
4. Où et quand est-ce que Chantal a participé à son premier marathon? (à Detroit, le 16 octobre 1988)
5. Elle a gagné? (Oui, elle a terminé première.)
6. Dans quelle université est-ce qu'elle va? (à l'Université d'Alberta à Edmonton)
7. Qu'est-ce qu'elle étudie à l'université? (l'histoire du Canada avec option en sciences politiques)
8. Où a-t-elle gagné une médaille de bronze? (à Tokyo)
9. Pour quelle épreuve? (le 800 mètres)
10. Qu'est-ce que Chantal espère? (que le 800 mètres devienne un sport officiel des Jeux olympiques d'Atlanta en 1996)

1 Lis cet article et réponds aux questions suivantes.

CHANTAL PETITCLERC : UN EXEMPLE DE COURAGE

Chantal Petitclerc prouve, hors de tout doute, que le sport en fauteuil roulant, c'est aussi excitant que n'importe quelle autre discipline

Tout le monde connaît dans sa vie des hauts et des bas, des succès et des échecs. Championne canadienne au marathon... en fauteuil roulant, médaillée de bronze sur 800 m aux Championnats mondiaux d'athlétisme à Tokyo, en 1991, Chantal Petitclerc a perdu l'usage de ses deux jambes à 13 ans en jouant avec des copains sur la ferme familiale, à Saint-Marc-des-Carrières. Une porte de grange lui est tombée sur le dos.

La natation

«Avant mon accident, je ne faisais pas tellement de sport. Grâce à l'aide de ma famille et de Gaston Jacques, un professeur d'éducation physique, j'ai commencé à faire de la natation. Monsieur Jacques s'est mis dans la tête de me montrer à nager. Ce n'est pas évident, lorsqu'on ne peut plus utiliser ses jambes», raconte Chantal.

Petit à petit, à force de volonté, Chantal a fait des progrès et, à la fin de son secondaire V, elle était en pleine forme grâce à la natation.

Comme André Viger était son athlète préféré, elle s'est tournée vers les compétitions d'athlétisme en fauteuil roulant. Dès le début, ses succès ont été étonnants. «Lors de mon premier marathon à Detroit, le 16 octobre 1988, j'ai terminé première en 2.29.49», dit Chantal. Compétition après compétition, ses performances devenaient de plus en plus exceptionnelles.

Jolie et intelligente, Chantal poursuit des études en histoire du Canada avec option en sciences politiques à l'Université d'Alberta, à Edmonton. En plus de ses études, elle s'entraîne 25 heures par semaine. Dotée d'un solide caractère, Chantal a toujours voulu être traitée comme une véritable athlète. «Beaucoup de personnes voient dans la pratique de l'athlétisme en fauteuil roulant une sorte de réadaptation. C'est plus que cela. Pour moi, c'est un mode de vie.»

La pratique de son sport lui a fait également découvrir plusieurs pays, dont le Japon. «Ma plus grande expérience a été lors des championnats mondiaux à Tokyo, l'année dernière. Courir le 800 m en

démonstration devant 55000 spectateurs, c'est très impressionnant. En gagnant une médaille de bronze, j'ai voulu montrer aux amateurs que le sport en fauteuil roulant c'était bien «tripant», avoue-t-elle.

Chantal souhaite ardemment que l'épreuve du 800 m devienne un sport officiel aux Jeux olympiques d'Atlanta en 1996. Une des meilleures au monde sur la distance, Chantal a disputé le 800 m (sport en démonstration) aux Jeux de Barcelone, au mois d'août.

Pour son gérant, Martin Chicoine, il n'y a pas d'athlètes féminines de son calibre au Québec. «Chantal doit se mesurer en compétition contre les meilleures au monde. Elle est de niveau international», ajoute-t-il.

Très confiante en elle, Chantal Petitclerc avoue qu'elle peut encore s'améliorer. «Si tu veux gagner, il faut que tu croies en toi.» Voilà un beau message de la part d'une athlète qui suscite le courage et l'admiration.

Vrai ou faux?

1. Chantal a toujours fait beaucoup de sport. faux
2. Gaston Jacques l'a encouragée à faire de la natation après son accident. vrai
3. Chantal a choisi de faire des compétitions d'athlétisme en fauteuil roulant parce que c'est plus facile que la natation. faux
4. Elle s'est spécialisée en éducation physique à l'Université d'Alberta. faux
5. Elle voudrait montrer à tout le monde que le sport en fauteuil roulant est vraiment délirant. vrai

316 *trois cent seize* CHAPITRE 12 Echanges sportifs et culturels

Language Notes

- Students might want to know the following vocabulary from *Un exemple de courage:* **fauteuil roulant** *(wheelchair)*; **doté(e)** *(endowed with)*; **ardemment** *(fervently);* **gérant** *(manager).*

- **A la fin de son secondaire V** refers to the last year of Canadian high school. The five years of secondary school in Canada are called **secondaire I, II, III, IV,** and **V.**
- The expression **C'est tripant** comes from the American slang expression *It's a trip.*

2 Ecoute Marion qui montre à ses amis les photos qu'elle a prises aux Jeux olympiques. De quelle photo est-ce qu'elle parle? 1. c 2. g 3. d 4. a 5. h 6. e 7. b 8. f

a.

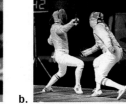
b.

c.

d.

e.

f.

g.

h.

3 Tes camarades et toi, vous allez assister aux Jeux olympiques. Il faut que vous choisissiez à l'avance les événements que vous voulez voir pour pouvoir acheter des places. Dis à tes camarades quels sports il te tarde de voir. Ils/Elles vont parler de ce qu'ils/elles voudraient voir. Essayez de vous mettre d'accord pour pouvoir y aller tous ensemble.

4 Un magazine français va offrir un voyage aux Jeux olympiques à la personne qui écrira le meilleur essai sur la raison pour laquelle elle voudrait y aller. Ecris un essai. N'oublie pas de parler des épreuves auxquelles tu voudrais assister et de mentionner les gens que tu voudrais rencontrer. Décris comment tu imagines que ça sera.

5

JEU DE ROLE

You and your partner are Olympic athletes. Choose the sports that you play and the countries you represent. Then, act out the following situations.

a. Imagine you're meeting each other in the Olympic village for the first time. Ask questions to find out about each other's country and interests.

b. You meet again on the last day. Tell each other how your competitions went. (One of you did very well and one of you did very badly.) Talk also about your other experiences and what you enjoyed about the Games.

For Individual Needs

2 Slower Pace Before you play the recording, describe the photos at random and have students give the corresponding letter.

2 Tactile/Auditory Learners Students might name the events represented by the photos and have a partner respond by pointing to the corresponding photo.

2 Challenge Play the recording a second time and have students tell whether the athlete did well or poorly in the event mentioned.

Teaching Suggestions

2 Have students suggest additional captions for these photos.

3 You might have students do this activity as if they were deciding which events to watch on TV. Have them refer to the schedules on page 305 and mention specific days and times in their conversations.

Portfolio

3 Oral This activity is appropriate for students' oral portfolios.

4 Written This activity is appropriate for students' written portfolios. For portfolio suggestions, see *Assessment Guide,* page 25.

MISE EN PRATIQUE

trois cent dix-sept **317**

QUE SAIS-JE?

This page is intended to help students prepare for the test. It is a brief checklist of the major points covered in the chapter. The students should be reminded that this is only a checklist and does not necessarily include everything that will appear on the test.

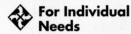 **For Individual Needs**

Auditory Learners Before students attempt to answer the questions in **Que sais-je?**, read aloud some of the answers at random (**C'est vraiment le pied!**) and have students tell which functions they serve (*expressing excitement*).

Teaching Suggestions

• Have partners or small groups do these activities together.
• Once students have answered the questions in **Que sais-je?**, have a volunteer act as the teacher. Give the student-teacher an answer key for the questions and have him or her call on individual students to answer them at random. Encourage the student-teacher to praise the other students. (**Excellent! Bravo!**)

Can you express anticipation? p. 304

Can you make suppositions? p. 304

Can you express certainty and doubt? p. 304

Can you inquire? p. 309

Can you express excitement and disappointment? p. 311

Can you use what you've learned in this chapter?

1 How would you express your anticipation if you were . . . *Possible answers:*
  1. going to watch the Olympic games? Vivement que je sois là-bas!
  2. about to be an exchange student in Switzerland? Il me tarde d'aller en Suisse!
  3. traveling to a foreign country? Je suis vraiment impatient(e) de partir!

2 What suppositions can you make about the following situations? See answers below.
  1. Your school team is going to compete in a state tournament.
  2. You have to tell your best friend you've lost his/her leather jacket.
  3. You're going to spend the summer working in a store.

3 Your friend asks you the following questions. How would you express your certainty? *Possible answers:*

Est-ce que l'équipe de basket-ball américaine va gagner la médaille d'or?
Oui, c'est sûr.

Est-ce qu'il y a une interro de maths demain?
Oui, j'en suis sûr(e).

Est-ce que c'est une bonne idée d'étudier une langue étrangère?
Oui, j'en suis certain(e).

4 How would you express doubt about the situations in number 3? See answers below.

5 You've just been introduced to an exchange student from a foreign country. What questions would you ask to find out . . .
  1. what life is like in that country? C'est comment, la vie là-bas?
  2. what people eat and wear there? Qu'est-ce qu'on y mange/porte comme vêtements?
  3. what is typical there? Qu'est-ce qui est typique de chez toi?

6 How would you express your excitement if . . . *Possible answers:*
  1. your school's basketball team won the state championship? Super!
  2. you got a perfect grade on a very difficult test? J'arrive pas à y croire!
  3. you received a birthday card with a $100 check inside? Youpi!

7 How would you express your disappointment if . . . *Possible answers:*
  1. you just missed first place in a competition? Les boules! **2.** Quelle angoisse!
  2. you arrived late and found that your friends had left without you?
  3. you received a lower grade than you had expected on a test? C'est pas juste.

318 *trois cent dix-huit*   CHAPITRE 12   Echanges sportifs et culturels

Possible answers
2 1. Ça doit être cool!
  2. Je parie qu'il/elle va être fâché(e).
  3. Je pourrai sûrement rencontrer des gens intéressants.
4 1. Ça m'étonnerait qu'ils gagnent la médaille d'or.
  2. Je ne pense pas qu'il y ait une interro.
  3. Je ne suis pas certain(e) que ce soit une bonne idée.

PREMIERE ETAPE

Sports and equipment

les anneaux (m.)   *the rings*
l'arc (m.)   *the bow*
l'aviron (m.)   *rowing*
la balle   *the ball*
le ballon   *the ball*
les barres asymétriques (f.)   *the uneven parallel bars*
le bâton   *the bat*
la boxe   *boxing*
le casque   *the helmet*
la course de fond   *long-distance running*
le cyclisme   *cycling*
l'entraîneur (m.)   *the coach*
l'épée (f.)   *the epee/the sword*
l'escrime (f.)   *fencing*
la flèche   *the arrow*
le frappeur   *the batter*
la gymnastique   *gymnastics*

les haltères (f.)   *weights*
l'haltérophilie (f.)   *weightlifting*
le judo   *judo*
le lancer du disque   *the discus throw*
le lanceur   *the pitcher*
la lutte   *wrestling*
le masque   *the mask*
le panier   *the basket*
le plongeoir   *the diving board*
le plongeon acrobatique   *diving*
plonger   *to dive*
la poutre   *the balance beam*
le saut à la perche   *the pole vault*
le saut en longueur   *the long jump*
les rames (f.)   *oars*
la tenue   *the outfit*
le tir à l'arc   *archery*
tirer   *to shoot*

Expressing anticipation

Il me tarde de...   *I can't wait to . . .*
Je suis vraiment impatient(e) de... !   *I can hardly wait to . . . !*
Vivement que... !   *I just can't wait . . . !*
Dès que je serai là,...   *As soon as I get there, . . .*
Quand je verrai...   *When I see . . .*

Expressing certainty and doubt

Ça, c'est sûr.   *That's for sure.*
Je n'en ai aucun doute.   *I have no doubt of it.*

Game

QUEL SPORT? Have students form small groups. In each group, one player chooses a sport. The other players ask him or her yes-no questions about the sport until one player can identify it. (**On a besoin d'un masque? On en fait en été ou en hiver?**) The first student to guess the player's sport takes the next turn.

Teaching Suggestion

To review countries, play the game "D'où viens-tu?" on page 295F.

DEUXIEME ETAPE

Places of origin

l'Afrique (f.) du Sud   *South Africa*
l'Algérie (f.)   *Algeria*
l'Allemagne (f.)   *Germany*
l'Angleterre (f.)   *England*
la Belgique   *Belgium*
le Brésil   *Brazil*
le Canada   *Canada*
la Chine   *China*
la Côte d'Ivoire   *the Republic of Côte d'Ivoire*
l'Espagne (f.)   *Spain*
les Etats-Unis (m.)   *the United States*
la Guadeloupe   *Guadeloupe*
Haïti (m.)   *Haiti*
l'Italie (f.)   *Italy*
le Japon   *Japan*
le Maroc   *Morocco*
le Mexique   *Mexico*
le Niger   *Niger*

la République centrafricaine   *the Central African Republic*
la Russie   *Russia*
le Sénégal   *Senegal*
la Suisse   *Switzerland*
la Tunisie   *Tunisia*
le Zaïre   *Zaire*

Inquiring

Tu es d'où?   *Where are you from?*
C'est comment, la vie là-bas?   *What's life like there?*
Qu'est-ce qu'on y...?   *What do you . . . there?*
On... chez toi?   *Do people . . . where you're from?*
Vous avez/Il y a... chez vous?   *Do you have/Are there . . . where you're from?*
Qu'est-ce qui est typique de chez toi?   *What's typical of where you're from?*

Expressing excitement and disappointment

C'est trop cool!   *That's too cool!*
J'arrive pas à y croire!   *I can't believe it!*
C'est pas possible!   *No way!*
C'est vraiment le pied!   *That's really neat!*
Youpi!   *Yippee!*
Les boules!   *Darn!*
J'en ai vraiment marre!   *I'm sick of this!*
J'ai vraiment pas de chance.   *I'm so unlucky.*
C'est pas juste.   *It's not fair.*
Quelle angoisse!   *This is the worst!*
Qu'est-ce que je peux être nul(le)!   *I just can't do anything right!*

CHAPTER 12 ASSESSMENT

CHAPTER TEST

• *Chapter Teaching Resources, Book 3* pp. 189–194
• *Assessment Guide,* Speaking Test, p. 33
• *Assessment Items,* Audiocassette 8B Audio CD 12

TEST GENERATOR, CHAPTER 12

ALTERNATIVE ASSESSMENT

Performance Assessment

You might want to use the **Jeu de rôle** (p. 317) as a cumulative performance assessment activity.

Portfolio Assessment

• **Written:** Mise en pratique, Activity 4, *Pupil's Edition,* p. 317
  Assessment Guide, p. 25
• **Oral:** Mise en pratique, Activity 3, *Pupil's Edition,* p. 317
  Assessment Guide, p. 25

FINAL EXAM

• *Assessment Guide,* pp. 49–56
• *Assessment Items,* Audiocassette 8B Audio CD 12

VOCABULAIRE   *trois cent dix-neuf*   **319**

Game

DIS-LE! Assign at least one sport listed on this page to each student. You might also want to include additional sports that students already know. Have students illustrate their sport(s) on one side of a large index card and write the French name of the sport on the reverse side. Then, form two teams (Team A and Team B) and have one student come forward. Show the illustration on one of the cards to the student from Team A and have him or her identify the name of the sport pictured. If the answer is correct, Team A receives a point; if the answer is incorrect, the player from Team B has the opportunity to answer. Continue until all the cards have been used. The team with the most points wins.

SUMMARY OF FUNCTIONS

Function is another word for the way in which you use language for a specific purpose. When you find yourself in a certain situation, such as in a restaurant, in a grocery store, or at school, you'll want to place an order, or make a purchase, or talk about your class schedule. In order to communicate in French, you have to "function" in the language.

Each chapter in this book focuses on language functions. You can easily find them in boxes labeled **Comment dit-on... ?** The other features in the chapter—grammar, vocabulary, culture notes—support the functions you're learning.

Here is a list of the functions presented in this book and their French expressions. You'll need them in order to communicate in a wide range of situations. Following each function are the numbers of the level, chapter, and page where the function was first introduced.

SOCIALIZING

Greeting people **I Ch. 1, p. 22**

Bonjour. Salut.

Saying goodbye **I Ch. 1, p. 22**

Salut.	A bientôt.
Au revoir.	A demain.
A tout à l'heure.	Tchao.

Asking how people are **I Ch. 1, p. 23**

(Comment) ça va? Et toi?

Telling how you are **I Ch. 1, p. 23**

Ça va.
Super!
Très bien.
Comme ci, comme ça.
Bof.
Pas mal.
Pas terrible.

Expressing thanks **I Ch. 3, p. 82**

Merci.

III Ch. 6, p. 149
Merci bien/infiniment/mille fois.
Je vous remercie.
C'est vraiment très gentil de votre part.

Responding to thanks **I Ch. 3, p. 82**

A votre service.

III Ch. 6, p. 149
De rien.
Je vous en prie.
(Il n'y a) pas de quoi.
C'est tout à fait normal.

Extending invitations **I Ch. 6, p. 159**

Allons... !	Tu viens?
Tu veux... ?	On peut...

Accepting invitations **I Ch. 6, p. 159**

Je veux bien.	D'accord.
Pourquoi pas?	Bonne idée.

Refusing invitations **I Ch. 6, p. 159**

Désolé(e), je suis occupé(e).
Ça ne me dit rien.
J'ai des trucs à faire.
Désolé(e), je ne peux pas.

Identifying people **I Ch. 7, p. 179**

C'est...	Voici...
Ce sont...	Voilà...

II Ch. 11, p. 273
Tu connais... ?
Bien sûr. C'est...
Je ne connais pas.

Introducing people **I Ch. 7, p. 183**

C'est...
Je te (vous) présente...
Très heureux (heureuse). (FORMAL)

Renewing old acquaintances **III Ch. 1, p. 9**

Ça fait longtemps qu'on ne s'est pas vu(e)s.
Ça fait...
Depuis...
Je suis content(e) de te revoir.
Qu'est-ce que tu deviens?
Quoi de neuf?
Toujours la même chose!
Rien (de spécial).

Seeing someone off **I Ch. 11, p. 296**

Bon voyage!	Amuse-toi bien!
Bonnes vacances!	Bonne chance!

Asking someone to convey good wishes **III Ch. 8, p. 194**

Embrasse... pour moi.
Fais mes amitiés à...

Salue... de ma part.
Dis à... que je vais lui écrire.
Dis à... que je pense à lui/elle.

Closing a letter III Ch. 8, p. 194

Bien des choses à...
Je t'embrasse bien fort.
Grosses bises.
Bisous à...

Welcoming someone II Ch. 2, p. 33

Bienvenue chez moi/chez nous.
Faites/Fais comme chez vous/toi.
Vous avez/Tu as fait bon voyage?

Responding to someone's welcome II Ch. 2, p. 33

Merci.
C'est gentil de votre/ta part.
Oui, excellent.
C'était fatigant!

Showing hospitality III Ch. 6, p. 149

Entrez, je vous en prie.
Ça me fait plaisir de vous voir.
Donnez-moi votre...
Mettez-vous à l'aise.
Asseyez-vous.
Je vous sers quelque chose?
Qu'est-ce que je peux vous offrir?

Responding to hospitality III Ch. 6, p. 149

Vous êtes bien aimable.
Moi aussi.
C'est gentil.
Je prendrais bien...
Vous auriez... ?

Extending good wishes II Ch. 3, p. 71

Bonne fête!
Joyeux (Bon) anniversaire!
Bonne fête de Hanoukka!
Joyeux Noël!
Bonne année!
Meilleurs vœux!
Félicitations!
Bon voyage!
Bonne route!
Bon rétablissement!

Congratulating someone II Ch. 5, p. 127

Félicitations!
Bravo!
Chapeau!

EXCHANGING INFORMATION

Asking someone's name and giving yours I Ch. 1, p. 24

Tu t'appelles comment?
Je m'appelle...

Asking and giving someone else's name I Ch. 1, p. 24

Il/Elle s'appelle comment?   Il/Elle s'appelle...

Asking someone's age and giving yours I Ch. 1, p. 25

Tu as quel âge?   J'ai... ans.

Inquiring III Ch. 12, p. 309

Tu es d'où?
C'est comment, la vie là-bas?
Qu'est-ce qu'on y...?
On... chez toi?
Vous avez/Il y a... chez vous?
Qu'est-ce qui est typique de chez toi?

Asking for information I Ch. 2, pp. 51, 54
(about classes)

Tu as quels cours... ?   Vous avez... ?
Tu as quoi... ?   Tu as... à quelle heure?

I Ch. 3, p. 82   *(at a store or restaurant)*
C'est combien?

II Ch. 6, p. 152   *(about travel)*
A quelle heure est-ce que le train (le car) pour... part?
De quel quai... ?
A quelle heure est-ce que vous ouvrez (fermez)?
Combien coûte... ?
C'est combien, l'entrée?

II Ch. 11, p. 280   *(about movies)*
Qu'est-ce qu'on joue comme film?
Ça passe où?
C'est avec qui?
Ça commence à quelle heure?

II Ch. 4, p. 90   *(about places)*
Où se trouve... ?
Qu'est-ce qu'il y a... ?
C'est comment?

Giving information I Ch. 2, pp. 51, 54
(about classes)

Nous avons...   J'ai...

II Ch. 6, p. 152   *(about travel)*
Du quai...
Je voudrais...
Un... , s'il vous plaît.
... tickets, s'il vous plaît.

II Ch. 11, p. 280   *(about movies)*
On joue...   C'est avec...
Ça passe à...   A...

II Ch. 12, p. 304   *(about places)*
... se trouve...
Il y a...
On peut...

Telling when you have class I Ch. 2, p. 54

à... heures	le soir
à... heures quinze	le lundi
à... heures trente	le mardi
à... heures	le mercredi
quarante-cinq	le jeudi
aujourd'hui	le vendredi
demain	le samedi
le matin	le dimanche
l'après-midi	

Writing a formal letter III Ch. 5, p. 127

Monsieur/Madame,
En réponse à votre lettre du...
Suite à notre conversation téléphonique,...
Je vous prie d'agréer, Monsieur/Madame, l'expression de mes sentiments distingués.

Requesting information III Ch. 5, p. 127

Pourriez-vous m'envoyer des renseignements sur... ?
Je voudrais savoir...
Vous serait-il possible de... ?

Asking for confirmation III Ch. 11, p. 276

toujours...	... , c'est ça?
bien...	Si je me souviens bien,...
... , déjà?	Si je ne me trompe pas,...

Asking for explanations III Ch. 11, p. 283

Qu'est-ce que c'est?
Comment est-ce qu'on appelle ça?
Qu'est-ce que ça veut dire,... ?
Qu'est-ce qu'il y a dans... ?
Comment est-ce qu'on fait... ?
D'où vient le mot... ?
Comment on dit... ?

Getting someone's attention I Ch. 3, p. 82

Pardon.	Excusez-moi.

I Ch. 5, p. 135

La carte, s'il vous	Madame!
plaît.	Mademoiselle!
Monsieur!	

Ordering food and beverages I Ch. 5, p. 135

Vous avez choisi?
Vous prenez?
Je voudrais...
Je vais prendre... , s'il vous plaît.
... , s'il vous plaît.
Donnez-moi... , s'il vous plaît.
Apportez-moi... , s'il vous plaît.
Vous avez... ?
Qu'est-ce que vous avez comme... ?

Ordering and asking for details III Ch. 1, p. 18

Vous avez décidé?
Non, pas encore.
Un instant, s'il vous plaît.
Que voulez-vous comme entrée?

Comme entrée, j'aimerais...
Et comme boisson?
Comment désirez-vous votre viande?
Saignante.
A point.
Bien cuite.
Qu'est-ce que vous me conseillez?
Qu'est-ce que c'est,... ?

Paying the check I Ch. 5, p. 139

L'addition, s'il vous plaît.
Oui, tout de suite.
Un moment, s'il vous plaît.
Ça fait combien, s'il vous plaît?
Ça fait... francs.
C'est combien,... ?
C'est... francs.

Exchanging information I Ch. 4, p. 104
(leisure activities)

Qu'est-ce que tu fais comme sport?
Qu'est-ce que tu fais pour t'amuser?
Je fais...
Je ne fais pas de...
Je (ne) joue (pas)...

II Ch. 1, p. 12
Qu'est-ce que tu aimes faire?
Qu'est-ce que tu fais comme sport?
Qu'est-ce que tu aimes comme musique?
Quel est ton/ta... préféré(e)?
Qui est ton/ta... préféré(e)?

Making plans I Ch. 6, p. 153

Qu'est-ce que tu vas faire... ?
Tu vas faire quoi... ?
Je vais...
Pas grand-chose.
Rien de spécial.

Arranging to meet someone I Ch. 6, p. 163

Quand (ça)?	et quart
tout de suite	moins le quart
Où (ça)?	moins cinq
devant...	midi (et demi)
au métro...	minuit (et demi)
chez...	vers...
dans...	On se retrouve...
Avec qui?	Rendez-vous...
A quelle heure?	Entendu.
et demie	

III Ch. 6, p. 141
Comment est-ce qu'on fait?
Quand est-ce qu'on se revoit?
Où est-ce qu'on se retrouve?
A quelle heure est-ce qu'on se donne rendez-vous?

Inquiring about future plans I Ch. 11, p. 289

Qu'est-ce que tu vas faire... ?
Où est-ce que tu vas aller... ?

Asking about intentions III Ch. 5, p. 117

Qu'est-ce que tu penses faire?
Qu'est-ce que tu as l'intention de faire?
Qu'est-ce que tu comptes faire?

Asking about future plans III Ch. 5, p. 124

Tu sais ce que tu veux faire?
Tu as des projets?
Qu'est-ce que tu veux faire plus tard?

Sharing future plans I Ch. 11, p. 289

J'ai l'intention de...   Je vais...

Expressing intentions III Ch. 5, p. 117

Je pense...
Je compte...
Je tiens à...

Expressing conditions and possibilities III Ch. 5,
p. 117

Si...   Il se peut que...
Peut-être que...   Il est possible que...

Describing and characterizing people I Ch. 7, p. 185

Il/Elle est comment?   Il/Elle est...
Ils/Elles sont   Ils/Elles sont...
  comment?

II Ch. 1, p. 10
avoir... ans   Je suis...
J'ai...   Il/Elle est...
Il/Elle a...   Ils/Elles sont...
Ils/Elles ont...

II Ch. 12, p. 314
Il avait faim.   J'étais...
Elle avait l'air...

Describing a place II Ch. 4, p. 90

dans le nord/sud/est/ouest
plus grand(e) que
moins grand(e) que
charmant(e)
coloré(e)
vivant(e)

II Ch. 12, p. 314
Il y avait...   Il était...

Making a telephone call I Ch. 9, p. 244

Bonjour.
Je suis bien chez... ?
C'est...
(Est-ce que)... est là, s'il vous plaît?
(Est-ce que) je peux parler à... ?
Je peux laisser un message?
Vous pouvez lui dire que j'ai téléphoné?
Ça ne répond pas.
C'est occupé.

Answering a telephone call I Ch. 9, p. 244

Allô?
Bonjour.
Qui est à l'appareil?
Une seconde, s'il vous plaît.
Bien sûr.
Vous pouvez rappeler plus tard?
D'accord.
Ne quittez pas.

Asking others what they need I Ch. 3, p. 74

Qu'est-ce qu'il te (vous) faut pour... ?

I Ch. 8, p. 210
De quoi est-ce que tu as besoin?
Qu'est-ce qu'il te faut?

Expressing need I Ch. 8, p. 210

Il me faut...   J'ai besoin de...

I Ch. 10, p. 265
(shopping)
Oui, vous avez... ?
Je cherche quelque chose pour...
J'aimerais... pour aller avec...
Non, merci, je regarde.

Making purchases II Ch. 3, p. 58

C'est combien, s'il vous plaît?
Combien coûte(nt)... ?
Combien en voulez-vous?
Je voudrais...
Je vais (en) prendre...
Ça fait combien?

Inquiring I Ch. 10, p. 265 *(shopping)*

(Est-ce que) je peux vous aider?
Vous désirez?
Je peux l'(les) essayer?
Je peux essayer... ?
C'est combien,... ?
Ça fait combien?
Vous avez ça en... ?

Asking which one(s) III Ch. 4, p. 88

Quel(s)/Quelle(s)... ?
Lequel/Laquelle/Lesquels/Lesquelles?

Pointing out and identifying people and things
III Ch. 4, p. 88

Ça, c'est...   Celui avec...
Celui-là/Celle-là.   Celle qui...
Ceux-là/Celles-là.   La fille au...
Le vert.   Là-bas, le garçon qui...
Celui du...

Pointing out places and things I Ch. 12, p. 317

Voici...
Là, tu vois, c'est...
Regarde, voilà...
Ça, c'est...
Là, c'est...

II Ch. 2, p. 39

A côté de...   à gauche de
Il y a...   à droite de
en face de   près de

Asking where things are   III Ch. 2, p. 43

Vous pourriez me dire où il y a... ?
Pardon, vous savez où se trouve... ?
Tu sais où sont... ?

Telling where things are   III Ch. 2, p. 43

Par là, au bout du couloir.
Juste là, à côté de...
En bas.
En haut.
Au fond.
Au rez-de-chaussée.
Au premier étage.
A l'entrée de...
En face de...

Asking for directions   I Ch. 12, p. 327

Pardon,... , s'il vous plaît?
Pardon,... . Où est... , s'il vous plaît?
Pardon,... . Je cherche... , s'il vous plaît.

III Ch. 2, p. 33

La route pour... , s'il vous plaît?
Comment on va à... ?

Giving directions   I Ch. 12, p. 327

Vous continuez jusqu'au prochain feu rouge.
Vous tournez...
Vous allez tout droit jusqu'à...
Prenez la rue... , puis traversez la rue...
Vous passez devant...
C'est tout de suite à...

II Ch. 2, p. 45

Traversez...
Prenez...
Puis, tournez à gauche dans...
Allez (continuez) tout droit.
sur la droite (gauche)

II Ch. 12, p. 304

C'est au nord/au sud/à l'est/à l'ouest de...
C'est dans le nord/le sud/l'est/l'ouest de...

III Ch. 2, p. 33

Pour (aller à)... , vous suivez la... pendant à peu
    près... kilomètres.
Vous allez voir un panneau qui indique l'entrée de
    l'autoroute.
Vous traversez...
Après... , vous allez tomber sur...
Cette route vous conduira au centre-ville.
Vous continuez tout droit, jusqu'au carrefour.

Inquiring about past events   I Ch. 9, p. 237

Tu as passé un bon week-end?

I Ch. 9, p. 238

Qu'est-ce que tu as fait... ?
Tu es allé(e) où?
Et après?
Qu'est-ce qui s'est passé?

I Ch. 11, p. 297

Tu as passé un bon... ?
Ça s'est bien passé?
Tu t'es bien amusé(e)?

II Ch. 5, p. 123

Comment ça s'est passé?
Comment s'est passée ta journée (hier)?
Comment s'est passé ton week-end?
Comment se sont passées tes vacances?

II Ch. 6, p. 144

C'était comment?
Ça t'a plu?
Tu t'es amusé(e)?

III Ch. 1, p. 10

C'était comment, tes vacances?

Exchanging information   III Ch. 1, p. 12
(about vacations)

Est-ce que tu es resté(e) ici?
Oui, je suis resté(e) ici tout le temps.
Non, je suis parti(e)...
Quand est-ce que tu y es allé(e)?
J'y suis allé(e) début/fin...
Avec qui est-ce que tu y es allé(e)?
J'y suis allé(e) seul(e)/avec...
Tu es parti(e) comment?
Je suis parti(e) en...
Où est-ce que tu as dormi?
A l'hôtel.
Chez...
Quel temps est-ce qu'il a fait?
Il a fait un temps...
Il a plu tout le temps.

Relating a series of events   I Ch. 9, p. 238

D'abord,...
Ensuite,...
Après,...
Je suis allé(e)...
Et après ça...
Enfin,...

II Ch. 1, p. 20

Puis,...

II Ch. 4, p. 99

Finalement,...
Vers... ,

Asking what things were like   II Ch. 8, p. 198

C'était comment?
C'était tellement différent?

Describing what things were like **II Ch. 8, p. 198**

    C'était...
    Il y avait...
    La vie était plus... , moins...

Reminiscing **II Ch. 8, p. 201**

    Quand j'étais petit(e),...
    Quand il/elle était petit(e),...
    Quand j'avais... ans,...

To tell what or whom you miss **II Ch. 8, p. 197**

    Je regrette...
    ... me manque.
    ... me manquent.
    Ce qui me manque, c'est...

Asking about a story **III Ch. 9, p. 234**

    De quoi ça parle?
    Comment est-ce que ça commence?
    Comment ça se termine?

Beginning a story **II Ch. 9, p. 235**

    A propos,...

Continuing a story **II Ch. 9, p. 235**

    Donc,...   C'est-à-dire que...
    Alors,...   ... , quoi.
    A ce moment-là,...   ... , tu vois.
    Bref,...

Ending a story **II Ch. 9, p. 235**

    Heureusement,...
    Malheureusement,...
    Finalement,...

Summarizing a story **II Ch. 11, p. 286**

    De quoi ça parle?
    Ça parle de...
    Qu'est-ce que ça raconte?
    C'est l'histoire de...

    III Ch. 9, p. 234
    Ça parle de...   Ça se passe,...
    C'est l'histoire de... Au début,...
    Il s'agit de...   A ce moment-là,...
    A la fin,...

Breaking some news **II Ch. 9, p. 231**

    Tu connais la nouvelle?
    Tu ne devineras jamais ce qui s'est passé.
    Tu sais qui... ?
    Tu sais ce que... ?
    Devine qui...
    Devine ce que...

    III Ch. 10, p. 259
    Tu savais que...?
    Tu connais la dernière?
    J'ai entendu dire que...

    Figure-toi que...
    Si tu avais vu...

Showing interest **II Ch. 9, p. 231**

    Raconte!
    Aucune idée.
    Dis vite!

    III Ch. 10, p. 259
    Oh là là!
    Qui t'a dit ça?
    Et alors?

Expressing disbelief and doubt **II Ch. 6, p. 148**

    Tu plaisantes!   C'est pas vrai!
    Pas possible!   N'importe quoi!
    Ça m'étonnerait!   Mon œil!

    III Ch. 10, p. 259
    Je n'en reviens pas.

Telling jokes **III Ch. 10, p. 261**

    J'en connais une bonne.
    Est-ce que tu connais l'histoire de... ?
    Quelle est la différence entre ... et... ?
    Quel est le point commun entre... et... ?
    C'est l'histoire d'un mec qui...
    ... et alors, il dit que...
    ... et l'autre lui répond...
    Elle est bien bonne!
    Elle est nulle, ta blague!

EXPRESSING FEELINGS AND EMOTIONS

Expressing likes and preferences about things
I Ch. 1, p. 26

    J'aime (bien)...   J'aime mieux...
    J'adore...   J' préfère...

    I Ch. 5, p. 138
    C'est...

Expressing dislikes about things **I Ch. 1, p. 26**

    Je n'aime pas...

    I Ch. 5, p. 138
    C'est...

Telling what you'd like and what you'd like to do
I Ch. 3, p. 77

    Je voudrais...
    Je voudrais acheter...

Telling how much you like or dislike something
I Ch. 4, p. 102

    Beaucoup.   Pas du tout.
    Pas beaucoup.   surtout
    Pas tellement.

Inquiring about likes and dislikes **I Ch. 1, p. 26**

Tu aimes...?

I Ch. 5, p. 138
Comment tu trouves ça?

Hesitating **I Ch. 10, p. 274**

Euh... J'hésite.
Je ne sais pas.
Il/Elle me plaît, mais il/elle est...

Making a decision **I Ch. 10, p. 274**

Vous avez décidé de prendre... ?
Vous avez choisi?
Vous le/la/les prenez?
Je le/la/les prends.
Non, c'est trop cher.

Expressing indecision **I Ch. 11, p. 289**

J'hésite.
Je ne sais pas.
Je n'en sais rien.
Je n'ai rien de prévu.

III Ch. 1, p. 17
Tout me tente.
Je n'arrive pas à me décider.
J'hésite entre... et...

III Ch. 5, p. 124
Pas vraiment.
Je ne sais pas trop.
Non, je me demande.
Je n'en ai aucune idée.
J'ai du mal à me décider.
Je ne sais plus ce que je veux.

Making suppositions **III Ch. 7, p. 169**

On pourrait sûrement...
Ça doit être...
Je parie que...
Il doit y avoir...

Expressing doubt **III Ch. 7, p. 169**

Ça m'étonnerait que...
Je ne suis pas sûr(e) que...
Je ne suis pas certain(e) que...
Je ne pense pas que...

Expressing certainty **III Ch. 7, p. 169**

Je suis certain(e) que...
Je suis sûr(e) que...
Je sais que...
Je suis convaincu(e) que...

III Ch. 12, p. 304
Ça, c'est sûr.
Je n'en ai aucun doute.

Wondering what happened and offering possible explanations **II Ch. 9, p. 228**

Je me demande...   Je crois que...
A mon avis,...   Je parie que...
Peut-être que...

Accepting explanations **II Ch. 9, p. 228**

Tu as peut-être raison.   Ça se voit.
C'est possible.   Evidemment.

Rejecting explanations **II Ch. 9, p. 228**

A mon avis, tu te trompes.
Ce n'est pas possible.
Je ne crois pas.

Expressing hopes and wishes **I Ch. 11, p. 289**

J'ai envie de...
Je voudrais bien...

III Ch. 5, p. 124
J'aimerais bien...
Ce qui me plairait, c'est de...
Mon rêve, c'est de...

III Ch. 8, p. 196
Si seulement je pouvais,...
Si j'avais le choix,...
Si c'était possible,...
Ça serait chouette si...
Qu'est-ce que j'aimerais... !

Expressing anticipation **III Ch. 12, p. 304**

Il me tarde de...
Je suis vraiment impatient(e) de...!
Vivement que... !
Dès que je serai là,...
Quand je verrai...

Asking how someone is feeling **II Ch. 2, p. 34**

Pas trop fatigué(e)?
Vous n'avez pas/Tu n'as pas faim?
Vous n'avez pas/Tu n'as pas soif?

Telling how you are feeling **II Ch. 2, p. 34**

Non, ça va.
Si, un peu.
Si, je suis crevé(e).
Si, j'ai très faim/soif!
Si, je meurs de faim/soif!

Expressing concern for someone **II Ch. 5, p. 119**

Ça n'a pas l'air d'aller.
Qu'est-ce qui se passe?
Qu'est-ce qui t'arrive?
Raconte!

II Ch. 7, p. 165
Quelque chose ne va pas?
Qu'est-ce que tu as?
Tu n'as pas l'air en forme.

Sympathizing with someone II Ch. 5, p. 125

Oh là là!
C'est pas de chance, ça!
Pauvre vieux (vieille)!

Sharing confidences I Ch. 9, p. 247

J'ai un petit problème.
Je peux te parler?
Tu as une minute?

II Ch. 10, p. 250

Je ne sais pas quoi faire.
Qu'est-ce qu'il y a?
Je t'écoute.
Qu'est-ce que je peux faire?

Consoling others I Ch. 9, p. 247

Ne t'en fais pas!
Je t'écoute.
Ça va aller mieux!
Qu'est-ce que je peux faire?

II Ch. 5, p. 125

Courage!
T'en fais pas.
C'est pas grave.

Expressing satisfaction II Ch. 5, p. 123

Ça s'est très bien passé!
C'était...
   incroyable!
   super!
   génial!
Quelle journée formidable!
Quel week-end formidable!

Expressing frustration II Ch. 5, p. 123

Quelle journée!
Quel week-end!
J'ai passé une journée horrible!
C'est pas mon jour!
Tout a été de travers!

Expressing impatience III Ch. 2, p. 36

Mais, qu'est-ce que tu fais?
Tu peux te dépêcher?
Grouille-toi!
On n'a pas le temps!
Je suis vraiment impatient(e) de...

Expressing annoyance III Ch. 8, p. 203

Non mais, vous vous prenez pour qui?
Non mais, surtout, ne vous gênez pas!
Ça va pas, non?!
Ça commence à bien faire, hein?
Dites donc, ça vous gênerait de... ?

Complaining II Ch. 7, p. 165

Je ne me sens pas bien.
Je suis tout(e) raplapla.

J'ai mal dormi.
J'ai mal partout!

II Ch. 12, p. 310

Je crève de faim!   Je suis fatigué(e).
Je meurs de soif!   J'ai peur de...

III Ch. 8, p. 203

C'est l'horreur!
C'est insupportable, à la fin!
J'en ai ras le bol!
Je commence à en avoir marre!

Quarreling III Ch. 6, p. 152

Rapporteur(-euse)!
Pleurnicheur(-euse)!
Tricheur(-euse)!
Tu es bête comme tes pieds!
Tu m'énerves, à la fin!
Tu es vraiment casse-pieds!
Tu me prends la tête!
Oh, ça va, hein?
Arrête!
Ça suffit!
Tu le fais exprès?
Mêle-toi de tes oignons!
Fiche-moi la paix!
Casse-toi!
Tant pis pour toi!
Ferme-la!
C'est toujours la même chose!
C'est lui/elle qui a commencé!
Il/Elle m'a traité(e) de... !
C'est toujours moi qui prends!

Expressing discouragement II Ch. 7, p. 174; II Ch. 12, p. 310

Je n'en peux plus!
J'abandonne.
Je craque!

Offering encouragement II Ch. 7, p. 174

Allez!
Encore un effort!
Tu y es presque!
Courage!

Expressing disappointment III Ch. 12, p. 311

Les boules!
J'en ai vraiment marre!
J'ai vraiment pas de chance.
C'est pas juste.
Quelle angoisse!
Qu'est-ce que je peux être nul(le)!

Expressing excitement III Ch. 12, p. 311

Génial!
C'est trop cool!
J'arrive pas à y croire!
C'est pas possible!
C'est vraiment le pied!
Youpi!

SUMMARY OF FUNCTIONS

Expressing astonishment **III Ch. 7, p. 177**

> Oh, dis donc!
> Ça alors!
> C'est pas vrai!
> Ouah!
> C'est le pied!
> Oh là là!
> Qu'est-ce que... !
> Quel... !
> Tiens! Regarde un peu!
> C'est fou comme... !
> Tu as vu comme... ?
> Je n'ai jamais vu un(e) aussi...

Expressing fear **III Ch. 7, p. 178**

> J'ai très peur de...
> J'ai peur que...
> J'ai la frousse!

Expressing relief **III Ch. 7, p. 178**

> On a eu de la chance!
> Ouf! On a eu chaud!
> On l'a échappé belle!

PERSUADING

Asking for recommendations **III Ch. 9, p. 233**
(movies)

> Qu'est-ce que tu as vu comme bon film?
> Qu'est-ce qu'il y a comme bons films en ce moment?

Making recommendations **III Ch. 9, p. 233**
(movies)

> Tu devrais aller voir...
> Je te recommande...
> Va voir... , c'est génial comme film.
> C'est à ne pas manquer!
> N'y va pas!
> Ça ne vaut pas le coup!
> Ne va surtout pas voir...
> Evite d'aller voir...

I Ch. 5, p. 132 *(food)*
> Prends...
> Prenez...

III Ch. 1, p. 17
> Tu devrais prendre...
> Pourquoi tu ne prends pas...
> Essaie...

Asking for suggestions **II Ch. 1, p. 18**

> Qu'est-ce qu'on fait?

II Ch. 4, p. 94
> Qu'est-ce qu'on peut faire?

Making suggestions **I Ch. 4, p. 110**

> On... ?

I Ch. 5, p. 129
> On va au café?

> On fait du ski?
> On joue au base-ball?

I Ch. 12, p. 322 *(how to get somewhere)*
> On peut y aller...
> On peut prendre...

II Ch. 1, p. 18
> Si tu veux, on peut...
> On pourrait...
> Tu as envie de... ?
> Ça te dit de... ?

II Ch. 4, p. 94
> On peut...
> Si on allait... ?

II Ch. 8, p. 209
> Si on achetait... ?
> Si on visitait... ?
> Si on jouait... ?

III Ch. 6, p. 141
> Ça t'intéresse de... ?
> Ça te plairait de... ?
> Tu ne voudrais pas... ?

Accepting suggestions **I Ch. 4, p. 110**

> D'accord.   Allons-y!
> Bonne idée.   Oui, c'est...

III Ch. 6, p. 141
> Ce serait sympa.
> Ça me plairait beaucoup.
> J'aimerais bien.

Turning down suggestions **I Ch. 4, p. 110**

> Non, c'est...
> Ça ne me dit rien.
> Désolé(e), mais je ne peux pas.

III Ch. 6, p. 141
> C'est gentil, mais j'ai un rendez-vous.
> Impossible, je suis pris(e).
> J'aimerais bien, mais...

Responding to suggestions **II Ch. 1, p. 18**

> C'est une bonne/excellente idée.
> Je veux bien.
> Je ne peux pas.
> Non, je préfère...
> Pas question!

II Ch. 8, p. 209
> Bof.
> Non, je ne veux pas.
> Comme tu veux.

Making excuses **I Ch. 5, p. 129**

> Désolé(e). J'ai des devoirs à faire.
> J'ai des courses à faire.
> J'ai des trucs à faire.
> J'ai des tas de choses à faire.

II Ch. 10, p. 255
J'ai quelque chose à faire.
Je n'ai pas le temps.
Je suis très occupé(e).
C'est impossible.

II Ch. 5, p. 127 *(school)*
... , c'est pas mon fort.
J'ai du mal à comprendre.
Je suis pas doué(e) pour...

Giving reasons II Ch. 5, p. 127
Je suis assez bon (bonne) en...
C'est en... que je suis le/la meilleur(e).
... , c'est mon fort!

Asking for permission I Ch. 7, p. 189
(Est-ce que) je peux... ?
Tu es d'accord?

III Ch. 3, p. 60
J'aimerais...
Tu veux bien que je... ?
Ça te dérange si... ?

Giving permission I Ch. 7, p. 189
Oui, si tu veux.
Pourquoi pas?
Oui, bien sûr.
D'accord, si tu... d'abord...

III Ch. 3, p. 60
Ça va pour cette fois.
Oui, si...

Refusing permission I Ch. 7, p. 189
Pas question!   Non, tu dois...
Non, c'est impossible.   Pas ce soir.

III Ch. 3, p. 60
Tu n'as pas le droit de...
Ce n'est pas possible.

Expressing obligation III Ch. 3, p. 60
Il faut que... d'abord.
Tu dois...

Reprimanding someone II Ch. 5, p. 127
C'est inadmissible.
Tu dois mieux travailler en classe.
Tu ne dois pas faire le clown en classe!
Ne recommence pas.

Making requests I Ch. 3, p. 72
Tu as... ?   Vous avez... ?

I Ch. 8, p. 212
Tu peux...
Tu me rapportes... ?

III Ch. 9, p. 227
Chut!

Tais-toi!
Ne parle pas si fort.
Tu pourrais faire moins de bruit?
Vous pourriez vous taire, s'il vous plaît?
Baisse/Monte le son.

Responding to requests I Ch. 3, p. 72
Voilà.
Je regrette.
Je n'ai pas de...

Accepting requests I Ch. 8, p. 212
Pourquoi pas?
Bon, d'accord.
Je veux bien.
J'y vais tout de suite.

I Ch. 12, p. 320
D'accord.
Si tu veux.

Declining requests I Ch. 8, p. 212
Je ne peux pas maintenant.
Je regrette, mais je n'ai pas le temps.
J'ai des tas de choses (trucs) à faire.

I Ch. 12, p. 320
Désolé(e), mais je n'ai pas le temps.

Asking a favor I Ch. 12, p. 320
Est-ce que tu peux... ?
Tu me rapportes... ?
Tu pourrais passer à... ?

II Ch. 10, p. 255
Tu peux m'aider?
Tu pourrais... ?
Ça t'ennuie de... ?
Ça t'embête de... ?

Granting a favor II Ch. 10, p. 255
Avec plaisir.   Bien sûr que non.
Bien sûr.   Pas du tout.
Pas de problème.

Telling someone what to do I Ch. 8, p. 212
Rapporte-moi...   Achète(-moi)...
Prends...   N'oublie pas de...

Asking for food II Ch. 3, p. 64
Je pourrais avoir... , s'il vous (te) plaît?
Vous pourriez (tu pourrais) me passer... ?

Offering food I Ch. 8, p. 219
Tu veux... ?   Tu prends... ?
Vous voulez... ?   Encore de... ?
Vous prenez ... ?

II Ch. 3, p. 64
Voilà.
Vous voulez (tu veux)... ?
Encore... ?
Tenez (tiens).

Accepting food I Ch. 8, p. 219

Oui, s'il vous (te) plaît.
Oui, avec plaisir.
Oui, j'en veux bien.

II Ch. 3, p. 64
Oui, je veux bien.

Refusing food I Ch. 8, p. 219

Non, merci.
Non, merci. Je n'ai plus faim.
Je n'en veux plus.

II Ch. 3, p. 64
Merci, ça va.
Je n'ai plus faim/soif.

Asking for advice I Ch. 9, p. 247 *(general)*

A ton avis, qu'est-ce que je fais?
Qu'est-ce que tu me conseilles?

II Ch. 10, p. 250
A ton avis, qu'est-ce que je dois faire?
Qu'est-ce que tu ferais, toi?

II Ch. 1, p. 15
Qu'est-ce que je dois... ?

III Ch. 7, p. 171
Tu crois que je devrais... ?
Tu penses qu'il vaudrait mieux... ?

I Ch. 10, p. 264 *(clothes)*
Je ne sais pas quoi mettre pour...
Qu'est-ce que je mets?

I Ch. 12, p. 322 *(directions)*
Comment est-ce qu'on y va?

II Ch. 3, p. 68 *(gifts)*
Tu as une idée de cadeau pour... ?
Qu'est-ce que je pourrais offrir à... ?

Giving advice I Ch. 9, p. 247

Oublie-le/-la/-les!
Téléphone-lui/-leur!
Tu devrais...
Pourquoi tu ne... pas?

I Ch. 10, p. 264
Pourquoi est-ce que tu ne mets pas... ?
Mets...

II Ch. 1, p. 15
Pense à prendre...
Prends...
N'oublie pas...

II Ch. 3, p. 68
Offre-lui (leur) ...
Tu pourrais lui (leur) offrir...
... , peut-être.

II Ch. 7, p. 173
Tu dois...
Tu ferais bien de...
Tu n'as qu'à...

II Ch. 10, p. 250
Invite-le/-la/-les.
Parle-lui/-leur.
Dis-lui/-leur que...
Ecris-lui/-leur.
Explique-lui/-leur.
Excuse-toi.

II Ch. 12, p. 312
Evite de...
Tu ne devrais pas...

III Ch. 5, p. 124
Tu ferais mieux de...
Il faudrait que tu...
Il vaudrait mieux que...

III Ch. 7, p. 171
Je crois que ça vaut mieux.
A mon avis, c'est plus sûr.
Ce n'est pas la peine.
Je ne crois pas que ce soit utile.
Il faudrait que...
Il est très important que...
Il est essentiel que...
Il est nécessaire que...

III Ch. 8, p. 196
Si c'était moi,...
Si j'étais toi,...
A ta place,...

Justifying your recommendations II Ch. 7, p. 178

C'est bon pour toi.
Ça te fera du bien.
C'est meilleur que de...

Accepting advice II Ch. 7, p. 173

Tu as raison.
Bonne idée!
D'accord.

Rejecting advice II Ch. 7, p. 173

Je ne peux pas.
Non, je n'ai pas très envie.
Non, je préfère...
Pas question!
Je n'ai pas le temps.
Ce n'est pas mon truc.

Advising against something II Ch. 7, p. 178

Evite de...
Ne saute pas...
Tu ne devrais pas...

Cautioning someone III Ch. 7, p. 178

Je vous signale que...
Il serait plus prudent de...

Faites gaffe!
Attention à... !
Méfiez-vous!
Ne bougez pas.

Forbidding III Ch. 3, p. 67

Il est interdit de...
Veuillez ne pas...
Prière de ne pas...
Interdiction de...
Défense de...

Reproaching someone II Ch. 10, p. 258

Tu aurais dû...
Tu aurais pu...

III Ch. 3, p. 69
Vous (ne) devriez (pas)...
Tu as tort de...
Ce n'est pas bien de...
Tu ferais mieux de ne pas...

Justifying your actions III Ch. 3, p. 69

Je suis quand même libre, non?
Tout le monde fait pareil.
Je ne suis pas le/la seul(e) à...

Rejecting others' excuses III Ch. 3, p. 69

Pense aux autres.
Ce n'est pas une raison.
Ce n'est pas parce que tout le monde... que tu dois
  le faire.

Reminding I Ch. 11, p. 293

N'oublie pas...
Tu n'as pas oublié... ?
Tu ne peux pas partir sans...
Tu prends... ?

Reassuring someone I Ch. 11, p. 293

Ne t'en fais pas.
J'ai pensé à tout.
Je n'ai rien oublié.

II Ch. 8, p. 197
Tu vas t'y faire.
Fais-toi une raison.
Tu vas te plaire ici.
Tu vas voir que...

III Ch. 2, p. 36
Ça ne va pas prendre longtemps!
Sois patient(e)!
On a largement le temps!
Il n'y a pas le feu.
Du calme, du calme.

III Ch. 4, p. 96
Crois-moi.
Je t'assure.
Fais-moi confiance.
Je ne dis pas ça pour te faire plaisir.

III Ch. 7, p. 178
Ne vous en faites pas!
N'ayez pas peur.
Calmez-vous!
Pas de panique!

Apologizing II Ch. 10, p. 258

C'est de ma faute.
Excuse-moi.
Désolé(e).
J'aurais dû...
J'aurais pu...
Tu ne m'en veux pas?

III Ch. 6, p. 143
Je m'excuse de...
Je suis vraiment désolé(e) de...
Pardonne-moi de...
Je m'en veux de...

Accepting an apology II Ch. 10, p. 258

Ça ne fait rien.
C'est pas grave.
Il n'y a pas de mal.
T'en fais pas.
Je ne t'en veux pas.

III Ch. 6, p. 143
Ne t'inquiète pas.
Ça arrive à tout le monde.

EXPRESSING ATTITUDES AND OPINIONS

Agreeing I Ch. 2, p. 50

Oui, beaucoup.
Moi aussi.
Moi non plus.

III Ch. 9, p. 225
Je suis d'accord   Tu l'as dit!
  avec toi.   Tout à fait!
Tu as raison.

III Ch. 11, p. 278
Ça, c'est sûr.

Disagreeing I Ch. 2, p. 50

Moi, non.
Moi, si.
Pas moi.
Non, pas trop.

III Ch. 9, p. 225
Pas du tout.
Tu parles!
Tu te fiches de moi?
Tu rigoles!
Tu as tort.

III Ch. 11, p. 278
Tu délires ou quoi?

Asking for opinions I Ch. 2, p. 57

Comment tu trouves...?
Comment tu trouves ça?

I Ch. 10, p. 270
Il/Elle me va... ?
Il/Elle te (vous) plaît... ?
Tu aimes mieux... ou... ?

III Ch. 4, p. 86
Tu n'aimes pas...?
Elle/Il te plaît,...?
Qu'est-ce que tu penses de... ?
Qu'en penses-tu?

III Ch. 11, p. 278
Ça te branche,... ?

Expressing opinions I Ch. 2, p. 57

C'est...

I Ch. 9, p. 237
Oui, très chouette.
Oui, excellent.
Oui, très bon.
Oui, ça a été.
Oh, pas mauvais.
C'était épouvantable.
Très mauvais.

I Ch. 11, p. 297
C'était formidable!
Non, pas vraiment.
C'était un véritable cauchemar!

II Ch. 11, p. 284
C'est drôle/amusant.
C'est une belle histoire.
C'est plein de rebondissements.
Il y a du suspense.
On ne s'ennuie pas.
C'est une histoire passionnante.
Je te le/la recommande.
Il n'y a pas d'histoire.
Ça casse pas des briques.
C'est...
    trop violent.
    trop long.
    déprimant.
    bête.
    un navet.
    du n'importe quoi.
    gentillet, sans plus.

III Ch. 4, p. 86
Je le/la trouve...
Je l'aime bien.
Elle/Il me plaît beaucoup.
C'est très bien, ça.
J'aime bien ce genre de...

Je ne l'aime pas tellement.
Elle/Il ne me plaît pas du tout.
Je trouve qu'ils/elles font...
Ça fait vraiment...

III Ch. 11, p. 278
Ça m'éclate.
Je n'écoute que ça.
Ça ne me branche pas trop.

Asking for judgments III Ch. 9, p. 233

C'était comment?
Comment tu as trouvé ça?

Making judgments III Ch. 9, p. 233

Ça m'a beaucoup plu.
J'ai trouvé ça pas mal/amusant.
Il y avait de...
Je ne me suis pas ennuyé(e) une seconde.
Ça m'a bien fait rire.
C'est nul/lourd.
C'est un navet.
Ça n'a aucun intérêt.
Je n'ai pas du tout aimé.
Ça ne m'a pas emballé(e).
Je me suis ennuyé(e) à mourir.

Making observations III Ch. 11, p. 286

Ce qui est intéressant/incroyable, c'est...
Ce qui saute aux yeux, c'est...
Ce qui me branche vraiment, c'est...
Ce que je trouve super, c'est...
Ce que j'adore/j'aime, c'est...

Giving impressions III Ch. 11, p. 286

On dirait que...
Il me semble que...
J'ai l'impression que...
Ils ont l'air de...

Making comparisons III Ch. 8, p. 204

Ce n'était pas comme ça.
Ici,... tandis que...
moins de... que
plus de... que
autant de... que...
plus... que...
moins... que...
aussi... que...

Bragging III Ch. 10, p. 251

C'est fastoche, ça!
C'est pas pour me vanter, mais moi,...
Oh, j'en ai vu d'autres.
C'est moi le/la meilleur(e).
C'est moi qui... le mieux.

Flattering III Ch. 10, p. 251

Tu es fortiche/calé(e).
Alors là, tu m'épates!
Tu en as, du courage.

Tu es vraiment le/la meilleur(e).
Tu es le/la... le/la plus... que je connaisse.

Teasing III Ch. 10, p. 254

Tu es amoureux(-euse) ou quoi?
Non mais, tu t'es pas regardé(e)!
Réveille-toi un peu!
Tu en rates pas une, toi!
Arrête de délirer!

Responding to teasing III Ch. 10, p. 254

Lâche-moi, tu veux?
Je t'ai pas demandé ton avis.
Oh, ça va, hein!
Qu'est-ce que tu en sais?
Ben, ça peut arriver à tout le monde.
Et toi, arrête de m'embêter!

Paying a compliment I Ch. 10, p. 270
(clothing)

C'est tout à fait ton/votre style.
Il/Elle te (vous) va très bien.
Il/Elle va très bien avec...
Je le/la/les trouve...
C'est parfait.

II Ch. 2, p. 40 *(general)*
Il/Elle est vraiment bien, ton/ta...
Il/Elle est cool, ton/ta...

II Ch. 3, p. 64 *(food)*
C'est vraiment bon!
Ç'était délicieux!

III Ch. 4, p. 96 *(clothing)*
Je te trouve très bien comme ça.
Ça fait très bien.
Que tu es... avec ça!
C'est tout à fait toi.
C'est assorti à...
Ça te va comme un gant.

Responding to compliments II Ch. 2, p. 40

Tu trouves?
C'est vrai? (Vraiment?)
C'est gentil!

II Ch. 3, p. 64
Ce n'est pas grand-chose.

III Ch. 4, p. 96
Ça te plaît, vraiment?
Tu crois?
Oh, c'est un vieux truc.
Oh, tu sais, je ne l'ai pas payé(e) cher.

Criticizing I Ch. 10, p. 270

Il/Elle ne te (vous) va pas du tout.
Il/Elle ne va pas du tout avec...
Il/Elle est (Ils/Elles sont) trop...
Je le/la/les trouve...

Expressing indifference II Ch. 6, p. 144

C'était...
   assez bien.
   comme ci, comme ça.
   pas mal.
Mouais.
Plus ou moins.

III Ch. 9, p. 225
Je m'en fiche.
Ça m'est vraiment égal.
Peu importe.

Emphasizing likes II Ch. 4, p. 96

Ce que j'aime bien, c'est...
Ce que je préfère, c'est...
Ce qui me plaît, c'est...

Emphasizing dislikes II Ch. 4, p. 96

Ce que je n'aime pas, c'est...
Ce qui m'ennuie, c'est...
Ce qui ne me plaît pas, c'est...

Expressing dissatisfaction II Ch. 6, p. 144

C'était...
   ennuyeux.
   mortel.
   nul.
   sinistre.
Sûrement pas!
Je me suis ennuyé(e).

III Ch. 1, p. 10
C'était pas terrible.
Pas trop bien.
Ça ne s'est pas très bien passé.

Expressing enthusiasm II Ch. 6, p. 144

C'était...
   magnifique.
   incroyable.
   superbe.
   sensas.
Ça m'a beaucoup plu.
Je me suis beaucoup amusé(e).

III Ch. 1, p. 10
C'était chouette!
Ça s'est très bien passé!
Super!

III Ch. 2, p. 41
Qu'est-ce que c'est... !
Ce que c'est bien!
C'est... comme tout!
Ça me branche!

Expressing boredom III Ch. 2, p. 41

Ça m'embête!
Ça me casse les pieds!
Ça m'ennuie à mourir!

SI TU AS OUBLIE...

This list presents vocabulary words that you've already learned in the Level 1 and Level 2 books, but may have forgotten. You may want to use them when you're working on the activities in the textbook and workbook. If you can't find the words you need here, try the English-French and French-English vocabulary lists beginning on page 359.

CLOTHING

un anorak   *ski jacket*
des baskets (f.)   *sneakers*
un blouson   *jacket*
des boucles d'oreilles (f.)   *earrings*
un bracelet   *bracelet*
un cardigan   *sweater*
une casquette   *cap*
une ceinture   *belt*
un chapeau   *hat*
des chaussettes (f.)   *socks*
des chaussures (f.)   *shoes*
un chemisier   *shirt (women's)*
une écharpe   *scarf*
un foulard   *scarf*
un jean   *pair of jeans*
une jupe   *skirt*
des lunettes (f.) de soleil   *sunglasses*
un maillot de bain   *bathing suit*
un manteau   *coat*
une montre   *watch*
un portefeuille   *wallet*
un pull   *pullover sweater*
des sandales (f.)   *sandals*
un short   *pair of shorts*
un sweat-shirt   *sweatshirt*
une veste   *suit jacket, blazer*

STYLES, FABRICS, AND COLORS

blanc(he)(s)   *white*
bleu(e)(s)   *blue*
en coton   *cotton*
en jean   *denim*
gris(e)(s)   *grey*
jaune(s)   *yellow*
marron (inv.)   *brown*
noir(e)(s)   *black*
orange (inv.)   *orange*
rose(s)   *pink*
rouge(s)   *red*
vert(e)(s)   *green*
violet(te)(s)   *purple*

DESCRIBING CLOTHES

à la mode   *in style*
branché(e)(s)   *cool*

chic   *chic*
court(e)(s)   *short*
démodé(e)(s)   *out of style*
grand(e)(s)   *big*
horrible(s)   *terrible*
large(s)   *baggy*
moche(s)   *ugly*
petit(e)(s)   *small*
rétro   *old-fashioned*
sensas   *fantastic*
serré(e)(s)   *tight*

FAMILY MEMBERS

le beau-père   *stepfather, father-in-law*
la belle-fille   *stepdaughter, daughter-in-law*
la belle-mère   *stepmother, mother-in-law*
le cousin (la cousine)   *cousin*
le demi-frère   *half-brother/stepbrother, brother-in-law*
la demi-sœur   *half-sister/stepsister, sister-in-law*
l'enfant unique   *only child*
la fille   *daughter*
le fils   *son*
le frère   *brother*
la grand-mère   *grandmother*
le grand-père   *grandfather*
la mère   *mother*
l'oncle (m.)   *uncle*
le père   *father*
la sœur   *sister*
la tante   *aunt*

FOODS AND BEVERAGES

les ananas (m.)   *pineapple*
les avocats (m.)   *avocados*
la baguette   *French bread*
les bananes (f.)   *bananas*
le beurre   *butter*
le bifteck   *steak*
le café   *coffee*
les carottes (f.)   *carrots*
les céréales (f.)   *cereal*
un chocolat   *hot chocolate*
un coca   *cola*
la confiture   *jam*
un croque-monsieur   *toasted cheese and ham sandwich*
une eau minérale   *mineral water*
la farine   *flour*

les fraises (f.) *strawberries*
le fromage *cheese*
le fruit *fruit*
le gâteau *cake*
les gombos (m.) *okra*
les haricots (m.) *beans*
les haricots verts (m.) *green beans*
un hot-dog *hot dog*
un jus d'orange *orange juice*
un jus de pomme *apple juice*
un jus de raisin *grape juice*
le lait *milk*
une limonade *sparkling lemon soda*
le maïs *corn*
les mangues (f.) *mangoes*
les noix de coco (f.) *coconuts*
les œufs (m.) *eggs*
les oranges (f.) *oranges*
le pain *bread*
les papayes (f.) *papayas*
les pâtes (f.) *pasta*
les pêches (f.) *peaches*
les petits pois (m.) *peas*
les poires (f.) *pears*
le poisson *fish*
les pommes (f.) *apples*
les pommes de terre (f.) *potatoes*
la salade *salad, lettuce*
un sandwich *sandwich*
le saucisson *salami*
le sel *salt*
les tomates (f.) *tomatoes*
la viande *meat*
le yaourt *yogurt*

SPORTS

faire de l'aérobic *to do aerobics*
faire du jogging *to jog*
faire de la musculation *to lift weights*
faire du patin à glace *to ice-skate*
faire de la randonnée *to go hiking*
faire du roller en ligne *to in-line skate*
faire du ski *to ski*
faire du ski nautique *to water-ski*
faire du vélo *to bike*
faire de la voile *to go sailing*
jouer au foot(ball) *to play soccer*
jouer au football américain *to play football*
jouer au golf *to play golf*
jouer au hockey *to play hockey*
jouer au tennis *to play tennis*
jouer au volley(-ball) *to play volleyball*

SI TU AS OUBLIE…

SUPPLEMENTARY VOCABULARY

This list presents extra vocabulary words you're not responsible for on tests that you may want to use when you're working on the activities in the textbook and workbook. If you can't find the words you need here, try the English-French and French-English vocabulary lists beginning on page 359.

ADJECTIVES

calm *calme*
cheerful *joyeux (joyeuse)*
cold *froid(e)*
cultured *cultivé(e)*
discrete *discret (discrète)*
easy to get along with *facile à vivre*
enthusiastic *enthousiaste*
exasperating *exaspérant(e)*
generous *généreux (généreuse)*
honest *honnête*
hypocritical *faux jeton*
independent *indépendant(e)*
likable *aimable*
loves to party *fêtard(e)*
moody *versatile*
not with it *pas futé(e)*
obnoxious *pénible*
open *ouvert(e)*
polite *poli(e)*
pretentious *prétentieux (prétentieuse)*
quick-witted *vif (vive)*
reserved *réservé(e)*
selfish *égoïste*
sensitive *sensible*
sincere *sincère*
shy *timide*
snobbish *snob*
sociable *sociable*
spontaneous *spontané(e)*
talkative *bavard(e)*
understanding *compréhensif (compréhensive)*
weird *bizarre*

ADVENTUROUS ACTIVITIES

to fly a plane *piloter un avion*
to go bungee jumping *faire du saut à l'élastique*
to go canoeing *faire du canoë*
to go mountain-climbing *faire de l'alpinisme*
to go on a photo safari *aller faire un safari-photo*
to go parachuting *sauter en parachute*
to go rafting *faire la descente d'une rivière*
to go rock-climbing *faire de l'escalade*
to go skydiving *sauter en chute libre*
to go spelunking *faire de la spéléologie*
to go surfing *faire du surf*
to race cars *faire des courses de voitures*
to ride in a helicopter *faire un tour en hélicoptère*

AT THE BEACH

to build sandcastles *faire des châteaux de sable*
to feed the seagulls *nourrir les mouettes* (f.)
to float *flotter*
to get sunburned *attraper un coup de soleil*
to look for seashells *chercher/ramasser des coquillages*
to play in the waves *sauter/jouer dans les vagues*
to put on suntan lotion *mettre de la crème solaire*
to sunbathe *prendre un bain de soleil*
to walk along the shore *se promener au bord de la mer*

CARS AND DRIVING

accident *un accident*
antifreeze *de l'antifreeze*
battery *la batterie*
to brake *freiner*
brake pedal *la pédale de frein*
bumper *le pare-chocs*
car seat *le siège*
clutch *la pédale d'embrayage*
dashboard *le tableau de bord*
entrance ramp *l'entrée de l'autoroute* (f.)
fender *l'aile* (f.)
gas pedal *la pédale d'accélération*
to get a ticket *avoir un P.V. (procès-verbal)*
headlights *les phares* (m.)
hood *le capot*
horn *le klaxon*
hubcap *l'enjoliveur* (m.)
jack *le cric*
license plate *la plaque d'immatriculation*
motor *le moteur*
muffler *le silencieux*
parking meter *le parcmètre*
radiator *le radiateur*
rearview mirror *le rétroviseur*
spark plugs *les bougies*
speed limit *la vitesse maximale (la vitesse est limitée à...)*
to stall *caler*
steering wheel *le volant*
sticker *un autocollant*
stop sign *un stop*
tow truck *une dépanneuse*
traffic light *un feu* (m.) *rouge*
transmission *la transmission*
trunk *le coffre*
turn signal *le clignotant*
windshield wipers *les essuie-glace* (m.)
to yield *laisser la priorité/céder le passage*

CLOTHING, FABRICS, COLORS

ankle boots   *des bottines* (f.)
beige   *beige*
bell bottoms   *un pattes d'eph*
button   *un bouton*
checked   *à carreaux*
collar   *un col*
colorful   *coloré(e), vif/vive*
dark   *foncé(e)*
eyeglasses   *des lunettes* (f.)
flowered   *à fleurs*
gold   *doré(e)*
handkerchief   *un mouchoir*
khaki   *kaki*
lace   *la dentelle*
light   *clair(e)*
linen   *en lin, en toile*
loafers   *des mocassins* (m.)
nylon   *en nylon*
pajamas   *un pyjama*
printed   *imprimé(e)*
raincoat   *un imperméable*
short/long sleeved   *à manches courtes/longues*
sleeve   *une manche*
slippers   *des pantoufles* (f.)
suede   *en daim*
suspenders   *des bretelles* (f.)
tank top   *un débardeur*
turquoise   *turquoise*
underwear   *les sous-vêtements* (m.)
velvet   *en velours*
windbreaker   *un coupe-vent*
zipper   *une fermeture éclair*

ENVIRONMENT

acid rain   *la pluie acide*
car exhaust   *l'échappement* (m.)
chemical-free   *sans produits chimiques*
destruction of the tropical rain forest   *la destruction de la forêt tropicale*
droughts   *les périodes* (f.) *de sécheresse*
endangered species   *les espèces* (f.) *en voie de disparition*
erosion   *l'érosion* (f.) *du sol*
extinct animals   *les espèces* (f.) *disparues*
famine   *la famine*
global warming   *le réchauffement de la planète*
greenhouse effect   *l'effet* (m.) *de serre*
industrial waste   *les déchets* (m.) *industriels*
landfills   *les décharges* (f.)
melting of the polar ice caps   *la fonte des glaces polaires*
nuclear waste   *les déchets* (m.) *nucléaires*
organic foods   *la nourriture biologique*
overpopulation   *la surpopulation*
ozone layer   *la couche d'ozone*
pesticides   *les pesticides* (m.)
pollution   *la pollution*

FARM LIFE

to bale hay   *emballoter le foin*
barn   *une grange*
cage   *une cage*

chicken coop   *un poulailler*
fence   *une barrière, une clôture*
to get up before dawn   *se lever à l'aube*
to groom the dogs   *toiletter les chiens*
to mill cotton   *filer le coton*
pen   *un enclos*
to plant crops   *planter des cultures*
to plow the fields   *labourer les champs*
to raise cattle   *élever du bétail*
stable   *une écurie*
to take the crops to market   *aller vendre les produits agricoles au marché*
tractor   *un tracteur*
trough   *un abreuvoir* (drink), *une auge* (food)
truck   *un camion*

FOODS AND BEVERAGES

asparagus   *des asperges* (f.)
bacon   *du bacon*
beef   *du bœuf*
bland   *doux (douce)*
Brussels sprouts   *des choux* (m.) *de Bruxelles*
cabbage   *du chou*
cauliflower   *du chou-fleur*
chestnut   *un marron*
cookie   *un biscuit*
cucumber   *un concombre*
cutlet   *une escalope*
doughnut   *un beignet*
duck   *un canard*
eggplant   *une aubergine*
fried eggs   *des œufs* (m.) *au plat*
garlic   *de l'ail* (m.)
grapefruit   *un pamplemousse*
hard-boiled egg   *un œuf dur*
honey   *du miel*
hot (spicy)   *fort(e), piquant(e)*
juicy (fruit)   *juteux (-euse);* (meat)   *moelleux (-euse); tendre*
lamb   *l'agneau* (m.)
liver   *du foie*
margarine   *de la margarine*
marshmallows   *des guimauves* (f.)
mayonnaise   *de la mayonnaise*
melon   *un melon*
mustard   *de la moutarde*
nuts   *des noix* (f.)
onion   *un oignon*
peanut butter   *du beurre de cacahouètes*
pepper (spice)   *du poivre;* (vegetable)   *un poivron*
pickle   *le cornichon*
popcorn   *du pop-corn*
potato chips   *des chips* (f.)
raspberry   *une framboise*
salmon   *du saumon*
scrambled eggs   *des œufs brouillés*
shellfish   *des fruits de mer* (m.)
soft-boiled egg   *un œuf à la coque*
spicy   *relevé(e)*
strawberry   *une fraise*
syrup   *du sirop*
tasty   *savoureux (savoureuse)*
veal   *du veau*
watermelon   *une pastèque*
yogurt   *un yaourt*
zucchini   *une courgette*

IN A RESTAURANT

bowl *un bol*
chef *le chef*
to clear the plates *enlever les assiettes*
cup *une tasse*
fork *une fourchette*
glass *un verre*
host/hostess *le maître-d'hôtel*
knife *un couteau*
napkin *une serviette*
pepper shaker *la poivrière*
plate *une assiette*
to refill the glass *remplir le verre*
reservation *une réservation*
salt shaker *la salière*
saucer *la soucoupe*
serving tray *le plateau*
spoon *une cuillère*
tablecloth *la nappe*
tip *un pourboire*

FRIENDSHIP

to be sorry *être désolé(e)*
to confide in someone *se confier à quelqu'un*
to feel guilty *se sentir coupable*
to get along with someone *bien s'entendre avec quelqu'un*
to help someone do something *aider quelqu'un à faire quelque chose*
to make friends *se faire des amis*
to meet after school *se retrouver après l'école*
to misunderstand *mal comprendre*
to take the first step *faire le premier pas*
to talk with friends *discuter avec des amis*
to trust someone *avoir confiance en quelqu'un*

LEISURE ACTIVITIES

to build a fire *faire un feu*
to collect butterflies *faire la collection des papillons*
to collect rocks *collectionner les pierres*
to collect stamps *collectionner les timbres*
to fly a kite *faire voler un cerf-volant*
to go to a botanical garden *aller au jardin botanique*
to go to a concert *aller au concert*
to go to a festival *aller à un festival*
to go fishing *aller à la pêche*
to go to a party *aller à une soirée/boum/fête*
to go to an art exhibit *aller voir une exposition*
to paint *faire de la peinture*
to pick wildflowers *cueillir des fleurs sauvages*
to play cards *jouer aux cartes*
to play checkers *jouer aux dames*
to play chess *jouer aux échecs*
to rent movies *louer des vidéos*
to ride a skateboard *faire du skateboard*
to sew *coudre; faire de la couture*
to sing around the campfire *chanter autour du feu de camp*
to visit friends *rendre visite à des amis*

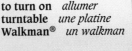

MAKEUP AND TOILETRIES

aftershave lotion *la lotion après-rasage*
bath towels *les serviettes de toilette* (f.)
blowdryer *le séchoir à cheveux*
brush *une brosse (à cheveux)*
comb *un peigne*
conditioner *l'après-shampooing* (m.)
cotton balls *des boules* (f.) *de coton*
cover stick *le correcteur de teint*
dental floss *le fil dentaire*
deodorant *le déodorant*
eyeshadow *l'ombre* (f.) *à paupières*
foundation *le fond de teint*
hair gel *le gel*
hair mousse *la mousse*
hairspray *la laque*
hand lotion *la crème pour les mains*
lipstick *le rouge à lèvres*
mascara *le mascara*
mouthwash *le bain de bouche*
razor *le rasoir*
rouge *le fard à joues*
shampoo *le shampooing*
shaving cream *la crème à raser*
soap *le savon*
toothbrush *la brosse à dents*
toothpaste *le dentifrice*
tweezers *la pince à épiler*
washcloth *le gant de toilette*

MUSICAL INSTRUMENTS AND EQUIPMENT

acoustic guitar *une guitare acoustique*
CD player *un lecteur CD*
cello *un violoncelle*
clarinet *une clarinette*
cymbals *des cymbales* (f.)
electric guitar *une guitare électrique*
harp *une harpe*
headphones *un casque, des écouteurs* (m.)
hit (song) *un tube*
mandolin *une mandoline*
oboe *un hautbois*
speakers *des enceintes* (f.), *des baffles* (m.)
trombone *un trombone*
tuba *un tuba*
to turn on *allumer*
turntable *une platine*
Walkman® *un walkman*

NATURE

bushes *des buissons* (m.)
cave *une grotte*
cliff *la falaise*
date palm *un dattier*
desert *le désert*
dunes *les dunes* (f.)
dust *la poussière*
fields *des champs* (m.)
insects *les insectes* (m.)

jungle *la jungle*
leaves *les feuilles* (f.)
mud *la boue*
oasis *l'oasis* (f.)
palm tree *un palmier*
plains *la plaine*
plateau *le plateau*
sand *le sable*
stream *un ruisseau*
swamp *un marais*
valley *une vallée*
vines *les vignes* (f.)
volcano *le volcan*
waves *les vagues* (f.)

PROFESSIONS

archeologist *un(e) archéologue*
athlete *un(e) athlète*
banker *un(e) banquier(-ière)*
businessman/businesswoman *un homme d'affaires (une femme d'affaires)*
carpenter *un menuisier*
commercial artist *un(e) dessinateur(-trice)*
dancer *un(e) danseur(-euse)*
diplomat *un(e) diplomate*
editor *un(e) rédacteur(-trice)*
electrician *un(e) électricien(ne)*
fashion model *un mannequin*
homemaker *un homme au foyer (une femme au foyer)*
insurance agent *un agent d'assurances*
judge *un juge*
manager (of a company) *le/la directeur (-trice);* (of a store or restaurant) *le/la gérant(e)*
painter *un peintre*
programmer *un(e) programmeur(-euse)*
psychiatrist *un(e) psychiatre*
real-estate agent *un agent immobilier*
scientist *un(e) scientifique, un(e) chercheur(-euse)*
social worker *un(e) assistant(e) social(e)*
soldier *un soldat*
surgeon *un chirurgien*
truck driver *un routier*
veterinarian *un(e) vétérinaire*

SEA LIFE AND EXPLORATION

air tank *une bouteille de plongée*
baracuda *un baracuda*
claws *les pinces* (f.)
current *le courant*
deep water *l'eau profonde* (f.), *les haut-fonds* (m.)
deep-sea fishing *la pêche hauturière, la pêche en haute mer*
dolphin *un dauphin*
fins (diving) *les palmes* (f.); (fish) *les nageoires* (f.); (shark) *l'aileron* (m.)
fishing line *la ligne de pêche*
flippers *les nageoires* (f.), *les palmes* (f.)
gills *les ouïes* (f.), *les branchies* (f.)
high tide *la marée haute*
piranha *un pirranha*
saltwater *l'eau* (f.) *de mer*
scales *les écailles* (f.)
scuba gear *l'équipement* (m.) *de plongée*
scuba mask *un masque de plongée*

seal *un phoque*
shallow water *l'eau peu profonde* (f.), *les bas-fonds* (m.)
snorkel *un tuba*
snorkeling *la plongée*
tentacles *les tentacules* (m.)
tropical fish *des poissons* (m.) *tropicaux*
walrus *un morse*
whale *une baleine*

TV AND MOVIES

action scenes *les scènes* (f.) *d'action*
actors *les acteurs*
actresses *les actrices*
car chase *une poursuite de voitures*
costumes *les costumes* (m.)
digital sound *le son digital*
direction *la mise en scène*
director *le metteur en scène, le réalisateur*
ending *le dénouement final*
hero *un héros*
laserdisc *un disque laser*
lighting *la lumière*
movie soundtrack *la bande originale d'un film*
producer *le producteur*
scenery *les décors* (m.)
sound effects *le bruitage*
special effects *les effets* (m.) *spéciaux*
star *une star, une vedette*
story *l'histoire* (f.)
stunts *les cascades* (f.)
villain *le méchant*

WILD ANIMALS

antelope *une antilope*
baboon *un babouin*
bat *une chauve-souris*
buffalo *un buffle*
chimpanzee *un chimpanzé*
crocodile *un crocodile*
flamingo *un flamant*
gazelle *une gazelle*
gorilla *un gorille*
gnu *un gnou*
hyena *une hyène*
leopard *un léopard*
lizard *un lézard*
ostrich *une autruche*
panther *une panthère*
squirrel *un écureuil*
tortoise *une tortue*
vulture *un vautour*

GEOGRAPHICAL TERMS
THE CONTINENTS

Africa *l'Afrique* (f.)
Antarctica *l'Antarctique* (f.)
Asia *l'Asie* (f.)
Australia *l'Australie* (f.)
Europe *l'Europe* (f.)
North America *l'Amérique* (f.) *du Nord*
South America *l'Amérique* (f.) *du Sud*

340 *trois cent quarante*

SUPPLEMENTARY VOCABULARY

COUNTRIES

Argentina   *l'Argentine* (f.)
Australia   *l'Australie* (f.)
Austria   *l'Autriche* (f.)
Cameroon   *le Cameroun*
Chad   *le Tchad*
Cuba   *Cuba (no article)*
Egypt   *l'Egypte* (f.)
Greece   *la Grèce*
Guinea   *la Guinée*
Holland   *la Hollande*
India   *l'Inde* (f.)
Ireland   *l'Irlande* (f.)
Israel   *Israël* (m.) *(no article)*
Jamaica   *la Jamaïque*
Jordan   *la Jordanie*
Lebanon   *le Liban*
Libya   *la Libye*
Luxembourg   *le Luxembourg*
Mexico   *le Mexique*
Monaco   *Monaco* (f.) *(no article)*
Netherlands   *les Pays-Bas* (m.)
North Korea   *la Corée du Nord*
Peru   *le Pérou*
Philippines   *les Philippines* (f.)
Poland   *la Pologne*
Portugal   *le Portugal*
Puerto Rico   *Porto Rico (no article)*
Republic of Côte d'Ivoire   *la République de Côte d'Ivoire*
South Korea   *la Corée du Sud*
Syria   *la Syrie*
Turkey   *la Turquie*
Vietnam   *le Viêt-nam*

STATES

Alabama   *l'Alabama* (m.)
Alaska   *l'Alaska* (m.)
Arizona   *l'Arizona* (m.)
Arkansas   *l'Arkansas* (m.)
California   *la Californie*
Colorado   *le Colorado*
Connecticut   *le Connecticut*
Delaware   *le Delaware*
Florida   *la Floride*
Georgia   *la Géorgie*
Hawaii   *Hawaii (no article)*
Idaho   *l'Idaho* (m.)
Illinois   *l'Illinois* (m.)
Indiana   *l'Indiana* (m.)
Iowa   *l'Iowa* (m.)
Kansas   *le Kansas*
Kentucky   *le Kentucky*
Louisiana   *la Louisiane*
Maine   *le Maine*
Maryland   *le Maryland*
Massachusetts   *le Massachusetts*
Michigan   *le Michigan*
Minnesota   *le Minnesota*
Mississippi   *le Mississippi*
Missouri   *le Missouri*
Montana   *le Montana*
Nebraska   *le Nebraska*
Nevada   *le Nevada*
New Hampshire   *le New Hampshire*

New Jersey   *le New Jersey*
New Mexico   *le Nouveau-Mexique*
New York   *l'Etat de New York*
North Carolina   *la Caroline du Nord*
North Dakota   *le Dakota du Nord*
Ohio   *l'Ohio* (m.)
Oklahoma   *l'Oklahoma* (m.)
Oregon   *l'Orégon* (m.)
Pennsylvania   *la Pennsylvanie*
Rhode Island   *le Rhode Island*
South Carolina   *la Caroline du Sud*
South Dakota   *le Dakota du Sud*
Tennessee   *le Tennessee*
Texas   *le Texas*
Utah   *l'Utah* (m.)
Vermont   *le Vermont*
Virginia   *la Virginie*
Washington   *l'Etat de Washington*
West Virginia   *la Virginie-Occidentale*
Wisconsin   *le Wisconsin*
Wyoming   *le Wyoming*

CITIES

Algiers   *Alger*
Brussels   *Bruxelles*
Cairo   *Le Caire*
Geneva   *Genève*
Lisbon   *Lisbonne*
London   *Londres*
Montreal   *Montréal*
Moscow   *Moscou*
New Orleans   *La Nouvelle-Orléans*
Quebec City   *Québec*
Tangier   *Tanger*
Venice   *Venise*
Vienna   *Vienne*

OTHER GEOGRAPHICAL TERMS

Alps   *les Alpes* (f.)
Atlantic Ocean   *l'Atlantique* (m.), *l'océan* (m.), *Atlantique*
border   *la frontière*
capital   *la capitale*
continent   *un continent*
country   *un pays*
English Channel   *la Manche*
hill   *une colline*
lake   *un lac*
latitude   *la latitude*
longitude   *la longitude*
Mediterranean Sea   *la mer Méditerranée*
North Africa   *l'Afrique* (f.) *du Nord*
the North Pole   *le pôle Nord*
ocean   *l'océan* (m.)
Pacific Ocean   *le Pacifique, l'océan* (m.) *Pacifique*
peninsula   *une presqu'île*
plain   *une plaine*
Pyrenees   *les Pyrénées* (f.)
river   *un fleuve*
Sahara desert   *le désert du Sahara*
sea   *la mer*
the South Pole   *le pôle Sud*
state   *un état*
valley   *une vallée*

PRONUNCIATION INDEX

SOUND	LETTER COMBINATION	IPA SYMBOL	EXAMPLE
The sounds [y] and [u]	the letter u the letter combination ou	/y/ /u/	une nous
The nasal sound [ɑ̃]	the letter combination an the letter combination am the letter combination en the letter combination em	/ɑ̃/	anglais jambon comment temps
The vowel sounds [ø] and [œ]	the letter combination eu the letter combination eu	/ø/ /œ/	deux heure
The nasal sounds [ɔ̃], [ɛ̃], and [œ̃]	the letter combination on the letter combination om the letter combination in the letter combination im the letter combination ain the letter combination aim the letter combination (i)en the letter combination un the letter combination um	/ɔ̃/ /ɛ̃/ /œ̃/	pardon nombre cousin impossible copain faim bien lundi humble
The sounds [o] and [ɔ]	the letter combination au the letter combination eau the letter ô the letter o	/o/ /ɔ/	jaune beau rôle carotte
The vowel sounds [e] and [ɛ]	the letter combination ez the letter combination er the letter combination ait the letter combination ais the letter combination ei the letter ê	/e/ /ɛ/	apportez trouver fait français neige bête
The glides [j], [w], and [ɥ]	the letter i the letter combination ill the letter combination oi the letter combination oui the letter combination ui	/j/ /w/ /ɥ/	mieux maillot moi Louis huit
h, th, ch, and gn	the letter h the letter combination th the letter combination ch the letter combination gn	/'/ /t/ /ʃ/ /ɲ/	les halls théâtre chocolat oignon
The r sound	the letter r	/ʀ/	rouge vert

NUMBERS

LES NOMBRES CARDINAUX

0	zéro	20	vingt	80	quatre-vingts
1	un(e)	21	vingt et un(e)	81	quatre-vingt-un(e)
2	deux	22	vingt-deux	82	quatre-vingt-deux
3	trois	23	vingt-trois	90	quatre-vingt-dix
4	quatre	24	vingt-quatre	91	quatre-vingt-onze
5	cinq	25	vingt-cinq	92	quatre-vingt-douze
6	six	26	vingt-six	100	cent
7	sept	27	vingt-sept	101	cent un
8	huit	28	vingt-huit	200	deux cents
9	neuf	29	vingt-neuf	300	trois cents
10	dix	30	trente	800	huit cents
11	onze	31	trente et un(e)	900	neuf cents
12	douze	32	trente-deux	1.000	mille
13	treize	40	quarante	2.000	deux mille
14	quatorze	50	cinquante	3.000	trois mille
15	quinze	60	soixante	10.000	dix mille
16	seize	70	soixante-dix	19.000	dix-neuf mille
17	dix-sept	71	soixante et onze	40.000	quarante mille
18	dix-huit	72	soixante-douze	500.000	cinq cent mille
19	dix-neuf	73	soixante-treize	1.000.000	un million

- The word **et** is used only in 21, 31, 41, 51, 61, and 71.
- **Vingt (trente, quarante,** and so on) **et une** is used when the number refers to a feminine noun: **trente et une cassettes.**
- The **s** is dropped from **quatre-vingts** and is not added to multiples of **cent** when these numbers are followed by another number: **quatre-vingt-cinq; deux cents,** *but* **deux cent six.** The number **mille** never takes an **s: deux mille insectes.**
- **Un million** is followed by **de** + a noun: **un million de francs.**
- In writing numbers, a period is used in French where a comma is used in English.

LES NOMBRES ORDINAUX

1er, 1ère	premier, première	9e	neuvième	17e	dix-septième
2e	deuxième	10e	dixième	18e	dix-huitième
3e	troisième	11e	onzième	19e	dix-neuvième
4e	quatrième	12e	douzième	20e	vingtième
5e	cinquième	13e	treizième	21e	vingt et unième
6e	sixième	14e	quatorzième	22e	vingt-deuxième
7e	septième	15e	quinzième	30e	trentième
8e	huitième	16e	seizième	40e	quarantième

GRAMMAR SUMMARY

ARTICLES

SINGULAR		PLURAL	
MASCULINE	FEMININE	MASCULINE	FEMININE
un frère un ami	une sœur une amie	des frères des amis	des sœurs des amies
le frère l'ami	la sœur l'amie	les frères les amis	les sœurs les amies
ce frère cet ami	cette sœur cette amie	ces frères ces amis	ces sœurs ces amies

CONTRACTIONS WITH à AND de

à or de + article =	CONTRACTION
à + le =	au
à + la =	à la (no contraction)
à + l' =	à l' (no contraction)
à + les =	aux
de + le =	du
de + la =	de la (no contraction)
de + l' =	de l' (no contraction)
de + les =	des

ADJECTIVES: FORMATION OF FEMININE

	MASCULINE	FEMININE
Most adjectives (add -e)	Il est brun.	Elle est brune.
Most adjectives ending in -é (add -e)	Il est démodé.	Elle est démodée.
All adjectives ending in an unaccented -e (no change)	Il est jeune.	Elle est jeune.
Most adjectives ending in -eux (-eux → -euse)	Il est furieux.	Elle est furieuse.
All adjectives ending in -ien (-ien → -ienne)	Il est tunisien.	Elle est tunisienne.

ADJECTIVES AND NOUNS: FORMATION OF PLURAL

		MASCULINE	FEMININE
Most noun and adjective forms (add -**s**)	Singular Plural	**un pantalon vert** **des pantalons verts**	**une jupe verte** **des jupes vertes**
Most masculine noun and adjective forms ending in -**al** (-**al** → -**aux**) Feminine forms add -**s**	Singular Plural	**le sport principal** **les sports principaux**	**la rue principale** **les rues principales**
All masculine noun and adjective forms ending in -**eau** (add -**x**) Feminine forms add -**s**	Singular Plural	**le nouveau manteau** **les nouveaux manteaux**	**la nouvelle robe** **les nouvelles robes**
All masculine noun and adjective forms ending in -**s** (no change in masculine form) Feminine forms add -**s**	Singular Plural	**un bus gris** **des bus gris**	**une maison grise** **des maisons grises**
All masculine adjective forms ending in -**x** (no change in masculine form) Feminine forms add -**s**	Singular Plural	**un garçon heureux** **des garçons heureux**	**une fille heureuse** **des filles heureuses**

POSSESSIVE ADJECTIVES

SINGULAR		PLURAL	
MASCULINE	FEMININE	MASCULINE	FEMININE
mon frère **mon ami** **ton frère** **ton ami** **son frère** **son ami**	**ma sœur** **mon amie** **ta sœur** **ton amie** **sa sœur** **son amie**	**mes frères** **mes amis** **tes frères** **tes amis** **ses frères** **ses amis**	**mes sœurs** **mes amies** **tes sœurs** **tes amies** **ses sœurs** **ses amies**
notre frère **notre ami** **votre frère** **votre ami** **leur frère** **leur ami**	**notre sœur** **notre amie** **votre sœur** **votre amie** **leur sœur** **leur amie**	**nos frères** **nos amis** **vos frères** **vos amis** **leurs frères** **leurs amis**	**nos sœurs** **nos amies** **vos sœurs** **vos amies** **leurs sœurs** **leurs amies**

PRONOUNS

INDEPENDENT PRONOUNS	SUBJECT PRONOUNS	DIRECT OBJECT PRONOUNS	INDIRECT OBJECT PRONOUNS	PRONOUN REPLACING à, dans, sur... + noun phrase	PRONOUN REPLACING de + noun phrase
moi toi lui elle	je (j') tu il elle on	me te le la	me te lui lui		
nous vous eux elles	nous vous ils elles	nous vous les les	nous vous leur leur	y	en

INTERROGATIVE PRONOUNS

	People	Things	People and Things
Subject of verb	qui qui est-ce qui	qu'est-ce qui	lequel
Object of verb	qui qui est-ce que	que qu'est-ce que	laquelle lesquels lesquelles
Object of preposition	de qui à qui	de quoi à quoi	

DEMONSTRATIVE PRONOUNS

	Masculine	Feminine
Singular	celui-là	celle-là
Plural	ceux-là	celles-là

INTERROGATIVE ADJECTIVES

	Masculine	Feminine
Singular	quel	quelle
Plural	quels	quelles

RELATIVE PRONOUNS: Qui and Que

	Qui Subject of verb in clause	**Que** Object of verb in clause
People	Laeticia parle avec une amie **qui** s'appelle Séverine.	Séverine sort avec un garçon **que** je ne connais pas.
Places	J'ai visité une ville **qui** est près de Strasbourg.	La ville **que** j'ai visitée était intéressante.
Things	C'est un arbre **qui** se trouve dans la forêt tropicale.	C'est une chanson **que** j'aime beaucoup.

RELATIVE PRONOUNS: Ce qui and ce que

	Subject of verb in clause	Object of verb in clause
The relative pronoun *what* Use **ce qui** or **ce que**	**Ce qui** est incroyable, c'est leurs masques. Tu ne comprends pas **ce qui** est important.	**Ce que** j'adore, c'est le jazz. Je ne sais pas **ce qu'**elle fait.

RELATIVE PRONOUN: Dont

The relative pronoun *whose* (Use **dont**)	C'est le garçon **dont** la sœur est une actrice célèbre.
The relative pronoun *whom: about/of/from whom* (Use **dont**)	Tu connais l'actrice **dont** il parle?

REGULAR VERBS: PRESENT TENSE

INFINITIVE	écouter	sortir	choisir	répondre
	STEM / ENDING	STEM / ENDING	STEM / ENDING	STEM / ENDING
PRESENT	écout { -e, -es, -e, -ons, -ez, -ent	sor { -s, -s, -t sort { -ons, -ez, -ent	chois { -is, -is, -it, -issons, -issez, -issent	répond { -s, -s, —, -ons, -ez, -ent
REQUESTS COMMANDS SUGGESTIONS	écout { -e, -ons, -ez	sor -s sort { -ons, -ez	chois { -is, -issons, -issez	répond { -s, -ons, -ez

REGULAR VERBS: COMPOUND TENSES

	PASSE COMPOSE (past)		PLUS-QUE-PARFAIT (past perfect)	
	Auxiliary	Past Participle	Auxiliary	Past Participle
with avoir	ai as a avons avez ont	jou -é chois -i attend -u	avais avais avait avions aviez avaient	jou -é chois -i attend -u
with être	suis es est sommes êtes sont	rentr -é(e)s sort -i(e)(s) descend -u(e)s	étais étais était étions étiez étaient	rentr -é(e)(s) sort -i(e)(s) descend -u(e)(s)

REFLEXIVE VERBS

PRESENT	PASSE COMPOSE (past)	INFINITIF
Je **me lave**.	Je **me suis lavé(e)**.	Je vais **me laver**.
Tu **te laves**.	Tu **t'es lavé(e)**.	Tu vas **te laver**.
Il **se lave**.	Il **s'est lavé**.	Il va **se laver**.
Elle **se lave**.	Elle **s'est lavée**.	Elle va **se laver**.
On **se lave**.	On **s'est lavé(e)(s)**.	On va **se laver**.
Nous **nous lavons**.	Nous **nous sommes lavé(e)s**.	Nous **allons nous laver**.
Vous **vous lavez**.	Vous **vous êtes lavé(e)(s)**.	Vous **allez vous laver**.
Ils **se lavent**.	Ils **se sont lavés**.	Ils **vont se laver**.
Elles **se lavent**.	Elles **se sont lavées**.	Elles **vont se laver**.

REQUESTS
COMMANDS } Lave-toi.   Ne te lave pas.
SUGGESTIONS Lavons-nous.   Ne nous lavons pas.
Lavez-vous.   Ne vous lavez pas.

REGULAR VERBS: IMPARFAIT (IMPERFECT)

Stem	Ending

Present tense **nous** form:
 	
    habit~~ons~~
    finiss~~ons~~
    entend~~ons~~
	-ais
	-ais
	-ait
	-ions
	-iez
	-aient

REGULAR VERBS: PRESENT SUBJUNCTIVE

Stem	Ending
Present tense **ils** form: habit~~ent~~ finiss~~ent~~ entend~~ent~~	-e -es -e -ions -iez -ent

REGULAR VERBS: CONDITIONAL

Stem	Ending
Infinitive: habiter finir entendr~~e~~	-ais -ais -ait -ions -iez -aient

REGULAR VERBS: FUTURE

Stem	Ending
Infinitive: habiter finir entendr~~e~~	-ai -as -a -ons -ez -ont

SEQUENCE OF TENSES IN SENTENCES WITH *SI* CLAUSES

Probable	**Si** + present →	present future
Less probable	**Si** + imperfect →	conditional
Impossible	**Si** + past perfect →	past conditional

EXPRESSIONS FOLLOWED BY *QUE* + THE SUBJUNCTIVE

Necessity	Il est nécessaire que... Il est essentiel que... Il est important que... Il faudrait que... Il vaudrait mieux que...	+ subjunctive
Doubt	Je ne crois pas que... Je ne pense pas que... Ça m'étonnerait que... Je ne suis pas sûr(e) que... Je ne suis pas certain(e) que...	+ subjunctive
Emotion	Je suis désolé(e) que... Je suis heureux (-euse) que... J'ai peur que...	+ subjunctive
Possibility	Il est possible que... Il est fort possible que... Il se peut que...	+ subjunctive
Wishes	Je veux que... Je voudrais que...	+ subjunctive

COMPARATIVE AND SUPERLATIVE

Comparative				Superlative					
moins **aussi** **plus**	+	adjective or adverb	+	**que**	le/la/les	+	**moins** **plus**	+	adjective or adverb	+	de

IRREGULAR COMPARATIVE AND SUPERLATIVE FORMS

		Comparative	Superlative
adjectives	bon(s), bonne(s) mauvais(e)(es)	meilleur(e)(s) plus mauvais(e)(es)	le/la/les meilleur(e)(s) le/la/les plus mauvais(e)(es) le/la/les pire(s)
adverbs	bien	mieux	le mieux

VERBS FOLLOWED BY AN INFINITIVE

aimer aller compter devoir penser pouvoir préférer savoir vouloir	+ infinitive

VERBS FOLLOWED BY à OR de WITH AN INFINITIVE

aider s'amuser apprendre arriver commencer inviter réussir	à	+ infinitive

s'arrêter conseiller décider demander essayer éviter finir oublier persuader promettre proposer refuser rêver	de	+ infinitive

VERBS THAT TAKE A DIRECT OR INDIRECT OBJECT

Verbs that take a direct object	Verbs that take an indirect object
appeler chercher écouter payer regarder	téléphoner à conseiller à répondre à dire à demander à écrire à parler à permettre à apprendre à offrir à

VERB INDEX

VERBS WITH STEM AND SPELLING CHANGES

Verbs listed in this section are not irregular, but they do show some stem and spelling changes. The forms in which the changes occur are printed in **boldface** type.

ACHETER *(to buy)*

PRESENT	IMPERFECT	SUBJUNCTIVE	CONDITIONAL	FUTURE	COMMANDS
achète	achetais	**achète**	**achèterais**	**achèterai**	
achètes	achetais	**achètes**	**achèterais**	**achèteras**	**achète**
achète	achetait	**achète**	**achèterait**	**achètera**	
achetons	achetions	achetions	**achèterions**	**achèterons**	achetons
achetez	achetiez	achetiez	**achèteriez**	**achèterez**	achetez
achètent	achetaient	**achètent**	**achèteraient**	**achèteront**	

Passé Composé: *Auxiliary:* avoir
Past Participle: acheté

APPELER *(to call)*

PRESENT	IMPERFECT	SUBJUNCTIVE	CONDITIONAL	FUTURE	COMMANDS
appelle	appelais	**appelle**	**appellerais**	**appellerai**	
appelles	appelais	**appelles**	**appellerais**	**appelleras**	**appelle**
appelle	appelait	**appelle**	**appellerait**	**appellera**	
appelons	appelions	appelions	**appellerions**	**appellerons**	appelons
appelez	appeliez	appeliez	**appelleriez**	**appellerez**	appelez
appellent	appelaient	**appellent**	**appelleraient**	**appelleront**	

Passé Composé: *Auxiliary:* avoir
Past Participle: appelé

COMMENCER *(to start, to begin)*

PRESENT	IMPERFECT	SUBJUNCTIVE	CONDITIONAL	FUTURE	COMMANDS
commence	**commençais**	commence	commencerais	commencerai	
commences	**commençais**	commences	commencerais	commenceras	commence
commence	**commençait**	commence	commencerait	commencera	
commençons	commencions	commencions	commencerions	commencerons	**commençons**
commencez	commenciez	commenciez	commenceriez	commencerez	commencez
commencent	**commençaient**	commencent	commenceraient	commenceront	

Passé Composé: *Auxiliary:* avoir
Past Participle: commencé

ESSAYER *(to try)*

PRESENT	IMPERFECT	SUBJUNCTIVE	CONDITIONAL	FUTURE	COMMANDS
essaie	essayais	**essaie**	**essaierais**	**essaierai**	
essaies	essayais	**essaies**	**essaierais**	**essaieras**	**essaie**
essaie	essayait	**essaie**	**essaierait**	**essaiera**	
essayons	essayions	essayions	**essaierions**	**essaierons**	essayons
essayez	essayiez	essayiez	**essaieriez**	**essaierez**	essayez
essaient	essayaient	**essaient**	**essaieraient**	**essaieront**	

Passé Composé: *Auxiliary:* avoir
                             Past Participle: essayé

MANGER *(to eat)*

PRESENT	IMPERFECT	SUBJUNCTIVE	CONDITIONAL	FUTURE	COMMANDS
mange	**mangeais**	mange	mangerais	mangerai	
manges	**mangeais**	manges	mangerais	mangeras	mange
mange	**mangeait**	mange	mangerait	mangera	
mangeons	mangions	mangions	mangerions	mangerons	**mangeons**
mangez	mangiez	mangiez	mangeriez	mangerez	mangez
mangent	**mangeaient**	mangent	mangeraient	mangeront	

Passé Composé: *Auxiliary:* avoir
                             Past Participle: mangé

PREFERER *(to prefer)*

PRESENT	IMPERFECT	SUBJUNCTIVE	CONDITIONAL	FUTURE	COMMANDS
préfère	préférais	**préfère**	préférerais	préférerai	
préfères	préférais	**préfères**	préférerais	préféreras	—
préfère	préférait	**préfère**	préférerait	préférera	
préférons	préférions	préférions	préférerions	préférerons	—
préférez	préfériez	préfériez	préféreriez	préférerez	—
préfèrent	préféraient	**préfèrent**	préféreraient	préféreront	

Passé Composé: *Auxiliary:* avoir
                             Past Participle: préféré

VERBS WITH IRREGULAR FORMS

Verbs listed in this section are those that do not follow the pattern of verbs like **aimer,** verbs like **choisir,** verbs like **sortir,** or verbs like **attendre.**

ALLER *(to go)*

PRESENT	IMPERFECT	SUBJUNCTIVE	CONDITIONAL	FUTURE	COMMANDS
vais	allais	aille	irais	irai	
vas	allais	ailles	irais	iras	va
va	allait	aille	irait	ira	
allons	allions	allions	irions	irons	allons
allez	alliez	alliez	iriez	irez	allez
vont	allaient	aillent	iraient	iront	

Passé Composé: *Auxiliary:* être
                             Past Participle: allé

AVOIR *(to have)*

PRESENT	IMPERFECT	SUBJUNCTIVE	CONDITIONAL	FUTURE	COMMANDS
ai	avais	aie	aurais	aurai	
as	avais	aies	aurais	auras	aie
a	avait	ait	aurait	aura	
avons	avions	ayons	aurions	aurons	ayons
avez	aviez	ayez	auriez	aurez	ayez
ont	avaient	aient	auraient	auront	

Passé Composé: *Auxiliary:* avoir
Past Participle: eu

BOIRE *(to drink)*

PRESENT	IMPERFECT	SUBJUNCTIVE	CONDITIONAL	FUTURE	COMMANDS
bois	buvais	boive	boirais	boirai	
bois	buvais	boives	boirais	boiras	bois
boit	buvait	boive	boirait	boira	
buvons	buvions	buvions	boirions	boirons	buvons
buvez	buviez	buviez	boiriez	boirez	buvez
boivent	buvaient	boivent	boiraient	boiront	

Passé Composé: *Auxiliary:* avoir
Past Participle: bu

CONDUIRE *(to drive)*

PRESENT	IMPERFECT	SUBJUNCTIVE	CONDITIONAL	FUTURE	COMMANDS
conduis	conduisais	conduise	conduirais	conduirai	
conduis	conduisais	conduises	conduirais	conduiras	conduis
conduit	conduisait	conduise	conduirait	conduira	
conduisons	conduisions	conduisions	conduirions	conduirons	conduisons
conduisez	conduisiez	conduisiez	conduiriez	conduirez	conduisez
conduisent	conduisaient	conduisent	conduiraient	conduiront	

Passé Composé: *Auxiliary:* avoir
Past Participle: conduit

CONNAITRE *(to know, to be acquainted with)*

PRESENT	IMPERFECT	SUBJUNCTIVE	CONDITIONAL	FUTURE	COMMANDS
connais	connaissais	connaisse	connaîtrais	connaîtrai	
connais	connaissais	connaisses	connaîtrais	connaîtras	—
connaît	connaissait	connaisse	connaîtrait	connaîtra	
connaissons	connaissions	connaissions	connaîtrions	connaîtrons	—
connaissez	connaissiez	connaissiez	connaîtriez	connaîtrez	—
connaissent	connaissaient	connaissent	connaîtraient	connaîtront	

Passé Composé: *Auxiliary:* avoir
Past Participle: connu

COURIR *(to run)*

PRESENT	IMPERFECT	SUBJUNCTIVE	CONDITIONAL	FUTURE	COMMANDS
cours	courais	coure	courrais	courrai	
cours	courais	coures	courrais	courras	cours
court	courait	coure	courrait	courra	
courons	courions	courions	courrions	courrons	courons
courez	couriez	couriez	courriez	courrez	courez
courent	couraient	courent	courraient	courront	

Passé Composé: *Auxiliary:* avoir
Past Participle: couru

CROIRE *(to believe)*

PRESENT	IMPERFECT	SUBJUNCTIVE	CONDITIONAL	FUTURE	COMMANDS
crois	croyais	croie	croirais	croirai	
crois	croyais	croies	croirais	croiras	crois
croit	croyait	croie	croirait	croira	
croyons	croyions	croyions	croirions	croirons	croyons
croyez	croyiez	croyiez	croiriez	croirez	croyez
croient	croyaient	croient	croiraient	croiront	

Passé Composé: *Auxiliary:* avoir
Past Participle: cru

DEVOIR *(to have to)*

PRESENT	IMPERFECT	SUBJUNCTIVE	CONDITIONAL	FUTURE	COMMANDS
dois	devais	doive	devrais	devrai	
dois	devais	doives	devrais	devras	—
doit	devait	doive	devrait	devra	
devons	devions	devions	devrions	devrons	—
devez	deviez	deviez	devriez	devrez	
doivent	devaient	doivent	devraient	devront	—

Passé Composé: *Auxiliary:* avoir
Past Participle: dû

DIRE *(to say, tell)*

PRESENT	IMPERFECT	SUBJUNCTIVE	CONDITIONAL	FUTURE	COMMANDS
dis	disais	dise	dirais	dirai	
dis	disais	dises	dirais	diras	dis
dit	disait	dise	dirait	dira	
disons	disions	disions	dirions	dirons	disons
dites	disiez	disiez	diriez	direz	dites
disent	disaient	disent	diraient	diront	

Passé Composé: *Auxiliary:* avoir
Past Participle: dit

ECRIRE *(to write)*

PRESENT	IMPERFECT	SUBJUNCTIVE	CONDITIONAL	FUTURE	COMMANDS
écris	écrivais	écrive	écrirais	écrirai	
écris	écrivais	écrives	écrirais	écriras	écris
écrit	écrivait	écrive	écrirait	écrira	
écrivons	écrivions	écrivions	écririons	écrirons	écrivons
écrivez	écriviez	écriviez	écririez	écrirez	écrivez
écrivent	écrivaient	écrivent	écriraient	écriront	

Passé Composé: *Auxiliary:* avoir
Past Participle: écrit

ETEINDRE *(to turn off)*

PRESENT	IMPERFECT	SUBJUNCTIVE	CONDITIONAL	FUTURE	COMMANDS
éteins	éteignais	éteigne	éteindrais	éteindrai	
éteins	éteignais	éteignes	éteindrais	éteindras	éteins
éteint	éteignait	éteigne	éteindrait	éteindra	
éteignons	éteignions	éteignions	éteindrions	éteindrons	éteignons
éteignez	éteigniez	éteigniez	éteindriez	éteindrez	éteignez
éteignent	éteignaient	éteignent	éteindraient	éteindront	

Passé Composé: *Auxiliary:* avoir
Past Participle: éteint

ETRE *(to be)*

PRESENT	IMPERFECT	SUBJUNCTIVE	CONDITIONAL	FUTURE	COMMANDS
suis	étais	sois	serais	serai	
es	étais	sois	serais	seras	sois
est	était	soit	serait	sera	
sommes	étions	soyons	serions	serons	soyons
êtes	étiez	soyez	seriez	serez	soyez
sont	étaient	soient	seraient	seront	

Passé Composé: *Auxiliary:* avoir
Past Participle: été

FAIRE *(to make, to do)*

PRESENT	IMPERFECT	SUBJUNCTIVE	CONDITIONAL	FUTURE	COMMANDS
fais	faisais	fasse	ferais	ferai	
fais	faisais	fasses	ferais	feras	fais
fait	faisait	fasse	ferait	fera	
faisons	faisions	fassions	ferions	ferons	faisons
faites	faisiez	fassiez	feriez	ferez	faites
font	faisaient	fassent	feraient	feront	

Passé Composé: *Auxiliary:* avoir
Past Participle: fait

LIRE *(to read)*

PRESENT	IMPERFECT	SUBJUNCTIVE	CONDITIONAL	FUTURE	COMMANDS
lis	lisais	lise	lirais	lirai	
lis	lisais	lises	lirais	liras	lis
lit	lisait	lise	lirait	lira	
lisons	lisions	lisions	lirions	lirons	lisons
lisez	lisiez	lisiez	liriez	lirez	lisez
lisent	lisaient	lisent	liraient	liront	

Passé Composé: *Auxiliary:* avoir
Past Participle: lu

METTRE *(to put, to put on)*

PRESENT	IMPERFECT	SUBJUNCTIVE	CONDITIONAL	FUTURE	COMMANDS
mets	mettais	mette	mettrais	mettrai	
mets	mettais	mettes	mettrais	mettras	mets
met	mettait	mette	mettrait	mettra	
mettons	mettions	mettions	mettrions	mettrons	mettons
mettez	mettiez	mettiez	mettriez	mettrez	mettez
mettent	mettaient	mettent	mettraient	mettront	

Passé Composé: *Auxiliary:* avoir
Past Participle: mis

POUVOIR *(to be able, can)*

PRESENT	IMPERFECT	SUBJUNCTIVE	CONDITIONAL	FUTURE	COMMANDS
peux	pouvais	puisse	pourrais	pourrai	
peux	pouvais	puisses	pourrais	pourras	—
peut	pouvait	puisse	pourrait	pourra	
pouvons	pouvions	puissions	pourrions	pourrons	—
pouvez	pouviez	puissiez	pourriez	pourrez	—
peuvent	pouvaient	puissent	pourraient	pourront	

Passé Composé: *Auxiliary:* avoir
Past Participle: pu

PRENDRE *(to take)*

PRESENT	IMPERFECT	SUBJUNCTIVE	CONDITIONAL	FUTURE	COMMANDS
prends	prenais	prenne	prendrais	prendrai	
prends	prenais	prennes	prendrais	prendras	prends
prend	prenait	prenne	prendrait	prendra	
prenons	prenions	prenions	prendrions	prendrons	prenons
prenez	preniez	preniez	prendriez	prendrez	prenez
prennent	prenaient	prennent	prendraient	prendront	

Passé Composé: *Auxiliary:* avoir
Past Participle: pris

SAVOIR *(to know)*

PRESENT	IMPERFECT	SUBJUNCTIVE	CONDITIONAL	FUTURE	COMMANDS
sais	savais	sache	saurais	saurai	
sais	savais	saches	saurais	sauras	sache
sait	savait	sache	saurait	saura	
savons	savions	sachions	saurions	saurons	sachons
savez	saviez	sachiez	sauriez	saurez	sachez
savent	savaient	sachent	sauraient	sauront	

Passé Composé: *Auxiliary:* avoir
Past Participle: su

VENIR *(to come)*

PRESENT	IMPERFECT	SUBJUNCTIVE	CONDITIONAL	FUTURE	COMMANDS
viens	venais	vienne	viendrais	viendrai	
viens	venais	viennes	viendrais	viendras	viens
vient	venait	vienne	viendrait	viendra	
venons	venions	venions	viendrions	viendrons	venons
venez	veniez	veniez	viendriez	viendrez	venez
viennent	venaient	viennent	viendraient	viendront	

Passé Composé: *Auxiliary:* être
Past Participle: venu

VOIR *(to see)*

PRESENT	IMPERFECT	SUBJUNCTIVE	CONDITIONAL	FUTURE	COMMANDS
vois	voyais	voie	verrais	verrai	
vois	voyais	voies	verrais	verras	vois
voit	voyait	voie	verrait	verra	
voyons	voyions	voyions	verrions	verrons	voyons
voyez	voyiez	voyiez	verriez	verrez	voyez
voient	voyaient	voient	verraient	verront	

Passé Composé: *Auxiliary:* avoir
Past Participle: vu

VOULOIR *(to want)*

PRESENT	IMPERFECT	SUBJUNCTIVE	CONDITIONAL	FUTURE	COMMANDS
veux	voulais	veuille	voudrais	voudrai	
veux	voulais	veuilles	voudrais	voudras	—
veut	voulait	veuille	voudrait	voudra	—
voulons	voulions	voulions	voudrions	voudrons	
voulez	vouliez	vouliez	voudriez	voudrez	veuillez
veulent	voulaient	veuillent	voudraient	voudront	

Passé Composé: *Auxiliary:* avoir
Past Participle: voulu

FRENCH-ENGLISH VOCABULARY

This list includes both active and passive vocabulary in this textbook. Active words and phrases are those listed in boxes labeled **Vocabulaire, Comment dit-on...?, Grammaire,** and **Note de grammaire,** as well as the **Vocabulaire** section at the end of each chapter. You are expected to know and be able to use active vocabulary. All entries in black heavy type in this list are active. All other words are passive. Passive vocabulary is for recognition only.

The number after each entry refers to the chapter where the word or phrase after each entry is introduced. Verbs are given in the infinitive. Phrases are alphabetized by the key word(s) in the phrase. Nouns are always given with an article. If it is not clear whether the noun is masculine or feminine, *m.* (masculine) or *f.* (feminine) follows the noun. An asterisk (*) before a word beginning with *h* indicates an aspirate *h.*

The following abbreviations are used in this vocabulary: pl. (plural), pp. (past participle), and inv. (invariable).

A

à *to, in (a city or place),* I, 11; **A bientôt.** *See you soon.* I, 1; **A côté de...** *Next to . . . ,* II, 2; **A demain.** *See you tomorrow.* I, 1; **A point.** *Medium rare.* III, 1; **A propos,...** *By the way, . . . ,* II, 9; **A quelle heure?** *At what time?* I, 6; **A tout à l'heure!** *See you later!* I, 1; **A votre service.** *At your service; You're welcome,* I, 3; à côté: Juste là, à côté de... *Right there, next to . . . ,* III, 2; **à droite de** *to the right of,* II, 2; **à gauche de** *to the left of,* II, 2; **à la mode** *in style,* I, 10; **à la** *to, at,* I, 6; à réaction *jet,* III, 3; **A... At . . . ,** II, 11

abandonner: **J'abandonne.** *I give up.* II, 7

les **abdominaux** (m.): **faire des abdominaux** *to do sit-ups,* II, 7

accabler *to blame,* III, 8

l' **accident** (m.): **avoir un accident** *to have an accident,* II, 9

l' **accord** (m.): **Bon, d'accord.** *Well, OK.* I, 8; **D'accord, si tu... d'abord.** *OK, if you . . . , first.* I, 7; **D'accord.** *OK.* I, 9; **Je ne suis pas d'accord.** *I don't agree.* I, 7; **Tu es d'accord?** *Is that OK with you?* I, 7

l' **accordéon** (m.) *accordion,* III, 11

accoucher *to give birth,* III, 8

Accrochez-vous! *Hang on!* III, 7

l' **accueil** (m.) *information desk,* III, 2

accueillant(e) *hospitable,* III, 6

accueillir *to welcome,* III, 6

acheter *to buy,* I, 9; **Achète(-moi)...** *Buy me . . . ,* I, 8; **s'acheter quelque chose** *to buy oneself something,* III, 10

l' **acteur** (m.) *actor,* III, 5

l' **actrice** (f.) *actress,* III, 5

l' actualité (f.) *the news,* III, 5

l' **addition** (f.): **L'addition, s'il vous plaît.** *The check please.* I, 5

adorer: **Ce que j'adore, c'est...** *What I like/love is . . . ,* III, 11; **J'adore...** *I adore . . . ,* I, 1

l' **aérobic** (m.): **faire de l'aérobic** *to do aerobics,* I, 4; II, 7

les **aérosols** (m.): **utiliser des aérosols** *to use aerosol sprays,* III, 3

les **affaires** (f.): **partager ses affaires** *to share,* III, 3

afin de *in order to,* I, 7

affranchir *to put a stamp on,* III, 3

affreux (affreuse) *hideous,* III, 4

africain(e) (adj.) *African,* II, 11

l' **Afrique** (f.) **du sud** *South Africa,* III, 12

âgé(e) *older,* I, 7

l' **âge** (m.): **Tu as quel âge?** *How old are you?* I, 1

agir *to act,* III, 6; **Il s'agit de...** *It's about . . . ,* III, 9

agréer: Je vous prie d'agréer, Monsieur/Madame, l'expression de mes sentiments distingués. *Very truly yours, . . . ,* III, 5

aider *to help,* II, 8; **(Est-ce que) je peux vous aider?** *May I help you?* I, 10; **aider les personnes âgées** *to help elderly people,* III, 3; **Tu peux m'aider?** *Can you help me?* II, 10

aimable: Vous êtes bien aimable. *That's kind of you.* III, 6

aimer *to like,* I, 1 *L1;* **Ce que j'aime, c'est...** *What I like/love is . . . ,* III, 11; **Ce que j'aime bien, c'est...** *What I like is . . . ,* II, 4; **Ce que je n'aime pas, c'est...** *What I don't like is . . . ,* II, 4; **J'aime bien...** *I like . . . ,* II, 1; **J'aime mieux...** *I prefer . . . ,* II, 1; **Je n'aime pas...** *I don't like . . . ,* I, 1; **Le prof ne m'aime pas.** *The teacher doesn't*

like me. II, 5; **Moi, j'aime (bien)...** *I (really) like . . . ,* I, 1; **Qu'est-ce que tu aimes comme musique?** *What music do you like?* II, 1; **Qu'est-ce que tu aimes faire?** *What do you like to do?* II, 1; **Tu aimes mieux... ou... ?** *Do you prefer . . . or . . . ?* I, 10; **Tu aimes... ?** *Do you like . . . ?* I, 1; **J'aimerais bien...** *I'd really like . . . ,* III, 5; **J'aimerais...** *I'd like . . . ,* III, 3; **J'aimerais... pour aller avec...** *I'd like . . . to go with . . . ,* I, 10; **Qu'est-ce que j'aimerais... !** *I'd really like to . . . !* III, 8

l' **aîné(e)** *the oldest child,* III, 6

l' **air** (m.): **avoir l'air... to seem . . . ,** II, 9; **Ça n'a pas l'air d'aller.** *Something's wrong.* II, 5; **Elle avait l'air...** *She seemed . . . ,* II, 12; **Ils ont l'air de...** *They look like . . . ,* III, 11; **mettre de l'air dans les pneus** *to put air in the tires,* III, 2; **Tu n'as pas l'air en forme.** *You don't seem too well.* II, 7

aise: Mettez-vous à l'aise. *Make yourself comfortable.* III, 6

ajouter *to add,* III, 3

l' **algèbre** (f.) *algebra,* I, 2

l' **Algérie** (f.) *Algeria,* III, 12

l' **algue** (f.) *seaweed,* III, 10

l' **Allemagne** (f.) *Germany,* III, 12

l' **allemand** (m.) *German (language),* I, 2

aller *to go,* I, 6; **l'aller simple** (m.) *a one-way ticket,* II, 6; **l'aller-retour** (m.) *a round-trip ticket,* II, 6; **aller à la pêche** *to go fishing,* II, 4; **Ça n'a pas l'air d'aller.** *Something's wrong.* II, 5; **Ça te dit d'aller... ?** *What do you think about going . . . ?* II, 4; **Ça va aller mieux!** *It's going to get better!* I, 9; *It'll get better.* II, 5; **On peut y aller...** *We can go there . . . ,* I, 12;

Allez tout droit. *Go straight ahead.* II, 2; **Allez au tableau!** *Go to the blackboard!* I, 0; **Allez! Come on!** II, 7; **Ça va pas, non?!** *Are you out of your mind?!* III, 8; **Ça va pour cette fois.** *OK, just this once.* III, 3; **Ça va très bien avec...** *It goes very well with . . . ,* I, 10; **N'y va pas!** *Don't go!* III, 9; **Oh, ça va, hein?** *Oh, cut it out!* III, 6; **Allons...** *Let's go . . .* I, 6; **Allons-y!** *Let's go!* I, 4

les **allergies** (f.): **J'ai des allergies.** *I have allergies.* II, 7

Allô? *Hello?* I, 9

les **allumettes** (f.) *matches,* II, 12

Alors,... *So . . . ,* II, 9; **Ça alors!** *How about that!* III, 7; **Et alors?** *And then?* III, 10

améliorer *to improve,* III, 3

américain(e) *American (adj.),* II, 11

les **amis** (m.) *friends,* I, 1

l' **amitié** (f.) *friendship,* III, 8; **Fais mes amitiés à...** *Give . . . my regards to . . .* III, 8

amoureux (amoureuse) *in love,* II, 9; **tomber amoureux(-euse) (de quelqu'un)** *to fall in love (with someone),* II, 9; **Tu es amoureux (-euse) ou quoi?** *Are you in love or what?* III, 10

amusant(e) *fun,* II, 11; *funny,* I, 7; II, 1; **J'ai trouvé ça amusant.** *It was funny.* III, 9

les **amuse-gueule** (m.): **préparer les amuse-gueule** *to make party snacks,* II, 10

s'amuser *to have fun,* II, 4; **Qu'est-ce que tu fais pour t'amuser?** *What do you do to have fun?* I, 4; **Amuse-toi bien!** *Have fun!* I, 11; **Je me suis beaucoup amusé(e).** *I had a lot of fun.* II, 6; III, 1; **Tu t'es amusé(e)?** *Did you have fun?* II, 6

l' **ananas** (m.) *pineapple,* I, 8; II, 4

l' **andouille** (f.) *andouille sausage,* III, 11

l' **anglais** (m.) *English (language),* I, 1

l' **Angleterre** (f.) *England,* III, 12

l' **angoisse** (f.): **Quelle angoisse!** *This is terrible!* III, 12

les **animaux** (m.): **nourrir les animaux** *to feed the animals,* II, 12

animé(e) *lively,* II, 8

les **anneaux** (m.) *rings (in gymnastics),* III, 12

l' **année** (f.): **Bonne année!** *Happy New Year!* II, 3

l' **anniversaire** (m.): **Joyeux (Bon) anniversaire!** *Happy birthday!* II, 3

l' **anorak** (m.) *ski jacket,* II, 1

antillais(e) *from the Antilles,* II, 11

l' **antilope** (f.) *antelope,* III, 7

l' **antre** (m.) *cave, lair,* III, 10

août *August,* I, 4

l' **appareil** (m.): **Qui est à l'appareil?** *Who's calling?* I, 9

l' **appareil-photo** (m.) *camera,* I, 11; II, 1

s'appeler: Comment est-ce qu'on appelle ça? *What is that called?* III, 11; **Il/Elle s'appelle comment?** *What's his/her name?* I, 1; **Il/Elle s'appelle...** *His/Her name is . . . ,* I, 1; **Je m'appelle...** *My name is . . . ,* I, 1; **Tu t'appelles comment?** *What's your name?* I, 1

apporter *to bring,* I, 9; **Apportez-moi... , s'il vous plaît.** *Please bring me . . .* I, 5

l' **apprentissage** (m.): **faire un apprentissage** *to do an apprenticeship,* III, 5

l' **après-midi** (m.) *in the afternoon,* I, 2; **l'après-midi libre** *afternoon off,* I, 2

après: Après ça... *After that . . . ,* II, 4; **Après, je suis sorti(e).** *Afterwards, I went out.* I, 9; **Et après?** *And afterwards?* I, 9

l' **araignée** (f.) *spider,* III, 7

l' **arbre** (m.) *tree,* III, 7; **planter un arbre** *to plant a tree,* III, 3; **mutiler les arbres** *to deface the trees,* II, 12

l' **arc** (m.) *bow,* III, 12

l' **architecte** (m./f.) *architect,* III, 5

l' **argent** (m.) *silver,* III, 6; **de l'argent** *money,* I, 11

l' **armoire** (f.) *armoire/wardrobe,* II, 2

l' **arrêt** (m.): **arrêt de bus** *bus stop,* III, 8

arrêter: arrêter ses études *to stop one's studies,* III, 5; **Arrête! Stop!** III, 6; **Et toi, arrête de m'embêter! Stop bothering me!** III, 10

l' **arrière-grand-mère** (f.) *great-grandmother,* III, 6

l' **arrière-grand-père** (m.) *great-grandfather,* III, 6

arriver *to arrive,* II, 5; **Ça peut arriver à tout le monde.** *It could happen to anyone.* III, 10; **Ça arrive à tout le monde.** *It happens to everybody.* III, 6; **J'arrive pas à y croire!** *I can't believe it.* III, 12; **Je n'arrive pas à me décider.** *I can't make up my mind.* III, 1; **Qu'est-ce qui t'arrive?** *What's wrong?* II, 5

arroser: arroser le jardin *to water the garden,* III, 3

l' **artisanat** (m.): **faire de l'artisanat** *to make crafts,* III, 8

les **arts** (m.) **plastiques** *art class,* I, 2

l' **aspirateur** (m.): **passer l'aspirateur** *to vacuum,* III, 3

Asseyez-vous! *Sit down!* I, 0; III, 6

assez *sort of,* II, 9; **assez bien** *OK,* II, 6

l' **assiette** (f.): **l'assiette de charcuterie** *plate of pâté, ham, and cold sausage,* III, 1; **assiette de crudités** *plate of raw vegetables with vinaigrette,* III, 1; **assiette de fromages** *a selection of cheeses,* III, 1

l' **assistant(e) social(e)** *social worker,* III, 5

assister: assister à un spectacle son et lumière *to attend a sound and light show,* II, 6

assorti: C'est assorti à... *That matches . . . ,* III, 4

assure: Je t'assure. *Really.* III, 4

l' **athlétisme** (m.): **faire de l'athlétisme** *to do track and field,* I, 4

l' **atout** (m.) *trump,* III, 12

attendre *to wait for,* I, 9

attention: Attention à... ! *Watch out for . . . !* III, 7

attentionné: être attentionné(e) *to be considerate,* III, 3

au *to, at,* I, 6; *to, in (before a masculine noun),* I, 11; **Au revoir!** *Goodbye!* I, 1; **au métro Saint-Michel** *at the Saint-Michel metro stop,* I, 6; **La fille au...** *The girl in the/with the . . . ,* III, 4

l' **aubaine** (f.) *godsend,* III, 12

l' **auberge** (f.): **l'auberge de jeunesse** *youth hostel,* II, 2

aucun(e): Ça n'a aucun intérêt. *It's not interesting.* III, 9; **Je n'en ai aucun doute.** *I have no doubt of it.* III, 12; **Aucune idée.** *No idea.* II, 9; **Je n'en ai aucune idée.** *I have no idea.* III, 5

aujourd'hui *today,* I, 2

aurais: J'aurais dû... *I should have . . . ,* II, 10; **J'aurais pu...** *I could have . . . ,* II, 10; **Tu aurais dû...** *You should have . . . ,* II, 10; **Tu aurais pu...** *You could have . . . ,* II, 10

auriez: Vous auriez... ? *Would you have . . . ?* III, 6

aussi *also,* I, 1; **aussi... que...** *as . . . as . . . ,* III, 8; **Je n'ai jamais vu un(e) aussi...** *I've never seen such a . . . ,* III, 7; **Moi aussi.** *Me too.* I, 2

autant: autant de... que... *as many/ as much . . . as . . . ,* III, 8

l' **automne** (m.) *autumn, fall,* I, 4; **en automne** *in the fall,* I, 4

autre: ... et l'autre lui répond... *. . . and then the other one answers . . . ,* III, 10; **Oh, j'en ai vu d'autres.** *I've done bigger and better things.* III, 10; **Pense aux autres.** *Think about other people.* III, 3

l' **autruche** (f.) *ostrich,* III, 7

avare *greedy,* III, 2

avec: avec moi *with me,* I, 6; **Avec qui?** *With whom?* I, 6; **C'est avec qui?** *Who's in it?* II, 11; **C'est avec...** *. . . is (are) in it.* II, 11; **J'y suis allé(e) avec...** *I went with . . . ,* III, 1

l' **avion** (m.): **en avion** *by plane,* I, 12

l' **aviron** (m.) *rowing,* III, 12

avis: A mon avis,... *In my opinion, . . . ,* II, 9; **A mon avis, c'est plus sûr.** *In my opinion, it's safer.* III, 7; **A mon avis, tu te trompes.** *In my opinion, you're mistaken.* II, 9; **A ton avis, qu'est-ce que je dois faire?** *In your opinion, what should I do?* II, 10; **A ton avis, qu'est-ce que je fais?** *In your opinion, what do I do?* I, 9

l' **avocat(e)** *lawyer,* III, 5

les **avocats** (m.) *avocados,* I, 8

avoir *to have* I, 2 ; **avoir (prendre) rendez-vous (avec quelqu'un)** *to have (make) a date (with someone),* II, 9; **avoir 8 en...** *to get an 8 in . . .* II, 5; **avoir des responsabilités** *to have responsibilities,* II, 8; **avoir des soucis** *to have worries,* II, 8; **avoir faim** *to be hungry,* I, 5; **avoir l'air...** *to seem . . . ,* I, 9; **avoir soif** *to be thirsty,* I, 5; **avoir un accident** *to have an accident,* II, 9; **avoir... ans** *to be . . . years old,* II, 1; **Oui, vous avez... ?** *Yes, do you have . . . ?* I, 10; **Qu'est-ce que vous avez comme... ?** *What kind of . . . do you have?* I, 5; **Vous avez... ?** *Do you have . . . ?* I, 2; **Quand j'avais... ans,...** *When I was . . . years old, . . . ,* II, 8; **Si j'avais le choix,...** *If I had a choice, . . . ,* III, 8; **Elle avait l'air...** *She seemed . . . ,* II, 12; **Il y avait de...** *There were . . . ,* III, 9

avril *April,* I, 4

B

le **babouin** *baboon,* III, 7

se **bagarrer** *to fight,* III, 10

les **bagues** (f.): **se faire enlever ses bagues** *to get one's braces off,* III, 10

la **baguette** *long, thin loaf of bread,* II, 3

se **baigner** *to go swimming,* II, 4

baisser: Baisse le son. *Turn down the volume.* III, 9

se **balader** *to take a walk,* III, 8

le **balcon** *balcony,* II, 2

la **balle** *ball,* III, 12

le **ballon** *ball,* III, 12

banal: C'est banal. *That's ordinary.* II, 3

les **bananes** (f.) *bananas,* I, 8

le **bananier** *banana tree,* II, 4

la **bande dessinée (une BD)** *a comic book ,* II, 11

la **banque** *bank,* I, 12

barbant *boring,* I, 2

la **barbe** *beard,* III, 4

barjo *nuts, crazy,* III, 12

les **barres asymétriques** (f.) *the uneven parallel bars,* III, 12

bas: En bas. *Downstairs.* III, 2

le **base-ball** *baseball,* I, 4; III, 12

le **basket-ball** *basketball,* I, 4; III, 12

les **baskets** (f.) *sneakers,* I, 3; II, 1

la **basse** *bass (guitar),* III, 11

le **bateau** *boat,* I, 12; **en bateau** *by boat,* I, 12; **faire du bateau** *to go boating,* I, 11

le **bâton** *baseball bat,* III, 12

la **batterie** *drums,* III, 11

battre *to beat,* III, 12

bavard(e) *talkative,* III, 6

beau *handsome,* II, 1; **Il fait beau.** *It's nice weather.* II, 1

beaucoup. *A lot.* I, 4; **Pas beaucoup.** *Not very much.* I, 4

bébé *childish, stupid,* III, 2

la **Belgique** *Belgium,* III, 12

belle *beautiful,* II, 1; **C'est une belle histoire.** *It's a great story.* II, 11; **On l'a échappé belle!** *That was close!* III, 7

le **benjamin (la benjamine)** *the youngest child,* III, 6

le **besoin: De quoi est-ce que tu as besoin?** *What do you need?* I, 8; **J'ai besoin de...** *I need . . . ,* I, 8

bête *stupid,* II, 1; **Tu es bête comme tes pieds!** *You're so stupid!* III, 6

les **bêtises** (f.): **faire des bêtises** *to do silly things,* II, 8

le **beurre** *butter,* I, 8; II, 3

la **bibliothèque** *library,* I, 6; II, 2

bien: bien... *really . . .* III, 11; **Bien des choses à...** *All the best to . . . ,* III, 8; **bien se nourrir** *eat well,* II, 7; **Ça commence à bien faire, hein?** *Enough is enough!* III, 8; **Ça te fera du bien.** *It'll do you good.* II, 7; **Ce n'est pas bien de...** *It's not good to . . . ,* III, 3; **Ce que c'est bien!** *Isn't it great!* III, 2; **Il/Elle est vraiment bien, ton/ta...** *Your . . . is really great.* II, 2 ; **J'aime bien...** *I like . . . ,* II, 1; **Je ne me sens pas bien.** *I don't feel well.* II, 7; **J'en veux bien.** *I'd like some.* I, 8; **Je veux bien.** *Gladly.* I, 8; *I'd really like to.* I, 6; **Merci bien.** *Thank you so much.* III, 6; **Moi, j'aime bien...** *I really like . . . ,* I, 1; **Très bien.** *Very well.* I, 1; **Tu ferais bien de...** *You would do well to . . . ,* III, 5; **Tu veux bien que je...** *Is it OK with you if . . . ?* III, 3; **Bien sûr.** *Certainly,* I, 9; *Of course,* I, 3; II, 10; **Bien sûr que non.** *Of course not.* II, 10

bientôt: A bientôt. *See you soon.* I, 1

bienvenue: Bienvenue chez moi (chez nous). *Welcome to my home (our home),* II, 2

le **bifteck** *steak,* I, 8; II, 3

les **bijoux** (m.) *jewelry,* III, 8

le **billet: billet d'avion** *plane ticket,* I, 11; II, 1; **billet de train** *train ticket,* I, 11

la **biographie** *biography,* II, 11

la **biologie** *biology,* I, 2

la **bise: Grosses bises.** *Hugs and kisses.* III, 8

Bisous à... *Kisses to . . . ,* III, 8

bisque: en bisque *bisque,* III, 11

bizarre *weird,* III, 6

la **blague: Elle est nulle, ta blague!** *What a stupid joke!* III, 10

blanc(he) *white,* I, 3

le **blé: cultiver le blé** *to grow wheat,* III, 8

blesser *to wound,* III, 8

bleu(e) *blue,* I, 3; II, 1

blond(e) *blond,* I, 7; II, 1

le **blouson** *jacket,* I, 10

le **blues** *blues,* II, 11; III, 11

Bof! *(expression of indifference),* I, 1; II, 8

la **boisson** *drink, beverage,* I, 5; **Et comme boisson?** *And to drink?* III, 1; **Qu'est-ce que vous avez comme boissons?** *What do you have to drink?* I, 5

la **boîte: boîte à rythmes** *drum machine,* III, 11; **boîte de chocolats** *box of chocolates,* II, 3; **une boîte de** *a can of,* I, 8; **les boîtes** (f.) *cans,* III, 3

bon(ne) *good,* I, 5; **Vous avez (Tu as) fait bon voyage?** *Did you have a good trip?* II, 2; **Bon voyage!** *Have a good trip!* I, 11; **Bon, d'accord.** *Well, OK.* I, 8; **C'est bon pour toi.** *It's good for you.* II, 7; **C'est vraiment bon!** *It's good!* II, 3; **Oui, très bon.** *Yes, very good.* I, 9; **pas bon** *not very good,* I, 5; **bon chic bon genre (BCBG)** *preppy,* III, 4; **bon marché** *cheap,* III, 4; **Bonne chance!** *Good luck!* I, 11; **Bonne idée.** *Good idea.* I, 4; **Bonnes vacances!** *Have a good vacation!* I, 11; **Bonne fête!** *Happy holiday! (Happy saint's day!),* II, 3; **Bonne fête de Hanoukka!** *Happy Hannukah,* II, 3; **Bonne idée!** *Good idea!* II, 7; **C'est une bonne (excellente) idée.** *That's a good (excellent) idea.,* II, 1; **de bonne humeur** *in a good mood,* II, 9; **Elle est bien bonne!** *That's a good one!* III, 10

les **bonbons** (m.) *candies,* II, 3

Bonjour *Hello,* I, 1

le **bord: au bord de la mer** *to/at the coast,* I, 11

les **bottes** (f.) *boots,* I, 10; II, 1

les **bottines** (f.) *ankle boots,* III, 4

la **boucherie** *butcher shop,* II, 3

les **boucles d'oreilles** (f.) *earrings,* I, 10

le **boudin** *blood sausage,* III, 3

bouger: Ne bougez pas. *Don't move.* III, 7

bouillir *to boil,* III, 11

la **boulangerie** *bakery,* I, 12; II, 3

Les boules! *Darn!* III, 12

bouleverser *to overturn,* III, 8

la **boum: faire une boum** *to give a party,* II, 10

bouquiner *to read,* III, 2

La Bourse *the stock market,* III, 2

bousculer *to bump into, to jostle,* III, 3

la boussole *compass,* II, 12

le bout: Par là, au bout du couloir. *Over there, at the end of the hallway.* III, 2

la bouteille: une bouteille de *a bottle of,* I, 8

la boutique de cadeaux *gift shop,* II, 3

les boutons (m.): avoir des boutons *to have acne,* III, 10

la boxe *boxing,* III, 12

le bracelet *bracelet,* I, 3

le braconnier *poacher,* III, 7

brancher: Ça me branche! *I'm crazy about that!* III, 2; Ça ne me branche pas. *I'm not into that.* III, 11; Ça te branche,... ? *Are you into . . . ?* III, 11; Ce qui me branche vraiment, c'est... *What I'm really crazy about is . . . ,* III, 11

le bras: J'ai mal au bras *My arm hurts.* II, 7

la brasse *breaststroke,* III, 12

brasser *to stir,* III, 11

brave *brave,* II, 1

Bravo! *Terrific!* II, 5

Bref,... *Anyway, . . . ,* II, 9

le Brésil *Brazil,* III, 12

les bretelles (f.) *straps,* III, 3; *suspenders,* III, 4

la brique: Ça casse pas des briques. *It's not earth-shattering.* II, 11

briser *to break,* III, 3

la brosse: les cheveux en brosse (m.) *a crew cut,* III, 4

se brosser: se brosser les dents *to brush one's teeth,* II, 4

le brouillon *rough draft,* III, 3

la brousse *the brush (bushes),* III, 7

le bruit: faire du bruit *to make noise,* III, 3; Tu pourrais faire moins de bruit? *Could you make less noise?* III, 9

brun(e) *brunette,* I, 7; *dark brown (hair),* II, 1

bruyant(e) *noisy,* II, 8

le buffle *buffalo,* III, 7

les bulles (f.) *speech bubbles,* III, 2

le bus: en bus *by bus,* I, 12; rater le bus *to miss the bus,* II, 5

le but *goal,* III, 7

C

ça: Ça fait combien, s'il vous plaît? *How much is it, please?* I, 5; Ça fait combien? *How much does that make?* II, 3; Ça fait... francs. *It's . . . francs.* I, 5; Ça ne me dit rien. *That doesn't interest me.,* II, 1; Ça se voit. *That's obvious.* II, 9; Ça te dit d'aller... ? *What do you think about going . . . ?* II, 4; Ça te dit de... ? *Does . . . sound good to you?*

II, 1; Ça va. *Fine.* I, 1; Ça, c'est... *This is . . . ,* II, 2; Comment ça s'est passé? *How did it go?* II, 5; Et après ça,... *And after that, . . . ,* I, 9; Merci, ça va. *No thank you, I've had enough.* II, 3; Non, ça va. *No, I'm fine.* II, 2; Oui, ça a été. *Yes, it was fine.* I, 9; Il/Elle me va? *Does it suit me?* I, 10; Il/Elle te/vous va très bien. *That suits you really well.* I, 10; Ça te va comme un gant. *That fits you like a glove.* III, 4

le cadeau *gift,* I, 11; Tu as une idée de cadeau pour... ? *Have you got a gift idea for. . . ?* II, 3; la boutique de cadeaux *gift shop,* II, 3

le cadet (la cadette) *the younger child,* III, 6

le cadre *photo frame,* II, 3

le café *coffee, café,* I, 5

la cafetière *coffee pot,* III, 6

le cahier *notebook,* I, 3

la calculatrice *calculator,* I, 3

calé: Tu es calé(e). *You're really good at that.* III, 10

le caleçon *leggings,* III, 4

le calme: Du calme, du calme. *Calm down.* III, 2; Calmez-vous! *Calm down!* III, 7

le caméscope *camcorder,* III, 7

la campagne: à la campagne *to/at the countryside,* I, 11

le camping: faire du camping *to go camping,* I, 11; II, 12; terrain de camping *campground,* II, 2

le Canada *Canada,* III, 12

canadien(ne) *Canadian (adj.),* II, 11

le canard *duck,* II, 12

le canari *canary,* I, 7

la canne à pêche *fishing pole,* II, 12

le canotage: faire du canotage *to go for a canoe ride,* II, 12

la cantine: à la cantine *at the school cafeteria,* I, 9

la capitale *capital,* II, 4

le cardigan *sweater,* I, 10

la carie *cavity,* III, 3

les carottes (f.) *carrots,* I, 8; carottes râpées *grated carrots with vinaigrette dressing,* III, 1

les carreaux (m.): à carreaux *checked,* III, 4

le carrefour: Vous continuez tout droit, jusqu'au carrefour. *Keep going straight ahead up to the intersection.* III, 2

la carte *map,* I, 0; La carte, s'il vous plaît. *The menu, please.* I, 5

la carte de crédit *credit card,* III, 7

le casque *helmet,* III, 12

la casquette *cap,* I, 10

casser (avec quelqu'un) *to break up (with someone),* II, 9; Tu es vraiment casse-pieds! *You're such a pain!* III, 6; Casse-toi! *Get*

out of here! III, 6; Ça casse pas des briques. *It's not earth-shattering.* II, 11; Ça me casse les pieds! *That's so boring!* III, 2

se casser... *to break one's . . . ,* II, 7; III, 10

la cassette *cassette tape,* I, 3

la cassette vidéo *videocassette,* III, 9

la cathédrale *cathedral,* II, 2

le cauchemar: C'était un véritable cauchemar! *It was a real nightmare!* I, 11

ce que: Ce que c'est bien! *Isn't it great!* III, 2; Ce que j'aime bien, c'est... *What I like is . . . ,* II, 4; Ce que je n'aime pas, c'est... *What I don't like is . . . ,* II, 4; Ce que je préfère, c'est... *What I prefer is . . . ,* II, 4; Tu sais ce que tu veux faire? *Do you know what you want to do?* III, 5; Tu sais ce que... ? *Do you know what . . . ?* II, 9

ce qui: Ce qui m'ennuie, c'est... *What bothers me is . . . ,* II, 4; Ce qui me plaît, c'est... *What I like is . . . ,* II, 4; Ce qui ne me plaît pas, c'est... *What I don't care for is . . . ,* II, 4

la ceinture *belt,* I, 10

le céleri rémoulade *grated celery root with mayonnaise and vinaigrette,* III, 1

célibataire *unmarried,* III, 6

celle: Celle qui... *The woman/girl /one who . . . ,* III, 4; Celle-là. *That one.* III, 4; Celles-là *Those.* III, 4

celui: Celui avec... *The man/guy/ one with . . . ,* III, 4; Celui du... *The one . . . ,* III, 4; Celui-là. *That one.* III, 4

le centre commercial *mall,* I, 6

les céréales (f.) *cereal,* II, 3

certain: Je (ne) suis (pas) certain(e) que... *I'm (not) certain that . . . ,* III, 7

cervelas *sausage made with pork meat and brains,* III, 1

C'est... *It's . . . ,* I, 2; II, 11; *This is . . . ,* I, 7; C'est comment? *What's it like?* II, 4; Ça, c'est... *This is . . . ,* II, 2; C'est-à-dire que... *That is, . . . ,* II, 9

ceux: Ceux-là *Those.* III, 4

la chaîne *channel,* III, 9

la chaîne stéréo *stereo,* II, 2

la chaise *chair,* I, 0

la chambre *bedroom,* II, 2; ranger ta chambre *to pick up your room,* I, 7

le chameau *camel,* III, 8

les champignons (m.) *mushrooms,* I, 8; III, 11

les champs (m.) *fields,* III, 7; les champs de canne à sucre (m.) *sugarcane fields,* II, 4

la chance: Bonne chance! *Good luck!* I, 11; C'est pas de chance, ça!

Tough luck! II, 5; **J'ai vraiment pas de chance.** *I'm so unlucky.* III, 12; **On a eu de la chance!** *We were lucky!* III, 7

la chanson *song,* II, 11

le chant *singing,* III, 11

chanter *to sing,* I, 9

le chanteur *(male) singer,* II, 11

la chanteuse *(female) singer,* II, 11

le chapeau *hat,* I, 10; **Chapeau!** *Well done!* II, 5

la charcuterie *delicatessen,* II, 3; **l'assiette (f.) de charcuterie** *plate of pâté, ham, and cold sausage,* III, 1

charmant(e) *charming,* II, 4

la chasse *hunting,* III, 7

le chat *cat,* I, 7

châtain (inv.) *brown (hair),* II, 1

chaud: Il fait chaud. *It's hot.* I, 4; **Ouf! On a eu chaud!** *Wow! That was a real scare!* III, 7

le chauffeur *driver,* III, 5

les chaussettes (f.) *socks,* I, 10

les chaussures (f.) *shoes,* I, 10

le chemin *path, way,* III, 10

la chemise *shirt (men's),* I, 10

le chemisier *shirt (women's),* I, 10

le chêne *oak,* III, 11

les chèques (m.) de voyage *traveler's checks,* II, 1

cher: C'est trop cher. *It's too expensive.* I, 10; II, 3

chercher *to look for,* I, 9; **Je cherche quelque chose pour...** *I'm looking for something for . . . ,* I, 10

les cheveux (m.) *hair,* II, 1; III, 4

la cheville: se fouler la cheville *to sprain one's ankle,* II, 7

la chèvre *goat,* III, 8

chez: Chez... *With . . . ,* III, 1; **chez...** *to/at . . . 's house,* I, 11; **Bienvenue chez moi (chez nous).** *Welcome to my home (our home),* II, 2; **chez le disquaire** *at the record store,* I, 12; **Faites/Fais comme chez vous/toi.** *Make yourself at home.* II, 2; **Je suis bien chez...?** *Is this . . . 's house?* I, 9; **On... chez toi?** *Do people . . . where you're from?* III, 12; **Qu'est-ce qui est typique de chez toi?** *What's typical of where you're from?* III, 12; **Vous avez/Il y a des... chez vous?** *Do you have/Are there . . . where you're from?* III, 12

chic *chic,* I, 10

le chien *dog,* I, 7; **promener le chien** *to walk the dog,* I, 7

le chignon *bun,* III, 4

la chimie *chemistry,* I, 2

la Chine *China,* III, 12

le chiot *puppy,* III, 9

le chocolat *chocolate,* I, 1; *hot chocolate,* I, 5

choisir *to choose, to pick,* I, 10; **choisir un métier** *to choose a career,* III, 5; **choisir la musique**

to choose the music, II, 10; **Vous avez choisi?** *Have you made your selection?* III, 1

le choix: Si j'avais le choix,... *If I had a choice, . . . ,* III, 8

le chômage: être au chômage *to be unemployed,* III, 5

la chorale *choir,* I, 2

la chose: C'est toujours la même chose! *It's always the same!* III, 6; **J'ai quelque chose à faire.** *I have something else to do.* II, 10; **Quelque chose ne va pas?** *Is something wrong?* II, 7; **Bien des choses à...** *All the best to . . . ,* III, 8; **J'ai des tas de choses à faire.** *I have lots of things to do.* I, 5

chouette *very cool,* II, 2; **Ça serait chouette si...** *It would be great if . . . ,* III, 8; **Oui, très chouette.** *Yes, very cool.* I, 9

Chut! *Shh!* III, 9

la chute d'eau *waterfall,* II, 4

les cigognes (f.) *storks,* III, 1

les cils (m.) *the eyelashes,* III, 4

le cinéma *the movies,* I, 1; *the movie theater,* I, 6

le circuit *tour,* III, 1; **faire un circuit des châteaux** *to tour some châteaux,* II, 6

la circulation *traffic,* III, 2

la cire *wax,* III, 1

la citation *quotation,* III, 10

clair *light,* III, 4

classe *classy,* III, 4

le classeur *loose-leaf binder,* I, 3

le (roman) classique *classic,* II, 11

cloche *goofy,* III, 4

le clou *nail,* III, 6

le clown: Il ne faut pas faire le clown en classe! *You can't be goofing off in class!* II, 5

le coca *cola,* I, 5

le cocotier *coconut tree,* II, 4

le cœur: J'ai mal au cœur. *I'm sick to my stomach.* II, 7

la coiffe *headdress,* III, 1

le coiffeur (la coiffeuse) *hair stylist,* III, 4

le coin: au coin de *on the corner of,* I, 12

le col roulé *turtleneck sweater,* III, 4

le col: à col en V *V-necked,* III, 4

le collant *hose,* I, 10; *tights,* III, 4

collé: être collé(e) *to have detention,* II, 5

la colonie: en colonie de vacances *to/at a summer camp,* I, 11

coloré(e) *colorful,* II, 4

combien: C'est combien, l'entrée? *How much is the entrance fee?* II, 6; **C'est combien,... ?** *How much is . . . ?* I, 5; **Ça fait combien, s'il vous plaît?** *How much is it, please?* I, 5; **Ça fait combien?** *How much does that make?* II, 3; **Combien coûte(nt)... ?** *How much is (are) . . . ?* II, 3; **Combien**

en voulez-vous? *How many (much) do you want?* II, 3

la comédie *comedy,* III, 9; **la comédie musicale** *musical comedy,* III, 9

commander *to order,* III, 1

comme: C'est bien comme... ? *Is it a nice . . . ?* III, 12; **C'est fou comme... !** *I can't believe how . . . !* III, 7; **Comme entrée, je voudrais . . .** *As an appetizer I would like . . . ,* III, 1; **Comme ci, comme ça.** *So-so.* I, 1; **Qu'est-ce que tu fais comme sport?** *What sports do you play?* I, 4; **Qu'est-ce que vous avez comme boissons?** *What do you have to drink?* I, 5; **Qu'est-ce que vous avez comme... ?** *What kind of . . . do you have?* I, 5; **Tu as vu comme... ?** *Did you see how . . . ?* III, 7; **C'est... comme tout!** *It's as . . . as anything!* III, 2

commencer *to begin, to start,* I, 9; **C'est lui/elle qui a commencé!** *He/She started it!* III, 6; **Ça commence à quelle heure?** *What time does it start?* II, 11; **Comment est-ce que ça commence?** *How does it start?* III, 9

comment *what,* I, 0; *how,* II, 5; **(Comment) ça va?** *How's it going?* I, 1; **C'est comment?** *What's it like?* II, 4; **C'était comment?** *How was it?* I, 6; III, 9; **Comment est-ce qu'on fait... ?** *How do you make . . . ?* III, 11; **Comment est-ce qu'on fait?** *How should we work this out?* III, 6; **Comment on dit... ?** *How do you say . . . ?* III, 11; **Comment tu as trouvé ça?** *How did you like it?* III, 9; **Comment tu trouves ça?** *What do you think of that/it?* I, 2; **Comment tu trouves... ?** *What do you think of . . . ?* I, 2; **Elle est comment?** *What is she like?* I, 7; **Il est comment?** *What is he like?* I, 7; **Ils/Elles sont comment?** *What are they like?* I, 7; **Tu t'appelles comment?** *What is your name?* I, 0; **Comment on va à... ?** *How do you get to . . . ?* III, 2

la commode *chest of drawers,* II, 2

commun: prendre les transports en commun *to take public transportation,* III, 3

le comportement *behavior,* III, 7

compréhensif (compréhensive) *understanding,* III, 6

comprendre *to understand,* II, 5; **J'ai du mal à comprendre.** *I have a hard time understanding.* II, 5

les comprimés (m.) *tablets,* III, 7

le comptable *accountant,* III, 5

compter: Je compte... *I'm planning on . . . ,* III, 5; **Qu'est-ce que tu comptes faire?** *What do you plan to do?* III, 5

les concerts (m.) *concerts,* I, 1

la condition: se mettre en condition *to get into shape,* II, 7

conduire *to drive,* III, 2; **conduire une voiture** *to drive a car,* II, 8; **Cette route vous conduira au centre-ville.** *This road will lead you into the center of town.* III, 2

la confiance: Fais-moi confiance. *Trust me.* III, 4

la confiserie *candy shop,* II, 3

la confiture *jam,* I, 8

connais: J'en connais une bonne. *I've got a good one.* III, 10; **Je ne connais pas.** *I'm not familiar with them (him/her).* II, 11; **Tu connais la dernière?** *Have you heard the latest?* III, 10; **Tu connais la nouvelle?** *Did you hear the latest?* II, 9; **Tu connais...** *Are you familiar with . . . ?* II, 11

connaisse: Tu es le/la... le/la plus... que je connaisse. *You're the . . . -est . . . I know.* III, 10

conseiller: Qu'est-ce que tu me conseilles? *What do you advise me to do?* I, 9 **Qu'est-ce que vous me conseillez?** *What do you recommend?* III, 1

les conseils (m.) *advice,* III, 4

consommer: consommer trop de sucre *to eat too much sugar,* II, 7

continuer: Vous continuez cette rue jusqu'au prochain feu rouge. *You go down this street to the next light.* I, 12; **Vous continuez tout droit, jusqu'au carrefour.** *Keep going straight ahead up to the intersection.* III, 2

convaincu: Je suis convaincu(e) que... *I'm convinced that . . . ,* III, 7

cool *cool,* I, 2; **C'est trop cool!** *That's too cool!* III, 12; **Il/Elle est cool, ton/ta...** *Your . . . is cool.* II, 2

le coquillage *shell,* III, 10

le corail *coral,* III, 10

la corne *horn,* III, 7

corriger *to correct,* III, 3

le costume *man's suit,* III, 4

le côté: à côté de *next to,* I, 12; II, 2; **Juste là, à côté de...** *Right there, next to . . . ,* II, 2

la côte *cutlet; chop,* III, 1

la côtelette de porc pâtes *porkchop with pasta,* III, 1

le coton: en coton *cotton,* I, 10

le cou: J'ai mal au cou *My neck hurts.* II, 7

se coucher *to go to bed,* II, 4

le coucher de soleil *sunset,* III, 8

couler: J'ai le nez qui coule. *I've got a runny nose.* II, 7

le country *country,* II, 11; III, 11

le coup de cœur *favorite,* III, 4

la coupe *haircut,* III, 4; **une coupe au carré** *square cut,* III, 4

le coupe-vent *windbreaker, jacket,* III, 4

couper: Tu t'es fait couper les cheveux? *Did you get your hair cut?* III, 4; **se couper le doigt** *to cut one's finger,* II, 7

le courage: Courage! *Hang in there!* II, 5; **Tu en as, du courage.** *You've really got courage.* III, 10

le courrier *mail,* III, 4

le cours *course,* I, 2; **cours de développement personnel et social (DPS)** *health,* I, 2; **Tu as quels cours... ?** *What classes do you have . . . ?* I, 2

la course de fond *long-distance running,* III, 12

les courses (f.) *shopping, errands,* I, 7; **faire les courses** *to do the shopping,* I, 7.

court(e) *short (objects),* I, 10; II, 1; **au court-bouillon** *boiled,* III, 11; **les cheveux courts** (m.) *short hair,* III, 4

le cousin *male cousin,* I, 7

la cousine *female cousin,* I, 7

coûte: Combien coûte(nt)... ? *How much is (are). . . ?* II, 3

le crabe *crab,* III, 1

cracher *to spit (out),* III, 6

craquer: Je craque! *I'm losing it!* II, 7

la cravate *a tie,* I, 10

le crayon *pencil,* I, 3

la crème: la crème caramel *caramel custard,* III, 1; **de la crème solaire** *sunscreen,* III, 7

la crémerie *dairy,* II, 3

crevé: avoir un pneu crevé *to have a flat tire,* II, 2; **Je suis crevé(e).** *I'm exhausted.* II, 2

crève: Je crève de faim! *I'm dying of hunger!* II, 12

la crevette *shrimp,* II, 3; III, 10

le cric *car jack,* III, 2

le crocodile *crocodile,* III, 7

croire: J'arrive pas à y croire! *I can't believe it.* III, 12; **Crois-moi.** *Believe me.* III, 4; **Je crois que ça vaut mieux.** *I think that's better.* III, 7; **Je crois que...** *I think that . . . ,* II, 9; **Je ne crois pas.** *I don't think so.* II, 9

les croissants (m.) *croissants,* II, 3

le croque-monsieur *toasted cheese and ham sandwich,* I, 5

les crudités (f.): **l'assiette de crudités** *plate of raw vegetables with vinaigrette,* III, 1

les crustacés (m.) *shellfish,* III, 11

la cueillette: faire la cueillette *to harvest fruits,* III, 8

cueillir *to harvest,* III, 8

le cuir: en cuir *leather,* I, 10

cuire *to cook,* III, 11

la cuisine *kitchen,* II, 2; **faire la cuisine** *to cook,* III, 3

cuite: Bien cuite. *Well done.* III, 1

le cuivre *brass, copper,* III, 8

cultiver: cultiver le blé *to grow wheat,* III, 8

le cyclisme *cycling,* III, 12

D

d'abord: D'abord,... *First, . . . ,* II, 12

d'accord: D'accord. *OK.* I, 4; II, 1; **D'accord, si tu... d'abord...** *OK, if you . . . , first.* I, 7; **Je ne suis pas d'accord.** *I don't agree.* I, 7; **Tu es d'accord?** *Is that OK with you?* I, 7

d'habitude *usually,* I, 4

le daim: en daim *suede,* III, 4

la dance *dance music,* III, 11

dangereux (dangereuse) *dangerous,* II, 8

dans *in,* I, 6; **C'est dans le nord/le sud/l'est/l'ouest de...** *It's in the northern/southern/eastern/western part of . . . ,* II, 12; **dans l'eau** *in the water,* III, 3; **Qu'est-ce qu'il y a dans... ?** *What's in . . . ?* III, 11

la danse *dance,* I, 2

danser *to dance,* I, 1; **danser le zouk** *to dance the zouk,* II, 4

la datte *date (fruit),* III, 8

le dattier *date palm tree,* III, 8

de *of,* I, 0; **de l'** *some,* I, 8; **de la** *some,* I, 8; **De rien.** *You're welcome.* III, 6; **de taille moyenne** *of medium height,* II, 1; **Je n'ai pas de...** *I don't have any . . . ,* I, 3; **Je ne fais pas de...** *I don't play/do . . . ,* I, 4

le débardeur *tank top,* III, 4

débarrasser la table *to clear the table,* I, 7

les débouchés (m.) *job prospects,* III, 5

le début: Au début... *At the beginning . . . ,* III, 9; **J'y suis allé(e) début...** *I went at the beginning of . . . ,* III, 1

le décalage *gap,* III, 12

décembre *December,* I, 4

les déchets (m.): **jeter (remporter) les déchets** *to throw away (to take with you) your trash,* II, 12

déchirer *to rip,* II, 5

décider: J'ai du mal à me décider. *I'm having trouble deciding.* III, 5; **Je n'arrive pas à me décider.** *I can't make up my mind.* III, 1

les décisions (f.): **prendre ses propres décisions** *to make up one's own mind,* III, 3

décontracté *relaxed,* III, 4

Défense de... *Do not . . . ,* III, 3

le défi *challenge,* III, 12

défoncer *to unwind,* III, 12

se défouler *to let off steam,* III, 12

dégoûtant *gross,* I, 5

déguster *to taste, enjoy,* II, 4

dehors *outside,* III, 4

déjà *already,* I, 9; **... , déjà?** *again,* III, 11; **Il/Elle en a déjà un(e).** *He/She already has one (of them).* II, 3 le **déjeuner** *lunch,* I, 2

déjeuner *to have lunch,* I, 9

délicieux (délicieuse) *delicious,* I, 5; **C'était délicieux!** *That was delicious!* II, 3

délirant(e) *wild,* III, 4

délirer: Arrête de délirer! *Stop being so silly!* III, 10; **Tu délires ou quoi?** *Are you crazy or what?* III, 11

le **deltaplane: faire du deltaplane** *to hang glide,* II, 4

demain *tomorrow,* I, 2; **A demain.** *See you tomorrow.* I, 1

demander: demander la permission à tes parents *to ask your parents' permission,* II, 10; **demander pardon à (quelqu'un)** *to ask (someone's) forgiveness,* II, 10; **Je t'ai pas demandé ton avis.** *I didn't ask your opinion.* III, 10

se demander: Je me demande... *I wonder . . . ,* II, 9

démarrer *to start up,* III, 10

déménager *to move,* III, 10

la **demeure** *residence,* III, 10

demie: et demie *half past,* I, 6; **demi: et demi** *half past (after midi and minuit),* I, 6

démodé(e) *old fashioned,* I, 10

la **dentelle** *lace,* III, 2

le/la **dentiste** *dentist,* III, 5

les **dents** (f.): **J'ai mal aux dents** *My teeth hurt.* II, 7

dépêcher: Tu peux te dépêcher? *Can you hurry up?* III, 2; **Dépêche-toi!** *Hurry up!* III, 2

déposer *to deposit,* I, 12

le **dépotoir** *dump,* III, 3

déprimant(e) *depressing ,* II, 11

déprimé(e) *depressed,* II, 9

Depuis... *Since . . . ,* III, 1

déranger *to bother, disturb,* III, 6; **Ça te dérange si...** *Do you mind if . . . ?* III, 3

dernièrement *recently,* III, 9

derrière *behind,* I, 12

dès que: Dès que je serai là,... *As soon as I get there, . . . ,* III, 12

descendre *to go down,* II, 6

le **désinfectant** *disinfectant,* III, 7

désirer: Comment désirez-vous votre viande? *How do you like your meat cooked?* III, 1; **Vous désirez?** *What would you like?* I, 10

Désolé(e). *Sorry.* II, 10; **Désolé(e), je suis occupé(e).** *Sorry, I'm busy.* I, 6; **Désolé(e), mais je ne peux pas.** *Sorry, but I can't.* I, 4

le **dessert** *dessert,* II, 3

dessiner *to draw,* III, 4

le **dessin animé** *cartoon,* III, 9

le **dessinateur (la dessinatrice)** *commercial artist,* III, 5

détoner *to detonate, explode,* III, 4

détruire *to destroy,* III, 7

dévalisé *stripped, robbed,* III, 2

devant *in front of,* I, 6

devenir *to become,* II, 6; **Qu'est-ce que tu deviens?** *What's going on with you?* III, 1

deviner *to guess,* III, 5; **Devine ce que...** *Guess what . . . ,* II, 9; **Devine qui...** *Guess who . . . ,* II, 9; **Tu ne devineras jamais ce qui s'est passé.** *You'll never guess what happened.* III, 10

les **devoirs** (m.) *homework,* I, 2; **J'ai des devoirs à faire.** *I've got homework to do,* I, 5

devoir *have to, must,* III, 3; **Ça doit être...** *It must be . . . ,* III, 7; **Il doit y avoir...** *There must be . . . ,* III, 7; **On doit...** *Everyone should . . . ,* II, 7; **Tu crois que je devrais... ?** *Do you think I should . . . ?* III, 7; **Tu devrais aller voir...** *You should go see . . . ,* III, 9; **Tu devrais...** *You should . . . ,* I, 9; **Tu ne devrais pas...** *You shouldn't . . . ,* II, 7

dévoué(e) *dedicated,* III, 5

la **diapositive** *slide (photograpy),* III, 10

le **dictionnaire** *dictionary,* I, 3

la **différence: Quelle est la différence entre ... et... ?** *What's the difference between . . . and . . . ?* III, 10

difficile *difficult,* I, 2

le **dimanche** *on Sundays,* I, 2

la **dinde: l'escalope de dinde purée** *sliced turkey breast with mashed potatoes,* III, 1

le **dîner** *dinner,* I, 8

dîner *to have dinner,* I, 9

dingue *wild, crazy, funny,* III, 2

le **diplôme: obtenir son diplôme** *to get one's diploma,* III, 5

dire: dire à (quelqu'un) que... *to tell (someone) that . . . ,* II, 10; **dire la vérité** *to tell the truth,* III, 3; **J'ai entendu dire que...** *I've heard that . . . ,* III, 10; **Qu'est-ce que ça veut dire,... ?** *What does . . . mean?* III, 11; **Vous pouvez lui dire que j'ai téléphoné?** *Can you tell her/him that I called?* I, 9; **Dis à... que je pense à lui/elle.** *Tell . . . that I'm thinking about him/her,* III, 8; **Dis à... que je vais lui écrire.** *Tell . . . that I'm going to write.* III, 8; **Dis vite!** *Let's hear it!* II, 9; **Dis-lui/-leur que...** *Tell him/her/them that . . . ,* II, 10; **Oh, dis donc!** *Wow!* III, 7; **... et alors il dit que...** *So he says . . . ,* III, 10; **Ça ne me dit rien.** *That doesn't interest me.* I, 4; II, 1; **Ça te dit d'aller... ?** *What do you think about going . . . ?* II, 4; **Ça te dit de...?** *Does . . . sound good to you?* II, 1; **Comment on dit... ?** *How do you say . . . ?* III, 11; **écouter ce qu'il/elle dit** *to listen to what he/she says,* II, 10; **Je ne t'ai pas dit?** *Didn't I tell you?* III, 10; **Qui t'a dit ça?** *Who told you that?* III, 10; **Tu l'as dit!** *You said it!* III, 9; **Dites donc, ça vous gênerait de... ?** *Hey, do you think*

you can . . . ? III, 8; **On dirait que... ** *It looks like . . . ,* III, 11

se disputer (avec quelqu'un) *to have an argument (with someone),* II, 9

le **disquaire: chez le disquaire** *at the record store,* I, 12

le **disque compact/le CD** *compact disc/ CD,* I, 3

divers *various,* III, 1

divorcé(e) *divorced,* III, 6

le **documentaire** *documentary,* III, 9

le **doigt: se couper le doigt** *to cut one's finger,* II, 7

Donc,... *Therefore, . . . ,* II, 9; **Oh, dis donc!** *Wow!* III, 7

donner: donner à manger aux animaux *to feed the animals,* II, 6; **Donnez-moi votre...** *Give me your . . . ,* III, 6; **Donnez-moi... , s'il vous plaît.** *Please give me . . .* I, 5

dormir *to sleep,* I, 1; **Où est-ce que tu as dormi?** *Where did you stay?* III, 1

le **dos: J'ai mal au dos** *My back hurts.* II, 7

le **doute: Je n'en ai aucun doute.** *I have no doubt of it.* III, 12

la **douzaine: une douzaine de** *a dozen,* I, 8

le **drame** *drama,* III, 9

le **droit: Tu n'as pas le droit de...** *You're not allowed to . . . ,* III, 3

droite: à droite *to the right,* I, 12; **à droite de** *to the right of,* II, 2; **sur la droite (gauche)** *on the right (left),* II, 2

drôle: C'est drôle (amusant). *It's funny.* II, 11

dû: J'aurais dû... *I should have . . . ,* II, 10; **Tu aurais dû...** *You should have . . . ,* II, 10

E

l' **eau** (f.) *water,* I, 5; **l'eau minérale** *mineral water,* I, 5; **la chute d'eau** *waterfall,* II, 4

échapper *to escape,* III, 7; **On l'a échappé belle!** *That was close!* III, 7

l' **écharpe** (f.) *scarf,* I, 10; II, 1

l' **échec** (m.) *failure,* III, 8

éclater: Ça m'éclate. *I'm wild about it.* III, 11

l' **école** (f.) *school,* I, 1; **faire une école technique** *to go to a technical school,* III, 5

écossais(e) *plaid,* III, 4

écouter: écouter ce qu'il/elle dit *to listen to what he/she says,* II, 10; **écouter de la musique** *to listen to music,* I, 1; **Ecoutez!** *Listen!* I, 0; **J'écoute que ça.** *That's all I listen to.* III, 11; **Je t'écoute.** *I'm listening.* I, 9; II, 10

l' écran (m.) *screen*, III, 9

les écrevisses (f.) *crawfish*, III, 11

l' écrivain (m.) *writer*, III, 5

l' écureuil (m.) *squirrel*, II, 12

l' édition (f.) *publishing*, III, 5

l' éducation (f.) physique et sportive (EPS) *physical education*, I, 2

l' effort (m.): Encore un effort! *One more try!* II, 7

égal: Ça m'est égal. *Whatever.* II, 8; Ça m'est vraiment égal. *It's really all the same to me.* III, 9

l' église (f.) *church*, II, 2

égoïste *selfish*, III, 6

élégant(e) *elegant, sophisticated*, III, 4

l' éléphant (m.) *elephant*, III, 7

l' élève (m./f.) *student*, I, 2

élever *to raise*, III, 8

éloignés *distant (relatives)*, III, 11

emballé: Ça ne m'a pas emballé(e). *It didn't do anything for me.* III, 9

embêtant(e) *annoying*, I, 7; II, 1

embêter *to pester, annoy*, III, 6; Et toi, arrête de m'embêter! *Stop bothering me!* III, 10; Ça m'embête! *That bores me!* III, 2; Ça t'embête de... ? *Would you mind . . . ?* II, 10

l' embouteillage (m.) *traffic jam*, III, 8

embrasser: Embrasse... pour moi. *Give . . . a kiss for me.* III, 8; Je t'embrasse bien fort. *Hugs and kisses.* III, 8

l' émincé (m.) *slice*, III, 1

l' émission (f.) *program*, III, 9; l'émission de variétés *variety show*, III, 9

emmener *to take (a person) with you*, III, 9

empêcher *to prevent, stop*, III, 12

emporter *to bring (with you)*, II, 12

emprunter *borrow*, I, 12

en *some, of it, of them, any, none*, I, 8; en *to, in (before a feminine noun)*, I, 11; en laine *wool*, III, 4; en soie *silk*, III, 4; Combien en voulez-vous? *How many (much) do you want?* II, 3; En bas. *Downstairs.* III, 2; en coton *cotton*, I, 10; en cuir *leather*, I, 10; en face de *across from*, II, 2; En haut. *Upstairs.* III, 2; en jean *denim*, I, 10; Il/Elle en a déjà un(e). *He/She already has one (of them).* II, 3; Je m'en veux de... *I feel bad for . . .* , III, 6; Je n'en peux plus! *I just can't do any more!* II, 7; Je n'en veux plus. *I don't want anymore*, I, 8; Je ne t'en veux pas. *No hard feelings.* II, 10; Je suis parti(e) en... *I went by . . .* , III, 1; Je vais (en) prendre... *I'll take . . .* , II, 3; T'en fais pas. *Don't worry.* II, 5; Tu n'as pas l'air en forme. *You don't seem too well.* II, 7; Tu ne m'en veux pas? *No hard feelings?* II, 10; Vous avez ça en... ? *Do you*

have that in . . . ? *(size, fabric, color)*, I, 10

encore: Encore de... ? *More . . . , ?* I, 8; Encore un effort! *One more try!* II, 7; Encore... ? *Some more . . . ?* II, 3; Pas encore. *Not yet.* III, 1

l' énergie (f.) *energy*, III, 3

énervé(e) *annoyed*, II, 9

énerver: Tu m'énerves, à la fin! *You're bugging me to death!* III, 6

Enfin,... *Finally, . . . ,* II, 1

enfoncer *to drive (a nail)*, III, 6

enlever: enlever la neige *to shovel snow*, III, 3; se faire enlever ses bagues *to get one's braces off*, III, 10

ennuyer *to bother*, II, 8; Ça m'ennuie à mourir! *That bores me to death!* III, 2; Ça t'ennuie de... ? *Would you mind . . . ?* II, 10; Ce qui m'ennuie, c'est... *What bothers me is . . .* , II, 4; On ne s'ennuie pas. *You're never bored.* II, 11; Je me suis ennuyé(e) à mourir. *I was bored to death.* III, 9; Je me suis ennuyé(e). *I was bored.* II, 6; Je ne me suis pas ennuyé une seconde. *I wasn't bored a second.* III, 9

ennuyeux (ennuyeuse) *boring*, II, 6; C'était ennuyeux. *It was boring.* I, 5

enregistrer *to record*, III, 9

Ensuite,... *Next, . . . ,* II, 1; *Then, . . . ,* II, 12

entendre: entendre le réveil *to hear the alarm clock*, II, 5; Entendu. *OK.* I, 6; J'ai entendu dire que... *I've heard that . . .* , III, 10

s'entraîner à... *to train for (a sport)*, II, 7

l' entraîneur (m.) *coach*, III, 12

entre *between*, I, 12; Quelle est la différence entre ... et... ? *What's the difference between . . . and . . . ?* III, 10

l' entrecôte grillée *rib steak*, III, 1

l' entrée (f.) *first course*, II, 3; C'est combien, l'entrée? *How much is the entrance fee?* II, 6; Que voulez-vous comme entrée? *What sort of appetizer would you like?*, III, 1; Comme entrée, j'aimerais... *For an appetizer, I would like . . .* III, 1; A l'entrée de... *At the entrance to . . .* , II, 2

entrer *to enter*, II, 6; entrer à l'université *to enter the university*, III, 5

l' enveloppe (f.) *envelope*, I, 12

envie: J'ai envie de... *I feel like . . .* , I, 11; Non, je n'ai pas très envie. *No, I don't feel like it.* II, 7; Tu as envie de... ? *Do you feel like . . . ?* II, 1

envoyer: envoyer des lettres *to send letters*, I, 12; envoyer les invitations *to send the invitations*,

II, 10; Pourriez-vous m'envoyer des renseignements sur... ? *Could you send me information on . . . ?* III, 5

épater: Alors, là, tu m'épates! *I'm really impressed!* III, 10

l' épée (f.) *an epee/a sword*, III, 12

épicé(e) *spicy*, III, 11

l' épicerie (f.) *grocery store*, I, 12

les épices (f.) *spices*, III, 11

les épinards (m.) *spinach*, III, 11

épouser *to marry*, III, 6

épouvantable: avoir une journée épouvantable *to have a horrible day*, II, 5; C'était épouvantable. *It was horrible.* I, 9; J'ai passé une journée épouvantable! *I had a terrible day!* II, 5

l' épreuve (f.) *event (sports)*, III, 12

l' équipe (f.) *a team*, III, 12

l' équitation (f.) *equestrian events*, III, 12; faire de l'équitation *to go horseback riding*, I, 1

l' escalope (f.) de dinde purée *sliced turkey breast with mashed potatoes*, III, 1

les escargots (m.) *snails*, I, 1; II, 3

l' escrime (f.) *fencing*, III, 12

l' espadon (m.) *swordfish*, III, 10

l' Espagne (f.) *Spain*, III, 12

l' espagnol (m.) *Spanish (language)*, I, 2

les espèces (f.) *species*, III, 7

l' essayage (m.) *fitting*, III, 4

essayer: Je peux essayer... ? *Can I try on . . . ?* I, 10; Je peux l'(les) essayer? *Can I try it (them) on ?* I, 10; Essaie... *Try . . . ,* III, 1

l' essence (f.) *gas*, III, 2

essentiel: Il est essentiel que... *It's essential to . . .* , III, 7

l' est (m): dans l'est *in the east*, II, 4; C'est à l'est de... *It's to the east of . . .* , II, 12

Est-ce que *(Introduces a yes-or-no question)*, I, 4; (Est-ce que) je peux... ? *May I . . . , ?* I, 7

l' étage (m.): Au premier étage. *On the second floor.* III, 2

les étagères (f.) *shelves*, II, 2

les Etats-Unis (m.) *United States*, III, 12

l' été (m.) *summer*, I, 4; en été *in the summer*, I, 4

éteindre *to turn off/out*, III, 3

l' étoile de mer (f.) *starfish*, III, 10

étonné(e) *surprised*, II, 9

étonner: Ça m'étonnerait que... *I'd be surprised if . . .* , III, 7; Ça m'étonnerait! *That would surprise me.* II, 6; III, 10

étouffée: à l'étouffée *steamed*, III, 11

être *to be*, I, 7; être collé(e) *to have detention*, II, 5; être en train de (+ infinitive) *to be in the process of (doing something)*, II, 9

l' étude (f.) *study hall*, I, 2; arrêter ses études *to stop one's studies*, III, 5

étudier *to study,* I, 1

les événements (m.) *events,* III, 10

Evidemment. *Obviously.* II, 9

éviter *to avoid,* III, 3; **Evite d'aller voir...** *Avoid seeing. . . ,* III, 9; **Evite de...** *Avoid . . . ,* II, 7

les examens (m.) *tests,* I, 1

excellent(e) *excellent,* I, 5; **Oui, excellent.** *Yes, excellent.* I, 9; II, 2

s'excuser *to apologize,* II, 10; **Excuse-moi.** *Forgive me.* II, 10; **Excuse-toi.** *Apologize.* II, 10; **Je m'excuse de...** *I'm sorry for . . . ,* III, 6

l' exercice (m.): **faire de l'exercice** *to exercise,* II, 7

exigeant *demanding,* III, 5

expliquer: expliquer ce qui s'est passé (à quelqu'un) *to explain what happened (to someone),* II, 10; **Explique-lui/-leur.** *Explain to him/her/them.* II, 10

exprès: Tu le fais exprès? *Are you doing that on purpose?* III, 6

F

face: en face de *across from,* I, 12; II, 12

fâché(e) *angry,* II, 9

facile *easy,* I, 2

la faim: avoir faim *to be hungry,* I, 5; **Je n'ai plus faim.** *I'm not hungry anymore.* II, 3; **Si, j'ai très faim!** *Yes, I'm very hungry.* II, 2; **Vous n'avez pas/Tu n'as pas faim?** *Aren't you hungry?* II, 2

faire *to do, to make, to play,* I, 4; **faire + infinitive** *to have done,* III, 4; **se faire enlever ses bagues** *to get one's braces off,* III, 10; **se faire percer les oreilles** *to have one's ears pierced,* III, 10; **se faire mal à ...** *to hurt one's . . . ,* II, 7; III, 10; **faire la tête** *to sulk,* II, 9; **faire le plein** *to fill it up,* III, 2; **faire les préparatifs** *to get ready,* II, 10; **Tu vas t'y faire.** *You'll get used to it.* II, 8; **fais: A ton avis, qu'est-ce que je fais?** *In your opinion, what do I do?* I, 9; **Est-ce que tu fais... ?** *Do you play/do . . . ?* I, 4; **Fais-toi une raison.** *Make the best of it.* II, 8; **Ne t'en fais pas!** *Don't worry!* I, 9; **Faites/Fais comme chez vous (toi).** *Make yourself at home.* II, 2; **Mais, qu'est-ce que tu fais?** *What are you doing?* III, 2; **Ne t'en fais pas.** *Don't worry.* I, 11; **Qu'est-ce que tu fais comme sport?** *What sports do you play?* II, 1; **Qu'est-ce que tu fais pour t'amuser?** *What do you do to have fun?* I, 4; **Qu'est-ce que tu fais quand... ?** *What do you do when . . . ?* I, 4; **Ça fait combien?**

How much does that make? II, 3; **Ça fait très bien.** *That looks good.* III, 4; **Ça fait vraiment...** *That looks really . . . ,* III, 4; **Ça fait...** *It's been . . . ,* III, 1; **Ça ne fait rien.** *It doesn't matter.* II, 10; **Comment est-ce qu'on fait?** *How should we work this out?* III, 6; **D'abord, j'ai fait...** *First, I did . . . ,* I, 9; **Il fait beau.** *It's nice weather.* I, 4; **Il fait frais.** *It's cool.* I, 4; **Il fait froid.** *It's cold.* I, 4; **Il fait chaud.** *It's hot.* I, 4; **Qu'est-ce qu'on fait?** *What should we do?* II, 1; **Faites/Fais comme chez vous/toi.** *Make yourself at home.* II, 2; **Faites gaffe!** *Look out!* III, 7

fameux (fameuse): pas fameux *not so great,* I, 5

fantaisiste *eccentric, whimsical,* III, 5

farci (à) *stuffed (with),* III, 11

la farine *flour,* I, 8

fastoche: C'est fastoche, ça! *That's so easy!* III, 10

fatigant: C'était fatigant! *It was tiring!* II, 2

fatigué(e): Je suis fatigué(e) *I'm tired.* II, 12; **Pas trop fatigué(e)?** *(You're) not too tired?* II, 2

faudrait: Il faudrait que tu... *You should . . . ,* III, 5; **Il faudrait que...** *You ought to . . . ,* III, 7

faut: Il faut mieux travailler en classe. *You have to do better in class.* II, 5; **Il faut que... d'abord.** *First, you have to . . . ,* III, 3; **Il me faut...** *I need . . . ,* I, 3; **Il ne faut pas...** *One should not . . . ,* III, 3; **Qu'est-ce qu'il te faut pour... ?** *What do you need for . . . ? (informal),* I, 3

la faute: C'est de ma faute. *It's my fault.* II, 10

Félicitations! *Congratulations!* II, 3

la femme *wife,* III, 6

la femme d'affaires *businesswoman,* III, 5

la fenêtre *window,* I, 0

fermer: Ferme-la! *Shut up!* III, 6; **A quelle heure est-ce que vous fermez?** *When do you close?* II, 6; **Fermez la porte.** *Close the door.* I, 0

féroce *ferocious,* III, 7

la fête: Bonne fête de Hanoukka! *Happy Hanukkah!* II, 3; **Bonne fête!** *Happy holiday! (Happy saint's day!),* II, 3

le feu: Il n'y a pas le feu. *Where's the fire?* III, 2

la feuille: une feuille de papier *a sheet of paper,* I, 0; **ramasser les feuilles** *to rake leaves,* III, 3

feuilleter *to leaf through ,* III, 2

le feuilleton *soap opera,* III, 9

février *February,* I, 4

se fiancer *to get engaged,* III, 10

ficher: Je m'en fiche. *I don't give a darn.* III, 9; **Fiche-moi la paix!** *Leave me alone!* III, 6; **Tu te fiches de moi?** *Are you kidding me?* III, 9

fier (fière) *proud,* III, 10; **Tu peux être fier (fière) de toi.** *You should be proud of yourself.* II, 5

la fièvre jaune *yellow fever,* III, 7

la figue *fig,* III, 8

figurer: Figure-toi que... *Can you imagine that . . . ,* III, 10

le filet de sole riz champignons *filet of sole with rice and mushrooms,* III, 1

le film: le film classique *classic movie,* II, 11; **le film comique** *comedy,* II, 11; **le film d'action** *action movie,* II, 11; **le film d'aventures** *adventure movie,* II, 11; **le film d'horreur** *horror movie,* II, 11; **le film de science-fiction** *science-fiction movie,* II, 11; **le film policier** *detective or mystery movie,* II, 11; **le film étranger** *foreign film,* III, 9; **le film historique** *historical movie,* III, 9; **le film de guerre** *war movie,* III, 9; **le film d'espionnage** *spy movie,* III, 9; **voir un film** *to see a movie,* I, 6; **Qu'est-ce qu'il y a comme bon film en ce moment?** *What good movies are out now?* III, 9; **Qu'est-ce que tu as vu comme bons films?** *What good movies have you seen?* III, 9

la fin: A la fin... *At the end . . . ,* III, 9; **C'est insupportable, à la fin!** *I won't put up with this!* III, 8; **Tu m'énerves, à la fin!** *You're bugging me to death!* III, 6

Finalement... *Finally . . . ,* II, 4

fixer: fixer la date *to choose the date,* II, 10

le flamant *flamingo,* III, 7

la flèche *arrow,* III, 12

le fleuret *foil (sword),* III, 12

le fleuriste *florist's shop,* II, 3

les fleurs (f.) *flowers,* II, 3

la flûte *flute,* III, 11

la fois: Ça va pour cette fois. *OK, just this once.* III, 3; **une fois par semaine** *once a week,* I, 4

foncé(e) *dark,* III, 4

le fonceur (la fonceuse) *a "go-getter," an ambitious person,* III, 12

le fond: Au fond. *Towards the back.* III, 2

le fond de teint *foundation,* III, 4

le foot(ball) *soccer,* I, 1; **le football américain** *football,* I, 4

la forêt: en forêt *to the forest,* I, 11; **la forêt tropicale** *tropical rainforest,* II, 4

la forme: Tu n'as pas l'air en forme. *You don't seem too well.* II, 7; **forme tunique** *tunic style,* III, 4

formidable: C'était formidable! *It was great!* I, 11

fort(e) *strong,* I, 7; II, 1; **Ce n'est pas mon fort.** *It's not my strong point.* II, 5; **Je t'embrasse bien fort.** *Hugs and kisses.* III, 8

fortiche: Tu es fortiche. *You're really strong.* III, 10

fou (folle) *crazy, funny,* III, 2; **C'est fou comme... !** *I can't believe how . . . !* III, 7

fouiller *to rummage around,* III, 6

la fougère *fern,* III, 10

le foulard *scarf,* II, 3; III, 4

la foule *crowd,* III, 8

se fouler: se fouler la cheville *to sprain one's ankle,* II, 7

la fourmi *ant,* III, 7

la fourrure *fur,* III, 7

les frais (m.) *fees,* III, 5

frais: Il fait frais. *It's cool.* I, 4

les fraises (f.) *strawberries,* I, 8

le franc *(the French monetary unit),* I, 3

le français *French (language),* I, 1

la frange *bangs,* III, 4

le frappeur *the batter (in baseball),* III, 12

les freins (m.) *the brakes,* III, 2

le frère *brother,* I, 7

frire *to fry,* III, 11

frisé: les cheveux frisés (m.) *curly hair,* III, 4

frit(e) *fried,* III, 11

les frites (f.) *French fries,* I, 1

froid: Il fait froid. *It's cold.* I, 4

le fromage *cheese,* I, 5; II, 3; **fromage de chèvre** *goat cheese,* III, 1

la frousse: J'ai la frousse! *I'm scared to death!* III, 7

les fruits de mer (m.) *seafood,* II, 3

fumer *to smoke,* III, 3

furieux (furieuse) *furious,* II, 9

la fusée *rocket,* III, 2

futé: pas futé(e) *not with it,* III, 6

G

gaffe: Faites gaffe! *Look out!* III, 7

gagner *to win,* I, 9; *to earn,* I, 9

le gant *glove,* III, 4; **Ça te va comme un gant.** *That fits you like a glove.* III, 4; **les gants** (m.) *a pair of gloves,* II, 1; III, 4

garder ta petite sœur *to look after your little sister,* I, 7

le gardien *warden, caretaker,* III, 7

la gare *train station,* II, 2

le gaspillage *waste,* III, 3

gaspiller *to waste,* III, 3

le gâteau *cake,* I, 8

gauche: à gauche *to the left,* I, 12; **à gauche de** *to the left of,* II, 2

la gazelle *gazelle,* III, 7

gêné(e) *embarrassed,* II, 9

gêner: Dites donc, ça vous gênerait de... ? *Hey, do you think you can . . . ?* III, 8; **Non mais, surtout, ne**

vous gênez pas! *Well just go right ahead!* III, 8

génial (e) *great,* I, 2; II, 2

le genre: J'aime bien ce genre de... *I like this type of . . . ,* III, 4

les gens (m.) *people,* III, 8

gentil (gentille) *nice,* I, 7; II, 1; **C'est gentil.** *That's nice of you.* III, 6; **C'est gentil de votre/ta part.** *That's so nice of you.* II, 2

gentillet: gentillet, sans plus *cute (but that's all) ,* II, 11

la géographie *geography,* I, 2

la géométrie *geometry,* I, 2

la gestion *management,* III, 5

le gilet *vest,* II, 11

la girafe *giraffe,* III, 7

la glace *ice cream,* I, 1; **faire du patin à glace** *to ice-skate,* I, 4

le glas *toll, knell,* III, 8

le gnon *blow,* III, 3

le gnou *gnu,* III, 7

le golf *golf,* I, 4; **jouer au golf** *to play golf,* I, 4

le gombo *gumbo,* III, 11; **les gombos okra,** I, 8

la gomme *eraser,* I, 3

gommer *to erase,* III, 4

la gorge: J'ai mal à la gorge *I have a sore throat.* II, 7

le gorille *gorilla,* III, 7

la gourde *canteen,* III, 7

gourmand(e) *someone who loves to eat,* II, 1

le goût *taste,* III, 4; **de mauvais goût** *in poor taste,* III, 2

le goûter *afternoon snack,* I, 8

les goyaves (f.) *guavas,* I, 8

grand(e) *tall, big,* I, 7; II, 1; **moins grand(e) que** *smaller than . . . ,* II, 4; **plus grand(e) que** *bigger than . . . ,* II, 4

grand-chose: Ce n'est pas grand-chose. *It's nothing special.* II, 3; **Pas grand-chose.** *Not much.* I, 6

la grand-mère *grandmother,* I, 7

le grand-père *grandfather,* I, 7

grandir *to grow,* I, 10

la grange *barn,* III, 11

le graphisme *graphic arts,* III, 5

le gratte-ciel *skyscraper,* III, 8

grave: C'est pas grave. *It's not serious.* II, 5

la gregue *a coffeepot (Cajun),* III, 11

grignoter: grignoter entre les repas *snacking between meals,* II, 7

grimper *to climb,* III, 3

la grippe: J'ai la grippe. *I've got the flu.* II, 7

gris(e) *grey,* I, 3

le grognement *growling,* III, 7

gros (grosse) *fat,* I, 7; **Grosses bises.** *Hugs and kisses.* III, 8

grossir *to gain weight,* I, 10

grouiller: Grouille-toi! *Get a move on!* III, 2

le groupe *(music) group,* II, 11

le grumeau *lump,* III, 11

la Guadeloupe *Guadeloupe,* III, 12

le guépard *cheetah,* III, 7

guidée: une visite guidée *a guided tour,* II, 6

la guitare *guitar,* III, 11

la gymnastique *gymnastics,* III, 12; **faire de la gymnastique** *to do gymnastics,* II, 7

H

habile *skillful,* III, 5

s'habiller *to get dressed,* II, 4

l' habitude (f.): **d'habitude** *usually,* I, 4

Haïti (m.) *(no article) Haiti,* III, 12

les haltères (m.) *barbells,* III, 12

l' haltérophilie (f.) *weightlifting,* III, 12

*les hamburgers (m.) *hamburgers,* I, 1

*le hareng *herring,* III, 1

*les haricots (m.) *beans,* I, 8; **haricots verts** *green beans,* I, 8

*haut: En haut. *Upstairs.* III, 2

*les hauts talons (m.) *high heels,* III, 4

l' herbe (f.) *grass,* III, 7

hésiter: Euh... J'hésite. *Oh, I'm not sure.* I, 10; **J'hésite entre... et...** *I can't decide between . . . and . . . ,* III, 1

l' heure (f.): I, 2; **A quelle heure?** *At what time?* I, 6; **A tout à l'heure!** *See you later!* I, 1; **Tu as... à quelle heure?** *At what time do you have . . . ?* I, 2; **à... heures** *at . . . o'clock,* I, 2; **à... heures quarante-cinq** *at . . . forty-five,* I, 2; **à... heures quinze** *at . . . fifteen,* I, 2; **à... heures trente** *at . . . thirty,* I, 2

Heureusement,... *Fortunately, . . . ,* II, 9

heureux: Très heureux (heureuse). *Pleased to meet you.* I, 7

l' hippocampe (m.) *seahorse,* III, 10

l' hippopotame (m.) *hippopotamus,* III, 7

*se hisser *to haul oneself up,* III, 10

l' histoire (f.) *history,* I, 2; **C'est l'histoire de...** *It's the story of . . . ,* II, 11; III, 9; **C'est une belle histoire.** *It's a great story.* II, 11; **C'est une histoire passionnante.** *It's an exciting story.* II, 11; **Est-ce que tu connais l'histoire de... ?** *Do you know the one about . . . ?* 10; **Il n'y a pas d'histoire.** *It has no plot.* II, 11; **l'histoire d'amour** *love story,* II, 9

l' hiver *winter,* I, 4; **en hiver** *in the winter,* I, 4

*le hockey *hockey,* I, 4

*le homard *lobster,* III, 10

l' homme (m.) **d'affaires** *businessman,* III, 5

*la honte: Oh la honte! *How embarrassing!* III, 11

l' horreur (f.): **C'est l'horreur!** *This is just horrible!* III, 8

horrible *terrible,* I, 10

'hors *outside,* III, 12

'les hors-d'œuvre (m.) *hors d'œuvre,* III, 11

'le hot-dog *hot dog,* I, 5

l' hôtel (m.): **A l'hôtel.** *In a hotel.* III, 1

l' huile (f.) *the oil,* III, 2; **mettre de l'huile dans le moteur** *to put oil in the motor,* III, 2

les huîtres (f.) *oysters,* II, 3; III, 11

l' humeur (f): **de mauvaise humeur** *in a bad mood,* II, 9; **de bonne humeur** *in a good mood,* II, 9

l' hyène (f.) *hyena,* III, 7

hyper-cool *super cool,* III, 4

I

ici: **Ici,... tandis que...** *Here, . . . whereas . . .* III, 8

l' idée (f.): **Bonne idée!** *Good idea!* II, 3; **C'est une bonne (excellente) idée.** *That's a good (excellent) idea.,* II, 1; **Je n'en ai aucune idée.** *I have no idea.* III, 5; **Tu as une idée de cadeau pour... ?** *Have you got a gift idea for. . . ?* II, 3

l' île (f.) *island,* II, 4

l' image (f.) *the picture,* III, 9

l' immeuble (m.) *building,* III, 8

impatient(e): **Je suis vraiment impatient(e) de... !** *I can hardly wait to . . . !* III, 12; *I'm really anxious to . . . !* III, 2

l' imperméable (m.) *raincoat,* II, 1

important: **Il est très important que...** *It's very important to . . . ,* III, 7

importer: **du n'importe quoi** *worthless,* II, 11; **N'importe quoi!** *That's ridiculous!* II, 6; *Yeah, right!* III, 10; **Peu importe.** *It doesn't matter.* III, 9

impossible: **C'est impossible.** *It's impossible.* II, 10

l' impression (f.): **J'ai l'impression que...** *I have the impression that . . . ,* III, 11

impressionner *to impress,* III, 10

imprimé(e) *printed,* III, 4

inadmissible: **C'est inadmissible.** *That's not acceptable.* II, 5

incroyable *incredible,* II, 6; **C'était incroyable!** *It was amazing/ unbelievably bad!* II, 5; **Ce qui est incroyable, c'est...** *What's incredible is . . . ,* III, 11

les indications (f.) *directions,* III, 2

infiniment: **Merci infiniment** *Thank you so much.* III, 6

l' infirmier (m.), l'infirmière (f.) *nurse,* III, 5

les informations (f.) *the news,* III, 9

l' informatique (f.) *computer science,* I, 2

l' ingénieur (m.) *engineer,* III, 5

inquiet (inquiète) *worried,* II, 9

s'inquiéter: **Ne t'inquiète pas!** *Don't worry!* III, 6

s'inscrire *to enroll,* III, 5

l' instant (m.): **Un instant, s'il vous plaît.** *One moment, please.* III, 1

l' instituteur (m.), l'institutrice (f.) *elementary school teacher,* III, 5

insupportable: **C'est insupportable, à la fin!** *I won't put up with this!* III, 8

intelligent(e) *smart,* I, 7; II, 1

l' intention (f.): **J'ai l'intention de...** *I intend to . . . ,* I, 11; III, 5; **Qu'est-ce que tu as l'intention de faire?** *What do you intend to do?* III, 5

l' interdiction (f.) *ban,* III, 3; **Interdiction de...** *. . . is not allowed,* III, 3

interdit: **Il est interdit de...** *It's forbidden to . . . ,* III, 3

intéressant *interesting,* I, 2; **Ce qui est intéressant/incroyable, c'est...** *What's interesting/incredible is . . . ,* III, 11

l' intérêt (m.): **Ça n'a aucun intérêt.** *It's not interesting.* III, 9

l' interro (f.) *quiz,* I, 9

les invitations (f.): **envoyer les invitations** *to send the invitations,* II, 10

isolé(e) *isolated,* II, 8

l' Italie (f.) *Italy,* III, 12

J

jamais: **ne... jamais** *never,* I, 4; **Je n'ai jamais vu un(e) aussi...** *I've never seen such a . . . ,* III, 7

le jambalaya *jambalaya,* III, 11

la jambe: **J'ai mal à la jambe** *My leg hurts.* II, 7

le jambon *ham,* I, 5; II, 3

janvier *January,* I, 4

le Japon *Japan,* III, 12

le jardin *yard,* II, 2

jaune *yellow,* I, 3

le jazz *jazz,* II, 11; III, 11

le jean *(a pair of) jeans,* I, 3; II, 1; **en jean** *denim,* I, 10

jeter: **jeter les déchets** *to throw away your trash,* II, 12; **jeter des ordures** *to throw trash,* III, 3

le jeu télévisé *game show,* III, 9

le jeudi *on Thursdays,* I, 2

jeune *young,* I, 7; II, 1

la jeunesse *youth,* III, 5; **l'auberge (f.) de jeunesse** *youth hostel,* II, 2

les jeux (m.): **jouer à des jeux vidéo** *to play video games,* I, 4

le jogging: **faire du jogging** *to jog,* I, 4

jouer *to play,* I, 4; **jouer à...** *to play . . . ,* I, 4; **Qu'est-ce qu'on joue comme film?** *What films are playing?* II, 11; **On joue... . . . is showing.** II, 11

le jour: **C'est pas mon jour!** *It's just not my day!* II, 5

le/la journaliste *journalist,* III, 5

la journée: **avoir une journée épou-**vantable *to have a horrible day,* II, 5; **Comment s'est passée ta journée (hier)?** *How was your day (yesterday)?* II, 5; **Quelle journée!** *What a bad day!* II, 5; **Quelle journée formidable!** *What a great day!* II, 5

joyeux (joyeuse) *cheerful,* III, 6; **Joyeux (Bon) anniversaire!** *Happy birthday!* II, 3; **Joyeux Noël!** *Merry Christmas!* II, 3

le judo *judo,* III, 12

le juge *judge,* III, 5

juillet *July,* I, 4

juin *June,* I, 4

les jumeaux (-elles) *twins,* III, 6

les jumelles (f.) *binoculars,* III, 7

la jupe *skirt,* I, 10

le jus: **le jus d'orange** *orange juice,* I, 5; **le jus de pomme** *apple juice,* I, 5

jusqu'à: **Vous allez tout droit jusqu'à...** *You go straight ahead until you get to . . . ,* 12

juste: **C'est pas juste.** *It's not fair.* III, 12; **Juste là, à côté de...** *Right there, next to . . . ,* III, 2

K

le kilo: **un kilo de** *a kilogram of,* I, 8

le klaxon *car horn,* III, 8

L

-là *there (noun suffix),* I, 3; **(Est-ce que)... est là, s'il vous plaît?** *Is . . . , there, please?* I, 9; **Là, c'est...** *Here (There) is . . . ,* II, 2; **C'est comment, la vie là-bas?** *What's life like there?* III, 12; **Là-bas, le garçon qui...** *Over there, the boy who . . . ,* III, 4

lâcher: **Lâche-moi, tu veux?** *Will you give me a break?* III, 10

laisser: **Je peux laisser un message?** *Can I leave a message?* I, 9

la laine: **en laine** *wool,* III, 4

le lait *milk,* I, 8; II, 3

la lampe *lamp,* II, 2; **la lampe de poche** *flashlight,* II, 12

le lancer du disque *the discus throw,* III, 12

le lanceur *the pitcher (baseball),* III, 12

Laquelle? *Which one?* III, 4

large *baggy,* I, 10

largement: **On a largement le temps!** *We've got plenty of time!* III, 2

le latin *Latin,* I, 2

laver: **laver la voiture** *to wash the car,* I, 7; **laver les vitres (f.)** *to wash the windows,* III, 3; **se laver** *to wash oneself,* II, 4;

les légumes (m.) *vegetables,* II, 7

Lequel? *Which one?* III, 4

Lesquels/Lesquelles? *Which ones?* III, 4

la lessive: faire la lessive *to do the laundry,* III, 3

se lever *to get up,* II, 4

lever: Levez la main! *Raise your hand!* I, 0; **Levez-vous!** *Stand up!* I, 0

la librairie *bookstore,* I, 12

libre: Je suis quand même libre, non? *I'm free, aren't I?* III, 3

la limonade *lemon soda,* I, 5

le lion *lion,* III, 7

lire *to read,* I, 1

le lit *bed,* II, 2; **faire son lit** *to make one's bed,* III, 3

le litre: un litre de *a liter of,* I, 8

la livre: une livre de *a pound of,* I, 8

le livre *book,* I, 3; **le livre de poésie** *book of poetry,* II, 11

loin: loin de *far from,* I, 12

long *long,* II, 1; **les cheveux longs (m.)** *long hair,* III, 4; **trop long** *too long,* II, 11

longtemps: Ça fait longtemps qu'on ne s'est pas vu(e)s. *It's been a long time since we've seen each other.* III, 1; **Ça ne va pas prendre longtemps!** *It's not going to take long!* III, 2

lorsque *when,* III, 3

la lotion anti-moustique(s) *mosquito repellent,* II, 7

loufoque *wild, crazy,* III, 2

le loup *wolf,* II, 12

lourd(e) *heavy,* III, 7; **C'est lourd.** *It's dull.* III, 9

luire *to gleam,* III, 10

les lumières (f.) *lights,* III, 3

le lundi *on Mondays,* I, 2

les lunettes de soleil (f.) *sunglasses,* I, 10

la lutte *wrestling,* III, 12

le lycée *high school,* II, 2

M

madame (Mme) *ma'am; Mrs,* I, 1; **Madame!** *Waitress!* I, 5; **Monsieur/Madame (to start a business letter)** *Sir/Madam,* III, 5

mademoiselle (Mlle) *miss; Miss,* I, 1; **Mademoiselle!** *Waitress!* I, 5

les magasins (m.) *stores,* I, 1; **faire les magasins** *to go shopping,* I, 1

le magazine *magazine,* I, 3; **magazine télévisé** *magazine show,* III, 9

le magnétoscope *videocassette recorder, VCR,* I, 0; III, 9

magnifique *beautiful,* II, 6

mai *May,* I, 4

maigrir *to lose weight,* I, 10

maigrichon *scrawny, skinny,* III, 2

le maillot de bain *a bathing suit,* I, 10

la main *hand,* I, 0; **J'ai mal à la main** *My hand hurts.*

mais *but,* I, 1; **Non mais, tu t'es pas regardé(e)!** *If you could see how you look!* III, 10

le maïs *corn,* I, 8

la Maison des jeunes et de la culture (MJC) *recreation center,* I, 6

mal: mal à l'aise *uncomfortable,* II, 9; **Il n'y a pas de mal.** *No harm done.* II, 10; **J'ai du mal à me décider.** *I'm having trouble deciding.* III, 5; **J'ai mal dormi.** *I didn't sleep well.* II, 7; **J'ai mal partout!** *I hurt all over!* II, 7; **J'ai mal... My . . . hurts.** II, 7; **J'ai trouvé ça pas mal.** *It was not bad.* III, 9; **Pas mal.** *Not bad.* I, 1; *all right,* II, 6; **se faire mal à...** *to hurt one's . . . ,* II, 7; III, 10; **mal élevé(e)** *rude,* III, 8

malade: Je suis malade. *I'm sick.* II, 7; **tomber malade** *to get sick,* III, 10

la malédiction *curse,* III, 8

le malentendu: un petit malentendu *a little misunderstanding,* II, 10

Malheureusement,... *Unfortunately, . . . ,* II, 9

malicieusement *mischievously,* III, 10

les manches (f.): à manches courtes/ longues *short/long-sleeved,* III, 4

manger *to eat,* I, 6; II, 7; **donner à manger aux animaux** *to feed the animals,* II, 6; **manger mieux** *to eat better,* III, 3

les mangues (f.) *mangoes,* I, 8

manier *to handle,* III, 5

le mannequin *model,* III, 5

manquer: C'est à ne pas manquer! *Don't miss it!* III, 9; **... me manque.** *I miss . . . (singular subject),* II, 8; **... me manquent.** *I miss . . . (plural subject),* II, 8; **Ce qui me manque, c'est...** *What I miss is . . . ,* II, 8

le manteau *coat,* I, 10

le maquillage *makeup,* III, 4

se maquiller *to put on makeup,* III, 4

le maquis *popular Ivorian outdoor restaurant,* II, 8

le marais *marsh, swamp,* III, 11

la marche: rater une marche *to miss a step,* II, 5

le mardi *on Tuesdays,* I, 2

le mari *husband,* III, 6

marié(e) *married,* III, 6

se marier *to get married,* III, 5

le Maroc *Morocco,* III, 12

la maroquinerie *leather-goods shop,* II, 3

marrant(e) *funny,* III, 2

marre: J'en ai vraiment marre! *I'm sick of this!* III, 12; **Je commence à en avoir marre!** *I've just about had it!* III, 8

marron *brown,* I, 3; II, 1

mars *March,* I, 4

le masque *mask,* II, 8; III, 12

m'as-tu-vu: être m'as-tu-vu *to be a show off,* III, 7

le match: regarder un match *to watch a game (on TV),* I, 6; **voir**

un match *to see a game (in person),* I, 6

les maths (f.) *math,* I, 1

les matières grasses (f.) *fat,* II, 7

le matin *in the morning,* I, 2

mauvais(e): de mauvais goût *in poor taste,* III, 2; **avoir une mauvaise note** *to get a bad grade,* II, 5; **de mauvaise humeur** *in a bad mood,* II, 9

le mec: C'est l'histoire d'un mec qui... *It's about a guy who . . . ,* III, 10

le mécanicien (la mécanicienne) *mechanic,* III, 5

méchant(e) *mean,* I, 7; II, 1

le médecin *doctor,* III, 5

les médicaments (m.) *medicine,* I, 12

la méduse *jellyfish,* III, 10

Méfiez-vous! *Be careful!* III, 7

meilleur(e): C'est meilleur que... *It's better than . . . ,* II, 7; **C'est moi le/la meilleur(e).** *I'm the best.* III, 10; **Tu es vraiment le/la meilleur(e).** *You're really the best.* III, 10; **Meilleurs vœux!** *Best wishes!* II, 3

mélanger *to mix,* III, 1

mêler *to mix,* III, 11; **Mêle-toi de tes oignons!** *Mind your own business!* III, 6

même: C'est toujours la même chose! *It's always the same!* III, 6; **Toujours la même chose!** *Same old thing!* III, 1

le ménage: faire le ménage *to do housework,* I, 1; II, 10

mener *to lead,* III, 2

mentir *to lie,* III, 6

le menu *fixed-price menu,* III, 1

le menuisier *carpenter,* III, 5

la mer *sea,* II, 4; **au bord de la mer** *to/at the coast,* I, 11

Merci. *Thank you,* I, 3; II, 2; **Merci bien/infiniment/mille fois.** *Thank you so much.* III, 6; **Merci, ça va.** *No thank you, I've had enough.* II, 3; **Non, merci.** *No, thank you.* I, 8

le mercredi *on Wednesdays,* I, 2

la mère *mother,* I, 7

la météo *the weather report,* III, 9

le métier *job, occupation,* III, 5; **choisir un métier** *to choose a career,* III, 5

le métissage *crossbreeding,* III, 4

le métro: au métro... *at the . . . metro stop,* I, 6; **en métro** *by subway,* I, 12

le metteur en scène *director,* III, 9

mettre *to put, to put on, to wear,* I, 10; **Je ne sais pas quoi mettre pour...** *I don't know what to wear for . . . ;* **mettre: mets: Qu'est-ce que je mets?** *What shall I wear?* I, 10; **mettre la table** *to set the table,* III, 3; **se mettre en condition** *to get into shape,* II, 7; **Mettez-vous à l'aise.** *Make yourself comfortable.* III, 6

se mettre à *to start,* III, 1

meurs: Je meurs de faim (soif)! *Yes, I'm dying of hunger (thirst)!* II, 2

le Mexique *Mexico,* III, 12

le micro (le microphone) *the mike, the microphone,* III, 11

midi *noon,* I, 6

mieux: C'est moi qui... le mieux. *I . . . the best.* III, 10; **Ça va aller mieux!** *It's going to get better!* I, 9; **J'aime mieux...** *I prefer . . . ,* II, 1; **manger mieux** *to eat better,* III, 3; **Tu ferais mieux de...** *You would do better to . . . ,* III, 5

mignon(ne) *cute,* I, 7; II, 1

mijoter *to simmer,* III, 11

militaire: faire son service militaire *to do one's military service,* III, 5

le mille-feuille *layered pastry,* II, 3

le millénaire *millenium, thousand-year-old,* III, 4

mince *slender,* I, 7

la mini-jupe *miniskirt,* III, 4

minuit *midnight,* I, 6

la minute: Tu as une minute? *Do you have a minute?* I, 9; II, 10

les mocassins (m.) *loafers,* III, 4

moche: Je le/la/les trouve moche(s). *I think it's (they're) really tacky.* I, 10

la mode: à la mode *in style,* I, 10

moi *me,* I, 2

moins: La vie était plus... moins... *Life was more . . . , less . . . ,* II, 8; **moins cinq** *five to,* I, 6; **moins de... que** *fewer . . . than . . . ,* III, 8; **moins grand(e) que** *smaller than . . . ,* II, 4; **moins le quart** *quarter to,* I, 6; **moins... que...** *less . . . than . . . ,* III, 8; **Plus ou moins.** *More or less.* II, 6

la moisson *harvest,* III, 1

le moment: A ce moment-là... *At that point . . . ,* II, 9; III, 9; **Un moment, s'il vous plaît.** *One moment, please.* I, 5

monsieur (M.) *sir; Mr.* I, 1; **Monsieur!** *Waiter!* I, 5; **Monsieur/Madame (to start a business letter)** *Sir/Madame,* III, 5

la montagne: à la montagne *to/at the mountains,* I, 11; **faire du vélo de montagne** *to go mountain-bike riding,* II, 12; **les montagnes russes** *the roller coaster,* II, 6

monter *to go up,* II, 6; **monter dans une tour** *to go up in a tower,* II, 6

la montre *watch,* I, 3

montrer *to show,* I, 9

se moquer de *to tease, make fun of,* III, 10

le morceau: un morceau de *a piece of,* I, 8

mort(e) *dead,* III, 1

mortel(le) *deadly boring,* II, 6; III, 2

la mosquée *mosque,* II, 8

la motivation *incentive,* III, 5

Mouais. *Yeah.* II, 6

la mouche *fly,* III, 7

la mouffette *skunk,* II, 12

mourir *to die,* II, 6; **Ça m'ennuie à mourir!** *That bores me to death!* III, 2; **Je me suis ennuyé(e) à mourir.** *I was bored to death.* III, 9

la moustache *mustache,* III, 4

le moustique *mosquito,* II, 4

le mouton *sheep,* III, 8

moyenne: de taille moyenne *of medium height,* II, 1

la musculation: faire de la musculation *to lift weights,* II, 7

le museau *muzzle, snout,* III, 1

le musée *museum,* I, 6; II, 2

le musicien (la musicienne) *musician,* II, 11

la musique *music,* I, 2; **la musique cajun** *Cajun music,* III, 11; **la musique classique** *classical music,* II, 11; III, 11; **écouter de la musique** *to listen to music,* I, 1; **Qu'est-ce que tu aimes comme musique?** *What music do you like?* II, 1

musulman *Muslim,* III, 8

mutiler: mutiler les arbres *to deface the trees,* II, 12

nager *to swim,* I, 1

naître *to be born,* II, 6

la natation *swimming,* III, 12; **faire de la natation** *to swim,* I, 4

la natte *braid,* III, 4

nautique: faire du ski nautique *to water ski,* I, 4

le navet: C'est un navet. *It stinks.* II, 11; *It's trash.* III, 9

ne: ne... pas *not,* I, 1; **ne... jamais** *never,* I, 4; **ne... pas encore** *not yet,* I, 9; **ne... aucun(e)** *no . . . ,* III, 9; **ne... ni... ni...** *neither . . . nor . . . ,* III, 9; **ne... nulle part** *nowhere,* III, 9; **ne... personne** *no one,* III, 9; **ne... rien** *nothing,* III, 9; **ne... que** *only,* III, 9; **Tu n'as qu'à...** *All you have to do is . . . ,* II, 7

nécessaire: Il est nécessaire que... *It's necessary to . . . ,* III, 7

néfaste *harmful,* III, 8

la neige: enlever la neige *to shovel snow,* III, 3; **Il neige.** *It's snowing.* I, 4

nettoyer: nettoyer la salle de bains *to clean the bathroom,* III, 3; **nettoyer le pare-brise** *to clean the windshield,* III, 2; **nettoyer le parquet** *to clean the floor,* III, 3

neuf: Quoi de neuf? *What's new?* III, 1

le neveu *nephew,* III, 6

le nez: J'ai le nez qui coule. *I've got a runny nose.* II, 7

la nièce *niece,* III, 6

Noël: Joyeux Noël! *Merry Christmas!* II, 3

noir(e) *black,* I, 3; II, 1

les noix de coco (f.) *coconuts,* I, 8

non *no,* I, 1; **Moi non plus.** *Neither do I.* I, 2; **Moi, non.** *I don't.* I, 2; **Non, pas trop.** *No, not too much.* I, 2

le nord: dans le nord *in the north,* II, 4; **C'est au nord de...** *It's to the north of . . . ,* II, 12

normal: C'est tout à fait normal. *You don't have to thank me.* III, 6

la note: avoir une mauvaise note *to get a bad grade,* II, 5

la nouille *noodle,* III, 1

se nourrir: bien se nourrir *eat well,* II, 7; **nourrir les animaux** *to feed the animals,* II, 12

nouveau (nouvelle) *new,* II, 2

novembre *November,* I, 4

nul (nulle) *useless,* I, 2; *worthless,* II, 8; **C'est nul.** *It's no good.* III, 9; **Qu'est-ce que je peux être nul(le)!** *I just can't do anything right!* III, 12

obtenir: obtenir son diplôme *to get one's diploma,* III, 5

occupé: C'est occupé. *It's busy.* I, 9; **Désolé(e), je suis occupé(e).** *Sorry, I'm busy.* I, 6

s'occuper de *to take care of,* III, 8

octobre *October,* I, 4

l' œil (m.) (pl. les yeux) *eye,* II, 1; **Mon œil!** *Yeah, right!* II, 6; *No way!* III, 10

les œufs (m.) *eggs,* I, 8; II, 3

l' office de tourisme (m.) *tourist information office,* II, 2

offrir (à quelqu'un) *to give (to someone),* II, 10; **Qu'est-ce que je peux vous offrir?** *What can I offer you?* III, 6; **Qu'est-ce que je pourrais offrir à... ?** *What could I give to . . . ?* II, 3; **Tu pourrais lui/leur offrir...** *You could give him/her . . . ,* II, 3; **Offre-lui/leur...** *Give him/her/them . . . ,* II, 3

oh: Oh là là! *Oh no!* II, 5; *Wow!* III, 10; **Oh dis donc!** *Wow,* III, 9

l' oiseau (m.) *bird,* III, 7

les okras (m.) *okra,* III, 11

l' olive (f.) *olive,* III, 8

l' olivier (m.) *olive tree,* III, 8

l' ombre à paupières (f.) *eyeshadow,* III, 4

on: On... ? *How about . . . ?* I, 4; **On pourrait...** *We could . . . ,* II, 1

l' oncle (m.) *uncle,* I, 7

l' onglet (m.) *prime cut of beef,* III, 1

opprimer *to oppress,* III, 8

orange (inv.) *orange,* I, 3

les oranges (f.) *oranges,* I, 8

l' ordinateur (m.) *computer,* I, 3

les ordures (f.): jeter des ordures *to throw trash,* III, 3

les oreilles (f.): J'ai mal aux oreilles *My ears hurt.* II, 7

original: C'est original. *That's unique.* II, 3

l' orignal (m.) *moose,* II, 12

l' orthographe *spelling,* III, 2

où: D'où vient le mot... ? *Where does the word . . . come from?* III, 11; Où ça? *Where?* I, 6; Où est-ce que tu vas aller... ? *Where are you going to go . . . ?* I, 11; Où est... s'il vous plaît? *Where is . . . , please?* II, 2; Où se trouve... ? *Where is . . . ?* II, 4; Tu es allé(e) où? *Where did you go?* I, 9; Tu es d'où? *Where are you from?* III, 12; Vous pourriez me dire où il y a... ? *Could you tell me where I could find . . . ?* III, 2

Ouah! *Wow!* III, 7

oublier *to forget,* I, 9; N'oublie pas de... *Don't forget to . . .* I, 8; II, 1; Oublie-le/-la/-les! *Forget him/her/them!* I, 9; II, 10; Je n'ai rien oublié. *I didn't forget anything.* I, 11; Tu n'as pas oublié... ? *You didn't forget . . . ?* I, 11

l' ouest (m.): dans l'ouest *in the west,* II, 4; C'est à l'ouest de... *It's to the west of . . . ,* II, 12

ouf: Ouf! On a eu chaud! *Whew! That was a real scare!* III, 7

oui *yes,* I, 1

l' ours (m.) *bear,* II, 12

l' ouvrier (l'ouvrière) *worker,* III, 5

ouvrir: A quelle heure est-ce que vous ouvrez? *When do you open?* II, 6; Ouvrez vos livres à la page... *Open your books to page . . . ,* I, 0

P

la page *page,* I, 0

le pagne *piece of Ivorian cloth,* II, 8

pailleté *sequined,* III, 10

le pain *bread,* I, 8; II, 3; pain au chocolat *croissant with a chocolate filling,* II, 3

la paix: Fiche-moi la paix! *Leave me alone!* III, 6

la palmeraie *palm grove,* III, 8

le palmier *palm tree,* II, 4

le paludisme *malaria,* III, 7

le panier (m.) *basket,* II, 12

la panique: Pas de panique! *Don't panic!* III, 7

panne: tomber en panne *to break down,* II, 9; tomber en panne d'essence *(to run out of gas),* III, 2

le panneau *sign,* III, 2; Vous allez voir un panneau qui indique l'entrée de l'autoroute. *You'll see a sign that points out the freeway entrance.* III, 2

les pansements (m.) *bandages,* III, 7

le pantalon *a pair of pants,* I, 10

les papayes (f.) *papayas,* I, 8

la papeterie *stationery store,* I, 12

le papier *paper,* I, 0; III, 3

le papillon *butterfly,* III, 7

le paquet: un paquet de *a carton/box of,* I, 8

par: Par là, au bout du couloir. *Over there, at the end of the hallway.* III, 2; par terre *on the ground,* III, 3

le parc *park,* I, 6; II, 2; visiter un parc d'attractions *to visit an amusement park,* II, 6

parce que: Ce n'est pas parce que tout le monde... que tu dois le faire. *Just because everyone else . . . doesn't mean you have to.* III, 3

Pardon *Pardon me,* I, 3; demander pardon à (quelqu'un) *to ask (someone's) forgiveness,* II, 10; Pardon, madame. *Excuse me, ma'am.* I, 12; Pardon, mademoiselle. Où est... , s'il vous plaît? *Excuse me, miss. Where is . . . Please?* I, 12; Pardon, monsieur. Je cherche... , s'il vous plaît. *Excuse me, sir. I'm looking for . . . , please.* I, 12; Pardonne-moi de... *Pardon me for . . . ,* III, 6

pardonner à (quelqu'un) *to forgive (someone),* II, 10

le pare-brise: nettoyer le pare-brise *to clean the windshield,* III, 2

pareil: Tout le monde fait pareil. *Everybody does it.* III, 3

parfait: C'est parfait. *It's perfect.* I, 10

parier: Je parie que... *I bet that . . . ,* II, 9

parler: (Est-ce que) je peux parler à... ? *Could I speak to . . . ?* I, 9; Je peux te parler? *Can I talk to you?* I, 9; parler au téléphone *to talk on the phone,* I, 1; Tu parles! *No way!* III, 9; Ça parle de... *It's about . . . ,* II, 11; De quoi ça parle? *What's it about?* II, 11; Ne parle pas si fort. *Don't speak so loudly.* III, 9; Parle-lui/-leur. *Talk to him/her/them.* II, 10

le parquet: nettoyer le parquet *to clean the floor,* III, 3

la part: C'est vraiment très gentil de votre part. *That's very nice of you.* III, 6

partager: partager ses affaires *to share,* III, 3; partager son véhicule *to share one's vehicle,* III, 3

particulière *private,* III, 8

partir *to leave,* I, 11; II, 6; Tu ne peux pas partir sans... *You can't leave without . . . ,* 11; Je suis parti(e) en... *I went by . . . ,* III, 1; Non, je suis parti(e)... *No, I went away for . . . ;* Tu es parti(e) comment? *How did you get there?* III, 1

partout: J'ai mal partout! *I hurt all over!* II, 7

pas: (Il n'y a) pas de quoi. *It's nothing.* III, 6; Pas du tout. *Not at all.* II, 10; III, 9; Pas mal. *Not bad.* I, 1; Pas mauvais *Not bad,* I, 9; Pas question! *Out of the question!* I, 7; *No way!,* II, 1; Pas super *not so hot,* I, 2; Pas terrible. *Not so great.* I, 1

le passage pour piétons *pedestrian crossing,* III, 8

le passeport *passport,* I, 11; II, 1

passer: Tu pourrais passer à... ? *Could you go by . . . ?* I, 12; Vous passez devant... *You'll pass . . . ,* 12; Ça passe à... *It's playing at . . . ,* II, 11; Ça passe où? *Where is that playing?* II, 11; Ça se passe... *It takes place . . . ,* III, 9; Qu'est-ce qui se passe? *What's going on?* II, 5; Ça s'est bien passé? *Did it go well?* I, 9; Ça s'est très bien passé! *It went really well!* II, 5; Comment ça s'est passé? *How did it go?* II, 5; expliquer ce qui s'est passé (à quelqu'un) *to explain what happened (to someone),* II, 10; J'ai passé une journée épouvantable! *I had a terrible day!* II, 5; Qu'est-ce qui s'est passé? *What happened?* I, 9; Tu as passé un bon week-end? *Did you have a good weekend?* I, 9

passionnant(e): *fascinating,* I, 2; C'est une histoire passionnante. *It's an exciting story.* II, 11

le pâté *paté,* II, 3

les pâtes (f.) *pasta,* II, 7

patient: Sois patient(e)! *Be patient!* III, 2

le patin: faire du patin à glace *to ice-skate,* I, 4

la pâtisserie *pastry shop,* I, 12; II, 3

le pattes d'eph *bell-bottoms,* III, 4

les pattes (f.) *sideburns,* III, 4

les paupières (f.) *the eyelids,* III, 4

pauvre: Pauvre vieille! *You poor thing!* II, 5

payer *to pay,* III, 4; Oh, tu sais, je ne l'ai pas payé(e) cher. *Oh, it wasn't expensive.* III, 4

le paysage *scenery, landscape,* III, 10

la peau *skin,* III, 7

la pêche: aller à la pêche *to go fishing,* II, 4

pêcher *to fish,* III, 8

les pêches (f.) *peaches,* I, 8

les pêcheurs: village de pêcheurs *fishing village,* II, 4

pédestre: faire une randonnée pédestre *to go for a hike,* II, 12

la peine: Ce n'est pas la peine. *It's not worth it.* III, 7

la pellicule *roll of film,* III, 7

la pelouse: tondre la pelouse *to mow the lawn,* III, 3

peluche *plush,* III, 11

pendant: Pour (aller à)... vous suivez la... pendant à peu près... kilomètres. *To get to . . . , follow . . . for about . . . kilometers.* III, 2

le pendentif *pendant,* III, 4

pénible *a pain in the neck,* I, 7; *a pain,* II, 1

penser *to think,* I, 11; **J'ai pensé à tout.** *I've thought of everything.* I, 11; **Je ne pense pas que...** *I don't think that . . . ,* III, 7; **Je pense...** *I think I'll . . . ,* III, 5; **Pense à prendre...** *Remember to take . . . ,* II, 1; **Pense aux autres.** *Think about other people.* III, 3; **Qu'en penses-tu?** *What do you think of it?* III, 4; **Qu'est-ce que tu penses de... ?** *What do you think of . . . ?* III, 4; *What do you say about . . . ?* III, 11; **Qu'est-ce que tu penses faire?** *What do you think you'll do?* III, 5

perdre *to lose,* II, 5; **perdre du poids** *to lose weight,* III, 10; **se perdre** *to get lost,* II, 9

le père *father,* I, 7

la permanente *perm,* III, 4

le permis: passer son permis de conduire *to get one's driver's license,* III, 5

la permission: demander la permission à tes parents *to ask your parents' permission,* II, 10

petit(e) *short (height),* I, 7; II, 1; *small,* I, 10; II, 1; **petit déjeuner** *breakfast,* I, 8; **le petit-fils** *grandson,* III, 6; **la petite-fille** *granddaughter,* III, 6; **Quand il/elle était petit(e),...** *When he/she was little, . . . ,* II, 8; **Quand j'étais petit(e),...** *When I was little, . . . ,* II, 8

les petits pois (m.) *peas,* I, 8

peu: Peu importe. *It doesn't matter.* III, 9; **Un peu.** *A little.* II, 2

la peur: J'ai peur (de la, du, des)... *I'm scared (of) . . . ,* II, 12; **J'ai peur que...** *I'm afraid that . . . ,* III, 7; **J'ai très peur de...** *I'm very afraid of . . . ,* III, 7; **N'ayez pas peur.** *Don't be afraid.* III, 7

peut-être *maybe,* II, 3; **Peut-être que...** *Maybe . . . ,* II, 9; III, 5; **Tu as peut-être raison.** *Maybe you're right.* II, 9

la pharmacie *drugstore,* I, 12

le/la pharmacien(ne) *pharmacist,* III, 5

les photos (f.): **faire des photos** *to take pictures,* I, 4

la physique *physics,* I, 2

le piano *piano,* III, 11

la pièce *room (of a house),* II, 2; **voir une pièce** *to see a play,* I, 6

le pied: à pied *on foot,* I, 12; **C'est le pied!** *Cool! Neat!* III, 7; **C'est vraiment le pied!** *That's really neat!* III, 12; **J'ai mal aux pieds** *My feet hurt.* II, 7

la pieuvre *octopus,* III, 10

le pilote *pilot,* III, 5

les pinces (f.): **à pinces** *pleated,* III, 4

le pique-nique: faire un pique-nique *to have a picnic,* I, 6; II, 6

la piqûre *shot,* III, 7

la piscine *swimming pool,* I, 6; II, 2

la pizza *pizza,* I, 1

la place: la place de stationnement *parking place,* III, 8; **A ta place,...** *If I were in your place, . . . ,* III, 8

la plage *beach,* I, 1; II, 4

plaire: Tu vas te plaire ici. *You're going to like it here.* II, 8; **Ça me plairait beaucoup.** *I'd like that a lot.* III, 6; **Ça te plairait de...** *Would you like to . . . ?* III, 6; **Ce qui me plairait, c'est de...** *What I would like is to . . . ,* III, 5; **Il/Elle me plaît, mais il/elle est cher.** *I like it, but it's expensive.* I, 10; **Il/Elle te/vous plaît?** *Do you like it?* I, 10; **Ce qui me plaît, c'est...** *What I like is . . . ,* II, 4; **Ce qui ne me plaît pas, c'est...** *What I don't care for is . . . ,* II, 4; **s'il vous/te plaît** *please,* I, 3; **Un... s'il vous plaît.** *A . . . , please.* II, 6

plaisanter *to joke,* III, 10; **Tu plaisantes!** *You're joking!* II, 6

plaisir: Avec plaisir. *With pleasure.* II, 10; **Ça me fait plaisir de vous voir.** *I'm happy to see you.* III, 6; **Je ne dis pas ça pour te faire plaisir.** *And I'm not just saying that.* III, 4; **Oui, avec plaisir.** *Yes, with pleasure.* I, 8

la planche: faire de la planche à voile *to go windsurfing,* I, 11; II, 4

planter: planter un arbre *to plant a tree,* III, 3; **planter la voiture** *to wreck the car,* III, 10

le plastique *plastic,* III, 3

les plats (m.) *main dishes,* III, 1; **le plat principal** *main course,* II, 3

plein: C'est plein de rebondissements. *It's full of plot twists.* II, 11; **faire le plein** *to fill it up,* III, 2

pleurer *to cry,* III, 1

Pleurnicheur (-euse)! *Crybaby!* III, 6

pleut: Il pleut. *It's raining.* I, 4

le plombier *plumber,* III, 5

la plongée: faire de la plongée avec un tuba *to snorkel,* II, 4; **faire de la plongée sous-marine** *to go scuba diving,* II, 4

le plongeoir *diving board,* III, 12

le plongeon acrobatique *diving,* III, 12

plonger *to dive,* III, 12

plu (pp. of plaire): **Ça m'a beaucoup plu.** *I liked it a lot.* III, 9; **Ça t'a plu?** *Did you like it?* II, 6

plu (pp. of pleuvoir): **Il a plu tout le temps.** *It rained the whole time.* III, 1

plus: Je n'en peux plus! *I just can't do any more!* II, 7; **Je n'en veux plus.** *I don't want anymore,* I, 8; **Je ne sais plus ce que je veux.** *I don't know what I want anymore.* III, 5; **plus tard** *later,* III, 5; **La vie était plus...** *Life was more . . . ,* II, 8; **Moi non plus.** *Neither do I.* I, 2; **Non, merci. Je n'ai plus faim.** *No thanks. I'm not hungry anymore.* I, 8; **plus de... que** *more . . . than . . . ,* III, 8; **plus grand(e) que** *bigger than . . . ,* II, 4; **Plus ou moins.** *More or less.* II, 6; **Tu es le/la... le/la plus... que je connaisse.** *You're the . . . -est . . . I know.* III, 10

plutôt *rather,* III, 9

les pneus (m.) *tires,* III, 2; **avoir un pneu crevé** *to have a flat tire,* III, 2

le po-boy *po-boy sandwich,* III, 11

la poêle *pan,* III, 11

le poids: perdre du poids *to lose weight,* III, 10

le point d'eau *watering hole,* III, 7; **A point.** *Medium rare.* III, 1; **Quel est le point commun entre... ?** *What do . . . and . . . have in common?* 10

les poireaux (m.) *leeks,* III, 1

les poires (f.) *pears,* I, 8

les pois (m.): **les petits pois** (m.) *peas,* I, 8; **à pois** *polka-dot,* III, 4

le poisson *fish,* I, 7; II, 3

la poissonnerie *fish shop,* II, 3

le poivron *pepper,* III, 1

poli(e) *polite,* III, 3

la pollution *pollution,* III, 8

le polo *polo shirt,* III, 4

les pommes (f.) *apples,* I, 8; **les pommes de terre** (f.) *potatoes,* I, 8; **les pommes mousseline** (f.) *mashed potatoes,* III, 1

les pompes (f.): **faire des pompes** *to do push-ups,* II, 7

le pompiste (la pompiste) *gas station attendant,* III, 2

le pop *popular, mainstream music,* II, 11

le porc *pork,* I, 8; III, 11; **la côtelette de porc pâtes** *porkchop with pasta,* III, 1

la porte *door,* I, 0

porter *to wear,* I, 10

le portefeuille *wallet,* I, 3; II, 3

possible: Pas possible! *No way!* II, 6; **C'est pas possible!** *No way!* III, 12; **Ce n'est pas possible.** *That's not possible.* II, 9; **C'est possible.** *That's possible.* II, 9; **Il est possible que...** *It's possible that . . . ,* III, 5; **Si c'était possible,...** *If it were possible, . . . ,* III, 8; **Vous serait-il possible de... ?** *Would it be possible for you to . . . ?* III, 5

la poste *post office,* I, 12; II, 12

le poster *poster,* I, 3; II, 2

le potage *soup,* III, 1

la poterie *pottery,* II, 8; III, 8

la potiche *oriental vase,* III, 9

la poubelle *trashcan,* I, 7; sortir la poubelle *to take out the trash,* I, 7

le pouce *inch,* III, 11

le pouding au pain *bread pudding,* III, 11

la poule *chicken,* III, 8

le poulet *chicken (meat),* I, 8; II, 3; le poulet haricots verts *roasted chicken with green beans,* III, 1

pour: Qu'est-ce qu'il te faut pour... ? *What do you need for . . . ? (informal),* I, 3; Qu'est-ce que tu fais pour t'amuser? *What do you do to have fun?* I, 4

pourquoi: Pourquoi est-ce que tu ne mets pas... ? *Why don't you wear . . . ?,* I, 10; Pourquoi pas? *Why not?* I, 6; Pourquoi tu ne... pas? *Why don't you . . . ?* I, 9; II, 7

pousser *to grow,* III, 3

pourtant *nevertheless, yet,* III, 7

la poussière: faire la poussière *to dust,* III, 3

la poutre *the balance beam,* III, 12

pouvoir *to be able to, can,* I, 8; Il se peut que... *It might be that . . . ,* III, 5; On peut... *We can . . . ,* II, 4; Je pourrais avoir... ? *May I have some . . . ?* II, 3; Tu pourrais... ? *Could you . . . ?* II, 10; Tu pourrais passer à... ? *Could you go by . . . ?* I, 12; On pourrait... *We could . . . ,* II, 1; On pourrait sûrement... *We'd be able to . . . for sure.* III, 7; Vous pourriez/tu pourrais me passer... *Would you pass . . . ,* II, 3; Vous pourriez me dire où il y a... ? *Could you tell me where I could find . . . ?* III, 2

préférer: Ce que je préfère, c'est... *What I prefer is . . . ,* II, 4; Je préfère *I prefer,* II, 1

préféré: Quel est ton... préféré(e)? *What is your favorite . . . ?* II, 1; Qui est ton... préféré(e)? *Who is your favorite . . . ?* II, 1

le premier étage *second floor,* II, 2

prendre *to take or to have (food or drink),* I, 5; prendre rendez-vous (avec quelqu'un) *to make a date (with someone),* II, 9; Ça ne va pas prendre longtemps! *It's not going to take long!* III, 2; Je vais (en) prendre... *I'll take . . . ,* I, 3; Je vais prendre... , s'il vous plaît. *I'm going to have . . . , please.* I, 5; Pense à prendre... *Remember to take . . . ,* II, 1; prendre les transports en commun *to take public transportation,* III, 3; prendre ses propres décisions *to make up one's own mind,* III, 3; prendre des leçons de conduite *to take driving lessons,* III, 10; Tu devrais prendre... *You should have . . . ,* III, 1; Vous

avez décidé de prendre... ? *Have you decided to have . . . ?* I, 10; Je prendrais bien... *I'd like some . . . ,* III, 6; Prends... *Have . . . ,* I, 5; Get . . . , I, 8; Take . . . , II, 1; C'est toujours moi qui prends! *I'm always the one who gets blamed!* III, 6; Je le/la/les prends. *I'll take it/them.* I, 10; Je prends... , s'il vous plaît. *I'll have . . . , please.* I, 5; Tu me prends la tête! *You're driving me crazy!* III, 6; Tu prends... ? *Will you have . . . , ?* I, 8; Are you having . . . ? I, 11; Prenez.. *Take . . . ,* II, 2; Non mais, vous vous prenez pour qui? *Who do you think you are?* III, 8; Prenez une feuille de papier. *Take out a sheet of paper.* I, 0; Vous le/la/les prenez? *Are you going to take it/them?* I, 10; Vous prenez? *What are you having?* I, 5; Vous prenez... ? *Will you have . . . , ?* I, 8; Prenez la rue... puis traversez la rue... *You take . . . Street, then cross . . . Street,* I, 12

les préparatifs (m.): faire les préparatifs *to get ready,* II, 10

préparer: préparer les amuse-gueule *to make party snacks,* II, 10

près: près de *close to,* I, 12; *near,* II, 2

présenter: Je te/vous présente... *I'd like you to meet . . . ,* I, 7

presque: Tu y es presque! *You're almost there!* II, 7; Tu y es (On y est) presque! *You're (we're) almost there!* II, 12

pressé(e) *in a hurry,* III, 8

la pression: la pression des pneus *the tire pressure,* III, 2

prêt(e) *ready,* III, 2

prévoyant *provident,* III, 5

prévu: Je n'ai rien de prévu. *I don't have any plans.* I, 11

prier: Entrez, je vous en prie. *Come in, please.* III, 6; Je vous en prie. *You're very welcome.* III, 6; Je vous prie d'agréer, Monsieur/Madame, l'expression de mes sentiments distingués. *Very truly yours, . . . ,* III, 5

la prière: Prière de ne pas... *Please do not . . . ,* III, 3

le printemps *spring,* I, 4; au printemps *in the spring,* I, 4

privé: être privé(e) de sortie *to be "grounded,"* II, 9

le problème: J'ai un petit problème. *I've got a problem.* I, 9; Pas de problème. *No problem.* II, 10

prochain: Vous continuez cette rue jusqu'au prochain feu rouge. *You go down this street to the next light.* I, 12

produire *to produce,* III, 11

le prof(esseur) *high school/college teacher,* I, 2; III, 5

le programme télé *TV guide/listing,* III, 9

le programmeur (la programmeuse) *computer programmer,* III, 5

la proie *prey,* III, 7

les projets (m.): Tu as des projets? *Do you have plans?* III, 5

la promenade: faire une promenade *to go for a walk,* I, 6

promener: promener le chien *to walk the dog,* I, 7; se promener *to go for a walk,* II, 4

les pronostics (m.) *predictions,* III, 12

propos: A propos,... *By the way, . . . ,* II, 9

propre *clean,* II, 8; prendre ses propres décisions *to make up one's own mind,* III, 3

prudemment: conduire prudemment *to drive safely,* III, 3

prudent(e) *careful, aware,* III, 3; Il serait plus prudent de... *It would be wise to . . . ,* III, 7

pu (pp. of pouvoir): J'aurais pu... *I could have . . . ,* II, 10; Tu aurais pu... *You could have . . . ,* II, 10

la publicité *commercial,* III, 9

puis: Puis,... *Then, . . . ,* II, 1; Puis, tournez à gauche dans... *Then, turn left on . . . ,* II, 2; Vous prenez la rue... puis la rue... *You take . . . Street, then . . . Street,* I, 12

le puits *well,* III, 8

le pull *sweater,* II, 1

le pull(-over) *pullover,* I, 3; II, 1

punir *to punish,* III, 6

Q

qu'est-ce que: Qu'est-ce que vous avez comme spécialités? *What kind of . . . do you have?* III, 1; Mais, qu'est-ce que tu fais? *What are you doing?* III, 2; Qu'est-ce que tu as? *What's wrong? ,* II, 7; Qu'est-ce qu'il y a... ? *What is there . . . ?* II, 4; Qu'est-ce qu'il y a? *What's wrong?* II, 10; Qu'est-ce qu'il y a dans... *What's in . . . ?* III, 11; Qu'est-ce qu'on fait? *What should we do?* II, 1; Qu'est-ce qu'on peut faire? *What can we do?* II, 4; Qu'est-ce que c'est,... ? *What is . . . ?* III, 1; Qu'est-ce que c'est... ! *That is so . . . !* III, 2; Qu'est-ce que c'est? *What's that?* III, 11; Qu'est-ce que j'aimerais... ! *I'd really like to . . . !* III, 8; Qu'est-ce que je peux faire? *What can I do?* I, 9; II, 10; Qu'est-ce que tu aimes faire? *What do you like to do?* II, 1; Qu'est-ce que tu as fait... ? *What did you do . . . ?* I, 9; Qu'est-ce que tu fais quand... ? *What do you do when . . . ?* I, 4; Qu'est-ce que tu fais... ? *What do you do . . . ?* I, 4; Qu'est-ce que tu

vas faire... ? *What are you going to do . . . ?* I, 6; **Qu'est-ce que vous avez comme boissons?** *What do you have to drink?* I, 5; **Qu'est-ce que vous avez comme... ?** *What kind of . . . do you have?* I, 5

Qu'est-ce qui: Qu'est-ce qui s'est passé? *What happened?* I, 9; **Qu'est-ce qui se passe?** *What's going on?* II, 5; **Qu'est-ce qui t'arrive?** *What's wrong?* II, 5

le quai: Du quai... *From platform . . . ,* II, 6; **De quel quai... ?** *From which platform . . . ?* II, 6

quand: Quand (ça)? *When?* I, 6; **Quand je verrai...** *When I see . . . ,* III, 12; **Quand est-ce que tu y es allé(e)?** *When did you go?* III, 1

le quart: et quart *quarter past,* I, 6; **moins le quart** *quarter to,* I, 6

quel(s): Quel(s)... *Which . . . ,* III, 4; **Quel week-end!** *What a bad weekend!* II, 5; **Quel est ton... préféré(e)?** *What is your favorite . . . ?* II, 1; **Tu as quel âge?** *How old are you?* I, 1; **Tu as quels cours... ?** *What classes do you have . . . ?* I, 2

quelle(s): Quelle(s)... *Which . . . ,* III, 4; **Quelle journée!** *What a bad day!* II, 5; **Tu as... à quelle heure?** *At what time do you have . . . ?* I, 2

quelque chose: J'ai quelque chose à faire. *I have something else to do.* II, 10; **Je cherche quelque chose pour...** *I'm looking for something for . . . ,* I, 10; **Quelque chose ne va pas?** *Is something wrong?* II, 7

quelquefois *sometimes,* I, 4

la question: Pas question! *Out of the question!* I, 7; *No way!,* II, 1

la queue de cheval *pony tail,* III, 4

qui: Avec qui? *With whom?* I, 6; **Qui est ton... préféré(e)?** *Who is your favorite . . . ?* II, 1

quitter: quitter sa famille *to leave one's family,* III, 5; **Ne quittez pas.** *Hold on.* I, 9

quoi: (Il n'y a) pas de quoi. *It's nothing.* III, 6; **... , quoi.** *. . . , you know.* II, 9; **De quoi ça parle?** *What's it about?* III, 9; **Je ne sais pas quoi faire.** *I don't know what to do.* II, 10; **Je ne sais pas quoi mettre pour...** *I don't know what to wear for . . . ,* I, 10; **N'importe quoi!** *That's ridiculous!* II, 6; **Tu as quoi... ?** *What do you have . . . ?* I, 2

R

raconter: Raconte! *Tell me!* II, 5; III, 10; **Qu'est-ce que ça raconte?** *What's the story?* II, 11

la radio *radio,* I, 3

raide: les cheveux raides (m.) *straight hair,* III, 4

le raifort *horseradish,* III, 1

le raisin *grapes,* I, 8; **les raisins secs** (m.) *raisins,* III, 11

la raison: Ce n'est pas une raison. *That's not a reason.* III, 3; **Fais-toi une raison.** *Make the best of it.* II, 8; **Tu as raison...** *You're right . . . ,* II, 3; III, 9

ramasser *to pick up,* III, 3; **ramasser les feuilles** *to rake leaves,* III, 3

les rames (f.) *oars,* III, 12

la randonnée: faire de la randonnée *to go hiking,* I, 11; **faire une randonnée en raquettes** *to go snow-shoeing,* II, 12; **faire une randonnée en skis** *to go cross-country skiing,* II, 12; **faire une randonnée pédestre** *to go for a hike,* II, 12

ranger: ranger ta chambre *to pick up your room,* I, 7

le rap *rap,* II, 11; III, 11

râpé: les carottes râpées *grated carrots with vinaigrette dressing,* III, 1

raplapla: Je suis tout(e) raplapla. *I'm "wiped" out.* II, 7

rappeler *to remind,* III, 3; **se rappeler** *to remember,* III, 6; **Vous pouvez rappeler plus tard?** *Can you call back later?* I, 9

rapporter: Rapporte-moi... *Bring me back . . . ,* I, 8; **Tu me rapportes... ?** *Will you bring me . . . , ?* I, 8

Rapporteur (-euse)! *Tattletale!* III, 6

les rapports (m.) *relationship,* III, 6

les raquettes (f.): **faire une randonnée en raquettes** *to go snow-shoeing,* II, 12

ras: J'en ai ras le bol! *I've had it!* III, 8

rasant(e) *boring,* III, 2; **C'est rasant!** *That's boring!* III, 2

se raser *to shave,* III, 4

rassurer *to reassure,* III, 4

rater: rater le bus *to miss the bus,* I, 9; II, 5; **rater un examen** *to fail a test,* I, 9; **rater une marche** *to miss a step,* II, 5; **Tu en rates pas une, toi!** *You're batting a thousand!* III, 10

le raton laveur *raccoon,* II, 12

les rayures (f.): **à rayures** *striped,* III, 4

la réalisation *production,* III, 6

les rebondissements (m.): **C'est plein de rebondissements.** *It's full of plot twists.* II, 11

recevoir: recevoir le bulletin trimestriel *to receive one's report card,* II, 5

recommander: Je te le recommande. *I recommend it.* II, 11; **Je te recommande...** *I recommend . . . ,* III, 9

recommencer: Ne recommence pas. *Don't do it again.* II, 5

réconcilier: se réconcilier avec (quelqu'un) *to make up (with someone),* II, 10

reconnaître *to recognize,* III, 1

la récréation *break,* I, 2

recycler *to recycle,* III, 3

rédiger *to write (a paper),* III, 3

regarder: regarder la télé *to watch TV,* I, 1; **regarder un match** *to watch a game (on TV),* I, 6; **Non mais, tu t'es pas regardé(e)!** *If you could see how you look!* III, 10; **Non, merci, je regarde.** *No, thanks, I'm just looking.* I, 10; **Tiens! Regarde un peu!** *Hey! Check it out!* III, 7

le reggae *reggae music,* II, 11

le régime: suivre un régime trop strict *follow a diet that's too strict.* II, 7

la règle *ruler,* I, 3

regretter: Je regrette. *Sorry,* I, 3; **Je regrette, mais je n'ai pas le temps.** *I'm sorry, but I don't have time.* I, 8; **Je regrette...** *I miss . . . ,* II, 8

rejoindre *to join,* III, 11

relax *relaxing,* II, 8

la religieuse *cream puff pastry,* II, 3

remarquer *to notice,* III, 6

remercier: Je vous remercie. *Thank you.* III, 6

rémoulade: le céleri rémoulade *grated celery root with mayonnaise and vinaigrette ,* III, 1

remplir *to fill out, fill in,* III, 3

la rémunération *payment,* III, 5

le renard *fox,* II, 12

rencontrer *to meet,* I, 9; II, 9

le rendez-vous: Rendez-vous... *We'll meet . . .* I, 6; **A quelle heure est-ce qu'on se donne rendez-vous?** *What time are we meeting?* III, 6; **avoir (prendre) rendez-vous (avec quelqu'un)** *to have (make) a date (with someone),* II, 9; **C'est gentil, mais j'ai un rendez-vous.** *That's nice of you, but I've got an appointment.* III, 6

rendre *to return something,* I, 12; **rendre les examens** *to return tests,* II, 5

la renommée *fame,* III, 1

renoncer *to give up,* III, 1

les renseignements (m.): **Pourriez-vous m'envoyer des renseignements sur... ?** *Could you send me information on . . . ?* III, 5

rentrer *to go back (home),* II, 6

renverser *to turn over,* III, 6

le repas: sauter un repas *to skip a meal,* II, 7

le repassage: faire le repassage *to do the ironing,* III, 3

répéter *to rehearse, to practice,* I, 9; **Répétez!** *Repeat!* I, 0

répondre *to answer,* I, 9; **Ça ne répond pas.** *There's no answer.* I, 9

le répondeur *answering machine,* III, 7

la réponse: En réponse à votre lettre

du... *In response to your letter of . . .*, III, 5

le reportage sportif *sportscast*, III, 9

la République centrafricaine *Central African Republic*, III, 12

la République de Côte d'Ivoire *the Republic of Côte d'Ivoire*, III, 12

le requin *shark*, III, 10

le réservoir *the gas tank*, III, 2

résoudre *to resolve*, III, 9

respecter: **respecter la nature** *to respect nature*, II, 12; **respecter ses profs et ses parents** *to respect one's teachers and one's parents*, III, 3

les responsabilités (f.): **avoir des responsabilités** *to have responsibilities*, II, 8

responsable *responsible*, III, 3

ressentir *to feel*, III, 8

ressortir: **faire ressortir** *to highlight*, III, 4

le restaurant *restaurant*, I, 6

la restauration *food service; catering*, III, 5

rester *to stay*, II, 6; **Est-ce que tu es resté(e) ici?** *Did you stay here?* III, 1; **Oui, je suis resté(e) ici tout le temps.** *Yes, I stayed here the whole time.* III, 1

le résumé *summary*, III, 9

le rétablissement: Bon rétablissement! *Get well soon!* II, 3

retirer: **retirer de l'argent** (m.) *to withdraw money*, I, 12

retourner *to return*, II, 6

rétro (inv.) *old-fashioned*, I, 10

les retrouvailles (f.) *reunion*, III, 1

retrouver: On se retrouve... *We'll meet . . .* I, 6; **Où est-ce qu'on se retrouve?** *Where are we meeting?* III, 6

réussir son bac *to pass one's baccalaureat exam*, III, 5

la revanche: en revanche *on the other hand*, III, 12; **une revanche à prendre** *to get revenge on somebody*, III, 12

rêvasser *to daydream*, III, 3

le rêve: Mon rêve, c'est de... *My dream is to . . ,* III, 5

le réveil: entendre le réveil *to hear the alarm clock*, II, 5

réveiller: **Réveille-toi un peu!** *Get with it!* III, 10

revenir *to come back*, II, 6; **Je n'en reviens pas.** *I don't believe it.* III, 10

revoir: **Je suis content(e) de te revoir.** *I'm glad to see you again.* III, 1; **Quand est-ce qu'on se revoit?** *When are we getting together?* III, 6

le rez-de-chaussée *first (ground) floor*, II, 2; III, 2

le rhinocéros *rhinoceros*, III, 7

le rhume: J'ai un rhume. *I've got a cold.* II, 7

rien: **Ça ne fait rien.** *It doesn't matter.* II, 10; **Ça ne me dit rien.** *That doesn't interest me.* I, 4; **De rien.** *You're welcome.* III, 6; **Je n'ai rien oublié.** *I didn't forget anything.* I, 11; **Rien (de spécial).** *Nothing (special).* I, 6; III, 1

rigoler: **Tu rigoles!** *You're joking!* III, 9

rigolo(te) *funny, hysterical*, III, 2

ringard(e) *corny*, III, 4

rire: **Ça m'a bien fait rire.** *It made me laugh.* III, 9

la rivière *river*, III, 7

le riz *rice*, I, 8

la robe *a dress*, I, 10

le robinet *the faucet*, III, 3

le rocher *rock*, III, 10

le rock *rock music*, II, 11; III, 11

le rognon *kidney*, III, 1

la roideur *stiffness, rigidity*, III, 4

le roller: faire du roller en ligne *to in-line skate*, I, 4

le roman *novel* , I, 3; **roman d'amour** *romance novel*, II, 11; **roman de science-fiction** *science-fiction novel*, II, 11; **roman policier (le polar)** *detective or mystery novel*, II, 11

rose *pink*, I, 3

le rôti de bœuf *roast beef*, II, 3

la roue: la grande roue *the ferris wheel*, II, 6

rouge *red*, I, 3

le rouge à lèvres *lipstick*, III, 4

la route: Bonne route! *Have a good (car) trip!* , II, 3; **Cette route vous conduira au centre-ville.** *This road will lead you into the center of town.* III, 2; **La route pour... s'il vous plaît?** *Could you tell me how to get to . . .* , III, 2

roux (rousse) *redheaded*, I, 7

russe: **les montagnes russes** *the roller coaster*, II, 6

la Russie *Russia*, III, 12

S

le sable *sand*, II, 4

le sac (à dos) *bag; backpack*, I, 3; **sac (à main)** *purse*, II, 3; III, 4

le sac de couchage *sleeping bag*, II, 12

Saignante. *Rare.* III, 1

la salade *salad, lettuce*, I, 8

sale *dirty*, II, 8

salé(e) *salty*, III, 11

les saletés (f.) *trash, junk*, III, 3

la salle: la salle à manger *dining room*, II, 2; **la salle de bains** *bathroom*, II, 2

le salon *living room*, II, 2

saluer: **Salue... de ma part.** *Tell . . . hi for me.* III, 8

Salut! *Hi! or Goodbye!* I, 1

le samedi *on Saturdays*, I, 2

les sandales (f.) *sandals*, I, 10

le sandre *pike perch*, III, 1

le sandwich *sandwich*, I, 5

sanguine *the color of blood*, III, 10

les saucisses (f.) *sausages*, III, 11

le saucisson *salami*, I, 5; II, 3

le saut à la perche *pole vault*, III, 12

le saut en longueur *long jump*, III, 12

sauter: **sauter un repas** *to skip a meal*, II, 7; **Ce qui saute aux yeux, c'est...** *What catches your eye is . . .* , III, 11

la savane *savannah*, III, 7

savoir: **Je voudrais savoir...** *I would like to know . . . ?* III, 5; **Je n'en sais rien.** *I have no idea.* I, 11; **Je ne sais pas quoi faire.** *I don't know what to do.* II, 10; **Je ne sais pas.** *I don't know.* I, 10; **Je ne sais pas trop.** *I really don't know.* III, 5; **Je sais que...** *I know that . . .* , III, 7; **Qu'est-ce que tu en sais?** *What do you know about it?* III, 10; **Tu sais ce que tu veux faire?** *Do you know what you want to do?* III, 5; **Tu sais où sont...** *Do you know where . . . are?* III, 2; **Tu sais qui... ?** *Do you know who . . . ?* II, 9; **Tu savais que... ?** *Did you know that . . . ?* III, 10; **Pardon, vous savez où se trouve...** *Excuse me, could you tell me where . . . is?* III, 2

le saxophone *saxophone*, III, 11

le scénario *screenplay*, III, 9

les sciences (f.) **naturelles** *natural science* , I, 2

la seconde: Une seconde, s'il vous plaît. *One second, please.* I, 9

le secrétaire (la secrétaire) *secretary*, III, 5

le sel *salt*, II, 7

la semaine: une fois par semaine *once a week*, I, 4

sembler: **Il me semble que...** *It seems to me that . . .* , III, 11

le Sénégal *Senegal*, III, 12

sensas (sensationnel) *fantastic*, I, 10; *sensational!* II, 6

sensible *sensitive*, III, 6

les sentiers (m.): **suivre les sentiers balisés** *to follow the marked trails*, II, 12

les sentiments (m.): **Je vous prie d'agréer, Monsieur/Madame, l'expression de mes sentiments distingués.** *Very truly yours, . . .* , III, 5

septembre *September*, I, 4

la série *series*, III, 9

sérieux (-euse) *conservative*, III, 4

le serpent *snake*, III, 7

serré(e) *tight*, I, 10

le serveur (la serveuse) *server*, III, 5

service: **A votre service.** *At your service; You're welcome*, I, 3; **(Est-ce que) tu pourrais me rendre un petit service?** *Could you do me a favor?* I, 8

servir: Je vous sers quelque chose? *Can I offer you something?* III, 6

seul(e): J'y suis allé(e) seul(e)... *I went alone . . . ,* III, 1; **Je ne suis pas le/la seul(e) à...** *I'm not the only person who . . . ,* III, 3

seulement: Si seulement je pouvais,... *If I could only, . . . ,* III, 8

le shampooing *(a) shampoo (in a salon),* III, 4

le short *(a pair of) shorts,* I, 3

si: Si... *If . . . ,* III, 5; **Moi, si.** *I do.* I, 2; **Si c'était moi,...** *If it were me, . . . ,* III, 8; **Si c'était possible,...** *If it were possible, . . . ,* III, 8; **Si j'étais toi,...** *If I were you, . . . ,* III, 8; **Si on achetait... ?** *How about buying . . . ?* II, 8; **Si on allait... ?** *How about going . . . ?* II, 4; **Si on jouait... ?** *How about playing . . . ?* II, 8; **Si on visitait... ?** *How about visiting . . . ?* II, 8; **Si tu veux, on peut...** *If you like, we can . . . ,* II, 1

la sieste: faire la sieste *to take a nap,* II, 8

signaler: Je vous signale que... *I'm warning you that . . . ,* III, 7

simple *simple,* II, 8

le singe *monkey,* III, 7

sinistre *awful,* II, 6; *deadly boring,* III, 12

le ski *skiing,* I, 1; **faire du ski** *to ski,* I, 4; **faire du ski nautique** *to water-ski,* I, 4; **faire une randonnée en skis** *to go cross-country skiing,* II, 12

sobre *plain,* III, 4

sociable *outgoing,* III, 6

la sœur *sister,* I, 7

la soif: avoir soif *to be thirsty,* I, 5; **Je n'ai plus soif.** *I'm not thirsty anymore.* II, 3; **J'ai très soif!** *I'm very thirsty.* II, 2; **Vous n'avez pas/Tu n'as pas soif?** *Aren't you thirsty?* II, 2

soigner *to take care of,* III, 6

le soir *evening; in the evening,* I, 4; **Pas ce soir.** *Not tonight.* I, 7

sois: Sois patient(e)! *Be patient!* III, 2

le soldat *soldier,* III, 5

le son *sound,* III, 9; **Monte le son.** *Turn up the volume.* III, 9

le sondage *poll,* III, 1

le songe *dream,* III, 2

la sonorité *tone,* III, 11

la sortie *dismissal,* III, 2; **être privé(e) de sortie** *to be "grounded",* II, 9

sortir *to go out,* II, 6; **sortir avec les copains** *to go out with friends,* I, 1; **sortir la poubelle** *to take out the trash,* I, 7; **sortir le chien** *to take out the dog,* III, 3

les soucis (m.): **avoir des soucis** *to have worries,* II, 8

le souhait *wish, desire,* III, 8

soumettre *to submit,* III, 1

les soupes (f.) *soups,* III, 11

souple *soft,* III, 4

les sourcils (m.) *eyebrows,* III, 4

sourire *to smile,* III, 7

sous-marine: faire de la plongée sous-marine *to scuba dive,* II, 4

souvent *often,* I, 4

se souvenir: Si je me souviens bien,... *If I remember correctly, . . . ?* III, 11

spécial: Rien de spécial. *Nothing special.* I, 6

le spectacle: assister à un spectacle son et lumière *to attend a sound and light show,* II, 6

le sport *sports,* I, 1; *gym (class),* I, 2; **faire du sport** *to play sports,* I, 1; **Qu'est-ce que tu fais comme sport?** *What sports do you play?* I, 4

le stade *stadium,* I, 6

le stage *training period, training course,* III, 5

la station: la station de métro *metro station,* III, 8; **la station-service** *a gas station,* III, 2

le steak-frites *steak and French fries,* I, 5; III, 1

le style: C'est tout à fait ton style. *It looks great on you!* I, 10; **Ce n'est pas son style.** *That's not his/her style.* II, 3

le stylo *pen,* I, 3

le sud: dans le sud *in the south,* II, 4; **C'est au sud de...** *It's to the south of . . . ,* II, 12

suffit: Ça suffit! *That's enough!* III, 6

la Suisse *Switzerland,* III, 12

la suite: C'est tout de suite à... *It's right there on the . . . ,* I, 12; **J'y vais tout de suite.** *I'll go right away.* I, 8; **Suite à notre conversation téléphonique,...** *Following our telephone conversation, . . . ,* III, 5; **tout de suite** *right away,* I, 6

suivre: suivre les sentiers balisés *to follow the marked trails,* II, 12; **suivre un régime trop strict** *to follow a diet that's too strict,* II, 7; **Pour (aller à)... vous suivez la... pendant à peu près... kilomètres.** *To get to . . . , follow . . . for about . . . kilometers.* III, 2

super (adj.) *super,* I, 2; (adv.) *really, ultra-,* II, 9; **Super!** *Great!* I, 1; **Super!** III, 12; **pas super** *not so hot,* I, 2; **le super** *regular leaded gasoline,* III, 2; **le super sans plomb** *unleaded gasoline,* III, 2

superbe *great,* II, 6

sûr: Bien sûr. *Of course.* II, 10; **Bien sûr.** *Of course. Ça, c'est sûr.* *That's for sure.* III, 11; **Je (ne) suis (pas) sûr(e) que...** *I'm (not) sure that . . . ,* III, 7

sur: sur la droite (gauche) *on the right (left),* II, 2

sûrement: On pourrait sûrement... *We'd be able to . . . for sure.* III, 7; **Sûrement pas!** *Definitely not!* II, 6

surtout *especially,* I, 1; **Ne va surtout pas voir...** *Really, don't go see . . . ,* III, 9; **Non mais, surtout, ne vous gênez pas!** *Well just go right ahead!* III, 8

susciter *to provoke, arouse,* III, 12

le suspense: Il y a du suspense. *It's suspenseful.* II, 11

le sweat(-shirt) *sweatshirt,* I, 3; II, 1

sympa (abbrev. of sympathique) (inv.) *nice,* I, 7; II, 1

le synthé (synthétiseur) *synthesizer,* III, 11

T

le tableau *blackboard,* I, 0; *chart,* III, 6

tacheté *spotted,* III, 7

la taille *the waist,* III, 4

le taille-crayon *pencil sharpener,* I, 3

taire: Vous pourriez vous taire, s'il vous plaît? *Could you please be quiet?* III, 9; **Tais-toi!** *Be quiet!* III, 9

le tam-tam *an African drum,* II, 8

tandis que: Ici,... tandis que... *Here . . . , whereas . . . ,* III, 8

tant: Tant pis pour toi! *Tough!* III, 6

tant que *as long as,* III, 1

la tante *aunt,* I, 7

tape-à-l'œil *gaudy,* III, 4

taper *to beat,* III, 3

le tapis *rug,* II, 2; III, 8

taquiner *to tease,* II, 8

tard *late,* II, 4; **plus tard** *later,* III, 5

tarder: Il me tarde de... *I can't wait to . . . ,* III, 12

la tarte *pie,* I, 8; **la tarte aux pommes** *apple tart,* II, 3; **les tartes aux fruits** *fruit pies/tarts,* III, 1

la tartine *bread, butter, and jam,* II, 3

le tas: J'ai des tas de choses à faire. *I have lots of things to do.* I, 5

le taux *rate,* III, 1

le taxi: en taxi *by taxi,* I, 12

Tchao! *Bye!* I, 1

le technicien (la technicienne) *technician,* III, 5

le tee-shirt *T-shirt,* I, 3; II, 1

teint: les cheveux teints (m.) *dyed hair,* III, 4

la télécommande *remote,* III, 9

le téléphone: parler au téléphone *to talk on the phone,* I, 1

téléphoner à (quelqu'un) *to call (someone),* II, 10; **Téléphone-lui/-leur!** *Call him/her/them!* I, 9

le téléviseur *television set,* III, 9

la télévision *television,* I, 3; **regarder la télé(vision)** *to watch TV,* I, 1

tellement: C'était tellement différent? *Was it really so different?*

II, 8; **Pas tellement.** *Not too much.* I, 4

le temps: de temps en temps *from time to time,* I, 4; **Je suis désolé(e), mais je n'ai pas le temps.** *Sorry, but I don't have time.* I, 12; **Il a fait un temps...** *The weather was . . .* III, 1; **On a largement le temps!** *We've got plenty of time!* III, 2; **On n'a pas le temps!** *We don't have time!* III, 2; **Quel temps est-ce qu'il a fait?** *What was the weather like?* III, 1

tenir: Tenez. *Here you are.* II, 3; **Tiens.** *Here you are.* II, 3; **Je tiens à...** *I really want to . . . ,* III, 5; **Tiens! Regarde un peu!** *Hey! Check it out!* III, 7

le tennis *tennis,* I, 4

la tente *tent,* II, 12

la tenue *outfit,* III, 12

terminer: Comment ça se termine? *How does it end?* III, 9

le terrain de camping *campground,* II, 2

la terre: par terre *on the ground,* III, 3

terrible: Pas terrible. *Not so great.* I, 1; **C'était pas terrible.** *It wasn't so great.* III, 1

la tête: faire la tête *to sulk,* II, 9; **J'ai mal à la tête** *My head hurts.* II, 7; **Tu me prends la tête!** *You're driving me crazy!* III, 6

le théâtre *theater,* I, 6; II, 12; **faire du théâtre** *to do drama,* I, 4

le thon *tuna,* III, 1

les tickets (m.): **Trois tickets, s'il vous plaît.** *Three (entrance) tickets, please.* II, 6

le timbre *stamp,* I, 12

timide *shy,* I, 7

le tir à l'arc *archery,* III, 12

tirer *to pull, to shoot,* III, 6, 12

le tisserin *a type of African bird,* III, 7

le tissu *fabric, cloth,* II, 8

la toile: en toile *linen,* III, 4

les toilettes (les W.-C.) (f.) *toilet, restroom,* II, 2

tolérant(e) *tolerant,* III, 3

les tomates (f.) *tomatoes,* I, 8

tomber *to fall,* II, 5; **Après... , vous allez tomber sur...** *After . . . , you'll come across . . . ,* III, 2; **tomber amoureux(-euse) (de quelqu'un)** *to fall in love (with someone),* II, 9; **tomber en panne** *to break down,* II, 9; **tomber en panne d'essence** *to run out of gas,* III, 2; **tomber malade** *to get sick,* III, 10

tondre: tondre la pelouse *to mow the lawn,* III, 3

la torche *flashlight,* III, 7

tort: Tu as tort. *You're wrong.* III, 9; **Tu as tort de...** *You're wrong to . . . ,* III, 3

la tortue *turtle,* III, 10

tôt *early,* II, 4

toujours: toujours... *still . . . ?* III, 11; **C'est toujours la même chose!** *It's always the same!* III, 6; **Toujours la même chose!** *Same old thing!* III, 1

la tour *tower,* II, 6

le tour: faire un tour sur la grande roue *to take a ride on the ferris wheel,* II, 6; **faire un tour sur les montagnes russes** *to take a ride on the roller coaster,* II, 6

tourner: Puis, tournez à gauche dans/sur... *Then, turn left on . . . ,* II, 2; **Vous tournez...** *You turn . . . ,* 12

tout à fait: Tout à fait! *Absolutely!* III, 9; **C'est tout à fait normal.** *You don't have to thank me.* III, 6; **C'est tout à fait toi.** *That's really you.* III, 4

tout le monde: Ça arrive à tout le monde. *It happens to everybody.* III, 6; **Ça peut arriver à tout le monde.** *It could happen to anyone.* III, 10; **Ce n'est pas parce que tout le monde... que tu dois le faire.** *Just because everyone else . . . doesn't mean you have to.* III, 3; **Tout le monde fait pareil.** *Everybody does it.* III, 3

tout: A tout à l'heure! *See you later!* I, 1; **Allez (continuez) tout droit.** *Go (keep going) straight ahead.* II, 2; **C'est... comme tout!** *It's as . . . as can be!* III, 2; **J'ai pensé à tout.** *I've thought of everything.* I, 11; **Je n'ai pas du tout aimé.** *I didn't like it at all.* III, 9; **Pas du tout.** *Not at all.* I, 4; II, 10; III, 9; **Il/Elle ne va pas du tout avec...** *It doesn't go at all with . . .* **Tout a été de travers!** *Everything went wrong!* II, 5; **Tout me tente.** *Everything looks tempting.* III, 1; **Tout à fait!** *Absolutely!* III, 9; **C'est tout à fait ton style.** *It looks great on you!* I, 10; **tout de suite** *right away,* I, 6; **C'est tout de suite à...** *It's right there on the . . . ,* 12; **J'y vais tout de suite.** *I'll go right away.* I, 8; **Vous allez tout droit jusqu'à...** *You go straight ahead until you get to . . . ,* 12

le trac: Tu as le trac? *Are you nervous?* III, 12

le train: en train *by train,* I, 12; **être en train de** *to be in the process of (doing something),* II, 9

traire: traire les vaches (f.) *to milk the cows,* III, 8

traiter: Il/Elle m'a traité(e) de... ! *He/She called me a . . . !* III, 6

la tranche: une tranche de *a slice of,* I, 8

tranquille *calm,* II, 8

le travail: trouver un travail *to find a job,* III, 5

travailler *to work,* I, 9; **Il faut mieux travailler en classe.** *You have to do better in class.* II, 5

les travaux (m.) **pratiques** *lab,* I, 2

travers: Tout a été de travers! *Everything went wrong!* II, 5

traverser: Traversez... *Cross . . . ,* II, 2; **Vous traversez...** *You cross . . . ,* III, 2

Tricheur (-euse)! *Cheater!* III, 6

la trompe *trunk,* III, 7

se tromper: A mon avis, tu te trompes. *In my opinion, you're mistaken.* II, 9; **Si je ne me trompe pas,...** *If I'm not mistaken, . . . ?* III, 11

la trompette *trumpet,* III, 11

trop: C'est trop cher. *It's too expensive.* II, 3; **Je ne sais pas trop.** *I really don't know.* III, 5; **Non, pas trop.** *No, not too much.* I, 2; **Pas trop bien.** *Not too well.* III, 1

le trottoir *sidewalk,* III, 8

le trou *hole,* III, 7

troué *hollowed out,* III, 11

le trouillard *coward, wimp,* III, 7

le troupeau *herd,* III, 7

la trousse *pencil case,* I, 3; **la trousse de premiers soins** *first-aid kit,* II, 12

trouver *to find,* I, 9; **se trouve... ...** *is located . . . ,* II, 12; **Ce que je trouve super, c'est...** *What I think is super is . . . ,* III, 11; **Je le/la/les trouve moche(s).** *I think it's (they're) really tacky.* I, 10; **Je te trouve très bien comme ça.** *I think you look very good like that.* III, 4; **Je trouve qu'il est...** *I think it's . . . ,* III, 4; **Je trouve qu'ils/elles font...** *I think they look . . . ,* III, 4; **Où se trouve... ?** *Where is . . . ?* II, 4; **Comment tu as trouvé ça?** *How did you like it?* III, 9; **J'ai trouvé ça pas mal/amusant.** *It was not bad/funny.* III, 9

le truc *thing,* I, 5; **Ce n'est pas mon truc.** *It's not my thing.* II, 7; **Oh, c'est un vieux truc.** *This old thing?* III, 4; **J'ai des tas de trucs à faire.** *I have lots of things to do.* I, 12; **J'ai des trucs à faire.** *I have some things to do.* I, 5

les truffes (f.) *truffles,* III, 1

la truite *trout,* III, 1

tuer *to kill,* III, 7

la Tunisie *Tunisia,* III, 12

typique: Qu'est-ce qui est typique de chez toi? *What's typical of where you're from?* III, 12

U

un *a; an,* I, 3

une *a; an,* I, 3

utile: Je ne crois pas que ce soit utile. *I don't think it's worthwhile.* III, 7

V

les vacances (f.) *vacation,* I, 1; **Bonnes vacances!** *Have a good vacation!* I, 11; **C'était comment, tes vacances?** *How was your vacation?* III, 1; **Comment se sont passées tes vacances?** *How was your vacation?* II, 5; **en colonie de vacances** *to/at a summer camp,* I, 11; **en vacances** *on vacation,* I, 4

vachement *really,* II, 9

la vaisselle: faire la vaisselle *to do the dishes,* I, 7

la valise *suitcase,* I, 11

la vanille: à la vanille *vanilla,* III, 1

se vanter *to brag,* III, 10; **C'est pas pour me vanter, mais moi...** *I'm not trying to brag, but . . . ,* III, 10

le vase *vase,* II, 3

vaudrait: Il vaudrait mieux que... *It would be better if . . . ,* III, 5; **Tu penses qu'il vaudrait mieux... ?** *Do you think it'd be better to . . . ?* III, 7

vaut: Ça ne vaut pas le coup! *It's not worth it!* III, 9; **Je crois que ça vaut mieux.** *I think that's better.* III, 7

le vautour *vulture,* III, 7

la végétation tropicale *tropical vegetation,* III, 7

le vélo *biking,* I, 1; **à vélo** *by bike,* I, 12; **faire du vélo** *to bike,* I, 4; **faire du vélo de montagne** *to go mountain-bike riding,* II, 12

le vélomoteur *moped,* III, 8

le vendredi *on Fridays,* I, 2

venir *to come,* II, 6

le ventre: J'ai mal au ventre *My stomach hurts.* II, 7

vérifier *to check,* III, 2

véritable: C'était un véritable cauchemar! *It was a real nightmare!* I, 11

la vérité: dire la vérité *to tell the truth,* III, 3

le verre *glass,* III, 3

vers *about,* I, 6; **Vers...** *About (a certain time) . . . ,* II, 4

versatile *moody,* III, 6

vert(e) *green,* I, 3; II, 1

la veste *suit jacket, blazer,* I, 10

le/la vétérinaire *veterinarian,* III, 5

veuf (veuve) *widowed,* III, 6

veuillez: Veuillez ne pas... *Please do not . . . ,* III, 3

la viande *meat,* I, 8; III, 11

la vidange: faire la vidange *to change the oil,* III, 2

la vidéo: faire de la vidéo *to make videos,* I, 4; **jouer à des jeux vidéo** *to play video games,* I, 4

la vidéocassette *videotape,* I, 3

le vidéoclip *music video,* III, 9

la vie: C'est comment la vie là-bas? *What's life like there?* III, 12; **La vie était plus... moins...** *Life was more . . . , less . . . ,* II, 8

vieux (vieille): Pauvre vieux/ vieille! *You poor thing!* II, 5

vif (vive) *quick (witted),* III, 6

le village de pêcheurs *fishing village,* II, 4

violent: trop violent *too violent,* II, 11

violet(te) *purple,* I, 3

le violon *violin,* III, 11

le virage *turn,* III, 12

viser *to aim at, to take aim,* III, 12

la visite: une visite guidée *a guided tour,* II, 6

visiter *to visit (a place),* I, 9; II, 6

vite: Dis vite! *Let's hear it!* II, 9

les vitres: laver les vitres (f.) *to wash the windows,* III, 3

les vitrines (f): **faire les vitrines** *to window-shop,* I, 6

vivant(e) *lively,* II, 4

vivement: Vivement que... ! *I just can't wait . . . !* III, 12

les vœux (m.): **Meilleurs vœux!** *Best wishes!* II, 3

Voici... *Here's . . . ,* I, 7

Voilà. *Here it is.* II, 3; *Here,* I, 3; **Voilà...** *There's . . . ,* I, 7; III, 12

la voile: faire de la planche à voile *to go windsurfing,* I, 11; **faire de la voile** *to go sailing,* I, 11

voir: Qu'est-ce qu'il y a à voir... *What is there to see . . . ?* II, 12; **Tu devrais aller voir...** *You should go see . . . ,* III, 9; **Tu vas voir que...** *You'll see that . . . ,* II, 8; **Va voir... c'est génial comme film.** *Go see . . . , it's a great movie.* III, 9; **voir un film** *to see a movie,* I, 6; **voir un match** *to see a game (in person),* I, 6; **voir une pièce** *to see a play,* I, 6; **... tu vois.** *. . . you see.* II, 9; **Ça se voit.** *That's obvious.* II, 9

le voisinage *neighborhood,* III, 11

la voiture: *car,* I, 7; **en voiture** *by car,* I, 12; **laver la voiture** *to wash the car,* I, 7; **planter la voiture** *to wreck the car,* III, 10

le volcan *volcano,* II, 4

le volley (-ball) *volleyball,* I, 4

vouloir *to want,* I, 6; **Je m'en veux de...** *I feel bad that . . . ,* III, 6; **Je ne t'en veux pas.** *No hard feelings.* II, 10; **Je veux bien.** *Gladly,* I, 12; *I'd like to.,* II, 1; *I'd really like to.* I, 6; **Non, je ne veux pas.** *No, I don't want to.* II, 8; **Oui, si tu veux.** *Yes, if you want to.* I, 7; **Si tu veux,**

on peut... *If you like, we can . . . ,* II, 1; **Tu ne m'en veux pas?** *No hard feelings?* II, 10; **Tu veux bien que je...** *Is it OK with you if . . . ?* III, 3; **Je voudrais acheter...** *I'd like to buy . . . ,* I, 3; **Je voudrais bien...** *I'd really like to . . . ,* 11; **Tu ne voudrais pas... ?** *Wouldn't you like to . . . ?* III, 6

le voyage: Bon voyage! *Have a good trip! (by plane, ship),* I, 11; II, 3; **Vous avez/Tu as fait bon voyage?** *Did you have a good trip?* II, 2

voyager *to travel,* I, 1

vrai: C'est pas vrai! *You're kidding!* II, 6; **C'est vrai?** *Really?* II, 2

vraiment: Vraiment? *Really?* II, 2; **C'est vraiment bon!** *It's good!* II, 3; **Il/Elle est vraiment bien, ton/ ta...** *Your . . . is really great.* II, 2 ; **Non, pas vraiment.** *No, not really.* I, 11

vulgaire *tasteless,* III, 4

W

le week-end *weekend; on weekends,* I, 4; **ce week-end** *this weekend,* I, 6; **Comment s'est passé ton week-end?** *How was your weekend?* II, 5

le western *western (movie),* II, 11

Y

y *there,* I, 12; **Allons-y!** *Let's go!* I, 4; **Comment est-ce qu'on y va?** *How can we get there?* I, 12; **Je n'y comprends rien.** *I don't understand anything about it.* II, 5; **N'y va pas!** *Don't go!* III, 9; **On peut y aller...** *We can go there . . . ,* 12; **Qu'est-ce qu'on y...?** *What do you . . . there?* III, 12; **Tu vas t'y faire.** *You'll get used to it.* II, 8

le yaourt *yogurt,* I, 8

les yeux (m.) *eyes,* II, 1

Youpi! *Yippee!* III, 12

Z

le Zaïre *Zaire,* III, 12

le zèbre *zebra,* III, 7

zéro *a waste of time,* I, 2

le zoo *zoo,* I, 6; II, 6

le zouk: danser le zouk *to dance the zouk,* II, 4

Zut! *Darn!,* I, 3

ENGLISH-FRENCH VOCABULARY

In this vocabulary, the English definitions of all active French words in the book have been listed, followed by the French. The numbers after each entry refer to the level and chapter where the word or phrase first appears, or where it becomes an active vocabulary word. It is important to use a French word in its correct context. The use of a word can be checked easily by referring to the chapter where it appears.

French words and phrases are presented in the same way as in the French-English vocabulary.

A

a *un, une,* I, 3
able: We'd be able to . . . for sure. *On pourrait sûrement... ,* III, 7
about: About (a certain time) . . . *Vers... ,* II, 4; **It's about . . .** *Ça parle de... ,* II, 11; III, 9; **It's about . . .** *Il s'agit de... ,* III, 9; **It's about a guy who . . .** *C'est l'histoire d'un mec qui... ,* III, 10; **What's it about?** *De quoi ça parle?* II, 11; III, 9
Absolutely! *Tout à fait!* III, 9
acceptable: That's not acceptable. *C'est inadmissible.* II, 5
accident: to have an accident *avoir un accident,* II, 9
accordion *l'accordéon* (m.), III, 11
accountant *comptable,* III, 5
acne: to have acne *avoir des boutons,* III, 10
across: across from *en face de,* I, 12; II, 2
action: action movie *un film d'action,* II, 11
actor *l'acteur* (m.), III, 5
actress *l'actrice* (f.), III, 5
adore: I adore... *J'adore... ,* I, 1
adventure: adventure movie *un film d'aventure,* II, 11
advise: What do you advise me to do? *Qu'est-ce que tu me conseilles?* I, 9
aerobics: to do aerobics *faire de l'aérobic,* I, 4; II, 7
aerosol: to use aerosol sprays *utiliser des aérosols,* III, 3
afraid: Don't be afraid. *N'ayez pas peur.* III, 7; **I'm afraid that . . .** *J'ai peur que... ,* III, 7; **I'm very afraid of . . .** *J'ai très peur de... ,* III, 7
African *africain(e),* II, 11
after: After that . . . *Après ça... ,* II, 4, 12; **And after that, . . .** *Et après ça... ,* I, 9
afternoon: afternoon off *l'après-midi libre,* I, 2; **in the afternoon** *l'après-midi,* I, 2
afterwards: Afterwards, I went out. *Après, je suis sorti(e),* I, 9; **And afterwards?** *Et après?* I, 9
again: . . . again *...déjà,* III, 11; **Don't do it again.** *Ne recommence pas.* II, 5
agree: I don't agree. *Je ne suis pas d'accord.* I, 7; **I agree with you.** *Je suis d'accord avec toi.* III, 9
ahead: Go (keep going) straight ahead. *Allez (continuez) tout droit,* II, 2; **Well just go right ahead!** *Non mais, surtout, ne vous gênez pas!* III, 8

air: to put air in the tires *mettre de l'air dans les pneus,* III, 2
alarm: to hear the alarm clock *entendre le réveil,* II, 8
algebra *l'algèbre* (f.), I, 2
Algeria *l'Algérie* (f.), III, 12
all: All you have to do is . . . *Tu n'as qu'à... ,* II, 7; **I didn't like it at all.** *Je n'ai pas du tout aimé.* III, 9; **Not at all.** *Pas du tout.* I, 4; II, 10; **I don't like that at all.** *Ça ne me plaît pas du tout.* III, 11; **That's all I listen to.** *Je n'écoute que ça.* III, 11
all over: I hurt all over! *J'ai mal partout!* II, 7
all right *pas mal,* II, 6
allergies: I have allergies. *J'ai des allergies.* II, 7
allowed: You're not allowed to . . . *Tu n'as pas le droit de... ,* III, 3
almost: You're (We're) almost there! *Tu y es (On y est) presque!* II, 12; **You're almost there!** *Tu y es presque!* II, 7
alone: I went alone . . . *J'y suis allé(e) seul(e)... ,* III, 1; **Leave me alone!** *Fiche-moi la paix!* III, 6
already *déjà,* I, 9; **He/She already has one (of them).** *Il/Elle en a déjà un(e).* II, 3
also *aussi,* I, 1
always: I'm always the one who gets blamed! *C'est toujours moi qui prends!* III, 6; **It's always the same!** *C'est toujours la même chose!* III, 6
am: I am . . . *Je suis... ,* II, 1
amazing: It was amazing/unbelievably bad! *C'était incroyable!* II, 5
American *américain(e),* II, 11
amusement park *un parc d'attractions,* II, 6
an *un, une,* I, 3
and *et,* I, 1
andouille sausage *l'andouille* (f.), III, 11
angry *fâché(e),* II, 9
ankle: to sprain one's ankle *se fouler la cheville,* II, 7
annoyed *énervé(e),* II, 9
annoying *embêtant(e),* I, 7; II, 1
answer *répondre,* I, 9; **There's no answer.** *Ça ne répond pas.* I, 9; **. . . and then the other one answers . . .** *. . . et l'autre lui répond... ,* III, 10
ant *la fourmi,* III, 7
anxious: I'm really anxious to . . . *Je suis vraiment impatient(e) de... ,* III, 2
any (of it) *en,* I, 8
any more: I don't want any more. *Je n'en veux plus.* I, 8; **I just can't do any more!** *Je n'en peux plus!* II, 7, 12

anymore: I don't know what I want anymore. *Je ne sais plus ce que je veux.* III, 5; **I'm not hungry (thirsty) anymore.** *Je n'ai plus faim (soif).* II, 3
anyone: It could happen to anyone. *Ça peut arriver à tout le monde.* III, 10
anything: I didn't forget anything. *Je n'ai rien oublié.* I, 11; **It didn't do anything for me.** *Ça ne m'a pas emballé.* III, 9; **I just can't do anything right!** *Qu'est-ce que je peux être nul(le)!* III, 12
Anyway, . . . *Bref,... ,* II, 9
apologize *s'excuser,* II, 10; **Apologize.** *Excuse-toi.* II, 10
appetizers *les entrées* (f.), III, 1; **What would you like for an appetizer?** *Que voulez-vous comme entrée?* III, 1
apples *des pommes* (f.), I, 8; **apple juice** *un jus de pomme,* I, 5; **apple tart** *la tarte aux pommes,* II, 3
appointment: That's nice of you, but I've got an appointment. *C'est gentil, mais j'ai un rendez-vous.* III, 6
apprenticeship: to do an apprenticeship *faire un apprentissage,* III, 5
April *avril,* I, 4
archery *le tir à l'arc,* III, 12
architect *architecte,* III, 5
are: There is/are . . . *Il y a... ,* II, 12; **They are . . .** *Ils/Elles sont... ,* II, 1
argument: to have an argument (with someone) *se disputer (avec quelqu'un),* II, 9
arm *le bras,* II, 7
armoire: armoire/wardrobe *l'armoire* (f.), II, 2
around *vers,* I, 6
arrive *arriver,* II, 5
arrow *la flèche,* III, 12
art class *les arts* (m.) *plastiques,* I, 2
as: as many/as much . . . as . . . *autant de... que... ,* III, 8; **as . . . as . . .** *aussi... que... ,* III, 8; **It's as . . . as can be!** *C'est... comme tout!* III, 2
ask: to ask (someone's) forgiveness *demander pardon à (quelqu'un),* II, 10; **to ask your parents' permission** *demander la permission à tes parents,* II, 10
at *à la, au,* II, 6; **At . . .** *A... ,* II, 11; **at . . . fifteen** *à... heures quinze,* I, 2; **at . . . forty-five** *à... heures quarante-cinq,* I, 2; **at my house** *chez moi,* I, 6; **At that point, . . .** *A ce moment-là,... ,* II, 9; **at the record store** *chez le disquaire,* I, 12; **At what time?** *A quelle heure?* I, 6
attend: to attend a sound and light show *assister à un spectacle son et lumière,* II, 6

attendant: gas station attendant *le/la pompiste*, III, 2

August *août*, I, 4

aunt *la tante*, I, 7

avocados *des avocats* (m.), I, 8

Avoid . . . *Évite de. . .* , II, 12; **Avoid . . .** *Évite(z) de. . .* , II, 7; **Avoid seeing . . .** *Évite d'aller voir. . .* , III, 9

aware *prudent(e)*, III, 3

away: No, I went away for . . . *Non, je suis parti(e). . .* , III, 1; **Yes, right away.** *Oui, tout de suite.* I, 5

awful *sinistre*, II, 6

B

back *le dos*, II, 7; **come back** *revenir*, II, 6; **go back (home)** *rentrer*, II, 6; **Towards the back.** *Au fond.* III, 2

backpack *un sac à dos*, I, 3

bad: I feel bad that . . . *Je m'en veux de. . .* , III, 6; **I'm bad in computer science.** *Je suis mauvais(e) en informatique.* II, 5; **It was amazing/unbelievably bad!** *C'était incroyable!* II, 5; **It was not bad/funny.** *J'ai trouvé ça pas mal/amusant.* III, 9; **not bad** *pas mal*, I, 2; **Oh, not bad** *Oh, pas mal.* I, 9; **What a bad day!** *Quelle journée!* II, 5; **What a bad weekend!** *Quel week-end!* II, 5

bag *un sac*, I, 3

baggy *large(s)*, I, 10

bakery *la boulangerie*, I, 12; II, 3

balance: the balance beam *la poutre*, III, 12

balcony *le balcon*, II, 2

ball *la balle*, II, 12; *le ballon*, III, 12

banana tree *un bananier*, II, 4

bananas *des bananes* (f.), I, 8

bandages *les pansements* (m.), III, 7

bangs *la frange*, III, 4

bank *la banque*, I, 12

baseball *le base-ball*, III, 12; **to play baseball** *jouer au base-ball*, I, 4

basketball *le basket-ball*, I, 4; III, 12; **to play basketball** *jouer au basket(-ball)*, I, 4

baskets *des paniers* (m.), II, 8; **basket (basketball)** *le panier*, III, 12

bass (guitar) *la basse*, III, 11

bat (baseball) *le bâton*, III, 12

bathing suit *un maillot de bain*, I, 10

bathroom *la salle de bains*, II, 2

batter (baseball) *le frappeur*, III, 12

batting: You're batting a thousand! *Tu en rates pas une, toi!* III, 10

be *être*, I, 7; **to be in the process of (doing something)** *être en train de* (+ infinitive), II, 9

be able to, can *pouvoir*, I, 8; **Can you . . . ?** *Est-ce que tu peux. . . ?* I, 12; **I can't** *Je ne peux pas.*

beach *la plage*, I, 1

beans *des haricots* (m.), I, 8

bear *un ours*, II, 12

beard *la barbe*, III, 4

beautiful *beau (belle)*, II, 2; *magnifique*, II, 6

because: Just because everyone else . . . doesn't mean you have to. *Ce n'est pas parce que tout le monde... que tu dois le faire.* III, 3

become *devenir*, II, 6

bed *le lit*, II, 2; **to go to bed** *se coucher*, II, 4; **to make one's bed** *faire son lit*, III, 3

bedroom *la chambre*, II, 2

been: It's been . . . *Ça fait. . .* , III, 1

begin, to start *commencer*, I, 9

beginning: At the beginning . . . *Au début. . .* , III, 9; **I went at the beginning of . . .** *J'y suis allé(e) début. . .* , III, 1

behind *derrière*, I, 12

Belgium *la Belgique*, III, 12

believe: Believe me. *Crois-moi.* III, 4; **I can't believe how . . . !** *C'est fou comme... !* III, 7; **I can't believe it.** *J'arrive pas à y croire!* III, 12; **I don't believe it.** *Je n'en reviens pas.* III, 10

belt *la ceinture*, I, 10

best: All the best to . . . *Bien des choses à. . .* , III, 8; **Best wishes!** *Meilleurs vœux!* II, 3; **I . . . the best.** *C'est moi qui... le mieux.* III, 10; **I'm the best.** *C'est moi le/la meilleur(e).* III, 10; **Make the best of it.** *Fais-toi une raison.* II, 8; **You're really the best.** *Tu es vraiment le/la meilleur(e).* III, 10

bet: I bet that . . . *Je parie que. . .* , II, 9

better: It would be better if . . . *Il vaudrait mieux que. . .* , III, 5; **It'll get better.** *Ça va aller mieux.* II, 5; **It's better than . . .** *C'est meilleur que. . .* , II, 7; **It's going to get better!** *Ça va aller mieux!* I, 9; **You have to do better in class.** *Il faut mieux travailler en classe.* II, 5; **You would do well/better to . . .** *Tu ferais bien/mieux de. . .* , III, 5

between *entre*, I, 12

big *grand(e)*, I, 10; **big (tall)** *grand(e)*, II, 1

bigger: bigger than . . . *plus grand(e) que*, II, 4; **I've done bigger and better things.** *Oh, j'en ai vu d'autres.* III, 10

bike *faire du vélo*, I, 4; **by bike** *à vélo*, I, 12

biking *le vélo*, I, 1

binder: loose-leaf binder *un classeur*, I, 3

binoculars *les jumelles* (f.), III, 7

biography *la biographie*, II, 11

biology *la biologie*, I, 2

bird *l'oiseau* (m.), III, 7

birthday: Happy birthday! *Joyeux (Bon) anniversaire!* II, 3

bisque *en bisque*, III, 11

black *noir(e)(s)*, I, 3; **black** *noir*, II, 1; **black hair** *les cheveux noirs*, II, 1

blackboard *le tableau*, I, 0; **Go to the blackboard** *Allez au tableau!*, I, 0

blamed: I'm always the one who gets blamed! *C'est toujours moi qui prends!* III, 6

blazer *la veste*, I, 10

blond *blond(e)*, I, 7; **blond hair** *les cheveux blonds*, II, 1

blue *bleu(e)(s)*, I, 3; *bleu*, II, 1

blues *le blues*, II, 11; III, 11

boat *le bateau*, I, 12; **by boat** *en bateau*, I, 12

boiled *au court-bouillon*, III, 11

book *le livre*, I, 0

bookstore *la librairie*, I, 12

boots *des bottes* (f.), I, 10; **pair of boots** *les bottes* (f.), II, 1

bored: I was bored: *Je me suis ennuyé(e).* II, 6; III, 1; **I was bored to death.** *Je me suis ennuyé(e) à mourir.* III, 9; **I wasn't bored a second.** *Je ne me suis pas ennuyé une seconde.* III, 9; **You're never bored.** *On ne s'ennuie pas.* II, 11

bores: That bores me to death! *Ça m'ennuie à mourir!* III, 2; **That bores me!** *Ça m'embête!* III, 2

boring *barbant*, I, 2; *ennuyeux (ennuyeuse)*, II, 6, 8; *rasoir*, III, 2; **It was boring.** *C'était ennuyeux.* I, 5; **deadly boring** *mortel(le)*, III, 2; **That's boring!** *C'est rasant!* III, 2; **That's so boring!** *Ça me casse les pieds!* III, 2

born: be born *naître*, II, 6

borrow *emprunter*, I, 12

bother *ennuyer*, II, 8; **What bothers me is . . .** *Ce qui m'ennuie, c'est. . .* , II, 4; **Stop bothering me!** *Et toi, arrête de m'embêter!* III, 10

bottle: a bottle of *une bouteille de*, I, 8

bow (in archery) *l'arc* (m.), III, 12

box: a carton/box of *un paquet de*, I, 8

boxing *la boxe*, III, 12

bracelet *le bracelet*, I, 3

braces: to get one's braces off *se faire enlever ses bagues*, III, 10

brag: I'm not trying to brag, but . . . *C'est pas pour me vanter, mais moi. . .* , III, 10

braid *la natte*, III, 4

brakes *les freins* (m.), III, 2

brass, copper *le cuivre*, III, 8

brave *brave*, II, 1

Brazil *le Brésil*, III, 12

Brazilian (adj.) *brésilien(ne)*, III, 12

bread *du pain*, I, 8; *le pain*, II, 3

bread pudding *le pouding au pain*, III, 11

break *la récréation*, I, 2; **Give me a break!** *Oh, ça va, hein!* III, 10; **Will you give me a break?** *Lâche-moi, tu veux?* III, 10; **to break one's . . .** *se casser le/la . . .* , II, 7; III, 10;

break down *tomber en panne*, II, 9; **to break down (run out of gas)** *tomber en panne (d'essence)*, III, 2

break up (with someone) *casser (avec quelqu'un)*, II, 9

breakfast *le petit déjeuner*, I, 8

bring *apporter*, I, 9; **Bring me back . . .** *Rapporte-moi. . .* , I, 8; **Please bring me . . .** *Apportez-moi. . . , s'il vous plaît.* I, 5; **to bring (with you)** *emporter*, II, 12; **Will you bring me . . . ?** *Tu me rapportes. . . ?* I, 8

brother *le frère*, I, 7

brown *marron*, I, 3; II, 1; **light brown hair** *châtain* (inv.) II, 1; **dark brown hair** *les cheveux bruns*, II, 1

brunette *brun(e)*, I, 7

brush (bushes) *la brousse*, III, 7; **to brush one's teeth** *se brosser les dents*, II, 4

buffalo *le buffle*, III, 7

bugging: You're bugging me to death! *Tu m'énerves, à la fin!* III, 6

building *l'immeuble* (m.), III, 8

bun (hairstyle) *le chignon*, III, 4

bus: by bus *en bus*, I, 12; **bus stop** *l'arrêt* (m.) *de bus*, III, 8

business: Mind your own business! *Mêle-toi de tes oignons!* III, 6; **businessman/woman** *homme/femme d'affaires*, III, 5

busy: I'm very busy. *Je suis très occupé(e).* II, 10; **It's busy.** *C'est occupé.* I, 9; **Sorry, I'm busy.** *Désolé(e), je suis occupé(e).* I, 6; *Je suis pris(e).* III, 6

but *mais,* I, 1

butcher shop *la boucherie,* II, 3

butter *du beurre,* I, 8; *le beurre,* II, 3

butterfly *le papillon,* III, 7

buy *acheter,* I, 9

buy: Buy me . . . *Achète(-moi)... ,* I, 8; **How about buying . . . ?** *Si on achetait... ?* II, 8; **to buy oneself something** *s'acheter quelque chose,* III, 10

by: By the way, . . . *A propos,... ,* II, 9

Bye! *Tchao!* I, 1

C

café *le café,* I, 5

cafeteria: at the school cafeteria *à la cantine,* I, 9

Cajun music *la musique cajun,* III, 11

cake *du gâteau,* I, 8

calculator *la calculatrice,* I, 3

call (someone) *téléphoner à (quelqu'un),* II, 10; **Call him/her/them!** *Téléphone-lui/-leur!* I, 9; **Can you call back later?** *Vous pouvez rappeler plus tard?* I, 9; **Then I called . . .** *Ensuite, j'ai téléphoné à... ,* I, 9; **called: He/She called me a . . . !** *Il/Elle m'a traité(e) de... !* III, 6; **called: What is that called?** *Comment est-ce qu'on appelle ça?* III, 11; **calling: Who's calling?** *Qui est à l'appareil?* I, 9

calm *tranquille,* II, 8; **Calm down!** *Calmez-vous!* III, 7; **Calm down.** *Du calme, du calme.* III, 2

camcorder *le caméscope,* III, 7

camel *le chameau,* III, 8

camera *l'appareil-photo* (m.), I, 11; II, 1

camp: to/at a summer camp *en colonie de vacances,* I, 11

campground *le terrain de camping,* II, 2

camping: to go camping *faire du camping,* I, 11; II, 2

can: a can of *la boîte de,* I, 8

can (to be able to): *pouvoir,* I, 8; **Can I . . . ?** *Je peux... ?* III, 3; **Can I try on . . . ?** *Je peux essayer... ?* I, 10; **Can you . . . ?** *Est-ce que tu peux... ?* I, 12; **I can't.** *Je ne peux pas.* II, 1, 7; **I can't right now.** *Je ne peux pas maintenant.* I, 8; **No, I can't.** *Non, je ne peux pas.* I, 12; **Can I talk to you?** *Je peux te parler?* II, 10; **If you like, we can . . .** *Si tu veux, on peut... ,* II, 1; **We can . . .** *On peut... ,* II, 4; **What can I do?** *Qu'est-ce que je peux faire?* II, 10; **What can we do?** *Qu'est-ce qu'on peut faire?* II, 4; **You can . . .** *On peut... ,* II, 12

Canada *le Canada,* III, 12

canary *le canari,* I, 7

candies *les bonbons* (m), II, 3

candy shop *la confiserie,* II, 3

canoe: to go for a canoe ride *faire du canotage,* II, 12

cans *les boîtes* (f.), III, 3

canteen *la gourde,* III, 7

cap *la casquette,* I, 10

capital *la capitale,* II, 4

car: by car *en voiture,* I, 12; **to wash the**

car *laver la voiture,* I, 7; **to wreck the car** *planter la voiture,* III, 10

caramel custard *la crème caramel,* III, 1

care:
What I don't care for is . . . *Ce qui ne me plaît pas, c'est... ,* II, 4

career: to choose a career *choisir un métier,* III, 5

careful *prudent(e),* III, 3; **Be careful!** *Méfiez-vous!* III, 7

carrots *les carottes* (f.), I, 8; **grated carrots with vinaigrette dressing** *les carottes râpées,* III, 1

carton: a carton/box of *un paquet de,* I, 8

cartoon *le dessin animé,* III, 9

cartoon book *une bande dessinée (une B. D.),* II, 11

cassette tape *la cassette,* I, 3

cat *le chat,* I, 7

catches: What catches your eye is . . . *Ce qui saute aux yeux, c'est... ,* III, 11

cathedral *la cathédrale,* II, 2

CD (compact disc) *un disque compact/un CD,* I, 3

celery: grated celery root with mayonnaise and vinaigrette *le céleri rémoulade,* III, 1

Central African Republic *la République centrafricaine,* III, 12

cereal *des céréales* (f.), II, 3

certain: I'm (not) certain that . . . *Je (ne) suis (pas) certain(e) que... ,* III, 7

Certainly. *Bien sûr.* I, 9

chair *la chaise,* I, 0

channel (TV) *la chaîne,* III, 9

charming *charmant(e),* II, 4

Cheater! *Tricheur (-euse)!* III, 6

check *vérifier,* III, 2; **check out: Hey! Check it out!** *Tiens! Regarde un peu!* III, 7; **The check please.** *L'addition, s'il vous plaît.* I, 5; **traveler's checks** *les chèques* (m.) *de voyage,* II, 1

cheese *le fromage,* I, 5; II, 3; **a selection of cheeses** *l'assiette de fromages,* III, 1; **goat cheese** *fromage de chèvre,* III, 1; **toasted cheese and ham sandwich** *un croque-monsieur,* I, 5

cheetah *le guépard,* III, 7

chemistry *la chimie,* I, 2

chest: chest of drawers *la commode,* II, 2

chic *chic,* I, 10

chicken *la poule,* I, 3; III, 8

chicken *le poulet* I, 8; **chicken meat** *du poulet,* I, 8; **live chickens** *des poules,* I, 8; **roasted chicken with green beans** *le poulet haricots verts,* III, 1

child: to have a child *avoir un enfant,* III, 5

childish *bébé,* II, 2

China *la Chine,* III, 12

chocolate *le chocolat,* I, 1; **box of chocolates** *la boîte de chocolats,* II, 3

choice: If I had a choice, . . . *Si j'avais le choix,... ,* III, 8

choir *la chorale,* I, 2

choose *choisir,* I, 10; **to choose a career** *choisir un métier,* III, 5; **to choose the date** *fixer la date,* II, 10; **to choose the music** *choisir la musique,* II, 10

Christmas: Merry Christmas! *Joyeux Noël!* II, 3

church *l'église* (f.), II, 2

class: What classes do you have . . . ? *Tu as quels cours... ?* I, 2

classic *un (roman) classique,* II, 11; **classic movie** *un film classique,* II, 11

classical music *la musique classique,* II, 11; III, 11

classy *classe,* III, 4

clean *propre,* II, 8

clean: to clean house *faire le ménage,* I, 7; **to clean the bathroom** *nettoyer la salle de bains,* III, 3; **to clean the floor** *nettoyer le parquet,* III, 3; **to clean the windshield** *nettoyer le pare-brise,* III, 2

clear: to clear the table *débarrasser la table,* I, 7

close to *près de,* I, 12

close: That was close! *On l'a échappé belle!* III, 7

close: Close the door! *Fermez la porte!,* I, 0; **When do you close?** *A quelle heure est-ce que vous fermez?* II, 6

cloth *le tissu,* II, 8

coach *l'entraîneur* (m.), III, 12

coast: to/at the coast *au bord de la mer,* I, 11

coat *un manteau,* I, 10

coconut tree *un cocotier,* II, 4

coconuts *des noix de coco* (f.), I, 8

coffee *le café,* I, 5

cola *un coca,* I, 5

cold: I've got a cold. *J'ai un rhume.* II, 7; **It's cold.** *Il fait froid.* I, 4

colorful *coloré(e),* II, 4

come *venir,* II, 6; **come across: After . . . , you'll come across . . .** *Après..., vous allez tomber sur...* III, 2; **come back** *revenir,* II, 6; **Come in, please.** *Entrez, je vous en prie.* III, 6; **Come on!** *Allez!* II, 12; **Come on!** *Allez!* II, 7; **Where does the word . . . come from?** *D'où vient le mot... ?* III, 11; **Will you come?** *Tu viens?* I, 6

comedy *la comédie,* III, 9; *le film comique,* II, 11

comfortable: Mettez-vous à l'aise. III, 6

commercial *la publicité,* III, 9

common: What do . . . and . . . have in common? *Quel est le point commun entre... ?* III, 10

compact disc/CD *un disque compact/un CD,* I, 3

compass *une boussole,* II, 12

competition *la compétition,* III, 12

computer *un ordinateur,* I, 3

computer science *l'informatique,* I, 2

concerts *les concerts* (m.), I, 1

Congratulations! *Félicitations!* II, 3; II, 5

conservative *sérieux (-euse),* III, 4

considerate: to be considerate *être attentionné,* III, 3

conversation: Following our telephone conversation, . . . *Suite à notre conversation téléphonique,... ,* III, 5

convinced: I'm convinced that . . . *Je suis convaincu(e) que... ,* III, 7

cooked: How do you like your meat cooked? *Comment désirez-vous votre viande?* III, 1

cool *cool,* I, 2; **Cool!** *C'est le pied!* III, 7; **It's cool.** *Il fait frais.* I, 4; **super cool** *hyper-cool,* III, 4; **That's too cool!** *C'est trop cool!* III, 12; **very cool** *chouette,* II, 2; **Yes, very cool.** *Oui, très chouette.* I, 9; I, 11; **Your . . . is cool.** *Il/Elle est cool, ton/ta... ,* II, 2

copper *le cuivre,* III, 8

coral *du corail*, III, 10
corn *du maïs*, I, 8
corner: on the corner of *au coin de*, I, 12
corny *ringard(e)*, III, 4
Côte d'Ivoire *la République de Côte d'Ivoire*, III, 12
cotton: in cotton *en coton*, I, 10
could: Could you . . . ? *Tu pourrais...?* II, 10; Could you go by . . . ? *Tu pourrais passer à... ?* I, 12; I could have . . . *J'aurais pu...* , II, 10; If I could, . . . *Si seulement je pouvais,...* , III, 8; We could . . . *On pourrait...* , II, 1; You could give him/her (them) . . . *Tu pourrais lui (leur) offrir...* , II, 3; You could have . . . *Tu aurais pu...* , II, 10
country music *le country*, II, 11; III, 11
country: to/at the countryside *à la campagne*, I, 11
courage: You've really got courage. *Tu en as, du courage.* III, 10
course (school) *le cours*, I, 2; (meal) first course *l'entrée*, II, 3; main course *le plat principal*, II, 3; Of course not. *Bien sûr que non.* I, 10; Of course. *Bien sûr.* I, 3; II, 10; Of course. They are (He/She is) . . . *Bien sûr. C'est...* , II, 11; Yes, of course. *Oui, bien sûr.* I, 7
cousin *le cousin (la cousine)* I, 7
crab *le crabe*, III, 10
crafts: to make crafts *faire de l'artisanat* (m.), III, 8
crawfish *les écrevisses* (f.), III, 11
crazy (funny) *fou/folle*, III, 2; (wild) *dingue*, III, 2; Are you crazy or what? *Tu délires ou quoi?* III, 11; I'm crazy about that! *Ça me branche!* III, 2; What I'm really crazy about is . . . *Ce qui me branche vraiment, c'est...* , III, 11; You're driving me crazy! *Tu me prends la tête!* III, 6
cream: cream puff pastry *la religieuse*, II, 3
credit card *la carte de crédit*, III, 7
crew: a crew cut *les cheveux en brosse* (m.), III, 4
crocodile *le crocodile*, III, 7
croissant *les croissants* (m.), II, 3; croissant with a chocolate filling *le pain au chocolat*, II, 3
cross-country: to go cross-country skiing *faire une randonnée à skis*, II, 12
cross: Cross . . . *Traversez..* , II, 2; You cross . . . *Vous traversez...* , III, 2
crowd *la foule*, III, 8
Crybaby! *Pleurnicheur (-euse)!* III, 6
curly: curly hair *les cheveux frisés* (m.), III, 4
cut: Oh, cut it out! *Oh, ça va, hein?* III, 6; a crew cut *les cheveux en brosse* (m.), III, 4; a square cut *une coupe au carré*, III, 4; Did you get your hair cut? *Tu t'es fait couper les cheveux?* III, 4; to cut one's finger *se couper le doigt*, II, 7
cute *mignon, mignonne*, I, 7; II, 1; cute, but that's all *gentillet, sans plus*, II, 11
cycling *le cyclisme*, III, 12

D

dairy *la crémerie*, II, 3
dance *danser*, I, 1; *la danse*, I, 2; dance music *la dance*, III, 11; to dance the zouk *danser le zouk*, II, 4

dangerous *dangereux (dangereuse)*, II, 8
Darn it! *Zut!* I, 3; *Zut, alors!* III, 7; *Les boules!* III, 12
date (fruit) *la datte*, III, 8
date: to have (make) a date (with someone) *avoir (prendre) rendez-vous (avec quelqu'un)*, II, 9
day: I had a terrible day! *J'ai passé une journée épouvantable!* II, 5; It's just not my day! *C'est pas mon jour!* II, 5; What a bad day! *Quelle journée!* II, 5
dead *mort(e)*, III, 6
deadly: deadly dull *mortel*, II, 6
death: I was bored to death. *Je me suis ennuyé(e) à mourir.* III, 9
December *décembre*, I, 4
decide: I can't decide between . . . and . . . *J'hésite entre... et...* , III, 1; Have you decided to take . . . ? *Vous avez décidé de prendre... ?* I, 10; I'm having trouble deciding. *J'ai du mal à me décider.* III, 5
deface: to deface the trees *mutiler les arbres*, II, 12
Definitely not! *Sûrement pas!* II, 6
delicatessen *la charcuterie*, II, 3
delicious *délicieux*, I, 5; That was delicious! *C'était délicieux!* II, 3
denim: in denim *en jean*, I, 10
dentist *dentiste* (m.), II, 5
deposit *déposer*, I, 12
depressed *déprimé(e)*, II, 9
depressing *déprimant*, II, 11
dessert *le dessert*, II, 3; III, 1
detective: detective or mystery movie *un film policier*, II, 11; detective or mystery novel *un roman policier (un polar)*, II, 11
detention: to have detention *être collé(e)*, II, 5
dictionary *le dictionnaire*, I, 3
did: First, I did . . . *D'abord, j'ai fait...* , I, 9
die *mourir*, II, 6
diet: to follow a diet that's too strict. *suivre un régime trop strict*, II, 7
difference: What's the difference between . . . and . . . ? *Quelle est la différence entre ... et... ?* III, 10
different: Was it really so different? *C'était tellement différent?* II, 8
dining room *la salle à manger*, II, 2
dinner *le dîner*, I, 8; to have dinner *dîner*, II, 2
diploma: to get one's diploma *obtenir son diplôme*, III, 5
dirty *sale*, II, 8
discus: the discus throw *le lancer du disque*, III, 12
dishes: to do the dishes *faire la vaisselle*, I, 7
disinfectant *le désinfectant*, III, 7
dismissal (when school gets out) *la sortie*, I, 2
dive *plonger*, III, 12; diving *le plongeon acrobatique*, III, 12; diving board *le plongeoir*, III, 12
divorced *divorcé(e)*, III, 6
do *faire*, I, 4; All you have to do is . . . *Tu n'as qu'à...* , II, 7; III, 5; Do you know what you want to do? *Tu sais ce que tu veux faire?* III, 5; Do you play/do . . . ? *Est-ce que tu fais... ?* I, 4; Don't do it again. *Ne recommence pas.* II, 5; I do. *Moi, si.* I, 2; I don't know what to do. *Je ne sais pas quoi faire.* II, 10; I

don't play/do . . . *Je ne fais pas de...* , I, 4; I have errands to do. *J'ai des courses à faire.* I, 5; I just can't do any more! *Je n'en peux plus!* II, 7; I play/do . . . *Je fais...* , I, 4; In your opinion, what do I do? *A ton avis, qu'est-ce que je fais?* I, 9; It didn't do anything for me. *Ça ne m'a pas emballé(e).* III, 9; It'll do you good. *Ça te fera du bien.* II, 7; to do homework *faire les devoirs*, I, 7; to do the dishes *faire la vaisselle*, I, 7; What are you going to do . . . ? *Qu'est-ce que tu vas faire... ?* I, 6; II, 1; *Tu vas faire quoi... ?* I, 6; What can I do? *Qu'est-ce que je peux faire?* I, 9; What can we do? *Qu'est-ce qu'on peut faire?* II, 4; What did you do? *Qu'est-ce que tu as fait?* I, 9; What do you advise me to do? *Qu'est-ce que tu me conseilles?* I, 9; What do you do (when). . . ? *Qu'est-ce que tu fais (quand)... ,?* I, 4; What do you like to do? *Qu'est-ce que tu aimes faire?* II, 1; What should we do? *Qu'est-ce qu'on fait?* II, 1; What are you doing? *Mais, qu'est-ce que tu fais?* III, 2
doctor *médecin* (m.), III, 5
documentary *le documentaire*, III, 9
dog *le chien*, I, 7; to walk the dog *promener le chien*, I, 7; *sortir le chien*, III, 3
don't: I don't. *Moi, non.* I, 2; What I don't like is . . . *Ce que je n'aime pas, c'est...* , II, 4; Why don't you . . . ? *Pourquoi tu ne... pas... ?* II, 7
done, made *fait (faire)*, I, 9
door *la porte*, I, 2
doubt: I have no doubt of it. *Je n'en ai aucun doute.* III, 12
down: go down *descendre*, II, 6; You go down this street to the next light. *Vous continuez cette rue jusqu'au prochain feu rouge.* I, 12; downstairs *en bas*, III, 2
dozen *la douzaine de*, I, 8
drama *le drame*, III, 9; to do drama *faire du théâtre*, I, 4
drawers: chest of drawers *la commode*, II, 2
dream: My dream is to . . . *Mon rêve, c'est de...* , III, 5
dress *la robe*, I, 10; to get dressed *s'habiller*, II, 4
drink *la boisson*, I, 5; And to drink? *Et comme boisson?* III, 1; What do you have to drink? *Qu'est-ce que vous avez comme boissons?* I, 5
drive *conduire*, III, 2; to drive a car *conduire une voiture*, II, 8; to drive safely *conduire prudemment*, III, 3
driver *chauffeur* (m.), III, 5; to get one's driver's license *passer son permis de conduire*, III, 5
driving: You're driving me crazy! *Tu me prends la tête!* III, 6; to take driving lessons *prendre des leçons de conduite*, III, 10
drugstore *la pharmacie*, I, 12
drum (from Africa) *un tam-tam*, II, 8; drum machine *la boîte à rythmes*, III, 11; drums *la batterie*, III, 11
duck *un canard*, II, 12
dull: It's no good/dull. *C'est nul/lourd.* III, 9
dust: to dust *faire la poussière*, III, 3
dyed: dyed hair *les cheveux teints* (m.), III, 4

dying: I'm dying of hunger! *Je crève de faim!* II, 12; I'm dying of thirst! *Je meurs de soif!* II, 12

E

early *tôt*, II, 4
earrings *des boucles d'oreilles* (f.), I, 10
ears *les oreilles* (f.), II, 7; to get one's ears pierced *se faire percer les oreilles*, III, 10
earth-shattering: It's not earth-shattering. *Ça casse pas des briques.* II, 11
east: in the east *dans l'est*, II, 4; It's to the east of . . . *C'est à l'est de...*, II, 12
eastern: It's in the eastern part of . . . *C'est dans l'est de...*, II, 12
easy *facile*, I, 2; That's so easy! *C'est fastoche, ça!* III, 10
eat *manger*, I, 6; II, 7; to eat too much sugar *consommer trop de sucre*, II, 7; someone who loves to eat *gourmand(e)*, II, 1; to eat better *manger mieux*, III, 3; to eat well *bien se nourrir*, II, 7
eggs *des œufs* (m.), I, 8; II, 3
elderly: to help elderly people *aider les personnes âgées*, III, 3
elegant *élégant(e)*, III, 4
elementary school teacher *instituteur (-trice)*, III, 5
elephant *l'éléphant* (m.), III, 7
else: I have something else to do. *J'ai quelque chose à faire.* II, 10
embarrassed *gêné(e)*, II, 9
end: At the end . . . *A la fin...*, III, 9; How does it end? *Comment ça se termine?* III, 9; I went at the end of (month)... *J'y suis allé(e) fin...*, III, 1; Over there, at the end of the hallway. *Par là, au bout du couloir.* II, 2
energy *l'énergie* (f.), III, 3
engaged: to get engaged *se fiancer*, III, 10
engineer *ingénieur* (m.), III, 5
England *l'Angleterre* (f.), III, 12
English (language) *l'anglais* (m.), I, 1
enjoy *déguster*, II, 4
enough: Enough is enough! *Ça commence à bien faire, hein?* III, 8; That's enough! *Ça suffit!* III, 6
enter *entrer*, II, 6; to enter the university *entrer à l'université*, III, 5
entrance: At the entrance to . . . *A l'entrée de...*, III, 2; How much is the entrance fee? *C'est combien, l'entrée?* II, 6
envelope *l'enveloppe* (f.), I, 12
epee (sword) *l'épée* (f.), III, 12
equestrian events *l'équitation* (f.), III, 12
eraser *la gomme*, I, 3
especially *surtout*, I, 1
essential: It's essential to . . . *Il est essentiel que...*, III, 7
evening: *le soir*, I, 2; in the evening *le soir*, I, 2
everybody: Everybody does it. *Tout le monde fait pareil.* III, 3; It happens to everybody. *Ça arrive à tout le monde.* III, 6
everyone: Everyone should . . . *On doit.* II, 7; Just because everyone else . . . doesn't mean you have to. *Ce n'est pas parce que tout le monde... que tu dois le faire.* III, 3

everything: Everything went wrong! *Tout a été de travers!* II, 5; I've thought of everything. *J'ai pensé à tout.* I, 11
exam *les examens* (m.), I, 1; to pass one's baccalaureat exam *réussir son bac*, III, 5
excellent *excellent*, I, 5, 9; II, 2
exciting: It's an exciting story. *C'est une histoire passionnante.* II, 11
excuse: Excuse me. *Excusez-moi.!* I, 3, 5; Excuse me, ma'am. . . . , please? *Pardon, madame. ... , s'il vous plaît?* I, 12; Excuse me, miss. Where is . . . , please? *Pardon, mademoiselle. Où est... , s'il vous plaît?* I, 12; Excuse me, sir. I'm looking for . . . , please. *Pardon, monsieur. Je cherche... , s'il vous plaît.* I, 12
exercise *faire de l'exercice*, II, 7
exhausted: I'm exhausted. *Je suis crevé(e).* II, 7
expensive: It's too expensive. *C'est trop cher.* II, 3; Oh, it wasn't expensive. *Oh, tu sais, je ne l'ai pas payé(e) cher.* III, 4
explain: Explain to him/her/them. *Explique-lui/leur.* II, 10; to explain what happened (to someone) *expliquer ce qui s'est passé (à quelqu'un)*, II, 10
eye *l'œil* (m.) (pl. *les yeux*), II, 1

F

fabric *le tissu*, II, 8
faded *délavé(e)*, III, 4
fail: to fail a test *rater un examen*, I, 9
fair: It's not fair. *C'est pas juste.* III, 12
fall *tomber*, II, 5; in the fall *en automne*, I, 4; to fall in love (with someone) *tomber amoureux (-euse) (de quelqu'un)*, III, 9
familiar: Are you familiar with . . . ? *Tu connais...*, II, 11; I'm not familiar with them (him/her). *Je ne connais pas.* II, 11
fantastic *sensas (sensationnel)*, I, 10
far from *loin de*, I, 12
fascinating *passionnant(e)*, I, 2
fat (adj.) *gros (grosse)*, I, 7; (noun) *les matières grasses* (f.), II, 7
father *le père*, I, 7
fault: It's my fault. *C'est de ma faute.* II, 10
favorite: What is your favorite . . . ? *Quel est ton... préféré(e)?* II, 1; Who is your favorite . . . ? *Qui est ton... préféré(e)?* II, 1
February *février*, I, 4
fee: How much is the entrance fee? *C'est combien, l'entrée?* II, 6
feed: to feed the animals *donner à manger aux animaux*, II, 6; *nourrir les animaux*, II, 6
feel: Do you feel like . . . ? *Tu as envie de... ?* II, 1; I don't feel well. *Je ne me sens pas bien.* II, 7; I feel bad for . . . *Je m'en veux de...*, III, 6; I feel like . . . *J'ai envie de...*, I, 11; No, I don't feel like it. *Non, je n'ai pas très envie.* II, 7
feelings: No hard feelings. *Je ne t'en veux pas.* II, 10; No hard feelings? *Tu ne m'en veux pas?* II, 10
fencing *l'escrime* (f.), III, 12
ferocious *féroce*, III, 7
ferris wheel *la grande roue*, II, 6

fewer: fewer . . . than . . . *moins de... que*, III, 8
fig *la figue*, III, 8
fight *se bagarrer*, III, 10
fill: to fill it up *faire le plein*, III, 2
film: foreign film *le film étranger*, III, 9; roll of film *la pellicule*, III, 7; What films are playing? *Qu'est-ce qu'on joue comme film?* II, 11
Finally . . . *Enfin,... ,* II, 1; *Finalement... ,* II, 4
find *trouver*, I, 9; Could you tell me where I could find . . *Vous pourriez me dire où il y a... ?* III, 2; to find a job *trouver un travail*, III, 5
finish: to finish one's studies *finir ses études* (f.), III, 5
Fine. *Ça va.* I, 1; Yes, it was fine. *Oui, ça a été.* I, 9
fire: Where's the fire? *Il n'y a pas le feu.* III, 2
first: First, . . . *D'abord,... ,* II, 12; First, I did . . . *D'abord, j'ai fait... ,* I, 9; First, I'm going to . . . *D'abord, je vais... ,* II, 1; OK, if you . . . first. *D'accord, si tu... d'abord... ,* I, 7
first-aid kit *une trousse de premiers soins*, II, 12; III, 7
fish *le poisson*, I, 7; II, 3; *du poisson*, I, 8; *pêcher*, III, 8; fish shop *la poissonnerie*, II, 3
fishing: fishing pole *une canne à pêche*, II, 12; fishing village *un village de pêcheurs*, II, 4; to go fishing *aller à la pêche*, II, 4
fits: That fits you like a glove. *Ça te va comme un gant.* III, 4
flashlight *une lampe de poche*, II, 12; *la torche*, III, 7
flat: to have a flat tire *avoir un pneu crevé*, III, 2
floor: first (ground) floor *le rez-de-chaussée*, II, 2; On the ground floor. *Au rez-de-chaussée.* III, 2; On the second floor. *Au premier étage.* III, 2; second floor *le premier étage*, II, 2; to clean the floor *nettoyer le parquet*, III, 3
florist's shop *le fleuriste*, II, 3
flour *de la farine*, I, 8
flu: I've got the flu. *J'ai la grippe.* II, 7
flute *la flûte*, III, 11
fly *la mouche*, III, 7
folk music *le folk*, II, 11; III, 11
follow: to follow a diet that's too strict. *suivre un régime trop strict*, II, 7; to follow the marked trails *suivre les sentiers balisés*, II, 12; To get to . . . , follow . . . for about . . . kilometers. *Pour (aller à)..., vous suivez la... pendant à peu près... kilomètres.* III, 2
following: Following our telephone conversation, . . . *Suite à notre conversation téléphonique,... ,* III, 5
foot *le pied*, II, 7; My foot hurts. *J'ai mal au pied.* II, 7; on foot *à pied*, I, 12
football: to play football *jouer au football américain*, I, 4
for: It's good for you. *C'est bon pour toi.* II, 7
forbidden: It's forbidden to . . . *Il est interdit de...*, III, 3
foreign: foreign film *le film étranger*, III, 9
forest: to the forest *en forêt*, I, 11
forget *oublier*, I, 9; Don't forget . . .

N'oublie pas... , II, 1; *N'oublie pas de...* I, 8; **Forget him/her/them!** *Oublie-le/-la/-les!* I, 9; II, 10; **I didn't forget anything.** *Je n'ai rien oublié.* I, 11; **You didn't forget your . . . ?** *Tu n'as pas oublié... ?* I, 11

forgive (someone) *pardonner à (quelqu'un),* II, 10; **Forgive me.** *Excuse-moi.* II, 10

forgiveness: to ask (someone's) forgiveness *demander pardon à (quelqu'un),* II, 10

Fortunately, . . . *Heureusement,... ,* II, 9

fox *un renard,* II, 12

frame: photo frame *le cadre,* II, 3

franc (the French monetary unit) *le franc,* I, 3

free: I'm free, aren't I? *Je suis libre, non?* III, 3

freeway: You'll see a sign that points out the freeway entrance. *Vous allez voir un panneau qui indique l'entrée de l'autoroute.* III, 2

French (language) *le français* 1; **French fries** *les frites* (f.), I, 1

Friday: on Fridays *le vendredi,* I, 2

fried *frit(e),* III, 11

friends *les ami(e)s* , I, 1; **to go out with friends** *sortir avec les copains,* I, 1

from: Do people . . . where you're from? *On... chez toi?* III, 12; **Do you have/Are there . . . where you're from?** *Vous avez/Il y a des... chez vous?* III, 12; **From platform . . .** *Du quai... ,* II, 6; **Where are you from?** *Tu es d'où?* III, 12

front: in front of *devant,* I, 6

fun *amusant(e),* II, 11; **Did you have fun?** *Tu t'es amusé(e)?* II, 6; *Tu t'es bien amusé(e)?* I, 11; III, 1; **Have fun!** *Amuse-toi bien!* I, 11; **I had a lot of fun.** *Je me suis beaucoup amusé(e).* II, 6; III, 1; **What do you do to have fun?** *Qu'est-ce que tu fais pour t'amuser?* I, 4

funny *amusant(e),* I, 7; II, 1; *marrant(e),* III, 2; **funny (crazy)** *fou/folle,* III, 2; **funny (hysterical)** *rigolo(te),* III, 2; **funny (wild)** *dingue,* III, 2; **It's funny.** *C'est drôle (amusant).* II, 11

furious *furieux (furieuse),* II, 9

G

gain: to gain weight *grossir,* I, 10

game (match) *le match,* III, 12; **game show** *le jeu télévisé,* III, 9; **to watch a game (on TV)** *regarder un match,* I, 6

gas *l'essence* (f.), III, 2; **gas station** *une station-service,* III, 2; **the gas tank** *le réservoir,* III, 2

gaudy *tape-à-l'œil,* III, 4

geography *la géographie,* I, 2

geometry *la géométrie,* I, 2

German (language) *l'allemand* (m.), I, 2; (adj.)

Germany *l'Allemagne* (f.), III, 12

get: As soon as I get there, . . . *Dès que je serai là,... ,* III, 12; **Get . . .** *Prends... ,* I, 8; **Get a move on!** *Grouille-toi!* III, 2; **Get out of here!** *Casse-toi!* III, 6; **Get well soon!** *Bon rétablissement!* II, 3; **Get with it!** *Réveille-toi un peu!* III, 10; **get up** *se lever,* II, 4; **How can I get to . . . ?** *Comment on va à... ?* III, 2; **How**

can we get there? *Comment est-ce qu'on y va?* I, 12; **How did you get there?** *Tu es parti(e) comment?* III, 1; **It'll get better.** *Ça va aller mieux.* II, 5; **To get to . . . , follow . . . for about . . . kilometers.** *Pour (aller à)..., vous suivez la... pendant à peu près... kilomètres.* III, 2; **to get a bad grade** *avoir une mauvaise note,* II, 5; **to get an 8 in . . .** *avoir 8 en... ,* II, 5; **to get lost** *se perdre,* II, 9; **to get ready** *faire les préparatifs,* II, 10; **You'll get used to it.** *Tu vas t'y faire.* II, 8

gift *le cadeau,* I, 11; **gift shop** *la boutique de cadeaux,* II, 3; **Have you got a gift idea for. . . ?** *Tu as une idée de cadeau pour... ?* II, 3

giraffe *la girafe,* III, 7

give: Give . . . a kiss for me. *Embrasse... pour moi.* III, 8; **Give . . . my regards.** *Fais mes amitiés à... ,* III, 8; **Give him/her (them) . . .** *Offre-lui (leur) ... ,* II, 3; **Give me your . . .** *Donnez-moi votre... ,* III, 6; **Please give me . . .** *Donnez-moi... , s'il vous plaît.* I, 5; **to give (to someone)** *offrir (à quelqu'un),* II, 10; **What could I give to . . . ?** *Qu'est-ce que je pourrais offrir à... ?* II, 3; **You could give him/her (them) . . .** *Tu pourrais lui (leur) offrir... ,* II, 3

give up: I give up. *J'abandonne.* II, 7

glad: I'm glad to see you again. *Je suis content(e) de te revoir.* III, 1

Gladly. *Je veux bien.* I, 8

glass *le verre,* III, 3

glove *le gant,* III, 12; **gloves** *les gants* (m.), I, 1; III, 4; **That fits you like a glove.** *Ça te va comme un gant.* III, 4

go *aller,* I, 6; **Go to the blackboard!** *Allez au tableau!,* I, 0; **Could you go by . . . ?** *Tu pourrais passer à... ?* I, 12; **Did it go well?** *Ça s'est bien passé?* I, 9; **Don't go!** *N'y va pas!* III, 9; **Go (keep going) straight ahead.** *Allez (continuez) tout droit,* II, 2; **How did it go?** *Comment ça s'est passé?* I, 9; **Let's go . . .** *Allons... ,* I, 6; **to go for a walk** *faire une promenade,* I, 6; **We can go there . . .** *On peut y aller... ,* I, 12; **Where did you go?** *Tu es allé(e) où?* I, 9; **You go down this street to the next light.** *Vous continuez cette rue jusqu'au prochain feu rouge.* I, 12

go back (home) *rentrer,* II, 6

go down *descendre,* II, 6

go out *sortir,* II, 6; **to go out with friends** *sortir avec les copains,* I, 1

go up *monter,* II, 6; **to go up in a tower** *monter dans une tour,* II, 6

go with: It doesn't go at all with . . . *Il/Elle ne va pas du tout avec... ,* I, 10; **It goes very well with . . .** *Il/Elle va très bien avec... ,* I, 10; **I'd like . . . to go with . . .** *J'aimerais... pour aller avec... ,* I, 10

goat *la chèvre,* III, 8; **goat cheese** *le fromage de chèvre,* III, 1

going: First, I'm going to . . . *D'abord, je vais... ,* II, 1; **How about going . . . ?** *Si on allait... ?* II, 4; **How's it going? (Comment) ça va?** I, 1; **I'm going . . .** *Je vais... ,* I, 6; **I'm going to . . .** *Je vais... ,* I, 11; **I'm going to have . . . , please.** *Je vais prendre... , s'il vous plaît.* I, 5; **What are you going to do . . . ?** *Qu'est-ce que tu vas faire . . . ?* I, 6; II, 1; **What do**

you think about going . . . ? *Ça te dit d'aller... ?* II, 4; **What's going on?** *Qu'est-ce qui se passe?* II, 5; **What's going on with you?** *Qu'est-ce que tu deviens?* III, 1; **Where are you going to go . . . ?** *Où est-ce que tu vas aller... ?* I, 11; **You're going to like it here.** *Tu vas te plaire ici.* II, 8

golf *le golf,* I, 4; **to play golf** *jouer au golf,* I, 4

good *bon,* I, 5; **Did you have a good . . . ?** *Tu as passé un bon... ?* I, 11; **Did you have a good trip?** *Vous avez (Tu as) fait bon voyage?* II, 2; **Good idea!** *Bonne idée!* II, 3; **I've got a good one.** *J'en connais une bonne.* III, 10; **It'll do you good.** *Ça te fera du bien.* II, 7; **It's good for you.** *C'est bon pour toi.* II, 7; **It's good!** *C'est vraiment bon!* II, 3; **not very good** *pas bon,* I, 5; **That's a good (excellent) idea.** *C'est une bonne (excellente) idée.* II, 1; **That's a good one!** *Elle est bien bonne!* III, 10; **Yes, very good.** *Oui, très bon.* I, 9; **You're really strong/good at that.** *Tu es fortiche/calé(e).* III, 10

Goodbye! *Au revoir!* I, 1; *Salut!* I, 1

goofing: You can't be goofing off in class! *Il ne faut pas faire le clown en classe!* II, 5

got (to have to): All you've got to do is . . . *Tu n'as qu'à... ,* III, 5; **No. You've got . . . to . . .** *Non, tu as... à... ,* I, 7

grade: to get a bad grade *avoir une mauvaise note,* II, 5

granddaughter *la petite-fille,* III, 6

grandfather *le grand-père,* I, 7

grandmother *la grand-mère,* I, 7

grandson *le petit-fils,* III, 6

grapes *du raisin,* I, 8

grass *l'herbe* (f.), III, 7

great *génial(e),* I, 2; II, 2; *superbe,* II, 6; **Great!** *Super!* I, 1; *Génial!* III, 12; **Isn't it great!** *Ce que c'est bien!* III, 2; **It was great!** *C'était formidable!* I, 11; *C'était chouette!* III, 1; **It wasn't so great.** *C'était pas terrible.* III, 1; **It would be great if . . .** *Ça serait chouette si... ,* III, 8; **Not so great.** *Pas terrible.* I, 1; **What a great day!** *Quelle journée formidable!* II, 5; **What a great weekend!** *Quel week-end formidable!* II, 5; **Your . . . is really great.** *Il/Elle est vraiment bien, ton/ta... ,* II, 2

great-grandfather *l'arrière-grand-père* (m.), III, 6

great-grandmother *l'arrière-grand-mère,* (f.), III, 6

green *vert(e)(s),* I, 3; II, 1; **green beans** *les haricots verts* (m.), I, 8

grey *gris(e)(s),* I, 3

grocery store *l'épicerie* (f.), I, 12

gross *dégoûtant,* I, 5

ground: on the ground *par terre,* III, 3; **On the ground floor.** *Au rez-de-chaussée.* III, 2

grounded: to be "grounded" *être privé(e) de sortie,* II, 9

group *un groupe,* II, 11

grow *grandir,* I, 10

to grow wheat *cultiver le blé,* III, 8

Guadeloupe *la Guadeloupe,* III, 12

guavas *des goyaves* (f.), I, 8

guess: Guess what . . . *Devine ce que... ,* II, 9; **Guess who . . .** *Devine qui... ,* II, 9; **You'll never guess what happened.**

Tu ne devineras jamais ce qui s'est passé. II, 9

guide: TV guide/listing *le programme télé,* III, 9

guided: to take a guided tour *faire une visite guidée,* II, 6

guitar *la guitare,* III, 11

gumbo *le gombo,* III, 11

guy: It's about a guy who . . . *C'est l'histoire d'un mec qui... ,* III, 10

gym *le sport,* I, 2

gymnastics *la gymnastique,* III, 12; **to do gymnastics** *faire de la gymnastique,* II, 7

H

had: I've really had it! *J'en ai ras le bol!* III, 8; **I've had it up to here!** *J'en ai jusque là!* III, 8; **I've just about had it!** *Je commence à en avoir marre!* III, 8

hair *les cheveux* (m.), II, 1; **black hair** *les cheveux noirs,* II, 1; **blond hair** *les cheveux blonds,* II, 1; **dark brown hair** *les cheveux bruns,* II, 1; **curly hair** *les cheveux frisés,* III, 4; **dyed hair** *les cheveux teints,* III, 4; **hair stylist** *un coiffeur (une coiffeuse),* III, 4; **long hair** *les cheveux longs,* II, 1; III, 4; **red hair** *les cheveux roux,* II, 1; **short hair** *les cheveux courts,* II, 1; III, 4; **straight hair** *les cheveux raides,* III, 4

haircut *la coupe,* III, 4

Haiti *Haïti* (m.), III, 12

half: half past *et demie,* I, 6; **half past (after midi and minuit)** *et demi,* I, 6

ham *le jambon,* I, 5; II, 3; **toasted cheese and ham sandwich** *un croque-monsieur,* I, 5

hamburgers *les hamburgers* (m.), I, 1

hand *la main,* I, 0; II, 7

handsome *beau,* II, 1

hang: Hang in there! *Courage!* II, 5

hang glide *faire du deltaplane,* II, 4

Hanukkah: Happy Hanukkah! *Bonne fête de Hanoukka!* II, 3

happen: It could happen to anyone. *Ça peut arriver à tout le monde.* III, 10

happened: What happened? *Qu'est-ce qui s'est passé?* I, 9; **to explain what happened (to someone)** *expliquer ce qui s'est passé (à quelqu'un),* II, 10; **What happened?** *Qu'est-ce qui s'est passé?* I, 9; **You'll never guess what happened.** *Tu ne devineras jamais ce qui s'est passé.* II, 9

happens: It happens to everybody. *Ça arrive à tout le monde.* III, 6

happy: Happy birthday! *Joyeux (Bon) anniversaire!* II, 3; **Happy Hanukkah!** *Bonne fête de Hanoukka!* II, 3; **Happy holiday! (Happy saint's day!)** *Bonne fête!* II, 3; **Happy New Year!** *Bonne année!* II, 3; **I'm happy to see you.** *Ça me fait plaisir de vous voir.* III, 6

hard *difficile,* I, 2; **No hard feelings.** *Je ne t'en veux pas.* II, 10; **No hard feelings?** *Tu ne m'en veux pas?* II, 10

harm: No harm done. *Il n'y a pas de mal.* II, 10

harvest: to harvest fruits *faire la cueillette,* III, 8

has: He/She has . . . *Il/Elle a... ,* II, 1

hat *un chapeau,* I, 10

have *avoir,* I, 2; **have fun** *s'amuser,* II, 4; **At what time do you have . . . ?** *Tu as... à quelle heure?* I, 2; **Do you have . . . ?** *Tu as... ?* I, 3; **Do you have . . . ?** *Vous avez... ?* I, 2; **Do you have that in . . . ? (size, fabric, color)** *Vous avez ça en... ?* I, 10; **Have . . . Prends... ,** I, 5; **Have a good (car) trip!** *Bonne route!* II, 3; **Have a good trip! (by plane, ship)** *Bon voyage!* II, 3; **He/She has . . .** *Il/Elle a... ,* II, 1; **I don't have . . .** *Je n'ai pas de... ,* I, 3; **I have some things to do.** *J'ai des trucs à faire.* I, 5; **I have...** *J'ai... ,* I, 5; II, 1; **I'll have . . . , please.** *Je prends... , s'il vous plaît.* I, 5; **I'm going to have . . . , please.** *Je vais prendre... , s'il vous plaît.* I, 5; **May I have some . . . ?** *Je pourrais avoir... ?* II, 3; **They have . . .** *Ils/Elles ont... ,* II, 1; **to have an accident** *avoir un accident,* II, 9; **to have an argument (with someone)** *se disputer (avec quelqu'un),* II, 9; **to have done** *faire + infinitive,* III, 4; **to take or to have (food or drink)** *prendre,* I, 5; **to have a child** *avoir un enfant,* III, 5; **We have . . .** *Nous avons... ,* I, 2; **What classes do you have . . . ?** *Tu as quels cours... ?* I, 2; **What do you have . . . ?** *Tu as quoi... ?* I, 2; **What kind of . . . do you have?** *Qu'est-ce que vous avez comme... ?* I, 5 L1; **Will you have . . . ?** *Tu prends... ?* I, 8; *Vous prenez ... ?* I, 8; **Would you have . . . ?** *Vous auriez... ?* III, 6; **Yes, do you have . . . ?** *Oui, vous avez... ?* I, 10; **Why don't you have . . . ?** *Pourquoi tu ne prends pas... ?* III, 1

have to: All you have to do is . . . *Tu n'as qu'à... ,* II, 7; **First you have to . . .** *Il faut que... d'abord.* III, 3; **You have to do better in class.** *Il faut mieux travailler en classe.* II, 5; **You have to . . .** *Tu dois... ,* III, 3

having: What are you having? *Vous prenez?* I, 5

head *la tête,* II, 7

health *le cours de développement personnel et social (DPS),* I, 2

hear: Did you hear the latest? *Tu connais la nouvelle?* II, 9; **Let's hear it!** *Dis vite!* II, 9; **to hear the alarm clock** *entendre le réveil,* I, 5

heard: Have you heard the latest? *Tu connais la dernière?* III, 10; **I've heard that . . .** *J'ai entendu dire que... ,* III, 10

heavy *lourd(e),* III, 7

height: of medium height *de taille moyenne,* II, 1

Hello *Bonjour* 1; **Hello? (on the phone)** *Allô?* I, 9

helmet *le casque,* III, 12

help *aider,* II, 8

Can you help me? *Tu peux m'aider?* II, 10; **May I help you?** *(Est-ce que) je peux vous aider?* I, 10; **to help elderly people** *aider les personnes âgées,* III, 3

her *la,* I, 9; **her** *son/sa/ses,* I, 7; *lui,* I, 9

here: Here. *Voilà.* I, 3; **Here's . . .** *Voici...* I, 7; **Here (There) is . . .** *Là, c'est... ,* II, 2; **Here . . . , whereas . . .** *Ici,... tandis que... ,* III, 8; **Here it is.** *Voilà.* II, 3; **Here you are.** *Tenez (tiens).* II, 3

Hey! Check it out! *Tiens! Regarde un peu!*

III, 7; **Hey, do you think you can . . . ?** *Dites donc, ça vous gênerait de . . . ?* III, 8

Hi! *Salut!* I, 1; **Tell . . . hi for me.** *Salue... de ma part.* III, 8

hideous *affreux (-euse),* III, 4

high heels *les hauts talons* (m.), III, 4

high school *le lycée,* II, 2; **high school/ college teacher** *professeur,* III, 5

hike: to go for a hike *faire une randonnée pédestre,* II, 12

hiking: to go hiking *faire de la randonnée,* I, 11

him *le,* I, 9; *lui,* I, 9

hippopotamus *l'hippopotame* (m.), III, 7

his *son/sa/ses,* I, 7

historical: historical movie *le film historique,* III, 9

history *l'histoire* (f.), I, 2

hockey: to play hockey *jouer au hockey,* I, 4

Hold on. *Ne quittez pas.* I, 9

holiday: Happy holiday! (Happy saint's day!) *Bonne fête!* II, 3

home: Make yourself at home. *Faites (Fais) comme chez vous (toi),* II, 2; **Welcome to my home (our home)** *Bienvenue chez moi (chez nous),* II, 2

homework *les devoirs* (m.), I, 2; **I've got homework to do.** *J'ai des devoirs à faire.* I, 5; **to do homework** *faire ses devoirs,* I, 7

horn *une corne,* III, 7

horrible: It was horrible. *C'était épouvantable.* I, 9; **This is just horrible!** *C'est l'horreur!* III, 8; **to have a horrible day** *avoir une journée épouvantable,* II, 5

horror movie *le film d'horreur,* II, 11

hors d'œuvre *les hors-d'œuvre,* III, 11

horseback: to go horseback riding *faire de l'équitation,* I, 1

hose *un collant,* I, 10

hostel: youth hostel *l'auberge de jeunesse (f.),* II, 2

hot: hot chocolate *un chocolat,* I, 5; **hot dog** *un hot-dog,* I, 5; **It's hot.** *Il fait chaud.* I, 4; **not so hot** *pas super,* I, 2

house: at my *chez moi,* I, 6; **Is this . . . 's house?** *Je suis bien chez... ?* I, 9; **to clean house** *faire le ménage,* I, 7; **to/ at . . . 's** *chez... ,* I, 11

housework: to do housework *faire le ménage,* I, 7; II, 10

how: Could you tell me how to get to . . . ? *La route pour..., s'il vous plaît?* III, 2; **Did you see how . . . ?** *Tu as vu comme... ?* III, 7; **How about . . . ?** *On... ?* I, 4; **How about buying . . . ?** *Si on achetait... ?* II, 8; **How about going . . . ?** *Si on allait... ?* II, 4; **How about playing . . . ?** *Si on jouait... ?* II, 8; **How about playing baseball?** *On joue au base-ball?* I, 5; **How about skiing?** *On fait du ski?* I, 5; **How about that!** *Ça alors!* III, 7; **How about visiting . . . ?** *Si on visitait... ?* II, 8; **How can I get to . . . ?** *Comment on va à... ?* III, 2; **How did it go?** *Comment ça s'est passé?* II, 5; **How do you like it?** *Comment tu trouves ça?* I, 5; **How do you say . . . ?** *Comment on dit... ?* III, 11; **How many (much) do you want?** *Combien en voulez-vous?* II, 3; **How much does that make?** *Ça fait combien?* II, 3; **How much is (are). . . ?** *Combien coûte(nt)... ?* II, 3; **How much is . . . ?**

C'est combien,... ? I, 5; **How much is it?** *C'est combien?* I, 3; *Ça fait combien?* I, 10; **How much is it, please?** *Ça fait combien, s'il vous plaît?* I, 5; **How old are you?** *Tu as quel âge?* I, 1; **How was it?** *C'était comment?* II, 6; **How was your day (yesterday)?** *Comment s'est passée ta journée (hier)?* II, 5; **How was your vacation?** *Comment se sont passées tes vacances?* II, 5; **How was your weekend?** *Comment s'est passé ton week-end?* II, 5; **How's it going?** *(Comment) ça va?* I, 1; **How . . . !** *Qu'est-ce que... !* III, 6

hugs: Hugs and kisses. *Grosses bises.* III, 8; *Je t'embrasse bien fort.* III, 8

hunger: I'm dying of hunger! *Je crève de faim!* II, 12; **Yes, I'm dying of hunger!** *Si, je meurs de faim!* II, 2

hungry: to be hungry *avoir faim,* I, 5; **Aren't you hungry?** *Vous n'avez pas (Tu n'as pas) faim?* II, 2; **I'm not hungry anymore.** *Je n'ai plus faim.* II, 3; **No thanks. I'm not hungry anymore.** *Non, merci. Je n'ai plus faim.* I, 8; **Yes, I'm very hungry** *Si, j'ai très faim!* II, 2

hurry: Can you hurry up? *Tu peux te dépêcher?* III, 2; **Hurry up!** *Dépêche-toi!* III, 2; **people in a hurry** *les gens pressés,* III, 8

hurt: I hurt all over! *J'ai mal partout!* II, 7; **My . . . hurts.** *J'ai mal... ,* II, 7; **to hurt one's . . .** *se faire mal à ... ,* II, 7; III, 10

husband *le mari,* III, 6

hysterical (funny) *rigolo(te),* III, 2

I

I *je,* I, 0

I'd: I'd like to buy . . . *Je voudrais acheter... ,* I, 3

ice: to ice-skate *faire du patin à glace,* I, 4

ice cream *la glace,* I, 1

idea: Good idea. *Bonne idée.* I, 4; II, 3; **That's a good (excellent) idea.** *C'est une bonne (excellente) idée.* II, 1; **I have no idea.** *Je n'en sais rien.* I, 11; *Je n'en ai aucune idée.* III, 5; **No idea.** *Aucune idée.* II, 9

if: If . . . *Si... ,* III, 5; **If I could, . . .** *Si seulement je pouvais,... ,* III, 8; **If I had a choice, . . .** *Si j'avais le choix,... ,* III, 8; **If I were in your place, . . .** *A ta place,... ,* III, 8; **If I were you, . . .** *Si j'étais toi,... ,* III, 8; **If it were me, . . .** *Si c'était moi,... ,* III, 8; **OK, if you . . . first.** *D'accord, si tu... d'abord.* I, 7; **Yes, if . . .** *Oui, si... ,* III, 3

imagine: Can you imagine that . . . *Figure-toi que... ,* III, 10

impolite: impolite people *les gens (m.) mal élevés,* III, 8

important: It's very important to . . . *Il est très important que... ,* III, 7

impossible: It's impossible. *C'est impossible.* II, 10

impressed: I'm really impressed! *Alors, là, tu m'épates!* III, 10

impression: I have the impression that . . . *J'ai l'impression que... ,* III, 11

in *dans,* I, 6; **. . . is (are) in it.** *C'est avec... ,* II, 11; **in (a city or place)** *à,* I, 11; **in (before a feminine noun)** *en,* I, 11; **in (before a masculine noun)** *au,* I, 11; **in (before a plural noun)** *aux,* I, 11; **In a hotel.** *A l'hôtel.* III, 1; **in front of** *devant,* I, 6; **in order to** *afin de,* I, 7; **in the afternoon** *l'après-midi,* I, 2; **in the evening** *le soir,* I, 2; **in the morning** *le matin,* I, 2; **in the water** *dans l'eau,* III, 3; **The girl in the/with the . . .** *La fille au... ,* III, 4; **What's in . . .?** *Qu'est-ce qu'il y a dans... ?* III, 11; **Who's in it?** *C'est avec qui?* II, 11

incredible *incroyable,* II, 6

indifference: (expression of indifference) *Bof!* I, 1; II, 8

information: Could you send me information on . . . ? *Pourriez-vous m'envoyer des renseignements sur... ?* III, 5

insect repellent *de la lotion anti-moustiques,* II, 12

intend: I intend to . . . *J'ai l'intention de... ,* I, 11; III, 5; **What do you intend to do?** *Qu'est-ce que tu as l'intention de faire?* III, 5

interest: That doesn't interest me. *Ça ne me dit rien.* I, 4; II, 1

interested: Would you be interested in . . . ? *Ça t'intéresse de... ,* III, 6

interesting *intéressant,* I, 2; **It's not interesting.** *Ça n'a aucun intérêt.* III, 9

into: Are you into . . .? *Ça te branche,... ?* III, 11; **I'm not into that.** *Ça ne me branche pas.* III, 11

invite: Invite him/her/them. *Invite-le/la/les.* II, 10

ironing: to do the ironing *faire le repassage,* III, 3

is: He/She is . . . *Il/Elle est... ,* II, 1; **There is/are . . .** *Il y a... ,* II, 12

island *l'île* (f.), II, 4

isn't: Isn't it great! *Ce que c'est bien!* III, 2

isolated *isolé(e),* II, 8

it *le, la,* I, 9

it's: It's . . . *C'est... ,* I, 2; II, 11; **It's . . . francs.** *Ça fait... francs.* I, 5

Italy *l'Italie* (f.), III, 12

J

jacket *le blouson,* I, 10; **ski jacket** *l'anorak* (m.), II, 1

jam *de la confiture,* I, 8

jambalaya *le jambalaya,* III, 11

January *janvier,* I, 4

Japan *le Japon,* III, 12

jazz *le jazz,* II, 11; III, 11

jeans: pair of jeans *un jean,* I, 3; II, 1

jellyfish *la méduse,* III, 10

jewelry *les bijoux* (m.), III, 8

job: to find a job *trouver un travail,* III, 5

jog *faire du jogging,* I, 4

joke: What a stupid joke! *Elle est nulle, ta blague!* III, 10

joking: You're joking! *Tu plaisantes!* II, 6; *Tu rigoles!* III, 9

journalist *journaliste,* III, 5

judo *le judo,* III, 12

July *juillet,* I, 4

June *juin,* I, 4

K

kidding: Are you kidding me? *Tu te fiches de moi?* III, 9; **You're kidding!** *C'est pas vrai!* II, 6

kilogram: a kilogram of *un kilo de,* I, 8

kind: That's kind of you. *Vous êtes bien aimable.* III, 6; **What kind of . . . do you have?** *Qu'est-ce que vous avez comme... ?* I, 5, III, 1

kiss: Give . . . a kiss for me. *Embrasse... pour moi.* III, 8

kisses: Hugs and kisses. *Je t'embrasse bien fort.* III, 8; **Kisses to . . .** *Bisous à... ,* III, 8

kitchen *la cuisine,* II, 2

know: Did you know that . . . ? *Tu savais que... ?* III, 10; **Do you know the one about . . . ?** *Est-ce que tu connais l'histoire de... ?* III, 10; **Do you know what . . . ?** *Tu sais ce que... ?* II, 9; **Do you know who . . . ?** *Tu sais qui... ?* II, 9; **I don't know what to do.** *Je ne sais pas quoi faire.* II, 10; **I don't know.** *Je ne sais pas.* I, 10; **I know that . . .** *Je sais que... ,* III, 7; **I really don't know.** *Je ne sais pas trop.* III, 5; **I would like to know . . .** *Je voudrais savoir... ,* III, 5; **What do you know about it?** *Qu'est-ce que tu en sais?* III, 10; **You're the . . . -est . . . I know.** *Tu es le/la... le/la plus... que je connaisse.* III, 10

L

lab *les travaux* (m.) *pratiques,* I, 2

lamp *la lampe,* II, 2

late *tard,* II, 4

later: Can you call back later? *Vous pouvez rappeler plus tard?* I, 9; **See you later!** *A tout à l'heure!* I, 1

latest: Did you hear the latest? *Tu connais la nouvelle?* II, 9; **Have you heard the latest?** *Tu connais la dernière?* III, 10

Latin *le latin,* I, 2

laugh: It really made me laugh. *Ça m'a bien fait rire.* III, 9

laundry: to do the laundry *faire la lessive,* III, 3

lawn: to mow the lawn *tondre la pelouse,* III, 3

lawyer *avocat(e),* III, 5

lead: This road will lead you into the center of town. *Cette route vous conduira au centre-ville.,* III, 2

leather: leather-goods shop *la maroquinerie,* II, 3; **in leather** *en cuir,* I, 10

leave *partir,* I, 11; II, 6; **Can I leave a message?** *Je peux laisser un message?* I, 9; **Leave me alone!** *Fiche-moi la paix!* III, 6; **to leave one's family** *quitter sa famille,* III, 5; **You can't leave without . . .** *Tu ne peux pas partir sans... ,* I, 11

left: to the left *à gauche,* I, 12; **to the left of** *à gauche de,* I, 12

leg *la jambe,* II, 7

leggings *un caleçon,* III, 4

lemon soda *la limonade,* I, 5

less: less . . . than . . . *moins... que... ,* III, 8; **Life was more . . . , less . . .** *La vie était plus... , moins... ,* II, 8; **More or less.** *Plus ou moins.* II, 6

let's: Let's go . . . *Allons... ,* I, 6; **Let's go!** *Allons-y!* I, 4; **Let's hear it!** *Dis vite!* II, 9

letter: to send letters *envoyer des lettres,* I, 12

library *la bibliothèque,* I, 6; II, 2

license: to get one's driver's license *passer son permis de conduire,* III, 5

life: Life was more . . . , less . . . *La vie était plus... moins... ,* II, 8

lift: to lift weights *faire de la musculation,* II, 7

lights *les lumières* (f.), III, 3

like *aimer,* I, 1; **Did you like it?** *Ça t'a plu?* II, 6; **Do you like . . . ?** *Tu aimes... ?* I, 1; **Do you like it?** *Il/Elle te/vous plaît?* I, 10; **Do you like this . . . ?** *Il/Elle te plaît,... ?* III, 4; **How did you like it?** *Comment tu as trouvé ça?* III, 9; **How do you like . . . ?** *Comment tu trouves... ?* I, 10; **How do you like it?** *Comment tu trouves ça?* I, 5; **I like it a lot.** *Il/Elle me plaît beaucoup.* III, 4; **I (really) like . . .** *Moi, j'aime (bien)... ,* I, 1; **I didn't like it at all.** *Je n'ai pas du tout aimé.* III, 9; **Don't you like . . . ?** *Tu n'aimes pas... ?* III, 4; **I don't like...** *Je n'aime pas... ,* I, 1; II, 1; **I like . . .** *J'aime bien... ,* II, 1; **I like it, but it's expensive.** *Il/Elle me plaît, mais il/elle est cher.* I, 10; **I like this type of . . .** *J'aime bien ce genre de... ,* III, 4; **I'd like . . .** *J'aimerais... ,* III, 3; *Je voudrais... ,* I, 3; II, 6; **I'd like some.** *J'en veux bien.* I, 8; **I'd like . . . to go with . . .** *J'aimerais... pour aller avec... ,* I, 10; **I'd like some.** *Je prendrais bien... ,* III, 6; **I'd like that a lot.** *Ça me plairait beaucoup.* III, 6; **I'd like to.** *Je veux bien.* II, 1; **I'd really like . . .** *J'aimerais bien... ,* III, 5; **I'd really like to . . .** *Je voudrais bien... ,* I, 11; **I'd really like to . . . !** *Qu'est-ce que j'aimerais... !* III, 8; **I'd really like to.** *Je veux bien.* I, 6; **If you like, we can . . .** *Si tu veux, on peut... ,* II, 1; **Is it like here?** *C'est pareil qu'ici?* III, 12; **It looks like . . .** *On dirait que... ,* III, 11; **It wasn't like this.** *Ce n'était pas comme ça.* III, 8; **The teacher doesn't like me.** *Le prof ne m'aime pas.* II, 5; **They look like . . .** *Ils ont l'air de... ,* III, 11; **What are they like?** *Ils sont comment?* I, 7; **What do you like to do?** *Qu'est-ce que tu aimes faire?* II, 1; **What I don't like is . . .** *Ce que je n'aime pas, c'est... ,* II, 4; **What I like is . . .** *Ce que j'aime bien, c'est... ,* II, 4; *Ce qui me plaît, c'est... ,* II, 4; **What I like/love is . . .** *Ce que j'adore/j'aime, c'est... ,* III, 11; **What I would like is to . . .** *Ce qui me plairait, c'est de... ,* III, 5; **What is he like?** *Il est comment?* I, 7; **What is she like?** *Elle est comment?* I, 7; **What music do you like?** *Qu'est-ce que tu aimes comme musique?* II, 1; **What was it like?** *C'était comment?* II, 8; **What would you like?** *Vous désirez?* I, 10; **What's life like there?** *C'est comment la vie là-bas?* III, 12; **Would you like to . . .?** *Ça te plairait de... ,* III, 6; **Wouldn't you like to . . .?** *Tu ne voudrais pas... ?* III, 6; **You're going to like it here.** *Tu vas te plaire ici.* II, 8

liked: I liked it a lot. *Ça m'a beaucoup plu.* III, 9; **I really liked it.** *Ça m'a beaucoup plu.* II, 6

lion *le lion,* III, 7

listen: Listen! *Ecoutez!,* I, 0; **to listen to music** *écouter de la musique,* I, 1; **to listen to what he/she says** *écouter ce qu'il/elle dit,* II, 10

listening: I'm listening. *Je t'écoute.* I, 9; II, 10

listing: TV guide/listing *le programme télé,* III, 9

liter: a liter of *un litre de,* I, 8

little: When he/she was little, . . . *Quand il/elle était petit(e),... ,* II, 8; **When I was little, . . .** *Quand j'étais petit(e),... ,* II, 8; **Yes, a little.** *Si, un peu.* II, 2

lively *vivant(e),* II, 4; *animé(e),* II, 8

living room *le salon,* II, 2

lobster *le homard,* III, 10

located: . . . is located . . . *... se trouve... ,* II, 12; **Where is . . . located?** *Où se trouve... ,* II, 12

long *long,* II, 11; **long-distance running** *la course de fond,* III, 12; **long-sleeved** *à manches longues,* III, 4; **It's been a long time since we've seen each other.** *Ça fait longtemps qu'on ne s'est pas vu(e)s.* III, 1; **It's not going to take long!** *Ça ne va pas prendre longtemps!* III, 2; **long hair** *les cheveux longs* (m.), II, 1; III, 4; **the long jump** *le saut en longueur,* III, 12

look: I think they look . . . *Je trouve qu'ils/elles font... ,* III, 4; **I think you look very good like that.** *Je te trouve très bien comme ça.* III, 4; **If you could see how you look!** *Non mais, tu t'es pas regardé(e)!* III, 10; **Look at the map!** *Regardez la carte!,* I, 0; **Look out!** *Faites gaffe!* III, 7; **Look, here's (there's) (it's) . . .** *Regarde, voilà... ,* I, 12; **That doesn't look good on you.** *Ça ne te (vous) va pas du tout.* I, 10; **That looks good.** *Ça fait très bien.* III, 4; **That looks really . . .** *Ça fait vraiment... ,* III, 4; **They look like . . .** *Ils ont l'air de... ,* III, 11; **to look after** *garder,* III, 3; **to look after your little sister** *garder ta petite sœur,* I, 7; **to look for** *chercher,* I, 9; **You look really . . . in that!** *Que tu es... avec ça!* III, 4

looking: I'm looking for something for . . . *Je cherche quelque chose pour... ,* I, 10; **No, thanks, I'm just looking.** *Non, merci, je regarde.* I, 10

looks: It looks great on you! *C'est tout à fait ton style.* I, 10; **It looks like . . .** *On dirait que... ,* III, 11

lose *perdre,* II, 5; III, 12; **to lose weight** *maigrir,* I, 10; *perdre du poids,* III, 10

losing: I'm losing it! *Je craque!* II, 7

lost: to get lost *se perdre,* II, 9

lot: A lot. *Beaucoup.* I, 4; **I had a lot of fun.** *Je me suis beaucoup amusé(e).* II, 6; **I liked it a lot.** *Ça m'a beaucoup plu.* III, 9; **I'd like that a lot.** *Ça me plairait beaucoup.* III, 6

lots: I have lots of things to do. *J'ai des tas de choses à faire.* I, 5

loudly: Don't speak so loudly. *Ne parle pas si fort.* III, 9

love: I love . . . *J'adore... ,* II, 1; **love: Are you in love or what?** *Tu es amoureux (-euse) ou quoi?* III, 10; **in love** *amoureux (amoureuse),* II, 9; **to fall in love (with someone)** *tomber amoureux(-euse) (de quelqu'un),* II, 9; **What I like/love is . . .** *Ce que j'adore/j'aime, c'est... ,* III, 11

luck: Good luck! *Bonne chance!* I, 11; **Tough luck!** *C'est pas de chance, ça!* II, 5

lucky: We were lucky! *On a eu de la chance!* III, 7

lunch *le déjeuner,* I, 2; **to have lunch** *déjeuner,* I, 9

M

ma'am *madame (Mme),* I, 1

madam *madame,* III, 5

made *fait (faire),* I, 9

magazine *un magazine,* I, 3; **magazine show** *le magazine télévisé,* III, 9

main dishes *les plats* (m.), III, 1

make *faire,* I, 4; **How do you make . . .?** *Comment est-ce qu'on fait... ?* III, 11; **How much does that make?** *Ça fait combien?* II, 3; **Make the best of it.** *Fais-toi une raison.* II, 8; **to have (make) a date (with someone)** *avoir (prendre) rendez-vous (avec quelqu'un),* II, 9; **to make one's bed** *faire son lit,* III, 3

make up: to make up (with someone) *se réconcilier avec (quelqu'un),* II, 10; **to make up one's own mind** *prendre ses propres décisions,* III, 3

mall *le centre commercial,* I, 6

mangoes *des mangues* (f.), I, 8

many: as many/as much . . . as . . . *autant de... que... ,* III, 8; **How many (much) do you want?** *Combien en voulez-vous?* II, 3

map *la carte,* I, 0

March *mars,* I, 4

married *marié(e),* III, 6; **to get married** *se marier,* III, 5

mask *le masque,* II, 8; III, 12

match (game) *le match,* III, 12

matches *les allumettes,* II, 12; **That matches . . .** *C'est assorti à... ,* III, 4

math *les maths* (f.), I, 1

matter: It doesn't matter. *Ça ne fait rien.* II, 10; *Peu importe.* III, 9

May *mai,* I, 4

may: May I . . . ? *(Est-ce que) je peux... ?* I, 7; **May I have some . . . ?** *Je pourrais avoir... ?* II, 3; **May I help you?** *(Est-ce que) je peux vous aider?* I, 10

maybe *peut-être,* II, 3; **Maybe . . .** *Peut-être que... ,* II, 9; III, 5; **Maybe you're right.** *Tu as peut-être raison.* II, 9

me *moi,* I, 2

meal *un repas,* II, 7

mean *méchant(e),* I, 7; II, 1; **What does . . . mean?** *Qu'est-ce que ça veut dire,... ?* III, 11

meat *la viande,* I, 8; III, 11

mechanic *mécanicien(ne),* III, 5

medicine *des médicaments* (m.), I, 12

medium: of medium height *de taille moyenne,* II, 1; **Medium rare.** *A point.* III, 1

meet *rencontrer,* I, 9; II, 9; **I'd like you to meet . . .** *Je te (vous) présente... ,* I, 7; **Pleased to meet you.** *Très heureux (heureuse).* I, 7; **We'll meet . . .** *On se retrouve... ,* I, 6; **We'll meet . . .** *Rendez-vous... ,* I, 6

meeting: What time are we meeting? *A quelle heure est-ce qu'on se donne rendez-vous?* III, 6; **Where are we meeting?** *Où est-ce qu'on se retrouve?* III, 6

menu: The menu, please. *La carte, s'il vous plaît.* I, 5

merry: Merry Christmas! *Joyeux Noël!* II, 3

message: Can I leave a message? *Je peux laisser un message?* I, 9

metro: at the . . . metro stop *au métro. . . ,* I, 6; **metro station** *la station de métro,* III, 8

Mexico *le Mexique,* III, 12

microphone *le microphone,* III, 11

midnight *minuit,* I, 6

might: It might be that . . . *Il se peut que. . . ,* III, 5

mike (microphone) *le micro,* III, 11

military: to do one's military service *faire son service militaire,* III, 5

milk *du lait,* I, 8; II, 3; **to milk the cows** *traire les vaches* (f.), III, 8

mind: Are you out of your mind?! *Ça va pas, non?!* III, 8; **Do you mind if . . . ?** *Ça te dérange si. . . ?,* III, 3; **I can't make up my mind.** *Je n'arrive pas à me décider.* III, 1; **Mind your own business!** *Mêle-toi de tes oignons!* III, 6; **to make up one's own mind** *prendre ses propres décisions,* III, 3; **Would you mind . . . ?** *Ça t'embête de. . . ?* II, 10; *Ça t'ennuie de. . . ?* II, 10

mineral water *l'eau minérale,* I, 5

miniskirt *la mini-jupe,* III, 4

minute: Do you have a minute? *Tu as une minute?* I, 9; II, 10

miss, Miss *mademoiselle (Mlle),* I, 1

miss: Don't miss it! *C'est à ne pas manquer!* III, 9; **I miss . . .** *Je regrette. . . ,* II, 8; **(plural subject) . . . me manquent.** II, 8; **(singular subject) . . . me manque.** II, 8; **to miss a step** *rater une marche,* II, 5; **to miss the bus** *rater le bus,* I, 9; **to miss the bus** *rater le bus,* II, 5; **What I miss is . . .** *Ce qui me manque, c'est. . . ,* II, 8

mistaken: If I'm not mistaken, . . . *Si je ne me trompe pas,. . . ,* III, 11; **In my opinion, you're mistaken.** *A mon avis, tu te trompes.* II, 9

misunderstanding: a little misunderstanding *un petit malentendu,* II, 10

moment: One moment, please. *Un moment, s'il vous plaît.* I, 5

Monday: on Mondays *le lundi,* I, 2

money *de l'argent,* I, 11

monkey *le singe,* III, 7

mood: in a bad mood *de mauvaise humeur,* II, 9; **in a good mood** *de bonne humeur,* II, 9

moose *un orignal,* II, 12

moped *le vélomoteur,* III, 8

more: More . . . ? *Encore de. . . ?* I, 8; **Some more . . . ?** *Encore. . . ?* II, 3; **I just can't do any more!** *Je n'en peux plus!* II, 7; **Life was more . . . , less . . .** *La vie était plus. . . moins. . . ,* II, 8; **more . . . than . . .** *plus de. . . que,* III, 8; **more . . . than . . .** *plus. . . que. . . ,* III, 8; **More or less.** *Plus ou moins.* II, 6; **One more try!** *Encore un effort!* II, 7

morning: in the morning *le matin,* I, 2

Morocco *le Maroc,* III, 12

mosque *une mosquée,* II, 8

mosquito *un moustique,* II, 4; **mosquito repellent** *de la lotion anti-moustique,* III, 7

mother *la mère,* I, 7

mountain: to go mountain-bike riding *faire du vélo de montagne,* II, 12; **to/at the mountains** *à la montagne,* I, 11

move *déménager,* III, 10; **Don't move.** *Ne bougez pas.* III, 7; **Get a move on!** *Grouille-toi!* III, 2

movie *le film,* I, 6; **the movies** *le cinéma,* I, 1; **movie theater** *le cinéma,* I, 6; **historical movie** *le film historique,* III, 9; **war movie** *le film de guerre,* III, 9; **What good movies are out?** *Qu'est-ce qu'il y a comme bons films en ce moment?* III, 9; **What good movies have you seen?** *Qu'est-ce que tu as vu comme bon film?* III, 9

mow: to mow the lawn *tondre la pelouse,* III, 3

Mr. *monsieur (M.),* I, 1

Mrs. *madame (Mme),* I, 1

much: as many/as much . . . as . . . *autant de. . . que. . . ,* III, 8; **How much is (are) . . . ?** *Combien coûte(nt). . . ?* II, 3; **How much is . . . ?** *C'est combien,. . . ?* I, 5; **How much is it, please?** *Ça fait combien, s'il vous plaît.* I, 5; **How much is it?** *C'est combien?* I, 3; **How much is the entrance fee?** *C'est combien, l'entrée?* II, 6; **No, not too much.** *Non, pas trop.* I, 2; **Not much.** *Pas grand-chose.* I, 6; **Not too much.** *Pas tellement.* I, 4; **Not very much.** *Pas beaucoup.* I, 4; **Yes, very much.** *Oui, beaucoup.* I, 2; **I don't like that very much.** *Je n'aime pas tellement ça.* III, 11

museum *le musée,* I, 6; II, 2

mushrooms *les champignons* (m.), I, 8; III, 11

music *la musique,* I, 2; **(music) group** *un groupe,* II, 11; **classical music** *la musique classique,* II, 11; **music video** *le vidéoclip,* III, 9; **What music do you like?** *Qu'est-ce que tu aimes comme musique?* II, 1

musical comedy *une comédie musicale,* III, 9

musician *musicien(ne),* II, 11

must: It must be . . . *Ça doit être. . . ,* III, 7; **There must be . . .** *Il doit y avoir. . . ,* III, 7

mustache *la moustache,* III, 4

my *mon/ma/mes,* I, 7; **It's just not my day!** *C'est pas mon jour!* II, 5

mystery: detective or mystery movie *un film policier,* II, 11

N

name: His/Her name is... *Il/Elle s'appelle. . . ,* I, 1; **My name is...** *Je m'appelle. . . ,* I, 1; **What's your name?** *Tu t'appelles comment?* I, 1

nap: to take a nap *faire la sieste,* II, 8

natural science *les sciences* (f.) *naturelles,* I, 2

near *près de,* II, 2

Neat! *C'est le pied!* III, 7; **That's really neat!** *C'est vraiment le pied!* III, 12

necessary: It's necessary that . . . *Il est nécessaire que. . . ,* III, 7

neck *le cou,* II, 7

necklace *le collier,* III, 4

need: I need . . . *Il me faut. . . ,* I, 3, 10; *J'ai besoin de. . . ,* I, 8; **What do you need for . . . ?** *Qu'est-ce qu'il vous (te) faut pour. . . ?* I, 3, 8; **What do you need?** *De quoi est-ce que tu as besoin?; Qu'est-ce qu'il te faut?* I, 8

neither: Neither do I. *Moi non plus.* I, 2; III, 9

nephew *le neveu,* III, 6

never *ne. . . jamais,* I, 4

new *nouveau (nouvelle),* II, 2; **Happy New Year!** *Bonne année!* II, 3; **What's new?** *Quoi de neuf?* III, 1

news *les informations* (f.), III, 9

next: Next, . . . *Ensuite, . . .* II, 1; **next to** *à côté de,* I, 12; II, 2; **Right there, next to . . .** *Juste là, à côté de. . . ,* III, 2

nice *gentil (gentille),* I, 7; II, 1; *sympa,* II, 1; **It's nice weather.** *Il fait beau.* I, 4; **That would be nice.** *Ce serait sympa.* III, 6; **That's nice of you.** *C'est gentil (à vous).* II, 2; III, 6; **That's so nice of you.** *C'est gentil de votre (ta) part,* II, 2; **That's very nice of you.** *C'est vraiment très gentil de votre part.* III, 6

niece *la nièce,* III, 6

Niger *le Niger,* III, 12

nightmare: It was a real nightmare! *C'était un véritable cauchemar!* I, 11

no *non,* I, 1; **No . . . ing** *Défense de. . . ,* III, 3; **It's no good.** *C'est nul* III, 9; **No way!** *C'est pas possible!* III, 12; *Mon œil!* III, 10; *Pas question!* II, 1; *Tu parles!* III, 9

noise *le bruit,* III, 8; **Could you make less noise?** *Tu pourrais faire moins de bruit?* III, 9; **to make noise** *faire du bruit,* III, 3

noisy *bruyant(e),* II, 8

none (of it) *en,* I, 8

noon *midi,* I, 6

north: in the north *dans le nord,,* II, 4; **It's to the north of . . .** *C'est au nord de. . . ,* II, 12

northern: It's in the northern part of . . . *C'est dans le nord de. . . ,* II, 12

nose: I've got a runny nose. *J'ai le nez qui coule.* II, 7

not *ne. . . pas,* I, 1; **. . . is not allowed** *Interdiction de. . . ,* III, 3; **Definitely not!** *Sûrement pas!* II, 6; **It was not bad.** *J'ai trouvé ça pas mal, ,* III, 9; **It's not good to . . .** *Ce n'est pas bien de. . . ,* III, 3; **Not at all.** *Pas du tout.* I, 4; II, 10; III, 9; **Oh, not bad.** *Oh, pas mal.* I, 9; **not so great** *pas fameux,* I, 5; **not very good** *pas bon,* I, 5; **not yet** *ne. . . pas encore,* I, 9; **One should not . . .** *Il ne faut pas. . . ,* III, 3; **Please do not . . .** *Prière de ne pas. . . ,; Veuillez ne pas. . . ,* III, 3; **You'd do better not to . . .** *Tu ferais mieux de ne pas. . . ,* III, 3

notebook *le cahier,* I, 0

nothing: It's nothing special. *Ce n'est pas grand-chose.* II, 3; **It's nothing.** *(Il n'y a) pas de quoi.* III, 6; **Nothing (special).** *Rien (de spécial).* I, 6; III, 1

novel *un roman,* I, 3

November *novembre,* I, 4

nurse *infirmier(-ière),* III, 5

O

oars *les rames* (f.), III, 12

obvious: That's obvious. *Ça se voit.* II, 9

obviously *évidemment,* II, 9

o'clock: at . . . o'clock *à... heures,* I, 2
October *octobre,* I, 4
octopus *la pieuvre,* III, 10
of *de,* I, 0; **Of course not.** *Bien sûr que non.* II, 10; **Of course.** *Bien sûr.* I, 3; II, 10; **of it** *en,* I, 8; **of them** *en,* I, 8
off: afternoon off *l'après-midi libre,* I, 2
offer: Can I offer you something? *Je vous sers quelque chose?* III, 6; **What can I offer you?** *Qu'est-ce que je peux vous offrir?* III, 6
often *souvent,* I, 4
oh: Oh no! *Oh là là!* II, 5
oil *l'huile* (f.), III, 2; **to put oil in the motor** *mettre de l'huile dans le moteur,* III, 2; **to check the oil** *vérifier l'huile,* III, 2; **to change the oil** *faire la vidange,* III, 2
OK. *assez bien,* II, 6; *D'accord.* I, 4; *Entendu.* I, 2; **Well, OK.** *Bon, d'accord.* I, 8; **Is it OK with you if . . . ?** *Tu veux bien que je... ?,* III, 3; **Is that OK with you?** *Tu es d'accord?* I, 7
okra *des okras* (m.), III, 11; *du gombo,* I, 8
old-fashioned *démodé(e),* I, 10
old: How old are you? *Tu as quel âge?* I, 1; **I am . . . years old.** *J'ai... ans.* I, 1; **This old thing?** *Oh, c'est un vieux truc.* III, 4; **to be . . . years old** *avoir... ans,* II, 1; **When I was . . . years old, . . .** *Quand j'avais... ans,... ,* II, 8
older *âgé(e),* I, 7
oldest: the oldest child *l'aîné(e),* III, 6
olive *l'olive* (f.), II, 8
on: Can I try on . . . ? *Je peux essayer... ?* I, 10; **on foot** *à pied,* I, 12; **on Fridays** *le vendredi,* I, 2; **on (day of the week) . . . s** *le + (day of the week),* I, 2
on the right (left) *sur la droite (gauche),* II, 2
once: OK, just this once. *Ça va pour cette fois.* III, 3; **once a week** *une fois par semaine,* I, 4
one-way: a one-way ticket *un aller simple,* II, 6
one: He/She already has one (of them). *Il/Elle en a déjà un(e).* II, 3; **That one.** *Celui-là/Celle-là,* III, 4; **The one . . .** *Celui du... ,* III, 4; **Which one?** *Lequel/Laquelle?* III, 4; **Which ones?** *Lesquels/Lesquelles?* III, 4
only: I'm not the only one who . . . *Je ne suis pas le/la seul(e) à... ,* III, 3
open: Open your books to page . . . *Ouvrez vos livres à la page...,* I, 0; **When do you open?** *A quelle heure est-ce que vous ouvrez?* II, 6
opinion: I didn't ask your opinion. *Je t'ai pas demandé ton avis.* III, 10; **In my opinion, . . .** *A mon avis,... ,* II, 9; **In my opinion, it's safer.** *A mon avis, c'est plus sûr.* III, 7; **In my opinion, you're mistaken.** *A mon avis, tu te trompes.* II, 9; **In your opinion, what do I do?** *A ton avis, qu'est-ce que je fais?* I, 9; **In your opinion, what should I do?** *A ton avis, qu'est-ce que je dois faire?* II, 10
orange (color) *orange,* I, 3; **orange juice** *un jus d'orange,* I, 5; **oranges** *des oranges* (f.), I, 8
ordinary: That's ordinary. *C'est banal.* II, 3
other: Think about other people. *Pense aux autres.* III, 3

ought: You ought to . . . *Il faudrait que tu...,* III, 5
our *notre, nos,* I, 7
out: to go out *sortir,* II, 6; **Out of the question!** *Pas question!* I, 7
outfit *la tenue,* III, 12
over there: Over there, the boy who . . . *Là-bas, le garçon qui... ,* III, 4
oysters *les huîtres* (f.), II, 3; III, 11

P

page *la page,* I, 0
pain: a pain (in the neck) *pénible,* I, 7; II, 1; **You're such a pain!** *Tu es vraiment casse-pieds!* III, 6
pair: a pair of jeans *un jean,* I, 3; II, 1; **of shorts** *un short,* I, 3; **of boots** *les bottes* (f.), II, 1; **of gloves** *les gants* (m.), II, 1; **of pants** *un pantalon,* I, 10; **of sneakers** *les baskets* (f.), II, 1
palm tree *un palmier,* II, 4
panic: Don't panic! *Pas de panique!* III, 7
pantyhose *un collant,* III, 4
papayas *des papayes* (f.), I, 8
paper *le papier,* I, 0; III, 3; **sheets of paper** *des feuilles* (f.) *de papier,* I, 3
parallel: the uneven parallel bars *les barres asymétriques* (f.), III, 12
pardon: Pardon me. *Pardon,* I, 3; **Pardon me for . . .** *Pardonne-moi de... ,* III, 6
park *le parc,* I, 6; II, 2
parking place *la place de stationnement,* III, 8
party: to give a party *faire une boum,* II, 10
pass: to pass one's baccalaureat exam *réussir son bac,* III, 5; **Would you pass . . . ?** *Vous pourriez (tu pourrais) me passer... ?,* II, 3; **You'll pass . . .** *Vous passez devant... ,* I, 12
passport *le passeport,* I, 11; II, 1; III, 7
pasta *des pâtes* (f.), II, 7
pastry *la pâtisserie,* I, 12; **pastry shop** *la pâtisserie,* I, 12; II, 3
paté *le pâté,* II, 3
patient: Be patient! *Sois patient(e)!* III, 2
peaches *des pêches* (f.), I, 8
pears *des poires* (f.), I, 8
peas *des petits pois* (m.), I, 8
pedestrian: pedestrian crossing *le passage pour piétons,* III, 8
pen *le stylo,* I, 0
pencil *un crayon,* I, 3; **pencil case** *la trousse,* I, 3; **pencil sharpener** *un taille-crayon,* I, 3
pendant *le pendentif,* III, 4
people: people in a hurry *les gens pressés,* III, 8
perfect: It's perfect. *C'est parfait.* I, 10
perm *la permanente,* III, 4
permission: to ask your parents' permission *demander la permission à tes parents,* II, 10
pharmacist *pharmacien(ne),* III, 5
phone: Phone him/her/them. *Téléphone-lui/-leur.* II, 10; **to talk on the phone** *parler au téléphone,* I, 1
photo: photo frame *le cadre,* II, 3
physical education *l'éducation* (f.) *physique et sportive (EPS),* I, 2
physics *la physique,* I, 2
piano *le piano,* III, 11

pick *choisir,* I, 10; **to pick up your room** *ranger ta chambre,* I, 7
picnic: to have a picnic *faire un pique-nique,* I, 6; II, 6
picture *l'image* (f.), III, 9; **to take pictures** *faire des photos,* I, 4
pie *de la tarte,* I, 8; **fruit pies/tarts** *les tartes aux fruits,* III, 1
piece: a piece of *un morceau de,* I, 8
pilot *pilote,* III, 5
pineapple *des ananas* (m.), I, 8; *un ananas,* II, 4
pink *rose,* I, 3
pitcher (baseball) *le lanceur,* III, 12
pizza *la pizza,* I, 1
plaid *écossais(e),* III, 4
plain *sobre,* III, 4
plan: What do you plan to do? *Qu'est-ce que tu comptes faire?* III, 5
plane: plane ticket *un billet d'avion,* I, 11; **by plane** *en avion,* I, 12
planning: I'm planning on . . . *Je compte... ,* III, 5
plans: Do you have plans? *Tu as des projets?* III, 5; **I don't have any plans.** *Je n'ai rien de prévu.* I, 11
plant: to plant a tree *planter un arbre,* III, 3
plastic *le plastique,* III, 3
plate: plate of pâté, ham, and cold sausage *l'assiette de charcuterie,* III, 1
platform: From platform . . . *Du quai... ,* II, 6; **From which platform . . . ?** *De quel quai... ?* II, 6
play *faire, jouer,* I, 4; **Do you play/do . . . ?** *Est-ce que tu fais... ?* I, 4; **How about playing . . . ?** *Si on jouait... ?* II, 8; **I don't play/do . . .** *Je ne fais pas de... ,* I, 4; **I play . . .** *Je joue... ,* I, 4; **I play/do . . .** *Je fais... ,* I, 4; **to play baseball** *jouer au base-ball,* I, 4; **to play basketball** *jouer au basket(-ball),* I, 4; **to play football** *jouer au football américain,* I, 4; **to play golf** *jouer au golf,* I, 4; **to play hockey** *jouer au hockey,* I, 4; **to play soccer** *jouer au foot(ball),* I, 4; **to play sports** *faire du sport,* I, 1; **to play tennis** *jouer au tennis,* I, 4; **to play volleyball** *jouer au volley(-ball),* I, 4; **What sports do you play?** *Qu'est-ce que tu fais comme sport?* I, 4; II, 1
playing: It's playing at . . . *Ça passe à... ,* II, 11; **What films are playing?** *Qu'est-ce qu'on joue comme film?* II, 11; **Where is that playing?** *Ça passe où?* II, 11
please *s'il vous (te) plaît,* I, 3; **A . . . , please.** *Un(e)... s'il vous plaît.* I, 6; **Pleased to meet you.** *Très heureux (heureuse).* I, 7
pleasure: Yes, with pleasure. *Oui, avec plaisir.* I, 8; *Avec plaisir.* II, 10
pleated *à pinces,* III, 4
plenty: We've got plenty of time! *On a largement le temps!* III, 2
plot: It has no plot. *Il n'y a pas d'histoire.* II, 11; **It's full of plot twists.** *C'est plein de rebondissements.* II, 11
plumber *plombier* (m.), III, 5
po-boy sandwich *le po-boy,* III, 11
poetry: book of poetry *un livre de poésie,* II, 11
point: At that point . . . *A ce moment-là... ,* II, 9; III, 9; **It's not my strong point.** *Ce n'est pas mon fort.* II, 5

pole: the pole vault *le saut à la perche,* III, 12

polite *poli(e),* III, 3

polka-dot *à pois,* III, 4

pollution *la pollution,* III, 8

pony tail *une queue de cheval,* III, 4

pool *la piscine,* II, 2

poor: You poor thing! *Pauvre vieux (vieille)!* II, 5

pop: popular, mainstream music *le pop,* II, 11

pork *du porc,* I, 8; III, 11; porkchop with pasta *la côtelette de porc pâtes,* III, 1

possible: If it were possible, . . . *Si c'était possible,... ,* III, 8; It's possible that . . . *Il est possible que... ,* III, 5; That's not possible. *Ce n'est pas possible.* II, 9; That's possible. *C'est possible.* II, 9; Would it be possible for you to . . . ? *Vous serait-il possible de... ?* III, 5

post office *la poste,* I, 12; II, 2

poster *le poster,* I, 0, 3; II, 2

potatoes *des pommes de terre* (f.), I, 8

pottery *la poterie,* II, 8; III, 8

pound: a pound of *une livre de,* I, 8

practice *répéter,* I, 9

prefer: Do you prefer . . . or . . . ? *Tu aimes mieux... ou... ?* I, 10; I prefer *Je préfère,* II, 1, 7, 8; *J'aime mieux... ,* I, 1; II, 1; What I prefer is . . . *Ce que je préfère, c'est... ,* II, 4

pressure: tire pressure *la pression des pneus* (m.), III, 2

prey *la proie,* III, 7

problem: I've got a problem. *J'ai un (petit) problème.* I, 9; II, 10; No problem. *Pas de problème.* II, 10

process: to be in the process of (doing something) *être en train de (+ infinitive),* II, 9

public: to take public transportation *prendre les transports en commun,* III, 3

pudding: bread pudding *le pouding au pain,* III, 11

pullover (sweater) *un pull-over,* I, 3

purple *violet(te),* I, 3

purpose: Are you doing that on purpose? *Tu le fais exprès?* III, 6

purse *le sac à main,* II, 3

push-ups: to do push-ups *faire des pompes,* II, 7

put *mettre,* I, 10; put on (clothing) *mettre,* I, 10; put up: I won't put up with this! *C'est insupportable, à la fin!* III, 8

Q

quarter: quarter past *et quart,* I, 6; quarter to *moins le quart,* I, 6

question: Out of the question! *Pas question!* I, 7

quiet: Be quiet! *Tais-toi!* III, 9; Could you please be quiet? *Vous pourriez vous taire, s'il vous plaît?* III, 9

quiz *l'interro* (f.), I, 9

R

raccoon *le raton laveur,* II, 12

radio *la radio,* I, 3

rain: It's raining. *Il pleut.* I, 4

raincoat *l'imperméable* (m.), II, 1

rained: It rained the whole time. *Il a plu tout le temps.* III, 1

rainforest: tropical rainforest *la forêt tropicale,* II, 4; III, 7

raise *élever,* III, 8; Raise your hand! *Levez la main!,* I, 0

raisins *les raisins secs,* III, 11

rake: to rake leaves *ramasser les feuilles,* III, 3

rap *le rap,* II, 11; III, 11

Rare. *Saignante.* III, 1

rather *plutôt,* II, 9; No, I'd rather. . . *Non, je préfère... ,* II, 1

read *lire,* I, 1; read (pp.) *lu* (pp. of lire), I, 9

ready: to get ready *faire les préparatifs,* II, 10

really *vachement,* II, 9; really . . . *bien... ,* III, 11; Really. *Je t'assure.* III, 4; Really? *C'est vrai? (Vraiment?),* II, 2; I (really) like... *Moi, j'aime (bien)... ,* I, 1; I really don't know. *Je ne sais pas trop.* III, 5; I really liked it. *Ça m'a beaucoup plu.* II, 6; I'd really like . . . *J'aimerais bien... ,* III, 5; I'd really like to . . . *Je voudrais bien... ,* I, 11; I'd really like to. *Je veux bien.* I, 6; No, not really. *Non, pas vraiment.* I, 11; That looks really . . . *Ça fait vraiment... ,* III, 4; That's really you. *C'est tout à fait toi.* III, 4; Was it really so different? *C'était tellement différent?* II, 8; Your . . . is really great. *Il/Elle est vraiment bien, ton/ta... ,* II, 2

reason: That's no reason. *Ce n'est pas une raison.* III, 3

receive: to receive one's report card *recevoir le bulletin trimestriel,* II, 5

recommend: I recommend . . . *Je te recommande... ,* III, 9; I recommend it. *Je te le recommande.* II, 11; What do you recommend? *Qu'est-ce que vous me conseillez?* III, 1

record: at the record store *chez le disquaire,* I, 12

recorder: videocassette recorder *le magnétoscope,* III, 9

recreation center *la Maison des jeunes et de la culture (MJC),* I, 6

recycle *recycler,* III, 3

red *rouge,* I, 3; red hair *les cheveux roux,* II, 1; redheaded *roux (rousse),* I, 7

regards: Give . . . my regards. *Fais mes amitiés à... ,* III, 8

reggae music *le reggae,* II, 11

regular: regular leaded (gasoline) *super,* III, 2

rehearse *répéter,* I, 9

relaxing *relax,* II, 8

remember: If I remember correctly, . . . *Si je me souviens bien,... ,* III, 11; Remember to take . . . *Pense à prendre... ,* II, 1

remote (control) *la télécommande,* III, 9

repeat: Repeat! *Répétez!,* I, 0

report card: to receive one's report card *recevoir le bulletin trimestriel,* II, 5

respect: to respect nature *respecter la nature,* II, 12; to respect one's teachers and one's parents *respecter ses profs et ses parents,* III, 3

response: In response to your letter of . . . *En réponse à votre lettre du... ,* III, 5

responsibilities: to have responsibilities *avoir des responsabilités,* II, 8

responsible *responsable,* III, 3

restaurant *le restaurant,* I, 6

restroom: *les toilettes (les W.-C.),* II, 2

return *retourner,* II, 6; to return something *rendre,* I, 12; to return tests *rendre les examens,* II, 5

rhinoceros *le rhinocéros,* III, 7

rice *du riz,* I, 8

ride: to take a ride on the ferris wheel *faire un tour sur la grande roue,* II, 6; to take a ride on the roller coaster *faire un tour sur les montagnes russes,* II, 6

ridiculous: That's ridiculous! *N'importe quoi!* II, 6

riding: to go horseback riding *faire de l'équitation,* I, 1

right: I can't right now. *Je ne peux pas maintenant.* I, 8; I'll go right away. *J'y vais tout de suite.* I, 8; It's right there on the . . . *C'est tout de suite à... ,* I, 12; on the right *sur la droite,* II, 2; right away *tout de suite,* I, 6; to the right *à droite,* I, 12; to the right of *à droite de,* II, 2; Yeah, right! *Mon œil!* II, 6; *N'importe quoi!* III, 10; You're right. *Tu as raison.* II, 3; III, 9; I just can't do anything right! *Qu'est-ce que je peux être nul(le)!* III, 12

ring: the rings (in gymnastics) *les anneaux* (m.), III, 12

rip *déchirer,* II, 5

river *la rivière,* III, 7

roast beef *le rôti de bœuf,* III, 3

rock (music) *le rock,* II, 11; III, 11

rocks *les rochers* (m.), III, 10

roll: roll of film *la pellicule,* III, 7

roller coaster *les montagnes russes,* II, 6

romance novel *un roman d'amour,* II, 11

romantic: romantic movie *une histoire* (f.) *d'amour,* II, 11

room (of a house) *la pièce,* II, 2; to pick up your room *ranger ta chambre,* I, 7

round-trip: a round-trip ticket *un aller-retour,* II, 6

rowing *l'aviron* (m.), III, 12

rug *le tapis,* II, 2; III, 8

ruler *la règle,* I, 3

running: long-distance running *la course de fond,* III, 12

runny: I've got a runny nose. *J'ai le nez qui coule.* II, 7

Russia *la Russie,* III, 12

S

safely: to drive safely *conduire prudemment,* III, 3

safer: In my opinion, it's safer. *A mon avis, c'est plus sûr.* III, 7

said: You said it! *Tu l'as dit!* III, 9

sailing: to go sailing *faire de la voile,* I, 11; *faire du bateau,* II, 1

salad *la salade verte,* III, 1; salad, lettuce *de la salade,* I, 8

salami *le saucisson,* I, 5; II, 3

salesperson *vendeur(-euse),* III, 5

salt *le sel,* II, 7

salty *salé(e),* III, 11

same: It's always the same! *C'est toujours la même chose!* III, 6; It's really all the same to me. *Ça m'est vraiment égal.* III, 9; Same old thing! *Toujours la même chose!* III, 1

sand *le sable*, II, 4
sandals *des sandales* (f.), I, 10
sandwich *un sandwich*, I, 5
Saturday: on Saturdays *le samedi*, I, 2
sausages *les saucisses* (f.), III, 11
savannah *la savane*, III, 7
saxophone *le saxophone*, III, 11
say: How do you say . . .? *Comment on dit... ?* III, 11; **What do you say about . . .?** *Qu'est-ce que tu penses de... ?* III, 11
saying: I'm not just saying that. *Je ne dis pas ça pour te faire plaisir.* III, 4
says: So he says . . . *... et alors, il dit que... ,* III, 10
scare: Wow! That was a real scare! *Ouf! On a eu chaud!* III, 7
scared: I'm scared (of) . . . *J'ai peur (de la, du, des)... ,* II, 12; **I'm scared to death!** *J'ai la frousse!* III, 7
scarf *l'écharpe* (f.), I, 10; II, 1; *le foulard*, II, 3
school *l'école* (f.), I, 1; **high school** *le lycée*, II, 2
science fiction: science-fiction novel *un roman de science-fiction*, II, 11; **science-fiction movie** *un film de science-fiction*, II, 11
score: to score . . . points *marquer... points*, III, 12
screen *l'écran* (m.), III, 9
scuba dive: to go scuba diving *faire de la plongée sous-marine*, II, 4
sea *la mer*, II, 4
seahorse *l'hippocampe* (m.), III, 10
seaweed *l'algue* (f.), III, 10
second: One second, please. *Une seconde, s'il vous plaît.* I, 9
secretary *secrétaire*, III, 5
see: Go see . . . it's a great movie. *Va voir... , c'est génial comme film.* III, 9; **Really, don't go see . . .** *Ne va surtout pas voir... ,* III, 9; **See you later!** *A tout à l'heure!* I, 1; **See you soon.** *A bientôt.* I, 1; **See you tomorrow.** *A demain.* I, 1; **to see a game (in person)** *voir un match*, I, 6; **to see a movie** *voir un film*, I, 6; **to see a play** *voir une pièce*, I, 6; **What is there to see . . .?** *Qu'est-ce qu'il y a à voir... ,* II, 12; **When I see . . .** *Quand je verrai... ,* III, 12; **You should go see . . .** *Tu devrais aller voir... ,* III, 9; **You'll see that . . .** *Tu vas voir que... ,* II, 8
seem: to seem . . . *avoir l'air... ,* II, 9; **You don't seem too well.** *Tu n'as pas l'air en forme.* II, 7
seemed: She seemed . . . *Elle avait l'air... ,* II, 12
seems: It seems to me that . . . *Il me semble que... ,* III, 11
seen (pp.) *vu* (pp. of *voir*), I, 9; **If you could have seen . . .!** *Si tu avais vu... ,* III, 10
selection: Have you made your selection? *Vous avez choisi?* III, 1
send: to send letters *envoyer des lettres*, I, 12; **to send the invitations** *envoyer les invitations*, II, 10
Senegal *le Sénégal*, III, 12
sensational! *sensas*, II, 6
September *septembre*, I, 4
series *la série*, III, 9
serious: It's not serious. *C'est pas grave.* II, 5

server *serveur (-euse)*, III, 5
service: At your service; You're welcome. *A votre service.* I, 3
set: to set the table *mettre la table*, III, 3
shall: Shall we go to the café? *On va au café?* I, 5
shampoo: a shampoo *un shampooing*, III, 4
shape: to get into shape *se mettre en condition*, II, 7
share *partager ses affaires*, III, 3; **to share one's vehicle** *partager son véhicule*, III, 3
shark *le requin*, III, 10
shave *se raser*, III, 4
sheep *le mouton*, III, 8
sheet: a sheet of paper *la feuille de papier*, I, 0
shell *le coquillage*, III, 10
shellfish *les crustacés* (m.), III, 11
shelves *les étagères*, II, 2
Shh! *Chut!* III, 9
shirt (men's) *la chemise*, I, 10; **(women's)** *le chemisier*, I, 10
shoes *les chaussures* (f.), I, 10
shoot *tirer*, III, 12
shop: to window-shop *faire les vitrines*, I, 6
shopping *les courses* (f.), I, 7; **to do the shopping** *faire les courses*, I, 7; **to go shopping** *faire les magasins*, I, 1; **Can you do the shopping?** *Tu peux aller faire les courses?* I, 8
short (objects) *court(e)*, I, 10; **short (height)** *petit(e)*, I, 7; II, 1; **short hair** *les cheveux courts* (m.), II, 1; III, 4
shorts: (a pair of) shorts *un short*, I, 3
should: Do you think I should . . .? *Tu crois que je devrais... ?* III, 7; **Everyone should . . .** *On doit.* II, 7; **I should have . . .** *J'aurais dû... ,* II, 10; **In your opinion, what should I do?** *A ton avis, qu'est-ce que je dois faire?* II, 10; **What do you think I should do?** *Qu'est-ce que tu me conseilles?* II, 10; **What should I . . .?** *Qu'est-ce que je dois... ,* II, 1; **What should I do?** *Qu'est-ce que je dois faire?* II, 12; **What should we do?** *Qu'est-ce qu'on fait?* II, 1; **You should . . .** *Il faudrait que tu... ,* III, 5; **You should . . .** *Tu devrais... ,* I, 9; II, 7; **You should be proud of yourself.** *Tu peux être fier (fière) de toi.* II, 5; **You should go see . . .** *Tu devrais aller voir... ,* III, 9; **You should have . . . (food or drink)** *Tu devrais prendre... ,* III, 1; **(ought to have)** *Tu aurais dû... ,* II, 10
shouldn't: You shouldn't . . . *Tu ne devrais pas... ,* II, 7; *Tu ne dois pas... ,* III, 3; **One should not . . .** *Il ne faut pas... ,* III, 3
shovel: to shovel snow *enlever la neige*, III, 3
show *montrer*, I, 9; **game show** *le jeu télévisé*, III, 9; **magazine show** *le magazine télévisé*, III, 9; **sound and light show** *un spectacle son et lumière*, II, 6
showing: . . . is showing. *On joue... ,* II, 11
shrimp *la crevette*, II, 3; III, 10
Shut up! *Ferme-la!* III, 6
shy *timide*, I, 7
sick: I'm sick of this! *J'en ai vraiment marre!* III, 12; **I'm sick to my stomach.** *J'ai mal au cœur.* II, 7; **I'm sick.** *Je suis malade.* II, 7

sideburns *des pattes* (f.), III, 4
sidewalk *le trottoir*, III, 8
silk *en soie*, III, 4
silly: Stop being so silly! *Arrête de délirer!* III, 10; **to do silly things** *faire des bêtises*, II, 8
simple *simple*, II, 8
Since . . . *Depuis... ,* III, 1
sing *chanter*, I, 9
singer *une chanteuse (un chanteur)*, II, 11
singing *le chant*, III, 11
single *célibataire*, III, 6
sir *monsieur (M.)*, I, 1; III, 5
sister *la sœur*, I, 7
sit-ups: to do sit-ups *faire des abdominaux*, II, 7
sit: Sit down. *Asseyez-vous.* III, 6
skate: to ice-skate *faire du patin à glace*, I, 4; **to in-line skate** *faire du roller en ligne*, I, 4
ski *faire du ski*, I, 4; **ski jacket** *l'anorak* (m.), II, 1; **to water ski** *faire du ski nautique*, I, 4
skiing *le ski*, I, 1
skip: Don't skip . . . *Ne saute pas... ,* II, 7
skipping: skipping a meal *sauter un repas*, II, 7
skirt *la jupe*, I, 10
skunk *une mouffette*, II, 12
skyscraper *le gratte-ciel*, III, 8
sleep *dormir*, I, 1; **I didn't sleep well.** *J'ai mal dormi.* II, 7
sleeping bag *un sac de couchage*, II, 12
slender *mince*, I, 7
slice: a slice of *la tranche de*, I, 8
small *petit(e) (s)*, I, 10; II, 1
smaller: smaller than . . . *moins grand(e) que*, II, 4
smart *intelligent(e)*, I, 7; II, 1
smoke *fumer*, III, 3
snack: afternoon snack *le goûter*, I, 8; **to make party snacks** *préparer les amuse-gueule*, II, 10
snacking: snacking between meals *grignoter entre les repas*, II, 7
snails *les escargots* (m.), I, 1; II, 3
snake *le serpent*, III, 7
sneakers *des baskets* (f.), I, 3; **pair of sneakers** *les baskets* (f.), II, 1
snorkel *faire de la plongée avec un tuba*, II, 4
snowing: It's snowing. *Il neige.* I, 4
snow-shoeing: to go snow-shoeing *faire une randonnée en raquettes*, II, 12
so: So . . . *Alors,... ,* II, 9; **so-so** *comme ci, comme ça*, I, 1; II, 6; **not so great** *pas fameux*, I, 5; **That is so . . .!** *Qu'est-ce que c'est... !* III, 2
soap opera *le feuilleton*, III, 9
soccer *le football*, I, 1; **to play soccer** *jouer au foot(ball)*, I, 4
socks *les chaussettes* (f.), I, 10
sole: filet of sole with rice and mushrooms *le filet de sole riz champignons*, III, 1
some *des*, I, 3; *; du, de la, de l', des, en*, I, 8; **I'd like some.** *J'en veux bien.* I, 8; **Some more . . .?** *Encore... ?* II, 3
sometimes *quelquefois*, I, 4
song *la chanson*, II, 11
soon: As soon as I get there, . . . *Dès que je serai là,... ,* III, 12; **See you soon.** *A bientôt.* I, 1
sophisticated *élégant(e)*, III, 4

sorry: Sorry. *Désolé(e).* II, 10; *Je regrette.* I, 3; **I'm sorry.** *Désolé(e).* II, 10; **I'm sorry for . . .** *Je m'excuse de... ,* III, 6

sort of *assez,* II, 9

sound *le son,* III, 9; **Does . . . sound good to you?** *Ça te dit de... ?* II, 1; **sound and light show** *un spectacle son et lumière,* II, 6

soups *les soupes* (f.), III, 11

south: in the south *dans le sud,* II, 4; **It's to the south of . . .** *C'est au sud de... ,* II, 12; **South Africa** *l'Afrique* (f.) *du sud,* III, 12; **South African** (adj.) *sud-africain(e),* III, 12

southern: It's in the southern part of . . . *C'est dans le sud de... ,* II, 12

Spain *l'Espagne* (f.), III, 12

Spanish (language) *l'espagnol* (m.), I, 2

speak: Could I speak to . . . ? *(Est-ce que) je peux parler à... ?* I, 9

special: It's nothing special. *Ce n'est pas grand-chose.* II, 3; **Nothing (special).** *Rien (de spécial).* I, 6; III, 1

spices *les épices* (f.), III, 11

spicy *épicé(e),* III, 11

spider *l'araignée* (f.), III, 7

spinach *les épinards* (m.), III, 11

sports *le sport,* I, 1; **to play sports** *faire du sport,* I, 1; **What sports do you play?** *Qu'est-ce que tu fais comme sport?* I, 4; II, 1

sportscast *le reportage sportif,* III, 9

sprain: to sprain one's ankle *se fouler la cheville,* II, 7; III, 10

spring: in the spring *au printemps,* I, 4

spy flick *le film d'espionnage,* III, 9

squirrel *un écureuil,* II, 12

stadium *le stade,* I, 6

stamp *un timbre,* I, 12

stand: Stand up! *Levez-vous!,* I, 0

starfish *l'étoile* (f.) *de mer,* III, 10

start *commencer,* I, 9; **How does it start?** *Comment est-ce que ça commence?* III, 9; **What time does it start?** *Ça commence à quelle heure?* II, 11

started: He/She started it! *C'est lui/elle qui a commencé!* III, 6

stationery store *la papeterie,* I, 12

stay *rester,* II, 6; **Did you stay here?** *Est-ce que tu es resté(e) ici?* III, 1; **Where did you stay?** *Où est-ce que tu as dormi?* III, 1

stayed: Yes, I stayed here the whole time. *Oui, je suis resté(e) ici tout le temps.* III, 1

steak *le bifteck,* I, 8; II, 3; **steak and French fries** *le steak-frites,* I, 5; III, 1

steamed *à la vapeur,* III, 11

step: to miss a step *rater une marche,* II, 5

stereo *la chaîne stéréo,* II, 2

still . . . *toujours... ,* III, 11

stinks: It stinks. *C'est un navet,* II, 11

stomach *le ventre,* II, 7; **I'm sick to my stomach.** *J'ai mal au cœur.* II, 7

stop: Stop! *Arrête!* III, 6; **at the . . . metro stop** *au métro... ,* I, 6; **to stop one's studies** *arrêter ses études,* III, 5

stores *les magasins* (m.), I, 1

story: It's a great story. *C'est une belle histoire.* II, 11; **It's the story of . . .** *C'est l'histoire de... ,* II, 11; III, 9; **What's the story?** *Qu'est-ce que ça raconte?* II, 11

straight: straight hair *les cheveux raides* (m.), III, 4

straight ahead: Go (keep going) straight ahead. *Allez (continuez) tout droit,* II, 2; **Keep going straight ahead up to the intersection.** *Vous continuez tout droit, jusqu'au carrefour. ,* III, 2; **You go straight ahead until you get to . . .** *Vous allez tout droit jusqu'à... ,* I, 12

strawberries *les fraises* (f.), I, 8

street: You go down this street to the next light. *Vous continuez cette rue jusqu'au prochain feu rouge.* I, 12; **You take . . . Street, then cross . . . Street.** *Prenez la rue... , puis prenez la rue... ,* I, 12

strict: to follow a diet that's too strict. *suivre un régime trop strict,* II, 7

striped *à rayures,* III, 4

strong *fort(e),* I, 7; II, 1; **It's not my strong point.** *Ce n'est pas mon fort.* II, 5; **You're really strong/good at that.** *Tu es fortiche/calé(e).* III, 10

student *l'élève* (m./f.), I, 2

studies: to stop one's studies *arrêter ses études,* III, 5

study *étudier,* I, 1; **study hall** *l'étude,* I, 2

stuffed (with) *farci (à),* III, 11

stupid *bête,* II, 1; **(childish)** *bébé,* III, 2; **What a stupid joke!** *Elle est nulle, ta blague!* III, 10; **You're so stupid!** *Tu es bête comme tes pieds!* III, 6; **That looks really stupid!** *Ça fait vraiment cloche!* III, 4

style: in style *à la mode,* I, 10; **style of the Forties or Fifties** *rétro,* I, 10; **That's not his/her style.** *Ce n'est pas son style.* II, 3

subway: by subway *en métro,* I, 12

such: I've never seen such a . . . *Je n'ai jamais vu un(e) aussi... ,* III, 7

sugar: sugarcane fields *des champs de canne à sucre,* II, 4

suit: man's suit *le costume,* III, 4; **suit jacket** *la veste,* I, 10; **Does it suit me?** *Ça me va?* I, 10

suitcase *la valise,* I, 11

suits: That suits you really well. *Ça te (vous) va très bien.* I, 10

sulk *faire la tête,* II, 9

summer: in the summer *en été,* I, 4

Sunday: on Sundays *le dimanche,* I, 2

sunglasses *des lunettes* (f.) *de soleil,* I, 10

sunscreen *de la crème solaire,* III, 7

super (adj.) *super,* I, 2; **Super!** *Super!* III, 1; **super cool** *hyper-cool,* III, 4; **What I think is super is . . .** *Ce que je trouve super, c'est... ,* III, 11

sure: I'm not sure. *J'hésite.* I, 11; **I'm (not) sure that . . .** *Je (ne) suis (pas) sûr(e) que... ,* III, 7; **Oh, I'm not sure.** *Euh... J'hésite.* I, 10; **That's for sure.** *Ça, c'est sûr.* III, 11; **We'd be able to . . . for sure.** *On pourrait sûrement... ,* III, 7

surprise: That would surprise me. *Ça m'étonnerait!* II, 6; III, 10

surprised *étonné(e),* II, 9; **I'd be surprised if . . .** *Ça m'étonnerait que... ,* III, 7

suspenseful: It's suspenseful. *Il y a du suspense.* II, 11

sweater *le cardigan,* I, 10; *le pull,* II, 1

sweatshirt *le sweat-shirt,* I, 3; *le sweat,* II, 1

swim *faire de la natation,* I, 4; *nager,* I, 1

swimming *la natation,* III, 12; **to go swimming** *se baigner,* II, 4; **swimming pool** *la piscine,* I, 6

Switzerland *la Suisse,* III, 12

sword *l'épée* (f.), III, 12

swordfish *l'espadon* (m.), III, 10

synthesizer *le synthé (le synthétiseur),* III, 11

T

T-shirt *le tee-shirt,* I, 3; II, 1

table: to clear the table *débarrasser la table,* I, 7

tacky: I think it's (they're) really tacky. *Je le/la/les trouve moche(s).* I, 10

tailor *tailleur (-euse),* III, 5

take: Are you going to take it/them? *Vous le/la/les prenez?* I, 10; **Have you decided to take . . . ?** *Vous avez décidé de prendre... ?* I, 10; **I'll take . . .** *Je vais (en) prendre... ,* II, 3; **I'll take . . . (of them).** *Je vais en prendre... ,* II, 3; **I'll take it/them.** *Je le/la/les prends.* I, 10; **It's not going to take long!** *Ça ne va pas prendre longtemps!* III, 2; **Remember to take . . .** *Pense à prendre... ,* II, 1; **Take . . .** *Prends... ,* II, 1; *Prenez..,* II, 2; **to take or to have (food or drink)** *prendre,* I, 5; **to take pictures** *faire des photos,* I, 4; **We can take . . .** *On peut prendre... ,* I, 12; **You take . . . Street, then cross . . . Street.** *Prenez la rue... , puis traversez la rue... ,* I, 12

take out: Take out a sheet of paper. *Prenez une feuille de papier.,* I, 0; **to take out the trash** *sortir la poubelle,* I, 7

takes place: It takes place . . . *Ça se passe... ,* III, 9

taking: Are you taking . . . ? *Tu prends... ?* I, 11

talk: Can I talk to you? *Je peux te parler?* I, 9; II, 10; **Talk to him/her/them.** *Parle-lui/leur.* II, 10; **to talk on the phone** *parler au téléphone,* I, 1

tall *grand(e),* I, 7; II, 1

tank: the gas tank *le réservoir,* III, 2

tart: apple tart *la tarte aux pommes,* II, 3; **fruit pies/tarts** *les tartes aux fruits,* III, 1

taste *déguster,* II, 4; **in poor taste** *de mauvais goût,* III, 4

tasteless *vulgaire,* III, 4

Tattletale! *Rapporteur (-euse)!* III, 6

taxi: by taxi *en taxi,* I, 12

teacher *le professeur,* I, 0

team *l'équipe* (f.), III, 12

tease *taquiner,* II, 8

technical: to go to a technical school *faire une école technique,* III, 5

technician *technicien(ne),* III, 5

teeth *les dents* (f.), I, 7

television *la télévision,* I, 0; **television set** *le téléviseur,* III, 9

tell: Can you tell her/him that I called? *Vous pouvez lui dire que j'ai téléphoné?* I, 9; **Didn't I tell you?** *Je ne t'ai pas dit?* III, 10; **Tell . . . hi for me.** *Salue... de ma part.* III, 8; **Tell . . . that I'm going to write.** *Dis à... que je vais lui écrire.* III, 8; **Tell . . . that I'm thinking about him/her** *Dis à... que je pense à lui/elle.* III, 8; **Tell him/her/them that . . .** *Dis-lui/-leur que... ,* II, 10; **Tell me!** *Raconte!* II, 5; III, 10; **to tell (someone) that . . .**

dire à (quelqu'un) que... , II, 10; **to tell the truth** dire la vérité, III, 3

tempting: Everything looks tempting. Tout me tente. III, 1

tennis: to play tennis jouer au tennis, I, 4

tent une tente, II, 12

terrible horrible, I, 10; **I had a terrible day!** J'ai passé une journée épouvantable! II, 5; **This is terrible!** Quelle angoisse! II, 12;

Terrific! Bravo! II, 5

tests les examens (m.), I, 1

than: bigger than . . . plus grand(e) que, II, 4; **fewer . . . than** . . . moins de... que, III, 8; **It's better than** . . . C'est meilleur que... , II, 7; **less . . . than** . . . moins... que... , III, 8; **more . . . than** . . . plus de... que, III, 8; plus... que... , III, 8; **smaller than** . . . moins grand(e) que, II, 4

thank you: Thank you. Merci. I, 3; II, 2; Je vous remercie. III, 6; **Thank you so much.** Merci bien/infiniment/mille fois. III, 6; **Yes, thank you.** Oui, s'il vous (te) plaît. I, 8; **No, thank you.** Non, merci. I, 8; **No thank you, I've had enough.** Merci, ça va. II, 3

thank: You don't have to thank me. C'est tout à fait normal. III, 6

thanks: No thanks. I'm not hungry anymore. Non, merci. Je n'ai plus faim., I, 8

that ce, cet, cette, I, 3; **That is so . . . !** Qu'est-ce que c'est... ! III, 2; **This/That is . . .** Ça, c'est... , I, 12; **That is, . . .** C'est-à-dire que... , II, 9

theater le théâtre, I, 6; II, 2

their leur/leurs, I, 7

them les, leur, I, 9

then: Then, . . . Ensuite,... , II, 12; Puis,... , II, 1; **And then?** Et alors? III, 10; **Then I called . . .** Ensuite, j'ai téléphoné à... , I, 9

there -là (noun suffix), I, 3; y, I, 12; **Here (There) is . . .** Là, c'est... , II, 2; **Is . . . there, please?** (Est-ce que)... est là, s'il vous plaît? I, 9; **Over there, at the end of the hallway.** Par là, au bout du couloir. III, 2; **Right there, next to . . .** Juste là, à côté de... , III, 2; **There is** . . . Il y a... , II, 2; **There's . . .** Voilà... , I, 7; **What do you . . . there?** Qu'est-ce qu'on y...? III, 12; **You're almost there!** Tu y es presque! II, 5

Therefore, . . . Donc,... , II, 9

these ces, I, 3; **These/Those are . . .** Ce sont... , I, 7

thing: It's not my thing. Ce n'est pas mon truc. II, 7; **This old thing?** Oh, c'est un vieux truc. III, 4

things: I have lots of things to do. J'ai des tas de choses à faire. I, 5; **I have some things to do.** J'ai des trucs à faire. I, 5

think: Do you think I should . . . ? Tu crois que je devrais... ? III, 7; **Do you think it'd be better to . . . ?** Tu penses qu'il vaudrait mieux... ? III, 7; **Do you think so?** Tu trouves? II, 2; **Hey, do you think you can . . . ?** Dites donc, ça vous gênerait de... ? III, 8; **I don't think so.** Je ne crois pas. II, 9; **I don't think that . . .** Je ne pense pas que... , III, 7; **I think I'll . . .** Je pense... , III, 5; **I think it's . . .** Je trouve qu'il est... , III, 4;

I think it's/they're . . . Je le/la/les trouve... , I, 10; **I think that . . .** Je crois que... , II, 9; **I think that's better.** Je crois que ça vaut mieux. III, 7; **What do you think about going . . . ?** Ça te dit d'aller... ? II, 4; **What do you think I should do?** Qu'est-ce que tu me conseilles? II, 10; **What do you think of . . . ?** Comment tu trouves... ? I, 2; Qu'est-ce que tu penses de... ? III, 12; **What do you think of it?** Qu'en penses-tu? III, 4; **What do you think of that/it?** Comment tu trouves ça? I, 2; **What do you think you'll do?** Qu'est-ce que tu penses faire? III, 5; **Who do you think you are?** Non mais, vous vous prenez pour qui? III, 8

thirst: I'm dying of thirst! Je meurs de soif! II, 12; **Yes, I'm dying of thirst!** Si, je meurs de soif! II, 2

thirsty: to be thirsty avoir soif, I, 5; **Aren't you thirsty?** Vous n'avez pas (Tu n'as pas) soif? II, 2; **I'm not thirsty anymore.** Je n'ai plus soif, II, 3

this ce, cet, cette, I, 3; **This is . . .** C'est... , I, 7; Ça, c'est... , II, 2; **This/That is . . .** Ça, c'est... , I, 12

those ces, I, 3; **Those.** Ceux-là/Celles-là, III, 4; **Those are . . .** Ce sont... , I, 7

thought: I've thought of everything. J'ai pensé à tout. I, 5

throat la gorge, II, 7

throw: to throw away your trash jeter les déchets, II, 12; **to throw the ball** lancer le ballon, III, 12; **to throw trash** jeter des ordures, III, 3

Thursday: on Thursdays le jeudi, I, 2

ticket: plane ticket un billet d'avion, I, 11; II, 1; **Three (entrance) tickets, please.** Trois tickets, s'il vous plaît. II, 6; **train ticket** un billet de train, I, 11

tie la cravate, I, 10; III, 4

tied: to be tied être à égalité, III, 12

tight serré(e)(s), I, 10

tights un collant, III, 4

time: a waste of time zéro, I, 2; **At what time do you have . . . ?** Tu as... à quelle heure? I, 2; **At what time?** A quelle heure? I, 6; **from time to time** de temps en temps, I, 4; **I don't have time.** Je n'ai pas le temps. II, 10; **I'm sorry, but I don't have time.** Je regrette, mais je n'ai pas le temps. I, 8; **Sorry, but I don't have time.** Je suis désolé(e), mais je n'ai pas le temps. I, 12; **We don't have time!** On n'a pas le temps! III, 2; **What time does it start?** Ça commence à quelle heure? II, 11; **What time does the train (the bus) for . . . leave?** A quelle heure est-ce que le train (le car) pour... part? II, 6

tire le pneu, III, 2; **tire pressure** la pression des pneus (m.), III, 2; **to have a flat tire** avoir un pneu crevé, III, 2

tired: I'm tired . Je suis fatigué(e), II, 12; **(You're) not too tired?** Pas trop fatigué(e)? II, 2

tiring: It was tiring! C'était fatigant! II, 2

to à la, I, 6; **(a city or place)** à, I, 11; **(before a feminine noun)** en, I, 11; **(before a masculine noun)** au, I, 11; **(before a plural noun)** aux, I, 11; **five to** moins cinq, I, 6

today aujourd'hui, I, 2

together: When are we getting together? Quand est-ce qu'on se revoit? III, 6

toilet les toilettes (les W.-C.), II, 2

told: Who told you that? Qui t'a dit ça? III, 10

tolerant tolérant(e), III, 3

tomato: tomato salad la salade de tomates, III, 1; **tomatoes** des tomates (f.), I, 8

tomorrow demain, I, 2; **See you tomorrow.** A demain. I, 1

tonight: Not tonight. Pas ce soir. I, 7

too: It's too expensive. C'est trop cher. II, 3; **Me too.** Moi aussi. I, 2; III, 9; **No, it's too expensive.** Non, c'est trop cher. I, 10; **No, not too much.** Non, pas trop. I, 2; **Not too much.** Pas tellement. I, 4; **too violent** trop violent, II, 11

took pris (pp. of prendre), I, 9

Tough! Tant pis pour toi! III, 6; **Tough luck!** C'est pas de chance, ça! II, 5

tour: to take a guided tour faire une visite guidée, II, 6; **to tour some châteaux** faire un circuit des châteaux, II, 6

tourist: tourist information office l'office de tourisme, II, 2

towards: Towards the back. Au fond. III, 2

tower: to go up in a tower monter dans une tour, II, 6

track and field l'athlétisme, III, 12; **to do track and field** faire de l'athlétisme, I, 4

traffic jam l'embouteillage (m.), III, 8

trails: to follow the marked trails suivre les sentiers balisés, II, 12

train s'entraîner, III, 12; **train for (a sport)** s'entraîner à... , II, 7

train (locomotive): by train en train, I, 12; **train station** la gare, II, 2; **train ticket** un billet de train, I, 11

trash: It's trash. C'est un navet. III, 9; **to take out the trash** sortir la poubelle, I, 7; **to throw trash** jeter des ordures, III, 3

trashcan la poubelle, I, 7

travel voyager, I, 1

tree l'arbre (m.), III, 7

trip: Did you have a good trip? Vous avez (Tu as) fait bon voyage? II, 2; **Have a good (car) trip!** Bonne route! II, 3; **Have a good trip! (by plane, ship)** Bon voyage! I, 11; II, 3

tropical rainforest la forêt tropicale, II, 4

trouble: I'm having trouble deciding. J'ai du mal à me décider. III, 5

truly: Very truly yours, . . . Je vous prie d'agréer, Monsieur/Madame, l'expression de mes sentiments distingués. III, 5

trumpet la trompette, III, 11

trunk la trompe, III, 7

trust: Trust me. Fais-moi confiance. III, 4

truth: to tell the truth dire la vérité, III, 3

try: Try . . . Essaie... , III, 1; **Can I try it (them) on ?** Je peux l'(les) essayer? I, 10; **One more try!** Encore un effort! II, 7

Tuesdays: on Tuesdays le mardi, I, 2

Tunisia la Tunisie, III, 12

turkey: sliced turkey breast with mashed potatoes l'escalope de dinde purée, III, 1

turn: Then, turn left on . . . Puis, tournez à gauche dans/sur... , II, 2; **to turn off/**

out *éteindre*, III, 3; **You turn . . .** *Vous tournez... ,* I, 12
turn down: Turn down the volume. *Baisse le son.* III, 9
turn up: Turn up the volume. *Monte le son.* III, 9
turtle *la tortue*, III, 10
turtleneck sweater *le col roulé*, III, 4
TV: TV guide/listing *le programme télé*, III, 9; **to watch TV** *regarder la télé(vision)*, I, 1
twins *les jumeaux(-elles)*, III, 6
twists: It's full of plot twists. *C'est plein de rebondissements.* II, 11
type: I like this type of . . . *J'aime bien ce genre de... ,* III, 4
typical: What's typical of where you're from? *Qu'est-ce qui est typique de chez toi?* III, 12

U

ultra- (adv.) *super*, I, 2
uncle *l'oncle* (m.), I, 7
uncomfortable *mal à l'aise*, II, 9
understanding: I have a hard time understanding. *J'ai du mal à comprendre.* II, 5
unemployed: to be unemployed *être au chômage*, III, 5
Unfortunately, . . . *Malheureusement,... ,* II, 9
unique: That's unique. *C'est original.* II, 3
United States *les Etats-Unis* (m.), III, 12
unleaded (gasoline) *super sans plomb*, III, 2
unlucky: I'm so unlucky. *J'ai vraiment pas de chance.* III, 12
up: to go up *monter*, II, 6
up to: I've had it up to here! *J'en ai ras le bol!* III, 8
Upstairs. *En haut.* III, 2
used: You'll get used to it. *Tu vas t'y faire.* II, 8
useless *nul*, I, 2
usually *d'habitude*, I, 4

V

V-necked *à col en V*, III, 4
vacation *les vacances* (f.), I, 1; **Have a good vacation!** *Bonnes vacances!* I, 11; **How was your vacation?** *C'était comment, tes vacances?* III, 1; **on vacation** *en vacances*, I, 4
vacuum: to vacuum *passer l'aspirateur*, III, 3
variety show *l'émission* (f.) *de variétés*, III, 9
vase *le vase*, II, 3
VCR (videocassette recorder) *le magnétoscope*, I, 0
vegetables *des légumes*, II, 7
vegetables: plate of raw vegetables with vinaigrette *l'assiette de crudités*, III, 4
vegetation: tropical vegetation *la végétation tropicale*, III, 7
very: not very good *pas bon*, I, 5; **very cool** *chouette*, II, 2; **Yes, very much.** *Oui, beaucoup.* I, 2
vest *le gilet*, III, 4
video: music video *le vidéoclip*, III, 9; **to**

make videos *faire de la vidéo*, I, 4; **to play video games** *jouer à des jeux vidéo*, I, 4
videocassette *la cassette vidéo*, III, 9; **videocassette recorder, VCR** *le magnétoscope*, I, 0; III, 9
videotape *la vidéocassette*, I, 3
village: fishing village *un village de pêcheurs*, II, 4
violent *violent*, II, 11
violin *le violon*, III, 11
visit (a place) *visiter*, I, 9; II, 6
visiting: How about visiting . . . ? *Si on visitait... ?* II, 8
volcano *le volcan*, II, 4
volleyball: to play volleyball *jouer au volley(-ball)*, I, 4

W

wait: I can hardly wait to . . . ! *Je suis vraiment impatient(e) de... !* III, 12; **I can't wait to . . .** *Il me tarde de... ,* III, 12; **I just can't wait . . . !** *Vivement que... !* III, 12
wait for *attendre*, I, 9
waiter *le serveur*, III, 5; **Waiter!** *Monsieur!* I, 5
waitress *la serveuse*, III, 5; **Waitress!** *Madame!* I, 5; *Mademoiselle!* I, 5
walk: to go for a walk *faire une promenade*, I, 6; *se promener*, II, 4; **to walk the dog** *promener le chien*, I, 7; *sortir le chien*, III, 3
wallet *le portefeuille*, I, 3; II, 3
want *vouloir*, I, 6; **Do you know what you want to do?** *Tu sais ce que tu veux faire?* III, 5; **Do you want . . . ?** *Vous voulez (tu veux)... ?* I, 6, II, 3; **I don't know what I want anymore.** *Je ne sais plus ce que je veux.* III, 5; **I really want to . . .** *Je tiens à... ,* III, 5; **If you want.** *Si tu veux.* I, 12; **No, I don't want to.** *Non, je ne veux pas.* II, 8; **Yes, if you want to.** *Oui, si tu veux.* I, 7
war movie *le film de guerre*, III, 9
wardrobe: armoire/wardrobe *l'armoire* (f.), II, 2
warning: I'm warning you that . . . *Je vous signale que... ,* III, 7
was: He was . . . *Il était... ,* II, 12; **How was it?** *C'était comment?* III, 9; **I was . . .** *J'étais... ,* II, 12; **It was . . .** *C'était... ,* II, 6; **It was amazing/unbelievably bad!** *C'était incroyable!* II, 5; **There was/were . . .** *Il y avait... ,* II, 12
wash: to wash oneself *se laver*, II, 4; **to wash the car** *laver la voiture*, I, 7; **to wash the windows** *laver les vitres*, III, 3
waste *gaspiller*, III, 3; **a waste of time** *zéro*, I, 2
watch *la montre*, I, 3
watch: to watch a game (on TV) *regarder un match*, I, 6; **to watch TV** *regarder la télé(vision)*, I, 1; **Watch out for . . . !** *Attention à... !* III, 7
water *l'eau* (f.), I, 5; **mineral water** *l'eau minérale*, I, 5; **to water ski** *faire du ski nautique*, I, 4; **to water the garden** *arroser le jardin*, III, 3; **Water, please.** *De l'eau, sil vous plaît.* III, 1
waterfall *une chute d'eau*, II, 4

watering hole *le point d'eau*, III, 7
way: a one-way ticket *un aller simple*, II, 6; **By the way, . . .** *A propos,... ,* II, 9; **No way!** *C'est pas possible!* III, 12; *Mon œil!* III, 10; *Pas possible!* II, 6; *Pas question!* II, 1; *Tu parles!* III, 9
wear *mettre, porter*, I, 10; **I don't know what to wear for . . .** *Je ne sais pas quoi mettre pour... ,* I, 10; **Wear . . .** *Mets... ,* I, 10; **What shall I wear?** *Qu'est-ce que je mets?* I, 10; **Why don't you wear . . . ?** *Pourquoi est-ce que tu ne mets pas... ?* I, 10
weather: The weather was great. *Il a fait un temps magnifique ,* III, 1; **weather report** *la météo*, III, 9; **What was the weather like?** *Quel temps est-ce qu'il a fait?* III, 1
Wednesday: on Wednesdays *le mercredi*, I, 2
weekend: Did you have a good weekend? *Tu as passé un bon week-end?* I, 9; **on weekends** *le week-end*, I, 4; **this weekend** *ce week-end*, I, 6; **What a bad weekend!** *Quel week-end!* II, 5
weight: to lose weight *maigrir*, I, 10; *perdre du poids*, III, 10
weights *les haltères* (m.), III, 12
weightlifting *l'haltérophilie* (f.), III, 12
welcome: At your service; You're welcome. *A votre service.* I, 3; **Welcome to my home (our home)** *Bienvenue chez moi (chez nous),* II, 2; **You're very welcome.** *Je vous en prie.* III, 6; **You're welcome.** *De rien.* III, 6
well: Did it go well? *Ça s'est bien passé?* I, 9; **It didn't go well.** *Ça ne s'est pas bien passé.* III, 1; **Get well soon!** *Bon rétablissement!* II, 3; **I don't feel well.** *Je ne me sens pas bien.* II, 7; **It went really well!** *Ça s'est très bien passé!* II, 5; **Very well.** *Très bien.* I, 1; **Well done!** *Chapeau!* II, 5; **well done (meat)** *bien cuite.* III, 1; **You don't seem too well.** *Tu n'as pas l'air en forme.* II, 7; **You would do well to . . .** *Tu ferais bien de... ,* II, 7; **You would do well/better to . . .** *Tu ferais bien/mieux de... ,* III, 5; **Not too well.** *Pas trop bien.* III, 1
went: Afterwards, I went out. *Après, je suis sorti(e).* I, 9; **I went . . .** *Je suis allé(e)... ,* I, 9; **I went by . . .** *Je suis parti(e) en... ,* III, 1; **It went really well!** *Ça s'est très bien passé!* II, 5
were: If I were in your place, . . . *A ta place,... ,* III, 8; **If I were you, . . .** *Si j'étais toi,... ,* III, 8; **If it were me, . . .** *Si c'était moi,... ,* III, 8; **If it were possible, . . .** *Si c'était possible,... ,* III, 8; **There was/were . . .** *Il y avait... ,* II, 12; **There were . . .** *Il y avait de... ,* III, 9
west: in the west *dans l'ouest*, II, 4; **It's to the west of . . .** *C'est à l'ouest de... ,* II, 12
western: western (film) *un western*, II, 11; III, 9; **It's in the western part of . . .** *C'est dans l'ouest de... ,* II, 12
what *comment*, I, 0; **What's interesting/incredible is . . .** *Ce qui est intéressant/incroyable, c'est... ,* III, 11; **I don't know what to do.** *Je ne sais pas quoi faire.* II, 10; **What are you doing?** *Mais, qu'est-ce que tu fais?* III, 2; **What are you going to do . . . ?** *Qu'est-ce que*

tu vas faire... ? I, 6; *Tu vas faire quoi... ?* I, 6; **What bothers me is . . .** *Ce qui m'ennuie, c'est...* , II, 4; **What can we do?** *Qu'est-ce qu'on peut faire?* II, 4; **What catches your eye is . . .** *Ce qui saute aux yeux, c'est...* , III, 11; **What do you have to drink?** *Qu'est-ce que vous avez comme boissons?* I, 5; **What do you need for . . . ?** (formal) *Qu'est-ce qu'il vous faut pour... ?* (informal) *Qu'est-ce qu'il te faut pour... ?* I, 3; **What do you think of . . . ?** *Comment tu trouves... ?* I, 2; **What do you think of that/it?** *Comment tu trouves ça?* I, 2; **What I don't like is . . .** *Ce que je n'aime pas, c'est...* , II, 4; **What I like is . . .** *Ce qui me plaît, c'est...* , II, 4; **What is . . . ?** *Qu'est-ce que c'est,... ?* III, 1; **What is that called?** *Comment est-ce qu'on appelle ça?* III, 11; **What is there . . . ?** *Qu'est-ce qu'il y a... ?* II, 4; **What is your name?** *Tu t'appelles comment?* I, 0; **What kind of . . . do you have?** *Qu'est-ce que vous avez comme...* ? I, 5; **What's going on?** *Qu'est-ce qui se passe?* II, 5; **What's his/her name?** *Il/Elle s'appelle comment?* I, 1; **What's it like?** *C'est comment?* II, 4; **What's that?** *Qu'est-ce que c'est?* III, 11; **What's wrong?** *Qu'est-ce qui t'arrive?* II, 5

whatever: Whatever. *Ça m'est égal.* II, 8

when: When? *Quand (ça)?* I, 6; **When do you open (close)?** *À quelle heure est-ce que vous ouvrez (fermez)?* II, 6; **When did you go there?** *Quand est-ce que tu y es allé(e)?* III, 1

where: Where? *Où ça?* I, 6; **Do you know where . . . are?** *Tu sais où sont...* , III, 2; **Excuse me, could you tell me where . . . is?** *Pardon, vous savez où se trouve... ?;* **Where did you go?** *Tu es allé(e) où?* I, 9; **Where is . . . , please?** *Où est..., s'il vous plaît?* II, 2; **Where is . . . ?** *Où se trouve...* ? II, 4; **Where is . . . located?** *Où se trouve...* , II, 12; **Where's the fire?** *Il n'y a pas le feu.* III, 2;

whereas: Here . . . whereas . . . *Ici,... tandis que...* , III, 8

which: Which . . . *Quel(s)/Quelle(s)...* , III, 4; **From which platform . . . ?** *De quel quai... ?* II, 6; **Which one?** *Lequel/Laquelle?* III, 4; **Which ones?** *Lesquels/Lesquelles?* III, 4

white *blanc(he),* I, 3

who: The woman/girl/one who . . . *Celle qui...* , III, 4; **Who's calling?** *Qui est à l'appareil?* I, 9

whom: With whom? *Avec qui?* I, 6

why: Why don't you . . . ? *Pourquoi tu ne... pas?* I, 9; II, 7; **Why not?** *Pourquoi pas?* I, 6

widowed *veuf (veuve),* III, 6

wife *la femme,* III, 6

wild *délirant(e),* III, 4; (crazy, funny) *dingue,* III, 2; **I'm wild about it.** *Ça m'éclate.* III, 11

win *gagner,* I, 9; III, 12

window *la fenêtre,* I, 0; **to window-shop** *faire les vitrines,* I, 6; **to wash the windows** *laver les vitres,* III, 3

windshield: to clean the windshield *nettoyer le pare-brise,* III, 2

windsurf *faire de la planche à voile,* I, 11, II, 4

winter: in the winter *en hiver,* I, 4

wiped out: I'm wiped out. *Je suis tout(e) raplapla.* II, 7

wise: It would be wise to . . . *Il serait plus prudent de...* , III, 7

wishes: Best wishes! *Meilleurs vœux!* II, 3

with: With . . . *Chez...* , III, 1; **I went with . . .** *J'y suis allé(e) avec...* , III, 1; **The girl in the/with the . . .** *La fille au...* , III, 4; **The man/guy/one with . . .** *Celui avec...* , III, 4; **with me** *avec moi,* I, 6; **With whom?** *Avec qui?* I, 6

withdraw: to withdraw money *retirer de l'argent* (m.), I, 12

without: You can't leave without . . . *Tu ne peux pas partir sans...* , I, 11

wolf *un loup,* II, 12

wonder: I wonder . . . *Je me demande...* , II, 9; III, 5

wool *en laine,* III, 4

word: Where does the word . . . come from? *D'où vient le mot... ?* III, 11

work *travailler,* I, 9

work out: How should we work this out? *Comment est-ce qu'on fait?* III, 6

worker *ouvrier(-ière),* III, 5

worried *inquiet (inquiète),* II, 9

worries: to have worries *avoir des soucis,* II, 8

worry: Don't worry! *Ne t'en fais pas!* I, 9; II, 5; *Ne vous en faites pas!* III, 7; **Don't worry about it!** *Ne t'inquiète pas.* III, 6

worth: It's not worth it! *Ça ne vaut pas le coup!* III, 9; *Ce n'est pas la peine.* III, 7

worthless *n'importe quoi,* II, 11; *nul (nulle),* II, 8

worthwhile: I don't think it's worthwhile. *Je ne crois pas que ce soit utile.* III, 7

would: It would be great if . . . *Ça serait chouette si...* , III, 8; **That would be nice.** *Ce serait sympa.* III, 6; **What would you do?** *Qu'est-ce que tu ferais, toi?* II, 10; **would like: I'd like to buy . . .** *Je*

voudrais acheter... , I, 3; **Would you mind . . . ?** *Ça t'embête de... ?* II, 10; *Ça t'ennuie de... ?* II, 10; **Would you pass . . .** *Vous pourriez (tu pourrais) me passer...* , I, 3; **Yes, I would.** *Oui, je veux bien.* II, 3; **You would do well to . . .** *Tu ferais bien de...* , II, 7;

Wow! *Oh, dis donc!* III, 7; *Ouah!* III, 7; **Wow! That was a real scare!** *Ouf! On a eu chaud!* III, 7

wreck: to wreck the car *planter la voiture,* III, 10

wrestling *la lutte,* III, 12

write: Write him/her/them. *Ecris-lui/leur.* II, 10

writer *un écrivain,* III, 5

wrong: Everything went wrong! *Tout a été de travers!* II, 5; **Is something wrong?** *Quelque chose ne va pas?* II, 7; **Something's wrong.** *Ça n'a pas l'air d'aller.* II, 5; **What's wrong?** *Qu'est-ce qui t'arrive?* II, 5; *Qu'est ce que tu as?* II, 7; *Qu'est-ce qu'il y a?* II, 10; **You're wrong to . . .** *Tu as tort de...* , III, 3; **You're wrong.** *Tu as tort.* III, 9

Y

yard *le jardin,* II, 2

yeah: Yeah. *Mouais.* II, 6; **Oh yeah? Yeah, right!** *Mon œil!* II, 6

year: I am . . . years old. *J'ai... ans.* I, 1; **When I was . . . years old, . . .** *Quand j'avais... ans,...* , II, 8

yellow *jaune,* I, 3

yes *oui,* I, 1

yet: not yet *ne... pas encore,* I, 9; **No, not yet.** *Non, pas encore.* III, 10

Yippee! *Youpi!* III, 12

yogurt *du yaourt,* I, 8

you *tu, vous,* I, 0; **And you?** *Et toi?* I, 1; **. . . you know.** *... quoi.* II, 9; **. . . you see.** *... tu vois.* II, 9

young *jeune,* I, 7; II, 1

younger: the younger child *le/la cadet(te),* III, 6

youngest: the youngest child *le/la benjamin(e),* III, 6

your *ton/ta/tes,* I, 7; *votre/vos,* I, 7

yours: Very truly yours, . . . *Je vous prie d'agréer, Monsieur/Madame, l'expression de mes sentiments distingués.* III, 5

Z

Zaire *le Zaïre,* III, 12

zebra *le zèbre,* III, 7

zoo *le zoo,* I, 6; II, 6

GRAMMAR INDEX

A

adjectives: formation of feminine adjectives (table),
p. 344; formation of plural adjective and nouns
(table), p. 345
agreement: agreement of past participles, p. 11
articles: definite and indefinite articles (table), p. 344

C

ça: replacing the subject of a sentence with **il, elle,** or
ça, p. 177
causative **faire,** p. 95
ce qui and **ce que,** p. 286; (table), p. 347
celle-là, celles-là, celui-là, ceux-là: demonstrative
pronouns, p. 89
commands: forming commands and suggestions, p. 37
comparative (explained), p. 204 (table), p. 350
conditional (explained), p. 125; (table), p. 349
conduire, p. 35
contractions with **à** and **de** (table), p. 344

D

demonstrative pronouns, p. 89
dès que with the future tense, p. 304
devoir (irregular), p. 60
direct object pronouns, p. 42
dont: relative pronouns (explained), p. 234; (table),
p. 347

E

elle: replacing the subject of a sentence with **il, elle,** or
ça, p. 177

F

faire: causative **faire,** p. 95; reflexive verbs with **faire,**
p. 95
feminine: formation of feminine adjectives (table), p. 344
future: future tense, p. 118; **quand** and **dès que** with
the future tense, p. 304

I

il: replacing the subject of a sentence with **il, elle,** or **ça,**
p. 177
indirect object pronouns, p. 42
infinitive: the past infinitive, p. 143
interrogative pronouns (explained), p. 89; (table), p. 346
inversion in questions, p. 127

L

lequel, laquelle, lesquels, lesquelles: interrogative
pronouns (explained), p. 89; (table), p. 346

N

negative expressions, p. 226
nouns: formation of plural (table), p. 345

O

on: using **on,** p. 143

P

passé composé (explained), p. 11; (table), p. 348
passive voice (avoiding), p. 283
past: past infinitive, p. 143; past participles, p. 11; past
perfect (explained), p. 259; (table), p. 348; using the
present tense to relate past events, p. 234
plural: formation of plural adjectives and nouns (table),
p. 345
possessive adjectives (table), p. 345
prepositions with countries, p. 302
present: using the present tense to relate past events,
p. 234
pronouns: interrogative and demonstrative pronouns:
(explained), p. 89; (tables), p. 346; omitting the object
pronoun in speech, p. 278; relative pronouns:
(explained), p. 234; (tables), p. 347; using on, p. 143

Q

quand with the future tense, p. 304
que: relative pronouns (explained), p. 234; (table),
p. 347
questions: inversion in questions, p. 127
qui: relative pronouns (explained), p. 234; (table),
p. 347

R

reciprocal verbs, p. 142
reflexive verbs with **faire,** p. 95
relative pronouns: **qui, que,** and **dont** (explained),
p. 234; (tables), p. 347; **ce qui** and **ce que** (explained), p. 286; (table), p. 347

S

si clauses (explained), p. 197; (table), p. 349
stems: irregular verb stems in the future tense, p. 118
subjunctive: irregular subjunctive forms, p. 179; review
of the subjunctive, p. 117; (table), p. 349; using the
subjunctive, p. 172; (table), p. 350
suggestions: forming commands and suggestions, p. 37
superlative (explained), p. 252; (table), p. 350

V

verbs: reciprocal verbs, p. 142

ACKNOWLEDGMENTS (continued from page ii)

The Center for Louisiana Studies, University of Southwestern Louisiana: "Hé, Américain!" by Jean Arceneaux, "Leçon du bon français!" by Dégât, "Parlez en Anglais?" by Frère Moreau, and "Le Gombo de Cadiens" by Isabelle Têche from *Acadie Tropicale.* Copyright © 1983 by the University of Southwestern Louisiana.

Centre Belge de la Bande Dessinée: Logo, hours of operation, photograph of entry room, photograph of rocketship, and two photographs of library from the *Centre Belge de la Bande Dessinée.*

Comité Français d'Education pour la Santé: Sticker, "Fumer, c'est pas ma nature!" Published and distributed by the Comité Français d'Education pour la Santé, 2, rue Auguste Comte, 92170, Vanves, France.

Département de l'intérieur, de l'environnement et des affaires régionales: "250 litres par personne et par jour." "Aidez-nous à protéger les eaux!," and from "Faire le bon geste" from *Voyage au bout de l'eau.*

Direction de l'Espace Rural et de la Forêt, ministère de l'agriculture et de la pêche République Française: Text from *Protégez la forêt.*

Dwight's Cajun Bar-B-Que: Advertisement, "Dwight's Cajun Bar-B-Que," from *Le Menu Français,* Volume I.

Editions Aventures et Voyages: Text and captions from "Zapping" from *Super,* no. 78, October 1994. Copyright © 1994 by Editions Aventures et Voyages.

Editions Bauer: From "Vanessa, Hélène, Charlotte, Shannen... Exploite leurs combines" from *Bravo Girl,* no. 56, April 25–May 8, 1994. Copyright © 1994 by Editions Bauer.

Editions Denoël: "Il faut être raisonnable" from *Les vacances du Petit Nicolas* by Sempé and Goscinny. Copyright © 1962 by Editions Denoël.

Editions Gallimard: From *La cause des femmes* by Gisèle Halimi. Copyright © 1973 by Editions Grasset & Fasquelle.

Editions L'Harmattan: French text only from *O'gaya* by Isabelle and Henri Cadoré, illustrations by Bernadette Coléno. Copyright © 1991 by Editions L'Harmattan.

Editorial Melhoramentos, São Paulo: "Tortoise and the Leopard" from *African American Tales* by Rogério Andrade Barbosa, illustrations by Ciça Fittipaldi. Copyright © 1987 by Rogério Andrade Barbosa and Comp. Melhoramentos de São Paulo, Indústrias de Papel. English translation copyright © 1993 by Volcano Press, Inc.

Fondation Carzou Manosque: Ticket, "Alpes de Haute-Provence."

Grand Théâtre de Bordeaux: Classified advertisement, "Concours de Recrutement," from *Libération,* Monday, March 21, 1994.

Hachette Livre: "La petite maison," "Le clou de Djeha," et "Les trois femmes du roi" from *Contes et histoires du Maghreb* by Jean-Paul Tauvel. Copyright © 1975 by Hachette Livre. From "La cuisine cajun" from "La Louisiane" from *Le guide du routard: Etats-Unis 1993/94.* Copyright © 1993 by Hachette Livre (Littérature Générale: Guides de Voyages). "La mosquée de la kasbah," from "La place Jemaa-el-Fna," "Le minaret de la Koutoubia," "Le palais de la Bahia," from "Les souks," "Les tombeaux saadiens," and front cover from *Le guide du routard: Maroc 1994–95.* Copyright © 1994 by Hachette Livre (Littérature Générale: Guides de Voyages).

Hôtel Bristol: L'Auberge: Adaptation of the L'Auberge menu.

Impact Médecin: Classified advertisement, "Maquettiste réf 001, Secrétaire de rédaction réf 002, Correcteur réf 003," from *Libération,* Monday, July 18, 1994.

INSEE: Table, "Les vacances des 14/19 ans" from *Insee,* 1990, partially updated 1991.

JACANA: Photographs from pages 40, 41, 43, 50, and 51 from *Images Doc,* no. 25, January 1991.

J.C. Penney Company, Inc.: Photograph on page 135 from catalog, Vol. C-94, *Celebrate Summer* by J.C. Penney. Copyright © 1994 by J.C. Penney Company. Inc. Photograph of vest from *1995 Fall/Winter* catalog. Copyright © 1995 by J.C. Penney Company, Inc.

Journal L'Alsace: "A la soupe les potaches" from *L'Alsace,* April 11–13, 1993. Copyright © 1993 by Journal L'Alsace.

J.S.I.: Tables, "Les divergences garçons-filles," "Parmi les choses suivantes, qu'est-ce qui vous paraît le plus important lorsqu'on a un emploi?," "Pensez-vous que dans les prochaines années il y a de grands risques que vous soyez chômeur?," "Pour un jeune comme vous, diriez-vous que pour trouver un emploi aujourd'hui, il vaut mieux:," and "Quand vous pensez au premier emploi pour un jeune comme vous, diriez-vous:," from *La Tribune Desfossés,* Monday, March 14, 1994. Copyright © 1994 by J.S.I.

Christian Lacroix: From "Bazar de Christian Lacroix: Automne-Hiver 1994–1995," from "Christian Lacroix Collection Haute-Couture: Automne-Hiver 1994/95," from "Christian Lacroix Prêt-à-Porter: Automne-Hiver 1994/1995," and four illustrations by Christian Lacroix.

Lafayette Convention & Visitors Commission: From "Calendrier des événements," from "La paroisse de Lafayette," "La paroisse de Saint Martin," and map of Acadiana from *Acadiana, c'est magnifique.*

La Fête de Lafayette: Advertisement, "La Fête de Lafayette," from *Le Menu Français,* Volume 1.

La Maison de Campagne: Advertisement, "La Maison de Campagne, Lafayette," from *Le Menu Français,* Volume 1.

La Source Quelle: Seven photographs, "le body/le pantalon," "Le tailleur entièrement doublé," "le tee-shirt depuis/le caleçon depuis," "le gilet depuis," "la robe depuis," "le pendentif," and "le sac," with descriptions from *La Source Quelle,* Spring-Summer 1994.

La Tribune Desfossés: Title, "Sondage: les jeunes pour un travail à tout prix," from *La Tribune Desfossés,* March 14, 1994, page 16.

La Visite des Calanques: Cover of *Promenade en mer: la visite des calanques.*

le soleil: Text from "De nouveaux professionnels sur le marché" from *le soleil,* July 20, 1993, vol. 24, no. 6936. Copyright © 1993 by le soleil. All rights reserved. *le soleil* is a Senegalese daily newspaper.

Les productions La Fête: Four photographs, Scene 83, and synopsis and production information from *FIERRO... L'été des secrets,* produced by Rock Demers, directed by André Melançon, from a story by Rodolfo Otero, screenplay by André Melançon and Geneviève Lefebvre, stills by Jean Demers. *FIERRO... L'été des secrets* is number 8 in the collection, *Tales for All.* Produced by Productions La Fête, 225 Roy Street East, Suite 203, Montreal, Quebec, Canada H2W 1M5.

Les Restaurants du Cœur: Classified advertisement, "Bénévoles (H/F)" from *Libération,* Monday, March 14, 1994.

Les III Balzac 2: Ticket for Les III Balzac 2.

Librairie Gründ: "Le cimetière des éléphants" from *Légendes et contes: Contes africains* by Vladislav Stanovsk, translated into French by Dagmar Doppia. Copyright © 1992 by Aventinum, Prague; French translation copyright © 1992 by Librairie Gründ.

L'Officiel des Spectacles: From "Ami africain (L')", from "Adventures d'un homme invisible (Les)," from "Famille Pierrafeu (La)," from "Henry V," and from "Patriotes (Les)," from "films en exclusivité" from *L'Officiel des Spectacles,* no. 2488, August 31–September 6, 1994. Copyright © 1994 by L'Officiel des Spectacles.

L'Union des écrivaines et écrivains québécois: Text and photograph from "La protection de l'environnement: ça regarde aussi les jeunes" by Francine Gagnon, photographs by Joseph Labbate from *Vidéo-Presse,* vol. XIX, no. 5, January 1990. Copyright © 1990 by UNEQ.

Madame au Foyer: From "Les femmes dans le monde" by Monique Roy from *Madame,* September 1994. Copyright © 1994 by Madame au Foyer.

Michelin Travel Publications: From Map No. 970, "Europe," 1994 edition, Permission No. 94–460. Copyright © 1994 by Michelin. From Map No. 409, "Belgique, Luxembourg, Belgium," 1994 edition, Permission No. 94–460. Copyright © 1994 by Michelin.

Moulinsart: Covers of *Coke en stock, L'oreille cassée,* and *Tintin au Tibet* from *Les aventures de Tintin* series by Hergé. Copyright © by Casterman.

Musée de la Dentelle: Advertisement, "Musée de la Dentelle: Marche-en-Famenne," from *Guides des attractions touristiques & musées: Belgique.*

Musée Rodin: Ticket, "Musée Rodin: Entrée-6F."

Office Municipal du Tourisme de Cassis et des Calanques: Cover of *Cassis : Plan de Cassis et des Calanques.*

Office National du Tourisme Tunisien: Photographs and text from pages 6, 10, 15, 16, 18, 34–36, 38, and 47 from *Tunisie amie: Tunisie. Le pays proche.*

Opéra de Paris: Ticket, "Béjart: Ballet de Lausanne," March 21, 1990.

Parc Astérix, S.A.: Classified advertisement, "Communication," from *Libération,* March 14, 1994.

Parc de Récréation Mont Mosan: Advertisement, "Parc de Récréation Mont Mosan," from *Guide des attractions touristiques & musées, Belgique.*

Pelican: Recipes, "Beignets de Banane" and "Crevettes et Jambon Jambalaya," from *Recettes Préférées de la Nouvelle-Orléans* by Suzanne Ormond, Mary E. Irvine, and Denyse Cantin. Copyright © 1979 by Suzanne Ormond, Mary E. Irvine, and Denyse Cantin.

Liliane Phung: Photographs from "Mannequins d'un jour : Liliane, une vraie beauté asiatique" from *OK! Podium,* no. 34, May 2–15, 1994.

Poor Boy's Riverside Inn: Advertisement, "Poor Boy's Riverside Inn: Sert la meilleure cuisine cajun depuis 1932," from *Le Menu Français,* Volume 1.

Poupart Bakery, Inc.: Advertisement, "Poupart Bakery, Inc.: 'La Boulangerie Française de Lafayette'," from *Le Menu Français,* Volume 1.

Prisma Presse: From "Barcelone 92 — La semaine de tous les records" by Sylvie Breton and Valérie Huck from *Télé Loisirs,* no. 335, August 1–7, 1992. Copyright © 1992 by Prisma Presse.

Randol's Seafood & Restaurant: Photographs and text from brochure, *Randol's Seafood & Restaurant: Lafayette, LA.*

Réunion des Musées Nationaux: Ticket, "Musées Nationaux: Entrée Tarif Réduit-12F."

Rhino Records, Inc.: Lyrics from "Cajun Telephone Stomp" by Michael L. Doucet and lyrics from "Le Chanky-Chank Français" by Michael L. Doucet from *Cajun Conga* by BeauSoleil. Copyright © 1991 by RNA Records, a Division of Rhino Records Inc. French lyrics from "Chez Denouse McGee" and "Freeman's Zydeco" from *L'Echo* by BeauSoleil. Published by Orange Skies Music/Do-Say Music BMI.

Scoop: From "Mannequins d'un jour: Liliane, une vraie beauté asiatique" from *OK! Podium,* no. 34, May 2–15, 1994. Copyright © 1994 by COGEDIPRESSE.

Didier Sorelli: Cover and illustrations by Didier Sorelli from *Protégez la forêt.*

Swiss Council for Accident Prevention, Berne, Switzerland: From "Equipement adéquat" and front cover from *Faire des randonnées en montagne, sûrement!*

SYGMA: Photograph of Vanessa Paradis by Bettina Rheims and photograph of Hélène Rolles by Jacques Bourget.

Trois Suisses: Photographs from pp. 28 ("la jupe droite"), 163 (pants), and 265 ("les gants"), photograph and description, "La chemise," p. 507; photograph and description, "La chemise à rayures," p. 496; photograph and description, "Le gilet sans manches 'Stop ou encore'," p. 72; photograph and description, "Le pull Lambswool double fil," p. 70; and photograph and description, "Les bottes drapées," p. 263 from *3 Suisses,* Autumn/Winter '92–'93.

TV 7 Jours: Cover, text from "Les Feuilletons" by Benoît Breton, and television listing from "Samedi, 10 Septembre" from *TV 7 Jours,* September 10–16, 1992. Copyright © 1992 by TV 7 Jours.

TV10 Angers: Classified advertisement, "TV10 Angers recherche pour ses émissions en direct animateurs (trices)..." from *Libération,* Monday, March 14, 1994.

UNEQ: From "Chantal Petitclerc: Un exemple de courage" by Pierre Latreille from *Vidéo Presse,* vol. XXII, no. 5, January 1993. Copyright © 1993 by Editions Paulines Inc. From "Cloutier: Spécialiste de la brasse" by Pierre Latreille from *Vidéo-Presse,* vol. XXIV, no. 2, October 1994. Copyright © 1994 by Editions Paulines Inc.

Winstub au Cygne: Adaptation of menu, "Le Cygne."

WWF® - World Wide Fund for Nature: From *Sauvegarder la nature, c'est assurer l'avenir de l'homme.*

WWF Suisse: "Je désire devenir membre du WWF" from *Les Îles,* vol. 14, no. 3, September 1981.

PHOTOGRAPHY CREDITS

Abbreviations used: (t) top, (c) center, (b) bottom, (l) left, (r) right, (bckgd) background, (bdr) border.

FRONT COVER: (tl), Robert Frerck/Panoramic Images; (tr), Daniel J. Schaefer; (b), C. Hergé/Casterman SA. **BACK COVER:** (tl), Deitrich Photography; (tr); SuperStock.

FRONT AND BACK COVER COLLAGE: HRW Photo by Andrew Yates.

CHAPTER OPENER PHOTOGRAPHS: HRW Photos by Scott Van Osdol.

TABLE OF CONTENTS: Page ix(tr), HRW Photo by May Polycarpe; ix(bl), Brian Seed/Tony Stone Images; v(t), David R. Frazier Photolibrary; v(cr), Emmanuel Rongiéras D'Usseau; vi(t), HRW Photo by Patrice Maurin-Berthier; vi(b), HRW Photo by Patrice Maurin-Berthier; vii(tl), HRW Photo by Patrice Maurin-Berthier; viii(tl), Michael Newman/PhotoEdit; viii(tr), Blaine Harrington; viii(br), Robert Fried; x(tl), Jean Whitney/Tony Stone Images; x(tr), Robert Frerck/Odyssey; xi(t), HRW Photo by Patrice Maurin-Berthier; xi(b), Adventure Photo; xii(tl), SuperStock; xii(tr), HRW Photo by Sam Dudgeon; xiii(tr), HRW Photo by May Polycarpe; xiii(bl), Wolfgang Kaehler; xiv(tl), Mauricio Handler/The Wildlife Collection; xiv(tr), Karl I. Wallin/FPG International; xv(tl), Dick Dietrich/Dietrich Photography; xv(b), Bob Krist/Leo de Wys, Inc.; xvi(tl), P. Rondeau/AllSport; xvi(cr), Mitchell B. Reibel/Sports Photo Masters.

UNIT ONE: Page xxiv–1, Phil Cantor/SuperStock; 2(tl), (bl), SuperStock; 2(cr), Blaine Harrington; 3(tl), Gary Cralle; 3(br), W. Gontscharff/SuperStock; 3(cr), SuperStock; 3(cl), P. and G. Bowater/Image Bank. **CHAPTER ONE:** Page 4(c), P.J. Sharpe/SuperStock; 5(t), David R. Frazier/Photolibrary; 5(b), Robert Fried; 6(tr), Jean-Marc Truchet/Tony Stone Worldwide; 6(c), Barry Iverson/Woodfin Camp & Associates; 6(b), Adina Tovy/Photo 20-20; 7(t), Rick Lee/SuperStock; 7(cl), David R. Frazier Photolibrary; 7(cr), F. Bouillot/Marco Polo/Photo Take; 7(bl), Leo de Wys/Bas van Beek; 7(b), Ph, Halle/Marco Polo/Photo Take; 12(l), M. Blanchard/Marco Polo/Photo Take; 12(c), David R. Frazier/Photolibrary; 14(tr), Emmanuel Rongiéras D'Usseau; 15(c), Catherine Ursillo/Photo Researchers; 16(l), HRW Photo by Marty Granger/Edge Productions; 16(r), HRW Photo by Louis Boireau; 16(c), HRW Photo by Marty Granger/Edge Productions. **CHAPTER TWO:** Page 28(b), Pierre Berger/Photo Researchers; 29-32(all), HRW Photo by Patrice Maurin-Berthier; 34(tc), F. Bouillot/Marco Polo/Photo Take; 34(cl), David Young-Wolf/PhotoEdit; 40(l), HRW Photo by Marty Granger/Edge Productions; 40(r), HRW Photo by Louis Boireau; 40(c), HRW Photo by Marty Granger/Edge Productions; 44(tl), HRW photo by Sam Dudgeon; 44(tc), Victor Englebert; 44(tr), Color Day Productions/The Image Bank; 44(cl), Messerschmdt/FPG; 44(c), John Darling/Tony Stone Worldwide; 44(cr), F. Bouillot/Marco Polo/Photo Take; 45(l), J. Wishnetsky/Comstock; 45(r), Victor Englebert; 45(cl), F. Bouillot/Marco Polo/Photo Take; 45(cr), Richard Pasley; 54(b), 55(t), Blaine Harrington; 55(b), HRW Photo by Patrice Maurin-Berthier. **CHAPTER THREE:** Page 56(cl), Blaine Harrington; 56(c), 56(cr), Mark Antman/Harbrace Photo; 56(br), Blaine Harrington; 57(cr), HRW Photo by May Polycarpe; 58(l), Michelle Bridwell/Frontera Fotos; 58(r), HRW Photo; 58(cl), Blaine Harrington; 58(cr), HRW Photo by Patrice Maurin-Berthier; 65-66, Blaine Harrington; 67(tr), (tc), (l), (r), (cl), (cr), (c), Daniel J. Schaefer; 67(tl), HRW Photo by Russell Dian; 68(l), HRW Photo by Louis Boireau; 68(r), (c), HRW Photo by Marty Granger/Edge Productions. **CHAPTER FOUR:** Page 80(b), Robert Fried; 81(t), HRW Photo by Patrice Maurin-Berthier; 81(b), Carol Simowitz; 90(tl), Peter Menzel/HBJ Photo; 90(tr), Charles Graham/Leo de Wys, Inc.; 91(l), 91(r), 91(c), HRW Photo by Marty Granger/Edge Productions; 92(l), Michael Newman/PhotoEdit; 92(r), Shirley Richards/SuperStock; 93(tl), Cathlyn Melloan/Tony Stone Images; 93(tr), Daniel J. Schaefer; 93(bl), Tony Freeman/PhotoEdit; 93(bc), Photo 20/20; 93(br), HRW Photo by Patrice Maurin-Berthier.

UNIT TWO: Page 106–107, Gill Copeland/Nawrocki Stock Photo, Inc; 108(tl), J. Deselliers/SuperStock; 108(tr), R. Campillo/The Stock Market, Inc.; 108(br), 109(tr), Gill Copeland/Nawrocki Stock Photo, Inc.; 109(cl), Charles G. Summers/Ron Kimball Stock Agency; 109(br), Dave G. Houser; 109(c) Rita Summers/Ron Kimball Stock Agency; 109(tl) Cliche. **CHAPTER FIVE:** Page